CHARACTER STUDIES IN THE FOURTH GOSPEL

Character Studies in the Fourth Gospel

Narrative Approaches to Seventy Figures in John

Edited by

Steven A. Hunt, D. Francois Tolmie *&* Ruben Zimmermann

WILLIAM B. EERDMANS PUBLISHING COMPANY
GRAND RAPIDS, MICHIGAN

Wm. B. Eerdmans Publishing Co.
2140 Oak Industrial Drive N.E., Grand Rapids, Michigan 49505
www.eerdmans.com

First published 2013 by
Mohr Siebeck, Tübingen
© 2013 Mohr Siebeck
Eerdmans edition published 2016

ISBN 978-0-8028-7392-7

Library of Congress Cataloging-in-Publication Data

Names: Hunt, Steven A., editor. | Tolmie, D. F. (D. Francois), editor. |
    Zimmermann, Ruben, 1968– editor.
Title: Character studies in the Fourth Gospel : narrative approaches to seventy figures in John /
    edited by Steven A. Hunt, D. Francois Tolmie & Ruben Zimmermann.
Description: Grand Rapids : Eerdmans Publishing Co., 2016. | Originally published:Tübingen :
    Mohr Siebeck, 2013. | Includes bibliographical references and index.
Identifiers: LCCN 2016024696 | ISBN 9780802873927 (pbk. : alk. paper)
Subjects: LCSH: Bible. John—Criticism, interpretation, etc. | Characters and characteristics in the
    Bible.
Classification: LCC BS2615.52 .C44 2016 | DDC 226.5/06—dc23
    LC record available at https://lccn.loc.gov/2016024696

Contents

Preface	xi
Foreword, *by Craig R. Koester*	xviii
An Introduction to Character and Characterization in John and Related New Testament Literature *Steven A. Hunt, D. Francois Tolmie, and Ruben Zimmermann*	1
Table on the Characters in the Fourth Gospel *Steven A. Hunt, D. Francois Tolmie, and Ruben Zimmermann*	34
John (the Baptist): The Witness on the Threshold *Catrin H. Williams*	46
The World: Promise and Unfulfilled Hope *Christopher W. Skinner*	61
"The Jews": Unreliable Figures or Unreliable Narration? *Ruben Zimmermann*	71
The Priests and Levites: Identity and Politics in the Search for a Messiah *Sherri Brown*	110
The Pharisees: A House Divided *Uta Poplutz*	116
The Disciples of John (the Baptist): Hearers of John, Followers of Jesus *Gary T. Manning, Jr.*	127
An Anonymous Disciple: A Type of Discipleship *Derek Tovey*	133
Andrew: The First Link in the Chain *Martinus C. de Boer*	137
Simon Peter: An Ambiguous Character and His Narrative Career *Michael Labahn*	151

Philip: A Connective Figure in Polyvalent Perspective — 168
Paul N. Anderson

Nathanael: Under the Fig Tree on the Fourth Day — 189
Steven A. Hunt

The Mother of Jesus: A Woman Possessed — 202
Mary L. Coloe

The Disciples: The "Now" and "Not Yet" of Belief in Jesus — 214
Susan E. Hylen

The Servants / Steward at Cana:
The "Whispering Wizard's" Wine-Bearers — 228
Mary L. Coloe

The Bridegroom at Cana: Ignorance is Bliss — 233
Edward W. Klink III

The Brothers of Jesus: All in the Family? — 238
Joel Nolette and Steven A. Hunt

The Animal Sellers / The Money Changers in the Temple:
Driven Out – But Why? — 245
Mark A. Matson

Nicodemus: The Travail of New Birth — 249
R. Alan Culpepper

"A Jew": A Search for the Identity and Role of an Anonymous Judean — 260
Mark Appold

The Samaritan Woman: A Woman Transformed — 268
Harold W. Attridge

The Men of the Samaritan Woman: Six of Sychar — 282
Steven A. Hunt

The Samaritans of Sychar: A Responsive Chorus — 292
Peter Phillips

The Galileans: Interpretive Possibilities and the Limits
of Narrative Critical Approaches — 299
Andy M. Reimer

The Royal Official: Not so Officious *Peter J. Judge*	306
The Son of the Royal Official: Incarnating the Life Giving Power of Jesus' Word *Gilbert Van Belle and Steven A. Hunt*	314
The Slaves of the Royal Official: Servants of the Word *Peter J. Judge*	329
The Ill and the Sick: Those Who Were Healed and Those Who Were Not *D. Francois Tolmie*	332
The Invalid at the Pool: The Man Who Merely Got Well *J. Ramsey Michaels*	337
The Crowd: A Faceless, Divided Mass *Cornelis Bennema*	347
The Boy with Loaves and Fish: Picnic, Plot, and Pattern *Dieter T. Roth*	356
Judas (the Betrayer): The Black Sheep of the Family *Cornelis Bennema*	360
The Authorities: Indeterminate Complex Identities *Susanne Luther*	373
The Chief Priests: Masterminds of Jesus' Death *Cornelis Bennema*	382
The Temple Police: Double Agents *Gary T. Manning, Jr.*	388
The Greeks: Jesus' Hour and the Weight of the World *Sherri Brown*	397
The Scribes and the Elders: Mirror Characterization of Jesus and His Opponents in the *Pericope Adulterae* *Chris Keith*	403
The Adulterous Woman: Nameless, Partnerless, Defenseless *Peter Phillips*	407

The Devil: Murderer, Liar, and Defeated Foe *Dave L. Mathewson*	421
The Man Born Blind: True Disciple of Jesus *Andy M. Reimer*	428
The Neighbors of the Man Born Blind: A Question of Identity *Matthew D. Montonini*	439
The Parents of the Man Born Blind: The Reason for Fear without True Reason *Michael Labahn*	446
The Believers Across the Jordan: On Location with Jesus *Ruben Zimmermann*	451
Lazarus: "Behold a Man Raised Up by Christ!" *Marianne Meye Thompson*	460
Mary (of Bethany): The Anointer of the Suffering Messiah *Susan Miller*	473
Martha: Seeing the Glory of God *Gail R. O'Day*	487
Thomas: Question Marks and Exclamation Marks *Thomas Popp*	504
Caiaphas and Annas: The Villains of the Piece? *Adele Reinhartz*	530
The Beloved Disciple: The Ideal Point of View *James L. Resseguie*	537
Judas (not Iscariot): What's in a Name? *Catrin H. Williams*	550
The Roman Soldiers at Jesus' Arrest: "You Are Dust, and to Dust You Shall Return" *Steven A. Hunt*	554
Malchus: Cutting Up in the Garden *Christopher W. Skinner*	568

People in the Courtyard: Escalating Darkness 573
Helen K. Bond

Pontius Pilate: Failing in More Ways Than One 578
D. Francois Tolmie

Barabbas: A Foil for Jesus, the Jewish Leadership, and Pilate 598
David L. Mathewson

The Soldiers Who Crucify: Fulfilling Scripture 601
Michael Labahn

The Co-Crucified Men: Shadows by His Cross 607
Chelsea N. Revell and Steven A. Hunt

The Women by the Cross: Creating Contrasts 618
D. Francois Tolmie

Mary Magdalene: Beginning at the End 626
Jaime Clark-Soles

The Mother of Jesus and the Beloved Disciple:
How a New Family is Established Under the Cross 641
Jean Zumstein

Joseph of Arimathea: One of "the Jews," But with a Fearful Secret! 646
William John Lyons

The Angels: Marking the Divine Presence 658
Jan van der Watt

The Sons of Zebedee and Two Other Disciples:
Two Pairs of Puzzling Acquaintances in the Johannine Dénouement 663
Christos Karakolis

List of Contributors 677

Index of References 679

Index of Modern Authors 701

Index of Subjects 710

Preface

The following volume on characters studies in John began, strangely enough, when two of the editors met (via email) because they shared a love for Paul's rhetoric in Galatians! Upon this discovery in late 2008, they soon realized they also thoroughly enjoyed literary studies related to the Fourth Gospel. However great the distance between Galatians and John, one point of convergence relates to "artistic" issues: the rhetorical art in Paul and the literary art in John are both explicitly persuasive (cf. Galatians *passim*; John 20:30–31). So emails passed between Gordon College near Boston, Massachusetts, and the University of the Free State in Bloemfontein, South Africa frequently in those days. The idea to do something with characters in John was the result of those early emails. When Ruben Zimmermann from the Johannes Gutenberg-University of Mainz in Germany joined the project in the spring of 2009, the team was complete. And during a delicious dinner in New Orleans at the Annual Meeting of the Society of Biblical Literature later that year, the contours of the book were worked out. Realizing that we did not know of any book like the one we were proposing (on the state of character studies in John at present, see more below), we knew that an ambitious project related to nearly all the characters in the Gospel was in order. Running the idea by a few different publishers who expressed some enthusiasm at that conference cemented in our minds the need for this book.

Since we desired to make a substantial contribution to the field of literary studies on the Fourth Gospel, we sketched out the following purpose statement for the volume before issuing any invitations to contribute:

> The purpose of this volume is to offer a comprehensive narrative-critical study of nearly every character Jesus (or, in some cases, only the reader) encounters in the narrative world of the Fourth Gospel. The emphasis is thus on a literary approach to the matter, in particular from the viewpoint of characterization as it is generally understood.

In light of the statement, we thought long and hard about *methodology* (on methodological issues related to character and characterization, see more below). While we insisted on a literary approach to the characters in John (as opposed to, for example, a strictly historical approach), we did not prescribe a certain method. In the end, our authors employed a variety of approaches: in several articles the approach chosen could be described simply as a close reading of the text which focuses especially on the way a character is portrayed in the narrative. In others, the approach could be described in broad terms, e. g., as a focus on intertextuality, intercharacterization, spatial semantics, polyvalence, participant reference, or speech act theory, to name only a few. One author even engaged in a dramatic rewriting of the text from the perspective of characterization. Other authors preferred to employ a specific model (in some instances, a combination of such models) developed for the analysis of characters in narrative texts. In this regard readers will find well-known names such as Robert Alter, Cornelis Bennema, Adele Berlin, Seymour Chatman, Joseph Ewen, E. M. Forster, W. J. Harvey, Uri Margolin, James Resseguie, and Victor Shklovsky.

We allowed for this openness with respect to methodology for three basic reasons: first, we believed that the contributors should determine the best course of action with respect to the character(s) they were studying. Literary criticism related to John over the years has shown definitively that there is no one particular methodology that works best with respect to so many different kinds of characters (and, of course, this conclusion holds true for character studies related to other works as well). Second, we believed that insisting on one particular methodology would make for formulaic chapters, lead to predetermined conclusions, and, quite frankly, result in boring reading. Instead, the authors here are as varied in their hermeneutical presuppositions and literary methodologies as they are in their conclusions. Readers will therefore observe firsthand the implementation of a wide variety of methods available for character studies, as well as the necessarily circular relationship between methods and conclusions. Third, as editors we are each committed to the notion that *openness* best suits the literary design and theological message of the Fourth Gospel itself. With regard to theological issues like Christology, for example, the Fourth Gospel likes playing with different titles, images, and traditions. As soon as someone wants to focus on a single name or decisive image, one clear conviction over the rest, that same one is inevitably confronted in the text by the one Mark Stibbe has aptly described, "the elusive Christ" (e. g., John 6:15; 8:59; 12:36);[1] it does not seem possible to harness the Fourth Gospel's openness. Indeed, since Jesus won't ride in his disciples' boat in John (cf. 6:21), we suspect he won't ride in ours either.

After drawing up the list of characters in John, we began to compile a list of scholars to approach for possible contributions. The response from those we invited could not have been more enthusiastic. We were delighted by their interest in the project and, subsequently, the way they went about their work. In the end, forty-four authors from eleven different countries and four different continents, contributed essays to this volume. Editors of volumes such as

---

[1] See Mark W. G. Stibbe, "The Elusive Christ: A New Reading of the Fourth Gospel," *JSNT* 44 (1991): 20–38.

this often speak about contributors as though working with them is akin to "herding cats." Our experience, however, has proved that old maxim (mostly!) untrue. We very much want to thank the authors for their contributions to this volume, as well as for their patience with us during this long process. Having worked on the project steadily for nearly four years (in the midst of other obligations and commitments), we have learned a great deal about what we have described as "inter-continental, cross-cultural, team exegesis." We remain committed to the notion that reading, interpreting, writing, and editing – as well as the process by which all of that gets repeated again and again – are all worthy endeavors.

In terms of the selection of characters included here, we deliberately avoided articles related to the deity; readers looking for articles on "God/Father,"[2] "Jesus,"[3] or "the Holy Spirit/Paraclete,"[4] or the titles, symbols, and images related specifically to them, will not find them here. Still, given their prominence in the Gospel, readers of this volume will encounter discussions of these three, especially Jesus, quite frequently. The authors of other recent publications on characters in John, especially those with titles like "encountering Jesus,"[5] understand this point very well. In terms of non-human "characters," we grouped together as one character, "the Devil, Satan, and the Ruler of this World," even though we could perhaps have split them profitably into separate studies;

---

[2] See further, Marianne Meye Thompson, *The God of the Gospel of John* (Grand Rapids, Mich.: Eerdmans, 2001); D. Francois Tolmie, "The Characterization of God in the Fourth Gospel," *JSNT* (1998) 20: 57–75.

[3] On Jesus specifically as a character in John, see most recently, Jason Sturdevant, *The Character of Jesus in the Fourth Gospel: The Adaptability of the Logos* (PhD Dissertation; Princeton Theological Seminary, 2013); see also, Steven A. Hunt, "And the Word Became Flesh – Again? Jesus and Abraham in John 8," in *Perspectives on Our Father Abraham* (ed. Steven A. Hunt; Grand Rapids, Mich.: Eerdmans, 2010), 81–109; Ruben Zimmermann, *Christologie der Bilder im Johannesevangelium* (WUNT 171; Tübingen: Mohr Siebeck, 2004), here "Chapter 8: Narrative Bildlichkeit," 197–217, 355–71; Mark W.G. Stibbe, "The Elusive Christ: A New Reading of the Fourth Gospel," *JSNT* 44 (1991): 20–38; J.A. du Rand, "The Characterization of Jesus as Depicted in the Narrative of the Fourth Gospel," *Neotestamentica* 19 (1985): 18–36; Gail O'Day, *Revelation in the Fourth Gospel: Narrative Mode and Theological Claim* (Philadelphia: Fortress Press, 1986); R. Alan Culpepper, *The Anatomy of the Fourth Gospel: A Study in Literary Design* (Philadelphia: Fortress Press, 1983), esp. 106–12.

[4] While not strictly narratological studies, see especially, Gitte Buch-Hansen, *"It is the Spirit that Gives Life": A Stoic Understanding of Pneuma in John's Gospel* (BZNW 173; Berlin: de Gruyter, 2010); Tricia Gates Brown, *Spirit in the Writings of John: Johannine Pneumatology in Social-Scientific Perspective* (JSNTSup 253; London: T&T Clark, 2003); and Gary M. Burge, *The Anointed Community: The Holy Spirit in the Johannine Community* (Grand Rapids, Mich.: Eerdmans, 1987) and the excellent bibliographies in all those works.

[5] See Peter Dschulnigg, *Jesus begegnen: Personen und ihre Bedeutung im Johannesevangelium* (2d ed.; Münster: LIT, 2002); Frances Taylor Gench, *Encounters with Jesus: Studies in the Gospel of John* (Louisville, Ky.: Westminster John Knox Press, 2007); Cornelis Bennema, *Encountering Jesus: Character Studies in the Gospel of John* (Milton Keynes: Paternoster, 2009).

and we included an essay on the Angels at Jesus' tomb. And while we included an essay on "the World" as a corporate character, we decided against an essay on "Scripture" as a character, even though a compelling case can be made for its personification in the Gospel.[6] Similarly, while we considered this option, in the end we did not include essays on "characters from the Hebrew Bible" who figure prominently in John (most notably, for example, Abraham, Jacob, Moses, and Isaiah).[7] We also decided against articles on the "We/I" in 1:14, 16; 21:24–25, since they do not actually operate as characters in the narrative world of the text. While some minor "implied" characters have been omitted from the volume ("the guests" who will presumably get "over-served" at the wedding in John 2; "inhabitants of Jerusalem" in 7:25; "a messenger" in 11:3, etc.), for various reasons a few others have been linked together in articles:

- "the Priests" and "the Levites"
- "Jesus' Disciples" and "the Twelve"
- "the Servants at Cana" and "the Steward at Cana"
- "the Money Changers in the Temple" and "the Animal Traders in the Temple"
- "the Ill at the Pool" and "the Sick at the Feeding"
- "the Scribes" and "the Elders" in the *Pericope Adulterae*
- "Caiaphas" and "Annas"
- "the Mother of Jesus" and "the Beloved Disciple"
- "the Sons of Zebedee" and "the Two Anonymous Disciples"

In the end, roughly seventy characters (or groups of characters) in John, no matter how major or minor, however round or flat, have been made the focus of an essay in this book. This number – seventy – is not to be understood in any absolute sense for a few fairly obvious reasons. First, how should one count corporate characters? So, for example, there are characters which speak and act or get acted upon like a single character and accordingly can be counted just as "one," even if they were "two" (consider in this regard the parents of the man born blind in John 9 or the co-crucified men in John 19). Others, like "the neighbors" in John 9 or "the many believers" in John 10, obviously defy

---

[6] See especially Michael Labahn's essay "Scripture *Talks* Because Jesus *Talks*: The Narrative Rhetoric of Persuading and Creativity in John's Use of Scripture," in *The Fourth Gospel in First-Century Media Culture* (ed. Anthony Le Donne and Tom Thatcher; LNTS 426; London: T&T Clark, 2011), 133–54; and Gary T. Manning, Jr., *The 'Character' of the Scriptures in the Fourth Gospel: A Literary Analysis* (paper presented at the "John Section" of the national meeting of the Evangelical Theological Society, Milwaukee, Wisc., Nov. 13–15, 2012).

[7] See, e. g., Michael Theobald, "Abraham – (Isaak –) Jakob: Israels Väter im Johannesevangelium," in *Israel und seine Heilstraditionen im Johannesevangelium* (ed. Michael Labahn et al.; FS J. Beutler SJ, Paderborn: Schöningh, 2004), 158–83; on Moses in particular see, Stan Harstine, *Moses as a Character in the Fourth Gospel: A Study of Ancient Reading Techniques* (JSNTSup 229; Sheffield: Sheffield Academic Press, 2002).

the numbers game entirely and sometimes split into further subgroups anyway, like "the crowds" in John 7. And while others like the "Women at the cross" in John 19 can be counted separately, it made sense to us to understand them as a single character in that scene.[8] This example in particular illustrates well the inherent subjectivity of the enterprise, since we also saw fit to group one of these women, Jesus' mother, with the disciple Jesus loved as yet another group character, all while commissioning separate essays on both as individual characters as well! Subjective? We are guilty as charged! We also included essays on the three characters that share the stage with Jesus in the *Pericope Adulterae* (John 7:53–8:11), even though the vast majority of scholars line up against that narrative's authenticity; and we asked that, when appropriate, our authors consider John 21 and the characters therein as integral to the process, even though the jury still appears to be out on whether or not this passage is a later addition to the Gospel. When one adds to all of this that there are clearly overlapping group characters, like "the Pharisees" and "the Jews" (or "the crowds" and "the Jews"), and perhaps even overlapping individual characters like the "anonymous disciple" in John 1:35 and the "Beloved Disciple" who emerges in John 13, that one will likely come to the conclusion, as we did, that any form of absolute counting is out of the question. Hence, *roughly* seventy characters.

Far from worrying about our inability to delimit these characters, we remain convinced that it would be a basic misunderstanding of Johannine style to attempt to circumscribe them at all. There is already a symbolism related to numbers in John (e. g., the counting of days, miracles, "I Am" sayings,[9] "a hundred and fifty-three" fish,[10] etc.) and in the end, such counting almost invariably leaves one pondering curious anomalies.[11] The patterns appear to be there of course, but how should they be counted? One gets the distinct impression

---

[8] Even here scholars differ on whether there were two, three, or four women at the cross! For a discussion of these issues, see D. Francois Tolmie, "Creating Contrasts: The Women Standing Near the Cross," in this volume.

[9] There are not only the seven "I Am" sayings, as they are so often described. During the "bread of life" discourse alone, we find four different ones (John 6:35, 41, 48, 51); furthermore, we must include the so called "absolute 'I Am' sayings" (e. g., 4:26; 6:20; 8:58 etc.), as well as the "I Am" saying of the man born blind (John 9:9); even John 18:37 may be seen as an inverted "I Am" saying; see on all these problems, Ruben Zimmermann, *Christologie der Bilder im Johannesevangelium* (WUNT 171; Tübingen: Mohr Siebeck 2004), 121–36.

[10] See, e. g., R. Alan Culpepper, "Designs for the Church in the Imagery of John 21:1–14," in *Imagery in the Gospel of John: Terms, Forms, Themes, and Theology of Johannine Figurative Language* (ed. Jörg Frey et al.; WUNT 200; Tübingen: Mohr Siebeck, 2006), 369–402, here 383–94 on "the 153 large fish;" Richard Bauckham, "The 153 Fish and the Unity of the Fourth Gospel," in *The Testimony of the Beloved Disciple: Narrative, History, and Theology in the Gospel of John* (Grand Rapids, Mich.: Baker Academic, 2007), 271–84.

[11] Cf. Maarten J. J. Menken, *Numerical Literary Techniques in John: The Fourth Evangelist's Use of Numbers of Words and Syllables* (NovTSup 55; Leiden: Brill, 1985).

that the text simply does not want to be pinned down. Starting and ending the Gospel with "anonymous disciples" (John 1:35; 21:2) should be enough to demonstrate that the puzzling openness and genuine flexibility of this Gospel probably also extends to its characters. Still, as editors, we had to draw the line somewhere. So we did. We hope the number and combinations of characters we fixed upon functions heuristically to demonstrate that there are many characters in John and, if thought about in another light or from another angle, probably more than we expect. We conclude the topic of character selection with a slightly revised form of Johannine wisdom: there are also many other characters who encountered Jesus; if every one of them were written down, we suppose that the world itself could not contain the books that would be written.

Two important details about the organization of the book and its chapters: the more or less seventy characters presented in this volume in sixty-two chapters are arranged here, with only a handful of exceptions, simply in the order of their first appearance in the Gospel (see the table of contents and the accompanying table). In the chapters themselves, authors have been asked to introduce their method, offer a brief history of research (if one is available), summarize the raw data related to the character in terms of narrative occurrences, actions, and speech, and finally to engage in character analysis of traits, development, interaction with others, etc. Of course, our authors were not limited to these kinds of issues and concerns, and many went much further in their studies, for example, considering the theological implications of their character's role in the text or the way their character was instrumental in the development of the Gospel's overall Christology.

In conclusion, we are delighted to publically acknowledge several individuals whose work on this volume will not soon be forgotten. We are grateful to Christopher Skinner for his frequent encouragement, especially early on while he was getting his own project off the ground,[12] as well as his timely and thoughtful contributions to our volume. We would like to recognize also the exceptional research, writing, and translation work of four Gordon College students (Sophie Buchanan, Laura Johnson, Joel Nolette, and Chelsea Revell), as well as several extraordinary "wissenschaftliche Mitarbeiter" associated with the Johannes Gutenberg-University at Mainz (Lena-Mareen Höllein, Jörg Röder, Dieter Roth, and Susanne Luther). Cornelis Bennema, whose own major work on several characters in John came out in 2009,[13] spent some research time at the Johannes Gutenberg-University in 2012. During this time he was involved in several aspects related to our project; we are exceedingly grateful that he was so keen to help out. We would like to thank Jörg Frey

---

[12] Christopher Skinner (ed.), *Characters and Characterization in the Gospel of John* (LNTS 461; London: T & T Clark, 2013).

[13] Bennema, *Encountering Jesus*.

who accepted this volume for Mohr Siebeck's WUNT series. We are delighted to be working with such a fine editor as well as with such an esteemed publisher. Ilse König did a phenomenal job managing the editorial process on the side of the publisher. We offer her our sincerest gratitude.

Finally, we have spent many hours with these figures in John; no doubt, many more than we realize. Attempting to live in their world, to see things through their eyes, we have embraced the object of our investigation. But it's very difficult to live in two worlds, especially when we consider that there are real figures in this one, figures near and dear to the editors' hearts who have stood by patiently, bearing much of the burden of our fascination with this Gospel. We would be entirely remiss, therefore, if we did not express our deep and abiding love for our wives, Bridget, Ansa, and Mirjam. We each consider ourselves blessed beyond measure. As fathers also, we want to thank our children for their love and support: Carmien (24), Francois (21), Nathaniel (20), Jordan (18), Rahel (18), Josua (16), Mialise (15), William (13), Rebekka (13), Lindsey (11), Ruth (11), and Parker (2). Like we said, blessed beyond measure!

Steven A. Hunt, Wenham, Mass., United States of America
D. Francois Tolmie, Bloemfontein, South Africa
Ruben Zimmermann, Mainz, Germany

Easter, 2013

Foreword

Character portrayal is one of the major ways that John's gospel engages the imagination of the readers. At first the soaring prose of the prologue takes readers to the dawn of creation, but immediately afterward the story unfolds through the interaction of people. There are direct questions and cryptic responses in the opening encounter of John the Baptist with a delegation of Jewish leaders. Then the circle grows to include Andrew, an anonymous disciple, and others, who exhibit curiosity, confusion, and an almost inexplicable willingness to follow. As the story continues, we find major figures, who take up entire chapters, and minor figures, who make only a single fleeting appearance before vanishing from the stage.

The present collection of studies of John's characters builds on the wealth of literary studies of the gospel that have been done in recent decades, offering the best in recent scholarship. At the same time, the studies are accessible, inviting a broad range of current readers to consider one of the most intriguing aspects of John's narrative: its portrayal of the people whose are lives are somehow intertwined with that of Jesus. The writer shows a keen interest in showing us who these people are and inviting us to ask how they see things.

It is striking that some of the longer episodes in the Fourth Gospel consist entirely of encounters between Jesus and individuals or groups. For example, when Nicodemus comes to Jesus by night or the Samaritan woman appears at midday, there is almost no action. Instead, what "happens" is conversation, and the way we understand the conversation is inextricably tied to the overall presentation of each character. Even when an episode includes a notable action, such as a sign, much of the narrative is still devoted to the depiction of the characters, who struggle to discern the meaning of the sign. For example, when Jesus heals a man born blind or raises Lazarus from the dead, each sign is recounted in just a few verses. The portrayal of the characters and their perceptions of Jesus' action take up the rest of each chapter.

John's gospel is meant to be read in the company of other people, and as we exchange our views about the characters, we are often reminded how difficult it can be to distinguish what is said in the text from what we supply in the process of reading. John may deftly sketch out the contours of characters, but we ourselves fill in the gaps—and the portrait I complete in my mind's eye may or may not correspond to what is pictured by other readers. At the wedding at Cana, Jesus' mother says, "They have wine," and when Jesus responds enigmatically about his "hour" not having come, she says, "Do whatever he tells you" (John 2:3–5). It is difficult to read her words without supplying a voice tone, but what sort of tone is appropriate to the text? Do we imagine her speaking with hushed sincerity or with utter exasperation? Or when Jesus engages the woman at the well in conversation about thirst and living water, do we picture her responses to Jesus as evasive or confrontational (4:7–15)? And when she finally says, "He couldn't be the Christ, could he?" (4:29), is she tending toward faith or skepticism? How can one tell?

The forty-four scholars who contributed to this volume are valuable conversation partners who help us deal with the kinds of questions noted above. They come from eleven countries on four continents, thus providing a rich variety of insights. They do not follow identical methods of interpretation, and the differences enhance the appeal of the collection. As a group, they draw us more deeply into dialogue about how to construe the narrative.

The initial chapter orients us to some of the methods that have been used in literary studies of the gospels. I commend the overview of methods to both specialists and nonspecialists, because all of us who read John make certain assumptions about the text and favor certain types of questions. What reflection on method does is heighten our self-awareness. It calls us to consider how our presuppositions and angle of vision inevitably shape our reading of the text, and what other options are available. At its best, a method both stimulates and disciplines thinking about a text.

In antiquity, the dominant framework for interpreting characters was developed by Aristotle. In his *Poetics* (6.19–24, 1450b) he observed that in drama, character or *ēthos* is not self-evident. Rather, character is disclosed when people face situations in which they have to respond—and not everyone will respond in the same way. That way of looking at the people portrayed in the Fourth Gospel can be helpful, since Jesus repeatedly says and does things that provoke very different responses from those he meets. When he raises Lazarus from the dead, Mary responds with gratitude and anoints Jesus' feet, while the Jewish authorities see the sign's potential to destabilize the political situation and determine to end his career. In each case, the response of a person or group discloses character.

The studies in the present volume also recognize that other interpretive frameworks are needed to encompass the range of characters in the narrative. Many modern readers are familiar with E. M. Forster's distinction between "round" and "flat" characters. Flat characters are types who personify a single quality or idea, and they do not exhibit any real change or development in the narrative. By way of contrast, round characters are more complex. They have multiple traits and do undergo change as the narrative unfolds. As a way of developing this framework, the studies in this volume generally favor the idea of a spectrum of possibilities for assessing characters in John's gospel. The contributors label the options differently, but they tend to see a continuum of perspectives ranging from more simple to more complex portrayals, and from depictions that seem more static to those that are more dynamic.

When approaching particular characters in the gospel, it is helpful to turn the spectrum of interpretive options into questions. For example, how clear or ambiguous is the depiction of a certain figure? In the past, studies of Johannine characters have tended to see people and groups as types, who exemplify positive and negative responses to Jesus. The gospel's dualistic language seems to invite such clear categorization by contrasting those who remain in darkness with those who come to the light, those who believe in Jesus and have life with those who do not believe and are condemned (3:19–21).

But more recent work has tended to draw out the ambiguous elements. It is striking that the dualistic contrast between light and darkness is part of Jesus' encounter with Nicodemus, who is one of the gospel's most enigmatic figures. The setting of the encounter is at night (3:2), but does that mean Nicodemus is simply in darkness or does the encounter suggest that he is coming to Jesus the light? His questions show that he does not understand Jesus, yet he does not reject Jesus. So where does that leave us as readers? Are we able to categorize him neatly or not? If not, what does that mean for our understanding of the gospel as a whole?

The tension between clarity and ambiguity plays a role in the study of other characters as well. Some, like John the Baptist, seem to have consistently positive roles, but what about Simon Peter? His confession of faith (6:68–69) is positive and his denial of Jesus (18:15–27) is negative, his response to the foot washing is well intended but misguided (13:6–9), and his response to the empty tomb seems inconclusive (20:1–10). The complexity in portrayal resists easy categorization and draws readers more deeply into the challenges facing such a disciple. The same complexity applies to the gospel's portrayal of the Jews. There are some passages in which they seem unequivocally hostile to Jesus, but at other points they show a lack of unanimity and greater openness to asking questions. Given the tensions within the portrayal, are readers simply to regard them as negative, or are they to see traces of genuine struggle within the group?

A second question that recurs in this collection of studies concerns the continuum from static to dynamic portrayals of character. Interpreters have regularly pointed out the aspect of development in a figure like the man born blind, who progresses from blindness and silence through conflict with Jewish leaders to worshiping Jesus as the Son of Man. The movement seems clear and it takes a full chapter to complete. But asking about development is also helpful when considering figures who are depicted more briefly. For example, the Galilean official appears in just nine verses, but in that short span of narrative he moves from desperation to hearing Jesus' promise and then to belief. By way of contrast, the invalid at Bethzatha appears in an episode of comparable length, but he seems incapable of change. His static quality is perhaps his most notable trait. That in turn invites reflection on why some characters seem capable of change while others are not; and the writers of these essays leave us as readers of the volume to explore that for ourselves.

One of the most valuable aspects of this collection is the extent of its coverage. In addition to the studies of major figures, there is careful attention to the cast of minor characters, who contribute to the narrative in ways we often overlook. Sometimes a minor character is mentioned in only one or two verses, in which the person says or does something that advances the story. Such brief references mean that the characterization will be simple rather than complex, and will not involve any real development. As readers, we naturally give our attention to those who are at the center of the story, but pausing to reflect on the minor figures—whom we so often overlook—encourages us to consider an encounter from multiple points of view. The exercise is valuable for scholars, teachers, and preachers, all of whom face the challenge of reading the text in fresh and stimulating ways.

At the wedding at Cana, for example, Jesus is the center of the episode (2:1–11). His mother plays a key supporting role by prompting his action and eliciting his comment about the coming "hour," and the disciples complete the scene by exhibiting belief. But what would it mean to give attention to the servants, who silently go about their work in the background? When we trouble ourselves to look at them, we find that a primary trait is responsiveness. They listen to Jesus' mother, and then to Jesus himself, as they are given successive tasks to perform. Another trait is insightfulness; they know the source of the wine. By way of contrast, the chief steward is a minor character who speaks but exhibits misplaced insight. He is correct that the wine is excellent but incorrect in assuming that the groom provided it. Finally, the bridegroom is a minor character who listens to the steward's incorrect assumption without saying anything. If we linger for a moment at the bridegroom's silence, we may find ourselves wanting to draw the servants more directly into the story, because they have the needed insight: It was not this bridegroom but Jesus who provides the gift.

Working with the minor characters helps us attend to details that we might otherwise overlook. For example, the account of Jesus' arrest is dominated by Jesus and the disciples, Judas, and the soldiers. But in the thick of the action is a slave, whose ear Peter cuts off. Initially the slave is anonymous, but later he receives a name, Malchus, which underscores a sense of identity (18:10). Later, in the high priest's courtyard, we learn that he had relatives in the area; he was part of a family network (18:26). During the arrest it is clear that Malchus belongs to the high priest and is therefore among Jesus' opponents, yet after Peter attacks Malchus, Jesus intervenes and identifies Peter as the one in the wrong (18:11). Focusing for a moment on Malchus calls attention to the bewildering shifts within the narrative as Jesus redefines the roles of victim and victimizer, and at the same time clarifies the nature of his own obedience to the will of his Father.

Studies of John's gospel have often given a central role to Christology, yet among these studies of seventy characters there is no specific chapter on Jesus. He is present throughout the collection but is not a topic of study in his own right. This omission does not downplay the importance of Jesus in the narrative, but it spreads our attention more widely, so perceptions of Jesus are consistently shaped by his interactions with other characters. This approach can be valuable for those whose primary interest is in the depiction of Jesus, because it ensures that any attempt to construct a portrait of him will need to synthesize multiple angles of vision. Jesus draws out character traits from those he encounters in the narrative, but the reverse is also true: the many characters—major and minor—also draw out aspects of Jesus' character. Studies of the characterization of Jesus can rightly develop insights that are presented here, asking how the gospel presents him not only in relation to his primary followers and opponents, but also in relation to the steward at the wedding banquet and to the high priest's slave in the garden.

The essays in this volume are contributions to the vibrant conversation about the characters in John's gospel. Each one offers valuable insights into the individuals and groups we encounter in the narrative, and each invites continuing reflection and dialogue in the future. This collection is organized in a way that provides a reference tool for those working on particular passages, while its multifaceted approach helps to stimulate the reader's ongoing engagement with the Fourth Gospel itself. The studies invite all of us to become participants in the process of reading and interpreting John's text.

CRAIG R. KOESTER

An Introduction to Character and Characterization in John and Related New Testament Literature

Steven A. Hunt, D. Francois Tolmie, and Ruben Zimmermann

1. Theoretical Approaches to Character and Characterization: A Brief Overview

Over the centuries scholars have grappled with the interpretation of character and characterization in texts. Issues that surfaced regularly include the relationship between character(s) and actions/plot; whether characters should be regarded as people or words, and how one should classify characters. This brief overview will highlight some of the responses to these and other issues.

For *Aristotle*, action was more important than character, because, according to him, one could not have a tragedy without action, but one could have a tragedy without character.[1] Accordingly, since antiquity it has become common to describe characters in terms of their actions in a narrative, for example by using terms such as "protagonist" for the main character, and "antagonist" for his/her most important opponent.[2] In the nineteenth century, more emphasis was placed on characters themselves, for example by *Leslie Stephen*, for whom the primary purpose of narrative was to reveal characters; and by *Henry James*, who argued that one could not separate characters and action, since they actually melted into one another.[3] In the nineteenth century the distinction between *direct* and *indirect characterization* also came to the fore, with some critics highlighting the fact that contemporary authors and readers seemed to prefer the latter.[4]

Early in the twentieth century *Edward M. Forster*[5] introduced the distinction between so-called "flat" and "round" characters. According to Forster,

---

[1] *Poetics* 1450a. Cf. Jens Eder, Fotis Jannidis and Ralf Schneider, *Characters in Fictional Worlds: Understanding Imaginary Beings in Literature, Film, and Other Media* (Revisionen 3; Berlin: De Gruyter, 2010), 20.

[2] Eder, Jannidis, Schneider, *Characters in Fictional Worlds*, 20.

[3] Horace P. Abbott, *The Cambridge Introduction to Narrative* (Cambridge: Cambridge University Press, 2002), 124.

[4] Fotis Jannidis, "Character," in *Handbook of Narratology* (ed. Peter Hühn et al.; Narratologia; Contributions to Narrative Theory 19; Berlin: De Gruyter, 2009), 21.

[5] Edward M. Forster, *Aspects of the Novel* (New York: Harcourt Brace, 1927), 67–78.

"flat" characters are caricatures or types that embody only a single idea or quality. Furthermore, they do not display any development in the course of the narrative. "Round characters," on the other hand, are complex characters who have more than one quality (trait) and who show signs of development. In order to establish a criterion for deciding whether a character should be classified as round or flat, Forster suggested that a character that is capable of surprising the reader in a convincing way, should be classified as a round character. In spite of criticism raised by scholars on the usefulness of this distinction,[6] it has remained one of the most popular classifications of character up to the present day.

Vladimir Propp[7] – considered by many as the founder of Structuralism – investigated 100 Russian folktales and identified a sequence of 31 events underlying all of them. Propp also distinguished eight character types in these tales: the hero, helper, villain, false hero, donor (the person who helps the hero by giving him something special), the dispatcher (the one who sends the hero on his mission), the princess and the princess' father. Propp's approach was later generalized by Greimas (see further, below)

In their well-known book, *Theory of Literature*, *René Wellek and Austin Warren*[8] discuss a large number of issues which are important for the study of literature in general. A section on narrative fiction is also included.[9] They point out that plot, character and setting are the three constituents of narrative fiction, with each of the three elements being determinant of the others. In their discussion of character, they focus primarily on characterization. For example, they point out that naming is the simplest form of characterization, but that many other modes of characterization exist, such as block characterization, introductory labels and mimicry. They also distinguish between static and dynamic (or developmental) characterization. These two categories overlap to a large degree with the distinction between flat and round characters which was introduced by Forster. Finally, they point out that there is a connection between characterization and characterology (theories of character and personality types) and that one often finds a "repertory company" in novels, namely the hero, heroine and the villain who function as the "character

---

[6] For example, that the criteria are formulated so vaguely that it really is very difficult to apply them fruitfully to Biblical texts, or that the distinction between "flat" and "round" may imply a moral judgment of the characters, in the sense that round characters are usually considered as being superior to flat characters. Cf. Klaus D. Beekman and Jan Fontijn, "Roman-Figuren I," *Spektator* 1 (1971): 406–13.

[7] Propp's study was published in 1928 in Russian, and thirty years later in English as Vladimir J. Propp, *Morphology of the Folktale* (Bloomington, Ind.: Research Center, Indiana Univ, 1958).

[8] René Wellek and Austin Warren, *Theory of Literature* (repr.; London: Jonathan Cape, 1961 [1949]).

[9] Wellek and Warren, *Theory of Literature*, 224–234.

actors." Other types of characters that are often used are "juveniles, and ingénues and the elderly."[10]

W. J. Harvey[11] devoted a whole book to character in the novel, based on a mimetic approach. In the first part[12] of this book, several constituents of character are discussed. He begins by indicating how important context is for interpreting character, in particular the various types of relationships that can exist between people and objects. In the next chapter[13] the human context is considered, which is approached from the perspective of depth, i. e., the extent to which characters stand out from other human beings. In this regard Harvey distinguishes between several categories of characters: on the one end of the scale are the protagonists (the important characters in the narrative), with background characters at the other end of the scale (their only function being to fulfill a role in the mechanics of the plot); while in between, two types of intermediary characters are found: cards (characters who approach greatness, but who are not cast into the role of protagonists) and *ficelles* (characterized more extensively than the background characters, yet only existing with the purpose of fulfilling certain functions within the narrative). The last constituent issue that Harvey discusses is the relationship between character and narration,[14] in particular the effect that reliable and unreliable narrators may have on the portrayal of characters.

Based on the work of Propp, *Algirdas J. Greimas*[15] proposed the actantial model, according to which all characters are viewed as expressions of an underlying structure, even if this implies that the same actant is manifested in more than one character, or that more than one character should be reduced to the same actant. The six actants are divided into three groups, each forming an actantial axis: the axis of desire (subject and object; the relationship between subject and object is called a junction); the axis of power (helper – the one who helps in achieving the junction, and opponent – the one who opposes the junction), and the axis of knowledge (sender – the one who instigates the action, and receiver – the one who benefits from the action). By means of actantial analysis the action in narrative texts may then be analyzed.

Robert Scholes and Robert Kellogg[16] argue that there are three different ways of representing reality, and that one can distinguish between three types of

---

[10] Wellek and Warren, *Theory of Literature*, 228.
[11] William J. Harvey, *Character and the Novel* (London: Chatto & Windus, 1965).
[12] Harvey, *Character and the Novel*, 30–51.
[13] Harvey, *Character and the Novel*, 52–73.
[14] Harvey, *Character and the Novel*, 74–79.
[15] Algirdas J. Greimas, *Sémantique structurale: Recherche de méthode* (Paris: Librairie Larousse, 1966), 172–91.
[16] Robert Scholes and Robert Kellogg, *The Nature of Narrative* (repr.; Oxford: Oxford University Press, 1975 [1966]), 87–91.

characterization: aesthetic, illustrative and mimetic. In the case of aesthetic characterization, characters are used as stock types; illustrative characterization is used when characters are employed to illustrate particular principles, but are not characterized in detail; mimetic characterization is used when characters are portrayed in a highly realistic fashion with numerous details. In another chapter,[17] they argue that one should not regard a particular order of characterization as being better than any other; for example "monolithic and stark"[18] characterization can be just as impressive as detailed characterization. They also point out that the notion of a developing character is a factor that only came to the fore rather late in the history of literature; characters in primitive stories were all flat, static and opaque. The importance of the portrayal of inward life in the type of characterization that is used in modern literature is also pointed out.

According to *Roland G. Barthes*,[19] characters in a narrative text should be regarded in terms of the web of "semes" (basic units of signification) that are attached to a particular proper name. In *S/Z*, his famous analysis of Balzac's novel *Sarrasine*, Barthes illustrates how a text may be analyzed in terms of the five codes or "voices" speaking from it at the same time, namely the proairetic, hermeneutic, referential, semic and symbolic codes.[20] Of these, the fourth one, the semic code (also known as the connotative code), is important for characterization. According to Barthes, the semic code in a text enables the reader to label persons in the text in an adjectival way as persons with certain traits. On the basis of the semic code, various semes in the text are collected and linked to a particular proper name, thereby constituting character.[21]

For *Jurij Lotman*,[22] a text is a stratified system which generates meaning by means of sets of similarities and oppositions. A character may thus be regarded as the sum of all its oppositions to other characters in the text. Furthermore, all the characters in a text form a collection of characters who either display similar traits or who manifest opposing traits.

Seymour Chatman[23] opts for an "open theory," treating characters as "autonomous beings," and not merely in terms of the functions that they fulfill in relation to the plot. He focuses on the way in which characters are con-

---

[17] Scholes and Kellogg, *Nature of Narrative*, 160–206.
[18] Scholes and Kellogg, *Nature of Narrative*, 163.
[19] Roland G. Barthes, *S/Z* (Paris: Seuil, 1970).
[20] Barthes, *S/Z*, XII (27–29).
[21] Barthes, *S/Z*, XL–XLVI (98–113).
[22] Cf. Jurij Lotman, *The Structure of the Artistic Text* (trans. G. Lenhoff and R. Vroon; Michigan Slavic Contributions 7; Ann Arbor: University of Michigan, 1977). The summary of Lotman's views above is based upon Jannidis, "Character," 16–17.
[23] Seymour Chatman, *Story and Discourse: Narrative Structure in Fiction and Film* (Ithaca, N. Y.: Cornell University Press, 1978), 121–30.

structed by the reader, and views a character as a "paradigm of traits" constructed by the reader, a trait being any relatively stable or abiding personal quality that is associated with a character. As such, the traits associated with a particular character may be unfolded, or replaced, or may even disappear in the course of the narrative.

Mieke Bal[24] distinguishes between actors (on the level of the *fabula* – the events organized and structured by aspects such as time, location and actors) and characters (on the level of the story, formed by aspects such as point of view, focalization and characters). For the analysis of the actors, she basically follows the distinctions made by Greimas, i. e., between subject and object, sender and receiver, and helper and opponent.[25] For the analysis of the characters, she emphasizes aspects such as the predictability of characters and the way in which the reader's attention is focused on the relevant traits of a particular character, namely by means of repetition, accumulation and the portrayal of its relationship with other characters.[26]

Baruch Hochman[27] agrees with Chatman on the process of abstracting characters from a text, further pointing out that there is a congruity between the way in which readers perceive characters in a text and the way in which they think of people in the real world. Hochman also stresses the large variety of ways in which information about characters is revealed in texts: "speech, gesture, actions, thoughts, dress, and surroundings; the company they keep and the objects and subjects they desire, abhor, and equivocate about; the images and associations they stir in our consciousness, including the epithets that we apply to them."[28] Furthermore, he proposes a different taxonomy for characters, consisting of eight categories, each representing a continuum with two polar opposites: stylization/naturalism, coherence/incoherence, wholeness/fragmentariness, literalness/symbolism, complexity/simplicity, transparency/opacity, dynamism/staticism and closure/openness.[29]

In her book on narratology, *Shlomith Rimmon-Kenan*[30] distinguishes between story, text and narration (as Mieke Bal does), with characters being considered on two levels, namely the level of the story, and that of the text. In

---

[24] Mieke Bal, *De Theorie van Vertellen en Verhalen: Inleiding in de Narratologie* (Muiderberg: Dick Coutinho, 1978), 33–46, 87–100. Newest (revised) English version: Mieke Bal, *Narratology: Introduction to the Theory of Narrative* (3d ed.; Toronto: University of Toronto Press, 2009).

[25] Bal, *De Theorie van Vertellen en Verhalen*, 33–46.

[26] Bal, *De Theorie van Vertellen en Verhalen*, 87–100.

[27] Baruch Hochman, *Character in Literature* (Ithaca, N. Y.: Cornell University Press, 1985), 16.

[28] Hochman, *Character in Literature*, 38.

[29] Hochman, *Character in Literature*, 89.

[30] Shlomith Rimmon-Kenan, *Narrative Fiction: Contemporary Poetics* (London: Metheuen, 1983), 29–42, 59–70. Second edition: Shlomith Rimmon-Kenan, *Narrative Fiction: Contemporary Poetics* (2d ed.; London: Routledge, 2002).

her discussion of characters on the level of the story, she follows Chatman: Characters are construed by the reader from the text in terms of a paradigm of traits associated with every character. She also points out that this is a process of generalization, in that elements are combined in "increasingly broader categories."[31] In this regard, cohesion is achieved by four aspects, namely repetition, similarity, contrast and implication of elements. With regard to character classification, she follows Joseph Ewen,[32] who classifies characters in terms of three continua, namely complexity, development and penetration into inner life.[33] On the level of the text, Rimmon-Kenan focuses on the process of characterization. Two issues are discussed.[34] First, a distinction is made between two types of textual indicators of character, namely direct definition (the naming of a character's qualities) and indirect presentation, which may be effectuated by the representation of action, speech, external appearance and the environment within which a character is portrayed. Secondly, reinforcement by analogy is discussed. Three ways in which characterization can be reinforced are mentioned: analogous names, analogous landscapes and analogy between characters.

Of the many contributions to the theoretical consideration of characterization made by *Uri Margolin*, the following three are highlighted: In one contribution, Margolin[35] points out that characters may be approached from three different theoretical perspectives: as literary figures (constructed by an author for a particular purpose), as individuals within a possible world, and as constructs in a reader's mind, based on a text. In another contribution,[36] Margolin focuses on the way in which readers ascribe mental properties to characters. In this regard he distinguishes between "characterization" and "character-building." The former refers to the inferences made by readers from the actions of characters, and is the primary process involved. The latter is a secondary process, which refers to the accumulation of individual properties, in particular to a process of "classification, hierarchisation and confrontation,"[37] and the combination of such properties into a unified constellation. In a further contribution,[38] Margolin outlines five conditions which need to be fulfilled if characters

---

[31] Rimmon-Kenan, *Narrative Fiction*, 39.
[32] Joseph Ewen, "The Theory of Character in Narrative Fiction (Hebrew)," *Hasifrut* 3 (1971): 1–30.
[33] Rimmon-Kenan, *Narrative Fiction*, 40–41.
[34] Rimmon-Kenan, *Narrative Fiction*, 59–70.
[35] Uri Margolin, "Character," in *The Cambridge Companion to Narrative* (ed. David Herman; Cambridge: Cambridge University Press, 2007), 66–79.
[36] Uri Margolin, "Characterization in Narrative: Some Theoretical Prolegomena," *Neophilologus* 67 (1983): 1–14.
[37] Margolin, "Characterization in Narrative," 4.
[38] Uri Margolin, "Introducing and Sustaining Characters in Literary Narrative," *Style* 21/1 (1987): 107–24.

are to be introduced and sustained in a narrative. Three examples: existential dimension (a character must "exist" in the narrative world), intentional dimension (a character must have some traits or properties), and uniqueness (a character must differ in some way from other characters).

In contrast to the structuralist and semiotic approaches that have dominated theoretical approaches to character, *James Phelan*[39] opts for a rhetorical approach, emphasizing the text as communication between author and reader, and the effect that narrative progression has on the way in which a reader understands characters, and is moved to various ways of relating to particular characters. In his view, characters are "multichromatic" – literary elements composed of three components, namely mimetic, thematic and synthetic elements, with the possibility of the first two elements being developed in different ways, and of the third element being foregrounded in different ways.[40] The mimetic element refers to the way in which characters are recognizable as images of real people; the thematic element to the way in which characters may express significant attitudes or be representative figures; while the synthetic element refers to the fact that characters are always artificial, in the sense that they are constructed from the text. In his discussion of narrative progression, Phelan also emphasizes "instabilities" in the text, of which he distinguishes two kinds, namely instabilities occurring within the story, for example instabilities between characters, and, secondly, instabilities created by the discourse, for example instabilities between the author and the reader.[41]

Fotis Jannidis[42] made quite a number of contributions to the study of character of which some are highlighted here: A character is defined as follows: "Die Figur ist ein mentales Modell eines Modell-Lesers, das inkremental im Fortgang des Textes gebildet wird."[43] According to Jannidis, this model presupposes a basic type according to which a distinction is made between internal being and external appearance, with external appearance being observable by other characters as well as the narrator, whereas internal being is observable to the narrator only. With regard to the nature of the information on characters that is provided in a text, Jannidis[44] identifies four important dimensions: reliability, mode, relevance and straightforwardness. The process of character-

---

[39] James Phelan, *Reading People, Reading Plots: Character, Progression, and the Interpretation of Narrative* (Chicago: University of Chicago Press, 1989), 1–23. See also James Phelan, *Narrative as Rhetoric: Technique, Audiences, Ethics, Ideology* (Columbus: Ohio State University Press, 1996).
[40] Phelan, *Narrative as Rhetoric*, 3.
[41] Phelan, *Narrative as Rhetoric*, 15.
[42] Fotis Jannidis, *Figur und Person: Beitrag zu einer historischen Narratologie* (Narratologia 3; Berlin: de Gruyter, 2004).
[43] Jannidis, *Figur und Person*, 240.
[44] Jannidis, *Figur und Person*, 201–207.

ization is also discussed in detail. According to Jannidis,[45] some of the issues that are important in this regard include how long and how often a particular character is characterized; the extent to which the sources of information with regard to a character are mixed; how often the same information about a character is provided; the order in which the information about a particular character is revealed; whether everything about a character is revealed at once or whether it is distributed throughout the text; how information about a character is linked to other information that is provided; and which information about a character is linked to other characters.

Jens Eder's[46] book is devoted to characters in films, but contains much about character analysis in general. The two basic theoretical issues that he discusses are how one can analyze characters in a systematic way and how one can explain the various ways in which viewers of films experience characters. The model that he proposes for character consists of four aspects, and is called a "clock" ("Uhr") of character.[47] The four aspects are: characters as artifacts, fictional beings, symbols and symptoms. If one focuses on characters as artifacts, the questions investigated typically concern composition and textual aspects, and characters are classified as realistic or multi-dimensional.[48] When characters are considered as fictional beings, the focus falls on the properties that characters possess and how they act within a fictional world.[49] When characters are analyzed as symbols, one asks the question as to whether characters stand for something, for example whether they represent a deeper or even an allegorical meaning.[50] When characters are considered in terms of symptoms, the focal issues is that of how characters are "caused;" in other words, which effects were used to produce them.[51] According to Eder, scholars tend to concentrate on one aspect only, namely characters as fictional beings. By means of the model that he proposes, one is encouraged to investigate other issues as well.

This brief overview has highlighted some of the developments and approaches with regard to characterization. Many of these have had an influence on the way in which Biblical scholars approach characterization. This will be illustrated in the next two sections.

---

[45] Jannidis, *Figur und Person*, 220–21.
[46] Jens Eder, *Die Figur im Film: Grundlagen der Figurenanalyse* (Marburg: Schüren, 2008).
[47] Eder, *Die Figur im Film*, 131–42.
[48] Eder, *Die Figur im Film*, 322–425.
[49] Eder, *Die Figur im Film*, 426–520.
[50] Eder, *Die Figur im Film*, 529–41.
[51] Eder, *Die Figur im Film*, 541–53.

2. Approaches to Character and Characterization in Biblical Studies

Over the years numerous studies of a more general nature dealing with characterization in Biblical literature have been published. In this section a brief overview of some of these studies will be offered, with a focus on the approach to characters/characterization that has been followed in each instance.

Robert Alter[52] points out the different ways in which a character may be revealed: through actions, appearance, gesture, posture, costume, the comments that a character makes about other characters, direct speech, inward speech, and statements by the narrator. Furthermore, he draws attention to the order of explicitness that can be detected in the way in which characters are presented: when only actions or appearance are narrated, one is in the realm of inference; when the direct speech of a character is reported, one moves from inference to the weighing of claims; when inward speech is narrated, one may be relatively certain that one's interpretation of a character is correct; and when a reliable narrator's statements are used for the purpose of characterization, one has certainty about this issue. Alter illustrates this by discussing 1 Sam 18, where Saul is characterized directly by the narrator, whereas David is characterized by means derived from the lower end of the scale.

In her study on the interpretation of Biblical narrative, *Adele Berlin*[53] focuses on two issues pertaining to character, namely character types and characterization. With regard to character types, she distinguishes between three types of characters, instead of the usual two types (flat and round characters): full-fledged characters (normally called "round characters"), types (normally called "flat characters") and functionaries (characters who are not characterized at all, and who only have to fulfill a particular role or function). With regard to characterization, she identifies a number of techniques that are used in this regard: description, portrayal of inner life, speech and actions and contrast. She also points out that in most cases in Biblical narrative, characterization is achieved by a combination of some or all of these techniques.

For *Meir Sternberg*,[54] the process of reading is important when characterization is considered. Such a reading process might be quite intricate: "So reading a character becomes a process of discovery, attended by all the biblical hallmarks: progressive reconstruction, tentative closure of discontinuities, frequent and sometimes painful reshaping in the face of the unexpected, and intractable pock-

---

[52] Robert Alter, *The Art of Biblical Narrative* (London: George Allen & Unwin, 1981), 114–30.
[53] Adele Berlin, *Poetics and Interpretation of Biblical Narrative* (Bible and Literature; Sheffield: Almond Press, 1983), 23–42.
[54] Meir Sternberg, *The Poetics of Biblical Narrative: Ideological Literature and the Drama of Reading* (Indiana Literary Biblical Studies; Bloomington, Ind.: Indiana University Press, 1985), 321–322.

ets of darkness."⁵⁵ He first focuses on direct characterization, *inter alia* by pointing out three varieties: "complete but stylized insight into a simple or simplified character," "partial revelation of a complex and otherwise opaque character," and "the depiction of externals, for which the transparent and the intricate are equally eligible."⁵⁶ In his discussion of indirect characterization, Sternberg⁵⁷ draws particular attention to the way in which indirect characterization may be used for portrayal that is aimed at moving beyond a characteristic that has already been indicated by means of an epithet, for example in cases where the indirect characterization is discontinuous with direct epithetic characterization.

For *Shimon Bar-Efrat*,⁵⁸ a character in literature is the "sum of the means used in the description;"⁵⁹ it is thus created by the portrayal. Accordingly, he focuses on the two ways in which characters may be shaped, namely directly and indirectly. With regard to direct shaping of characters, two techniques are discussed and illustrated, namely that of outward appearance and that of inner personality.⁶⁰ With regard to indirect shaping of characters, three techniques are identified, namely portrayal of speech, actions and subsidiary characters.⁶¹

*Mark Allan Powell*⁶² points out that characters are constructs of an implied author and that they are created in order to play a particular role in the narrative. Several issues with regard to characterization are then discussed in more detail. The distinction between telling and showing is highlighted; and it is also pointed out that in the Gospels, the technique of showing is favored to a large extent. Furthermore, the evaluative point of view that a character or group of characters in a narrative may have is discussed. Powell also endorses Chatman's definition of characters in terms of a paradigm of traits. With regard to the classification of characters, Powell follows Forster's well-known definition, adding one type, the stock character⁶³ (a character having a single trait only). Lastly, he indicates how empathy, sympathy, and antipathy towards characters are created.

In their discussion of character in the Hebrew Bible, *David Gunn and Danna Nolan Fewell*⁶⁴ proceed from the assumption that characters are not

---

[55] Sternberg, *Poetics of Biblical Narrative*, 323–24.
[56] Sternberg, *Poetics of Biblical Narrative*, 326.
[57] Sternberg, *Poetics of Biblical Narrative*, 342–64.
[58] Shimon Bar-Efrat, *Narrative Art in the Bible* (JSOT 17; Sheffield: Almond, 1989). This study was first published in Hebrew in 1979. First English publication: 1989.
[59] Bar-Efrat, *Narrative Art*, 48.
[60] Bar-Efrat, *Narrative Art*, 48–63.
[61] Bar-Efrat, *Narrative Art*, 64–91.
[62] Mark Allan Powell, *What Is Narrative Criticism?* (Guides to Biblical Scholarship; Minneapolis: Fortress, 1990), 51–61.
[63] Powell here follows Meyer H. Abrams, *A Glossary of Literary Terms* (4th ed.; New York: Holt, Rhinehart and Winston, 1981), 185.
[64] David M. Gunn and Danna N. Fewell, *Narrative in the Hebrew Bible* (Oxford Bible Series; Oxford: Oxford University Press, 1993), 51.

real people, but are constructed from the text. They then highlight the two sources of information pertaining to character, namely the narrator and the characters themselves. With regard to the narrator's role, three aspects are pointed out: the relationship between the reliability of the narrator and characterization; how description by the narrator may be used to characterize; and the possible effect of the evaluation of characters by the narrator.[65] With regard to characterization by characters themselves, three issues are distinguished: first, the possible role that may be played by a character's speech, as well as by the context and the use of contrast; secondly, how the responses by characters and their reliability influence characterization; and, thirdly, the effect of issues such as contradiction between various sources of information about a character, difference in points of view between narrator and character(s), and irony.[66] Finally, Forster's distinction between round and flat characters is adopted, followed by two remarks, namely that readers relate more easily to round characters, and that a character that may be a flat character in one episode may be a round character in the next.[67]

Jan Fokkelman[68] highlights the relationship between characters and the narrator who is "the boss of the complete circus,"[69] "the veritable ringmaster."[70] After a discussion and several illustrations of the fact that narrator and characters operate at different levels, the various ways in which readers may discover the deceit of characters are discussed.[71] This is followed by a discussion of the difference between character text (direct speech of characters) and the narrator's text.[72]

In their contribution to the analysis of characters in Biblical texts, *Daniel Marguerat and Yvan Bourquin*[73] attempt to combine two approaches, namely that of regarding characters as agents (as, for example Propp has done) and that of viewing characters as autonomous beings (as Chatman has done). For the classification of characters, the models of Forster and Greimas are recommended.[74] Another issue that is dealt with is the question as to why readers are captivated by characters. According to Marguerat and Bourquin, the more

---

[65] Gunn and Fewell, *Narrative in the Hebrew Bible*, 53–63.
[66] Gunn and Fewell, *Narrative in the Hebrew Bible*, 63–75.
[67] Gunn and Fewell, *Narrative in the Hebrew Bible*, 75–76.
[68] Jan Fokkelman, *Reading Biblical Narrative: An Introductory Guide* (trans. I. Smit; Louisville, Ky.: Westminster John Knox, 1999). Originally published in Dutch, 1995. First English publication: 1999.
[69] Fokkelman, *Reading Biblical Narrative*, 55.
[70] Fokkelman, *Reading Biblical Narrative*, 56.
[71] Fokkelman, *Reading Biblical Narrative*, 60–67.
[72] Fokkelman, *Reading Biblical Narrative*, 67–72.
[73] Daniel Marguerat and Yvan Bourquin, *How to Read Bible Stories: An Introduction to Narrative Criticism* (London: SCM, 1999), 58–59.
[74] Marguerat and Bourquin, *How to Read Bible Stories*, 62–63.

characters resemble real beings, the more attractive they become to readers.[75] Two further issues that are discussed concern the use of an evaluative point of view by the narrator to influence readers' perception of characters, and the well-known difference between telling and showing of characters.[76] Finally, the relative positions of readers vis-à-vis characters in terms of knowing more than, less than, or just as much as a character knows are identified, and the way in which focalization and the focalized may be used in characterization is discussed.[77]

Francois Tolmie's[78] approach to the study of characters in Biblical narratives is based on that of Rimmon-Kenan. Two issues are discussed and illustrated, namely the process of characterization and the classification of characters. With regard to the process of characterization, Chatman's definition of character as a paradigm of traits is adopted, and techniques of direct and indirect characterization are discussed.[79] With regard to the classification of characters, four different systems are discussed and illustrated, namely those of Forster, Harvey, Ewen and Greimas.[80]

In her contribution, *Yairah Amit*[81] focuses on three aspects: the classification of characters, the process of characterization, and the role of the reader. With regard to classification she follows Berlin, distinguishing between types, flat characters, and round characters. With regard to characterization she discusses the difference between direct and indirect characterization and provides examples of each. In her discussion of the role of the reader, she focuses on the way in which a reader can determine who the main character in a narrative is, namely by concentrating on four aspects: the focus of interest, as well as quantitative, structural and thematic indications.

James L. Resseguie[82] first discusses aspects of characterization. He begins with Forster's distinction between round and flat characters, adding three other character types, namely stocks, foils, and walk-ons.[83] This is followed by a distinction between dynamic and static characters.[84] Subsequently, the distinction between showing and telling is considered. In this regard, Chatman's

---

[75] Marguerat and Bourquin, *How to Read Bible Stories*, 65–66.
[76] Marguerat and Bourquin, *How to Read Bible Stories*, 68–70.
[77] Marguerat and Bourquin, *How to Read Bible Stories*, 71–72.
[78] D. Francois Tolmie, *Narratology and Biblical Narratives: A Practical Guide* (San Francisco: International Scholars Publications, 1999).
[79] Tolmie, *Narratology*, 41–52.
[80] Tolmie, *Narratology*, 53–60.
[81] Yairah Amit, *Reading Biblical Narratives: Literary Criticism and the Hebrew Bible* (Minneapolis: Fortress, 2001), 69–92.
[82] James L. Resseguie, *Narrative Criticism of the New Testament: An Introduction* (Grand Rapids, Mich.: Baker Academic, 2005).
[83] Resseguie, *Narrative Criticism*, 123–25.
[84] Resseguie, *Narrative Criticism*, 126–27.

definition of character traits is also introduced.[85] Finally, the focus falls on Alter's scale of means, according to which a distinction is made between more and less explicit forms of characterization.[86] In the illustration of the analysis of Biblical characters that follows, Resseguie highlights two aspects, namely marginalized and dominant characters.[87]

After providing a thorough overview of the way scholars approach the analysis of character, *Sönke Finnern*[88] proposes a methodology for the analysis of Biblical characters that focuses on the following six aspects: 1. collection of and relationship between characters (issues relating to the identification of characters in a particular scene and classification of characters in terms of main and subsidiary figures); 2. character traits (issues that are relevant to the traits associated with characters and the personality of characters); 3. constellation of figures (pertaining to aspects such as the particular group to which characters belong and the hierarchy between characters); 4. character and action (issues such as the importance of a particular character for the events that are narrated and the function that a particular character fulfills); 5. characterization (issues such as the techniques used to characterize and the extent to which characterization is convincing); and 6. conceptualization[89] of characters (issues such as whether a character is flat or round).

3. Studies on Character and Characterization in the Synoptic Gospels and Acts

Since the 1980s several hundred narrative-critical/narratological studies of the Gospels and Acts have been published. Some of these are highlighted below. Since it is impossible to provide a comprehensive overview of all the studies that have been conducted in this regard in a brief survey such as this, no attempt will be made to do so. Instead, the emphasis will fall on a different objective, namely to illustrate the different approaches to characterization that have been followed, as well as the wide scope of characters that have already been investigated.

---

[85] Resseguie, *Narrative Criticism*, 126–30.
[86] Resseguie, *Narrative Criticism*, 130–32.
[87] Resseguie, *Narrative Criticism*, 137–65.
[88] Sönke Finnern, *Narratologie und Biblische Exegese: Eine integrative Methode der Erzählanalyse und ihr Ertrag am Beispiel von Matthäus* (WUNT 285; Tübingen: Mohr Siebeck, 2010), 162–64.
[89] Our translation of "Figurenkonzeption"; Finnern, *Narratologie und Biblische Exegese*, 164.

3.1 The Four Gospels and Acts

James L. Resseguie[90] approaches characterization in terms of "defamiliarization," i. e., the techniques that are used to make what is well-known appear unfamiliar. According to him, when one applies this to the Gospels, one should be on the lookout for "a perceptible clash between the expected and the unexpected, the ordinary and the habitual, the novel and the strange."[91] He then shows how techniques of defamiliarization are used in the Four Gospels to characterize, and distinguishes and illustrates three types in this regard: comic defamiliarization, ironic defamiliarization and voluntary status reversal.[92]

One of the issues investigated by *Helen K. Bond*[93] in her study on Pontius Pilate pertains to the different ways in which he is characterized in the Four Gospels (and also by Philo and Josephus). According to her, the Pilate of Mark's Gospel is a skilful politician who manipulates the crowd; Mathew's Pilate is indifferent to Jesus and allows the Jewish leaders to do with him as they wish; Luke's Pilate represents Roman law, which officially declares Jesus innocent, yet also allows the leaders of the Jewish nation to force him to condemn Jesus despite his innocence; and John's Pilate is manipulative, derisive and very much aware of the authority that he has over Jesus.[94]

In his study of the characterization of Peter in the Four Gospels, *Timothy Wiarda*[95] focuses on two aspects, namely distance and individualization. The first aspect refers to the level of involvement between Peter and the reader. The second aspect is linked to the traits associated with Peter in each Gospel, which are classified in terms of five levels, namely information about group, class or occupational type; stereotypical traits/feelings; distinctive external information; distinctive traits/feelings, and distinctive complexity.[96] On the basis of this approach, Wiarda compiles a list of eighteen traits of Peter in the Four Gospels.[97]

In a contribution on "characters in the making," *Petri Merenlahti*[98] argues that the characters in the Gospels are quite often not complete, and either "increase" or "decrease," depending on the extent to which they relate to the

---

[90] James L. Resseguie, "Defamiliarization and the Gospels," *BTB* 20/4 (1990): 147–53.
[91] Resseguie, "Defamiliarization," 148.
[92] Resseguie, "Defamiliarization," 150–52.
[93] Helen K. Bond, *Pontius Pilate in History and Interpretation* (MSSNTS 100; Cambridge: Cambridge University Press, 1998).
[94] Bond, *Pontius Pilate*, 205–207.
[95] Timothy Wiarda, *Peter in the Gospels: Pattern, Personality and Relationship* (WUNT II/127; Tübingen: Mohr Siebeck, 2000), 65–119.
[96] Wiarda, *Peter in the Gospels*, 66–67.
[97] Wiarda, *Peter in the Gospels*, 117–18.
[98] Petri Merenlahti, *Poetics for the Gospels? Rethinking Narrative Criticism* (London: T&T Clark, 2002), 77–98.

ideology of a Gospel and/or the ideology of its readers. According to Merenlahti, this should prevent one from engaging in a quest for static and harmonious interpretations of characters. This argument is illustrated by means of several examples from the Gospels, such as Peter, Judas and the haemorrhaging woman.

Justin Howell[99] draws attention to the characterization of Jesus in a particular manuscript, namely Codex Washingtonianus, a manuscript which seems to have been produced in Egypt. By investigating some of the singular and sub-singular readings in this manuscript, he shows how the scribe amplified the image of Jesus as a teacher who was well received, approachable, and non-threatening, a picture which fitted the context of early Christian polemics.

3.2 The Gospel of Mark

One of the aspects considered by *David Rhoads and Donald Michie*[100] in their narrative analysis of Mark is its characters. After considering several theoretical issues such as telling and showing, the way in which the reader is guided to measure characters against certain standards, and the assignment of traits, they discuss the following characters: Jesus, the authorities, the disciples, and the little people. One example: In the case of Jesus, several traits are discussed, for example his authority, integrity, faith, and his service to others.[101]

Elizabeth Struthers Malbon has made a number of valuable contributions to the study of characterization in Mark's Gospel, as the following example illustrates: In an article on the disciples and crowds in Mark,[102] she shows how the disciples are portrayed with both strong and weak points in order to serve as realistic models for the readers. She also points out that the crowds are portrayed both positively and negatively in terms of their relationship to Jesus, thereby complementing the disciples.

Of the many studies in which the minor characters in Mark are discussed, two examples will be mentioned here: *Joel F. Williams*[103] argues that one can detect a pattern in the way in which Mark presents minor characters: from

---

[99] Justin R. Howell, "The Characterization of Jesus in Codex W," *JECS* 14/1 (2006): 47–75.

[100] David Rhoads and Donald Michie, *Mark as Story: An Introduction to the Narrative of a Gospel* (Philadelphia: Fortress, 1982), 101–35. 2d ed.: David Rhoads, Joanna Dewey and Donald Michie, *Mark as Story: An Introduction to the Narrative of a Gospel* (2d ed.; Minneapolis: Fortress, 1999).

[101] Rhoads and Michie, *Mark as Story*, 103–16.

[102] Elizabeth S. Malbon, "Disciples/Crowds/Whoever: Markan Characters and Readers," *NT* 28/2 (1986): 104–30. Cf. also Elizabeth S. Malbon, *In the Company of Jesus: Characters in Mark's Gospel* (Louisville, Ky.: Westminster John Knox, 2000), and Elizabeth S. Malbon, *Mark's Jesus: Characterization as Narrative Christology* (Waco, Tex.: Baylor University Press, 2009).

[103] Joel F. Williams, "Discipleship and Minor Characters in Mark's Gospel," *BS* 153/611 (1996): 332–43.

suppliants in the first part of the narrative (1:1–10:45), to exemplars in the second part of the narrative (10:46–16:7), to negative examples in 16:8. *Martin Ebner*[104] focuses on a different aspect, namely the use of minor characters as "contrast" characters. He shows how the disciples (the important characters) are portrayed in the Gospel in an ambivalent way, and how the minor characters such as the Syrophoenician woman and the Roman centurion at the cross are portrayed in such a way that they "step out of the shadows" of the disciples and win the sympathy of the reader.

David du Toit[105] draws attention to a very interesting aspect of the way in which Jesus is characterized in Mark's Gospel, namely the manipulation of temporal aspects in the narrative ("Anachronie"). In particular, he shows how prolepses are used to characterize Jesus as an eschatological prophet from God, and as a prophet like Moses. According to Du Toit, in this way Mark succeeds in linking Jesus both to the past and the future.

Paul Danove has published several studies on characterization in Mark's Gospel. In one of these,[106] he analyzes the characterization of God. He begins by categorizing all the references to God in terms of semantic functions (for example God as agent, experience, and source), and then focuses on the role of repetition. Danove argues that the narrative function of all of these strategies is to initially encourage readers to link Jesus with God, and subsequently to encourage them to identify closely with Jesus.

According to *Abraham Smith*,[107] Mark's characterization of Herod Antipas (6:14–29) shows clear signs of "tyrant typology," in that the author makes use of certain typical stock features of tyrants in portraying this character, for example his fear of the Baptist, his use of a bodyguard, and the fact that he was a man of excess. Smith argues that this approach was not only used to expose Herod Antipas as a tyrant, but also to admonish the disciples not to lord it over others.

Geoff R. Webb[108] applies categories developed by Mikhail Bakhtin to characterization in Mark. The two Bakhtinian categories that he uses are "chronotope" (the way time and space are represented in literature) and "carnival" (the context in which different voices are heard and interact, and threshold situa-

---

[104] Martin Ebner, "Im Schatten der Großen: Kleine Erzählfiguren im Markusevangelium," *BZ* 44/1 (2000): 56–76.

[105] David S. du Toit, "Prolepsis als Prophetie: Zur christologischen Funktion narrativer Anachronie im Markusevangelium," *WuD* 26 (2001): 165–89.

[106] Paul Danove, "The Narrative Function of Mark's Characterization of God," *NT* 43/1 (2001): 12–30. Cf. also Paul Danove, *The Rhetoric of the Characterization of God, Jesus, and Jesus' Disciples in the Gospel of Mark* (New York: T&T Clark, 2005).

[107] Abraham Smith, "Tyranny Exposed: Mark's Typological Characterization of Herod Antipas (Mark 6:14–29)," *BibInt* 14/3 (2006): 259–93.

[108] Geoff R. Webb, *Mark at the Threshold: Applying Bakhtinian Categories to Markan Characterisation* (Biblical Interpretation Series 95; Leiden: Brill, 2008).

tions are created). Applying these two categories to Mark, Webb discusses several different types: adventure chronotope and comic carnival (for example the cleansed leper in 1:40–45),[109] threshold chronotope and comic carnival (for example the beheaded Baptizer in 6:14–29),[110] road chronotope and comic carnival (for example the transfigured Jesus in 9:2–8),[111] and threshold chronotope and tragic carnival (the characters playing a role in Jesus' betrayal, trial and crucifixion in 14:43–15:41).[112]

3.3 The Gospel of Matthew

In his analysis of the characterization of God in Matthew, *Fred W. Burnett*[113] shows how the implied author employs the narrator and Jesus (as the main character) to portray God in such a way that the reader is moved to a position where the exclusiveness of Jesus' sonship is accepted; in other words, the readers are moved to a position where they side with Jesus against "the Jews," and accept that God is not the Father of "the Jews."

Janice Capel Anderson[114] discusses the characterization of two individual characters in Matthew, the Baptist and Peter, as well as the characterization of the Jewish leaders. The particular issue that she highlights is the role that repetition plays in the characterization of these characters. In this regard, several recurring types of characterization are identified, for example, the repetition of labels or epithets that are used to characterize, the repeated depiction of actions of a character, and double stories.

Mark Allan Powell[115] takes Boris Uspensky's contribution regarding the phraseological plane (one of the planes on which information about characters is communicated to the reader) as his point of departure, and investigates the extent to which this plays a role in the characterization of Jesus, the disciples, and the religious leaders. In the case of Jesus, Powell shows that the phraseological plane is not the primary means by which Jesus is characterized, but that it is used to confirm the characterization established through other means. Furthermore, Powell shows that Jesus' phraseology is absolutely reliable in terms of his characterization, and that the distinction between direct and indirect phraseology does not play any role in his case.

---

[109] Webb, *Mark at the Threshold*, 71–105.
[110] Webb, *Mark at the Threshold*, 107–49.
[111] Webb, *Mark at the Threshold*, 151–80.
[112] Webb, *Mark at the Threshold*, 181–230.
[113] Fred W. Burnett, "Exposing the Anti-Jewish Ideology of Matthew's Implied Author: The Characterization of God as Father," *Semeia* 59 (1992): 155–91.
[114] Janice C. Anderson, *Matthew's Narrative Web: Over, and Over, and Over Again* (JSNTSup 91; Sheffield: Sheffield Academic Press, 1994), 78–132.
[115] Mark A. Powell, "Characterization on the Phraseological Plane in the Gospel of Matthew," in *Treasures New and Old: Recent Contributions to Matthean Studies* (ed. David R. Bauer and Mark A. Powell; Atlanta: Scholars Press, 1996), 161–77.

David R. Bauer[116] discusses some of the major characters in Matthew: Jesus, the disciples and Israel (i. e., the crowds and the religious leaders). In the case of the disciples, he highlights three aspects: Firstly, Matthew makes the nature of discipleship clear and specifies what is expected of disciples. Secondly, he shows how the disciples actually perform. This is a mixed portrait: They display both positive and negative characteristics. Thirdly, he also devotes attention to the future of the disciples in the period between the resurrection and the Parousia, focusing on aspects such as the continuing opposition and the threat of apostasy, the importance of endurance, and mission work.

Talvikki Mattila[117] approaches Matthew's narrative world from the angle of gender, with particular reference to the women characters in the Passion Narrative. Several characters are discussed: the two female servants and Pilate's wife (26:69–75; 27:11–26), the women at the cross and at the tomb (27:54–66; 28:1–8), and the women sent to the disciples (28:8–10, 16–20). Mattila argues that the women in the Passion Narrative are portrayed as "representatives of prophetic commitment and communication … insiders who are 'outsiders'."[118]

In her discussion of the "peripheral characters" ("Randfiguren") in Matthew, *Uta Poplutz*[119] shows how the characters in this Gospel can be grouped into two broad categories, namely helpers and opponents, depending on the basic question of whether they are for or against Jesus. She goes on to pose the interesting question as to whether there are minor characters who break this pattern by their behavior. Of the many minor characters in the Gospel, she then identifies and discusses five characters who are "Grenzgänger" and who behave differently from what the reader would expect:[120] the Roman officer (8:5–13), a scribe (8:19–29), the Canaanite woman (15:21–28), Pilate's wife (27:19), and the Roman officer and the soldiers (27:54).

3.4 The Gospel of Luke and Luke-Acts

John Darr offers an approach to character studies which is based on the models of reader-response-criticism. He states that "a reader-response critic reads

---

[116] David R. Bauer, "The Major Characters of Matthew's Story: Their Function and Significance," in *Gospel Interpretation: Narrative-Critical & Social-Scientific Approaches* (ed. Jack D. Kingsbury; Harrisburg, Pa.: Trinity Press International, 1997), 27–37.

[117] Talvikki Mattila, "Naming the Nameless: Gender and Discipleship in Matthew's Passion Narrative," in *Characterization in the Gospels: Reconceiving Narrative Criticism* (ed. David Rhoads and Kari Syreeni; JSNTSup 184, Sheffield: Sheffield Academic Press, 1999), 153–79.

[118] Mattila, "Naming the Nameless," 178.

[119] Uta Poplutz, *Erzählte Welt: Narratologische Studien zum Matthäusevangelium* (Neukirchen-Vluyn: Neukirchener, 2008), 57–100. In another contribution in this book, she also discusses the crowd, the disciples and the authorities in Matthew (ibid., 101–39).

[120] Poplutz, *Erzählte Welt*, 80–100.

the reader reading the text."[121] Concerning Luke-Acts, Darr tries to reconstruct a Lukan reader on the basis of the text, questioning: "What did a reader have to bring to a text in order to actualize it competently?"[122] He then analyzes Lukan characters in their context (plot, setting and other characters), sequence, and cumulatively: the reader develops the character during the act of reading and it consists of the sum of its character traits.[123] According to Darr, in a pragmatic-rhetorical sense, a character can be understood as a sender of a special message. Darr also points out that readers have to speculate and anticipate, since they perceive characters as similar to real persons.[124] He states: "Characters are not just words ... or textual functions, but rather, affective and realistic personal images generated by text and reader."[125]

Ronald D. Witherup[126] introduces the concept "functional redundancy" and argues that the "redundancy" in Acts 9, 22 and 26 is actually part of a purposeful characterization of Paul. According to Witherup, the three passages serve as the main pillars in the characterization of Paul as a witness to the gospel. With each passage the role of Ananias and Paul's companions decreases, whereas Paul's stature increases. In this way, the reader is shown how Paul changes "from a persecutor, to a blind and helpless convert, to an eloquent spokesperson for the faith."[127]

According to *James M. Dawsey*,[128] Luke uses the way in which characters address or do not address Jesus to differentiate between them. In particular, he highlights three aspects: the way in which Luke distinguishes between characters by letting them refer to Jesus in different ways (Son of Man, teacher, Lord, and Son of God), Luke's use of different designations for Jesus, not only to characterize Jesus, but also to characterize other characters in the story, and Luke's use of third-person narration in order to control the way in which his story will be interpreted.

Adaoma M. Okorie[129] investigates the characterization of Jesus, the disciples and the public in Luke. Characterization is viewed in terms of a continuum

---

[121] John A. Darr, *On Character Building: The Reader and the Rhetoric of Characterization* (Louisville, Ky.: Westminster John Knox, 1992), 20. Cf. in application on Herod, John A. Darr, *Herod the Fox. Audience Criticism and Lukan Characterization* (JSNTSup 163; Sheffield: Sheffield Academic Press, 1998).
[122] Darr, *Character Building*, 26.
[123] Darr, *Character Building*, 38–44.
[124] Darr, *Character Building*, 45–47.
[125] Darr, *Character Building*, 47.
[126] Ronald D. Witherup, "Functional Redundancy in the Acts of the Apostles: A Case Study," *JSNT* 48 (1992): 67–86.
[127] Witherup, "Functional Redundancy," 70.
[128] James M. Dawsey, "What's in a Name? Characterization in Luke," *BTB* 16/4 (1986): 143–47.
[129] Adaoma M. Okorie, "The Art of Characterisation in the Lukan Narrative: Jesus, the Disciples and the Populace," *Religion & Theology* 2/3 (1995): 274–82.

ranging from flat, nameless characters to characters that are developed fully. According to Okorie, Jesus is the only character in Luke who can be regarded as a fully developed character. The disciples are classified as intermediate characters serving as a point of identification for the reader. The public functions primarily in terms of the plot of the Gospel, and helps to extend Jesus' identity.

In his theological reading of Luke, *David Lee*[130] combines insights from the work of Hans Frei (new critical reading and reading for the *sensus literalis*) and narratology. The narratological insights are based on the work of Mieke Bal. These insights are applied to the characterization of Jesus in the seven "acts" that Lee distinguishes in the Gospel. This is done from two perspectives, the narrator's characterization of Jesus and Jesus' self-characterization. In the discussion of the narrator's characterization of Jesus, theological aspects that are highlighted include Jesus as the One obedient to the will of God, Jesus as the One in whom God is at work, and Jesus as God's ambassador to the Gentiles.[131]

As part of his "dynamic" reading of the Holy Spirit in Luke-Acts, *Ju Hur*[132] considers the characterization of the Holy Spirit. On the basis of various approaches to characterization (amongst others that of Rimmon-Kenan), he develops a model focusing on two aspects: firstly, that of focusing on direct definition and indirect presentation (speech, action, external appearance, environment) and secondly, that of analogy (repetition and similarity, and comparison and contrast).[133] According to Hur, the two most important aspects of the characterization of the Holy Spirit in Luke-Acts are its characterization as the Spirit promised by God in the Jewish Bible, and its association with Jesus who is Messiah and Lord.[134]

Claire Clivaz[135] analyzes the characterization of Judas in Luke 22, in particular in vss. 21–22. Clivaz warns against the tendency of modern readers to "psychologize" the character of Judas, and argues that in ancient Greek literature the emphasis was on actions and not on character.[136] Accordingly, Judas is analyzed in terms of his function in the plot and the references to "the hand of Judas." One of the aspects that is emphasized is the fact that Judas is a symbolic character who reflects Luke's daring anthropology.[137]

---

[130] David Lee, *Luke's Stories of Jesus: Theological Reading of Gospel Narrative and the Legacy of Hans Frei* (JSNTSup 185; Sheffield: Sheffield Academic Press, 1999).

[131] Lee, *Luke's Stories*, 243–45.

[132] Ju Hur, *A Dynamic Reading of the Holy Spirit in Luke-Acts* (JSNTSup 211; Sheffield: Sheffield Academic Press, 2001).

[133] Hur, *Dynamic Reading*, 127–28.

[134] Hur, *Dynamic Reading*, 178–80.

[135] Claire Clivaz, "Douze noms pour une main: nouveaux regards sur Judas à partir de Lc 22.21-2," *NTS* 48/3 (2002): 400–16.

[136] Clivaz, "Douze noms," 404.

[137] Clivaz, "Douze noms," 410–16.

Christoph Gregor Müller[138] draws attention to an aspect that often plays a role in characterization in the New Testament, namely the characters' clothing. After an overview of the way in which this aspect functioned in antiquity, several cases in which clothing is used in Luke-Acts are considered. According to Müller, clothing is used in various ways in this work, for example to indicate basic human needs, decoration, an office/important social position, or personal traits.

Several studies focus on the way in which physical aspects are used in Luke-Acts as a means of characterization. Two examples: *Mikeal C. Parsons*[139] shows that the description of Zacchaeus as "short in stature" should be understood in terms of the broad consciousness of physiognomics in the ancient world, according to which such descriptions were often used as a way of ridiculing other people. In the case of Zacchaeus this description is used together with other epithets such as "rich" and "tax collector" to characterize Zacchaeus as traitorous, small-minded and greedy; a picture that is then reversed by Luke to show that he is also a "son of Abraham." *Chad Hartsock*[140] begins his study on blindness in Luke-Acts with an overview of physiognomy and blindness in the Old Testament, Second-Temple Judaism, the New Testament and other early Christian literature.[141] Hartsock argues that Luke was aware of ancient physiognomic notions, and used and often subverted them. He shows that for Luke, the opening of the eyes of the blind was one of the characteristic aspects of Jesus' ministry (Luke 4). Hartsock then illustrates how this notion forms a narrative thread throughout Luke-Acts, for example in the case of the blind man at Jericho, the calling of Paul, and Bar-Jesus.[142]

Christian Dionne[143] investigates the characterization of God in Acts, in particular in the Petrine discourses (2:14–40; 3:12–26; 4:8–12; 5:29–32; and 10:34–43). Utilizing narrative criticism, Dionne focuses on issues such as the traits associated with God, how they are developed or modified, how the portrayal of God as a character develops, and how this is related to other characters and the plot.[144] On the basis of this analysis, Dionne highlights several important aspects in the characterization of God in the Petrine speeches, for

---

[138] Christoph G. Müller, "Kleidung als Element der Charakterzeichnung im Neuen Testament und seiner Umwelt: Ein Streifzug durch das lukanische Erzählwerk," SNTU 28 (2003): 187–214.

[139] Mikeal C. Parsons, "'Short in Stature': Luke's Physical Description of Zacchaeus," NTS 47/1 (2002): 50–57.

[140] Chad Hartsock, *Sight and Blindness in Luke-Acts: The Use of Physical Features in Characterization* (Biblical Interpretation Series 94; Leiden: Brill, 2008).

[141] Hartsock, *Sight and Blindness*, 83–166.

[142] Hartsock, *Sight and Blindness*, 167–206.

[143] Christian Dionne, *La Bonne Nouvelle de Dieu: Une analyse de la figure narrative de Dieu dans les discours Pétriniens d'évangélisation des Actes des Apôtres* (LeDiv; Paris: Cerf, 2004).

[144] Dionne, *La Bonne Nouvelle de Dieu*, 61–330.

example his omnipresence and his portrayal as a God of relationships and mediation, and as a discreet but acting God.[145]

Richard P. Thompson[146] discusses the church as a narrative character in Acts. In his approach to character in ancient narrative, he focuses on the following aspects of character: indirect description, direct description, the manner or categories in terms of which characters are presented, the accumulation of pictures and effects and the interaction with other characters.[147] The Jerusalem church, the churches in Jerusalem and beyond, and the churches in the Roman Empire are then discussed systematically.[148] The most important traits of the church that are identified by Thompson are its oneness of spirit and purpose, its commitment to meeting the needs of fellow believers, receptivity to the word and presence of God, Christ and the Spirit, and a vision for expansion which includes both Jewish and Gentile believers.[149]

Paul Borgman[150] contends that major patterns of repetition, as for any biblical narrative, are primary contexts within Luke-Acts. He argues that ancient texts rely more on ancient rhetorical practice, much of it circling backward by way of patterns, than on modern notions of plot, character, and theme. Close reading attention to hearing cues reveals (1) that each volume requires the other for full understanding; and that (2) embedded in the narrative is a twofold meaning of Jesus: he is, first, God's word-bearer, proven to be Messiah and only prophet raised from a violent death; and, second, he is the sender of the Holy Spirit. The latter is essential, since empowerment to do the word Jesus taught is essential for human salvation.[151] Borgman also emphasizes interlocking patterns in the narratives. So he points, for example, to Peter and Paul in Acts, each with seven speeches, which in turn touch on parallel themes such as repentance, forgiveness (yet without atonement via the cross), resurrection, and Spirit.[152]

In her narratological study of Acts, *Ute Eisen*[153] also discusses character analysis. She begins with a methodological overview, distinguishing between two issues: classification of characters and techniques of characterization. In the first instance she focuses on four aspects: status, complexity, function and

---

[145] Dionne, *La Bonne Nouvelle de Dieu*, 332–47.
[146] Richard P. Thompson, *Keeping the Church in its Place: The Church as Narrative Character in Acts* (New York: T&T Clark, 2006).
[147] Thompson, *The Church as Narrative Character*, 18–28.
[148] Thompson, *The Church as Narrative Character*, 29–240.
[149] Thompson, *The Church as Narrative Character*, 241–49.
[150] Paul Borgman, *The Way according to Luke: Hearing the Whole Story of Luke-Acts* (Grand Rapids, Mich.: Eerdmans, 2006).
[151] Borgman, *Hearing the Whole Story*, 1–7.
[152] Borgman, *Hearing the Whole Story*, 11–15.
[153] Ute Eisen, *Die Poetik der Apostelgeschichte. Eine narratologische Studie* (NTOA 58; Göttingen: Vandenhoeck & Ruprecht, 2006).

attributes.[154] With regard to characterization, she discusses the following aspects: explicit/implict and auctorial/figurative characterization.[155] In the analysis that follows characters are analyzed in terms of a broad narratological approach, with a particular focus on Peter and Paul as protagonists.[156] According to Eisen,[157] by focusing on these characters, one can get a very good grasp of the difficult transformative process through which the early followers of Jesus went.

4. Character and Characterization in the Gospel of John

There have also been character studies in the Gospel of John over the last fifty years.[158] We have divided this history of research into three parts: (4.1) scholars who have a general or broad view on Johannine characters; (4.2) scholars who have examined characters from a gender perspective; (4.3) scholars who present a particular perspective on Johannine characterization, such as minor characters, anonymous characters, or ambiguous characters. In each section, we have presented the scholars in chronological order.

4.1 Early and General Studies

One of the earliest studies on Johannine characters is an article from 1956 by *Eva Krafft*.[159] Influenced by Bultmann's commentary on John, she argues that John made his characters typically transparent and that they personify a certain attitude to Jesus. Then, in 1976, *Raymond Collins* wrote a lengthy article on Johannine characters, which was reprinted in 1990, and added a second essay in 1995.[160] According to Collins, through interaction with Jesus as the protagonist, characters can be seen to play roles of widely disparate importance. Whereas some characters, such as John (the Baptizer), Nicodemus, the Samaritan woman, the invalid, the man born blind, Peter and the Beloved Disciple, participate in the unfolding of the plot, others simply play minor roles in the story. Examining about fifteen characters, Collins argues that these characters are type-cast, i. e., they represent a particular type of faith-response to Jesus.

---

[154] Eisen, *Poetik der Apostelgeschichte*, 133–135.
[155] Eisen, *Poetik der Apostelgeschichte*, 136–137.
[156] Eisen, *Poetik der Apostelgeschichte*, 170–172.
[157] Eisen, *Poetik der Apostelgeschichte*, 226.
[158] We are deeply grateful to Cornelis Bennema for his help on this survey.
[159] Eva Krafft, "Die Personen des Johannesevangeliums," *EvT* 16 (1956): 18–32.
[160] Raymond F. Collins, "Representative Figures," in idem, *These Things Have Been Written: Studies on the Fourth Gospel* (LTPM 2; Louvain: Peeters, 1990), 1–45 (originally in *Downside Review* 94 [1976]: 26–46; 95 [1976]: 118–32); idem, "From John to the Beloved Disciples: An Essay on Johannine characters," *Int* 49 (1995): 359–69.

The first book-length treatment of John's Gospel as a literary work is *Alan Culpepper*'s seminal work *Anatomy of the Fourth Gospel* in which he devotes one chapter to roughly twenty-four Johannine characters.[161] He provides a brief theoretical discussion on characterization, arguing that John draws from both Greek and Hebrew models of character, although most Johannine characters represent particular ethical types (as in Greek literature). Like Collins, Culpepper contends that most of John's minor characters are types which the reader can recognize easily. Because Johannine characters respond to Jesus differently, Culpepper is able to produce an extensive taxonomy of belief-responses in which characters are seen to progress or regress from one response to another.

When we come to the 1990s, *Margaret Davies* undertakes a comprehensive reading of John's Gospel, mainly using structuralism and reader-response criticism, and dedicates one chapter to twenty Johannine characters.[162] Similar to Krafft, Collins, and Culpepper, she contends that most of the characters are flat caricatures, having a single trait, and showing little or no development. *Mark Stibbe* did some important work on characterization in John 8, 11 and 18–19 to show how narrative criticism can be applied to John's Gospel, and he was the first to present a number of characters, like Pilate and Peter, as more complicated than had previously been assumed.[163] Stibbe provided brief theoretical considerations on characterization, stressing that readers must (i) construct character by inference from fragmentary information in the text (like in ancient Hebrew narratives); (ii) analyze characters with reference to history rather than according to the laws of fiction; and (iii) consider the Gospel's ideological point of view, expressed in 20:31.[164] In addition, Stibbe produced a narratological commentary on John's Gospel, highlighting how John portrays the various characters in his gospel.[165]

The Roman Catholic New Testament scholar *Peter Dschulnigg*, well-known for his studies of the Gospel of John's language and style,[166] broadened earlier

---

[161] R. Alan Culpepper, *Anatomy of the Fourth Gospel: A Study in Literary Design* (Philadelphia: Fortress, 1983), 99–148.

[162] Margaret Davies, *Rhetoric and Reference in the Fourth Gospel* (JSNTS 69; Sheffield: JSOT Press, 1992), 316–49. Elsewhere, she also refers to the world, "the Jews" and Pilate (*Rhetoric*, 154–58, 313–15).

[163] Mark W. G. Stibbe, *John as Storyteller: Narrative Criticism and the Fourth Gospel* (SNTSMS 73; Cambridge: Cambridge University Press, 1992), 97–99, 106–13, 119; idem, *John's Gospel* (London: Routledge, 1994), 90–96, 121–25.

[164] Stibbe, *Storyteller*, 24–25, 28; idem, *John's Gospel*, 10–11.

[165] Mark W. G. Stibbe, *John* (Sheffield: JSOT Press, 1993).

[166] Eugen Ruckstuhl and Peter Dschulnigg, *Stilkritik und Verfasserfrage im Johannesevangelium: Die johanneischen Sprachmerkmale auf dem Hintergrund des Neuen Testaments und des zeitgenössischen hellenistischen Schrifttums* (NTOA 17; Freiburg: Universitätsverlag, 1991).

studies on individual characters[167] and presented a comprehensive work on the "Personen" in John's Gospel.[168] His use of the term "persons" (in German: "Personen") instead of "characters" (in German: "Figuren") reveals that he is not approaching his study with a strictly narratological method; rather, he presents a close reading of 21 characters. The selection is built on the criterion that the characters play a major role in the plot, accordingly most of them occur in more than one passage.[169] The characters are presented, according to Dschulnigg, in "typisierender Absicht ... um an ihnen unterschiedliche Reaktionen auf Jesus darzustellen und diese den LeserInnen vor Augen zu führen, damit sie sich orientieren und ihre eigene Antwort auf Jesus finden und realisieren können."[170]

Interest in Johannine characters increased in the current century. In 2001, *James Resseguie* produced a monograph on point of view in John's Gospel.[171] In chapter three, he explores various characters from a material point of view and classifies them according to their dominance or social presence in society rather than their faith-response.[172] For example, Nicodemus, who represents the dominant culture, abandons his material perspective for a spiritual one, and the lame man, who represents the marginalized of society, is freed from the constraints of the dominant culture and even acts counter-culturally by violating the sabbath. Resseguie claims that the characters' material points of view contribute or relate to the Gospel's overall ideology.[173]

In a provocative article, *Colleen Conway* challenges the consensus view that Johannine characters represent particular belief-responses.[174] She criticizes the "flattening" of characters and argues that Johannine characters show varying degrees of ambiguity and do more to complicate the clear choice between belief and unbelief than to illustrate it. Instead of positioning the minor characters on a spectrum of negative to positive faith-responses, she claims that they appear unstable in relation to Jesus. In doing so, the characters challenge,

---

[167] See Peter Dschulnigg, *Petrus im Johannesevangelium* (Stuttgart: Katholisches Bibelwerk, 1996); idem, "Nikodemus im Johannesevangelium," *SNT.A* 24 (1999): 103–18.

[168] Peter Dschulnigg, *Jesus begegnen: Personen und ihre Bedeutung im Johannesevangelium* (Münster: LIT, 2000; 2d ed.; Münster: LIT, 2002).

[169] See Dschulnigg, *Jesus begegnen*, 4: "(Die Einzelperson soll) handelnd auftreten, sei es an verschiedenen Stellen oder an einer Stelle in relativer Breite."

[170] Dschulnigg, *Jesus begegnen*, 1–2.

[171] James L. Resseguie, *The Strange Gospel: Narrative Design and Point of View in John* (BIS 56; Leiden: Brill, 2001).

[172] Resseguie, *Strange Gospel*, 109–68.

[173] In an introductory book on narrative criticism, Resseguie treats a few other Johannine characters, such as the crowd, Judas, the man born blind and Mary Magdalene (idem, *Narrative Criticism of the New Testament: An Introduction* [Grand Rapids, Mich.: Baker Academic, 2005], ch. 4).

[174] Colleen M. Conway, "Speaking through Ambiguity: Minor Characters in the Fourth Gospel," *BibInt* 10 (2002): 324–41.

undercut and subvert the dualistic world of the Gospel because they do not line up on either side of the belief/unbelief divide.

In his book *Symbolism in the Fourth Gospel*, Craig Koester has a chapter on characterization, subscribing to the idea that each of John's characters represents a particular faith-response.[175] He first examines the character of Jesus and then explores fourteen characters who meet Jesus. Koester's strength is that he interprets the Johannine characters on the basis of the text and its historical context. He sees many parallels between John's story and ancient Greek drama or tragedy, where characters are types who convey general truths by representing a moral choice.

In an introductory study of the Gospel of John entitled "Encounters with Jesus," *Frances Taylor Gench* utilizes the church's lectionary to examine thirteen central texts. Most of the chapters deal with various Johannine characters, such as Nicodemus (ch. 3), the Samaritan woman (ch. 4), the woman accused of adultery (ch. 6), the man born blind (ch. 7), the Bethany family (ch. 8), Pilate (ch. 11) and Mary Magdalene and Thomas (ch. 12).[176] Gench describes the encounters on a basic level, not using specific narratological methods.

For *Judith Hartenstein*, the particular constellation of characters in John, especially the interaction of individual figures with Jesus in comparison with other characters, take center stage in her Habilitationsschrift.[177] In an introduction on methodology she tries to link narrative criticism to historical questions. According to Hartenstein, the narrative cannot be isolated from history. "Die Figuren der Erzählung sind nicht unbedingt neu entworfen, sondern sie sind historisch (oder literarisch) schon vorhanden. Das hat Konsequenzen für die Interpretation, weil die Wechselwirkungen zwischen der Darstellung im JohEv und den außerhalb vorhandenen Vorstellungen einbezogen werden müssen."[178] Accordingly the author explores the characters not only synchronically within the Gospel, but also diachronically by comparing the Johannine text with texts which demonstrate how the figures are developed in later apocryphal literature. In the first part she deals with characterization in John in general (ch. 2), giving a survey on various characters, distinguished by direct presentation and then by indirect presentation focussing on actions and speeches. In the following she concentrates her analysis on Mary Magdalene (ch. 3), Peter (ch. 4), Thomas (ch. 5), and the mother of Jesus (ch. 6). In the end, she contends that the characters are ambigous: "Sie sind zu vielschichtig

---

[175] Craig R. Koester, *Symbolism in the Fourth Gospel: Meaning, Mystery, Community* (2d ed.; Minneapolis: Fortress, 2003), 33–77.

[176] Frances Taylor Gench, *Encounters with Jesus: Studies in the Gospel of John* (Louisville, Ky.: Westminster John Knox, 2007).

[177] Judith Hartenstein, *Charakterisierung im Dialog: Maria Magdalena, Petrus, Thomas und die Mutter Jesu im Johannesevangelium im Kontext frühchristlicher Darstellungen* (NTOA/SUNT 64; Göttingen: Vandenhoeck & Ruprecht, 2007).

[178] Hartenstein, *Charakterisierung*, 37.

und zu reich an Spannungen und Wendungen, um sich klar sortieren und einordnen zu lassen ... Vielleicht liegt die Absicht gerade darin, den LeserInnen die Offenheit aller Figuren zu vermitteln."[179]

In 2009, *Cornelis Bennema* produced a twofold work on Johannine characters where he seeks to reverse the consensus view that Johannine characters are types, have little complexity and show little or no development.[180] Arguing that the differences in characterization in the Hebrew Bible, ancient Greek literature, and modern fiction are differences in emphases rather than kind, Bennema suggests that it is better to speak of degrees of characterization along a continuum.[181] He then outlines a comprehensive theory of character that comprises three aspects: (i) the study of character in text and context, using information from the text and other sources; (ii) the analysis and classification of characters along Ewen's three dimensions (complexity, development, inner life), and plotting the resulting character on a continuum of degree of characterization (from agent to type to personality to individuality); (iii) the evaluation of characters in relation to John's point of view, purpose and dualistic worldview. Bennema then applies his theory to John's Gospel, showing that only eight out of twenty-three characters are "types."

4.2 Gender Studies

Many scholars have observed that John gives special attention to women, resulting in a large number of gender-focused studies. In 1975, *Raymond Brown* examined John's Gospel to determine the roles of women in the Johannine community.[182] Except for Martha's role of serving at the table (John 12:2), which possibly alludes to the office of deacon that already existed in the late 90s, Brown contends that other passages are concerned with the general position of women in the Johannine community. Brown concludes that discipleship is the primary Johannine category and that women are included as first-class disciples.

Sandra Schneiders studies women in John's Gospel in order to aid the imagination of contemporary Christians as they deal with the issue of women in

---

[179] Hartenstein, *Charakterisierung*, 303.
[180] Cornelis Bennema, "A Theory of Character in the Fourth Gospel with Reference to Ancient and Modern Literature," *BibInt* 17 (2009): 375–421; Cornelis Bennema, *Encountering Jesus: Character Studies in the Gospel of John* (Milton Keynes: Paternoster, 2009). Bennema has recently sharpened his theory further in "A Comprehensive Approach to Understanding Character in the Gospel of John," in *Characters and Characterization in the Gospel of John* (ed. Christopher Skinner; LNTS 461; London: T&T Clark, 2013).
[181] Bennema is especially indebted to Fred W. Burnett, who has excellently argued this case in "Characterization and Reader Construction of Characters in the Gospels," *Semeia* 63 (1993): 3–28.
[182] Raymond E. Brown, "Roles of Women in the Fourth Gospel," *TS* 36 (1975): 688–99.

the church today.[183] Schneiders observes that: (i) all the women in John's Gospel are presented positively and in intimate relation to Jesus; (ii) John's positive portrayal of women is neither one-dimensional nor stereotypical; (iii) the women play unconventional roles. Schneiders concludes that if leadership is a function of creative initiative and decisive action, the Johannine women qualify well for the role. A year later, *Elisabeth Schüssler Fiorenza* produced her landmark study in which she briefly looked at women in John's Gospel.[184] Although she does not undertake in-depth character studies, she argues that Jesus' mother, the Samaritan woman, Martha and Mary of Bethany, and Mary Magdalene are paradigms of women's apostolic and ministerial leadership in the Johannine communities. Moreover, they function as paradigms of true discipleship for all believers.

Turid Karlsen Seim aims to paint a coherent picture of the roles and functions of women in John's Gospel.[185] Seim observes that the Johannine women are presented independent of men and that they are almost always favourably portrayed. Yet, there is an impressive individual differentiation and originality so that each of the women is presented as a person in her own right. Seim's question thus is whether John wants to emphasize the women as representative examples of discipleship (so Schüssler Fiorenza) or as women. Seim's argument is that the "sexual" aspect is of importance when one considers the role of women in this Gospel. In exploring the various love relationships in John's Gospel, *Sjef van Tilborg* also pays attention to Jesus' mother, the Samaritan woman, Martha and Mary of Bethany, and Mary Magdalene.[186] He argues that the relationship between Jesus and his mother is seen most clearly when Jesus obeys his mother and Jesus' mother does not abandon her son. When it comes to the other women in John's Gospel, however, van Tilborg finds a negative portrayal: in the beginning of the various stories Jesus is inviting and open to women but each time there is a phase in the story where this openness dissipates and Jesus retreats from this relation to women and returns to the male partners.

Robert Maccini analyzes John's Gospel as a rhetorical work that uses the metaphor of a trial in order to persuade readers that the Messiah is Jesus.[187] Examining John's presentation of Jesus' mother, the Samaritan woman,

---

[183] Sandra M. Schneiders, "Women in the Fourth Gospel and the Role of Women in the Contemporary Church," *BTB* 12 (1982): 35–45.

[184] Elisabeth Schüssler Fiorenza, *In Memory of Her: A Feminist Theological Reconstruction of Christian Origins* (London: SCM, 1983), 323–33.

[185] Turid Karlsen Seim, "Roles of Women in the Gospel of John," in *Aspects on the Johannine Literature* (ed. Lars Hartman and Birger Olsson; ConBNT 18; Uppsala: University Press, 1987), 56–73.

[186] Sjef van Tilborg, *Imaginative Love in John* (BIS 2; Leiden: Brill, 1993), ch. 1 and ch. 4.

[187] Robert G. Maccini, *Her Testimony is True: Women as Witnesses according to John* (JSNTS 125; Sheffield: Sheffield Academic Press, 1996).

Martha and Mary of Bethany, and Mary Magdalene as witnesses in this trial, Maccini argues that their role follows no stereotypical pattern but that they, like the men, are treated as individuals, not as a class. Like Maccini, *Adeline Fehribach* also examines the five women in John's Gospel, arguing that their primary function is to support the portrayal of Jesus as the messianic bridegroom.[188] She draws on character types in the Hebrew Bible, Hellenistic-Jewish literature, and Graeco-Roman literature in her analysis of Johannine women. Driven by a feminist agenda to expose the patriarchy and androcentrism of John's gospel (and the culture of that time), she concludes that the egalitarianism of the community or school behind the text was not extended to women.

Colleen Conway also looks at Johannine characterization from the perspective of gender, asking whether men and women are presented differently.[189] Analysing five female and five male characters, she concludes that throughout John's Gospel women are presented positively while male characters present a different, inconsistent pattern – Nicodemus, Pilate and Peter are depicted negatively, while the man born blind and the Beloved Disciple are presented positively. Conway also provides an informed theoretical discussion of character in which she leans toward the contemporary theories of Chatman and Hochman (although she does not utilize the latter's classification), and includes Hebrew techniques of characterization (but leaves out character in ancient Greek literature).

Ruth Edwards has devoted one chapter in her book to Johannine characters.[190] Although this chapter is short and offers only sketches, she recognizes that many Johannine characters are not stereotypical or "flat." She is particularly interested in whether John portrays women and men differently and therefore treats them in different sections. Although she touches on all female characters, she has not looked at prominent male characters such as John (the Baptizer), the lame man and Pilate.

Margaret Beirne examines six gender pairs of characters – Jesus' mother and the royal official, Nicodemus and the Samaritan woman, the man born blind and Martha, Mary of Bethany and Judas, Jesus' mother and the Beloved Disciple, Mary Magdalene and Thomas – and concludes that women and men are equal in terms of the nature and value of discipleship.[191] She recognizes that "these gender pairs serve as a foil for Jesus" ongoing self-revelation and demonstrate a range of faith responses with which the reader may identify. In

---

[188] Adeline Fehribach, *The Women in the Life of the Bridegroom: A Feminist Historical-Literary Analysis of the Female Characters in the Fourth Gospel* (Collegeville, Minn.: Liturgical Press, 1998).

[189] Colleen M. Conway, *Men and Women in the Fourth Gospel: Gender and Johannine Characterization* (SBLDS 167; Atlanta: SBL, 1999).

[190] Ruth Edwards, *Discovering John* (London: SPCK, 2003), ch. 10.

[191] Margaret M. Beirne, *Women and Men in the Fourth Gospel: A Genuine Discipleship of Equals* (JSNTS 242; London: SAP, 2003).

order to thus engage the reader, and thereby fulfil the Gospel's stated purpose (20:31), the evangelist has portrayed them not as mere functionaries, but as engaging and varied characters.[192] Beirne repeatedly points out that although many Johannine characters are representative of a particular belief-response, they are also characters in their own right and cannot be type-cast or stereotyped.

4.3 Special Focus Studies

In his narratological analysis of John 13–17, *Francois Tolmie* also examines the characters who play prominent roles in the discourse.[193] He undergirds his study with an extensive theoretical discussion. He follows the narratological model of Shlomith Rimmon-Kenan (who in turn draws on Seymour Chatman), and utilizes the actantial model of Greimas and the character classification of Ewen (but also refers to those of Forster and Harvey). Tolmie discusses only contemporary fiction and does not consider character in ancient Hebrew and Greek literature. With the exception of God, Jesus, and the Spirit, Tolmie evaluates all characters in John 13–17 as flat – they have a single trait or are not complex, show no development, and reveal no inner life.

David Beck explores the concept of anonymity in relation to discipleship, arguing that only the unnamed characters serve as models of appropriate responses to Jesus.[194] He provides a brief theoretical discussion on character, deciding to adopt Darr's[195] model which considers how characterization entices readers into fuller participation in the narrative. According to Beck, anonymity facilitates readers' identification with, and imitation of, characters in John's Gospel. Beck concludes that the unnamed characters most closely model the paradigm of discipleship, of appropriate response to Jesus, whereas named characters, even with a degree of positive approval, are inappropriate models for reader identification and imitation.

Ingrid Kitzberger challenges the traditional views of the relationship between the Synoptics and John, and traces the presence of Synoptic female characters in John who are not visible at first sight.[196] For her analysis, she combines Seymour Chatman's view of character, Wolfgang's Müller's "interfi-

---

[192] Beirne, *Women and Men*, 219; cf. 25–26.

[193] D. Francois Tolmie, *Jesus' Farewell to the Disciples: John 13:1–17:26 in Narratological Perspective* (BIS 12; Leiden: Brill, 1995), 117–44.

[194] David R. Beck, *The Discipleship Paradigm: Readers and Anonymous Characters in the Fourth Gospel* (BIS 27; Leiden: Brill, 1997). Beck's monograph builds on his earlier essay, "The Narrative Function of Anonymity in Fourth Gospel Characterization," *Semeia* 63 (1993): 143–58.

[195] J. A. Darr, *On Character Building: The Reader and the Rhetoric of Characterization in Luke-Acts* (LCBI; Louisville, Ky.: Westminster John Knox, 1992).

[196] Ingrid Rosa Kitzberger, "Synoptic Women in John: Interfigural Readings," in *Transformative Encounters: Jesus and Women Re-viewed* (ed. idem; BIS 43; Leiden: Brill, 2000), 77–111.

gural" view of character (i. e., interrelations that exist between characters of different texts), and a reader-response approach. Kitzberger contends that some text signals in the Nicodemus narratives open up these texts to Synoptic intertexts and hence relate Nicodemus to Synoptic women. For example, Nicodemus's question to Jesus, "How can this be?", relates to Mary's question, "How shall this be?", when the angel Gabriel announced the conception of Jesus. She also connects the Johannine story of Jesus' mother at the cross and the Lukan widow of Nain, in that both receive a son. Kitzberger concludes that "interfigural encounters create a network of relationships, between characters in different texts, and between characters and readers reading characters."[197]

Whereas most of the numerous studies on "the Jews" in the Fourth Gospel deal with historical questions[198] there are some studies which concentrate on the Ἰουδαῖοι as a group character. The French scholar *Gérald Caron* wants to know how "the Jews" are "fabricated"[199] by the Evangelist. In his literary approach he explores the role of "the Jews" in John 5 (ch. 2) and John 8 (ch. 3) and concludes that the conflict between Jesus and "the Jews" is always related to feasts in Jerusalem and on general religious issues like temple, Sabbath and law. Thus "the Jews" represent the "'pseudo-Judaism' official de Jérusalem."[200] Like the world (which is interpreted as an "attitude" of darkness) the character of "the Jews" therefore is symbolized and represents something abstract more than concrete. *Tobias Nicklas* also investigates the role of "the Jews" together with the disciples as character within the Gospel of John.[201] Combining narrative criticism with reader response criticism he concentrates on detailed analysis of John 1, 3, 5, and 9. The particular value of his study lies in the fact that Nicklas eases the tension of, for German scholarship, the particularly delicate question of "anti-Judaism in John" in that "the Jews" are no longer considered as a historical group, but rather as a stylized, literary constellation. Nicklas concludes: "In den untersuchten Partien des Textes bilden die 'Juden' als Charaktere der erzählten Welt die Negativfolien, vor deren Hintergrund die Identifikation des Lesers mit Gestalten, die sich auf den Weg zum Glauben an Jesus

---

Although Kitzberger could be classified under gender studies, in our view, her special focus on interfigurality outweighs that of gender.

[197] Kitzberger, "Synoptic Women," 108–109.

[198] See for instance the more recent monographs of Raimo Hakola, *Identity Matters: John, the Jews and Jewishness* (NovTSup 118; Leiden: Brill, 2005); and Lars Kierspel, The *Jews and the World in the Fourth Gospel: Parallelism, Function, and Context* (WUNT II/220; Tübingen: Mohr Siebeck, 2006).

[199] Gérald Caron, *Qui sont les Juifs de l'Évanglie de Jean?* (Recherches 35; Quebec: Bellarmin, 1997), 53.

[200] Caron, *Qui sont les Juifs*, 285.

[201] Tobias Nicklas, *Ablösung und Verstrickung: "Juden" und Jüngergestalten als Charaktere der erzählten Welt des Johannesevangeliums und ihre Wirkung auf den impliziten Leser* (RST 60; Frankfurt am Main: Lang, 2001).

machen, erleichtert wird."[202] Whereas "the Jews" are drawn as a flat character or even "type," the disciples are complex individuals which invite the reader to follow in their footsteps towards Jesus. For Nicklas, the intended transformation from the literal world to reality (of the reader), has a dramatic negative aspect: Also the typical presentation of "the Jews" has been transferred to real Jewish persons and groups in the world of the reader. Thus the literal and reader orientated presentation of "the Jews" as characters also takes responsibility for the anti-Judaism derived from John. *Manfred Diefenbach* also approaches "the Jews" with synchronic methods.[203] To avoid an anachronistic misreading he refuses to use modern theories on narratology, but takes only antique theories on drama into account. "The Jews" are presented as a figure in a drama, which is characterized by means of actions rather than identity matters or direct presentation.[204] Diefenbach comes to the conclusion that the negative portrayal of "the Jews" is based on their behavior, and not on their identity.[205]

Similar to Diefenbach, but not limited to "the Jews" *Jo-Ann Brant* also interprets the Johannine characters against the backdrop of Greek drama.[206] According to Brant, "the Jews" are not actors in the Johannine drama but function as the deliberating chorus in a Greek drama – a corporate voice at the sidelines, witnesses to the action. As such the deliberation of "the Jews" and their response of unbelief provides the believing audience an opportunity to look into the mind of the other, whose perspective it does not share. Brant deliberately refrains from evaluating the Johannine characters. Drawing parallels with ancient Greek tragedy, Brant argues that readers are not members of a jury, evaluating characters as right or wrong, innocent or guilty, or answering christological questions about Jesus' identity, but are called to join the Fourth Evangelist in commemorating Jesus' life.

James Howard investigates how some of the minor characters (Jesus' mother, the royal official, the man born blind, the invalid, Mary and Martha of Bethany) contribute to the development of the plot and the purpose of John's Gospel.[207] Examining these minor characters and their responses to Jesus' miraculous signs, Howard concludes that, in line with John's purpose, each of the characters represent either belief or unbelief. Moreover, each char-

---

[202] Nicklas, *Ablösung und Verstrickung*, 409.

[203] Manfred Diefenbach, *Der Konflikt Jesu mit den "Juden": Ein Versuch zur Lösung der johanneischen Antijudaismus. Diskussion mit Hilfe des antiken Handlungsverständnisses* (NTAbh 41; Münster: Aschendorff Verlag, 2002).

[204] Diefenbach calls this focus "Primat der Handlung," meaning that the identity questions are less important than the action of the character, see Diefenbach, *Der Konflikt Jesu*, 59, 61, 68.

[205] Diefenbach, *Der Konflikt Jesu*, 269–70.

[206] Jo-Ann A. Brant, *Dialogue and Drama: Elements of Greek Tragedy in the Fourth Gospel* (Peabody, Mass.: Hendrickson, 2004), 159–232.

[207] James M. Howard, "The Significance of Minor Characters in the Gospel of John," *BibSac* 163 (2006): 63–78.

acter reveals the Messiah in a different way and reflects some degree of change (either positively or negatively) as a result of his or her encounter with Jesus.

Christopher Skinner uses misunderstanding as a lens through which to read the Johannine characters.[208] Considering the Prologue as the greatest source of information about Jesus, Skinner contends that "[e]ach character in the narrative approaches Jesus with varying levels of understanding but no one approaches him fully comprehending the truths that have been revealed to the reader in the prologue. Thus, it is possible for the reader to evaluate the correctness of every character's interaction with Jesus on the basis of what has been revealed in the prologue."[209] Examining six male characters (Thomas, Peter, Andrew, Philip, Judas [not Iscariot] and Nicodemus), three female characters (the Samaritan woman, Martha and Mary) and one male character group (the twelve disciples), Skinner shows that all characters are uncomprehending to a degree.

Susan Hylen identifies the following problem in Johannine character studies: while many interpreters read most Johannine characters as flat, embodying a single trait and representing a type of believer, the sheer variety of interpretations proves that it is difficult to evaluate John's characters.[210] She presents an alternative strategy for reading characters in John's Gospel, arguing that John's characters display various kinds of ambiguity. For example, Nicodemus's ambiguity lies in the uncertainty of what he understands or believes. The Samaritan woman, the disciples, Martha, the Beloved Disciple and "the Jews" display a more prominent ambiguity, namely that of belief in Jesus mixed with disbelief and misunderstanding. Finally, although Jesus' character is unambiguously positive, it is at the same time ambiguous through the many metaphors John uses to characterize Jesus.

---

[208] Christopher W. Skinner, *John and Thomas – Gospels in Conflict? Johannine Characterization and the Thomas Question* (PTMS 115; Eugene, Oreg.: Wipf and Stock, 2009).

[209] Skinner, *John and Thomas*, 37.

[210] Susan E. Hylen, *Imperfect Believers: Ambiguous Characters in the Gospel of John* (Louisville, Ky.: Westminster John Knox, 2009).

Table on the Characters in the Fourth Gospel
(in order of first appearance)

Steven A. Hunt, D. Francois Tolmie, and Ruben Zimmermann

Character	Narrative Scenes	Textual References	Interactions
John (the Baptist)	John 1:6–18, 19–36; 3:22–36	Ἰωάννης = 18×: John 1:6, 15, 19, 26, 28, 32, 35, 40; 3:23–27; 4:1; 5:33, 36; 10:40–41	Priests, Levites, Jesus, Two Disciples (including Andrew), A "Jew," Other Disciples
The World	John 1:1–18; 29–34; 3:16–21; 4:28–42; 6:1–15, 25–59; 7:1–9; 8:12–30; 9:1–12, 35–41; 10:22–39; 11:7–27; 12:12–19, 20–36, 44–50; 13:1–17:26; 18:19–24, 33–38a; 21:24–25	κόσμος = 78×: John 1:9, 10(3×), 29; 3:16, 17(3×), 19; 4:42; 6:14, 33, 51; 7:4, 7; 8:12, 23*bis*, 26; 9:5*bis*, 39; 10:36; 11:9, 27; 12:19, 25, 31*bis*, 46, 47*bis*; 13:1*bis*; 14:17, 19, 22, 27, 30–31; 15:18, 19(5×); 16:8, 11, 20–21, 28*bis*, 33*bis*; 17:5–6, 9, 11*bis*, 13, 14(3×), 15, 16*bis*, 18*bis*, 21, 23–25; 18:20, 36*bis*, 37; 21:25	Jesus, "The Jews," The Ruler of This World, Jesus' "Own Who Were in the World," "Those Whom You Gave Me from the World"
"The Jews"	John 1:19–28; 2:13–25; 5:1–47; 6:41–59; 7:1–36; 8:21–59; 9:1–41; 10:7–21, 22–42; 11:1–12:11; 18:12–27, 28–19:16, 17–37, 38–42; 20:19–23	οἱ Ἰουδαῖοι = 67×: John 1:19; 2:6, 13, 18, 20; 3:1; 4:9, 22; 5:1, 10, 15–16, 18; 6:4, 41, 52; 7:1–2, 11, 13, 15, 35; 8:22, 31, 48, 52, 57; 9:18, 22*bis*; 10:19, 24, 31, 33; 11:8, 19, 31, 33, 36, 45, 54–55; 12:9, 11; 13:33; 18:12, 14, 20, 31, 33, 36, 38–39; 19:3, 7, 12, 14, 19–20, 21(3×), 31, 38, 40, 42; 20:19	The World, Priests, Levites, Pharisees, Simon Peter, Disciples of Jesus, The Twelve, Animal Sellers, Nicodemus, The Invalid at the Pool of Bethzatha, The Crowd, Greeks, Devil, Man Born Blind, Parents of Man Born Blind, Lazarus, Mary, Martha, Thomas, Annas, Pilate, Barrabas, Joseph of Arimathea

Table on the Characters in the Fourth Gospel

Character	Narrative Scenes	Textual References	Interactions
Priests	John 1:19–28	ἱερεῖς = 1×: John 1:19	"The Jews," Levites, John, The Pharisees, "One Whom You Do Not Know"
Levites	John 1:19–28	Λευίται = 1×: John 1:19	"The Jews," Priests, John, The Pharisees, "One Whom You Do Not Know"
Pharisees	John 1:19–28; 3:1–21; 4:1–3; 7:32–36, 45–52; 7:53–8:11; 8:12–30; 9:13–10:21; 11:45–57; 12:12–19, 36b–43; 18:1–11	Φαρισαῖοι = 20×: John 1:24; 3:1; 4:1; 7:32bis, 45, 47–48; 8:3, 13; 9:13, 15–16, 40; 11:46–47, 57; 12:19, 42; 18:3	"The Jews," Priests, Levites, Nicodemus, The Crowd, Temple Police, Chief Priests, The Authorities, Scribes, Adulterous Woman, Jesus, Elders, Man Born Blind, The Parents of the Man Born Blind, The World
Disciples of John	John 1:35–36; 3:25–36	μαθηταί = 2×: John 1:35; 3:25	John, Jesus, Andrew, An Anonymous Disciple, A "Jew"
An Anonymous Disciple	John 1:35–41 (21:2?); see also "Beloved Disciple" and "Disciples" below		John, Jesus, The World, Andrew, Jesus' Disciples (Jesus' Mother? Jesus' Brothers?)
Andrew	John 1:35–42 (21:2?)	Ἀνδρέας = 5×: John 1:40, 44; 6:8; 12:22bis	John, Jesus, The World, An Anonymous Disciple, Simon Peter, Jesus' Disciples, (Jesus' Mother? Jesus' Brothers?), The Crowd, A Boy With Loaves and Fish, People, Philip, Greeks

Character	Narrative Scenes	Textual References	Interactions
Simon Peter: – Peter – Simon – Cephas	John 1:35–42; 6:1–15, 60–68; 13:1–17:26, 18:1–11, 18:12–27, 20:1–10, 21:1–25	Πέτρος = 34×: John 1:40, 42, 44; 6:8, 68; 13:6, 8–9, 24, 36, 37; 18:10–11, 15, 16bis, 17–18, 25–27; 20:2–4, 6; 21:2–3, 7bis, 11, 15, 17, 20–21 Σίμων = 25×: John 1:40–42; 6:8, 68, 71; 13:2, 6, 9, 24, 26, 36; 18:10; 15, 25; 20:2, 6; 21:2–3, 7, 11, 15bis, 16–17 Κηφᾶς = 1×: John 1:42	Andrew, Jesus, Jesus' Disciples, The Twelve, Judas Iscariot, Beloved Disciple, Temple Police, Pharisees, Malchus, Soldiers, Another Disciple, People in the Courtyard, Mary Magdalene, Thomas, Nathanael, Sons of Zebedee, Two Others of Jesus' Disciples
Philip	John 1:43–46; 6:1–15; 12:20–26; 13:31–14:30	Φίλιππος = 12×: John 1:43–46, 48; 6:5, 7; 12:21, 22bis; 14:8–9	Jesus, Nathanael, Jesus' Disciples (Jesus' Mother? Jesus' Brothers?), The Crowd, Greeks
Nathanael	John 1:45–51; 21:1–23	Ναθαναήλ = 6×: John 1:45–49; 21:2	Philip, Jesus, Angels, Jesus' Disciples (Jesus' Mother? Jesus' Brothers?), Simon Peter, Thomas, Sons of Zebedee, Two Others of Jesus' Disciples
Mother of Jesus: – The Mother of Jesus – His Mother – Mother – Your Mother	John 2:1–12; 6:41–51; 19:25b–27	ἡ μήτηρ τοῦ Ἰησοῦ = 2×: John 2:1, 3 ἡ μήτηρ αὐτοῦ = 4×: John 2:5, 12, 19:25bis μήτηρ = 3×: John 6:42; 19:26bis ἡ μήτηρ σου = 1×: John 19:27	Jesus, Jesus' Disciples, Jesus' Brothers (Her Sons?), Servants at Cana, Bridegroom at Cana; Jesus' Mother's Sister, Mary the Wife of Clopas, Mary Magdalene, Beloved Disciple

Table on the Characters in the Fourth Gospel

Character	Narrative Scenes	Textual References	Interactions
Disciples of Jesus: – Disciples – The Twelve	John 2:1–12; 2:13–25; 3:22–36; 4:1–42; 6:1–15; 6:16–21; 6:22–59; 7:1–9; 9:1–41; 11:1–44; 11:54; 12:1–11; 12:12–19; 13:1–17:26; 18:1–11/12; 20:11–18; 20:19–31; 21:1–25	μαθηταί = 56×: John 2:2, 11–12, 17, 22; 3:22; 4:1–2, 8, 27, 31, 33; 6:3, 8, 12, 16, 22bis, 24, 60–61, 66; 7:3; 9:2; 11:7–8, 12, 54; 12:4, 16; 13:5, 22–23, 35; 15:8; 16:17, 29; 18:1bis, 2, 17, 19, 25; 20:10, 18–20, 25–26, 30; 21:1–2, 4, 8, 12, 14 οἱ δώδεκα = 4×: John 6:67, 70–71; 20:24	Mother of Jesus, Jesus, Servants at Cana, Steward at Cana, Bridegroom, Jesus' Brothers, Animal Sellers and "Money-Changers," "The Jews," Samaritan Woman, Samaritans, The Crowd, The Boy With the Loaves and Fish, Man Born Blind, Neighbors of the Man Born Blind, Pharisees, Martha, Mary, Lazarus, Temple Police, Malchus, Soldiers, Mary Magdalene
Servants at Cana	John 2:1–11	διάκονοι = 2×: John 2:5, 9	Jesus' Mother, Jesus, Steward at Cana
Steward at Cana	John 2:1–11	ἀρχιτρίκλινος = 3×: John 2:8, 9bis	Jesus, Servants at Cana, The Bridegroom at Cana
Bridegroom	John 2:1–11	νυμφίος = 1×: John 2:9	Jesus, Jesus' Mother, Jesus' Disciples, Steward at Cana
Brothers of Jesus	John 2:12	ἀδελφοί = 4×: John 2:12; 7:3, 5, 10	Jesus, Jesus' Mother, Jesus' Disciples
Animal Sellers: – People Selling Cattle and Sheep and Doves – Money Changers – People Selling Doves	John 2:13–21	οἱ πωλοῦντες βόας καὶ πρόβατα καὶ περιστεράς = 1×: John 2:14 κερματισταί = 1×: John 2:14 κολλυβισταί = 1×: John 2:15 οἱ τὰς περιστεράς πωλοῦσιν = 1×: John 2:16	Jesus, Jesus' Disciples, "The Jews"

Character	Narrative Scenes	Textual References	Interactions
Nicodemus	John 3:1–21; 7:45–52; 8:12–30; (9:16b?); (10:21?); (12:42–43?); 19:38–42	Νικόδημος = 5×: John 3:1, 4, 9; 7:50; 19:39	Pharisees, "The Jews," Jesus, Temple Police, Chief Priests, Authorities
A "Jew"	John 3:25–36	Ἰουδαῖος = 1×: John 3:25	John's Disciples
Samaritan Woman	John 4:7–42	γυνή = 13×: John 4:7, 9bis, 11, 15, 17, 19, 21, 25, 27–28, 39, 42	Jesus, Husbands of the Samaritan Woman, Current Man of the Samaritan Woman, Jesus' Disciples, Samaritans of Sychar
Men of the Samaritan Woman: – Former Men – Current Man of the Samaritan Woman	John 4:16–30	ἄνδρες = 4×: John 4:16, 17bis, 18 ἀνήρ = 1×: John 4:18	The Samaritan Woman
Samaritans of Sychar: – People – Many of the Samaritans – Samaritans	John 4:28–30, 39–42	ἄνθρωποι = 1×: John 4:28 πολλοὶ τῶν Σαμαριτῶν = 1×: John 4:39 Σαμαρῖται = 1×: John 4:40	The Samaritan Woman, Jesus, Jesus' Disciples
Galileans	John 4:43–45	Γαλιλαῖοι = 1×: John 4:45	Jesus
Royal Official: – Man – Father	John 4:46–54	βασιλικός = 2×: John 4:46, 49 ἄνθρωπος = 1×: John 4:50 πατήρ = 1×: John 4:53	The Royal Official's Son, Jesus, (Jesus' Disciples?), The Official's Slaves, The Official's Household

Table on the Characters in the Fourth Gospel

Character	Narrative Scenes	Textual References	Interactions
Son of the Royal Official: – Son – Little Boy – Boy	John 4:46–54	υἱός = 4×: John 4:46, 47, 50, 53 παιδίον = 1×: John 4:49 παῖς = 1×: John 4:51	Royal Official, Slaves of the Royal Official, Household of the Royal Official
Slaves of the Royal Official / Household of the Royal Official	John 4:50b–54	δοῦλοι = 1×: John 4:51 ἡ οἰκία = 1×: John 4:53	Royal Official, The Official's Son
The Ill at the Pool of Bethzatha	John 5:2–9	οἱ ἀσθενοῦντες = 1×: John 5:3	The Invalid at the Pool, Jesus
The Invalid at the Pool of Bethzatha: – A Certain Man – The Sick Man – Man – The Man Who Had Been Cured – The Man Who Had Been Healed	John 5:5–15	τις ἄνθρωπος = 1×: John 5:5 ὁ ἀσθενῶν = 1×: John 5:7 ἄνθρωπος = 2×: John 5:9, 15 ὁ τεθεραπευμένος = 1×: John 5:10 ὁ ἰαθείς = 1×: John 5:13	The Ill at the Pool, Jesus, The Crowd, "The Jews"
The Crowd	John 5:10–18; 6:1–15, 22–59; 7:10–52; 11:28–45; 12:9–50	ὄχλος = 20×: John 5:13; 6:2, 5, 22, 24; 7:12*bis*, 20, 31–32, 40, 43, 49; 11:42; 12:9, 12, 17–18, 29, 34	Jesus, The Invalid at the Pool, (Philip? Andrew? The Boy with the Loaves and Fish?), Jesus' Disciples, "The Jews"
The Boy with the Loaves and Fish	John 6:1–15	παιδάριον = 1×: John 6:9	Andrew, Jesus, The Crowd

Character	Narrative Scenes	Textual References	Interactions
Judas (the Betrayer)	John 6:60–71; 12:1–8; 13:1–30; 18:1–14	Ἰούδας = 8×: John 6:71; 12:4; 13:2, 26, 29; 18:2–3, 5	Jesus, Jesus' Disciples/ The Twelve, Simon Peter, Mary, Martha, Lazarus, The Poor, The Beloved Disciple, Devil/ Satan, Temple Police, Soldiers, Pharisees, (Malchus? Annas? Caiaphas?)
Authorities	John 7:10–52	ἄρχοντες = 3×: John 7:26, 48; 12:42	Jesus, Pharisees
Chief Priests	John 7:45–52; 11:45–53; 18:1–11; 18:28–19:37	ἀρχιερεῖς = 10×: John 7:32, 45; 11:47, 57; 12:10; 18:3, 35, 19:6, 15, 21	Temple Police, Pharisees, Nicodemus, Caiaphas, Pilate, Jesus
Temple Police	John 7:32, 45–52; 18:1–27; 18:28–19:16	ὑπηρέται = 8×: John 7:32, 45, 46; 18:3, 12, 18, 22, 19:6	Chief Priests, Pharisees, Jesus, Nicodemus, Judas, Jesus' Disciples, Soldiers, Simon Peter, Malchus, The Officer (of the Temple Police), Annas, Slaves, High Priest, Pilate
Greeks	John 7:10–52; 12:20–50	Ἕλληνές = 2×: John 7:35, 12:20	"The Jews," Philip, Andrew, Jesus
Scribes	John 8:1–11	γραμματεῖς = 1×: John 8:3	Pharisees, Adulterous Woman, Jesus, Elders
The Adulterous Woman: – A Woman Who Had Been Caught in Adultery – Woman	John 8:1–11	γυνὴ ἐν μοιχείᾳ καταλήφθεισα = 1×: John 8:3 γυνή = 3×: John 8:4, 9, 10	The People, Jesus, Scribes, Pharisees, Elders
Elders	John 8:1–11	πρεσβύτεροι = 1×: John 8:9	Scribes, Pharisees, Adulterous Woman, Jesus

Table on the Characters in the Fourth Gospel 41

Character	Narrative Scenes	Textual References	Interactions
The Devil: – Satan – Ruler of This World	John 8:21–59; 13:1–30; 14:1–31	διάβολος = 2×: John 8:44; 13:2 Σατανᾶς = 1×: John 13:27 ὁ ἄρχων τοῦ κόσμου τούτου = 2×: John 12:31, 16:11 ὁ τοῦ κόσμου ἄρχων = 1×: John 14:30	Jesus, "The Jews," Judas Iscariot, Jesus' Disciples
Man Born Blind: – Beggar – The Man Who Used To Sit and Beg – The Man Who Had Been Formerly Blind – Blind Man – The Man Who Had Received His Sight – Son – The Man Who Had Been Blind – A Disciple of That Man – Man	John 9:1–41	ἄνθρωπος τυφλὸς ἐκ γενετῆς = 1×: John 9:1 προσαίτης = 1×: John 9:8 ὁ καθήμενος καὶ προσαιτῶν = 1×: John 9:8 ὁ ποτε τυφλός = 1×: John 9:13 τυφλός = 1×: John 9:17 ὁ ἀναβλέψας = 1×: John 9:18 υἱός = 2×: John 9:19–20 ὁ ἄνθρωπος ὃς ἦν τυφλός = 1×: John 9:24 μαθητὴς ἐκείνου = 1×: John 9:28 ἄνθρωπος = 1×: John 9:30	Jesus, Jesus' Disciples, Neighbors, Pharisees, "The Jews," Parents of the Man Born Blind
Neighbors of the Man Born Blind: – The People Who Had Seen Him Before As a Beggar	John 9:1–41	γείτονες = 1×: John 9:8 οἱ θεωροῦντες αὐτὸν τὸ πρότερον ὅτι προσαίτης ἦν = 1×: John 9:8	Man Born Blind, Pharisees
Parents of Man Born Blind	John 9:1–41	γονεῖς = 6×: John 9:2, 3, 18, 20, 22, 23	"The Jews," Man Born Blind

Character	Narrative Scenes	Textual References	Interactions
Believers across the Jordan: Many	John 10:40–42	πολλοί = 2×: John 10:41, 42	Jesus, John the Baptist
Lazarus:	John 11:1–44; 12:1–11, 12–19	Λάζαρος ἀπὸ Βηθανίας = 1×: John 11:1	Mary, Martha, Jesus, Disciples, "The Jews," Judas Iscariot, The Crowd
– Lazarus		Λάζαρος = 10×: John 11:2, 5, 11, 14, 43; 12:1, 2, 9, 10, 17	
– Brother		ἀδελφός = 5×: John 11:2, 19, 21, 23, 32	
– He Whom You Love		ὃν φιλεῖς = 1×: John 11:3	
– Our Friend		ὁ φίλος ἡμῶν = 1×: John 11:11	
– The Dead Man		ὁ τετελευτηκώς = 1×: John 11:39	
– The Dead Man		ὁ τεθνηκώς = 1×: John 11:44	
Mary (of Bethany):	John 11:1–44, 45–57; 12:1–11		Lazarus, Martha, Jesus, Disciples, "The Jews," Judas Iscariot
– Mary		Μαρία = 1×: John 11:1	
– Mary		Μαριάμ = 8×: John 11:2, 19, 20, 28, 31, 32, 45; 12:3	
– Sisters		ἀδελφαί = 1×: John 11:3	
– Sister		ἀδελφή = 2×: John 11:5, 28	
Martha:	John 11:1–44; 12:1–11		Lazarus, Mary, Jesus, Disciples, "The Jews," Judas Iscariot
– Martha		Μάρθα = 9×: John 11:1, 5, 19, 20, 21, 24, 30, 39; 12:2	
– Sister		ἀδελφή = 1×: John 11:1	
– Sisters		ἀδελφαί = 1×: John 11:3	
– Sister of the Dead Man		ἀδελφὴ τοῦ τετελευτηκότος = 1×: John 11:39	

Table on the Characters in the Fourth Gospel

Character	Narrative Scenes	Textual References	Interactions
Thomas Twin	John 11:1–44; 14:1–31; 20:24–25; 20:26–29	Θωμᾶς = 7×: John 11:16; 14:5; 20:24, 26, 27, 28; 21:2 Δίδυμος =3×: John 11:16; 20:24; 21:2	Jesus, Disciples, Mary, Martha, Lazarus, "The Jews," Nathanael, Sons of Zebedee, Two Other Disciples
Caiaphas High Priest	John 11:45–57; 18:12–27; 18:28–19:16	Καϊάφας = 5×: John 11:49; 18:13, 14; 18:24, 28 ἀρχιερεύς = 4×: John 11:49, 51; 18:13, 24	Chief Priests, Pharisees, Jesus, Annas
The Beloved Disciple: - Two of His (=John the Baptist's) Disciples - One of the Disciples – the One Whom Jesus Loved - Another Disciple - The Disciple Whom He Loved - Your Son - Disciple - The One Whom Jesus Loved - The Two Disciples - The Sons of Zebedee and Two of His Other Disciples	John 1:35–40 (?); 13:21–30; 18:15–16 (?); 19:26–27; 19:35, 20:1–10; 21:1–23; 21:24–25	ἐκ τῶν μαθητῶν αὐτοῦ (= ὁ Ἰωάννης) δύο (?) = 1×: John 1:35 εἷς ἐκ τῶν μαθητῶν … ὃν ἠγάπα ὁ Ἰησοῦς = 1×: John 13:23 ἄλλος μαθητής = 5×: John 18:15 (?); 20:2, 3, 4, 8 ὁ μαθητής …ὃν ἠγάπα = 3×: John 19:26; 21:7, 20 υἱός σου = 1×: John 19:26 μαθητής = 4×: John 19:27bis; 21:23, 24 ὃν ἐφίλει ὁ Ἰησοῦς = 1×: John 20:2 οἱ δύο = 1×: John 20:4 μαθηταί = 1×: John 20:10 οἱ τοῦ Ζεβεδαίου καὶ ἄλλοι ἐκ τῶν μαθητῶν αὐτοῦ δύο = 1×: John 21:2 (?)	John the Baptist (?), Jesus, Andrew (?), John's Disciples, Jesus' Disciples, Simon Peter, Judas Iscariot, High Priest, The Woman Who Guarded the Gate, The Mother of Jesus, Mary Magdalene, Thomas, Nathanael, "Sons of Zebedee and Two Others of His Disciples" (?)
Judas (not Iscariot)	John 14:1–31	Ἰούδας, οὐχ ὁ Ἰσκαριώτης = 1×: John 14:22	Jesus, Jesus' Disciples

Character	Narrative Scenes	Textual References	Interactions
Annas: - Father-in-Law of Caiaphas - High Priest	John 18:12–27	Ἄννας = 2×: John 18:13, 24 πενθερὸς τοῦ Καϊάφα = 1×: John 18:13 ἀρχιερεύς = 6×: John 18:15bis, 16, 19, 22, 26	Soldiers, Temple Police, Officer (of the Temple Police), "The Jews," Caiaphas, Jesus, Another Disciple
Roman Soldiers at Jesus' Arrest: - Cohort	John 18:1–11, 12–15	σπεῖρα = 2×: John 18:3, 12	Judas Iscariot, Temple Police, Jesus, Officer (of the Temple Police), Annas
Malchus: - The Slave of the High Priest - Slave - Malchus	John 18:1–11	τοῦ ἀρχιερέως δοῦλος = 1×: John 18:10 δοῦλος = 1×: John 18:10 Μάλχος = 1×: John 18:10	Simon Peter, Jesus
People in the Courtyard: - The Woman Who Guarded The Gate - Servant Girl - Slaves - One of the Slaves of the High Priest, a Relative of the Man Whose Ear Peter Had Cut Off	John 18:12–26	θυρωρός = 2×: John 18:16, 17 παιδίσκη = 1×: John 18:17 δοῦλοι = 1×: John 18:18 εἷς ἐκ τῶν δούλων τοῦ ἀρχιερέως, συγγενὴς ὢν οὗ ἀπέκοψεν Πέτρος τὸ ὠτίον = 1×: John 18:26	Another Disciple, Simon Peter
Pontius Pilate	John 18:28–19:16; 19:17–37, 38–42	Πιλᾶτος = 20×: John 18:29, 31, 33, 35, 37, 38; 19:1, 4, 6, 8, 10, 12, 13, 15, 19, 21, 22, 31, 38bis	Jesus, "The Jews," Chief Priests, Temple Police, Joseph of Arimathea
Barabbas	John 18:28–19:16	Βαραββᾶς = 2×: John 18:40bis	Pilate, "The Jews," Jesus

Table on the Characters in the Fourth Gospel 45

Character	Narrative Scenes	Textual References	Interactions
Soldiers Who Crucified: - Soldiers	John 19:17–37	στρατιῶται = 5×: John 19:2, 23, 24, 32, 34	Jesus, Women by the Cross (?), Co-Crucified
The Co-Crucified Men: - Two Others - Co-Crucified	John 19:17–37	ἄλλοι δύο = 1×: John 19:18 συσταυρωθείς = 1×: John 19:32	Jesus, Soldiers
Women by the Cross: - His Mother - The Sister of His Mother - Mary of Clopas - Mary Magdalene	John 19:17–37	ἡ μήτηρ αὐτοῦ = 1×: John 19:25 ἡ ἀδελφὴ τῆς μητρὸς αὐτοῦ = 1×: John 19:25 Μαρία ἡ τοῦ Κλωπᾶ = 1×: John 19:25 Μαρία ἡ Μαγδαληνή = 1×: John 19:25	Jesus, Soldiers (?), Beloved Disciple
Mary Magdalene: - Mary - Woman - Mary - Mary Magdalene	John 19:17–37; 20:1–10, 11–18	Μαρία ἡ Μαγδαληνή = 2×: John 19:25; 20:1 Μαρία = 1×: John 20:11 γύνη = 2×: John 20:13, 15 Μαριάμ = 1×: John 20:16 Μαριάμ ἡ Μαγδαληνή = 1×: John 20:18	Jesus, The Mother of Jesus, Mary of Clopas, Mary Magdalene, Simon Peter, Other Disciple (= Beloved Disciple?), Two Angels, Jesus' Disciples
Joseph of Arimathea	John 19:38–42	Ἰωσὴφ ἀπὸ Ἁριμαθαίας = 1×: John 19:38	Pilate, Nicodemus, Jesus, "The Jews"
Angels	John 20:11–18	ἄγγελοι = 1×: John 20:12 (cf. also 1:51)	Mary Magdalene
Sons of Zebedee	John 21:1–14	οἱ τοῦ Ζεβεδαίου = 1×: John 21:2	Simon Peter, Thomas, Nathanael, Two Other Disciples (Beloved Disciple included?), Jesus
Two Others of His Disciples	John 21:1–14	ἄλλοι ἐκ τῶν μαθητῶν αὐτοῦ δύο = 1×: John 21:2	Simon Peter, Thomas, Nathanael, Sons of Zebedee (Beloved Disciple included?), Jesus

John (the Baptist):
The Witness on the Threshold

Catrin H. Williams

John the Baptist stands considerably apart from the other characters who encounter Jesus in the narrated world of the Fourth Gospel. He is ascribed more direct speech than any other figure apart from Jesus, and, like Jesus, he is the subject of evocative imagery in his own self-declarations and in descriptions of him offered by others. John[1] is undoubtedly a decisive figure in the first half of the narrative, especially in the first chapter; his story and voice emerge clearly as early as the prologue (1:6–8, 15), only for both to be brought firmly to earth, and amplified, in a three-day account of his testimony and witnessing activity (1:19–28, 29–34, 35–37, 40). Recapitulation follows (3:22–30[31–36]) and, after John's final appearance, there is retrospective evaluation of his testimony (5:33–36) and of its efficacy in drawing people to Jesus (10:40–42).

What evidently binds together these episodes is John's identity and function as witness, so much so that it has become commonplace to claim that his character portrait in the Fourth Gospel is almost totally restricted to that of a witness on behalf of Jesus.[2] Several conspicuous textual features have prompted scholars to reach this conclusion. First, only the bare essentials are provided as far as John's character profile is concerned; well-known "Synoptic" features such as his designation as a "prophet" and his role as a preacher of repentance are striking for their absence from the Johannine narrative (cf. Mark 1:4, 11:32; Matt 3:11; 11:9; Luke 3:3), as are references to his diet and physical appearance (Mark 1:6; Matt 3:4).[3] Secondly, what remains of John's otherwise well-known

---
[1] Because the Fourth Gospel, in contrast to the Synoptic Gospels, does not use the designation "the Baptist" as his identity marker, this essay will refer to him as "John" or occasionally as "John (the Baptist)."

[2] See especially R. Alan Culpepper, *Anatomy of the Fourth Gospel: A Study in Literary Design* (Philadelphia: Fortress, 1983), 132–33; cf. Josef Ernst, *Johannes der Täufer: Interpretation – Geschichte – Wirkungsgeschichte* (BZNW 53; Berlin: Walter de Gruyter, 1989), 186–216; Raymond F. Collins, "From John to the Beloved Disciple: An Essay on Johannine Characters," *Int* 49 (1995): 359–69, here 361–62.

[3] On the presentation of John the Baptist in Synoptic traditions, see, for example, Josef Ernst, *Johannes der Täufer – der Lehrer Jesu?* (Biblische Bücher 2; Freiburg: Herder, 1994), 11–50; Ulrich B. Müller, *Johannes der Täufer: Jüdischer Prophet und Wegbereiter Jesu* (Biblische Gestalten 6; Leipzig: Evangelische Verlagsanstalt, 2002), 100–62. See also Knut Backhaus, "Echoes from the Wilderness: The Historical John the Baptist," in *The Study of Jesus*

characteristics now informs his characterization as a key witness to Jesus. Although the appellation "the Baptist" and an account of Jesus' baptism do not occur in the Fourth Gospel, John's water-baptism is explicitly identified as the occasion for Jesus to be revealed to Israel (John 1:31, 33). Thirdly, in all but the final scene in which John is mentioned (10:40–42), the language of "witnessing" permeates his description, either with the aid of the verb μαρτυρέω (1:7, 8, 15, 32, 34; 3:26; 5:33) or the noun μαρτυρία (1:7, 19; 5:34, 36). Fourthly, John's role as witness is given expression not only through his own speech and actions, but also in what other characters (5:33–36; 10:41) as well as the narrator (1:6–8, 15, 19) say about him.

The carefully constructed presentation of John (the Baptist) in the Johannine narrative has led to his narrative-critical categorization as a "flat" character, as one who displays the single consistent trait of bearing witness to Jesus.[4] However, one of the inevitable consequences of pigeonholing John into the category of "flat character" is that it implies a wholly monochromic figure lacking any signs of individuality.[5] More recently, Cornelis Bennema has proposed that John's characterization in the Fourth Gospel is more complex, hovering between "type" and "personality."[6] John, it is remarked, displays personal qualities such as loyalty and humility, and although he possesses one primary trait (= witness) under which all secondary traits are subsumed (= baptizer, herald, teacher, best man, lamp), the latter help to elaborate upon, adding further dimensions to, his character portrait.[7]

Bennema aptly delineates the multifaceted nature of John's role as witness, although his decision to focus exclusively on John's "character indicators"

(ed. Tom Holmén and Stanley E. Porter; vol. 2 of *Handbook for the Study of the Historical Jesus*; Leiden: Brill, 2011), 1747–85.

[4] Collins, "Beloved Disciple," 368, fn. 19; Colleen M. Conway, "Speaking through Ambiguity: Minor Characters in the Fourth Gospel," *BibInt* 10 (2002): 324–41, here 330. Edward M. Forster, *Aspects of the Novel* (Harmondsworth, Middlesex: Penguin, 1962), 73–81, used the phrase "flat characters" to describe predictable and one-dimensional characters constructed around a single idea or quality, and "round characters" for those who possess more than one quality and show signs of development.

[5] For the view that Forster's classification is too rigid, "obliterating the degrees and nuances found in actual works of narrative fiction," see Shlomith Rimmon-Kenan, *Narrative Fiction: Contemporary Poetics* (New York: Methuen, 1983), 40–41 (quotation on p. 40). See further D. Francois Tolmie, *Narratology and Biblical Narratives: A Practical Guide* (San Francisco: International Scholars Publication, 1999), 54–55.

[6] Cornelis Bennema, *Encountering Jesus: Character Studies in the Gospel of John* (Milton Keynes: Paternoster, 2009), 30. Bennema employs the term "type" to classify characters possessing a single trait, and "personality" for characters who display development and a measure of complexity but are not fully round; see idem, "A Theory of Character in the Fourth Gospel with Reference to Ancient and Modern Literature," *BibInt* 17 (2009): 375–421, here 407. On "types," see Horace Porter Abbott, *The Cambridge Introduction to Narrative* (2d ed.; Cambridge: Cambridge University Press, 2008), 136–38, who states that "characterization by type can accommodate a great deal of human complexity" (137).

[7] See Bennema, "Theory of Character," 403.

through his actions and designations[8] overlooks the close symbiotic relationship between "character" and "characterization" in the text's literary strategy.[9] Studying a "character" involves reconstruction and classification in the light of his/her given traits, but "characterization" entails analyzing the methods employed by an author to construct a character and, as a result, to work out his/her function in a text. Examining *how* a character is created proves to be a particularly fruitful exercise in the case of the "Johannine John (the Baptist)," for although he does not display conflicting traits and is not "capable of surprising [the reader] in a convincing way,"[10] the dynamics of his characterization are both varied and striking. This essay seeks to bring John's "character" and "characterization" into direct conversation with each other, in order to examine how various literary techniques such as telling and focalization, structural patterns and setting, shape his presentation as a decisive witness to Jesus.

The "Telling" of the Witness and his Testimony (1:6–8, 15)

Observing how a character is introduced into a narrative is an essential aspect of the study of characterization; it frequently operates as the platform for establishing a character's defining features and as the lens through which that character should be viewed. From within the cosmic setting of the initial verses of the prologue (1:1–5), John (the Baptist) comes directly into view as a human witness who provides the historical anchoring for the story of the eternal Logos and light. The narrator engages in a process of "telling," through a direct form of characterization,[11] and highlights the human facets of John's identity by using them to frame the divine origin of his commission: "There was a man (ἐγένετο ἄνθρωπος), sent from God (ἀπεσταλμένος παρὰ Θεοῦ), whose name was John (ὄνομα αὐτῷ Ἰωάννης)" (1:6). Articulating the relationship between his (human) identity and (divine) mission figures prominently, as we shall see, in later scenes involving John, but it is also striking that all three initial clauses about him are clothed in language echoing the scriptural introduction to figures "sent from God" in Israel's past (cf. Exod 3:10–12; I Sam 1:1; Isa 6:8).[12] Thus, already in the opening statement, John is characterized as a connecting link – on the threshold – between the heavenly and the earthly, the eternal and the historical, the old and the new.

---

[8] Bennema, *Encountering Jesus*, 22–30.
[9] On the formation of "character" in relation to techniques of "characterization," see especially Rimmon-Kenan, *Narrative Fiction*, 59–71.
[10] Forster, *Aspects of the Novel*, 81.
[11] On "direct characterization," see Tolmie, *Narratology and Biblical Narratives*, 42–44.
[12] See Hartwig Thyen, *Das Johannesevangelium* (HNT 6; Tübingen: Mohr Siebeck, 2005), 75–76; and Rudolf Schnackenburg, *The Gospel according to St. John: Volume 1* (trans. K. Smyth; New York: Herder & Herder, 1968), 250.

Having established the source of John's mission, its nature and purpose is now carefully outlined: he came to bear witness to the light (1:7a, 8b) so that all might believe (in the light) through him (1:7b). The narrator's evaluative point of view is set out unequivocally at this juncture; while presenting John's witness for the first time, the focus is clearly on Jesus, as corroborated by the statement of qualification that John himself was not the light (1:8a).

The narrator picks up the central theme of 1:6–8 in 1:15 (Ἰωάννης μαρτυρεῖ περὶ αὐτοῦ), this time to introduce John's boldly stated testimony (κέκραγεν λέγων) as affirmation and explanation why he is not the light: he may have precedence in terms of the timing of his earthly mission, but Jesus is superior to him because of his eternal priority (πρῶτός μου ἦν). The close "fit" between the prologue's two sections about John aligns the narrator's words to those of John, so that John affirms the validity of what has earlier been said about him. In other words, the divinely ordained witness gives explicit expression to what the narrator has already intimated through a series of contrasting parallels: John came into being (1:6: ἐγένετο), but the Logos was (ἦν) in the beginning (1:1); John is a man (1:6), the Logos is "God" (1:1); God has sent John (1:6), the Logos is with God (1:1); John is a witness to the light (1:7–8), the Logos is the light (1:4); people come to faith in the Logos (1:12) through John (1:7).

There is one notable difference between 1:6–8 and 1:15. The former section represents John as a figure who appeared at a specific point of time in the past (1:6–8 is dominated by aorist verbal forms), but in 1:15 John speaks from the present (μαρτυρεῖ), offering a retrospective assessment (οὗτος ἦν) of Jesus' earthly mission.[13] John's testimony, now embedded within the "we" statements of the present community (1:14–16),[14] thus continues to be of enduring significance, even though he himself is a figure belonging to the past.

An examination of John's initial characterization demonstrates that, whatever the compositional history of the prologue, 1:6–8 and 15 are well integrated into their present context. What can be said of their overall function? Morna Hooker has cogently argued that both references occur at turning points in the prologue's two main sections (1:1–13, 14–18) to present John as the one who substantiates the truth of earlier statements: he testifies that the Logos is indeed the light shining in the darkness (1:1–5), the one whose incarnate glory has been seen (1:14).[15] Nevertheless, from a narratological perspective, the declaratory

---

[13] See Martin Stowasser, *Johannes der Täufer im vierten Evangelium: Eine Untersuchung zu seiner Bedeutung für die johanneische Gemeinde* (ÖBS 12; Klosterneuburg: Österreichisches Katholisches Bibelwerk, 1992), 47; Michael Theobald, *Das Evangelium nach Johannes: Kapitel 1–12* (RNT; Regensburg: Friedrich Pustet, 2009), 131; cf. C. Kingsley Barrett, *The Gospel According to St John: An Introduction with Commentary and Notes on the Greek Text* (2d ed.; London: SPCK, 1978), 167.

[14] See in particular Andrew T. Lincoln, *Truth on Trial: The Lawsuit Motif in the Fourth Gospel* (Peabody, Mass.: Hendrickson, 2000), 59–60.

[15] See Morna D. Hooker, "John the Baptist and the Johannine Prologue," NTS 16 (1970): 354–58, here 356–57.

statements in 1:6–8 and 15 also possess an anticipatory function, providing a link between the prologue and what follows, and, most importantly, outlining the main contours of John's character. As has been widely recognized, 1:6–8 offers a "threefold *schema* that controls subsequent sections dealing with the Baptist,"[16] especially 1:19–37 but also other parts of the narrative:

a) John was not the light (1:8a; see 1:19–21; 3:28; 10:41).
b) He came to bear witness to the light (1:7a, 8b; see 1:29–34, 36; 3:26; 5:33; 10:41).
c) He bore witness so that all might believe in the light (1:7b; see 1:35–37; 3:26; 5:34; 10:41–42).

Given that John's testimony (1:15) confirms and elaborates upon the narrator's earlier statements, especially a) and b), a fourth aspect from the prologue should be added:

d) John is subordinate to Jesus (1:15; see 1:27, 30; 3:28–30; 5:34–35).

As we shall see, the prologue's statements about John are determinative for his characterization elsewhere in the text. The four features noted above establish a recognizable pattern, albeit with different configurations, which sum up the narrator's point of view and which are intended as a guide for the implied reader in his/her evaluation of John. The prologue, in this respect, engages in a process of "telling,"[17] focusing on key features and character traits that pass as an evaluative blueprint for John's characterization in other parts of the narrative. The narrator undoubtedly relies on him – and other characters – to both "show" and "tell" his traits and motives in subsequent scenes, but all the basic ingredients have been outlined in the prologue; some embellishment may be detected around the edges, but the implied reader's perception of John will not change.

John's Testimony Over Three Days (1:19–28, 29–34, 35–42)

After the "telling" of John and his witness in the prologue, the narrator shifts, with considerable ease (a simple καί), to offer a new introduction that picks up and focuses on the core subject of 1:6–8 and 15: "*This* is the testimony (καὶ

---

[16] Charles H. Dodd, *Historical Tradition in the Fourth Gospel* (Cambridge: Cambridge University Press, 1963), 248–49. See also Ernst, *Johannes der Täufer,* 197; Mark W. G. Stibbe, *John* (Sheffield: JSOT Press, 1993), 31.

[17] On the narratological techniques of "telling" and "showing," see Wayne C. Booth, *The Rhetoric of Fiction* (Chicago: University of Chicago Press, 1961), 3–16; Mark A. Powell, *What is Narrative Criticism? A New Approach to the Bible* (London: SPCK, 1993), 52–53; James L. Resseguie, *Narrative Criticism of the New Testament: An Introduction* (Grand Rapids, Mich.: Baker Academic, 2005), 126–30.

αὕτη ἐστὶν ἡ μαρτυρία) of John" (1:19). Once again, John functions as a bridge bringing together the historical past and the living present. The continuing significance of his testimony, first communicated at a concrete time and place (cf. 1:19: ὅτε),[18] is encapsulated by the use of the present tense in the opening statement (ἐστίν; cf. 1:15). Furthermore, although John's central character traits have already been set out in the prologue, his characterization in the rest of the first chapter highlights his crucial role in plot development. Through temporal sequences and causal links, the nature, scope and purpose of John's testimony over three days are made unquestionably apparent: John outlines his own limitations and role as a witness to a nameless figure (1:19–28), one whose appearance "the next day" prompts John to offer a witnessing monologue (1:29–34), with the result that, on the following day, two of his disciples become followers of Jesus (1:35–36).

Despite significant demarcation markers, there is no doubt that, as far as the characterization of John is concerned, emphasis should be placed on the unity of these three scenes. The temporal signals (τῇ ἐπαύριον) may point to a change of time/scene, but they also establish continuity for John's testimony over three days, whereas the spotlight on his witness is conveyed by the "witnessing" *inclusio* framing the beginning of the first scene (1:19) and the end of the second (1:34).[19] Repetition links together John's three-stage testimony (1:29, 36), and several commentators have noted that his threefold denial about his own significance (1:20–21: not the Messiah, Elijah, or the prophet) "parallels" his three-part proclamation about Jesus' identity (1:30, 33, 34: Lamb of God, Spirit-baptizer, Chosen/Son of God).[20]

Regarding John's character presentation on the first day (1:19–28), certain narrative strategies are identifiable which show him redirecting attention away from himself towards Jesus. The initial focus is clearly on John, whom the Jewish religious authorities question in the starkest possible terms: "Who are you?" (1:19). And yet, while John does offer a bold and unequivocal response with reference to his own identity,[21] the formulation itself, "*I* am not the Mes-

---

[18] In particular see Theobald, *Das Evangelium nach Johannes*, 272–73.

[19] As noted by, among others, Raymond E. Brown, *The Gospel According to John I (i–xii)*, (AB 29; New York: Doubleday, 1966), 67; Tobias Nicklas, *Ablösung und Verstrickung: "Juden" und Jüngergestalten als Charaktere der erzählten Welt des Johannesevangeliums und ihre Wirkung auf den impliziten Leser* (RST 60; Frankfurt am Main: Peter Lang, 2001), 100.

[20] Cf. Stibbe, *John*, 34; Johannes Rinke, *Kerygma und Autopsie: Der christologische Disput als Spiegel johanneischer Gemeindegeschichte* (Herders Biblische Studien 12; Freiburg: Herder, 1997), 272.

[21] Boldness of speech is one of John's character traits (cf. 1:15, 23), as indicated by the narrator's introduction to his first disavowal: "He confessed and did not deny it, but confessed ..." (1:20). The pleonastic form of this statement suggests that, integral to this scene's judicial atmosphere, is John's unwavering witness before the religious authorities (cf. 9:22; 12:42; 13:38; 18:25, 27). On placing John as witness within the Johannine framework of a cosmic lawsuit, see Anthony E. Harvey, *Jesus on Trial: A Study in the Fourth Gospel* (London:

siah" (ἐγὼ οὐκ εἰμὶ ὁ χριστός), with its likely emphatic ἐγώ, already indicates that there is another figure to whom this title belongs, but who, at this point, remains in the shadows of the narrative.

Further probing by the Jewish delegation (1:21: "Are you Elijah?;" "Are you the prophet?") leads to other, progressively brief,[22] denials by John (1:21: οὐκ εἰμί ... οὔ), before he makes the first positive pronouncement about his identity with the aid of Isaiah 40:3: "I am the voice of one crying out in the wilderness, 'Make straight the way of the Lord,' as the prophet Isaiah said" (1:23). This declaration contributes to the character portrait of John in a number of significant ways. He is the only figure in the Fourth Gospel to appropriate and actualize the words of Scripture for the purpose of self-description. Indeed, in view of the judicial character of this scene, with its emphasis on witness, interrogation, confession and lack of denial (1:20), John's self-testimony is joined to Isaiah's testimony to give it validity and authority.[23] Through Isaiah's words, John overtly identifies himself with the herald who proclaims God's message of imminent salvation (Isa 40:3–5). Thus, despite his eagerness to deflect attention away from himself, he is not stripped of all significance.[24] John's embodiment as the Isaianic voice is, in fact, integral to his characterization as the divinely appointed witness, because it is precisely through his testimony to Jesus that he makes straight the way of the Lord. The implied reader, who knows from the outset that John's exclusive role is to bear witness to Jesus, will make this connection with relative ease. Even the setting "in the wilderness" connotes a character trait that has already been established in the prologue; from a literary and theological perspective, the wilderness symbolizes the "in-between space,"[25] between captivity and freedom, between the past and the future. The wilderness can also serve as a temporary dwelling place,[26] which, as a metonym for John's status, indicates that he will not be the subject of debate for long. Given that the Isaianic "way of the Lord" in the Fourth Gospel

---

SPCK, 1976); and Lincoln, *Truth on Trial*, who describes John as "the first witness called in the trial proceedings" (58).

[22] For the view that John's three decreasing replies (1:20–21) amount to a "faint evoking of a process of self-emptying" (cf. 3:30), see Thomas L. Brodie, *The Gospel According to John: A Literary and Theological Commentary* (Oxford: Oxford University Press, 1993), 150.

[23] With Isaiah as his co-witness ("as the prophet Isaiah said"), John's testimony accords with the Jewish legal requirement for at least two witnesses (Num 35:30; Deut 17:6; 19:15). However, because John has been "sent" by God (1:6), the implied reader *expects* him to be an authentic witness.

[24] *Pace* Collins, "Beloved Disciple," 361: "only a voice."

[25] A phrase coined by Resseguie, *Narrative Criticism*, 95. For ancient Jewish traditions on the wilderness as a (temporary) place of preparation, see, for example, Richard A. Horsley & Jonathan A. Draper, *Whoever Hears You Hears Me: Prophets, Performance, and Tradition in Q* (Harrisburg: Trinity Press International, 1999), 264–65.

[26] See Resseguie, *Narrative Criticism*, 96.

is realized in the coming of *Jesus*,[27] the one to whom John bears witness, albeit indirectly at this stage, is increasingly coming into focus.

A more pronounced shift occurs in 1:24–26, when John's interlocutors proceed to ask him about the significance of his baptism. No explicit connection is made at this point between John's water-baptism and Jesus (cf. 1:31), but he immediately shifts attention away from his own activity: "Among you stands one whom you do not know" (1:26). For the first time, reference is made in veiled fashion to an unnamed "other," one whose superiority explains why John must rule out any role for himself other than as the herald for the "coming one." Jesus may remain physically concealed, but his presence gradually infiltrates John's testimony on the first day.[28]

The nature of John's testimony does change when Jesus makes his first appearance (1:29–34), although Jesus remains "der große Schweigende" throughout this scene.[29] When the narrator remarks that John sees Jesus coming towards him, the implied reader is simply left to speculate why he approaches John; it evidently provides an occasion for the next instalment of testimony, but it also acts as an instant illustration of how John "makes straight the way of the Lord" by pointing and testifying to Jesus (cf. 1:23). The description of actions (1:29: John sees Jesus approaching) can be defined, in narratological terms, as an example of external focalization; that is, the narrator provides the lens through which events or characters are seen.[30] More or less immediately, however, the focus turns to John's observations on Jesus, who now becomes the object of internal – or character-bound – focalization.[31] Until the end of this encounter (1:29–34), and briefly during the early stages of the next scene (1:36), John remains the vehicle for focalization, and the rich monologue that follows is narrated entirely from his perspective.

---

[27] See in particular Catrin H. Williams, "Isaiah in John's Gospel," in *Isaiah in the New Testament* (ed. Steven Moyise and Maarten J. J. Menken; London: T&T Clark, 2005), 100–16, here 103–04.

[28] T. Francis Glasson, "John the Baptist in the Fourth Gospel," *ExpTim* 67 (1955–56): 245–46, here 245. Following Nestle-Aland (27th edition) one notes that John's succinct negations about his own identity (eight words in total) are replaced by increasingly longer positive statements of i) self-identification (1:23: fifteen words) and ii) a description of Jesus (1:26–27: twenty-six words).

[29] Michael Theobald, *Die Fleischwerdung des Logos: Studien zum Verhältnis des Johannesprologs zum Corpus des 4. Evangeliums und zum 1. Johannesbrief* (NTAbh 20; Münster: Aschendorff, 1988), 275.

[30] On focalization, see especially Rimmon-Kenan, *Narrative Fiction*, 72–86; Abbott, *Introduction to Narrative*, 73–74, 233; Mieke Bal, *Narratology: Introduction to the Theory of Narrative* (3d ed.; Toronto: University of Toronto Press, 2009), 145–65.

[31] See further Rinke, *Kerygma und Autopsie*, 272; Judith Hartenstein, *Charakterisierung im Dialog: Maria Magdalena, Petrus, Thomas und die Mutter Jesu im Johannesevangelium im Kontext anderer frühchristlicher Darstellungen* (NTOA/SUNT 64; Göttingen: Vandenhoeck & Ruprecht, 2007), 41.

This shift to John as focalizer operates as a significant literary strategy as far as his characterization is concerned. In contrast to the previous scene, John's testimony to Jesus possesses a strong visual-optical dimension in 1:29b–34. The action is to be observed through his eyes, and the implied reader's gaze is aligned with John's point of observation, in the knowledge that he is a divinely commissioned witness (1:33; cf. 1:6). One clear focalizing marker is the use of ἴδε in the exclamation, "Behold the Lamb of God who takes away the sin of the world" (1:29; cf. 1:36). John, through an act of speech, points to and encourages unspecified others to look at the one who has hitherto been hidden. Through a scripturally saturated statement, in which Passover lamb imagery (cf. 19:14, 29, 36) has, in all likelihood, been combined with echoes of the description of the Servant of God (Isa 53:4, 7, 12 LXX), John already looks ahead to Jesus' way of dealing with sin.[32] The threefold use of the demonstrative phrase οὗτός ἐστιν (1:30, 33, 34) provides yet another focalizing marker, binding together John's claim that the now visibly present Jesus is the one whose pre-eminence he has already declared (1:30; cf. 1:27), the one whose baptism with the Holy Spirit has earlier been announced to John by God (1:33), the one who is "the Chosen One of God" (1:34).[33]

What evidently undergirds John's witnessing gaze on Jesus in this scene is his own earlier experience,[34] particularly what he himself *saw* when the Spirit descended on Jesus, presumably on the occasion of his baptism (1:32: τεθέαμαι; 1:33: ἐφ' ὃν ἂν ἴδῃς; 1:34: κἀγὼ ἑώρακα). In the previous scene John's baptizing activity only gradually comes into view (1:25, 26, 28), and his response to the Jewish delegation's question about its significance is delayed until the following day: the purpose of John's water-baptism is to reveal Jesus to Israel (1:31). Given that the verb φανερόω in the Fourth Gospel repeatedly connotes "an emergence from concealment and obscurity to disclosure,"[35] John's baptism parallels the narrative function, through focalization, of his spoken testimony: the hidden one is unveiled and, when seen, is made known.[36]

---

[32] As aptly remarked by Ruben Zimmermann, *Christologie der Bilder im Johannesevangelium: Die Christopoetik des vierten Evangeliums unter besonderer Berücksichtigung von Joh 10* (WUNT 171; Tübingen: Mohr Siebeck, 2004), 114–15, the rich scriptural background and sacrificial connotations of the "lamb" metaphor prompt the reader to identify a connection with Jesus' death.

[33] For the view that the reading ὁ ἐκλεκτὸς τοῦ θεοῦ ("Chosen One of God") is to be preferred over ὁ υἱὸς τοῦ θεοῦ ("the Son of God"), see Tze-Ming Quek, "A Text-Critical Study of John 1.34," NTS 55 (2009): 22–34. Isaianic echoes can be detected in the declaration that Jesus is the Chosen One of God (Isa 42:1) upon whom the Spirit remained (11:2; 42:1; 61:1).

[34] As highlighted by Angelika Ottillinger, *Vorläufer, Vorbild oder Zeuge? Zum Wandel des Täuferbildes im Johannesevangelium* (Dissertationen: Theologische Reihe 45; St Ottilien: EOS Verlag, 1991), 85.

[35] Stibbe, *John*, 35. Cf. John 2:11; 3:21; 7:4; 9:3.

[36] The enduring significance of John's testimony (cf. 1:15, 19) is again suggested at the end of this scene by the use of two perfect tenses: "And I myself have seen (ἑώρακα) and testified (μεμαρτύρηκα) that this is the Chosen One (or Son) of God" (1:34).

The third scene (1:35–42) opens with another instance of external focalization as the narrator depicts John seeing Jesus walking by. John once again, albeit only fleetingly, becomes the narrative's perspectival filter (1:36: "Behold the Lamb of God"). The narrator, however, quickly resumes the position of focalizer to state that, as a consequence of John's testimony, two of his disciples gravitate towards Jesus, who turns and, for the first time, speaks: "What are you looking for?" (1:38). John at this point simply disappears from the scene, and the one further reference to him in this chapter (1:40) already points back to his *earlier* witnessing activity; his work is nearly done and Jesus is now visibly on centre stage.

The Last Testimony of John (3:22–30[31–36])

John makes his next (and last) appearance, as speaker, when Jesus departs to the Judaean countryside to engage in a baptizing ministry with his disciples (3:22; cf. 4:2). No direct encounter is mentioned, but the scene is shaped in a way that highlights certain affinities between John and Jesus: both baptize in a similar, but geographically separate, setting (3:22–24) and both have disciples (3:22, 25) who address them as "Rabbi" (3:26; cf. 1:49; 3:2). These parallels serve as a platform for a discussion of their relationship, which John addresses directly in his final testimony (3:27–30, 31–36).

Like their master before them, John's disciples "point" to Jesus (3:26: ἴδε οὗτος), although their outlook on him is coloured by two new features: Jesus is now well-known and "all are going to him" (3:26). The suspicion bubbling under the surface, that "Jesus' growth in fame and reputation comes at the expense of John and his disciples,"[37] is later corroborated by the Pharisees: "Jesus is making and baptizing more disciples than John" (4:1). Donning the mantle of the rabbi, John therefore teaches his disciples that Jesus' growing popularity is of divine origin (3:27: "given from heaven") as indeed is his own diminution.

John's role, narratologically, is once again to shift the focus away from himself, this time by revisiting his original testimony. The repetition of his earlier denial, "I am not the Messiah" (3:28; cf. 1:20), invites the implied reader to include consistency among his "paradigm of traits."[38] Repetition can have many literary functions,[39] but the large number of analeptic echoes in John's

---

[37] Jerome H. Neyrey, "'He Must Increase, I Must Decrease' (John 3:30)," in *The Gospel of John in Cultural and Rhetorical Perspective* (Grand Rapids, Mich.: Eerdmans, 2009), 123–142, here 125.
[38] See further Seymour Chatman, *Story and Discourse: Narrative Structure in Fiction and Film* (Ithaca, N. Y.: Cornell University Press, 1978), 126–27.
[39] Resseguie, *Narrative Criticism*, 42, notes the use of repetition as a stylistic device for the

speech projects the image of a reliable witness, whose oft-repeated declarations about Jesus' superiority (1:15, 26, 30) and his own limitations as a forerunner (3:28; cf. 1:20, 27, 30) are borne out by the reported movement of followers from John to Jesus. John's testimony may continue to have impact (3:26: μεμαρτύρηκας), but the scene's emphasis on the reiteration of past words, as well as his disciples' role as a fresh link in the chain of witnesses, suggest that his witnessing activity is something that increasingly belongs to the past.[40]

A new element is, admittedly, introduced into John's reflections on his role: he is the friend of the bridegroom whose joy is fulfilled when he stands and hears the bridegroom's voice (3:29). Intriguingly, this metaphorical description of John's positive reception of Jesus ("hearing his voice;" cf. 5:25; 10:3–4, 16) bears little resemblance to his earlier characterization, where the emphasis has fallen on what John has seen rather than heard. Nevertheless, the wide-ranging duties of the bridegroom's friend in Jewish marriage traditions help to reinforce John's ascribed role as the loyal witness who joyfully acknowledges Jesus' growing success.[41] This scene, in fact, offers several anticipatory indicators of John's pithy declaration, "He must increase, but I must decrease" (3:30). The disciples' remark that "all are going to him [Jesus]" (3:26; cf. 4:1) has been the catalyst for John to admit that the time for his withdrawal has arrived, as already signalled by the parenthetical comment that "John, of course, had not yet been thrown into prison" (3:24). In addition to situating these events before the Galilean phase of Jesus' ministry (cf. Mark 1:14–15), the comment acts as a signal to the implied reader that John's imprisonment – and demise – is imminent.

His departure is not narrated at this point, but neither is it made clear that his spoken testimony is over. Despite many theories about the status of 3:31–36, the lack of a compelling reason for positing a different speaker suggests that it can be read as John's uninterrupted explication of his words in 3:27–30.[42] John explicitly contrasts how he, like all human beings, is "of the earth," while Jesus alone is "from above" (3:31) and faith in him leads to eternal life (3:36). Because what Jesus offers is of a wholly different order, John willingly embraces Jesus' increase and his own decrease through this "swan song" testimony.

---

purpose of emphasis, for adding force or clarity to a statement, and for identifying narrative structure and design.

[40] Cf. Brodie, *John*, 206.

[41] Mirjam and Ruben Zimmermann, "Der Freund des Bräutigams (Joh 3,29): Deflorations- oder Christuszeuge?," *ZNW* 90 (1999): 123–28; Mary L. Coloe, "Witness and Friend: Symbolism Associated with John the Baptiser," in *Imagery in the Gospel of John: Terms, Forms, Themes, and Theology of Johannine Figurative Language* (ed. Jörg Frey et al.; WUNT 200; Tübingen: Mohr Siebeck, 2006), 319–32, here 324–26.

[42] This is the view adopted, for example, by Barrett, *John*, 224; Jeffrey Wilson, "The Integrity of John 3:22–36," *JSNT* 10 (1981): 36–40. Cf. however Stowasser, *Johannes der Täufer*, 159–61.

The Narrative Dwindling and Departure of John (5:33–36; 10:40–42)

Only after John's final appearance does Jesus, for the first time, speak directly about the one sent ahead of him. He is among an array of witnesses invoked by Jesus when he informs "the Jews" that his testimony does not stand alone, but is legitimated by his works, the Scriptures, and by the Father (5:31–39). His interlocutors are reminded that they sent a delegation to John (5:33; cf. 1:19–27), thereby attaching some importance to his role as witness. Jesus himself acknowledges that John bore enduring witness to the truth (5:33: μεμαρτύρηκεν) and that his testimony can lead to faith and salvation (5:34; cf. 1:7, 37; 10:41–42). However, Jesus does not need to rely on, or appeal to, that testimony (5:34), because a human witness like John can only testify to, not legitimate, the works of God.[43] At this point, Jesus confirms what has earlier been intimated about John's identity (cf. 1:6): he is a human being sent by God, who, by his own admission, is "of the earth" (3:31).

The limitations of John's testimony are then articulated in a number of subtle ways. For Jesus to describe him as a "burning and shining lamp" (5:35: λύχνος) confirms what the implied reader has known since the prologue: John is not the true light (1:8–9). His witness helps to diffuse the light, but God initiates or "kindles" his testimony (5:35: ὁ καιόμενος).[44] Similarly, the pastness of his witnessing activity is accentuated (5:35: ἦν), as is its transitoriness (πρὸς ὥραν). On one level, Jesus' estimation of John is somewhat surprising, as considerable importance has been attached to his testimony during the early stages of the narrative. And yet, this assessment is not at odds with the earlier characterization of John; if anything it substantiates the reliability of his witness, since from the outset he has been depicted as being under no illusion about Jesus' superiority as well as his own restricted role.

Striking a fine balance between asserting John's significance and limitations is maintained in 10:40–42, which offers a key transitional point now that Jesus' public ministry draws to an end. The setting is of course significant, because the initial reference to Jesus' withdrawal to the place where John had earlier been baptizing (10:40; cf. 1:28) takes Jesus "back to the beginning."[45] He may have returned to the same location, but this time it is marked by John's absence not his presence. Though a figure of the past (10:41: ἐποίησεν ... εἶπεν; cf. 5:33–36), his witness remains alive because many believe in Jesus *on*

---

[43] Cf. Stowasser, *Johannes der Täufer*, 227–28; Müller, *Johannes der Täufer*, 181–82; Klaus Wengst, *Das Johannesevangelium: 1. Teilband: Kapitel 1–10* (2d ed.; Theologischer Kommentar zum Neuen Testament 4, 1; Stuttgart: W. Kohlhammer, 2004), 216.

[44] Cf. Barrett, *John*, 265; Francis J. Moloney, *Signs and Shadows: Reading John 5–12* (Minneapolis: Fortress, 1996), 21.

[45] Herman N. Ridderbos, *The Gospel of John: A Theological Commentary* (trans. J. Vriend; Grand Rapids, Mich.: Eerdmans, 1997), 378. Cf. Stowasser, *Johannes der Täufer*, 232–33.

the basis of John's testimony (10:41–42). An implied contrast with Jesus, who performs many signs, is suggested by the crowd's remark that "John did no sign" (10:41), but their immediately subsequent affirmation, "Everything that John said about this man was true," demonstrates that his testimony in fact serves to corroborate Jesus' signs.[46]

To the end, John plays his role as witness. Taken back to the narrative beginning, the implied reader recognizes that all the ingredients of "telling" from the prologue now recur through "showing" in this epilogue: John's mission was to bear witness to Jesus; he was not the light (he did no sign), but people come to faith through his enduring and reliable testimony. 10:40–42 thus offers "closure" on John;[47] all the expectations raised earlier about him have been satisfactorily met. Admittedly, what one encounters at the end of John 10 is character closure, not narrative closure. The Johannine story of Jesus continues and, in the absence of a replacement witness within the narrative – at least until the appearance of the Beloved Disciple (13:23–26; 19:35; 20:8; 21:7, 24) – readers are themselves encouraged to take up the witnessing role while "the cosmic lawsuit continues to unfold."[48] However, as far as John's character portrait is concerned, there are no more loose ends, no gaps to be filled; John has no further role to play in the text.

The Character of John (the Baptist)

The Fourth Gospel offers a consistent and highly controlled presentation of John. Neither the narrator nor the narrated characters veer at all from his representation as a key witness to Jesus. Indeed, the sparseness of character details, the unswerving focus on the scope and purpose of his testimony, as well as the repeated avowals of his limitations (1:8, 20; 3:28; 5:35; 10:41) and subordination to Jesus (1:15, 27, 30; 3:29–30), can give the impression that he is more of a functional agent than an individual personality.[49] John's stable and recurring qualities have the effect, moreover, of lending certain predictability to his characterization. The validity of his testimony is repeatedly accentuated (5:33–35; 10:41–42), whereas his boldness of speech (1:15, 20, 23)

---

[46] Andrew T. Lincoln, *The Gospel According to St John* (BNTC; Peabody, Mass.: Hendrickson, 2005), 312–13.
[47] Abbott, *Introduction to Narrative*, 230: "When a narrative ends in such a way as to satisfy the expectations and answer the questions that it has raised, it is said to close, or to have closure."
[48] Lincoln, *Truth on Trial*, 175.
[49] See in particular Colleen M. Conway, *Men and Women in the Fourth Gospel: Gender and Johannine Characterization* (SBLDS 167; Atlanta: Society of Biblical Literature, 1999), 52–53.

and frequently noted reliability, through analeptic echoes of earlier claims, project the image of a loyal and credible witness.

John's character may not be sufficiently unpredictable to allow one to categorize him as a complex and multilayered figure, but this is not to deprive him of some degree of movement and individualization within the narrative. A brief glimpse into his inner life is given in 1:33, by virtue of an embedded analepsis[50] in which John recalls his earlier transition from ignorance to knowledge following his vision of the Spirit's descent on Jesus. John's evaluative point of view thus changes as a result of divine revelation. Moreover, there are occasional hints that some prior knowledge of John is assumed on the part of the implied reader, who, in turn, is encouraged to fill in certain gaps.[51] When the narrator states, "John, of course, had not yet been thrown into prison" (3:24), it is taken for granted that the story of John's imprisonment (and death) is already well known, suggesting that the world behind the text is being evoked at this point.[52] This is not to deny that the characterization of John does, by and large, possess a self-referential quality containable within the narrative text.

While the highly stylized nature of John's character in the Fourth Gospel suggests that he functions as a type with a single overarching trait, it does not follow that he is also a typical figure. It is not uncommon for him to be tagged as a "representative figure," even as a paradigm of the Christian preacher/ believer,[53] but usually without probing further into the appropriateness of the terms "representative" and "paradigm" with reference to his characterization. Insofar as John "sees" Jesus and bears witness to him, he undoubtedly sets an example to be followed by others. He also betrays certain affinities with the Beloved Disciple, whose own "true" testimony similarly leads to faith (19:35; 21:24).[54] However, the differences between them in their capacity as "model witnesses" should not be overlooked. As far as the plot is concerned, John provides an early and decisive link in a chain of witnesses, and the focus of interest is not his belief-response resulting from a face-to-face encounter with Jesus but what he sees as a result of divine commission.

John's unique features as a witness should also not be underestimated. No other "disciple" in the Fourth Gospel reveals such a deep understanding of Jesus' true identity. He is the only human witness to declare Jesus' pre-existence (1:15, 30) and to anticipate the significance of his earthly mission in its entirety, including what he accomplishes through his death, as the Lamb of

---

[50] For this term, see Tolmie, *Narratology and Biblical Narratives*, 90.
[51] Cf. Tolmie, *Narratology and Biblical Narratives*, 40.
[52] See Bennema, "Theory of Character," 399–402.
[53] See Ernst, *Johannes der Täufer*, 215; Raymond F. Collins, *These Things Have Been Written: Studies on the Fourth Gospel* (Louvain: Peeters, 1990), 11.
[54] Cf. Zimmermann, "Der Freund des Bräutigams," 129; Lincoln, *Truth on Trial*, 65.

God (1:29), and through his resurrection, as the one who baptizes with the Spirit (1:33; cf. 7:38–39; 20:22). That John's profound christological insights stem from divine revelation is suggested by the narrative's clear emphasis on God as the source of his witnessing mission. He is the only character other than Jesus and the Paraclete to be described as "sent" by God (1:6, 33), and, as the recipient of heavenly communication (1:32–33), his status is clearly different from that conferred on other Johannine "earthly" characters.

John's characterization as a divinely authorized figure aligns him more closely, in this respect, to key prophetic figures like Moses (Exod 3:10–15) and Isaiah (6:8), both of whom are depicted in the Fourth Gospel as witnesses to Jesus (1:45; 5:46; 12:41; cf. 8:56). John may deny that he is "the prophet" in an eschatological sense (1:21),[55] but the origin and nature of his mission bears close resemblance to that of past prophets. His "prophetic" status may even explain his curious lack of direct interaction with Jesus; like Moses, he bears witness to the protagonist without any suggestion that he converses directly with him,[56] and, like Isaiah, he speaks about, rather than with, Jesus (12:41). In fact, of all the narrated Johannine characters, it is with Isaiah that John shares the most striking similarities. Already at an early stage of his mission, he overtly binds his testimony to that of Isaiah (1:23) and several of his christological testimonies are steeped in Isaianic language (1:29, 32, 34).[57] John, like Isaiah, testifies to what he has seen (12:41), even using the words of his predecessor to furnish his testimony with content and prophetic authority.

John's distinctively prophetic contours in the Fourth Gospel are part and parcel of his characterization as one who belongs to the "in-between" times. With his sound witnessing credentials, John stands on the threshold between promise and fulfilment, between the old and the new. He may be closely linked to significant figures from the past, but his testimony, at the same time, looks forward to what Jesus will accomplish through his life, death and resurrection. Straddling the divide is one of John's most distinguishing features and, for that reason, it is difficult to "place" him or pin him down. After the "telling" of the prologue, he emerges at a point of transition – both spatially (in the wilderness) and chronologically (on the first day) – embodying the Isaianic voice and announcing the appearance of "the coming one." Through his witnessing activity John is able usher in and point to Jesus, but, once Jesus' public ministry is underway and the in-between stage is passing, John's fate is to diminish and fade away. His legacy as a character is that he fulfils a bridge-like role. John's earthly mission belongs firmly to the past, but his testimony still speaks loudly in the present.

---

[55] Cf. Maarten J. J. Menken, *Old Testament Quotations in the Fourth Gospel: Studies in Textual Form* (Biblical Exegesis and Theology 15; Kampen: Kok Pharos, 1996), 133.

[56] See Hartenstein, *Charakterisierung im Dialog*, 112.

[57] See further Williams, "Isaiah in John's Gospel," 104–106.

The World:
Promise and Unfulfilled Hope

Christopher W. Skinner

Introduction

Within the story of the incarnate *Logos*, the Fourth Gospel introduces its readers to the multi-layered and theologically significant term, ὁ κόσμος ("the world").[1] In Hellenistic Greek, κόσμος carries a range of meanings, several of which are employed by the Fourth Evangelist.[2] The term is used to refer to the material reality of the created world,[3] the physical realm into which Jesus has entered,[4] and the object of God's affection and salvific intentions.[5] However, of greater importance for the present study is the term's metonymical function as a symbol for humanity. In at least eight instances in John, κόσμος emerges as a technical term for the human race and in those contexts is presented with a "distinctly pejorative meaning."[6] This nuance is especially important for the unfolding story of the Johannine Jesus.

While many commentators have analyzed the significance of the term κόσμος in John, few have written examining the world as a character or character group. Both Lars Kierspel[7] and Cornelis Bennema[8] have treated the world as a

---

[1] The term is used 78 times in the Fourth Gospel and appears in all but four chapters (chs. 2, 5, 19, and 20).

[2] See H. Sasse, "κόσμος," *TDNT* 3:868–98; BDAG, s. v. κόσμος, 561–63.

[3] Most notably 1:10b: ὁ κόσμος δι' αὐτοῦ ἐγένετο.

[4] The Fourth Gospel presents Jesus as the one who has come "from above." Thus, his departure from the Father represents his entrance into "the world," the realm of "below." On this, see 1:9, 10a, 3:17ab, 19; 6:14.

[5] See, among others, 1:29; 3:16, 17c; 4:42; 6:51.

[6] "'Obscure' though its etymology remains to this day, κόσμος is still beyond doubt one of the principal concepts of Greek thought. It was, to be sure, the richness of its various meanings that fitted it for the role it played in Greco-Hellenistic philosophy ... For in this variety of meanings lay its potential to become 'one of the most important terms in Greek philosophy' and 'one of the great original creations of the Greek spirit.' It is, therefore, doubly puzzling that κόσμος comes to have a *distinctly pejorative meaning* in the NT, and particularly in the Gospel of John" (Stanley B. Marrow, "Κόσμος in John," *CBQ* 64 [2002]: 90) (emphasis added).

[7] Lars Kierspel, *The Jews and the World in the Fourth Gospel: Parallelism, Function, and Context* (WUNT II/220; Tübingen: Mohr Siebeck, 2006), especially chs. 3 and 4.

[8] Cornelis Bennema, *Encountering Jesus: Character Studies in the Gospel of John* (Milton Keynes: Paternoster, 2009), 31–37.

character in John, though both focus too narrowly on the connection between "the Jews" (οἱ Ἰουδαῖοι) and "the world" (ὁ κόσμος) that emerges in the latter stages of the Gospel story. In my opinion this identification is too restrictive and more discussion should be devoted to understanding parallel characteristics exhibited by both the world and other characters in the Fourth Gospel. Such an examination has the potential to yield fresh insights about the world as a character, but also runs the risk of flattening out a robust and complex Johannine concept. We must be careful to emphasize at the outset of our study that a character study of the world is not the same as a comprehensive analysis of the κόσμος concept in John. Such a study would take us far afield from the focus of the present volume. To be sure, for John the world is a beautiful place created by God, as well as a place capable of great evils. These complementary ideas stand side-by-side in the Fourth Gospel and should be kept in mind in the face of the exclusively negative presentation that follows.

Despite the previous criticism of their work, both Kierspel and Bennema provide, at the very least, a satisfactory foundation for treating κόσμος as a character. They note that in the Gospel, the world is described as having human emotions and responses to Jesus; even though the reader is never formally introduced to the world as a character, the narrator's depiction of the world establishes its impact upon events and other characters in the story.[9]

This essay will plow a narrow swath through the text of the Fourth Gospel, focusing specifically on those places where the world, as a character, represents a human race that is at odds with the plan of God as inaugurated by Jesus. In what follows, I will argue that κόσμος, when used of humanity, is macrocosmic, referring to all humanity within John's story world, and to individual Johannine characters in particular. After a discussion of κόσμος in the Johannine Prologue, the remainder of this essay will use narrative exegesis to focus on five examples in John that illustrate the relationship between Jesus and ὁ κόσμος: (1) the world hates Jesus and his followers (7:1–7; 15:18–21; 17:14–15), (2) the world follows Jesus in ignorance (12:19), (3) the world rejects the Spirit of truth (14:15–17), (4) the world rejoices at Jesus' departure (16:20), and (5) the world does not know the Father (17:25). These categories will be used to illustrate the promise and unfulfilled hope displayed by the world in the Fourth Gospel.

---

[9] At first glance it might seem strange to treat the world as a character alongside other established Johannine figures such as Peter, Mary, Martha, and Nicodemus. In recent years a handful of studies have appeared that examine other entities in narrative literature and consider their role as characters. A very good example of this recent approach in Johannine studies is Stan Harstine, *Moses as a Character in the Fourth Gospel: A Study of Ancient Reading Techniques* (JSNTSup 229; Sheffield: Sheffield Academic Press, 2002). Harstine treats Moses as an actual character, though he only appears in references to OT passages and in metonymical references to Torah.

The World in the Prologue

It is widely recognized that the Johannine Prologue (1:1–18) sets both the literary and theological agendas for the Gospel story. There, the reader learns that Jesus is the agent of all creation, including the totality of humanity (1:3, 10–11). Because of its unique relationship to God through Jesus, the world carries the promise of great things, most of which never materialize. Among the most important of these is the promise of knowing the God whom Jesus reveals.[10] In this regard, Barrett has written, "The world made through the Word is a world capable of knowing, or of reprehensibly not knowing, its Maker."[11] The failure of the world to know God is demonstrated explicitly in the passages considered below, and implicitly in numerous interactions between Jesus and other uncomprehending characters. There can be little doubt that misunderstanding is one of the key themes in John's presentation of Jesus' life and mission.[12] Throughout the Fourth Gospel Jesus is met with a steady stream of characters whose most consistent trait is an inability to know him in a way that would be deemed legitimate by Johannine standards. Many characters fail to comprehend even the most transparent elements of his message, mission, or identity. Though there is not space here to develop this argument in greater detail, it must be kept in mind nonetheless. Two proleptic statements from the Prologue describe this unfolding reality in the story:

1:10 – He was in the world (ἐν τῷ κοσμῷ), and though the world (ὁ κόσμος) was created through him, the world (ὁ κόσμος) did not know him.

Three different nuances seem to be present in this verse. The first use of κόσμος refers to the physical realm into which Jesus has entered. The second occurrence refers to the created order while the third refers to humanity. This statement prepares the reader for the world's rejection of Jesus and builds upon 1:5, where the narrator comments that "the darkness has not comprehended the light" (ἡ σκοτία αὐτὸ οὐ κατέλαβεν). Verse 11 reiterates what v. 10 communicated:

1:11 – He came to his own place (τὰ ἴδια) and his own people (οἱ ἴδιοι) did not receive him.

---

[10] One important facet of Jesus' mission in John is his role of "the revealer of God" (cf. 1:18).

[11] C. Kingsley Barrett, *The Gospel According to St John: An Introduction with Commentary and Notes on the Greek Text* (2d ed.; London: SPCK, 1978), 161.

[12] With the exception of the Beloved Disciple, all other Johannine characters display some inability to understand Jesus' identity, message, or mission. Misunderstood statements, ironic speech, and *double entendre* are the means by which the narrator brings about these instances of misunderstanding. When characters misunderstand Jesus it often leads to one of the Fourth Gospel's theological discourses, and these are the means by which the evangelist clarifies the misunderstood elements of Jesus' mission or identity.

The neuter plural use of ἴδιος in the first half of the verse is a reference to the world as the physical realm into which Jesus has entered. The masculine plural use of ἴδιος in the second half of the verse refers to humanity. Together, these two verses function in much the same manner as the synthetic parallelism in poetic passages of the Hebrew Bible. Specifically, the second verse reiterates and clarifies the meaning of the first.

Together, these two programmatic statements describe a future reality that will unfold throughout the narrative, especially in Jesus' interactions with human characters. As a character in the Fourth Gospel, the world represents the comprehension, internal orientation, and outward behavior of all who oppose the light (cf. 1:5). As a character that opposes and misunderstands Jesus' mission, the κόσμος has a number of representatives in John's Gospel – "the Jews," the crowds, individuals such as Nicodemus, and even the disciples. For the purposes of this essay, κόσμος is defined as the representative totality of humanity in John's story world, characterized by an internal disposition and outward response of misunderstanding and hostility toward Jesus. Though there are exceptions in the Fourth Gospel, this is the general rule for defining humanity's response to Jesus. We proceed now to an examination of passages where the world as a character is explicitly described or depicted.

Jesus and the World

The World Hates Jesus and His Followers (7:1–7; 15:18–21; 17:14–15)

The first of three references to the world's hatred for Jesus comes in the context of a conversation between Jesus and his brothers about the impending Feast of Tabernacles. In 7:1–4 Jesus is in Galilee when his brothers encourage him to travel to Judea to make his ministry public (φανέρωσον σεαυτὸν τῷ κόσμῳ, v. 4) at the upcoming feast. That this advice is driven by their derision is made clear in v. 5: "For his brothers did not believe in him." Jesus responds to their challenge by contrasting his divinely appointed time, which has yet to come, with their ability to come and go on the basis of any human whim (ὁ καιρὸς ὁ ἐμὸς οὔπω πάρεστιν ὁ δὲ καιρὸς ὁ ὑμέτερος πάντοτέ ἐστιν ἕτοιμος, v. 6). In v. 7 Jesus describes the world in two ways: (1) it is characterized by evil deeds, and (2) it hates Jesus because he bears witness to its evil deeds. This hatred will manifest itself in a number of ways, one of which is complicity in Jesus' condemnation and death.

The other two references to the world's hatred of Jesus occur in the Farewell Discourse (13:1–17:26). In that section of the Gospel, Jesus prepares the disciples for his departure by encouraging them to persevere, providing insights into forthcoming events, and praying for his disciples and all future believers.

In John 15 Jesus speaks to his disciples at length about the necessity of abiding in him as a means to both accomplishing God's will and remaining in his love (vss. 1-17). In this context Jesus again speaks of the world's hatred for him. Because the world hates Jesus, it will also hate those who follow him (εἰ ὁ κόσμος ὑμᾶς μισεῖ, γινώσκετε ὅτι ἐμὲ πρῶτον ὑμῶν μεμίσηκεν, v. 18). This does not mean that the world is fully incapable of showing love. On the contrary, the world loves those whose perspectives and choices mirror its own (εἰ ἐκ τοῦ κόσμου ἦτε ὁ κόσμος ἂν τὸ ἴδιον ἐφίλει, v. 19). Jesus cautions his disciples that the world will treat his followers in the same way they have treated him (vss. 20-21). This warning is not only a prediction of future persecution for the disciples but also an implicit exhortation to perseverance. Again it is clear that the world is characterized by hostility toward Jesus and those who are associated with him.

The third reference to the world's hatred comes during Jesus' prayer in John 17. In 15:18-21 Jesus warned that the world would persecute his followers simply because of their association with him. Picking up on this theme once again, Jesus acknowledges that the world hates his followers because he has given them the Father's message (ἐγὼ δέδωκα αὐτοῖς τὸν λόγον σου καὶ ὁ κόσμος ἐμίσησεν αὐτούς, v. 14a) and because they are not of the world (ὅτι οὐκ εἰσὶν ἐκ τοῦ κόσμου, v. 14b). It is noteworthy that Jesus asks the Father not to remove them from the world, but rather to protect them from the evil one (ἐκ τοῦ πονηροῦ, v. 15). This protection will be necessary because "after Jesus' departure from the world, the story of *the disciples and the world* begins."[13] In order for the Johannine disciples – as well as the future believers for which Jesus prays – to continue facing the hatred of the world, it will require a special protection from the wiles of the evil one.

One of the distinctive features of Johannine discourse is the use of dualistic contrasts (e. g., light vs. darkness, truth vs. lie) to make a theological point. In these three passages, another contrast emerges: one can be associated either with Jesus or the world, but not both.[14] This contrast unveils the extreme opposition between the two, and further explains the reason for the world's hatred of Jesus and his followers. The world's unrighteousness and hostility toward Jesus are several stitches in a much larger tapestry of its rejection of God and the one whom he has sent.

---

[13] Bennema, *Encountering Jesus*, 31 (emphasis added).

[14] This dualism seems to have been characteristic of the teaching in the Johannine community. See, for instance, 1 John 2:15-16, "Do not love the world (κόσμος) or anything in the world. If anyone loves the world, the love of the Father is not in him. For all the things in the world – the lust of the flesh, the lust of the eyes, and the pride of life – are not from the Father but the world."

The World Follows Jesus in Ignorance (12:19)[15]

Along with its hatred of Jesus, the world is also ignorant of his origins and mission. The Prologue unveils many facts about Jesus: he is from above and existed before time (1:1–2), he is the agent of creation (1:3), the light of humanity (1:4), the giver of authority (1:12), the incarnate λόγος (1:14), and the revealer of the Father to humanity (1:18). While the reader navigates the Fourth Gospel with an awareness of these themes, most characters within the story are unaware and therefore have difficulty coming to terms with Jesus' identity. Their moments of misunderstanding provide opportunities for the Johannine discourses, where Jesus often clarifies elements of his mission and identity. There are occasions, however, when the world, or one of its representatives, confesses something of significance about Jesus. While these insights often occur in the context of Jesus' sign-miracles,[16] this is problematic because the Fourth Evangelist does not regard a signs-faith as a legitimate response to Jesus. Rather, belief in Jesus' word is legitimate while belief in his works falls short of the mark.[17]

The events of John 11:38–44 mark the turning point of the Fourth Gospel and usher in a series of responses to Jesus' last and greatest sign. In 11:41–43, Jesus performs his seventh and final σημεῖον in raising Lazarus from the dead – an act that not only foreshadows his own resurrection and power over death, but also serves as the impetus for his crucifixion at the hands of οἱ Ἰουδαῖοι. The anger of the Jewish leaders and their plan to kill Jesus are recounted in 11:45–57. Then, in 12:1–19 the narrator describes a series of positive responses to Jesus: in vss. 3–8 Mary anoints Jesus and is praised for her actions; in v. 9 a large crowd of "Jews" (ὄχλος πολὺς ἐκ τῶν Ἰουδαίων) comes to see both Jesus and Lazarus; in vss. 12–19 that same crowd appears, waving palm branches and acclaiming Jesus as a messianic king. Each of these responses to Jesus is a source of dismay for the Jewish leaders, though the final response causes the Pharisees

---

[15] I recognize that this instance, unlike the other occurrences of κόσμος discussed in this essay, arises from the estimation of Pharisees rather than the narrator. However, the characters in the Gospel story generally share the evaluative point of view of the narrator. Thus, it makes sense to consider this example of the κόσμος concept in the same context as the other occurrences in the Fourth Gospel.

[16] The Johannine *semeia* have traditionally been identified as follows: 2:1–12 (changing of water to wine); 4:46–54 (healing of an official's son); 5:1–9 (healing at the pool of Bethesda); 6:1–15 (multiplication of loaves and fish); 6:16–21 (walking on the water); 9:1–12 (healing of the man born blind), and 11:38–44 (the raising of Lazarus). Though his position has garnered little support, Andreas Köstenberger (idem, "Seventh Johannine Sign: A Study in John's Christology," *BBR* 5 [1995]: 87–103) departs from the traditional listing of *semeia* by replacing the walking on water (6:16–21) with the cleansing of the temple (2:13–22).

[17] On the contrast between belief in Jesus' works vs. belief in Jesus' word, see this theme as it unfolds in three volumes by Francis J. Moloney, *Belief in the Word: Reading John 1–4* (Minneapolis: Fortress, 1993); *Signs and Shadows: Reading John 5–12* (Minneapolis: Fortress, 1996); and *Glory Not Dishonor: Reading John 13–21* (Minneapolis: Fortress, 1998).

to remark, "Look, *the world* has run off after him" (ἴδε ὁ κόσμος ὀπίσω αὐτοῦ ἀπῆλθεν, v. 19). Though this statement is probably to be understood as hyperbole, it is significant that when the κόσμος is described as following Jesus, it does so on the basis of what it has seen (Jesus' works) rather than what it has heard and internalized (Jesus' word). For the purposes of the evangelist, this response amounts to following Jesus in ignorance.[18] The world may be following after Jesus, but it eventually stops when the works it seeks cease to occur.

Though this is seemingly a more positive moment for the world than the three previous examples we have examined, the world's pursuit of Jesus will not last. Ultimately, nearly everyone will abandon Jesus, providing further proof that the signs-faith the world has expressed is not genuine (Johannine) belief. The world runs after Jesus, but only because it hopes to gain that which the world values. Against the backdrop of Jesus' death, the world's abandonment of him reveals that it was following in ignorance all along.

The World Rejects the Spirit of Truth (14:15–17)

In 14:15 Jesus exhorts his disciples to demonstrate their love for him by keeping his commands. If they do, Jesus promises to petition the Father to send another advocate (ἄλλον παράκλητον) to remain with them during his absence. Throughout the history of Johannine research, much has been written about the παράκλητος, though the importance of ἄλλος is often overlooked. It is a given that παράκλητος is John's unique term for the Holy Spirit. Numerous translations have been proposed – "helper," "representative," "advocate," "comforter," "intercessor" – though it is difficult to translate the term faithfully with an economy of words.[19] While more is intended than any one of these definitions communicates on its own, the reader progressively understands that παράκλητος is John's technical term for the coming Spirit that will assist his followers after his departure to the Father.

Of greater relevance to our argument here is the evangelist's use of the term ἄλλος. Prior to the Hellenistic period ἄλλος was used to refer to "another of the same kind," in contradistinction to ἕτερος, which denoted "another of a different kind."[20] Though this distinction appears to have faded somewhat during the Hellenistic era – and particularly in the semitized Greek of the Gospels – there is evidence of its use in the NT.[21] John employs ἄλλος 33 times

---

[18] It should be noted that in 7:49 the Pharisees suggest something similar about the crowds that follow Jesus (ἀλλὰ ὁ ὄχλος οὗτος ὁ μὴ γινώσκων τὸν νόμον ἐπάρετοί εἰσιν).

[19] For more detailed information, see BDAG, 766 and TDNT, 5:804.

[20] See LSJ, s. v. ἕτερος (especially section III, which provides several attested examples of the contrast between ἕτερος and ἄλλος).

[21] An important example of this contrast is found in Galatians 1:6–7, where Paul refers to the gospel which the Judaizers preach as "another gospel" (ἕτερον εὐαγγέλιον) which is really not another (ὃ οὐκ ἔστιν ἄλλο).

while the term ἕτερος appears once (19:37), but seemingly without the specific nuance stated above. However, given John's penchant for synonyms (e. g., φιλέω/ἀγαπάω, ἀποστέλλω/πέμπω, etc.), there is good reason to believe ἄλλος has been chosen and maintained almost exclusively throughout the Gospel for a specific reason. Thus, the use of ἄλλον παράκλητον communicates that the promised παράκλητος is of the same kind (or nature) as both the Father and Son.[22] The advocate – to whom Jesus also refers as the Spirit of truth (τὸ πνεῦμα τῆς ἀληθείας) – is intimately related to both the Father and Son, and will come to assist Jesus' followers in the same ways they have.

We have already seen that the world does not receive Jesus. In 14:17 the reader further learns that the world is not able to receive the παράκλητος. This realization adds a new dimension to the world's rejection of God and those he sends. It is not simply a case of the world choosing to oppose God. Rather, the world is unable to receive the things of God. The world neither sees nor knows God (14:17c) and therefore opposes God as a natural outworking of its internal orientation. By its very nature, the world rejects God, and by extension, both Jesus and the Paraclete.

The World Rejoices at Jesus' Departure (16:20)

By now, the implied reader of the Gospel is aware that it is necessary for Jesus to return to the Father in order to complete the mission for which he was sent. Though the end result of his departure (resurrection) will ultimately be a cause of rejoicing for his followers, Jesus knows that in the interim they will weep and mourn (ἀμὴν ἀμὴν λέγω ὑμῖν ὅτι κλαύσετε καὶ θρηνήσετε ὑμεῖς, 16:20a). However, the world, which has been continuously characterized by its opposition to Jesus, will rejoice at Jesus' departure. Since the world does not know Jesus, its rejoicing over his departure is rooted in its ignorance. Jesus' crucifixion, to which the Evangelist refers as his glorification, will initially appear to the world as the silencing of Jesus once and for all. But, this event will ultimately be a triumph over which the disciples will rejoice. In this regard, Moloney comments:

The reader knows that a death through being lifted up on a cross lies in the immediate future. This death will bear all the appearances of a victory for the forces which are lining up against Jesus. But their rejoicing will be short-lived as, for this author, the brute facts of history do not reflect the true significance of the death of Jesus. The departure of Jesus through the cross will create the *mikron* when Jesus will not be seen, but the sorrow of the disciples will be turned into joy.[23]

---

[22] There is no denying that this language, along with other imagery from the Fourth Gospel, served as a repository for later Trinitarian formulations in the first four centuries of the church.

[23] Moloney, *Glory Not Dishonor*, 91.

When the world rejoices over Jesus' departure it does so because it hates Jesus (7:1-7; 15:18-21; 17:14-15), fails to understand him (12:19), and rejects the God who sent him (14:15-17). Against the backdrop of this accumulated information, what else should the implied reader expect than the world's shallow satisfaction at their perceived victory over Jesus?

The World Does Not Know the Father (17:25)

At the very end of his farewell discourse, Jesus mentions the world once again, almost in passing. After a lengthy speech in which he has sought to prepare his followers for his departure, Jesus closes by offering a final supplication. John 17 consists of one long prayer in which Jesus prays for his own glorification (vss. 1-5), the perseverance and protection of his disciples (vss. 6-19), and the benefit of all future believers (vss. 20-26). In v. 24 Jesus prays that future disciples, those given to him by the Father, may be with him and behold his glory. His next statement pits the world against himself and the future believers for whom he has just prayed (καὶ ὁ κόσμος σε οὐκ ἔγνω, ἐγὼ δέ σε ἔγνων, καὶ οὗτοι ἔγνωσαν ὅτι σύ με ἀπέστειλας, "Even though the world does not know you, I know you and these [the disciples] know that you sent me").[24] This simple statement reiterates what the reader has already learned about the world – it has no transformative knowledge about the things of God. This ignorance keeps the world in the dark about the Father and his representatives – the Son and the Paraclete. In this context γινώσκω refers to more than simple knowledge.[25] The knowledge Jesus describes is one rooted in experience. The disciples have experienced God in the person of Jesus, the revealer of the Father (cf. 1:18). Because of its inward orientation, the world has never truly experienced God and therefore has no access to the same type of knowledge possessed by Jesus' followers.

Conclusion

The Jesus of John's Gospel has come down from above while the Johannine κόσμος consists of both the realm and the people in the sphere below. This simple positional contrast is symbolic of the greater divide that exists between

---

[24] Though this is not formally structured as a conditional sentence, some translations render it with a conditional force. In light of the cumulative argument of this essay, I translate the initial καί as "even though" rather than "even if."

[25] "To know God is to have eternal life (17.3); to know the truth is to be set free (8.32). Knowledge, then, is a way of entrance into salvation and life. Jesus himself knows the Father, and his ministry may be summed up as the communication of this knowledge (1.18; 17.26). ... [K]nowledge itself implies relationship in addition to cognition; to know God is to be united with him" (Barrett, *John*, 81-82).

Jesus and the world (as character) in John's Gospel. The two are at odds, but only insofar as the world conspires to bring this existential situation about. As the one who comes from above, Jesus has set off on a mission to make God known to humanity. He is both the creator and savior of humanity though the world will ultimately reject and destroy him. The world's rejection of Jesus amounts to a rejection of the Father who sent him, and by extension, the coming Paraclete and Jesus' followers. Thus, as a character in the Fourth Gospel, the world represents the human forces that stand in opposition to Jesus, and in this way, functions even if surreptitiously, as the story's primary antagonist. As a character, the world carries the promise of great things but consistently betrays that promise for a darkened perspective that opposes rather than celebrates the plans and purposes of God.

"The Jews":
Unreliable Figures or Unreliable Narration?

Ruben Zimmermann

A First Approach:
"The Jews" in John – Complex and Difficult Material

The use of οἱ Ἰουδαῖοι in the Fourth Gospel is a popular research field.[1] The questions associated with this field are as diverse as the methods used to examine and answer them.[2] Within *the historical perspective*, the question is to which group or partial group in first century Judaism the term refers. Is it the "Jews in general" as an ethnic-religious group or is it the common people? Or a religious party such as the Pharisees?[3] Perhaps the term refers to a specific group of Jewish authorities and officials in Jerusalem (e. g., "temple partisans"[4]) even though they are identified across the board as "Jews"? And to which time period is the reader referred? Is it a Jewish group during the life of Jesus and, therefore, the narrated world (*erzählte Welt*)? Or are οἱ Ἰουδαῖοι

---

[1] See Urban C. von Wahlde, "The Johannine 'Jews': A Critical Survey," *NTS* 28 (1982): 33–60; idem, "The 'Jews' in the Gospel of John: Fifteen Years of Research (1983–1998)," *ETL* 76 (2000): 30–55; see further the broad section on "The Jews," in *Anti-Judaism and the Fourth Gospel: Papers of the Leuven Colloquium 2000* (ed. Reimund Bieringer et al.; Jewish and Christian Heritage Series 1; Assen: van Gorcum, 2001), 229–356; and more recently, Lars Kierspel, *The Jews and the World in the Fourth Gospel: Parallelism, Function, and Context* (WUNT II/220; Tübingen: Mohr Siebeck, 2006), 13–62.

[2] Von Wahlde structured his survey in 1) narrative criticism; 2) social science criticism; 3) psychological approach; 4) traditional historical critical approach; 5) textual criticism; see von Wahlde, "Jews," 30–55.

[3] For example, Klaus Wengst, *Das Johannesevangelium. Teilbd. 1: Kapitel 1–10* (2d ed.; Theologischer Kommentar zum Neuen Testament 4/1; Stuttgart: Kohlhammer, 2004), 30: "Von den jüdischen Gruppen treten im Johannesevangelium praktisch nur noch die Pharisäer auf; das in ihm begegnende Judentum ist ein pharisäisch bestimmtes Judentum." For Wengst, the Gospel of John is about an "Abgrenzungsprozess zwischen der rabbinisch geleiteten Mehrheit und einer auf Jesus bezogenen Minderheit (der Juden)" (Wengst, *Johannesevangelium 1*, 30); see more recently, Maria Neubrand, "Das Johannesevangelium und 'die Juden': Antijudaismus im vierten Evangelium," *TGl* 99 (2009): 205–17, here 213: "[E]s dominiert die Verwendung der Pluralbildung οἱ Ἰουδαῖοι im Sinn einer kleinen pharisäisch ausgerichteten Gruppe."

[4] See Cornelis Bennema, "The Identity and Composition of OI IOYΔAIOI in the Gospel of John," *TynBul* 60 (2009): 239–63, here 245; see also Cornelis Bennema, *Encountering Jesus: Character Studies in the Gospel of John* (Milton Keynes: Paternoster, 2009), 38–46.

a Jewish party at the time during which the Gospel was written – the world in which the author and his readers live (*Erzählwelt*).[5] Or are the two time aspects specifically connected, as J. Louis Martyn and others suggested? In other words, is there a "two-level-drama" in John,[6] with the consequence that a conflict in the Johannine Community at the time when the Gospel emerged is projected backwards in such a way that the enemies of the Community are stylized as Jesus' opponents? However, precisely such a "conflict between the Johannine group and emerging rabbinic Judaism" was vehemently contested by Raimo Hakola.[7]

The questions with respect to reference are closely connected to those of the *terminology and semantics*. What exactly does the term οἱ Ἰουδαῖοι mean? Malcolm Lowe advocated, with lasting impact, for a geographic meaning – οἱ Ἰουδαῖοι stands for the "inhabitants of the Judean countryside," "the Judeans."[8] In his arguments, he refers to the dominant language use of the time (e. g., in the case of Josephus[9]) as well as to the use of the term Ἰουδαία, which always refers analogously to "Judea" in contrast to the countryside of Samaria and Galilee (4:3, 47, 54; 7:1, 3; 11:7), as well as to the term ἑορτὴ τῶν Ἰουδαίων (2:13; 5:1; 7:2–3; 11:5) which was always used for the feasts in Jerusalem. However, formulations such as κατὰ τὸν καθαρισμὸν τῶν Ἰουδαίων (2:6) or πάσχα τῶν Ἰουδαίων (6:4) show that the translation "Judeans" can hardly be used here. Taking up Lowe's ideas, von Wahlde pointed out that the term οἱ Ἰουδαῖοι has three different meanings, which can be linked to different editions of the Gospel. In the first edition the term refers to "Judeans," in the second edition to "hostile religious authorities," and the third use of the term is one that refers to "the Jewish people as a whole."[10]

---

[5] Daniel Boyarin, "The Ioudaioi in John and the Prehistory of 'Judaism'," in *Pauline Conversations in Context: Essays in Honor of Calvin J. Roetzel* (ed. Janice C. Anderson et al.; JSNTSup 221; Sheffield: SAP, 2002), 216–39; Jörg Frey, "Das Bild der Juden im vierten Evangelium und die Geschichte der johanneischen Gemeinde," in *Israel und seine Heilstraditionen im vierten Evangelium* (ed. Michael Labahn et al.; FS Johannes Beutler; Paderborn: Schöningh, 2004), 33–53, who explores a background in Asia Minor.

[6] See James Louis Martyn, *History and Theology in the Fourth Gospel* (2d ed.; Nashville: Abingdon, 1979), 30, 38–62. Of central importance for Martyn is the insertion of the so-called "Blessing on the Heretics" (Birkat ha-Minim) in the Amidah (The Standing Prayer) that he identifies with the synagogue committee (ἀποσυνάγωγος; see John 9:22; 12:42; 16:2). Similarly, Klaus Wengst assumed that rabbinical Judaism is reflected in the image of "the Jews" in the Fourth Gospel, see Wengst, *Johannesevangelium 1*, 30.

[7] See Raimo Hakola, *Identity Matters: John, the Jews and Jewishness* (NovTSup 118; Leiden: Brill, 2005).

[8] See Malcome Lowe, "Who Were the ΙΟΥΔΑΙΟΙ," *NovT* 18 (1976): 101–30.

[9] See the references in Lowe, "ΙΟΥΔΑΙΟΙ," 105, fn. 13–15.

[10] See most recently Urban C. von Wahlde, *The Gospel and Letters of John, Vol. 1: Introduction, Analysis, and Reference* (3 vols.; Grand Rapids, Mich.: Eerdmans, 2010), 70–71, 91–93, 144–49, as well as idem, "Survey," 42–60.

Most exegetes, however, are in favor of a multifaceted semantic, in which case οἱ Ἰουδαῖοι means
1) an ethnic-cultural group (i. e., "the Jews" in contrast to the Romans);
2) a geographical group (i. e., the people of Judea in contrast to the Galileans);
3) a traditio-historical group (i. e., descendants of the line of Judah);
4) a religious-theological group (e. g., "adherence to the Judean religion"[11]);
5) a functional group (e. g., the religious authorities in Jerusalem).

Some exegetes also add other specific meanings such as "Jesusfeinde und Repräsentanten des Unglaubens"[12] or "Dialogpartner bzw. Stichwortgeber."[13]

The variety of meanings grows if we add intersections with other groups and terminologies. In that case there are close parallels (or overlapping moments) with the Pharisees, the crowd (ὄχλος),[14] the world (κόσμος), the Levites and priests (1:19) or high priests (οἱ ἀρχιερεῖς; 19:21) and authorities (ἄρχων; 3:1) or the people of Jerusalem (7:25). Moloney classified οἱ Ἰουδαῖοι within their broader literary and narrative context and also added "Israel," "Israelite," "people" (ὁ λαός), and "nation" (τὸ ἔθνος).[15]

Finally, the question of "the Jews" in the Gospel of John cannot be posed neutrally (i. e., disregarding the *hermeneutical standpoint*), especially by a German exegete.[16] "The discussion of the meaning of the term 'Jews' (…) has broad implications for the question whether the Gospel is anti-Jewish and, if it is anti-Jewish, for the question of scripture as normative for the believing community."[17] Because parts of the Gospel such as 8:44 ("You are from your father the devil") were abused by the anti-Semitism of the National Socialists, an unburdened analysis of this text is no longer possible. Is the Gospel of John – precisely because of its image of Jews – "the most anti-Jewish docu-

---

[11] Bennema, "Identity," 242.

[12] Udo Schnelle, "Die Juden im Johannesevangelium," in *Gedenkt an das Wort: Festschrift für Werner Vogler zum 65. Geburtstag* (Leipzig: Evangelische Verlagsanstalt, 1999), 217–30, here 219.

[13] Schnelle, "Die Juden im Johannesevangelium," 219. See also Rudolf Schnackenburg, *Das Johannesevangelium: Teil 1: Kommentar zu Kapitel 1–4* (6th ed.; HTKNT IV; Freiburg: Herder, 1986), 275–76.

[14] Contra Koester, who states that John identifies the crowd as "the Jews" in 6:41, 52; see Craig Koester, *Symbolism in the Fourth Gospel: Meaning, Mystery, Community* (Minneapolis: Fortress, 2003), 57–58.

[15] See Francis J. Moloney, "'The Jews' in the Fourth Gospel: Another Perspective," *Pacifica* 15 (2002): 16–36.

[16] See Ferdinand Hahn, "Theologie nach Auschwitz: Ihre Bedeutung für die neutestamentliche Exegese: Eine Thesenreihe," in *Die Verwurzelung des Christentums im Judentum: Exegetische Beiträge zum christlich-jüdischen Gespräch* (ed. Ciliers Breytenbach; Neukirchen-Vluyn: Neukirchener Verlag, 1996), 49–54.

[17] Von Wahlde, "Jews," 51.

ment in the Christian Canon"[18] from which anti-Semitism was derived or with which it was even abetted?

Some exegetes affirm this position and call for critical assessment of the Gospel of John. Others attempt to identify this Gospel as a Jewish work with intra-Jewish polemic and thus protect it against later misinterpretation. On this view, the term οἱ Ἰουδαῖοι is narrowly limited to the Jewish authorities who were against Jesus, whereas it is used as an ethnic-religious group in statements such as John 4:22 ("Salvation is from the Jews"). Or do we need to put "the Jews" in quotation marks in order to identify that this is a literary group and not an historical one?[19]

In complete consciousness of this unavoidable hermeneutical context, this narratological study will attempt to reduce this complex material to οἱ Ἰουδαῖοι as a character in the narrated world of the Gospel. At first it may be a relief to attempt to consider οἱ Ἰουδαῖοι as a purely literary group, as narrative characters who act in the world of the text but who do not need to be connected to an historical-empirical group. Nevertheless, exegetes have objected that a hidden anti-Semitism can also be present in stylizing "the Jews" as "types" and thus dealing with them in this way as a whole.[20] Furthermore, cognitivistic approaches to characterization have questioned a mere structuralist approach. The author as well as the reader uses his/her knowledge about the world in which they live to interlink and to augment the textual information about the characters as "mental models."[21] However, heuristically it is possible to focus on the narrated world. It is not the literary approach and classification but rather the application of this description to real-empirical groups that leads to anti-Judaism.

---

[18] See Micha Brumlik, "Johannes: Das judenfeindliche Evangelium," in *Teufelskinder oder Heilsbringer – Die Juden im Johannes-Evangelium* (ed. Dietrich Neuhaus; Arndoldshainer Texte 64; Frankfurt: Haag und Herrchen, 1990), 6–21.

[19] The Jewish scholar Reinhartz refuses this option for several reasons; see Adele Reinhartz, "'The Jews' and the Jews in the Fourth Gospel," in *Anti-Judaism and the Fourth Gospel* (ed. Reimund Bieringer et al.), 341–56. Nevertheless, in spite of acknowledging her argument I consider it better to use the quotation marks to make the hermeneutical problem at least visible.

[20] See Peter von der Osten-Sacken, "Leistung und Grenze der johanneischen Kreuzestheologie," *EvT* 36 (1976): 154–76, here 168: "Gerade die Stilisierung der Juden zu Typen ist zu allen Zeiten Kennzeichen von Antijudaismus gewesen."

[21] See Fotis Jannidis, *Figur und Person: Beitrag zu einer historischen Narratologie* (Narratologia 3; Berlin: de Gruyter, 2004), 177–85.

History of Research and Methodological Approach

"The Jews" as Characters? Synchronic Approaches to οἱ Ἰουδαῖοι *in John*

There are a number of works that have examined the role of "the Jews" from non-historical perspectives. With a certain justification, we can even point to Bultmann's commentary on John, in which he saw in "the Jews" typified and stylized representatives of unbelief, even though fundamentally he carried out a diachronic analysis without narratological methods.

"Das für den Evglisten (sic!) charakteristische οἱ Ἰουδαῖοι faßt die Juden in ihrer Gesamtheit zusammen, so wie sie als Vertreter des Unglaubens (und damit, wie sich zeigen wird, der ungläubigen 'Welt' überhaupt) vom christlichen Glauben aus gesehen werden. [D]ementsprechend erscheint jemand, in dem sich der Glaube oder auch nur das Fragen nach Jesus regt, im Gegensatz zu den 'Juden', auch wenn er selbst Jude ist. (…) Die Ἰουδαῖοι 'sind eben das jüdische Volk nicht in seinem empirischen Bestande (…).'"[22]

However, it was *R. Alan Culpepper* who first described οἱ Ἰουδαῖοι as "characters" in his seminal narratological study of the Gospel of John.[23] "Just as the Johannine characters carry representative value, so do the Jews."[24] According to Culpepper, οἱ Ἰουδαῖοι are "integrally related to the advancement of the plot (…). There is generally an escalation of hostility from one episode to another."[25] Culpepper is conscious of the "divisions within the Jews;"[26] however, they are nevertheless "representatives of unbelief:"[27] "Through the Jews, John explores the heart and soul of unbelief."[28] Because they are thus portrayed stereotypically, the character gains figurative and symbolic traits. In the same way that Jesus as the Lamb must carry the sins of the world, "the Jews" – now clearly understood as an historical group – are given the task to "carry the burden of the unbelief of 'the world' in John."[29]

Gérald Caron[30] also chooses a literary approach, arguing that the text should be understood as a unit and not only as a source of historical facts. In

---

[22] Rudolf Bultmann, *Das Evangelium des Johannes* (21st ed.; KEK 2; Göttingen: Vandenhoeck & Ruprecht, 1986), 59. For a similar interpretation, see Robert Kysar, *John: The Maverick Gospel* (Atlanta: John Knox Press, 1976), 57: "types of unbelief."

[23] See R. Alan Culpepper, *Anatomy of the Fourth Gospel: A Study in Literary Design* (Philadelphia: Fortress, ²1987), 125–32; see also R. Alan Culpepper, "The Gospel of John and the Jews," *RevExp* 84 (1987): 273–88.

[24] Culpepper, *Anatomy of the Fourth Gospel*, 128.
[25] Culpepper, *Anatomy of the Fourth Gospel*, 127.
[26] Culpepper, *Anatomy of the Fourth Gospel*, 128.
[27] Culpepper, *Anatomy of the Fourth Gospel*, 129.
[28] Culpepper, *Anatomy of the Fourth Gospel*, 129.
[29] Culpepper, *Anatomy of the Fourth Gospel*, 130.
[30] Gérald Caron, *Qui sont les Juifs de l'Évangile de Jean?* (Recherches 35; Quebec: Bellarmin, 1997).

his leading question *Qui sont les Juifs de l'Évangile de Jean?*, he brings out that the term οἱ Ἰουδαῖοι does not refer to the Jewish people, the Jewish race in general, or a particular group such as the Pharisees. Instead it stands for the "pseudo-Judaisme officiel de Jérusalem."[31] He bases his argument in particular on a reduced text base in the analysis of John 5 and John 8. Although Caron assumes a more structuralist construction of the characters,[32] his final chapter also demonstrates his hermeneutical interest in a consciously non-anti-Jewish interpretation of the Gospel of John.

Tobias Nicklas examines the "'Jews' and the disciples as characters of the narrated world"[33] in John 1, 3, 5 and 9. He links narratology with reader response criticism by simultaneously studying the effect on the reader. Drawing on the system of A. Berlin,[34] he classifies οἱ Ἰουδαῖοι as a "type" or flat character who, as soon as they appear as a group, represent non-understanding for Jesus' claim.[35] "The Jews" thus become a negative foil on the background of which the "Jüngergestalten" stand out, shown in a "mehr oder weniger differenzierten Entwicklungsprozess"[36] although they are also Jewish. Precisely these disciples invite the reader to identify with the characters who take up the path to belief in Jesus.[37] However, with this intended transferral to the "real world," the typified portrayal of "the Jews" has gone awry: "(Die Darstellung der Juden ermöglicht) fataler weise die Übertragung ihrer Zeichnung als Charaktere der erzählten Welt auf jüdische Personen und Gruppen des realen Lebens."[38] Thus the narrative abstraction of οἱ Ἰουδαῖοι can contribute to the development of anti-Judaism.[39]

Stephen Motyer considers his "reception-based interpretative strategy"[40] to be a new start in the issue of οἱ Ἰουδαῖοι. He appeals for a much more subtle

---

[31] Caron, *Qui sont les Juifs*, 285.

[32] Caron, *Qui sont les Juifs*, 53: "(l'auteur) fabrique ses personages."

[33] Tobias Nicklas, *Ablösung und Verstrickung: 'Juden' und Jüngergestalten als Charaktere der erzählten Welt des Johannesevangeliums und ihre Wirkung auf den impliziten Leser* (RST 60; Frankfurt: Peter Lang, 2001).

[34] See Adele Berlin, *Poetics and Interpretation of Biblical Narrative* (Bible and Literature Series 9; Sheffield: Almond, 1983). She distinguishes three categories: agent, type, and complex character (see for details the introduction to this volume).

[35] Nicklas, *Ablösung und Verstrickung*, 399: "von vornherein Unverständnis gegenüber dem Anspruch Jesu."

[36] Nicklas, *Ablösung und Verstrickung*, 401.

[37] Nicklas, *Ablösung und Verstrickung*, 409: "Identifikation des Lesers mit Gestalten, die sich auf den Weg zum Glauben an Jesus machen."

[38] Nicklas, *Ablösung und Verstrickung*, 409.

[39] This converges with the thesis of Adele Reinhartz, who considers the Fourth Gospel not to be a reaction but as a starting point "for anti-Jewish emotions and attitudes." See Reinhartz, "Jews," 356.

[40] See Stephen Motyer, "The Fourth Gospel and the Salvation of Israel: An Appeal for a New Start," in *Anti-Judaism and the Fourth Gospel* (ed. Reimund Bieringer et al.), 92–110; summarizing the argument of the earlier book. Idem, *Your Father the Devil? A New Approach*

"portrayal of 'the Jews'" that is derived from the use of passages that emphasize the positive side of "the Jews" (such as 4:22; 11:45). Therefore, despite his partiality for a connection of οἱ Ἰουδαῖοι to "late first-century Judaism,"[41] he cannot share the negative evaluation of οἱ Ἰουδαῖοι across the board. Instead the narratively presented dividedness of "the Jews," the positive statements about them and finally the polemical speech as part of a prophetic appeal,[42] have the goal of convincing "the Jews" of the message of the Gospel. "The narrative seeks to lure readers into its perspective, and into accepting that he (= Jesus) really is the raised Temple around which the scattered people of God can be gathered into one."[43]

There is also a series of individual works that draw on the narratological approach, of which I will mention four. *Udo Schnelle* also assumes "daß in der literarischen Welt des Johannesevangeliums der Schlüssel zum Verständnis von Ἰουδαῖοι liegt."[44] The placement, in particular, of οἱ Ἰουδαῖοι within the Gospel as a whole reveals the dramaturgy of the Evangelist because the references to οἱ Ἰουδαῖοι are concentrated in the middle and at the end of the Gospel and thus become a definitive element of the intensifying conflict. Because of both the positive and negative semantic of οἱ Ἰουδαῖοι, "sind die Juden gleichermaßen Repräsentanten des Unglaubens und des Glaubens (...). Negativ erscheinen die Juden bei Johannes – wie alle Menschen – nur dann, wenn sie im Unglauben verharren."[45]

With his "narratological perspective," *D. Francois Tolmie* diverts the attention from the question of identity which, in his opinion, is also undercut by the implied author because the "distinctions/borders among the various groups are blurred."[46] Using a precise analysis of the various scenes with regard to the character traits, he brings out the tensions and incongruities in the portrayal of "the Jews" which do not enable a unilinear development and classification. Thus, according to the implied author "in terms of the characterization of the Ἰουδαῖοι and the other groups closely associated with them, what is important is not *who* they are, but what they *do* in the narrative world."[47]

---

to John and 'the Jews' (Paternoster Biblical and Theological Monographs; London: Paternoster Press, 1997).

[41] Motyer, *Your Father the Devil*, 54–55, 153–54, 213: "Judea-based, Torah-loyal adherents of the Yavneh-ideals, the direct heirs of pre-70 Pharisaism."

[42] John 8 is to be compared with Hosea; see Motyer, *Your Father the Devil*, 146–48.

[43] Motyer, "Fourth Gospel and the Salvation," 108.

[44] See Schnelle, "Die Juden im Johannesevangelium," 227.

[45] Schnelle, "Die Juden im Johannesevangelium," 230.

[46] D. Francois Tolmie, "The ΙΟΥΔΑΙΟΙ in the Fourth Gospel: A Narratological Perspective," in *Theology and Christology in the Fourth Gospel: Essays by Members of the SNTS Johannine Writings Seminar* (ed. Gilbert Van Belle et al.; BETL 184, Louvain: Peeters, 2005), 377–98, here 395.

[47] Tolmie, "ΙΟΥΔΑΙΟΙ," 395.

In his 2009 article, *Cornelis Bennema* tries to combine the historical and narratological approaches. He deals in particular with the "referent" of οἱ Ἰουδαῖοι and comes to the result that the Evangelist "had a single referent in mind – albeit the referent is a composite group which does not present a uniform response."[48] Beginning with an understanding of "the Jews" as a "particular religious group of Torah- and temple partisans,"[49] which according to Bennema already existed in Second Temple Judaism, he examines in particular the relationship of "the Jews" to the Judean authorities and works out a complex organizational system of the various groups under the leadership of the chief priests. With few exceptions, "the Jews" are continuously portrayed as being hostile toward Jesus, although a development or "a shift in hostility from a religious-theological conflict with the Pharisees in the middle of Jesus' ministry towards a religious-political conflict with the chief priests at the end of Jesus' ministry"[50] takes place.

Finally, in a chapter about "the Jews" in her monograph, *Susan Hylen* hopes "in approaching 'the Jews' as a character … to open up some new interpretative possibilities."[51] First she emphasizes that "the Jews" are not portrayed as uniformly negative but rather are "characterized as both believing and unbelieving."[52] The evangelist's portrayal of "the Jews" is often ironic, which shows up particularly through misunderstandings which in the end are meant to lead to a deeper understanding for the reader. Thus, the presentation of "the Jews" fulfils a strategic function in the narrative process. Because "the Jews" are portrayed as an "ambiguous character," the option remains open "that John's intended reader would self-identify as Jewish."[53] Overall she detects a surprising proximity between the group character of the disciples and that of "the Jews." It is precisely these parallels that enable the modern reader to see "the Jews" as an example. Thus, reading "the Jews" as a character "offers a different way of addressing anti-Jewish prejudice in contemporary preaching and scholarship."[54]

In summary, we can state that the existing narratological studies examine the role of "the Jews" in the macro structure of the Gospel; then they either a) deal with the identity issue "text-inherently" or use a combination of methods; or b) move the actions or plot to the center and analyze the pragmatic function of the words and deeds of "the Jews." Authors often attempt to harmonize the disparate results into a clear picture.

---

[48] Bennema, "Identity," 262.
[49] Bennema, "Identity," 245.
[50] Bennema, "Identity," 260.
[51] See Susan Hylen, *Imperfect Believers: Ambiguous Characters in the Gospel of John* (Louisville, Ky.: Westminster Knox Press, 2009), 113–34, here 113.
[52] Hylen, *Imperfect Believers*, 119, here with regard to John 6.
[53] Hylen, *Imperfect Believers*, 127.
[54] Hylen, *Imperfect Believers*, 128.

Methodological Presuppositions

Within narratological theory we differentiate between a strict stucturalist and a cognitive-mimetic model of character analysis. In the latter, the "Weltwissen" ("knowledge of the world") is a definitive factor in the constitution of characters, while the former refers purely to the text level. In the heuristic sense, we will take a more structuralist position in differentiation from historical or hermeneutical models of interpretation. This leads to the fundamental statement – "the Jews" as narrated characters are not historical people. "They are fabricated creatures made up from fantasy, imitation, memory: paper people, without flesh and blood. (...) The character is not a human being, but it resembles one. It has no real psyche, personality, ideology, or competence to act, but it does possess characteristics which make psychological and ideological descriptions possible."[55] On the basis of such an insight, "the Jews" in John can first be observed and described on their own on the level of the plot. A synchronic narratological analysis frees the exegesis from the historical construction of hypotheses and from ideological partisanship.

In the 67 references to "the Jews," there are many passages in which "the Jews" are mentioned only within the framework of a speech or narrator's remark or belong to the inventory of characters but in which they themselves do not act. On the other hand, there are also scenes in which "the Jews" truly act in the narrative world or perform on the stage of events.[56] In order to appropriately portray this important aspect, I would like to return to one of the fundamental distinctions of narratology which in a broader sense must be classified within the aspect of focalization and point of view.[57] The central question is: How is this character narrated? One can differentiate between *direct presentation* and *indirect presentation*, or "telling" and "showing."[58] In

---

[55] Mieke Bal, *Narratology: Introduction to the Theory of Narrative* (2d ed.; Toronto: University of Toronto Press, 2007), 115; see also Seymour Chatman, *Story and Discourse: Narrative Structure in Fiction and Film* (Ithaca, N. Y.: Cornell University Press, 1978), 138: "Characters do not have 'lives'."

[56] See also Uta Poplutz, *Erzählte Welt: Narratologische Studien zum Matthäusevangelium* (BThS 100; Neukirchen-Vluyn: Neukirchener Verlag, 2008), 66 with reference to Manfred Pfister, *Das Drama: Theorie und Analyse* (11th ed.; München: Fink, 2001), 225–26.

[57] See for instance Gérard Genette, *Die Erzählung* (2d ed.; München: Fink, 1998), 115–88, who differenciates between "Modus" and "Stimme"; the latter consists of "Distanz" and "Fokalisierung"; Bal, *Narratology*, 156–60; see on "Perspektivenanalyse" Sönke Finnern, *Narratologie und Biblische Exegese: Eine integrative Methode der Erzählanalyse und ihr Ertrag am Beispiel von Matthäus 28* (WUNT II/285; Tübingen: Mohr Siebeck, 2010), 164–86.

[58] See on this Shlomith Rimmon-Kenan, *Narrative Fiction: Contemporary Poetics* (London: Methuen, 1983), 60–67, 106–108; the brief introduction in James L. Resseguie, *Narrative Criticism of the New Testament: An Introduction* (Grand Rapids, Mich.: Baker Academic, 2005), 126–30; further Judith Hartenstein, *Charakterisierung im Dialog: Maria Magdalena,*

"telling" (direct presentation) the character is described in direct terms and by means of *epitheta* by the author (e. g.,"Judas was a thief"; 12:6). In "showing" (indirect presentation or dramatic method), the character who is speaking or acting, and the area and constellation of the inter-action with others or insights into their "inner life" (such as interior monologue) are at the forefront and enable readers to create an image of the character. The two forms of character presentation can complement and strengthen each other but can also come into conflict.

In analyzing "the Jews" in detail as a character, I will draw on Sönke Finnern's model of character analysis[59] within his narratological study. However, his six-element schema of analysis will be reduced to four and the order will be modified: 1) *inventory and constellation of characters*: where do "the Jews" appear and with which other characters do they interact? 2) *Character and plot*: what does the character do or say or where does he/she appear as the object of the actions of other characters? Which role does he/she take with relation to the plot? Is he/she a main character/protagonist or a minor/secondary character? Is he/she a walk-on character or a part of a chorus? 3) *Character traits*: which traits identify the character? One can differentiate among physical, mental and social categories of analysis.[60] And in which way does the implied reader experience these traits? Explicitly through identification by the auctorial narrator or other characters (= telling) or implicitly through action and speech of the character him/herself (= showing)? 4) *Character concept*: finally, one can categorize characters comparatively. Drawing on Jens Eder,[61] Finnern identified opposing pairs between which the characters can be positioned. For example, "Change in the character: static – dynamic;"[62] "Detail of the character: scarce – detailed;"[63] "Dimensionality of the character: one dimensional – multi-dimensional;"[64] "Conventionality of the character: typical – individual,"[65] etc. In the analysis of the individual passages, these four

---

Petrus, Thomas und die Mutter Jesu im Johannesevangelium im Kontext anderer frühchristlicher Darstellungen (NTOA/SUNT 64; Göttingen: Vandenhoeck & Ruprecht, 2007), 34–36 and the application; ibid., 58–109.

[59] See Finnern, *Narratologie und Biblische Exegese*, 125–63. Finnern distinguishes between 1. "Figurenbestand und -konfiguration;" 2. "Figurenmerkmale;" 3. "Figurenkonstellation;" 4. "Figur und Handlung;" 5. "Figurendarstellung;" and 6. "Figurenkonzeption."

[60] See the list of twelve different categories in Finnern, *Narratologie und Biblische Exegese*, 134.

[61] See Jens Eder, *Die Figur im Film: Grundlagen der Figurenanalyse* (Marburg: Schüren, 2008), 375–99. Bennema takes the three axes by which a character may be situated from Yosef Ewen: complexity; development; penetration into the inner life, see Cornelis Bennema, "A Theory of Character in the Fourth Gospel with Reference to Ancient and Modern Literature," *BibInt*17 (2009): 375–421, here 392.

[62] Finnern, *Narratologie und Biblische Exegese*, 157.
[63] Finnern, *Narratologie und Biblische Exegese*, 157.
[64] Finnern, *Narratologie und Biblische Exegese*, 158.
[65] Finnern, *Narratologie und Biblische Exegese*, 158.

aspects will not be discussed in order, but rather will be intermingled according to the text. The character traits and entire conceptualization will be summarized in the final systematic section of this article.

A second question pertains to the group character. Although character analysis of individual characters is a desideratum of research,[66] this problem intensifies with regard to the analysis of group characters. Even though the narratological analysis does not greatly differ in most aspects from that of the individual characters, there are a few particularities.[67] 1) *Identification of the groups*: the implied reader can speak of a group only if a group is identified as such with a *nomen appellativum*. The term – here οἱ Ἰουδαῖοι – makes a recognizable group character out of an entity of the narrated world. In the Gospel of John there are various groups such as the "Pharisees," "priests," "soldiers" and even "women at the cross."[68] In each case, different relationships (e. g., "disciples" *of Jesus*, the [sons] *of Zebedee*), characteristics (e. g., believers, ill and sick) or professions (e. g., money changers, temple police) characterize the groups. 2) *Relationships of individual characters to the group or parts of the group*: individual characters can be portrayed in proximity to or at a distance from the group. Thus, the group of disciples consists of individual characters that represent the group (e. g., Thomas in 11:16) or that distance themselves from it (e. g., Judas in 6:71). Finally, 3) *Identity and unity of the group*: identification with a name does not mean that the group character is also presented as a unit. Instead we can recognize various aspects. Which traits bring the group together as a unit? What differentiates this group from another and thus gives it an identity?

Οἱ Ἰουδαῖοι in the Fourth Gospel –
A Descriptive Approach and Analysis of Texts

Of the total of 71 uses of the usually nominative adjective Ἰουδαῖος (= "Jewish") in the Fourth Gospel, only four are in the singular.[69] The remaining 67 are, in their grammatical usage, plural.[70] "The Jews" are thus a group character. What

---

[66] See Poplutz, *Erzählte Welt*, 60–61; and Bal, *Narratology*, 225; Jannidis, *Figur und Person*, 2.
[67] See Poplutz, *Erzählte Welt*, 131–39.
[68] See the table in this volume.
[69] See 3:22 where it is used as attribute: "into the Judean countryside" (εἰς τὴν Ἰουδαίαν γῆν); 3:25 where it is used to refer to an anonymous Jew (see the article of Mark Appold in this volume); in 4:9 Jesus is addressed as a "Jew" (σὺ Ἰουδαῖος) by the Samaritan woman; in 18:35 Pilate denies being a Jew/Jewish (μήτι ἐγὼ Ἰουδαῖός εἰμι).
[70] The calculation of the number of references to οἱ Ἰουδαῖοι or "the Jews" in the Gospel is imprecise, because the group may just as well be represented by personal pronouns and

does the reader learn about this character? How is it introduced and described? How does it act?

In the inductive description carried out here, we will draw heuristically on the difference between "telling" and "showing" (see above). We can recognize a direct characterization in many statements that refer to "the Jews" in general. These will be covered comprehensively in the first section. Direct and indirect presentation interlock in statements about "the Jews" directly involved in the plot. In the analysis of such concrete plot characters, I follow the course of the Gospel in the second section.

Telling About "the Jews" (in General)

Let us begin with statements *about* "the Jews" made by others, in particular by the narrator. In such cases "the Jews" appear most often grammatically as the object. We can differentiate between two levels. On one level there are statements about "the Jews" and their concrete actions, which are made, for example, by other characters in meeting scenes or which refer to earlier narrated events. In this way, the disciples recall that "the Jews" wanted to stone Jesus (11:18) or the narrator mentions the reason that "the Jews" went to Mary and Martha – they had come to console them about their brother (11:19). In these occurrences "the Jews" refer to a clearly defined group of acting "Jews," mentioned earlier in the Gospel. On the other level, information about "the Jews" which identifies life habits, traditions, etc., is introduced by the narrator. In such cases, the subject is "the Jews" in a general sense without reference to concrete representatives in the plot. So, for example, the burial habits of "the Jews" are reported in this way (19:40).

We will first consider the latter field of direct presentation with regard to a more general group of "Jews." Following the course of the Gospel, the beginning tells of "the Jews'" laws of ritual purification in connection with the jars of stone of Cana (2:6). Jesus' first trip to Jerusalem is introduced with the reference to the "Passover of the Jews" (2:13: τὸ πάσχα τῶν Ἰουδαίων) which itself introduces a series of similar comments about Sabbath and feasts that are repeatedly called "the feast of the Jews" (e. g., 6:4: ἡ ἑορτὴ τῶν Ἰουδαίων; cf. 7:2; 11:55). After crucifixion, Jesus' body is dealt with according to the "burial customs of 'the Jews'." They wrapped it with spices in linen cloths (19:40). The last remark of this kind is in 19:42 where "the Jews'" "day of preparation" is mentioned, a reference to the day of preparation for the Passover Feast.

---

verbs including reference to the group as its subject. Nevertheless, as far as I could determine, there is no scene in which "the Jews" are referred to without the term being used somewhere in it.

In the conversation with the Samaritan woman (ch. 4), Jesus himself is identified as "a Jew" (4:9) but "the Jews" as a group character about which others speak occur only as a unit in the background. Thus, in the meeting with the protagonists, ethnic-religious conflicts that have already been alluded to are extended to the group: "For 'the Jews' do not share things in common with Samaritans" (4:9). Thus, "the Jews" as a religious-ethnic entity are to be distinguished from "the Samaritans." In the further conversation about places of worship we find the well-known sentence: ἡ σωτηρία ἐκ τῶν Ἰουδαίων ἐστίν (4:22). Jesus as speaker refers in this section several times to a future and self-fulfilling time (4:21, 23), so that "the Jews" can be best understood here as sources of salvation and bearers of the promise, similar to "Israel."[71]

Finally, the title "King of the Jews" (ὁ βασιλεὺς τῶν Ἰουδαίων, 18:33, 39; 19:3, 19, 21), which appears frequently within the Passion narrative, can be added. The stereotypically utilized title reveals the genitive object "of the Jews" as a unit of tradition. This is reinforced by the fact that the title is introduced with the supplement "King *of Israel*" (ὁ βασιλεὺς τοῦ Ἰσραήλ; 1:49; 12:13; cf. 12:15) over the course of the Gospel. This title is taken from tradition, which is made evident by means of the Old Testament quotations of Zeph 3:15 (12:13) and Zech 9:9 (12:15) referred to in the narration on Jesus' entry into Jerusalem. Indeed, it is not only the change from "of Israel" to "of the Jews" that is astonishing. In Pilate's speech, the traditional title is linked to the present. In his question about kingship, Pilate was certainly not interested in a purely interreligious conflict over the title (18:33); this link to the present becomes obvious in the last scene of the trial. Pilate says "Behold *your* King!" (ὁ βασιλεὺς ὑμῶν; 19:14, cf. v. 15) and the pronoun clearly refers to "the Jews." However, it is precisely this declaration that "the Jews" want to avoid and thus they are led into the blasphemous statement that they have no other king than the Emperor (19:15). Later in the conflict about the *titulus crucis*, Pilate's title for Jesus is called into question again (19:21).

The direct characterizations mentioned up to now show "the Jews" as an ethnic-religious group that constitutes itself through rituals (e. g., marriage and burial), issues related to the calendar (e. g., Sabbath and feasts), as well as through the expectations of a king. In terms of focalization the characterization takes a more distanced perspective – the customs are generally identified by the narrator on an informative level without being assigned a particular value. Only in 4:22 does the positive statement that salvation comes from "the Jews" issue from Jesus' mouth. The usage of the title "King of the Jews" revealed that in some ways the division line cannot be drawn sharply between

---

[71] See Moloney, "Jews," 31: "(…) the man whom the woman had earlier called 'a Jew' (v. 9) is also the one in whom the revelation of God to Israel reaches its fulfillment. (…) the notion of 'Israel' (has) been expanded to indicate that both Jews and non-Jews can be regarded as belonging to Israel on the basis of their belief."

the direct presentation of a general group – in the sense of an ethnic-religious group – and the concretely acting characters.

Telling About and Showing "the Jews" as a Concretely Acting Character

When οἱ Ἰουδαῖοι appear as a concretely acting character, they can be directly characterized when the narrator or another character identifies character traits. What is dominant here are statements from Jesus with which he refers to "the Jews" and often speaks directly to them. In addition to this, indirect characterization takes place by means of the actions and statements of "the Jews" themselves.

In view of the overlap with other group characters, there are, of course, varying assessments of which scenes should be considered here.[72] Below I will carry out a more minimalistic reduction using the lexical evidence. Only the scenes in which "the Jews" are explicitly mentioned will be analyzed. Of course, this cannot be limited to the verses in which the word Ἰουδαῖοι appears because the characters are frequently mentioned in subsequent verses only by means of personal pronouns. Nevertheless, the internal references must clearly reveal that Jesus' conversational partners are "the Jews" and no other group.[73]

The first occurrence of "the Jews" is in the first verse after the prologue, *John 1:19*. As soon as the action begins, "the Jews" are mentioned. To be exact, they are the first characters who act because the reference to John has more the character of a title ("This is the testimony of John"). Although they are the subject of the sentence, "the Jews" themselves do not appear because the scene takes place in Bethany on the other side of the Jordan river (1:28). Their action lies in the past in the narrative perspective because the subsequent dialogue begins with the question, "Who are you?" Over a very short space, various aspects of "the Jews" are recounted – they come "from Jerusalem," they send "priests and Levites" (ἀπέστειλαν), which means that they not only have a close connection to these representatives of the cult but also have the authority to send them out. They want to know who John (the Baptist) is. As the following dialogue is carried out with the priests and Levites, one can expand the constellation of characters related to "the Jews" in v. 24: the sending of those leading the conversation with John is here attributed to the Pharisees which permits the identification of the Pharisees and "the Jews" at this point.[74]

---

[72] See Tolmie, who also includes 6:1–40 where only the crowd is mentioned explicitly, see Tolmie, "ΙΟΥΔΑΙΟΙ," 383–84.

[73] This is clearly to be seen in 5:19–47. In 5:18 οἱ Ἰουδαῖοι are mentioned explicitly, thus the following pronoun αὐτοῖς (5:19: "Jesus said to *them*") must be linked to "the Jews" as no other group appearing is mentioned. Later on in the same speech Jesus also refers to an action, which referred to "the Jews" as subject (5:33: "You sent messengers to John," see 1:19).

[74] On the interrelatedness of "the Jews" and the Pharisees see below; furthermore, see the article from Uta Poplutz in this volume.

The next explicit mention of "the Jews" as characters of action is in the "cleansing of the temple" (*John 2:13–25*). After the "cleansing," "the Jews" appear suddenly and demand that Jesus justify his actions. The implied reader not only knows that the scene takes place in Jerusalem (2:13) but can conclude from the use of the personal pronoun ("Can you show *us*?") that they have a close connection to the temple. This also becomes clear in the next sentence when "the Jews" prove themselves to be knowledgeable of the temple's history of construction (2:20). At this point, the first of many so-called "Johannine misunderstandings" takes place. Thus are "the Jews" put squarely into the role of those who misunderstand.

One of the strongest sections in regard to direct characterization by Jesus is the expanded monologue in *John 5:19–47* which explicitly addresses "the Jews"[75] after being introduced with a brief remark on the actions of "the Jews" and two comments by the narrator. After the healing of the lame man at the pool of Bethesda (5:1–9), "the Jews" appear and ask the healed man about the identity of the miracle worker. Both comments by the narrator not only mention the conflict with Jesus, but also clarify the reasons: 1) they started persecuting Jesus, because he broke the Sabbath (5:16); and 2) "This was why 'the Jews' sought all the more to kill him because … he called God his Father, making himself equal with God" (5:18). In the following speech, quite a number of traits are revealed by means of direct characterization from Jesus' perspective. As Tolmie correctly summarizes, eight traits are to be mentioned: "The Ἰουδαῖοι 1. have never heard God's voice (5:37); 2. have never seen God (5:37); 3. do not have God's word in their hearts (5:38); 4. search the Scripture without finding eternal life (5:39); 5. do not possess the love of God (5:42); 6. are willing to accept one who comes in his own name (5:43); 7. seek the honor of people and not that of God (5:44); and 8. have set their hope on Moses, yet do not believe in him (5:47)."[76]

This quite negative characterization calls into question most Jewish traditions related to their having received God's word, as well as their love for and study of the Scripture. They fail to follow these traditions because they "refuse to come to Jesus" (5:40), they do not believe in him (5:38) and have not received him (5:43). In John 5, "the Jews" are thus clearly presented in a negative light by means of direct characterization. The reliability of the characterization of "the Jews" is created in two ways: First it is the narrator who describes their hostile attitude toward Jesus (e. g., they persecute Jesus and intend to kill him) and mentions the breaking of the Sabbath and the equation with God as the reasons. Subsequently, the focus shifts to Jesus, whose statements about "the Jews" must be considered to be true based on the authority of his person.

---

[75] See 5:18–19, 33; on the addressee of John 5, see below.
[76] See Tolmie, "ΟΙ ΙΟΥΔΑΙΟΙ," 383 (the occurrences have been added by myself – RZ); similarly Culpepper, *Anatomy of the Fourth Gospel*, 129.

In the miracle of the loaves and fishes in *John 6*, the crowd (ὄχλος) is identified as a collective counterpart in the first section; however, the term Ἰουδαῖοι does not appear again until 6:41. For Bennema, "the Jews" set themselves apart from the crowd precisely at the moment when the conversation "becomes particularly hostile."[77] At the very least it is striking that the previous dialogue now fails and comes to an end. "The Jews" no longer speak *to* Jesus but rather *about* him.[78] They grumble about the statement on the bread and they question Jesus' declaration that he came down "from heaven" (6:41–42). The use of the verb γογγύζω recalls the grumbling of the Israelites during their desert migration in Exodus (Ex 17:3; Num 14:27–29), which is further demonstrated by the reference to the provision of manna in the wilderness (Ex 16; see John 6:31, 49). In this way, indirect characterization completes a parallelization between "the Jews" and the Israelites in the desert.[79] This connection is made even clearer when in Numbers 14:29 death is mentioned despite the provision of manna. Of course, this issue is also addressed by Jesus (6:49, 58), while reference to the bread of Jesus, which he is himself, notably is linked to eternal life (vss. 51, 56–58).[80] "The Jews" misunderstand Jesus' words and even come into conflict with each other (v. 52). Nevertheless, the actions of "the Jews" in John 6 are in no way as hostile as is often assumed. They may often doubt Jesus' heavenly origins but the reference to his worldly origins (vss. 41–42) is expressly formulated as a question. The grumbling is relativized by the connection back to the Israelites. Jesus understands their "grumbling" as not primarily directed against himself or the Father (as in Num 14). Instead, he speaks of "grumbling among yourselves" (v. 43), which anticipates the internal conflict (v. 52) and even creates a connection to the disciples and their divisions (vss. 61, 66). Thus, unlike in John 5, the statements in John 6:41–59 seem to be more an invitation than a judgment. Although "the Jews" exist in the tradition of the fathers (see "your fathers," v. 49), Jesus does not reproach them for their incomprehension for it is the deeds of the fathers and sons that call forth life (v. 44). "The Jews" share this lack of understanding with all people (see 6:44: "no one" – οὐδείς; 6:46: "any one" – τις). The frequently used participles (v.

---

[77] Bennema, "Identity," 256.

[78] See also Michael Theobald, *Das Evangelium nach Johannes: Kapitel 1–12* (RNT; Regensburg: Pustet, 2009), 469: "Die Verschärfung der Konfrontation, die durch den Terminus 'die Juden' angezeigt sein könnte, äußert sich auch darin, dass sie von nun an keine *direkte* Frage mehr an Jesus richten, sondern '*untereinander* murren,' der Dialog also zum Erliegen kommt."

[79] See Hylen, *Imperfect Believers*, 120: "The Jews are thus characterized as similar to the Israelites." For Hylen this has several implications for the character of "the Jews"; e. g., "the Jews' response is not necessarily hostile here … Their response to Jesus is the same response that the Israelites had to God's salvation in the wilderness" (120).

[80] See on the close connection of (eternal) life and bread in John 6, Mira Stare, *Durch ihn leben: Die Lebensthematik in Joh 6* (NTAbh 49; Münster: Aschendorff, 2004), 265–68 and 280–82.

45: ὁ ἀκούσας, v. 47: ὁ πιστεύων, vss. 54, 56, 58: ὁ τρώγων – ὁ πίνων) leave space for integration in the sense of "anyone who …," which of course also includes "the Jews." Nevertheless, one of the specific privileges of "the Jews," being inheritors of their Jewish tradition, is thus subtly relativized and made redundant.

The conflict intensifies in the next scene, which lasts dramaturgically from *John 7–10*[81] and, specifically from 7:14–10:39, in Jerusalem. It takes place frequently in the temple and temple forecourt and is framed by two Jewish feasts (7: Feast of Tabernacles; 10: Feast of Dedication). If we first concentrate on *John 7* with regard to the "character inventory," we can see a close interweaving of "the Jews" with "the crowd," the "Pharisees," with "some of the people of Jerusalem" (7:25), the "temple police" (7:45) and finally with Nicodemus (7:50).[82] With regard to the traits, certain existing attributes are intensified or expanded. "The Jews'" intention to kill Jesus, which we are familiar with from John 5:18, is repeated right at the beginning (7:1). Because Jesus first travels secretly – and not with his brothers – to the feast, it is not necessarily noteworthy that "the Jews" search for him (7:11). The people are not forthcoming with information because of their "fear of the Jews" (7:13), which creates a distance between "the Jews" and the crowd and strengthens the thesis that "the Jews" here denotes the Jewish authorities.[83] Although Jesus' own anxiety due to the persecution and death threats may have been expected, it is surprising that the people are now "afraid." This is a motif that is taken up repeatedly until the end of the Gospel (9:22; 19:38; 20:19). "The Jews" are thus characterized as powerful authorities who are feared by others.

The meeting between Jesus and "the Jews" is located in the temple (7:14–19). The reader learns that "the Jews" claim authority for the interpretation of scripture when they call Jesus' own understanding of scripture into question. This confirms that the Law of Moses has been given to "the Jews" (v. 19a). The proximity to the Law that is postulated here intensifies the existing traits that are introduced through the laws of purity (John 2) and the Sabbath (John 5) – keeping the Torah can be counted as a characteristic of "the Jews." However, Jesus challenges exactly this fact by stating that they do not follow the law (v. 19b: καὶ οὐδεὶς ἐξ ὑμῶν ποιεῖ τὸν νόμον). Jesus' judgment creates distance between the law (of "the Jews") and his own teaching authority, which is an aspect that is taken up later with the possessive pronoun "your law" (see also 8:17; 10:34; 15:25).

Jesus' dialogue is now continued with the people (v. 20) and with the Pharisees (v. 32) and 7:35–36 again reports on a conversation of "the Jews" "among themselves" in which they express their renewed incomprehension related to

---

[81] See Ludger Schenke, "Joh 7–10: Eine dramatische Szene," *ZNW* 80 (1989): 172–92.
[82] See Tolmie, "ΙΟΥΔΑΙΟΙ," 384–86; and Bennema, "Crowd," in this volume.
[83] See for instance, von Wahlde, *John*, 149.

Jesus' statement that he is going away. "The Jews" now take that which was said previously to the Pharisees (v. 32) and literally repeat it to themselves (v. 36). Although this is one of the Johannine misunderstandings, it is precisely the contrast created between the Greeks and "the Jews" which could be helpful in giving meaning to Johannine irony. "The dispersion among the Greeks" (v. 35) refers primarily to "the Jews" living in the diaspora, although this narrow scope is expanded. Jesus' teaching authority which is addressed in 7:15–16 is now extended in general to the Greeks. Will Jesus also teach the Greeks?

The well-known saying of Jesus, that he is going away (see 7:35; 7:36), is repeated a third time (8:21). It differs only slightly with the announcement that the addressees will die in their sins. According to 8:13, the Pharisees are addressed here, but the following verse makes it obvious that "Jews" are at least present in the scene. They reply with another interpretation asking whether Jesus will commit suicide. This idea is even more absurd than the first which considered the diaspora and thus confirms the trait of misunderstanding. At the same time the trait – "intention to kill" – comes to the fore again. But it is driven to a grotesque and ironic twist. The implied author demonstrates that "the Jews" think only about Jesus' death; they are obsessed with or possessed by the idea that Jesus should be killed. Therefore they even conclude that he might kill himself. The most intensive dialogue between Jesus and "the Jews" within the whole Gospel begins in v. 21. According to Theobald, *John 8* is the center of the conflict between Jesus and "the Jews" within the whole passage John 7–10.[84] The passage can be structured in three subsections: 8:21–30 (dialogue with four statements of Jesus, two of "the Jews," and two comments by the narrator on "the Jews"); 8:31–47 (four statements of Jesus, and three of "the Jews"); 8:48–59 (three statements of Jesus, and three of "the Jews"). In the first section we realize a sharp contradiction between the final direct presentation of "the Jews" and what is reported before. At the end of the section the narrator tells that many (of "the Jews") believed in him (v. 30). This characterization is surprising after Jesus created a clear contrast between their origin (from below, from this world) and his own (from above, not from this world) (8:23)[85] and spoke of their death unless they believed in him. Obviously they do not, which is made clear by their action. Right after he told them who he is (ἐγώ εἰμι; v. 24), they asked, "Who are you?" Accordingly, the narrator states that they did not understand (v. 27). In the face of this incomprehension Jesus announced a time when they will know exactly who he is. "It is the lifting

---

[84] See Theobald, *Johannes*, 609: "Joh 8 ist das Zentrum und der Höhepunkt der Jerusalemer Auseinandersetzung Jesu mit 'den Juden', wie sie der Evangelist im großen dramatischen Spannungsbogen der Kap. 7–10 zur Darstellung bringt."

[85] The meaning of κόσμος (as sinful, dark, etc.) is used here to qualify "the Jews;" see Caron, *Qui sont les Juifs*, 166–67, 283.

up on the cross that will be the means by which the divine identity and glory of Jesus ... will be revealed."[86] However, this hopeful announcement includes a severe accusation, which is mostly ignored by interpreters: "When *you* have lifted up the Son of Man ...". Jesus tells "the Jews" that they will be the actors who will lift him up, a lifting up which will be explained as crucifixion later in 12:33. Is this the action to be expected of people who believe? This statement of faith should thus not be overemphasized when considering the overall characterization of "the Jews," especially when one considers the context.

This is even more true with regard to the next passage (8:31–47), which is addressed to the "believing Jews" (πρὸς τοὺς πεπιστευκότας αὐτῷ Ἰουδαίους; the present perfect is best to be understood as an ongoing result, not stating anteriority[87]). Jesus, however, challenges their belief, considering it insufficient with regard to his person and word. It is especially belief in his word, as an indicator of true discipleship, which is obviously lacking for "the Jews." They declare that they are descendants of Abraham (vss. 33, 39) and children of God (v. 41), but by not knowing (v. 43), loving (v. 42), and listening to Jesus (vss. 43, 47), and even more in their wish to kill him (vss. 37, 40), they demonstrate their unbelief (vss. 45–46). Hence, instead of having God as their father (v. 41) Jesus tells them polemically: "You are of your father, the devil" (v. 44). The sharp contrast in the first passage (above – below) is extended to an extreme and polemic opposition: God – Jesus – truth *versus* lie – "Jews" – Devil. This statement can be read against the background of apocalyptic polemic in Early Judaism.[88] Nevertheless it is doubtless one of the most fatalistic sentences of the New Testament, the abuse of which has led to anti-Jewish excesses.[89] However, it is difficult to argue that this passage is just an inner conflict of "Johannine Judaism."[90] From a narrative perspective "the Jews" are said to be on the wrong side. Both of their arguments (being children of Abraham as well as of God; vss. 8:33, 41) fail in not acknowledging Jesus' ministry and his being from God.

---

[86] Andrew T. Lincoln, *The Gospel According to John* (Peabody, Mass.: Hendrickson, 2006), 269.

[87] Some exegetes translate "had believed"; see, e. g., Leon Morris, *The Gospel According to John* (NICNT; Grand Rapids, Mich.: Eerdmans, 1989), 455; on the arguments for the present meaning, see Theobald, *Johannes*, 588–89.

[88] See Hakola, *Identity Matters*, 197–210; see also Urban C. von Wahlde, "'You Are of Your Father the Devil' in its Context: Stereotyped Apocalyptic Polemic in John 8:38–47," in *Anti-Judaism and the Fourth Gospel* (ed. Reimund Bieringer et al.), 418–44.

[89] See more recently a brief survey on the *Wirkungsgeschichte* of 8:44, Neubrand, "Antijudaismus," 206–209.

[90] See von Wahlde, "Father," 440: "Rather than being anti-Jewish, the polemic was 'anti-opposition'." It is hard to agree that "the author is not saying that the Jewish perspective is wrong," (442), but von Wahlde points out correctly that the dispute is on the right interpretation of Abraham and the child-relationship of God and Jesus.

In the final section of 8:48–59 once again "the Jews" misunderstand Jesus' status when they claim that he is a Samaritan and possessed by a demon. Readers will remember that in 4:9 they were told that Jesus is "a Jew," not a Samaritan.

Coming back to the statement in v. 31, Jesus proclaims that keeping his words leads to eternal life (v. 52). Although "the Jews" still misunderstand, taking Jesus' pronouncement literally with regard to the mortality of Abraham (v. 53), they ask in the right direction: "Are you greater than our father Abraham?" (v. 53), and furthermore: "Have you seen Abraham?" (v. 57). "The Jews" mean this rhetorically and expect the negative answer, "Of course not;" however, a positive answer would proclaim the truth understood by the implied reader.[91] Indeed, Jesus is before Abraham (v. 58). Only now "the Jews" start to realize who Jesus is claiming to be (cf. v. 53). In taking up stones they find him guilty of blasphemy. By doing so they demonstrate that the fundamental dissonance between themselves and Jesus relates to his claim that he comes from God. Is the claim of being equal to God (5:18) just a lie, the statement of a possessed man – or is it the truth, which leads to eternal life? Thus the conflict is rooted in deep christological concerns, which are linked to Jewish traditions.

Finally the character trait which we could describe as "intention to kill" is also explored in the passage. It is exactly the point which explains why "the Jews" differ from Abraham. As Steven Hunt has clearly pointed out, John 8 refers to the *Akedah* in Gen 22.[92] Thus, the works of Abraham refer not only to what Abraham did, but also to what he did not do – that is, he did not kill his son. Against this background Jesus' words sound different: "If you were Abraham's children, you would do what Abraham did, but now you seek to kill me …" (v. 39). Instead of desisting from killing like Abraham, they "seek to kill" him (vss. 37, 40). By their wishes and works they made themselves "children of a murderer" (v. 44).

John 8 presents "the Jews" both by means of direct and indirect presentation as fully aware of Jewish traditional confessions, but not willing to link them to Jesus or follow Jesus' words. Having started to be presented as believers, they end as a "murderous" mob, who have yet to succeed.

In the account of the man born blind in *John 9:1–41*, "the Jews" are encountered together with a whole series of characters: Jesus, the disciples, the

---

[91] See also Steven A. Hunt, "And the Word Became Flesh – Again? Jesus and Abraham in John 8:31–59," in *Perspectives on Our Father Abraham* (ed. Steven A. Hunt; Grand Rapids, Mich.: Eerdmans, 2010), 81–109, who reads this against the background of John's irony: "So while 'the Jews' clearly assume a negative answer to the question, the narrator intends for readers to answer in the affirmative. Yes, Jesus did see Abraham" (104).

[92] For details, including verbal connections to the LXX, see Hunt, "Word Became Flesh," 96–101.

blind man, neighbors, the parents of the man born blind, etc.[93] A significant difference from the constellation of characters in the scenes up to this point is that in John 9 the primary contact of "the Jews" is with other characters and not with Jesus. A close connection, indeed a certain superimposition of "the Jews" onto the Pharisees exists in this chapter. In fact, numerous exegetes view οἱ Ἰουδαῖοι as synonymous with the Pharisees here,[94] since in vss. 13, 15, 16, and 40 οἱ Φαρισαῖοι are explicitly mentioned, whereas in between the final two references (vss. 18 and 22), without any indication of a change in the scene, reference is made to οἱ Ἰουδαῖοι. A strong argument for this thesis can be found in the fact that v. 24 recounts a second summoning (ἐκ δευτέρου) of the blind man and that up to this point, only the Pharisees had questioned him (vss. 15–17). At the same time, however, the notion of "the Jews" as an independent group of characters is supported by the questioning of the healed man by different groups: first the neighbors (vss. 8–12), then the Pharisees (vss. 13–17), and finally "the Jews" (vss. 24–34). The sequence of these interrogations reveal a certain parallel structure as the conversations increase in length and lead to more poignant concluding confessions (v. 11: ἄνθρωπος ὁ λεγόμενος Ἰησοῦς; v. 17: προφήτης ἐστίν; v. 33: οὗτος παρὰ θεοῦ). In this way the different groups of characters form a contrasting foil which aids in guiding the healed man through a process of recognition leading to faith (v. 38: πιστεύω, κύριε· καὶ προσεκύνησεν αὐτῷ).[95] Furthermore, certain characteristics of these adversaries assist in distinguishing the groups of characters. "The Jews" are explicitly named in the final dialogue (vss. 18–34) and the first comment of the narrator (v. 18) creates a double contrast – on the one hand with the faith of the man born blind and on the other hand with the statement of the believing "Jews" in the previous chapter (8:31). The skepticism of "the Jews" is initially directed towards the previous blindness, concerning which – as seen in the manner in which the account progresses – faith is fundamentally determinative (see vss. 25, 30). In the questioning of the parents one reads of the "fear of the Jews" (v. 22; cf. 7:13); however, this trait of "fear" is now founded upon the threat of exclusion from the synagogue: "Anyone who confessed that he was Christ would be put out of synagogue" (v. 22). The varying

---

[93] For a recent narratival analysis, see Jörg Frey, "Sehen oder Nicht-Sehen? (Die Heilung des blind Geborenen) Joh 9,1–41," in *Kompendium der frühchristlichen Wundererzählungen, Vol. 1: Die Wunder Jesu* (ed. Ruben Zimmermann et al.; Gütersloh: Gütersloher Verlagshaus, 2013), 725–41, here 726–34.

[94] See, for instance, Uta Poplutz on the Pharisees in this volume: "The Pharisees and 'the Jews' are one and the same in John 9:13–41."

[95] Concerning this process, see Michael Labahn, "Der Weg eines Namenlosen – Vom Hilflosen zum Vorbild (Joh 9): Ansätze zu einer narrativen Ethik der sozialen Verantwortung im vierten Evangelium," in *Die bleibende Gegenwart des Evangeliums* (ed. Roland Gebauer and Martin Meiser; FS Otto Merk; Marburger Theologische Studien 76; Marburg: Elwert, 2003), 63–80.

hypotheses concerning this exclusion from the synagogue will not be discussed here.[96] Yet, from a narratological perspective it is noteworthy that a motif is here introduced that will be taken up repeatedly (9:34–35; 12:42; 16:2; see below). It is significant, and ultimately determinative, that within the plot of the pericope this fear is a reality. The implied reader initially must think that such an exclusion is a hyperbolic exaggeration; but, in 9:34–35 it is recounted that the formerly blind man actually is thrown out of the synagogue. Apparently his final statements fulfilled the conditions for the previous decree to go into effect. The confession that Jesus is "from God" (v. 33) thus effectively means the same thing as confessing him as Christ (v. 22).

The close connection between John 9 and *John 10* has often been noted in Johannine scholarship.[97] From a narratological perspective in particular, no scene change can be discovered so that the implied reader must assume that Jesus is still speaking to the same group of people. Though the Pharisees are the last named group (9:40), there is no mention of the departure of "the Jews" (9:22) so that they are also assumed to be among those who were "divided" (10:19) on account of Jesus' words. In the two large sections (9:39–10:21 and 10:22–42) and four cycles of dialogue in this extended pericope,[98] "the Jews" are particularly prominent in the third (vss. 22–31) and fourth (vss. 32–42) dialogues.[99] The dialogue takes place in the Temple during the Festival of the Dedication. "The Jews" literally press Jesus, they "gather around" him (v. 25) and want an unambiguous answer to their question: "If you are the Christ, tell us plainly" (v. 24). In the first part of the shepherd discourse, Jesus had already claimed his equality with God. Whereas the shepherd metaphor tradition always reserves the possession of the flock for God, Jesus now presents a claim to this possession (as "my sheep").[100] On account of their knowledge of this tradition, "the Jews" could easily have comprehended the significance of this shift. Now, instead of speaking in images (ἐν παροιμίαι) Jesus should speak plainly. Jesus obliges by initially interpreting the shepherd speech and then utilizing a citation from the Psalms (Ps 82:6) in order to arrive at the pointed concluding statements: "I and the Father are one" (v. 30) and "the Father is in

---

[96] See, for instance, Martyn, *History and Theology*, 31–41; critically Michael Theobald, "Exkurs: Der Synagogenausschluss und die sog. Birkat-ha-minim," in idem, *Johannes*, 647–49.

[97] See Francis J. Moloney, *Signs and Shadows: Reading John 5–12* (Minneapolis: Fortress, 1996), who comments on John 9–10 in one single chapter (pp. 117–42).

[98] See the outline of the structure in my article on "Many Believers" in this volume.

[99] See Ruben Zimmermann, *Christologie der Bilder im Johannesevangelium: Die Christopoetik des vierten Evangeliums unter besonderer Berücksichtigung von Joh 10* (WUNT 171; Tübingen: Mohr Siebeck, 2004), 269–76.

[100] Concerning the "Shepherd-King or -Messiah-Bildfeld," see Ruben Zimmermann, "Jesus im Bild Gottes: Anspielungen auf das Alte Testament im Johannesevangelium am Beispiel der Hirtenbildfelder in Joh 10," in *Kontexte des Johannesevangeliums: Das vierte Evangelium in religions- und traditionsgeschichtlicher Perspektive* (ed. Jörg Frey and Udo Schnelle; WUNT 175; Tübingen: Mohr Siebeck 2004), 81–116.

me and I am in the Father" (v. 38). The invitation found in the introduction to this final statement, namely "That you might learn and know" (v. 38a), is particularly significant. As opposed to the previous radical denial of "the Jews'" ability to understand, this verse offers hope. This is also underscored in the parallel scene. Whereas the conclusion to the third dialogue is entirely negative (v. 31: they attempt to stone him), the verses following the fourth dialogue relate a divided reaction: some attempted to apprehend him (v. 39), though many believed in him (v. 42).

"The Jews" encountered in *John 11–12* present the reader with a rather different picture of this group than the one sketched of them up to this point. Though initially there is a reminder of the intention of the hostile "Jews" to kill Jesus (v. 8), the narrator then relates that "many Jews" came to Mary and Martha in order to comfort them (v. 19). These play a completely different role from "the Jews" who entered into disputes with Jesus. "The Jews" are staged within this complex and carefully composed chapter[101] like a chorus in classical drama: they observe and comment upon that which occurs. The narrator recounts how Mary gets up and goes out as it is seen through the eyes of "the Jews" (v. 31). They observe and comment – though erroneously – upon her action. They misunderstand that Mary goes to Jesus.

They also comment upon the weeping of Jesus as a sign of his love for Lazarus (v. 35) and pose the question, to a certain extent in the place of the implied reader, why Jesus could heal the blind but was not able to heal his sick friend (v. 37). It is almost stereotypically repeated that "the Jews" "came" (vss. 19, 33, 45). They have fellowship in the home with Mary (v. 31) and see "what Jesus did" (v. 45). After the long lead-in, in which the openness of "the Jews" to Jesus' deeds and the lack of ability to hear or see was criticized, the conclusion is almost superfluous. When "the Jews" now "come and see," they also believe (v. 45).

At the same time, however, the group is once again divided. Some of them (v. 46) denounce Jesus to the Pharisees, which leads to an intensifying resolve to put Jesus to death. The actual decree to seek Jesus' death, however, is made by the High Priest, the Pharisees, and the chief council without explicitly mentioning οἱ Ἰουδαῖοι. Nevertheless, the following statement that Jesus "no longer walked openly among 'the Jews'" can only be understood if "the Jews" are also implicated in the decision to pursue Jesus.

---

[101] See e. g., Andrew T. Lincoln, "The Lazarus Story: A Literary Perspective," in *The Gospel of John and Christian Theology* (ed. Richard Bauckham and Carl Mosser; Grand Rapids, Mich.: Eerdmans, 2008), 229–31; Ruben Zimmermann, "The Narrative Hermeneutics of Joh 11: Learning with Lazarus How to Understand Death, Life, and Resurrection," in *The Resurrection of Jesus in the Gospel of John* (ed. Craig R. Koester and Reimund Bieringer; WUNT 222; Tübingen: Mohr Siebeck, 2008), 75–101.

The change of scene to Bethany once again takes up the positive thread from v. 45. A large crowd of "Jews" comes to the home of Lazarus (12:9) and many "Jews" "were believing in Jesus" (12:11).

"The Jews" play a central role in the passion narrative, especially in Jesus' trial (*John 18:28 – 19:16*). The determination of the exact identity of the group is hindered because they are mentioned in close connection with other characters who, according to the construction of the scene and parallel formulations, in part suggest a synonymous use of the terms. The separately named group of "Jewish police/officers" (18:12; cf. 18:18, 22) who carry out the arrest in Gethsemane can be clearly identified as a functional sub-group. However, it is unclear who "the Jews" are who appear in Jesus' trial before Pilate. Are they the high priests of "the Jews" (οἱ ἀρχιερεῖς τῶν Ἰουδαίων), who according to 18:12–24 carry out the first interrogation and then are identified again in 19:4–8 synonymously with "the Jews" (19:6; cf. v. 15)? It is also the high priests who negotiate with Pilate in the dispute about the inscription on the cross (19:21)? Or are they the emissaries of the high priests, such that we should translate οἱ Ἰουδαῖοι here as Klaus Wengst does as "the Jews leading the complaint?"[102] In 18:28 on the way from the house of Caiaphas to the praetorium, no *nomen agentis* is explicitly mentioned (just ἄγουσιν οὖν τὸν Ἰησοῦν). The reader is not told who exactly led Jesus to the *praetorium*. Later on the narrator mentions οἱ Ἰουδαῖοι (18:31, 38; 19:7, 12, 14) in general.

In particular in the "choral termination" at the end of the trial before Pilate should we imagine, with Haenchen, the entire Jewish people as the "hostile and shouting masses?"[103] However, there is no mention of ὄχλος in 18:28–19:16. As is explicitly stated in 19:6 of the high priest, also a couple of men can shout. However, does one not picture in one's inner eye the so-called "Passover amnesty" as a mass of people, as it is known from the Synoptics?[104]

Then the passage ends as vaguely as it began. Pilate "handed him over *to them*" (19:16). According to 18:36 (παραδοθῶ τοῖς Ἰουδαίοις, cf. 19:11), we must assume that it is "the Jews" to whom Jesus is handed over, which makes no sense from an historical perspective because they would not have been able to carry out the crucifixion. However, questions remain in the narrative plot because despite the handover, "the Jews" remain dependent on Pilate. Later

---

[102] See Wengst, *Das Johannesevangelium. Teilbd. 2: Kapitel 11–21* (Theologischer Kommentar zum Neuen Testament 4/2; Stuttgart: Kohlhammer, 2001), 213–14; see here 216: "Wer sind in der Sicht des Johannes die jüdischen Ankläger? Obwohl er in diesem Zusammenhang mehrfach von 'den Juden' spricht (Joh 18,31.38; 19,7.12.14), hat er dabei doch nur bestimmte Juden im Blick. (…) Beauftragte des Hohenpriesters Kaijafas, die Diener als Wachmannschaft und die Oberpriester als Vertreter der Anklage."

[103] Ernst Haenchen, *Das Johannesevangelium: Ein Kommentar* (ed. Ulrich Busse; Tübingen: Mohr Siebeck, 1980), 545: "die feindliche und brüllende Menge."

[104] The synoptic Gospels explicitly speak of the "crowd," see Mark 15:6–8; Matt 27:15, 24.

they must also request permission to take the dead bodies off the crosses (19:31).

As Tolmie previously indicated, the issue of identity, which to a certain extent cannot be resolved, is far less interesting than the actions of the characters.[105] This is also true of the trial. If one observes the characters and their constellation in semantic space, something significant emerges. In seven scenes, six of them with parallel arrangements,[106] the space *in front of* and *in the praetorium* is used in order to create contrasting pairs of binary opposition.[107] The reader learns of the categorical evaluation right at the beginning. "The Jews" do not want to enter the house of the non-Jewish Roman in order not to be defiled, so that they might eat the Passover (18:28). Thus the classification of "outside-pure" and "inside-impure" is created. The interpretative process is now accelerated by the introduction of further opposing pairs which are revealed implicitly or explicitly in the text: Jewish – Roman (18:35), King (of "the Jews") (vss. 33, 39; 19:3, 19) – Emperor (of Rome) (19:12, 15), law (of "the Jews") (18:31; 19:7) and law of the Romans (as a legal basis), human being (19:5) – Son of God (19:7), guilty – innocent, free – captive, true – untrue (18:37).

Following Lotman's sense of semantic space,[108] the distribution of the spaces can be used as an organizational system for the political and religious dimensions which thus gain specific meaning. However there are breakdowns. "The Jews" remain consistently outside and Jesus is shown on the inside in the middle scenes. Pilate, however, goes back and forth. This semantic space allows the characters to gain importance simultaneously. Pilate, in the role of the judge, fluctuates back and forth and at the end asks a question instead of issuing a verdict (19:15). Jesus, the accused, remains confident and plays a leading role in the dialogue. "The Jews," Jesus' accusers, who want to strictly follow the laws of purity, actually violate the highest law by recognizing the Emperor as the only king instead of God (19:15[109]) and thus find themselves guilty of blasphemy. "The Jews" misunderstand their own law also in that they want to kill Jesus according to the law. They want to eat the Passover lamb and

---

[105] See Tolmie, "ΙΟΥΔΑΙΟΙ," 395.

[106] See with others, Raymond E. Brown, *The Gospel According to John (xiii–xxi)* (AB 29a; London: Chapman, 1984), 858–59; on the dramatic reading of John 18 also for detail Ludger Schenke, *Johannes: Kommentar* (Düsseldorf: Patmos, 1998), 346–56.

[107] The beginning verbs ἐξέρχομαι and εἰσέρχομαι clearly indicate this. See for details and a table of the scenes Ruben Zimmermann, "Deuten heißt 'Erzählen' und 'Übertragen': Narrativität und Metaphorik als zentrale Sprachformen historischer Sinnbildung zum Tod Jesu," in *Deutungen des Todes Jesu im Neuen Testament* (ed. Jörg Frey and Jens Schröter; WUNT 181; Tübingen: Mohr Siebeck, Studienausgabe, 2011), 315–73, here 339–51.

[108] Jurij M. Lotman, *Die Struktur literarischer Texte* (4th ed.; München: Fink, 1993), 316.

[109] Here the chief priests answered, whereas "the Jews" were addressed with Pilate's saying (v. 14).

do not realize that the "Lamb of God" can exonerate even if he appears impure and helpless. Dirk Gniesmer[110] interpreted this multiple confusion of roles with Ricœur's category of threefold "mimesis" that reveals how the reader can reassign the roles in the process of "refiguration" (= mimesis III). Only one role that is obligatory in the trial remains unfilled – that of the witness. Here the reader can clearly "take part" in the trial and answer the open question: "What is truth?" (18:38) by remembering what is told from the beginning (1:17) and in the I-am-Saying (14:6).

The final time that "the Jews" are mentioned is found in the crucifixion scene and in the removal of the bodies from the crosses (*John 19:19–42*). The discussion concerning the title "King of the Jews" is, once again, taken up, but this time in relation to the sign on the cross. "The Jews" reading it are initially presented as a group. The mentioning of the proximity to the city (ἐγγὺς ἦν ὁ τόπος τῆς πόλεως, v. 20) suggests that reference is being made to the inhabitants of Jerusalem. In v. 21 the sub-group, "chief priests of the Jews," is named, and these once again contest the legitimacy of Jesus' claim to the title of "king." In this way the character trait is taken up again that "the Jews" contradict Jesus' own claim.

In the crucifixion scene numerous rituals of "the Jews" are named, whether with a view towards the Sabbath (v. 31), burial (v. 40), or Passover (vss. 31, 42). Because of the day of preparation, "the Jews" demand the *crurifragium* (which would accelerate the onset of death) as well as the removal of the bodies before the Sabbath (v. 31). The narrator's comment, including the citation of Exod 12:10, 46 ("Not a bone of him shall be broken") creates a link to the Passover lamb, which retrospectively condemns the request of "the Jews." They (still) have not understood that Jesus is the true Passover lamb for otherwise they could not have called for the breaking of his bones. Scripture, however, testifies for Jesus (v. 36) and against them (cf. 5:45–47).

Finally, the "fear of the Jews" continues after the death of Jesus. Joseph of Arimathea cannot publically reveal his discipleship (v. 38) and the disciples keep the door locked out of fear (20:19). Significantly the final occurrence of "the Jews" as characters in the narrative world illustrates two well-known traits of this group, firstly breaking the Sabbath, by their request to take down the corpses of the crucified (19:31; see 5:16), and secondly contesting the claim to Jesus' identity (now as "King" – 19:21; cf. 5:18). Thus, "the Jews" ultimately exit the stage in a somber light as they have started.

---

[110] See Dirk F. Gniesmer, *In den Prozeß verwickelt: Erzähltextanalytische und textpragmatische Erwägungen zur Erzählung vom Prozeß Jesu vor Pilatus (Joh 18,28–19,16a.b)* (Europäische Hochschulschriften: Theologie 23/688; Frankfurt: Lang, 2000), 370–74.

"The Jews" as a Character in John – A Systematic Approach

Character Inventory: Where Do "the Jews" Appear?

The term οἱ Ἰουδαῖοι is used as a *nomen appellativum* which makes a group character to be recognized by the implied reader within the narrated world. As "the Jews" appear throughout the entire narrative of the Fourth Gospel we can consider their role in the development of the plot. One significant observation is that the statistical evidence demonstrates how the frequency of their appearance in various episodes is markedly different. Although only 8 references to "the Jews" are to be found in the first four chapters,[111] there are 36 references in chapters 5–12 and 22 references in 19–20.[112] Apart from one occurrence (13:33) no reference to "the Jews" is to be found in the so-called farewell discourse (chs. 13–17)[113] nor in ch. 21. "The Jews" turn up, therefore, in the developing conflict as well as in the passion narrative but are missing in Galilee and on the other side of the Jordan as well as in the speech to the disciples.

These results are linked to the observation that "the Jews" are topographically connected to *Jerusalem* and often to the temple. In some cases they appear there in larger numbers and in some cases Jerusalem is explicitly mentioned (see 1:19; 2:13; 5:1, etc). With regard to semantic space in the Gospel, Jerusalem carries negative connotations as the location of Jesus' death. This suggests the conclusion that, in the dramatic composition of the Johannine narration, "the Jews" play a definitive role in the conflict that leads to Jesus' death.[114]

Character Constellation: Identity and Interaction of "the Jews"

If we attempt to determine the *group identity* of "the Jews" at the level of the narrative, we see that the name alone hardly suffices to constitute a homogenous group. The character's parallels, overlaps, and subsets produce a complex system of classification that can scarcely lead to clear results in the text. To a certain extent it is the decision of the exegete whether a personal pronoun that has been used over long stretches still refers to "the Jews" or whether he or she proposes varying referents for the same lexeme. One can only note that there are close relationships with other character groups who are identified by name,

---

[111] Of the eleven total occurrences of Ἰουδαῖος in John 1–4, 3:22 refers to Jewish land, 3:25 to a single anonymous Jew, and 4:9 to Jesus as "a Jew."

[112] In 18:35 Pilate asks whether he also is a "Jew."

[113] See the exception in 13:33, where "the Jews" are mentioned as having been addressed previously by Jesus (see below).

[114] See also Schnelle, "Die Juden im Johannesevangelium," 220; Bennema "Identity," 259–60.

such as the Pharisees,[115] the priests (and high priests) and Levites, or the authorities in Jerusalem. The textual evidence, however, is not clear as to whether these groups can be identified with each other, so that terms may be used synonymously, or whether one group is a subgroup of the other, or whether the groups retain their distinctiveness. For example, the reader is told first that the priests and Levites have been sent by "the Jews" (1:19). Only a few verses later one reads that "they had been sent from the Pharisees" (1:24). Then, in 5:33 "the Jews" are again addressed as the ones who had done the sending. Once again in John 8 and 9 the two groups – if indeed they are two groups – are not easily separated. On the other hand, according to 11:46, the reader should assume that there are two groups to be distinguished since "some of them (= 'the Jews') went to the Pharisees ..." A further example can be found in that although there is a clearly recognizable overlap between οἱ Ἰουδαῖοι and the religious authorities (in Jerusalem), e. g., during the trial of Jesus, it is obvious that not every occurrence of the term refers to authorities, e. g., customs and feasts "of the Jews," which cannot be limited to authorities.[116] Cornelis Bennema, in particular, examined the relationship of the various Jewish groups and attempted to represent them in a Venn diagram.[117] The crowd[118] and the world (κόσμος)[119] also present intersections with "the Jews," which makes it even more difficult to describe the identity of the group. In addition, individual characters are explicitly identified as "Jews" or as representative of a group of "Jews" (e. g., Nicodemus as one of the elders of "the Jews;" 3:1).

Their unity as a group is mentioned in 18:20, which speaks of the comprehensive unity of "the Jews" with regard to the synagogues and temple community. Jesus' discourse is thus directed at all of "the Jews" (πάντες οἱ Ἰουδαῖοι). The concretely acting group of "Jews" identify themselves, however, through a lack of homogeneity. There are frequent reports of subsets "of the Jews," in particular "many" or "some of 'the Jews'" (11:45–46; 12:9; 19:20). Nevertheless, there is internal communication (πρὸς ἑαυτούς; 7:35) which strengthens the idea of their unity; however, this conversation does not always proceed harmoniously. "The Jews" "grumble" (6:43) or argue among themselves (6:52), and divisions occur because of Jesus (Σχίσμα πάλιν ἐγένετο ἐν τοῖς Ἰουδαίοις διὰ τοὺς λόγους τούτους, 10:19) leading to parallels with the Pharisees (9:16) and the people (7:43). John 12:11 reports that "many Jews" who believe were going

---

[115] See for instance the parallelism with regard to the expulsion of the synagogue which mentions "the Jews" in 9:22 and the Pharisees in 12:42 in nearly identical formulations.

[116] With Bennema, "Identity," 256.

[117] See Bennema, "Identity," 246–55 and 259–62 (the diagram on p. 260).

[118] See John 6 or the direct grammatical link in 12:9: ὁ ὄχλος πολὺς ἐκ τῶν Ἰουδαίων.

[119] See on this complex connection Kierspel, *Jews and the World*, ch. 3, where he lists all of the parallels between "the Jews" and "the world;" see 76–110, as well as the "Function of 'the world' in relation to 'the Jews'" (ibid., ch. 4, 111–54).

away ("were deserting and believing in Jesus;" 12:11). Does this indicate that there has been a definitive separation within this group? If so, why did the implied author not record that more plainly when he takes up this language again in the trial; e. g., by naming the aggressive group of "the Jews" differently? Once again, it is just "the Jews" who act.

If we observe the *character interaction* with other, clearly definable groups or individuals, we can distinguish between various levels of interaction. On the one hand, in direct contact, there are characters with whom "the Jews" appear together or with whom they are linked through actions (e. g., they speak with the parents of the man born blind). On the other hand, an indirect contact is often created by means of a scenic or personal framework. Thus, the dialogue with the healed man (5:15–16) is not about the man himself but about Jesus. This mediating contact is characteristic of interaction with "the Jews." They ask the Baptist through an emissary (1:19) and they question the parents of the man who was born blind (9:19) about their son and him about Jesus. In addition, even in direct contact with Jesus, formulations are often in the third person ("is he …;" "how can he …," see 6:42; 7:15), which produces distance. This distance creates the impression of a group working indirectly in the background, which intensifies the threat. At the same time, such background activity stands in contrast with Jesus' discourse in which he spoke plainly before the entire world and before all of "the Jews," as he states explicitly in the interrogation with the high priests (παρρησίᾳ λελάληκα; 18:20).

In most cases, "the Jews" are in dialogue with Jesus and speak about him or he speaks to them. The relationship enacted here is primarily hostile. The dominance of this opposition in the narrative is supported by various forms of portrayal and frequently with the medium of "showing," in which miscommunication (speaking about and not with one another) and misunderstandings occur or in which "the Jews" enter into a concrete argument with Jesus. The contrast is also sharpened through direct presentation: "By not having heard or seen the Father, they are Jesus' opposite; in their response to Jesus they are the opposite of the disciples."[120] In the introduction to the farewell discourse Jesus creates an analogy between his speech to "the Jews" and his speech to the disciples: "As I said to 'the Jews' so now I say to you" (13:33). Although this suggests an opposition (there "the Jews"– here the disciples), a parallel is also expressed (see below). One can see in John 6 how a process of distancing commences with the appearance of "the Jews." While 6:31 speaks in the manna narrative of "our fathers," after the appearance of "the Jews" it is explicitly "your fathers" (6:49), although the Exodus as the field of reference has not changed.

---

[120] Culpepper, *Anatomy of the Fourth Gospel*, 129.

"The Jews" interact with many other characters within the narrative. However, all of these contacts are clearly concentrated on Jesus. The majority of interactions take place between "the Jews" and Jesus himself, but most of them demonstrate misunderstanding and failed communication. Thus, the interaction focus demonstrates a paradox: Despite many conversations, there remains a lack of real and meaningful contact. They appear to talk past one another, and the relational distance between them grows with virtually every encounter.

Character and Actions: What Do "the Jews" Do?

The entire discussion about "the Jews" in the Gospel of John has frequently been dominated by the question of the reference to and the identity of "the Jews." With its observation of the levels of action, the narratological method produced an important shift of emphasis.[121] Let us first simply describe in detail what "the Jews" do. In doing this we can consider the verbs of action that are used with οἱ Ἰουδαῖοι as the subject.[122] Most of these statements are provided as indirect characterization by the narrator; however, some figural statements (e. g., by Jesus, Pilate) telling about actions of "the Jews" are also taken into account.

They speak: "The Jews" are often identified as the speakers (they talk, speak, answer[123]) who are in dialogue with others.

They ask questions: The number of questions that are asked by "the Jews" and that refer to Jesus is striking.[124] In 10:24 this questioning attitude leads to the "Christological question:" Are you the Christ?

They are surprised, misunderstand and do not know: "The Jews" are closely linked to the Johannine technique of misunderstanding. Their fundamental

---

[121] See Tolmie, "ΙΟΥΔΑΙΟΙ," 395; see also Martinus C. de Boer, "The Depiction of 'the Jews' in John's Gospel: Matters of Behavior and Identity," in *Anti-Judaism and the Fourth Gospel* (ed. Reimund Bieringer et al.), 260–80, who distinguishes the aspect of behavior from that of identity.

[122] Οἱ Ἰουδαῖοι are the subject of the sentence in approximately half of the occurrences of the term.

[123] The following verbs are used: "say" – λέγω in John 2:18, 20; 5:10; 6:41, 52; 7:11, 15, 35; 8:22, 48, 52, 57; 10:24; 11:36; 18:31; 18:40; 19:12 (in total 16 times); "answer" – ἀποκρίνομαι in John 2:18; 8:48; 10:33; 19:7; "cry (out)" – κραυγάζω in John 18:40; 19:12, 15.

[124] Indirectly in John 1:19: "Who are you?" (cf. 1:21, 25); John 5:12: "Who is the man who said to you 'Take up your pallet, and walk'?;" 6:42: "Is not this Jesus, the son of Joseph, whose father and mother we know?;" 7:11: "Where is he?;" 7:15: "The Jews" are marveled at it, saying, "How is it that this man has learning, when he has never studied?;" 7:35: "Where does this man intend to go that we shall not find him?;" 8:22: "Is he going to kill himself?;" 8:25: "Who are you?;" 8:33: "How do you say, that 'You will become free'?" 8:48: "Do we not say that you are a Samaritan and have a demon?;" 8:53: "Are you greater than our Father Abraham? ... Who do you make yourself to be?;" 8:57: "... you have seen Abraham?;" 9:19 (to the parents of the man born blind): "Is this your son ...;" 9:26 (to the man born blind): "What did he do for you?;" 10:24: "How long will you keep us in suspense?"

lack of comprehension as well as an ironic note in the portrayal of this character[125] clearly make them the preferred candidates in passages highlighting misunderstandings.[126] In most of the scenes their questions and statements demonstrate that they totally missed the point of Jesus' sayings. In addition to this indirect characterization, the reader is directly told by the narrator that "the Jews" were astonished (7:15) and that they do not understand (8:27) or know (stated by the formerly blind man, 8:30; cf. 9:29). Jesus himself confirms this trait, saying: "Why do you not understand what I say?" (8:43)

They know and decide: "The Jews" are depicted as having knowledge (9:29), which informs their deeds. Thus, they act deliberately and not only spontaneously.[127] Correspondingly, they make a deliberate decision to seek Jesus' death (5:18) and bring about an expulsion from the synagogue (9:22).

They grumble, argue and are divisive: John 6 alludes to an internal conflict (grumble: 6:41; argue: 6:52) that leads to division (10:19).

They persecute, and surround; they stone and accuse: Their hostile attitude toward Jesus and their intention to kill him are expressed with various actions and verbs. 5:16 speaks about persecution, and according to 8:37, 40, they "seek to kill." In 10:24 they surround Jesus before they pick up stones to stone him (10:31–33; cf. 8:59; 11:8). The behavior in the trial follows that line (see 18:29, 31: they accuse Jesus and seek the death penalty[128]).

They revile and drive out (of the synagogue): The verbs used for the hostile behavior of "the Jews" differ with respect to the addressee (Jesus or others). Whereas the persecution towards Jesus is more aggressive, including the intention to kill, the pressure on Jesus' followers is realized through reviling (9:28) and casting out (9:34). Most of the conflicts, however, between "the Jews" and the disciples are narrated from the perspective of Jesus' followers and do not present "the Jews" as subject (e. g., the "fear of the Jews;" see below).

They comfort: The behavior of "the Jews" in connection with the death of Lazarus in John 11–12 reveals a completely different side of this group. They come and they comfort the sisters.

They believe and do not believe: There are contradictory statements related to their belief (in Christ). According to 8:30–31; 11:45; 12:11, there is faith among "the Jews;" however, the instances in which they do not believe predominate (e. g., 9:18; 10:37). This unbelief is closely linked to Jesus' words and deeds. In 10:25–26 it is Jesus himself who states twice that "the Jews" do not

---

[125] See Hylen, *Imperfect Believers*, 124–26; Hunt, "Word Became Flesh," 104.

[126] See, for instance, 7:35 (They think Jesus intends to go the Dispersion among the Greeks); 8:22 (They think that Jesus wants to kill himself); 11:31 (They think that Mary was going to the tomb), etc.

[127] Nevertheless, there are spontaneous actions, like the attempt to stone Jesus, which Hunt describes as a "mob-lynching" (Hunt, "Word Became Flesh," 90).

[128] Pilate gives an overarching direct declaration of the action of "the Jews:" τίνα κατηγορίαν φέρετε [κατὰ] τοῦ ἀνθρώπου τούτου; see 19:29.

believe. In having asked the question concerning the identity of the Christ before (v. 24), it is exactly this claim made by Jesus that they do not believe. In v. 27 Jesus disclosed that they do not believe because they do not belong to his flock.

Character Traits: Neutral, Negative, and Positive Characterization?

A common pattern of classification of "the Jews" is threefold: There are neutral, negative, and positive traits[129] which reveal different aspects of this group character. At first glance, this seems to be a helpful grid to describe the complexity of statements and highlight the positive aspects in particular. Thus, we start in following this path.

One seems to be able to distinguish *general statements*, that is "neutral" characterization, about the feasts/festivals, Torah observance, and rituals of "the Jews" from their concrete actions. Scholarship has used such a differentiation in order to postulate that the group of "the Jews" as an ethnic-religious unit is to be distinguished from the group of the hostile Jewish authorities or Judeans in Jerusalem. The analysis of the concrete conflicts and their motivations has revealed, however, that such a division is an oversimplification and is misleading. The concrete issues of contention between Jesus and "the Jews" are related to broad and fundamental conceptions such as the understanding of the Torah, the tradition of the Fathers (Moses, Abraham), the keeping of the Sabbath or the Passover tradition. Even someone who relates the characterization of "the Jews" exclusively to their actions can come to the same conclusion, because it is the intention to kill, which contradicts for example the keeping of the Law (7:19) or their descent from Abraham (8:37). The direct characterization that takes place through the "telling" in particular by Jesus (see 5:8) reveals the link between the "Jews" who act and the religious traditions and rituals. This link culminates in the transfer of the title "King of Israel/of the Jews" to Jesus.

In this it is not the general, basic Jewish elements such as Scripture, Law, Feasts, etc., that are criticized as such, but only their incorrect or insufficient interpretation. "The Jews" are identified as descendants of the Israelites fed with Manna (6:49); the law of Moses is given to "the Jews" (7:19); and they are descendents of Abraham (8:37). One can also add the positive statement of 4:22 (salvation comes from "the Jews") to this positive acknowledgement of Jewish identity. "The Jews" are the true recipients of God's promises and salvation. These elements, however, are the basis for the confession of Jesus as the Christ for anyone who understands them correctly. The controversies with

---

[129] See, e. g., Frey, "Sehen oder Nicht-Sehen," 735–37; Schnelle, "Die Juden im Johannesevangelium," 218–19.

Jesus center around the claim that the true interpretation of the Jewish tradition must lead to the confession of Jesus as Christ.

Secondly, without a doubt, "the Jews" are presented as a *hostile power* and therefore characterized *negatively*. This is seen first through their interaction with several figures, most of them followers of Jesus. Their covert communication and interrogation practices, enactment of the decree with reference of the expulsion from the synagogue, practices of persecution, and intention to kill all engender fear. The "fear of the Jews"[130] is mentioned explicitly four times: in 7:13 speaking about Jesus in public does not take place due to the fear of "the Jews;" the parents of the man born blind are fearful (9:22) because "the Jews" have agreed to throw anyone who confesses Christ out of the synagogue (this, in fact, occurs later on, see 9:34). Furthermore, Joseph of Arimathea, who conceals that he is a disciple (19:38), has fear of "the Jews." Finally, the disciples lock the doors of their houses on the day of resurrection "for fear of the Jews" (20:19). At the end of the Gospel, this character trait is again intensified through the mention of fear in chapters 19 and 20. In each case a confession of Jesus as the Christ or a mere statement concerning Jesus motivates fear.

Thus, it is shown that the hostile attitude of "the Jews" is ultimately rooted in their rejection of Jesus. Hence, secondly, the fundamental conflict exists between "the Jews" and Jesus, particularly with regard to the understanding of his being and ministry. Since chapter 5, the voice of the narrator, which engenders reliability, has talked about "the Jews'" persecution of Jesus and their intention to kill (5:18; 7:1). Jesus himself confirms their desire to kill in his criticism of the law (7:19) although the people have not yet realized this intention (7:20). In an ironic reversal, "the Jews" ask whether Jesus wants to kill himself (8:22) before the conflict escalates within the Abraham dialogue. Three times Jesus blames "the Jews" for their intention to kill him (8:28, 37, 40), and in calling them children of the devil (8:44) they are said to be children of the principle murderer (8:44b: "He was a murderer from the beginning"). It is by their "seeking to kill" (8:37, 40) that "the Jews" are described as not doing Abraham's works, a father who did not kill his son. The controversy ends up in the first attempt to stone him (8:52). After the speech about the good shepherd and the avowal of unity with the Father, "the Jews" again attempted to stone him (10:31) and to seize him (10:39). The disciples explicitly recall this intention to kill (11:19). Finally, "the Jews" play an important role in the arrest (temple police of "the Jews"), the interrogation, and the trial before Pilate, as well as in the demand for crucifixion and the handing over from Pilate (19:16). The fundamental conflict is carried here to an extreme as is seen in the conflict

---

[130] Steven A. Hunt, "Nicodemus, Lazarus, and the Fear of 'the Jews' in the Fourth Gospel," in *Repetitions and Variations in the Fourth Gospel: Style, Text, Interpretation* (ed. Gilbert Van Belle et al.; BETL 223; Louvain: Peeters, 2009), 199–212.

about the title ("King of the Jews"), the use of the law, and as the underlying fundamental aspect: the question of the Christ. While for Jesus, the action of the law precludes his death (7:19), "the Jews" infer the death penalty from the law. The demand for death is then justified theologically and such a connection is made when their decision to kill Jesus is mentioned in 5:18. Something similar happens in the middle of the Gospel (8:53; 10:33). "The Jews" accuse Jesus of self-deification, which is according to their traditions blasphemy deserving death. Within the trial it is demonstrated clearly. "The Jews" misunderstand up to the end of the story Jesus' words and deeds, and his Christological claim. Instead, by means of declaring the emperor as their only king, it is clear (indirect presentation) that they are guilty themselves of blasphemy.

In this regard the plot unrolls continuously until Jesus' crucifixion, but there is little development in respect of "the Jews" as character. Their intention to kill Jesus is noted repeatedly from chapters 5 to 19. However, the reason is not simply to demonstrate a negative intention of "the Jews" in following anti-Jewish polemics generally or to draw these characters as sociopaths and misanthropes, lusting to shed blood. Nor it is related to the fact that they are identified with the powerful Jerusalem temple authorities. During the whole conflict from the beginning up to the end, "the Jews" argue in terms of their tradition, they accuse Jesus of being a liar, a possessed man, and a sinner in their honorable wish to fulfill the law.

Before the reader wraps "the Jews" in an exclusively negative mantle,[131] relativizing and *positive traits* must be perceived according to which "the Jews" are shown as a more complex character. In addition to the clearly hostile attitude, "the Jews" are also portrayed as knowing, questioning, and seeking. Clearly they are interested in insight – they send for John (the Baptist) in order to discover his identity; they search for Jesus several times (5:18; 7:1[132]); frequently they ask for Jesus' identity. Individual representatives like Nicodemus and Joseph of Arimathea represent at least a part of "the Jews" in their interest in Jesus, although the conversation with Nicodemus remains in the dark, and the discipleship of Joseph is kept secretly. In particular, the use of some significant Johannine verbs like "send" (1:19), "know" (9:34) "come and see" (11:33, 45) or even "believe" (12:11) engender positive connotations. Are "the Jews" on their way to Jesus like many other "ambiguous believers?" Are these positive-sounding character traits used simply in order to make them foils in the end? Do they "send" only out of animosity, do they "seek" in order to kill, does even the initial "belief" reveal that they are "children of the devil" (8:31, 44)?

---

[131] See in that way Reinhartz, "Jews," 220, who claims that the term Ἰουδαῖος "is never used of a figure who is a believer."

[132] Twice they seek to kill him.

Indeed the fundamental statement about salvation from "the Jews" (4:22) is made by Jesus without relativization.[133] However, read in the Johannine context this is only the starting point for the salvation of the world. Within the encounter with the Samaritans Jesus is developed from a Jewish man (4:9) to the redeemer of the world (4:42). Thus, the statement of salvation can be interpreted along the same lines as the other dimensions of Jewish traditions, like the fathers, the law, and the feasts. All of this is not questioned in general, but "christianized." The Johannine Jesus and "the Jews" represent different interpretations of these traditions, and even opposite understandings concerning the Christ confession.

Furthermore the reference to the belief of "the Jews" in 8:31 ("who have come to believe in him" – πεπιστευκότας αὐτῷ) is ambivalent in view of the continuation of the chapter. Humane characteristics are also visible in the Lazarus pericope, a story in which they come in order to comfort the sisters from Bethany (11:19, 31, 33). However, right after "many Jews" came to a belief in Jesus (11:45), "some of them" went to the Pharisees to "denounce" what Jesus did (11:46). Obviously the belief of "the Jews" is "only" based on the Lazarus miracle (12:11), not on their confession of Christ. Their belief should thus be viewed as deficient, because it has been brought about by a miracle whereas the close parallels between the destiny of Lazarus and that of Jesus are disregarded. Anyone who comes to belief in view of the death and resurrection of Lazarus should already have understood the fundamentals of the cross of Jesus.

Finally, Susan Hylen has pointed out a structural parallel between "the Jews" and the disciples. They are not a foil for the disciples; rather, the ambivalence, the doubt, even the grumbling and the misunderstanding turn both equally into "ambiguous believers."[134] But what about the explicit statement on the unbelief of "the Jews?" "The Jews" are presented as an "ambiguous character;" however, doubt remains whether they may correctly be classified as "believers." Those among "the Jews" who believe are cast out (9:34–38), and the believers depart to the other side (10:41; 12:11).[135] With regard to verb analysis there is intersection with the disciples; however, exactly the vocabulary with positive connotation regarding faith and discipleship is missing: "the Jews" do not "listen," they do not "follow," they do not "abide." On the contrary, the only scene where discipleship of "the Jews" is discussed explicitly in 9:27–29, they deny vehemently to be disciples of Jesus: "You are his disciple,

---

[133] See the profound contribution on this verse by Gilbert Van Belle, "'Salvation is from the Jews:' The Parenthesis in John 4:22b," in *Anti-Judaism and the Fourth Gospel* (ed. Reimund Bieringer et al.), 370–400.

[134] Hylen, *Imperfect Believers*, 129. See for instance parallel statements like 8:27 ("The Jews" did not understand) and 12:16 (The disciples did not understand).

[135] See on this space semantics my article on the "many believers" in this volume.

but we are disciples of Moses" (9:28). There are seeds of positive traits, but as soon as one tries to explore them, they slip away and are lost in the blinding light of the Christological questions. Within Jesus' last words directly addressed to "the Jews" there is hope for true belief and discipleship ("Even though you do not believe me, believe the works ...," 10:38a); however, the content of this belief is nothing less than the immanent reciprocity of Father and Son (10:38b).

To sum up, the structure of positive, neutral, and negative statements does not stand a close reading of the texts where these aspects occur within their context and functional purposes. The so called "neutral" traits are closely linked to concrete actions, which normally are assumed to be negative. The "negative" attitudes are rooted in otherwise positive intentions with regard to keeping traditions. The "positive" traits sometimes are insufficient and ultimately fail with regard to the confession of Christ. Simple classification of "the Jews" is not possible due to the interlaced aspects of their characterization. How then, shall the reader fabricate a mental model of "the Jews?"

Character Conception: "The Jews" as a Complex and Open Character

"The Jews" in the Fourth Gospel present puzzles to the reader. There are indubitably traits that come to the forefront through direct and indirect characterization. The interactions and character constellations also reveal clear affinities (e. g., between the authorities in Jerusalem and "the Jews") or delineations (e. g., between "the Jews" and the disciples).

Seen as a whole, we must note their constant hostility towards Jesus and – according to the narrator – the misinterpretation of their own tradition. The main issue is that most of "the Jews" do not believe in Christ. The intention to persecute and kill as well as their motivation therefore appears with remarkable continuity. There are precisely two aspects mentioned at the beginning of the conflict with "the Jews" (ch. 5) that are taken up in the final scene (ch. 19), namely breaking the Sabbath (5:16 and 19:31) and the claim of Jesus (5:18 and 19:20–21). The intention to kill Jesus is mentioned stereotypically in almost every scene.

This deadly conflict with Jesus also affects other characters. Beginning with the interrogation of John (the Baptist), the man born blind in the middle, and then Joseph of Arimathea in the end– all of the characters who have contact with Jesus or are Jesus' disciples are put under pressure and suffer from "fear of the Jews." The arrangement of the macro structure of the Gospel such as the lack of references to "the Jews" in the farewell discourse (chs. 13–17) or the concentration in the passion (chs. 18–19) also confirm this impression.

However, there remain awkward statements that defy a clear and flat character conception. That starts with the arguments for their conflict with Jesus.

"The Jews" are faithless toward Christ, but still reliable to their traditions. To put it distinctly: on account of their keeping law, religious customs, and responsibility they are in conflict with Jesus and his disciples. Furthermore the group dissolves into partial groups, divisions and inconsistencies. If we want to recognize a development at all, then we can state within the section from John 5 to 12 that exactly this part of "the Jews," who start to believe, is steadily increasing. The "telling" of Jesus in John 5 seems to be hopeless; however, the last word of Jesus to "the Jews" in 10:38 indicates that they still can learn and know about Jesus' close relationship to God. In 10:42 the reader is told that "many" believe; according to 12:9 a "numerous crowd of the Jews" (ὄχλος πολὺς ἐκ τῶν Ἰουδαίων) came; and finally "many of the Jews" were believing in Jesus (12:11). Hence, is there a development from the unbelieving, questioning, and finally believing Jews? Is it the final goal of this text to make the unbelieving part of "the Jews" jealous, or to provoke "that they might learn and know" (10:38) about Jesus? Does the implied author renew "his longstanding invitation to 'believe'"[136] by means of these last words of Jesus to "the Jews" in direct speech? But the story with "the Jews" did not continue to a "happy ending." Within the trial these hopeful traits seem to fully disappear. Are there other "Jews" acting in Jerusalem toward Jesus as before in Bethany?

Seen thus, the group character of "the Jews" is the most complex character in the entire Gospel. However, even this statement causes opposition. As a corporate character "the Jews" are to a certain extent "flat" and "static," hostile "opponents *par excellence*."[137] The binary-coded pairs pointed out by Finnern[138] fall short in a determination of the character conception of "the Jews." The presentation of "the Jews" is to be classified "round" as well as "flat," "dynamic" and "static," "complex" and "simple" at the same time.

Conclusions: "The Jews" and Unreliable Narration

The discourse on "the Jews" as a character in the Fourth Gospel demonstrates great complexity and diversity. Even if we limit ourselves to the passages in which "the Jews" appear as actors, the statements often remain manifold and even contradictory. However, it has become clear that such a limitation on an

---

[136] See J. Ramsey Michaels, *The Gospel of John* (NICNT; Grand Rapids, Mich.: Eerdmans, 2010), 593 (translation), furthermore 606: "He can still end with an open invitation to believe."

[137] See Bennema, *Encountering Jesus*, 38. Nevertheless in his final classification he classifies "the Jews" as a "complex character" and "corporate personality" (46).

[138] See Finnern, *Narratologie und Biblische Exegese*, 157–61: "statisch – dynamisch," "knapp – detailliert," "eindimensional – mehrdimensional," "typisch – individuell," "geschlossen – offen," "realistisch – unrealistisch," "kohärent – inkohärent," "transpsychologisch – psychologisch."

acting group of characters is made practically impossible by the interweaving of the direct and indirect characterization within the narrative. "Neutral" statements on "the Jews" in general (with regard to traditions, customs, etc.) are closely linked to "negative" statements within concrete dialogues. In between some positive and hopeful statements can be found. Thus, the separation of "sense" and "reference" which has been suggested by some exegetes[139] or the differentiating categorizations of certain Jewish groups (e. g., the Judeans, the authorities in Jerusalem, or Torah and temple partisans) are not consistently possible.

As a reader in need of harmony or a scholar seeking consistency it is difficult to bear up under these tensions. One tends to resolve them hastily using operations from source criticism[140] or textual criticism.[141] Admittedly, in such cases one's own perception of a homogenous concept is then read into the text instead of interpreting the existing text.

However, the ideal of a consistent narrative concept is in no way compulsory. A lively discussion about so-called "unreliable narration"[142] has recently developed within narratology. Although this concept is being investigated in modern literature, it can also be transferred heuristically to the Fourth Gospel. According to Chatman, "in 'unreliable narration' the narrator's account is at odds with the implied reader's surmises about the story's real intentions."[143] The implied author turns out to be "unreliable" with regard to a coherent concept of "the Jews." In some cases, traits can be condensed into a final interpretation and lines of development can be drawn. The history of the research presents a checkered image as to what these positively or negatively judgmental character concepts look like. At the same time, the diversity of these researched constructs reveals that each of them disregards some aspects or bends to their presuppositions. The reader is thus left insecure – how should

---

[139] See John Ashton, "The Identity and Function of the Ἰουδαῖοι in the Fourth Gospel," *NovT* 27 (1985): 40–75, followed by Bennema, "Identity," 240.

[140] See, e. g., Ashton with regard to the "believing Jews," see Ashton, "Identity and Function," 62; von Wahlde, *John*, passim.

[141] See the suggestion of John C. O'Neill, "The Jews in the Fourth Gospel," *IBSt* 18 (1996): 58–74.

[142] First introduced by Wayne C. Booth, *The Rhetoric of Fiction* (Chicago: Chicago UP, 1961), the concept turned from a marginal into a central issue of narratological debate. See Renate Hof, *Das Spiel des "unreliable narrator:" Aspekte unglaubwürdigen Erzählens im Werk von Vladimir Nabokov* (München: Fink, 1984); Ansgar Nünning (ed.), *Unreliable Narration: Studien zur Theorie und Praxis unglaubwürdigen Erzählens in der englischsprachigen Erzählliteratur* (Trier: Wissenschaftlicher Verlag Trier, 1998); Fabienne Liptay, Yvonne Wolf (eds.), *Was stimmt denn jetzt? Unzuverlässiges Erzählen in Literatur und Film* (München: Edition Text + Kritik, 2005); Gaby Allrath, *Engendering Unreliable Narration: A Feminist-Narratological Theory and Analysis of Unreliability in Contemporary Women's Novels* (Trier: Wissenschaftlicher Verlag, 2005); Tilmann Köppe and Tom Kindt (Guest Editors), Special Issue "Unreliable Narration," *Journal of Literary Theory* 5.1 (2011).

[143] Chatman, *Story and Discourse*, 233.

he or she finally perceive and evaluate "the Jews?" The implied author did not solve these problems. To a certain extent, the narrator remains an "unreliable narrator." These incoherencies cannot at all be resolved on the level of text. As current cognitive theories on the "unreliable narration" have pointed out, the category of "unreliability" itself is not to be separated from the "interactive model of the reading process."[144] Unreliable narration depends on "both sensorially perceived information located in the text and extratextual conceptual information located in the reader's mind."[145] While some of the assumptions of this cognitive grounding of narrative analysis is contradictory to a pragmatic approach,[146] both theories agree in the statement that the narrative system is a communication model, which produces unreliability.[147]

Thus, the concept of "unreliable narration" links the textual evidences back to the reader's mind and opens the horizons for both. At first the reader may be annoyed at such insecurity of the textual presentation of "the Jews." Insofar, however, as the narrator remains ambiguous and open, the reader should also abstain from a final judgment about "the Jews." This vagueness may at first be unsatisfactory; however, it is decidedly better than – as was found most often in the history of interpretation – an unambiguously anti-Jewish interpretation of "the Jews."

---

[144] See John W. Harker, "Information Processing and the Reading of Literary Texts," *New Literary History* 20 (1989): 465–81, here 471.

[145] Harker, "Information Processing," 476; see also Ansgar Nünning, "Unreliable Narration zur Einführung," in *Unreliable Narration* (ed. Ansgar Nünning), 3–39, here 23: "Bei 'unreliable narration' (handelt es sich) nicht um ein rein textimmanentes – sei es strukturelles oder semantisches – Phänomen ..., sondern um ein relationales bzw. interaktionales, bei dem die Information und Strukturen des Textes und das von Rezipienten an den Text herangetragenes Weltwissen und Werte- und Normensysteme gleichermaßen zu berücksichtigen sind."

[146] See for instance Theresa Heyd, "Unreliability: The Pragmatic Perspective Revisited," *Journal of Literary Theory* 5 (2011): 3–18.

[147] Heyd, "Unreliability," 4. In terms of a communication model, she points out a "double sendership: thus literary narrative is uttered by the author and the narrator simultaneously. Crucially, the reader of fiction is always more or less aware of this duality. This duality ... is the fundamental mechanism that creates ... unreliability" (9).

The Priests and Levites:
Identity and Politics in the Search for a Messiah

Sherri Brown

John 1:19–28 presents the first day of the Gospel narrative during which John the Baptist emerges as the central character who testifies just as the prologue articulates he was sent to do. The detail of John's witness over the three-day progression in which he appears directly parallels the pattern set forth in vss. 6–8. On day one John declares he is not the light (vss. 19–28), on day two he witnesses positively to the light (vss. 29–34), and on day three people begin to believe through him (vss. 35–42).[1] On the first day John is approached by a delegation from Jerusalem and finds himself in dialogue with them over his identity. This delegation is characterized corporately as "priests and Levites" (ἱερεῖς καὶ Λευίτας; v. 19) and they proceed to speak and act as one body, with no individual agency. In their initial encounter, the priests and Levites instigate contact to inquire who John is and what he is trying to accomplish. In so doing, however, they largely assert misconceptions; thus, their interaction is largely negative. Nonetheless, these minor characters from the ritual establishment of Jerusalem do serve a key role in launching the Gospel story.

Who Are You and Who Aren't You?
Testimony and the Question of Identity

The opening of v. 19 directly connects the action of the day at hand with information provided in the prologue: "And this is the testimony (ἡ μαρτυρία) of John." Readers are pointed to John's mission as stated in the prologue while their attention is focused on the beginning of the action proper. The one who is sent from God (ἀπεσταλμένος παρὰ θεοῦ, v. 6), John, is first interrogated by a delegation "sent from Jerusalem" (ἀπέστειλαν … ἐξ Ἱεροσολύμων, v. 19). That they are identified as "priests and Levites" alerts readers that they will very likely be interested in John's activity as it pertains to ritual purity and

---

[1] Charles H. Dodd, *Historical Tradition in the Fourth Gospel* (Cambridge: Cambridge University Press, 1976), 248; Dirk G. van der Merwe, "The Historical and Theological Significance of John the Baptist as He Is Portrayed in John 1," *Neot* 33 (1999): 276–92, here 273, fn. 18.

any purification rites that he may be initiating.² They approach him with the question that will mark these first days, and indeed, the first part of the body of the Gospel, "Who are you?"³ Their use of a pronoun in direct speech, the personal pronoun σύ, lends emphasis and focuses attention on the person of John and the identity in question.

The beginning of John's testimony is a response that characterizes what he is not. "He confessed, and did not deny it, but confessed, 'I am not the Christ'" (v. 20). The narrator's strong pleonastic introductory formula of John's first direct speech correlates the content of the testimony (ἡ μαρτυρία, v. 19) with the act of confessing (ὡμολόγησεν, v. 20). When confronted with official interrogation, the witness can choose to confess or deny his identity and self-understanding – John chooses to confess.⁴ The recitative ὅτι marks John's first statement. In response to their general question, "Who are you?" John chooses to turn the dialogue to the question of Christology.⁵ He asserts, "I am not the Christ." Using his own deictic pronoun ἐγώ, John points negatively to his own character and mission in a manner that will correspond to the positive claim that Jesus will make time and again over the course of the Gospel.⁶ This first response is the most expansive denial that the Baptist will provide his interrogators in this interaction. Further, by first stating who he is not in this unofficial trial scene, John distances himself from all contemporary Jewish expectations, including those of the priests and Levites.⁷

The delegation continues with its quest for identification, "What then?" (τί οὖν, v. 21). Even as they take the lead suggesting possible titular claims, dialogically they continue to point emphatically to the identity of John's role with the personal pronoun: "Are you Elijah? ... Are you the prophet?" (σὺ Ἠλίας

---

² Raymond E. Brown, *The Gospel According to John I (i–xii)*, (AB 29; New York: Doubleday, 1966), 43.

³ The delegation asks John this question here at 1:19, then again at 1:22. This question of identity is put in various ways to Jesus or to others about Jesus throughout his public ministry (see 5:12; 8:25; 9:13–41; 10:24; 12:34).

⁴ Francis J. Moloney (*The Gospel According to John* [SP 4; Collegeville, Minn.: Liturgical Press, 1998], 58) further correlates this act of confessing with the Johannine community readership's situation where "uncompromising confession of Jesus as the Messiah was leading to exclusion from the synagogue." The verb ὁμολογέω appears elsewhere in the Gospel only at 9:22 and 12:42, "in which some form of exclusion from the synagogue is at stake."

⁵ Although historically it is likely that questions of the Baptist's messianic claims had circulated and thus specifically spurred this delegation (see C. Kingsley Barrett, *The Gospel According to St John: An Introduction with Commentary and Notes on the Greek Text* [2d ed.; London: SPCK, 1978], 172), the rhetorical force of giving John the agency of turning the dialogue to the question of Christology allows the evangelist to affirm the Baptist's role as the witness sent from God.

⁶ ἐγώ εἰμι; see 4:26; 6:20, 35, 41, 48, 51; 8:12, 18, 24, 28, 58; 10:7, 9, 11, 14; 11:25; 13:19; 14:6; 15:1, 5; 18:5, 8. So Barrett, *John*, 172.

⁷ Thomas L. Brodie, *The Gospel According to John: A Literary and Theological Commentary* (Oxford: Oxford University Press, 1993), 150; Brown, *John*, 45–46.

εἶ; … ὁ προφήτης εἶ σύ;). After unambiguously denying that he is the Messiah/Christ in v. 20, the Baptist's succeeding denials progress more concisely, cutting short any designs his interlocutors' may have for information or even the dialogical upper hand: "And he said, 'I am not'… And he answered, 'No.'"[8] With the transitional conjunction οὖν of v. 22, a favorite of the evangelist, one can then almost feel the frustration of the interrogators as they find themselves where they began, "Who are you?"[9] They must have an answer "for those who sent" them (referring back to "the Jews from Jerusalem"), and they concede all the power to identify, and thus the dialogical lead, to John: "What do you say about yourself?" In so doing, the priests and Levites reveal something of their disposition and motive. The self-distancing that results from both shifting the onus to their authorities and conceding the lead in the dialogue indicates that they may not really be interested in John's identity so much as managing a political imperative dictated by the bureaucracy in Jerusalem.[10]

Only then does John testify positively as to who he is by accepting the role of the Isaian voice (v. 23; see Isa 40:3).[11] Unlike the Synoptic Evangelists who narrate this identification, the Fourth Evangelist allows John the witnessing agency to give voice to his own self-identification. The Baptist "says" (ἔφη) that he is the "voice" (φωνή) "crying out in the wilderness" in order to prepare the people to "make straight the way of the Lord." He allies his own voice with that in the book of the prophet Isaiah and finally positively asserts his testimonial role. For their part, the priests and Levites give no reaction, a further indication that they are not genuinely interested in John's identity, but with an answer that fits within the political categories their "senders" from Jerusalem expect. As Thomas Brodie astutely notes, "They live in a world which has concerns other than those of making straight the way of the Lord."[12]

Verse 24 provides an interlude to the dialogue of this first day. By way of a periphrastic perfect passive the narrator states, "and they had been sent from the Pharisees."[13] The Evangelist uses this terminology to take the reader

---

[8] For discussion of the Jewish expectations for the eschatological figures of the Messiah, Elijah, and the prophet (like Moses) and their relationship to one another, see Brown, *John*, 46–50. Regardless of the conception of him in Christian tradition, the Baptist gives no indication of having thought himself in the role of Elijah. See John A. T. Robinson, "Elijah, John and Jesus: an Essay in Detection," NTS 4 (1957–58): 263–81.

[9] With regard to the conjunction, Daniel B. Wallace (*Greek Grammar Beyond the Basics* [Grand Rapids, Mich.: Zondervan, 1996], 674) notes the "transitional force of οὖν sometimes comes close to the inferential force, as here." See other occurrences in John 2:18, 20; 3:25; 4:33, 46; 5:19; 6:60, 67; 7:25, 28, 33, 35, 40; 8:13, 21, 22, 25, 31, 57; 9:10, 16.

[10] Brodie, *John*, 150–51.

[11] For a detailed study of John's quotation and the LXX of Isa 40:3, see Maarten J. J. Menken, "The Quotation from Isa 40:3 in John 1:23," Bib 66 (1985): 190–205.

[12] Brodie, *John*, 151.

[13] Wallace, *Greek Grammar*, 585.

"behind the scenes."[14] This back-grounding technique allies the audience with the narrator who continues to share information that will aid their understanding and decision-making. Translators and commentators differ on whether this phrase indicates the arrival of a second delegation (see, e. g., the NAB) or simply further characterization of the first (and only) delegation (see, e. g., the NRSV). On its own the phrase would suggest the latter, that "the Jews from Jerusalem" who had sent these priests and Levites could be identified as Pharisees. But herein lies the problem: many scholars assert there would be no context in which Pharisees would collude with priests and Levites to form such a fact-finding mission.[15] Therefore, this could be a second, independent delegation whose concerns coincide with those of the first. Narratively, however, this aside does serve to ally the priests and Levites as well as the Pharisees with "the Jews from Jerusalem" (v. 19) who will often be identified across the rest of the story as the opponents of Jesus and his christological mission (2:18–20; 5:10–18; 6:41–59; 7:11–53; 8:20–59; 10:19–42; 18:31–19:42). Therefore, the full range of the opposition to the good news is laid out on this first day.

The emissaries initiate one further dialogue exchange in v. 25. Repeating the Baptist's three-part denial of vss. 20–21, they ask him why, then, he is baptizing. This first reference to baptism indicates indirectly what prompted the delegation in the first place. John's practice of baptizing must have brought him to the attention of the Jerusalem authorities and has now given him the opportunity to fulfill his particular testimonial role in this Gospel narrative. The interrogators question why, if John the Baptist does not claim any recognizable eschatological identity of the messianic era, is he performing an act of purification like baptism?[16] Although there is no sound first-century evidence apart from the Gospel that links the practice of baptism to these eschatological roles, from a narrative perspective the question does serve to keep the christological issue before the readers.[17] In addition, the exchange furthers the characterization of the interrogators as those who cannot hear responses outside their preconceived categories.

John's response affirms his baptizing role, even as he continues to witness to the one who is coming after him (vss. 26–27). John's apocalyptic allusion to

---

[14] Archibald T. Robertson, *A Grammar of the Greek New Testament in the Light of Historical Research* (4th ed.; New York: Hodder & Stoughton, 1923), 904–05.

[15] Because of the textual instability of this verse, a number of scholars have argued that v. 24 is an indicator of the Gospel's literary prehistory and suggest that a second delegation is indicated here. The historical question is that priest and Levites would typically belong to the Sadducees and would scarcely have partnered with Pharisees to send forth a delegation. See Rudolf Bultmann, *The Gospel of John: A Commentary* (trans. G. R. Beasley-Murray; Philadelphia: Westminster, 1971), 58; Marie-Émile Boismard, "Les Traditions Johanniques concernant le Baptiste," *RB* 70 (1963): 5–42; and Bas M. F. van Iersel, "Tradition und Redaktion in Joh. i 19–36," *NovT* 5 (1962): 245–67. See the general discussion in Brown, *John*, 67–71.

[16] Brown, *John*, 51.

[17] Moloney, *John*, 51–53.

the hidden one to come emphasizes what the interrogators "do not know," and the Messiah they will be hard-pressed to recognize and receive in the narrative to come. The first day is concluded by the narrator geographically by situating these events in "Bethany across the Jordan" (v. 28; see also 3:26; 10:40). Closing an episode with this sort of index of setting is common in the Fourth Gospel (2:12; 4:54; 6:59; 8:20; 9:54) as the evangelist draws the readers into the place inhabited by the characters and points them to space beyond the current sphere of activity. John's witness continues in terms of fulfillment the very next day (τῇ ἐπαύριον, v. 29) when he points verbally to the promised coming one (ἐρχόμενος, v. 27) as he sees Jesus coming toward him (ἐρχόμενον πρὸς αὐτόν). The first day's testimonial dialogue becomes a monologue on this second day of promise fulfillment. John's interlocutors have faded from the scene and he bears witness to any and all who would hear.

The Narrative Force of the Priests and Levites in the Gospel of John

Although priests and Levites are frequently presented together as a sociological and narrative pattern in Jewish literature (see 1 Kgs 8:4–5; Ezek 44:15; Ezra 2:70; 7:7; 10:5; 1QM 2:1; 5:6), they appear as a corporate character only once in the Gospel of John. As emissaries of "the Jews of Jerusalem," their encounter with John the Baptist in 1:19–28 launches the body of the narrative. The priests and Levites function in constellation with other characters in this scene: "the Jews," John the Baptist, and the Pharisees. Their dialogue is dominated by the Baptist, but we can nonetheless construct a brief paradigm of traits.[18] Directly, these actants in the narrative are characterized as priests and Levites who originate from Jerusalem and are sent on this mission by the Jewish authorities, possibly in collusion with some Pharisees. Along this same line, their trait of being "sent" links them with the larger sending metaphor of the Gospel, in this instance as representatives of "the Jews" of Jerusalem.[19] Indirectly, their questions regarding ritual activity characterizes them as part of the religious establishment with concern for rigid categories of worship and practice. In addition, the insistent manner of their questioning could lead readers

---

[18] For a full discussion of compiling a trait paradigm, see D. Francois Tolmie, *Narratology and Biblical Narratives: A Practical Guide* (San Francisco: International Scholars Publications, 1999), 39–62. He notes that traits are "any relatively stable or abiding personal quality associated with a character" (41). The process by which an implied author characterizes may be direct, indirect, or both (42–47).

[19] Jan-Adolf Bühner, *Der Gesandte und sein Weg im viertem Evangelium* (WUNT II/2; Tübingen: Mohr Siebeck, 1977); Ruben Zimmermann, "Metaphoric Networks as Hermeneutic Keys in the Gospel of John: Using the Example of the Mission Imagery," in *Repetitions and Variations in the Gospel of John: Style, Text, Interpretation* (ed. Michael Labahn et al.; BETL 223; Louvain: Peeters, 2009), 381–402.

to deduce their character as persistent, even tenacious, at least in form if not conviction. More importantly, their focus on identity reinforces the limits of their perspective from within the cultural expectations of first century messianic hopes. When the Baptist refuses to accept even the role of the precursor, they fade from the scene without closure. Nonetheless their categorical messianic expectations will be called to mind as Jesus comes to the fore of the narrative and encounters the resistance, lack of understanding, and even violence of the priests and other representatives of the Jewish establishment (see 7:32, 45; 11:47, 57; 12:10; 18:3, 35; 19:6, 15, 21). These priests and Levites thus also function in constellation with those later characters in the narrative.

Although this trait paradigm is brief, it allows for the classification of the corporate character of the priests and Levites as well as for the implication of their narrative force in the Gospel. The priests and Levites are background characters who are neither complex nor developed in the plot, and readers are given only minor penetration into their inner lives.[20] Thus, according to Greimas's actantial model, the priests and Levites are classified as "senders" who initiate and/or enable an event in the advancement of the plot, in this case the launching of the narrative and the clarification of John's role as neither Messiah nor messianic precursor, but rather as the witness identified in the Prologue as sent from God to testify to the coming of Jesus Christ.[21] Furthermore, readers are presented more insight on Jesus' role as the coming one who is already among them whom these representatives "do not know" and for whom these offered titles of "prophet" and "Messiah/Christ" *will* apply (1:26; see 1:41; 4:19, 44; 6:14; 7:26–27, 40, 52; 9:17; 10:24; 11:27; 17:3; 20:31).

---

[20] William J. Harvey uses the category of "background characters" (*Character and the Novel* [London: Chatto & Windus, 1965]) and Joseph Ewen employs the three axes of complexity, development, and penetration ("The Theory of Character in Narrative Fiction," *Hasifrut* 3 [1974]: 1–30). See the discussion in Tolmie, *Narratology and Biblical Narratives*, 53–57.

[21] For Greimas' model of six general categories of actants in narrative texts, see Algirdas J. Greimas, *Sémantique structural. Recherche dé méthode* (Paris: Librairie Larousse, 1966), 172–91.

The Pharisees: A House Divided[1]

Uta Poplutz

The Problem: Vague Characterization of the Pharisees

Characters are the life of a story. Their words and deeds give narratives much of their meaning. As opponents of the protagonist Jesus in the Gospel of John, the Pharisees propel the plot and add depth. But analyzing the Pharisees is difficult: an accurate narratological classification of the Pharisees as a specific group character is not always possible.

On the one hand, the Pharisees, chief priests, Levites and scribes belong to the Ἰουδαῖοι, the most important opponents of Jesus in the Fourth Gospel.[2] However, the Pharisees also appear as a distinct group when confronting Jesus.

The dialogue between John the Baptist and the delegation from Jerusalem in John 1:19–29 reveals the problem:

And this is the testimony of John, when *the Jews* (οἱ Ἰουδαῖοι) sent *priests and Levites* (ἱερεῖς καὶ Λευίτας) from Jerusalem to ask him, "Who are you?" (John 1:19)

Two identifiable Jewish group characters, the *"priests and Levites,"* are sent by "the Jews" from Jerusalem, who are introduced here for the first time in the Gospel. Priests, Levites and "the Jews" are given different names, but are closely connected delegations.

Further interrogation of John the Baptist illustrates the narrative vagueness: during the dialogue the narrator parenthetically supplies the information that the delegation was not in fact sent by "the (nonspecific) Jews" (1:19) but by "the Pharisees" in particular:

Now they had been sent from the *Pharisees* (ἐκ τῶν Φαρισαίων) (John 1:24).

---

[1] Cf. also my contribution, Uta Poplutz, "Die Pharisäer als literarische Figurengruppe im Johannesevangelium," in *Narrativität und Theologie im Johannesevangelium* (ed. Jörg Frey and Uta Poplutz; BThSt 130; Neukirchen-Vluyn: Neukirchener Theologie, 2012), 19–39. I am grateful to Laura Johnson from Gordon College for polishing the English in my essay.

[2] The term "the Jews" occurs sixty-six times in John's Gospel, making them one of the most important characters. For the different meanings connected with Ἰουδαῖοι, cf. Urban C. von Wahlde, "The Terms for Religious Authorities in the Fourth Gospel: A Key to Literary Strata?," *JBL* 98 (1979): 231–53; R. Alan Culpepper, *Anatomy of the Fourth Gospel: A Study in Literary Design* (repr., Philadelphia: Fortress, 1996), 125–30.

One may solve the problem by hypothesizing a second delegation, but this only obscures the deeper issue. The imprecise narration becomes part of the Pharisees' identity: it seems that the narrator is not interested in an accurate differentiation. This significantly hinders a thorough characterization of the Pharisees.

A final observation concerning the problem is that different groups of the Jewish authorities can enter the stage separately, with the exception of the Levites in John 1:19, yet they can also appear in alternating coalitions. The narrator combines the chief priests, scribes and Pharisees into various pairs without any differentiation in their speech or actions.

Thus the starting position is complex and poses a special challenge for the application of narrative approaches. However, I think this vagueness of characterization is significant. It may be possible to show that this unspecific classification of the Pharisees within the other Jewish groups actually determines them in a particular way and contributes to their characterization.

Theory: Narrative Analysis of Group Characters

A fundamental feature of characters is their description by means of limited information.[3] The narrator is selective in what he writes, for only some events and speeches can be narrated, and only these can be analyzed.[4] In contrast to real people, the information about a literary character is not expandable. As a result, any information may serve as an important character indicator.

A character can be defined as the sum of all pieces of information, with characterization being the method of linking this information together. This not only entails naming a character's qualities (*direct characterization*) but also indicating qualities by portraying the behaviour of the character through his or her action and speech (*indirect characterization*).[5]

Some specific issues must be considered in analyzing group characters like the Pharisees.[6] It is helpful to observe three related aspects:

---

[3] Manfred Pfister, *Das Drama: Theorie und Analyse* (11th ed.; München: Fink, 2001), 221–22; Seymour Chatman, *Story and Discourse: Narrative Structure in Fiction and Film* (Ithaca, N. Y.: Cornell University Press, 1978), 138: "Characters do not have 'lives'; we endow them with 'personality' only to the extent that personality is a structure familiar to us in life and art."

[4] James L. Resseguie, *Narrative Criticism of the New Testament: An Introduction* (Grand Rapids, Mich.: Baker Academic, 2005), 121.

[5] Shlomith Rimmon-Kenan, *Narrative Fiction: Contemporary Poetics, New Accents* (2d ed.; London: Routledge, 2003), 57–71; in detail also Uta Poplutz, "Kleine Leute? Von der narrativen Bedeutung so genannter 'Randfiguren' im Matthäusevangelium," in *Erzählte Welt: Narratologische Studien zum Mattäusevangelium* (ed. Uta Poplutz; BThSt 100; Neukirchen-Vluyn: Neukirchener, 2008), 57–100.

[6] Uta Poplutz, "Volk – Jünger – Autoritäten: Überlegungen zur Konzeption und Charak-

1. The *designation*[7] of the group distinguishes it from other entities in the story world and is a hint to the connective feature that combines single characters into a group character. With the naming as οἱ Φαρισαῖοι[8] they belong to "the Jews" and are related to them in function as Jesus' opponents. They also play a privileged role, signalled by the "Weltwissen" (world knowledge) of the ancient readers as well as by the way the Pharisees act within the story. In the narrated world, they are allied with the chief priests and gather council with them (John 11:45–53, 57), are consulted on specific cultic questions like the Sabbath observance (John 9:13–16), and control the synagogue and the judicial process by which opposing members are expelled (John 12:42–43). As we have seen in John 1:19, 24, they send delegations,[9] so we can presume that they are an officially powerful group. Because the readers develop a character model on the basis of the information given in the text and their preformed "Weltwissen," they understand the Pharisees as the most important representatives of Judaism in the Fourth Gospel, second only to the chief priests. The synoptic comparison confirms this: while the Sadducees and scribes are integral to the plots of the other Gospels, John excludes the Sadducees from his plot altogether and hardly mentions the scribes.[10] They only occur in connection with the Pharisees in John 8:3, a non-Johannine interpolation.[11]

2. The *identity*[12] of the group character in the narrative is pivotal for its constitution. They have to be portrayed in such a way that they may be identified by the reader as the same wherever they appear in the narrative.

---

terisierung von Figurengruppen im Matthäusevangelium," in *Erzählte Welt* (ed. Poplutz), 101–39.

[7] Chatman, *Story and Discourse*, 131: "Names are deictic, that is, pointing, marked out as definite, ('de-finited') or cut out of infinity, hypostatized, and catalogued (be it ever so minimally). Thus, narratives do not need proper names in the strict sense." With regard to the function of names for the characterization, cf. Thomas Koch, *Literarische Menschendarstellung: Studien zu ihrer Theorie und Praxis (Retz, La Bruyère, Balzac, Flaubert, Proust, Lainé)* (Romanica et Comparatistica 18; Tübingen: Stauffenburg Verlag, 1991), 129–31; David R. Beck, *The Discipleship Paradigm: Readers and Anonymous Characters in the Fourth Gospel* (Biblical Interpretation Series 27; Leiden: Brill, 1997), 10–12.

[8] They occur in the following scenes and roles. As acting characters: John 7:32, 45–52; 8:3–9, 13–21; 9:13–17, 40–41; 11:46–53, 57; 12:19; as background information: John 1:24; 4:1; 12:42–43; 18:3; as single characters: John 3:1 (also 7:50; 19:39). For comparison: "the Pharisees" occurs twelve times in Mark, thirty times in Matthew, twenty-seven times in Luke, and nine times in Acts.

[9] John 5:33; 7:32; 18:24; Culpepper, *Anatomy of the Fourth Gospel*, 131: "From the very beginning, therefore, there is the hint that the Jewish authorities are rival 'senders'."

[10] Anthony J. Saldarini, *Pharisees, Scribes and Sadducees in Palestinian Society: A Sociological Approach* (The Biblical Resource Series; Grand Rapids, Mich.: Eerdmans, 2001), 188, fn. 25: "The Pharisees in John fill the roles of the Markan scribes and Pharisees."

[11] Michael Theobald, *Das Evangelium nach Johannes: Kapitel 1–12* (RNT; Regensburg: Pustet, 2009), 548–53.

[12] "Identity" is not an ontological or semantic category but the linguistic construction of a character by means of communicative references: The reader has to be told of which character

For the Pharisees, this is achieved with their designation and by presenting them as types, involving a specific categorization. As *"types"* they have limited traits and qualities so that the reader can recognize them easily. This is essential for group characters because they consist of several individuals that must nevertheless speak and act as a single one.[13] In the case of the Pharisees this is achieved by the fact that the narrator does not use complicated traits.

There is a second, closely related aspect to be mentioned in this context: the *"social categorization"* of the Pharisees as a collective. I mean by this the fact that the Pharisees are subject to strict role assignments, both with regard to their characterization and their dramatic function as a group. As "Pharisees" they belong to the group of "the Jews" as well as to their own group (the so-called *"group category"*), and their most often invoked dramatic function is their acting as "opponents" to the main character, Jesus (the so-called *"role category"*). The fact that the Pharisees' own group category is so strongly delineated here is the main reason why the already mentioned narrative blurring of lines between the Pharisees and "the Jews" can occur: because of certain behaviours by the group, which are easily recognizable to recipients, the labels "Pharisees" and "Jews" can oscillate. A less attentive reader will not necessarily pick up on this subtlety at all.

In fact, it is difficult to separate "the Jews" precisely from the Pharisees, and in several episodes they are synonymous. In addition to the aforementioned interrogation of John the Baptist (John 1:19–28), the narrator also uses the two designations interchangeably in chapter 8. In 8:13, Jesus debates with the Pharisees (8:13–19, 21), but "the Jews" answer him in 8:22. From 8:28 it is clear that "the Jews" are the elites from Jerusalem who are, from the narrator's perspective, responsible for the crucifixion of Jesus. Both designations can be used as synonyms. Likewise, the Pharisees and "the Jews" are one and the same in John 9:13–41. But elsewhere the narrator differentiates the two groups: as John 11:45–47 shows, both character groups can be perceived separately.[14]

On the basis of these techniques and the limited character information, a coherent identity of character groups emerges. The reader can imagine the "typical Pharisee," a model completed with text-external information. That the coalitions between the groups change is rooted in the said ambiguity while simultaneously demonstrating their fundamental belonging to the all-encompassing character group of "the Jews."

3. One must also consider the *assignment* of single characters to the group. In John's Gospel, this is important for the only Pharisee who is mentioned by name.

---

is spoken about, cf. Fotis Jannidis, *Figur und Person: Beitrag zu einer historischen Narratologie* (Narratologia 3; Berlin: de Gruyter, 2004), 147.

[13] Jack D. Kingsbury, *Matthew as Story* (2d ed.; Philadelphia: Fortress, 1988), 9: "Groups of persons … may function as a single character."

[14] See Cornelis Bennema, *Encountering Jesus: Character Studies in the Gospel of John* (Milton Keynes: Paternoster, 2009), 41.

Now there was a man of the Pharisees named Nicodemus, a leader (ἄρχων) of the Jews (John 3:1; cf. 3:10; 7:50; 19:39).

Because of his denomination as "Pharisee and leader," he is introduced as a representative of the group. This means that he must be taken into account for the characterization of the Pharisees as a group character. But one must question whether he acts as an individual character that represents the collective or whether he serves as a renegade to show that the group is not completely homogeneous.

Analysis: The Pharisees in the Gospel of John

The Pharisees as a Powerful Religious Authority

The Pharisees are introduced in John 1:19, 24 as a very influential group of "the Jews": they have not entered the stage of the narrative yet, but the reader is informed that the Pharisees can act with power and influence through others, like the delegation. The local link to Jerusalem (John 1:19) underlines this assessment. This background information is the first indicator of the privileged status of the Pharisees.

In John 1:24 as well as in other central passages like 7:32 or 18:3, the Pharisees, in these cases together with chief priests, send out delegations to lay hold of Jesus. The Pharisees control the temple police[15] and are well-informed about what is happening in the crowd, even what is spoken in secret.[16] Even the leaders (ἄρχοντες, John 12:42), people in higher positions, stand in awe of them and are afraid to confess their faith in Jesus openly.

Two conclusions emerge from these incidents: the Pharisees have enough personal or institutional power to command supporting staff to seek information and execute orders, and they are distant from Jesus. In sending delegations or servants they avoid confrontation with and being questioned by Jesus.[17] As John 7:45–52 illustrates, this causes arguments between the senders and the sent. Both the returning servants and Nicodemus, who come out from the Pharisees, are struck by direct contact with Jesus. Thus, the Pharisees accuse the servants of having also been deceived (John 7:47: μὴ καὶ ὑμεῖς πεπλάνησθε;), and Nicodemus, "one of them" (John 7:50), criticizes the Phar-

---

[15] Von Wahlde, "Religious Authorities in the Fourth Gospel?," 233, fn. 6.

[16] Rudolf Schnackenburg, *Das Johannesevangelium: Teil 2: Kommentar zu Kapitel 5–12* (HTKNT IV; Freiburg: Herder, 2001), 206: "Die Pharisäer haben guten Kontakt zum Volk, sind überall anwesend und hören das Gerede der Leute."

[17] It is the same principle in John 4:1: "Now when Jesus learned that the Pharisees had heard that Jesus was making and baptizing more disciples than John … he left Judea and departed again for Galilee." The Pharisees' distance to Jesus corresponds to his leaving in John 4:1. This is a sort of background information for the characterization.

isees. The law, he reminds them, does not judge a man without first giving him a hearing and learning what he has really done (John 7:51). This implies that the Pharisees as guardians of the law do not act according to the law themselves. Predictably, the open-minded servants and sceptical Nicodemus provoke vituperation from the Pharisees: they realize that Jesus has the power to convince. They eventually cry out in frustration:

"You see that you are gaining nothing! Look, the world has gone after him!" (John 12:19)

John 9:13–16 characterizes the Pharisees as an institution that observes the religious order. This order may be threatened by Jesus, as exemplified by his healing the man born blind on the Sabbath.

The Pharisees exert the authority of summoning the accused to a hearing (John 9:18, 24), which causes fear among participants, even the leaders (John 9:22; 12:42). An atmosphere of fear accompanies this group that both wields and is jealous for power.

The Pharisees' vulnerability is further manifested in John 11:45–53. Some of "the Jews" who have come to Mary and witness the resurrection of Lazarus (cf. John 11:19) report this to the Pharisees. Consequently, the "chief priests and Pharisees" gather a council (John 11:47: Συνήγαγον οὖν οἱ ἀρχιερεῖς καὶ οἱ Φαρισαῖοι συνέδριον).[18]

As in the Synoptic accounts, the chief priests are named prior to the Pharisees[19] (cf. John 7:32), but the latter play a special role as addressees for news, even of denouncing content. Perhaps, as a movement of laymen, they were easier to address than the distinguished upper class Sadducees, for example. The Pharisees thus provided a link between the people and the priestly aristocracy. In this position they exerted considerable influence in both directions.

However, there seems to be a growing consensus that the Pharisees in Jesus' time had the power of influence rather than control. They were not only able to influence the common people but also those who had the power of control and policy making. We therefore include the Pharisees among the religious authorities, though not as the main leaders.[20]

In John 12:42–43, the Pharisees also appear as a normative authority, pronouncing that members who have turned toward Jesus be excluded from the synagogue. Here they can even have their way against members of the Sanhedrin, proving their influence.

---

[18] "'Gathered council' implies a meeting of the Sanhedrin, the highest ruling authority in Jerusalem other than Romans, but the absence of the definite article suggests that it may not have been a formal meeting of the whole body" (J. Ramsey Michaels, *The Gospel of John* [NICNT; Grand Rapids, Mich.: Eerdmans, 2010], 648).

[19] Cf. John 7:45; 11:57; 18:3.

[20] Cornelis Bennema, "The Identity and Composition of ΟΙ ΙΟΥΔΑΙΟΙ in the Gospel of John," *TynBul* 60 (2009): 239–63, here 246–47.

Overall, the conflict between Jesus and the Pharisees gradually increases throughout the course of the Fourth Gospel. Though they keep their distance initially, the Pharisees become increasingly more engaged in direct confrontation. However, their prominence tapers off during Jesus' passion. They are frequently mentioned in chapters 7–10, whereas the chief priests dominate the Sanhedrin and thus the action taken against Jesus from ch. 11 onwards (diff. John 7:45–52).

While the Pharisees first act by means of delegations (cf. John 1:24; 7:32), they step into direct confrontation with Jesus for the first time in John 8:12–20.[21]

Again Jesus spoke to them, saying: I am the light of the world. Whoever follows me will not walk in darkness, but will have the light of life. So the Pharisees said to him: You are bearing witness about yourself; your testimony is not true (σὺ περὶ σεαυτοῦ μαρτυρεῖς· ἡ μαρτυρία σου οὐκ ἔστιν ἀληθής)! (John 8:12–13)

The Pharisees act according to judicial standards when they state that Jesus' claim to be the "light of the world" has no credibility without witnesses. Such testimony is not valid in court. Their expertise fuels this legal debate.[22] However, as with the chief priests, their underlying intention is to arrest and kill Jesus rather than uphold the law (John 7:32, 47; 11:53, 57; 18:3).

It is striking that the Pharisees play no role in the Johannine passion narrative. This further illumines their character: they take a leading part regarding religious questions and have great influence over the people, but they do not represent the highest religious-political authority among "the Jews." This position is undoubtedly held by the chief priests, with whom the Pharisees are allied throughout the Gospel. The chief priests probably replace the Synoptic Sanhedrin, the council of chief priests, elders, and scribes, but they do not surpass it.

The consequent nominal priority of the chief priests in alliances and the leading part they take in the passion events demonstrates that the narrator regards the chief priests as the leading Jewish elite.[23]

---

[21] John 8:3–11 is a non-Johannine interpolation.

[22] Saldarini, *Pharisees, Scribes and Sadducees*, 191: "Usually the Pharisees do not legitimate Jesus by treating him as an equal. Rather, they maintain a superior position based on social recognition on their learning, their influence with the people and their political power in conjunction with the chief priests."

[23] A. J. Saldarini, "Pharisees," *ABD* 5:289–303, here 297: "That they are not the highest authorities is clear in the account of Jesus' condemnation to death, during which the Pharisees drop from view. Thus, John follows the Synoptic Gospels in the passion account in assigning the highest leadership and contact with the Romans to the chief priests."

The Pharisees as a Consistent Group Character

The Pharisees are not easily set apart from the circle of "the Jews" as an independently acting group because of their lack of narrated character traits and vague designation. Therefore, the issue of delimiting the Pharisees as a consistent, homogeneous group from a narratological perspective is yet to be dealt with more precisely.

The only Pharisee who notably steps out of the group character and is introduced by name is Nicodemus, who is a member of the Jewish authority (John 3:1). Although a distanced attitude is characteristic behavior of the Pharisees toward Jesus early in the Gospel, Nicodemus acts contrary to the stereotype: he seeks out Jesus and engages in an intimate conversation with him at night. Nicodemus appears twice more in the Gospel: in 7:50–51, defending Jesus' right to a hearing before the Pharisees, his own group, and in 19:39, bringing myrrh and aloes to anoint Jesus.

Since Nicodemus is explicitly referred to as ἄνθρωπος ἐκ τῶν Φαρισαίων, as one of the Pharisees, in John 3:1, his characterization must represent the entire group.[24] Further passages support this conclusion. First, John 7:40–53, a narratively elaborate passage, must be taken into account again. 7:43 mentions that the different opinions about Jesus have caused "a division" (σχίσμα) among the people, which even threatens to affect the servants sent by the chief priests and Pharisees (John 7:46: "No one ever spoke like this man!"). Because the servants, fascinated by Jesus' speech, have not fulfilled their task of seizing him, the Pharisees rebuke them in 7:47–48:

"Have you also been deceived? Have any of *the authorities* or the *Pharisees* believed in him?"

With a note about Nicodemus the narrative reveals that this assessment of the situation is not fully correct (John 7:50):

Nicodemus, who had gone to him [sc. Jesus] before, and *who was one of them*, said to them ...

Nicodemus carries the external division among the people right into the ranks of the Pharisees. It is unclear whether Nicodemus has come to believe in Jesus primarily as a consequence of their nighttime conversation or later interactions (John 3; 19:39).[25] Nevertheless, this passage adds to the growing characterization of the Pharisees. They are not an isolated group, as is shown by the character of Nicodemus, who belongs to three different groups at once. He is a

---

[24] The preposition ἐκ signals the connection with the group character.
[25] Instead Nicodemus is shown (John 2:23–25) as one of the "many" sympathizers of Jesus who come to him because of the "signs," cf. Jörg Frey, *Die eschatologische Verkündigung in den johanneischen Texten* (vol. 3 of *Die johanneische Eschatologie*; WUNT 117; Tübingen: Mohr Siebeck, 2000), 255.

Pharisee and one of the leading authorities, but he is also, though limited by the "signs," a believer in Jesus. Nicodemus even defends him before the Pharisees who wish to do away with him quickly.

Here the dual consideration of the Pharisees as both individuals and a type yields further insight: the division regarding Jesus that has splintered the people (John 7:43; also 11:45–46) also infects the Pharisees. This shows that they are more closely associated with the people than with the aristocracy of chief priests, as hinted at in John 7:32.

In John 12:42 the Pharisees' statement from 7:48 is once again exposed as wrong judgment or even a lie:

Nevertheless, many even *of the authorities* believed in him, but for fear of the Pharisees they did not confess it …

Could this be a reference to Nicodemus, who is then marked as a crypto-Christian, one who came to believe in Jesus but feared to confess to the larger group?

However, the Pharisees are no homogeneous entity, a description they have in common with "the Jews." This is also revealed in 9:16. When the man born blind shows himself healed to the Pharisees, their reactions to Jesus vary considerably:

Some of the Pharisees said: "This man is not from God, for he does not keep the Sabbath." But *others* said: "How can a man who is a sinner do such signs?" And there was a division (σχίσμα) among them.

Here the division among the group is addressed explicitly. The continuation of the story in 9:39–41 is interesting, for it mentions "*some of the Pharisees near him.*" Although this might simply indicate that some Pharisees were standing near Jesus, an inconsistency of location on a narrative level suggests a deeper interpretation. In 9:34 the Pharisees have sent away the healed man, yet in the next verse Jesus finds him again. So where do the Pharisees come from, of whom it is said:

Some of the Pharisees near him (μετ' αὐτοῦ) heard these things, and said to him: "Are we also blind?" (John 9:40)

It is not unlikely that this verse once more hints at the division among the group of the Pharisees. Is John indicating that not only some of the authorities but also Pharisees might be found among Jesus' followers, maybe to learn more like Nicodemus?[26]

The narrator does not report this explicitly, therefore these considerations are only speculative. Nevertheless, the text does support the idea of a group

---

[26] Cf. John 1:39–40: "So they came and saw where he was staying, and they stayed with him (παρ' αὐτῷ) that day …"; also John 11:16.

that is not homogeneous, thus allowing for both Nicodemus and the internal debate surrounding Jesus.

It is reasonable to treat the Pharisees, including Nicodemus, as one consistent group. Thus, the renegades, the critics, and those who belong to different groups also contribute to the characterization of the Pharisees.

The Pharisees are styled as opponents of Jesus, but their ranks are not closed. This allows for the historical question of whether the character of Nicodemus and the disputing Pharisees serve as an affirmation of and reference to the situation in the Evangelist's community. Did the Christians of the Johannine community view the powerful Pharisees, who dominated the restructuring of the Jewish society after 70 C. E. and were considered the prototypical Jewish opponents, as the impenetrable front that had caused their traumatic expulsion from the synagogue? Or were there individuals who, if not convinced by the Christian faith, could at least be regarded as genuinely interested interlocutors in a discussion?

Conclusion

By means of alternating group compositions (the Pharisees alone, together with the chief priests or the scribes, or "the Jews") the narrator counteracts a differentiated perception of the larger group, "the Jews." Consequently, the reader perceives the Pharisees, together with "the Jews," as massive opposition to Jesus who voice their lack of understanding along defined, typical lines.

Nevertheless, what I think has not always been perceived is that this conclusion is qualified by the Pharisees' not always acting and speaking with one voice as a *single character*.

We presuppose that within a limited set of narrated character traits, each detail is likely to be meaningful. Therefore, the vagueness of designation concerning the group of Pharisees can be interpreted as intentional and thus significant.

In addition to the construction of a threatening opposition to Jesus, group relevance is created.[27]

If we read John's Gospel as a *"grand récit"* ("master narration"), the group relevance is obvious. The author tells his version of the story of Jesus on the basis of experience: his experience in the community and that of the narrated time. Furthermore, he generates a new experience for his recipients. A memory is established, and, more than that, the narrator creates a new collective awareness.

---

[27] Barbara Schaff, "Erzählen und kollektive Identität," in *Handbuch Erzählliteratur: Theorie, Analyse, Geschichte* (ed. Matías Martínez; Stuttgart: Metzler, 2011), 89–97, here 90.

The character group of the Pharisees plays an important role in this context. The Pharisees are the ones to advance the plot of the Gospel, and yet they represent the opponents in John's own community. As characters, they stand for all that the local synagogue had to experience and endure, paralleling Jesus' earlier experience. The imprecise alternation of the terms "the Jews" and "the Pharisees" is then no coincidence but rather reflects the perception of the Johannine community at the end of the first century C. E. Where Pharisaic Judaism claims the leading role, the terms are interchangeable: "the Jews" and "the Pharisees" are one and the same. Clear character delimitations are redundant and would be counterproductive for the narrative strategy.

Because the literary representation of social groups like the Pharisees is situated between fictionality and extra-textual references, the narrative of the Gospel has a stabilizing effect.

It exerts a mimetic sociocultural function by legitimizing existing social groups. The group of the Pharisees has always posed a threatening opposition to Jesus and Christians. The community's present experience of threat is therefore by no means new but linked with the decision to follow Jesus. At the same time, the opposition crumbles through a division within. Here a subtle thread of hope is woven into the difficult situation of the time. There is no doubt that the Pharisees are the most influential opponents regarding the history of the community,[28] but this does not have to be the last word. Maybe the time would come when one of the leaders joins the Christian community and a Pharisee like Nicodemus would not come to Jesus secretly but rather openly and confess his faith. Obviously, this also strikes a slightly ironical note.

---

[28] Saldarini, *Pharisees, Scribes and Sadducees*, 197: "The Pharisees were a major opposition group for the johannine community because some Pharisees had great influence in Jerusalem and so some control of who was accepted as a Jew in good standing and allowed into the assembly (synagogue)."

The Disciples of John (the Baptist): Hearers of John, Followers of Jesus

Gary T. Manning, Jr.

The disciples of John the Baptist make two appearances in the Fourth Gospel. In the first scene (1:35–40), two unnamed disciples of John hear his declaration that Jesus is "the Lamb of God." They leave John, follow Jesus, ask him where he is staying, and then remain with him. One of these disciples is revealed as Andrew, who brings others to Jesus and eventually becomes one of the Twelve.

The second scene (3:25–30) also begins with unnamed disciples of John. The disciples have a discussion with a "Jew" about purification. While this discussion is never detailed, it results in the disciples' complaining to John about Jesus' success in baptizing disciples. John explains to them that his role is to testify to Jesus; it is only appropriate that Jesus must increase, and John must decrease. Nothing further is recorded about these disciples. They are not named, and the reader is not informed about their response to John's message, or their future.

These characters appear only briefly; each group has only one line of dialogue and minimal narration. However, they serve as contrasting examples of the characterization scheme inaugurated in John's prologue. The Gospel of John begins with a graded dualistic characterization scheme.[1] On the one hand is the "darkness:" those of merely human birth, who cannot understand or accept the light (1:5, 10–13); in fact, they are already judged because of their evil deeds and their hatred for the light (3:18–20). On the other hand are the children of God: those who receive and believe the light, who are born from God (1:12–13); their works are "in God" and they are not judged (3:18, 21).

While John's characterization scheme is dualistic, it is neither simplistic nor static. The "darkness" includes some who are completely hostile to Jesus (Caiaphas, the Pharisees, Judas), some who are informants (the lame man), and some

---

[1] R. Alan Culpepper, *Anatomy of the Fourth Gospel: A Study in Literary Design* (Philadelphia: Fortress, 1983), 104; Mark Allan Powell, *What is Narrative Criticism?* (Guides to Biblical Scholarship; Minneapolis: Fortress, 1990), 54. For an overview of John the Baptist material in all four Gospels, see Knut Backhaus, "Echoes from the Wilderness: The Historical John the Baptist," in *The Study of Jesus* (ed. Tom Holmén and Stanley E. Porter; vol. 2 of *Handbook for the Study of the Historical Jesus*; Leiden: Brill, 2011), 1747–85.

who merely reject Jesus' message (the disciples who leave Jesus). The "children of God" include some who make great confessions of faith (Peter, Martha), some who bring others to Jesus (the Samaritan woman, Andrew), and some who make simplistic but true declarations of faith in Jesus (the blind man, the nobleman). In addition, characters can develop in those qualities that establish them as darkness or light, displaying greater faith in Jesus or increasing in hostility towards him. Characters also sometimes possess qualities from the other domain. Nicodemus, for example, is part of the darkness at his first appearance, but he defends Jesus (7:50–52). Believing characters regularly misunderstand Jesus, and non-believers occasionally give unwitting testimony to Jesus.

A Study in Contrasts

The author crafts the two scenes involving John's disciples so that the characters in each are placed on opposite sides of the author's dualistic characterization scheme. Clearly the first two disciples become disciples of Jesus while the second group does not; but the first two are also better disciples of John because they listen to him (1:37). John *implicitly* praises them as those who possess truth (3:33). In contrast, John *explicitly* rebukes the second group for failing to listen ("You yourselves are witnesses that I said …"; 3:28).

The orientation of the two sets of characters is also informative. The first group is oriented away from John, whom they only hear, and toward Jesus. They talk with Jesus, follow him and remain with him. They address Jesus as "Rabbi" (1:37) and "Messiah" (1:41), while giving John no titles at all. The second group of disciples is oriented entirely toward John in their actions and dialogue; they are among the very few characters in John who have no encounter with Jesus at all. They call John "Rabbi" (every other occurrence of "Rabbi" in John is addressed to Jesus); their question emphasizes John rather than Jesus (σὺ μεμαρτύρηκας); and they pointedly avoid mentioning Jesus' name or giving him any adequate title ("the one who was with you across the Jordan, to whom you testified," 3:26).

The author uses "showing" (as opposed to "telling") to contrast the two groups. In the first scene, seven verbs, some repeated, show that the two are ideal disciples.

hear John	1:37, 1:41
follow Jesus	1:37, 1:41
seek Jesus	1:38
come and *see*	1:39 (twice)
remain with Jesus	1:39–40 (three times)
finds his brother	1:41

The Fourth Gospel regularly uses these seven verbs to "show" ideal discipleship.[2] Even *remain* (μένω), which at first reading seems to be non-theological, is revealed as incipient Johannine *abiding* (15:4–10) upon repeated re-readings of the Gospel.[3] By piling up these seven verbs, the narrator "shows" the reader that these are ideal disciples of John first and then Jesus, and thus creates idealistic empathy with the characters.[4]

The author then uses "showing" to create antipathy towards the second group of disciples. The only verbs associated with them, "they *came* to John and *said*," are mundane. The scene begins with their dispute (ζήτησις) over purification, creating a contrast with the first group of disciples, who seek (ζητέω) Jesus. To the careful reader of John's Gospel, their concern over purification is passé,[5] since Jesus' "good wine" has now replaced purification water (2:9–10).

Readers are inclined to begin with a sense of empathy towards both sets of characters, since they are allied with John, the greatest witness to Jesus. However, the narrator crafts a sense of antipathy towards the second set of disciples by hinting at alliances between these disciples and Johannine antagonists. They are involved in a discussion with a "Jew," which creates ambiguity, since "the Jews" are often negatively portrayed in John. Their complaint to John, "all are coming to him" (3:26) allies them with the Pharisees, who warn that "all will believe in him" (11:48, cf. 4:1),[6] and with the chief priests, who plot against Jesus because "many of the Jews ... were leaving and believing in Jesus" (12:11). Their role as informants against Jesus places them in direct contrast to the positive witnesses to Jesus (Andrew, Philip, the Samaritan woman, the blind man) and allies them with other informants against Jesus (the lame man, the anonymous "Jews" of 11:46, and Judas).

The conclusions of the two accounts further the contrast between the two sets of disciples. In the first account, one of the disciples is identified as Andrew, a prominent disciple who displays ideal discipleship by giving an ade-

---

[2] Randall Adkisson calls these first disciples "models of adequate believing" (idem, "An Examination of the Concept of Believing as a Dominant Motif in the Gospel of John" [Ph.D. diss.; New Orleans: Baptist Theological Seminary, 1990], 110). Anthony Hopkins points out that the first disciples have adequate volitional belief, but are lacking cognitive aspects (idem, "A Narratological Approach to the Development of Faith in the Gospel of John" [Ph.D. diss.; Louisville, Ky.: Southern Baptist Theological Seminary, 1992], 98, 139). Cf. Culpepper, *Anatomy of the Fourth Gospel*, 116; Cornelis Bennema, *Encountering Jesus: Character Studies in the Gospel of John* (Milton Keynes: Paternoster, 2009), 51–52.

[3] Bennema, *Encountering Jesus*, 48.

[4] Idealistic empathy is the desire created in the reader to emulate a character, often "established on the basis of common evaluative point of view and character traits" (Powell, *Narrative Criticism*, 56).

[5] Andreas J. Köstenberger, *John* (BECNT; Grand Rapids, Mich.: Baker Academic, 2004), 136–37.

[6] Köstenberger, *John*, 137.

quate title to Jesus and testifying to others about Jesus. Both disciples enter into the stream of the narrative of the Fourth Gospel. The repetition of the phrase "two of his disciples" (ἐκ τῶν μαθητῶν αὐτοῦ δύο) at the beginning and end (1:35; 21:3) of John is a narrative framing device suggesting their continued presence with Jesus. The narrative of the second group of disciples is truncated. Their dispute over purification is not detailed, explained or resolved. Their response to John's correction is not recorded, suggesting that they neither "receive his testimony" (3:32) nor "obey the Son" (3:36). They have no future in John's Gospel.

Character Depth

Using Ewen's model for analyzing character depth (complexity, development, and penetration into inner life),[7] the first group of disciples is more rounded than the second. The complexity of both groups is minimal, but the characteristics of the first group (simplicity, enthusiasm, and belief) are designed to gain the reader's interest more than the characteristics of the second group (dullness, entrenchment, and unbelief). The narrator includes additional details in the first narrative to increase interest: the time of day, the amount of disciples, and their purposeful activity. The first group shows development as they leave John, become disciples of Jesus, and lose their anonymity.[8] The second group displays no development at all: they did not understand John after his first testimony or his final testimony, and they remain anonymous. The author gives minimal penetration into the inner lives of either group, since none of their thoughts are presented. However, the first group of disciples is slightly more transparent, as their actions and words cohere to demonstrate their identity as true disciples.

The two groups of characters are *ficelles*; that is, they are minimally developed, serving primarily as plot functionaries and transitional agents.[9] The first disciples are transitional agents between John and Jesus. The prologue "tells" the readers that John is the supreme witness to Jesus, so that "all might believe through him" (1:6–8). The first two disciples "show" that the prologue was correct: John faithfully testified to Jesus, and the two believed through the witness of John. Still, the Fourth Gospel preserves tension in its characterization

---

[7] D. Francois Tolmie, *Narratology and Biblical Narratives: A Practical Guide* (San Francisco: International Scholars Publication, 1999), 56; citing Joseph Ewen, "The Theory of Character in Narrative Fiction," *Hasifrut* 3 (1974): 1–30.

[8] Development in a character "often provides a clue to the direction and meaning of the plot and theme" (James L. Resseguie, *Narrative Criticism of the New Testament: An Introduction* [Grand Rapids, Mich.: Baker Academic, 2005], 126).

[9] Tolmie, *Narratology and Biblical Narratives*, 55–56, relying on William J. Harvey, *Character and the Novel* (London: Chatto and Windus, 1965).

of John. On the one hand, he is the greatest witness to Jesus, included in the prologue as the third character after the Word and God; on the other hand, he is not the light, not the Prophet, not the Christ, not the bridegroom, and he is destined to decrease. The first two disciples assist in preserving this tension, as they faithfully listen to John, but do not follow him. In this way, they also serve as positive foils both to John and Jesus.

The second group serves as transitional agents between John and "the world." They represent those who misunderstand John's claims. The priests and Levites who question John think that he is claiming to be the Messiah (1:19–28); similarly, John's disciples seem to think that John is the light, rather than a witness to the light (a claim countered in the prologue, 1:8). The second group thus serves as a negative foil to John. Their failure to accept John's testimony gives John the opportunity to correct them and clarify his role as the one who must decrease.

The Role of Anonymity

Anonymity can have many functions in a narrative. In the first episode involving John's disciples, anonymity helps the reader perceive them as primarily plot agents and foils.[10] The lack of names keeps the reader focused on the characters with names, John and Jesus.[11] Anonymity also serves as a tool for reader identification: since the characters have no name, readers are free to see themselves in the narrative or to idealize the two disciples as models of acceptable belief.[12] Ultimately, anonymity in the first episode allows the identification of Andrew to serve as a naming event (juxtaposed with the naming of Peter). By delaying reader awareness of the name of Andrew, the author allows anonymity to accomplish his narrative purposes. John's other disciple remains technically anonymous. However, several details suggest (but do not insist) that the other disciple is in fact the "beloved disciple," the author of the Gospel: the general similarity to other accounts of the "beloved disciple," the presence of eyewitness details ("the tenth hour," 1:39), his association with named disciples, and his significant role as an early follower of Jesus.[13]

---

[10] Adele Reinhartz, "Anonymity and Character in the Book of Samuel," *Semeia* 63 (1993): 117–41, here 120–21, 127.

[11] David Beck, "The Narrative Function of Anonymity in Fourth Gospel Characterization," *Semeia* 63 (1993): 143–58, here 147.

[12] Beck, "Narrative Function," 247; Hopkins, "Development of Faith," 255; Culpepper, *Anatomy of the Fourth Gospel*, 115.

[13] The identification of this disciple as the apostle John goes back at least as far as Theodore of Mopsuestia (*Commentary on John* 1.1.39–41, cited in Joel C. Elowsky, ed., *Ancient Christian Commentary on Scripture IVa: John 1–10* [Downers Grove, Ill.: InterVarsity Press, 2006], 80).

In the second episode, anonymity may function to devalue the characters.[14] The second set of disciples is more anonymous than the first: no names, no number, few actions, and they begin the scene associated with another anonymous character. Some anonymous characters in John acquire tremendous importance, but in doing so, they usually acquire a title that functions as a name: the Samaritan woman, the blind man. In the case of these disciples of John, their anonymity and their unimportance remains.

Rhetorical Strategy

The strong contrast between the two sets of characters suggests the use of the ancient rhetorical category *genus syncrisis*, a literary device whereby two real groups were compared by means of representative members.[15] In this case, the Fourth Gospel compares two groups of John's disciples: one group who heard John and followed Jesus, and another group who remained with John and thus did not really hear him. It is hard to avoid the sense that the second episode is aimed at a continuing John the Baptist sect.[16]

If so, then the Fourth Evangelist's point is clear: true disciples of John will leave him to become true disciples of Jesus. Those who persist in following John have not really heard John. Their jealousy of Jesus' success allies them with the enemies of Jesus, and their continued focus on purification renders them passé in view of the cleansing that Jesus brings. True discipleship involves seeking, following and remaining with Jesus, and finding others to bring to Jesus.

---

[14] Resseguie, *Narrative Criticism*, 129–30.
[15] Michael Martin, *Judas and the Rhetoric of Comparison in the Fourth Gospel* (Sheffield: Sheffield Phoenix, 2010), 29–36.
[16] The continued existence of a John the Baptist sect is suggested by Acts 18:25; 19:1-7, as well as references in later works such as the *Pseudo-Clementine Recognitions* and the Mandean literature.

An Anonymous Disciple: A Type of Discipleship

Derek Tovey

In John 1:35 the narrator introduces two disciples of John who are unnamed. One, however, is soon identified as Andrew, Simon Peter's brother (1:40). The other disciple remains anonymous and it is with this disciple that this article is concerned. Where commentators do speculate upon the identity of this disciple, they often suggest that he is either John, the son of Zebedee (generally by assimilating the information in John's Gospel with that in the Synoptic Gospels), or "the disciple whom Jesus loved."[1] Frequently, the Evangelist, John the son of Zebedee, and the Beloved Disciple are considered to be one and the same, and identified with this anonymous disciple. A few commentators identify this disciple as Philip, primarily because the Gospel story subsequently links Philip with Andrew (see, for example, John 6:7–8; 12:20–22) but this suggestion meets a difficulty in 1:43.[2]

Among scholars who develop a "character study" of the Beloved Disciple, many either ignore or dismiss 1:35 as a reference to this disciple, or merely note it as a possibility.[3] David Beck, who has written a monograph on anon-

---

[1] See, for example. C. Kingsley Barrett, *The Gospel According to St John: An Introduction with Commentary and Notes on the Greek Text* (2d ed.; London: SPCK, 1978), 181 (on v. 41); John H. Bernard, *A Critical and Exegetical Commentary on the Gospel According to St. John* (ed. Alan H. McNeile; 2 vols.; ICC; Edinburgh: T&T Clark, 1928), 53; Raymond E. Brown, *The Gospel According to John I (I–XII)* (AB 29; New York: Doubleday, 1966), 73 (raised as a question); Gary M. Burge, *John* (NIV Application Commentary; Grand Rapids, Mich.: Zondervan, 2000), 75; Donald A. Carson, *The Gospel According to John* (Leicester: InterVarsity Press, 1991), 154, 157; Andreas J. Köstenberger, *John* (Baker Exegetical Commentary on the New Testament; Grand Rapids, Mich.: Baker Academic, 2004), 76.

[2] For the identification with Philip, see Marie-Émile Boismard, *Moses or Jesus: An Essay in Johannine Christology* (trans. B. T. Viviano; Minneapolis: Fortress, 1993), 23–24. For a fuller discussion of the possibilities here, see Kevin Quast, *Peter and the Beloved Disciple: Figures for a Community in Crisis* (JSNTSup 32; Sheffield: JSOT Press, 1989), 31–35; Quast leaves the identity of this other disciple open. A full discussion of the issues may be found in Frans Neirynck, "The Anonymous Disciple in John 1," in *Evangelica II, 1982–1991, Collected Essays by Frans Neirynck* (ed. Frans van Segbroek; BETL 99; Louvain: Leuven University Press, 1991), 617–49; originally published in *ETL* 66 (1990): 5–37.

[3] See e. g., Susan E. Hylen, *Imperfect Believers: Ambiguous Characters in the Gospel of John* (Louisville, Ky.: Westminster John Knox, 2009), 93; and Colleen M. Conway, *Men and Women in the Fourth Gospel: Gender and Johannine Characterisation* (SBLDS 167; Atlanta: Society of Biblical Literature, 1999), 179 (ignore); Bradford B. Blaine, Jr., *Peter in the Gospel*

ymous characters in the Fourth Gospel, scarcely considers this character at all, beyond summarising readers' attempts to identify this disciple with specific characters.[4] He writes, "the 'anonymous disciple' with Andrew in 1:35–39 is never presented as an individual in the text."[5]

However, some scholars who clearly identify the anonymous disciple with the Beloved Disciple, and whose discussion may be taken as contributing towards a delineation of this character, are Richard Bauckham, Cornelis Bennema and Sjef van Tilborg.[6] Taken together, their work shows that 1:35–40 contributes the following aspects to the wider characterization of the Beloved Disciple: (a) that the Beloved Disciple has been a member of Jesus' discipleband since the beginning and has come to know Jesus well, (b) that the Beloved Disciple can testify himself to Jesus as "the Lamb of God" having heard John's testimony (1:35), and that (c) the Beloved Disciple is, therefore, a perceptive and "ideal" witness.

I shall return to the question of the identity of this anonymous disciple with the Beloved Disciple shortly. First, however, we must consider this character within the locale of 1:35–40 to discern what character traits emerge that determine the function of this anonymous character. We may note, briefly, that here he appears, in company with Andrew, as a disciple of John. Upon hearing John proclaim Jesus as "the Lamb of God," he and Andrew leave John to follow Jesus. When asked by Jesus what they are seeking, they reply with their own question: "Rabbi, where are you staying?" (1:38b, NRSV). Jesus invites them to "come and see" and they remain with Jesus the rest of that day (the

---

of John: The Making of an Authentic Disciple (SBL Academia Biblica 27; Atlanta: Society of Biblical Literature, 2007), 28 (dismiss); Margaret M. Beirne, *Women and Men in the Fourth Gospel: A Genuine Discipleship of Equals* (JSNTSup 242; London: Sheffield Academic Press, 2003), 186, fn. 61 ("cannot be determined"); James L. Resseguie, *The Strange Gospel: Narrative Design and Point of View in John* (Biblical Interpretation Series 56; Leiden: Brill, 2001), 156, fn. 55 ("possible").

[4] David R. Beck, *The Discipleship Paradigm: Readers and Anonymous Characters in the Fourth Gospel* (Biblical Interpretation Series 27; Leiden: Brill, 1997), 46.

[5] David R. Beck, *The Discipleship Paradigm*, 33; he does not accept a link with the Beloved Disciple. He does, however, understand this disciple's function as providing an opportunity for readers to "include themselves among [Jesus'] followers" (44).

[6] See Richard Bauckham, "The Beloved Disciple as Ideal Author," in his *The Testimony of the Beloved Disciple: Narrative, History, and Theology in the Gospel of John* (Grand Rapids, Mich.: Baker Academic, 2007), 73–91; repr. from *JBL* 49 (1993): 21–44; also idem, *Jesus and the Eyewitnesses: The Gospels and Eyewitness Testimony* (Grand Rapids, Mich.: Eerdmans, 2006), 390–93; Cornelis Bennema, *Encountering Jesus: Character Studies in the Gospel of John* (Milton Keynes: Paternoster, 2009), 209, especially 171–75; Sjef van Tilborg, *Imaginative Love in John* (Biblical Interpretation Series 2; Leiden: Brill, 1993), especially 87–88, 99–100. See also Michael Theobald, "Der Jünger, den Jesus liebte. Beobachtungen zum narrativen Konzept der johanneischen Redaktion," in *Geschichte – Tradition – Reflexion: Festschrift für Martin Hengel zum 70. Geburtstag; Bd. 3: Frühes Christentum* (ed. Hubert Cancik et al.; Tübingen: Mohr Siebeck, 1996), 219–55, here 221–22, 225–26, 245, 248 (pertinent to a reading of the text as it currently stands, whatever redactional history it may have had).

narrator notes that it was the tenth hour, or "about four o'clock in the afternoon," 1:39c, NRSV).

The anonymous disciple, then, functions here as a "ficelle," or a type, whose character is shaped by the following traits and functions. First, this character's anonymity means that a reader may more easily identify with him. Thus, his presence may provide a space within the narrative for the implied reader to inhabit. Certainly, this feature invites readers' participation in the narrative's world and its depiction of discipleship.[7] Second, as a disciple of John, he implicitly bolsters John's function as a witness to Jesus. He is a disciple who believes in, and follows Jesus, on account of John's word: this role as a witness, the disciple will also be called upon to fulfil (15:27; cf. 17:20). Third, as many commentators note, the language used by the implied author here represents the language of discipleship.[8] Thus, this disciple becomes a disciple of Jesus, and represents, with Andrew, the nature of discipleship as one who seeks and follows (1:37–38; ἠκολούθησαν τῷ Ἰησοῦ ... λέγει αὐτοῖς· τί ζητεῖτε;) and remains (1:39; παρ' αὐτῷ ἔμειναν).

The cameo scene in which this anonymous disciple appears also serves to introduce an important theme in the Gospel, that of the question of Jesus' origins, and where he "resides." The question, "Rabbi/Teacher, where are you staying?" (ποῦ μένεις;) will play out later in the Gospel with ironic effect as other characters seek Jesus and attempt to discern his origins (cf. 7:25–36, 40–43, 52; 8:21–23; 9:29; 11:55–56; 19:9). Hence, the anonymous disciple may be said to be a ficelle, or type (or an agent), who supports the protagonist Jesus (and John the Baptist's characterization), helping to get the plot going, introducing a significant theme, and functioning to support the implied author's depiction of discipleship as that of seeking, following, remaining and witnessing.

Finally, I argue that this anonymous disciple is to be associated with the Beloved Disciple. The grounds for this is the *inclusio* with 1:35–40, created by the appearance of two unnamed disciples in 21:2, and by the "implicature" provided by the structure of each passage and the use of certain words.[9] We may note, first of all, the linguistic correspondence between 1:35 and 21:2.

1:35 καὶ ἐκ τῶν μαθητῶν αὐτοῦ δύο: "and two of his disciples" (NRSV).
21:2 καὶ ἄλλοι ἐκ τῶν μαθητῶν αὐτοῦ δύο: "and two others of his disciples"

---

[7] See David R. Beck, *The Discipleship Paradigm*, 44, 144–45 (if my argument holds, then this disciple becomes one who receives "more than just a brief mention," and thus counters Beck's reluctance to consider him).

[8] Barrett, *John*, 180–81; Brown, *John*, 74–75. 78–79; Burge, *John*, 75; Barnabas Lindars, *The Gospel of John* (NCB; Grand Rapids, Mich.: Eerdmans, 1972), 113.

[9] I use the (speech-act) term "implicature" to refer to a dynamic of literary communication whereby statements, or narrative devices, achieve their purpose by implying connections or suggesting associations (see further, Derek Tovey, *Narrative Art and Act in the Fourth Gospel* [JSNTSup 151; Sheffield: Sheffield Academic Press, 1997], 75–76).

Furthermore, within the wider context of each passage (i. e., 1:35–40; 21:1–7), we find that while one of the disciples is identified, the other remains unidentified. In 1:40 Andrew is named as one of the two initially anonymous disciples; and, I submit, in 21:7, it is the Beloved Disciple who is here identified as one of the two anonymous disciples, while Andrew remains unidentified. I have argued elsewhere that the "other" [ἄλλος] disciple of 18:15 is to be identified with the Beloved Disciple because of the implicature provided by the fact that this descriptor is associated with the Beloved Disciple in 20:2.[10] In this case, there may well be a further implication (*inclusio*, perhaps?) in the use of the word ἄλλοι ("others") to include the two anonymous disciples in the fishing party.

Should it be objected that the implied author gives no indication in 1:35–40 that the Beloved Disciple is in view (after all he is not mentioned by this descriptor until 13:23), I would reply that under the dynamics of narrative, an understanding of a character's profile must be built up over the course of the narrative by recalling information provided earlier (and implicature is one way in which an implied author aids this process), and through "rereading," that is, understanding earlier information in the light of information gleaned later in the narrative. Let it be remembered that this applies equally to the process of understanding themes and motifs (and indeed, *Tendenz* or redactional tendencies, for that matter).[11]

If this argument holds, then a further dimension of this anonymous disciple emerges. For his characterization may be gathered up into that of the Beloved Disciple. Importantly, also, the appearance of this anonymous disciple in 1:35 provides a narrative corroboration of the Beloved Disciple's function as a witness to Jesus who has been with him "from the beginning" (see 15:27).

---

[10] Space forbids elaboration of this argument here; see Tovey, *Narrative Art*, 129–33; or idem, *Jesus, Story of God: John's Story of Jesus* (Hindmarsh: ATF Press, 2007), 30–31.

[11] Cf. van Tilborg, *Imaginative Love*, 87–88.

Andrew:
The First Link in the Chain

Martinus C. de Boer

The Gospel of John (henceforth GJohn)[1] refers five times to someone named Andrew (1:40, 44; 6:8; twice in 12:22).[2] These five instances occur in four discrete literary units: 1:35–42; 1:43–51; 6:1–14; and 12:20–26. The units are narratives, i. e., they tell a story in which this Andrew plays a role. In this article, we shall be interested in answering three questions in particular: How is Andrew described? What does he do and say? What is his function in the story?

In answering these questions, we shall be guided primarily by the narrative-critical methodology used in the classic work of R. Alan Culpepper.[3] Culpepper defines "characterization as the art and techniques by which an author fashions a convincing portrait of a person within a more or less unified piece of writing. Even if one is disposed to see real, historical persons behind every character in John and actual events in every episode, the question of how the author chose to portray the person still arises ... It is, therefore, for our present purposes, immaterial whether the literary character has its origin in historical tradition, memory, or imagination. The writer has a distinct understanding of a person and his or her role in a significant sequence of events."[4] Taken strictly, Culpepper's approach is ahistorical.

In a recent full-length study of characters in GJohn, Cornelis Bennema regards Culpepper's work as "the most comprehensive and significant contribution on the subject to date,"[5] but he also wants to qualify Culpepper's approach by taking seriously the character of GJohn as "a non-fictional narra-

---

[1] I use this designation to prevent confusion below with characters in the Gospel who are called John.
[2] There are eight references to Andrew in the Synoptics and Acts (Matt 4:18; 10:2; Mark 1:16, 29; 3:18; 13:3; Luke 6:14; Acts 1:13). In Mark 3:18; Matt 10:2; Luke 6:14, he is listed as one of the twelve disciples of Jesus (in the latter two passages, these twelve are referred to as "apostles," cf. also Acts 1:13 with 1:26).
[3] R. Alan Culpepper, *Anatomy of the Fourth Gospel: A Study in Literary Design* (Philadelphia: Fortress, 1983), esp. 99–148.
[4] Culpepper, *Anatomy of the Fourth Gospel*, 105.
[5] Cornelis Bennema, *Encountering Jesus: Character Studies in the Gospel of John* (Milton Keynes: Paternoster, 2009), 11.

tive" whose characters have "historical referents."[6] Bennema regards the Gospel as the product of "a reliable eyewitness for the events recorded,"[7] though he acknowledges that the evangelist "may have 'fictionalized' or embellished aspects of his characters by leaving out, changing or adding certain details from his sources"; Gospels, he notes, "need not necessarily be historically accurate in every detail."[8] Bennema also insists that the characters "must be interpreted within the socio-historical first-century Jewish context and not just on the basis of the text itself."[9] He has a point since it cannot be ignored that the stories told are set in the first century C. E. and reflect a specifically Jewish milieu.[10] A narrative-critical approach combined with attention to the social, cultural, and religious historical setting of the Gospel is required.[11] Nevertheless, the concern of this study is neither with the historicity nor with the historical reliability of the accounts in which Andrew occurs. Following Culpepper, the focus remains on "how the author chose to portray the person" in question.

With respect to fictional literature (e. g., a novel), a narrative-critical methodology maintains a distinction between the narrator (story-teller), implied author, and real author, on the one hand, and between the narratee ("the one who hears the narrator"[12]), implied reader, and real reader on the other. The implied author is the image of the author created by the text, by the way the story is told; the same counts for the implied reader.[13] Like the narrator and the narratee, the implied author and reader are "internal" to the text, whereas the real author and reader are "external" to the text. These distinctions, though extremely helpful, are difficult to apply without further ado in a narrative-cri-

---

[6] Bennema, *Encountering Jesus*, 13. For Bennema these historical referents concern the time of Jesus only. He explicitly prescinds from any attempt "to discover historical referents for the Johannine characters in John's own time and setting" (idem, *Encountering Jesus*, 208, fn. 7), rejecting the works of Raymond E. Brown, *The Community of the Beloved Disciple* (New York: Paulist, 1979) and J. Louis Martyn, *History and Theology in the Fourth Gospel* (3d ed.; Louisville, Ky.: Westminster John Knox, 2003). See the review of Francis J. Moloney in *Review of Biblical Literature 03/2011*.

[7] Bennema, *Encountering Jesus*, 13; cf. 181: the author of the Fourth Gospel is the Beloved Disciple whom Bennema thinks was probably John the son of Zebedee (or, as a somewhat lesser possibility, John the Elder).

[8] Bennema, *Encountering Jesus*, 13.

[9] Bennema, *Encountering Jesus*, 13. See Culpepper, *Anatomy of the Fourth Gospel*, 207.

[10] See Raymond E. Brown, *The Gospel According to John I (i–xii)* (AB 29; New York: Doubleday, 1966); Martyn, *History and Theology*. Bennema simply takes the Jewish socio-historical context of the Fourth Gospel as a given from the start and he does not relate this context to the setting in which the Gospel itself was composed.

[11] See my article "Narrative Criticism, Historical Criticism, and the Gospel of John," *JSNT* 47 (1992): 21–34. Cf. Bennema, *Encountering Jesus*, 12.

[12] Culpepper, *Anatomy of the Fourth Gospel*, 206.

[13] See Culpepper, *Anatomy of the Fourth Gospel*, 15–16; 205–27. The reader, whether implied or real, may be collective, i. e., a group or a community.

tical analysis of GJohn since, as Culpepper writes: "In John the implied reader is scarcely distinguishable from the narratee, just as the implied author can hardly be separated from the narrator."[14] Moreover, according to Culpepper, "there is no reason to suspect any difference in the ideological, spatial, temporal, or phraseological points of view of the narrator, the implied author, and the author."[15] A similar conclusion applies to the narratee, the implied reader, and the real reader.[16]

The category of the real reader, however, needs clarification with respect to GJohn. In a narrative-critical analysis of fiction the real reader is a contemporary reader, but for a narrative-critical analysis of GJohn, which is not fiction though it may contain fictional elements, the real reader must in the first instance be construed as someone or a group from the first century C. E. (explicitly represented in GJohn by the plural "you" of 19:35 and 20:31). The "real reader" is here "the *intended* reader."[17] The establishment of the latter's identity is largely dependent on the profile of the reader implied by the text of GJohn itself, there being no other reliable sources of information about the intended reader of GJohn. As indicated in the previous paragraph, there is no reason to suspect that the intended first-century reader of GJohn has a profile significantly different from the reader implied by the Gospel narrative itself. The real, intended reader, we may assume, largely corresponds to the implied reader. For our purposes it is relevant to indicate some of the conclusions to which Culpepper comes in his investigation of the relationship between the implied and the real, intended reader: According to Culpepper, the implied and thus intended reader "has extensive knowledge of the Old Testament and a general understanding of Jewish groups and beliefs,"[18] including "especially expectations of messianic figures."[19] The implied and thus intended reader is also "certainly familiar with Christian beliefs and the Christian story."[20] "This readership" also "shares a common idiom and the ability to appreciate the gospel's use of particular images, ironies, and symbols."[21] On the whole, Culpep-

---

[14] Culpepper, *Anatomy of the Fourth Gospel*, 8; cf. 206. Similarly, Culpepper observes that "there is no real difference between the point of view of the narrator, i. e., the voice which tells the story, and the perspective of the implied author which is projected by the text" (Culpepper, *Anatomy of the Fourth Gospel*, 7).

[15] Culpepper, *Anatomy of the Fourth Gospel*, 43.

[16] Culpepper, *Anatomy of the Fourth Gospel*, 211–27.

[17] Culpepper, *Anatomy of the Fourth Gospel*, 224 (emphasis added). The real historical, intended reader is to be distinguished from the real reader today (cf. Culpepper, *Anatomy of the Fourth Gospel*, 207–208); the former is "culturally, historically, and philosophically distant" from the latter (208).

[18] Culpepper, *Anatomy of the Fourth Gospel*, 222.

[19] Culpepper, *Anatomy of the Fourth Gospel*, 224.

[20] Culpepper, *Anatomy of the Fourth Gospel*, 223; cf. 224–25.

[21] Culpepper, *Anatomy of the Fourth Gospel*, 225.

per concludes, "a remarkably coherent and consistent picture of the intended reader emerges from the narrator's comments."[22]

Consistent with a narrative-critical methodology, we shall refer below simply to "the narrator" or "the story-teller" rather than to "the author," whether implied or real, even though (as indicated above) the voice of the narrator is for all intents and purposes also the voice of both. Corresponding to the narrator is the narratee, but we shall instead refer below simply to "the reader," meaning in the first instance the implied reader who (as indicated above) can scarcely be meaningfully differentiated from the narratee on the one hand or the real (historically intended) reader on the other.[23]

Andrew in 1:35–42[24]

This passage is worth quoting in full:

[35]The next day again John was standing with two of his disciples, [36]and he looked at Jesus as he walked, and says, "Behold, the Lamb of God!" [37]And the two disciples heard him say this, and they followed Jesus. [38]Jesus turned and saw them following him, and says to them, "What do you seek?" They said to him, "Rabbi" (which means Teacher), "where are you staying?" [39]He says to them, "Come and see." They then came and saw where he was staying; and they stayed with him that day; it was about the tenth hour. [40]Andrew, Simon Peter's brother, was one of the two who had heard from John, and had followed him (Ἦν Ἀνδρέας ὁ ἀδελφὸς Σίμωνος Πέτρου εἷς ἐκ τῶν δύο τῶν ἀκουσάντων παρὰ Ἰωάννου καὶ ἀκολουθησάντων αὐτῷ·).[25] [41]He first finds his own brother, Simon, and says to him, "We have found the Messiah" (which means Christ). [42]He brought him to Jesus. Jesus looked at him, and said, "You are Simon the son of John; you shall be called Cephas" (which means Peter).

Andrew first appears by name in v. 40, where he is identified in two ways, as "Simon Peter's brother" and as "one of the two who had heard [something

---

[22] Culpepper, *Anatomy of the Fourth Gospel*, 224. This does not mean that there are no tensions, inconsistencies, or ambiguities in the profile of the implied and intended reader, especially in connection with "the presumption of familiarity with the Jewish festivals, especially in the discourses, and explanatory comments which make the gospel intelligible to readers unfamiliar with Judaism" (Culpepper, *Anatomy of the Fourth Gospel*, 225; cf. 220–21). Culpepper himself entertains the possibility that the Gospel has gone through several stages of composition whereby the intended audience changed from predominantly Jewish to predominantly Gentile.

[23] Some of what will be said about this reader may well apply to any reader, including a reader today, but I will not address that issue in this study.

[24] Translations take the RSV as the point of departure, but modifications have been made where necessary to bring the translation into line with the underlying Greek text, especially in verses concerning Andrew.

[25] Cf. NIV, NAB, following the Greek word order. RSV translates v. 40 as follows: "One of the two who heard John speak and followed him, was Andrew, Simon Peter's brother" (cf. KJV, NRSV).

about Jesus] from John [the Baptist] and [as a result] had followed him [i. e., Jesus]". The first identification is traditional (cf. Matt 4:18; 10:2; Mark 1:16; Luke 6:14) and it signifies that Andrew is defined by his relationship to Simon Peter who is assumed to be a well-known figure[26] (the latter is not introduced as a character in the narrative until the following verse). The second identification harks back to v. 37: "The two disciples [of John] heard him [John] say this [about Jesus] and they followed Jesus". This verse in turn refers back to vss. 35–36 where John is depicted as standing with "two of his disciples" and then declaring Jesus to be "the Lamb of God" (cf. 1:29 where John declares Jesus to be "the Lamb of God, who takes away the sin of the world"). On the basis of this declaration, the two disciples of John, one of them being Andrew, go and "follow" Jesus. In doing so, Andrew and his anonymous companion ask Jesus where he is staying (1:38); Jesus responds by inviting them to "come and see," which they do; and they stay "with him that day" (1:39). The verb "follow" is to be taken both literally and metaphorically: the two disciples of John literally follow Jesus on his travels, as vss. 37–39 show, and they become his followers in a deeper sense (cf. 8:12; 10:4, 27; 12:26; 13:36; 21:19, 22), as Andrew's subsequent christological confession in v. 41 indicates.[27] It is worth emphasizing that the two disciples of John are not "called" by Jesus to "follow" him (contrast Mark 1:16-20 par.)[28]; rather, they "follow" Jesus because they have been directed to him by John and his proclamation of Jesus as God's Lamb.[29] As indicated above, the reader does not know before v. 40 that one of the two disciples of John in vss. 35–37 is in fact Andrew. Narratively speaking, then, he gets a name

---

[26] That is, the narrator assumes that the reader shares this knowledge.

[27] Many interpreters would also attribute a deeper meaning to the verb μένω ("stay"), which occurs three times in 1:38–39. There are another thirty-seven instances in GJohn, often with a deeper theological meaning ("abide"). In most of those cases, however, the verb is accompanied by the preposition ἐν ("in"), e. g., to "abide in" Jesus or his word (cf. 5:38; 6:56; 15:4–6, 10). But that is not the case in 1:38–39. Two instances concern Jesus himself staying (lodging) somewhere in an evidently mundane way (for similar usage, cf. 2:12; 11:6). The third instance, which concerns Andrew and his companion "staying with (σύν)" (rather than "in") Jesus, has a temporal limitation ("that day"), and that is unlike the notion of "abiding in" elsewhere in GJohn, where the idea is ongoing union between the believer and Christ.

[28] Contrast Andreas J. Köstenberger, who concludes his otherwise helpful book with the claim: "From the beginning to the end of the Fourth Gospel, the disciples are called to follow Jesus" (idem, *The Missions of Jesus and the Disciples according to the Fourth Gospel* [Grand Rapids, Mich.: Eerdmans, 1998], 220; emphasis removed). It is a disappointing feature of Köstenberger's investigation that it fails to analyze this passage and thus misses its distinctive contribution to the theme of his study.

[29] As Craig Koester points out, this difference from the Synoptics is "congruent with the experience of a later generation of Christians, who came to faith through the witness of others (17:20)" (idem, *Symbolism in the Fourth Gospel: Meaning, Mystery, Community* [2d ed.; Minneapolis: Fortress, 2003], 62–63). See fn. 6 above.

only when he has become a follower of Jesus. Along with the other disciple, who remains anonymous,[30] Andrew counts as the first follower of Jesus.[31] He is the first named link in a chain of disciples that extends in Chapter 1 through Simon Peter and Philip to Nathanael (1:45–51).

The significance of describing Andrew as in the first place the brother of Simon Peter in v. 40 becomes evident in v. 41, where the narrator reports that Andrew "first finds his own brother, Simon, and says to him, 'We have found the Messiah'." Andrew is not only the first (named) disciple of Jesus, who makes the first open confession of faith in Jesus as the Messiah, he is also the first missionary.[32] Having found his brother and announced to him that Jesus is the Messiah, Andrew brings him to Jesus who proceeds to give Simon a new name, Cephas/Peter (v. 42; cf. Matt 16:18). Peter goes on to play a crucial role later as the spokesman of the Twelve (cf. 6:67–69; 13:6–10, 24, 36–38; 18:10–11, 15–18, 25–27; 20:2–10; 21:1–14, 15–23), something of which the reader is apparently already aware at this stage of the narrative. Andrew's bringing Peter to Jesus has played a decisive role in this important development.

The narrator evidently wants the reader to think that the encounter with Jesus as described in v. 39, where Jesus invites Andrew and his anonymous companion to "come and see," caused them to embrace Jesus as the Messiah in v. 41. Only that assumption can explain why Andrew is subsequently depicted as going and finding his brother and announcing to him: "We[33] have found the Messiah" (εὑρήκαμεν τὸν Μεσσίαν). Moreover, this confessional formulation compels the reader to conclude that Andrew and the anonymous disciple, as portrayed, "already hold certain well-known messianic expectations" and that "these expectations" have found their "fulfillment in Jesus of Nazareth. *He* is ... the expected Messiah."[34] In the hands of the story-teller, Andrew "like John the Baptist, points to Jesus, so that those who have been brought up on the traditional Jewish expectations [such as his brother, Simon

---

[30] Is he perhaps the disciple whom Jesus loved (cf. 13:23; 19:26; 20:2; 21:7, 20) and/or John the son of Zebedee (21:2)? The narrator does not divulge his identity and it may not be relevant. See fn. 33 below.

[31] It is not until 2:2 that Andrew and the other new followers of Jesus (Andrew's anonymous companion, Simon Peter, Philip, and Nathanael) are called "his disciples." The only instances of the term "disciple" (μαθητής) in John 1 occurs in connection with the two followers of John the Baptist in this passage (1:35, 37; cf. 3:25).

[32] Cf. Mark W. G. Stibbe, *John* (Sheffield: JSOT Press, 1993), 43: Andrew's role is that of "witness and evangelist."

[33] The use of the first person plural points to the narrative function of the anonymous disciple alongside Andrew in the narrative prior to this verse: He is needed to give Andrew's confession a communal cast.

[34] J. Louis Martyn, "Glimpses into the History of the Johannine Community," in *History and Theology in the Fourth Gospel* (3d ed.; The New Testament Library; Louisville, Ky.: Westminster John Knox, 2003), 149–75, here 149 (emphasis original).

Peter] may now find the one so long expected."[35] As a disciple of John, Andrew had been a Jew with certain well-formed messianic expectations; in contrast to other disciples of the Baptist, he found these expectations fulfilled in Jesus of Nazareth (cf. 1:19–25; 3:28).

The narrative observation that Andrew "*first* finds his *own* brother, Simon" presents difficulties for interpretation. The adverb "first" (πρῶτον)[36] appears to imply that Andrew did something "second" (δεύτερον), while the reference to "his *own* (ἴδιον) brother" appears at first glance to be emphatic, implying that Andrew subsequently found someone else's brother. The issue is complicated by the fact that there is a significant alternate reading for πρῶτον, namely πρῶτος (attested *inter alia* by the first hand of א), a predicate adjective modifying the subject. This reading would yield the following translation: "He (Andrew) was the first one to find his own brother, Simon." As C. K. Barrett observes, this reading would "imply that after Andrew found his brother the other disciple found his; he therefore belonged to another pair of brother disciples, and must have been one of the sons of Zebedee, James or John."[37] The use of the adjective ἴδιον can support this line of interpretation further: Andrew was the first one to find his *own* brother, which could then imply that the other disciple subsequently found *his* own brother. But aside from the fact that the Fourth Gospel says nothing explicit about the anonymous follower of Jesus finding his own brother, the adjective ἴδιον is not necessarily emphatic; it can mean simply "his".[38] Furthermore, the reading πρῶτον has "early and diversified support" (p[66] p[75] A B et al) and is to be preferred.[39] This adverb may signify simply that "Andrew found Simon before he did anything else,"[40] though that is not the most natural way to understand it. The residual implication that Andrew may still have done something "second" is a matter that may be relevant for the interpretation of v. 43 below.

---

[35] Martyn, "History of the Johannine Community," 149–50.

[36] Cf. 2:10; 7:51; 10:40; 12:16; 15:18; 18:13; 19:39.

[37] C. Kingsley Barrett, *The Gospel According to St John: An Introduction with Commentary and Notes on the Greek Text* (2d ed.; London: SPCK, 1978), 181. Note the reference to "the sons of Zebedee" in John 21:2.

[38] See Friedrich Blass, Albert Debrunner, and Robert W. Funk. *A Greek Grammar of the New Testament and Other Early Christian Literature* (Chicago: University of Chicago Press, 1961), #286:1.

[39] Bruce M. Metzger, *A Textual Commentary on the Greek New Testament* (2d ed.; Stuttgart: Deutsche Bibelgesellschaft, 1994), 172.

[40] Barrett, *John*, 181–82.

Andrew in 1:43–51

The first three verses of this passage are particularly relevant for our investigation[41]:

⁴³The next day he wanted to go into Galilee, and he finds Philip. And Jesus says to him, "Follow me." ⁴⁴Now Philip was from Bethsaida, the city of Andrew and Peter (ἦν δὲ ὁ Φίλιππος ἀπὸ Βηθσαϊδά, ἐκ τῆς πόλεως ᾿Ανδρέου καὶ Πέτρου). ⁴⁵Philip finds Nathanael, and says to him: "We have found him of whom Moses wrote in the law (also the prophets), Jesus, the son of Joseph, from Nazareth."

The name "Andrew" appears in v. 44 only to indicate that Bethsaida, the city from which Philip came, was apparently also the hometown or the residence of Andrew and his brother, Simon Peter (cf. 12:21).[42] However, Andrew may also appear as a character in the ongoing narrative in v. 43 since the subject here is unclear: "The next day *he* wanted to go into Galilee and *he* finds Philip" (Τῇ ἐπαύριον ἠθέλησεν ἐξελθεῖν εἰς τὴν Γαλιλαίαν καὶ εὑρίσκει Φίλιππον). Does "he" refer to Jesus,[43] to Peter, or to Andrew? Raymond Brown comments: "Peter was last mentioned and so grammatically would be the best choice for subject. However, while John might tell us that Peter found Philip, he would scarcely stop to tell us that Peter wanted to go to Galilee. In the present sequence Jesus is probably meant to be the subject, although *in an earlier stage of the narrative Andrew may be have been subject.*"[44] According to Rudolf Bultmann, "it is strange that Jesus himself should find Philip; for this ... runs contrary to the idea, that is evidently consciously worked into the rest of the account, that one disciple brings the next disciple to Jesus." If Jesus found Philip, "there would ... be no reason for the πρῶτον or πρῶτος ['first'], which is said of Andrew in v. 41." Bultmann continues: "All becomes clear if the subject of εὑρίσκει ['he finds'] in v. 43 was originally one of the disciples who had already been called, either *Andrew*, who first finds Simon and then Philip, or else the disciple called at the same time as Andrew, who then finds Philip." Bultmann thinks Andrew must originally have been the subject of εὑρίσκει if πρῶτον is the correct reading in v. 41 (see above).[45] As Brown goes on to

---

[41] Beginning with v. 46, Nathanael takes center stage and Andrew, like Philip, disappears from the narrative.

[42] Capernaum appears to be their hometown in Mark 1:21, 29.

[43] Cf. RSV, NRSV: "The next day Jesus decided to go to Galilee. And he found Philip and said to him, 'Follow me'"; NIV: "The next day Jesus decided to leave for Galilee. Finding Philip, he said to him, 'Follow me.'" The NAB leaves the ambiguity intact: "The next day he decided to go to Galilee, and he found Philip. And Jesus said to him, 'Follow me.'"

[44] Brown, *John*, 81 (emphasis added).

[45] Rudolf Bultmann, *The Gospel of John: A Commentary* (trans. G. R. Beasley-Murray; Philadelphia: Westminster, 1971), 98; cf. 101, fn. 3: "If in v. 43 Andrew was the subj. of εὑρίσκει, then πρῶτον is demanded in v. 41; if it was Andrew's companion, then we must read πρῶτος." Bultmann considers the latter more probable (idem, *John*, 98, fn. 4). I have argued above that πρῶτον is the more probable reading in v. 41.

observe, following Bultmann, "the passage would make more sense if Andrew was the one to find Philip. ... this would explain the enigmatic v. 41: Andrew *first* found his brother Simon; then he found Philip."[46] Brown, like Bultmann, thinks that the evangelist has altered the text to make "Jesus the subject who now finds Philip," whereby "Jesus [now] takes the initiative."[47] Even in the text as it now stands, however, it is not at all certain that Jesus is the intended subject. Andrew can still be construed as the intended subject of v. 43a, given the (continuing) presence of the adverb πρῶτον ("first") in v. 41 in the final text of the Fourth Gospel: Andrew "first finds" Peter; he then wanted to go to Galilee where he (secondly) "finds" Philip who, like Andrew and Peter, came from Bethsaida (1:44; 12:21). If this is correct, then the reader must assume that Andrew told Philip what he had earlier told Simon about Jesus as the Messiah and then brought him to Jesus, as he earlier had brought Simon. As to why Andrew would "want to go to Galilee,"[48] the answer is to be found in the fact that, according to 12:21, Bethsaida is located there.[49]

In the first chapter of the Fourth Gospel, then, Andrew is the first link in the chain of (named) disciples who come to and find Jesus to be the fulfillment of Jewish messianic expectations. This chain extends from Andrew (1:35–41) through Simon Peter (1:41–42) and Philip (1:43–45) to Nathanael (1:45–51) whom Jesus declares to be the "Israelite in whom there is no guile" (1:47), who in turn acclaims Jesus as "the Son of God" and the "King of Israel" (1:48), who then receives Jesus' promise that he "will see greater things than these" (1:50), and to whom Jesus finally utters a promise meant for them all: "Truly, truly, I say to you (pl.), you (pl.) will see the heaven opened and the angels of God ascending and descending upon the Son of Man!" (1:51).

---

[46] Brown, *John*, 85.

[47] Ibid. For an impressive and largely convincing attempt to reconstruct a previous version of v. 43, see J. Louis Martyn, "We Have Found Elijah," in *The Gospel of John in Christian History: Essays for Interpreters* (New York: Paulist, 1979), 9–54. Martyn argues that v. 43 may once have read approximately as follows: "He (Andrew, secondly) finds Philip and says to him, 'We have found Elijah who comes to restore all things.' He brought Philip to Jesus. And looking at him, Jesus says, 'Follow me.'" This reconstruction is based partly on the fact that John the Baptist denies in 1:20–21 that he is the (a) Christ, (b) Elijah, and (c) "the prophet," i. e., the prophet-like-Moses promised in Deut 18:15 ("The Lord your God will raise up a prophet like me from among you"). New followers of Jesus find him to be (a) the Christ (Andrew in 1:41) and (c) "him of whom Moses wrote in the law," namely, "the prophet" (Philip in 1:45). The Fourth Gospel may originally have contained a reference to a new disciple finding Jesus to be (b) Elijah (*ex hypothesi* Andrew in 1:43). The writer of the text in its current form deleted the confession of Jesus as Elijah to conform with his own high Christology: the identification of Jesus as Elijah would problematically imply that the Word "experienced successive incarnations" (ibid., 52).

[48] The previous activity evidently took place in the Jordan Valley (cf. 1:28).

[49] Geographically Bethsaida was considered part of Galilee though politically it was then part of Gaulinitis. See Brown, *John*, 82; J. F. Strange, "Bethsaida," *ABD* 1:692–93.

Andrew in 6:1–14

In John 6, as in ch. 12, Andrew is briefly brought back on stage, once again along with Philip.[50] The order of their appearance is reversed, however: In contrast to ch. 1, Andrew appears after Philip in both passages, rather than before him.

John 6:1–14 depicts the Gospel's version of the Feeding of the Five Thousand (cf. Matt 14:13–21; Mark 6:32–44; Luke 9:10b–17; cf. Matt 15:32–39; Mark 8:1–10). Only in GJohn does Andrew play a role in this event, as does Philip. In the story, Jesus goes up a mountain and sits down with "his disciples" (6:3); Andrew and Philip evidently form part of this group (cf. 2:2). Both characters are portrayed as expressing the seemingly insurmountable problem of feeding the multitude that is coming to Jesus (6:4). When he sees the multitude, Jesus asks Philip: "Where shall we buy loaves of bread that these people may eat?" (6:5). A good question under the circumstances, but the narrator comments that Jesus said "these things in order to test him [Philip], for he [Jesus] knew what he was about to do." Philip fails the test for he answers with a realistic appraisal of the situation: Two hundred denarii (a substantial sum), he observes, would not be sufficient to buy enough to give each person even a little bread (6:7). Andrew, once again identified as the brother of Simon Peter (6:8), then pipes up and informs Jesus that "there is a lad here who has five barley loaves and two fish,"[51] and concludes with his own realistic appraisal of the situation: "but what are these things for so many?" (6:9).[52] Upon hearing this, Jesus utters a command that is evidently directed to both Philip and Andrew, since he uses a plural imperative: "Make (ποιήσατε) the people sit down" (6:10). Jesus then goes on to perform the multiplication of the loaves and the fishes so that all have more than enough; there is even enough bread fragments left over to fill twelve baskets (6:10–13). Jesus is subsequently proclaimed by those present to be "the prophet who is to come into the world" (6:14), which Jesus evidently understands as an attempt to "make him king" (6:15). Andrew's role in the story, like Philip's, serves merely to heighten the miraculous nature of the "sign" (6:14) Jesus performs. The effect on the reader is to suggest that Andrew and Philip have not understood the full implications

---

[50] This fact causes Bennema to treat the two characters together (Bennema, *Encountering Jesus*, 47–52). Philip appears once more, in 14:8–9, without Andrew.

[51] The text does not say that Andrew "brings" (Bennema, *Encountering Jesus*, 52; Stibbe, *John*, 37) or "introduces" the lad to Jesus (Culpepper, *Anatomy of the Fourth Gospel*, 120). Andrew merely indicates his presence to Jesus. There is no indication of any interaction between Jesus and the lad. Besides, as part of the multitude, the lad had "come" (6:3) to Jesus without the intervention of the disciples.

[52] On the basis of this verse, Bennema labels Andrew "resourceful" (Bennema, *Encountering Jesus*, 52), but that is surely overdrawn given Andrew's rhetorical question.

of the magnificent confessions they have made at the beginning, when Andrew found Jesus to be the Messiah (1:41) and Philip found him to be the prophet like Moses (1:45). The significance of noting once again that Andrew is Simon Peter's brother becomes evident in this light, for it was to the latter that Andrew had proclaimed, "We have found the Messiah!" Andrew, like Philip, evidently still has much to learn. They, along with the reader, will learn in the subsequent discourse that Jesus himself is the Bread of Life who has come down from heaven (6:35, 38, 41, 50) and that they must not "labor for the food that perishes, but for the food that remains to eternal life, which the Son of Man will give" to them (6:27; cf. 1:51; 6:53–58).

Andrew in 12:20–26

In this passage, Andrew (along with Philip) appears in a scene toward the end of Jesus' public ministry in connection with the desire of "certain Greeks" ("Ἕλληνές τινες) to "see Jesus" (cf. 1:39) at the Feast of Passover in Jerusalem (12:20–21; cf. 13:1). These "Greeks" come to Jesus of their own volition (thus not as the result of missionary activity on the part of Andrew or other disciples of Jesus) and are most probably to be identified as Gentile God-fearers who have some affinity with Judaism since they are described as "going up [to Jerusalem] in order that they might worship at the Feast" (12:20).[53] The "Greeks" first approach Philip, "the one from Bethsaida of Galilee" (cf. 1:44), who in turn reports (12:22a) their desire to see Jesus to Andrew (ἔρχεται ὁ Φίλιππος καὶ λέγει τῷ Ἀνδρέᾳ, lit., "Philip comes and tells Andrew"). Andrew and Philip then go and report this desire to Jesus (12:22b), though Andrew is given pride of place in the process, for the text literally reads "Andrew comes, also Philip, and they tell Jesus" (ἔρχεται Ἀνδρέας καὶ Φίλιππος καὶ λέγουσιν τῷ Ἰησοῦ). Jesus responds by making an oblique reference to his death as a form of glorification, once again referring to himself as the Son of Man: "The hour has come for the Son of Man to be glorified" (12:23). He continues: "Truly, truly I say to you, unless a grain of wheat falls in the earth and dies, it remains alone. But if it dies, it bears much fruit ..." (12:24; cf. 12:25–26). Verse 32 from the next unit may also be relevant here, where Jesus says: "And I, when I am

---

[53] See Martinus C. de Boer, *Johannine Perspectives on the Death of Jesus* (Contributions to Biblical Exegesis & Theology 17; Kampen: Kok Pharos, 1996), 190–191; idem, "The Depiction of 'the Jews' in John's Gospel: Matters of Behavior and Identity," in *Anti-Judaism and the Fourth Gospel* (ed. Reimund Bieringer et al.; Louisville, Ky.: Westminster John Knox, 2001), 141-57, here 144, fn. 17; J. Louis Martyn, "A Gentile Mission That Replaced an Earlier Jewish Mission?," in *Exploring the Gospel of John: In Honor of D. Moody Smith* (ed. R. Alan Culpepper and C. Clifton Black; Louisville, Ky.: Westminster John Knox, 1996), 124-44, esp. 131-33; J. McRay, "Greece," *ABD* 2:1092–98 (esp. 1093).

lifted up[54] from the earth, will draw *all people* to myself." Verse 34 in turn shows that Jesus will be "lifted up" or "exalted" as the Son of Man (cf. 3:14; 8:28).[55] Through his exaltation and glorification on the cross, Jesus, the Son of Man, will "draw" not only Jews but also Gentiles, here represented by a group of God-fearing "Greeks."

Summary and Conclusion

At the beginning of this study, we posed three questions: How is Andrew described? What does he do and say? What is his function in the story? The answers can be summarized as follows:

1. *How is Andrew described*? Andrew is described as the brother of Simon Peter (1:40; 6:8) and as a former disciple of John the Baptist whose testimony that Jesus is the Lamb of God caused Andrew to follow Jesus (1:35–40). He evidently comes from Bethsaida (1:44). He is subsequently included in the group of followers known as "his disciples" (2:2; 6:3). It may also be worth noting here that Andrew is the first (named) disciple in the public ministry of Jesus (1:41) and also the last named disciple in that public ministry (12:22).[56]

2. *What does Andrew do and say*? In 1:35–42, Andrew, along with an anonymous companion, follows Jesus upon hearing the testimony of John the Baptist, asks Jesus where he is staying, comes and sees, and stays with Jesus for a day. He finds his brother, Simon Peter, and says to him that he and his anonymous companion have found Jesus to be the Messiah. Andrew then brought his brother to Jesus. In one possible interpretation of 1:43, Andrew also wanted to go to Galilee where he finds Philip, who also comes from Bethsaida, under-

---

[54] The verb is ὑψόω which can mean "to lift up" and "to exalt" (cf. Acts 2:32–26; 5:30–31; Phil 2:9–11).

[55] See Martinus C. de Boer, "Johannine History and Johannine Theology: The Death of Jesus as the Exaltation and Glorification of the Son of Man," in *The Death of Jesus in the Fourth Gospel* (ed. Gilbert Van Belle; BETL 200; Louvain: Leuven University Press, 2007), 293–326.

[56] Andrew's distinctive prominence in the narrative has sometimes led to claims that he may in fact be the Beloved Disciple. So Klaus Berger, *Im Anfang war Johannes, Datierung und Theologie des vierten Evangeliums* (Stuttgart: Quell, 1997), 96–106, and earlier Ernst C. J. Lützelberger, *Die kirchliche Tradition über den Apostel Johannes und seine Schriften in ihrer Grundlosigkeit* (Leipzig: Brockhaus, 1840); for a summary of his views, see James H. Charlesworth, *The Beloved Disciple: Whose Witness Validates the Gospel of John?* (Valley Forge, Pa.: Trinity Press International, 1995), 179–80. This is very difficult to prove (Andrew is mentioned by name only in John 1–12 and the BD only in John 13–21) and overlooks Andrew's lesser role in 6:1–14, which would seem to count against the identification. Berger claims that Andrew became the disciple whom Jesus loved because he was "der Erstberufene" (the first one called) (Berger, *Im Anfang war Johannes*, 99). But Andrew in GJohn is not "called" by Jesus (see fn. 28 above). In none of the passages mentioning Andrew by name is there a hint of a special bond between him and Jesus.

stood by the narrator to be in Galilee (12:21). In 6:1-14, Andrew, who along with the other disciples is sitting with Jesus on a mountain while a large crowd is coming toward him, calls Jesus' attention to the presence of a lad with five barley loaves and two fish, while openly wondering about the adequacy of these supplies for such a large crowd (6:8-9). Andrew, along with Philip, makes the people gathered sit down (6:9), whereupon Jesus performs the "sign" of the multiplication of the loaves (and the fish). In 12:20-26, Andrew hears from Philip that certain Greeks want to see Jesus, whereupon he, accompanied by Philip, informs Jesus (12:22)

3. *What is his function (or role) in the story?* In 1:35-42, Andrew (together with an anonymous companion) functions as the first link in the chain of disciples that will eventually include his brother Simon Peter, Philip, and Nathanael (1:35-51). He (along with his anonymous companion) is the first person to confess Jesus as the Messiah of Jewish expectation (1:41). He does so to his brother Simon Peter whom he then brings to Jesus. In one possible reading of 1:43, he also finds Philip to whom by implication he also confessed his newfound faith in Jesus as the Messiah and whom he then also brought to Jesus. Andrew's role is not only to be the first follower of Jesus as the presumed Messiah, he is also the first missionary. In this double role, he probably functions as a paradigm for the reader,[57] who is also a disciple.[58] In 6:8-9, Andrew's realistic appraisal of the value of the five barley loaves and two fish for feeding a huge multitude functions as a foil for the miracle ("sign") Jesus is about to perform. With respect to the reader, Andrew functions to indicate that being a disciple involves learning that Jesus is more than the foundational messianic confession made by Andrew in 1:41 would indicate. In 12:22, Andrew, like Philip, functions not as a missionary who brings people to Jesus but as a messenger on behalf of "certain Greeks" who desire to "see Jesus" on their own. For the reader, he functions as a model intermediary between people who are attracted to Jesus and Jesus himself.

We may conclude, with Bennema, that Andrew in GJohn is not a complex personality but a "flat" one; he does not develop and his inner life remains completely hidden; Andrew is a one-dimensional "type" rather than an independent personality.[59] Only in ch. 1 does he reveal some traits: in 1:35-44, Andrew's "main trait is the ability to find people and bring them to Jesus,"[60] but that is not the case in chs. 6 and 12. Similarly, in ch. 1, he comes across as

---

[57] Cf. Culpepper, *Anatomy of the Fourth Gospel*, 120: "Like his more famous brother, though in a different way, he too is an appropriate model of the disciple that bears much fruit"; Bennema, *Encountering Jesus*, 51: Both Andrew and Philip in John 1 are "exemplary disciple-makers."

[58] John 6:60, 66-71 shows that "disciples" are not limited to the circle of the Twelve. A disciple is any believer.

[59] Bennema, *Encountering Jesus*, 203; cf. 13.

[60] Bennema, *Encountering Jesus*, 52.

"inquiring" (1:39) and "perceptive" (1:41),[61] but that cannot be said of his subsequent appearances. By being twice characterized as the brother of Simon Peter (1:40; 6:8) Andrew clearly remains in the latter's shadow.[62] But more importantly he remains in Jesus' shadow, the Jesus who is the mysterious, heavenly Son of Man who will be exalted and glorified on the cross. What the reader (and we may here include the contemporary reader) learns from the role of Andrew in the context of the four stories in which he appears in GJohn is that the confession of Jesus as the Messiah of Israel provides a good starting point for faith but does not fully capture the mystery of who He is.

---

[61] Bennema, *Encountering Jesus*, 52.
[62] Culpepper, *Anatomy of the Fourth Gospel*, 119.

Simon Peter:
An Ambiguous Character and His Narrative Career*

Michael Labahn

Peter and the Complexities of Becoming a Spokesman and a Shepherd of Jesus' Flock – Introductory Remarks

Peter, a fisherman (John 21:2–3) and perhaps the owner of a fishing boat (21:3), son of "John" (1:42), brother of Andrew (1:40), and originally called "Kephas" (1:42), is one of the most interesting and challenging characters in the Johannine story.[1] The Johannine Peter is a complex narrative figure[2] who appears in a number of episodes that depict him in positive, neutral, and negative ways. Thus, Peter serves an exemplary function as spokesman for the disciples in John 6:68–69, but is elsewhere depicted as a betrayer (18:15–27) who requires a belated reconciliation (21:15–17). In the final version of the Johannine narrative, Peter rises above his up-and-down characterization to become the shepherd of Jesus' flock, a role that Jesus attributes to himself in John 10.

---

* My thanks are extended to Tom Thatcher for checking the English in this essay.

[1] A number of studies have focused on Peter's characterization in the Gospel of John, e. g., Bradford B. Blaine, *Peter in the Gospel of John: The Making of an Authentic Disciple* (Academia Biblica 27; Atlanta: SBL, 2007); Judith Hartenstein, *Charakterisierung im Dialog: Maria Magdalena, Petrus, Thomas und die Mutter Jesu im Johannesevangelium im Kontext anderer frühchristlicher Darstellungen* (NTOA/SUNT 64; Göttingen: Vandenhoeck & Ruprecht, 2007); Patrick J. Hartin, "The Role of Peter in the Fourth Gospel," *Neot* 24 (1990): 49–61; Arthur H. Maynard, "The Role of Peter in the Fourth Gospel," *NTS* 30 (1984): 531–48; Joachim Kügler, "Der 'gegürtete' Hirte: Zum Petrusbild des Johannesevangeliums," *BK* 67 (2012): 221–26; Tanja Schultheiß, *Das Petrusbild im Johannesevangelium* (WUNT II/329; Tübingen: Mohr Siebeck, 2012); Lutz Simon, *Petrus und der Lieblingsjünger im Johannesevangelium: Amt und Autorität* (EHS.T 498; Frankfurt am Main: Lang, 1994); Timothy Wiarda, *Peter in the Gospels: Pattern, Personality and Relationship* (Tübingen: Mohr Siebeck, 2000); Ansgar Wucherpfennig, "Das Petrusamt im Johannesevangelium," in *Neutestamentliche Ämtermodelle im Kontext* (ed. Thomas Schmeller et al.; QD 239; Freiburg: Herder, 2010), 72–100.

[2] Cf. R. Alan Culpepper, *Anatomy of the Fourth Gospel: A Study in Literary Design* (repr.; Philadelphia: Fortress, 1987), 120: "Next to Jesus, Peter is the most complex character."

Peter in Jesus' Public Life

The Rock Identified

The call of Peter in the Gospel of John is a unique episode. The reader who is aware of the Synoptic call stories (Mark 1:16–20 par.) may be disappointed by John's suggestion that Peter was not the first disciple. Yet Peter is mentioned before he is officially acknowledged and called into discipleship by Jesus. In the Fourth Gospel, it is John the Baptist who first affects the story of discipleship in the Gospel by alerting two of his own followers to the presence of Jesus, the "Lamb of God" (John 1:36): "the two disciples heard him saying this and followed Jesus" (v. 37: … καὶ ἠκολούθησαν τῷ Ἰησοῦ). Jesus sees and accepts them, inviting them "to come and see!" (v. 39). Andrew, one of these two formerly anonymous disciples, is then introduced by reference to his brother, Simon Peter (v. 40). This is a fairly clear indication that the text presupposes an informed (implied) reader who knows something about Peter beyond what the text states[3] – it is a reference to the cultural memory of a potential reader.[4] It also is a reference to the first step in Peter's story. Andrew goes to his brother, and now he, like the Baptist before him, points Peter to Jesus as the Messiah (v. 41) and leads him to Jesus. Now it is Jesus who acknowledges Peter by identifying him as "Simon, the son of John."

In John, there is no Synoptic-like call for Peter to follow Jesus as a disciple, but rather a presentation of a new name: "You shall be called Kephas" (v. 42). In a typically Johannine manner, the narrator adds that Kephas means "rock," Greek "petros" (σὺ κληθήσῃ Κηφᾶς, ὃ ἑρμηνεύεται Πέτρος), the same word used earlier in the designation "Simon *Peter*" (v. 40). The translation here is a bit awkward, and it may be that a tradition similar to Matt 16:18 lies in the background of Peter's call-story. The narrator's reference, however, indicates that Simon Peter is called into discipleship as the "rock." Although John does not follow Matt in suggesting that Peter will be a rock for his community, it could be assumed that such a role is implicitly affirmed. In making a basic confession for all the disciples in John 6:68–69, Peter acts according to this role. He also takes the role of a spokesman on behalf of the other disciples in

---

[3] E. g., Hartenstein, *Charakterisierung im Dialog*, 158, 171. According to Hartenstein, *ibid.*, 173–209, the Johannine characterization as a whole is related to an informed reader who acknowledges different Early Christian traditions about Peter which are *essential* for a new understanding of Peter (206). It might be true that the Johannine Peter is an ambiguous character (on ambiguity in Johannine characterization, cf. Colleen M. Conway, "Speaking through Ambiguity: Minor Characters in the Fourth Gospel," *BibInt* 10 [2002]: 324–41) and that the narrator plays with the knowledge of his implied reader but it is a character that develops its meaning within the Johannine story according to its special post-Easter perspective.

[4] According to Schultheiß, *Petrusbild im Johannesevangelium*, 87, John 1:40 indicates a "vorausgesetzte (größere) Bekanntheit bzw. Bedeutung des Petrus."

13:24 (via the Beloved Disciple [v. 25]; 21:3). Further, even if John 21 is a later addition to the Gospel's narrative, Peter's fundamental role in Jesus' flock is already implied in his initial calling.[5] The call secures Peter's leading role without ignoring his subsequent misunderstanding and defection in John 13:6–20:10. In 20:19–23 (as a part of the group of disciples), and especially in 21:15–19, Peter's leading role among the disciples is acknowledged.[6] John's presentation, however, does not portray a psychological development of Peter's character.[7] In each scene, Peter is qualified by his own activity or by the activity of Jesus; in the first scene he is a passive narrative character mostly defined by receiving a new name through Jesus.[8]

Is there any hint as to why Peter is not the first disciple called in John, when he seems to play a leading role among the disciples later in the narrative?[9] The answer seems to lie in John's larger narrative strategy concerning the presentation of John the Baptist. The Fourth Gospel consistently portrays John the Baptist as subordinate to Jesus. In the call story, the Baptist, the "witness" already mentioned in the introductory logos-hymn, testifies to his own followers in order to deliver them to Jesus. Yet it is not John's witness, but rather Jesus' invitation, that makes them disciples. Similarly, as in the synoptic call stories, the Baptist is not involved directly in Peter's calling. John thus locates Peter's calling at a very early stage in the narrative while making it clear that Jesus, not John the Baptist, was responsible for Peter's faith.

Taking these observations together, Peter is of special importance for the narrative characterization of the disciples. He is mentioned as early as possible in the story, but is not directly associated with the Baptist. He gets a new symbolic name that corresponds to his Greek name: he is the "rock," and as such is

---

[5] With different reason Schultheiß, *Petrusbild im Johannesevangelium*, 87, argues by reference to the difference between "Erzählzeit" (story time) und "erzählter Zeit" (narrated time), that John 1:40–42 already opens a development which aims at the post-Easter ecclesiological role of Peter. In Schultheiß the interpretation of John 1:40–42 and 21:19, 22 are interrelated (Schultheiß, *Petrusbild im Johannesevangelium*, 89).

[6] D. Francois Tolmie, "The (not so) Good Shepherd. The Use of Shepherd Imagery in the Characterisation of Peter in the Fourth Gospel," in *Imagery in the Gospel of John: Terms, Forms, Themes, and Theology of Johannine Figurative Language* (ed. Jörg Frey et al.; WUNT 200; Tübingen: Mohr Siebeck, 2006), 353–67, here 357.

[7] As implied, e. g., by Tolmie, "The (not so) Good Shepherd," (see also figure on p. 362), Blaine, *Peter in the Gospel of John*, 38, and Ulrich Busse, *Das Johannesevangelium: Bildlichkeit, Diskurs und Ritual: Mit einer Bibliographie über den Zeitraum 1986–1998* (BETL 162; Louvain: Peeters, 2002), 83.

[8] Tobias Nicklas, *Ablösung und Verstrickung: "Juden" und Jüngergestalten als Charaktere der erzählten Welt des Johannesevangeliums und ihre Wirkung auf den impliziten Leser* (RST 60; Frankfurt am Main: Lang, 2001), 174.

[9] Christfried Böttrich, *Petrus: Fischer, Fels und Funktionär* (Biblische Gestalten 2; Leipzig: Evangelische Verlagsanstalt, 2001), 242, sees in the later calling of Peter a signal which is indicative of its importance in the Fourth Gospel.

qualified to be the spokesman for the others (and even to become the shepherd of Jesus' flock in the final shape of the narrative). Further, the narrative seems to assume some knowledge of Peter's portrayal in the Synoptics, although not in a way that necessarily implies direct dependence.

From the outset, then, the reader anticipates that Peter will be a strong character, an expectation that is only partially fulfilled. Peter appears more frequently in the Johannine story than most other figures, but the positive elements of his presentation are shadowed by his weaknesses, particularly his denial of his hero.

Peter, the Steady Confessor

Peter next appears in John 6. The narrator uses a technique similar to that employed in John 1 to highlight Peter's role in the episode.[10] The bread of life discourse follows a two-miracle cycle. Jesus provides real bread and fish to the crowd and then saves his disciples from distress in the storm on the Sea of Tiberias. In doing this, Jesus illustrates his identity as the life-giving bread that leads into eternal life. What is the role of Peter, formerly introduced as the "rock," in this episode?

Peter is first mentioned indirectly. Developing the problem that introduces the miracle story,[11] Jesus asks where they may buy bread for the crowd. The narrator indicates that this is a "test" of Philip (6:6: πειράζων αὐτόν) as a representative of the disciples, inasmuch as Jesus already knows what he intends to do. Two disciples respond: Philip, who informs both Jesus and the reader that 200 denarii would not buy enough food to feed the crowd (v. 7), and Andrew, who is again introduced as "the brother of Simon Peter" (v. 8). Andrew refers to a young man who has food (v. 9); Jesus blesses the food and delivers it (v. 11). The focus of the episode rests entirely on Jesus.

One might suggest that Peter is mentioned here simply to identify Andrew, but this reading overlooks the larger movement of the narrative. The reference to Peter at 6:8 is linked to the narrator's characterization of the episode as a "test." After the two miracles and the bread of life discourse (vss. 1–59), there is a schism among the disciples, here a larger group than the twelve who stay with Jesus (vss. 60–66). This division over Jesus provides a backdrop to display the results of the earlier "test," and here Peter plays the lead role as the model disciple, in specific contrast to opposing figures like "the Jews," the crowd, and the schismatic disciples, who clearly fail the test. Jesus asks the twelve if they

---

[10] See also Hartenstein, *Charakterisierung im Dialog*, 158, fn. 4.
[11] On my own interpretation of John 6, cf. Michael Labahn, *Offenbarung in Zeichen und Wort: Untersuchungen zur Vorgeschichte von Joh 6,1–25a und seiner Rezeption in der Brotrede* (WUNT II/117; Tübingen: Mohr Siebeck, 2000).

also plan to leave (v. 67). Peter, acting as their spokesman,[12] draws the right conclusion from the whole episode about Jesus' deeds and his self-revelation as the bread of eternal life, thereby demonstrating what it means to pass the test. He confesses exemplarily that Jesus is the one who "has words of eternal life (ῥήματα ζωῆς αἰωνίου ἔχεις). We believe and have come to know that you are the Holy One of God (εἶ ὁ ἅγιος τοῦ θεοῦ)" (6:68–69). Peter makes Christological claims that include a statement about the soteriological function of Jesus as Logos and Son. As presented throughout the story by the narrator and in his own words, Christ is the Holy One from God who provides eternal life.[13] Peter's reply adds another element that should not be overlooked. The confession of Jesus as the Holy One from God is based on "belief" and "understanding" (ἡμεῖς πεπιστεύκαμεν καὶ ἐγνώκαμεν, v. 69); both terms are Johannine markers of discipleship. Believing and understanding are the behavior of a model disciple, and here it is Peter, the "rock," who both confesses who Jesus is and illustrates what a true disciple does.

Peter's confession thus forms an *inclusio* with Jesus' question in 6:5. The correct answer to Jesus' test is to believe and to understand that there is no need to buy bread,[14] because Jesus himself is the bread that leads into eternal life and, building on the preceding miracle stories, the one who provides for the needs and dangers of the present life. At the same time, discipleship is an endangered way of living. The schism over Jesus' words not only separates true and false disciples, but also introduces another character who shows that believing and understanding is not a one-time decision but rather something that must continue throughout a true Christian's lifetime: Judas, one of the chosen twelve, is actually a "devil" (v. 70: εἷς διάβολός ἐστιν).[15] The narrator explains this appellation by noting that Judas Iscariot will betray Jesus, repeating a second time that this character is one of the twelve (v. 71: εἷς ἐκ τῶν δώδεκα). Both Peter and Judas belong to the twelve, but one of them is a devil; they thus serve as opposing figures within the characterization of the twelve.

Overall, John 6 is not only a story about Jesus' soteriological objectives but also a lesson for the reader on how to respond to the claims of Christ. In the episode about Jesus as bread of eternal life, Peter becomes a *model for the read-*

---

[12] Cf. Schultheiß, *Petrusbild im Johannesevangelium*, 98, 102.

[13] See also Cornelis Bennema, *Encountering Jesus: Character Studies in the Gospel of John* (Milton Keynes: Paternoster, 2009), 54–55.

[14] Differently, see Tom Thatcher, "Jesus, Judas, and Peter: Character by contrast in the Fourth Gospel," *BSac* 153 (1996): 435–38, who correctly raises the question of control, which is of basic importance for understanding Peter as a Johannine character. On John 6:68, Thatcher judges that Peter, "though genuine, was imperceptive. He was unable to please His Master because he did not understand the control structure of the relationship." As far as the confession of Peter could be related to Jesus' testing in 6:6, this confession is caused or even controlled by Jesus' activity.

[15] Cf. Schultheiß, *Petrusbild im Johannesevangelium*, 103; the reference to Judas also includes a theological interpretation of the historical situation behind the Fourth Gospel.

er. Interestingly, despite Peter's role as a rock and a model of faith, John does not show him in a consistently positive light, as will be seen in the following discussion.

Peter and the Passion – Strong Words and Severe Failure

From ch. 13 on, Peter is associated with the figure of the Beloved Disciple. This character seems to accept the authority of Peter (20:4–5), but is also portrayed as a special authority himself, representing the Johannine understanding of Jesus' death and resurrection. In contrast, Peter illustrates the need for a correct understanding of Jesus' death and resurrection through his misunderstandings and failures.

Too Quick to the Point: Peter's Misunderstanding in the Johannine Foot-Washing Episode (John 13:6–10)

Within the foot-washing episode of John 13, Peter is portrayed as a pseudo-hero whose words come quicker than his understanding (13:6–10). Of course, his misunderstanding of Jesus' actions is not to be taken as a historical reminiscence, but is rather a narrative-rhetorical strategy that leads readers into a Johannine understanding of Jesus. Following this strategy, Peter is presented as the disciple who acknowledges Jesus' role as master but does not accept Christ in the Johannine way. So Jesus and Peter become (at least partly) opponents in John 13:6–10, with the tension between them serving to produce a better understanding of Johannine Christology and ethics.

The subject of the story is indicated explicitly in John 13:1. This verse not only serves as a headline for the passion narrative – note that the language here is taken up and brought to its ultimate meaning in Jesus' final cry from the cross (John 19:28)[16] – but also defines the meaning of the foot-washing as a symbolic act of love that is related to the passion as an illustration of "a love to the end."[17] Indeed, the whole scene is explicitly connected to "the end;" Jesus knows that the devil has entered Judas, that God has handed all things over to him, and that he is returning to his Father (vss. 2–4). Against this backdrop, he begins to wash his disciples' feet (vss. 4–5). Peter, however, resists by questioning Jesus' actions: "O Master, are you going to wash my

---

[16] Cf. Michael Labahn, "'Verlassen' oder 'Vollendet': Ps 22 in der 'Johannespassion' zwischen Intratextualität und Intertextualität," in *Psalm 22 und die Passionsgeschichten der Evangelien* (ed. Dieter Sänger; BThSt 88; Neukirchen-Vluyn: Neukirchener Verlag, 2007), 111–53, here 136–41.

[17] Cf. Udo Schnelle, *Das Evangelium nach Johannes* (3d ed.; ThKNT 4; Leipzig: Evangelische Verlagsanstalt, 2004), 235.

feet?" (v. 6: κύριε, σύ μου νίπτεις τοὺς πόδας;). This resistance is in accordance with ancient social hierarchy: normally, only an inferior person may wash the feet of a superior. Yet in questioning Jesus, Peter ironically violates the very rules of honor and shame on which his objection is based: the disciple criticizes his master for not behaving as a master should. Peter's interruption stops the story so that the reader may gain insight into the point of Jesus' action: the footwashing defines the terms "master and servant." According to Peter's thinking, the true "master" (cf. Thomas' confession at 20:28: "my master and my God" [ὁ κύριός μου καὶ ὁ θεός μου]) cannot act like a servant. This reasoning, however, is not in line with the larger message of the Johannine foot-washing story, where Jesus' servile behavior symbolizes his "love to the end."

Jesus' reply reflects a post-Easter understanding of his act,[18] which Peter obviously cannot comprehend at this point in the narrative (v. 7). While Peter is not able to understand, the reader, encountering the narrative in post-Easter time and perspective, should understand the implication of Jesus' words: Christ is clearly referring to his impending death. Peter, unaware of the events to follow, remains unimpressed by Jesus' ambiguous explanation, and replies even more sharply: "Never will you wash my feet" (v. 8: οὐ μὴ νίψῃς μου τοὺς πόδας εἰς τὸν αἰῶνα). According to Jesus, however, the foot-washing is essential for people to become part of him. The symbolic act by which the master must do a servant's work is necessary for the disciple's salvation. As an act of love, the washing refers to the fellowship with Jesus that is established by his death on the cross (cf. 13:1), an act that also establishes a society of brotherly love within the community (13:34).

In response to Jesus' threat, Peter changes his posture, contradicting his own earlier word and actions in comic fashion. Whereas he previously forbade Jesus from washing his feet, he now commands Christ to bathe his entire body: κύριε, μὴ τοὺς πόδας μου μόνον ἀλλὰ καὶ τὰς χεῖρας καὶ τὴν κεφαλήν ("Master, do not wash only my feet, but also my hands and my head"). Again, Peter's reply provides an opportunity for Jesus to explain the foot-washing. Peter's words still operate on a material level,[19] indicating his failure to understand that the washing is a symbolic act with a deeper meaning. Further, by asking Jesus to do more than he is willing to do, Peter again tries to control the actions of his master.[20] Peter's comic behavior is an aid for the reader to follow the hints of the narrative and its leading character Jesus.

---

[18] See also Schultheiß, *Petrusbild im Johannesevangelium*, 123. On the Johannine post-Easter hermeneutic, cf. Christina Hoegen-Rohls, *Der nachösterliche Johannes: Die Abschiedsreden als hermeneutischer Schlüssel zum vierten Evangelium* (WUNT II/84; Tübingen: Mohr Siebeck, 1996). Peter Dschulnigg, *Jesus begegnen: Personen und ihre Bedeutung im Johannesevangelium* (Theologie 30; Münster: LIT, 2000), 57.

[19] See also Bennema, *Encountering Jesus*, 56.

[20] See also Thatcher, "Jesus, Judas, and Peter," 443.

Peter's role in this short scene is very limited. His vivid antics portray him as a sort of pseudo-hero who provides an opportunity for the real hero of the story to offer an interpretation of the foot-washing. Peter does not understand its meaning; and his mistake proceeds from a misconception of honor and shame and betrays a rigidly literalistic view of Jesus' words. But the Johannine Lord must *serve* his disciples in an act of love.

Only a Secondary Spokesman: Peter and the Beloved Disciple (John 13:21–30)

Peter appears a second time within the narrative frame of Jesus' final dinner with his disciples (13:21–30). In the privacy of a common meal, Jesus identifies his traitor, Judas. Jesus' proclamation that one of his own will betray him (v. 20) confuses the disciples (v. 21). As in John 6, Peter acts as spokesman for the group, but in this context he does not serve as the vehicle for the revelation of the clue to the betrayer's identity.[21] Rather, another character takes over this lead role: the Beloved Disciple, who reclines on Jesus' breast (v. 23), the most intimate place at the table and, importantly, the place Jesus himself occupied with the Father before the incarnation (1:18). In this case, the spokesman does not ask Jesus himself, but rather the privileged Beloved Disciple, to identify the traitor: "Simon Peter gestured to him to ask 'Who is the one of whom he is talking about?'" (νεύει οὖν τούτῳ Σίμων Πέτρος πυθέσθαι τίς ἂν εἴη περὶ οὗ λέγει). Peter's request is reported by the narrator and indirect speech is used.

From such an artificial narrative construction, it becomes evident that this episode serves not only to identify the traitor but also to establish the relationship between Peter and the Beloved Disciple within (and perhaps beyond[22]) the narrative. Is Peter now "subordinated"[23] or cast in a "supporting role,"[24] as claimed by Francis Moloney and Udo Schnelle? Or does John mean to suggest, as Craig Keener argues, only that a "friendly competition"[25] has surfaced between the two disciples? The characterization of Peter in the Fourth Gospel may play on the historical knowledge of John's real readers, and as such may represent John's reflection on authority structures in the church of his own time. Whether or not this is the case, within the world of the story, while Peter's courage and authority are not denied, the Beloved Disciple clearly

---

[21] See also Kügler, "Der 'gegürtete' Hirte," 221.

[22] It is highly debated whether Peter and the Beloved Disciple stand as ciphers for different trajectories of early Christianity, e. g., the Beloved Disciple representing Johannine Christianity and Peter another branch of mainstream Christianity; see Raymond E. Brown, *The Community of the Beloved Disciple* (New York: Paulist Press, 1979), 81–88.

[23] Francis J. Moloney, *The Gospel of John* (SP 4; Collegeville, Minn.: Liturgical Press, 1998), 383.

[24] Schnelle, *Evangelium nach Johannes*, 243.

[25] Craig S. Keener, *The Gospel of John: A Commentary* (2 vols., Peabody, Mass.: Hendrickson, 2003), 2.917.

comes to a quicker and better understanding of Jesus' death (cf. 19:25–27, 35). In the present context, as François Tolmie has noted, "the spokesman is forced to use another spokesman,"[26] and the Beloved Disciple becomes the primary spokesman who has more direct access to Jesus.

Greatest Loyalty and Greatest Misunderstanding

Peter appears a third time in John 13, now after the meal. Judas has left the room, and Jesus announces once again that he has been, and will be, glorified (13:31–32). Therefore, he must go to a place where his disciples cannot follow (v. 33), and before going there he leaves them with the new commandment to love (vss. 34–35).

Peter dares to ask Jesus directly where he is going. Jesus repeats that the disciples cannot follow him now, but will follow him later (13:36–37). As in the foot-washing scene, Peter ignores this vague explanation and resists a second time, demanding a more precise answer and claiming that he will give his life for his master in the same terms that Jesus had earlier used in describing himself as the "Good Shepherd:" "I will lay down my life for you" (cf. John 13:37c: **τὴν ψυχήν** μου **ὑπὲρ** σοῦ θήσω with John 10:11: Ἐγώ εἰμι ὁ ποιμὴν ὁ καλός. ὁ ποιμὴν ὁ καλὸς **τὴν ψυχὴν** αὐτοῦ τίθησιν **ὑπὲρ** τῶν προβάτων·).[27] Although the terms of Peter's declaration reflect the language of courage and loyalty within ancient discussions of state and friendship ethics,[28] he clearly misunderstands Jesus once again (see 13:6–10).[29] Peter's remark fails to take Jesus' claim seriously, and his error is highlighted immediately, as Jesus proclaims that Peter will deny him three times before the cock crows.

As noted below, both aspects of Peter's bold declaration, courage and failure, will be reflected in his subsequent appearances in the story. In view of this fact, Jesus' prediction concerning the denial, which silences Peter's protests for the time being, is not merely a caricature,[30] but rather will serve to lead the reader once again into a deeper understanding. Jesus' passion is not an accident caused by a failure of human courage or a lack of loyalty (cf. 18:4–9).

---

[26] Tolmie, "The (not so) Good Shepherd," 358.
[27] See here Tolmie, "The (not so) Good Shepherd," 364.
[28] Cf. e. g., Jens Schröter, "Sterben für die Freunde: Überlegungen zur Deutung des Todes Jesu im Johannesevangelium," in *Religionsgeschichte des Neuen Testaments* (ed. Axel von Dobbeler et al.; FS Klaus Berger; Tübingen: Francke, 2000), 263–87; Klaus Scholtissek, "'Eine größere Liebe als diese hat niemand, als wenn einer sein Leben hingibt für seine Freunde' (Joh 15,13): Die hellenistische Freundschaftsethik und das Johannesevangelium," in *Kontexte des Johannesevangeliums: Das vierte Evangelium in religions- und traditionsgeschichtlicher Perspektive* (ed. Jörg Frey et al.; WUNT 175; Tübingen: Mohr Siebeck, 2004), 413–39.
[29] According to Schultheiß, *Das Petrusbild im Johannesevangelium*, 103, Peter becomes a personification of misunderstanding "das von dem im Johannesevangelium vermittelten nachösterlichen Verständnis, und damit den Adressaten selbst, bereits überflügelt ist."
[30] So Schnelle, *Evangelium nach Johannes*, 247.

Further, giving one's life for others is a key element of Jesus' task and mission (cf. 10:11, 15; 15:13), but not a task of his disciple (cf. 3:15). Peter's willingness to give his life for Jesus is not in accordance with God's will but is rather a human idea that reflects Peter's unwillingness to accept Christ's words, an incomprehension that will soon be highlighted by Peter's denial and failure. In ch. 21, a possible re-reading (or "re-lecture") of the Johannine narrative by a later author, Peter will be presented after Jesus' earthly mission has ended as a shepherd of Christ's flock who finally gives his life as a follower of Jesus (21:18–19).

Misguided Courage (John 18:10–11)

In his narration of the garden arrest scene, John gives a name to a figure who remains anonymous in the synoptic tradition, designating Peter as the violent individual who raises the sword against the servant of the High Priest (cf. Mark 14:47 par.). John 18:10–11 shows once again that Peter is a loyal but misguided individual who is ready to take courage and risk his life for his master. The scene reflects Peter's own claim of 13:37, but also shows that he does not understand Jesus' rebuke of 13:38. Peter's completely misguided act is highlighted by its location in the narrative sequence: his resistance is irrelevant, in view of the fact that Jesus has already shown himself master of the situation by surrendering himself to be arrested and securing safe conduct for his followers (cf. 18:4–9).

Peter's aggressiveness is a human act that contradicts the motivation of the whole scene. He is not a hero but once again a pseudo-hero who misses the true point. The true point is marked by Jesus' closing rhetorical question, "The cup which the Father has given to me, shall I not drink it?" (v. 11).[31] While Jesus acts in accordance with his Father's will, Peter acts in accordance with his own will and thereby opposes Jesus. Here again, Peter represents a pre-Easter-understanding[32] that does not comprehend the true meaning of what is happening.

Losing his Courage: Peter as Threefold Denier (John 18:15–27)

The low point of Peter's career comes in the scene that follows Jesus' arrest. With the assistance of the Beloved Disciple (vss. 15, 16[33]), Peter enters the courtyard of the high priest. While Peter's desire to be close to his master

---

[31] See also Wiarda, *Peter in the Gospels*, 110.
[32] Differently Dschulnigg, *Jesus begegnen*, 62, who claims that Peter acts as a typical disciple not understanding the passion of the Son of Man.
[33] The anonymous "other disciple" (ἄλλος μαθητής) is best understood as another designation for the Beloved Disciple.

might be taken as a sign of courage, he utterly fails when invited to confess his relationship to Jesus (18:15–18, 25–27).

Peter is introduced in this sequence as a follower of Jesus (v. 15: ἠκολούθει δὲ τῷ Ἰησοῦ). In terms of physical location, he is first portrayed as an "outsider" (εἱστήκει … ἔξω), inasmuch as he cannot enter the courtyard of the house where Jesus has been taken. The "other disciple" provides access so that Peter can physically come inside ("he brought Peter in": εἰσήγαγεν τὸν Πέτρον; v. 16). Once inside, however, Peter's courage fails, and he not only refuses to confess Jesus but in fact denies his own discipleship. As he goes through the gate, the female doorkeeper asks if he "is one of this man's disciples" (ἐκ τῶν μαθητῶν εἶ τοῦ ἀνθρώπου τούτου); Peter replies, "I am not" (v. 17). In v. 18 Peter stands together with servants and officers of the high priest (μετ' αὐτῶν) at a charcoal fire. That means in narrative terms Peter becomes a companion of Jesus' opponents as Judas did previously in the arrest scene (cf. 18:5: … καὶ Ἰούδας ὁ παραδιδοὺς αὐτὸν μετ' αὐτῶν).

John now switches to another setting (18:19–24), in which Jesus refuses to answer the High Priest's questions about his disciples and his teaching. No such answers are necessary, because Jesus has always been entirely transparent,[34] as his accusers may readily discover by interrogating anyone who has heard him. One such listener, Peter, is standing in the courtyard, perhaps in close proximity to his master.[35] But Peter immediately undermines Jesus' self-defense by denying Christ once again, not under questioning by the High Priest, but rather at the simple inquiry of a bystander. The bystander's question follows the formula of the servant girl's earlier inquiry: "Aren't you also one of his disciples?" (μὴ καὶ σὺ ἐκ τῶν μαθητῶν αὐτοῦ;). Peter responds, as before, "I am not" (v. 25). Here, Peter is not only a hearer of Jesus' frank proclamation, but also a follower who refuses to testify for his master when asked to do so.[36] Peter's third denial is narrated without direct discourse. The brother

---

[34] The Greek term here is παρρησία, "frankness." During his public proclamation Jesus has always come across in all frankness to his hearers, who have accepted his preaching or dismissed it; cf. Michael Labahn, "Die παρρησία des Gottessohnes im Johannesevangelium: Theologische Hermeneutik und philosophisches Selbstverständnis," in *Kontexte des Johannesevangeliums* (ed. Frey et al.), 321–63, here 338–41.

[35] See here Ludger Schenke, *Johannes: Kommentar* (Kommentare zu den Evangelien; Düsseldorf: Patmos, 1998), 345. "Hearers of what I (=Jesus) said" (ἀκηκοότας τί ἐλάλησα αὐτοῖς) stand nearby around the charcoal fire, and this group includes Peter, who earlier had clearly articulated the Johannine confession (6:68–69).

[36] The question might be raised if Peter here is not only placed with opposing figures in the Johannine narrative but also portrayed in opposition to positive characters such as the Beloved Disciple, who enters the garden but does not deny Jesus; cf. Steven A. Hunt, "Nicodemus, Lazarus and the Fear of 'the Jews' in the Fourth Gospel," in *Repetition and Variation in the Fourth Gospel: Style, Text, Interpretation* (ed. Gilbert Van Belle et al.; BETL 223; Louvain: Peeters, 2009), 199–212, here 211, who finds that the other disciple has already made a confession; for a different interpretation of the relationship between the disciple and Peter, see, e. g., Hartenstein, *Charakterisierung im Dialog*, 166–67.

of the man who earlier had been injured by Peter's sword identifies him as a disciple of Jesus; Peter again as a highpoint of the storyline denies any connection with Jesus and, in accordance with Christ's prediction, "immediately a cock crowed" (18:27; cf. 13:38).

In this scene, Peter is shown to be willing to follow Jesus (although he can only do so with the help of the Beloved Disciple), but he crucially fails by denying his own discipleship and placing himself among the opponents of Jesus. He is not ready to follow Jesus and testify for him, and still clearly represents a limited, pre-Easter understanding. The Spirit-Paraclete has not been given because Jesus has not yet been glorified on the cross (cf. 20:22). This low point in Peter's career, then, does not function to demonstrate his psychological development as a narrative character, but rather serves the larger rhetorical function of helping John's reader understand the implications of Jesus' passion and crucifixion. Particularly here, the reader, viewing Peter's failure from a post-Easter perspective, clearly sees the differences in faith and discipleship before and after the cross.[37]

After Easter – What?

Peter re-appears in the narrative after the crucifixion and burial of Jesus. While his first appearance continues his prior characterization, he eventually receives a completely new role.

Still a Leader in Need of Understanding (John 20:2–10, 19–23)

Mary Magdalene finds Jesus' tomb open and empty and reports this information to the disciples. Peter again appears as the spokesman for the group and is mentioned before the Beloved Disciple (20:2)[38] when Mary addresses them. Both disciples quickly proceed to the tomb, and though the Beloved Disciple arrives first he waits for Peter, who enters first. This sequence might be read as a sign of the Beloved Disciple's ongoing respect for Peter. Once Peter sees that the grave is empty, the narrator notes the details and then allows the other disciple to enter, indicating that he "saw and believed." Because John makes no comparable statement regarding Peter, Cornelis Bennema finds no indication that Peter or the Beloved Disciple have "reached resurrection faith." Following this reading, John 20 is an instance of Johannine misunderstanding,

---

[37] With a slightly different argument see also, Schultheiß, *Das Petrusbild im Johannesevangelium*, 134.

[38] Cf. Tolmie, "The (not so) Good Shepherd," 359.

with both disciples returning to their homes because they fail to perceive the significance of what they have seen.[39]

Indeed, Peter seems to be puzzled, but not yet a believer.[40] Like the other disciples (possibly excluding the Beloved Disciple about whom the narrator comments: καὶ ἐπίστευσεν [v. 8b][41]), he needs an encounter with the risen Jesus, which is provided in a subsequent scene: 20:19–29, which leads him to post-Easter understanding. This encounter is the moment when the disciples experience eschatological joy (20:20). Now they are sent by Jesus, just as Jesus was sent by his Father, and they receive the Spirit-Paraclete (vss. 21–23) that guides into a post-Easter Johannine understanding of the Jesus story. Here, the reader finds a Johannine interpretation of Peter being the "rock" (1:42). Any knowledge about the special importance of Peter beyond the text finds its first Johannine re-interpretation by the disciples being sent and receiving the Spirit-Paraclete after Easter. However, in John 1–20, Peter is still simply one of the other disciples, regardless of his prior confessions and denials. After Easter, the disciples including Peter receive the Spirit as promised by Jesus and are ready to testify on Jesus' behalf.

No More a Sinner, but a True Shepherd (John 21:1–14, 15–19)

With good reason, scholars have often suggested that the Gospel of John originally ended with ch. 20. In its present form, however, the narrative contains two more episodes involving Peter, which strategically fill gaps left by the earlier chapters.[42] John 21 *relectures* John 1–20 by adding two new episodes.

The first episode, located on the shore of the Sea of Tiberias (John 21:1–14), narrates the third appearance of Jesus to his disciples after his resurrection.[43] It may well be read as a missionary commission, as symbolized by the miraculous catch of fish.[44] Within this narrative frame, Peter, acting again as spokes-

---

[39] Bennema, *Encountering Jesus*, 57.

[40] See also, e. g., Dschulnigg, *Jesus begegnen*, 66.

[41] According to Hartenstein, *Charakterisierung im Dialog*, 168, Peter does not believe, yet becomes a foil for the Beloved Disciple.

[42] According to Bennema, *Encountering Jesus*, 58, John 21 "concludes the story of Peter."

[43] See also Michael Labahn, "Beim Mahl am Kohlenfeuer trifft man sich wieder (Die Offenbarung beim wunderbaren Fischfang): Joh 21,1-14," in *Kompendium der frühchristlichen Wundererzählungen I: Die Wunder Jesu* (ed. Ruben Zimmermann et al.; Gütersloh: Gütersloher Verlagshaus, 2013), 778–91.

[44] See Thomas Söding, "Erscheinung, Vergebung und Sendung: Joh 21 als Zeugnis entwickelten Osterglaubens," in *Resurrection in the New Testament* (ed. Reimund Bieringer et al.; FS Jan Lambrecht; BETL 165; Louvain: Peeters, 2002), 207–32, here 209–10. For a somewhat different reading, see R. Alan Culpepper, "Designs for the Church in the Imagery of John 21:1-14," in *Imagery in the Gospel of John: Terms, Forms, Themes, and Theology of Johannine Figurative Language* (ed. Jörg Frey et al.; WUNT 200; Tübingen: Mohr Siebeck, 2006), 369–402, who points to an "ecclesiological imagery" in ch. 21 that may include "the preaching mission."

man for a group of disciples (v. 2), decides to go fishing; the others follow (v. 3). Their efforts, however, are unsuccessful (v. 3) until Jesus appears on the shore and tells them to drop their net on the other side of the boat (vss. 4–6). The Beloved Disciple identifies the stranger as Jesus and reports to Peter, whose leading role is thus highlighted: "it is the master." Upon hearing this news, Peter becomes aware of his nakedness and puts on his clothes. While Peter's nakedness is obviously explained by the fact that he is fishing, the narrator may intend an allusion here to his former sin of denial. Therefore, John 21:7 may refer to the shame of Peter's sin, which has been left unresolved in the preceding Johannine story.[45]

The episode ends with fishing success and then a common meal. Peter is again part of the community of Jesus' disciples (vss. 2–3 as Peter was in 20:19–23), who are invited to "catch" people by bringing them into the community (21:11). Peter's leading role in this enterprise is suggested by his act of dragging the net full of fish to shore (21:11). It is perhaps unsurprising that the narrative setting of John 21 borrows terms and motifs from John 6,[46] inasmuch as Peter's position here is similar to the role he has already taken in John 6.

A further *relecture* of the Johannine story provides a second episode that clarifies the relationships between Peter and Jesus and between Peter and the Beloved Disciple (21:15–25),[47] who was presented as a privileged mediator in the earlier fishing story. Peter's encounter with Jesus here builds on the narrative setting of the fishing story but repeats, varies, and adds new implications to the denial scene in the High Priest's courtyard in ch. 18. The short dialogue may suggest that Peter is becoming the shepherd of Jesus' flock, and thereby in some way stepping into Jesus' role as the Good Shepherd (John 10:1–18). The interplay of the characters within the dialogue, however, suggests that John 21:15–19 is aiming first at another issue, the problem of Peter's denial. The dialogue answers questions about Peter's failure that the earlier narratives have left open.

In an intimate scene, separating Jesus and Peter from the other disciples, Jesus addresses Peter by his full name, "Simon, son of John," so that the follow-

---

[45] Cf. Michael Labahn, "Fishing for Meaning: The Miraculous Catch of Fish in John 21," in *Wonders Never Cease: The Purpose of Narrating Miracle Stories in the New Testament and Its Religious Environment* (ed. idem et al.; European Studies on Christian origins/Library of New Testament Studies 288; London: T&T Clark, 2006), 125–45, here 137; Jean Zumstein, "Die Endredaktion des Johannesevangeliums (am Beispiel von Kapitel 21)," in idem, *Kreative Erinnerung: Relecture und Auslegung im Johannesevangelium* (2d ed.; ATANT 84; Zürich: Theologischer Verlag, 2004), 291–315, here 310.

[46] Cf. Martin Hasitschka, "Die beiden 'Zeichen' am See von Tiberias: Interpretation von Joh 6 in Verbindung mit Joh 21,1–14," *SNTU* 24 (1999): 85–102.

[47] See also Michael Labahn, "Peter's Rehabilitation (John 21:15-19) and the Adoption of Sinners: Remembering Jesus and Relecturing John," in *John, Jesus, and History, Vol. 2. Aspects of Historicity in John* (ed. Paul N. Anderson et al.; SBLSymS 44; Atlanta: Society of Biblical Literature, 2009), 335–48.

ing question receives special weight: "Do you love me more than those others?" Peter replies, "You know, Lord, I love you." This confession is answered by the charge to shepherd Jesus' lambs. Up to this point, nothing in the discussion has referred to Peter's denial. It seems to be a dialogue about Peter's special future role or symbolic function as shepherd for the early Christian community in relation to other disciples, as indicated by "more than these" (πλέον τούτων). Verse 16 repeats, as explicitly marked by the narrator, Jesus' cheerful question. Now it comes to the surface that the dialogue is not only about the charge to Peter to shepherd lambs. Jesus now simply asks, without reference to the other disciples, "Do you love me?" The reader has already been alerted that something special must be behind the discussion when the question is raised a third time. Again, the narrator marks the question with τὸ τρίτον, which explicitly refers back to another threefold action: Peter's three denials. This time the question uses another word for "to love" (φιλεῖς με) but otherwise simply repeats the content of v. 16: "Do you love me? (ἀγαπᾷς με;)." Repeatedly raising the question of one's love offends any loving partner and leads to sorrow, as the narrator now states explicitly: Peter felt sad because Jesus asked him for the third time, "Do you love me?" This third exchange ends like the two previous, but with Peter now heightening the emphasis on Jesus' knowledge and showing that he has moved from denial into deep love, as is well known to Jesus and now also to the readers, who accept Peter as a shepherd. Such a change represents a strong rehabilitation of Peter's character.[48]

In vss. 18–19 the dialogue comes to an end with a reference to Peter's death, which seems only loosely connected to the preceding context. However, these two verses add significantly to the exchange in vss. 15–17. Again, motifs and material from John 1–20 are taken up. In John 12:32–33, Jesus refers to his own death on the cross, and there are sufficient verbal agreements between 12:32–34 and John 21:18–19 to suggest a varied repetition of the announcement of the death of Peter, who, according to early Christian tradition (*Acts Pet.* 36–41; Tertullian *Scorp.* 15:3; Eusebius *Hist. eccl.* 2.25.8, 3.1.2), also died on a cross. At John 13:36 Peter professes his readiness to die for his master, which is questioned in 13:38. Now, it is Jesus who refers to Peter's death for the sake of his flock and it is Jesus who asks Peter to follow him, in contrast to Peter's own decision to "follow" Jesus at 18:15.

The inner logic of John 21:18–19 is that Peter will become a good shepherd by imitating Jesus' death: "The good shepherd lays down his life for the sheep" (10:11). Peter's earlier willingness to die for his master will thus finally be fulfilled, but under Jesus' control.[49] The reader may perhaps note one difference: while Peter dies as the shepherd *of* Jesus' flock, Jesus is still the "Good Shep-

---

[48] See also Dschulnigg, *Jesus begegnen*, 70.
[49] See also Bennema, *Encountering Jesus*, 60.

herd" who gives his life *for* his flock. Insofar the dialogue does not show much interest in serving the strategy of post-Easter hermeneutics as we have seen in the scene in John 1–20.

Jesus' address to Peter is a rehabilitation of Peter, a restoration that represents a forgiveness of the sin of denial and that will culminate in Peter's own death for the flock because of his faith in Jesus. He becomes a reliable follower and shepherd who is ready to die as his master's shepherd. Through this restoration, a former betrayer becomes a symbol of later church leaders' responsibility for their communities.

Still Second Place: A Final Note on Peter and the Beloved Disciple (21:20–23)

In a final narrative scene of the Fourth Gospel, the omniscient narrator states that Peter sees the Beloved Disciple following Jesus referring back to another scene of the Gospel, the identification of the traitor (v. 20). Referring back to ch. 13, the whole Johannine passion and resurrection narratives including the special role of the disciple as a witness beneath the cross and his believing returning out of the empty tomb is recalled. The Beloved Disciple is thus recalled as representative of Johannine faith who truly follows Jesus (ἀκολουθοῦντα).[50] In contrast to 13:24 (the identity of the traitor) now, Peter, the shepherd, asks Jesus directly for the future role of the Beloved Disciple (v. 21). Jesus' answer about the future life of the Beloved Disciple is of less interest for the characterization of Peter – after all, the final scene is more about the characterization of the Beloved Disciple than of Peter. However, it becomes clear that Peter the shepherd has no authority over him.[51] Even as the shepherd of Jesus' flock, Peter has to accept the Beloved Disciple's special role (21:21–23). The reappraisal of the character of Peter in John 21, thus, goes hand in hand with a revaluation of the Beloved disciple.

Summary

Peter is one of the most vividly portrayed characters in the Gospel of John. He is a complex figure who is driven by his desire, loyalty, and zeal for the main character of the narrative, Jesus. In each of his appearances, Peter is somehow related to Jesus. When the story centers on Jesus' questioning by the high

---

[50] In 18:15 Peter follows Jesus into the courtyard of the high priest and he fails. Even after his rehabilitation and after his new career as shepherd there is a reminder to his career low point. This reminder highlights again the role of the Beloved Disciple.

[51] Schnelle, *Evangelium nach Johannes*, 344: "Jesu Antwort hat zurückweisenden Charakter, das weitere Schicksal des Lieblingsjüngers geht Petrus nichts an, er hat keine Befugnis über ihn."

priest, Jesus refers to those who have heard his frank proclamation, obviously including Peter. In John 20:3–10 Peter is related to the absent (risen) Jesus.

Peter's path through the Fourth Gospel is characterized by ambiguity, leading him from his vocation and confession as a model for the reader into the depth of denial and finally into a post-Easter disciple guided by the Spirit-Paraclete (20:22) and into a leading role in the post-Easter community of Jesus (21:15–19). Within the Gospel narrative, Peter acts as a spokesman full of courage and also full of failure. Finally, Peter is the Rock and becomes the Pastor who loves Jesus and who is loved by Jesus even if he had failed from time to time – as such, he serves as a reminder for anyone who holds authority in a Christian community. Although he is portrayed as a loyal figure, his loyalty leads him to oppose his hero. He shows his belief and his disbelief and is portrayed in his limits and by the trust of his master.

There is no psychological development in Peter's figure, which often serves the larger rhetorical strategy of the story. Peter's misunderstandings and failures arise from his own human perception and activity, while his successes and leading role are products of Jesus' calling and activity (the confession of Peter might be an exception, but this must be read against his re-naming as the "rock"). When Peter acts on his own pre-Easter understanding, he fails; when he is called to follow, he plays a positive role as a model disciple or church leader (cf. 21:19 in contrast to 18:15). In this way, Peter plays a major role in the development of the Johannine post-Easter hermeneutic.

Philip:
A Connective Figure in Polyvalent Perspective

Paul N. Anderson

While Philip plays no special role in the Synoptics, he plays more of a central role in the Fourth Gospel. Aside from references to Peter and the Beloved Disciple, Philip is mentioned in John more often (a dozen times) than any of the other followers of Jesus – either male or female. Interestingly, he plays a connective role in the narrative, and in several ways.[1] At the outset of the Gospel, during the calling narrative, Philip plays the role of an intermediary, connecting Nathanael with Jesus (John 1:43–48). At the beginning of the feeding narrative, Philip is asked by Jesus to feed the crowd (6:5–7), a request that correlates with his hailing from the nearby town, Bethsaida. At the end of Jesus' public ministry, Philip plays a pivotal role in connecting Greek seekers with Jesus, leading to Jesus' declaration that his hour is fulfilled (12:21–23). And, leading into the first of the final discourses, Philip asks Jesus to show the disciples the Father (14:8–9), whereupon Jesus invites all to a connection with God. As such, Philip provides a bridge between others and Jesus at pivotal points, playing a prominent ambassadorial role. This essay will suggest how that is so in terms of polyvalent characterological analysis, leading to interpretive considerations.

Characterological Analysis
and a Polyvalent Reading of the Johannine Text

As an approach to the subject, I want to advocate a polyvalent reading of the Johannine text, as the way one approaches some of the Johannine riddles invariably impacts one's treatment of others.[2] Therefore, literary, historical,

---

[1] Cornelis Bennema rightly refers to Andrew and Philip as "finders of people" in his *Encountering Jesus: Character Studies in the Gospel of John* (Milton Keynes: Paternoster, 2009), 47–53.

[2] Indeed, one of the main reasons leading Johannine scholars have disagreed with each other regarding John's composition and development is the lack of agreement over how to approach the Johannine riddles. Cf. Paul N. Anderson, *The Riddles of the Fourth Gospel: An Introduction to John* (Minneapolis: Fortress, 2011). For a polyvalent approach to John's lit-

and theological issues must be considered together, at least to some degree. First, however, a brief treatment of characterization and approaches to John may be serviceable. Indeed, a rich diversity of characterological studies of the Fourth Gospel has surfaced in the last three decades, following Alan Culpepper's pivotal 1983 literary analysis,[3] which I still consider the most important single work in Johannine studies since the Martyn-Brown illumination of the Johannine situation a decade or two earlier.[4] As great strides have been made by new-literary gospel approaches in both important monographs[5] and collections,[6] I am less concerned than Cornelis Bennema regarding the dearth of, or need for, standardization in characterological studies, although I do appreciate

---

erary, historical, and theological dialectics, see Paul N. Anderson, "From One Dialogue to Another: Johannine Polyvalence From Origins to Receptions," in *Anatomies of Literary Criticism: The Past, Present and Futures of the Fourth Gospel as Literature* (ed. Tom Thatcher and Stephen D. Moore; Atlanta: SBL Press, 2008), 93–119.

[3] R. Alan Culpepper, *Anatomy of the Fourth Gospel: A Study in Literary Design* (Philadelphia: Fortress, 1983); following, of course, David Wead, *The Literary Devices of John's Gospel* (TD 4; Basel: Friedrich Reinhardt, 1970). Note the important studies following within a decade or so of Culpepper's work: Gail O'Day, *Revelation in the Fourth Gospel: Narrative Mode and Theological Claim* (Minneapolis: Fortress, 1986); Jeffrey L. Staley, *The Print's First Kiss: A Rhetorical Investigation of the Implied Reader in the Fourth Gospel* (SBLDS 82; Atlanta: SBL Press, 1988); Mark Stibbe, *John as Storyteller: Narrative Criticism and the Fourth Gospel* (Cambridge: Cambridge University Press, 1992). These books were followed by several important literary-critical collections, including *Semeia 53: The Fourth Gospel from a Literary Perspective* (ed. R. Alan Culpepper et al.; Atlanta: SBL Press, 1991); and the two volumes edited by Fernando Segovia, *What is John? Volume I: Readers and Readings of the Fourth Gospel*; and *What is John? Volume II: Literary and Social Readings of the Fourth Gospel* (Atlanta: SBL Press, 1996 and 1998).

[4] Paul N. Anderson, "Beyond the Shade of the Oak Tree: Recent Growth in Johannine Studies," *ExpTim* 119/8 (2008): 365–73. Note also the important interdisciplinary characteristics of Culpepper's work in pages 95–96 of Anderson, "From One Dialogue to Another."

[5] Note, for instance, the important advances in Johannine characterological studies sure to inform present and future investigations: Norman R. Peterson, *The Gospel of John and the Sociology of Light: Language and Characterization in the Fourth Gospel* (Valley Forge, Pa.; Trinity Press International, 1993); David R. Beck, *The Discipleship Paradigm: Readers and Anonymous Characters in the Fourth Gospel* (Biblical Interpretation Series 27; Leiden: E. J. Brill, 1997); Colleen M. Conway, *Men and Women in the Fourth Gospel: Gender and Johannine Characterization* (SBLDS 167; Atlanta: SBL Press 1999); Stan Harstine, *Moses as a Character in the Fourth Gospel: A Study of Ancient Reading Technique* (JSNTSup 229; London: Sheffield Academic Press, 2002).

[6] Additional important collections related to Johannine characterization studies include *The Gospel of John as Literature: An Anthology of Twentieth-Century Perspectives* (ed. Mark Stibbe; NTTS 17; Leiden: E. J. Brill, 1993); *Characterization in Biblical Literature* (ed. Elizabeth Struthers Malbon and Adele Berlin; Semeia 63; Atlanta: Scholars Press, 1993); *New Readings in John: Literary and Theological Perspectives: Essays from the Scandinavian Conference on the Fourth Gospel in Århus 1997* (ed. Johannes and Sigfred Pedersen; JSNTSup 182; Sheffield: Sheffield Academic Press, 1999); *Word, Theology, and Community in John; Festschrift for Robert Kysar* (ed. John Painter et al.; St. Louis, Mo.: Chalice Press, 2002); *A Feminist Companion to John* (ed. Amy-Jill Levine; 2 vols., Feminist Companion to the New Testament and Early Christian Writings 4 and 5; Sheffield: Sheffield Academic Press, 2003).

both the clarity and the nuance he and others bring to the discipline.[7] Characterological studies of course build upon other literary critical approaches,[8] and several book-length treatments of the characters in the Fourth Gospel have begun to treat the issue comprehensively, posing a great help to interpretation.[9]

Over and against many other literary analyses of John, however, part of what an interdisciplinary approach might contribute is a feel for how the characterization of Philip in the Johannine narrative might have been perceived and experienced by its original audiences. If Philip as a historical figure might have been familiar to late first-century audiences in Palestine or Asia Minor (or elsewhere), how might that inform his presentation in the Johannine story? Literature, especially religious literature, is far more polyvalent than a singular discipline will allow, so I want to argue for an interdisciplinary approach, even to characterological Gospel analysis, as a reflective consideration alongside other serviceable ways forward.

Against monovalent literary analyses alone, though such can be profitable in and of themselves,[10] a polyvalent analysis of the Johannine narrative focuses

---

[7] Cornelis Bennema, "A Theory of Character in the Fourth Gospel with Reference to Ancient and Modern Literature," BibInt 17/4 (2009): 375–421. I really appreciate his correct assertion that characters in the Fourth Gospel are rarely "flat" – they are more "round" in their presentation, as even minor characters play more than a singular role. On this matter, Bennema's appropriation of Yosef Ewen's continua of complexity, development, and penetration of characters for their analysis in the Fourth Gospel is highly serviceable, and that comes through in his work.

[8] On literary devices and operations in John, some of the most helpful works are Paul D. Duke, *Irony in the Fourth Gospel* (Louisville, Ky.: John Knox Press, 1985); Craig R. Koester, *Symbolism in the Fourth Gospel: Meaning, Mystery, Community* (2d ed.; Minneapolis: Fortress, 2003), esp. his chapter on representative figures, 33–77. An excellent collection of essays addressing a variety of related studies is *Interpretation* 49.1 on the Gospel of John (Oct. 1995), including Gail R. O'Day, "Toward a Narrative-Critical Reading of John" (341–46); R. Alan Culpepper, "The Plot of John's Story of Jesus" (347–58); Raymond F. Collins, "From John to the Beloved Disciple: An Essay on Johannine Characters" (359–69); Fernando F. Segovia, "The Significance of the Social Location in Reading John's Story" (370–78); and Urban C. von Wahlde, "The History and Social Context of the Johannine Community" (379–89).

[9] One of the first comprehensive treatments of characters in the Fourth Gospel was performed by Raymond F. Collins, *These Things Have Been Written: Studies on the Fourth Gospel* (Louvain Theological and Pastoral Monographs 2; Louvain: Peeters, 1990); followed by Adeline Fehribach, *The Women in the Life of the Bridegroom: A Feminist Historical-Literary Analysis of Female Characters in the Fourth Gospel* (Collegeville, Minn.: The Liturgical Press, 1998); Frances Taylor Gench, *Encounters with Jesus: Studies in the Gospel of John* (Louisville, Ky.: Westminster John Knox Press, 2007); Nicolas Farelly, *The Disciples in the Fourth Gospel: A Narrative Analysis of their Faith and Understanding* (WUNT II/290; Tübingen: Mohr Siebeck, 2010).

[10] Indeed, the integration of interdisciplinary inquiry can only proceed on the basis of more focused, limited disciplinary studies, having first ascertained the best approaches to particular issues and having conducted effective critical analyses of particular data. There is no substitute for narrow and disciplined approaches as foundations for further inquiry. However,

critically on the primary categories of the Johannine riddles, which are literary, historical, and theological.¹¹ Here one is reminded by Mikhail Bakhtin that literature itself is highly polyvalent in its origin, development, and operation.¹² Indeed, in narrative there is never a first word, nor a last word, as we ourselves are involved in the making of meaning – and dialogically so. And yet, various levels of dialogical operation deserve consideration, even when performing characterological analysis within Johannine fields of inquiry.¹³

Literary Issues

Literarily, while it is indeed perilous to infer too facilely a text's authorial purpose, the Johannine narrator *does* declare a purpose in John 20:31 and does so more clearly than any other biblical text.¹⁴ If the narrative is written to facilitate belief – both initial and abiding – the first characterological question is

---

the weakness lies with the conducting of one type of Gospel analysis to the exclusion of other worthy (and related) approaches. On this matter, Donald A. Carson's critical analysis of the recent Johannine secondary literature is worth noting: "The Challenge of the Balkanization of Johannine Studies," in *John, Jesus, and History, Vol. 1: Critical Assessments of Critical Views* (ed. Paul N. Anderson et al.; Symposium Series 44; Atlanta: SBL Press, 2007), 133–159.

¹¹ Having outlined eighteen major Johannine riddles in 2008 ("Polyvalence," 96–106), I expanded the lists to a dozen in each category and discussed them in greater detail in *Riddles*, 25–90, moving from theological, to historical, to literary riddles. For interpretation, though, the order must be reversed. The literary facts of the text must be considered first, followed by dealing with a host of history-related issues. Only then can theological subjects be understood and interpreted adequately and profitably. That being the case, characterological literary analyses precede historical considerations, and theological inferences hinge upon having done the earlier, foundational work well.

¹² In that sense, historical narrative functions identically to fictive narrative; both are rhetorical in their thrusts, employing characterological devices. Mikhail Bakhtin, *The Dialogic Imagination* (ed. Michael Holquist; Austin: University of Texas Press, 1981); see especially his essay, "Discourse in the Novel" (259–422), where he explores the multi-leveled character of living discourse within narrative.

¹³ In addition to characterological analysis, the following levels of dialogue apply to all of John's literary features, as noted by Paul D. Duke, *Irony in the Fourth Gospel* (Louisville, Ky.: John Knox Press, 1985); Craig R. Koester, *Symbolism in the Fourth Gospel: Meaning, Mystery, Community* (2d ed.; Minneapolis: Fortress, 2003), 33–77.

¹⁴ The dangers of the intentionalist fallacy are well noted by William K. Wimsatt, Jr. and Monroe C. Beardsley, "The Intentional Fallacy," in *The Verbal Icon: Studies in the Meaning of Poetry* (ed. William K. Wimsatt, Jr.; Lexington, Ky.: University of Kentucky Press, 1954), 3–18, and some Gospel scholars thus claim the Fourth Evangelist's purpose cannot be known and should not be sought. While appreciating the phenomenology of the text itself is a point worth making, the literary problem with such a judgment is the literary fact that the narrator declares his purpose in writing in John 20:31 – "These [things] are written that you might believe." Therefore, the signs, the witnesses, and the fulfilled word all contribute a basis for the reader's belief in Jesus as the Messiah/Christ (cf. Paul Anderson, *Navigating the Living Waters of the Gospel of John – On Wading with Children and Swimming with Elephants* [Pendle Hill Pamphlet 352; Wallingford, Pa.: Pendle Hill, 2000]), and characterization also plays a role in furthering that narrative purpose. The question is, how so?

what role characters in the narrative play in furthering (or detracting from) such a narratological goal.[15] Second, as the narrator draws the hearer/reader into the community of the author/editor dialogically, using corporate and personal references to the text's testimony ("we," "our," "his" claims, etc.), how is the audience drawn into the narrative personally and *identificationally* via characterological presentations? Put in reader-response terms, do characters play an attractive function or a repulsive one – or both? Third, how do the actions and words of characters *function rhetorically* as a means of furthering the plot of the narrative? More pointedly, when characters get it right, they offer positive examples to follow; when they misunderstand or get it wrong, they pose negative examples to be rejected by later audiences.[16] All three of these features are highly dialogical in their operations, so considering the apologetic, identificational, and rhetorical features of characterization in John poses valuable ways forward in terms of its literary analysis.

Historical Issues

Historically, characters also assume several levels of dialogical operation. First, *intratraditional dialogue* is also evident within the Johannine tradition, as earlier insights and perceptions are affirmed or amended by the narrator or a later editor. Therefore, character associations may also have shifted between earlier and later phases of the Johannine tradition, although establishing such distinctions is a notoriously difficult challenge. Nonetheless, if the later material included at least the Prologue, chapters 6, 15–17, 21, and eyewitness/Beloved Disciple references,[17] a literary basis for such judgments can be inferred in addition to explanatory asides. Second, *intertraditional dialogue* may be dis-

---

[15] Here Raymond Brown (*The Gospel According to John I [i–xii]*, [AB 29; New York: Doubleday, 1966], 1055–1061, and elsewhere) errs in pitting an appeal to abide (continuing faith) against a call to the gospel (initial faith), as though the presence of the former displaces the latter. While pastoral concerns are present, a plausible two-edition theory of composition exposes the fact that the main loci of the Johannine calls to abide are found in the later material (1:1–18; chs. 6, 15–17, 21; and "Beloved Disciple" and "eyewitness" references), leading to the likelihood that the first edition of the Johannine Gospel was apologetic in its call to faith, while the later material (addressing divisions in the community as exposed in the Johannine Epistles) calls for solidarity with Jesus and his community (Anderson, *Riddles*, 85–87). Therefore, the *purposes* of the Fourth Gospel were apologetic *and* pastoral.

[16] For an analysis of revelation and rhetoric, two dialogical modes in the Johannine narrative, see Paul N. Anderson, *The Christology of the Fourth Gospel: Its Unity and Disunity in the Light of John 6* (WUNT II/78; Tübingen: Mohr Siebeck, 1996; third printing with a new introduction, outlines, and epilogue. Eugene, Oreg.: Cascade Books, 2010), 194–97; and 17–24 of Paul N. Anderson, "The *Sitz im Leben* of the Johannine Bread of Life Discourse and Its Evolving Context," in *Critical Readings of John 6* (ed. R. Alan Culpepper; Biblical Interpretation Series; Leiden: E. J. Brill, 1997), 1–59.

[17] Of all the composition theories I am aware of, that of Barnabas Lindars accounts for John's major aporias in the most efficient and compelling way: *The Gospel of John* (NCB;

cerned where Johannine similarities and/or differences with other traditions seem telling. Of course, the Johannine narrators could not have had access to the full-fledged Synoptic traditions as we now know them, although at least general familiarity with some form of Mark is plausible.[18] While the Johannine tradition is pervasively autonomous and not dependent on alien sources or other traditions, differences may imply augmentation of or an alternative to Mark – with intentionality – at times dialectically so.[19] Third, *the history of the Johannine situation* plausibly informs the tension between history and theology in the Johannine narrative, and special sensitivity to the relation between the narratological presentation of characters and issues being faced by later audiences.[20]

Theological Issues

Theologically, several dialogical operations are also at work. First, the *dialectical thinking of the evangelist* must be kept in mind when performing any analysis of Johannine themes or subjects.[21] Rarely does the Fourth Evangelist address any one theme with unoffending consistency; he nearly always presents his subjects in both-and ways instead of either-or ones. This is why Johannine characters are rarely flat (with Bennema); the evangelist invariably presents textured portraits of individuals and groups, defying monodimensional portraitures. Second, as the *agency of the Revealer* within the divine-human discourse is the *Leitmotif* of the Johannine evangel, noting how characters embrace or reject the Mosaic Prophet[22] becomes a key for understanding their roles within the narra-

---

London: Oliphants, 1972), 47–54. John Ashton independently came to the same conclusion regarding Lindars' work in his *Understanding the Fourth Gospel* (Oxford: Oxford University Press, 1991), 199–204.

[18] For an analysis of John's intratraditional and intertraditional developments using John 6 as a case study, see Anderson, *Christology,* 167–251. For an outlining of an overall theory of John's composition and development and its *dialogical autonomy,* see Anderson, *Riddles,* 125–155.

[19] For sketches of the Johannine dialectical situation, see Anderson, *Christology,* 119–27 and 194–251; *Sitz im Leben,* 24–57; *Riddles,* 134–141.

[20] For an interdisciplinary analysis of how the rhetorical design of the Johannine dialogues likely functioned within the dialectical Johannine situation involving seven crises over seven decades, see Paul N. Anderson, "Bakhtin's Dialogism and the Corrective Rhetoric of the Johannine Misunderstanding Dialogue: Exposing Seven Crises in the Johannine Situation," in *Bakhtin and Genre Theory in Biblical Studies* (ed. Roland Boer; SemeiaSt 63; Atlanta: SBL Press, 2007), 133–59.

[21] On the dialectical thinking of the evangelist, see C. Kingsley Barrett, "The Dialectical Theology of St John," in his *New Testament Essays* (London: SPCK, 1972), 49–69; and Anderson, *Christology,* 137–165. See also the polarities regarding twelve major theological themes in John: Anderson, *Riddles,* 25–43.

[22] For twenty-four points of contact between the Johannine Father-Son relationship and the Prophet-like-Moses agency schema of Deuteronomy 18:15–22, see Paul N. Anderson, "The Having-Sent-Me Father – Aspects of Irony, Agency, and Encounter in the Johannine

tive. Put otherwise, those who are scandalized by the divine initiative are usually exposed as bearing fixations upon that which is of human initiative – the world, the religious, the political, the conventional; to respond in faith to that which is from above, one must first release one's grip on that which is of creaturely origin. Third, the intended overall effect of these dialogical operations is to evoke a personal response to the divine initiative on behalf of the hearer/reader. Therefore, the *existential response* to truth and its revelation within the human-divine discourse becomes the final interest of characterological analysis, but such cannot be ascertained effectively from a distance. It can only be embraced or rejected as a personal factor of authentic faith. To read the Johannine text well, therefore, will inevitably lead to crisis, and the degree to which a literary paradigm facilitates such an existential engagement could be seen as a measure of its hermeneutical value.

Revelation and Rhetoric

While all of these dialogical operations and levels are important factors to consider within Johannine interpretation, they need not be engaged in a linear way to be drawn effectively into one's analysis. In fact, one means of getting at several of them is to consider two dialogical modes within the narrative: *revelation* and *rhetoric*.[23] As the divine initiative scandalizes all that is of creaturely origin, so the Revealer, Moses, the Scriptures, the Baptizer, witnesses, the Father, Jesus' words and works, and the Spirit convey the saving/redeeming truth of God's love and light to the world. When human actants and discussants in the narrative respond in faith to God's agencies, from the narrator's perspective the result is life-producing; disbelief is conversely death-producing. Most of the narrative actions and discourses of Jesus in John are revelational – inviting audiences to make a response for or against the Revealer.[24] However, when the initiative shifts to a discussant or an actant – as people proclaim their self-assured knowledge or take bold actions – they are often exposed as unbelieving, or at least miscomprehending. And, in narrative, miscomprehension is always rhetorical, and correctively so.[25]

Therefore, when characters respond in faith to Jesus, or other divine agents in the narrative, they pose exemplary views and stances to be embraced and

---

Father-Son Relationship," 33–57 in *Semeia* 85 (1999). See also the rhetorical operations of the evangelist in creating a "sociology of light" in service to that goal in Peterson, *Sociology*.

[23] In addition to sources mentioned in fn. 16 and fn. 20, see Anderson, *Riddles*, 150–152.

[24] So Rudolf Bultmann puts it well regarding Jesus' Bread-of-Life declaration in John 6:35 (*The Gospel of John: A Commentary* [trans. G. R. Beasley-Murray, Philadelphia: Westminster, 1971], 227): "Jesus *gives* the bread of life in that he *is* the bread of life".

[25] With Mikhail Bakhtin, *Dialogic Imagination*, 403, stupidity and incomprehension in narrative rip the masks off of lofty characters in narrative, exposing flaws in their thinking and acting with ironic potency.

imitated. Negative or partial responses conversely expose flawed views and stances to be eschewed. And, when characters seize the initiative in speech or action, reader beware! That figure is likely to be exposed as miscomprehending, not only of the Revealer, but of the character of divine-human discourse, itself. Such representations are often crafted ironically, with corresponding embellishment. In performing characterological analyses of Gospel narratives, the following questions will thus be serviceable: a) How is a character presented on the surface level of the text, in terms of frequency and extent of presentation, and how does he or she further the apologetic thrust of the narrative? b) What is the character's relation to the protagonist and other characters in the narrative in relation to the development of its plot? c) How is a character presented in relation to other contemporary texts, and does the Johannine rendering cohere with or seem at odds with parallel or related traditions? d) What is the rhetorical thrust of a character's presentation, and how would such have been received by targeted audiences in the Johannine situation? In considering the characterization of Philip in the Fourth Gospel, these and other issues begin to be addressed in polyvalent ways.

The Characterization of Philip in John – the Surface Level of the Text

Before considering the rhetorical presentation of Philip in John, however, a few preliminary points deserve to be made about his presentation on the surface level of the text. These, of course, involve literary, historical, and theological considerations, and such are distinctive for every character analyzed.

Literary Levels

On a surface literary level, Philip is introduced in the four passages mentioned above, yet none of these describes him in lengthy ways. He is only mentioned directly in a total of eleven verses in John, and three of the four passages reference him only within a two- or three-sentence section. On the other hand, Philip plays an important set of roles with relation to the protagonist, Jesus and appears within larger, important scenarios. He brings disciples to Jesus (John 1:19–51), is tested by Jesus (John 6:1–71), brings Greek seekers to Jesus (John 12:9–50) and plays a leading support-role, asking Jesus a question as a means of providing a rhetorical platform on which to launch into the first of his farewell discourses (John 14:1–31). In these ways, Philip furthers the plot of the narrative consistently and progressively. Is his presentation, though, positive, negative, or a mixture?

Pivotally, Philip's first appearance heralds themes that are echoed later in the narrative. Jesus' introductory invitation for him to "follow me" is matched by a climactic exhortation for Peter to do the same – as book-ends of the narrative (John 1:43; 21:19, 22). As Jesus' true sheep know his voice and follow him (John 10:27), and as to serve Jesus is to follow him (John 12:26), Philip's recognizing and following Jesus at the outset signals the exemplary path for others to follow. While the narrator is silent on whether or not Philip follows Jesus directly, not only does he declare to Nathanael that Jesus is "the one of whom Moses and the prophets wrote," as Jesus claims of himself later (John 1:45; 5:46), but Nathanael proclaims Jesus "King of Israel," even as the crowd does at the triumphal entry (John 1:49; 12:13). Philip refers to Jesus also as the familiar "son of Joseph," as do others (John 1:45; 6:42), but in contrast to the miscomprehending Judean and Galilean crowds, Philip and Nathanael get it right. As striking evidence of his authentic responsiveness, Philip echoes the very words of Jesus as his imitative witness, declaring to Nathanael: "Come and see" (John 1:39, 46).[26] Philip is thus presented in the opening scene not only as a willing follower of Jesus but as an effective and imitative agent of the Lord.

The presentation of Philip in John 6 bears intra- and intertraditional implications. Within the Johannine tradition, the reader is reminded again that Philip and Andrew (and thus Peter) are connected (John 1:44; 6:5–7; 12:22), and one is reminded of the Bethsaida link intertraditionally in Mark (mentioned in both Markan feeding narratives, Mark 6:45; 8:22) and intratraditionally in John 1:44 and 12:21. While a similarity exists between the Johannine and Markan feeding narratives regarding the cost of feeding the multitude being 200 denarii (Mark 6:37; John 6:7), in Mark the disciples reference the cost as an objecting question; in John, Philip simply asserts that such an amount of food would not be enough for each to have even a bit. The Markan thrust features the disciples' anxiety over perceived insufficiency of funds; the Johannine notes a realism-oriented concern over the insufficiency of loaves to satisfy such a multitude, even if purchased. Might these two very different sentiments reflect a Johannine knowing contrast to Mark's rendering?[27] Another distinctive fea-

---

[26] Likewise, the Samaritan woman issues the same invitation to her townspeople in John 4:29 and they believe. And, the crowd's caring for Jesus is echoed by an invitation to "come and see" the tomb of Lazarus in 11:34, after which Jesus weeps.

[27] Here John's differences with Mark seem to reflect simply a different rendering of the account, although other differences with Mark may suggest a knowing set of contrasts in ways designed to either provide an alternative view, or at times, to set the record straight; with Richard Bauckham, "John for Readers of Mark," in *The Gospel for All Christians: Rethinking the Gospel Audiences* (Grand Rapids, Mich.: Eerdmans, 1998), 147–71; cf. Paul N. Anderson, *The Fourth Gospel and the Quest for Jesus: Modern Foundations Reconsidered* (Library of New Testament Studies 321; London: T&T Clark), 104–112, 128–173. If familiarity with Mark can be inferred (cf. Steven A. Hunt, *Rewriting the Feeding of Five Thousand: John 6.1–15 as a Test Case for Johannine Dependence on the Synoptic Gospels*; SBL 125; New York: Peter Lang, 2011), John's presentation of Philip is less negative than Mark's, as he is presented as simply commenting on the realism of the feeding challenge rather than objecting to the instruction to feed the crowd.

ture is that while the Synoptic Jesus is often tested by religious leaders, here Jesus tests Philip.[28] Andrew brings meager assistance, connecting Jesus with a lad having five loaves and two fishes, which Jesus multiplies, and by which the crowd is satisfied.

Chapter 12 presents another pivotal scene where Philip connects Greek seekers of Jesus with the Lord, after which Jesus declares the completion of his mission and time for the Son of Man to be glorified (John 12:20–23).[29] Ironically, whereas the Judean leaders question whether Jesus might launch a mission to the Greeks in the Diaspora (John 7:35), here Greeks come to him seeking redemption. The second Johannine mention of Bethsaida here also offers a clue to cross-cultural associations with Philip, pointing also to cross-cultural features of Jesus' own mission.[30] If the appointing of twelve disciples (Mark 3:14) had anything to do with restoring the rest of the twelve lost tribes of Israel scattered in the Diaspora, the linking of Hellenic Bethsaida with the cross-cultural reception of Greeks visiting Jerusalem at Passover is telling. In the Synoptics and John alike, Jesus can be seen to have a vision for the restoration of the fallen house of Israel, and in John Philip plays a central role in that cross-cultural mission.

The final scene in which Philip appears in the Johannine narrative (although he may be implicitly referenced as one of "two other disciples" mentioned in John 21:2) shows him providing a platform for Jesus to declare his relation to the Father as the opening thrust of his final discourses. As Thomas had just asked how to know the way, whereupon Jesus declares that he is the way, the truth, and the life, Philip serves a similar role. Following on Jesus' declaring the visibility of the Father through his revelatory work, Philip requests a clearer rendering of the Father's image (John 14:7–8). Jesus then declares his revelation of the Father through his works and words, promising also that the Holy Spirit would continue that disclosure process even after his own departure. Again, on a surface, literary level of the text, Philip plays a connective role between Jesus and others – now connecting past and future audiences, becoming an effective agent of Jesus' own mission and ministering effectively on his behalf.

---

[28] In John, rather than Jesus being tested by religious leaders, as in the Synoptics and the *Pericope Adulterae* (Matt 16:1; 19:3; 22:18, 35; Mark 8:11; 10:2; 12:15; Luke 10:25; 11:16; John 8:6), Jesus is the one who tests his followers (John 6:6).

[29] For the leading analysis of quest narratives in the Fourth Gospel, see John Painter's important work: *The Quest for the Messiah: The History, Literature and Theology of the Johannine Community* (2d ed., rev. and enl.: London: T&T Clark, 2006).

[30] Here John and Mark, the Bi-Optic Gospels, corroborate the cross-cultural mission of Jesus in ways similar-yet-distinctive (as they do a variety of other issues, cf. Anderson, *Quest*, 128–145). Just as the Markan Jesus ministered among the Greco-Roman Decapolis cities (Mark 5:20; 7:31), took his disciples to "the other side" of the lake to the land of the Gerasenes (emphasizing alterity, Mark 4:35–5:1), ministered to the Syrophoenecian Gentile woman (Mark 7:26), and invited Peter's confession at the polytheistic worship site of Caesarea Philippi (Mark 8:27–29), so the Johannine Jesus climactically reaches out to the Greek seekers.

Historical Levels

On the first level of history, the repeated linking of Philip with Bethsaida (John 1:44; 12:21) is significant. Josephus (*Ant.* 18:27) claims that around 30 C.E. the town of Bethsaida was elevated to the status of a "city" (πόλις) by Philip, son of Herod the Great, and that he renamed it Julias, after the Emperor's daughter or wife.[31] Four years later, Philip is reported to have died and been buried in Julias (thus, Bethsaida, *Ant.* 18:108), and the prominence of the city would have been impressive at the time. These references by Josephus are corroborated by archaeological finds at the primary site associated with Bethsaida, to the east of the Jordan River, on the north shore of the Sea of Galilee. In addition, fishing equipment has been found (hooks, weights, etc.), so this is a likely site for fishermen such as Peter and Andrew to have lived (John 1:44).[32] It is also understandable that Jesus would have asked him to procure food for the crowd to eat before the feeding in John 6 (see also references to Bethsaida in Mark 6:45 and 8:22).

If indeed Philip had Hellenistic societal connections, with a recognizably Greek name, it is no wonder that Greeks came specifically to Philip in John 12, looking for Jesus.[33] The repeated mention of Bethsaida (John 12:21) thus points to such a cross-cultural role and associative link. This event is also pivotal in the narrative, as the Pharisees had just exclaimed in dismay that "the whole world" is going after Jesus (John 12:19), and it is followed by Jesus' declaration that the hour had come for the Son of Man to be glorified (John 12:23). While the implications here are highly theological, something of the cross-cultural thrust of Jesus' mission here becomes palpable.

The final scene in which Philip is explicitly present in the Johannine narrative follows the last supper, where the question of Thomas is followed by his request: "Lord, show us the Father, and we shall be satisfied" (John 14:8). Jesus employs this request as a platform to emphasize his agency from the Father and the sending of the Spirit. Despite being rendered in distinctive terms, the

---

[31] Josephus' first reference is to the wife of the Emperor, although he later in the same passage connects the name Julias with his daughter. In the view of Nikos Kokkinos, "The Foundation of Bethsaida-Julias by Philip the Tetrarch," *JJS* 59/2 (2008): 236–51, the name change refers to the daughter of Caesar, not the wife.

[32] See the collections of essays edited by Rami Arav and Richard A. Freund, *Bethsaida: A City by the North Shore of the Sea of Galilee*; Vols. 1–4 (Kirksville, Mo.: Truman State University Press, 1995, 1999, 2004, 2009), although some scholars have proposed alternative sites to the south or east. While the sediment of the river has built up over the years, so that the village site is now over a mile from the shore, archaeological finds have produced incense shovels and a temple area, suggesting Greco-Roman cultic practices and worship sites.

[33] As a common Greek name, especially following Philip II, king of Macedonia and father of Alexander the Great, it is not surprising that the son of Herod would have been given the name Philip, and the inclusion of a Galilean Jew with a Hellenistic name among the twelve suggests something of the cross-cultural intentionality of Jesus' mission.

Johannine Jesus promises the ongoing guidance of the Spirit (John 14–16) in ways parallel to the promise of the Spirit's guidance in the Synoptics (Matt 10:17–20; Mark 13:11; Luke 12:11–12), expanding a promise of Jesus upon the platform Philip's request provides. While Philip's role here is highly theological, with Synoptic literary parallels, it is simply interesting to note Johannine alternative presentations of traditional Jesus-sayings – evoked by Philip's request.

Theological Levels

Theologically, Philip plays a role of extending the agency of the Son not only to the world, but also to diverse peoples in the world. As one who echoes the calls to discipleship of Jesus, trusts the Lord authentically, connects seekers with the Jewish Messiah, and provides a platform for Jesus' final teachings, Philip extends the reconciling work of the redeemer to other individuals and groups. As such, he further becomes a connective bridge between the narrative texts and later audiences in different phases of the tradition's development, reaching also Hellenistic audiences as well as Jewish ones on behalf of Jesus.

On these levels, it is not problematic to see Philip portrayed characterologically as a real person from the cross-cultural town of Bethsaida, who played particular roles within the narrative serving both literary and theological purposes. Whether the first level of the text's narrative bears any historical claim is impossible to ascertain – or to deny; it is, nonetheless, realistic in its rendering. In that sense, it also coheres with other presentations of Philip elsewhere in the New Testament and also in the writings of Eusebius.

Philip's Presentation in the Synoptics, Acts, and Eusebius – A Familiar Figure

Given that Philip is presented as coming from the Greek village, Bethsaida, in John 1, it is not surprising that he is also presented as a cross-cultural bridge in such church histories as Acts (only incidentally in the Synoptics) and the writings of Eusebius. Therefore, a brief noting of parallel presentations outside of John may suggest aspects of familiarity for later audiences.[34]

---

[34] For an overall theory of interfluentiality between the Johannine and the Synoptic traditions, see Anderson, *Quest*, 101–26. Within this larger theory, (a) early pre-Markan and Johannine traditions likely had some interfluential contact, (b) the first edition of John appears to augment and provide an alternative to written Mark (perhaps heard by the evangelist as it was delivered among the churches); (c) Luke departs from Mark and sides with John no fewer than six dozen times, reflecting Luke's access to the Johannine tradition, probably in its oral stages of delivery; (d) as the Q tradition shows some affinities with the Johannine tradition, even including Johannine language on the Father-Son relationship, the early Johan-

The Synoptics

Philip appears in other Gospel narratives only in the Markan calling narrative (Mark 3:18; cf. Matt 10:3; Luke 6:14) and simply is listed alongside the other twelve: between Andrew and Bartholomew in Mark and between John and Bartholomew in Matthew and Luke. Might the extensive presentation of Philip in the Fourth Gospel have influenced Matthew's and Luke's shifting of the association of Philip with John instead of Andrew? Perhaps, although Philip is also presented alongside Andrew several times in John, so that likelihood is not impressive. Of interest is the far more extensive presentation of such disciples as Philip and Andrew in the Fourth Gospel in contrast to the Synoptics, as well as the featuring of Nathanael, who is mentioned by name only in the Fourth Gospel.[35]

Acts 1

Acts 1:13 connects Philip with Andrew, as he is likewise paired in Mark 3:18 and John 1:44; 6:5–7; 12:22. This may be simply a factor of an association, as the Johannine narrator mentions twice that Philip (likewise Andrew and Peter) is a resident of the town of Bethsaida, but if Philip indeed had a cross-cultural background, it is noteworthy that in Acts he also connects representatives of various people groups with Jesus and his movement. The distinctively cross-cultural bridge-work of Philip's connecting the Greeks to Jesus in John 12 and the rest of Acts is intriguing indeed!

Acts 6

A heightened featuring of Philip's cross-cultural identity and work is featured in Acts 6, where a disciple named "Philip" is chosen as a "deacon" by the "apostles" in order to care for the Hellenistic Jewish believers. While modern scholars have distinguished Philip the apostle from Philip the deacon and evangelist in Acts, such a distinction is nowhere made within Acts, nor is it asserted in the early church. After Philip's first appearance with the eleven apostles in Jerusalem after the ascension of Jesus (Acts 1:9–14), the next appearance of a person named "Philip" is in Jerusalem, where, in response to

---

nine tradition may have played a formative role in the development of the Q tradition; (e) later Matthean and Johannine traditions appear to have some interfluential contact involving dialectical exchanges over Christian mission and modes of church governance. Whether or not the Q tradition follows the Johannine rendering in associating John and Philip together, Luke appears to follow either Mark or the Johannine tradition when linking Philip and Andrew together again in Acts 1:13.

[35] On this associative basis some interpreters have connected Nathanael in John with Bartholomew, but this can be nothing more than a guess, however, perhaps in the interest of inferring Nathanael's being one of the twelve.

the Hellenists' feeling that their widows were being neglected by the Hebrews in the daily distribution of food, "the twelve" invite seven deacons to be chosen, stipulating that they be "of good standing, full of the Spirit and of wisdom" (Acts 6:1–7). One of those chosen is named "Philip," listed between Stephen (the main character in the next chapter) and Prochorus (associated in later traditions with John of Patmos). Is this the same person as the apostle, though, or is it another Philip?[36]

Acts 8

The next appearances of Philip occur in Acts 8, where he comes "down from Jerusalem" and preaches about Jesus as the Messiah/Christ (Acts 8:5–13). As a result of his preaching, exorcisms and healings, many Samaritans come to believe in Jesus and are baptized, although some do not receive the Holy Spirit until Peter and John lay their hands upon them (Acts 8:14–25). Meanwhile, Philip is sent away by an angel to the Gaza road, where he encounters the Ethiopian eunuch – an official of the Queen's court – to whom he ministers successfully (Acts 8:26–39). Philip subsequently finds himself at Azotus, and he preaches at various villages until he arrives at Caesarea (Acts 8:40).

Acts 21

Philip is later visited by Paul and Luke after traveling to Caesarea from Tyre and Ptolemais (Acts 21:8–9); they stay with "Philip the evangelist" and his four daughters, who have the gift of prophecy (affirming Joel 2:28–32; Acts 2:17). Here Philip continues to serve as a connection-builder; he indirectly connects Paul with the apostolic leadership back in Jerusalem, which marks a pivotal turn, then, in Paul's final witness-journey to Rome.

While the identification of Philip the evangelist as one of the seven deacons in Acts 6 is made explicitly in Acts 21:8, this does not necessarily deny his identification as one of the apostles, as described explicitly in Acts 1 and implicitly in Acts 8. One can appreciate how later traditions debated whether to distinguish Philip the deacon/evangelist from Philip the apostle, and yet the second-century tradition that Philip the apostle traveled throughout Asia Minor, along with his prophesying daughters (Acts 21:9) remains strong. Given that Philip's Martyrium in Hierapolis, near Colossae and Laodicea, would have associated the apostle's cross-cultural ministry to have extended to Asia Minor, his role as a connective intermediary continues beyond his representations in John and Acts.

---

[36] While "the apostles" pray for those chosen in Acts 6:6, the text does not directly support a dichotomous distinguishing of these two groups.

Eusebius and Characterological Receptions of Philip in Asia Minor

While modern critical scholarship has assumed that Philip the apostle and Philip the deacon/evangelist were conflated into one, the reverse is actually true. Eusebius did not "confuse" two Philips – there never were two Philips in early church memory; modern scholars have "truncated" a single Philip – perplexed over Luke's somewhat ambiguous presentation of a single Philip in Acts, but wrongly so. Neither Eusebius nor his sources, however, make such a move. In four sections of *Church History* Eusebius associates *Philip the apostle* with ministering in Hierapolis, having prophesying daughters (connecting Acts 1 and 6 with Acts 8 and 21).[37]

The point here is not to argue for the "historical" Philip, but to focus on how the characterization of Philip in the Fourth Gospel would have been received and associated in ancient memory with the same Christian leader who ministered and died in Hierapolis, less than one hundred miles from Ephesus in Asia Minor. This might account for three things in the Johannine narrative: a) how such a figure might have been known to some extended members of the Johannine audience (if indeed the Johannine Gospel were delivered and circulated among the Asia Minor churches), b) how a cross-cultural figure such as Philip may have been remembered as continuing a ministry of connecting the message of the Jewish Jesus with Hellenistic audiences, and c) how the characterological presentation of Philip in the Johannine narrative may have continued to serve as a rhetorical means of connecting later audiences with its protagonist, Jesus.

Therefore, audiences in such a Hellenistic setting, within which the Johannine narrative was likely delivered and preserved in written form, would probably have been familiar with Philip's continuing, connective ministries. Not only did he connect actants in the Johannine narrative with the ministry of Jesus, but he continued to be a cross-cultural bridge between the Jesus-mission in Palestine with the mission to the Gentiles in the broader Hellenistic world.

---

[37] Cf. Eusebius, *Hist. Eccl.* 2.1.10–13; 3.31.1–5; 3.37.1; 3.39.9; 5.25.2. Also, Christopher R. Matthews, *Philip: Apostle and Evangelist: Configurations of a Tradition* (NovTSup105; Leiden: E. J. Brill, 2002), argues convincingly that the apostle and the evangelist are the same Philip, despite some early and modern attempts to differentiate the two. Indeed, the Epistle of Polycrates, as cited twice by Eusebius (*Hist. Eccl.* 3.31.2–3; 5.24.1–2), declares that two great apostolic "lights" (Philip and John) are dead and buried in Asia Minor (Hierapolis and Ephesus). The point here is that Philip would have been familiar to at least some audiences in Galilee and Judea; he would also have been familiar to at least some audiences in Asia Minor. On both levels of the text, Philip continues to play a cross-cultural, connective role.

The Characterization of Philip in John –
Revelation and Rhetoric in Dialogical Context

On the second level of the text, the presentation of Philip as a bridge-connector figure would have played rhetorically in several powerful ways. Whether his portraiture on the first level of the text is rooted in historical or traditional knowledge, or whether it simply reflects an associative interest on the part of the narrator,[38] his characterization certainly functions to build bridges between later hearers/readers and Jesus. As the dialectical Johannine situation involved development among audiences over at least three phases within the Johannine situation, first in Palestine and later in a Hellenistic setting such as Asia Minor, the cross-cultural role of Philip in the narrative would have served a similar function within the evolving Johannine dialogical context.

Comprehension and Incomprehension

As comprehension in narrative is normally exemplary, incomprehension and stupidity are nearly always corrective. Both presentations function rhetorically, and sometimes the same character in the Johannine narrative acts or speaks in ways suggesting positive examples to emulate as well as negative examples to eschew. In Philip's case, his following Jesus and bringing Nathanael to Jesus in John 1 provides a positive example for others to follow.[39] Just as he had come to believe that Jesus was indeed the Messiah, he also draws others into that circle of conviction, and on behalf of Philip's authentic witness, Nathanael too becomes a follower of Jesus. The same can be said of Philip's serving as a bridge between the seeking Hellenists and Jesus in John 12. Whereas they are presented as authentic seekers, coming and declaring their desire to see Jesus, Philip is the one who connects them with Jesus (along with Andrew),[40] and

---

[38] The thesis of Petri Merenlahti, of course, is that the ideological inclination of the narrator is the primary factor in the presentation of characters in his "Characters in the Making: Individuality and Ideology in the Gospels," in *Characterization in the Gospels: Reconceiving Narrative Criticism* (ed. David Rhoads and Kari Syreeni; London: T&T Clark, 2004), 49–72; the same would be true of historical narrative as well as fiction.

[39] While some might infer that the narrator's silence on whether or not Philip actually followed Jesus, his faithful response is featured in the next sentence where he not only follows Jesus personally, but he even echoes the Lord's invitation to "come and see" by issuing the same invitation to Nathanael (John 1:39, 46).

[40] A comparison with Andrew may be significant. Like Philip, Andrew also is featured with greater prominence in John than in the other Gospels, often alongside Philip. Just as Andrew brings Peter to the Lord in John 1, so Philip brings Nathanael; whereas Jesus tests Philip at the feeding, Andrew finds a lad with loaves and fishes; while Philip and Andrew introduce the Greeks to Philip, it is Philip to whom they have come, and without his bridge-work, Andrew would not have had a role to play in John 12. Therefore, the characterological roles of Andrew and Philip in John are complementary rather than elevating

later hearers and readers are thereby encouraged to bring seekers to the Lord, however the opportunity might present itself.

On the other hand, Philip's responses to Jesus in John 6 and 14 appear to be incomprehending, yet they both provide platforms for Jesus to perform a sign or deliver a discourse, thereby advancing his mission. When considered alongside the first Markan feeding narrative, there the disciples object to the cost of feeding the crowd; in John, Philip questions whether human provision itself would suffice. Therefore, Jesus' "testing" Philip becomes a case study in trust. Will future followers of Jesus trust in divine provision, or will they feel limited by their own resources or the lack thereof (Mark 6:37; John 6:7)? In John 14, Philip asks Jesus to show them the Father, to which Jesus replies that he has been doing so all along. On one hand, Philip's request hints at incomprehension; if Philip has not seen the Father in Jesus' ministry so far, where has he been? Then again, Philip's asking the right question, that Jesus show his followers the Father, becomes a means of accentuating the representative mission of Jesus as the one who is sent from the Father as the true Mosaic agent (Deut 18:15–22) from the beginning – continuing on through the ministry of the Holy Spirit (John 14–16). In both of these instances, Philip's role within his brief dialogues with Jesus serves as a platform for Jesus to demonstrate his glory and to fulfill his representative mission from the Father.

The Connective Function of Philip for the Johannine Audiences – Characterization in Received Contexts

Within the three phases of the Johannine situation, the characterization of Philip as a connective agent would speak clearly to later audiences, inviting their identification with him as an exemplary character within the narrative. During the first phase (the Palestinian Phase, 30–70 C. E.) featuring dialogical engagements between northern Galileans and southern Judeans and between followers of Jesus and the Baptizer, Philip's characterization would challenge conventional sensibilities directly. For Judean leaders advocating a Judean Messianism rooted in David's city, believing that Jerusalem might be a light to the nations (Isa 60:3), Philip shows that Jesus is already reaching "the nations" by their coming to him, as the Jewish Messiah, *in* Jerusalem. And, for followers of the Baptist, Andrew's leaving him and following Jesus, along with Philip and others, points the way as even a fulfillment of John's self-declared mission: the whole reason he came was to point to Jesus (John 1:31).

---

one at the expense of the other. If Nathanael is conceived of as a disciple, though not one of the twelve, the connective roles of Andrew and Philip might have been understood as bridges between Jesus and the twelve (Andrew) and Jesus and the rest of his followers (Philip) respectively.

Following a move to one of the churches in the Gentile mission during the destruction of Jerusalem by the Romans, the Johannine evangelist found himself addressing audiences involving both Jewish and Gentile members. During the first Asia-Minor phase (70–85 C. E., and there is no more conducive setting than the traditional memory of Ephesus), the characterization of Philip would have pointed local members of the synagogue to Jesus as the Messiah, given his testimony: "We have found him about whom Moses in the law and also the prophets wrote, Jesus son of Joseph from Nazareth" (John 1:45). In the light of a second crisis during this phase, involving the Roman presence during the reign of Domitian (81–96 C. E.), Philip's bringing Nathanael to Jesus, confessing "Rabbi, you are the Son of God! You are the King of Israel!" (John 1:49), this confession would have challenged the pressures of the imperial cult. Philip indeed came from a royal village, Bethsaida, so Rome-based divine and royal honors faced a direct challenge in Philip's witness to the divinely commissioned mission and identity of Jesus.

During the third phase (the second Asia-Minor phase) of the Johannine situation (85–100 C. E.) the rhetorical effect of Philip's characterization would have been most pointed in its thrust. Within the larger mission to the Gentiles, Philip's role in bringing Hellenistic seekers to Jesus would have inspired the Johannine mission to the Greeks within its new setting.[41] Just as Philip came from a cross-cultural village, the cross-cultural mission among the Pauline churches had an apostolic precedent. Further, members of the emerging Christian movement within the Lycus Valley may have known or heard of Philip, who was buried in Hierapolis, three days' walk from Ephesus, so Philip's role within the narrative may have even connected with audiences' contemporary familiarity with Philip and his later ministry. Whatever the case, Philip's connecting Greek seekers with Jesus would have inspired the Johannine mission to the Gentiles, encouraging others to take up the mantle of becoming cross-cultural connectives to Jesus. Regarding engagements with other Christian communities and leaders in the region (such as Diotrephes and his kin, 3 John 1:9–10), Philip would have pointed the way to Jesus and the Spirit, who convey the will of the Father for the Church in directly mediated ways (John 14–17) without need of human (hierarchical) intermediaries.

Therefore, in each of the six crises discernible within the three main phases of the Johannine situation (including a seventh, if engagements with other Gospel traditions are included), Philip plays an important rhetorical role for later audiences. Not only does he point the way for others to point the way to

---

[41] Kiyoshi Tsuchido, ""Ἕλλην in the Gospel of John: Tradition and Redaction in John 12:20–24," in *The Conversation Continues: Studies in Paul & John: In Honor of J. Louis Martyn* (ed. Robert T. Fortna and Beverly R. Gaventa; Nashville: Abingdon, 1990), 348–356.

Jesus cross-culturally, but he also becomes an extension of Jesus' agency, inviting later seekers of the truth to "come and see" for themselves.

Dialogism, Identification, and Meaning

As the dialogical function of the Johannine narrative and its dialogues is designed to facilitate an imaginary dialogue with Jesus within the perception and experience of later audiences, the question is how that might happen for later readers of the text. As the Johannine community can attest: *we* have seen his glory, *we* have received from his fullness grace upon grace, and *we* know the Beloved Disciple's testimony is true (John 1:14, 16; 21:24), the use of the first-person plural pronoun in association with Philip likewise bears identificational overtones.[42] First, his declaration to Nathanael, "*We* have found him about whom Moses in the law and also the prophets wrote, Jesus son of Joseph from Nazareth" (John 1:45) becomes an invitation to future audiences to receive Jesus as such – entering the community of first followers of Jesus: Philip, Andrew, Peter, Nathanael, and an unnamed disciple. Second, Jesus invites Philip (and those identifying with him) into partnership with him as his friends in the furthering of his mission and work: "Where are *we* to buy bread for these people to eat?" (John 6:5; 15:14–15). Third, in the Greek seekers' coming to Philip on their way to Jesus, hearers and readers are welcomed to identify with seekers who would profess in later settings also: "Sir, *we* wish to see Jesus" (John 12:21). Fourth, in requesting "Lord, show us the Father, and *we* will be satisfied" (John 14:8), Philip elevates the spiritual interest of subsequent believers to the front-and-center stage of Jesus' final words. In the promise of ongoing revelation of the Father's way and will in the world, future followers of Jesus are thereby sustained by the agency of the Son and the Spirit sent by the Father and by Jesus (John 14:16, 26; 15:26; 16:7).

In these and other ways, the dialogical presentation of Philip in the Johannine narrative engages later audiences as a facilitator of transformative encounter. As the reflective dialogue between perception and experience is provoked by the exemplary characterization of Philip in the narrative, later audiences are drawn into the world of the text in ways that lead to the discovery of meaning. In identifying with Philip and other communities presented in the text, the meaning of the narrative becomes personal, and the hearer/reader is drawn experientially into its world. In so doing, the invitation to "come and see" moves the experience of the hearer/reader from an observer to a participant within the narrative as a continuing and unfolding story.

---

[42] Note how the Johannine narrative draws readers into the community of the text experientially, either as waders or swimmers, helping them feel included without becoming exclusive; Anderson, *Riddles*, 1–5, 240–41.

Conclusion

While fictive approaches to characterological Gospel studies can be serviceable in and of themselves, the genre of the canonical Gospels fits better within the genres of Jewish and Greco-Roman biographical accounts.[43] Therefore, considerations of originative and developing histories must accompany delivery-situation analyses in considering the tradition history of the material as well as its final rhetorical operations. Historical narrative, like its fictive counterparts, involves characterological crafting of actants in the narrative, but they are also ordered by perceived historical realities, or at least associative perceptions. Remarkably, the Johannine presentation of Philip matches his cross-cultural representations in Acts and the sources of Eusebius, so at least we have corroborative associations – if not historical memory – here at work. Therefore, a polyvalent analysis of his presentation in John is all the more important, as it helps us consider not only the narrative designs of the narrator, but also the narrative associations likely to have been effected among the targeted audiences of the evolving Johannine situation.

The characterization of Philip in the Fourth Gospel thus presents him as a connective bridge between others and Jesus in ways that further the plot and thrust of the narrative within its delivered contexts. Considered in polyvalent analysis, from a *literary* standpoint, Philip's characterization furthers the narrator's purpose – leading audiences to initial and continuing belief in Jesus as the Christ, creates identificational connections with later audiences drawing them into association with the ministry of Philip, and poses an exemplary case study in faithful discipleship for later generations of believers seeking also to be authentic followers of Jesus. From a *historical* standpoint, Philip grounds the Johannine narrative in the Galilean ministry of Jesus – connected from the outset with the cross-cultural history and repute of Bethsaida. Philip's presentation in John also corrects the relative dearth of his treatment in Mark and the Synoptics, and it shows his ministry to be far more apostolic and cross-cultural, which is also taken further in Acts. As a result, the presentation of Philip in the emerging history of the Johannine situation would have connected with audiences during all three of its phases, plausibly even engaging regional memories of Philip and his ministries *among* the Hellenistic-mission churches, familiar at least to Christians in Asia Minor. From a *theological* standpoint, Philip affirms Jesus' representative divine agency, bolstering further chapters of Johannine cross-cultural mission, inviting later audiences

---

[43] Richard A. Burridge, *What Are the Gospels?: A Comparison with Graeco-Roman Biography* (2d ed., Grand Rapids, Mich.: Eerdmans, 2004), 213–32; see also Jo-Ann A. Brant, *Dialogue and Drama: Elements of Greek Tragedy in the Fourth Gospel* (Peabody, Mass.: Hendrickson, 2004).

not only to be connective agents as witnesses in their settings but also to welcome experiential encounter with the subject of the narrative – Jesus – as audiences in every generation and setting are invited to "*come and see.*"

Nathanael:
Under the Fig Tree on the Fourth Day

Steven A. Hunt

Introduction

Several contributors to the recent volume, *Anatomies of Narrative Criticism: The Past, Present, and Futures of the Fourth Gospel as Literature*, wrestled with the difficulties related to readings of John which took seriously both historical concerns and literary issues.[1] Indeed many scholars today are not only attempting to surmount the divide between diachronic and synchronic readings, they are arguing that such a course is the only way forward when studying an ancient text like the Fourth Gospel. Out ahead of the curve, Cornelis Bennema recently outlined a methodology he describes as "historical narrative criticism,"[2] while Udo Schnelle argued "for a combination of diachronic and synchronic interpretation" when studying John.[3]

I agree and intend in this essay to make use of synthetic methodologies in my character study of Nathanael, one of Jesus' disciples in John. After some preliminary matters then, the following study will employ methodologies which focus on the *narrative setting* of Nathanael's story in the Gospel as well as his *narrative voice* within it. An *intercharacterizational* analysis will focus on Nathanael's character when juxtaposed with other characters, particularly Simon Peter and Philip. And an *intertextual* analysis will concentrate on allusions between this narrative and other earlier narratives.

Nathanael – The Questions of Identity and Historicity

Absent from the Synoptic lists of the twelve disciples (Matt 10:2–4; Mark 3:16–19; Luke 6:14–16), readers encounter Nathanael only in the Gospel of John,

---

[1] *Anatomies of Narrative Criticism: The Past, Present, and Futures of the Fourth Gospel as Literature* (ed. Tom Thatcher and Stephen D. Moore; Atlanta: Society of Biblical Literature, 2008).

[2] Cornelis Bennema, "A Theory of Character in the Fourth Gospel with Reference to Ancient and Modern Literature," *BibInt* 17 (2009): 375–421.

[3] Udo Schnelle, "Recent Views of John's Gospel," *WW* 21 (2001): 352–359, here 355.

and there only briefly in 1:45–51 and 21:2. Several attempts have been made to identify Nathanael with one of Jesus' disciples in the Synoptics; Bartholomew,[4] Matthew,[5] and James of Alphaeus[6] appear to be the top contenders. These are, of course, tenuous identifications: the narrator shows little interest in "the twelve," who are not explicitly mentioned until 6:67, approximately a year (in narrative time) after the stories in chapter 1 (cf. 2:13; 6:4).[7] Ultimately, a broader range of disciples and a more expansive understanding of discipleship seems to be in view throughout John.[8]

As to Nathanael's historicity, several scholars make much of the fact that the Talmud makes reference to a certain *"Netzer"* as one of Jesus' disciples (*b. Sanh.* 43a). Since this name is perhaps a pun on the name *"Nittai,"* which in turn is a hypocorism of the name Nathanael, these scholars suggest that Nathanael is more likely to be an actual disciple of Jesus, rather than simply a fictitious or idealized disciple.[9] Ultimately, historical conclusions about characters in the Gospel of John are most often simply the by-product of the investigator's presuppositions about the text.

Nathanael – Basic Characterization

In terms of exegesis, scholars are primarily interested in the following: Nathanael's location "under the fig tree" (1:48, 50),[10] the narrator's use of the Jacob story in Genesis and Jewish traditions as intertexts,[11] Nathanael's confession

---

[4] See the review of this tradition in Urban Holzmeister, "Nathanael fuitne idem ac S. Bartholomaeus Apostolus?," *Bib* 21 (1940): 28–39. On the patronym "Bartholomew," see Edeltraut Leidig, "Natanael, ein Sohn des Tholomäus," *TZ* 36 (1980): 374–75.

[5] See, e. g., Karel Hanhart, "The Structure of John I 35–IV 54," in *Studies in John: Presented to Prof. J. N. Sevenster on the Occasion of His Seventieth Birthday* (NovTSup 24; Leiden: E. J. Brill, 1970), 22–46.

[6] See Charles E. Hill, "The Identity of John's Nathanael," *JSNT* 67 (1997): 45–61.

[7] Note further this group's portrayal in John, where reference to them occurs in the context of defection (6:67), betrayal (6:70–71), and doubt (20:24).

[8] So also Cornelis Bennema, *Encountering Jesus: Character Studies in the Gospel of John* (Milton Keynes: Paternoster, 2009), 65.

[9] See Richard Bauckham, *The Testimony of the Beloved Disciple: Narrative, History, and Theology in the Gospel of John* (Grand Rapids, Mich.: Baker Book House, 2007), 168–69.

[10] See, e. g., Craig R. Koester, "Messianic Exegesis and the Call of Nathanael," *JSNT* 39 (1990): 23–34; Charles F. D. Moule, "A Note on 'Under the Fig Tree' in John I.48, 50," *JTS* 5 (1954): 210–11; Tobias Nicklas, "Unter dem Feigenbaum: Die Rolle des Lesers im Dialog zwischen Jesus und Natanael (Joh 1.45–50)," *NTS* 46 (2000): 193–203, here 200–202; J. Ramsey Michaels, "Nathanael Under the Fig Tree," *ExpTim* 78 (1967): 182–83; Wolfgang Fenske, "Unter dem Feigenbaum sah ich dich," *SThZ* 54/3 (1998): 210–27.

[11] See, e. g., Christopher Rowland, "John 1:51, Jewish Apocalyptic and Targumic Tradition," *NTS* 30 (1984): 498–507; Jerome H. Neyrey, *The Gospel of John in Cultural and Rhetorical Perspective* (Grand Rapids, Mich.: Eerdmans, 2009), 87–122.

(1:49),[12] and Jesus' response (1:50–51).[13] Since all of these issues, particularly as exegetical concerns, lie beyond the purview of this paper, we will not pursue them at any length.

In terms of literary characterization, Nathanael is merely a "flat" character, personifying a positive response to Jesus.[14] In the summary that follows, we simply identify Nathanael's possible traits based on the narrator's portrayal of his actions and speech. We note that these are mostly *inferred* traits, based on indirect characterization and predicated on apparent "gaps" in the text.

At the end of the Gospel, the narrator points out that Nathanael is from Cana in Galilee (21:2; cf. 2:1-11; 4:46–54). Upon re-reading the text then, readers might conclude from his introduction in chapter 1 that Nathanael is far from home, associated with the Baptist's ministry near the Jordan (on this, see below). Based on Philip's invitation in 1:45 and Nathanael's location "under the fig tree" (i. e., a traditional location for studying scripture[15]), scholars sometimes suggest that the narrator portrays Nathanael as a serious student of scripture.[16] More plainly, in response to Philip (and those for whom he speaks: "we have found ..."), Nathanael first expresses incredulity and/or doubt,[17] showing a certain amount of gumption when he does not immediately respond to Philip's invitation. But when prodded further, he becomes responsive and physically active when he goes to find Jesus. That Nathanael does not immediately turn to the law when responding to Philip's law-based invitation is suggestive, pitting him against "the Jews" who "search the scriptures" to find eternal life (5:39; cf. 7:52). Nathanael's "going to" Jesus is exemplary, especially given the description of true disciples elsewhere as those who "follow" (ἀκολουθέω).[18]

The trustworthiness of Jesus' confession relative to Nathanael ("here is truly an Israelite in whom there is no deceit") may actually emerge in Nathanael's second response in the narrative: "Where did you get to know me?" In other

---

[12] See, e. g., Rush Rhees, "The Confession of Nathanael," *JBL* 17 (1898): 21–30.

[13] See, e. g., the summary of views here in Francis J. Moloney, *The Johannine Son of Man* (BSRel 14; Rome: LAS, 1976), 23–41; and Anselm Steiger, "Nathanael: ein Israelit, an dem kein Falsch ist," *BTZ* 9 (1992): 50–73.

[14] On "flat" and "round" characters, see Edward M. Forster, *Aspects of the Novel* (New York: Penguin Books, 1962), 54–84.

[15] See the review of literature in Koester, "Messianic Exegesis," 31, fn. 3.

[16] So, e. g., Rudolf Schnackenburg, *The Gospel According to St. John* (trans. K. Smyth; London: Burns & Oates, 1968–82), 1.315, 317.

[17] Brown's "disparaging" (Raymond E. Brown, *The Gospel According to John* [AB 29–29A; New York: Doubleday, 1966–70], 1.86), Barrett's "scornful" (C. Kingsley Barrett, *The Gospel According to St John: An Introduction with Commentary and Notes on the Greek Text* [2d ed.; London: SPCK, 1978], 184), and Duke's "cynical" (Paul D. Duke, *Irony in the Fourth Gospel* [Atlanta: John Knox Press, 1985], 54), each in reference to Nathanael's question, create too negative of an assessment.

[18] Cf. John 1:37–38, 43; 6:2(?); 8:12; 10:4–5, 27; 12:26; 13:36–37; 18:15; 21:19–20, 22.

words, he responds forthrightly, without false (i. e., deceitful) humility or obsequious action. Lastly, when confronted with Jesus' supernatural knowledge of his previous whereabouts,[19] Nathanael's final response exhibits astonishment and discernment when he offers a profound confession of faith. Nathanael "is in every respect the model Israelite, John's designation for the true or faithful Jew."[20]

While certainly a positive male character in the Gospel, Nathanael remains "flat." Readers observe no real development in Nathanael's character; they have no access to his inner life. His confession "surprises," to be sure, but not necessarily because it is "out of character." While some of his character traits seem obvious (e. g., he is incredulous, forthright, active, etc.), others appear more speculative (e. g., he is devoted to scripture, etc.). Still, one-time manifestations of so-called "traits" do not a "round" character make – Nathanael remains a type, not an individual.[21] The point notwithstanding, readers can draw out much more from the narrator's use of this character, particularly as his story feeds into pervasive and tendentious themes in the Gospel. We pursue some of these themes in what follows.

The Johannine Cosmological Setting and Nathanael's Entrance on the Fourth Day

After a relatively timeless prologue (1:1–18) which clearly alludes to Genesis 1:1 in its opening line and includes other connections to that cosmogony, the narrator of John's Gospel begins by situating the first scene by a river (1:28; cf. Gen 2:10) and proceeds to draw subtle attention to a week of days (1:29, 35, 43; 2:1; cf. Gen 1:3–2:3).[22] The Gospel moves towards its climax similarly with a pas-

---

[19] On Jesus' supernatural knowledge as a "sign" in John, see Urban C. von Wahlde, *The Gospels and Letters of John* (Eerdmans Critical Commentary; Grand Rapids, Mich.: Eerdmans, 2010), 2.78–79.

[20] R. Alan Culpepper, *Anatomy of the Fourth Gospel: A Study in Literary Design* (Philadelphia: Fortress, 1983), 123. Similarly, Raymond F. Collins observes that Nathanael "represent[s] the authentic Israel" (idem, *These Things Have Been Written: Studies on the Fourth Gospel* [Louvain Theological and Pastoral Monographs 2; Louvain: Peeters, 1990], 13).

[21] So also Bennema, *Encountering Jesus*, 68.

[22] Whether readers are to count six, seven, or even eight days is virtually irrelevant. The fact that the text stops noting a succession of days after 2:1, as the text does after the original week in Genesis, should settle the issue. Talbert makes much of these "days" as well (Charles H. Talbert, *Reading John: A Literary and Theological Commentary on the Fourth Gospel and the Johannine Epistles* [New York: Crossroad, 1992], 83–88). See the review of scholarly opinions on the issue in Craig S. Keener, *The Gospel of John: A Commentary* (Peabody, Mass.: Hendrickson, 2003), 1.496–98. Because the days call to mind the original days in Genesis does not rule out other meanings. On the polysemic nature of symbols in John, see Craig R. Koester, *Symbolism in the Fourth Gospel: Meaning, Mystery, Community* (2d ed.; Minneapolis: Fortress, 2003), 25–27.

sion week (12:1), which details an arrest in a garden (18:1–12; cf. Gen 2:8),[23] the crucifixion of three men with Jesus "in the middle" (μέσος; cf. LXX Gen 2:9), and a burial in an unused garden tomb (19:41; cf. Gen 3:23–24). It notes specifically that Jesus was raised "on the first day of the week" (20:1, 19; cf. Gen 1:5) and subsequently mistaken for a gardener (20:15; cf. Gen 2:8–9, 15). More, the major motif related to the Spirit in John resolves when Jesus "breathed on" (ἐνεφύσησεν) his disciples (20:22), a moment deliberately echoing the primeval moment when God "breathed on" (LXX: ἐνεφύσησεν) Adam in Genesis 2:7.[24]

It is on the fourth day in the narrative world of John, then, that readers are introduced to Nathanael. Given the Gospel's prolific connections to Genesis, his appearance on the fourth day may be significant. Readers should at least be open to such possibilities, even if they are pursued only as an exercise in reader-response.

The fourth day in Genesis involves the creation of sun, moon, and stars which are to separate "the day from the night" (1:14) and "the light from the darkness" (1:18). Of course, pronounced oppositions figure prominently in John as well, especially in the motif of light and darkness, and their counterparts, day and night.[25] The fourth day in John 1:43–51 feeds into some of these dualisms as well. So, for example, where light and darkness are primary symbols in the Gospel, sight and blindness are related, but secondary. Our narrator's repeated use of words related to sight[26] therefore continues the development of a theme begun already in 1:14: "The Word became flesh … and we have *seen* his glory."

Additionally, when Jesus says of Nathanael, "Here is truly an Israelite in whom there is no deceit" (1:47b), the use of the adverb "truly" (ἀληθῶς) and the noun "deceit" (δόλος) might be used to link this narrative to the dualism concerned with truth and falsehood in the Gospel, especially as they come together so clearly in chapter 8.[27] Similarly, when Jesus describes Nathanael as

---

[23] See further, Ruben Zimmermann, "Symbolic Communication Between John and His Reader: The Garden Symbolism in John 19–20," in *Anatomies of Narrative Criticism: The Past, Present, and Futures of the Fourth Gospel as Literature* (ed. Tom Thatcher and Stephen D. Moore; Atlanta: Society of Biblical Literature, 2008), 221–35.

[24] I trace the Fourth Gospel's allusions to the cosmogony in Genesis in greater detail in another chapter in this volume. See my, "The Roman Soldiers at Jesus' Arrest: 'You Are Dust, and to Dust You Shall Return.'" On the Spirit in John, see Gary M. Burge, *The Anointed Community: The Holy Spirit in the Johannine Tradition* (Grand Rapids, Mich.: Eerdmans, 1987).

[25] Craig Koester suggests that "images of light and darkness pervade the Fourth Gospel, creating what is probably its most striking motif" (idem, *Symbolism*, 141; see esp. 141–73).

[26] Not only does the narrator use forms of the verb "see" (ὁράω) six times in 1:45–51, but he uses the particle "look" (ἴδε) once and the semantically related term "find" (εὑρίσκω) twice.

[27] See further, Andrew T. Lincoln, *Truth on Trial: The Lawsuit Motif in the Fourth Gospel* (Peabody, Mass.: Hendrickson, 2000), esp. 222–31.

an "Israelite," the description sets him against Jesus' main opponents in the Gospel – "the Jews."[28]

The lights in Genesis 1:14–19 are "to give light upon the earth" (1:15) and "to be for signs ..." (1:14; LXX: ἔστωσαν εἰς σημεῖα). It should go without saying, of course, that Jesus is "the light of the world" (8:12; cf. 1:4–5, 9). Readers might note, however, the conjunction of Nathanael's story in 1:45–51 and the story that follows when Jesus does the first of his "signs" (σημείων) at a wedding in Cana (2:11). A link between the text in Genesis 1:14 on the one hand, and Nathanael and the sign mentioned in John 2:11 on the other, could be pursued on the basis that Nathanael is from Cana himself (21:2). Whether one imagines him as a relative of the bride or groom, or the groom himself (all matters for speculation), readers ought to be thinking of Nathanael as one of the five disciples (at least) who attended the wedding with Jesus, saw his glory and believed (2:12). More, they should see this sign as a preliminary yet direct fulfillment of Jesus' words when he told Nathanael that he "would see greater things than these" (1:50).

Finally, God created the "lights in the dome of the sky" in Genesis 1:14 "to rule over the day and over the night" (1:18). The declaration that these lights are "to rule" (LXX: ἄρχειν; cf. 1:16) links well with related Johannine themes which suggest, to put the matter baldly, that Jesus has come to drive out (12:31) and condemn "the ruler of this world" (16:11; ὁ ἄρχων τοῦ κόσμου) in order to be installed as its rightful king. While the Baptist's (1:20–36) and Andrew's (1:41) witness concerning Jesus anticipates these ideas, Nathanael's confession (1:49) and Jesus' response (1:50–51) on this fourth day bring the theme into sharp relief, as we will see more clearly below.

Nathanael, from Cana, a Follower of the Baptist and Gift of God

The tightly constructed, minimally narrated story in 1:19–51 leaves ample room for the reader's imagination. Numerous gaps in the narrative allow for any number of readings. Perhaps one of the more intriguing of these would suggest that Jesus and all the other men in this chapter were originally disciples of the Baptist. That Jesus decides to go to Galilee and *then* calls Philip (1:43), who hails from Bethsaida (1:44), does not necessarily entail that he was

---

[28] The latter designation, "the Jews," is used already in 1:19 (cf. 1:11), the first verse of the post-prologue narrative. On the former term, Lincoln writes, "This is the only time the term 'Israelite' is employed in the Gospel and it has none of the more dubious connotations that will be attached to the term 'Jew'" (Andrew T. Lincoln, *The Gospel According to Saint John* [BNTC; London: Continuum, 2005], 120). On the use of "the Jews" in John, always in quotations in my work, see Steven A. Hunt, "And the Word Became Flesh – Again? Jesus and Abraham in John 8:31–59," in *Perspectives on Our Father Abraham* (ed. idem; Grand Rapids, Mich.: Eerdmans, 2010), 81–109, here 85–86, fn. 14.

found there by Jesus, much less that Philip found Nathanael there (1:45).[29] More naturally, after deciding to return to Galilee (with Andrew, an unnamed follower, and Simon), Jesus found another of the Baptist's disciples, Philip, who in turn found one more, Nathanael. The whole scene anticipates this: Jesus increased, John decreased (cf. 3:30). The group, following Jesus now, departed for Galilee together, where readers find them at a wedding in the next scene. The chronological notice, "on the third day," in 2:1 seems to support this view, assuming, at least on a mundane level, the typical travel time from Judea to Galilee.[30]

Positing such a relationship between the Baptist and these men, and recognizing that Jesus was, in one sense anyway, from Nazareth (1:45) and Andrew, Simon Peter, and Philip were from Bethsaida (1:44) – towns all in Galilee – suggests no small measure of devotion to this counter-temple, anti-establishment ministry across the Jordan (1:28).[31] Such an association would complement a major theme in John's Gospel whereby Jesus replaces the temple in Jerusalem and becomes the true temple of God.[32] Since Nathanael hails from a Galilean town (21:2) and is drawn to the Baptist's ministry, he presumably also has a negative attitude towards the establishment in Jerusalem. Of course, Nathanael does not give explicit voice to or act out on this antagonism in the Gospel, but other disciples do (cf. 11:16; 18:10). Moreover, the detail about Nathanael's hometown goes some way toward explaining his initial incredulity at Philip's suggestion that Jesus *from Nazareth* is the one about whom Moses and the prophets wrote (1:46). Michaels explains: "Nathanael's skepticism [arises] … out of a stubborn provincialism in reverse that refuses to see anything great or glorious in that which is familiar or close to home."[33] Nathanael's question therefore intends only this: the Messiah could no more come from Nazareth, than he could come from Cana. And since, in John's Gospel, Jesus is "from above," Nathanael is right![34]

Nathanael's name in Hebrew means "gift of God." Since the narrator explicitly translated three other words in the preceding scene (1:38, 41, 42), yet does

---

[29] So Schnackenburg, *John*, 1.314.

[30] Cf. Josephus, *Life*, 52. To be sure, a number of other possible meanings may be found in this detail as well.

[31] While the counter-temple ministry of the Baptist is not as prominent here as it is the Synoptics (where, e. g., he baptizes "for the forgiveness of sins" in Mark 1:4), it is still detectable, for example, when he proclaims Jesus "the lamb of God who takes away the sin of the world!" (1:29) and in the narrator's notice that the Baptist was imprisoned (3:24).

[32] See further, Mary L. Coloe, *God Dwells with Us: Temple Symbolism in the Fourth Gospel* (Collegeville, Minn.: Liturgical Press, 2001) or her recent overview of that study in "Temple Imagery in John," *Int* 63 (2009): 368–81.

[33] J. Ramsey Michaels, *The Gospel of John* (NICNT; Grand Rapids: Eerdmans, 2010), 129. Cf. Mark 6:4; Luke 4:24; John 4:44.

[34] Cf. Duke, *Irony*, 54. See also his discussion of ironic questions like Nathanael's in the Gospel (90–91).

not provide a translation here, most scholars do not think we ought to make anything of this fact.³⁵ They may be right. Still, one could as well argue that because the narrator has tipped readers to the importance of names and titles and their meanings on the previous day (in fact, *three* times on the *third* day), readers ought to be thinking about their potency in the remainder of the narrative as well.³⁶

If his name is significant then, readers ought to be thinking that Nathanael represents those disciples who have been "given" to Jesus by the Father, a major theme in the Gospel which begins to resolve in 18:8–9 (when readers learn that Jesus has not lost those given to him) and finally climaxes in 19:26–27 (when Jesus gives his mother and Beloved Disciple to one another). On the other hand, and more to the point in the narrative in John 1, the narrator understands Nathanael to represent those disciples (note the twice-repeated plural "you" in 1:51) who are promised their own gift – a vision of the Son of Man in an opened heaven, a vision at least partially realized in the very next scene when Jesus revealed his glory to his disciples (2:11).

Calling Nathanael (and Andrew, Simon, and Philip)

Two features of Nathanael's call stand out prominently and the first has implications mostly for Philip who "found" him (1:45). But Philip's characterization, as one who repeatedly introduces people to Jesus (along with Andrew; 1:40–44; 6:5–9; 12:21–23), lies outside the scope of this paper. The second feature, however, relates to the broader structure of the "call narratives" in chapter 1. Early in the story, Jesus saw two disciples of the Baptist following him and invited them to "come and see" where he was staying (1:38–39). Jesus speaks first, initiating the actual encounter; in other words, he "found" them (cf. 5:14, 9:35). The verbal differences with the two subsequent "finding" narratives in 1:41, 45 are inconsequential, amounting to nothing more than the playful differences so characteristic of this Gospel (so, for example, the narrator refers to Nathanael being "found" in 1:45 and being "called" in 1:48).

One of the first disciples that Jesus found, Andrew, then "found" (εὑρίσκει) his brother Simon. After telling Simon that "we found" (εὑρήκαμεν) the Messiah, Andrew brought his brother to Jesus (1:41–42). Before the parallel scene begins in 1:43b–45, the narrator inserts a hinge, noting that Jesus decided to go to Galilee (1:43a). Once the parallel scene begins, then, the narrator records that Jesus "found" (εὑρίσκει) Philip and then Philip "found" (εὑρίσκει) Natha-

---

³⁵ So, Michaels, *John*, 127, fn. 39.
³⁶ The narrator translates three terms similarly in the climax of the Gospel (19:13, 17; 20:16; see also, 9:7; cf. 4:25; 11:16; 19:19–20; 20:24; 21:2).

nael. Next, Philip tells Nathanael that "we found" (εὑρήκαμεν) "him about whom Moses in the law and also the prophets wrote, Jesus ... from Nazareth." After a brief discussion, Nathanael goes to find Jesus. Essentially, the two scenes look like this:

A – Jesus finds Andrew
   B – Andrew "finds" Simon, saying "we found ..."
      C – Andrew brings Simon to Jesus
         D – Jesus speaks to Simon
            Hinge – "The next day Jesus decided to go to Galilee..."

A – Jesus finds Philip
   B – Philip "finds" Nathanael, saying "we found..."
      C – Nathanael goes to Jesus
         D – Jesus speaks to Nathanael

The well-balanced scene breaks down precisely at "C": where Andrew brings Simon to Jesus, Nathanael goes to Jesus on his own. Since Simon Peter and Nathanael are the last ones "found" in each cycle, it is useful to compare them to each other.[37] And, as is often the case, when juxtaposed with someone else in this Gospel, it is Peter who looks the poorer for it.[38]

First, Peter remains entirely passive in 1:41–42. He says nothing, does nothing and will not until 6:68; the text notes that Andrew "led him to Jesus." Does he go eagerly? Or with reluctance? The narrator does not say. Nor does Peter respond to Jesus or to his changed name in any way. Does he remain with Jesus, as Andrew had earlier that day (1:39)? Again, readers have no idea. Like other episodes, the narrative ends focusing on Jesus and his word. Peter simply disappears from the scene (cf., e. g., Nicodemus in chapter 3). Ultimately, in terms of narrative space, Peter simply appears as an "extra" in someone else's story.[39]

Nathanael, on the other hand, is the "co-star" in his scene; he is active, responding both in speech and movement. He engages, sparring with Philip. Not led by the one who found him, he goes to Jesus of his own accord. And, most importantly, his movement toward Jesus leads to Jesus' proclamation

---

[37] See Nicklas, "Unter dem Feigenbaum," 194–95; and Brodie's juxtaposition of Nathanael and Nicodemus (Thomas L. Brodie, *The Gospel According to John* [Oxford: Oxford University Press, 1993], 169).

[38] See especially Peter's negative characterization when juxtaposed with the Beloved Disciple in the Gospel. For a summary of these juxtapositions, see Raymond E. Brown, *The Community of the Beloved Disciple: The Life, Loves, and Hates of an Individual Church in New Testament Times* (New York: Paulist Press, 1979), 82–83. See the detailed response to this consensus view in Bradford B. Blaine, *Peter in the Gospel of John: The Making of an Authentic Disciple* (Academia Biblica; Atlanta: Society of Biblical Literature, 2007).

[39] So Michaels, *John*, 123. On Peter's passivity, see further Brodie, *John*, 161–62.

about him. In other words, *he is a "true Israelite" precisely because he goes to Jesus.* Upon his arrival, he questions Jesus. And upon Jesus' answer, he offers a startling confession which accords with the narrator's overall purpose for the Gospel (20:31). Nathanael's implied belief ("Jesus answered, 'Do you believe *because* …'"; 1:50[40]) makes him the first in the story to manifest this most important quality. Unlike Peter on the third day, it is Nathanael on day four who holds center stage with Jesus.

As an aside, note Philip's supporting role in this scene. Should readers question why, when Jesus has explicitly instructed him to "follow," Philip is next seen speaking with Nathanael who is explicitly not with Jesus (cf. 21:19–20)? Why does he refer to Jesus as "son of Joseph" (cf. 6:42), especially in light of Nathanael's impending confession (i. e., "You are the Son of God!") in v. 49? Does Philip even go with Nathanael when the latter goes to Jesus? Since the narrator focuses here only on Nathanael, readers do not yet know. In a Gospel which often presents discipleship in stark and simple terms (e. g., Jesus "said to them, 'Come and see.' They came and saw …"; 1:39), the narrator's subtlety here may be telling, especially given Philip's appearances later in the Gospel (6:7; 12:21–22; 14:8–14).[41] Nevertheless, Philip's overall positive role in this story becomes clear when he invites Nathanael to "come and see," employing the very phrase Jesus used the previous day (1:39; cf. 4:29; 11:34).

Second, having been invited, Nathanael is next seen by Jesus "coming toward him" (1:47). In addition to being exemplary (again, disciples "follow" Jesus), and in contrast to Peter's passivity, Nathanael's movement toward Jesus recalls Jesus' own movement toward the Baptist in 1:29 (cf. 1:36). And in both narratives, once seen by those they approach, a pronouncement follows: in 1:29, the Baptist sees Jesus and says, "Behold (Ἴδε), the lamb of God …!" In 1:47, Jesus sees Nathanael and says, "Behold (Ἴδε), an Israelite indeed …!" (RSV). Obviously, when a character is implicitly compared to the hero in this Gospel, it bodes well in terms of their overall characterization.

Third, when Jesus declares with reference to Nathanael, "Here is truly an Israelite in whom there is no deceit!" (1:47), readers ought rather obviously to be hearing echoes of Jacob's story in Genesis.[42] Not only does "Israelite" for Nathanael refer back to the story of Jacob (Gen 32:28), but the narrator's use of the word "deceit" (δόλος; only here in John) also echoes Jacob's story in Genesis when Isaac says to his son Esau, "your brother [Jacob] came deceitfully (LXX: δόλου), and he has taken away your blessing" (27:35; cf. 34:13). Jacob's

---

[40] Cf. Barrett, *John*, 186.

[41] In our scene, Jesus tells Philip to follow and instead Philip goes and tells Nathanael; in John 12, Greeks ask Philip if they might see Jesus and instead of taking them directly, he goes and finds Andrew.

[42] So Brown, *John*, 1.87; contra Schnackenburg, *John*, 1.316. On Jacob allusions in this narrative, see Neyrey, *John in Cultural and Rhetorical Perspective*, esp. 87–106.

deceptions in Genesis are legendary, to be sure. We note only the way our narrator implicitly *contrasts* Nathanael with him. Unlike Jacob, Nathanael is a true Israelite without deceit. Unlike Jacob, Nathanael's name will not be changed.

Simon's name, on the other hand, does get changed by Jesus: "You are to be called[43] Cephas" (1:42). That his name is changed precisely in a narrative where he is being contrasted with Nathanael, the anti-Jacob,[44] is intriguing. That his new name merits translation by the narrator makes it even more interesting, for Jacob's new name "Israel" is similarly translated in Genesis 32:28. In addition, once Jacob's name is changed in Genesis 32, he will name the place of his encounter with God "Peniel," saying, "I have seen God face to face" (v. 30). Our Gospel suggests in the prologue that "No one has ever seen God" but that the Son "has made him known" (1:18). Jesus' promise, therefore, that Nathanael would see "greater things" anticipates the fullness of Jesus' revelation of the Father (in ways which are thematically linked to the story of Jacob) while it continues to contrast Nathanael with Simon, for whom there is no such promise.

Latent Possibilities:
Nazareth, the Branch, and Nathanael Under the Fig Tree

We already noted how on the mundane level Nathanael's question, "Can anything good come out of Nazareth?" (1:46a), indicates a reverse provincialism. But from the narrator's perspective, Nathanael's question works well in two further ways. First, it begins to construct a framework for the later debates about Jesus' true origin, a major motif of this Gospel (see, e. g., 6:41–42; 7:27–29; 8:14).[45] Where Nathanael expresses doubt – not that Jesus is the one of whom Moses and the Prophets wrote, but that such an important figure comes from Nazareth – Jesus' opponents go one step further, doubting that Jesus is the one for whom they have been waiting precisely because they wrongly assume his origin in Galilee generally (7:41, 52) or Nazareth specifically (18:5, 7; 19:19). They do not accept his true origin "from above" (3:31).

Second, Nathanael's question, following on the heels of Philip's confession, repeats the word "Nazareth." The twice-repeated reference to Nazareth in 1:44–45 is interesting particularly in light of Nathanael's two-fold description of Jesus as "Son of God" and "King of Israel" (1:49), as well as the twice-repeated notice that Nathanael was "under the fig tree" (1:48, 50). All of these interlocking aspects of the narrative, I suggest, are anticipating one very

---

[43] κληθήσῃ; cf. LXX: κληθήσεται in Gen 32:28.
[44] Cf. Bruce who concludes that Nathanael is "one who is all Israel and no Jacob" (Frederick F. Bruce, *The Gospel of John* [Grand Rapids, Mich.: Eerdmans, 1983], 60).
[45] Cf. Lincoln, *John*, 120.

important moment in the Gospel. We attempt to unpack this complex motif only briefly in what follows.

Mary Coloe has argued that "recent excavations have shown that the word Nazareth has its root meaning in the word *netzer* (נצר) describing the future royal branch from the house of David."[46] Drawing on texts which describe this Branch (e. g., Isaiah, Zechariah, Qumran, the Targums), she maintains that in the Fourth Gospel, "the term Nazarene is not a name derived from a place, but is a title that leads to Jesus' arrest and execution."[47] She observes that only in John does the placard add "the Nazarene" (ὁ Ναζωραῖος) to the inscription, "Jesus *the Nazarene*, the King of the Jews" (19:19; cf. Matt 27:37; Mark 15:26; Luke 23:38). In light of Jewish expectations then, she concludes: "the title 'Nazarene' above the head of Jesus is a reference to his messianic role as builder of the eschatological temple."[48] To bring these points together, I would contend that in keeping with the narrator's penchant for irony, when Jesus hangs on the cross, Pilate unwittingly confesses the truth: "Jesus [is] the Branch, the king of the Jews."

How does all of this relate to Nathanael[49] and the narrative in John 1:45–51? First, in light of the understanding suggested by "the Nazarene" above, the twice-repeated reference to "Nazareth" (Ναζαρέτ) in 1:45 and 1:46 (the repetition suggesting emphasis) is likewise full of potential, especially given that this is the first of two scenes which verbally foreshadow the title in 19:19. The second scene takes place at Jesus' arrest in chapter 18. In both, Jesus' kingship is the primary issue, as it is in the superscription above the cross. In our narrative, Jesus' kingship comes to the fore explicitly in Nathanael's confession.[50] In the second, the arresting party, when prompted by Jesus, says twice (again, repetition for emphasis) that they are looking for Jesus "the Nazarene" (18:5, 7; τὸν Ναζωραῖον). The narrator obviously betrays an agenda when this armed cohort (18:3) steps back and falls to the ground when Jesus responds (18:6). Thus, the narrator only uses the words "Nazareth" and "Nazarene" in these two scenes prior to 19:19. In both, the word gets repeated a second time for emphasis, and ideas related to Jesus' kingship are explored. When the placard is put on the cross, proclaiming Jesus "the Nazarene" (i. e., the Branch of Jewish expectation) and king of the Jews (and, therefore, true temple builder), this motif as part of the narrator's overall story resolves.

---

[46] Mary L. Coloe, "The Nazarene King: Pilate's Title as the Key to John's Crucifixion," in *The Death of Jesus in the Fourth Gospel* (ed. Gilbert Van Belle; BETL 200; Louvain: Leuven University Press, 2007), 839–48, here 843.

[47] Coloe, "The Nazarene King," 846.

[48] Coloe, "The Nazarene King," 846.

[49] Should we at this point recall that the Talmud mentions one of Jesus' disciples named *Netzer*, a likely pun on a hypocoristic form of Nathanael's name? See our section above on historicity.

[50] On the singular intent in Nathanael's confession, see esp. Barrett, *John*, 185–86.

Nathanael's presence "under the fig tree" in 1:48, 50 strengthens the preceding point.[51] Scholars have long pointed to biblical parallels or Rabbinic traditions when commenting on Nathanael's location.[52] What they do not typically point out is the narrator's varied description of it:

1:48: ὑπὸ τὴν συκῆν
1:50: ὑποκάτω τῆς συκῆς

Following Robert Alter's rule, readers should always be keen to note *variation in repetition* in biblical narratives.[53] We observe then that the second reference to Nathanael's location employs the adverb ὑποκάτω (a hapax in John) and switches from the accusative to the genitive case. Why?

While LXX Mic 4:1–4 offers an interesting parallel, a more significant one surfaces in Zech 3:10 with its reference to one "under a fig tree" (LXX: ὑποκάτω συκῆς). This parallel is more important because the context of Zechariah's vision describes the LORD's servant as "the Branch"[54] and claims additionally that the LORD will remove "the guilt of this land in a single day" (3:9; LXX: πᾶσαν τὴν ἀδικίαν τῆς γῆς ἐκείνης ἐν ἡμέρᾳ μιᾷ). In John, Jesus' "hour" and "that day" are important to the unfolding drama; and the Baptist's early confession that Jesus is the lamb of God who takes away "the sin of the world" (1:29; τὴν ἁμαρτίαν τοῦ κόσμου) goes some way to setting the plot for the Gospel. That "the Branch" is later described in Zech 6:12 as one who "shall build the temple of the LORD" makes the swirl of these connections more interesting still.

In sum, the explicit kingship motif in John 1:45–51, in conjunction with twice repeated references to Nazareth (which, along with 18:5, 7, offers a verbal foreshadowing of John 19:19) and twice repeated references to Nathanael's location under the fig tree (in language identical to that in Zech 3 which, among other things, envisions the LORD's servant "the Branch"), suggests that the narrator employs Nathanael's character in subtle and not so subtle ways to further develop important kingship and temple motifs in the Gospel.

---

[51] As I add my own suggestion to the chorus of interpretations here, I am mindful of Brown's assessment: "We are far from exhausting the suggestions, all of which are pure speculation" (*John*, 1.83)!

[52] See the references cited above in fn. 10. Brodie simply suggests that the tree's shade serves well Nathanael's dark mood; thus, Nathanael represents "moving from darkness to light" (*John*, 167–68).

[53] Robert Alter, *The Art of Biblical Narrative* (New York: Basic Books, 1981), 97–113.

[54] Coloe discusses at length the two Hebrew words (*netzer* and *tzamah*) standing behind the word translated "Branch" in English editions of the Hebrew Bible and shows that by the time of Qumran, the two terms were synonymous (Coloe, "The Nazarene King," 844–45). That Zechariah employs the term *tzamah* does not detract from our case. See further, Rudolf Pesch, "He Will Be Called a Nazorean: Messianic Exegesis in Matthew 1–2," in *The Gospels and the Scriptures of Israel* (ed. Craig A. Evans and W. Richard Stegner; Sheffield: Sheffield Academic Press, 1994), 129–78, here 174–75.

The Mother of Jesus: A Woman Possessed

Mary L. Coloe

Characterization and Theology

Since the rise of New Criticism, to speak of characterization in narrative fiction invites vigorous debate as "character" is dissolved into a cipher to be understood solely within the text itself with little relationship to external considerations such as the historical circumstances of the text, or biographical information about the author, or the possible author's intention for writing the text.[1] To raise the issue of characterization in a Gospel is particularly problematic due to the ideological goal of the evangelist, which is made explicit in the Gospel of John. "These things have been written that you may believe that Jesus is the Christ the Son of God, and that believing you may have life in his name" (20:31).

There is also concern whether modern theories of narrative criticism and characterization are applicable when considering ancient texts. In the words of Mark Allen Powell, "[N]arrative critics may be charged with anachronistically applying modern concepts to ancient literature or with treating the Gospels as though they were novels or works of fiction."[2] Merenlahti and Hakola ask, "whether narrative-critical readings do justice to the nature of the Gospel

---

[1] A helpful introduction to various approaches in narrative criticism can be found in Elizabeth Struthers Malbon's analysis of Markan characters. See Elizabeth Struthers Malbon, *In the Company of Jesus: Characters in Mark's Gospel* (Louisville, Ky.: Westminster John Knox, 2000), ch. 1. See also the brief overview of the origins and development of narrative criticism in Petri Merenlahti and Raimo Hakola, "Reconceiving Narrative Criticism," in *Characterization in the Gospels: Reconceiving Narrative Criticism* (ed. David Rhoads and Kari Syreeni; London: T&T Clark, 1999), 17–23.

[2] Mark Allan Powell, "Narrative Criticism," in *Hearing the New Testament: Strategies for Interpretation* (ed. Joel B. Green; Grand Rapids, Mich.: Eerdmans, 1995), 239–55, here 254. A similar concern is raised by Cornelis Bennema in his study when he asks, "whether it is legitimate to apply modern methods used in fiction to ancient narratives and whether we can compare Hebrew and Greek literature regarding character" (idem, "A Theory of Character in the Fourth Gospel with Reference to Ancient and Modern Literature," *BibInt* 17 [2009]: 380). Bennema concludes that it is appropriate to apply modern methods of analysis to ancient narratives providing necessary precautions are taken such as being aware that by using modern methods "we fuse the modern and ancient horizon, and use modern terminology to understand characters in ancient literature" (ibid., 396).

narratives," since a narrative approach emphasizes the poetic/artistic nature of the work, measured in terms of "aesthetic standards" but the Gospels are "not only literary artefacts" but also "ideological discourse that originated in a particular real-life context."[3] They continue: "The primary goal of the Gospels was not beauty but truth."[4]

The recent study by Cornelis Bennema (fn. 2), on characterization in John makes a start in developing not simply a method or language for analyzing characters, but a comprehensive theory of character. In addition to the explicit characterization in Gospel texts, Merenlahti and Hakola draw attention to the way readers try to "fill the gaps"[5] by drawing on what is known about the events and circumstances. "What readers of a non-fictional narrative think of a character depends not only on what the narrator reveals but also on what else the readers may know about the person who is portrayed as a character in the narrative."[6] This comment is particularly pertinent when dealing with non-fiction narratives, such as the Gospels, where the narrative world needs to relate to the first-century setting. Yet another aspect of contemporary narrative criticism, important in Gospel studies, is called "the point of view," for as Bennema notes, "a narrative is not neutral since it has an inbuilt perspective."[7] In the case of the Fourth Gospel, this perspective is made explicit (20:31) but it can also operate implicitly within the deeper structural levels. The ideological point of view includes "the beliefs, norms, evaluations and value system of the text."[8] Resseguie asks how a narrator uses "setting, rhetoric, character, and plot to persuade the reader to adopt his evaluative point of view."[9]

In this essay, I will take up some of these approaches in my analysis of the characterization of the Mother of Jesus,[10] in particular I will make use of the insight of Resseguie and those other narrative critics who consider not only the

---

[3] Merenlahti and Hakola, "Reconceiving Narrative Criticism," 14–17.

[4] Merenlahti and Hakola, "Reconceiving Narrative Criticism," 32. For further on the truth claims of the Gospel that are extrinsic to the text itself, see pp. 33–34. Since the Gospels make truth claims that refer to the historical reality beyond the text, these claims are quite different to the claims of fictional works, and this makes a difference in the reading experience.

[5] Meir Sternberg seems to have been the first to speak of "filling the gaps" in examining the story of David. See Meir Sternberg, "The King through Ironic Eyes: Biblical Narrative and the Literary Reading Process," *Poetics Today* 7 (1986): 275–322. This was originally published in Hebrew in *Ha-Sifrut* 1.2 (1968): 263–92.

[6] Merenlahti and Hakola, "Reconceiving Narrative Criticism," 40.

[7] Bennema, "Theory of Character," 394.

[8] James L. Resseguie has undertaken an analysis of the Fourth Gospel examining ways in which the narrator communicates his point of view to the reader. In this study, he considers the spatial, phraseological, temporal, psychological, and ideological point of view (idem, *The Strange Gospel: Narrative Design and Point of View in John* [BIS 56; Leiden: Brill, 2001], 4–5).

[9] Resseguie, *The Strange Gospel*, 2.

[10] Where the term "mother" is used as a title to replace the personal name Mary, "mother" is capitalized, e. g. the Mother of Jesus; similarly the title "Woman."

quality of the characterization as such, but also raise the deeper question of how this characterization serves the ideological purpose or "point of view" of the writer since it is the characters "who transmit the significance and values of the narrative to the reader."[11] In other words, my interest is how the character "works" to contribute to the theological perspective of the Gospel.[12]

The questions I bring to the text are: why is the Mother of Jesus never given her personal name? Does it make a difference that she is present at Cana and the cross? Could her place in these scenes be substituted by any other character, male or female? Given that she speaks fewer than ten words, is she essential to the Johannine plot?

The Wedding at Cana[13]

The first character introduced in this scene is the Mother of Jesus, signaling her importance.[14] Her initial words, "They have no wine" (2:3), and Jesus' first response, "What [is this] to me and you, Woman" appear to be simply statements of fact. As guests at the wedding, the supply of wine is not a matter for

---

[11] Shimon Bar-Efrat, *Narrative Art in the Bible* (JSOTSup 70; Sheffield: Sheffield Academic Press, 1992), 47. Petri Merenlahti also emphasizes the importance of considering characterization in relation to the ideological or theological perspective of the Gospel. "Rather than static elements of design picked by a master author to fill a distinct literary or rhetorical purpose, they [characters] are constantly being reshaped by distinct ideological dynamics. This ideologically attuned nature of character presents a challenge for any theory or model of characterization for the Gospel narrative ... analysis of ideology should be an integral part of the analysis of the formal features of narrative" (idem, "Characters in the Making: Individuality and Ideology in the Gospels," in *Characterization in the Gospels: Reconceiving Narrative Criticism* [ed. David Rhoads and Kari Syreeni; London: T&T Clark, 1999], 49–72, here 50).

[12] In this essay, due to limits of space, it is not possible to engage with the positions taken by other scholars in their studies of the role of the Mother of Jesus in John. In this note I can only mention some of the more significant recent studies. Judith M. Lieu, "The Mother of the Son in the Fourth Gospel," *JBL* 117 (1998): 61–76. In this article, in addition to the Cana miracle and the cross, Lieu discusses the figure of the woman in labour in John 16:2. This present study focuses on the two explicit appearances of the Mother of Jesus, where both scenes are linked by the characters, mother and son, and by the mention of the "Hour." See also the very poignant reflection on the Mother standing at the cross by Ingrid R. Kitzberger, "Stabat Mater? Re-birth at the Foot of the Cross," *BibInt* 11 (2003): 468–87.

[13] In his study, Calum M. Carmichael, connects Cana with the second day of creation in Genesis 1 (idem, *The Story of Creation: Its Origin and Its Interpretation in Philo and the Fourth Gospel* [Ithaca, N. Y.: Cornell University Press, 1996]). I do not find his arguments convincing and follow the suggestion of Francis Moloney in linking "the third day" reference to the revelation of God's glory "on the third day" (Exod 19:11^{x2}, 15, 16) at Sinai which was commemorated in the Jewish Festival of Pentecost. See Mary L. Coloe, "The Johannine Pentecost: John 1:19–2:12," *ABR* 55 (2007): 41–56.

[14] Lieu notes, "John generally uses the formula 'there was ...' to introduce an individual who plays a significant role in the ensuing scene" (idem, "The Mother of the Son," 50).

their concern.[15] As the narrative will later reveal, it is the bridegroom's responsibility to provide wine. Jesus' further words, "my hour has not yet come" (2:4), indicate that he has heard in his mother's words more than a simple statement of facts. He has heard a request to do something about this issue. This is an example of the need for the reader to "fill the gaps." "Being given only sparse and ambiguous information, the reader simply has to infer, make guesses and interpretations."[16] At this point, the work of the sociolinguist Deborah Tannen on gender related modes of communication can add to our understanding of the interplay between the Mother and Son. Tannen describes her work as "discourse analysis" which "focuses on connected language 'beyond the sentence'."[17]

The Mother's apparently neutral comment, "they have no wine," can be understood as a linguistic strategy of indirectness where without making an explicit request, she presumes, because of her relationship with her son, that he will hear the implied request. Jesus' response indicates that her presumption is correct. He hears the implicit request. Tannen comments that "those who feel entitled to make demands may prefer not to, seeking the payoff in rapport."[18] She also notes that cultures vary in their use of indirect communication as an appropriate communication strategy.

One of the deeply puzzling aspects of the Cana episode is the sharp response Jesus makes to his mother when she indicates that the wine has run out; it reads literally, "What to me and to you?" (2:4).[19] In all its uses in the LXX[20] this statement has a corrective, if not harsh, tone in a situation "in which two parties have nothing in common, or no relationship to each other."[21] The reply to his mother is strange, but then the puzzle deepens when Jesus acts in accordance with her wishes. There is more to this dialogue than meets the eye. Tanner cautions about the tendency for scholars to see only one aspect of a

---

[15] Similarly, Ritva H. Williams, "The Mother of Jesus at Cana: A Social-Science Interpretation of John 2:1–12," CBQ 59 (1997): 679–92, here 688.

[16] Merenlahti, "Characters in the Making," 53.

[17] Deborah Tannen, *Gender and Discourse* (New York: Oxford University Press, 1994, 1996), 5. I wish to acknowledge the unpublished work of one of my Master's students, Sandra Jebb, who introduced me to Tannen's work and how it can contribute to understanding the implied nuances of language when gendered relationships are taken into account.

[18] Tannen, *Gender and Discourse*, 32.

[19] The use of the vocative, "Woman" when addressing his mother will be discussed in the next section in examining the scene at the foot of the cross.

[20] Judg 11:12; 2 Sam 16:10; 19:22; 1 Kgs 17:18; 2 Kgs 3:13; 2 Chr 35:21. Similarly in the New Testament it has the negative sense "leave me alone" (Matt 8:29; Mark 1:24; 5:7; Luke 4:34; 8:28).

[21] Arthur H. Maynard, "TI EMOI KAI SOI," NTS 31 (1985): 582–86, here 584. For a discussion of its use in the LXX and the possible Semitism lying behind the expression, see Jean-Paul Michaud, "Le signe de Cana dans son contexte johannique," *Laval Théologique et Philosophique* 18 (1962): 247–53. Williams cautions that context is important to interpret the meaning of this exchange and not presume that words and phrases remain constant over time or remain constant regardless of context (idem, "The Mother of Jesus at Cana," 687).

conversation between men and women when in fact there is ambiguity and the polysemy of both power and solidarity.[22] The contradiction between Jesus' words and his later actions suggest that his response is not simply a rebuff of his mother's request. Tannen notes that many cultures see "arguing as a pleasurable sign of intimacy" and in this context she notes that among men and women of Jewish backgrounds "a friendly argument is a means of being sociable" and that when a Jewish couple appear to be arguing, "they are staging a kind of public sparring match, where both fighters are on the same team."[23]

In spite of the seemingly harsh response of Jesus, there must be a deeper level of intimacy, as Tanner suggests, within this exchange, for with no further rejoinder, the Mother turns to the servants and says, "Do whatever he tells you" (2:5). Clearly, she presumes that Jesus will act. Whatever the apparent harshness at the surface level of the dialogue with her son, at a deeper level she has understood his compliance with her implied request. When commenting on indirectness as a strategy used between men and women, Tanner states, "The interpretation of a given utterance, and the likely response to it, depends on the setting, on individuals' status and their relationship with each other, and also on the linguistic conventions that are ritualized in the cultural context."[24] As a twenty-first century Western woman, trying to make sense of this exchange when I only have a text, I need to be aware of possible cultural conventions operating here that I may never fully grasp. Jane Kopas' comments express the demands placed on the modern interpreter when seeking to make sense of this exchange.

> [T]he level of understanding that exists between them transcends the words exchanged. In one sense, they seem to be talking past each other, and one gets the impression of a lack of real contact. On the other hand, Mary's reaction suggests that she understands all as she tells the servants to do whatever he tells them. As we ponder the kind of communication that was going on, we realize that there was an exchange of invitation and response, initiated and answered from each side. The words themselves are not the most important vehicle of meaning; the relationship is. The degree to which the relationship yields its meaning depends upon the willingness and ability of the participants to hear more than what was spoken, and to let the communication unfold in its own way.[25]

The very strangeness of the exchange draws the readers' attention to the relationship between Jesus and his mother and to the indication that this relationship will be particularly significant in the future, when "the Hour" arrives.[26]

---

[22] Tannen, *Gender and Discourse*, 46.
[23] Tannen, *Gender and Discourse*, 44.
[24] Tannen, *Gender and Discourse*, 34.
[25] Jane Kopas, "Jesus and Women: John's Gospel," *ThTo* 41 (1985): 202.
[26] The theme of Jesus' "Hour" will develop across the narrative and take on a meaning related to the Passion, as the "Hour" of Jesus' death, exaltation and glorification (7:30; 8:20; 12:23, 27; 13:1; 17:1). The presence of the Woman/Mother at Cana and at the cross link these two scenes and require that the "Hour" named here be understood in terms of the Passion.

Considering Jesus' subsequent actions in changing the water into wine, his words to his mother must be understood primarily as a narrative strategy directing the reader's attention to the future "Hour."[27] It is then that the relationship between Jesus and his mother will be critical. The importance of her relationship as mother of Jesus, in this Gospel, will only be revealed in "the Hour." The Cana miracle happens, but Jesus' apparent reprimand creates a puzzle that will not be resolved until the Passion.

As the Cana episode develops, the words of the steward to the bridegroom indicate that it was the role of the bridegroom to provide the wine for the wedding (2:10). This exchange implicitly identifies Jesus as the real bridegroom in this scene, which John the Baptizer will later confirm (3:28–30).[28] Since Jesus is the bridegroom, then his mother becomes the "mother of the bridegroom." The Mother's role at Cana concludes with the narrator's comment, "After this he went down to Capernaum, with his mother and his brothers and sisters and his disciples; and they dwelt there for a few days" (2:12). A household is being formed around Jesus and his mother. This narrative comment proleptically introduces a theme that will be further developed at the cross.[29]

To summarize: In this episode, the Mother of Jesus is portrayed as an active agent. She is introduced first indicating her significance; she then notices the lack of wine, initiates the miracle by speaking to her son (implicitly making a request), and then gives explicit directives to the servants. The "gaps" in the discourse between mother and son, and the directives to the servants suggest a deeper communication that depends upon their relational intimacy. The strangeness of Jesus' response points ahead to a future time, "my Hour." There is no report on the Mother's response to this miracle, as there is the disciples' (2:11) but the episode concludes with Jesus, his mother, his family and disciples together at Capernaum. Her role at this time is finished. What she has done and said is sufficient – for now!

The Hour

The Mother of Jesus returns to the narrative at the foot of the cross. Here she says nothing. But this scene marks the climax of the Gospel, for immediately

---

[27] So also Lieu: "we are led to look for a deeper meaning that has yet to be revealed. There is unfinished business" ("The Mother of the Son," 66).

[28] See in this same volume, Mary L. Coloe, "The Servants and Steward at Cana."

[29] I have developed in greater detail the significance of the nuptial theme in John 1 and 2 in an earlier study. See Mary L. Coloe, "Witness and Friend: Symbolism associated with John the Baptiser," in *Imagery in the Gospel of John: Terms, Forms, Themes and Theology of Figurative Language* (ed. Jörg Frey et al.; WUNT 200; Tübingen: Mohr Siebeck, 2006), 319–32.

following it the narrator states: "After this, knowing that everything had been finished (τετέλεσται) so that the scriptures might be fulfilled, Jesus said, 'I thirst.' After taking the vinegar Jesus then spoke aloud, 'It is finished (τετέλεσται),' and bowing his head he delivered over the spirit" (19:30).[30]

These words of completion, following the scene with his mother, emphasize the importance of this scene where Jesus changes the relationship between his mother and the Beloved Disciple: "Woman, behold your son" (19:26), "Behold your mother" (19:27). Jesus' words are frequently interpreted as simply a dying son showing filial care for his mother in seeing that she is given into the care of another.[31] Such an interpretation does little justice to the significance of the scene and Jesus' ensuing judgment "τετέλεσται."[32]

When Jesus turns to his mother, and says, "Woman, behold your son," and then turns to the Beloved Disciple and says, "Behold your mother," he effectively alters their relationship. The double use of the term "behold" (ἴδε; vss. 26, 27) informs the reader that Jesus' words are a prophetic revelation, while the form of words is very similar to the formula of adoption.[33] The woman is now "mother" to the Beloved Disciple, and the disciple is now "son." But with this change, the disciple's relationship with Jesus also changes. If they now have the same "mother" then the disciple is now brother to Jesus and therefore participates in Jesus' relationship with God.[34] This is the moment of divine filiation when disciples become brothers/sisters to Jesus and children of God.[35]

---

[30] On the importance of the use of τελέω following this scene (19:28, 30), see Jean Zumstein, *Kreative Erinnerung* (ATANT 84; Zürich: Theologischer Verlag Zürich, 2004), 266–68, and Klaus Scholtissek, *In Ihm sein und bleiben: Die Sprache der Immanenz in den johanneischen Schriften* (Herders Biblische Studien 21; Freiburg: Herder, 2000), 237. Both scholars show that this statement gives Jesus' words to his mother and the Beloved Disciple the character of a Last Testament.

[31] See for example C. Kingsley Barrett, *The Gospel According to St John* (2d ed.; London: SPCK, 1978), 552.

[32] Raymond E. Brown comments, "we doubt that Jesus' filial solicitude is the main import of the Johannine scene. Such a non-theological interpretation would make this episode a misfit amid the highly symbolic episodes that surround it in the crucifixion episode" (idem, *The Gospel According to John* [2 vols.; AB 29–29a; New York: Doubleday, 1966, 1970], 2:923).

[33] Michel de Goedt proposes that ἴδε introduces a revelatory formula (idem, "Un Scheme de revelation dans la quatrieme évangile," NTS 8 [1961–62]: 142–50). Barrett states that the words are both revelatory and adoptive (idem, *John*, 552).

[34] "[L]e disciple bien-aimé est adopté par Jésus comme frère" (De Goedt, *Un scheme de revelation*, 145). Without specifying the mutual change of relationships, Zumstein also concludes that the crucifixion constitutes a new family (idem, *Kreative Erinnerung*, 273). The scholar who has done some of the most significant work on the "family" metaphor and its significance in the Fourth Gospel is Jan G. van der Watt. He writes, "The extent to which the family imagery is developed in the Gospel, clearly gives priority to the idea of being born as a child of God, living in the family of a Father, as the basic, and most important image used to metaphorize the believers" (idem, *Family of the King: Dynamics of Metaphor in the Gospel according to John* [BIS 47; Leiden: Brill, 2000], 432).

[35] Following the gift of *the* Spirit (19:30), the Father of Jesus is called the Father of the

In fact the Prologue had already hinted that this was the ultimate goal of the narrative when it stated, "He came to his own (εἰς τὰ ἴδια) but his own did not receive him. But to all who received him, who believed in his name, he gave power to become children of God" (1:11–12). The phrase, "εἰς τὰ ἴδια" (1:11) is repeated at the cross, "and from that hour the disciple took her" (εἰς τὰ ἴδια; 19:27). The *inclusio* formed by this phrase indicates that what was promised in the Prologue is brought to completion at the cross. The Beloved Disciple, representative of all disciples, is born anew as a child of God.[36]

This scene of Jesus' death and the bestowal of the Spirit is also a scene depicting the disciple being born anew of the Spirit (3:3, 5), born into the household of God.[37] The flow of blood and water from the pierced side of Jesus (19:34) is evocative of birth when the mother's waters break at the onset of labor and the flow of blood in which the new child is born.[38] Lee comments, "The connection between the flow of blood and water and childbirth is not one that is generally made by commentators … Yet with an understanding of the flexible nature of Jesus' flesh as it is symbolically presented in the Fourth Gospel, and its capacity to take on cosmic significance, the imagery makes perfect sense – of the elements themselves … and the significance of the crucifixion as

---

disciples, "go to my brothers and sisters (τοὺς ἀδελφούς μου) and say to them, I am ascending to my Father and *your Father*, to my God and your God" (20:17). I read τοὺς ἀδελφούς μου as an inclusive expression since Mary Magdalene is surely included in "your Father."

[36] Scholtissek also links what happens at the cross to the statement in the Prologue (1:12–13) and so calls the scene at the cross the "*semantische Achse*" of the Gospel (idem, *Sein und Bleiben*, 238).

[37] This has been a theme of my work, see in particular Mary L. Coloe, *God Dwells with Us: Temple Symbolism in the Fourth Gospel* (Collegeville, Minn.: Liturgical Press, 2001), ch. 9. Where I use the term "household" Jan van der Watt uses "family" (idem, *Family of the King*, 432) and Ruben Zimmermann identifies the household/family as one of the major metaphorical concepts of the Gospel (idem, *Christologie der Bilder im Johannesevangelium: Die Christopoetik des vierten Evangeliums unter besonderer Berücksichtigung von Joh 10* [WUNT 171; Tübingen: Mohr Siebeck, 2004], 172–83).

[38] On the birth imagery in this scene see Dorothy A. Lee, *Flesh and Glory: Symbolism, Gender and Theology in the Gospel of John* (New York: Crossroad, 2002), 152–59. Brown identifies Jesus' mother as the New Eve and Lady Zion "giving birth to a new people in the messianic age" (Brown, *John*, 2:926). While I agree that the titles "Woman" and "Mother" are part of a constellation of images that evoke the Genesis creation narrative, I see the Johannine imagery pointing more towards God as the one "giving birth" in the Hour. Here, we need to allow Johannine imagery to have greater subtlety and even obscurity than allegorization, rather than looking for exact one-to-one equivalence. As R. Alan Culpepper explains, "Symbols … often span the gap between knowledge, or sensible reality, and mystery. They call for explanation and simultaneously resist it" (idem, *Anatomy of the Fourth Gospel: A Study in Literary Design* [Philadelphia: Fortress, 1983], 183). The flesh of ὁ Λόγος makes visible in history, the presence of ὁ Θέος (1:1, 14). The blood and water flowing from the flesh of Jesus symbolizes the rebirth of disciples, as children, born of God (1:14). Ingrid R. Kitzberger also speaks of the cross as a moment of birthing ("Synoptic Women in John: Interfigural Readings," in *Transformative Encounters: Jesus and Women Re-viewed* [ed. idem; BIS 43; Leiden: Brill, 2000], 107).

life-giving."[39] Jesus, as the one whose flesh makes God known, depicts the birthing moment when children are born of God. In his "labor" of death, Jesus' work is now finished (τετέλεσται, 19:28, 30; cf. Gal 4:19).

The verb τελέω reiterates God's judgment at the completion of his six days creative work – "thus the heavens and the earth were finished (συνετελέσθησαν) ... And on the seventh day God finished (συνετέλεσεν) the work" (Gen 2:1–2).[40] God's work, which was begun in creation, is brought to its completion at the cross as Jesus dies and breathes down the Spirit to the couple standing beneath the cross. In the next verse we are told that it was the day of Preparation before the Passover and the eve of Sabbath, and the narrator notes "that Sabbath was a great Sabbath" (19:31), the seventh day of blessing and rest when God's work of creation is ended. "So God blessed the seventh day and hallowed it, because on it God rested from all his work which he had done in creation" (Gen 2:3). But, throughout the Fourth Gospel Jesus had claimed that God in fact was still working (5:17), that the creative work of God had not yet been completed, and that he has been sent to complete (τελέω) this work (4:34; 5:36; 17:4). In the Hour, Jesus brings the work he was sent to accomplish to its conclusion. It is only with the death of Jesus that creation can truly hear the word "τετέλεσταί" and this word ushers in the great Sabbath, marking the completion of God's creative work that has been in process since the dawn of time "in the beginning" (Gen 1:1; John 1:1).

Woman and Mother

At both Cana and the cross, only two titles are given to this woman, known in the Synoptics as "Mary." In the Fourth Gospel in both scenes, she is described by the narrator using the title, "Mother" (2:1, 19:25) and spoken to by Jesus, with the title, "Woman" (2:4; 19:26). These two titles were names given to the first woman: "She shall be called Woman" (Gen 2:23). "The man called his wife's name Eve, because she was the *mother* of all the living" (Gen 3:20). These two titles, when considered with other unique features of the Johannine

---

[39] Lee, *Flesh and Glory*, 80. One ancient commentator who perceived birth symbolism in the flow of blood and water was Jacob of Sarug (450–520), who wrote, "Christ came and opened up baptism by his cross, so that it should be a mother of life for the world in place of Eve, water and blood for the fashioning of spiritual infants flowed forth from it, and baptism became the mother of life" (Homily on Three Baptisms), cited in Joel C. Elowsky, ed., *John 11–21* (Ancient Christian Commentary on Scripture: New Testament IVb; Downers Grove, Ill.: IVP, 2007), 328.

[40] Martin Hengel, "The Old Testament in the Fourth Gospel," in *The Gospels and the Scriptures of Israel* (JSNTSup 104; Sheffield: Sheffield Academic Press, 1994), 380–95, here 393–94.

Passion, suggest a deliberate evocation of the primordial Garden of Eden, and a theology of creation.[41]

Only in this Gospel, is Jesus arrested and buried in a garden (18:1; 19:41). As Frédéric Manns notes, "The symbol of the garden frames this section."[42] John emphasizes that the cross is in the center, "So they took Jesus ... to the place called the place of a skull ... There they crucified him, and with him two others, one on either side, and Jesus in the middle" (19:17-18).[43] The Johannine addition, "in the middle (μέσον)" echoes the phrase in Genesis where God plants "the tree of life in the middle of the garden" (LXX Gen 2:9: ἐν μέσῳ τῷ παραδείσῳ).[44] The evangelist depicts the crucifixion with the iconography of Gen 2: there is a garden, and in the middle of the garden is the cross, the tree of life, and at the foot of the cross stand a man, the Beloved Disciple and a woman, who is never named but called only "Woman" (John 2:4; 19:26) and "Mother," (2:1; 19:25), echoing the names given to the first woman (Gen 2:23; 3:20).

The Mother of Jesus: Her Characterization

The characterization of this woman from the ideological point of view of the Gospel lies in her two titles: Mother and Woman. The title "the Mother of Jesus" by which she is first introduced immediately emphasizes her relation-

---

[41] The theme of "creation" and "recreation" then continues in John 20 where Jesus is misunderstood to be the "gardener" by Mary Magdalene, the naming of the day as the first day of the week (20:1, 19), and "eight days" later (20:26), and when Jesus breathed (ἐνεφύσησεν) the Spirit upon his disciples with the same expression used in Genesis when God breathed (ἐνεφύσησεν) life into the face of the earth creature, and Adam becomes a living being (Gen 2:7). For more on the use of creation symbolism in John 20 see Mary L. Coloe, "Theological Reflections on Creation in the Gospel of John," *Pacifica* 24 (2011): 1-12; Jeannine K. Brown, "Creation's Renewal in the Gospel of John," *CBQ* 72 (2010): 275-90; Ruben Zimmermann, "Symbolic Communication between John and His Readers: Garden Symbolism in John 19–20," in *Anatomies of Narrative Criticism: The Past, Present, and Future of the Fourth Gospel as Literature* (ed. Tom Thatcher and Stephen D. Moore; Resources for Biblical Study 55; Atlanta: SBL, 2008], 221-35).

[42] The theme of creation is very richly developed in Frédéric Manns, *L'évangile de Jean à la lumière du judaïsme* (SBFA 33; Jerusalem: Franciscan Printing Press, 1991), 401-29 (quotation p. 409). He draws attention to many Genesis motifs within the Johannine Passion: the Kedron torrent (18:1), the tree of life in the middle of the garden (cf. 19:18), the rabbinic location of Eden beside the Jerusalem Temple. See also Margaret Barker, *The Gate of Heaven: The History and Symbolism of the Temple in Jerusalem* (London: SPCK, 1991), 57-95.

[43] The Synoptic Gospels mention the two criminals crucified with Jesus "one on the right and one on the left" (Mark 15:27; Matt 27:38; Luke 23:33), but only John adds, "and Jesus in the middle."

[44] The phrase, "in the middle of the garden" is repeated in Gen 3:3 (Marie-Émile Boismard and Arnaud Lamouille, *L'évangile de Jean* [Synopse des quatre Évangiles en Français 3; Paris: Cerf, 1977], 452; Manns, *L'évangile de Jean*, 426-27).

ship with Jesus. At Cana, because of this relationship, she presumes to speak to him about the wine shortage, which, ordinarily, should be no concern either to her or to Jesus. Jesus' strange "distancing" response sets up a dilemma for the reader, for while appearing to rebuff her, he then acts in accordance with her implicit request. The strangeness of his response also highlights his words that his Hour has *not yet* come, suggesting that there will be a time in the future when the relationship between mother and son will be important. Similarly, the use of the term "Woman" when Jesus speaks to his mother is strange. While it is not necessarily impolite, since it is the way Jesus later speaks to the Samaritan Woman (4:21), and Mary Magdalene (20:15),[45] it is unusual and again seems to suggest a distance between son and mother. Paradoxically the apparent "distancing" only emphasizes the relationship between Jesus and his mother.

At Cana, the two titles therefore arouse some discomfort in the reader due to Jesus' form of response.[46] This discomfort is not resolved until the cross where, in conjunction with other aspects of the Johannine crucifixion recalling the garden and tree of life (Gen 2) the titles "Mother" and "Woman" are part of a narrative strategy where the Johannine crucifixion is portrayed as an act of re-creation. And here, in this scene, the Mother's presence is crucial. Given that the Gospel is a narrative, the change in the status of the believer from disciple to brother of Jesus and child of God, could only be depicted in such a scene which has similarities to the formal process of adoption which bring about a change of relationship between two people.[47] From this point on disciples are children of God.[48]

---

[45] See also the woman caught in adultery (8:10).

[46] Resseguie identifies a narrative strategy he calls, "phraseological point of view" where there is ambiguity or strangeness in how the narrator or a character speaks. Names and titles are one aspect of this strategy (idem, *The Strange* Gospel, 10-15).

[47] Barrett states: "The form of words [your son] recalls formulas of adoption ... Adoption means the creation of a new relationship; the formula reveals what the new relationship is to be" (idem, *John*, 552; also Kitzberger, "Synoptic Women in John," 101).

[48] Karl Olav Sandnes studied ancient households and the importance of ties of kinship and friendship in relation to conversion to Judaism and Christianity. His primary focus was the sociological implications of conversion and the need to transfer bonds of kinship from one's birth family to the new community one is joining, which becomes like a family (idem, *A New Family: Conversion and Ecclesiology in the Early Church with Cross-Cultural Comparisons* [Studies in the Intercultural History of Christianity 91; Bern: Peter Lang, 1994). While not disagreeing with Sandnes on the social significance of the family metaphor for the Christian community, I am arguing that the Fourth Gospel directs this metaphor to the believers' relationship with God. The believer, in being drawn into the family of Jesus, is drawn into the communion of life with God, what Scholtissek names "die *Koinonia mit dem Vater und dem Sohn* (1 Joh 1, 3)" (Scholtissek, *Sein und Bleiben*, 239). The Fourth Gospel therefore takes this familial metaphor even further than the Pauline and Synoptic usage in describing believers as being "born anew" (3:5, 7), and participating in ζωὴ αἰώνιον – i. e., the very life of God in eternity (e. g., 3:15, 16, 36). The scene at the cross depicts this moment of rebirth, a moment of divine filiation.

Following Jesus' words, the narrator states, "from that hour the disciple took her" (εἰς τὰ ἴδια; 19:27). These words, are frequently understood in terms of the Beloved Disciple taking the Mother of Jesus, now his "mother," into his care. Such interpretations miss the theological and ecclesiological point of this passage. This phrase form an *inclusio* with it earlier use in the Prologue, "He came to his own (εἰς τὰ ἴδια) but his own did not receive him" (1:11). Here at the cross, this statement in the Prologue is brought to fulfillment and the plot of the narrative reaches its conclusion – believers become children of God. The characterization of the Mother of Jesus plays an essential role in this plot. In fact, the Mother's relationship to her son initiates his public ministry at Cana, and then enables it to be brought to fulfillment at the cross. For this reason Jean Zumstein speaks of the presence of the Mother at Cana as the ἀρχή and at the cross as the τέλος of Jesus' revelatory mission.[49]

In discussing characterization, Merenlahti places an emphasis on characters "in the process of becoming,"[50] rather than static "types" such as the heroes of Greek epics.[51] He makes use of the characterization of Judas across the four Gospels as a way of illustrating this claim. He states: "Both Luke and John report the exact moment when Judas the man, a greedy thief who stole from the common purse of the disciples (John 12:6), turns into Judas the betrayer occupied by Satan (Luke 22:3; John 13:27) – an intriguing case of a character *becoming possessed by his narrative role*" (italics mine).[52] This final phase aptly describes the significance of the Mother of Jesus. On one level, her explicit characterization declines. At Cana, she is active: she initiates, she responds, she directs. At the cross, she is passive: she stands, she says nothing, she receives directives. But when considering her characterization in relation to the ideological point of view of the Gospel, her role at the cross is where *she is possessed by her narrative role*. At the cross, there is no need for her to do or say anything. Her presence, her being "Woman and Mother" is sufficient for the theological goal of the narrative to be completed as disciples become children of God (1:12). Apart from Jesus, no other character is as important to the ideological point of view of this Gospel's narrative, than the Mother of Jesus.[53]

---

[49] Zumstein, *Kreative Erinnerung*, 271.
[50] Merenlahti, "Characters in the Making," 54.
[51] "Thus in the Gospels, characters are only in the process of becoming what they are" (Merenlahti, "Characters in the Making," 50).
[52] Merenlahti, "Characters in the Making," 61.
[53] Important though the Beloved Disciple is as eye witness, here at the cross, any disciple could have been present to achieve the ideological goal of divine filiation, but, by virtue of her unique relationship with her son, the Mother of Jesus was essential.

The Disciples:
The "Now" and "Not Yet" of Belief in Jesus

Susan E. Hylen

Interpreters often describe the disciples in John's Gospel as representatives of belief. Toward the end of the Farewell Discourse, Jesus says to his disciples, "The Father himself loves you, because you have loved me and have believed that I came from God" (16:27).[1] This straightforward declaration that the disciples have loved and believed in Jesus corresponds with many readers' expectations of the disciples as a character. In the words of R. Alan Culpepper, the disciples are "marked especially by their recognition of Jesus and belief in his claims."[2]

Such statements about the belief of the disciples always come with qualifications, however, because John's disciples are not whole-hearted in their belief. The verses that follow 16:27–28 bring the disciples' belief into question. Although Jesus has just said the disciples have believed he came from God, they indicate they only believe this now: "Yes, now you are speaking plainly, not in any figure of speech! Now we know that you know all things, and do not need to have anyone question you; by this we believe that you came from God" (16:29–30). The disciples' word choice, "now we know," suggests that something has recently changed in their understanding, that this belief is new. Their speech creates a tension with what Jesus has said.

Even more surprisingly, Jesus' subsequent words clash with his prior certainty about the disciples' love and belief. He says, "Do you now believe? The hour is coming, indeed it has come, when you will be scattered, each to his own home, and you will leave me alone" (vss. 31–32). Jesus questions the disciples' belief and predicts their desertion of him at the crucifixion.

---

[1] Translations are from the NRSV.
[2] R. Alan Culpepper, *Anatomy of the Fourth Gospel: A Study in Literary Design* (Philadelphia: Fortress, 1983), 115. See also Rudolf Bultmann, *The Gospel of John* (trans. G. R. Beasley-Murray; Philadelphia: Westminster, 1971), 589; Claude Coulot, "Les figures du maître et ses disciples dans les premieres communautés chrétiennes," *RevScRel* 59/1 (1985): 1–11, here 10; Rudolf Schnackenburg, *The Gospel According to St. John* (3 vols.; New York: Seabury, 1982–1990), 3:206; Fernando F. Segovia, "'Peace I Leave with You; My Peace I Give to You': Discipleship in the Fourth Gospel," in *Discipleship in the New Testament* (ed. Fernando F. Segovia; Philadelphia: Fortress, 1985), 78, 90.

Discontinuities such as these work against a "flat" assessment of the disciples as simple believers.³ Jesus' words in 16:31–32 conflict with what he has said earlier. He declares the disciples' love and belief and questions their certainty. The disciples' words create a similar tension. Their declaration of newfound faith contradicts Jesus' prior statement that they have believed. Such complexity in the disciples' character creates a rich opportunity for exploration, both of the character of the disciples and of John's message about the nature of discipleship.

Assessing the Character of the Disciples

John 16:27–32 is an example of the complex choices a reader faces when evaluating John's characters. The approach the reader takes in studying the disciples will affect the evaluation of their character. For example, in the mid- to late-20th century, source criticism allowed scholars to limit the verses considered relevant for a given character. This could affect the way the disciples were understood as a character, because some portions of the text (chapter 21, for example) were commonly eliminated from consideration.⁴ My approach in this study, following other literary critics, is to read the Gospel as a whole. The goal is not to speculate about the history of the production of the text, but to interpret the text as it stands. Reading the text as a literary whole makes it more likely that the reader will encounter discontinuities in the disciples' character. Here I discuss two other important elements of character study.

First, I assess the character of the disciples by identifying all of the elements of the Gospel that contribute to their characterization. I draw on David Gowler's description of modes of characterization, which he classifies in two categories, direct and indirect.⁵ Direct modes of characterization assign character traits through the voice of a reliable narrator. Luke's description of Simeon as

---

³ For the classic treatment of characters as "flat" and "round," see Edward M. Forster, *Aspects of the Novel* (New York: Harcourt, Brace & World, 1927), chs. 3–4. William J. Harvey's work has also influenced the interpretation of John's characters. He identified the "ficelle" as a type of character, one that serves a particular function in the plot, or that has a representative quality (idem, *Character and the Novel* [London: Chatto & Windus, 1965], ch. 3). For an example of the influence of Forster and Harvey on the interpretation of John's characters, see Culpepper, *Anatomy of the Fourth Gospel*, 102–4.

⁴ For example, Fernando Segovia eliminated chapters 15–17, 21 and parts of chapter 13 from consideration ("Peace," 79). Similarly, Rudolf Bultmann re-ordered the text, placing the disciples' rejection of Jesus in John 6 at the end of the Book of Signs (Bultmann, *John*, 443–51).

⁵ For a discussion of direct and indirect modes of characterization, see David B. Gowler, *Host, Guest, Enemy and Friend* (ed. Vernon K. Robbins; New York: Peter Lang, 1991), 55–75. Judith Hartenstein employs a similar method in *Charakterisierung im Dialog: Maria Magdalena, Petrus, Thomas und die Mutter Jesu im Johannesevangelium* (NTOA 64; Göttingen: Vandenhoeck & Ruprecht, 2007), 54–108.

"righteous and devout" (Luke 2:25) is an example of direct characterization. John describes John the Baptist as "sent from God" (1:6), but much more often employs indirect modes of characterization: what a character does; what a character says; what others say; the environment; and comparison with other characters. Evaluation of indirect modes of characterization is a complex task that requires considerable judgment. To arrive at an overall understanding of the disciples as a character, the reader must weigh Jesus' and the narrator's words about the disciples, their own words and actions, and elements of the Gospel's setting, keeping in mind potential comparisons with other characters in the narrative.

A second methodological decision addresses the boundaries of a character. In this study, I treat the disciples as a corporate character. Because the disciples often speak and act in unison, they may be viewed as a single character. "The disciples" (οἱ μαθηταί) are a group of indeterminate number first introduced in 2:2.[6] As I identify modes of characterization of the disciples, I look only for instances where "the disciples" are mentioned as being present in the story.[7] Individual disciples, including named disciples and the "one Jesus loved," contribute to the portrait of the disciples through the indirect mode of characterization, comparison with other characters. Similarly the group of disciples, "the Twelve" (6:67–71, 20:24) may also be explored as a separate character that the reader may draw on to understand the character of the disciples.[8] When characters act in similar ways, or when their differences are juxtaposed, the reader may perceive something about the character of the disciples. For example, Thomas's question in 14:5 voices confusion that seems familiar from the disciples' previous interactions with Jesus (e. g., in 4:33). Thus, his question may contribute to the reader's perception of the disciples' understanding of Jesus, as well as of Thomas' individual understanding. Individual disciples may have distinct functions in the Gospel, and may be treated on their own, just as it is useful to study "the disciples" as a separate character.

In this essay I present evidence regarding the character of the disciples according to these modes of characterization.[9] Part of the ambiguity in the

---

[6] The word "disciples" occurs prior to this in reference to the disciples of John the Baptist (1:35, 37).

[7] By contrast, in Cornelis Bennema's treatment of "the twelve," any individual disciple or group contributes directly to the character of the twelve. Bennema's decision to give preference to the twelve privileges the tradition of Jesus' twelve disciples over John's language, which rarely mentions the twelve and more commonly refers to this unnumbered group, "the disciples." See Cornelis Bennema, *Encountering Jesus: Character Studies in the Gospel of John* (Colorado Springs: Paternoster, 2009), ch. 14.

[8] See my discussion below under "Comparison with Other Characters."

[9] See also my chapter on the disciples in Susan E. Hylen, *Imperfect Believers: Ambiguous Characters in the Gospel of John* (Louisville, Ky.: Westminster John Knox, 2009), ch. 4. In that chapter, I present the evidence for the disciples' character in narrative order.

character of the disciples comes through the different signals the reader gets from these modes of characterization. Assessing the character in this way may help the reader to notice diverse aspects of the disciples' character.

What the Disciples Do

Very few actions are attributed to the disciples as a corporate character. Notably, the first verb that characterizes them as a group is their belief in Jesus (2:11). In 2:12, they also "remain" (μένω) with Jesus, a verb used frequently in John as a metaphor for discipleship. Thus, at the beginning a positive portrait of the disciples emerges. They believe and remain.

Many of the disciples' actions simply show their presence with and response to Jesus. They went with him (3:22), and they baptize (4:2), apparently on Jesus' behalf. They go to buy his food (4:8) and urge him to eat (4:31). They gather up the bread fragments at Jesus' command (6:12). They enter the garden with Jesus before his arrest (18:1), and they rejoice upon seeing him in the resurrection (20:20). These actions may implicitly characterize the disciples as those who remain with Jesus.

There are two small segments of the story where the disciples have sustained action. Both occur in chapter 6 (vss. 16–21; 60–71). The first of these is the sea-crossing story, in which the disciples' actions suggest both their understanding and their misunderstanding of Jesus. After the feeding miracle, the disciples went down to the sea, got into a boat, and started across (6:16–17). They saw Jesus walking toward them and they were terrified (v. 19). Being reassured by him, they wanted to take him into the boat (v. 21). In the Synoptic version of the story, the disciples think they see a ghost (cf. Matt 14:26; Mark 6:49). John's disciples, by contrast, "saw Jesus" walking on the sea (v. 19). They are not afraid because they think Jesus is a ghost. Instead, their fear suggests they understand that God's power is manifest in Jesus. Fear is a common biblical response to a theophany, as is Jesus' reassurance, "do not be afraid" (6:20).[10] John crafts the story in a way that suggests that the disciples experience Jesus' walking on water as an embodiment of the power of God.[11] Thus the actions of the disciples characterize them as understanding something significant about Jesus, something that contributes to the reader's developing understanding of who Jesus is. At the same time, their desire to

---

[10] Cf. Gen 15:1; 26:24; Dan 10:12, 19; Matt 28:5; Luke 1:3, 30; 2:10; Acts 27:24; Rev 1:17.

[11] For a lengthier treatment of the topic, see Susan Hylen, *Allusion and Meaning in John 6* (Berlin: de Gruyter, 2005), 131–34; Gail R. O'Day, "John 6:15–21: Jesus Walking on Water as Narrative Embodiment of Johannine Christology," in *Critical Readings of John 6* (ed. R. Alan Culpepper; BibInt 22; Leiden: Brill, 1997), 151–55.

take Jesus into the boat (v. 21) seems misplaced. This may suggest a misunderstanding on their part, as they formulate a desire that is not fulfilled by Jesus.

A different picture emerges in 6:60–71. Here the disciples are "complaining" about Jesus' teachings (v. 61; γογγύζω). In the context of this lengthy discussion about the manna (6:31–58), the word "complain" functions as an additional allusion to the manna story. It echoes the Israelites' "complaint" against Moses and God in the wilderness (cf. Exod 16:7; 17:3; Num 14:2, 27, 36).[12] Through the allusion, the disciples are characterized indirectly as the Israelites of the Exodus story. Although they have experienced God's power over the waters and believed in God (cf. Exod 14:31), they quickly began to complain, a sign of distrust.[13]

In these verses, John also characterizes the disciples as divided. After hearing Jesus address them, "many of his disciples turned back and no longer went about with him." Many interpreters have understood this rift as a division between true and false disciples, those who understand and believe, and those who fail to do so. The designation of "many of his disciples" (vss. 60, 66) reinforces this interpretive choice. Ludger Schenke, for example, argues that the disciples who turn away are no longer disciples but are Jews, characterized by unbelief.[14] However, it is also possible to read the dissention among the disciples as something that characterizes the disciples as a corporate character. In v. 61, Jesus is "aware that the disciples were complaining." That is, the group as a whole is characterized by the action of complaint. Even when some turn away, John continues to identify them as disciples: "many of his disciples turned back." Thus, instead of interpreting this division as a rift between true and false believers, the act of turning back may contribute to the disciples' character.[15] The disciples' actions in chapter 6 create a mixed impression: they both believe in Jesus and turn away from following him.

The Disciples' Speech

In contrast to their actions, the disciples' speech almost uniformly characterizes them as misunderstanding Jesus. As a group, the disciples speak relatively infrequently, but when they do they show blatant incomprehension. Twice the disciples do not understand Jesus' metaphorical speech (4:33;

---

[12] The LXX uses the related words διαγογγύζω and ὁ γογγυζμός.

[13] See my discussion in Hylen, *Allusion*, 146–52.

[14] Ludger Schenke, "Das johanneische Schisma und die 'Zwölf' (Johannes 6:60–71)," NTS 38 (1992): 105–21.

[15] I discuss this division within the disciples in relationship to the characters "the Jews" and "the crowd." See "Comparison to Other Characters," below.

11:12–13). Elsewhere, they question his teaching (6:60) and his decision to go to Lazarus (11:8). And while the narrative does not criticize their question about the blind man (9:2), Jesus rejects the options they present in favor of one they have not considered. Thus, the disciples' words consistently characterize them as misunderstanding.

The disciples' speech in the Farewell Discourse continues to portray them as lacking understanding. They respond to Jesus' teaching with confusion. In one instance, the disciples muse over and ponder Jesus' words, without apparent comprehension: "Then some of his disciples said to one another, 'What does he mean by saying to us,' 'A little while, and you will no longer see me, and again a little while, and you will see me;' and 'Because I am going to the Father?' They said 'What does he mean by this *a little while*? We do not know what he is talking about'" (16:17–18).[16] John's repetition of Jesus' words lengthens this interaction, drawing attention to their confusion and seeming to mimic the way the disciples are turning Jesus' words over in their minds. Later in this chapter, they speak once to declare their faith: "Yes, now you are speaking plainly, not in any figure of speech! Now we know that you know all things, and do not need to have anyone question you; by this we believe that you came from God" (16:29–30).[17] These words contrast with what Jesus has just said: "The hour is coming when I will no longer speak to you in figures, but will tell you plainly of the Father" (16:25). Although Jesus has spoken of this speech as a future event, the disciples see it as a present reality. And, as I noted above, Jesus immediately draws attention to their failure to respond to his message (vss. 31–32). These discontinuities raise questions about the disciples' understanding, even as they declare their belief.

On the other hand, the disciples' unequivocal Easter declaration: "We have seen the Lord" (20:25) characterizes them as understanding. These are the last words spoken by the disciples as a corporate character. They represent the disciples' witness to their experience of Jesus. Their words contribute to the perception that the disciples have some level of understanding following Jesus' resurrection.

What the Narrator Says

John constructs a narrator who gives frequent insight into the disciples' inner life. On the negative side, the narrator underscores the disciples' misunder-

---

[16] I also discuss this verse below under "Comparison with Other Characters."
[17] For a discussion of the meaning of the term "figures of speech" (Greek: παροιμίαι) in the Fourth Gospel, see Ruben Zimmermann, *Christologie der Bilder im Johannesevangelium: Die Christopoetik des vierten Evangeliums unter besonderer Berücksichtigung von Joh 10* (WUNT 171; Tübingen: Mohr Siebeck, 2004), 44–45.

standing of Jesus and their reluctance to ask Jesus questions. Yet the narrator also points forward to a later time when the disciples' remembrance of Jesus and his words provide important insights.

In a number of cases, the narrator points out the disciples' lack of understanding. For example, in 11:12, the disciples say regarding Lazarus, "Lord, if he has fallen asleep, he will be all right" (v. 12). The words "he will be all right" translate the Greek word σωθήσεται, which also means "he will be saved." The disciples' words might be interpreted as evidence that they understand that Lazarus has died but will nonetheless be saved. However, the narrator's comment eliminates this possibility: "Jesus, however, had been speaking about his death, but they thought he was referring merely to sleep" (v. 13). The narrator establishes the disciples' misunderstanding of Jesus' words.

Similarly, in 13:28 and 21:4, the narrator intervenes to describe misunderstanding by the disciples. In 13:21, Jesus initiates a conversation with the disciples about his betrayal. His identification of the betrayer comes in 13:28, but "no one at the table" understands. Similarly, in 21:4, the disciples are fishing and see Jesus on the shore, "but the disciples did not know that it was Jesus." Although the disciples' lack of knowledge may be excusable in both cases, it is noteworthy that the narrative asides specifically inform the reader about their lack of understanding.

The narrator also points out the disciples' reluctance to ask questions. In 4:27, the disciples are astonished to see Jesus conversing openly with the Samaritan woman, "but no one said, 'What do you want?' or 'Why are you speaking with her?'" The disciples' reluctance to ask contrasts with the bold questioning of the Samaritan, whose interaction with Jesus leads to greater understanding and to the faith of many (4:39–42). Something similar happens following 16:16–19, cited above, where the disciples formulate questions but do not ask.

The disciples' hesitation remains after the resurrection. The phrasing of 21:12 is unique: "Jesus said to them, 'Come and have breakfast.' Now none of the disciples dared to ask him 'Who are you?' because they knew it was the Lord." The narrator affirms that the disciples know it is Jesus but also formulates the question they dare not ask. This characterizes the disciples as simultaneously knowing and uncertain.

The narrator's foreknowledge of the disciples' future characterizes them in a positive light. The narrator points forward to a time when the disciples will remember and understand the events of Jesus' life. The cleansing of the Temple (2:22) and the entry into Jerusalem (12:16) are two events that the disciples do not understand during the narrative time. But the narrator indicates they will remember and reach greater understanding of these events after his resurrection. These insertions create an expectation for the reader that the disciples' story is not complete, and that greater understanding lies outside of the narrative time.[18]

What Jesus Says

Jesus' speech is important because he is a highly reliable character. Yet Jesus' words to and about the disciples create a mixed impression. Sometimes he suggests that the disciples believe, other times that they disbelieve. When he speaks metaphorically to describe his relationship with his followers, the disciples appear in a positive light as those who obey and bear fruit. Jesus also speaks of the disciples' future in glowing terms.

Many of Jesus' statements in the Farewell Discourse create the impression that the disciples believe in Jesus or understand important things about him. For example, Jesus says "You know the way to the place where I am going" (14:4) and "You know [the Advocate] because he abides with you and he will be in you" (14:17). Such statements suggest that the disciples already know a good deal during the course of the narrative. In addition, the verb tenses of Jesus' words create an impression that the disciples' faith is an accomplished fact. For example, when he says "the Father himself loves you, because you have loved me and have believed that I came from God" (16:27), "have loved" and "have believed" are in the perfect tense, which in the Greek represents an on-going state of affairs.[19] Other sentences suggest the disciples' belief or knowledge is complete. For example, the use of the aorist when the disciples' belief is introduced in 2:11 suggests that the narrator views their belief as a completed event. In these cases, Jesus' words suggest the disciples' firm belief.

However, in other cases Jesus' words call the disciples' belief into question. As I noted above, the disciples' declaration of their belief in 16:30 is followed by Jesus' question: "Do you now believe? The hour is coming, indeed it has come, when you will be scattered, each one to his own home, and you will leave me alone" (16:31). And although some verb tenses reinforce the disciples' belief, at other times verb tenses point toward their disbelief. In a number of cases, the use of the aorist subjunctive suggests that the disciples' belief may be completed in the future. For example, Jesus says, "For your sake I am glad I was not there, so that you may believe" (11:14). This pattern of speaking of the disciples' belief

---

[18] Jesus also anticipates the disciples' future understanding in 13:7; 16:4.

[19] The same is true of 17:8, where the aorist tense suggests the disciples' state of belief. Stanley Porter's notion that the perfect tense "frontgrounds" or highlights the action may also emphasize the disciples' state of belief. See e. g., Stanley E. Porter et al., *Fundamentals of New Testament Greek* (Grand Rapids, Mich.: Eerdmans, 2010), 315–24; Stanley E. Porter and Donald A. Carson, *Biblical Greek Language and Linguistics: Open Questions in Current Research* (JSNTSup 80; Sheffield: Sheffield Academic Press, 1993).

as an expectation of the future is repeated a number of times (cf. 13:19; 14:28, 29). The phrasing creates ambiguity about the disciples' current belief.

Jesus' metaphorical speech characterizes the disciples as having a close relationship to him. Jesus speaks metaphorically of the disciples several times, either in direct speech to them ("I have called you friends," 15:15; "you are the branches," 15:5), or indirectly (of sheep, 10:2–5). The metaphors show aspects of what it means to be a follower of Jesus: the friends do what he commands (15:14), the branches bear fruit and abide (15:2, 4, 5), and the sheep hear and follow (10:3, 4). In this way, the metaphors shed a positive light on the disciples' character, implying that they also do these things. Notably, the metaphors do not indicate the cognitive dimension of the disciples' belief (i. e., what they believe about Jesus) but point to its effects.

Many of Jesus' most positive statements about the disciples describe their future. For example, Jesus says, "In a little while the world will no longer see me, but you will see me; because I live, you also will live. On that day you will know that I am in my Father, and you in me, and I in you" (14:19–20). Jesus says the disciples will later be taught by the Holy Spirit (14:26), bear witness to Jesus (15:27; 17:20), and rejoice (16:22). Jesus' words characterize the disciples as people who will fully believe and understand in the future.

Jesus' speech also repeatedly characterizes the disciples as "chosen." For example, in 15:16, Jesus says, "You did not choose me but I chose you, and I appointed you to go and bear fruit" (cf. 13:18; 15:19). This idea of the disciples being chosen is consistent with language elsewhere in the Gospel that describes some as being "given" to Jesus (6:39; 10:29; 17:2, 24) or "drawn" to Jesus by God (6:43). These descriptions place the action of making disciples in the hands of Jesus or God. Disciples do not choose, but are chosen by Jesus.

The Environment

Elements of the character's environment may contribute to the reader's evaluation. For example, in the first resurrection appearances, the disciples are together in a locked room (20:19, 26). John indicates the disciples are there because of fear, lending a negative element to the characterization of the disciples (contrast Jesus' words about speaking openly in 18:20). Jesus' appearance (20:19–23) and the disciples' proclamation to Thomas (20:25) do not immediately change the situation, as they remain behind locked doors again a week later in 20:26. Likewise, many readers interpret the disciples' fishing in 21:1–3 as an indication that they have not fully understood the implications of the resurrection.[20] Such elements of the narrative are not clearly related to

---

[20] Bennema, *Encountering Jesus*, 120; Raymond E. Brown, *The Gospel According to John*

an individual character, and making such connections can be perilous. Many interpreters choose not to relate these elements directly to a character.[21]

Comparison with Other Characters

There are many possibilities for comparisons between characters, and I can treat only a few of them here. Many interpreters notice an implicit comparison between the Samaritan woman and the disciples.[22] Although the Samaritan woman's curiosity and bold questions lead to the faith of her whole community, the disciples hesitate to ask Jesus their questions (4:27). The disciples' question, "Surely no one has brought him something to eat?" (4:33), fails to engage Jesus' words on a metaphorical level, while the Samaritan woman's questions bring her closer to understanding (4:11–15). Jesus' words suggest that the disciples "have entered into" the labor of the eschatological harvest (4:38), but the "sowers" in the harvest of Samaritan believers are Jesus and the woman.

In a number of cases the disciples' behavior is strikingly similar to that of "the Jews." The complaining and division of the disciples in chapter 6 also characterizes the crowd and "the Jews." John employs the word "complaining" in this passage to characterize "the Jews'" response to Jesus (vss. 41, 43). Likewise, the crowd complains about him in 7:12. The crowd (7:12, 43) and "the Jews" (10:19–21; cf. 8:31 and 8:59) also appear to be divided in chapters 7–10. The division in the disciples parallels the condition of these other groups. These similarities are striking, because many interpreters have understood "the Jews" and the disciples as opposites: "the Jews" are representatives of disbelief, the disciples, of belief. Yet in these instances, John characterizes them with the same actions.[23]

At the end of chapter 6, comparison to "the twelve" reinforces the view of the disciples as divided. The twelve are introduced in 6:67 for the first time as a corporate character. Simon Peter steps forward with a collective confession of faith, "We have come to believe and know that you are the Holy One of God" (6:69), which contributes to the characterization of the twelve as believing. Yet the narrator steps aside to underscore Jesus' knowledge that the twelve also includes Judas Iscariot, who would betray Jesus (6:70–71). On the heels of the

---

(2 vols., AB 29 & 29A; New York: Doubleday, 1966, 1970), 2:1068–69; Edwyn Clement Hoskyns, *The Fourth Gospel* (ed. Francis N. Davey; London: Faber & Faber, 1947), 552.

[21] On the question of the disciples going fishing, see e.g., Francis J. Moloney, *The Gospel of John* (SP 4; Collegeville, Minn.: Liturgical, 1988), 549; Gail R. O'Day, *The Gospel of John* (NIB 9; Nashville: Abingdon, 1995), 857.

[22] See e. g., Élian Cuvillier, "La Figure des disciples en Jean 4," NTS 42 (1996): 245–59, here 253.

[23] Similarly, the question the disciples ask Jesus about where he is going (14:5; 16:17–18) echoes those of the Jews in 7:35–36 and 8:22.

departure of many of the disciples, the interchange with the inner circle reinforces the perception that the disciples are divided.

Many individual disciples also provide points of comparison for the disciples as a group. The individual disciples show insight and faith (e. g., Nathanael in 1:49; Peter in 6:69; Thomas in 20:28), yet they also display their lack of understanding (e. g., Thomas in 11:16; Peter in 13:36). At the end of the Gospel, the narrator points forward in time to the faithful witness of both Peter (21:19) and the Beloved Disciple (21:24). These two exemplify the potential that is promised of other disciples, yet the completion of their witness lies outside the narrative timeframe of the Gospel.[24]

As a whole, comparison with other characters leaves a mixed impression. The disciples are workers in the harvest, but they are not bold seekers. They reflect the pattern of disbelief of Israel and "the Jews." They believe and fail to understand, though their witness becomes important in the future time outside of the Gospel.

Evaluating the Evidence for the Disciples' Character

All interpreters recognize the disciples' frequent misunderstandings. Yet the most common assessment of the disciples is positive: they represent those who believe in Jesus. The idea that John's worldview is dualistic has strongly shaped this evaluation of the disciples. Interpreters have argued that John's characters are presented with an either/or choice to believe in or reject Jesus.[25] Characters must ultimately fall into one of two categories: belief or disbelief. If these are the only options available, it is not surprising that the disciples are evaluated as believers, even given their many failures and misunderstandings.

Yet interpreters' assessments of the disciples reflect the difficulty of making them fit neatly into dualistic categories. Many who evaluate the disciples as believers continue to reflect the tensions in the disciples' character. Culpepper follows his argument that the disciples are marked by their recognition of and belief in Jesus by this statement: "Yet they are not exemplars of perfect faith, but of positive responses and typical misunderstandings."[26] Cornelis Bennema presents the disciples as those who are "firmly on Jesus' side,"[27] even though a primary characteristic is their lack of understanding. These interpreters seem to prioritize the believing elements of the disciples, even though they recognize significant failures to do so.

---

[24] See my discussion of the Beloved Disciple (Hylen, *Imperfect Believers*, ch. 6).

[25] See for example the classic formulation in Culpepper, *Anatomy of the Fourth Gospel*, 104.

[26] Culpepper, *Anatomy of the Fourth Gospel*, 115.

[27] Bennema, *Encountering Jesus*, 121. Cf. 119–25.

An alternative approach is to let the discontinuities in the disciples' character stand. They believe in Jesus, yet their speech shows significant misunderstanding. They "remain" with Jesus, except at the most difficult hour of his crucifixion, when they scatter. Jesus attributes belief to the disciples, and creates great expectation for their future, yet he also questions their current belief. Read in this way, the disciples are a deeply ambiguous character. To suggest that they are representatives of belief implies that their primary or most important characteristic is belief. Yet the disciples believe and doubt, abide and scatter, know and misunderstand.

When John's disciples are read as an ambiguous character, the reader must make sense of these discontinuities. For example, how does it make sense that Jesus attributes both faith and disbelief to the disciples? His words seem contradictory at times. How can Jesus remain a reliable character? In addition, how does it make sense that the disciples misunderstand now but will understand everything later? Interpreters have found a number of ways to provide answers to such questions.

A popular approach is to interpret the disciples' character with a theory of progress. The disciples do not understand Jesus during his lifetime. Indeed, real understanding is not possible until Jesus' glorification. The promises of the Farewell Discourse point to future knowledge, belief, and love that disciples will fully inhabit with the assistance of the Holy Spirit.[28] Although the disciples do not live up to the Gospel's standards during Jesus' lifetime, the expectation is that they do so shortly thereafter.

Theologically, the implication is that full comprehension of Jesus should be possible for disciples, and such is required of all who truly believe. Although the disciples did not understand fully in Jesus' lifetime, their mistakes should allow later believers to avoid such problems as they believe and follow Jesus. Fernando Segovia argues, for example, that the promises of the Farewell Discourse are made only to those who believe in Jesus.[29] Read in this way, if the disciples do not achieve perfect belief at some point, Jesus' promises will never be fulfilled.

Another possibility is to maintain that the disciples never meet the Gospel's high standards for belief, abiding, and love. The image of the disciples as perfect believers is something that Jesus promises for the future, but from a narrative perspective it always remains in the future as well. In their final appearances of John 20–21, the disciples do not clearly develop into such perfect believers. They remain behind locked doors (20:26). They witness only to Tho-

---

[28] E. g., Bennema, *Encountering Jesus*, 121–24; Culpepper, *Anatomy of the Fourth Gospel*, 118; Segovia, "Peace," 81, 89–90; Fernando F. Segovia, "The Structure, Tendenz, and Sitz im Leben of John 13:31–14:31," JBL 104 (1985): 471–93, here 475.

[29] Segovia, "Structure," 478, 486.

mas, who does not believe them (20:24–25).[30] They do not dare to ask Jesus questions (21:12). Jesus promises great things for the disciples, but the reader never sees them happen. The fulfillment of these promises always lies just outside the completion of the Gospel story.

Read in this way, the disciples are an eschatological character. Their perfection is promised in a future time known only to Jesus. In the timeframe that lies within the reader's view, the disciples are always struggling to believe, to understand Jesus' identity and teachings, and to abide in his word. Discipleship is not the possession of those who have arrived at perfection, but is a journey of the imperfect – even, sometimes, of those who fail to live up to the Gospel's standards.

Understanding the disciples as ambiguous is difficult because of the common perception that John has a dualistic worldview, in which everything must fall into two polarized categories: e. g., light and darkness, above and below, belief and unbelief. In my analysis of the evidence, however, the disciples do not fit comfortably on either side of this divide. Instead of trying to make them fit, the disciples give interpreters reason to reassess the question of John's dualism. I have argued that the contrasts of the Gospel's language may instead function as standards for behavior.[31] Although the disciples are unable to meet the standards perfectly, the contrasting language may establish ideals for behavior and point toward a divine existence that exceeds the human capacity to understand or act. Disciples do not perfectly meet those standards, but they are nonetheless considered disciples.

The view that the disciples progress to perfection and my interpretation, in which their perfection is always unrealized, represent different choices regarding the language of the Gospel. Both are good interpretations, and each may be useful in different social contexts. The narrative of progress may help to motivate changes in behavior for those who would be disciples of Jesus. They must avoid darkness and come to the light (3:19–21). They must love as Jesus loved (13:34). They must believe that Jesus is "the Messiah, the Son of God" (20:31). Only when they do will they experience such promises as unity with God and Jesus (17:22–23).

Reading the disciples as an ambiguous character responds to different social and theological contexts. For example, one peril of reading the disciples as "true believers" is that it may contribute to a perception that believers are "insiders" who have already achieved perfect belief, knowledge, or behavior. Reading the disciples as ambiguous underscores a different view of discipleship, in which disciples are people who always seek to gain understanding. This perspective sees the Gospel as a rich resource for understanding Jesus, to

---

[30] Culpepper, *Anatomy of the Fourth Gospel*, 119.
[31] Hylen, *Imperfect Believers*. See especially 6–7, 158–59.

which readers may return again and again without achieving perfect understanding or belief. It suggests that standards like love or "coming to the light" are not the natural habitat of believers but are goals disciples should work toward. When the disciples are viewed as imperfect, believers may understand themselves as deeply flawed, yet called to persevere in discipleship toward the goals of belief, abiding, and love.

The Servants/Steward at Cana: The "Whispering Wizard's" Wine-Bearers

Mary L. Coloe

"Many of the views embodied in the narrative are expressed through the characters, and more specifically, through their speech and fate."[1]

These words of Shimon Bar-Efrat are particularly apt when considering the Gospel of John. This narrative has an explicit ideological point of view,[2] "that believing you may have life in his name" (20:31). All characters, even minor ones, participate in this narrative ideological goal. When considering the minor characters, Bar-Efrat cautions that it is "not always possible to make a clear and unequivocal distinction between a primary and a secondary character"[3] since an apparently "minor" character may have a significant function. The servants, and particularly the steward, at Cana exemplify the need for such caution.

The servants fulfill a technical role by complying to a guest's request, even if it appears strange. They fill the available jars with water, and then take some to the steward (2:7–8). When the steward's judgment is given to the bridegroom, these servants, along with Jesus and his Mother, are the only ones who know the origins of this "good wine." The narrator makes no mention of the servants' response to this knowledge. The reader is not told that they came to faith or exhibited wonder, even though they obey Jesus' words as a servant might obey the words of a guest. Their role complete, they disappear into the background.[4]

The steward of the feast, though apparently only a minor character, in fact has great significance when considering the "sign" value of the miracle. By many standards of character analysis he is a "flat" character, or a "type."[5] But

---

[1] Shimon Bar-Efrat, *Narrative Art in the Bible* (JSOTSup 70; Sheffield: Sheffield Academic Press, 1992), 47.

[2] James L. Resseguie provides a systematic study of the "point of view" in John (idem, *The Strange Gospel: Narrative Design and Point of View in John* [BIS 56; Leiden: Brill, 2001]; see pp. 4–5 for "ideological point of view").

[3] Bar-Efrat, *Narrative Art*, 86.

[4] Cornelis Bennema describes such characters as agents, actants, or walk-ons ("A Theory of Character in the Fourth Gospel with Reference to Ancient and Modern Literature," *BibInt* 17 [2009]: 375–421, here 407).

[5] Bennema considers the steward to be an agent (idem, "Theory of Character," 407); I prefer the designation "type" because he fulfills a function in the episode consistent with his title.

when this episode is read allowing the narrative to offer an implicit commentary through its symbolizing,[6] then this character plays a major role. To appreciate the significance of his role the Johannine clues must first be explicated.

Setting

The opening verse contains crucial information for interpreting the significance of the miraculous change of water to wine, and the role of the steward. The reader is told the temporal setting, "the third day," and the social context "there was a marriage." This apparently straight-forward information, when read with an understanding of first century Jewish religious festivals, is part of the implicit ideological perspective, which is often conveyed in the deeper symbolic resonances of the text.

What seems clear and simple on the surface is never so simple for the perceptive reader because of the opacity and complexity of the gospel's sub-surface signals. Various textual features, principally the misunderstandings, irony, and symbolism, constantly lead the reader to view the story from a higher vantage point and share the judgment which the "whispering wizard" conveys.[7]

In the Cana episode, there are a number of indications that situate this marriage within the Jewish Festival of Pentecost.[8] Francis Moloney and Birger Olsson have argued that the use of the phrase "the third day," the concluding expression that this was the first time Jesus "manifested his glory" and the words of the Mother of Jesus to the servants to "do whatever he tells you" suggest a deliberate allusion to the revelation of God's glory, on the third day at Sinai (Exod 19–24) during which the Israelites affirm, "Everything that the LORD has spoken we will do" (Exod 19:8; 24:3, 7).[9] At Sinai, Moses is instructed that the people are to be consecrated and prepared "for the third day" (Exod 19:11).[10] The narrative continues, "On the morning of the third

---

[6] "The symbols, like the images, metaphors, motifs, and themes to which they are related, often carry the principal burden of the narrative and provide implicit commentary and directional signals for the reader" (R. Alan Culpepper, *Anatomy of the Fourth Gospel: A Study in Literary Design* [Philadelphia: Fortress, 1983], 181).

[7] Culpepper, *Anatomy of the Fourth Gospel*, 151.

[8] Mary L. Coloe, *Dwelling in the Household of God: Johannine Ecclesiology and Spirituality* (Collegeville, Minn.: Liturgical Press, 2007), 39–43.

[9] Birger Olsson, *Structure and Meaning in the Fourth Gospel: A Text-Linguistic Analysis of John 2:1–11 and 4:1–42* (ConBNT 6; Lund: Gleerup, 1974), 102–9; Francis J. Moloney, *The Gospel According to John* (SP 4; Collegeville, Minn.: Liturgical Press, 1998), 65–74.

[10] Ruben Zimmermann notes that the expression found in Exod 19:11, "Consecrate them," was understood in later Rabbinic tradition as a formula of betrothal between God and Israel (idem, *Christologie der Bilder im Johannesevangelium: Die Christopoetik des vierten Evangeliums unter besonderer Berücksichtigung von Joh 10* [WUNT 171; Tübingen: Mohr Siebeck, 2004], 211). While the Rabbinic traditions are later, already in the OT Israel's covenant

day there was thunder and lightning, as well as a thick cloud upon the mountain" (Exod 19:16). Following the covenant ceremony in chapter 24, Moses ascends the mountain and God's glory settles on the mountain (Exod 24:16, 17).[11] The juxtaposition of the revelation of God's *glory* on the *third day* and the people's faith acclamation that they will do "everything that the LORD has spoken" provides an Old Testament background for the revelation of Jesus' glory on the third day.

By New Testament times the Sinai event was linked to the annual pilgrim Festival of Weeks, which is also known as "First Fruits" and in the later Greek books as "Pentecost."[12] In the celebration of Weeks the three days of Exod 19 were prefaced by four days of remote preparation.[13] The fourth day of this remote preparation is also the first of three days of immediate preparation according to the Exodus account. These preparations culminate therefore on "the third day," or the sixth from the beginning of the sequence. Moloney, correctly in my opinion, concludes that "[t]his time-scheme shapes the order of the events reported in John 1:19–2:12"[14] and explains the introductory phrase, "on the third day."[15]

Day 1 (vss. 19–28) John's testimony to the Jerusalem delegation.
Day 2 (vss. 29–34) John's testimony to Jesus' baptism.
Day 3 (vss. 35–42) Two of John's disciples follow Jesus. Andrew brings Peter to Jesus.
Day 4/1 (vss. 43–51) Day 1 of the Exodus 3 days of preparation. Philip and Nathanael.
Day 5/2
Day 6/3 (2:1-12) The revelation of Jesus' glory in Cana.[16]

---

relationship with God was likened to that of a marriage, with God as Israel's bridegroom (Isa 62:5; Jer 2:2; Hos 2:16). At Cana, the social context of a wedding alludes to these covenant traditions.

[11] Within the LXX, the term glory (*doxa*) is a technical expression reserved to translate the Hebrew word *kabod*, which is associated with weightiness in the sense of a person's honor. In English, this becomes "glory." Within the LXX, the term *doxa* comes to mean the divine revelation of God's essential nature in the created world. See Robert G. Bratcher, "What does 'glory' mean in relation to Jesus? Translating *doxa* and *doxazo* in John," BT 42 (1991): 401–408; Ceslas Spicq, "Δόξα, Δοξάζω, Συνδοξάζω," in *Theological Lexicon of the New Testament* (3 vols.; Peabody, Mass.: Hendrickson, 1994), 1:362–79; G. von Rad and G. Kittel, "Δόξα," TDNT 2:238–46.

[12] Feast of the Harvest (Exod 23:16), Feast of Weeks (Deut 16:10), day of the First Fruits (Num 28:26; Exod 23:16; 34:22; Lev 23:17), Pentecost (Tob 2:1; 2 Macc 12:32). See J. C. VanderKam, "Weeks, Festival of," ABD 6:895. The name "Feast of the harvest" may have been its original title (J. C. Rylaarsdam, "Weeks, Feast of," IDB 4:827).

[13] Moloney, *John*, 50.

[14] Moloney, *John*, 50.

[15] I am explaining this sequence in some detail, to emphasize the covenantal link with Sinai and to argue against interpretations that suggest a seven-day creation motif in John 1:19–2:12.

[16] This sequencing of days across the celebration of the Festivals is also found in the Mekhilta (ca. 250 C. E.) on Exod 19:10–11: "Go to the people and sanctify them today, that is, the 4th day. And tomorrow, that is, the 5th day. And they must be prepared for the third

The Steward and the Sign of Cana

The actions and words of the steward play a critical role in bringing to the surface the "sign" value of this episode. When the steward discovers the miraculously provided wine, he goes to the bridegroom and comments, "you have kept the good wine until now" (2:10).[17] His statement indicates that it was the role of the bridegroom to provide the wine, thus the steward implicitly reveals Jesus' identity as the bridegroom, since it was Jesus who provided the bountiful supply of good wine.[18] Later in the Gospel, John the Baptizer will explicitly name himself as the bridegroom's friend, and in this way confirm that Jesus is the bridegroom (3:29–30).

At Cana, when the narrator comments that this was the first of his signs, the word "sign" is not simply a synonym for miracle.[19] The sign of Cana points to the deeper identity of Jesus.[20] The episode begins by situating this event "on the third day" and concludes with the statement that this was the first time Jesus "manifested his glory." The opening and closing phrases frame the peri-

---

day, that is the 6th day, when the Torah was given" (see Jakob Winter and August Wünsche, *Mechiltha: Ein tannaitischer Midrasch zu Exodus* [Leipzig: Hinrichs, 1909], 199). A similar enumeration of days occurs in *Tg. Ps.-J. Exodus* 19 leading to the statement, "on the third day, on the sixth of the month ... the Lord was revealed on Mount Sinai." For further details of this see Coloe, *Dwelling in the Household of God*, 41–45.

[17] Without "hearing" these words, it is difficult to interpret any nuances other than a statement of fact. George R. Beasley-Murray suggests that these words may be ironical or humorous (*John* [WBC 36; Waco, Tex.: Word, 1987], 35). Zimmermann considers that the steward is critical of the bridegroom, and thus indirectly criticizing Jesus (*Christologie der Bilder*, 210). Zimmermann also makes a comparison between the steward and the Mother of Jesus, as usually it would be the steward who would give orders to the servants, but in this passage Jesus' Mother gives directions to the servants.

[18] For further detailed analysis of John's role see my "Witness and Friend: Symbolism associated with John the Baptiser," in *Imagery in the Gospel of John: Terms, Forms, Themes and Theology of Figurative Language* (ed. Jörg Frey et al.; WUNT 200; Tübingen: Mohr Siebeck 2006), 319–32; Marie-Émile Boismard, "L'ami de l'Époux (Jo. 3:29)," in *A la rencontre de Dieu: Mémorial Albert Gelin* (ed. A. Barucq et al.; Bibliothèque de la Faculté Catholique de Théologie de Lyon 8; Le Puy: Xavier Mappus, 1961), 289–95.

[19] See Frédéric Manns, "L'emploi du terme, sêmeion pour parler des miracles est un indice permettant de constater que le langage de Jean s'est enrichi d'un symbolism présent dans tout L'Evangile" (idem, *L'Evangile de Jean à la Lumière du Judaïsme* [SBFA 33; Jerusalem: Franciscan Printing Press, 1991], 111). On the significance of "signs" as a witness to divine authorization see Marie-Émile Boismard, *Moses or Jesus: An Essay in Johannine Christology* (trans. B. T. Viviano; Minneapolis: Fortress, 1993), 55–59.

[20] Many commentators overlook this aspect of the "sign" at Cana and interpret this passage in various ways: the miracle indicates the change of the waters of Judaism to the good wine of Christianity (Leon Morris, *The Gospel According To John* [rev. ed.; NICNT; Grand Rapids, Mich.: Eerdmans, 1995], 155); the comments of the steward proclaim the advent of the messianic era (Raymond E. Brown, *The Gospel According to John* [2 vols.; AB 29–29a; New York: Doubleday, 1966, 1970], 1:105). Barnabas Lindars links the "third day" to the resurrection (idem, *The Gospel of John* [NCB; London: Oliphants, 1972], 124).

cope with allusions to Exod 19, as discussed above. The covenanting God of Israel whose glory was once revealed at Sinai is now present in Jesus who comes as the covenant/bridegroom providing abundant wine. The steward is the character in this episode whose words provide the clue to the reader to make this identification. Thus, while apparently a minor character, his role is critical for understanding this first Johannine sign.[21]

---

[21] Zimmermann correctly identifies this scene as a "Jesuphanie" corresponding to the theophany at Sinai (*Christologie der Bilder*, 211).

The Bridegroom at Cana:
Ignorance is Bliss

Edward W. Klink III

At a wedding in Cana of Galilee the bridegroom, a necessary component for a wedding to exist, is conspicuously minimized in the narrative. He is given no name or voice: the only time he is mentioned is in v. 9, and he is only implied in v. 10 as the person to whom the master of ceremonies speaks. The implicitness of the bridegroom has resulted in his relative obscurity in studies on this pericope.[1] There is nothing about him that draws the reader toward him. Even the stone water jars receive more attention than the bridegroom. On the continuum of characterization the bridegroom is best defined as an "agent," a character given the least degree of complexity, development, and penetration into the inner life.[2] An agent is a plot functionary, a character that fulfills a function in the plot. To analyze the character of the bridegroom, therefore, we must understand the agent in relation to the plot. In a sense, the analysis of an agent character overlaps with an analysis of characterization, even though character (what a character is) and characterization (author's techniques of constructing character) are two different tasks. Although an agent character is a true character, the agency of the character is entirely motorized by and can only find meaning in the plot. This explains, then, our method for analyzing the bridegroom at Cana. The overlap between character and plot creates a poetic ambiguity that, in the language of Sternberg, "involves a two-way traffic" between the two.[3] As Sternberg explains, "in the absence of any preliminary givens, we first move from the action to the agent's character and then back

---

[1] Several studies have, however, made mention of the bridegroom in reference to the motif of marriage in the Gospel. For example, see Jocelyn McWhirter, *The Bridegroom Messiah and the People of God: Marriage in the Fourth Gospel* (SNTSMS 138; Cambridge: Cambridge University Press, 2006), 47–50, 79; Adeline Fehribach, *The Women in the Life of the Bridegroom: A Feminist Historical-Literary Analysis of the Female Characters in the Fourth Gospel* (Collegeville, Minn.: Liturgical Press, 1998), 23–43.

[2] The theory of characterization adopted here is taken from Cornelis Bennema, "A Theory of Character in the Fourth Gospel with Reference to Ancient and Modern Literature," *BibInt* 17 (2009): 375–421. See also Bennema's own analysis on characters in John in his *Encountering Jesus: Character Studies in the Gospel of John* (Milton Keynes: Paternoster, 2009).

[3] Meir Sternberg, *The Poetics of Biblical Narrative: Ideological Literature and the Drama of Reading* (Bloomington, Ind.: Indiana University Press, 1985), 344.

and forth ..."[4] The interplay between character and plot is a necessary component of dramatic irony, which is clearly at work in this pericope.[5] For this reason it is necessary to develop the plot in 2:1–11 so as to have handles to grasp the character of the bridegroom.[6]

Although the context for the pericope is a wedding, the conflict made clear from the beginning (v. 3) is the lack of wine. Wine was a standard part of daily life in the ancient Mediterranean world, but was an important, even necessary, part of festive occasions, especially at weddings.[7] Since weddings in the first century were not about two people but about two families, the social dynamics were more comprehensive and intense. For this reason to run out of wine during wedding celebrations was likely to have caused a loss of family honor and status, and possibly even financial loss through legal means.[8] Thus, by v. 3 the reader is present at a wedding and is feeling the social pressure that has emerged due to the lack of wine. But the climax of the conflict is not the lack of wine; rather, it is the burden of those responsible for the wedding to provide wine. And by the end of v. 3 we find out that the Mother of Jesus is somehow connected to those who bear the responsibility. Jesus himself, therefore, is at the center of the conflict. The climax of the conflict is presented in v. 4 when Jesus distances himself from the problem at this wedding, and in a very Johannine way unites himself to a much larger problem.

From v. 5 onward the narrative is caught between the strange irony that is common to John. As much as Jesus will do what his mother asks, it is an entirely secondary task that is, if nothing else, parabolic of that which is to come. Although the Mother of Jesus wanted the wedding at Cana to reach its end without embarrassment, especially for the family involved, Jesus, thinking of a much grander wedding feast and a much larger family (1:12), knew that embarrassment (the cross) is required for his wedding to reach its ultimate conclusion. The narrative's emplotment does all it can to give the reader a taste of the irony. A wonderful coincidence occurs in v. 6 with the close proximity of six stone water jars used for Jewish purification. That they are stone makes clear that they are both permanently clean and intimately tied to purification.

---

[4] Sternberg, *Poetics of Biblical Narrative*, 344.

[5] R. Alan Culpepper, *Anatomy of the Fourth Gospel: A Study in Literary Design* (Philadelphia: Fortress, 1983), 168, 176. Although Culpepper locates the dramatic irony surrounding the master of the banquet, the bridegroom is not only a necessary component in the scene in which he appears (2:9–11), but also in the larger significance of the pericope, even the entire gospel.

[6] For a fuller development of the plot of this pericope see Edward W. Klink III, *John* (ZECNT 4; Grand Rapids, Mich.: Zondervan, forthcoming).

[7] Craig S. Keener, *The Gospel of John: A Commentary* (2 vols.; Peabody, Mass.: Hendrickson, 2003), 1:500.

[8] Bruce J. Malina and Richard L. Rohrbaugh, *Social-Science Commentary on the Gospel of John* (Minneapolis: Fortress, 1998), 70–71.

In this way they become useful for what would initially be taken as an entirely different purpose: wine jars. The vessels previously used to contain the requirements for purification were now to contain the celebratory drink. The relation between purity and celebration finds an uncanny connection to the person and work of Jesus. The stated crisis at this wedding is being refracted to envisage the greater crisis – and both find their solution in this one act of Jesus. This wedding in Cana, this need for wine, and this moment in time simultaneously reflect something much greater and more important. The greatness of the celebration is emphasized by the fact that the jars were filled to the brim with water. The imagery is just too potent. In the presence of Jesus, a collection of pure (stone) water jars for the ceremonial washing of many people serve to herald the fulfillment ("to the brim") of the entire ceremonial purification of Judaism. Finally, in v. 8 the resolution to the problem is presented to the master of the banquet, the one selected to oversee and preside over the celebration, who would confirm not only the amount but also the quality of the wine.

The conflict has been presented and the resolution made manifest and still the narrative has not yet mentioned the bridegroom. While a bridegroom's role in a wedding is traditionally an essential component, in this wedding he has been eclipsed. The delay of his introduction, therefore, is highly suggestive. It is interesting to note that four different characters are portrayed as connected to the lack of wine, and in the following order: the Mother of Jesus, Jesus, the master of the banquet, and the bridegroom.[9] Of the four only Jesus is named, which signals his more overarching importance to the Gospel; and of the four only the bridegroom does not speak. It is possible for an agent character to speak, but the silence of the bridegroom allows him to be entirely formed by the narrative's emplotment. While the responses of the Mother of Jesus and the master of the banquet to Jesus create a distance between themselves and Jesus, the bridegroom is able to serve as an impressionable image in which Jesus (and his mission) is reflected. Just as the Mother of Jesus is clueless regarding the larger conflict to which Jesus refers (vss. 3–5), so also the master of the banquet is clueless regarding the origin of the wine (v. 9). It is ironic that the master of the banquet, the person who should have the most intimate and accurate knowledge of the source and quality of the wine for the wedding, was surprised by what he was responsible for. It is for this reason that the bridegroom is called upon. The bridegroom remains silent, but plays one central role in the actual circumstances of the scene: he receives the exclamatory announcement from the master of the banquet regarding the wine, an announcement of commendation that should have been addressed to Jesus. The statement ends the scene and serves to explain the meaning and signifi-

---

[9] We exclude the servants since they are portrayed as insiders (cf. v. 9), that is, ideal readers.

cance of the pericope. An ironic implication is suggested when the master of the banquet places the responsibility for this act on the bridegroom: "but *you* have kept the good wine until now." The bridegroom gets the credit for what Jesus has done. At this moment the silence of the bridegroom is deafening. The narrative does not provide a response, even though it might have given even further evidence that someone unknown to them both provided the wine. The exclusion can only be intentional. The irony demands that Jesus be seen as fulfilling the role of the bridegroom.[10] The master of the banquet is surprised that the bridegroom would have served such a good wine, especially so far into the wedding celebration. Refracted through the person and work of Jesus the image of purification is now made clear: what Jesus brings at the end of the process is nothing but "grace in place of grace" (1:16), which surprisingly comes strongest at the end. The plot ends with this statement. Although Jesus' status as the bridegroom is officially "not yet," his role as the true bridegroom is bursting through the narrative's significance and imagery, and will be announced by John in the following chapter (3:27–30). The narrative has performed a metaphorical interaction and roll exchange between and across the characters, so that their identities become intentionally intertwined.[11] It is with the full weight of the pericope's significance that the action of the pericope ends, with the two primary actors in this wedding, the master of the banquet and the bridegroom, discussing with astonishment the provisions for a wedding that, as the reader knows, is even greater than they understand.

The interplay between character and plot in this pericope provides insight into the agent character of the bridegroom at Cana. The narrative agency of the bridegroom is to employ the situational irony to a theological end, guiding the reader to see that Jesus performed the role of the bridegroom at the wedding in Cana so as to establish in 3:29 his role as the eschatological bridegroom. In spite of himself, the bridegroom of Cana provides a perfect characterization of the situation of the true bridegroom. The agency of the bridegroom serves to highlight the person and work of Jesus. The context of the wedding, the imagery of purification, and large amount of water-to-wine all forge in the minds of the readers the significance of Jesus, a significance that extends well beyond things seen and understood. We can only imagine that the wedding in Cana on this day went on as it should have. Public shame was avoided when refills of wine for the entire wedding party was followed by praise for the quality of the wine. The historical bridegroom may well have been the center of the attention on that day. But an "hour" (v. 4) was coming

---

[10] By his provision of wine, Jesus is also fulfilling at least in part the role of the master of ceremonies.

[11] Ruben Zimmermann, *Christologie der Bilder im Johannesevangelium: Die Christopoetik des vierten Evangeliums unter besonderer Berücksichtigung von Joh 10* (WUNT 171; Tübingen: Mohr Siebeck, 2004), 208–15.

when the true bridegroom would be made known. Unlike what he prevented from happening in Cana, on his day the true bridegroom will receive shame from those in attendance. And unlike the servants in Cana, not even those on the inside will understand the significance of what is taking place. And it is for this reason, as John bears witness, that he must increase and we must decrease (3:30). John's exhortation encourages us all to become like the bridegroom, an agent character who is entirely anonymous and passive, serving as a pure reflection of Jesus.

The Brothers of Jesus:
All in the Family?

Joel Nolette and Steven A. Hunt

Many of the characters in the Gospel of John do not simply embody one type of response or reaction to Jesus, but rather are ambiguous, serving as counterbalances to the pervasive dualisms in the Gospel.[1] It is hard to determine, for example, what single "type" a character like Nicodemus or Pilate represent. Their interactions with Jesus lend themselves to various readings.[2]

The brothers of Jesus in the Gospel, however, are anything but ambiguous. They appear only twice in the Gospel. They are first introduced in an "itinerary fragment"[3] in 2:12, where they are seen leaving Cana with Jesus, his mother, and the disciples after Jesus turned the water into wine. They reappear briefly to share center stage with Jesus before the Feast of Tabernacles in 7:1–9, where they instruct him to go up to Jerusalem to reveal himself "to the world." Before unpacking the significance of this confrontation as the key to their characterization in the Gospel, we must first pursue two other details.

Few topics in Johannine studies have proved as difficult as the one related to the Fourth Gospel's use of sources. Notwithstanding the diversity of opinions on this subject, the most productive way forward is to postulate the author's direct dependence on the Synoptics.[4] This working methodological hypothesis is important when considering the characterization of Jesus' brothers, because the scene where they figure most prominently in the Gospel (6:59–7:9) is most likely a rewriting of the "rejection at Capernaum" found in Matt 13:54–58 and Mark 6:1–6.[5] Apart from the fact that the three accounts are situated in the same town, the verbal parallels with respect to the crowd's

---

[1] Cf. Colleen M. Conway, "Speaking Through Ambiguity: Minor Characters in the Fourth Gospel," *BibInt* 10 (2002): 321–41, here 325.

[2] See, e. g., Conway's critique of the divergent interpretations of the character Nicodemus on pp. 329–30.

[3] Mark W. G. Stibbe, *John* (Sheffield: JSOT Press, 1993), 48.

[4] See further, Steven A. Hunt, *Rewriting the Feeding of Five Thousand: John 6.1–15 as a Test Case for Johannine Dependence on the Synoptic Gospels* (SBL 125; New York: Peter Lang, 2011).

[5] So Barnabas Lindars, *The Gospel of John* (NCB; Grand Rapids, Mich.: Eerdmans, 1972), 281. While Luke presents a similar rejection story specifically in Nazareth (4:16), Matt (13:54) and Mark (6:1–2) suggest simply that the rejection took place in Jesus' "hometown" (πατρίδα), a location elsewhere identified as Capernaum (Matt 4:13; Mark 2:1).

response to Jesus makes this identification quite plausible.[6] It is thus interesting to note in John that the narrator does not mention Jesus' brothers in connection with this rejection, reserving their appearance instead for the passage that follows Peter's confession of faith on behalf of the disciples in 6:69. This modification of source material and its rationale becomes apparent when the introduction of the brothers in 2:12 is briefly examined.

Immediately after the wedding at Cana the narrator notes that "[Jesus] went down to Capernaum, he and his mother and his brothers and his disciples." Since Jesus' brothers had not been mentioned at the wedding (unlike the others), their appearance here is clearly awkward; given the number of variant readings, apparently scribes thought so too. The evidence favors the textual reading in the UBS[4] – not least since their absence at the wedding makes their unexplained presence in the short travelogue following it a more difficult reading.[7] The fact that Jesus' disciples "believed in him" (ἐπίστευσαν εἰς αὐτόν) in 2:11 and declare their faith through Peter (πεπιστεύκαμεν) in 6:69 – events directly preceding the only appearances of Jesus' brothers in the Gospel – suggests that the narrator wants to juxtapose the brothers with the disciples, specifically in scenes where the latter have been portrayed positively. Clearly, the brothers come out on the negative side of this juxtaposition. A brief look at their portrayal in 7:3–5 makes their negative characterization clearer still.

Ironically, the response of Jesus' brothers to his self-imposed exile in Galilee is, at first glance, quite sensible. After all, Jesus himself earlier had proclaimed, "The one who does the truth comes to the light in order that his works might be seen, that they have been done in God" (3:20–21). The brothers appear to be exhorting Jesus to live up to his own word: Jesus belongs in Jerusalem, especially during feast-time, so that he might reveal himself to the people instead of hiding in Galilee. As Brown puts it, their advice is a "theological challenge to the Light to show himself to the world."[8] Note that they do not question Jesus' ability outright, posing their challenge instead with a condition: "If you do these things, reveal yourself to the world!" (7:4). If they had witnessed the previous scene wherein a large number of disciples (πολλοί) left Jesus in 6:66, they could be advising him to "fish or cut bait" – either be serious and go to Jeru-

---

[6] For example, compare where the author combines and condenses Mark 6:3 and Matt 13:55–56 in John 6:42.

[7] 𝔓[66], A, B, and the Majority Text, as well as Origen, Augustine, and Chrysostom, mention all three figures as leaving Cana with Jesus. Cf. Bruce M. Metzger, *A Textual Commentary on the Greek New Testament* (2d ed.; Stuttgart: Deutsche Bibelgesellschaft, 1994), 173. A handful of Old Latin mss. as well as ℵ omit mention of the disciples, possibly indicating that "his brothers" referred to the disciples who were actually at the wedding (2:2, cf. 20:17). A few MSS, including a 3rd century Coptic MS, omit "brothers" while retaining "disciples." Cf. the discussion in Raymond E. Brown, *The Gospel According to John I (i–xii)* (AB 29; New York: Doubleday, 1966), 112.

[8] Brown, *John*, 306.

salem or stop pretending while hiding in Galilee. Perhaps worse, on at least one ancient reading, the brothers are guilty of acting only in self-interest: "Jesus' brothers want him to go up to the festival in Jerusalem so they can share the limelight with him [and] so that they might also be glorified through him."[9] Similarly, Thomas Brodie suggests that the brothers here resemble the crowd in 6:15 who wanted to make Jesus king: "[T]hey seek to turn his mission into a spectacle which may suit their own purposes."[10]

In any case, the narrator is quick to dispel any possibility of a positive reading, explaining that theirs was not helpful brotherly advice, but issued instead from a lack of faith in Jesus.[11] The very presence of imperatives demonstrates their disrespectful tone: "[T]hey speak to him almost as if he were a slave."[12] A closer inspection of the Gospel as a whole turns up a number of other details that suggest the brothers are not just guilty of faithlessness but of explicit hostility.

Note, for example, the brothers' effort to force Jesus to go to Jerusalem. Readers of the Gospel recall that in 5:18 "the Jews" of Jerusalem (in this instance, Jewish authorities) wanted to kill Jesus for Sabbath-breaking and for provocative statements about his identity. The fact that the narrator reached back to this detail to remind readers in 7:1 that Jesus was in Galilee because "the Jews" were seeking to kill him, suggests that the brothers' words are to be read not as helpful advice but as disingenuous manipulation that betrays a secret desire that Jesus be arrested and perhaps even killed.[13] Compare, for instance, their desire that Jesus go to Jerusalem to the disciples' reaction when they learn Jesus wants to go up to Judea later in the narrative: "Rabbi, the Jews were just now seeking to stone you, and yet you go there again?" (11:8; cf. 11:16).

As a number of commentators have recognized, their words also echo one of the temptations Jesus faced during his testing in the wilderness (Cf. Matt 4:5–7//Luke 4:9–12): "Jesus' brothers duplicate Satan's temptation of Jesus at the beginning of his ministry by interpreting Jesus' messianic calling in self-

---

[9] Theodore, in *John 1–10* (ed. Joel C. Elowsky and Thomas Oden; vol. 4a of ACCS; Downers Grove, Ill.: InterVarsity Press, 2006), 250.

[10] Thomas L. Brodie, *The Gospel According to John: A Literary and Theological Commentary* (Oxford: Oxford University Press, 1993), 311.

[11] Note that this is ἐπίστευον εἰς αὐτόν, a construction that indicates the gravity of their faithlessness, as this is the most important "type" of faith in John. Cf. Charles H. Dodd, *The Interpretation of the Fourth Gospel* (Cambridge: Cambridge University Press, 1953), 179–86.

[12] Brodie, *John*, 311.

[13] *Pace* J. Ramsey Michaels, *The Gospel of John* (NICNT; Grand Rapids, Mich.: Eerdmans, 2010), 420, 426: "His brothers, apparently ignorant of the danger, urge him to go....There is no reason to doubt their good brotherly intentions – no implication, for example, that they wanted him to go to Judea so that he would be arrested and killed." While this might be true relative to any possible historicity behind the passage, as the story has been appropriated in John it clearly seems to cast the brothers as malevolent.

seeking terms."[14] Such an interesting parallel between the temptation of Satan in Matthew and Luke and the "advice" of Jesus' brothers here in John, suggests that they are being portrayed in a starkly negative light. While the Devil does not speak in John, Jesus' brothers do and, one might say, they speak on his behalf!

The complex theme related to Jesus' "open" revelation occurs a number of times throughout the Gospel. The brothers' critique that "no one does anything in secret (κρυπτῷ) while seeking to be known openly (παρρησίᾳ)" shows them to be ignorant of Jesus' revelation and puts them in the company of hostile "Jews" in the temple during another feast in 10:24: "If you are the Christ, say so to us openly (παρρησίᾳ)!" Before his inquisitors, in fact, Jesus declares, "I have spoken openly (παρρησίᾳ) to the world…and in secret (κρυπτῷ) I have spoken nothing" (18:20) – a defense which would have worked also with his brothers in chapter 7. The crowd at the Feast of Tabernacles attests to this as well for they remark that "he speaks openly (παρρησίᾳ) and no one says anything to him" (7:26). The brothers' ignorance of Jesus' revelation puts them on the side of those who are seeking to kill him (cf. 10:31). By way of contrast, the disciples do not demand that Jesus reveal himself; nevertheless they receive his revelation because of their faith: "the hour comes when … I will proclaim to you openly (παρρησίᾳ) concerning the Father" (16:25), to which they respond, "Behold, now you speak openly (παρρησίᾳ) … this is why we believe" (vss. 29–30).

A subtle shift occurs during the encounter between Jesus and his brothers with respect to Jesus' relationship to "the world." On the one hand, the world is simply the stage upon which the events of the Gospel unfold (cf. 1:9); it is also, however, a character in its own right which, over the course of the Gospel, has an ambiguous and sometimes tense relationship with Jesus. Excluding the ominous reference in 1:10, the rest of the references to the world up until this point in the narrative are positive in orientation: God loves the world (3:16); the Son has come to save the world (cf. 1:29; 3:17); the Bread of God came down to give life to the world (cf. 6:33, 51). Now, however, with the brothers' words to Jesus, the world transforms, becoming a hostile character: "The world cannot hate you, but it hates me, because I testify concerning it that its deeds are evil" (7:7).[15] After this, readers will learn that the world is in the process of being judged (12:31), that it hates Jesus' disciples (15:19), and

---

[14] Andreas J. Köstenberger, "John," in *Commentary on the New Testament Use of the Old Testament* (ed. Greagory K. Beale and Donald A. Carson; Grand Rapids, Mich.: Baker Academic, 2007), 414–512, here 452. In fact, Brown suggests that this type of story in John forms part of the historical background for the temptation narratives in the Synoptics: "Matthew and Luke are giving in dramatic form the type of temptations that Jesus actually faced in a more prosaic way during his ministry" (Brown, *John*, 308). Cf. also George R. Beasley-Murray, *John* (WBC; Waco, Tex.: Word Books, 1987), 106–107.

[15] "Through the confrontation between Jesus and his brothers it may be seen that … [Jesus'] revelation will confront the world's unbelief …" (Brodie, *John*, 312).

that eventually Jesus will conquer it (16:33). Ironically, therefore, the brothers starkly exemplify the prologue's notion that "the world did not know him" (1:10). That the world *cannot* hate the brothers indicates that they belong to it, for "the world loves its own" (15:19),[16] and it once again links them with hostile "Jews" in the Gospel who are also "of this world" (8:23; cf. 8:59).[17] Their disingenuous tone, made clear by the narrator's aside about their unbelief, indicates that they are guilty of the fundamental sin in the Gospel.[18] There is no ambiguity in John on this point: "The one who does not believe has already been judged, because he has not believed in the name of the one and only Son of God" (3:18).

Interestingly, Jesus' encounter with his mother at Cana (2:3–9) and his brothers here follow a similar pattern of request/command, refusal by Jesus, followed by subsequent performance of the request/command.[19] While the Mother of Jesus responds with (believing) expectation (2:5), the brothers do not. Other characters have at least believed on account of the signs Jesus did (cf. 2:23; 4:48; 6:2; 20:29) and Jesus himself encourages just such belief in 10:38. The brothers' recognition of the deeds of Jesus coupled with their failure to believe, indicates that the narrator clearly intends to portray them in a very negative light.

The last that readers see of the brothers is when they go up to Jerusalem for the Feast of Tabernacles (7:10), which demonstrates, as Calvin noted, that they "are on friendly terms with unbelievers, and therefore walk without any alarm."[20] It is as if, in going up to the Feast of Tabernacles – a Feast of "the Jews" (7:2; cf. 2:13; 5:1; 6:4) – they disappear into the crowd of "Jews," the very group with whom Jesus would soon come into open conflict (cf. 8:31–59). Are his brothers among those who attempt to stone him in 8:59? Given that sibling

---

[16] Cf. Beasley-Murray, *John*, 107; Michaels, *John*, 427.

[17] Michaels, *John*, 427. Cf. Brown, *John*, 307, who notes that "the Jews are also the spokesmen of a wider opposition on the part of the world, an opposition quite evident in the evangelist's time."

[18] On the variant that inserts a "then" into v. 5, Lindars is likely right to suggest that this was added to harmonize the state of the brothers in this Gospel (which was "back then") with the words in Acts 1:14 that indicate that his brothers became believers (Lindars, *John*, 283).

[19] Cf. Cornelis Bennema, *Encountering Jesus* (Milton Keynes: Paternoster, 2009), 70. There are other parallels between the two family encounters. For example, in both accounts, after refusing, Jesus seems to act in secret, without the knowledge of others in the scene. In both scenes, Jesus' refusal relates to time (2:4; 7:6). In both places, it appears that Jesus' family is at cross-purposes with him, suggesting things to him that only the Father can commission him to do (cf. 5:30). This pattern, a "Johannine motif" (Lindars, *John*, 281), also occurs in modified form with the healing of the official's son (4:46–54) and the raising of Lazarus (11:1–44). It is noteworthy therefore that among the occurrences of this pattern, the brothers are the only ones who do not exhibit belief in Jesus.

[20] John Calvin, *Commentary on the Holy Gospel of Jesus Christ, According to John* (trans. W. Pringle; Grand Rapids, Mich.: Baker Books, 1999, reprint), 286.

rivalry and even fratricide are such common themes in Scripture,[21] readers should not summarily reject such a possibility.

While the Fourth Gospel characterizes the brothers of Jesus as unbelievers,[22] there is another group, however, that appears as Jesus' "brothers" later in the Gospel – namely, the circle of Jesus' followers. The narrator establishes, then, a "supersessionist" view of Jesus' brothers: while his kin "from below" do not believe, his "true brothers" do.[23] This motif is further magnified when Jesus gives his mother to the Beloved Disciple and the Beloved Disciple to his mother while on the cross (19:26–27). Jesus' brothers "according to the flesh" are conspicuous only for their absence from this critical scene. They remain estranged from their crucified brother because of their unbelief. Similarly, after the resurrection, when Jesus instructs Mary Magdalene to "go *to my brothers* and say to them, 'I am ascending to my Father and your Father, to my God and your God,'" the narrator's intention along these lines becomes focused and explicit. For in the very next verse Mary does not go to Jesus' brothers by birth, but instead "went and announced *to the disciples*, 'I have seen the Lord'" (20:17–18).

Apart from these more obvious examples, one more curious detail from the Gospel could be understood to support the argument that the narrator depicts Jesus' actual brothers negatively in order to identify disciples as "true brothers." In John 14:22, during Jesus' final discourse, a disciple named Judas (specifically, not Iscariot) appears for the only time in the Gospel to ask Jesus, "Lord, how is it that you will reveal yourself to us (ἐμφανίζειν σεαυτόν) and not to the world (τῷ κόσμῳ)?" His question parallels the brothers' earlier command, when they directed Jesus to "reveal yourself to the world" (φανέρωσον σεαυτὸν τῷ κόσμῳ). Again, given our working hypothesis regarding the author's use of the Synoptics, this unique detail in John may be suggestive. Judas is only named as a disciple in Luke 16:16 and Acts 1:13. In the other Synoptic lists of Jesus' disciples this Judas is presumably the disciple named Thaddaeus (Matt 10:3; Mark 3:18). Interestingly, however, in Matthew and Mark, one of the brothers of Jesus is named Judas (Matt 13:55; Mark 6:3). Traditionally, this brother has been identified with the disciple mentioned in Luke-Acts, as well as the author of the epistle Jude. In the case of the Gospel of

---

[21] See, e. g., Cain and Abel (Gen 4:1–15); Isaac and Ishmael (Gen 21:1–13); Jacob and Esau (Gen 27:41–45); Joseph and his brothers (Gen 37, esp. v. 11); Moses, Miriam, and Aaron (Num 12); the sons of Gideon (Judg 9); David and Eliab (1 Sam 17:12–30); Solomon and Adonijah (1 Kgs 1:5–53, 2:13–25); *inter alios.*

[22] Contra George D. Kilpatrick, "Jesus, His Family, and His Disciples," *JSNT* 15 (1982): 3–19, here 19, who states, "in John, the evidence for the alienation of Jesus from his family disappears almost entirely ..."

[23] John 21:23 also uses ἀδελφούς to refer to the disciples, probably in light of the displacement of Jesus' physical brothers in the text proper: "The 'brothers' ... now seems to refer (as in 1 John) to the entire Christian community" (Michaels, *John*, 1052). Cf. Matt 28:10.

John, one may suppose that the author intentionally chose this obscure disciple – who was for the purposes of the Gospel not identified as Jesus' brother, despite their later conflation – in order to remind the audience of the brothers' rejection by putting nearly identical words into the mouth of a disciple (i. e., "true brother") who shared names with a physical brother of Jesus. The difference between these "brothers," then, is this: while a "physical brother" commands Jesus with suspicious intentions and from a position of unbelief, a "true brother" respectfully asks a question which acknowledges Jesus as Lord as well as the reality of his revelation.

Conclusion

The brothers of Jesus are negative characters in the Gospel of John, the most concrete expression of the prologue's notion that the Word "came unto his own, and his own did not receive him" (1:11).[24] While modern readers may be tempted to draw historical conclusions relative to this characterization (for example, as part of a sectarian group, the author of the Fourth Gospel was intentionally trying to slander the physical brothers of Jesus and their position of leadership in the Jerusalem church), they should be mindful that, as Susan Hylen has noted, "Characters [in John] are not easily equated with their flesh-and-blood counterparts."[25] Historical conclusions about characters in the Gospel of John are often nothing more than the by-product of the investigator's presuppositions about the text. The point relative to historicity and John notwithstanding, the literary (and theological) purpose of the narrator is clear: "These things are written so that you may believe ..." (20:31). Thus when family betrays and sides with those who dissociate, oppose, abuse, or even seek to kill, those who have believed in Jesus can take comfort that they have a family beyond the constraints of the world and the confines of flesh-and-blood, a family initiated by one who had experienced the pain of rejection and risen above it: "In the world you have trouble: but be courageous, I have conquered the world" (16:33).

---

[24] Stibbe, *John*, 160.
[25] Susan Hylen, *Imperfect Believers: Ambiguous Characters in the Gospel of John* (Louisville, Ky.: Westminster John Knox Press, 2009), 5.

The Animal Sellers / The Money Changers in the Temple: Driven Out – But Why?

Mark A. Matson

John's account of the incident in the temple, often called the temple "cleansing," is a somewhat complex scene that is actually bifurcated into two distinct acts with different characters. Act one is the actual disruptive incident in the temple, and the main characters in that act are Jesus and various merchants: money changers and people selling pigeons, oxen, and sheep. Act two, which closely follows the temple incident, consists of a dialogue about the meaning of the incident, and here the main characters are Jesus and "the Jews," who serve as the main interlocutors of Jesus. In addition to Jesus and (a) the merchants in the temple, (b) "the Jews," the disciples make an appearance, although the disciples' role is exclusively that of "after-the-fact" recollection and interpretation of the events. In act one the disciples later connect the disruption to Ps 69:10; in act two, the disciples are reported to have recalled Jesus' words about the temple after he was raised from the dead, and upon recalling this "believed." In other words, the disciples' role is purely one of observation and subsequent reflection about the meaning of the events.

Jesus finds the money changers and those selling animals in the temple immediately upon entering the temple, and what follows is a series of actions involving them: he makes a whip of cords to drive the sheep and oxen out of the temple and he pours out the coins of the money changers and overturns their tables.[1] And following the actions he makes one statement, directed at the pigeon sellers, commanding that "these things" (ταῦτα) be removed and a prohibition against making the temple (my Father's house) a house of trade.

The very brief mention of money changers and animal sellers in John 2 does severely limit the degree of characterization possible. The characters are essentially defined by and limited to their function in the story.[2] The money

---

[1] On this understanding that Jesus uses his constructed whip to drive out only the sheep and goats (and not the sellers or moneychangers), see N. Clayton Croy, "The Messianic Whippersnapper: Did Jesus Use a Whip on People in the Temple (John 2:15)?," *JBL* 128 (2009): 555–68.

[2] The temple cleansing primarily serves to initiate conflict between Jesus and Jewish leaders, and thus establish a major feature of the plot: the conflict with the "Jews." Pace Ruben Zimmermann, *Christologie der Bilder im Johannesevangelium: Die Christopoetik des vierten Evangeliums unter besonderer Berücksichtigung von Joh 10* (WUNT 171; Tübingen: Mohr Sie-

changers change money; that seems to be all we learn about them. The sellers of animals sell animals, and we learn nothing else about them. The characters seem to serve little else than to drive the plot, and thus function in the very limited way that Aristotle describes characters: an agent that does something (πράττειν).³ To put it another way, the characters are remarkably flat: we see no aspects of them except the activity that names them, and an insufficient pattern of activity with which to assign traits.⁴

But of course even Aristotle understood that agency allows for some consideration of ethos, since certain character traits (e. g., σπουδαῖος or φαῦλος) align with certain actions.⁵ So while the characters in John's temple incident have limited descriptions, is there an implied character that is developed by the nature of their agency? The question of any implied *ethos* attached to the sellers could rest on prior information or knowledge the reader would bring to the text, especially if we privilege the earliest readers. Specifically, was the presence of money changers or animal sellers on the temple grounds considered inappropriate? While it has frequently been asserted that such activity would constitute "desecration," there is little or no evidence that it would have been considered as such.⁶ Moreover, since this incident takes place immediately before the Passover, the presence of merchants in or near the temple courts could be expected: the changing of money for payment of the temple tax and selling of sacrificial animals would have been beneficial to pilgrims and supported the temple activity. While the term "money changer" now has negative connotations to modern readers, there is no indication that the various terms had such connotations for early readers. Indeed John uses two different terms for this role. The first term, κερματιστάς, unique to John in the Gospels, simply suggests one who converts a currency into smaller units (the κέρμα that were scattered on the ground). But the evangelist also uses the more common term, κολλυβιστής, which was used commonly in antiquity with no implication that it was an improper activity. It is also possible that readers would have sensed an intertextual resonance with Zech 14:21 in Jesus' declaration that there should be no trader in the temple. Such an intertextual reading would undoubtedly suggest an apocalyptic expectation of the temple's destruction

---

beck, 2004), 363–67, I don't see this temple incident as closely linked to subsequent temple actions, i. e. his actions in the feast of Dedication. Still it is true, as Zimmermann notes, that the temple is a critical component of the overall story of Jesus in the Fourth Gospel.

³ Aristotle, *Poet.*, II.1, 1448a.

⁴ See Edward M. Forster, *Aspects of the Novel* (New York: Harcourt, 1927), 103–18. On traits, see Seymour Chatman, *Story and Discourse: Narrative Structure in Fiction and Film* (Ithaca, N. Y.: Cornell University Press, 1978), 119–34.

⁵ See also Chatman, *Story and Discourse*, 109.

⁶ See the discussion in Ed Parish Sanders, *Jesus and Judaism* (Philadelphia: Fortress, 1985), 62–69.

and re-building. But this intertextual echo is not strong, and it is not clear readers would immediately call to mind Zech 14.

Without a clear indication that ancient readers would have understood the activity in the temple as "bad," however, we are left with the perception the implied reader would have gained from the actual story. Since these characters' agency involves selling animals and changing money, the prohibitions in v. 16, "take these things away; stop making my Father's house a house of trade" may suggest that the activities themselves are wrong, and thus the characters by implication also bad. But the very nature of the incident as portrayed in John is very matter of fact: the selling and trading activity does not "surprise" Jesus, and the prohibition is conveyed seemingly without any animus. Furthermore, Jesus seems to only use force (i. e., use of a whip to drive out) on the sheep and cattle; with respect to the people selling doves he simply instructs them to take away their birds. And, indeed, "the Jews'" request for further information about his actions in v. 18 seems to suggest that Jesus was introducing a new stricture, a new prohibition for which some authority is needed. Simply on the basis of the narrative itself, there is little to imply either nobility or baseness to the sellers.

In the temple incident, as noted above, the money changers and animal sellers are apparently distinct from "the Jews" in the second part of the story. But how far should we push this distinction? Clearly the exchange over the money-changing and selling of animals in the first act of the story sets up the second act and the response by "the Jews." And, as I have argued before, this incident itself is not only a unified story, but also is integral to the plot which the Fourth Evangelist develops in the next series of chapters in John, one which sees increasing tension between Jesus and "the Jews."[7] The question posed by "the Jews" in 2:18, "what sign would you show us for doing these things?" does not seem to be critical of Jesus on the face of it. Indeed at this stage of John's story, "the Jews" are portrayed as interested in his teaching, as the Nicodemus story that follows in chapter 3 implies. What that means, then, is that "the Jews" are not portrayed as either defending temple practices with regard to the selling of animals, nor are they critical of it. Rather the activity itself, and thus the characterization of those changing money and selling animals, is neutral and open to interpretation. The reaction of "the Jews" to the action in the temple does not sustain a negative portrayal of the money changers.

The characters of the money changers and sellers of animals in the temple in John chapter 2 are ultimately defined by Jesus' reaction to them. As indicated above, Jesus' action in the temple seems to point to the prohibition he

---

[7] Mark Matson, "The Temple Incident: An Integral Element in the Fourth Gospel's Narrative," in *Jesus in Johannine Tradition* (ed. Robert T. Fortna and Tom Thatcher; Louisville, Ky.: Westminster John Knox, 2001), 144–53.

gives to the sellers of pigeons to cease all such activity in the temple. But this statement itself is then interpreted by Jesus' later response to "the Jews:" the sign to support his action in the temple involves the destruction of the temple and its rebuilding, a sign which is further interpreted after his death by the disciples as meaning his death and resurrection. This subsequent interpretation of the action thus suggests that the cessation of economic activity in the temple is connected to its destruction, and this in turn to the larger issue of Jesus' own death and resurrection. The characters of money changer and seller of animals are thus part of a complex of symbols denoting a system destined for destruction, but not as symbols of corruption or desecration.

Nicodemus:
The Travail of New Birth

R. Alan Culpepper

Character and theme are at times closely interrelated so that a theme is developed or extended through a particular character, and a character illustrates or even personifies one of the Gospel's themes. In the case of Nicodemus, we find that the character is tied to the theme of birth from above and the related themes of recognizing Jesus' true identity, knowledge of God, the Spirit, and the Kingdom of God. At the same time, the character is never merely a cipher for a statement about a theme, and as a character Nicodemus transcends the themes with which he is linked.

Nicodemus emerges from the dark of night, but never completely. He appears only in the Gospel of John, and there only briefly – at three points: when he comes to Jesus at night (3:1–12), when he reminds the chief priests and Pharisees that legal procedure requires a hearing before they can pass judgment on Jesus (7:50–52), and when he joins Joseph of Arimathea in burying Jesus (19:39–42). All three passages contribute to the characterization of Nicodemus, but they leave unclear whether Nicodemus is a static character, or whether there is development in his character from one scene to the next. Does his act of assisting in the burial of Jesus mean that he has become a disciple or follower of Jesus? Interpreters have viewed Nicodemus alternatively as "the prime example of one whose expression of faith is dictated by his fear of 'the Jews,'"[1] a member of the religious establishment confronting a fringe movement,[2] or a "secret believer."[3] This essay will examine the literary devices used to characterize Nicodemus, the history of interpretation, and current perspectives on Nicodemus.

---

[1] Steven A. Hunt, "Nicodemus, Lazarus, and the Fear of 'the Jews' in the Fourth Gospel," in *Repetitions and Variations in the Fourth Gospel: Style, Text, Interpretation* (ed. Gilbert Van Belle et al.; BETL 223; Louvain: Peeters, 2009), 199–212, here 201; cf. Peter Dschulnigg, *Jesus begegnen: Personen und ihre Bedeutung im Johannesevangelium* (Münster: LIT, 2002), 116.

[2] David K. Rensberger, *Johannine Faith and Liberating Community* (Philadelphia: Westminster, 1988), 115.

[3] J. Louis Martyn, *History and Theology in the Fourth Gospel* (3d ed.; Nashville: Abingdon 2003), 88, 113; Paul D. Duke, *Irony in the Fourth Gospel* (Louisville, Ky.: Westminster John Knox, 1985), 152.

The openness of the text and the impulse of the reader to fill gaps in the text stand in tension, and John's brief evocations of Nicodemus have fueled a stream of insightful readings that fill the gaps in various ways. In the end all we can do in this essay is chronicle some of the high points of this history, show why the Gospel is open to various constructions of this character, and offer a reading of the text with the hope that others will find it illuminating also.

A review of the history of interpretation reveals three distinct eras: interpretation of Nicodemus as (1) a historical person, (2) a representative figure, and (3) a character within the Gospel narrative. Westcott, Godet, and Zahn are representative of the first era.[4] All three discuss the suggestion put forward by John Lightfoot in the seventeenth century, and then taken up by Delitzsch: that Nicodemus was Naqdimon ben Gurion, who is mentioned in the Talmud (*b. Taanith 20a*) as one of Jesus' disciples,[5] but all three reject the identification on the grounds that his "great age"[6] at the time of Jesus' ministry means he would not have been alive at the time of the destruction of Jerusalem. Bernard manages the span of decades by suggesting that the data accord well with the idea that John has in mind the "young ruler" of Luke 18:18.[7] Robinson argued that John's Nicodemus was the grandfather of Naqdimon ben Gurion.[8] More recently, in a definitive study of the Gurion family in the Talmudic tradition, Bauckham suggested that Nicodemus was his uncle.[9]

Bultmann rejected efforts to give psychological interpretations of Nicodemus, and saw him instead as representative of Judaism in his question about salvation, and as representative of humanity confronted with "the miracle of rebirth."[10] Nicodemus's question in 3:9 "accurately represents the inadequacy of the way in which man puts his questions."[11] Barrett too finds Nicodemus to be a representative character, commenting that "we are made to hear not a conversation between two persons but the dialogue of Church and Synago-

---

[4] Brooke F. Westcott, *The Gospel according to St. John* (orig. 1881; repr., Grand Rapids, Mich.: Eerdmans, 1971), 47–48; Frédéric Louis Godet, *Commentaire sur l'Évangile de Saint Jean* (3d ed.; Paris, 1886), 374, and Theodor von Zahn, *Das Evangelium des Johannes* (5th and 6th ed.; Leipzig: Deichert, 1921), 184, fn. 32.

[5] John Lightfoot, *A Commentary on the New Testament from the Talmud and Hebraica* (4 vols.; Peabody, Mass.: Hendrickson, 1997), 3:262–63; Franz Delitzsch, *Zeitschrift für Luth. Theologie*, 643 (cited by Westcott, *Gospel*, 48).

[6] Godet, *Jean*, 374.

[7] John H. Bernard, *Critical and Exegetical Commentary on the Gospel according to St. John* (ICC; Edinburgh: T&T Clark, 1928), 99–100.

[8] John A. T. Robinson, *The Priority of John* (ed. J. F. Coakley; London: SCM, 1985), 284–87.

[9] Richard Bauckham, "Nicodemus and the Gurion Family," *JTS* 47 (1996): 1–37, 34.

[10] Rudolf Bultmann, *The Gospel of John* (trans. G. R. Beasley-Murray; Philadelphia: Westminster, 1971), 134, 143–44.

[11] Bultmann, *John*, 143.

gue."[12] Similarly, Martyn saw Nicodemus as "typical of those in the Gerousia who secretly believe."[13] Rensberger developed further the interpretation of Nicodemus as "a *communal* symbolic figure:"[14] "Throughout the gospel, then, Nicodemus appears as a man of inadequate faith and inadequate courage, and as such he represents a *group* that the author wishes to characterize in this way," namely the secret believers at the time of the composition of the Gospel.[15] Provocatively, Rensberger adds that Nicodemus faced the choice of whether or not to side with a group that was being oppressed by members of his own rank and class.[16] Schnackenburg, although he recognizes that Nicodemus is "to some extent a typical figure," resists reducing him to a type and insists that he "retains some quite personal traits."[17] Schnackenburg further allows the possibility that the later references to Nicodemus in John "indicate his gradual progress to the faith."[18]

Brown anticipates more recent attention to Nicodemus's function within the Gospel, observing that "John obviously intends Nicodemus to illustrate a partial faith in Jesus on the basis of signs and has prepared the way for this with ii 23–25."[19] Meeks set the literary function of Nicodemus in its broader context, observing that "Nicodemus plays a well-known role: that of the rather stupid disciple whose maladroit questions provide the occasion (a) for the reader to feel superior and (b) for the sage who is questioned to deliver a discourse. The genre is widespread in the Greco-Roman world."[20] Meeks also labels Nicodemus's appearances later in the Gospel as "fraught with ambiguity," and claims that "this ambiguity is doubtless an important and deliberate part of the portrait of this obscure figure."[21]

Over the past forty years interpreters have turned repeatedly to ambiguity as the byword for Nicodemus's role in John. As examples we may cite the following titles:

---

[12] C. Kingsley Barrett, *The Gospel according to St. John* (London: SPCK, 1955), 169.

[13] J. Louis Martyn, *History and Theology in the Fourth Gospel* (Nashville: Abingdon, 1968), 75.

[14] David K. Rensberger, *Johannine Faith and Liberating Community* (Philadelphia: Westminster, 1988), 38.

[15] Rensberger, *Johannine Faith*, 40.

[16] Rensberger, *Johannine Faith*, 115.

[17] Rudolf Schnackenburg, *The Gospel according to St. John* (Volume 1; trans. K. Smyth; HTCNT; New York: Herder and Herder, 1968), 364.

[18] Schnackenburg, *John*, 365.

[19] Raymond E. Brown, *The Gospel According to John (i–xii)* (AB 29; Garden City, NY: Doubleday, 1966), 135.

[20] Wayne A. Meeks, who cites as parallels 4 Ezra 4:1-11, 20-21; Diogenes Laertius 1.34; Ps. Callisthenes, *Life of Alexander* 1.14 (idem, "The Man from Heaven in Johannine Sectarianism," *JBL* 91 [1972]: 53).

[21] Meeks, "Man from Heaven," 54.

Bassler, "Mixed Signals: Nicodemus in the Fourth Gospel," claims, "Nicodemus's Primary characteristic is ambiguity;"[22]

Donaldson, "Nicodemus: A Figure of Ambiguity in a Gospel of Certainty;"[23]

Schneiders: "Probably no passage in John's admittedly mysterious Gospel is more ambiguous than the dialogue between Jesus and Nicodemus in John 3:1–15. Frustrating as that may seem, however, the ambiguity is the clue to how the passage functions;"[24]

Severin, "The Nicodemus Enigma: The Characterization and Function of an Ambiguous Actor of the Fourth Gospel;"[25]

Renz, "Nicodemus: An Ambiguous Disciple? A Narrative Sensitive Investigation" says "an essential feature of Nicodemus is his ambiguity;"[26]

Bennema: "Nicodemus – In the Twilight Zone" comments, "John does not redeem Nicodemus of [sic] his ambiguity;"[27]

Hylen, *Imperfect Believers: Ambiguous Characters in the Gospel of John*, states, "In my view, Nicodemus is simply an ambiguous character."[28]

The observation that Nicodemus is an ambiguous character has become so prevalent that one now finds various interpretations of the function of this ambiguity. Bassler interpreted the importance of the ambiguity of the character in terms of its effect on the reader. The ambiguity creates a cognitive gap and forces the reader to "bring closure beyond the text."[29] Sevrin finds that through Nicodemus the Gospel establishes an "in-between" that is "neither on the side of those who reject nor on the side of those who believe … One could think that the Fourth Gospel develops the character of Nicodemus as a way to leave an opening to the Jews in their relation to Jesus."[30] Renz argues that there is no in-between in John. The ambiguity must be resolved in the third scene, but both positive and negative readings of Nicodemus's role at the burial of Jesus are possible: "Both readings can do full justice to the text and both readings support the function of the book to persuade the audience to become devoted disciples of Christ."[31]

---

[22] Jouette M. Bassler, "Mixed Signals: Nicodemus in the Fourth Gospel," *JBL* 108 (1989): 635–46, here 645.

[23] Terence L. Donaldson, "Nicodemus: A Figure of Ambiguity in a Gospel of Certainty," *Consensus* 24 (1998): 121–24.

[24] Sandra M. Schneiders, *Written That You May Believe: Encountering Jesus in the Fourth Gospel* (New York: Crossroad, 1999), 117.

[25] Jean Marie Sevrin, "The Nicodemus Enigma: The Characterization and Function of an Ambiguous Actor of the Fourth Gospel," in *Anti-Judaism and the Fourth Gospel: Papers of the Leuven Colloquium, 2000* (ed. Reimund Bieringer et al.; Assen: van Gorcum, 2001), 357–69.

[26] Gabi Renz, "Nicodemus: An Ambiguous Disciple? A Narrative Sensitive Investigation," in *Challenging Perspectives on the Gospel of John* (ed. John Lierman; WUNT 219; Tübingen: Mohr Siebeck, 2006), 255–81, here 255.

[27] Cornelis Bennema, *Encountering Jesus: Character Studies in the Gospel of John* (Milton Keynes: Paternoster, 2009), 84.

[28] Susan E. Hylen, *Imperfect Believers: Ambiguous Characters in the Gospel of John* (Louisville, Ky.: Westminster John Knox, 2009).

[29] Bassler, "Mixed Signals," 644.

[30] Sevrin, "Nicodemus Enigma," 369.

[31] Renz, "Nicodemus," 283.

The issue focused by this review of interpretations of Nicodemus is how this character, and the ambiguity that surrounds him, functions within the Gospel's narrative design. In an effort to gain a fresh perspective on this question we will review the way Nicodemus is evoked in the three passages in which he appears through a close reading of these verses, consideration of the setting of these passages in the rhetoric of the Gospel, and reflections on the function of Nicodemus as a model for readers who wrestle with how to respond to the Gospel's presentation of Jesus.

John 3:1–12: Nicodemus's Encounter with Jesus

Although Nicodemus is formally introduced in v. 1, some interpreters take 2:23–25 as the introduction to the dialogue between Jesus and Nicodemus.[32] Fittingly, the narrative moves on after his conversation with Jesus without a clearly demarcated conclusion, just as his ultimate response to Jesus is not clearly defined. The last clear address to Nicodemus (σοι) is in v. 11. Verse 12 seems to continue the address to Nicodemus, but now as a member of a larger group (ὑμῖν), the Pharisees, "the Jews," or better, all who struggle to respond to Jesus.[33]

The stage is set for Nicodemus's introduction by the immediately preceding transitional summary in 2:23–25. Here the narrator reports that many in Jerusalem "believed in his name" because they saw the signs that he was doing. This phrase echoes the norm set in the prologue for those who were authorized to become children of God (1:12). The following statement, that Jesus would not entrust himself to them because he knew what was "in the human person" (ἐν τῷ ἀνθρώπῳ), poses a question the reader cannot answer based on information communicated to this point in the Gospel: Why would Jesus not entrust himself to one who "believed in his name?" The question is especially mystifying since in 2:11 the narrator reported that the disciples believed in Jesus after they saw the first of the signs he did in Galilee.

Nicodemus is connected with 2:23–25 by (1) the fact that he is introduced immediately thereafter with a repetition of the last words of 2:25 – "There was a man" (ἦν δὲ ἄνθρωπος); (2) the way his reference to Jesus' signs echoes 2:23 (τὰ σημεῖα ἃ ἐποίει, 2:23; τὰ σημεῖα ποιεῖν ἃ σὺ ποιεῖς, 3:2), and (3) by the fact that Jesus rebuffs Nicodemus's confession, providing a specific example of the

---

[32] Martin Schmidl, *Jesus und Nikodemus: Gespräch zur johanneischen Christologie: Joh 3 in schichtenspezifischer Sicht* (BU 28; Regensburg: Pustet, 1998), 82–84; Bennema, *Encountering Jesus*, 79.

[33] Schmidl takes v. 12 as the end of the first part of 3:1–21 (Schmidl, *Jesus und Nikodemus*, 122–24). Bennema says John presents Nicodemus as "the representative of a larger group with the same faith-stance" (Bennema, *Encountering Jesus*, 79).

refusal to entrust himself to one of those who believed in him because of the signs he was doing.

The next item of information the reader is given is that Nicodemus was "from the Pharisees," which may mean either that he was sent by the Pharisees or that he was one of the Pharisees. The only previous reference to the Pharisees is in John 1:24, where the same phrase occurs, ἐκ τῶν Φαρισαίων; i. e., some were sent from or by the Pharisees. His name is supplied the same way John the Baptist is introduced in 1:6, but here there is a parallel between his name and his status – a fact that has drawn surprisingly little notice from commentators.[34] His name is Nicodemus, which means victor, conqueror, or ruler of the people, and his status is "ruler" or leader of "the Jews." Earlier, "the Jews" had sent emissaries to interrogate John (1:19) in the Gospel's opening scene, and in the previous chapter they had asked Jesus for a sign (2:18). It is unclear, therefore, whether Nicodemus sought Jesus out of his own accord or was sent by the Pharisees to question him further about what he was doing, and his signs.

The next verse adds that Nicodemus came to Jesus at night. Readers familiar with the Gospel will suspect immediately that this temporal reference carries symbolic significance in John's dualism of light and darkness, just as it does in later references to "night" in John (9:4; 11:10; 13:30; 21:3). The symbolic freight of the reference is further suggested by its repetition when Nicodemus is reintroduced in John 19:39. The only previous preparation the reader has is supplied by the light and darkness imagery in the prologue (1:4–5, 9).

In his first words, Nicodemus speaks as a representative, either of the Pharisees, "the Jews," or the people: "Rabbi, we know that you are a teacher who has come (or, been sent) from God," with emphasis by position placed on "from God" (3:2). Nicodemus has come from (ἐκ) the Pharisees; Jesus has come from (ἀπό) God. This opening statement lacks the Christological titles and more oblique references that appear in the confessions and initial statements offered by other characters to this point – John the Baptist (1:26, 29, 34, 36), Andrew (1:41), Philip (1:45), Nathanael (1:49) – instead identifying Jesus merely as a "rabbi" and teacher. On the other hand, the recognition that he is "from God" (ἀπὸ θεοῦ) is reminiscent of the introduction of John in 1:6 as one sent "from God" (παρὰ θεοῦ; cf. 9:16) and the prologue's references to the one who was "with God" (1:1) and is "close to the Father's heart" (1:18, NRSV). The claim "we know" will at times be pressed into the service of John's irony later, when the presumed knowledge of Jesus' interlocutors is exposed as ignorance (9:24; 16:30), but here it seems to express only confidence and authority, and perhaps flattery. The irony comes later (3:8–10), when Nicodemus fails to understand the parable of the wind. He hears its sound but does not understand "whence"

---

[34] See however Dschulnigg, *Jesus begegnen*, 116.

it comes and "whither" it goes, even though he began by confessing that Jesus had come from God. The signs confirm that Jesus is not only "from God" but that "God is with him" (3:2). It was commonly held that God's presence and power is demonstrated by both wonders and wisdom (Mark 6:2; 1 Cor 1:22). Nicodemus recognized Jesus' signs, but he fails to understand his wisdom.

Up to John 2:23–25 there has been no complication about receiving, believing in, or coming to Jesus. Characters either received him or they did not. With Nicodemus, however, the reader is introduced to a character that complicates the matter of positive responses to Jesus.

Jesus' first response to Nicodemus is a striking non-sequitur, illustrating the wry comment that in John Jesus seems to be congenitally incapable of giving a straight answer.[35] Nicodemus has not asked a question, so Jesus responds to his statement, a statement about Jesus' identity. The implication of Jesus' response, at least for readers, is that confession that Jesus came from God, or perhaps any confession, is not sufficient. The alternative is that one must find a deficiency in Nicodemus's confession, but in view of the narrator's statement in 2:23–35 the deficiency is not in the confession but in the person (ἐν τῷ ἀνθρώπῳ), and Jesus moves immediately to that point. In order to see the Kingdom of God one must be born ἄνωθεν. Jesus' declaration is radical: one does not enter the Kingdom of God by being born into the people of the covenant or by obedience to the covenant. Entry into the Kingdom is individual, not corporate. By this simple assertion, therefore, the whole basis for the architecture of the temple – with its courts for Gentiles, women, and Israel respectively – is swept aside (see 2:19–21). Nicodemus's motivation in coming to Jesus no longer matters. Jesus has repositioned the conversation, either responding to Nicodemus's implied interest or taking the conversation to a higher level. Nicodemus does not resist the declaration of this topic, even while playing the role of the uncomprehending pupil. Obtuse as Nicodemus's response is, its meaning may range from a scoffing rejection of the possibility of a new birth to the wistful hope that such a new beginning is possible.

Jesus' second response moves to clarify both the nature of the new birth and the means by which it occurs. The new birth requires the agency of the Spirit; it is not of one's own doing. The emphasis on Spirit is clear in John 3:5; the question is the import of "water and," which has been interpreted naturally (physical birth), sacramentally (baptism), or metaphorically as a hendiadys linking water and Spirit. The first (physical birth) is the weakest interpretation; the emphasis still falls on the new birth by the Spirit. The reference to the Spirit also picks up the double meaning of ἄνωθεν (i. e., from above) since the understood assumption is that the Spirit comes from above.

---

[35] Anthony D. Nuttall, *Overheard by God: Fiction and Prayer in Herbert, Milton, Dante and St. John* (London: Methuen, 1980), 131.

Verse 6 supplies the logic of the demand for a new birth. The dualism of the realms of flesh and Spirit means that one belongs to one or the other. Birth from above, from the Spirit, is therefore required if one is to be able to comprehend or enter into the realm of the Spirit (i. e., the Kingdom of God). Following the principle that like is known by like,[36] that which is of the flesh can never know that which is of the Spirit apart from a new birth by the Spirit. Unaided, Nicodemus, who now represents humanity in its quest for God, could never enter the realm of the divine or attain to the knowledge of God (see John 17:3). Through Nicodemus, therefore, John introduces the question of how one moves from the flesh to the Spirit, from below to above, from the world to the Kingdom of God, from this life to eternal life – a question to which responses will be given throughout the Gospel. Here the important elements are a new birth, from above, by the Spirit.

The parable of the wind in verse 8 points to the reality of the Spirit but also its incomprehensibility: we hear it and feel its presence, but we do not know where it comes from or where it goes. Remarkably, this is true not only for those who are of the flesh but for everyone who has been born of the Spirit. Being born of the Spirit enables one to know its presence but not to know from whence it comes or whither it goes. Even for those who are born from above, the divine remains a mystery.

Nicodemus's third and final response in this scene is the shortest: "How can these things be?" (3:9). The brevity of his response fits the pattern of economy in biblical narrative in which second and third responses that repeat the initial response become increasingly shorter (e. g., see the three accounts of Paul's experience on the road to Damascus in Acts 9:3–16; 22:6–16; 26:12–18). This pattern occurs elsewhere in John in the blind man's responses in 9:11, 15, 17. It also serves to show that Nicodemus is fading from the scene; hereafter the spotlight is exclusively on Jesus. Nicodemus's third response expresses a complete lack of comprehension, yet it is so general that one cannot say just what part of Jesus' discourse Nicodemus has not understood. Jesus' response underscores Nicodemus's lack of understanding, while pointing to the irony that "a teacher of Israel" does not understand "these things" – a parable about the wind, the dualism of flesh and Spirit, the need for a new birth, or the role of the Spirit. On the other hand, although Jesus' question implies that Nicodemus should understand, the central point of the conversation has been that apart from the new birth, he could not understand. At this point Nicodemus fades into the background, while Jesus' discourse continues. The reader is not told how Nicodemus responds to Jesus, nor when exactly he leaves the scene. The reader is there-

---

[36] Karl Olav Sandnes, "Whence and Whither: A Narrative Perspective on Birth ἄνωθεν (John 3,3–8)," *Bib* 86 (2005): 158–62.

fore left with Jesus' rebuke; the character through whom the theme of the necessity of a new birth, from above, is developed does not move beyond the earthly things Jesus has told him. By implication moving on to believe not only the earthly things but the heavenly things as well is either a requirement for or a manifestation of the new birth.

John 7:50–52: Nicodemus's Response to the Pharisees

Nicodemus re-emerges at the end of John 7, where he responds to the Pharisees who condemned those in the crowd who believed in Jesus. Nicodemus's reappearance here is set up in verse 48 by the Pharisees' rebuke of the officers by means of the question, "Has any one of the authorities or of the Pharisees believed in him?" The expected answer is "no." The question, more subtly, employs the two terms used to introduce Nicodemus in John 3:1 – he is both an "authority" (ἄρχων) and a Pharisee. Nicodemus is further tagged as "one of them" (7:50). His appearance therefore carries some level of implication that he believes in Jesus, even if his response to the Pharisees stops short of a confession. Nicodemus reminds the other Pharisees that "our law," by the negative answer implied by the syntax of the question, does not judge (or condemn) a person without first making "a thorough inquiry" and giving the accused a fair hearing. This legal principle is stated in Deut 1:16; 17:4; 19:16–18a. Nicodemus's question unmasks the other members of the council as unqualified interpreters of the Law.[37] Hunt offers the provocative suggestion that in two subsequent passages (9:16 and 10:21) some of the Pharisees raise questions that reflect Nicodemus's response to Jesus: "perhaps Nicodemus serves as a spokesman for these Pharisees in ch. 9, as he did in chs. 3 and 7."[38] Alternatively, one might say that Nicodemus personifies for the reader the division among the Pharisees. Having been introduced to Nicodemus as one of the Pharisees (3:1), readers understand the response of the minority of the Pharisees when it is expressed later in the narrative.

As Pancaro noted, Nicodemus's words can carry a deeper meaning. The verb "to hear" can mean to hear with understanding or even to obey.[39] On this level, only those who believe in Jesus follow the Law, which bears witness to Jesus, and only they understand that what Jesus has been doing are the "works" that the Father has given him to do. They are the signs that bear witness to him (John 5:19, 36). It is unlikely that the reader is meant to assume that Nicodemus is aware of this Johannine level of meaning in his words, but

---

[37] Dschulnigg, *Jesus begegnen*, 115, 120; Renz, "Nicodemus," 265.

[38] Steven A. Hunt, "Nicodemus, Lazarus, and the Fear," 203.

[39] Severino Pancaro, "The Metamorphosis of a Legal Principle in the Fourth Gospel: A Closer Look at Jn 7,51," *Bib* 53 (1972): 340–61.

the reader may see this further meaning.[40] The ironies are thick, as Pancaro observes: "the condemnation of Jesus which, for the Pharisees, is the defense and triumph of the Law is in reality its violation."[41] The Law as it is applied in the condemnation of Jesus is "a false criterion" (361). Therefore, Pancaro concludes, "*Jn brings this home in 7,51 by having the Law of the Jews establish conditions for the judgment of Jesus which can be met only by those who believe on him; by presenting faith in Jesus as demanded by the Law!*"[42] The Pharisees' derogatory response, "Surely you are not also from Galilee, are you?" (7:52) is tantamount to an accusation that Nicodemus too is one of Jesus' disciples. The implication is there, but again John leaves Nicodemus's status unresolved.

John 19:38–42: Nicodemus and Joseph of Arimathea

Nicodemus is introduced a third and final time in John 19:39, perhaps significantly, not until after Joseph of Arimathea, who is presented as a disciple in secret, has already secured permission to bury Jesus' body. Why did Nicodemus not go to Pilate with Joseph? Did he not want his role to be known publicly?[43] Was he afraid of the Romans? Or, given the approach of the Sabbath, was it his role to buy the spices while Joseph secured the body? Nicodemus is introduced by way of a reminder that he is the one who came to Jesus the first time at night, and this time he comes bringing a hundred pounds of spices for Jesus' burial. The anointing for burial resonates with both the reference to Lazarus' grave wrappings in John 11 and Mary's anointing of Jesus' feet with expensive ointment in John 12:1–8.[44] Joseph and Nicodemus follow the Jewish customs by wrapping Jesus' body in cloths with the spices.

Nicodemus does not speak in this scene, so any further inferences about his character must be based on associations and actions. Is Nicodemus to be seen now as a secret believer also (cf. 12:42)? If so, why is this not stated explicitly, as it is for Joseph of Arimathea? Does his coming forward to bury Jesus constitute a public confession of his discipleship? This implication is weakened by the fact that his companion is still introduced as a secret believer. Does the lavish burial of Jesus constitute a confession of his kingship,[45] or a failure to understand Jesus' life beyond death?[46] Does the lavish quantity of spices have

---

[40] Renz, "Nicodemus," 269.
[41] Pancaro, "Metamorphosis," 341.
[42] Pancaro, "Metamorphosis," 361 (original emphasis).
[43] Steven A. Hunt, "Nicodemus, Lazarus, and the Fear," 205.
[44] So esp. Sevrin, "Nicodemus Enigma," 365–67.
[45] Bauckham, "Nicodemus," 29–32; Hylen, *Imperfect Believers*, 36.
[46] Marinus de Jonge, "Nicodemus and Jesus: Some Observations on Misunderstanding and Understanding in the Fourth Gospel," *BJRL* 53 (1971): 343; Meeks, "Man from Heaven," 55, fn. 39; R. Alan Culpepper, *Anatomy of the Fourth Gospel: A Study in Literary Design* (Phi-

other meanings? Is it Nicodemus's penance for not having done more to protect Jesus? Is it akin to Judas' flinging the thirty pieces of silver back at the priests (cf. Matthew 27:4-5)?

The bar is set high by Nicodemus's encounter with Jesus and Jesus' declaration of the requirement of a new birth from above. Nicodemus seems to be moving toward Jesus with each appearance, coming to Jesus first at night, responding to his fellow Pharisees in Jesus' defense, and then joining with a secret disciple in the burial of Jesus. The reader has good reason to be hopeful about Nicodemus, as much of the history of interpretation attests.[47] On the other hand, Nicodemus never ceases to be "one of them" (7:50), one who came to Jesus at night (19:39), and perhaps, like Joseph of Arimathea, a "secret believer" (19:38). John leaves his status unresolved. Nicodemus remains, appropriately, identified with the complexity of becoming one of the "children of God," for whom both belief in his name and birth from above are required.

---

ladephia: Fortress, 1983), 136; Dennis D. Sylva, "Nicodemus and His Spices," NTS 34 (1988): 148-49.

[47] Renz, "Nicodemus," 272-74; so also Dschulnigg, who ventures that the burial demonstrates that Joseph and Nicodemus have definitively found faith in the Messiah (Dschulnigg, *Jesus begegnen*, 120-21).

"A Jew":
A Search for the Identity and Role of an Anonymous Judean

Mark Appold

The scene in John 3:22–30 pairs the baptizing ministry of Jesus and his disciples with that of John the Baptist and his disciples. Within this setting an isolated reference is made in 3:25 to "a Jew" who is depicted as engaging in an argument with the disciples of John. The reference to "a Jew" seems odd since all who are pictured in this scene, both Jesus and John and their disciples, are Jews. Odd also is the fact that this argument scene seems detached and appears to lack any further reference.[1] The aim of this study is to identify and to characterize this anonymous "Jew" who is given neither a recorded speaking part nor any background or other biographical description. Instead, this person is simply and generically introduced without the definite article as Ἰουδαῖος, an identity marker used in the Fourth Gospel seventy-one times to denote a person of Jewish background. The narrator, however, does not intend the reader to see this person in isolation. Instead, this nameless "Jew" serves as an important counter balance to the followers of John the Baptist, who are instructed by their Rabbi John (3:26) to recognize the pre-eminence of Jesus.[2] Furthermore, this pericope does not stand in isolation but contextually is matched by a repetitive, chiastically structured doublet in John 1:19–31 where John the Baptist affirms that he is not the Messiah and that the one who comes after him, namely Jesus, is greater than he is. In the first passage religious authorities from Jerusalem are sent to question John about Jesus. Such finely tuned pairings are typical for John's Gospel, marked by rhetorical devices, double *entendres*, irony, and multi-dimensional characterizations. It should therefore not be surprising that this pericope promises to present formative challenges and to render unexpected results beneath a surface reading of the text.

---

[1] "The curious thing is that it leads to nothing" (Charles H. Dodd, *Historical Tradition in the Fourth Gospel* [Cambridge: Cambridge University Press, 1963], 280).

[2] An interesting unrelated parallel, demonstrating how literary devices may be used, can be seen in Charles Bernstein's contemporary poem entitled "The Jew" who is never introduced or further described and yet who serves as a continuous foil for addressing whole series of critical issues (idem, *Harpers Magazine* [December 2012]: 21–23). In John's Gospel all of the persons introduced "spielen neben der Hauptperson Jesus nur eine untergeordnete Rolle" (Peter Dschulnigg, *Jesus begegnen: Personen und ihre Bedeutung im Johannesevangelium* [Münster: LIT, 2002], 1).

The first problem is the mixed manuscript attestation for the usage of the singular μετά Ἰουδαίου.³ The Greek text has equally ancient support for both a singular (𝔓11 and ℵ²) and a plural reading (𝔓66 and ℵ*), although the singular appears as the preferred reading since it is unlikely that the plural would have been changed into the more difficult reading of a singular as a scribal correction. It may be possible to understand the singular as a collective for many or for a group, although the evidence for this is scant. The closest parallel may be found in Zechariah, a text known to the Evangelist (2:16 and 19:37), where "ten men ... shall take hold of 'a Jew'" (Zech 8:23), although the Hebrew, יהודי, in this and similar cases is used attributively with איש, a man. We are left with the difficult, yet preferable reading of the singular in the Greek text for "a Jew" as one individual.⁴ Of the unusually high occurrences of the noun, Ἰουδαῖος, in the Fourth Gospel only three appear in the singular, once when the Samaritan woman asks Jesus, "How is it that you, 'a Jew,' ask a drink of me ...?" (4:9) and once when Pilate responds with the disclaimer, "I am not 'a Jew'" (19:35). The third appearance is the text here under consideration where a dispute unfolds between John's disciples and "a Jew" who is not given any explicit further identification.

At this point, the issue of translation presents a formidable challenge. The Greek word Ἰουδαῖοι is almost without exception equated in translations with "Jews." Even a cursory examination of the Johannine text reveals, however, a multi-dimensional usage that recognizes significant differences between ethnic, geographic, and religious usages. The implied author of John refers to Ἰουδαῖοι in varieties of ways, indicating, on the one hand, that "salvation is from 'the Jews'" (4:22) or referring to "Jews" "who had believed in him (Jesus)" (8:31) or to Galileans (who) welcomed him (4:45). On the other hand, the narrative presents "Jews" in a strongly negative way predisposed to unbelief and rejection.⁵ For this reason the Gospel of John has often been seen as the source for medieval and modern religious anti-Judaism as well as anti-Semitism which ultimately led to the Holocaust.⁶ This polarity is clearly present but does not exhaust the multi-valent use of the term in its positive, neutral, and negative forms. To translate Ἰουδαῖοι uniformly with "Judeans" would soften or even

---

³ "Joh 3,25 dürfte zu den dunkelsten Passus der johanneischen Literatur überhaupt gehören" (Knut Backhaus, *Die Jüngerkreise des Täufers Johannes* [Paderborn: Schöningh, 1991], 256).

⁴ Some scholars have suggested that the text was corrupted and originally read Ἰησοῦ or τοῦ Ἰησοῦ or τῶν Ἰησοῦ. Attractive as these suggestions may be, there is no textual support for them. Cf. C. Kingsley Barrett, *The Gospel According to St John: An Introduction with Commentary and Notes on the Greek Text* (2d ed.; London: SPCK, 1978), 184.

⁵ For a fuller discussion of this issue, cf. Robert Kysar, *Voyages with John* (Waco, Tex.: Baylor University Press, 2005), 147–59.

⁶ So Geza Vermes, *The Religion of Jesus the Jew* (Minneapolis: Fortress, 1993), 213; Jacob Neusner, *A Rabbi Talks with Jesus* (Montreal: McGill-Queen's University Press, 2000), 28.

eliminate the element of hostility, thereby, however, undercutting the Johannine dialectic present in this word. While the term may indeed geographically refer to the people of Judea, it is not equally applicable to Diaspora Jews, whether they be of Alexandria, Antioch or Jews in the Galilee or, for that matter, Jewish authorities of Jerusalem.[7] How then should the Ἰουδαῖος of 3:25 be understood? All depends on how the narrator provides contextual details.

The process of characterization may be applied in different ways. For some the narrative is not evaluated in terms of historical reference but exclusively in terms of the overall literary effect of the work.[8] Others make it clear that a "purist" approach does not necessarily exclude a "realistic" approach[9] suggesting a kind of interdependence. It is this kind of interdependence between literary and historical dimensions that will be used in this study. Although the author of the Gospel provides no *explicit* information about the anonymous Ἰουδαῖος of 3:25, enough *implicit* data is provided to make the case for identifying this person as a Judean. It should also be noted that the uniqueness of the text will be honored by seeking an interpretation on the text's terms, viewing it not as reportage but rather as interpretive historical narrative[10] interwoven with theological perspectives and literary motifs. With this approach we find enough clues implicit in the text, allowing a characterization of the Judean on the following three levels – first as *seeker*, then as *contender*, and finally as *witness*.

The introduction of the Judean is set, first of all, into the context of two parallel baptismal movements – one by Jesus and his disciples and the other by John the Baptist and his disciples. None of the followers of either Jesus or John are named, although previously five Galilean Jews, disciples of Jesus, had been introduced with one unnamed (1:35–51) and with the indication that some had previous connections with John the Baptist. It is a mixed picture with some common ground and yet with emerging sharp differences. The differences begin to be underscored by divergent geographical locations cited for the activity of Jesus and John. Jesus and his disciples' entry into the largely undefined Ἰουδαίαν γῆν, Judean territory, is framed at the beginning by his departure from Jerusalem at the time of the Passover including his visit with the high ranking Pharisee, Nicodemus (3:1–21). On the other end, Jesus

---

[7] A comprehensive analysis of the Johannine Jews is given by John Ashton in his extensive article on "The Identity and Function of the Ἰουδαῖοι in the Fourth Gospel," *NovT* 27/1 (1985): 40–75.

[8] This is the approach mandated by Mark Allan Powell, *What is Narrative Criticism?* (Minneapolis: Fortress, 1990). Powell speaks of the referential fallacy suggesting that the characters do not "stand for" any real people (idem, *Narrative Criticism*, 66).

[9] So D. Francois Tolmie, *Narratology and Biblical Narratives* (Bethesda, Md.: International Scholars Publications, 1999), 39–59.

[10] Cf. "poetische Geschichte" (Tobias Nicklas, *Ablösung und Verstrickung* [Frankfurt am Main: Peter Lang, 2001], 69).

returns to Jerusalem for the Sabbath (5:1). In between these two time and place markers Jesus leaves the city, enters the countryside, spends time with his disciples and baptizes (3:22).[11] This scene is immediately paralleled by reference to the baptizing activity of John at Aenon near Salim "because there was much water there."[12] This reference to the abundance of water may well be an inverse reflection on the one who baptizes with more than water, namely with the Holy Spirit (1:33). In any case, out of the three possible locations for Aenon,[13] one in particular, along with the added reference to "Bethany on the other side of the Jordan" (1:28), carries the further dimension of embracing the prophetic traditions of Israel's premier prophet, Elijah, along with Isaiah's declaration referring to "the voice of one crying in the wilderness" (Is 40:3). Of primary significance for this scene, however, are the growing numbers of unnamed people coming to the baptismal movements of both Jesus ("all are going to him;" v. 26) and John the Baptist ("people kept coming and were being baptized" (v. 23). At this point, not a group but a single unnamed person is introduced (v. 25), bracketed[14] on both sides by Jesus' activity in Jerusalem (ch. 2:13–3:21 and ch. 5). The evangelist's intimation is clear, allowing the unnamed Ἰουδαῖος to be identified as a Judean coming from Israel's heartland and acquainted with Jerusalem in conformity with the Markan description where "people from the whole Judean countryside and all the people of Jerusalem were going out to him" (1:5).

What could the motivation have been for the Judean to leave the comforts of settled life in Jerusalem and journey out into the harshness of the wilderness to check out newly reported baptismal movements? The disciples of John at this point are presented as a unified group at variance with the lone Judean who, though appearing without introduction, has a position to represent and an argument to pursue. That capacity suggests prior experiences in his search for spiritual answers. Since his focus is on both Jesus and John the Baptist, one

---

[11] The Fourth Evangelist's narrative leaves the door open for a pre-Galilean baptismal ministry of Jesus (3:22, 26). A later redactor closes the door on this tradition (4:2) perhaps wishing to adjust to the Synoptic tradition. Cf. Raymond E. Brown, *The Gospel according to John (i–xii)* (AB 29; Garden City, N.Y.: Doubleday, 1966), 164.

[12] A further example of parallelism in John's Gospel is the mention of Aenon by Salim (3:22) and "Bethany on the other side of the Jordan" (1:28). Both places, Bethany in the south and Aenon in the north (the famous 6th century C.E. Madaba Mosaic map has two Aenons), have long histories of problematic locations. This is not unusual for John's Gospel since the mention of other sites in this Gospel have slipped from historical view. It could hardly be said that these places are literary creations or inventions. More likely they were remembered as locales for early Christian communities, baptismal movements, or pilgrimage sites. For an extensive study of this issue, see Karl Kundsin, *Topologische Überlieferungsstoffe im Johannes-Evangelium* (Göttingen: Vandenhoeck & Ruprecht, 1925).

[13] Cf. Brown, *John*, 151.

[14] This bracketing seems intentional since many commentators argue that ch. 5 actually belongs after ch. 6.

could conclude that it was in Jerusalem where he had some prior level of exposure to and interaction with Jesus followers and/or with Jesus himself.[15] The same could be maintained for John the Baptist. A longstanding tradition placed the home of John in the outskirts of Jerusalem, in the hill country of the area around Ain Kerem. Recent archaeological excavations in the Suba cave in that area have brought dramatic evidence to light linking rites of purification with water baptism.[16] Although the activity of John as an ascetic and apocalyptic prophet announcing an imminent day of wrath and calling people to repentance followed by baptism took place in the Judean wilderness, it was his earlier life that would qualify him as a potential link with the Judean of 3:25. With a prior link to both John the Baptist and Jesus, the Judean serves as a parallel to the Galilean Andrew and the unnamed disciple (1:35–37) who for a time were followers of John the Baptist before their subsequent new alignment with Jesus.[17] One final point can be made here. Should the multi-layered compositional theories that advocate an early Jerusalem tradition in the Johannine authorship of this Gospel be on target, then added support is given to the background of the Judean as one already knowledgeable about the movements of John the Baptist and Jesus.

As a seeker, searching for resolution and answers, the Judean found himself turning to the Jesus movement and connecting with the Jesus who himself had parted ways with the Baptist while at the same time maintaining that "no one is greater than John" (Luke 7:28). With this new orientation, the Judean seeker becomes a contender by clashing with John's disciples and engaging in debate with them. Here his character becomes more complex. He is one against a group. The nature of this encounter is described as a ζήτησις. While this Greek term can mean a "discussion," its more basic and frequent usage suggests argument and disagreement.[18] The issue in the dispute is identified generically (without the article) as καθαρισμός, namely, purification. Could this be a debate over the relative merits and power of the contrasting baptismal practices of Jesus and John? The issues of purification and cleansing were central in Jewish life and practice ranging from temple rituals to daily purifications,

---

[15] Because of its frequent references to times Jesus spent in Jerusalem, the Fourth Gospel, in comparison to the Synoptics, is often referred to as the "Jerusalem Gospel."

[16] Shimon Gibson, *The Cave of John the Baptist* (New York: Doubleday, 2004).

[17] So Rudolf Bultmann, *Das Evangelium des Johannes* (Göttingen: Vandenhoeck & Ruprecht, 1965), 123 ("Im Zshg. kann man nur verstehen, daß sich die Johannes-Jünger an einen Juden halten, der sich von Jesus hat taufen lassen oder taufen lassen will") and Ernst Haenchen, *John* (Hermeneia; Philadelphia: Fortress, 1984), 210 with his reference to "a Jew baptized by Jesus," which, however, he finds contextually problematic.

[18] Although, e. g., the NRSV translates the term as "discussion," the majority of commentators use such terms as "dispute" (Barrett, *John*, 184), "controversy" (Brown, *John*, 150), "quarrel" (Rudolf Schnackenburg, *The Gospel according to St. John: Volume 1* [trans. K. Smyth; New York: Herder & Herder, 1968], 413), and "conflict" (Craig Keener, *The Gospel of John: A Commentary* [2 vols.; Peabody, Mass.: Hendrickson, 2003], 1:577, fn. 410).

rites with food and washings. Practices could vary from group to group, from Essenes to Pharisees to Levites (Mal 3:3) to the everyday person. Impurities and their opposites could be physical or ritual or moral. They covered every aspect of life. To the surprise of the reader none of these issues emerges as the object of the dispute. Then how should the reference to purification be understood?

It is clear that the narrator uses the term "purification" in a double sense, first as flat and one-dimensional with its apparent reference to essential Jewish rites and practices as demonstrated with the ritually cleansed "six stone water jars" in the wedding at Cana (2:6). By contrast, the foot-washing scene of Peter (13:1–20) unfolds in a fuller or rounder sense, where the foot-washing serves also as a symbol for baptism. Here the cleansing power is not lodged in ritual but in the *word of Jesus* ("you are clean [καθαροί]"; 3:10). The same is reaffirmed in the true vine discourse (15:3) where Jesus declares: "You have already been cleansed (καθαροί) *by the word* that I have spoken to you." These "purification" acts are conceptually related to "holiness" expressed in the terms of consecration and sanctification as derived from the root term ἁγιάζειν. Holiness is the characteristic of God. By extension all those who belong to God become holy (Lev 19:2). In this way Jesus prays, "Holy Father, protect them in your name" (17:11). In the Bread of Life discourse (John 6), Peter extends the same to Jesus and declares, "You have the words of eternal life … You are the Holy One of God" (vss. 69, 70). Consequently, Jesus in his Great Prayer in chapter 17 can implore His Father on behalf of the believing community and pray, "Sanctify them (make them holy) in the truth, your word is truth … and for their sakes I sanctify myself so that they also may be sanctified in truth" (17:17–19).

When the disciples of John and the anonymous Judean[19] approach John the Baptist for what one would expect to be a resolution of the purification dispute, the reader is surprised instead to learn that the question now revolves around the baptizing work of Jesus and the fact that "all are going to him." This startling disconnect holds if the reader continues to see the account on a flat one-dimensional level. Only when the fuller and deeper intent of "purification" and its connection to the cleansing and sanctifying work of the "Holy One of God" who acts "by his word" because of his oneness with the "Holy Father," does the response of John appear coherent and in line with the high Christology of the Fourth Gospel. John's response is the high point of this passage. Turning to his disciples and to the Judean, he makes two formative statements: "You yourselves are my witnesses" and "I am not the Messiah." If John

---

[19] Although some commentators restrict the plural form of the verb "came" (ἦλθον) to the disciples of John, the stronger contextual reading would be inclusive, embracing both the Judean and the disciples of John.

is not the Messiah, then what is his role? The reply is unequivocal. "No one can receive anything except what has been given from heaven." It is God's decree that John should be sent "ahead" of Jesus. As such he is a witness but more than a witness. He is the witness par excellence.[20] Now John's disciples as well as the Judean can in turn be addressed as witnesses. From seeker to contender, the Judean now emerges as a witness to the pre-eminence of Jesus as testified by John the Baptist.

The fact that the Judean is distinguished from the followers of John the Baptist is noteworthy. Why would he remain anonymous? A close reading of the Fourth Gospel reveals that anonymity is a frequent literary device[21] used in diverse ways to underscore a point of significance or primal status. The most outstanding use of this device is apparent in the question of the identity of the Johannine author/narrator. The traditional view ascribing authorship to the Galilean fisherman, John the son of Zebedee (John 21:20–24) has given way to more complex reconstructions in line with external evidence and the complexity of the text.[22] Reviving the work of many previous scholars, Martin Hengel[23] has compellingly argued for a fresh look at the importance of the earliest external witness (2nd century C. E.) of Papias and Polycrates who are unified in their view that John the Elder was the pivotal person in the composition of the Fourth Gospel. This John, later known as "the theologian" (ὁ θεολόγος) and head of the "Johannine school" in Asia Minor, was a Judean who as a young man came into close contact with Jesus in Jerusalem and became a disciple, although not one of the twelve.[24] While the ideal author remains the Galilean John, the real author of the Fourth Gospel would be the Judean John of Jerusalem and later Asia Minor. Could the Judean of our text have had his initial and continuing contact with the very one who would be the principal author of the text? Significant, however, is the fact that the author(s) together with final editors all want the riddle to remain unsolved. Anonymity serves to keep attention focused on the central figure, in this case, Jesus. For the same reason anonymity is used intentionally at times in identifying the disciples of Jesus. While the Synoptics cite names for each of "the twelve," the Fourth Evangelist provides names for only seven (nine, if the "sons of Zebedee"

---

[20] Cf. Cornelis Bennema, *Encountering Jesus: Character Studies in the Gospel of John* (Milton Keynes: Paternoster, 2009), 22–29.

[21] For further development of this point, see Richard Bauckham, *The Testimony of the Beloved Disciple* (Grand Rapids, Mich.: Baker Academic, 2007), 90–91.

[22] In his comprehensive overview of scholarly proposals for identifying the author of the Fourth Gospel, James Charlesworth examines twenty-one different possibilities in cases argued by scholars. He himself makes a case for Thomas (Ibid, *The Beloved Disciple* [Valley Forge, Pa.: Trinity, 1995], 127–224).

[23] Martin Hengel, *The Johannine Question* (Philadelphia: Trinity, 1989).

[24] Hengel, *Question*, 131. See also Bauckham, *Testimony* for further development of this position.

[21:2] are counted) and gives speaking parts to some who otherwise are only named. While the Synoptics additionally identify the twelve as "apostles"[25] that term never appears in John where discipleship is broadened to include all who hear and believe the word. With this as background, one could easily understand the anonymous Judean as one whose name is withheld in order not to detract from either the primacy of Jesus (whom he follows) or from John the Baptist's position as the prime witness to Jesus, whom the Judean may initially have followed.

These relationships are secured by a parable with allegorical traits that draw on Jewish marriage customs (v. 29). This parable-like sequel serves as a summary statement of the preceding and is a coherent integral part of the text. At its heart is the interaction between the bridegroom and his friend, namely, the groomsman or best man. When the "best man" hears the voice of the bridegroom, his joy is realized and is complete. The application is clear. Jesus is the bridegroom who has the bride (Rev 19:7). It is the relationship between the bridegroom and his best man (John the Baptist) which is at stake. The special function of the groomsman is to act on behalf of the bridegroom and to keep watch outside the bridal chamber. With these comparisons the vital yet secondary role of the Baptist is underscored. An interesting twist to these figures of speech comes from actual practice in Jewish weddings which call for two groomsmen to be attendants at the wedding.[26] Could the anonymous Judean by implication fit this role? He too, along with John the Baptist, fits the part of those whose personal status fades in order to give witness to the superiority of Jesus and to hear the voice of him who is one with the Father.

---

[25] Luke tends to restrict this designation only for the Twelve.

[26] Str-B 1:500–504. For full treatment of the friend of the bridegroom see Mirjam and Ruben Zimmerman, "Der Freund des Bräutigams (Joh 3,29): Deflorations- oder Christuszeuge?," *ZNW* 90 (1999): 123–30.

The Samaritan Woman:
A Woman Transformed

Harold W. Attridge

The "character" of the Samaritan Woman in John 4 is, like many characters in a drama, open to different readings. Stereotypes and literary intertexts hint at, but do not fully determine the ways in which the potential might be realized. However she is initially read, her dialogue with Jesus transforms her. The potentially coquettish object of attraction finds herself attracted to the mysterious stranger and comes more actively to pursue engagement with him as her curiosity drives her to plumb the mystery of his identity. As curiosity changes to wonder, the focus of her life shifts from eros to mission, and she engages in a successful apostolic outreach to her fellow Samaritans. The character of this Woman, like that of other women prominent in the Gospel, thus offers a model of transformative encounter with Jesus.

Although earlier commentators have noted aspects of the "characters" of the Fourth Gospel,[1] formal study of the topic, which began with the rise of contemporary literary-critical approaches to the text, reached a new and informed systematic level with the work of Cornelis Bennema,[2] who has forcefully argued that many of the characters in the Fourth Gospel are not simply types or conventional figures deployed to make a theological point about how one can or should encounter Jesus. Instead, by the varying degrees of complexity of their characterization, they contribute to the shaping of the narrative and the allure of the Gospel as a work of engaging narrative. So the Samaritan Woman is more than simply a model of a repentant sinner

---

[1] So, e. g., Raymond E. Brown, *The Gospel According to John (i–xii)* (AB 29; New York: Doubleday, 1966) 175–76, "And if we analyze the repartee at the well, we find quite true-to-life the characterization of the woman as mincing and coy, with a certain light grace (Lagrange, pl. 101). Though characters like Nicodemus, this woman, the paralytic of ch. V, and the blind man of ch. X are – to a certain extent – foils used by the evangelist to permit Jesus to unfold his revelation, still each has his or her own personal characteristics and fitting lines of dialogue."

[2] Cornelis Bennema, *Encountering Jesus: Character Studies in the Gospel of John* (Milton Keynes: Paternoster, 2009). Bennema provides a useful review of the many treatments of character in contemporary critical literature.

or enthusiastic apostle,[3] not simply a representative of the marginalized or the "other,"[4] but a woman with a personality whose interaction with Jesus can lead to significant insights into the dynamics of this Gospel. Bennema is surely right in this regard and this brief contribution will, I hope, build on his approach, although it will take a slightly different tack, because there remains a good deal of ambiguity about the personality of this character.

I begin with three preliminary observations, and one methodological suggestion. First, the characterization of the Samaritan Woman, known to orthodox tradition as Photina (or Photeine),[5] is sketched in succinct and somewhat ambivalent terms. Resolving the ambiguity depends primarily on the ways in which her dramatic dialogue with Jesus is to be construed, or, as I shall suggest, "played." Readers do not hear her inner thoughts and have no information about the development of her personality apart from the interaction in this one episode. Second, the dialogue between Jesus and the Woman, and, in turn, the "character" of the dialogue partners, has been a subject of considerable attention among commentators through the ages, who have in fact "read" the Samaritan Woman in a variety of ways.[6] Third, one's perception of the ways in which the dialogue is to be construed is, in part at least, shaped by how a reader construes the overall narrative, what kind of scene it is and what the expectations are that generic qualities may conjure up.

Since interactive dialogue is the primary mode of conveying information about the character, we need to take that dialogue quite seriously. Following the lead of various scholars who have pointed to the "dramatic" dimensions

---

[3] On the importance of the theme of mission in the pericope see Teresa Okure, *The Johannine Approach to Mission: A Contextual Study of John 4:1–42* (WUNT II/31; Tübingen: Mohr, 1988). See also Hubert Ritt, "Die Frau als Glaubensbotin: um Verständnis der Samaritanerin von Joh 4,1–42," in *Vom Urchristentum zu Jesus: FS J. Gnilka* (ed. Hubert Frankemölle and Klaus Kertelge; Freiburg: Herder, 1988), 287–306.

[4] For readings of the Samaritan Woman from a feminist perspective, see Sandra M. Schneiders, "Women in the Fourth Gospel and the Role of Women in the Contemporary Church," *BTB* 12 (1982): 40; idem, "A Case Study: A Feminist Interpretation of John 4:1–42," in idem, *The Revelatory Text: Interpreting the New Testament as Sacred Scripture* (San Francisco: Harper, 1991), 188–89; Elisabeth Schüssler-Fiorenza, *In Memory of Her* (New York: Crossroad, 1983), 326; Adeline Fehribach, *The Women in the Life of the Bridegroom: A Feminist Historical-Literary Analysis of the Female Characters in the Fourth Gospel* (Collegeville, Minn.: Liturgical Press, 1998), 45–81. While most feminist readings emphasize the role of the Woman as a disciple or apostle, Fehribach's elaborate reading highlights the Woman's representative role as symbolic Samaritan bride for her bridegroom.

[5] See Janeth Norfleete Day, *The Woman at the Well: Interpretation of John 4:1–42 in Retrospect and Prospect* (BIS 41; Leiden: Brill, 2002), 17.

[6] Day provides a very useful summary of the ways in which both literary commentators (*The Woman at the Well*, 7–41) and visual artists (idem, *The Woman at the Well*, 43–12) have interpreted her character. For another useful summary, see Andrea Link, *Was redest du mit ihr? Eine Studie zur Exegese-, Redaktions-, und Theologiegeschichte von Joh 4,1–42* (BU 24; Regensburg: Pustet, 1992).

of the Gospel,[7] it may be suggestive to construe John 4 as a dramatic script, rendered somewhat loosely. Such a construal invites reflection on the challenges that confront a director of the *performance* of this dramatic scene. How precisely is the actor playing the Samaritan Woman to play her part? What should be the inflection of her voice; the look of her eyes? Should her statements be simple and naïve or should they be laced with irony and innuendo? This approach, which defines the "implied reader" in a specific way,[8] will, I hope, illustrate the difficulty of too facile a *reading* of the character. The long history of literary and visual interpretation, helpfully traced by Janeth Norfleete Day, abundantly confirms the rich potential of the story. Readers and commentators on this text, like directors of a dramatic script, have made choices about how the part should be played, how the character works. While all have some foundation in the text, what the various directors bring to the text strongly influences what the see in it. Intertextual allusions offer some hints about how the part is to be played, but they do not fully determine the characterization of the Samaritan Woman.

---

[7] Brown, *John*, 176, appreciated the dramatic qualities of the Gospel, "If, as we suspect, there is a substratum of traditional material, the evangelist has taken it and with his masterful sense of drama and the various techniques of stage setting, has formed it into a superb theological scenario." More recently and in more detail, see Mark W. G. Stibbe, *John as Storyteller: Narrative Criticism and the Fourth Gospel* (SNTSMS 73; Cambridge: Cambridge University Press, 1992); Ludger Schenke, *Johanneskommentar* (Düsseldorf: Patmos, 1998); Jo-Ann A. Brant, *Dialogue and Drama: Elements of Greek Tragedy in the Fourth Gospel* (Peabody, Mass.: Hendrickson, 2004); George Parsenios, *Departure and Consolation: The Proliferation of Genres in John 13–17: The Johannine Farewell Discourses in Light of Greco-Roman Literature* (NovTSup 117; Leiden: Brill, 2005); idem, *Rhetoric and Drama in the Johannine Lawsuit Motif* (WUNT 258; Mohr Siebeck: Tübingen, 2010).

[8] The "implied reader" well known to narratological critics, can come in a variety of forms. A "reader" may be explicitly constructed in the text, as, for instance, Theophilus, addressed in the prefaces to Luke's two volumes (Luke 1:3; Acts 1:10), or the "you," called upon to believe in the Fourth Gospel (John 19:35; 20:31). The possible characteristics of that reader may, of course, differ from those who actually take the text in hand. Or the reader may be more subtly implied by the kinds of appeals and assumptions that are built into a text. As those appeals and assumptions become more tenuous and opaque, the image of the "implied reader" becomes more subject to the imaginative construction of the real reader who offers an interpretation or "reading" of the text. My "director," whose notes constitute the bulk of this article, is such a "reader," "implied" by the dramatic character of the episode, but constructed by the imagination of this interpreter. This construct suggests how much leeway the "reader" has in making sense of this narrative.

John 4 as a Script

Characters:
Jesus
A Samaritan Woman
The Disciples
The Townsfolk
The Narrator

I have blocked out the script into eight segments,[9] some clearly delineated by formal features, such as a narrator's intervention, or by an abrupt change in the thematic focus of the dialogue. Understanding the possible motivation for such changes will be one important question to address.

1. Setting

Jesus is on the road from Judea to Galilee and passes through Samaria, stopping around noon at a town called Sychar, famous as the site of Jacob's well.[10] With his disciples away fetching lunch in town, he stops, wearied and thirsty, at the well. A Samaritan woman comes to draw water.

Director's Note

As many readers of the story of have noted, the setting by a well evokes several episodes in the Hebrew Bible, Gen 24:11; 29:2; Exod 2:15, where a patriarchal

---

[9] Brown, *John*, 166–68, construes the chapter as a little drama with two scenes, the first portraying the interaction between Jesus and the woman, 4:6–26, and the second, that between Jesus and the disciples, 4:27–38, with an introduction, 4:1–6a, and conclusion, 4:39–41.

[10] Some commentators suspect that the text here may be corrupt and the town should in fact be Shechem, near the site of the traditional location of Jacob's well. See Brown, *John*, 169. Such commentators may, however, be influenced by later traditions about the location of Jacob's well and Sychar may be the correct original reading. See Hartwig Thyen, *Das Johannesevangelium* (HNT 6; Tübingen: Mohr Siebeck, 2005), 241–44.

[11] See, e. g., John Bligh, "Jesus in Samaria," *HeyJ* 3 (1962): 329–46, here 332, noted by Brown, *John*, 171, as a "curious interpretation." Many, however, have followed suit. See Annie Jaubert, "La symbolique de puits de Jacob: Jean 4,12," in *L'Homme devant Dieu: Mélanges offerts au Père Henri de Lubac* (3 vols.; Theologie 56; Lyon: Aubier, 1963), 1:70–71; Norman R. Bonneau, "The Woman at the Well, John 4 and Genesis 24," *Bible Today* 67 (1973): 1252–59; Jerome Neyrey, "Jacob Traditions and the Interpretation of John 4:10–26," *CBQ* 41 (1979): 436–37; Calum M. Carmichael, "Marriage and the Samaritan Woman," *NTS* 26 (1980): 332–46; P. Joseph Cahill, "Narrative Art in John IV," *Religious Studies Bulletin* 2 (1982): 41–48; Lyle Eslinger, "The Wooing of the Woman at the Well," *Literature and Theology* 1 (1987): 167–83, reprinted in Mark W. G. Stibbe, *The Gospel of John as Literature: An Anthology of Twentieth-Century Perspectives* (Leiden: Brill, 1993), 165–82; from a more general theoretical perspective, Jo-Ann A. Brant, "Husband Hunting: Characterization and Narrative Art in the Gospel of John," *BibInt* 4 (1996): 205–23; Danna Nolan Fewell and Gary A. Phillips, "Drawn

hero finds a bride.[11] As many note, Jesus has already been labeled the "bridegroom" in John 3:29, perhaps anticipating the current scene. The "type scene," as it is often dubbed, creates expectations of an erotic encounter of some sort, though how those expectations might be realized remains to be seen.

The script offers no hints about how the Samaritan Woman is to be attired or what demeanor she displays in coming to the well. The artistic tradition in visualizing the scene has generally portrayed her modestly, although a few artists play on the scene's erotic potential with somewhat provocative apparel, although these are in a distinct minority.[12] The actor playing the Woman might be instructed to saunter provocatively up to the well, or to move with simple nonchalance across the stage.

Some readers have taken a cue from the time of the encounter that the Samaritan is perhaps of loose morals,[13] and hence to be imagined as something of a hussy, since the normal times for drawing water would not be at the sixth hour (probably around noon[14]). But the data are ambiguous, it might be shame that sends the Woman out at an unusual hour, or it might be modesty or simple necessity. If shame motivates the timing of her trip, she might be asked to move with head bowed, dispirited and defensive in her demeanor.[15]

2. Initial Question

Jesus: "Give me something to drink."
SW: "How is it that you, a Jew, ask me, a Samaritan woman, for a drink?"
Narrator: Jews and Samaritans don't have any use for one another.

---

to Excess, or Reading Beyond Betrothal," *Semeia* 77 (1997): 23–59; Fehribach, *The Women in the Life of the Bridegroom*, 49–52; Mirjam and Ruben Zimmermann, "Brautwerbung in Samarien? Von der moralischen zur metaphorischen Interpretation von Joh 4," ZNT 1 (1998): 40–50; Ellen Aitken, "At the Well of Living Water: Jacob Traditions in John 4," in *The Interpretation of Scripture in Early Judaism and Christianity* (ed. Craig A. Evans; Sheffield: Sheffield Academic Press, 2000), 342–52. Others see the episode as a parody of the Old Testament type scene. See Jeffrey Lloyd Staley, *The Print's First Kiss: A Rhetorical Investigation of the Implied Reader in the Fourth Gospel* (Atlanta: Scholars Press, 1988), 99–103.

[12] See Day, *The Woman at the Well*, 103–109, for discussion of the visual treatments of the scene by Sebastiano Ricci (1659–1734), where the Samaritan's loose dresses and exposed flesh suggest a woman of somewhat loose morals. An interesting alternative is the depiction by Edouard von Gebhardt (1914), who portrays her as a robust and spirited but somewhat "earthy" character. See Day, *The Woman at the Well*, 112.

[13] See the extensive discussion in Craig S. Keener, *The Gospel of John: A Commentary* (2 vols.; Peabody, Mass.: Hendrickson, 2003), 1:593–96, with reference to earlier literature. See also Day, *The Woman at the Well*, 160.

[14] The text says the "sixth hour," which would be noon on a reckoning of the "hours" of the day from dawn to sunset. There are other, weakly attested, reckonings, beginning with midnight or noon, which would make this either 6:00 a. m. or 6:00 p. m. See Keener, *John*, 1:591–92.

[15] This suggestion comes from an "associate director," a. k. a., a reader of the manuscript.

Director's Note

Interpreters of the story, whether learned commentators or simple readers, here come to the second major fork in the road. What is the tone of the Woman's response? Is she pleasantly surprised? Does she politely say, in effect, "How is it, good sir, that a Jew such as yourself is asking me, a Samaritan woman, for a drink?" Or is there a little edge to her question? "So what's a Jew like you doing asking a Samaritan like me for a drink?"[16] Or is there a hint of flirtation? One might ask the actor to play it *a la* Mae West: "So, Jew, you wanna nice Samaritan to give you a drink?" We might ask our character actor to convey that with a gesture or a glance. She might respond looking over her shoulder while bending over to pull up her pail, perhaps with her quivering eyes glancing sideways.[17]

3. Living Water?

Jesus: "If you knew God's gift and who is asking for a drink, you would have made a request to him and he would have given you 'living water.'"

SW: "Sir, you don't have anything with which to draw water and the well is pretty deep. Where are you going to get 'living water'? Are you better than our ancestor Jacob, who provided us the well and drank from it himself along with his sons and his cattle?"

Jesus: "Anyone who drinks this water will be thirsty again, but whoever drinks the water that I give will never thirst. The water that I shall give will become in the one who receives it a well that springs up to eternal life."

SW: "Sir, give me this water, so I won't be thirsty and won't have to come all this way to draw water."

Director's Note

The same question that emerged in the first block resurfaces in the second, set off from the first by the narrator's remark. In this block the Samaritan Woman speaks twice, each time in response to a remark by Jesus. The first comment could also be read or performed in at least two ways. The Woman could be

---

[16] So Francis Moloney suggests that "The woman responds with mocking surprise" (idem, *The Gospel of John* [SP 4; Collegeville, Minn.: Liturgical Press, 1998], 115). He later suggests that the response is "arrogant." The warrants for that judgment are not particularly clear. If anything, the abrupt request from Jesus might easily be characterized as arrogant. For an alternative psychological analysis, see Wilhelm H. Wuellner and Robert C. Leslie, *The Surprising Gospel: Intriguing Psychological Insights from the New Testament* (Nashville: Abingdon, 1984), 40, noted by Day, *The Woman at the Well*, 164, who take the response to indicate that the Woman is a "defensive person."

[17] Some commentators, such as Keener, *John*, 1:605, realize the potential in the scene and suggest that the Woman misunderstands Jesus' request as an advance.

simply expressing astonishment at the bold claim of Jesus, however understood, that he is the one who can provide a good drink.[18] Some commentators want to find here a hint of movement toward Jesus on the part of the Woman.[19] Perhaps we would want the actor to say something like, "I just don't see how you are going to do that, and provide something better than what Jacob gave us." Or, again, her comment could be read in a more pointed way, perhaps with the intonation of a "valley girl," "Do you really think that you can do better than our famous ancestor Jacob? You don't even have a pail. *What* are you *thinking*?" In any case, if there was any erotic tone in the previous exchange, the wording here seems to provide little opportunity for continuing it, unless the actor playing Jesus uses a very lurid tone in talking about "living water."[20]

How the Woman's part is played will depend on how the part of Jesus is played and what connotations might be conveyed by the promise of "living water." If there is any possibility that there is an erotic *double entendre* here, as in Prov 5:15–18, or Song 4:12–15, her response would have to take on a flirtatious tone.[21]

The next claim of Jesus ups the ante. Not only, he says, can he provide her some fresh, "living" water. What he can give offers truly lasting satisfaction. A sip from him and she'll have her own internal fountain (πηγή, better than a

---

[18] Commentators regularly note the play on "living water." There is disagreement about whether the Woman understands Jesus to be talking on a metaphorical or spiritual level and rejects that or simply misunderstands his claim about the spiritual water of his teaching in terms of fresh, physical water. Her final remark seems to suggest the latter, unless she is being very ironic.

[19] Moloney, *John*, 123, cites Birger Olsson, *Structure and Meaning in the Fourth Gospel* (Lund: Gleerup, 1974), 182–83; Carmichael, "Marriage," 337–43, and Xavier Léon-Dufour, *Lecture de l'évangile selon Jean* (3 vols.; Parole de Dieu; Paris: Éditions du Seuil, 1988, 1990, 1993), 1:419, as finding the response positive. He rejects the notion: "The context demands, however, that the woman be judged in terms of her acceptance or refusal of the word of Jesus. On this criterion, 'the first round in the conversation ends in complete failure. The woman remains level-headed, incredulous' (citing Hendrikus Boers, *Neither on This Mountain Nor in Jerusalem: A Study of John 4* [SBLMS 35; Atlanta: Scholars, 1988], 169)." I doubt that the context is quite so demanding, except for a director who wants to emphasize the problematic character of the Woman.

[20] Day, *The Woman at the Well*, 165, recognizes the difficulties in sorting out the possibilities for reading the character: "Here we have one of those narrative occurrences where our inability to evaluate the intent of the discourse by observing gestures and facial expression or hearing vocal intonation requires that we as readers infer meaning." The situation that she describes here obtains for the whole of the episode.

[21] On this possibility, see Carmichael, "Marriage," 339–40, and Eslinger, "Wooing," 168–70, noted by Fehribach, *The Women in the Life of the Bridegroom*, 54. For more on the symbolic potential of "water" see Larry Paul Jones, *The Symbol of Water in the Gospel of John* (JSNTSup 145; Sheffield: Sheffield Academic Press, 1997); Ruben Zimmermann, *Christologie der Bilder im Johannesevangelium: Die Christopoetik des vierten Evangeliums unter besonderer Berücksichtigung von Joh 10* (WUNT 171; Tübingen: Mohr Siebeck, 2004), 142–44.

well?²²). The performance instruction for the Woman's next line depends on how this claim of Jesus is read. Does she respond with a kind of pious hope, "Yes, that would be wonderful! Do give me some of what you can provide, so that I won't experience thirst again." Such a response would seem to suggest that she gets the deeper meaning of Jesus' promise of "living water," whatever that may be. The conclusion of the remark, however, suggests that a different tone is required. The Woman seems to take Jesus at his word, which would be rather absurd when taken at face value. So her response can be read as somewhat dismissive: "By all means, do go ahead and give me some of this very special water. I would be happy not to have to walk down here every day."²³

Or does the erotic flirtation continue? Does the suggestion that the "living water" that Jesus provides will create something new for the recipient hint at what might happen after a sexual encounter?²⁴ If so, should the Woman respond in a tone that has a hint of amused but skeptical irony, continuing the banter? "I would certainly love it if you could give me a source of never ending water. That would spare me a lot of lugging. If only you could do something like that!"

What suggests that the director should coax out of the character actor something more than a straightforward response is the abrupt change in the dialogue that follows. The conversation between Jesus and the Samaritan Woman has reached an impasse. He promises something extraordinary, with perhaps more than one level of meaning;²⁵ she dismisses him, but the nature of the dismissal remains open to more than one actualization, within a band of emotion ranging from disdainful to wistful.²⁶

---

²² See the discussion of the possible distinction between "well" and "fountain" in Brown, *John*, 170, For some commentators, such as Moloney, *John*, 123, the change is likely to be simply stylistic.

²³ Commentators wrestle with the level of irony involved. See Gail O'Day, *Revelation in the Fourth Gospel: Narrative Mode and Theological Claim* (Philadelphia: Fortress, 1986), 64, noted by Thyen, *Johannesevangelium*, 252: "Her ignorance highlights the irony of her response, for the comprehending reader knows that the woman is making the correct request in spite of herself."

²⁴ The possible *double entendre* might be more obvious if Jesus had used the language that appears in John 7:38 where he promises that water will flow from the "belly" (κοιλία) of the believer.

²⁵ The precise referent of the "living water" is, as one might expect, elusive and debated. Candidates include one or more of the following: the Holy Spirit, eternal life, Jesus' teaching and the knowledge of God that it provides, the sacraments of baptism and eucharist. The commentators, Brown, *John*, 178–80; Moloney, *John*, 117–18, discuss the various possibilities. Our director need not limit the possibilities.

²⁶ Some commentators would limit the range of possibilities here. So Moloney, *John*, 119, "The words of Jesus have been misunderstood in a physical and selfish sense. As 'the Jews' rejected the words of Jesus in 2:20, so does the Samaritan woman in 4:15. She too is presented, at the conclusion of this first moment of her encounter with Jesus, as having no faith."

4. Is There a Hubby?

Jesus: "Go, call your husband and come here."
SW: "I don't have a husband."
Jesus: "Right, since you have had five, and the one you have now is not your husband. You spoke the truth, all right."

Director's Note

The next exchange between Jesus and the Woman is much more focused and abrupt than any of the preceding. Without any apparent motivation, Jesus tells the Woman to call her husband. If there had been any sexual banter in the previous conversation, it is now gone, and Jesus' remark has the feel of a rebuke. The Woman, in any case, says that she does not have a husband.[27] In response, Jesus reveals that he knows much more about her than anything in their previous dialogue would suggest. Whether the Woman has been arrogantly dismissive of Jesus or more playfully flirting with him, she is taken by surprise at this development. The fact that she will allude to this exchange later shows how significant it was for her.[28] It is indeed the pivot on which the whole dialogue turns. The fact that it turns on precisely the point of her marital status might suggest that the earlier readings of her exchanges need to be performed in a more flirtatious way. Flirtation ends when Jesus indicates his knowledge of her unavailability, yet at the same time her attraction to him becomes more serious.

The response of Jesus to the Woman, noting that she has had five husbands and is now with a man who is not her husband, has been the focal point of two major readings of the story. One ekes out an allegorical meaning, finding, for instance, an allusion to the Samaritan belief in only the five books of Moses,[29] or to the supposed five gods of the ancient Samaritans.[30] Whatever the merits of this approach, it does not illuminate the character of the Woman. The other reading – by far the more common – finds in the facts of marital history evidence of immorality,[31] leading to such odd moves as the identification of the Samaritan with the woman caught in adultery who appears in chapter 8.

---

[27] An associate director suggests the interesting possibility that the Woman winks as she delivers this line.

[28] As Moloney, *John*, 127 notes, "Jesus' knowledge of these 'facts' (scil. of her marital history) is the turning point of the narrative."

[29] Origen, *In Joh*. 13.8. See Brown, *John*, 171.

[30] 2 Kgs 17:24ff reports on the foreign colonists who came from five cities with their gods, though the number of the gods (vss. 30–31) was seven. As Brown, *John*, 171, notes, Josephus, *Ant*. 9.14.3, 288, reduced the number of gods to five.

[31] Moloney, *John*, 127, is typical: "She has lived an irregular married life and is currently in a sinful situation, but the point of v. 18 is not to lay bare her sinfulness." Some readers, stressing the theme of immorality, wonder whether the Woman was really married to these

Yet a history of five marriages is not a sure pointer to the Woman's character. She may have been unfortunate enough to have been married young to a series of older gentlemen who died before their time. Her current status could perhaps be simply a stage toward husband number 6. Her subsequent comments suggest nothing about repenting of past behavior, only amazement that Jesus knew all that he did about her. The tone going forward needs to be one of astonished fascination on the part of the Woman as she becomes more and more enthralled by her mysterious interlocutor.[32]

5. Where Does Real Worship Happen?

SW: "Sir, I have the sense that you are a prophet. Now, our ancestors worshipped on this mountain and you say that Jerusalem is the place where people should worship."

Jesus: "Ma'am, believe me, the time is coming when you will worship the Father neither on this mountain nor in Jerusalem. You worship what you do not know; we worship what we do know, for salvation is from the Jews. But the time is coming, and is upon us already, when true worshippers will worship the Father in spirit and truth. For that is the kind of worshipper that the Father seeks. God, you see, is spirit and those who worship him must worship in spirit and truth."

SW: "I know that the Messiah, the one who is called the Christ, is coming. When he comes, he will tell us everything."

Jesus: "The one who is speaking with you is that person."

Director's Note

The Woman, now forced from rather light-hearted banter to more serious conversation, changes the subject from her marital status to a perennial religious question. She asks, "Who is right, Jews or Samaritans in their claims about the place where God is truly worshipped?" There is a limited range of options from which to choose. The options available in the early part of the discourse have been limited by the abrupt turn caused by the question about marital status. The Woman, though perhaps trying to avoid discussion of a potentially embarrassing topic, asks a serious question.

---

husbands. See Cantwell, "Immortal Longings," 78–79, noted in Fehribach, *The Women in the Life of the Bridegroom*, 64.

[32] Stephen Moore, who reads the encounter as one steeped in eros, encapsulates the dynamic involved graphically, perhaps with a bit more verve than is warranted: "Jesus thirsts to arouse her thirst. His desire is to arouse her desire, to be himself desired. His desire is to be the desire of this woman, to have her recognize in him that which she herself lacks. His desire is to fill up her lack. Only thus can his own deeper thirst be assuaged, his own lack be filled." See Stephen Moore, *Poststructuralism and the New Testament: Derrida and Foucault at the Foot of the Cross* (Minneapolis: Fortress, 1994), 44.

Jesus is presented with a dilemma by his now surprisingly thoughtful interlocutor. To affirm the Samaritan option for legitimate worship would ingratiate himself with the Woman but would put him outside the boundaries of his own community. To affirm the Jewish/Judaean claim would probably be a final conversation stopper. Jesus refuses to be caught on the horns of the dilemma, and challenges the Woman to understand that worship of the God who is Spirit is not dependent on locale, but on the spirit and truth of the worshipper.[33]

The Woman responds with another change of subject, from true worship to the identity of God's eschatological agent. There may well be echoes of Samaritan belief in her description of the Messiah as the "one who will tell all,"[34] although that is not particularly relevant to the dynamics of the drama. The question probably functions as a way of deflecting the attempt by Jesus to tell her something about true worship and conclude the discussion. "Well," she says in effect, "we'll find out the answers to all these questions when the Messiah comes, since he will tell us what we need to know." Again, something of a dismissive tone might be called for. But, perhaps to her surprise, Jesus responds by identifying himself with that expected figure, something that should not surprise her, since he has told her all about herself.

6. Aftermath: Disciples and Townspeople

Narrator: The disciples return and do not ask about the Woman, who goes to the people of her town, leaving her water jar behind.

SW: "Come, see a man who told me everything that I ever did. Can he be the Christ?"

Narrator: The townspeople go out of the city.

Director's Note

As many commentators have suggested, whatever their view of the character of the Woman, it is clear by now that she is involved in at least a halting recognition of the significance of the one whom she encountered at the well. The abandonment of her water jar suggests that she is no longer concerned with literal "water," but whatever it is that Jesus can provide. Her question to the townspeople may reflect her own hesitant consideration of his special status or it may be a way of framing her own belief in a deferential fashion that

---

[33] On the variety of meanings that these terms have, the commentators have much to say. See Keener, *John*, 1:615–19. This intriguing issue need not detain us here.

[34] See Wayne Meeks, *The Prophet-King: Moses Traditions and the Johannine Christology* (NovTSup 14; Leiden: Brill, 1967). For more recent literature, and some doubts about the relevance of expectation of a Ta'eb, see Moloney, *John*, 133.

invites her fellow citizens to share it. In either case, the actor playing the Woman would want to render this line in a positive, upbeat manner.

7. Jesus and the Disciples

Disc.: "Eat, Rabbi."
    Jesus: "I have food that you don't know about."
    Disc.: "Has someone brought him something to eat?"
    Jesus: "My food is to do the will of the one who sent me and to accomplish his work. Don't say that there still four months to the harvest. See, I tell you, lift up your eyes and see the fields, already white for harvest. The one who reaps receives a wage and gathers fruit for eternal life. The one who sows and the one who reaps may then rejoice together. That's what the saying means, 'One sows and another reaps.' I sent you to reap what you have not worked at. Others have labored and you have simply joined them."

Director's Note

The scene is of interest, with its anticipation of "eating" themes in chapter 6, but it is not relevant to the portrayal of the character of the Woman.

8. The Townsfolk Arrive

Narrator: And they believed in him because of the testimony of the Woman that, "He told me everything I ever did." They listened to him, believed, and said:
    Townsfolk: "Now we believe, not because of what you said, for we have heard for ourselves and know that this is indeed the Savior of the World."
    Narrator: After two days Jesus left for Galilee.

Director's Note

In the final scene in Samaria, the Woman is silent, though the narrator recalls her earlier testimony, the effects of which are clear. The Samaritans who have heard of the remarkable prophetic ability of Jesus have experienced it themselves and come to believe that he is more than a prophet. The Woman now seems to have a certain standing in the community. If her initial portrayal had been one of marginalized shame, she too would have undergone a transformation.[35]

---

[35] Another intriguing suggestion of the associate director.

Concluding Reflections

The role of the Samaritan Woman in this little drama is open to various interpretive renditions, the initial stages of which will emphasize either her shame or her feistiness and provocative, somewhat flirtatious approach to life, or perhaps a bit of both. As the scene develops and she encounters someone who knows her as well as she knows herself, there is a change in her demeanor, but the gumption evident in her initial interaction with Jesus remains and is turned to the service of the mission of telling others about this marvelous stranger.

If those who would highlight the potential erotic dimensions of the scene are correct, there is another element at work in this transformation of the role of the Woman. As we have noted, whatever her initial stance, when she learns how much Jesus knows about her, she is attracted to him in a new way, looking for him to solve a vexing issue that involves the relationship of God to humankind. The resolution that Jesus proposed was not what she expected, but she embraces it, however tentatively. In that embrace, whatever eros lurked in and around the scene was transformed to apostolic service. Did this apostle become, like the Thecla or Mygdonia of later Christian novels, a celibate? The scene gives no hint.

The transformation recalls other models from antiquity in which simple eros is sublimated. The most famous example, of course, is Plato's *Symposium*, where the revelatory speech of the prophetess Diotima elevates the conversation about love onto a new plane.[36] Diotima's insistence that true love is the love of beauty that manifests itself in the efforts of the true lover to reproduce the beautiful, or, more specifically, to inculcate virtue in the souls of the beloved is then exemplified in the account by Alcibiades about his relations with Socrates.[37] Alcibiades, in a reversal of traditional patterns, had, during their military service together, tried to seduce Socrates, but to no avail. The older and wiser man, with his eyes on the more transcendent beauty of which Diotima spoke, tried, without apparent success, to inculcate virtue in the soul of Alcibiades. In that process, Socrates, like Aristotle's god, "moved as an object of desire"[38] attracting the youth to him, but not for his own sake, but for the cause of virtue. There is at least a loose analogy with the interaction of Jesus and the Samaritan Woman.[39] She moves from a position ripe with erotic

---

[36] Plato, *Symposium*, 201E–212A.
[37] Plato, *Symposium*, 215A–222C.
[38] Aristotle, *Metaphysics*, 12.7.
[39] Not many commentators make any connection with Socratic traditions. Keener, *John*, 1:608, is an exception, though he calls attention not to Plato's *Symposium*, but to the portrait of Socrates in Xenophon's *Memorabilia* 3.9.18, which describes Socrates' unwillingness to relate to a particular woman like the many men who pursued her. Keener, *John*, 1:608,

overtones, exemplifying a character that might well take advantage of such a situation, to a position where she has abandoned thought of herself and serves to bring a message of salvation to her neighbors. She is a character who learns from her encounter with Jesus a new meaning for her own life.

---

fn. 262, suggests "this may be comparable to stories about his academic concern for Alcibiades, in whom most men had other (sexual) interests."

The Men of the Samaritan Woman: Six of Sychar

Steven A. Hunt

Beside a well Lord Jesus, God and man,
Spoke in reproving the Samaritan:
"For thou hast had five husbands," thus said he;
"And he whom thou hast now to be with thee
Is not thine husband," thus he said that day,
But what He meant thereby, I cannot say.[1]

During a conversation with a Samaritan Woman just outside the town of Sychar, Jesus directed the Woman to call her husband and come back (John 4:16). The Woman, evidently something of a social outcast in her town (on which, see more below), replied that she had no husband (v. 17). Her intentions with this comment are not clear. What is clear is that she had not been entirely forthcoming about her situation.[2] But in a perfect example of the fact that "Jesus knew what was in everyone" (2:25; cf. 1:48; 6:6, 64, etc.), he immediately let the Woman know that he also knew about her previous five husbands and the man with whom she was currently cohabiting (4:18). No doubt astonished, the Woman verified Jesus' statement when she referred to him as a prophet (v. 19).

Thus are readers introduced to five men, plus one – the six men of Sychar. These six men, only briefly and tantalizingly mentioned in the narrative, raise for readers (implied or real) far more questions than they answer. As figures standing "behind" the narrative, they do nothing and say nothing. Indeed, as characters, they only exist in this verse off-stage and, interestingly, only in relation to the Samaritan Woman. So, Jesus says, "Go call *your husband*" (v. 16) and the Woman responds, "*I have* no husband" (v. 17). After this, note what Jesus does *not* say: "You have been a wife to five men and the man who currently has you has not made you his wife." Instead, he points out that *She has had* five husbands and the one *She presently has* is not *Her* husband either

---

[1] Geoffrey Chaucer, "The Wife of Bath's Tale" (*Canterbury Tales*; trans. J. U. Nicolson; Franklin Center, Pa.: Franklin Library, 1974), 351.

[2] Schnackenburg maintains that the Woman "answers evasively" (Rudolf Schnackenburg, *The Gospel According to St. John* [trans. K. Smyth and C. Hastings; London: Burns & Oates, 1968–82], 1.433).

(v. 18; cf. 1 Cor 5:1). Again, this is the only explicit information readers are given about these men: the five are her former husbands; the sixth, her current man. Ultimately then, these six men remain entirely flat characters whose only narrative role is to add to the story of the Samaritan Woman. In what way, then, do they contribute to her characterization?

Ancient readers might have drawn certain conclusions about these men given their defined relationships to the Woman. Reading between the lines, they may have been able to fill in the huge "gaps" in the narrative in historically plausible ways. Our "gap-filling" work, some twenty centuries later, can be nothing more than suggestive. Employing reader-response criticism (informed such as it is by socio-historical work on the Gospel), then, we will ask several questions and suggest a few provocative answers related to these six men. Our project, therefore, drags these men on to the stage if only for a moment, and does so with an eye towards considering their impact on the Woman's characterization.

We begin with the Woman's five former husbands. Our essay's title indicates that all these men were from Sychar, but we do not even know that.[3] Perhaps after the five husbands, the Woman relocated to Sychar, hoping to make a fresh start in a new town, or moved back to Sychar, closer to family. Both are possible readings.[4]

But let's stipulate for our reconstruction's sake that they all hail from Sychar originally. Again, questions come easily enough. What happened to these men? Did they *all* die? Or, did they *all* divorce the Woman? Of course, to frame the options this way obscures the possibility that some died and some divorced (or deserted or evicted) her, in any number of possible combinations. Still, to keep the process simple (and more dramatic), we will stick with the extreme positions.

We begin then assuming they all died. If so, one interesting possibility here would suggest that these men are all brothers, who, upon the death of their older brother, attempted to obey Moses' command with respect to levirate marriage (Deut 25:5-6; cf. Gen 38:6-26; Ruth 3-4). While the levirate law "does not appear to have been much practiced in NT times,"[5] nevertheless, stories related to the practice were common enough and the Mishnah dedicates an entire tractate to the subject (*Yebamoth*). So, for example, the Saddu-

---

[3] I just liked the alliteration that presented itself when assuming that they did!

[4] Consider Ruth's migration (with Naomi) from Moab to Bethlehem in Judah after the death of her husband (Ruth 1:6-22); or Joseph and Mary's journey from Bethlehem to Egypt and eventual relocation in Nazareth when facing persecution (Matt 2:13-23). It is most likely not relevant in any case that the Woman in John 4 describes herself as merely "a woman of Samaria" and not "a woman of Sychar" in v. 9.

[5] William D. Davies and Dale C. Allison, *Matthew* (ICC; Edinburgh: T&T Clark, 1988-97), 3.225.

cees explicitly refer to the Mosaic legislation regarding levirate marriage when they confront Jesus regarding marriage and the resurrection (Matt 22:23–33; Mark 12:18–27; Luke 20:27–40). Their question in particular very likely springs from a knowledge of the legendary story of Tobit's relative Sarah, who married seven brothers (Tobit 3:7–9).[6]

Since the Samaritans revered their own version of the Pentateuch,[7] and "were intensely religious,"[8] the reference to five former husbands may suggest the narrator's desire to portray them as obedient to the law of Moses. Indeed, this seems more than possible given that the Woman speaks to Samaritan traditions relative to the patriarchs (v. 12), temple (v. 20), and coming Messiah (v. 25; cf. v. 29), as well as to Jewish traditions about ritual purity (v. 9).[9] If the narrator intends to show that she had a basic familiarity with essential Mosaic teachings, one may assume that her husbands did too – wives often learned from their husbands.[10] In short, the important point relates to the expectation created within the story world of the text: historical questions aside, does the narrator expect readers to understand the story in light of Moses' teaching on levirate marriage? One cannot rule out such a possibility.

Once the possibility is granted, one must wonder if this reconstruction intends to portray the brothers/husbands as religiously observant in other areas of life. The implications for the characterization of the Woman here are hugely significant, especially as many readers (and the majority of commentators) often consider her morally suspect. Because she was living with a man who was not her husband (v. 18), she must be immoral – so the reasoning goes. Should readers at least consider an alternative understanding of that detail?

---

[6] Tobit does not specify that they were brothers; nevertheless, see e. g., Davies and Allison, *Matthew*, 3.225, fn. 27. Note further that the Sadducees raise the issue in Matthew as though it is a real-life scenario: "Now there were seven brothers *among us*..." (22:25).

[7] On the Samaritan Pentateuch generally, see Robert T. Anderson and Terry Giles, *The Keepers: An Introduction to the History and Culture of the Samaritans* (Peabody, Mass.: Hendrickson Publishers, 2002), 105–16. They note that the most pronounced differences between the Jewish Pentateuch and Samaritan Pentateuch "relate to the Samaritan concern to establish the priority of mount Gerizim" (107).

[8] Craig S. Keener, *The Gospel of John: A Commentary* (Peabody, Mass.: Hendrickson, 2003), 1.593. Anderson and Giles note: "While often incensed over the manner in which they observed matters of ritual cleanness..., the talmudic sources rarely criticize the ethical behavior of the Samaritans" (idem, *Samaritans*, 44).

[9] On the purity issues in this story, see the helpful essay on Samaritan women by David Daube in *The New Testament and Rabbinic Judaism* (London: University of London Press, 1956), 373–82.

[10] Cf. 1 Cor 14:34–35; see further, Craig S. Keener, "Learning in the Assemblies: 1 Corinthians 14:34–35," in *Discovering Biblical Equality: Complementarity Without Hierarchy*, ed. Ronald W. Pierce and Rebecca Merrill Groothuis (Downers Grove, Ill.: InterVarsity Press, 2004), 161–71.

But what if the narrator only intends to show that the brothers/husbands are duty bound to family, dedicated to carrying on their older brother's name and lineage? Maybe they are wholeheartedly devoted only to family, not Moses. And religious or not, are these husbands devoted to the Woman at all? The most extensive legislation in the Pentateuch concerning the levirate law assumes that implementation of the law will be difficult for younger brothers as well as for widows and for similar reasons (Deut 25:7–10; cf. Gen 38:11, 14, 26).

Consider the Woman, the widow now in this scenario: Has she really been widowed five times? Has she been ritually unclean so often (Num 19:11–22)? Wept so bitterly, so frequently (cf. John 11:33)? Been in the tombs or among the graves, doing what women do, so routinely (cf. 20:1, 11–12)?[11] This poor Woman has been marked more by death than by life. Each of her weddings seemingly ended with a funeral, another buried husband – five dead and decaying bodies. She lived life with ever present memories of loss, constant reminders of her own inevitable fate. She was probably shunned by her society as she would have been thought to be cursed by God, a sinner from birth.[12] Moreover, she no doubt believed she was solely responsible for decimating a family. Maybe she is cohabiting when she meets Jesus because there were no more brothers left to marry! And what man in his right mind would marry this cursed Woman anyway? So, having once been loved by a husband, having been part of a respected family which took seriously religious and/or familial commitments, she now plays the part of a concubine or prostitute.[13] As a Samaritan, the Woman would not necessarily have been familiar with stories about Job. Still, assuming this situation or one similar to it, she would no doubt have understood when he cursed the day he was born (Job 3:1–19; cf. Tobit 3:10–15).

---

[11] To provide some context, consider that at the death of her *one* husband, Judith "remained as a widow for three years and four months at home where she set up a tent for herself on the roof her house. She fasted all the days of her widowhood, except the day before the Sabbath and the Sabbath itself, the day before the new moon and the day of the new moon, and the festivals and days of rejoicing of the house of Israel" (Judith 8:4–6).

[12] Cf. John 9:2; listen to a maid excoriate Sarah (the relative of Tobit who lost seven husbands): "You are the one who kills your husbands! See, you have already been married to seven husbands and have not borne the name of a single one of them ... Go with them! May we never see a son or a daughter of yours!" (Tobit 3:8–9).

[13] Keener observes: "To illustrate the odium that would have attached to [the Woman and her cohabiting partner's] relationship among Samaritans with stricter moral commitments, the semantic range of the Hebrew term translated 'prostitute' included adultery and probably would have also included this woman living with the man without marriage" (Keener, *John*, 1.608). On concubinage and prostitution generally in the ancient world, see the helpful article (and sources cited therein) by Craig S. Keener, "Adultery, Divorce," in *Dictionary of New Testament Background* (ed. Craig A. Evans and Stanley E. Porter; Downers Grove, Ill.: InterVarsity Press, 2000), esp. 11–12.

What if she is not a widow, however, but a divorcee? Has she really been divorced five times? Since, as Schnackenburg notes, "Jews held that a woman could only marry twice, or three times at most ... the Samaritans must also have considered such frequent re-marriage as dishonourable and illegitimate."[14] And, as Keener observes, "Rightly or wrongly, most ancient readers would have drawn moral connotations from the number of her marriages."[15] Assuming this scenario and the inevitable question related to the Woman's morality, then, what do these multiple marriages suggest about the men who divorced her?

The short answer is, not much. Based on the legislation in Deuteronomy, the five men must have found something "objectionable about her" (Deut 24:1). But what? Given the common understanding of divorce which allowed a man to divorce his wife for any cause (cf. Matt 19:3–12), the "objection" could have been ever so slight – perhaps her culinary skills left something to be desired! A famous passage from the Mishnah records:

> The School of Shammai say: A man may not divorce his wife unless he has found unchastity in her, for it is written, Because he hath found in her indecency in anything. And the School of Hillel say: [He may divorce her] even if she spoiled a dish for him, for it is written, Because he hath found in her indecency in anything. R. Akiba says: Even if he found another fairer than she, for it is written, And it shall be if she find no favour in his eyes ...[16]

A woman's apparent infertility could also have been grounds for divorce, since according to the Rabbis "no man may abstain from keeping the law *'Be fruitful and multiply.'"*[17]

If obedient to Moses then, they would have given this Woman a certificate of divorce and simply sent her away out of the house (Deut 24:1–4) either back to family or to fend for herself. While *most* moderns rightly view this misogynistic practice with abhorrence, much less the attitudes toward women that undergird it, the men might not have been viewed in a negative light for having divorced this Woman at all. In fact, Sirach 25:26 orders that if a wife "does not go as you direct, separate [divorce] her from yourself." After all, "From a woman sin had its beginning, and because of her we all die."[18]

---

[14] Schnackenburg, *John*, 1.433. On divorce generally, see Raymond F. Collins, *Divorce in the New Testament* (Collegeville, Minn.: Liturgical Press, 1992); William Loader, *Sexuality and the Jesus Tradition* (Grand Rapids, Mich.: Eerdmans, 2005), esp. 61–120; David Instone-Brewer, *Divorce and Remarriage in the Bible: The Social and Literary Context* (Grand Rapids, Mich.: Eerdmans, 2002).

[15] Keener, *John*, 1.607.

[16] *M. Gittin* 9.10; emphasis original to the Danby translation (321).

[17] *M. Yebamoth* 6.6 (cited in translation by Danby, 227); the ruling goes on to suggest that a man must divorce his wife after ten years if she has not succeeded in giving him children.

[18] Sirach 25:24; cf. Gen 3:1–24; 1 Tim 2:13–14; 2 Cor 11:3; but see also Rom 5:12–21.

Less clear is the stigma, if any, attached to a man who married a divorced woman. The Mosaic code allowed for divorce (Deut 24:1–4) and only priests were forbidden from marrying divorced women (Lev 21:7, 14). Moreover, the only explicit restrictions placed on a man's right to divorce his wife related to crimes he committed against her reputation (Deut 22:13–19) or person (Deut 22:28–29) at the onset of their relationship.

To be sure, if the divorced Samaritan Woman were known to be a woman of questionable morality, then her husbands' virtue would naturally be called into question as well. "The figurative and effective antithesis of the dependable wife and supportive mother, the loose woman embraces all that male society pronounces unacceptable in women."[19] Thus we cannot characterize the Woman's first husband or even her second husband in this story negatively unless we knew that they knew in advance that they were marrying a less than virtuous woman. As for the final two or three husbands, however, ancient readers might have assumed that they were less than honorable themselves for having been married to this divorcee at all.

Considering the Woman's characterization in the Gospel in light of five divorces creates some interesting possibilities as well, especially for modern readers. On the one hand, if readers assume she was divorced for completely arbitrary reasons (see above), perhaps she could be viewed sympathetically.[20] While her acquaintances no doubt viewed her contemptuously, as her former husbands would have framed the matter in such a way that maintained their honor, this Woman probably felt quite abused by the various men in her life. She lived in a man's world, among men who were evidently quite capricious. She "walked on eggshells," going through life tense and intimidated, constantly fearing when she might next be found "objectionable," subsequently divorced, and homeless. Instead of a woman of honor and value, "more precious than jewels" (Prov 31:10), she found herself a prisoner of the ruthless whims of cruel men. Viewed in this light, her conversation with Jesus by the well stands in stark contrast to the conversations she has very likely had with other men and women who treated her with disdain.

---

[19] Carole R. Fontaine, *Smooth Words: Women, Proverbs and Performance in Biblical Wisdom* (London: T&T Clark, 2004), 42. Jewish wisdom traditions frequently encourage men to keep their distance from dishonorable or immoral women (e. g., Prov 2:16–19; 5:3–23; 6:23–35; etc.; of course, some of those traditions serve metaphorically to dissuade the righteous from religious deviation or cultural assimilation of any kind; see, e. g., the book of Hosea). See further, Claudia V. Camp, *Wisdom and the Feminine in the Book of Proverbs* (Bible and Literature 11; Sheffield: Almond, 1985), 112–20. Certainly, a number of the social dynamics at play here might be construed differently if one assumes a Greco-Roman background related to these issues (on that background, see especially, Bruce W. Winter, *Roman Wives, Roman Widows: The Appearance of New Women and the Pauline Communities* [Grand Rapids, Mich.: Eerdmans, 2003]).

[20] Cf. Sandra M. Schneiders, "A Case Study: A Feminist Interpretation of John 4:1–42," in *The Interpretation of John* (ed. John Ashton; Edinburgh: T&T Clark, 1997), 235–59.

On the other hand, perhaps she was divorced each time for moral failings. Chrysostom, in his homilies on John, referred to her explicitly as a "harlot."[21] That Jesus spoke of the man she currently "has" (v. 18; ἔχεις) implies at least a sexual relationship.[22] Even though punishments were more severe for adultery (i. e., a man's intercourse with a married or betrothed woman), "indications abound that for men [and women] any sexual relations outside of marriage were viewed as prohibited."[23] If divorced for moral failings, failings that would have been widely known in her community, she would have been despised by the women whose marriages she offended and ostracized by others hoping to protect their own. Promiscuous women were shunned by nearly everyone, save the men willing to use and abuse them. If she was this Woman, it is no wonder she went alone to the well and at noon (4:6–7, 27).[24] Assuming this scenario, then, the dénouement of the story, when "many Samaritans from that city believed in him *because of the woman's testimony*" (v. 39), becomes all the more remarkable – what an unexpected reversal for this Woman!

In a volume such as this, I would be remiss if I did not mention the possibility that Jesus was not speaking literally about the Woman's marital history but figuratively about Samaritan history generally.[25] In such a reading, the "five husbands" may represent the five nations imported by the Assyrians after the destruction of the northern kingdom in 722 B. C. E. 2 Kings 17:24 records: "The king of Assyria brought people from Babylon, Cuthah, Avva, Hamath, and Sepharvaim and placed them in the cities of Samaria in place of the people of Israel; they took possession of Samaria, and settled in its cities." According to Jewish polemic in the first century, the Samaritans emerged as a people

---

[21] *Hom. John* 12 [NPNF¹ 4.42].

[22] Cf. the use of the same verb in 1 Cor 5:1. Strictly speaking, read against the background of Jewish marriage customs, the story here in John 4 creates something of a contradiction. When a couple lives together or has a sexual relationship, they are husband and wife (cf. *mQid* 1.1; *bQid* 9b). How can one "have" a man without having a husband at the same time? The idea of "illicit" or "immoral" living together outside of marriage is a modern, mostly western phenomenon. See further, Mirjam Zimmermann and Ruben Zimmermann, "Brautwerbung in Samarien? Von der moralischen zur metaphorischen Interpretation von Joh 4," *ZNT* 1 (1998): 40–51.

[23] David W. Chapman, "Marriage and Family in Second Temple Judaism," in *Marriage and Family in the Biblical World* (ed. Ken M. Campbell; Downers Grove, Ill.: InterVarsity Press, 2003), 183–239, 222.

[24] Keener writes, "Since she had come to the well alone in the hottest time of day (rather than in other women's company), she probably could assume that Jesus knew that she was not accepted in her community" (Keener, *John*, 1.606).

[25] In arguing against the tendency, Michaels notes that "the 'five husbands' have lent themselves persistently to an allegorical interpretation" (J. Ramsey Michaels, *The Gospel of John* [NICNT; Grand Rapids, Mich.: Eerdmans, 2010], 247). So, e. g., Keener draws attention both to Origen (*Commentary on John* 13.43–51) who understood "the current man as the law and the five husbands as the five senses" and more recently Friedhelm Wessel ("Die fünf Männer der Samaritanerin. Jesus und die Tora nach Joh 4,16–19," *BN* 68 [1993]: 26–34), who understood "the five husbands as the five books of Torah" (Keener, *John*, 1.606, fn. 241).

when these five nations were brought into the land, intermarrying with the people who remained.²⁶ Josephus, for example, who explicitly referred to the five nations, observed that Samaritans variously claimed or rejected Jewish ancestry when it suited them.²⁷ How does the unmarried sixth man to whom Jesus refers figure into such an allegorical interpretation then? Craig Koester explains: "Herod the Great continued the pattern of colonization by settling thousands of foreigners in the Samaritan capital ... The Samaritans lived alongside the foreigners, but did not intermarry with them as extensively as before. The woman's personal history of marriage to five husbands and cohabitation with a sixth parallels the colonial history of Samaria."²⁸

Given that the Johannine Jesus rarely speaks literally and that the men drop from view entirely because the topic switches immediately to religious and political differences between Jews and Samaritans, such a reading ought not to be dismissed hastily.²⁹ To be sure, some object to this reading on the grounds that later in the narrative the Woman says to the people of her town: "Come and see a man who told me everything I have ever done!" (v. 29; cf. v. 39). Is she not speaking of her marital history at this point? Not necessarily: following Jesus' lead, she too could be speaking figuratively. In other words, she might be saying something along these lines: "Come and see a man who told me (a representative of the Samaritan people) our entire history!"³⁰

What about the unmarried sixth man? We assume that the man, like the Woman, was from Sychar.³¹ How would the townsfolk view a man who was living with a Woman previously married five times? It is very doubtful that he would have been a man of any standing in the community. As we noted above, a sexual relationship specifically outside the confines of marriage would have been widely regarded as immoral. Therefore, the man was more than likely something of an outsider himself, an outcast like the Woman with whom he lived. We can only guess as to why he did not marry her. Perhaps she was not

---

²⁶ On the complicated origins of the Samaritan people, see the extensive discussion in Anderson and Giles, *Samaritans*, esp. 9–34.

²⁷ See esp. his history in *Ant.* 9.14.3.

²⁸ Craig Koester, *Symbolism in the Fourth Gospel: Meaning, Mystery, Community* (Minneapolis: Fortress, 2003), 49.

²⁹ Most scholars who reject such an interpretation or similar ones do so on the grounds that the imported five nations had seven gods. So, e. g., see Schnackenburg, *John*, 1.433; C. Kingsley Barrett, *The Gospel According to St John: An Introduction with Commentary and Notes on the Greek Text* (2d ed.; London: SPCK, 1978), 235; Raymond E. Brown, *The Gospel According to John (i–xii)* (AB 29; New York: Doubleday, 1966), 1.171; Leon Morris, *The Gospel According to John* (rev. ed.; NICNT; Grand Rapids, Mich.: Eerdmans, 1995), 235; Lincoln, who does not explicitly favor a symbolic approach, cautions against a too simplistic rejection of one on these grounds (Andrew T. Lincoln, *The Gospel According to John* (BNTC; Peabody, Mass.: Hendrickson, 2005), 175–76).

³⁰ Cf., e. g., Schneiders, "Feminist Interpretation of John 4:1–42," 249.

³¹ Or did they move to Sychar together to begin a new life or avoid persecution (cf. Matt 2:21–23)?

free to marry. Did the fifth husband refuse to divorce her? Maybe the sixth man feared marriage with or refused marriage to this Woman (as the sixth brother? Cf. the story in Gen 38). Perhaps he believed that this Woman, with so many funerals (or divorces) in her background, must be cursed. What if he rejected marriage and only desired a domestic and/or sexual slave?[32]

What about the Woman – how did she view her live-in man? At first, she denied that she had a husband when Jesus asked. But to what end? Why does she not mention the man with whom she was cohabiting? Is she ashamed of her situation, or the man himself, or is she dissembling in order simply to keep her options open with this new man at the well? Since scholars have long noted that the entire story can be understood as a play on the "woman-at-the-well" type scene, with all of the romantic associations pertaining thereto, readers should not discount this latter possibility.[33] Jesus, after all, was just proclaimed "the bridegroom" in 3:29.

Finally, what becomes of this sixth man? Later in the narrative, "many" of the townsfolk believed in Jesus and confessed him as "the Savior of the world" (vss. 41–42). Is this man among them? Where we can hardly answer any of the questions we have posed so far, the natural answer to this question is, "of course!" He is most naturally one of the "people" who responds to her testimony, leaving the town to go find Jesus (v. 30). And it makes sense then that he is one of those to whom Jesus refers when he told the disciples to "look around … see how the fields are ripe for harvesting" (v. 35). Maybe he is even among those who invited Jesus to stay, a moment which draws on important language relative to hospitality in the Gospel (v. 40).[34] Did the Samaritan Woman and her man provide Jesus with lodging during his two days in Sychar (cf. 4:40, 43)? That we remain unable to make decisions with respect to the morality of this Woman's situation ultimately relates to the remarkable fact that Jesus never did (cf. 8:11*v. l.*). Given Jesus' reputation and activity in the Gospels generally (Matt 9:10–13; 11:19; Luke 7:36–50; 19:1–10), and the notion

---

[32] Tolstoy plays with yet another variant on the theme of a "kept" woman in his novel, *Anna Karenina*. Upon hearing of his wife's unfaithfulness, the cold, calculating husband Alexei Alexandrovich pondered his options. After contemplating and then refusing the idea of a duel with his wife's lover, Vronsky (a military officer!), he then rejected the possibility of divorce or separation: either of those options "flung his wife into the arms of Vronsky" and "neither she nor he ought to be happy." At one point, he decided the best way to punish Anna Karenina was to *keep* her (Leo Tolstoy, *Anna Karenina* [trans. C. Garnett; New York: The Heritage Press, 1952], 323–29, quotes 328).

[33] See especially, Zimmermann and Zimmermann, "Brautwerbung in Samarien?," 40–51; on betrothal scenes generally, see Robert Alter, *The Art of Biblical Narrative* (New York: Basic Books, 1981), 51–62.

[34] On hospitality in John, see my "And the Word Became Flesh – Again? Jesus and Abraham in John 8:31–59," in *Perspectives on Our Father Abraham* [ed. Steven A. Hunt; Grand Rapids, Mich.: Eerdmans, 2010), 81–109.

that he was already willing to share a drink with her (4:7), this Woman's home seems like precisely the type of place he would have stayed.

In terms of the man's relationship with the Woman then, readers should assume that because the narrative distinguishes between those who came to faith because of the Woman's testimony (v. 39) and those who came because of Jesus' word (v. 41), that he is among the former. In short, the man came to know Jesus as the Savior of the world because of the Woman with whom he cohabited. Thus Jesus' imperative in v. 16 ("Go, call your husband, and come back") anticipates the man's coming in v. 30 and the notice of his faith in v. 39. In the end, the Woman was obedient to Jesus' command, even if it was not her husband but a live-in man with whom she returned!

The Samaritans of Sychar:
A Responsive Chorus

Peter Phillips

How does one explore the characterization of such minor characters as the Samaritans of Sychar? The trick, of course, is not to mirror-read, to allow the characters to stand as a narrative identity in their own right. But in what way are they a character at all? One possible way forward might be to see the Samaritans acting as a chorus responding to the Samaritan Woman, like a chorus in a Greek drama. It may be that this understanding might provide readers with a way to discuss the narrative role of the Samaritans in their own right. We will return to this idea after a little ground-clearing.

If one wanted to flesh out the Samaritans as characters, it would be possible to say quite a bit about them. We could inventively create a narrative identity for them bound up in the identity of the Samaritan Woman (Sam). We could see her neighbours through (our interpretation of) Sam's point of view, giving them some more depth and distinction, rather than leaving them to their choral anonymity. But since Sam's identity remains somewhat ambiguous, at least in reception history, tending towards charges of immorality and exclusion, this necessarily paints the Samaritan community from which she comes as exclusive and alienating.[1] According to Theodor Zahn's infamous depiction, what is exposed is the woman's "immoral life, which has exhibited profligacy and unbridled passions for a long time."[2] Indeed, Jane Webster has suggested that the woman represents the "Strange Woman" tradition, the antithesis of Wisdom: adulterous, foreign and foolish.[3] Does this provide an interpretation for Sam's arrival, "wearing the clothes of Strange Woman," at the well in the mid-

---

[1] A good example of such characterization can be found in Andrew T. Lincoln, *The Gospel According to John* (BNTC; Peabody, Mass.: Hendrickson, 2005), 175–76: "Anyone in the woman's situation would be bound to have been viewed as morally suspect…She is there by herself at an unusual hour and this suggests she has been shunned by other women for what they perceived to be deviant behaviour." The majority of commentators characterize the woman as immoral.

[2] Zahn's outburst is quoted by Stephen Moore, "Are there Impurities in the Living Water the Johannine Jesus Dispenses?," in *A Feminist Companion to John: Volume 1* (ed. Amy-Jill Levine; Sheffield: Sheffield Academic Press, 2003), 78–97, here 82 (with a good exploration of similar critiques of the woman in fn. 18).

[3] Jane Webster, "Transcending Alteriety: Strange Woman to Samaritan Woman," in Levine, ed., *Feminist Companion*, 126–42.

dle of the day. Does the reader assume social ostracism rather than just oversleeping? If so, is it the Samaritans of Sychar who have done the ostracizing? Does the Samaritan chorus appear robed as discriminating gossips!

Sandra Schneiders has warned against such a tradition: "the treatment of the Samaritan woman in the history of interpretation is a textbook case of the trivialization, marginalization, and even sexual demonization of biblical women, which reflects and promotes the parallel treatment of real women in the church."[4] So if we approach the woman more gracefully, like Schneiders or Gail O'Day[5] or Ingrid Kitzberger[6], and question the layers of textual abuse hurled at her across the years, then perhaps the Samaritans act much more compassionately rather than like caricatures in a morality play?[7] What if she simply overslept? What if her previous husbands have died naturally, tragically, in their sleep? What of levirate marriage? What of theological metaphors? What if the point isn't in the woman's immorality at all?[8] In those terms, perhaps the Samaritans need to be read in their own (less lurid) light rather than through the refracted limelight shone by the interaction between Jesus and the Samaritan woman or even by the reception history of the lady of the well?

But if we are to avoid reading the Samaritans through the woman's eyes, are we still doomed to read them through the Masters' eyes, through what Jesus and the Fourth Evangelist have said?[9] What do we make of the Jewish/Samaritan stereotypes? Choruses tend to represent constituencies with specific views which tend towards caricature.[10] Are the Samaritans bound to conform to stereotypical patterns of Jewish understandings about outcast sinners, patterns which the woman herself seems to accept (4:9)? Jesus paints them in negative terms, highlighting what they don't know about worship and in contrast to the Jews from whom salvation comes (4:22). Have they got to act as a kind of Jewish caricature – just as the Samaritan is expected to act as a caricature in the Lucan Parable, with his heavily ironic epithet – as if any Samaritan could be good?

---

[4] Sandra Schneiders, *Written That You May Believe: Encountering Jesus in the Fourth Gospel* (New York: Herder & Herder, 1999), 137.

[5] Gail O'Day and Susan Hylen, *John* (Louisville, Ky.: Westminster John Knox, 2006), 296.

[6] Ingrid Kitzberger, "Border Crossing and Meeting Jesus at the Well: An Autobiographical Re-reading of the Samaritan Woman's Story in John 4:1-44," in *The Personal Voice in Biblical Interpretation* (ed. Ingrid Kitzberger; London: Routledge, 1999), 120.

[7] O'Day and Hylen, *John*, 296.

[8] Ruben and Mirjam Zimmermann, "Brautwerbung in Samarien? Von der moralischen zur metaphorischen Interpretation von Joh 4," *ZNT* 2 (1998): 40–51.

[9] Sung Uk Lim talks of the Samaritan Woman as spokeswoman for the colonized Samaritans and of Jesus the spokesman for the colonized oppressors ("*Speak My Name*: Anti-Colonial Mimicry and the Samaritan Woman in John 4:1–42," *USQR* 62.3-4 [2010]: 36).

[10] Helen Bacon, "The Chorus in Greek Life and Drama," *Arion* 3.3.1 (1995): 6–24, here 9.

Although, perhaps they also burst out of this caricature as the other characters speak about them. The woman talks of her people with a kind of pride – my people descended from "our father Jacob" (4:12); they are a people who believe in a prophet (4:19) and have maintained their traditional worship on Mount Gerizim (4:20) and even Jesus seems to open up the possibility that they could be included among the worshippers of the true Spirit (4:24). Are they really conforming to a caricature? Or, as Robert Maccini has suggested, have we misunderstood the whole relationship between the Samaritans and Jews in the first place?[11] Should we de-layer the text and re-appraise the Jewish-Samaritan problem as a later interpolation into the story?[12] Possibly. But, what we are interested in here is the role which the Samaritans play in this narrative and it is not necessary to do all the textual archaeology to explore that. Indeed, we would just be creating another narrative by deconstructing this one.

The problem, of course, is the paucity of information about them. The narrator of the Fourth Gospel offers us not a fully worked characterization of the Samaritans, but a hastily drawn sketch of a responsive chorus. In her discussion of the role of dramatic imagery within the Fourth Gospel, Jo-Ann Brant notes the similarity between transitions in Greek Drama and in the Fourth Gospel. She notes that often dramatists use a choral ode to make the transition (*stasimon*) between one scene and another. Often the *stasimon* will offer some form of reflection on what has happened and act as bridge into the next section. Brant lists the appearance of the Samaritans in John 4:29–30 and 39–42 as just such a choral transition.[13]

If, indeed, the Samaritans are a form of chorus, then it is clear that the model of chorus is quite different from that of Attic tragedy of the fifth and fourth century B.C.E. In that dramatic form, the chorus was a key part of the whole production, often present throughout.[14] Here, the chorus appears, comments briefly on their acceptance of the woman's testimony and on their belief in Jesus, and then disappears. Many commentators would agree with Schneiders' comment that the Samaritans' words seem to reflect "a postglorification Johannine formation of Christian faith in Jesus" reflecting a *Sitz im Leben* outside of Jesus' own ministry.[15] But it is important to note that choruses often provide an a-temporal reaction to what is happening on the stage. So, in her

---

[11] The traditional reading of the relationship is summarized in C. Kingsley Barrett, *The Gospel According to St John: An Introduction with Commentary and Notes on the Greek Text* (2d ed.; London: SPCK, 1978), 232; Robert Gordon Maccini, "A Re-assessment of the Woman at the Well in John 4 in Light of the Samaritan Context," *JSNT* 53 (1994): 35–46.

[12] So, for example, Lincoln, *John*, 181.

[13] Jo-Ann Brant, *Dialogue and Drama: Elements of Greek Tragedy in the Fourth Gospel* (Peabody, Mass.: Hendrickson, 2004), 31–32.

[14] Bacon, "Chorus," 6–10.

[15] Schneiders, *Encountering Jesus*, 137.

study of the role of the chorus in Greek tragedy, Helen Bacon focuses on the importance of the chorus as respondents to the action and speech of the key protagonists in the drama. By their response, the chorus allows the audience to respond in a similar fashion – almost showing what an appropriate response might be:[16]

> The dramatic chorus ... recreates a natural and traditional response to what was imagined to be an actual past event important enough to have implications which need to be reaffirmed or assimilated and understood by society as a whole and by posterity ... Re-enactment in dramatic choral performance made the ordeals of Oedipus and Jocasta, of Agamemnon, Clytemnestra, Electra and Orestes, or Hecuba and the women of Troy, with all their freight of human meaning, the common possession of the people of Athens and of all later audiences who make the imaginative effort to grasp them in their full choral richness.

So, whether or not the Samaritans represent flesh and blood people living in the vicinity of Sychar or not, the point is that they play a representational role, representing a real community and its ongoing response to the scene before them. The Samaritans may be a relatively two dimensional group character, just a sketch compared to the rounded depth needed for the Samaritan woman or Jesus, but even so this takes away none of their importance as respondents from real communities.[17] It is their response to the Samaritan woman which in some way both substantiates her own "conversion" and affirms the identity of Jesus in going beyond her words to encounter the man himself, who they come to know as the Savior of the World (John 4:39–42). Again, Bacon makes the point:[18]

> A choral performance is an action, a response to a significant event, and in some way integral to that event. Without the victory ode neither the athlete nor his fellow citizens would experience the glory which this achievement sheds on him and on his city. It is in the act of celebration, shared by performers and audience that the evanescent moment of victory achieves some kind of permanence and meaning ... As Plato points out, such choral acts give to events the coherence and meaning that constitute civilization.

We have already seen that the generalized comments about the Samaritans appear within the central dialogue between Jesus and the Samaritan Woman. The first is the narrator's comment that Jews do not associate with Samaritans (4:9). Of course, there is little information to corroborate the evangelist's viewpoint. Robert Maccini has challenged the suggestion on a complete divide between the two communities, drawing on later Samaritan texts.[19] Part of the

---

[16] Bacon, "Chorus," 18.
[17] Bacon, "Chorus," 17. Earlier in the essay, Bacon tells of an impromptu expression of choral grief recorded in a small contemporary Greek community (idem, "Chorus," 12–13).
[18] Bacon, "Chorus," 18.
[19] Maccini argues for a much more ambivalent relationship between the two communities ("Re-assessment," 45).

problem is the reconstruction needed to determine who the Samaritans were in the time of Jesus and the relationship between the two communities.[20] It is clear that although there may have been the kind of interpersonal rapprochement suggested by Maccini, the overall relationship was strained.

Whatever that relationship, Jesus later portrays the Samaritans as ignorant ("you worship what you do not know") both theologically and liturgically, in distinction to the Jews who both know who they worship and that they are the source of salvation (4:22). Here, Jesus acts as the colonizer, demeaning the Samaritans as ignorant outsiders.[21] In turn, the Samaritans will later demean the woman by claiming that their faith is based not just on her words but rather on his words, or rather on their hearing of those words (4:42). So, Jerome Neyrey has questioned a lot of the power plays within this text and queried whether we really understand the different levels of authority represented within it.[22]

It is true that, despite the negativity and colonizing aspects of the text towards the Samaritans there are also key aspects of the dialogue which give honour to the Samaritans' beliefs and culture, such as the references to their heritage (4:12, 19, 20). These references respect/honour Samaritan heritage and thus the Samaritans are portrayed in positive terms. But still Jesus seems to suggest throughout that the Samaritan beliefs and understanding are temporary, passing, inadequate in some way. When the woman asks whether Jesus is greater than "our father Jacob" (4:12), the suggestion from Jesus is that what Jacob has provided pales in significance compared to his gift, and whether the woman is responding sarcastically or not,[23] by the end of the dialogue, she seems to have begun to move over to Jesus' own way of thinking, even though as the commentators make clear, there are still signs of questioning within her statement to her fellow Samaritans ("Could this be …?"; 4:29). The shift in her understanding of Jesus and her willingness to share her understanding with her fellow Samaritans distinguishes the woman from Nicodemus in the previous chapter who simply fades into the background of the narrative. In contrast, the woman seems to embrace her new symbolic/representative role as a disciple/apostle, as Schneiders calls it.[24] In turn, she offers that hope to her neighbours. The hope for the Samaritans is that there is coming a time when

---

[20] For the background to the Samaritan sect, see Robert Anderson and Terry Giles, *The Keepers: An Introduction to the History and Culture of the Samaritans* (Peabody, Mass.: Hendrickson, 2002), 35–49; Lincoln, *John*, 172. George Beasley-Murray, *John* (2d ed.; WBC 36; Nashville: Thomas Nelson, 1999), 60, maintains a more traditional reading without any *apologia*.

[21] Sung Uk Lim, "*Speak My Name*," 47.

[22] Jerome Neyrey, *The Gospel of John in Cultural and Rhetorical Perspective* (Grand Rapids, Mich.: Eerdmans, 2009), 143–71.

[23] Neyrey, *John*, 160–161.

[24] Schneiders, *Encountering Jesus*, 137.

they can be embraced within the new dispensation of true spiritual worship (4:24) which will focus neither on Jerusalem or Mount Gerizim. If we reflect back into the Temple cleansing narrative, we realize that the focus will be Jesus himself (2:21), linking with Jesus' use of "I am He" in 4:26, and the Samaritans' faith in him rather than in the Samaritan Woman (4:42). Everything focuses back on Jesus.

As such, when the Samaritans first appear on stage (4:29), the narrator has told us to think of them as somewhat imperfect, as relics of a bygone age, as neither Gentile nor Jew, transient, temporary, ignorant but also as potential converts to Jesus. So what do they do? Interestingly, they receive the message passively. It is the woman who still holds the active role – she tells them the message about Jesus. That message is intriguingly offered in Johannine terms but with a Samaritan subtext. On the one hand, having encountered the Christ herself, she immediately calls her neighbours to "come and see" Jesus, reflecting the calling of the first disciples (1:36, 39, 43, 46). This is pure Johannine evangelism in action. But her invitation is based upon his prophetic knowledge "of all that she has done" (not just her relationships) and possible messianic identity ("Could he really be the Christ?")[25] – on Jesus as the Taheb (4:29).[26] In response to her words, the people come from the city and make their way towards Jesus – again reflecting the response of the early disciples to turn and follow Jesus (1:37, 42, 49). Indeed, their actions from this point onwards seem to reflect the practice of *apantesis*, in which a delegation is sent out from a town to welcome an approaching (royal) dignitary and escort them back for festivities and celebrations. The process is seen in 1 Thess where Christians will meet the (royal) Christ in the air and escort him back to earth and also in the parable of the ten virgins in Matt 25, where the virgins go out to meet the bridegroom and, presumably, escort him into the celebrations.[27] If this is correct, then the chorus confirms the woman's testimony through its actions.

After a brief interlude, the Samaritans reappear in v. 29 with a brief review of the woman's testimony. The response of the Samaritans is to draw Jesus into their community – for him to come and stay with them. We have already seen that this reflects the civic honour practice of *apantesis*. However, the invitation also picks up on the well-documented betrothal imagery used throughout the narrative as here the family of the potential bride welcomes the suitor

---

[25] Andreas J. Köstenberger, *John* (BECNT; Grand Rapids, Mich.: Baker Academic, 2004), 160, notes the widespread discussion amongst the commentators that μήτι signifies at least a hesitant question; Ramsey Michaels, *John* (NICNT; Grand Rapids, Mich.: Eerdmans, 2010), 259.

[26] Beasley-Murray, *John*, 63–65; Lincoln, *John*, 179; Köstenberger, *John*, 157–58.

[27] Nicholas Thomas Wright, *Paul in Fresh Perspective* (Minneapolis: Fortress, 2005), 54–56; James D. G. Dunn, *The Theology of Paul the Apostle* (London: T&T Clark, 1998), 299–300 and fn. 25, although here and in *TDNT* 5:859–60, the much more familiar technical term *parousia* is used. Many thanks to Steven Hunt for this excellent insight.

into their midst.[28] The response also makes use of another key Johannine term, "to abide" (4:40).[29] Just as the woman has begun to speak in Johannine terms, so the Samaritans begin to act in Johannine ways. They have become assimilated into the Johannine community already. So, while Schneiders talks of the apostolic role of the woman who, like the disciples abandoning their (Synoptic) nets, leaves her (Johannine) jar to evangelize the town, Neyrey talks of the development of a new fictive kinship group developed initially through the words of the Samaritan Woman but then by the embrace of Jesus in their midst.[30] The transient nature of the Samaritans, their potential for conversion, developed throughout the narrative, now becomes enfleshed in their own words as they come to Jesus and believe that he is the Savior of the world (4:42). Their response then is the archetypal discipleship response for the Gospel. They are invited to come and see and they do (4:29); they invite Jesus to abide with them, and he does (4:40); they replace their mediated faith through the woman, with an unmediated faith in Jesus himself based on personal encounter and a community of believers is formed (4:42).

Conclusion

The Samaritan chorus provides us with the correct response to the drama's unfolding narrative. This is normal role for a dramatic chorus. Not only do they comment on the words of the main actors, they also provide the exemplary response to that action – faith in Jesus. As Bacon made clear: "such choral acts give to events the coherence and meaning that constitute civilization."[31] The chorus of the Samaritans, therefore, affirms the Johannine narrative process itself by becoming the embodiment of that narrative process. As the woman encounters Jesus and, arguably, is transformed by the encounter, so the Samaritan chorus affirms her response by being transformed themselves. The suggestion is, as always with John, that the reader should act in the same way.

---

[28] For the betrothal imagery, see, for example, Lincoln, *John*, 170–178; Michaels, *John*, 238; Zimmermann and Zimmermann, "Brautwerbung," 42, 48.

[29] Barrett, *John*, 242; Neyrey, *John*, 169; Michaels, *John*, 268 ("a kind of bonding takes place between Jesus and those who view him as the Christ and a community of believers comes into being"). However, Köstenberger, *John*, 164, asserts there is probably no "spiritual overtones" in its use.

[30] Schneiders, *Encountering Jesus*, 141; Neyrey, *John*, 167–69. Michaels, *John*, 258, notes Chrysostom's words: "They, when they were called, left their nets; she of her own accord leaves her water pot, and winged by joy performs the office of Evangelists. And she calls not one or two, as did Andrew and Philip, but having aroused a whole city and people, so brought them to him." Again, this is all reminiscent of *apantesis*.

[31] Bacon, "Chorus," 18.

The Galileans:
Interpretive Possibilities
and the Limits of Narrative Critical Approaches

Andy M. Reimer

"The Galileans" as a group character in the Gospel of John provide an excellent case study on both the potential and the limits of narrative critical reading strategies applied to biblical texts.[1] Simply put, any attempt to apply narrative critical interpretive methodology to the Galileans as a character in the Gospel will rapidly devolve into questions about the methodology itself.[2] When applied as an interpretive strategy, it clarifies the factors that might shape a reader's determination of the nature of the Galileans as a character. However, if narrative critical methods are applied in a self-critical fashion, it becomes equally clear that this methodology cannot overcome the indeterminacy that afflicts other interpretive strategies that might wrestle with the Galileans in this Gospel. A narrative critical interpretation of the Galileans will produce a series of well defined options for reading this character, but it cannot provide the criteria for selecting a "correct reading."[3]

Galilee and the Galileans in the Johannine Narrative

"The Galileans" as a *named* group character appear only once in the narrative at 4:45:

---

[1] Standard introductions to narrative criticism appeared within a decade of its appearance within the biblical studies guild including those by Mark Allan Powell (*What is Narrative Criticism?* [Minneapolis: Fortress, 1990]) and Daniel Marguerat and Yvan Bourquin (*How to Read Bible Stories* [London: SCM, 1999]).

[2] Criticism of narrative critical methodology has come from a number of angles. From the standpoint of more traditional historical critical scholarship, John Ashton's withering critique of narrative criticism and Gospel scholarship (and especially Johannine scholarship) is a tour de force (idem, *Studying John: Approaches to the Fourth Gospel* [Oxford: Clarendon, 1994], 155–65). From a post-structuralist standpoint, Stephen Moore's *Literary Criticism and the Gospels: The Theoretical Challenge* (New Haven: Yale University Press, 1989) represents an early and thorough "demythologizing" of narrative critical interpretations.

[3] I owe this insight to William John Lyons who has made this point on a number of occasions, beginning with "The Words of Gamaliel (Acts 5:38–39) and the Irony of Indeterminacy," *JSNT* 68 (1997): 23–49.

When the two days were over, he went from that place to Galilee (for Jesus himself had testified that a prophet has no honor in the prophet's own country). When he came to Galilee, the Galileans welcomed him, since they had seen all that he had done in Jerusalem at the festival; for they too had gone to the festival. (4:43–45; NRSV)

Arguably, "the Galileans" (or at least a representative subset of this group character) are also the antecedents for the plural "you" of 4:48:

Then he came again to Cana in Galilee where he had changed the water into wine. Now there was a royal official whose son lay ill in Capernaum. When he heard that Jesus had come from Judea to Galilee, he went and begged him to come down and heal his son, for he was at the point of death. Then Jesus said to him, "Unless you (plural) see signs and wonders you (plural) will not believe" (4:46–48).

This text strongly hints that characterization in this case is inextricably linked with issues of spatial setting and plot. In terms of spatial setting, Galilee is a meaning-rich location alongside other meaning-rich spatial settings in the Gospels such as heaven/above, the world, Jerusalem, Judea, and Samaria. In terms of plot, much of the Gospel is driven by a *traveling* Jesus who engages in a series of dialogues (or rather disputes) at various destinations. If the plot is to be treated as a continuous whole, any one of these spatially set "scenes" must be read in terms of where it sits in the travel narrative as a whole.

Following the Gospel's introductory prologue, Jesus appears in Bethany "across the Jordan" being seen by John and attracting John's disciples for himself including Andrew and later his brother Peter (1:28–42). The next day he decides to go to Galilee, where he picks up Philip in Bethsaida, hometown to Andrew and Peter (1:43–44). This leads to an encounter with Nathanael in the same location. This encounter includes a supernatural act, an expression of belief as a result of that act, and a qualifier that more significant supernatural events are to follow (1:45–51). The third day sees Jesus in Cana *of Galilee* (2:1, 11), performing "the first of his signs" that "revealed his glory" provoking belief from his disciples (2:11). He remains on in Galilee in Capernaum with his mother, brothers and disciples (2:12). Then back to Jerusalem for the Passover and temple encounter. The Jerusalem crowds believe "because they saw the signs that he was doing" (2:23). However, Jesus' supernatural insight into people gives him pause in returning their belief (2:24–25). Nicodemus is one member of this Jerusalem crowd that believes in Jesus as a result of the supernatural signs (3:1-1), a "Pharisee … [and] leader of the Jews/Judeans" who becomes Jesus' night time dialogue partner. Following the Jerusalem conflict and dialogue, Jesus returns to John's territory in the "Judean countryside" (3:22). However, following "the Pharisees'" discovery that Jesus' circle is baptizing more disciples than John, Jesus makes the decision to go to Galilee (4:1–3). However, en route he has an encounter with a woman in Samaria, a geographical region replete with Jacob and Joseph connections (4:5–6). Here we have the Samaritans initially believing in Jesus due to his supernatural insight into the woman's life

(4:39–42). Jesus stays on three days as a result. And this brings us then to the text in question, with Jesus finally arriving in Galilee as was his plan back in 4:3.

Interpretive Possibilities

What the narrative has offered us to this point creates a set of rich interpretive possibilities for 4:43–45. However, in multiplying possibilities, it also creates an irresolvable indeterminacy in how we are to characterize the Galileans.

1. Is the implied reader of 4:43 to read Galilee as Jesus' home country (πατρίς) where he can expect to be short changed on honour? Or does the implied reader take his home country to be Jerusalem and Judea (where he has already met with dishonour)?[4] Or both (i. e., any territory where there are Jerusalem-centred Jews)?

2. Once our fearless implied reader has reached a decision on Jesus' home country, then a decision must be reached on whether the narrator's description of the Galilean welcome *confirms*, *overturns*, or *modifies* the expectations created by the proverb.[5]

3. The Galileans are identified by the narrator as attendees of the Jerusalem festival of John 2. Is the implied reader to associate them with the crowds of 2:23–25?[6] Does Jesus' lack of belief in the Jerusalem believers back there extend to the present Galileans in the crowd?

---

[4] Andrew T. Lincoln, citing Barrett, states that "the narrator has already indicated that Jesus' own country is not Galilee in 4:43–44" (idem, *Truth on Trial: The Lawsuit Motif in the Fourth Gospel* [Peabody, Mass.: Hendrickson, 2000], 237). C. Kingsley Barrett contrasts Mark's use of this proverb with John's use – "in John the πατρίς seems to be Judea, or Jerusalem" (idem, *The Gospel According to St John: An Introduction with Commentary and Notes on the Greek Text* [2d ed.; London: SPCK, 1978], 245–46). When Andrew T. Lincoln writes his commentary some years later he has changed his mind. Here he states "readers ... would most naturally assume Galilee to be his home territory" (idem, *The Gospel according to Saint John* [BNTC 4; Peabody, Mass.: Hendrickson, 2005], 184–85).

[5] Gail R. O'Day and Susan E. Hylen are a pair of real readers who fit the expectation that if one reads the home country as Judea, the Galilean welcome can be read as sincere and reinforcing the proverb (idem, *John* [Louisville, Ky.: Westminster John Knox, 2006], 58–59). Raymond E. Brown represents the flip side of that expectation where the Galileans are the home town folks but their welcome is "superficial ... based on enthusiasm for miracles [which is] no real *honor*" (idem, *The Gospel according to John (i–xii)* [AB 29; New York: Doubleday, 1966], 187 [italics original]). However, as (3) illustrates, the Galilean welcome may well be tainted even if the "home country" is Judea given the Galilean crowds are immediately associated with the Jerusalem crowds. Lincoln offers a third explanatory model (although he may not be committed to it) – Jesus wants a reprieve from the attention he received in Jerusalem that came with the unwanted scrutiny of the Pharisees and is hoping going to his home country (where he can expect a tepid reception) is just what is needed (Lincoln, *John*, 185). In this case their welcome is genuine but unexpected.

[6] Lincoln, *John*, 185.

4. As such, what is Jesus' tone in 4:48? Exasperated? Merely didactic? Positively revelatory?[7]

5. Is the "royal official" of Galilee Jewish or Gentile? And if Gentile, are we moving in circles further and further from the Jerusalem-centric universe (i. e., Jerusalem, Judean country-side, through Samaria, to a quasi-diasporic setting where Jews live alongside Gentiles)? Note that later in the text when the Greeks wish to see Jesus, they approach "Philip, who was from Bethsaida in Galilee" (12:21).

6. Both (1) and (5) point outside the narrative of John to a problematic debate within narrative critical methodology. Namely, what knowledge of other biblical materials or early Christian narratives does our real and/or implied narrator expect of his real and/or implied narratee/reader and how should this shape a narrative critical reading?[8]

7. And finally, the whole matter of signs and belief provoked by signs creates something of a theological quandary not as easily bracketed out as practitioners of narrative critical methodology might hope. Are signs and belief based on signs a positive step en route to full appreciation and belief in the identity of Jesus in this Gospel?[9] Or does belief based on signs signal an immature and deficient belief that must be overcome like an unhealthy addiction?[10] Since strong arguments for both can be constructed from the narrative, it is more likely that an interpreter's predisposition on the matter rather than the text itself will determine this matter.

Further Textual Indeterminacy

With respect to whether Jesus' home country is Galilee, the narrator teases us with one further bit of information in 7:40–44 and 7:52. There the Jerusalem crowd declares that based on their knowledge of the Scriptures, the Messiah must come from Bethlehem, not Galilee. The Jerusalem crowd certainly regards Galilee as Jesus' home country. However, given the frequency with which characters in John are prone to very ironic misunderstandings, the

---

[7] A fragmented interpretive "logic tree" like this is also applicable to the wedding at Cana where knowing the tone of Jesus' words to his mother would be incredibly helpful (2:4).

[8] Lincoln's earlier work when commenting on 7:42 while referencing 4:43–44 suggests an "implied reader is ... expected to know of the traditions that Jesus was in fact born in Bethlehem" (idem, *Truth on Trial*, 237).

[9] See for example O'Day and Hylen – they take Jesus' home country to be Judea, the Galilean welcome to be genuine, and are very positive on the role of signs (idem, *John*, 59).

[10] See for example Brown – who takes Jesus' home country to be Galilee but the Galilean welcome to be "superficial" as they illustrate an "unsatisfactory faith ... based on a crude dependence on signs and wonders (vs. 48)" (Brown, *John*, 187).

question of what this tells us about Jesus' home country remains unanswerable. The misunderstanding here could be any one of the following:

1. Jesus is from Galilee, but a diligent reader of the Jewish scriptures would know sign-working prophets that even raise the dead do come from Galilee (e. g., Elijah and Elisha).
2. Jesus is from Galilee, but ultimately it is his heavenly origins (as per the prologue) that determine his status.[11]
3. Jesus is actually "from Judea" as all insider readers familiar with the Christian stories of Jesus know.
4. Jesus is actually "from Judea" (as per insider knowledge) *and* he is from above (as per the prologue), making the crowd wrong on two fronts.

All this text can tell us about "Galilee" (and by extension "Galilean" characterization) is that Galilee is not highly regarded by southern Jews and that it is possible (but by no means certain) that we are to read Galilee as Jesus' home country.

Methodological Indeterminacy

With John 7:40–44, 52 as with John 4:43–54, we are confronted with the issue of what knowledge we are to attribute to the narratee/implied reader of the Gospel of John. Do we hermetically seal the text from other early Christian literature that provide a glimpse of what readers familiar with this literature might bring to their reading of John?[12] One of the more interesting debates on narrative critical methodology was waged between Darr and Gowler on the characterization of the Pharisees in the Book of Acts. The question revolved around whether the Lukan characterization could and should be extended to the Book of Acts or if the latter text should be read independently.[13] John Lyons pointed out that there is no external arbiter on a debate such as this. It really comes down to who is making up the rules on an interpretive methodology and where one chooses to draw the boundaries of the narrative.[14] Raymond Brown likewise makes an interesting point on the application of narrative critical methodology in discussing the handing over of Jesus

---

[11] See further the discussion in Barrett, who includes Bultmann and Lightfoot in his consideration of these options (Barrett, *John*, 246).

[12] John Ashton finds this feature (among others) of the typical narrative critical endeavour galling (Ashton, *Studying John*, 155–65).

[13] David B. Gowler, *Host, Guest, Enemy, and Friend: Portraits of the Pharisees in Luke and in Acts* (New York: Peter Lang, 1991) and John A. Darr, *On Character Building: The Reader and the Rhetoric of Characterization in Luke–Acts* (Louisville, Ky.: Westminster John Knox, 1992).

[14] Lyons, "Words of Gamaliel," esp. 43–45.

in Luke. Technically, the antecedent of the "they" who lead Jesus away to be crucified are the chief priests and rulers and the people of Luke 23:13. Brown argues that the familiarity of the story of Jesus' passion amongst early Gospel readers make such an interpretation all but impossible – "all Christians learned from the start that Jesus was crucified by the Romans."[15]

There are hints that the narrator of the Gospel implies a reader already familiar with other Christian narratives about Jesus – a fact used by Richard Bauckham to argue that the (real) writer of John is writing on the presumption that some of his readers are familiar with the Gospel of Mark.[16] In John 3:24, the narrator offers an aside on the timing of the event by stating that "John, of course, had not yet been thrown into prison." As this event is not narrated in the Gospel itself, it would appear that the implied reader (or at least a subset of the implied readership) would have previous knowledge of this event for the aside to have any explanatory value.[17] Likewise, Bauckham argues the introduction of Lazarus, Martha and Mary (as the "one who anointed the Lord with perfume and wiped his feet with her hair") is best explained by an implied reader with knowledge of Mark.[18] Should we presume that such an implied reader would equally know that a proverb about a prophet without honour in their home country was applied in other Christian literature to Jesus' reception in Galilee (e. g., Mark 6:4)? While Bauckham's particular argument is that the Gospel writer is signalling familiarity with Mark but not Matthew or Luke, familiarity with Markan material arguably opens the door to readers familiar with stories of Jesus' Davidic origins complete with a Bethlehem birth (Rom 1:3; Luke 2:1–7; Matt 2:1).[19] And if one is convinced, as Steven Hunt is in a recent study, that the writer betrays having read Luke and Matthew as well, creating readers unfamiliar with these traditions begins to feel artificial.[20] Once a reader with existing background knowledge of the story of Jesus is implied, interpretive possibilities multiply.

---

[15] Raymond E. Brown, *The Death of the Messiah: From Gethsemane to the Grave* (Vol. 1; New York: Doubleday, 1994), 8, 10. The subject of the limits of narrative critical readings was raised by Brown more extensively following the publication of the two volume work during his Manson Memorial Lecture at the University of Manchester in 1995.

[16] Richard Bauckham, "John for Readers of Mark," in *The Gospel for All Christians: Rethinking the Gospel Audiences* (ed. Richard Bauckham; Edinburgh: T&T Clark, 1998), 147–71.

[17] Bauckham, "John," 153.

[18] Bauckham, "John," 164.

[19] The Gospel of Mark does not supply either of these explicitly, but nor does it exclude these as possibilities. The point is simply that once one introduces background knowledge (i. e., application of the proverb to the Galileans), it rapidly becomes arbitrary to limit it to Mark, which itself appears to presume knowledgeable readers in places where it creates "gaps." The "implied reader" is a slippery character indeed.

[20] Steven A. Hunt, *Rewriting the Feeding of Five Thousand: John 6.1–15 as a Test Case for Johannine Dependence on the Synoptic Gospels* (Studies in Biblical Literature 125; New York: Peter Lang, 2011).

Two Distinct Possibilities

In very broad brush strokes, *at least* two rather distinct characterizations of the Galileans emerge based on how one constructs one's approach to narrative criticism and, quite possibly, one's theological predilections especially as it pertains to signs and the construction of belief.

Perhaps the narrator is casting the Galileans in a predominantly negative role. Whether or not the expectation of dishonour in the home country is applied to the Judeans or the Galileans or both, the Galileans are as untrustworthy as the Jerusalem crowds. In narrative critical terms, the Galileans and Judeans are fundamentally parallel characters who will ultimately play the role of antagonist. They are jubilant about Jesus but it is an attitude based on a thirst for miraculous signs which, as Jesus already knows, will not translate into a deep seated belief in his true identity. While not openly hostile at this point, they too will turn on him. For the moment, Jesus will capitulate to their need for signs even as it exasperates him (4:48).

Perhaps the narrator is casting the Galileans in a predominantly positive role, serving as a contrasting group character to the Judeans. Jesus has fled the Judeans because "his own" have rejected him there (as the prologue predicted). In a foreshadowing irony, as he moves further from Jerusalem, the reception becomes ever more positive. In Jerusalem it is a sole Judean coming to him secretly at night who probes belief in Jesus. In Samaria it is a whole city coming to belief. The Galileans, representing a location where Jews and Gentiles share social and religious space, turn out to be a much more receptive audience as well. As such, they also turn out to be the recipients of the first two numbered signs (2:11, 5:54), both of which end in belief rather than controversy (2:11, 4:53). One additional later sign performed in Galilee is the feeding of the five thousand. Again the result there is a powerful declaration of belief in Jesus' identity (6:14), while the subsequent controversy is with the Ἰουδαῖοι (6:41) – "Jews" or, perhaps better, "Judeans"! It is hardly surprising Galilee is preferred by Jesus over Judea that is thick with plots to kill him (7:1).

While the application of a narrative critical methodology will not arbitrate between these two interpretive possibilities (and, indeed, these could be multiplied), it does help frame and clarify the points at which divergent interpretive decisions determine multiple interpretive outcomes. Whether this indeterminacy is a case of narrative design or inherent in the gap when real readers are distant from ideal readers is a problem better left for another day.

The Royal Official: Not so Officious

Peter J. Judge

The royal official (βασιλικός) of John 4:46–54 is indeed "one of the overlooked characters of the gospel."[1] He appears just once in a short episode in which he seeks a healing for his son from Jesus, who has returned to Galilee after an interlude in Samaria and about whom the official has heard. The narrator informs the reader that Jesus has returned to Cana in Galilee and recalls the wine miracle that took place there. The official, resident at Capernaum, goes to Cana to meet Jesus. He asks Jesus to come down to Capernaum to heal his son who is at the point of death. Jesus replies with what seems an exasperated refusal: "Unless you (pl.) see signs and wonders you will not believe" (v. 48). Like the mother of Jesus in the first Cana story, however, the official ignores or looks beyond this refusal and implores Jesus: "Lord, come down before my little child (παιδίον) dies" (v. 49). Jesus does not go to Capernaum but responds positively this time, instructing the man: "Go; your son (υἱός) lives" (v. 50a). Now like the servants in the earlier Cana story, the official does what Jesus tells him; he believes Jesus' word and departs. While on his way, he is met by his servants who, echoing Jesus' words, inform him that his son is living, whereupon he learns from them that the boy's fever broke at the very hour when Jesus had spoken these words. As a result, we are told that the man and his whole household believed/became believers (ἐπίστευσεν) (v. 53). We never hear further about this man in the Gospel.

As a character in the Gospel narrative, the official has been seen as a representative "type" of responder to Jesus who demonstrates a degree of adequate faith in Jesus. Thus, in his oft-cited article, "The Representative Figures in the Fourth Gospel," Raymond Collins concludes that "the royal official of the Fourth Gospel stands as a representative of those who believe in Jesus' word, the word which alone brings life."[2] For Collins, various individuals in John

---

[1] R. Alan Culpepper, *Anatomy of the Fourth Gospel: A Study in Literary Design* (Philadelphia: Fortress, 1983), 137.
[2] Raymond F. Collins, "Representative Figures," in *These Things Have Been Written: Studies on the Fourth Gospel* (Louvain Theological & Pastoral Monographs 2; Louvain: Peeters, 1990), 1–45, here 20; repr. from *DRev* 94 (1976): 26–46 (published there with the longer title above).

have been "type cast" to represent a typical response to Jesus, one of either faith or lack of it. "It is therefore from the perspective of his/her representative capacity that the appearance of each of these personages in the Fourth Gospel must be understood."³ For R. Alan Culpepper, in his seminal narrative-critical study of the Fourth Gospel, the βασιλικός "exemplifies those who believe because of the signs but show themselves ready to believe the words of Jesus. Theirs is an authentic faith, and they will have the life it gives (cf. 20:30–31)".⁴ In his general view, nearly all the characters in John are ficelles, whose purpose is to "appear on the literary stage only long enough to fulfill their role in the evangelist's representation of Jesus and the responses to him."⁵ The individuality of all the characters (except Jesus himself) is determined by their encounter with Jesus and they represent a spectrum of responses with which the reader might identify or struggle.⁶ Sandra Schneiders prefers to call Collins' representative figures "symbolic characters" but emphasizes that they personify features or traits associated with historical persons, likely drawn from Jesus' actual life. "The reader identifies with the character, positively or negatively, and thus enters into the dynamic of the narrative in a deeply personal way."⁷ According to Schneiders, the Gospel stories cannot properly be understood by a detached reader but only by one who is existentially caught up in each character's choice either to believe or not.⁸ The royal official is one of these characters and thus not merely a cipher for a type of response.

This signals a direction we want to pursue further in understanding the rather minor figure of the βασιλικός as a real character in the Fourth Gospel. Methodologically, Cornelis Bennema has recently challenged many scholars' reduction of the characters in John to "flat" or typical figures whose only purpose is to highlight the protagonist Jesus and exemplify responses to him. Instead, Bennema thinks that "most Johannine characters are more complex and 'round.'"⁹ With his careful study, Bennema attempts (successfully in my

---

³ Collins, "Representative Figures," 7–8.
⁴ Culpepper, *Anatomy of the Fourth Gospel*, 137.
⁵ Culpepper, *Anatomy of the Fourth Gospel*, 102.
⁶ Culpepper, *Anatomy of the Fourth Gospel*, 104
⁷ Sandra M. Schneiders, *Written That You May Believe: Encountering Jesus in the Fourth Gospel* (New York: Crossroad, 1999), 75.
⁸ Schneiders, *Encountering Jesus*, 77.
⁹ Cornelis Bennema, "A Theory of Character in the Fourth Gospel with Reference to Ancient and Modern Literature," *BibInt* 17 (2009): 375–421, here 377. Most will recognize the terms "flat" and "round" as the terms coined by Edward M. Forster in his 1927 work, *Aspects of the Novel*; cf. Bennema, "Theory of Character," 376, and particularly 391: "Flat characters or types are built around a single trait and do not develop, whereas round characters are complex characters that have multiple traits and can develop in the course of action. Forster's criterion for deciding whether a character is round or flat is whether it is capable of surprising the reader." See also the reference to Forster in Culpepper, *Anatomy of the Fourth Gospel*, 102.
¹⁰ Bennema, "Theory of Character," 399.

opinion) to demonstrate that "a typical or representative belief-response does not necessarily reduce the character to a type."[10] Their *responses* might be typical but as *characters* in a narrative a reader can appreciate those making the responses with more or less depth of personality and individuality that existentially conveys what the evangelist wants the reader to embrace or avoid.[11] In fact, using a more refined "continuum of *degree of characterization*," each character in the Gospel can be analyzed, he suggests, with regard to complexity,[12] development,[13] and penetration into his or her inner life.[14] Thus, contrary especially to Culpepper, Johannine characters cannot be reduced simply to their responses to Jesus. A further attractive feature of Bennema's approach is his recognition of the need for a "form of historical narrative criticism" – a literary reading of the text with attention to the cues the text gives us that refer to the world outside or "behind" the text.[15]

What, then, can we know about and learn from the royal official?[16] He is introduced as βασιλικός – an adjective being used here as a noun meaning, literally, a royal man, not a royal person himself[17] but a royal "possession," someone in the service of a king, either civilian or military.[18] He is clearly a person of some authority but for the rest his identity is rather ambiguous. This man's story is very similar to the one in Matt 8:5–13/Luke 7:1–10 where Jesus likewise heals the son/servant of a centurion at Capernaum without going to

---

[11] Bennema, "Theory of Character," 392, 402–409. Bennema draws the three "continua or axes upon which a character may be situated" from the work, in Hebrew, of Yosef Ewen as represented by Shlomith Rimmon-Kenan in *Narrative Fiction: Contemporary Poetics* (2d ed.; London: Routledge, 2002), 41–42 (cf. Bennema, "Theory of Character," 392, fn. 78).

[12] "The continuum of *complexity* would range from characters with a single trait to those who have one dominant trait and some secondary traits to those who have multiple traits" (Bennema, "Theory of Character," 403).

[13] "The continuum of *development* ranges from characters with no development (they are static, unchanging) to those who display some development to those who change dramatically" (Bennema, "Theory of Character," 403).

[14] This is a bit more difficult to discern. Nevertheless, the "inner life of characters gives the reader insight into their thoughts, emotions and motivations, and is usually conveyed by the narrator and sometimes by other characters … The Fourth Evangelist thus employs a variety of means to convey aspects of the inner life of his characters" (Bennema, "Theory of Character," 405–407).

[15] Bennema, "Theory of Character," 401–402: "In other words, we should reconstruct the Johannine characters from the information that the text of the Fourth Gospel provides and supplement it with relevant information from other sources."

[16] In these next several paragraphs I draw heavily on my earlier work, Peter J. Judge, "The Royal Official and the Historical Jesus," in *Aspects of Historicity in the Fourth Gospel* (Vol. 2 of *John, Jesus, and History*; ed. Paul N. Anderson et al.; Atlanta: Society of Biblical Literature, 2009), 83–92.

[17] Codex Bezae and a few versions have βασιλίσκος, a petty king, but no one accepts this reading as genuine.

[18] Most commentators refer to Josephus's use of the word to designate the retainers (both military and civilian) of Herod Antipas, ruler of Galilee in the time of Jesus, whom the NT regularly refers to as βασιλεύς.

the man's home. While it seems to be of central importance in the Synoptics that the man is a Gentile, in John we are not completely sure. Frank Moloney is representative of the position that in John, too, the official is a Gentile – "a final example [in Jn 4] of the reception of the word of Jesus from the non-Jewish world."[19] John Meier, on the other hand, is just as insistent that the official is Jewish: "[N]o Gentile speaks directly to Jesus during the public ministry" until the arrival of some Greeks seeking Jesus in John 12,20–26 brings about the arrival of Jesus' "hour."[20] Nevertheless, as Meier points out, *historically* the officer's ethnicity is ambiguous at best, given the situation in Capernaum as a Galilean border town under the control of Herod Antipas.[21]

The officer's ethnic/religious identity is not the point as much as the fact that he is a Galilean, and the narrator, I suggest, leaves his historical identity *intentionally* ambiguous for the reader.[22] At the end of John 4, the βασιλικός steps out from among a new group who respond to Jesus – the Galileans – a group of mixed background, marginalized, mongrelized, and (like the Samaritans) theologically suspect as far as Judeans were concerned. In parallel to the report that the Samaritans came to Jesus because they heard about him but then advanced to a fuller faith because they themselves heard Jesus' word (4:39–42), in this story a Galilean approaches Jesus after hearing about him but advances to full faith on the same basis (4:43–54). The nature of this faith must be shown to be genuine in the Johannine narrator's perspective, and the ensuing sign story forms another parallel – this time with the opening sign at Cana where, after a certain expression of hesitancy on the part of Jesus, those who "see" the sign come to full faith in him (2:1–11). These two Cana episodes

---

[19] Francis J. Moloney, *The Gospel of John* (SP 4; Collegeville, Minn.: Liturgical Press, 1998), 153. See also idem, *Belief in the Word: Reading John 1-4* (Minneapolis: Fortress, 1993), 183: while "the *basilikos* may be either Jewish or Gentile," the implied reader of the Gospel knows that Jesus has left the world of Judaism behind and traveled through Samaria and now to Galilee where "the reader accepts this figure from Capernaum, a town where a military presence was called for, as a Gentile."

[20] John P. Meier, *A Marginal Jew: Rethinking the Historical Jesus. Vol. II: Mentor, Message, and Miracles* (ABRL; New York: Doubleday, 1994), 722.

[21] Meier, *Marginal Jew*, 2:721-22: "Matters are not quite so clear in John, who does not specify the ethnic origin of the royal official. Yet the overall redactional theology of John makes it likely that the Fourth Evangelist understands the official to be a Jew."

[22] See Tobias Nicklas, "Jesu Zweites Zeichen (Joh 4,43–45.46–54): Abgründe einer Glaubensgeschichte," in *Miracles and Imagery in Luke and John* (ed. Joseph Verheyden et al.; BETL 218; Louvain: Peeters, 2008), 89–104, esp. 98: It is conceivable that the alternative "Jewish"/ "Gentile" "ist zumindest für den Text hier nicht bedeutsam, ja vielleicht 'bewusst ausgeklammert'" (quotation from Jörn-Michael Schröder, *Das eschatologische Israel im Johannesevangelium: Eine Untersuchung der johanneischen Israelkonzeption in Joh 2-4 und Joh* [Neutestamentliche Entwürfe zur Theologie 3; Tübingen: Francke, 2003]; with reference also to J. Ramsey Michaels, *John* [NIBCNT; Peabody, Mass.: Hendrickson, 1989]). For Nicklas, the ambiguity of the official's identity is one part of the way the narrative opens different interpretive possibilities to the reader (cf. "Jesu Zweites Zeichen," 103-104).

[23] Moloney, *Belief in the Word*, 178-79; Moloney, *John*, 151.

bracket a series of episodes that illustrate what genuine faith in Jesus is and what it is not.[23]

Jesus testifies that "a prophet has no honor in the prophet's own country" (4:44), a difficult saying to be sure. Jesus is known throughout the Gospel of John to be from Galilee/Nazareth (1:45–46; 6:42; 7:3, 41–42, 52; 18:5, 7; 19:19) so that if the saying is used with the same meaning as in the Synoptic parallels (Matt 13:37; Mark 6:4; Luke 4:24) it produces something of a non-sequitur between Jesus going to the very place where he says he will find no honor (4:43) and the report in the following verse that "the Galileans welcomed him" (4:45). This leads to the frequent interpretation that, since we are told at the very beginning (1:11) that Jesus came to his own who did not accept him, "his own" are the Judeans / "the Jews" (οἱ Ἰουδαῖοι) and the πατρίς of Jesus is Israel in general. Moreover, since at this point in John's Gospel Jesus has already spent a good amount of time in Judea, it would seem that he comes from there as far as the story is concerned.[24] On the other hand, if we can read the γάρ of v. 44 with an anticipatory sense, as Gilbert van Belle has shown, it would carry the meaning "now," "yet," "admittedly," or even "although."[25] There is then no contradiction between Jesus' saying and the reception the Galileans give him. The saying does not explain why Jesus leaves Judea for Galilee, nor does it set up a contrast between Judea and Galilee, but rather expresses something especially Johannine, giving a rather different twist to the Synoptic understanding of the saying. We are told in John that Jesus does not seek honor in the usual sense of that word (cf. 5:41). Therefore, the saying in 4:44 is not about Jesus' concern over having *no* honor but about the *kind* of honor the Galileans will accord him.

> Verse 44 can be understood as an important hint for the reader about the faith of the Galileans. It is on the occasion of Jesus' return to Galilee that the evangelist reminds us of His saying that a prophet is not honoured in his own country. The saying explains why the Galileans do not honour Jesus suitably; their faith is insufficient because it relies on signs. True faith consists in believing in His word. This word is then illustrated in the story of the βασιλικός.[26]

The recollection of the feast in Jerusalem (4:45) recalls the suspicion of Jesus in 2:23–25, and so, as we see in the ensuing episode with the royal official, the faith of the Galileans must be tested and not accepted immediately *prima facie*. Just as Nicodemus steps out from among those who saw Jesus' signs in Jerusalem and expresses a faith that needs correction (3:1–2 following on 2:23–25),

---

[24] Moloney, *Belief in the Word*, 181; idem, *John*, 152; Craig Keener, *The Gospel of John: A Commentary* (2 vols.; Peabody, Mass.: Hendrickson, 2003), 629.

[25] Gilbert Van Belle, "The Faith of the Galileans: The Parenthesis in Jn 4,44," ETL 74 (1998): 27–44, esp. 36–39. He draws on an impressive history of interpretation in support of this view.

[26] Van Belle, "Faith of the Galileans," 35.

so the official steps out from among the Galileans whose acceptance of Jesus "might exemplify the same unreliable miracle-faith Jesus encountered in Jerusalem" and so must be tested.[27] The Galilean official undergoes and passes the test and moves to a deeper level of faith based on Jesus' word, just as the Samaritans did in vss. 41–42.[28]

The royal official comes to Jesus because he "heard that Jesus had come from Judea to Galilee." Like the Samaritans who came to Jesus because they heard from the woman in the previous episode, the official also "hears" of Jesus. Verse 47a is closely linked in the narrative with v. 45 – the official approaches Jesus because he heard from the Galileans of all that Jesus had done in Jerusalem. Like the Samaritans, the official's faith is deepened because of his own hearing of Jesus' word (cp. vss. 41–42 with 50, 53[29]). This is an important theme in the Fourth Gospel, as Craig Koester has demonstrated:[30] for example, the disciples in John 2:11, 22 are confirmed in a genuine faith because they believe the word Jesus spoke.

Unlike with the Samaritans, however, Jesus seems at first to respond negatively to the request, indeed he rebukes the man and with him the surrounding Galileans – warning "you people" against the need for "signs and wonders" (v. 48), i. e., warning that true faith cannot be based on witnessing signs (cf. 3:3). "This rebuke enables the author to state clearly the major theme of the passage: authentic belief."[31] Here we begin to perceive the truly Johannine character of the story, the structuring of which was aptly described by Charles

---

[27] Craig Koester, *Symbolism in the Fourth Gospel: Meaning, Mystery, Community* (Minneapolis: Fortress, 2003), 51.

[28] Van Belle, "Faith of the Galileans," esp. 34–35. See also Frans Neirynck, *Jean et les Synoptiques: Examen Critique de l'Exégèse de M.-É. Boismard* (BETL 49; Louvain: Leuven University Press, 1979), 114–16, and Raymond E. Brown, *The Gospel According to John (i–xii)* (AB 29; Garden City: Doubleday, 1966), 188, "[I]n their estimation of enthusiasm based on miracle, iv 44–45 and ii 23–25 have much in common. These two passages also have a similar function in the outline of John. After the description in ii 23–25 of those in Jerusalem who believed in Jesus because of his signs, one of these 'believers,' Nicodemus, came to Jesus with his inadequate understanding of Jesus' powers. Jesus had to explain to Nicodemus that he was really one who had come from above to give eternal life. So also, after the description in iv 44–45 of the Galileans who welcomed Jesus because of his works, a royal official from Galilee comes to Jesus with an inadequate understanding of Jesus' power. Jesus will lead the man to a deeper understanding of his function as a giver of life."

[29] Cf. Moloney, *Belief in the Word*, 187.

[30] Craig Koester, "Hearing, Seeing, and Believing in the Gospel of John," *Bib* 70 (1989): 327–48.

[31] Moloney, *John*, 153.

[32] Charles H. Giblin, "Suggestion, Negative Response, and Positive Action in St John's Portrayal of Jesus (John 2.1–11; 4.46–54; 7.2–14; 11.1–44)," *NTS* 26 (1979–80): 197–211, esp. 204–206; Moloney, *Belief in the Word*, 184–91; idem, *John*, 153–56; John Painter, "Inclined to God: The Quest for Eternal Life – Bultmannian Hermeneutics and the Theology of the Fourth Gospel," in *Exploring the Gospel of John: Essays in Honor of D. Moody Smith* (ed. R. Alan Culpepper and Clifton C. Black; Louisville, Ky.: Westminster John Knox, 1996), 357–61.

Giblin 30 years ago and more recently reiterated by Frank Moloney and John Painter.[32] As with the first Cana sign, there is an initial request to Jesus, who replies with a testing objection that is overcome in some way by the quester. Jesus then complies with the request but in his own way that makes clear that the reader can move with the evangelist/narrator to a new level of significance.

If we now apply Bennema's adaptation of Ewen's categories for character classification to the royal official, we can make the following observations:[33] With regard to *complexity*, his chief traits are that he is a persistent *seeker* of a healing: indeed, a *father* who is driven by his concern for his "little boy" (παιδίον). At the beginning of the story, the term βασιλικός cues the reader that the seeker is an *authoritative figure*, emboldened by his position to make his request rather confidently. Based on knowledge thus far of other authoritative figures in the narrative – priests and Levites from Jerusalem (1:19), Pharisees (1:24; 4:1), Nicodemus (ch. 3) – the reader might be inclined to be wary of him. By the end of the story, however, his "authority" is of a softer, moral nature: his whole household believes along with him. We learn along the way that he is also a *person who trusts and is obedient*. Indeed, like the servants in the first Cana story, he does what Jesus tells him (v. 50; cf. 2:5). This modicum of complexity guides the reader to an increasing sympathy and identification with the official.

As for *development*, the reader first encounters this character as a βασιλικός, an *official;* a description of his occupation and social status, an authoritative figure, as mentioned above. His own use of the affectionate παιδίον, however, softens his image for us (v. 49), and the narrator calls him a *man,* a *human being* (ἄνθρωπος) who puts his faith in Jesus' word (v. 50). By the time he meets his servants on the road and he realizes just what has happened, he is described as a *father* (πατήρ) who not only has obtained the gift of life for his son but whose belief brings the gift of Life to his household (v. 53). He has indeed developed as a character from being defined by his work to being defined by his relationships with both household and Jesus.[34]

Finally, some key verbs give the reader a clue to this character's *inner life*. He comes to Jesus because he *heard* about him from the Galileans (v. 47), like the Samaritans who heard from the woman (v. 39). He is curious and, apparently, desperate. After their initial exchange, however, it is clear that he HEARS Jesus, for he *believes* in Jesus' word, he takes it to heart, and puts it into action.

---

[33] Unfortunately, I was unable to obtain and consult Bennema's expanded study of the Johannine characters: Cornelis Bennema, *Encountering Jesus: Character Studies in the Gospel of John* (Milton Keynes: Paternoster, 2009).

[34] Cf. Moloney, *Belief in the Word,* 188; Moloney, *John,* 155; he in turn acknowledges "taking a hint" from Robert H. Lightfoot: cf. Lightfoot, *St. John's Gospel* (ed. Christopher F. Evans; Oxford: Oxford University Press, 1956), 129. See also Nicklas, "Jesu Zweites Zeichen," 101.

Moreover, when his servants confirm the time of the healing, he *knows* – in the sense of grasping the significance of or fully comprehending what has taken place.³⁵ Again, like the Samaritans, who "believed because of his word" and "know" who Jesus truly is (vss. 41–42), the reader understands that and what the official *knows*: he fully grasps the connection between Jesus' word of life and his own trust in it. His knowledge validates his belief (like the first disciples of Jesus in John 2:11, who, in witnessing the sign, have their belief confirmed, not engendered for the first time) and, seeing that, all his household come to belief as well (v. 53).³⁶

Thus, the royal official is more than a type of positive faith-response to Jesus. Rather we know him as an individual – or at least as a character who reveals some individuality. We readers learn something of his genuine faith through his character, in fact, and by entering existentially into both his dilemma and his response

---

³⁵ Cf. Frederick W. Danker (ed.), "γινώσκω" in *BDAG* (s. v., #3).
³⁶ Cf. Moloney, *Belief in the Word*, 188; idem, *John*, 155–56.

The Son of the Royal Official: Incarnating the Life Giving Power of Jesus' Word

Gilbert Van Belle and Steven A. Hunt

Introduction

In the introduction to her contribution on "Children in the Gospel of John," Marianne Meye Thompson notes, "Children are essentially missing from the pages of the Gospel of John. [The Gospel] lacks the stories and metaphors, so clear from the other Gospels, that have undergirded Christian understanding of children for years." Moreover, she observes that "[f]ew persons or characters in the Gospel of John ... even seem to have children" and contends that the metaphor "Children of God" in the Fourth Gospel "does not denote children as those who are young, but refers to any and all persons as children of God."[1] Of course, the major exception here is the son of the royal official in John 4:46–54.[2]

Most "character studies" on the Fourth Gospel do not deal with this child and (to our knowledge) only Raymond F. Collins mentions him in a list of characters in the Gospel.[3] In this contribution we wish to explore this son's characterization. Although he is not present in the scene between his father and Jesus, he is an important minor character nevertheless. Before we deal with the boy's characterization, we shall first examine the context, structure and plot, and characteristics of the story in which he appears. We will conclude by attempting to define the son's narrative role in concretizing or, perhaps better, incarnating the life-giving power of Jesus' word.

---

[1] Marianne Meye Thompson, "Children in the Gospel of John," in *The Child in the Bible* (ed. Marcia J. Bunge et al.; Grand Rapids, Mich.: Eerdmans, 2008), 195–214, here 195. Clearly, the primary focus of father son relationships in the Gospel is that of God and Jesus. See further, Ruben Zimmermann, *Christologie der Bilder im Johannesevangelium: Die Christopoetik des vierten Evangeliums unter besonderer Berücksichtigung von Joh 10* (WUNT 171; Tübingen: Mohr Siebeck, 2004), 176–83.

[2] One should perhaps also consider the boy with the loaves and fish in John 6:9.

[3] Raymond F. Collins, "From John to the Beloved Disciple: An Essay on Johannine Characters," *Int* 49 (1995): 353–69, see 360.

Context of John 4:46–54[4]

Following Mark Stibbe's lead, we can describe the context of the miracle story in which the son gets healed quite simply: "Jesus now completes the first itinerary of the Gospel. Having begun at Cana in 2.1, he now returns to Cana. His travels have taken him from Cana to Jerusalem, from Jerusalem into Judea, from Judea into Samaria, and from Samaria back to Cana. The circle of his first missionary journey is now complete."[5] The narrator highlights the four stages of Jesus' itinerary by means of four important bridge passages as well (2:12; 3:22; 4:1–3; 4:43–45).

The section "From Cana to Cana" in John 2:1–4:54 is carefully structured.[6] The evangelist makes an explicit reference to the wine miracle of the first narrative (2:1–11) at the onset of the second, ensuring that readers do not miss that Jesus is in the same location: "Then he came again to Cana in Galilee where he had changed the water into wine" (4:46). In addition to the identification of place, the two stories employ similar indications of time. In 4:43 the narrator specifically notes that Jesus travelled *after* two days in Sychar to Galilee, evidently arriving in Cana on the third day.[7] The wine miracle also took place "on the third day" (2:1). The connection between the two narratives becomes more obvious still in the concluding verses to each of the narratives:

John 2:11: "Jesus did this, the first of his signs, in Cana of Galilee."
John 4:54: "Now this was the second sign Jesus did after coming from Judea to Galilee."

The enumeration of only two signs in the Gospel, both performed in Cana, serves to link the son's healing to the earlier wine miracle.

---

[4] For a full analysis of the preceding and following context of the story, see esp. André Feuillet, "The Theological Significance of the Second Cana Miracle (John iv: 46–54)," in *Johannine Studies* (trans. T. E. Crane; Staten Island, N. Y.: Alba House, 1965), 39–51; Wolfgang J. Bittner, *Jesu Zeichen im Johannesevangelium: Die Messias-Erkenntnis im Johannesevangelium vor ihrem jüdischen Hintergrund* (WUNT II/26, Tübingen: Mohr Siebeck, 1987), 128–34; Tobias Nicklas, "Jesu zweites Zeichen (Joh 4,43–45.46–54): Abgründe einer Glaubensgeschichte," in *Miracles and Imagery in Luke and John: In honor of Ulrich Busse* (ed. Joseph Verheyden et al.; BETL 218, Louvain: Peeters, 2008), 89–104; more recently, see Jan G. van der Watt, "Vollkommener Glaube heilt vollkommen (Die Heilung des Sohnes des königlichen Beamten) Joh 4,46–54," in *Die Wunder Jesu* (Vol. 1 of *Kompendium der frühchristlichen Wundererzählungen*; ed. Ruben Zimmermann et al., Gütersloh: Gütersloher Verlagshaus, 2013), 681–89.

[5] Mark W. G. Stibbe, *John* (Sheffield: JSOT Press, 1993), 70.

[6] See esp. Francis J. Moloney, "From Cana to Cana (Jn 2:1–4:54) and the Fourth Evangelist's Concept of Correct (and Incorrect) Faith," *Sal* 40 (1978): 817–43; see also his *Belief in the Word: Reading John 1–4* (Minneapolis: Fortress, 1993), 192–97; and *The Gospel of John* (SP 4; Collegeville, Minn.: The Liturgical Press, 1998), 63–65. Cf. Gilbert Van Belle, "The Prophetic Power of the Word of Jesus: A Study of John 4:43–54," in *Prophecy, Wisdom, and Spirit in the Johannine Literature / Prophétisme, Sagesse et Esprit dans la littérature johannique* (ed. Baudouin Decharneux et al.; Bruxelles-Fernelmont: E. M. E., 2013).

[7] See Moloney, *John*, 159.

The two stories are further linked by two carefully embedded allusions to the story of the widow at Zarephath in 1 Kgs 17:8–24.[8] In the story, Elijah ministers to a widow and her son during a time of famine. After noting that their physical need for food was met by miraculous provision, the narrator records that the widow's son took ill and died (17:17, 20, 21). Obviously despondent, the widow questions Elijah accusingly, saying, "What have you against me …?" (17:18). Elijah, however, prays to God (17:20–21) and the child revives (17:22). Elijah gives the child to his mother, saying, "See, your son is alive" (17:23). The widow's question in the LXX is simply τί ἐμοὶ καὶ σοί (17:18). Of course, this question is exactly the question Jesus asks his mother during the first Cana story in John 2:4. Again, in the LXX, when Elijah gives the resuscitated child to the widow, he says ζῇ ὁ υἱός σου (1 Kgs 17:23). And this announcement closely approximates Jesus' announcement when he heals the royal official's son during the second Cana story in John 4:50, 53 (ὁ υἱός σου ζῇ). This remarkable use of Septuagintal language here and in John 2:4 can hardly be fortuitous, especially given the other more obvious ways in which the narrator so carefully structured this section to link the two Cana stories together.

Furthermore, the structure of the two Cana narratives contains six striking parallels.[9] (1) Confronted by a problem (2:3; 4:46), (2) Jesus' mother and the official each approach Jesus with a request (2:3; 4:47). (3) Jesus initially rejects their requests (2:4; 4:48); (4) while his mother ignores his rejection (2:5), the official renews his request more urgently (4:49). (5) In both stories, then, Jesus does a "sign" (resolving the problem) which (6) leads to the disciples' faith in the former (2:11) and to the official and his household's faith in the latter (4:50, 53).

Finally, the entire section of 2:1–4:54 presents various responses to Jesus. The section's beginning (the wine miracle in 2:1–11) and ending (the healing of the official's son in 4:46–54) form an *inclusio*, as we have seen. Both narratives describe a person who comes to believe fully: the mother of Jesus (with his disciples) and the royal official (with the members of his household). Between these two narratives the evangelist considers pairs of groups and/or individuals who show disbelief (the Jews in 2:12–22 and the Samaritan woman in 4:1–15), partial faith (Nicodemus in 3:1–21 and the Samaritan woman in 4:16–29), and complete faith (John the Baptist in 3:22–26 and the Samaritans of Sychar in 4:27–30, 39–42). These responses (disbelief, partial faith, complete faith) take place in both a Jewish milieu (2:12–3:26) and a non-Jewish milieu (4:1–42). Indeed, the two Cana narratives themselves occur in Jewish (2:1–11) and non-Jewish milieus (4:43–54). Moreover, the evangelist's own commen-

---

[8] For the Old Testament background, see below, fn. 55.
[9] See Moloney, "Cana to Cana," 826; as well as his *John*, 63–65 and 156–59.

tary is placed symmetrically: 2:23–25 appears *after* the first example of disbelief (the Jews) and 4:43–45 appears *before* the last example of faith in the section (the Royal Official).[10]

Structure and Plot of John 4:46–54

The plot, or "systematization of the events which make up the story,"[11] can be clarified by "the quinary" scheme.[12] This scheme divides the narrative into five stages:

(1) *Initial situation or exposition* (vss. 46b–47): A royal official, whose son lay ill in Capernaum, heard that Jesus had come to Judea from Galilee. He went to Jesus in Cana (see v. 46a) and "begged him to come down and heal his son, for he was at the point of death" (v. 47).

(2) *Complication* (v. 48): Jesus responds to the official and the Galileans (and potentially his disciples also) with what appears to be a harsh rebuke: "Unless you see signs and wonders you will not believe" (v. 48).

(3) *Transforming action* (vss. 49–50): The official repeats his request (v. 49: "Sir, come down before my little boy dies"), whereupon Jesus acknowledges the man with his life-giving word: "Go; your son will live" (v. 50a). With this short dialogue the plot reaches its peak: the official is, unexpectedly, confronted with Jesus' divine power right there in Cana. Thus, Jesus performs his miracle by speaking a healing word from a distance, whereas the official had twice asked Jesus to come down to Capernaum to help his son. The official's response shows that he believes now that Jesus' powerful word gives life, even at a distance: "The man believed the word that Jesus spoke to him and started on his way" (v. 50b).

(4) *Denouement (or resolution)* (vss. 51–53a): The narrator informs the reader that the father learned that his son had been healed as he was still making his way back to Capernaum: "As he was going down, his slaves met him and told him that his child was alive. So he asked them the hour when he began to recover, and they said to him, 'Yesterday at one in the afternoon the fever left him.' The father realized that this was the hour when Jesus had said to him, 'Your son will live.'" The timing proves conclusive – the official's son was healed through Jesus' powerful word spoken at a distance.

(5) *Final situation* (v. 53b): "So he himself believed, along with his whole household." Just as Jesus' disciples responded with belief when they saw the

---

[10] Our presentation of this symmetry differs slightly from Moloney; see his, "Cana to Cana," 839–43; and *John*, 64, 66–67 and 158.

[11] Daniel Marguerat and Yvan Bourquin, *How to Read Bible Stories: An Introduction to Narrative Criticism* (trans. J. Bowden; London: SCM Press, 1999), 41.

[12] Marguerat and Bourquin, *How to Read Bible Stories*, 43–49.

sign Jesus did at the wedding in Cana, so the father responds here. This quinary scheme of the second miracle in Cana in Galilee is, as we have noted above, framed by references to the wine miracle. Through the use of explicit comments or asides in 4:46a and 4:54, the narrator makes a clear connection between the second and the first Cana miracle.[13]

Some Particular Johannine Characteristics of John 4:46–54[14]

Some of the characteristics of this textual unit bear on our understanding of John's characterization of the royal official's son. Indeed, the several repetitions and variations of particular words and themes play an important role not only in 4:46–54, but also in the previous context (2:1–4:45), the following context (5:1–6:59) and in the first conclusion of the Gospel (20:30–31).[15] We emphasize four of these, "Life and Death," "Signs," "Belief," and "The Word of Jesus" in what follows.

"Life and Death" – The narrator's interest in "life" has been clear since the prologue (1:4). The contracted form of ζάω ("to live") is used in relation to the healing of the son three times (4:50, 51, 53). The same verb appears a number of times in the immediate and broader context: so, for example, compare the "living water" in 4:10, 11 (cf. 7:38); the life-giving "voice" of the Son of Man (5:25); the "living bread" which makes one "live forever" when eaten and is given "for the life of the world" (6:51); the "living Father," the living Son, and the life offered to the one who eats the Son (6:57); and the life offered to those

---

[13] Gilbert Van Belle, *Les parenthèses dans l'évangile de Jean: Aperçu historique et classification: Texte grec de Jean* (SNTA 11; Louvain: Leuven University Press, 1985), 67, 72–73 and 110–11.

[14] We have consulted the lists of Johannine style characteristics in Eduard Schweizer (1939, ²1965), Eugen Ruckstuhl (1951, ²1987), Willem Nicol (1972), Marie-Émile Boismard and Arnaud Lamouille (1977), Eugen Ruckstuhl and Peter Dschulnigg (1991) and Wolfgang Schenk (1993). See also the lists in Frans Neirynck, *Jean et les synoptiques: Examen critique de l'exégèse de M.-E. Boismard* (BETL 49; Louvain: Leuven University Press, 1979), 45–66; Gilbert Van Belle, *De sèmeia-bron in het vierde evangelie: Ontstaan en groei van een hypothese* (SNTA 10; Louvain: Leuven University Press, 1975), 149–53; idem, *Les parenthèses dans l'évangile de Jean*, 124–55; idem, *The Signs Source in the Fourth Gospel: Historical Survey and Critical Evaluation of the Semeia Hypothesis* (BETL 116; Louvain: Peeters, 1994), 405–20.

[15] On repetitions and variations, see Gilbert Van Belle, "Theory of Repetitions and Variations in the Fourth Gospel: A Neglected Field of Research?," in *Repetitions and Variations in the Fourth Gospel: Style, Text, Interpretation* (ed. Gilbert Van Belle et al.; BETL 223; Louvain: Peeters, 2009), 13–32. On the Gospel's first conclusion, see Gilbert Van Belle, "The Meaning of σημεῖα in Jn 20,30–31," *ETL* 74 (1998): 300–25; idem, "Christology and Soteriology in the Fourth Gospel: The Conclusion to the Gospel of John Revisited," in *Theology and Christology in the Fourth Gospel* (ed. Gilbert Van Belle et al.; BETL 184; Louvain: Peeters, 2006), 483–502.

who eat the bread from heaven (6:58).[16] In addition, the substantive ζωή is frequently used in John and in the immediate context of our story.[17]

The motif of "life" becomes more pronounced when placed in opposition to "death." The official's son is "at the point of death" (v. 47) and, after initially being rebuffed, the official said to Jesus: "Sir, come down before my little boy dies" (v. 49). In both verses the verb ἀποθνῄσκω is used. The construction in v. 47, ἤμελλεν ἀποθνῄσκειν,[18] and in v. 49, πρὶν ἀποθανεῖν,[19] betray Johannine characteristics as well. In the immediate context the word θάνατος is only used in 5:24.[20]

"*Signs*"[21] – In our story, the theme related to "signs" is emphasized in vss. 48, 54 and is hinted at in v. 46. Clearly, it is a central theme in the Fourth Gospel (20:30–31). Of its seventeen occurrences, σημεῖον appears fourteen times in the construction ποιέω σημεῖον or σημεῖα.[22] In several instances, the word σημεῖον is, as in 4:48, connected with *verba videndi* related to seeing (ὁράω, εἶδον,[23] θεωρέω[24]) and hearing (ἀκούω).[25] Along with θεάομαι[26] and βλέπω,[27] these verbs of seeing play an important role in the Fourth Gospel.[28]

"*Belief*" – The narrator emphasizes the belief "the man" displayed in "the word that Jesus spoke to him" (4:50; cf. v. 53). The verb πιστεύω is used three times in 4:46–54 (vss. 48, 50, 53) and is clearly a primary motif in John.[29]

---

[16] See the use of the verb in 11:25, 26; 14:19*bis*. See also the verb ζωοποιέω (3x) meaning "to make alive" in 5:21*bis* and 6:63.

[17] The word appears in the following constructions: (1) ζωὴ αἰώνιος (17x): 3:15, 16, 36; 4:14, 36; 5:24, 39; 6:27, 40, 47, 54, 68; 10:28; 12:25, 50; 17:2, 3; (2) ζωὴν δίδωμι (3x): 6:33; 10:28; 17:2; (3) ζωὴν ἔχω (14x): 3:15, 16, 36; 5:24, 26*bis*, 39, 40; 6:40, 47, 53, 54; 10:10; 20:31. See also the other instances of ζωή: 1:4*bis*; 3:36; 5:24, 29; 6:35, 48, 51, 63; 8:12; 11:25; 14:6.

[18] Cf. 11:51, 12:33, and 18:32, where it is used in reference to Jesus.

[19] Note that πρίν is also used in 8:58 and 14:29; other instances of ἀποθνῄσκω in John are: 6:49, 50, 58; 8:21, 24*bis*, 52, 53*bis*; 11:14, 16, 21, 25, 26, 32, 37, 50, 51; 12:24*bis*; 18:14; 19:7; 21:23*bis*.

[20] See further, 8:51, 52; 11:4, 13; 12:33; 18:32; 21:19.

[21] On σημεῖον, see Van Belle, *The Signs Source*, 381–89.

[22] Five times in the singular: 4:54; 6:14, 30; 10:41; 12:18; and 9x in the plural: 2:11; 2:23; 3:2; 6:2; 7:31; 9:16; 11:47; 12:37; 20:30.

[23] See 4:48; 6:2*v. l.*, 14, 26, 30.

[24] See 2:23; 6:2.

[25] See 12:18; the use of ἔμπροσθεν αὐτῶν in 12:37 and ἐνώπιον τῶν μαθητῶν in 20:30 may be interpreted similarly.

[26] See 1:14, 32, 38; 4:35; 6:5; [8:10*v. l.*]; 11:45.

[27] See 1:29; 5:19; 9:7, 15, 19, 21, 25, 39(3x), 41; 11:9; 13:22; 20:1, 5; 21:9, 20.

[28] On this important motif in the Gospel, see Cor Traets, *Voir Jésus et le Père en lui selon l'évangile de saint Jean* (AnGr 159; Rome: Libreria editrice dell' Università Gregoriana, 1967).

[29] The verb occurs 95x in John; typical constructions follow: πιστεύω + dative referring to a person (12x: 4:21; 5:24, 38, 46*bis*; 6:30; 8:31, 45, 46; 10:37, 38; 14:11); πιστεύω + dative referring to an object (5x: 2:22; 4:50; 5:47*bis*; 10:38); πιστεύω διά with accusative (4x: 4:39, 41, 42; 14:11) or with genitive (2x: 1:7; 17:20); πιστεύω εἰς (36x: 1:12; 2:11, 23; 3:16, 18*bis*, 36; 4:39; 6:29, 35, 40; 7:5, 31, 38, 39, 48; 8:30; 9:35, 36; 10:42; 11:25, 26, 45, 48; 12:11, 36, 37, 42, 44*bis*, 46; 14:1*bis*, 12; 16:9; 17:20); πιστεύω εἰς τὸ ὄνομα (3x: 1:12; 2:23; 3:18); πιστεύω ὅτι

"The Word of Jesus" – Note also the use of ὁ λόγος in 4:50. The construction ὁ λόγος ὃν εἶπεν is characteristic of the Fourth Gospel.[30] Consider also the frequency of expressions such as ὁ λόγος μου,[31] and ὁ λόγος ὁ ἐμός (with respect to Jesus' word),[32] as well as expressions such as ἵνα ὁ λόγος πληρωθῇ (with respect to the fulfillment of either Scripture or Jesus' word)[33] and τηρέω τὸν λόγον (with respect to keeping the word of the Father, Jesus, or even the disciples).[34]

The Characterization of the Official's Son

As in the preceding texts (2:1–4:42), our narrative (4:46–54) focuses simply on an encounter with Jesus: a father begs Jesus to heal his son. The following characters – present or absent during the encounter – appear in the story: Jesus, Jesus' disciples, the royal official, the son of the official, the Galileans, the official's servants, and the official's household.

As in the whole Gospel, *Jesus* is the main character. He is named six times in 4:46–54.[35] Although Jesus' *disciples* are not mentioned, we may presume that they are still present: they accompany Jesus on his route from Cana to Cana.[36]

The βασιλικός (v. 46), a *royal official*, "a servant of King Herod, tetrarch of Galilee,"[37] and the representative of *the Galileans* (see the plural in v. 48; cf. v. 45: οἱ Γαλιλαῖοι)[38] is carefully presented in four ways.[39] *First*, his status is

---

(13x: 6:69; 8:24; 9:18; 11:27, 42; 13:19; 14:10, 11; 16:27, 30; 17:8, 21; 20:31); ὁ πιστεύων (18x: 1:12; 3:15, 16, 18*bis*, 36; 5:24; 6:35, 40, 47, 64; 7:38; 11:25, 26; 12:44, 46; 14:12; 17:20); πολλοί ἐπίστευσαν (8x: 2:23; 4:39; 7:31; 8:30; 10:42; 11:45; 12:11, 42); ὁράω + πιστεύω (8x: 4:48; 6:30, 36; 11:40; 20:8, 25, 29*bis*). Other instances of πιστεύω: 1:50; 3:12*bis*; 4:53; 5:44; 6:64; 10:25, 26; 11:15, 26; 12:39; 14:29; 16:31; 19:35; 20:31. See also πιστός in 20:27.

[30] Six times: 2:22; 4:50; 7:36; 12:38; 18:9, 32; see also 15:20 (τοῦ λόγου οὗ ἐγὼ εἶπον).
[31] Five times: 5:24; 8:52; 14:23, 24; 15:20.
[32] Four times: 8:31, 37, 43, 51.
[33] Four times: 12:38; 15:25; 18:9, 32.
[34] Eight times: 8:51, 52, 55; 14:23, 24; 15:20*bis*; 17:6.
[35] See 4:47, 48, 50*bis*, 53, 54.
[36] Cf. 2:2, 11, 12, 17, 22; 3:22; 4:8, 27, 31, 33; through to this point in the narrative, the narrator has referred explicitly to four named disciples (Andrew, Simon Peter, Philip, and Nathanael) and one anonymous disciple of Jesus. Presumably others have become his disciples as well (cf. 3:25–30; 4:1).
[37] Stibbe, *John*, 72; Richard Bauckham (*Gospel Women: Studies of the Named Women in the Gospels* [Grand Rapids, Mich.: Eerdmans, 2002], 138) considers it nothing more than a "possibility" that this royal official is Chuza, the ἐπίτροπος of Herod Antipas in Luke 8:3. On Chuza, and the historical reliability of the Lukan identification with respect to him, see Bauckham's thorough discussion in *Gospel Women*, 150–61.
[38] See Gilbert Van Belle, "The Faith of the Galileans: The Parenthesis in Jn 4, 44," *ETL* 74 (1998): 27–44.
[39] See among others, Stibbe, *John*, 72.

stressed (he is a royal administrator; v. 46), and his social standing described (he has multiple servants; v. 51). *Second*, the narrator gives him a representative function by calling him ὁ ἄνθρωπος in v. 50. *Third*, he is a father ("the father," ὁ πατήρ) who, we may infer, dearly loves his child: having travelled from Capernaum to Cana, "he begged" (ἠρώτα) Jesus to help his son (v. 47). *Finally*, he is the head of the household (ἡ οἰκία; v. 53), clearly meaning "the family consisting of those related by blood and marriage, as well as slaves and servants, living in the same house or homestead."[40]

As the father is characterized with three different substantives ("royal official," "the man," and "the father"), so too the son.[41] *First*, he is presented four times as "*the son*" of the official (vss. 46, 47, 50, 53). Nothing in these references would give readers any indication of the son's age. But then, *second*, in the father's second request, the son is called "my little child" (v. 49; τὸ παιδίον μου). By using παιδίον, the diminutive of παῖς, the reader is informed that the son is "*a child*," probably "below the age of puberty."[42] Brooke F. Westcott rightly remarks that the diminutive is "significantly used" and notes that "the faith, however imperfect, which springs out of a fatherly love is unshaken."[43] Moloney considers the change from "the son" to "my little child" "... an interesting remark, particularly in light of the shift from *basilikos* (vss. 46,49) to *ho anthrōpos* (v. 50) to *ho patēr* (v. 53)."[44] One wonders whether Stibbe might be right when he supposes that "it is probable that the word *paidion* is to be taken as a catalyst for Jesus' change of attitude."[45] *Third*, the son is called a "child" by the narrator (v. 51: ὁ παῖς αὐτοῦ).[46] The substantive παῖς means "one's own immediate offspring, child as 'son' or 'daughter'"[47] and "develops the internal theme of the status of the official emerging since his use of *paidion* in v. 49, and the narrator's description of him as 'the man' (v. 50b) and 'the father' (v. 53)."[48]

The child belongs to the "household" of the royal official (v. 53).[49] The narrator does not inform the reader about the other members of the family that

---

[40] Johannes P. Louw and Eugene A. Nida (ed.), "οἶκος," L&N (2 vols.; New York: United Bible Society, 1989), 1.113 (domain 10.8).

[41] For the synoptic background of the use of υἱός, παιδίον, and παῖς in John 4:46-54, see Neirynck, *Jean et les synoptiques*, 99-100; more generally Stephan Landis, *Das Verhältnis des Johannesevangeliums zu den Synoptikern: Am Beispiel von Mt 8,5-13, Lk 7,1-10, Joh 4,46-54* (BZNW 74, Berlin, 1994).

[42] Louw and Nida (ed.), "παιδίον," L&N, 1.110 (domain 9.42).

[43] Brooke F. Westcott, *The Gospel According to St. John* (London: John Murray, 1903), 79.

[44] Moloney, *John*, 161.

[45] Stibbe, *John*, 72.

[46] On the important *varia lectio* in v. 51, see further, Edwin D. Freed, "John iv.51: Παῖς or Υἱός?," *JTS* 16 (1965): 448-49; and George D. Kilpatrick, "John iv.51: Παῖς or Υἱός," *JTS* 14 (1963): 393.

[47] Frederick W. Danker (ed.), "παῖς," *BDAG*, 750a.

[48] Moloney, *John*, 162.

[49] Cf. Hans-Josef Klauck, *Hausgemeinde und Hauskirche im frühen Christentum* (SBS 103; Stuttgart: Katholisches Bibelwerk, 1981), 53. Barnabas Lindars (*The Gospel of John* [NCB;

are related by blood and marriage. Nor do we know if he is an only child, although this may be so based on the use of the verb ἐρωτάω in v. 47 and the diminutive παιδίον in v. 49, through which the narrator stresses the father's love for his boy. John F. McHugh rightly observes that "the diminutive τὸ παιδίον μου (contrast the narrator's formal τὸν υἱόν in v. 47) is as affectionate as it is natural, and is placed, for emphasis, at the end of the sentence."[50]

The sickness of the boy is described progressively. *First*, the narrator tells us that the son of a royal official is sick (v. 46: τις βασιλικὸς οὗ ὁ υἱὸς ἠσθένει). The verb ἀσθενέω is typical of John and means "to suffer a debilitating illness, *be sick*."[51] The disease is not mentioned (on the son's symptomatic fever, see below). *Second*, at the official's first request, readers are informed that the son "was at the point of death" (v. 47: ἤμελλεν γὰρ ἀποθνῄσκειν). By using the present tense ἀποθνῄσκειν, the royal official "brings out clearly that the boy would soon *be dying*."[52] *Third*, the threat to the boy's life is repeated for emphasis in the second request: "Sir, come down before my little boy dies" (v. 49). Here, "the aorist in πρὶν ἀποθανεῖν contrasts sharply with the present infinitive ἀποθνῄσκειν in v. 47."[53] *Fourth*, only after the healing is noted do readers learn that the boy's sickness provoked "the fever" (v. 52: ἀφῆκεν αὐτὸν ὁ πυρετός).

Although the son is mentioned several times throughout the story, he is not present when the father encounters Jesus, because he "lay ill in Capernaum" (v. 46: καὶ ἦν τις βασιλικὸς οὗ ὁ υἱὸς ἠσθένει ἐν Καφαρναούμ). Thus the son does not appear in their scene, although his faith will be noted with the rest of the household in v. 53. The encounter takes place in Cana, and the routes travelled by Jesus and the royal official are minimally, yet carefully, described. On the one hand, Jesus, who had travelled from Judea to Galilee in the company of his disciples (4:1–3, 43–46), returns to Cana in Galilee, where he had earlier changed the water into wine (4:46, 54; cf. 2:1–12). On the other, having "heard that Jesus had come from Judea to Galilee," the official "went" to Jesus and begged him "to come down" (v. 47).[54] After Jesus' rebuke in v. 48 and the offi-

---

Grand Rapids, Mich.: Eerdmans, 1972], 205), rightly notes that "household" is "a word from the vocabulary of Christian mission." Cf. Acts 10:2; 11:14; 16:15, 31–34; 18:8; Rom 16:5; 1 Cor 1:16. On "his whole household," see esp. Markus Öhler, "Das ganze Haus: Antike Alltagsreligiosität und die Apostelgeschichte," *ZNW* 102 (2011): 201–34.

[50] John F. McHugh, *A Critical and Exegetical Commentary on John 1–4* (ICC; London: T&T Clark, 2009), 319.

[51] Frederick W. Danker (ed.), "ἀσθενέω," *BDAG*, 142b.

[52] McHugh, *John 1–4*, 318.

[53] McHugh, *John 1–4*, 319.

[54] With regard to καταβαίνω Stibbe (*John*, 73) may be right when he states: "The Father's request for Jesus' *katabasis* to Capernaum helps to keep the overall U-shaped plot of the Gospel (the descent and ascent of Jesus) in the mind of the reader." Indeed, we find the verb καταβαίνω three times in the story (4:47, 49, 51); various phrases relating to the Spirit's or Jesus' descent from heaven are common in John (cf. 1:32; 3:13; 6:33, 38, 41, 42, 50, 51, 58).

cial's repeated request in v. 49 (κύριε, κατάβηθι πρὶν ἀποθανεῖν τὸ παιδίον μου), Jesus still does not accompany the official. Instead he pronounces the healing word from a distance in Cana (v. 50: πορεύου, ὁ υἱός σου ζῇ).[55] Believing the word that Jesus spoke, the man begins to return, presumably, to Capernaum (v. 50). The next day, he will learn that his son is alive when his servants meet him with the good news on his return journey (vss. 51–53).

The threefold repetition of Jesus' life giving word in the verb ζάω counters the use of the verb ἀσθενέω (v. 46) as well as the twofold use of the verb ἀποθνήσκω (vss. 47, 49) in the description of the boy's sickness:

4:50: λέγει αὐτῷ ὁ Ἰησοῦς, πορεύου, ὁ υἱός σου ζῇ.
4:51: οἱ δοῦλοι αὐτοῦ ὑπήντησαν αὐτῷ λέγοντες ὅτι ὁ παῖς αὐτοῦ ζῇ.
4:53: ἔγνω οὖν ὁ πατὴρ ὅτι [ἐν] ἐκείνῃ τῇ ὥρᾳ ἐν ᾗ εἶπεν αὐτῷ ὁ Ἰησοῦς, ὁ υἱός σου ζῇ.

Compared to some translations (e. g., RSV, NRSV, NEB, NAB, NJB, etc.) that translate the present ζῇ as "will live," we prefer to translate it as a statement of fact in the present ("Your son lives" or "your son is living"), because, as Barnabas Lindars remarks, "it is a declaration, rather than a promise."[56] Moreover, as it is stated three times that the son is living, so it is also stressed three times that the son had passed from death to life in the hour that Jesus spoke his life-giving word:[57]

4:52: ἐπύθετο οὖν τὴν ὥραν παρ' αὐτῶν ἐν ᾗ κομψότερον ἔσχεν·
4:52: εἶπαν οὖν αὐτῷ ὅτι ἐχθὲς ὥραν ἑβδόμην ἀφῆκεν αὐτὸν ὁ πυρετός.
4:53: ἔγνω οὖν ὁ πατὴρ ὅτι [ἐν] ἐκείνῃ τῇ ὥρᾳ ἐν ᾗ εἶπεν αὐτῷ ὁ Ἰησοῦς, ὁ υἱός σου ζῇ.

The Royal Official's Son and the Life-Giving Power of Jesus' Word

We have demonstrated above that the second Cana miracle is closely connected with the rest of the Gospel through the context, structure, plot, characterization and an intrinsic network of Johannine characteristics (vocabulary, grammatical constructions, repetitions, variations, and themes). What can we now conclude with regard to the narrator's use of this "minor" character – the royal official's son? What is the relationship between the life-giving power of

---

[55] For the Old Testament background of ὁ υἱός σου ζῇ, see Neirynck, *Jean et les synoptiques*, 102–06.
[56] Lindars, *John*, 204; see also Moloney, *John*, 161.
[57] Cf. James L. Resseguie, *The Strange Gospel: Narrative Design and Point of View in John* (Biblical Interpretation Series 56; Leiden: E. J. Brill, 2001), 132–33. "On the seventh hour" probably means "at one o'clock in the afternoon." For various symbolical interpretations, see Bernard P. Robinson, "The Meaning and Significance of 'The Seventh Hour' in John 4:52," in *Studia Biblica II: Papers on the Gospels: Sixth International Congress on Biblical Studies, Oxford 3–7 April 1978* (ed. Elizabeth A. Livingstone; JSNTSup 2; Sheffield: Academic Press, 1980), 255–62.

Jesus illustrated in this second Cana miracle and the characterization of the son? We attempt to give a balanced answer by considering *three* important Johannine motifs: "signs as demonstrations of Jesus' life-giving power," "the life-giving power of Jesus' word," and "the revelation of the Father and the proclamation of the Gospel."

"Signs as Demonstrations of Jesus' Life-Giving Power" – First, the narrator of John's Gospel has clearly formulated the purpose of his writing in 20:30–31. He chose from the many signs that Jesus performed, writing down only a few of them, so that readers may "come to believe" (πιστεύσητε) or "continue to believe" (πιστεύητε)[58] that Jesus is the Messiah, the Son of God, and that through this believing may have life in his name. As Jesus' signs proved to be a source of his disciples' faith (2:11), and thus a means by which they received eternal life during his dwelling on earth with them, so the narrator's words that were written down in the Gospel for later generations of Christians can have the same effect. Signs point beyond themselves to a greater reality, a deeper truth. Once encountered, signs may arouse true faith, and when they do, faith engenders real life. The meaning of the signs in John can be described as follows: "… the signs are revelatory of the glory of God inasmuch as they show God's power at work through the person of Jesus. That power can be defined as life-giving power that involves the physical universe and the elements necessary for life."[59]

The second Cana sign clearly demonstrates this life-giving power of Jesus through the healing of a human body, a little boy at the point of death, and describes this healing as the restoration of life (see further below). The careful composition of the prologue (1:1–18), as well as the cycle "from Cana to Cana" in 2:1–4:54, prepares for this life-giving sign quite well.[60] We abridge R. Alan Culpepper's helpful table, presenting the theme "Jesus as Giver of Life" in 1:1–4:54 in what follows:

1:1–18: "In him was life" (1:4); 2:1–12: "Jesus provides wine at a wedding. Both wine and weddings were associated with the celebration of life and with eschatological hopes. Jesus' coming meant new life;" 2:13–25: "When Jesus was raised from the dead, his disciples would see that he was the new temple;" 3:1–21: "The necessity for new life: 'You must be born [again/from above]'" (3:7); "God sent his only Son, so that 'whoever believes in him may have eternal life' (3:15–16);" 3:22–30: "Jesus is the bridegroom" (3:29); 3:31–36: "Whoever believes in the Son has eternal life" (3:36); 4:1–42: "The water

---

[58] On the *varia lectio* here, see most recently the comments by Frederick D. Bruner, *The Gospel of John* (Grand Rapids, Mich.: Eerdmans, 2012), 1198–99 and J. Ramsey Michaels, *The Gospel of John* (NICNT; Grand Rapids, Mich.: Eerdmans, 2010), 1022. Both tend to minimize the significance of the differences between the two verbs.

[59] Van Belle, *The Signs Source*, 389–90.

[60] R. Alan Culpepper (*The Gospel and Letters of John* [Interpreting Biblical Texts; Nashville: Abingdon, 1998], 144) rightly remarks on 1:1–4:43 that "[in] a more subtle fashion, it advances the theme that has been important throughout this section: Jesus is the one who gives life."

that I will give will become in them a spring of water gushing up to eternal life" (4:14); 4:43–54: "Your son will live" (4:50).[61]

Moreover, we note with Stephen S. Smalley that there is a special connection of the discourse of 4:7–26 with 3:5 and 4:46–54: "This discourse, concerning the water of life [4:7–26], looks backwards to the discussion with Nicodemus about new birth through water and Spirit (3:5), and forwards to the new life given at a distance to the official's son."[62] In other words, Jesus' revolutionary teaching in 3:5, further developed in 4:7–26, becomes embodied in the sign of 4:50 – "Your son lives."

The evangelist also clarifies the meaning of the second Cana miracle by means of the discourses that follow it. If 4:46–54 is anticipated in Jesus' word of living water in 4:13b–14, one can presume that the meaning of the second sign in John is deepened by the two later similar words on living water in John 6:35 and 7:37b–38.[63]

Our narrative, however, is not only better understood retrospectively in the light of chs. 6 and 7, but also in the light of the discourse in ch. 5, as has been stressed by Marianne Meye Thompson: "There are thematic links between the story of the healing of the official's son, with its emphasis on the very hour when Jesus gave life to the little boy (4:50–53), and the discourse about the Son's life-giving authority in 5:19–47 (5:21, 25–26)."[64] Both emphasize the life-giving word of Jesus, as well as hearing and believing in that word. Thus the discourse in ch. 5, particularly in 5:19–29, comments not only on the healing of the invalid who had been sick for thirty eight years (5:1–18), but also on the healing of the royal official's son: "Both narratives illustrate that Jesus has power over life and death, and that he, who is prophet (4:19, 44), has been sent by the Father (5:23–24; compare 5:36–37), as he is the Son of man (5:27) and the Son of God (5:25; compare υἱός in 5:19bis, 20, 21, 22, 23bis, 26)."[65] The contrast then between the two signs in chs. 4 and 5 relates primarily to the response of those most immediately impacted by them. Thus the father whose

---

[61] Culpepper, *The Gospel and Letters of John*, 144.

[62] Stephen S. Smalley, *John – Evangelist and Interpreter* (Exeter: The Paternoster Press, 1978), 89.

[63] See further, Gilbert Van Belle, "The Imagery of Eating and Drinking in John 6:35," in *Imagery in the Gospel of John: Terms, Forms, Themes, and Theology of Johannine Figurative Language* (ed. Jörg Frey et al.; WUNT 200; Tübingen: Mohr Siebeck, 2006), 333–52; see esp., 341–45.

[64] Marianne Meye Thompson, *The Humanity of Jesus in the Fourth Gospel* (Philadelphia: Fortress, 1988), 143, fn. 11.

[65] Quoted from Van Belle, "The Prophetic Power of the Word of Jesus" (forthcoming, 2013); see esp. Feuillet, "Theological Significance," 44–51; see also, Thompson, *Humanity of Jesus*, 83: "The signs do not merely symbolize the revelation of God's glory; they embody it in visible manifestations. Thus Jesus is revealed to be the Son who gives life (4:46–54; 5:19–29) in perfect harmony with the will of God (5:19–36);" and Craig R. Koester, *Symbolism in the Fourth Gospel: Meaning, Mystery, Community* (2d ed.; Minneapolis: Fortress, 2003), 89–94.

son lives in ch. 4 "believed, along with his household" (v. 53), while the invalid who gets healed in ch. 5 simply reports Jesus to "the Jews" (v. 15), who, in turn, "started persecuting Jesus" (v. 16). Signs do not always lead to faith, and from there on to life in John.

Finally, Jesus' signs are not only explained by the discourses in John, but also by Jesus' ἐγώ εἰμι sayings. Thus, the healing of the son "at the point of death" (4:47) and the raising of the "dead man" (11:44) Lazarus, may together be considered the preeminent signs confirming the truth of the ἐγώ εἰμι sayings about life in 11:25 (ἐγώ εἰμι ἡ ἀνάστασις καὶ ἡ ζωή) and 14:6 (ἐγώ εἰμι ἡ ὁδὸς καὶ ἡ ἀλήθεια καὶ ἡ ζωή). While Lazarus was dead in ch. 11, the father's little boy in ch. 4 was as good as dead (vss. 47, 49). And while the father first believed that Jesus needed to walk in "the way" that led down to Capernaum to give life to his son, he came to believe "the truth" that Jesus was "the life" himself.

"The Life-Giving Power of Jesus' Word" – Second, the threefold repetition of Jesus' life-giving word (4:50, 51, 53), together with the threefold description of the boy's recovery (4:51, 52*bis*), contrast strongly with the threefold description of the deathly ill boy at the beginning of the story (4:46, 47, 49). Thus does the narrator stress the theme of *the life-giving power of Jesus' word* and, more subtly, the theme of *hearing and believing in Jesus' word*. The same themes emerge, as we have already seen, in the previous stories detailing Jesus' encounters with Nicodemus and the Samaritan woman: Jesus' teaching relative to "water and Spirit" (in 3:5) and his offer relative to living water (in 4:7–26) anticipates the life he gives to the deathly ill little boy.

But more specifically with regard to the Samaritans, the narrator especially emphasizes that their belief is based not only on the woman's testimony, but because they have heard Jesus himself speak: "And many more believed because of his word. They said to the woman, '*It is no longer because of what you said that we believe, for we have heard for ourselves*, and we know that this is truly the Savior of the world'" (4:41–42). And from that time to the present, later generations of Christians have benefited from this *compounding* testimony: the woman's, and the Samaritans', not to mention the life-giving power of Jesus' words in the Gospel: "These things are written so that … you may have life in his name" (20:31).

The royal official too believes in the life-giving word of Jesus, a word which transcends the space-time continuum as it did at the primeval moment of creation (cf. 1:3,10). Thus he does not insist after hearing Jesus' word of life that Jesus still must come down to his home: "Jesus *said* to him, '*Go; your son will live.*' The man *believed the word that Jesus spoke to him* and started on his way" (4:50; cf. 4:53). Thus, ch. 4 informs readers about true faith.[66] Interest-

---

[66] Van Belle, "The Faith of the Galileans," 35.

ingly, it is in the father's movement *away* from Jesus and towards his son, that he clearly shows his faith.

The Royal Official's Son, the Revelation of the Father, and the Proclamation of the Gospel

Finally, although the healed son is not present in the narrative when his father meets Jesus, he is carefully designated. His entire characterization, as described above, functions as a sign to demonstrate the life-giving power of Jesus' word. Moreover, the "physical" description and the "factual reality" of the illness and recovery of boy, together with the use of synonyms to express the relationship between the official and his "son" (i. e. "boy" or "little boy") in the household, may point to the evangelist's understanding of the sign:

> The cure of someone mortally ill manifests Jesus's power of giving "life" (cf. vss. 50, 51, 53). This Christological symbolism also holds [the evangelist's] attention at the healing of the man born blind (ch. 9, Jesus the light of the world) and the raising of Lazarus (ch. 11, Jesus the resurrection and the life). At the same time, the factual reality of the event is to be made clear, as is true of all the major miracles in John. It is precisely in the "flesh" of his earthly coming that the incarnate Logos reveals the underlying divinity and his significance for man.[67]

In other words, we may presume with Gail R. O'Day that "in the flesh and blood of the incarnation, the fullness of God is available to humanity, but only if one is able to see the visible as pointing to the invisible (1:18). In the healing of a sick boy, the fullness of God is also available. The physical healing provides a glimpse of the character of God in Jesus."[68] Jesus' signs, therefore, are clear glimpses of the God "no one has ever seen" (1:18).

The Christological symbolism embedded in the description of the healed boy encompasses yet another aspect. The boy is clearly presented as "the son" of the royal official and this son is characterized as "living." In the words of J. Ramsey Michaels: "Within the story, 'Your son lives' is a kind of refrain accomplishing the child's healing ... [but] in the Gospel's larger framework the association of 'son' and 'lives' evokes the notion that 'the Son' and 'life' go together (see 3:36; 1 John 5:12,20). Freed from its immediate narrative context, it becomes a word of praise to God ('Your son lives'), proclaiming nothing less than the resurrection of Jesus himself (see 5:26; 6:57; 14:19). Is it too much to suspect that such a thought might have crossed the minds of some of the

---

[67] Rudolf Schnackenburg, *The Gospel According to St. John* (trans. K. Smyth; London: Burns & Oates, 1968–82), 1.476.

[68] Gail R. O'Day, "The Gospel of John: Introduction, Commentary, and Reflections," (NIB 9; Nashville: Abingdon, 1995), 576.

story's first readers?"[69] Since the narrator repeats Jesus' word, "Your son lives" (v. 53) verbatim, yet without the command, "Go," which preceded the first pronouncement (v. 50), he may have hoped that readers would make some such connection between Jesus' life-giving word and the Word of life.

---

[69] Michaels, *John*, 285.

The Slaves of the Royal Official: Servants of the Word

Peter J. Judge

Most commentators overlook the servants of the royal official (John 4:51–52). They have the simple role of meeting the man on his way home from his encounter with Jesus. Recall that the official had entreated Jesus to come to Capernaum and heal his son who was deathly ill. Jesus instead reassuringly dismisses him saying, "Go, your son lives" (4:50).[1] The servants come from the house and greet him with the news that "his child lives" (4:51). The fact that they are described as servants (δοῦλοι) confirms the authoritative position of their master, whom the reader knows as a βασιλικός, but says little about them other than that they are part of his household. Yet, the reader begins to sense that they are more than simply bearers of happy news about the boy's condition. The narrator presents them as servants of the Word.

The good news they bring their master is told in indirect address with the same expression as Jesus' own direct address pronouncement: ὁ υἱός σου ζῇ / ὁ παῖς αὐτοῦ ζῇ (v. 50/51). Some few MSS. have υἱός in v. 51, probably due to assimilation, but παῖς is the best attested reading here. From a narrative point of view, as the word used by the servants, παῖς (child) perhaps reflects their understanding of the father's own tender concern for his little child reflected in his use of τὸ παιδίον μου in v. 49. This language conveys the sense to the reader that the servants are clearly concerned about the official, their master, whom they know and respect as a loving father. This could also be implied by the fact that they have obviously travelled some distance to find the man and tell him what has happened – we hear that the healing took place "yesterday" (v. 52). As far as the narrative logic is concerned, they unwittingly re-announce the word of Jesus in which the official placed his trust – "your son lives." As the man verifies the hour of the healing from them, the servants, having not

---

[1] Many modern English versions translate Jesus' words ὁ υἱός σου ζῇ with a future sense (RSV, NRSV, NAB, NEB, NJB) but this is really a statement of fact and not just a promise that things will get better. The Common English Bible (2010) thus has: "Jesus replied, 'Go home. Your son lives.'" Cf. Francis J. Moloney, *Belief in the Word: Reading John 1–4* (Minneapolis: Fortress, 1993), 185.

[2] Rudolf Bultmann, *The Gospel of John: A Commentary* (trans. G. R. Beasley-Murray; Philadelphia: Westminster, 1971), 208.

been present when the official and Jesus met, are unimpeachable witnesses to the fact of the healing[2] and catalysts of the man's knowledge that it occurred at the very hour when Jesus spoke these words of life/Life. In fact, Jesus' words are directly quoted once again in v. 53. This three-fold repetition of Jesus' pronouncement "keeps the primacy of the word of Jesus before the reader. Faith in the word of Jesus has led to knowledge."[3]

Mention of the "hour" and the presence of servants bring to the reader's mind in an implicit way what the author has otherwise explicitly recalled for the reader: the fact that the encounter between Jesus and the official took place at "Cana in Galilee where [Jesus] had changed the water into wine" (4:46) and that this was now "the second sign that Jesus did after coming from Judea to Galilee" (4:54). The narrator clearly wants the reader to link this miracle story with that of the first one at Cana (2:1–11). They are "signs" that point beyond the face value of a miraculous happening to something about authentic faith – for both the characters in the narrative and the reader. In the first story, Jesus reacts negatively to his mother's observation that "they have no wine" (most readers take this as an implied request that Jesus do something about the situation) by saying that his "hour" has not yet come. Nevertheless, she directs the servants (διάκονοι) to "do whatever he tells you" (2:5). They indeed do what Jesus tells them and the miracle of the wine ensues and we are told that the servants *knew* what had happened. The narrator tells us that, as a result, Jesus revealed his glory and his disciples believed in him (2:11). This appears to be a genuine faith. As the narrative continues, however, the reader comes to realize that the genuine faith of the disciples is not merely a matter of being impressed or convinced by a miraculous happening, as we learn from Jesus' reaction to the Jerusalem crowd or to Nicodemus (cf. 2:23–25; 3:1–21). Genuine faith sees beyond or behind the miracle to realize in it something significant about the miracle worker himself. In John 4:46–54, servants (this time δοῦλοι) are once again present to verify that a transformation has taken place. The official asks them about the "hour" in which the boy began to improve and we learn that it was precisely the seventh hour – a number not without implications in the Bible, signifying wholeness or completion. Moreover, the three-fold use of the word "hour" in vss. 52–53 certainly emphasizes it and puts the reader in mind of Jesus' own reference to his hour in the first Cana story that the narrator recalls in the very next verse. As the Gospel of John unfolds, the reader is well aware that in almost every case the word "hour" refers to Jesus' revealing his

---

[3] Moloney, *Belief in the Word*, 187. See also the entry above in this work on the Royal Official.

[4] Of the 26 times "hour" ὥρα is used in the Gospel of John, aside from the 3 occurrences in 4:52–53 only 3 others designate a time of day (1:39; 4:6; 19:14). Yet even these can carry a significance beyond a time indicator; see 19:14, for example, where the condemnation of Jesus, the Lamb of God (cf. 1:29, 36), coincides with the activities of the day of Preparation for Passover at noon.

glory and the saving presence of God in accordance with the will of the Father who sent him.⁴ Thus, the royal official's servants bring good news and at the same time bring Good News. The reader can recognize that, while the coincidence of time indeed provides the confirmation of the miracle worked by Jesus with a word of life, this emphasis on the "hour" points beyond the healing itself to recognition that in his "hour" Jesus reveals his glory as that of the Father's only Son (1:14), in whom is Life (1:4), with a Word of Life. Like the disciples in 2:11, the official and his household affirm and embrace this.⁵

The final statement of v. 53 indicates that the royal official's servants do more than *deliver* the word/Word. The conclusion of the story informs us that they, presumably as members of the household, embrace the Word themselves, moved by their master's comprehension and full faith in Jesus. Thus, these servants might appear on the surface to be very flat characters, agents whose only function is to move the plot of the story along.⁶ Yet, they fulfill a role in the narrative that subtly catalyzes the reader's sympathy for the official; cues the reader to attend to the higher level of meaning in Jesus' words, "your son lives," and the significance of the "hour;" and demonstrates that genuine faith in Jesus has overflown to bring others to faith.

---

⁵ See Tobias Nicklas, "Jesu Zweites Zeichen (Joh 4,43–45.46–54): Abgründe einer Glaubensgeschichte," in *Miracles and Imagery in Luke and John* (ed. Joseph Verheyden; BETL 218; Louvain: Peeters, 2008), 89–104, here 103.

⁶ Cornelis Bennema, "A Theory of Character in the Fourth Gospel with Reference to Ancient and Modern Literature," *BibInt* 17 (2009): 375–421, here 407.

The Ill and the Sick:
Those Who Were Healed and Those Who Were Not

D. Francois Tolmie

It is often noted that the Fourth Gospel's approach to healing differs from that of the Synoptic Gospels.[1] In narrative-critical terms, this difference can be described by pointing out that in the narrative world of the Fourth Gospel, the reader does not find any exorcisms, healing by the laying on of hands, or cleansing of lepers.[2] As John Pilch[3] puts it:

> Terms for healing appear twenty-five times in Luke, seventeen times in Matthew, and eight times in Mark. By contrast, there are only three healing stories in the entire Gospel of John (4:46–54; 5:1–20; 9:1–41). Moreover, none of these healing stories actually underscores Jesus' reputation. Rather, healing in John reveals Jesus' true identity, and the focus of the interaction surrounding the healing report rests on controversy with opponents. This controversy is always revealing since it makes even clearer who Jesus really is. The healing event itself fades into the background.

As a group, the ill and the sick are referred to only twice in the Gospel. In 5:3, they briefly appear in the narrative world (ἐν ταύταις κατέκειτο πλῆθος τῶν ἀσθενούντων, τυφλῶν, χωλῶν, ξηρῶν), only to disappear from view as the focus shifts to a particular individual in the group, namely the man who had been paralyzed for 38 years. In 6:2, the ill and the sick do not actually appear in the narrative world, and are only referred to indirectly: A large crowd was following Jesus because they had seen the signs that he had been performing on the sick (ἠκολούθει δὲ αὐτῷ ὄχλος πολύς, ὅτι ἐθεώρουν τὰ σημεῖα ἃ ἐποίει ἐπὶ τῶν ἀσθενούντων).

Let us first look at the terminology used to describe this group character. In both instances the word ἀσθενοῦντες is used, denoting people who are ill or sick.[4] In 5:3, the generic term ἀσθενοῦντες is further specified[5] as τυφλοί, χωλοί, ξηροί,[6] namely the blind, lame and "paralyzed."[7]

---

[1] Cf., for example, James K. Howard, *Disease and Healing in the New Testament: An Analysis and Interpretation* (Lanham, Md.: University Press of America, 2001), 171.

[2] Larry P. Hogan, *Healing in the Second Temple Period* (NTOA 21; Freiburg: Universitätsverlag, 1992), 277.

[3] John Pilch, *Healing in the New Testament: Insights from Medical and Mediterranean Anthropology* (Minneapolis: Fortress, 2000), 119. To the three healing stories one could also add the raising of Lazarus, as Pilch also acknowledges (138).

In the case of 5:3, scholarly interest rarely focuses on the group as such, and when it does, it is the desperate situation of the people clustered around the pool that is usually noted. So, for example, Thomas Brodie describes the scene as one of "swarming suffering,"[8] John Christopher Thomas refers to the sufferers as "society's abandoned,"[9] while John Pilch calls them "the socially expendable, the unclean 'throw-away' peoples that could be found in every pre-industrial city."[10] In the case of 6:2, scholars often register surprise that such a great crowd suddenly appears in the narrative. For example, Ernst Haenchen[11] notes that this aspect does not follow logically from the story up to this point in the Gospel, and suggests that this detail comes from the synoptic tradition, thus reflecting knowledge of a widespread healing ministry by Jesus in Galilee, which is not portrayed in the Fourth Gospel. One could also formulate this in terms of a narrative framework, as Steven A. Hunt[12] does: "John's narrative forces the reader to assume that Jesus has healed many others in addition to those mentioned in chapter 4 and 5."

What further observations can be made from a narrative-critical perspective? To my mind, three additional aspects deserve attention:

---

[4] L&N, *Greek-English Lexicon of the New Testament Based on Semantic Domains: Volume 1: Introduction and Domains* (New York: United Bible Societies, 1988), 23:144, place the word in Domain 23 (Physiological processes and states) and translate it as "ill," while BDAG (ἀσθενέω) explains it as "to suffer a debilitating illness, be sick." I am aware of the distinctions made in scholarly literature between sickness/illness and disease, e. g., by Pilch, *Healing in the New Testament*, 24–25. In this article, I use the terms "the ill and the sick" as blanket terms to refer to human beings undergoing experiences of disease and illness. The term "healing" is also used in the sense in which it is explained by Pilch, *Healing in the New Testament*, 25: "Healing is directed towards illness, that is, the attempt to provide personal and social meaning for the life problems created by sickness. Treatment, of course, can be concerned with one or the other aspect of a human problem (disease or illness), and either or both can be successfully treated."

[5] Thus, correctly, Barclay M. Newman and Eugene A. Nida, *A Translator's Handbook on the Gospel of John* (Helps for Translators; London: United Bible Societies, 1980), 145.

[6] Some manuscripts (e. g., D a b) add παραλυτικοί – "a good example of the Western text's inability to know when to stop," as C. Kingsley Barrett, *The Gospel According to St John: An Introduction with Commentary and Notes on the Greek Text* (2^d ed.; London: SPCK, 1978), 253, puts it.

[7] For the English translation of these terms, I follow L&N and BDAG.

[8] Thomas L. Brodie, *The Gospel According to John: A Literary and Theological Commentary* (Oxford: Oxford University Press, 1993), 235.

[9] John C. Thomas, "'Stop Sinning Lest Something Worse Come upon You': The Man at the Pool in John 5," *JSNT* 59 (1995): 3–20, here 6.

[10] Pilch, *Healing in the New Testament*, 128.

[11] Ernst Haenchen, *Das Johannesevangelium: Ein Kommentar aus den nachgelassenen Manuskripten* (ed. Ulrich Busse; Tübingen: Mohr Siebeck, 1980), 300.

[12] Steven A. Hunt, *Rewriting the Feeding of Five Thousand: John 6.1–15 as a Test Case for Johannine Dependence on the Synoptic Gospels* (Studies in Biblical Literature 125; New York: Peter Lang, 2011), 241.

First, it should be pointed out that the ill and the sick in the Fourth Gospel are an example of the type of narrative characters who "*only just*" exist in a narrative world. From a theoretical perspective, one could explain this by referring to the work of Uri Margolin,[13] who identifies five conditions that need to be fulfilled in order for a character to exist in a narrative world. As a group character, the ill and the sick in the Fourth Gospel barely meet these conditions, as can be seen from the comments in brackets: Existential dimension (it is possible to identify them unequivocally as a group of individuals in the narrative world), intentional dimension (they possess a trait or property; in fact, they only possess a single trait, namely that they are/were ill), uniqueness (one can distinguish them from other characters in the story), paradigmatic unity of features (one can identify the kind of characters they are, namely people in need of healing), and, finally, syntagmatic continuity (in this case, comprising an instance of zero change, since no development occurs). The fact that this group character *only just* exists in the narrative world can also be illustrated in another way, namely by posing the question as to how one would classify the ill and the sick in terms of available categories for the classification of characters. In terms of the most popular distinction, namely the distinction between major and minor characters, they would be classified as minor characters. However, one intuitively feels that classifying them in this way bestows a more important position to them than they actually occupy in the narrative world. It might thus be better to use systems that have more than two categories, and which distinguish more precisely between various types of minor characters. For example, one could describe their function in the narrative more accurately by means of categories such as "background characters" (W. J. Harvey[14]), "functionaries" (Adele Berlin[15]) or "walk-ons" (James L. Resseguie[16]).

Secondly, from a narrative-critical perspective, the importance of setting should be highlighted. Very often, the setting within which characters appear

---

[13] Uri Margolin, "Introducing and Sustaining Characters in Literary Narrative," *Style* 21/1 (1987): 107–24.

[14] William J. Harvey, *Character and the Novel* (London: Chatto & Windus, 1965), 52–73, distinguishes between several categories of characters: at one end of the scale are the protagonists (the important characters in the narrative), with background characters at the other end (their only function being to fulfil a role in the mechanics of the plot); while in between, two types of intermediary characters are found: cards (characters who approach greatness, but who are not cast into the role of protagonists) and ficelles (characterized more extensively than the background characters, yet only existing for the purpose of fulfilling certain functions within the narrative).

[15] Adele Berlin, *Poetics and Interpretation of Biblical Narrative* (Bible and Literature; Sheffield: Almond Press, 1983), 23–42, distinguishes between three types of characters: full-fledged characters (normally called "round characters"), types (normally referred to as "flat characters") and functionaries (characters who are not characterized at all, and who merely have to fulfil a particular role or function).

[16] James L. Resseguie, *Narrative Criticism of the New Testament: An Introduction* (Grand Rapids, Mich.: Baker Academic, 2005), 122–25, uses Forster's well-known distinction between

may be of significance. The ill and the sick mentioned in 5:3 are situated next to a pool of water; and as Thomas[17] quite rightly points out, thus far in the Gospel, water has always been mentioned in remarkable contexts: John's baptism (1:25–28, 33; 3:23), the turning of water into wine at Cana (2:1–11), the emphasis on the necessity of being born of water and Spirit (3:5), the fact that Jesus/his disciples had baptized people (4:2), and the discussion on living water between Jesus and the Samaritan woman (4:19–25). Thus, the appearance of the ill and the sick next to water may serve to heighten "the reader's expectancy level."[18] To this, I would add that a note of irony may possibly also be detected in the setting in 5:3: If one keeps in mind that water functions symbolically in the Fourth Gospel as an indication of the abundance of life brought by the Son of God, and if one then notes the stark contrast between the state of the people pictured here and the symbolic overtones of the setting within which they are portrayed, the irony is striking.

In the case of 6:2, the narrator portrays a different setting – across Lake Galilee, up a hill, where a large crowd has followed Jesus, because of the fact that he has healed the ill and the sick. However, this setting only refers to the crowd following Jesus; the exact setting within which the ill and the sick had been healed is unclear, since the only information that is provided by the narrator in this instance is that this happened sometime earlier on in the narrative. Accordingly, readers are left with a gap to be filled. This could be accomplished in different ways. One way of doing so is to imagine a group of healings at various locations in Galilee; these are not narrated in the Gospel, but are presupposed by the narrator (as pointed out above). Another way is to imagine healings in Judea and Galilee, with the two healings that have been narrated explicitly thus far (the healing of the official's son in Cana and the healing of the paralytic at the pool in Jerusalem) functioning as *partes pro toto* for all the healings presupposed here. This is the approach followed by Hartwig Thyen.[19] What is important, though, is to realize that, regardless of the way in which readers choose to imagine a setting (or settings) for the healing of the ill and the sick who are mentioned as a group character in 6:2, the setting in question would *not* be the pool in Jerusalem, since only one person (the paralytic) had been healed at the pool, whereas *all* the ill and the sick mentioned in 6:2 were healed. To put it in another way: the ill and the sick of 6:2 and the ill and the sick of 5:3 cannot be the same people, since those referred

---

round and flat characters, but adds other character types, namely stocks, foils and walk-ons. Following Seymour Chatman, *Story and Discourse: Narrative Structure in Fiction and Film* (Ithaca, N. Y.: Cornell University Press, 1978), 141, Resseguie describes walk-ons as characters "that are not fully delineated and individualized; rather they are part of the background or setting of the narrative" (125).

[17] Thomas, "The Man at the Pool," 6–7.
[18] Thomas, "The Man at the Pool," 6.
[19] Hartwig Thyen, *Das Johannesevangelium* (HNT 6; Tübingen: Mohr Siebeck, 2005), 335.

to in 5:3 (with the exception of one person) had *not* been healed, whereas those referred to in 6:2 had all been healed.

This brings me to the third point: the analysis that we have been conducting in the previous paragraph could be described as an instance of reading against the grain of the narrative. As background characters/functionaries/walk-ons, the ill and the sick at the pool in 5:3 were probably meant to "disappear" from the scene as the focus shifted onto the paralytic. Similarly, in 6:2, attention is only briefly fixed on (a different group of) ill and sick people, not so much for their own sake, but merely in order to provide a reason for the large crowd following Jesus. Nevertheless, the fact that the word ἀσθενοῦντες appears in both instances could prompt readers to link the two references. Making sense of this could then be approached in one of two ways:

First, readers could simply ignore the fact that the first group of ἀσθενοῦντες (except the paralytic) were not healed, and allow them to fade into the background, so to speak, and concentrate on the second group who were, in fact, healed, interpreting this as a further confirmation of Jesus' identity, and as an allusion to the many other signs that he performed (20:31).

A second option would be to try to balance the two references to the ill and the sick in the narrative world; in other words, not to mentally lose sight of either of the two groups. On the basis of such an approach, one would automatically contrast the different fates of these two groups. Readers would then start pondering questions such as: What happened to the ill and the sick at the pool who were not healed? Did they stay on at the pool, waiting without success for healing? More importantly, did they miss the Water of Life?

Perhaps readers who follow such an approach are putting the wrong questions to the text. Should one rather imagine a different kind of reader? Would it perhaps be advisable to envisage readers for whom the restoration of mobility and sight is beside the point – as John Pilch does?

> For persons in John's group whose relatives are ill or who themselves suffer from forms of immobility and blindness, the experience of the living Jesus in the midst of the group brings restoration. It is access to the resurrected Messiah of Israel in an altered state of consciousness (ASC) that enables results such as those reported in the significant healing interactions of Jesus.[20]

---

[20] Pilch, *Healing in the New Testament*, 138.

The Invalid at the Pool:
The Man Who Merely Got Well

J. Ramsey Michaels

He is seen first through the narrator's eyes, then through Jesus' eyes, a sick man lying beside a pool in a scene sketched in remarkable detail. Jesus and his disciples have come to the Holy City from Cana in Galilee to worship at an unnamed "festival of the Jews" (John 5:1). They are presumably on their way to the temple, when the narrator pauses to describe the everyday goings-on at a well-known place of healing in the city (v. 2)[1] – quite possibly things still going on decades later when the Gospel was written. There, in the pool's five porticoes, "a multitude of the sick, blind, lame, or shriveled up," would lie day after day. Just so we understand, later scribes have supplied two "Helps to the Reader." The first explains that they were all "waiting for the moving of the water" (v. 3b); the second explains what is meant by "the moving of the water" (v. 4): "For an angel of the Lord would come down from time to time in the pool and stir up the water. The first one in after the stirring of the water would get well from whatever disease he had." While it is doubtful that either reading is original,[2] they have been part and parcel of the story as read and interpreted in the church for centuries, and in all likelihood they do tell us what was commonly believed at the time about the pool and its healing qualities.

The Sick Man

Attention quickly centers on "a certain man there who was thirty-eight years in his sickness" (v. 5). The nature of his "sickness" is not stated, although the narrative presupposes that he belongs among those described as "lame" or

---

[1] The most important ancient witnesses (including $\mathfrak{P}^{75}$, B, the Vulgate, and Coptic versions) give the name as "Bethsaida" ($\mathfrak{P}^{66}$ offers a slight variation of this). Others (including ℵ and 33) have "Bethzatha," and still others "Belzetha" (D, and the old Latin), or "Bethesda" (A, C, and the majority of later manuscripts, as well as most English versions).

[2] Some early manuscripts have the first of these but not the second; others, the second without the first, but the majority of later witnesses (followed by the KJV) have both. Our earliest and most reliable witnesses (including $\mathfrak{P}^{66}$, $\mathfrak{P}^{75}$, ℵ and B), have neither. These readings seem to have been added to help explain the sick man's reference in v. 7 to the water being "stirred up." The presence of an "angel of the Lord" lends a certain validity to the pool's supposed healing powers, and defenders of the longer readings could argue that they were suppressed precisely to avoid acknowledging such powers.

"shriveled up." It is not unusual in healing stories to measure the seriousness of someone's affliction by how long it has lasted. A woman in Mark had "suffered from hemorrhages for twelve years" (Mark 5:43); another in Luke had been crippled "for eighteen years" (Luke 13:11); Aeneas in the book of Acts had been "bedridden for eight years" (Acts 9:33); the blind man in John was blind "from birth" (John 9:1; see also Acts 3:2, "lame from his mother's womb"). An omniscient narrator knows such things, and in this instance Jesus too "found out that he had been like that for a long time."[3] "Do you want to get well?" Jesus asks him (v. 6), the first of five references in the story to "getting well" (ὑγιὴς γενέσθαι) or being "made well" (ποιεῖν ὑγιής):

"Do you want to get well?" (v. 6).
"And all at once the man got well" (v. 9).
"The one who made me well" (v. 11).
"Look, you have gotten well" (v. 14).
"The man [announced] that Jesus is the one who made him well" (v. 15).

It is tempting – and many have yielded to the temptation – to find some hidden psychological analysis in Jesus' question, as if he were asking, "Do you *really* want to get well, or have you become quite comfortable in your life of dependency all these years?"[4] But the question is straightforward, probably just as straightforward as his question to blind Bartimaeus in Mark: "What do you want me to do for you?" (Mark 10:51). Bartimaeus had an answer ready ("that I might see," v. 51b), but here Jesus himself supplies the obvious answer. Of course he wants to "get well." To "get well" is as generalized and unspecific as being "sick." John's Gospel is not interested in the clinical details of the illnesses Jesus cures (compare 4:46, 11:2), only in his ability to make things right by giving life to those in need, whatever their affliction might be.

The "sick" man hears Jesus words simply as an offer of help from a kind stranger. To him "getting well" means getting into the pool, so he suggests something Jesus might do for him: "Sir, I have no man to put me into the pool when the water is stirred up. Whenever I get there, someone else goes down ahead of me" (v. 7).[5] He needs "a man" (probably male), either a slave[6] or a

---

[3] "Found out" is literally "knew" (γνούς), or "came to know" (aorist). Jesus probably "knew" this not by virtue of his omniscience, but by finding it out – presumably by inquiry. His knowledge is not supernatural (as in 2:25, where the verb "to know" is imperfect), but natural (as in 4:1, where it is aorist, as here). Yet this does not explain why he would have asked about this particular man. That he did so suggests that his attention was focused from the start on this man, and on what he intended to do for him.

[4] Perhaps the most convincing development of this line of thought is that of Charles H. Dodd, *Historical Tradition in the Fourth Gospel* (Cambridge: Cambridge University Press, 1963), 177.

[5] The scribes responsible for the explanation added in later manuscripts (see fn. 2) have interpreted this to mean that only the "first one" (πρῶτος) into the pool after the stirring of the water would be healed.

[6] On ἄνθρωπος, literally "man," as a slave or servant, see *BDAG, s.v.*, 81.

good friend, to assist him. A modern reader familiar with all the Gospels will remember the well-known story in Mark where a man who was paralyzed had not one but *four* faithful companions to carry him to the roof and let him down from there to be healed (Mark 2:3–4). The contrast is striking, and the reader will inevitably wonder if the author of John's Gospel knows this story and is tacitly acknowledging the contrast. Closer to home, the more immediate contrast is with a boy in Capernaum who was also "sick" (4:46), but had servants to watch over him, and a father eager to plead with Jesus for his healing. Unlike both of these, the sick man at the pool is on his own, and he seizes the opportunity to enlist Jesus as his friend and helper. Nothing in the text suggests that he knows of Jesus' supernatural powers, or who Jesus is. Instead he is asking (literally) for a "helping hand."

His motives are suspect. Unless others in the "multitude of the sick, blind, lame, or shriveled up" had a slave or a friend by their side, they were in the same situation as he, and no such healthy companions are mentioned in the opening scene (v. 3).[7] So we are left wondering if, in trying to recruit Jesus to help him, he is seeking an unfair advantage. His complaint, with its close juxtaposition of an emphatic "I" and "someone else," sounds whining and self-centered: "whenever *I* get there [ἐν ᾧ δὲ ἔρχομαι ἐγώ], *someone else* [ἄλλος] goes down ahead of me." Jesus will have none of it. Ignoring the pool and its supposed healing powers, he tells the man, "Get up, pick up your mat and walk" (ἔγειρε ἆρον τὸν κράβαττόν σου καὶ περιπάτει, v. 8). The setting of the incident, so elaborately introduced (vss. 2–3), is abruptly forgotten. Jesus and the sick man are still at the pool, but it no longer matters. They could be anywhere. They could, for example, be at a house in Capernaum surrounded by curiosity seekers, as the story of the paralytic in Mark again comes to mind. There Jesus uttered exactly the same words, "Get up, pick up your mat and walk" (ἔγειρε ἆρον τὸν κράβαττόν σου καὶ περιπάτει, Mark 2:9). In both accounts the healing is immediate, and the ensuing action agrees almost word for word. The paralytic in Mark "got up and at once picked up his mat and went out" (2:12), while in our story, "all at once the man got well, and he picked up his mat and walked" (v. 9). Whatever the doubts about the man's motives, Jesus knows that he truly wants to "get well," and he grants his wish unreservedly, with no requirement, or even any mention, of "faith" or "believing."[8]

---

[7] Thornton Wilder, however, in his short twentieth century fantasy based on this passage (idem, *The Angel That Troubled the Waters and Other Plays* [London: Longmans, Green and Co., 1928], 103), envisions in his stage directions just such healthy companions: "A door leads out upon the porch where the attendants of the sick are playing at dice, waiting for the call to fling their masters into the water when the angel of healing stirs the pool."

[8] This in contrast both to the story of the paralytic, in which Jesus saw the "faith" (Mark 2:5) of those who brought him through the roof, and the story of the royal official's son in Capernaum, where the father first "believed the word Jesus said to him" (4:50), and later "believed, he and his whole family" (4:53).

The natural question to ask of both stories is, Why mention the mat?[9] Why not just say "Get up and walk"? On a first reading, the mat seems more at home in Mark than here, for it was mentioned already when the paralytic's companions carried him to the roof and "let down the mat" on which he lay (2:4). In John's Gospel no mat has been mentioned, though one could be inferred from the description of the man "lying there" (v. 6) among the sick, the blind and the lame. This could mean that a recollection of the Markan story has shaped in some respects the telling of the story in John. Yet as soon as we learn – belatedly – that "it was the Sabbath that day" (v. 9), it becomes clear that the reverse is true. The mat, and the carrying of it, is going to be *more* significant in John than in Mark, not less. If there is a literary relationship, it now appears more likely that some form of John's story has influenced Mark's than the other way around. In John the mention of the mat is a way of setting the stage for a Sabbath controversy, a function it surely did not have in the Markan story. From here on the Sabbath will be the overriding issue.

The Sabbath Question

As if on cue, "the Jews," that is the religious authorities in Jerusalem, make their appearance, saying to "him who had been cured,[10] 'It is the Sabbath, and it is not lawful for you to pick up your mat.'" (v. 10). It was part of the oral law that "taking out from one domain into another" was one of thirty-nine activities considered to be work forbidden on the Sabbath,[11] and it is probably to some version of that law that "the Jews" are referring. But are we to conclude that Jesus knew this when he told the sick man, "Get up, pick up your mat and walk?" Was he deliberately provoking a confrontation? At the time he seemed only to be saying, "Get up, leave this place and take your mat with you, because you aren't coming back." In other words, so much for the pool and its supposed healing powers. That is undoubtedly the case, and yet we know that nothing ever takes Jesus by surprise in the Gospel of John. The likelihood, therefore, is that in giving this command he knew exactly what he was doing so far as the Sabbath laws were concerned. Whatever else it was, "pick up your

---

[9] A "mat" (κράβαττος, as here) was a poor man's bed that could also serve as a pallet or stretcher (see BDAG, s. v., 563). Matthew and Luke prefer other terms, such as κλίνη (Matt 9:2, 6; Luke 5:18), or its diminutive κλινίδιον (Luke 5:19, 24).

[10] The man is designated differently as the story unfolds: first as "a certain man" (τις ἄνθρωπος, v. 5), then as "the sick man" (ὁ ἀσθενῶν, v. 7), then simply as "the man" (ὁ ἄνθρωπος, v. 9), now after the healing as "him who had been cured" (τῷ τεθεραπευμένῳ, v. 10) and "he who had been healed" (ὁ ἰαθείς, v. 13), and finally again as "the man" (ὁ ἄνθρωπος, v. 15).

[11] M. Šabb. 7.2.

mat and walk" was a deliberate challenge to those laws and to the religious authorities whose job it was to enforce them. If the man had been "thirty-eight years in his sickness," after all (v. 5), waiting another day would have done little harm.

As quick as ever to make excuses, the man tells the Jewish authorities, "The one who made me well, he told me, 'Pick up your mat and walk'" (v. 11). The authorities are quite willing to accept his excuse, evidently in the hope that it will lead them to the real target of their investigation. They seem to have someone in mind that they are looking for, possibly for other reasons. They have crossed paths with Jesus once before, when they challenged his act of driving the money changers from the temple (2:18–20), and now we sense that they are on his trail again. They have no interest in the healing, only in the Sabbath violation. Instead of asking, "Who is the one who made you well," building on what the man has just said, they ask, "Who is the man who told you 'Pick up and walk'?" (v. 12). They are looking for a Sabbath breaker, not a healer or miracle worker, and they seem to want either a name or a face to face identification. Already the issue is subtly shifting, as it will explicitly later in the chapter (vss. 16–18), from the Sabbath to the issue of Jesus' identity. The question, "Who is the man?" (τίς ἐστιν ὁ ἄνθρωπος)[12] will echo and re-echo through the Gospel of John in various ways, and with multilayered answers. The man who was made well cannot provide a name, for "he did not know who it was," and he is unable to point Jesus out because Jesus is nowhere to be seen. He had "ducked out" (ἐξένευσεν),[13] we are told, because of the "crowd in the place" (v. 13).[14] The implication is that otherwise the man would have been quite willing to turn Jesus in to save himself from prosecution as a Sabbath breaker. He need not have worried, for he was *not* the one in the crosshairs of the religious establishment.

The Second Encounter

The story could have ended here, but there is more. "After these things" (v. 14) signals a break in the narrative, as Jesus moves on to what must have been his destination in the first place, the temple. There he "finds" (εὑρίσκει) once more the man he had healed, just as he first "found" Philip (1:43) when he enlisted

---

[12] Jesus is repeatedly called a "man" or "this man," particularly by his enemies (7:46; 9:16, 24; 10:33; 11:47; 18:17, 29; 19:5). The last answer to the question, "Who is the man?" (τίς ἐστιν ὁ ἄνθρωπος) is Pilate's "Here is the man" (ἰδοὺ ὁ ἄνθρωπος, 19:5).

[13] Colloquial English ("ducked out") captures quite well the sense of the verb, which suggests a dodge or a turning of the head (compare νεύει, 13:24).

[14] This is the first of several instances in the Gospel in which Jesus escapes potential arrest or even stoning (7:30; 8:20, 59; 10:39; 12:36).

him as a disciple, just as Andrew "found" Simon Peter (1:41) and Philip "found" Nathanael (1:45), and just as Jesus later "found" the man born blind, when he asked him, "Do you believe in the Son of man?" (9:35). But here, instead of "Do you believe?" or "Follow me" (see 1:43), he makes a more modest – yet more ominous – demand. After reminding the man of the miracle ("Look, you have gotten well"), he adds the thinly-veiled warning, "Don't sin any more, lest something worse happen to you" (μηκέτι ἁμάρτανε, ἵνα μὴ χεῖρόν σοί τι γένηται. v. 14). If the belated notice that it was the Sabbath caught the reader up short and changed the course of the story (v. 9), so too does this belated warning from Jesus. "Look, you have gotten well" is exactly what we would have expected (see vss. 6, 9, 11, 15). "Don't sin any more, lest something worse happen to you," is not. It sounds as if it belongs in that other story, the one in which Jesus said to the paralytic, "Your sins are forgiven" (Mark 2:5), and then demonstrated dramatically that "Your sins are forgiven" and "Get up, pick up your mat and walk" amount to the same thing (Mark 2:9–12). No such demonstration has taken place here, yet the man Jesus healed is supposed to understand that "Look, you have gotten well" is equivalent to "Look, your sins are forgiven." Or at least the reader is expected to. Once again this story in John and the story in Mark appear to be intertwined in the tradition. At least one detail – the picking up of the mat – turned out to be more at home in this story than in the other, because of the issue of the Sabbath. Now we find that another – the link between healing and the forgiveness of sins – was integral to the Markan story from the start, but comes in here almost as an afterthought.

Even though Jesus was identified from the start as "the Lamb of God who takes away the sin of the world" (John 1:29), the notion of the forgiveness of sins is conspicuously absent throughout most of the Gospel of John.[15] Jesus' first disciples are called to follow him, but are never identified as sinners or said to be forgiven. Nathanael, on the contrary, is "a true Israelite, in whom is no deceit" (1:47). Nicodemus needs to be born from above, but is not asked to repent or seek forgiveness for his sins. Nor did the healing of the royal official's son address any sins of either the child or the father. The Samaritan woman, with her "five husbands," and a partner not her husband (4:18), is arguably a "sinner," yet Jesus never explicitly identifies her as such, or condemns her, or for that matter, forgives her. The Pharisees charge the man born blind with being "born altogether in sins" (9:34), but according to Jesus, "Neither this man sinned nor his parents" (9:3). For the most part, "sin" in the Gospel of John is defined very narrowly as unbelief, or rejection of the One whom God has sent. The "sinners" are simply those who reject and oppose Jesus (see 8:21,

---

[15] Forgiveness is never mentioned until the next-to-last chapter, when the risen Jesus appears to his disciples, confers on them the Holy Spirit, and promises, "Whosoever sins you forgive, they are forgiven to them; whosoever you retain, they are retained" (20:23).

24, "you will die in your sin[s]"; 8:34, "everyone who commits sin is a slave of sin"; 9:41, "your sin remains"; 15:22, "If I had not come and spoken to them, they would not have sin, but now they have no cloak for their sin"). That is why Jesus' warning, "Don't sin any more, or something worse will happen to you," sounds out of place here. The man in this story has not thrown in his lot with Jesus' enemies, not yet at least. He has "gotten well." He is potentially a disciple. And yet he alone, of all the actual or potential disciples in this Gospel, is identified – albeit implicitly – as a "sinner."[16]

The apparent intrusion of the issue of sin and forgiveness could suggest that John is familiar with Mark's account of the paralytic in some form. Yet this is by no means certain, and it is safer to proceed as if it were not the case. Without help from Mark, what do we make of Jesus' warning to the man he had healed? Certainly it implies some connection between sickness and personal sin. Jesus' disciples will raise just such a possibility four chapters later on encountering the blind beggar: "Rabbi, who sinned, this man or his parents, that he should be born blind?" (9:2). And Jesus will not claim that such a connection is unthinkable, only that it does not apply in the blind man's case (9:3). Perhaps the best solution is to define "getting well" (ὑγιὴς γενέσθαι) as holistic healing, the restoration of the whole person. This could be implied in 7:21–23, when Jesus at another Jewish festival refers back to this healing at the Bethsaida pool as making "a whole man well on the Sabbath?" (v. 23). It is difficult to be sure because at one level Jesus is simply contrasting circumcision, viewed as the "healing" of a bodily member, with the healing of a man's whole body. Yet the phrase, "a whole man" (ὅλον ἄνθρωπον), seems to imply more than just the physical body, and being "made well," therefore, more than mere physical healing.

If this is the case, it is fair to assume that the healing of the man at the pool involved in some way the healing of the whole person, not just the strengthening of his useless limbs – in short the healing of his heart, the forgiveness of his sins.[17] This is obviously a presupposition of the story of the paralytic in Mark, and it may well be the presupposition of all New Testament healings.

---

[16] The only possible exception is the woman caught in adultery, to whom Jesus says, "Neither do I condemn you. Go, and from now on sin no more" (μηκέτι ἁμάρτανε). But this comes within a story generally agreed to be a later addition to the Gospel. Possibly the language of our story has influenced the ending of that one, although Jesus says nothing to the woman of "something worse."

[17] So Heinrich Seesemann, on ὅλος, in *TDNT*, 5:175: "In this light Jn 7:23 means that by healing Jesus has made the sick man healthy in his whole being. The healings which Jesus performs are healings of the whole man ... Similarly, forgiveness of sins is a healing of the whole man ... Hence we have to take the ὅλος of Jn 7:23 in this broad sense." It is worth adding that when Jesus wants to speak merely of "the whole body" (ὅλον τὸ σῶμα) he is quite capable of doing so, and even when he does, it is arguable that the whole person, not just the body, is in view (see Matt 5:29–30, 6:22–23; Luke 11:34, 36).

In James, for example, it is said of the one anointed by the elders of the congregation that "the Lord will raise him up, and if he has committed sins, he will be forgiven" (Jas 5:15). At the same time, the distinctive Johannine understanding of sin as unbelief is also in play. If Jesus is defining sin in that way, then "Don't sin any more, or something worse will happen to you" is more or less equivalent to what he will later say to Thomas after the resurrection, "be no longer faithless but faithful" (μὴ γίνου ἄπιστος ἀλλὰ πιστός, 20:27) – an implicit invitation to believe. It is in its own way equivalent, if not to "Follow me," at least to "Do you believe in the Son of man?" (9:35), or something similar. The alternative is "something worse" (χεῖρόν τι), and there can be little doubt that death is meant. If sickness leads to physical death, sin leads to spiritual or eternal death. Jesus will warn his antagonists at a later festival that "unless you believe that I am, you will die in your sins" (8:24). And throughout this Gospel unbelief leads to death just as surely as belief leads to life.

The response of the man who has "gotten well" to Jesus' warning is the single most important clue to his character. There have been other clues along the way. He was a "sick man" (v. 7) who had spent "thirty-eight years in his sickness" (v. 5),[18] and even those who are unaware that the Greek words for "sick" and "sickness" also mean, respectively, "weak" and "weakness"[19] will have sensed all along a weakness in his character, a certain selfishness and duplicity, in sharp contrast to the man born blind four chapters later. This is evident, as we have seen, in his whining complaint to Jesus that "I have no one to put me into the pool when the water is stirred up, and whenever I get there, someone else goes down ahead of me" (v. 7), and his willingness to implicate Jesus instead of taking responsibility for his own actions in carrying his mat on the Sabbath (v. 11). He is, moreover, from a literary standpoint a "flat" character, at least in comparison to the Samaritan woman and the man born blind.[20] George Beasley-Murray calls him "a colorless individual, without faith or hope."[21] Yet now that he has "gotten well," he has an opportunity for a fresh start, and significant character development. We are eager to learn his response, and it is not long in coming.

So far as Jesus is concerned it is no response at all. The man remained silent and "went away [ἀπῆλθεν] and announced to the Jews that Jesus is the one who made him well" (v. 15). There was no reason why he had to do this. He himself was in the clear so far as the charge of Sabbath breaking was con-

---

[18] That is, ὁ ἀσθενῶν, "the sick man" (v. 7), and ἐν τῇ ἀσθενείᾳ αὐτοῦ, "in his sickness" (v. 5).

[19] See *BDAG*, *s.v.*, 142–43.

[20] Flat, but not a stereotype. As John P. Meier recognizes, his attitude and actions "hardly fit the stock character of many stereotyped narratives" (idem, *A Marginal Jew: Rethinking the Historical Jesus* [New York: Doubleday, 1994], 2:681).

[21] George R. Beasley-Murray, *John* (WBC 36; Waco, Tex.: Word, 1987), 72.

cerned. He had told the authorities he did not know who had told him to pick up his mat, and that could have ended it. Yet now, having met Jesus in the temple, he suddenly becomes very scrupulous about the unfinished business, returning to volunteer information he had been unable to supply before. Somehow (we don't know how) he has learned Jesus' name, and he becomes in the end an informant. Andrew Lincoln comments that "at no stage of the story has the narrator been interested in the man's motivations in relation to Jesus, and that does not change here. The main purpose of the narrator's statement is to strengthen the connection between the miracle story and a direct confrontation between Jesus and the Jews."[22] The outcome is that "on account of this the Jews began pursuing Jesus, because he did such things on the Sabbath" (v. 16). A comparable scenario plays out again long afterward when some of those who had witnessed the raising of Lazarus "went away [ἀπῆλθον] to the Pharisees and told them the things Jesus had done" (11:46), so that the Pharisees, with the chief priests, "gathered council" and came to the decision that Jesus must be put to death (11:47–53).

Here, however, the vocabulary is noteworthy. The man does not merely "tell" the authorities; he "announces" (ἀνήγγειλεν), a verb suggesting something close to a formal declaration or proclamation (see 4:25, where the Samaritan woman claims that the Messiah will "announce [ἀναγγελεῖ] to us all things," and 16:13, where Jesus promises that the Spirit of truth "will announce [ἀναγγελεῖ] to you the things to come").[23] As to the content of the "announcement," it looks, superficially, like something akin to a formal confession of faith: "that Jesus is ... the one who made him well" (ὅτι Ἰησοῦς ἐστιν ὁ ποιήσας αὐτόν ὑγιῆ). "That Jesus is" (ὅτι Ἰησοῦς ἐστιν) recalls the confession that the Gospel of John wants every reader to make: "*that Jesus is* [ὅτι Ἰησοῦς ἐστιν] the Christ, the Son of God, and that believing you might have life in his name" (20:31), or the confessions in 1 John "*that Jesus is* the Son of God" (1 John 4:15, 5:5), or "*that Jesus is* the Christ" (1 John 5:1, italics added). These would have been the proper confessional answers to the authorities' question, "Who is the man?" (v. 12). But the great "announcement" is merely "that Jesus is the one who made him well" – true enough, but no confession of faith, more like a feeble parody of a real confession.

His intent may not have been malicious. According to Barnabas Lindars, "it is by no means clear that John imagined that the man was deliberately betraying Jesus to his enemies. He had cited Jesus as his authority for the breach of

---

[22] Andrew T. Lincoln, *The Gospel According to John* (BNTC; Peabody, Mass.: Hendrickson, 2005), 196.

[23] See also 1 John 1:5, "And this is the message which we have heard from him and announce [ἀναγγέλλομεν] to you, that God is light and in him is no darkness at all"; 1 Pet 1:12, "And now it has been announced [ἀνηγγέλη] to you through those who brought you the gospel with the Holy Spirit sent from heaven."

the Sabbath (v. 11), and the dispute could only be settled by a discussion between Jesus and the Jews; and until that had been done his own position would be ambiguous."[24] He might even have wanted to give credit, naively, to "the one who made him well." If so, he is naïve indeed, for his backhanded "confession" identifies Jesus as a Sabbath breaker whom the Jewish authorities will from here on "seek to kill" (v. 18). As Alan Culpepper observes, "To what extent his 'naivete' or 'dullness' is culpable may be debatable, but there is little with which to excuse him," adding that he "represents those whom even the signs cannot lead to authentic faith."[25] Raymond Brown speaks of his "obtuseness," "real dullness," and "persistent naiveté," especially in contrast to the man born blind in chapter 9. While acknowledging that "A character such as this could have been invented," Brown adds that "one would expect to see clearer motivation for such a creation."[26] More likely, he was not invented, but was based rather on the memory of a real man who once crossed Jesus' path and was not heard from again. All that can be said of him is what is said over and over again in the text – that he "got well." No faith, no new birth, no lasting forgiveness. Any of these – or on the contrary, "something worse" – *could* lie in his future, but it is all left to the reader's imagination because the Gospel writer himself does not know. From a purely literary standpoint, the prospects do not look promising.

---

[24] Barnabas Lindars, *The Gospel of John* (NCB; Grand Rapids, Mich.: Eerdmans, 1972), 217.

[25] R. Alan Culpepper, *Anatomy of the Fourth Gospel: A Study in Literary Design* (Philadelphia: Fortress, 1983), 138.

[26] Raymond E. Brown, *The Gospel According to John (i–xii)* (AB 29; New York: Doubleday, 1966), 209. While these examples are typical of most commentators, there are a few dissenting voices. Thomas Brodie, for example, argues that while the man's action "does have a possible negative interpretation – that the man is an ungrateful informer," it is also "sufficiently ambiguous to be open to a positive interpretation: the man has finally come to mature (repentant) recognition of Jesus, and he is announcing the good news to the Jews" (idem, *The Gospel According to John: A Literary and Theological Commentary* [Oxford: Oxford University Press, 1993], 238). And Jeffrey Staley notices that "neither the narrator nor Jesus condemns him, either explicitly or implicitly," adding that "Perhaps he is not a tattle-tale, but a character who serves in his own way, with his own theological argument, as a faithful witness to the sign performed" (idem, "Stumbling in the Dark, Reaching for the Light: Reading Character in John 5 and 9," *Semeia* 53 [1991]: 63).

The Crowd:
A Faceless, Divided Mass

Cornelis Bennema

Identity and Role of the Crowd

The crowd (ὄχλος) embodies, of course, the largest number of people, yet it is not an obvious character and has received virtually no attention from Johannine scholarship.[1] The crowd has a dominant presence in John 6, 7, and 12 (90% of all occurrences).[2] A quick glance, however, reveals that these crowds are not the same but differ in geographical location and composition, so we must first examine the identity and behavior of each crowd.

A Galilean Crowd of Common People in John 6

John 6 contains the account of Jesus miraculously feeding the crowd and the subsequent discourse in which he reveals himself as the true bread from heaven who gives life to the world. The setting for the story is Galilee, where the crowd gets a positive introduction (6:1-2). The crowd following Jesus because of his miraculous signs echoes the "believing" group in 2:23 (although 2:24-25 reveals the inadequacy of its "belief"). Besides, John often uses the verb "to follow" to suggest discipleship, thus creating the expectation that this crowd might come to believe in Jesus and become true followers. What is important for John is that people not only come to Jesus but also remain with him in discipleship.

With the miraculous feeding of the crowd in 6:10-15, Jesus begins to test its willingness or ability "to follow." Jesus performs this miracle not simply to provide a free meal but to reveal something of his identity and mission – that if he can miraculously provide physical food he can also provide spiritual

---

[1] Except for R. Alan Culpepper (*Anatomy of the Fourth Gospel: A Study in Literary Design* [Philadelphia: Fortress, 1983], 131-32) and Craig R. Koester (*Symbolism in the Fourth Gospel: Meaning, Mystery, Community* [2d ed.; Minneapolis: Fortress, 2003], 54-62), no one deals with the crowd. James L. Resseguie even contends that the crowd is part of the setting rather than a character in its own right (idem, *Narrative Criticism of the New Testament: An Introduction* [Grand Rapids, Mich.: Baker Academic, 2005], 125). I understand a crowd to be a large gathering of people, whereas a mob or throng denote particular types of crowd.

[2] The only references to the crowd outside John 6-7, 12 are in 5:13 and 11:42.

nourishment. The crowd builds on its promising start by recognizing something of Jesus' identity – he is the Prophet like Moses of Deuteronomy 18:15–18 (6:14). However, their intention to make him some sort of national leader is too worldly – "from below" – and causes Jesus to withdraw (6:15).[3]

Jesus escapes to the other side of the Sea of Galilee but the crowd keeps following him (6:22–25). Although this appears commendable, Jesus knows their intentions are still worldly – they simply want another free lunch (6:26). Even to have continued seeking Jesus because of his signs, as they initially did (6:2), would have been more spiritual; hence, their faith hardly seems "faith" at all. Typically, Jesus moves from a material to a spiritual level but the crowd misunderstands him (6:27–29). The crowd is stuck at an earthly level, thinking of Jesus merely as a miracle worker and demanding a greater miracle, similar to what Moses did (6:30–31). Nevertheless, the crowd progresses in understanding by setting the feeding and the bread within the theological framework of the manna in the wilderness (6:31).

In 6:32–33, Jesus corrects the crowd's misinterpretation of the true bread from heaven but they continue to think at an earthly level, hoping for a continual supply of this miraculous bread (6:34). Jesus then explains that he is the bread of life, the one who will sustain those who believe in him, knowing all the while that the crowd will not believe (6:35–36; cf. 2:24–25).

From 6:41 onwards, the debate between Jesus and his audience intensifies and becomes hostile. It is important to note that the term "the Jews" is used in 6:41, 52 instead of "the crowd." In John's Gospel, "the Jews" refers to a particular religious group of Torah- and temple-loyalists found especially, but not exclusively, in Judea.[4] While it is possible that the crowd consists of "the Jews," it is more likely that from among the crowd of common Galileans a group of "the Jews" emerges and becomes openly hostile towards Jesus.[5] Although "the Jews" start out as part of the crowd, their emerging from it and their increased hostility demand that they be distinguished from the crowd.[6] Besides, there is probably also a shift in location, from the shore of Capernaum in 6:25–40 to its synagogue in 6:41–59, and the crowd thus disappears into the background. Although this crowd initially shows signs-faith and potential discipleship, it

---

[3] Steven Hunt points out that Jesus' withdrawal to the mountain, where the large crowd does not follow him, may allude to the situation in Ex 19 where the Israelite crowd was not allowed to go up or touch Mount Sinai. This may not be farfetched since most scholars interpret John 6 against the backdrop of God's miraculous providence of manna during Israel's journey in the wilderness.

[4] Cornelis Bennema, "The Identity and Composition of οἱ Ἰουδαῖοι in the Gospel of John," *TynBul* 60 (2009): 239–63.

[5] These "Jews" in 6:41, 52 could be Pharisees travelling from Jerusalem or Pharisees residing in Galilee (Bennema, "Identity," 256).

[6] Contra Koester, who states that John identifies the crowd as "the Jews" in 6:41, 52 (Koester, *Symbolism*, 57–58).

follows Jesus for the wrong reasons, is slow to understand, and eventually fails to believe.

A Jerusalem Crowd of Common People in John 7

The setting for John 7 is the temple during the Feast of Tabernacles – one of the three great Jewish festivals that required Jews to make a pilgrimage to Jerusalem. Hence, besides local residents, the crowd probably includes Jews from all over Palestine. Throughout John 7, Jesus' audience is a mix of the crowd (the common people), "the Jews" (the particular Torah- and temple-loyalists), and the leaders of "the Jews" (the Pharisees, the chief priests or "rulers/authorities," and the temple police). The crowd is clearly distinct from "the Jews" and their leaders because 7:11–13 mentions the former's fear of the latter, then in 7:26 common Jerusalemites distinguish themselves from the religious authorities, and finally in 7:49 the Sanhedrin authorities contemptuously label the crowd as ignorant rabble.[7]

Before Jesus appears on the scene, the crowd is already divided on who he is but they are too afraid of "the Jews" to discuss the issue publicly (7:12–13). Like "the Jews" in 6:41, the crowd grumbles (7:12, 32) and it resembles Israel's grumbling in the wilderness (Exod 15:24; 16:2–12; Num 14:26–27). Jesus' teaching is met with incomprehension and aggravation (7:20). In fact, the crowd comes close to siding with "the Jews" when it accuses Jesus of being demon-possessed (cf. 7:20; 8:48, 52). The crowd claims to know Jesus' origin (7:25–27) but he firmly refutes this claim saying they lack knowledge of God – and hence of him (7:28–29).[8] Jesus' reply causes division: some try to arrest Jesus while others believe in him, reasoning that Jesus' miraculous signs prove that he is the Messiah (7:30–31). However, this "belief" may be viewed with caution because a similar miracle-based belief of a Jerusalem "crowd" was deficient (2:23–24). Jesus' invitation on the last day of the festival (7:37–38) seems attractive but once again causes division in the crowd (7:40–43).

Thus, throughout John 7, the crowd remains divided, unable to make up its mind about Jesus (7:12, 30–31, 40–43). Nevertheless, this division shows that Jesus is able to penetrate the crowd with his teaching and elicit some positive (though probably inadequate) responses. The crowd seems a microcosm of humanity, and the reactions and divisions in the crowd represent the responses of acceptance and rejection that humankind can make (cf. 1:10–13; 3:18, 36). Although the crowd in John 7 is primarily a divided one, it also shows an unflattering resemblance to "the Jews": (i) both "the Jews" and the

---

[7] Cf. Rudolf Bultmann, *The Gospel of John* (trans. G. R. Beasley-Murray; Philadelphia: Westminster, 1971), 310–11, fn. 5; R. Meyer, "ὄχλος," in *TDNT* 5:589–90.

[8] Although the term "Jerusalemites" rather than "crowd" is used in 7:25, they probably belong to the crowd since they distinguish themselves from "the authorities" in 7:26.

crowd grumble about Jesus (6:41; 7:12, 32); (ii) both accuse him of being demon-possessed (7:20; 8:48, 52).

A Jerusalem Crowd of Particular Religious Partisans in John 12

Whereas the crowds in John 6 and 7 consist of common people, John 12 presents a different one.[9] It is not a crowd of common Jerusalemites because John identifies this crowd as "the great crowd of 'the Jews'" (12:9). Nor is it a crowd of the religious authorities because the crowd in 12:9 is contrasted with the religious authorities in 12:10–11, 18–19.[10] The crowd in 12:9 is more likely a great crowd of Judean Torah- and temple-loyalists, corresponding to the "many people from the countryside" who went up to the Passover feast of "the Jews" in Jerusalem (11:55).[11] Although initially this crowd of "the Jews" is favorable to Jesus (12:12–19), soon its attitude changes and ultimately it responds with rejection and unbelief (12:27–40) – typical of "the Jews" throughout. In fact, this crowd displays an attitude similar to the Galilean crowd. I will elaborate.

Just as in 6:14, 26, 30, the crowd of "the Jews" is focused on the spectacular: they have come to see the controversial Jesus and the resurrected Lazarus (12:9, 18). The Jewish authorities are afraid that seeing Lazarus, the crowd may believe in Jesus – just as many of "the Jews" did when Lazarus was raised – therefore they plan to kill Lazarus too (12:10–11; cf. 11:45). When the crowd hears that Jesus is approaching Jerusalem, it hails him as the long-awaited messianic king (12:12–13). Jesus is given this rousing welcome because of the raising of Lazarus (12:17–18). While the crowd expects Jesus to be a political messianic leader who would liberate them from Roman oppression, Jesus' action in 12:14–15 serves to correct their misunderstanding. Against the backdrop of Zech 9:9–10, Jesus is depicted not as a warrior-king but as a king who will destroy Israel's war tools (including the war horse), and establish peace. Hence, the devotion and expectations of the crowd seem rather misplaced (cf. 6:14–15).

Jesus attempts to help the crowd overcome their misunderstanding and unbelief (12:29–30) but in vain. When he speaks of his impending salvific

---

[9] Besides the crowd in John 7, Koester surprisingly also considers the audience in John 8 as the Jerusalem crowd (whereas 8:12–59 clearly presents an audience of Pharisees and "the Jews") but ignores John 12, where a Jerusalem crowd is present (Koester, *Symbolism*, 59–62).

[10] John 12:17–18 depicts different crowds: the crowd in 12:17 is the same as in 11:42, whereas the crowd in 12:18 has only *heard* of the miracle and corresponds to the crowd in 11:55; 12:9, 12, 29, 34 (cf. Meyer, "ὄχλος," 5:588–89; *pace* Bultmann, *John*, 419).

[11] Cf. the crowd in 11:42, which consists of "the Jews" who had come to console Mary and Martha (11:19, 31, 33, 36, 45). However, the crowd in 11:42 is different from the one in 12:9 (see fn. 10, above).

death, the crowd is scandalized but once again Jesus urges the crowd to understand and believe in him lest the darkness overtake them (12:31–36; cf. 1:5; 8:12; 11:9–10). Finally, Jesus withdraws and John reveals that for all Jesus' admonitions and miraculous signs, the crowd at large does not believe in him (12:37; cf. 6:36). The crowd's unbelief fulfills the prophecy in Isaiah 53:1, which speaks of the messianic Servant who is rejected (12:38). John then reveals in 12:39–40 the reason for the crowd's unbelief: The closed minds of "the Jews" prevent understanding, repentance, and salvation, and by rejecting Jesus and his message they remain blind, or, are plunged further into darkness (cf. 9:39–41).

Nevertheless, John mentions that while the crowd at large is unbelieving, many from the crowd "believe" in Jesus (12:42). However, this "belief" appears inadequate. First, it is a "secret" belief since the fear of expulsion from the synagogue prevents them from publicly confessing their belief (12:42). John implicitly criticizes such an attitude in John 9, by contrasting the bold testimony of the formerly blind man before the religious authorities with the denial of his fearful parents. Second, these "secret believers" are more concerned with winning human praise than God's (12:43). Such an attitude, Jesus points out to "the Jews" in 5:44, is an obstacle to true faith. Thus, the crowd in John 12 as a whole is ultimately an unbelieving crowd. They move from enthusiasm to misunderstanding to aggravation to rejection and unbelief. This is not surprising since this crowd consists of "the Jews," who primarily represent the attitude of hostility and disbelief. The crowd makes no appearance beyond John 12.

So, although the crowd occurs in different geographical locations (Galilee in John 6; Jerusalem in John 7 and 12) and has different referents (common people in John 6 and 7; "the Jews" in John 12), in each instance it shows similar behavior and hence I suggest that the crowd should be treated as a single, corporate character.[12]

Character Analysis of the Crowd

Many scholars use a reductionist method of character analysis – some do not specify their criteria for character analysis; others only analyze characters in terms of their traits; still others do not classify or evaluate the characters. This is partly due to the lack of a suitable theory of character. I developed a comprehensive theory of character, which in its most succinct form is this: I will *analyze* the crowd along three dimensions (complexity, development, and inner life), *classify* the resulting character on a continuum of degree of charac-

---

[12] The setting of John 7 and 12 as a Jewish festival that requires a pilgrimage to Jerusalem makes it highly likely that the "Jerusalem" crowd includes Jews from all over Palestine.

terization (from agent to type to personality to individuality), and *evaluate* the character according to John's point of view.[13]

Character Complexity

The degree of a character's complexity has to do with its traits. As Seymour Chatman asserts, we reconstruct a character by inferring its traits from the information in the text, whereby trait is a "relatively stable or abiding personal quality."[14] Characters may vary from those displaying a single trait to those displaying a complex nexus of traits, and there can be various degrees of complexity in between.

The Galilean crowd in John 6 makes a promising start: it gives the impression that it will become true disciples (6:2), shows determination and eagerness (6:22–25, 28, 34), and demonstrates some discernment and ability to reason theologically (6:14, 30–31). However, this expectation is short-lived as it becomes clear that it follows Jesus for the wrong reasons, misunderstands him (6:25–34), and as Jesus foretells, fails to believe (6:36). In John 7, the Jerusalem crowd of commoners is divided about Jesus (7:12, 30–31, 40–43). This divided crowd is a microcosm of the world – representing the responses of acceptance and rejection that humankind can make. At the same time, this crowd imitates the negative attitude of "the Jews" in that they grumble, accuse Jesus of being demon-possessed, and are aggressive (7:12, 20, 32, 44). Yet, the crowd also shows some theological discernment (7:25–27, 31, 40–41). In John 12, we encounter a crowd of "the Jews" that is initially enthusiastic about Jesus (12:12–19), but it proves to be motivated by a desire for the spectacular (12:9, 18). Besides, its expectations are misplaced because it has misunderstood the nature of Jesus' mission (12:13–14). This continued misunderstanding eventually leads to rejection and unbelief because this crowd is "blind" (12:27–40; cf. 6:36).

Even though John presents different crowds – a Galilean crowd of common people in John 6, a Jerusalem crowd of common people in John 7, and a Jerusalem crowd of particular religious partisans in John 12 – they have similar characteristics and emerge as a consistent, corporate character. The crowd's main trait is its divisibility, while displaying various sub-traits: it is sympathetic, patriotic, enthusiastic, even sensationalist (6:14–15; 7:31, 40–41a; 12:9, 12–13, 18), has some determination and theological discernment, and shows potential for belief and discipleship; yet, it also displays misunderstanding,

---

[13] For a detailed explanation of my comprehensive theory of character, see Cornelis Bennema, "A Theory of Character in the Fourth Gospel with Reference to Ancient and Modern Literature," *BibInt* 17 (2009): 375–421. For a summary, see my chapter on Judas elsewhere in this book.

[14] Seymour Chatman, *Story and Discourse: Narrative Structure in Fiction and Film* (Ithaca, N.Y.: Cornell University Press, 1978), 119, 126 (quotation from p. 126).

complaining, aggression, rejection, and unbelief. In sum, the crowd is complex, having multiple traits.

Character Development

Character development is not simply the addition of a trait that the reader infers further along the text continuum or a character's progress in his or her understanding of Jesus.[15] Development is revealed in the character's ability to surprise the reader, when a newly found trait replaces another or does not fit neatly into the existing set of traits, implying that the character has changed. By and large, the crowd is consistent in its traits and behavior, and as such shows no development.

Inner Life

The inner life of a character gives the reader insight into the character's thoughts, emotions, and motivations, and is conveyed usually by the narrator and sometimes by the characters themselves.[16] In John's Gospel, however, Jesus also reveals the inner life of some characters, which should not surprise us since he is the revealer *par excellence*, who knows all people and what is in them (2:24–25; cf. 6:64; 13:11; 16:30; 21:17). Regarding inner life, characters range from those who allow us a peek inside their minds to those whose minds remain opaque. When it comes to the crowd, there is some penetration into their inner life: Jesus reveals that it desires the spectacular, will not believe, and does not know him (6:26, 36; 7:28), while the crowd itself claims to know Jesus' origins (7:27). Sometimes, the crowd's style of speaking is comparable to a soliloquy – an "inner monologue" (7:12, 40–42).

Characterization and Evaluation of the Crowd

After this character analysis, we can classify the character of the crowd by positioning it on the characterization continuum. Considering its location on the axes of complexity (complex, multiple traits), development (none), and inner life (some), I suggest to identify the character of the crowd as a corporate personality.[17]

---

[15] Contra Resseguie, *Narrative Criticism*, 153.

[16] Cf. Adele Berlin, *Poetics and Interpretation of Biblical Narrative* (Sheffield: Almond, 1983), 38.

[17] We should not understand the personality of the crowd in a modern individualistic sense but as a "group-oriented personality" (cf. Bruce J. Malina, *The New Testament World: Insights from Cultural Anthropology* [3d ed.; Louisville, Ky.: Westminster John Knox, 2001], 60–67).

From John's evaluative point of view, which is informed by his overall purpose of eliciting and increasing faith in the life-giving Jesus amongst his readers (20:31), the crowd must be evaluated negatively. John 6 eventually depicts an unbelieving crowd, out of which the hostile "Jews" emerge; John 7 presents a divided crowd which shares characteristics with "the Jews"; and John 12 portrays an unbelieving crowd of "Jews." The crowds in John 6, 7, and 12 all show promise but eventually reject Jesus and fail to believe. Although the crowd and "the Jews" are distinct characters, the crowd closely resembles "the Jews."[18] Thus, the crowd as a group or corporate character remains in darkness and chooses to respond with unbelief.[19] Besides, at the level of discourse, John "shows" the crowd in John 6–7 as grumbling Israel in the wilderness, thus subtly informing the reader how to read the Johannine crowd.

Despite the crowd's negative attitude overall, Jesus is able to break through and elicit positive responses, even belief, from some people. Besides, while the crowd has a cognitive problem – it does not understand Jesus and his teaching – and develops a hostile and unbelieving attitude, it can nevertheless think theologically (6:14, 28–31; 7:25–27, 31, 40–43; 12:34) – though the religious authorities, ironically, consider them incapable of doing so (7:49). However, the belief-responses do not stand scrutiny. In 7:31, the "belief" of many in the crowd is perhaps just that Jesus is a miracle worker – and Jesus has already been critical of such belief of the crowd (2:23–25). Next, though many from the crowd believe in Jesus (12:42), John is critical of these so-called "secret believers" who are afraid to confess publicly. Thus, the Johannine crowd at large is on a negative course, and even though Jesus is able to penetrate this group with his teaching, causing controversy and division, and elicit positive responses, these appear inadequate.[20] Nevertheless, though the "belief" of individuals in the crowd is questionable, the point is that the crowd is not uniform in its response to Jesus; some responses can be designated as "positive" (though inadequate).

---

[18] Contra those who argue that John has blurred the distinctions between the crowd and "the Jews" (Reginald Fuller, "The 'Jews' in the Fourth Gospel," *Dialog* 16 [1977]: 32–33; Koester, *Symbolism*, 59–62; R. Hakola, *Identity Matters: John, the Jews and Jewishness* [NovTSup 118; Leiden: Brill, 2005], 160–62, 226–31).

[19] In Jewish antiquity, the crowd was also perceived negatively. Josephus mentions the crowd's desire for the spectacular (*Ant.* 7.286–287; cf. John 6:26; 12:9, 18), its susceptibility to deception (*Ant.* 20.160, 167; cf. John 7:12b), its ignorance (*Ag. Ap.* 2.224; cf. John 7:49), and its function as a hiding place (*Ant.* 2.255; cf. John 5:13). Philo speaks negatively of the crowd as "a misguided multitude of ordinary careless people" (*Her.* 1.303), unstable (*Mos.* 1.197; *Leg.* 1.67), easily deceived (*Abr.* 1.22), lazy, disorderly, erring, blameable (*Praem.* 1.20), and unable to produce wisdom or pursue what is genuine (*Ios.* 1.59[–66]).

[20] Cf. Culpepper's conclusion that "[t]he crowd represents the struggle of those who are open to believing, but neither the scriptures nor the signs lead them to authentic faith" (Culpepper, *Anatomy of the Fourth Gospel*, 132).

If "plot" is the logical and causal sequence of events, the plot of John's Gospel relates to the revelation of the Father and Son in terms of their identity, character, mission, and relationship, and people's response to this revelation.[21] The Gospel's plot is affected by John's strategy to persuade the reader to believe that Jesus is the Christ and the source of everlasting life or salvation (20:31).[22] The crowd advances the plot a little in that their questioning and theological reasoning about Jesus' identity provides Jesus an opportunity to elaborate.

Finally, we must determine the crowd's significance for today. The crowd as a character has not received much attention because, typically, it seems a mass of "grey," faceless people. So also in life, many people prefer to remain anonymous, moving with the crowd. The crowd represents people who are initially enthusiastic and show potential for discipleship but who tend toward sensationalism, division, and misunderstanding, and eventually reject Jesus. Even though some may make positive responses, these must be evaluated. Some people in the crowd may show superficial faith in Jesus as a miracle worker, which disappears when it is challenged; others "believe" but are afraid to acknowledge this publicly. For John, a true believer is someone who publicly confesses belief in Jesus, so remaining in the crowd as a "secret believer" is inadequate.

---

[21] Cf. Culpepper, *Anatomy of the Fourth Gospel*, 79–98; Andrew T. Lincoln, *The Gospel according to Saint John* (BNTC 4; London: Continuum, 2005), 11–12; Nicolas Farelly, *The Disciples in the Fourth Gospel: A Narrative Analysis of their Faith and Understanding* (WUNT II/290; Tübingen: Mohr Siebeck, 2010), 168–69.

[22] Cf. Culpepper, *Anatomy of the Fourth Gospel*, 98.

The Boy with Loaves and Fish: Picnic, Plot, and Pattern

Dieter T. Roth

In R. Alan Culpepper's important study, *Anatomy of the Fourth Gospel: A Study in Literary Design,* he notes "One of the most interesting elements of any story is the cast of characters which populate it. Characters are defined by what they do (action) and what they say (dialogue) as well as what is said about them by the narrator or by other characters."[1] Though this observation is undoubtedly correct, it raises the question of just how interesting a character can be who does not explicitly do anything, who speaks no word, and about whom the narrator says next to nothing. The apparent insignificance of such a character may well explain why a survey of commentaries on John reveals that apart from the occasional discussion on the meaning of the term παιδάριον, there are rarely any comments on the boy with the five barley loaves and two fish in John 6:9.[2] Though simple and undeveloped, this character nevertheless, from the perspective of a plot analysis, is significant for the narrative.[3] At the same time, his implied action and his bread and fish implicitly embody certain Johannine themes and images.

In the account of the miraculous feeding in John, a plot analysis according to the quinary scheme unfolds as follows.[4] In the *initial situation,* Jesus is on

---

[1] R. Alan Culpepper, *Anatomy of the Fourth Gospel: A Study in Literary Design* (Philadelphia: Fortress, 1983), 7.

[2] An exception is found in Thomas L. Brodie, *The Gospel According to John: A Literary and Theological Commentary* (Oxford: Oxford University Press, 1993), 261–62. One can also mention the comments by Arthur John Gossip, which, though at some points rather imaginative, also strongly integrate this character into the narrative (idem, *John* [IB 8; New York: Abingdon, 1952], 555). On the other hand, even when the character is mentioned, at times the reference only serves to minimize, or perhaps even to denigrate, his role. This occurs, e. g., when Michael Labahn states that the boy "ist keine *persona dramatis*" and goes on to compare him to a "stummer Diener" (idem, *Jesus als Lebensspender: Untersuchungen zu einer Geschichte der johanneischen Tradition anhand ihrer Wundergeschichten* [BZNW 98; Berlin: de Gruyter, 1999], 270).

[3] For an examination of how a Gospel writer can utilize minor characters to influence the reader, see Joel F. Williams, *Other Followers of Jesus: Minor Characters as Major Figures in Mark's Gospel* (JSNTSup 102; Sheffield: JSOT, 1994).

[4] For a helpful overview of plot analysis, see Daniel Marguerat and Yvan Bourquin, *How to Read Bible Stories: An Introduction to Narrative Criticism* (trans. J. Bowden; London: SCM,

the move, is followed by a large crowd, and sits down with his disciples on a mountain (John 6:1-3). The *complication* is introduced as Jesus asks Philip "Where are we to buy bread for these people to eat?" (John 6:5). Through an example of "zero focalization,"[5] the narrator informs the reader that Jesus knew what he was going to do and that this question is a test (v. 6), a test which Philip appears to fail with his response (v. 7).[6] At the outset of the *transforming action,* Andrew, the disciple who elsewhere also functions as an individual introducing characters to Jesus (John 1:41-42; 12:21-22), here presents a boy "who has five barley loaves and two fish," though also, harkening back to the complication, adds "But what are they among so many people?" (v. 9). In this rather inauspicious manner, the boy is introduced as a character in the narrative. Jesus, however, initially does not respond to this introduction, instead saying "Make the people sit down" (v. 10). Only then does he take the loaves and fish from the boy and distribute them to all the people (v. 11). In the *denouement,* the crowd eats its fill and the disciples collect twelve baskets full of the fragments of leftover bread (vss. 12-13), and in the *final situation* the crowd proclaims that Jesus is the Prophet who is to come into the world (v. 14).

Though the boy disappears from the narrative just as quickly as he appeared, within the context of the transforming action it is he who provides the "little" that Jesus makes to be enough "for so many." In this way, the boy can be understood within the plot as embodying the "helper" facet within the actantial model advanced by A. J. Greimas.[7] That is to say, it is the boy who stands at a key point in the plot and provides the means for the transition from "there's no way we can buy enough bread" to the miraculous provision of the crowd with twelve baskets left over. In his imaginative commentary on the pericope, Arthur John Gossip concludes with the thought that on "that night he [the boy] burst into his home, with his eyes shining and his cheeks on fire, to tell them of the miracle that 'I and Jesus' wrought! And his bold

---

1999), 40-57. The discussion above utilizes the labels for the five components of the quinary scheme found in this text (p. 43).

[5] Different from "internal focalization," where a narrative says only that which a character knows, and "external focalization," where the narrative reveals less than what a character knows, "zero focalization" refers to the situation when a narrator says or reveals more than any of the characters in the narrative knows.

[6] Culpepper comments that Philip fails his "bread" test (6:5-7) and later fails his "Greek" test (12:21-22), though he begins well by bringing Nathanael to Jesus (Culpepper, *Anatomy of the Fourth Gospel,* 120).

[7] See Algirdas J. Greimas, *Sémantique structural: Recherche et méthode* (Paris: Larousse, 1966). Though stringently structuralist models have rightly been criticized (cf. the helpful survey in Fotis Jannidis, "Character," in *Handbook of Narratology* [ed. Peter Hühn et al.; Berlin: de Gruyter, 2009], 14-29), there is still benefit in considering the place a character has simply within the plot, especially when the character can hardly be considered from any other perspective.

claim was true."⁸ As Thomas L. Brodie observes, though this nameless boy is "hidden behind the figure of Andrew" he is "ahead of the action" and "does all he can" leading to the important observation: "[H]is role is decisive."⁹ In this way a minor and at first glance unimportant character is actually revealed to be a key figure in the narrative.

Having considered the significance of the boy for the plot of this miracle story, further observations are worth making regarding the possible intertexual shaping of this character, as well as his having given Jesus "bread" and "fish." First, the boy is called a παιδάριον, a double diminutive of παῖς and a term that occurs only here in the NT.¹⁰ Its meaning is equivocal, and can be used of a "youth," but not necessarily a young boy (cf. its use in the LXX for Joseph in Gen 37:30), or a "young slave" (cf. its use in *Mart. Pol.* 6:1; 7:1). C. K. Barrett, positing an intertextual connection with 2 Kgs 4:42–44, where Elisha is assisted by a servant in his miraculous feeding of one hundred men, suggests that John may have drawn intertextually on this servant being called a παιδάριον in LXX 2 Kgs 4:38, 41.¹¹ Second, there are interesting potential connections to patterns and themes in John relating to "bread" and "fish." Though the text explicitly states only that Jesus took (ἔλαβεν) the bread and fish (v. 11), one can legitimately infer that the boy gave the food which he had to Jesus.¹² Though the point is not developed in this pericope, it is at least interesting to note the way in which this youth fits into the pattern of bread being "given" in John. Jesus does not create bread *ex nihilo,* as it were, but multiplies bread that is "given" to him. Later in John 6, Jesus criticizes the multitudes for pursuing him "not because you saw signs, but because you ate your fill of the loaves" (6:26), which leads into the admonition not to labor for food that perishes, but the food that endures to eternal life (v. 27). The remainder of John 6 revolves around the theme of the bread from heaven, Jesus himself, which the Father gives (v. 32). The boy gave bread that Jesus used to fill stomachs; God gave the bread from heaven to provide eternal life. In the narrative, the provi-

---

⁸ Gossip, *John,* 555.

⁹ Brodie, *John,* 262.

¹⁰ Cf. Jan G. van der Watt, *Family of the King: Dynamics of Metaphor in the Gospel According to John* (BIS 47; Leiden: Brill, 2000) for a consideration of the way in which family, including "son"/"child," plays an important metaphorical role in the Johannine narrative.

¹¹ C. Kingsley Barrett, *The Gospel According to St. John: An Introduction with Commentary and Notes on the Greek Text* (2d ed.; Philadelphia: Westminster, 1978), 275. It should be noted, however, that in the actual "feeding" pericope, the servant is called a λειτουργός (v. 43), and it is in the previous pericope where the servant is called a παιδάριον. Cf. also Steven A. Hunt, *Rewriting the Feeding of Five Thousand: John 6:1–15 as a Test Case for Johannine Dependence on the Synoptic Gospels* (SBL 125; New York: Peter Lang, 2011), 254–55.

¹² At several points in John the act of receiving something is clearly linked to it having been given (e. g., John 3:27 and 17:8). Furthermore, it is also worth noting that though the narrative indicates that Andrew pointed out the boy and his resources, it does not indicate that Andrew gave the bread and fish to Jesus.

sion in the former instance allows for the transition to the teaching of the latter. In addition, the boy gives not only bread, but also fish (ὀψάρια). In the NT, this term occurs only in John 6:9, 11 and in John 21. In the last chapter of John, it is Jesus who has prepared bread and fish (21:9) and who gives both to the disciples (21:13). Within the twenty-one chapter form of John, upon a second reading the action of the boy in John 6 anticipates the action of Jesus himself in John 21.[13]

This brief consideration of the boy with the loaves and fish in John 6 has revealed the way in which even a silent and flat character in John can have relative importance. In the plot, this "helper" is vital for the narrative's development and without this character the miracle cannot take place in its present narrated form. In addition, his presence may carry intertextual echoes from the OT and he embodies at least some important Johannine themes and images. Thus, though one may legitimately identify the boy with the loaves and fish as a "minor character" he certainly may not be spoken of as an "insignificant character."

---

[13] As is well known, John 21 is often viewed as an appendix to a Gospel originally ending at 20:31. It is worth considering, however, that Paul S. Minear, "The Original Functions of John 21," *JBL* 102 (1983): 85–98 has argued that the chapter always was a crucial part of the design of the text and Richard Bauckham has pointed out that though chapter 21 could be regarded as an epilogue, "an epilogue need not be an afterthought: it may be integral to the design of the work" (*The Testimony of the Beloved Disciple: Narrative, History, and Theology in the Gospel of John* [Grand Rapids, Mich.: Baker Academic, 2007], 78). For example, "[T]his epilogue completes the double story of Peter and the beloved disciple, which began in chapter 13" (ibid.). Cf. also Hartwig Thyen, *Das Johannesevangelium* (HNT 6; Tübingen: Mohr Siebeck, 2005), 4–5, 771–96.

Judas (the Betrayer):
The Black Sheep of the Family

Cornelis Bennema

Identity and Role of Judas

In the Gospel of John, the name of Judas appears in three forms: (i) "Judas" (13:29; 18:2–3, 5); (ii) "Judas (the) Iscariot" (12:4); (iii) "Judas, [son] of Simon Iscariot" (6:71; 13:2, 26). Judas, the Greek variant of the Hebrew Judah, one of the patriarchs of the twelve tribes of Israel, was a popular name in first-century Palestine.[1] There is more uncertainty about the name "Iscariot." Most scholars hold that it refers to Judas's hometown Kerioth, presumably in southern Judea but some have suggested Moab.[2] A few have suggested that "Iscariot" indicates Judas was one of the Sicarii or "dagger-men" – urban assassins who attacked the Jewish aristocracy.[3] However, the Sicarii only surfaced in the 50s and became prominent during the first Jewish war, too late for Judas to have belonged to this group. Others have argued that "Iscariot" is an Aramaic occupational surname, meaning "(red) dyer."[4] This divergence of theories prevents us from inferring too much about Judas's name.[5] In the character analysis that follows, I shall unpack other epithets given to Judas: "devil" (6:70), "betrayer" (literally, ὁ παραδιδούς [6:71; 12:4; 13:11; 18:2, 5]), "thief" (12:4), and "son of perdition" (17:12). Additional clues to Judas's identity show that he belonged to Jesus' inner group of disciples, called "the Twelve" (6:71; 12:4), and within this group, he was the treasurer (12:6; 13:29).

Judas has certainly made a mark in history. According to the Oxford English dictionary, a Judas is "a person who betrays a friend" – a traitor. Traditionally, Judas is infamous for having betrayed Jesus but William Klassen challenges this view.[6] He argues that Judas's act of "handing over" was not one of

---

[1] William Klassen, *Judas: Betrayer or Friend of Jesus?* (Minneapolis: Fortress, 1996), 29–30.

[2] R. Alan Culpepper, *Anatomy of the Fourth Gospel: A Study in Literary Design* (Philadelphia: Fortress, 1983), 124; Andreas J. Köstenberger, *John* (BECNT; Grand Rapids, Mich.: Baker Academic, 2004), 222. Cf. the scholars mentioned by Klassen, *Judas*, 32–33.

[3] E. g., Oscar Cullmann, *Jesus and the Revolutionaries* (New York: Scribner's, 1970), 21–23.

[4] Albert Ehrman, "Judas Iscariot and Abba Saqqara," *JBL* 97 (1978): 572–73; Yoel Arbeitman, "The Suffix of Iscariot," *JBL* 99 (1980): 122–24.

[5] Klassen, *Judas*, 34.

betrayal but of informing the temple authorities – an act authorized by Jesus in line with God's purposes.[7] Central to Klassen's case is his discussion on the meaning of the verb παραδιδόναι. According to him, παραδιδόναι, which is virtually always translated "to betray" in connection with Judas's act, *never* connotes "betray" in Greek literature – whether in classical Greek, the Septuagint, Josephus, or the New Testament – but simply means "to hand over."[8] A critique of Klassen's linguistic study of παραδιδόναι in Greek literature is beyond the scope of this essay – and perhaps unnecessary; I only need to examine how the term is used in the Johannine narrative.[9] Although the basic lexical sense of παραδιδόναι is "to give over, to hand over," I must determine how *John* uses the term and whether it has connotations of betrayal.

The verb παραδιδόναι occurs fifteen times in John's Gospel. It is used in a neutral sense only once – in 19:30, to refer to Jesus' handing over the Spirit as his life-force. Four times, there are negative implications for Jesus but no sense of betrayal (18:30, 35, 36; 19:16). The ten remaining occurrences, referring to Judas's act of handing Jesus over (6:64, 71; 12:4; 13:2, 11, 21; 18:2, 5; 19:11; 21:20), clearly have negative connotations with the force of "to betray." In 6:70–71, for example, Judas who will "hand Jesus over" is designated a devil, and, in contrast to true disciples, is juxtaposed with those who do not believe (6:64). Jesus identifies the one who will "hand him over" as unclean (13:11) and thinking of him causes agitation (13:21). Judas's act of handing Jesus over to the Jewish temple police and a Roman cohort of soldiers obviously has negative consequences since the Jewish authorities have already plotted Jesus' death (11:47–53). In 19:11, when Jesus declares to Pilate that the one who "handed him over" has a greater sin, Jesus probably means Judas.[10] Thus, con-

---

[6] Klassen, *Judas, passim*. The apocryphal *Gospel of Judas* seems to support Klassen's case. Wilhelm Pratscher, for example, claims that the *Gospel of Judas* enables a better understanding of the historical Judas ("Judas Iskariot im Neuen Testament und im Judasevangelium," *NovT* 52 [2010]: 1–23). For a more sober assessment of the use of the *Gospel of Judas* in relation to early Christianity, see Simon Gathercole, *The Gospel of Judas: Rewriting Early Christianity* (Oxford: Oxford University Press, 2007).

[7] Klassen, *Judas*, 62–74.

[8] Klassen, *Judas*, 47–58. Cf. Klaus Beckmann, "Funktion und Gestalt des Judas Iskarioth im Johannesevangelium," *BTZ* 11 (1994): 181–200 (he prefers the term "dahingeben" ["to give away"] for παραδιδόναι); Anthony Cane, *The Place of Judas Iscariot in Christology* (Aldershot: Ashgate, 2005), 19–24; Pratscher, "Judas," 11–12. Similarly, Martin Meiser claims that παραδιδόναι acquired the sense "to betray" only after Judas's act (idem, *Judas Iskariot: Einer von uns* [Leipzig: Evangelische Verlagsanstalt, 2004], 49). Examining various options, Meiser then remains agnostic about what Judas actually has done (Meiser, *Judas Iskariot*, 50–57).

[9] In fact, F. A. Gosling evaluates Klassen's lexicographical study and observes that the rendering "to betray" for παραδιδόναι is found in classical Greek, the Septuagint, Josephus, and the New Testament (idem, "O Judas! What Have You Done?," *EvQ* 71 [1999]: 117–25).

[10] The majority of occurrences of παραδιδόναι refer to Judas. Judas's sin is greater than Pilate's because unlike Pilate (19:11) Judas has no divine authority; rather, his "authority" to betray Jesus comes from the devil (cf. 13:2, 27). Alternatively, the reference may be to "the Jews" who hand Jesus over to Pilate (18:30, 35) (Jesus' use of the singular is perhaps generic)

tra Klassen, Judas's act of handing Jesus over to the Jewish and Roman authorities is depicted by John as a negative act – an act of betrayal. Even though παραδιδόναι does not mean "to betray," *John* unmistakably attaches the nuance of betrayal to the verb when he uses it in connection with Judas's act.[11]

Character Analysis of Judas

Method

I must explain my method of character analysis before reconstructing the character of Judas from the Johannine text. If John's Gospel is the story of Jesus Christ, it will consist of a plot, events, and characters. While much has been written on plot and events, character appears to be the neglected child. There is no comprehensive theory of character in either literary theory or biblical criticism, and therefore no consensus amongst scholars on how to analyze, classify, and evaluate characters.[12] Most scholars provide only a few theoretical considerations or describe most Johannine characters in reductionistic terms as simply "flat" or representative types.[13] Using the comprehensive theory of character that I recently developed, I will (i) *analyze* the character of Judas along three dimensions (complexity, development, and inner life), (ii) *classify* the resulting character on a continuum of degree of characterization (from agent to type to personality to individuality), and (iii) *evaluate* the character according to John's point of view.[14] This needs further clarification.

---

or to Caiaphas as the leader of "the Jews" (although "to hand over" is never used with reference to him, he is the leading voice in 11:47–53).

[11] Cf. Harry T. Fleddermann, "Review of W. Klassen, *Judas: Betrayer or Friend of Jesus?* (Minneapolis: Fortress, 1996)," *CBQ* 59 (1997): 772; Lyle Eslinger, "Judas Game: The Biology of Combat in the Gospel of John," *JSNT* 77 (2000): 45–73, here 57, fn. 34; William M. Wright, "Greco-Roman Character Typing and the Presentation of Judas in the Fourth Gospel," *CBQ* 71 (2009): 544–59, here 551, fn. 22.

[12] Notable exceptions are, in literary and media theory, Fotis Jannidis, *Figur und Person: Beitrag zu einer historischen Narratologie* (Berlin: De Gruyter, 2004); Jens Eder, *Die Figur im Film: Grundlagen der Figurenanalye* (Marburg: Schüren, 2008), and in biblical criticism, Sönke Finnern, *Narratologie und biblische Exegese: Eine integrative Methode der Erzählanalyse und ihr Ertrag am Beispiel von Matthäus 28* (WUNT II/285; Tübingen: Mohr Siebeck, 2010), 125–64. However, Finnern seems to provide more of a comprehensive overview of aspects of character (mainly relying on Jens Eder's work on character in film) than a coherent, robust theory.

[13] See the overview of Johannine scholarship in Cornelis Bennema, *Encountering Jesus: Character Studies in the Gospel of John* (Milton Keynes: Paternoster, 2009), 2–12. Cf. Jerome H. Neyrey, who still adheres to the Aristotelian view that the Johannine characters are types that represent a particular trait (idem, *The Gospel of John* [NCBC; Cambridge: Cambridge University Press, 2007], 5–6). Wright also analyzes Judas against the backdrop of Greco-Roman moral character typing, resulting in Judas being a one-dimensional character (Wright, "Character Typing," 544–59). However, characterization in ancient Greco-Roman literature was more complex and varied – characters could be round and developing, albeit not to the extent that we see in modern literature (see my article in fn. 14 below).

[14] Cornelis Bennema, "A Theory of Character in the Fourth Gospel with Reference to

Analysis. Instead of placing a character in fixed categories (flat/round, static/dynamic, simple/complex), I suggest that character moves along a continuum or various continua. Hence, it is better to speak of degrees of characterization. I analyze the Johannine characters, using the non-reductionist model of Jewish scholar Yosef Ewen. He advocates three continua or axes upon which a character may be situated:
- Complexity: characters range from those displaying a single trait to those displaying a complex web of traits, with varying degrees of complexity in between;
- Development: characters may vary from those who show no development to those who are fully developed;
- Penetration into the inner life: characters range from those who, via the narrator, allow us a peek inside their minds to those whose minds remain opaque.[15]

Classification. After analyzing the character along these three continua, I plot the resulting character on a continuum of degree of characterization as (i) an agent, actant, or walk-on; (ii) a type, stock, or flat character; (iii) a character with personality; or (iv) an individual or person.[16]

Evaluation. Besides analyzing and classifying a character, I also evaluate it from the author's ideological point of view. Any meaningful communication, whether verbal or non-verbal, has a particular purpose – a message that the sender wants to get across to the receiver. In line with its salvific purpose (20:30–31), John tells his story from a particular perspective called "point of view."[17] Stephen Moore defines point of view as "the rhetorical activity of an author as he or she attempts, from a position within some socially shared system of assumptions and convictions, to impose a story-world upon an audience by the manipulation of narrative perspective."[18] James Resseguie states that point of view is "the *mode* or *angle of vision* from which characters, dialo-

---

Ancient and Modern Literature," *BibInt* 17 (2009): 375–421. I have recently sharpened my theory further in Cornelis Bennema, "A Comprehensive Approach to Understanding Character in the Gospel of John," in *Characters and Characterization in the Gospel of John* (ed. Christopher W. Skinner; LNTS 461; New York: T&T Clark, 2013), 36–58.

[15] Ewen's works are only available in Hebrew but his theory is summarized in Shlomith Rimmon-Kenan, *Narrative Fiction: Contemporary Poetics* (New York: Methuen, 1983), 41–42.

[16] The categories "personality" and "individual/person" to classify ancient characters refer to a "collectivist identity" or "group-oriented personality," where the person's identity is *embedded* in a larger group or community, rather than to a modern autonomous individual (cf. Bruce J. Malina, *The New Testament World: Insights from Cultural Anthropology* [3d ed.; Louisville, Ky.: Westminster John Knox, 2001], 60–67).

[17] Others prefer the term "focalization" (Rimmon-Kenan, *Narrative Fiction*, 72; D. Francois Tolmie, *Jesus' Farewell to the Disciples: John 13:1-17:26 in Narratological Perspective* [BIS 12; Leiden: Brill, 1995], 170).

[18] Stephen D. Moore, *Literary Criticism and the Gospels: The Theoretical Challenge* (New Haven: Yale University Press, 1989), 181.

gue, actions, setting, and events are considered or observed. But also point of view is the narrator's *attitude towards* or *evaluation of* characters, dialogue, actions, setting and events."[19] The implication is that a narrative is not neutral since it has an inbuilt perspective that is communicated to the reader, and hence we must evaluate Judas's character in the light of John's evaluative point of view.

In the remainder of this section, I will carry out the character analysis of Judas along the three dimensions that I just outlined, while the classification and evaluation of Judas's character occur in the final section.

Character Complexity

The degree of a character's complexity has to do with its traits. As Seymour Chatman asserts, we reconstruct character by inferring traits from the information in the text, in which trait is a "relatively stable or abiding personal quality."[20] The character traits of Judas are revealed both by "showing" and "telling," i. e., they are inferred from Judas's interaction with other characters and from the information mentioned by the narrator.[21] In the following analysis, I will demonstrate that Judas is a complex character whose dominant traits are betrayal and apostasy, but who also shows secondary traits of indifference, hypocrisy, unreliability, dishonesty, and disloyalty.

Betrayal. John's primary characterization of Judas as "the one who betrays him [Jesus]" indicates Judas's main trait. Judas's betrayal of Jesus is foretold on numerous occasions by both Jesus (6:64; 13:21) and the narrator (6:71; 12:4; 13:2, 11; 18:2, 5), while 18:1–12 describes Judas's concrete act of betrayal, precipitating Jesus' arrest. I observe that his act is clearly premeditated. First, Judas uses his inside knowledge of Jesus' habits to reveal his whereabouts (18:2). Second, he brings with him a cohort of Roman soldiers and the temple police of the Jewish religious authorities to arrest Jesus (18:3).[22] Judas thus aligns himself

---

[19] James L. Resseguie, *The Strange Gospel: Narrative Design and Point of View in John* (BIS 56; Leiden: Brill, 2001), 1 (original emphasis).

[20] Seymour Chatman, *Story and Discourse: Narrative Structure in Fiction and Film* (Ithaca, N.Y.: Cornell University Press, 1978), 119, 126 (quotation from p. 126). Elsewhere, Chatman defines trait more extensively as "a narrative adjective out of the vernacular labeling a personal quality of a character, as it persists over part or whole of the story" (Chatman, *Story and Discourse*, 125). When we infer a character's traits from the deep structure of an ancient text, it is inevitable that we use trait-names that are familiar to our modern world. Using modern terminology to analyze and describe characters in ancient literature is acceptable provided that we remember that we use categories unknown to the ancient authors and audiences (Bennema, "Theory of Character," 394, fn. 86, 396–97).

[21] Cf. James L. Resseguie, *Narrative Criticism of the New Testament: An Introduction* (Grand Rapids, Mich.: Baker Academic, 2005), 126–28.

[22] The failed attempts of the temple police to arrest Jesus (7:32, 44–45; cf. 7:30; 8:20, 59; 10:39) may explain why Judas brought an unusually large number of soldiers and police to arrest a single man.

with "the Jews" (Jesus' main opponents) and the Roman oppressors.²³ The narrator's telling that Judas "stood with them" (18:5) also indicates that he no longer was with Jesus, in contrast to those who "stood with Jesus" (3:29; 19:25). In fact, Judas and "the Jews" are linked in that they are both controlled by the devil (8:44; 13:2, 27). In the final section, I will show that betrayal is Judas's overarching trait rather than one in isolation of his other traits.²⁴

Apostasy. In the Johannine context, apostasy is the defection from Jesus to the opposition – the devil. Judas is characterized by apostasy both in his being identified as a "devil" (6:71) and "son of perdition" (17:12), as well as in his behavior (13:1–30). I start with the epithet "devil" to describe Judas. At a crucial time when many of his disciples start defecting, Jesus challenges "the Twelve" on their loyalty to him and Peter assures him that they will stick with him (6:60–69).²⁵ What Peter does not know, and Jesus reveals, is that even among "the Twelve" there is a devil (6:70) – Judas, who will betray Jesus, as the narrator clarifies (6:71).²⁶ The reference to Judas as a devil probably implies that he will side with the devil or that his behavior resembles that of the devil. The devil's main occupation is to lie and kill (8:44). Similarly, Judas lies (12:5–6) and, through his betrayal, abets the killing of Jesus (John 18–19). The devil, who plants the idea of betraying Jesus, uses Judas as his instrument (13:2, 27).²⁷

---

²³ Cf. Beckmann, who sees Judas as a representative of "the Jews," albeit not in a negative sense ("Funktion und Gestalt des Judas," 198–200).

²⁴ Steven Hunt helpfully points out that even though Judas only betrays Jesus once and hence one could object that this constitutes a trait, it probably does because the narrator keeps referring to it.

²⁵ Seeing a parallel with Jesus' rebuke of Peter in Mark 8:33, some suggest that John seeks to improve on Peter by putting an anti-Judas spin on this story (Klassen, *Judas*, 140; Hans-Josef Klauck, *Judas: Ein Jünger des Herrn* [QD 111; Freiburg: Herder, 1987], 74–75). However, I have rejected such an interpretation (Bennema, *Encountering Jesus*, 55).

²⁶ Klassen's interpretation of 6:70–71 that Judas is an adversary in the legal sense at Jesus' right hand to present evidence, just as the διάβολος did in Job 1, Zechariah 3:1, and Psalm 108:6 (LXX) (Klassen, *Judas*, 141), seems far-fetched. Considering 6:64, James V. Brownson argues that Judas is even characterized as an unbelieving insider who rejects the christological claims regarding Jesus' divine identity and origin (idem, "Neutralizing the Intimate Enemy: The Portrayal of Judas in the Fourth Gospel," SBLSP 31 [1992]: 50–51). Although 6:64 may simply indicate that Jesus knew those who did not believe *and* the one who was going to betray him, the juxtaposition of unbelief and betrayal suggests a relation between the two. Besides, if Jesus' reply in 6:70 implicitly corrects the "we know" in Peter's confession in 6:69, then Judas is marked by unbelief (cf. Dongsue Kim, *An Exegesis of Apostasy Embedded in John's Narratives of Peter and Judas against the Synoptic Parallels* [SBEC 61; Lewiston: Edwin Mellen, 2004], 154–55, 159; Klauck, *Judas*, 72, 74).

²⁷ Klauck's remark that Judas harbored his criminal plans from the beginning (i. e., when he joined Jesus) is unwarranted (Klauck, *Judas*, 73). Similarly, Margaret Davies contends that Jesus knew whom he had chosen (13:18) and, by implication, that he chose Judas so that Scripture might be fulfilled (idem, *Rhetoric and Reference in the Fourth Gospel* [JSNTSup 69; Sheffield: JSOT Press, 1992], 331). However, I prefer to distinguish between Jesus' foreknowledge of Judas's inclination and actions, and Judas's own development in this role. Although

Regarding the epithet "son of destruction" for Judas (17:12), I believe James Brownson is correct in understanding the term as a genitive of origin rather than a genitive of purpose ("son destined for destruction") or an adjectival genitive ("destroying son").[28] Brownson thus argues that the Greek term ἀπώλεια ("destruction") probably stands for the Hebrew *Abaddon*, a term used for hell (Prov 15:11; 27:20; 1QH 3:16, 19, 32) or hell personified, the devil (Job 28:22). And this reference to Judas as "son of hell" is in keeping with similar phrases in Jewish apocalyptic and early Christian literature.[29] Indeed, the reference to Judas as "son of destruction/hell" corresponds to the earlier description of Judas as "devil" (6:71). The epithet may also evoke the image of the thief who comes to destroy in 10:10 since the word for "thief" occurs only in 10:1, 8, 10 and then again in 12:6 specifically with reference to Judas.[30] Thus, Jesus' reference to Judas in 17:12 as "son of destruction" implies that Judas is an agent of the devil, in that he belongs to the devil and acts like him.

Judas's apostate behavior is tragically described in John 13. The narrator clearly informs the reader in 13:2 that Judas is going to betray Jesus. What is less clear is whose "heart" is in view in 13:2 – whether the devil had already decided in *his* heart that Judas should betray Jesus or that the devil had put it in *Judas's* heart to betray Jesus. I favor the latter interpretation because Jesus' comment to his disciples, "And you are clean, but not all of you," should be understood in the light of Judas's betrayal – it suggests that Judas is not clean (13:10b–11).[31]

---

not impossible, I consider it unlikely that Judas joined Jesus' group as a thief and devil, with the premeditated plan to betray Jesus.

[28] Brownson, "Enemy," 52. Cf. Klassen, *Judas*, 152. Contra those who interpret the term as Judas being (pre)destined for destruction (Raymond E. Brown, *The Gospel According to John* [AB 29; London: Chapman, 1971], 2:760; C. Kingsley Barrett, *The Gospel According to St John: An Introduction with Commentary and Notes on the Greek Text* [2d ed.; London: SPCK, 1978], 508; Kim, *Exegesis of Apostasy*, 152, 178). Whether Judas was (pre)destined for destruction was probably not an issue for John. See also the discussion in Wolfgang Fenske, *Brauchte Gott den Verräter? Die Gestalt des Judas in Theologie, Unterricht und Gottesdienst* (Göttingen: Vandenhoeck & Ruprecht, 2000), 69–72.

[29] Brownson, "Enemy," 52. Cf. Klassen, *Judas*, 152–53, 158, fn. 53; Klauck, *Judas*, 87–88; Donald A. Carson, *The Gospel According to John* (Leicester: InterVarsity Press, 1991), 563.

[30] For a detailed analysis of "thieves" in John 10, see Ruben Zimmermann, *Christologie der Bilder im Johannesevangelium: Die Christopoetik des vierten Evangelium unter besonderer Berücksichtigung von Joh 10* (WUNT 171; Tübingen: Mohr Siebeck, 2004), 259–65, 312–16, 340–44.

[31] Cf. Rudolf Bultmann, *The Gospel of John: A Commentary* (trans. G. R. Beasley-Murray; Philadelphia: Westminster, 1971), 464, fn. 2. Amongst those who favor the former interpretation, are Brownson, "Enemy," 52; Francis J. Moloney, *The Gospel of John* (SP 4; Collegeville, Minn.: Liturgical Press, 1998), 378; Kim, *Exegesis of Apostasy*, 190–91. There is no suggestion that Judas was excluded from the footwashing – it simply did not benefit him. Klassen deals poorly with Judas's uncleanness, arguing that John, like the Essenes, views purity in broad terms as including financial matters and ritual purity (Klassen, *Judas*, 151–52). The footwashing clearly has salvific overtones – it foreshadows Jesus' death on the cross and the completion of the disciples' spiritual cleansing. Judas, however, is not clean and will not partake in Jesus' salvific death. Although Cane perceptively raises the issue of how it is that Jesus' foot-

But even if Judas was unaware of the devil's plan in 13:2, he quickly learned of it because his sudden departure in 13:30 indicates that he understood Jesus' gesture and comment in 13:26–27. In 13:18, Jesus refers again to Judas's imminent betrayal, using the phrase "The one who eats my bread has lifted his heel against me," which is better translated as "The one with whom I shared a close relationship has opposed me." Jesus speaks of this event as a fulfilment of Psalm 41:9, where David speaks of being betrayed by an intimate friend whom he trusted and had table-fellowship with.[32] In 13:21–30, a similar scene is played out between Jesus and Judas. Besides serving to identify Judas as the betrayer, Jesus' gesture of sharing bread in 13:26 may also represent a last effort to restore fellowship.[33] In 13:1, John states that Jesus loves people to the end, and here we see Jesus showing his love for Judas until the very "end," when Satan enters into Judas after he takes the piece of bread (13:27).[34] Judas's "end" is then secured: not only does the devil prompt Judas (13:2), he also indwells him (13:27).[35] Judas, indwelled by the devil, stands in sharp contrast to the disciples, who are indwelled by the Father and Son (14:23; cf. 17:21–23). Judas has become a devil or his embodiment (cf. 6:70–71), a defector and apostate, switching his allegiance from Jesus to Satan. After receiving the piece of bread from Jesus, Judas leaves immediately – literally, but also symbolically, leaving the fellowship of Jesus (13:30). The dramatic, abrupt sentence, "And it was night," in 13:30 reinforces the solemnity: besides being a literal reference to late evening, it also refers to a spiritual reality, namely, the darkness caused by Satan in driving Judas to his act of betrayal.[36] Judas's being indwelled by the devil and leaving

---

washing is unable to cleanse Judas from the devil's influence, his conclusion that Judas is either treated unjustly or is evidence of a salvific failure (Cane, *Judas*, 36–37) seems unwarranted. Cf. Culpepper, who remarks with reference to 13:11 and 17:12 that Judas's loss was Jesus' failure (Culpepper, *Anatomy of the Fourth Gospel*, 125). Others, however, claim that Judas's loss was not due to any deficiency on the part of Jesus (Andrew T. Lincoln, *The Gospel According to John* [BNTC; Peabody, Mass.: Hendrickson, 2005], 437; Nicolas Farelly, *The Disciples in the Fourth Gospel: A Narrative Analysis of Their Faith and Understanding* [WUNT II/290; Tübingen: Mohr Siebeck, 2010], 114).

[32] Kim contends that John might have had in mind Ahithophel's betrayal of David, and he also sees an allusion to the "heel" motif of Genesis 3:15 which prophesies the cosmic conflict between Satan and the Son of God (Kim, *Exegesis of Apostasy*, 183–88).

[33] Cf. Beckmann, who states that, against the backdrop of 6:1–15, Jesus is in 13:26 "unmittelbar als Geber des Brotes präsent" (Beckmann, "Funktion und Gestalt des Judas," 187–88). Referring to ancient seating arrangements, Craig S. Keener suggests that the Beloved Disciple and Judas held the honored positions on either side of Jesus (idem, *The Gospel of John: A Commentary* [2 vols.; Peabody, Mass.: Hendrickson, 2003], 915–16).

[34] Cf. Eva Krafft, who states that Judas has twice witnessed acts of love – Mary's devotion of Jesus in John 12 and Jesus' footwashing in John 13 – but also twice closed himself from them (idem, "Die Personen des Johannesevangeliums," *EvT* 16 [1956]: 29–30).

[35] Contra Kim, who contends that Judas is not so much influenced by the devil to betray Jesus as he wilfully hardens his heart and invites the devil to work through him (Kim, *Exegesis of Apostasy*, 191–92).

[36] Hence, Raymond F. Collins calls Judas "a figure of the night" (idem, "Representative

the presence of Jesus heralds the approaching darkness precipitated by the devil. So, this passage records the tragic defection and apostasy of Judas in a context that promotes discipleship. While Jesus exhorts his disciples to emulate him and to exemplify humility and service (13:1–20), the devil prompts Judas to defect and negate discipleship. The character of Judas embodies the most negative of all responses to Jesus: defection, apostasy, and betrayal.

Indifference, Unreliability, Hypocrisy, Dishonesty, Disloyalty. During a dinner given in Lazarus's home in honor of Jesus, Mary's devotion is contrasted by the early stages of Judas's defection (12:1–8). Although we have known since 6:70–71 that Judas will betray Jesus, it is only in John 12–13 that the character and role of Judas emerge. After reminding his readers that Judas will betray Jesus (12:4), John says that Judas is a thief (12:6).[37] As the treasurer of the group, Judas would have preferred to receive the large sum of money that the perfume could fetch, so he could keep a part for himself (12:6). Learning that Judas *as the treasurer* is a thief highlights his dishonesty and disloyalty to the group – he betrays their trust. The word for "thief" occurs only here and in 10:1, 8, 10, and perhaps John deliberately portrays Judas as a false shepherd whose intention is to steal, kill, and destroy. It is unlikely, however, that Judas illegitimately found his way into Jesus' group of disciples and joined Jesus *as a thief*; he probably became one along the way. The point of comparison between the thief in John 10 and Judas in John 12 is probably the thief's *behavior* of stealing, killing, and destroying rather than his entry into the sheepfold.[38] Besides, Judas is a liar or hypocrite – his question in 12:5 feigns a concern for the poor, which the narrator quickly falsifies.[39] In this, Judas emulates the devil who is characterized as a liar (8:44). Jesus' reprimand in 12:7–8 reveals that Judas does not recognize Jesus' uniqueness and instead believes that Mary showed excessive devotion to Jesus.[40]

Character Development

Character development is not simply the addition of a trait that the reader infers further along the text continuum or a character's progress in his or her

---

Figures," in *These Things Have Been Written: Studies on the Fourth Gospel* [LTPM 2; Grand Rapids, Mich.: Eerdmans, 1990], 1–45, here 30).

[37] Klassen cannot accept John's allegation that Judas is a thief (Klassen, *Judas*, 146; cf. Pratscher, "Judas," 12). However, the Synoptics also hint at Judas's greed for money in Matthew 26:14–15; 27:3–10; Mark 14:10–11; Luke 22:3–5 (Rudolf Schnackenburg, *The Gospel According to St John* [3 vols; London: Burns & Oates, 1968–1982], 2:368; Kim, *Exegesis of Apostasy*, 171–72).

[38] Gail R. O'Day also notes that Judas exhibits a lack of care – whether for the poor (12:6) or the sheep (10:13) (idem, *The Gospel of John* [NIB 9; Nashville: Abingdon, 1995], 702).

[39] Farelly aptly remarks that "on the only occasion when Judas speaks, he cannot be trusted" (Farelly, *Disciples in the Fourth Gospel*, 116).

[40] Cf. Brownson, "Enemy," 51; Kim, *Exegesis of Apostasy*, 168.

understanding of Jesus.[41] Development is revealed in a character's ability to surprise the reader, when a newly found trait replaces another or does not fit neatly into the existing set of traits, implying that the character has changed.[42] Judas shows significant development in that his behavior shocks the reader and new traits replace old ones.[43] The revelation in 6:70–71 should shock the reader because it indicates that Judas will develop from being one of Jesus' intimate friends to a betrayer. When Jesus repeats this information in 13:21, the disciples are shocked, indicating that Judas has shown unexpected development.[44] Even when Jesus provides a clue to the identity of the betrayer in 13:26–27, the disciples are too stunned to grasp it (13:28–29).

When the narrator mentions in 12:6 that Judas is a thief, I suggested that he became a thief somewhere *along the way* rather than that he joined Jesus as a thief. A chapter later, we are privy to Judas's rapid development from one being influenced by the devil (13:2) to one being indwelled by the devil (13:27); from one leaving the fellowship of Jesus and entering into the darkness (13:30) to one eventually arranging Jesus' arrest – in short, the catastrophic development from being a disciple of Jesus to becoming a disciple of Satan. This negative development reveals that Judas was unreliable – he was a thief, a defector, a betrayer, and a disciple of the devil. The reader should thus notice the replacement of traits signifying the change in Judas. Since 12:6 mentions that Judas was a thief while being the treasurer of the group (a position of trust), traits of honesty and reliability are being replaced by dishonesty and unreliability. Then, with the switch of allegiance from Jesus to Satan, traits of intimacy and following Jesus disappear, and alienation and defection emerge.

Inner Life

The inner life of a character gives the reader insight into the character's thoughts, emotions, and motivations, and is conveyed usually by the narrator and sometimes by the characters themselves.[45] In John's Gospel, however,

---

[41] Contra Resseguie, *Narrative Criticism*, 153.

[42] Cf. Edward M. Forster, *Aspects of the Novel* (New York: Penguin, 1976; orig. publ. 1927), 73–81; Rimmon-Kenan, *Narrative Fiction*, 39.

[43] Contra Klauck, who contends that the character of Judas does not show development since he harbored evil plans from the beginning (Klauck, *Judas*, 73). However, even though Judas is characterized by negative traits already at his first appearance in the narrative (6:70–71), this should nevertheless shock the reader because such characterization of one in Jesus' inner circle is not expected.

[44] Contra Klassen's view that "the disciples are not bewildered by the announcement that someone will hand him over. They take it in stride … when Judas acted, he acted for everyone" (Klassen, *Judas*, 150). John 13:22 indicates that the disciples were clearly "at a loss" or "in consternation" (cf. 13:28).

[45] Cf. Adele Berlin, *Poetics and Interpretation of Biblical Narrative* (Sheffield: Almond, 1983), 38.

Jesus also reveals the inner life of some characters, which should not surprise us since he is the revealer *par excellence*, who knows all people and what is in them (2:24–25; cf. 6:64; 13:11; 16:30; 21:17). Indeed, both the narrator and Jesus disclose many aspects of Judas's inner life. The narrator reveals that Judas is indifferent, hypocritical, and dishonest (12:6), influenced in his mind by the devil (13:2), and that he is going to betray Jesus (6:71; 12:4), by virtue of the fact that he knows where Jesus normally goes (18:3). Additionally, Jesus reveals that Judas is a devil (6:70), unclean (13:10), and will betray him (13:21). Thus, John clearly informs the reader about Judas's motives and rationale for his actions by consistently revealing aspects of his inner life.[46] This aids the reader in evaluating Judas.

Characterization and Evaluation of Judas

After this character analysis, we can classify the character of Judas by positioning him on the characterization continuum. Considering his location on the axes of complexity (complex, multiple traits), development (some), and inner life (much), I suggest to identify the character of Judas as an individual. Since individuals in antiquity were not autonomous persons (as in modernity) but embedded in a group (see fn. 16), Judas was first embedded in Jesus' inner group of disciples ("the Twelve"), which in turn was embedded in the family of God, but with his apostasy, Judas became embedded in the family of the devil. Many scholars perceive Judas as a flat, one-dimensional character who shows no development,[47] but this is simplistic. Judas is a complex character whose dominant traits are betrayal and apostasy, but he also has secondary traits such as indifference, hypocrisy, unreliability, dishonesty, and disloyalty.

From John's evaluative point of view, which is informed by his overall purpose of eliciting and increasing faith in the life-giving Jesus amongst his readers (20:31), Judas must be evaluated negatively.[48] Judas's defection is permanent and a case of apostasy – he ceases to be a disciple of Jesus and joins the opposition, becoming a disciple of the devil. Judas mimics the characteristics

---

[46] Cf. Tom Thatcher, "Jesus, Judas, and Peter: Character by Contrast in the Fourth Gospel," *BSac* 153 (1996): 435–48, here 448.

[47] E. g., Tolmie, *Jesus' Farewell*, 142; Davies, *Rhetoric and Reference*, 332; Eslinger, "Judas Game," 72; Resseguie, *Narrative Criticism*, 159, 164; Wright, "Character Typing," 559. Similarly, Kim Paffenroth's assertion that "[a]ll attempt to understand him [Judas] as a human character has dropped out, and he becomes merely an illustration of John's ideas about evil" is too reductionistic (idem, *Judas: Images of the Lost Disciple* [Louisville, Ky.: Westminster John Knox, 2001], 36). Farelly thus correctly critiques Paffenroth, stating that "the narrator does take time to present Judas as a real human" (Farelly, *Disciples in the Fourth Gospel*, 108).

[48] Contra Moloney, who claims that John makes no final judgment upon Judas. Moloney contends that "son of perdition" in 17:12 is Satan, not Judas, and that Judas is included in the "I did not lose one" in 17:12 and 18:9 (Moloney, *John*, 483–85).

and actions of the devil: he lies about his concern for the poor (12:5-6); he steals money from the treasury (12:6); he plays an important role in the killing of Jesus by precipitating Jesus' arrest. Judas is an instrument and embodiment of the devil, in that the devil uses him for his evil purposes and indwells him. Judas's apostasy was the climax of a gradual, negative development rather than an abrupt turnaround, so he had opportunities to choose to do otherwise.[49]

Judas's betrayal is not limited to the premeditated act of handing Jesus over to the judicial authorities at his arrest but is a behavioral pattern that emerged over time. As a thief and then as a defector and apostate, he betrays the trust of both Jesus and his fellow disciples. He belonged to Jesus' inner circle of disciples, had an intimate relationship with Jesus, but eventually chose to join the opposition. Judas's betrayal therefore includes deceiving Jesus and his fellow disciples, being disloyal and letting down his master, and finally handing him over to the opposition. It is as thief, apostate, and the one who hands Jesus over to his enemies that Judas is the betrayer. At the heart of betrayal is relationship; you can only betray someone with whom you share a relationship. Since betrayal presupposes belonging, Judas is the betrayer *as an intimate friend and disciple of Jesus.*[50] Since his betrayal and apostasy result in a transfer of allegiance from the family of God to the family of the devil, Judas is the black sheep of the family.[51]

If "plot" is the logical and causal sequence of events, the plot of John's Gospel relates to the revelation of the Father and Son in terms of their identity, character, mission, and relationship, and people's response to this revelation.[52] The Gospel's plot is affected by John's strategy to persuade the reader to

---

[49] Cf. Craig R. Koester, who remarks that the narrator "holds Judas accountable to accepted standards for human conduct" (idem, *Symbolism in the Fourth Gospel: Meaning, Mystery, Community* [2d ed.; Minneapolis: Fortress, 2003], 73). See also Eslinger, "Judas Game," 59-60. Contra Klassen's evaluation that "Judas appears more like an automaton than a free, willing person" (Klassen, *Judas*, 153). Resseguie also reduces Judas's responsibility, asserting that he is passive and "little more than a pawn in a cosmic chess match [between God and Satan]" (Resseguie, *Strange Gospel*, 165-66; cf. idem, *Narrative Criticism*, 163).

[50] Cf. Brownson, "Enemy," 50. See also Wright, who views Judas's betrayal in the context of ancient Greco-Roman teacher-student relationship and friendship where loyalty or fidelity was the most important component (Wright, "Character Typing," 552-53). Contra Paffenroth, who claims that Judas never belonged to Jesus since Jesus cannot lose his own (Pfaffenroth, *Judas*, 35). Similarly, Hans-Josef Klauck also denies that Judas ever belonged to Jesus because from the beginning Judas belonged to those who did not believe (6:64) (idem, "Judas der Verräter? Eine exegetische und wirkungsgeschichtliche Studie," *ANRW* II 26.1 [1992]: 728-29). However, the εἰ μή ("except") clause in Jesus' statements regarding Judas (13:10; 17:12) shows that Judas did belong prior to his apostasy - Jesus' claims that all are clean and all are kept *except* Judas actually demonstrates that he was included in the "all" before he defected.

[51] Contra Klassen, who asserts that "it may be time to ... bury once and for all the belief that Judas was a thief or was motivated by demonic forces. Not for a moment does it seem credible that the Johannine portrait of Judas could be authentic" (Klassen, *Judas*, 146).

[52] Cf. Culpepper, *Anatomy of the Fourth Gospel*, 79-98; Lincoln, *John*, 11-12; Farelly, *Disciples in the Fourth Gospel*, 168-69.

believe that Jesus is the Christ and the source of everlasting life or salvation (20:31).[53] Judas significantly advances the plot in that his betrayal of Jesus sets in motion the plan of the chief priests and "the Jews" to kill Jesus. Jesus' death is climactic to the plot because the cross is where (i) Jesus is exalted and finishes his salvific mission (3:14; 12:32; 19:30); (ii) Jesus ultimately provides life for the life of the world (6:51); and (iii) God ultimately reveals his love for the world in the giving of his son (3:16). Thus, in the process from being Jesus' friend to becoming his foe, Judas propels the plot to its climax and resolution.[54]

Having evaluated Judas in terms of his response to Jesus and his role in the plot, we must determine his significance for today. Since John seeks to win his readers over to his point of view using a broad array of characters that interact with Jesus, we must reflect on how these characters and their responses have representative value for readers in other contexts. The Johannine characters are therefore representative figures in that they have a symbolic or illustrative value beyond the narrative but not in a reductionist, "typical" sense. I contend that the representative value across cultures and time lies in the *totality* of each character – traits, development, *and* response. The reader is thus invited to identify with (aspects of) one or more of the characters, learn from them and then make his or her own response to Jesus – preferably one that the author approves of. Conversely, the reader may already have made a response to Jesus and can now evaluate that response against those of the characters. When it comes to Judas, he represents those who belonged to Jesus but have defected and joined the opposition – the devil – and thus serves as a negative example.[55]

---

[53] Cf. Culpepper, *Anatomy of the Fourth Gospel*, 98.
[54] Cf. Lincoln, *John*, 11–12.
[55] Many scholars have also considered Judas's representative value for John's own time. For example, in view of the many antichrists who left the Johannine community and went out into the dark world (1 John 2:18–19; 4:1), Culpepper characterizes Judas as "the representative defector" (Culpepper, *Anatomy of the Fourth Gospel*, 124–25; cf. Resseguie, *Narrative Criticism*, 165). Referring to the ancient rhetorical device of "syncrisis," Michael W. Martin presents a similar case, arguing that Judas as the consummate defector is a representative of the schismatics described in 1–3 John who broke away from the Johannine community (idem, *Judas and the Rhetoric of Comparison in the Fourth Gospel* [NTM 25; Sheffield: Sheffield Phoenix, 2010]). See also Peter Dschulnigg, *Jesus begegnen: Personen und ihre Bedeutung im Johannesevangelium* (Münster: LIT, 2002), 179. Kim's contention that "John deliberately alludes to the historical situation of the church in which apostate-disciples become henchmen of Satan in delivering Christian brothers into the hands of Synagogue authorities and think that they are offering a service to God (16:2)" is perhaps overstated (Kim, *Exegesis of Apostasy*, 211). For Judas's representation throughout history, see Meiser, *Judas Iskariot*, 112–87.

The Authorities:
Indeterminate Complex Identities

Susanne Luther

E. M. Forster's criteria for round and flat characters have often been utilized to clearly divide the characters in the Gospel of John into two types according to their complexity:[1] Round characters are characters portrayed in detail, showing conflicting traits and are lifelike, able to surprise the reader; flat characters appear marginally in the plot of the narrative, they are reduced to one single trait and their portrayal lacks complexity.[2] This easily leads to the conclusion, that "[m]ajor characters are generally round and minor characters are generally flat," but – as Resseguie notices – this paradigm does not always hold true.[3] The following analysis of "the authorities" (οἱ ἄρχοντες) highlights the manner in which minor characters can be portrayed as complex and dynamic in the Gospel of John and in which ways they can contribute to the plot narrative.[4]

The Johannine "Authorities" in their Literary Context

The authorities (οἱ ἄρχοντες) appear only marginally within the Gospel's plot in John 7:26, 48 and John 12:42.[5] The narrative context of the first occurrence of οἱ ἄρχοντες (John 7:26) is the Jewish feast of the Tabernacles, where a controversy arises between Jesus on the one hand and "the Jews" and "the people" on the other hand (John 7:1-13, 14-36). John 7:25 narrates the astonished reaction of τινες ἐκ τῶν Ἱεροσολυμιτῶν towards Jesus' unimpeded public teaching in the Temple (v. 28). The Jerusalem characters, who remain unspe-

---

[1] Cf. Edward M. Forster, *Aspects of the Novel* (New York: Harcourt, 1927), 67-78.
[2] Cf. Forster, *Aspects of the Novel*, 78.
[3] Cf. James L. Resseguie, *Narrative Criticism of the New Testament: An Introduction* (Grand Rapids, Mich.: Baker Academic, 2005), 123.
[4] Cf. Colleen M. Conway, "Speaking through Ambiguity: Minor Characters in the Fourth Gospel," *BibInt* 10 (2002): 324-42.
[5] The singular ἄρχων occurs in John 12:31; 14:30 and 16:11 in the context of sayings addressing the final judgement and the power of ὁ ἄρχων τοῦ κόσμου (τούτου), thus referring to the devil and adding a decisively negative connotation to the term οἱ ἄρχοντες. However, this negative association is relativized by the authorities' assumed belief in Jesus, cf. below fn. 25.

cified, wonder what the reason for Jesus' unopposed presence might be. They assume that some of the Jewish authorities (οἱ ἄρχοντες) have become loyal to Jesus, are acknowledging him as Messiah (ὁ χριστός, v. 26) and therefore do not oppose his public teaching.[6] The topic is resumed in John 7:45–52, where the servants (οἱ ὑπηρέται) approach the chief priests and Pharisees and are rebuked for not having arrested Jesus for his public teaching on the last day of the feast (v. 45). The Pharisees presume from the servants' response, that their lenient conduct is due to their loyalty to Jesus (v. 46) and counter this with the position that the Sanhedrin communicates to the outside world: none of the ἄρχοντες or Pharisees has come to believe in Jesus (vss. 47–48). Only the crowd (ὁ ὄχλος), who do not know the Law, have been fooled into believing in Jesus' teaching (v. 49). The assessment of the Pharisees, as reported in v. 48, indicates that they assume or pretend that none of the members of the Jewish ruling authorities have come to faith in Jesus. In employing the term ἄρχοντες in this context, however, the narrator might hint at the fact that the speakers are mistaken in this matter, they either do not recognize the internal schisms within the ruling class or are trying to cover them up.[7] The third occurrence of οἱ ἄρχοντες in 12:42 is placed within a short note about the prevailing unbelief within the Jewish crowd (ὁ ὄχλος, v. 34) as opposed to the belief of ἐκ τῶν ἀρχόντων πολλοί (v. 42). V. 42 also provides the reason why this fact is not known or communicated openly: the believers among the authorities fear being excluded from the synagogue if the Pharisees discover their allegiance to Jesus (cf. also John 9:22).[8]

As a character, the ἄρχοντες appear as a group and not as individuals. As such, the identity of the group is difficult to pin down. It may be that characters in the Gospel narratives do not represent "any real people in the world *outside the story*, but are constructs of the implied author designed to fulfil a

---

[6] Hartwig Thyen points out the distance the Jerusalem characters create between themselves and the authorities by not using a formulation like "our leaders" but rather the impersonal "the leaders" (idem, *Das Johannesevangelium* [HNT 6; Tübingen: Mohr Siebeck, 2005], 394).

[7] This might be inferred from the other instances in which the term is employed in the Gospel of John, where it always implies the authorities' affiliation with Jesus (cf. below).

[8] Cf. Michael Theobald, *Evangelium nach Johannes Kap. 1–12* (Regensburg: Pustet, 2009), 300–301 and 525. Theobald suggests tracing the critical evaluation of the believers mentioned in v. 42 back to the evangelist's intention: "Vielleicht gab es ja Jesus-Gläubige in den Synagogen *aus Überzeugung*, für die der Glaube an den Messias Jesus *kein* Grund war, die angestammte Glaubensheimat zu verlassen. Dann hätten die Urteile des Evangelisten über diese Menschen einen genau kalkulierten Zweck, nämlich den, die im Kreis der eigenen Gemeinde erlittene Trennung von der Synagoge durch den Aufweis zu bekräftigen, dass christliche Existenz *in* der Synagoge unglaubwürdig werden müsse" (Theobald, *Johannes*, 831; original emphasis). Klaus Wengst also interprets the reference concerning the ejection from the synagogal community as an impact of contemporary experiences at the time of the composition of John's Gospel (idem, *Das Johannesevangelium* [2d ed.; THKNT 4/2; Stuttgart: Kohlhammer, 2007], 78).

particular role *in the story*".⁹ Although the question of historical referentiality could hence be left unconsidered in a study of characters within a narrative, the embeddedness of the Johannine narrative within a particular historical situation allows insight into the identity of the characters and their role within the narrative. In John 7:26 οἱ ἄρχοντες are not clearly defined: Within the spectrum of narrative characters in the Gospel, the term might refer to the temple authorities, either generally to members of the Sanhedrin or more specifically to the chief priests.¹⁰ In John 7:48 οἱ ἄρχοντες are explicitly distinguished from the Pharisees (οἱ Φαρισαῖοι); with reference to v. 45, where a meeting of the chief priests and Pharisees is narrated, οἱ ἄρχοντες in v. 48 might refer to the chief priests. John 12:42 speaks of οἱ ἄρχοντες, who are afraid of the Pharisees because of their belief in Jesus. It is difficult to determine whether οἱ ἄρχοντες in this instance refers to the chief priests, who are afraid of the Pharisees or to Pharisees who are afraid of other Pharisees: both options are feasible and therefore a definite decision is not possible.¹¹ John 3:1 describes Nicodemus as ἄνθρωπος ἐκ τῶν Φαρισαίων and, at the same time, as ἄρχων τῶν Ἰουδαίων. This use of the terminology in the Gospel of John supports an interpretation of οἱ ἄρχοντες generally as members of the "ruling Jerusalem body of οἱ Ἰουδαῖοι, the Sanhedrin"¹² and thus as either Pharisees or chief priests or as members of both parties.¹³ This conclusion is of major significance for character analysis, for it underlines the relation between "the authorities" and other (groups of) characters. As Sönke Finnern states, the relationship between characters allows the identification and classification of characters and indicates hierarchies.¹⁴ With a view to οἱ ἄρχοντες, they do not constitute a group of clearly defined characters or a clearly defined group; they

---

⁹ Mark A. Powell, *What is Narrative Criticism?* (Minneapolis: Fortress, 1990), 66 (original emphasis).
¹⁰ Cf. Theobald who points out that the Sanhedrin was actually constituted of chief priests, elders and scribes. In the Fourth Gospel the term Sanhedrin is not used, but rather the substituting formula "the chief priests and Pharisees" (cf., e. g., 7:32), which might reflect the situation after 70 C.E. (Theobald, *Johannes*, 530).
¹¹ Cf. Cornelis Bennema, "The Identity and Composition of ΟΙ ΙΟΥΔΑΙΟΙ in the Gospel of John," *TynBul* 60 (2009): 239–63, especially 251–53 for remarks concerning the reason οἱ ἄρχοντες might have been afraid of the Pharisees. Bennema concludes that "οἱ ἄρχοντες (whether chief priests or Pharisees) were afraid that if the Pharisees came to know about their sympathy towards Jesus, they would report it to the Sanhedrin or to the wider body of οἱ Ἰουδαῖοι" (Bennema, "Identity," 252).
¹² Cf. Bennema, "Identity," 253.
¹³ Cf. Uta Poplutz, "Die Pharisäer als literarische Figurengruppe im Johannesevangelium," in *Narrativität und Theologie im Johannesevangelium* (ed. Jörg Frey and Uta Poplutz; BThS 130; Neukirchen-Vluyn: Neukirchener, 2012), 19–39, esp. 21–22 concerning the problematic identification of the Pharisees.
¹⁴ Cf. Sönke Finnern, *Narratologie und Biblische Exegese: Eine integrative Methode der Erzählanalyse und ihr Ertrag am Beispiel von Matthäus* (WUNT 285; Tübingen: Mohr Siebeck, 2010), 147–48 and 162–64.

constitute an indeterminate group consisting of persons who are identified by their – either assumed or suspected or definite – allegiance to Jesus. Thus these minor characters form an independent group of marginal characters, but as they are composed of individuals belonging to the groups of "the Jews" (οἱ Ἰουδαῖοι), the chief priests (οἱ ἀρχιερεῖς) and the Pharisees (οἱ Φαρισαῖοι), οἱ ἄρχοντες stand in close relation to these three groups of major characters depicting the leading Jewish authorities in Jerusalem.[15] Constituting a subgroup, οἱ ἄρχοντες acquire their status as an autonomous minor character through their antagonistic relationship with these groups of major characters and through their ambivalent characterization as (potential) believers.

The use of the terminology in John's Gospel reveals that the Jewish authorities are always labelled ἄρχοντες when the narrative places them within the context of authorities believing in Jesus.[16] Οἱ ἄρχοντες play an important role within the Johannine plot, as they prove that the Jewish ruling elite, the Sanhedrin consisting of Pharisees and chief priests, must not be regarded as one unified and powerful opponent to Jesus, but that precisely these rulers, who try very hard to uphold the impression of being powerful and united, are actually internally divided and split into opposing groups. That οἱ ἄρχοντες are not an explicitly defined group (consisting of specific, identifiable individual members)[17] is part of the author's technique of displaying this group as a subliminal and secret movement within the Jewish ruling authorities. According to the actantial model proposed by A. J. Greimas, the authorities are hence part of the underlying structure of the Gospel plot and although they do not play any active part in the narration, they have the potential to undermine the plan to kill Jesus.[18] However, the climactic development of the appearance of οἱ ἄρχοντες in John's Gospel promotes the progress of the narrative indirectly: in 7:26 their allegiance to Jesus is formulated as a vague question, in 7:48 their loyalty is negated through the use of a rhetorical question expecting a negative answer (μή), while 12:42 openly states that a group of the ruling class, the authorities, have turned to Jesus in secret. This presentation produces the effect of the strengthening of their position and hence also of a growing schism

---

[15] Cf. Urban C. von Wahlde, "The Terms for Religious Authorities in the Fourth Gospel: A Key to Literary-Strata?," *JBL* 98 (1979): 231–53, esp. 235 for the presentation of the highly diverse use of terminology with reference to the Jewish authorities. Von Wahlde's observation that this phenomenon contrasts with the undefined use of the term Ἰουδαῖοι and his literary-critical suggestion that the reason is to be found in the interweaving of two separate literary strata does not seem convincing.

[16] See also the general analysis of the term Ἰουδαῖοι for the Jewish authorities (Urban C. von Wahlde, "The Johannine 'Jews': A Critical Survey," *NTS* 28 [1982]: 33–60, esp. 41–42).

[17] With the exception of Nicodemus (see below).

[18] Cf. Algirdas J. Greimas, *Sémantique structurale: Recherche de méthode* (Paris: Larousse, 1966), 172–91. In Greimas's terminology the authorities might be identified as "opponents," although their actions are not reported, but only assumed by other actants (i. e., their influence is presumed when Jesus is not harmed, cf. John 7:26).

within the group of Jesus' opponents. Remaining unknown for fear of being expelled from the synagogue, they constitute an immense threat to the Jewish ruling class as well as to the plot of the Gospel, which leads towards the passion, death and resurrection of Jesus.

Traits of Character and Techniques of Characterization

Any characterization has to rely on the conveyance of information about the character in question.[19] Although no inner monologues or insight from an omniscient narrator are presented and even though "the authorities" do not act or speak within the narrative, some of the characters' traits and inner life can be inferred from context information, from the words of other characters in the narrative as well as from the reaction they cause among their contemporaries within the narrative. Hence Seymour Chatman and more recently Uri Margolin have emphasized the construction of character in the reader's mind from the traits mentioned in the text.[20] The re/construction of the traits of character of οἱ ἄρχοντες and their function within the plot must also be derived through inference based on fragmentary information in the Gospel text.[21] Although only scarce information about οἱ ἄρχοντες is provided in the

---

[19] For the well-known categories of showing and telling, see, e. g., Resseguie, *Narrative Criticism*, 126–30; Baruch Hochman, *Character in Literature* (Ithaca, N. Y.: Cornell University Press, 1985), 38. See also the work of Cornelis Bennema for a more detailed theory of character analysis, using the categories of complexity, development and penetration into inner life (idem, *Encountering Jesus: Character Studies in the Gospel of John* [Milton Keynes: Paternoster, 2009], 12–15; idem, "A Theory of Character in the Fourth Gospel with Reference to Ancient and Modern Literature," *BibInt* 17 [2009]: 375–421, esp. 402–10). Cf. also Daniel Marguerat and Yvan Bourquin, *Pour lire les récits bibliques: Initiation à l'analyse narrative* (4th ed.; Paris: Cerf, 2009), 94–97.

[20] Seymour Chatman, *Story and Discourse: Narrative Structure in Fiction and Film* (Ithaca, N. Y.: Cornell University Press, 1978), 121–30. Chatman's theory proves very helpful when arguing that even scarcely developed characters may be considered as complex characters with autonomous traits. Cf. also Uri Margolin, "Character," in *The Cambridge Companion to Narrative* (ed. David Herman; Cambridge: Cambridge University Press, 2007), 66–79; idem, "Characterization in Narrative: Some Theoretical Prolegomena," *NP* 67 (1983): 1–14. In the field of biblical studies cf. esp. Fred W. Burnett, "Characterization and Reader Construction of Characters in the Gospels," *Semeia* 93 (1999): 3–28; Adele Berlin, *Poetics and Interpretation of Biblical Narrative* (Sheffield: Almond Press, 1983), 36–38, and Petri Merenlahti, "Characters in the Making: Individuality and Ideology in the Gospels," in *Characterization in the Gospels: Reconceiving Narrative Criticism* (ed. David Rhoads and Kari Syreeni; JSNTSup 184; Sheffield: Sheffield Academic Press, 1999), 49–72, esp. 52–53: the "reticence in characterization invites the reader to play an active part in the making of characters. Being given only sparse and ambiguous information, the reader simply has to infer, make guesses and interpretations, and correct those guesses and interpretations whenever his or her expectations are not fulfilled in the course of the narrative."

[21] Cf. Robert Alter, *The Art of Biblical Narrative* (New York: Basic Books, 1981), 116–17.

Gospel narrative, the reader can draw on the aspects mentioned and construct a character that can be classified as complex and dynamic.[22]

The auctorial narrator presents the character of "the authorities" through the perception and speech of the different parties involved: the people (John 7:26), the ruling classes (John 7:48) and his own evaluation (John 12:42). In this characterization, the narrator is drawing on the literary technique of contrast:[23] Οἱ ἄρχοντες are presented as a marginal group composed of members of different circles of Jewish rulers. At the same time they are always mentioned in ways which are suggestive of a possible affiliation with Jesus. Like Nicodemus, the only known member of the group, the authorities move in the darkness, they believe but do not dare to confess openly.[24] They remain incognito for fear of being expelled from the synagogue community. This conduct characterizes them as unstable and unpredictable characters: they move in both camps, pretending to be what they are not and hiding what they are.[25] As the group remains in complete opacity, their contours in reference to their belief, their intentions, their strength and number continue to be unknown and therefore they may be perceived as threateningly unpredictable. Their identity is in deep crisis between the known religious institutions and the new teaching they find convincing.[26] The encounter with Jesus or his teaching has changed their allegiance, their attitude, but not yet their action and their confession.[27]

---

[22] For the process of revelation of the traits of character cf. D. Francois Tolmie, *Narratology and Biblical Narratives: A Practical Guide* (Bethesda, Md.: International Scholars Publications, 1999), 42–53.

[23] Berlin mentions three types of contrast: "1) contrast with another character, 2) contrast with an earlier action, and 3) contrast with the expected norm" (Berlin, *Poetics*, 40). Berlin stresses that "sometimes the contrast is not so evident on the surface of the discourse, but is implicit in the story." Cf. also Hochman, *Character in Literature*, 68.

[24] Cf. R. Alan Culpepper, who characterizes the authorities as "acceptance without open commitment" (idem, *Anatomy of the Fourth Gospel: A Study in Literary Design* [Philadelphia: Fortress 1983], 146).

[25] Cf. Jo-Ann A. Brant, *Dialogue and Drama: Elements of Greek Tragedy in the Fourth Gospel* (Peabody, Mass.: Hendrickson, 2004), 193: "In classical drama, confusion about identity is limited to the dramatic axis. In a performance in which actors wear masks, it is necessary to identify them clearly in each scene. The Fourth Evangelist perhaps plays a modern game when he flouts the conventions of the theatrical axis by withholding the identity ... If the audience is intentionally trapped, is the preconception with which the evangelist plays our capacity to name authorities? ... The evangelist, or his representative the narrator, demonstrates a consistent disregard for distinctions between Jewish leaders."

[26] The correlation between the authorities' assumed, secret belief in Jesus and the terminological association with ὁ ἄρχων τοῦ κόσμου leads to several possible interpretations: the ἄρχοντες may be regarded as midway between two rulers – Jesus and the "ruler of this world." They might also form a positive terminological counterpart to the ruler of this world as being (though only secret) believers in high positions; their conduct, however, might also allow for an interpretation that contrasts the power of ὁ ἄρχων τοῦ κόσμου with the powerlessness of Jesus and his adherents.

[27] Thyen ascribes this to their failure "das Ansehen vor den Menschen höher zu achten als den Ruhm, den Gott verleiht" (Thyen, *Johannesevangelium*, 575).

As οἱ ἄρχοντες are mentioned so few times in the Fourth Gospel, no gradual change in character is depicted on the narrative level. However, although the gradual change may not be described, it can be inferred from the different aspects mentioned about the characters' words or actions – in this case it is rather an inner development and dynamic, which has to be inferred from the inner wrestling of the authorities with their loyalty to the old religious system and the new belief. This kind of dynamic does not have to be described at length but can nevertheless evoke a dynamic, complex character. The character development initiated by the encounter with Jesus has not been completed, for the development has stagnated on the inner level of personal conviction but has not yet had any impact on their outward conduct. This dilemma renders them unable to act and therefore outwardly static; nevertheless, at the same time, the dilemma itself connotes a complex inner life.[28]

Thus, οἱ ἄρχοντες are ambiguous characters: they are not easy to grasp as individuals; they show aspects of complex character changes still in progress; they are not assessed explicitly or precisely within the narrative. The ἄρχοντες are indicative of an internal debate within the group of Jewish ruling authorities. They express confusion within the group of the ruling class and thus create confusion for the reader who is trying to interpret their character.[29] They are confusing because individuals belonging to the different groups of major characters in the Gospel suddenly change their attitude to Jesus and, thus, turn one of their basic characteristic traits as opponents into the trait of allegiance to Jesus. This change, however, is not made explicit. Nevertheless, such individuals not only suddenly become indefinable and unintelligible, they also implicitly change the perception of the major characters of Pharisees and chief priests within the Gospel narrative. Οἱ ἄρχοντες are autonomous characters with their own ambiguous and complex traits, but – with the exception of Nicodemus[30] – unidentifiable as singular personalities. Their characteristic traits are not openly revealed by the narrator, but have to be inferred from their conduct, which is not narrated but only reported and speculated about in the narrative, and from the effect of this conduct on their contemporaries within the narrative. They do not appear as characters interacting with other characters or engaging openly in the plot. It can rather be stated that the paradox of the characters' conduct is mirrored in the narrative strategies adopted

---

[28] Cf. the distinction between marginalized and dominant characters in Resseguie, *Narrative Criticism*, 137–65.

[29] Brant, *Dialogue*, 182.

[30] Nicodemus, however, is also seen to be an ambiguous character: e. g., Raymond F. Collins considers him "clearly marked as a representative of official Judaism, [who] has become for the Evangelist a type of the unbeliever" ("The Representative Figures of the Fourth Gospel I," *DRev* 94 [1976]: 26–46, 37); Culpepper describes Joseph of Arimathea and Nicodemus as "secret disciples" (*Anatomy of the Fourth Gospel*, 135–36; cf. Udo Schnelle, *Das Evangelium nach Johannes* [4th ed.; THKNT 4; Leipzig: Evangelische Verlagsanstalt, 2009], 208, fn. 38).

for their presentation: As the characters remain in the dark within the Gospel plot because of their belief in Jesus, they also remain in the dark concerning their identity and characterization.

Theological Implications

According to Robert Scholes and Robert Kellog,[31] characters can be used to illustrate certain principles or notions. Throughout the history of research, οἱ ἄρχοντες – as minor characters in the Gospel of John in general – have been interpreted as symbolic or representative characters, as flat characters with the single trait of being "representatives of belief or unbelief."[32] Raymond Collins, e. g., views the minor characters in the Gospel of John in close relation to Johannine symbolism, where they are placed into the narrative as "individuals who have been type-cast. In their individuality they represent a type of faith-response (or lack of faith-response) to Jesus who is the Christ and Son of God."[33] According to this approach οἱ ἄρχοντες represent character types conveying the Johannine dualistic theme of true faith versus unbelief.[34] On a didactic level the characters portrayed in the Gospel of John are conceived as positive or negative role models for the reader, which convey the Gospel's central purpose, namely, providing an account that is to result in faith in Jesus. The reader may identify with οἱ ἄρχοντες and conceive of the fact that hidden faith is not evaluated positively – the authorities oscillate between evoking the empathy (because of the fear of being expelled from the synagogue) and the antipathy (because of the fear of openly confessing and presenting a clear identity) of the reader. This literary technique allows the reader to experience the impact and perception of this kind of conduct, the ambiguity and threat arising from this behaviour and its negative evaluation.

---

[31] Robert Scholes and Robert Kellogg, *The Nature of Narrative* (Oxford: Oxford University Press, 1975). Cf. also Jens Eder, *Die Figur im Film: Grundlagen der Figurenanalyse* (Marburg: Schüren, 2008).
[32] For an overview of the history of research, see Conway, "Speaking through Ambiguity," 326–28 (quote from p. 324). Cf. for this approach Collins, "Representative Figures I," 26–46; idem, "The Representative Figures of the Fourth Gospel II," *DRev* 95 (1976): 118–32; Culpepper, *Anatomy of the Fourth Gospel*.
[33] Collins, "Representative Figures I," 31.
[34] Craig R. Koester, *Symbolism in the Fourth Gospel: Meaning, Mystery, Community* (2d ed.; Minneapolis: Fortress, 2003), 33: "The supporting characters rarely interact with one another, but draw out facets of Jesus' identity through their responses to his words and actions. They present a spectrum of possible responses to Jesus, helping to attract readers to positive exemplars of faith, move them beyond inadequate faith responses, and alienate them from characters who reject Jesus". Cf. also Koester, *Symbolism*, 37: "Through positive and negative examples he directed readers towards his own stated goal, that they might believe and have life in Jesus' name (20:30–31)."

However, the character analysis of οἱ ἄρχοντες shows that this representative interpretation of Johannine characters has to be challenged due to the tension created by the evangelist in his portrayal of most minor characters through displaying their complex and ambiguous traits, thus constructing many minor characters as obscure marginal figures. Colleen Conway, e. g., stresses that most Johannine characters show "ambivalence and ambiguity in their relationship to Jesus;"[35] their character traits are not predictable and static, but dynamic.[36] In the case of οἱ ἄρχοντες, the character is portrayed as complex and lifelike,[37] rather than representing a mere type or symbolic character; οἱ ἄρχοντες specifically testify to the painful, irritating process of inner struggle and the problematic progress of identity formation within the confines of an non-sympathetic environment.

This analysis of "the authorities" (οἱ ἄρχοντες) has shown the manner in which literary techniques are employed to portray minor characters as complex and dynamic in the Gospel of John: they stand in close relationship with other characters or groups of characters and are part of the Gospel plot in that their mere presence creates a more complex and intricate plot narrative. Moreover, their portrayal as lifelike, complex characters and at the same time the concealment and indeterminacy of their identities offer the reader ample scope for construction, interpretation and identification.

---

[35] Conway, "Speaking through Ambiguity," 332.
[36] Cf. here for a systematic approach Bennema, "Theory of Character," esp. 394–410.
[37] Cf. Conway, "Speaking through Ambiguity," 325: "minor characters of the Fourth Gospel do more to complicate the clear choice between belief and unbelief than to illustrate it. In so doing, the Gospel's minor characters play a major role in undercutting the dualism of the Gospel."

The Chief Priests:
Masterminds of Jesus' Death

Cornelis Bennema

Identity and Role of the Chief Priests

In John's Gospel, the term ἀρχιερεύς occurs eleven times in the singular to denote the high priest (Caiaphas/Annas) and ten times in the plural to denote the chief priests. I will concentrate on the latter as a corporate character, i. e., a group that is homogeneous in its identity and behavior. The chief priests have received little or no attention because scholars tend to focus more on "the Jews" (sixty-six occurrences) and the Pharisees (twenty occurrences).[1] This has resulted in two tendencies. First, many scholars treat "the Jews" as a homogeneous group, both in their identity and behavior.[2] Second, many argue (or simply assume) that the Pharisees were the leaders or the core of "the Jews."[3] I have attempted elsewhere to correct these inclinations, arguing that (i) "the Jews" were a composite group of Torah- and temple-loyalists with the chief priests as their main leaders and the Pharisees as the influential laity, and (ii) "the Jews" were not homogeneous in their response to Jesus.[4]

There is general agreement that the chief priests were members or heads of the various highpriestly families – the priestly aristocracy – and the high priest

---

[1] In fact, I am not aware of a single study on the chief priests in John's Gospel.

[2] Most scholars contend that "the Jews" simply refers to the religious authorities and fail to distinguish between the chief priests and Pharisees. Differently, Stephen Motyer does not mention the chief priests and hence virtually treats "the Jews" as a homogeneous group consisting of the Pharisees (idem, *Your Father the Devil? A New Approach to John and "the Jews"* [Carlisle: Paternoster, 1997]). Regarding the role of "the Jews" in the Johannine narrative, Rudolf Bultmann's view that they represent the unbelieving world in general in its hostility towards Jesus is virtually the consensus (idem, *The Gospel of John* [Philadelphia: Westminster, 1971], 86–87).

[3] E. g., R. Alan Culpepper, *Anatomy of the Fourth Gospel: A Study in Literary Design* (Philadelphia: Fortress, 1983), 130–31; D. Moody Smith, *The Theology of the Gospel of John* (Cambridge: Cambridge University Press, 1995), 48–50, 171; Motyer, *Father*, 56; Daniel Boyarin, "The Ioudaioi in John and the Prehistory of 'Judaism,'" in *Pauline Conversations in Context: Essays in Honor of Calvin J. Roetzel* (ed. Janice C. Anderson et al.; JSNTSup 221; Sheffield: Sheffield University Press, 2002), 233–36.

[4] Cornelis Bennema, "The Identity and Composition of οἱ Ἰουδαῖοι in the Gospel of John," *TynBul* 60 (2009): 239–63; Cornelis Bennema, *Encountering Jesus: Character Studies in the Gospel of John* (Milton Keynes: Paternoster, 2009), 38–46.

was the leading chief priest (ἀρχιερεύς denotes both "chief priest" and "high priest"). As such, the chief priests were the temple authorities or "clergy," and they had the power to convene the Sanhedrin on judicial-religious matters. They were the political and religious authorities, the ones with the power to control and make policy (cf. Josephus, *Ant.* 20:250-251).[5] In contrast, the Pharisees were laity and had the power of influence rather than control, although some notable Pharisees could belong to the Sanhedrin.[6] In John's Gospel, the priority of the chief priests in the frequent phrase "the chief priests and the Pharisees" (7:32, 45; 11:47, 57; 18:3) confirms this pecking order. Besides, while the Pharisees identify themselves as "disciples of Moses" and "children of Abraham," and debate with Jesus on various religious-theological issues (law, sabbath, Moses, Abraham, blasphemy), the conflict between the chief priests and Jesus is more religious-political in nature, in that the chief priests perceive Jesus to be a political threat to their operational power base, the temple in Jerusalem (cf. 11:48).

The chief priests occur in three sections of the Johannine narrative. They first appear in John 7, together with the Pharisees in a meeting of the Sanhedrin, but the Pharisees are the dominant voice (7:32, 45-52).[7] The second appearance of the chief priests occurs in John 11-12, towards the end of Jesus' ministry in the commotional aftermath of the raising of Lazarus. There, in another Sanhedrin meeting with the Pharisees, the chief priests come to the fore, plotting Jesus' death because they perceive him as a political threat. The final appearance of the chief priests, now accompanied by "the Jews," is in John 18-19 where they orchestrate Jesus' death during his trial before Pilate. In the sequence of their appearances in the Johannine narrative, the chief priests become increasingly vocal – being virtually silent in the first scene (7:45-52), debating in the second (11:45-53), and shouting in the third (19:6, 15) – and domineering. John holds "the Jews" in general and their main leaders, the chief priests, in particular (cf. the phrase οἱ ἀρχιερεῖς τῶν Ἰουδαίων in 19:21) responsible for Jesus' death.

---

[5] Cf. Joachim Jeremias, *Jerusalem in the Time of Jesus* (London: SCM, 1969), 160-98; Gottlob Schrenk, "ἱερός-ἀρχιερεύς," *TDNT*, 3:221-83, esp. 265-83; Steve N. Mason, *Josephus and the New Testament* (Peabody, Mass.: Hendrickson, 1992), 118-31.

[6] Cf. Bennema, "Identity," 246-49.

[7] The meeting of οἱ ἀρχιερεῖς καὶ οἱ Φαρισαῖοι in 7:45 is explicitly called συνέδριον in 11:47, and although συνέδριον can simply refer to a local town council or assembly, the "town" in 11:45-53 is Jerusalem, so that it must refer to the Jewish supreme court – the Sanhedrin.

Character Analysis of the Chief Priests

Many scholars use a reductionist method of character analysis – some do not specify their criteria for character analysis; others only analyze characters in terms of their traits; still others do not classify or evaluate the characters. This is partly due to the lack of a suitable theory of character. I recently developed a comprehensive theory of character, which in its most succinct form is this: I will *analyze* the chief priests along three dimensions (complexity, development, and inner life), *classify* the resulting character on a continuum of degree of characterization (from agent to type to personality to individuality), and *evaluate* the character according to John's point of view.[8]

Character Complexity

The degree of a character's complexity has to do with its traits. As Seymour Chatman asserts, we reconstruct a character by inferring its traits – "relatively stable or abiding personal qualit[ies]" – from the information in the text.[9] Characters may vary from those displaying a single trait to those displaying a complex nexus of traits, and there can be various degrees of complexity in between. The character traits of the chief priests are revealed both by "showing" and "telling," i. e., they are inferred from their interaction with other characters and from the information mentioned by the narrator.[10] The chief priests have a broad relational network: indirect relations with Jesus, Lazarus, and Judas, and direct relations with the Pharisees, the temple police, "the Jews," and Pilate.

Examining the chief priests' three clusters of appearances in the Johannine narrative, I infer the following traits. First, at the Feast of Tabernacles, when the Pharisees learn that many people are beginning to consider Jesus as the Messiah, the chief priests and Pharisees mobilize the temple police to arrest Jesus (7:25–32). This shows that the chief priests are *proactive* and *alert*. When the temple police return empty-handed, the question posed by the chief priests (and Pharisees), "Why did you not arrest him?," reveals their *annoyance*. Second, Jesus' raising of Lazarus, the resulting change of allegiance of many fellow "Jews" to Jesus (11:45; 12:11), and the fear that Jesus' gaining more followers

---

[8] For a detailed explanation of my comprehensive theory of character, see Cornelis Bennema, "A Theory of Character in the Fourth Gospel with Reference to Ancient and Modern Literature," *BibInt* 17 (2009): 375–421. For a summary, see my chapter on Judas elsewhere in this book.

[9] Seymour Chatman, *Story and Discourse: Narrative Structure in Fiction and Film* (Ithaca, N. Y.: Cornell University Press, 1978), 119, 126 (quotation from p. 126). Traits include cognitive, behavioral, and emotional qualities of a character.

[10] Cf. James L. Resseguie, *Narrative Criticism of the New Testament: An Introduction* (Grand Rapids, Mich.: Baker Academic, 2005), 126–28.

could cause a Roman intervention that could potentially endanger their position, rouse the chief priests to drastic action (11:47–53). While they are *uncertain, anxious,* and *upset* (11:47–48), they are also *proactive, decisive, organized,* and have *murderous intent* (11:47, 53, 57). Their decision to kill Lazarus due to the large number of defecting "Jews" (12:10–11) also shows them to be *conspiratorial* and *calculating*. Finally, during Jesus' trial, the chief priests are *hostile, violent, exasperated,* and *murderous* (19:6, 15). They even show *disloyalty* to their own religious traditions in order to secure Jesus' death (19:15). In complaining to Pilate about the precise wording of the inscription on the cross, the chief priests appear *punctilious* and *dissatisfied* (19:21). In sum, the chief priests have multiple traits, indicating a complex corporate character.[11]

Character Development

Character development is not simply the addition of a trait that the reader infers further along the text continuum or a character's progress in his or her understanding of Jesus.[12] Development is revealed in the character's ability to surprise the reader, when a newly found trait replaces another or does not fit neatly into the existing set of traits, implying that the character has changed. By and large, the chief priests are consistent in their traits and behavior. The only event where they are able to surprise the reader is in 19:15. After having endured Pilate's prolonged taunting in their efforts to secure Jesus' death, the chief priests finally find a way to force Pilate's hand. When Pilate tries to release Jesus and the chief priests see their plans beginning to backfire, they corner Pilate by questioning his loyalty to the emperor (19:12). Knowing that he has been trapped, Pilate decides to tax the chief priests with a heavy price. By tauntingly asking them whether he shall crucify their king, Pilate is able to exact their allegiance to Rome and to make them sacrifice their religious and national hopes (19:15). The chief priests surprisingly choose to be disloyal to their religious traditions in order to secure Jesus' death and hence their own political survival.[13]

Inner Life

The inner life of a character gives the reader insight into the character's thoughts, emotions, and motivations, and is conveyed usually by the narrator

---

[11] While certain personal qualities or behavioral features of the chief priests recur (e. g., their hostility and murderous intent), others occur only once and one could question whether these constitute a trait. On the other hand, how often does a particular personal quality need to occur before we can call it a trait? What if a character only has a few appearances in the narrative and "has no opportunity" to show certain characteristics again?

[12] Contra Resseguie, *Narrative Criticism,* 153.

[13] For this analysis of Jesus' trial before Pilate, see Bennema, *Encountering Jesus,* 183–89.

and sometimes by the characters themselves.[14] In John's Gospel, however, Jesus also reveals the inner life of some characters, which should not surprise us since he is the revealer *par excellence*, who knows all people and what is in them (2:24–25; cf. 6:64; 13:11; 16:30; 21:17). Regarding inner life, characters range from those who, via the narrator or Jesus, allow us a peek inside their minds to those whose minds remain opaque. When it comes to the chief priests, there is some penetration into their inner life:

- they are *upset* and *anxious* about the possible implications of Jesus' raising of Lazarus (11:47–48);
- they are first *uncertain* about what to do (11:47–48) but then *resolve* to kill both Jesus (11:53) and Lazarus (12:10);
- their shouting shows that they are *exasperated* by Pilate's handling of the case (19:6, 15);
- their remark to Pilate regarding the inscription on the cross implies *dissatisfaction* (19:21).

It may be unsurprising that aspects of the chief priests' inner life relate to their traits. For example, their frustration with Pilate's taunts is caused by their hostility and murderous intent regarding Jesus; their dissatisfaction about the precise wording of the inscription on the cross arises from (or reveals) their being punctilious.

Characterization and Evaluation of the Chief Priests

After this character analysis, we can classify the character of the chief priests by positioning them on the characterization continuum. Considering their location on the axes of complexity (complex, multiple traits), development (little), and inner life (some), I suggest to identify the resulting character as a corporate personality. That is, as a homogeneous group, the chief priests act as a singular character that shows personality but falls short of individuality. We must not understand the corporate personality of the chief priests in a modern individualistic sense but as a "group-oriented personality," where the chief priests' identity is embedded in the larger group of "the Jews."

In relation to the plot of John's Gospel, the chief priests propel it forward significantly through their masterminding and executing Jesus' death.[15] The raising of Lazarus proved to be crucial because this event and its aftermath

---

[14] Cf. Adele Berlin, *Poetics and Interpretation of Biblical Narrative* (Sheffield: Almond, 1983), 38.

[15] Cf. Andrew T. Lincoln, stating that the chief priests, as part of Jesus' opponents, provide for the complication or element of conflict in the plot (idem, *The Gospel according to Saint John* [BNTC 4; London: Continuum, 2005], 11–12).

caught the attention of the chief priests, who swiftly and decisively planned to remove Jesus from the scene. In this process of securing their own political survival, they were even prepared to sacrifice their own religious traditions and messianic hopes by feigning allegiance to Caesar. From John's evaluative point of view, informed by the salvific purpose of his Gospel (20:31), it is thus evident that the chief priests, in terms of their response to Jesus, must be evaluated negatively. With regard to the possible contemporary significance or representative value of the chief priests beyond John's narrative world, they could represent religious leaders who are so concerned about their status and survival that they are prepared to eliminate those whom they perceive as a threat at all costs.

The Temple Police: Double Agents

Gary T. Manning, Jr.

The temple police (ὑπηρέται, often translated as "officers") appear in four scenes in the Gospel of John. Although technically anonymous, the officers function as a consistent group, much like the anonymous chief priests and Pharisees, with whom the temple police are always associated. In the first scene (7:32, 45–49), the Pharisees and chief priests send the officers to arrest Jesus. Impressed by Jesus' words, the officers return empty-handed, and are rebuked by the Pharisees. In the second scene (18:1–13), Judas brings the temple police and Roman soldiers to arrest Jesus in the garden. After an exchange with Jesus, the temple police fall to the ground, allow Jesus' disciples to depart, and then take Jesus into custody. In the third scene (18:18–25), the temple police are with Jesus and Peter in the courtyard of the high priest. One officer strikes Jesus during his interrogation, while other officers question Peter as they warm themselves by a fire. In the final scene, the temple police act in unity with the chief priests, accusing Jesus before Pilate and calling for his crucifixion (18:28–31, 19:6).

Scene 1: Failed Arrest (John 7:32, 45–49)

The temple police are introduced during the conflict over Jesus' identity at the feast of Tabernacles. The narrator presents the police with some ambivalence in this scene, alternately creating reader antipathy and empathy. Narrators often build empathy with a character through positive characteristics or through alliances with other positive characters. Conversely, narrators build antipathy ("feelings of alienation or disdain") through alliances with other negative characters or through hostility towards empathetic characters.[1] Readers begin with a sense of antipathy towards the temple police, since they are agents[2] of the chief

---

[1] Mark Allan Powell, *What is Narrative Criticism?* (GBS; Minneapolis: Fortress, 1990), 56–57.

[2] In this essay, I use "agent" to refer to one who acts on behalf of the protagonist or the antagonists. The temple police can also be described as "transitional agents," characters who

priests and Pharisees, sent to arrest Jesus; they are thus allied with the main antagonists of the Fourth Gospel. The officers' possible inclusion with the divided crowd (7:44–44) adds to this negative characterization. On the other hand, the police do not carry out their orders; after hearing Jesus' words, they return empty-handed, unwilling to arrest Jesus. Their positive response to Jesus presents them as empathetic characters. But the reader is left with uncertainty over even this positive portrayal: were the police truly unwilling to arrest Jesus? Or were they unable?

One of John's marks of discipleship is witness to Jesus. Andrew, the Samaritan woman and the blind man (among others) are portrayed as ideal disciples as they attest to Jesus' identity, words or signs. Others in John are informants rather than witnesses, giving information about Jesus, but with a desire to hinder him rather than follow him. The anonymous disciples of John (3:25–26), the lame man (5:10–16), the "Jews" who report the raising of Lazarus (11:45–46), Caiaphas (11:49–53) and ultimately Judas (18:2–3) give correct information about Jesus, but are informants rather than witnesses. By speaking positively about Jesus against the wishes of the antagonists, the temple police function as witnesses rather than informants in this scene.

This positive aspect of the temple police is confirmed by their attention to Jesus' words. In John, those who respond to Jesus' words are favored over those who respond only to his signs (4:39–41, 48). The temple police fail to arrest Jesus because "never has a man spoken like this" (7:46). The positive depiction of the temple police continues as the Pharisees persecute them. The Pharisees reject the officers' opinion and heap verbal abuse on them: the officers are deceived, they are not thinking in accord with the rulers and Pharisees, and like the crowd, they do not understand the Law and are thus cursed (7:47–49). This persecution associates the temple police with other positive figures such as the blind man (9:34).

The officers' failure to arrest Jesus accomplishes another narrative function: revealing that Jesus is completely in charge of his destiny. It is not yet Jesus' hour to be arrested (7:30, 44; 8:20, 59). Jesus' cryptic "I am not ascending at this feast (ἐγὼ οὐκ ἀναβαίνω εἰς τὴν ἑορτὴν ταύτην), for my time is not yet fulfilled" (7:8) is possibly a *double entendre* indicating that Jesus will "ascend" at another feast (cp. 6:62, 20:17).[3] The temple police thus are unknowing

---

mediate in any way between other characters. D. Francois Tolmie, *Narratology and Biblical Narratives: A Practical Guide* (San Francisco: International Scholars, 1999), 55–56, relying on William J. Harvey, *Character and the Novel* (London: Chatto and Windus, 1965).

[3] This view of John 7:7 is not widespread, but Craig Keener suggests it as a possibility (idem, *The Gospel of John: A Commentary* [Peabody, Mass.: Hendrickson, 2003], 702). Without specifically discussing the double meaning, Augustine (*Tract. John* 28.5–8) and Chrysostom (*Tract. John* 28.8) also thought of this passage as primarily about a delay of glory until a later feast.

agents of the protagonist, as they delay the arrest of Jesus until his "hour" at Passover.

Despite the positive testimony of the temple police, the narrator does not label them as believers or apply any other discipleship terminology to them. Their amazement at Jesus' words seems almost forced – they are more unable rather than unwilling to arrest him.[4] Their lack of any title for Jesus ("never has a man spoken like this," 7:46) suggests lack of belief and understanding, since all believing characters give adequate titles to Jesus. The final associations of the temple police in this passage are ambivalent. The Pharisees correctly associate the police with the crowd; at the feast of Tabernacles, the crowd alternates between belief, confusion and hostility towards Jesus. The narrator also associates the officers with Nicodemus by their shared tentative defense of Jesus (7:50–52). This association with Nicodemus confirms the ambiguous status of the temple police, since astute readers are doubtful of Nicodemus' belief. The temple police emerge from the scene outwardly as agents of the antagonists, but secretly serve as agents of the protagonist both by their unwitting cooperation with Jesus' "hour" and by their tentative witness to Jesus. Their loyalties are divided.

Scene 2: Successful Arrest (John 18:1–13)

In the second scene, the temple police continue to function as "double agents," but now their loyalties are undivided. In the first scene, there was some ambiguity, as the actions of the temple police linked them both with the protagonist and with the antagonists. In the second scene, the temple police are depicted entirely negatively. There is no longer any willing defense of Jesus.

The narrator firmly establishes antipathy towards the temple police in the second scene by allying them with all of the major antagonists. Judas, "the one who betrayed him," brings the police; with them is the Roman cohort (or a contingent from the cohort). Throughout the scene, the police are treated together with the soldiers as a single group, identified primarily by third-person verbs and pronouns. The scene introduces them as "officers from the chief priests and Pharisees" (18:3).[5] At the end of the scene, they are described as

---

[4] Anthony Hopkins suggests that Johannine faith requires both cognitive and volitional components. Because the temple police express no clear statements about Jesus and their admiration of Jesus' words seems almost forced, the narrator does not seem to be presenting them as believers (idem, "A Narratological Approach to the Development of Faith in the Gospel of John" [Ph.D. diss.; Louisville, Ky.: Southern Baptist Theological Seminary, 1992], 247).

[5] John's word order (ἐκ τῶν ἀρχιερέων καὶ ἐκ τῶν Φαρισαίων ὑπηρέτας) emphasizes the chief priests and Pharisees, suggesting that the temple police serve as agents fulfilling their senders' wishes.

"the officers of the Jews" (οἱ ὑπηρέται τῶν Ἰουδαίων, 18:12). While "the Jews" is a famously ambivalent term in John, it is clearly used for the enemies of Jesus by this point in the narrative, and is perhaps synonymous with the chief priests (see 18:14, 31, 36, 38). The bearing of torches, lamps and weapons is the final detail emphasizing their hostility toward the protagonist. The torches and lamps are also an ironic touch. The temple police are part of the darkness that tries to overcome the Light (1:5); here they meet Jesus at night (cf. 3:2, 4:6-7) and bring their own insufficient light.

Readers might expect that an arrest scene would depict the arresting officers as firmly in charge, and the arrested as a victim. However, the author narrates the scene to reveal that Jesus is in charge of his arrest. Jesus goes out to meet the arresting officers, questions them and gives them orders.

The repeated exchange between Jesus and the officers is compelling. Jesus' question, "Whom do you seek?" (τίνα ζητεῖτε) invites them to respond properly to him. Jesus asks similar questions to the first disciples (τί ζητεῖτε, 1:38) and to Mary Magdalene (τίνα ζητεῖτε, 20:6), and is called rabbi and Lord in response. The response of the officers, "Jesus the Nazarene" is technically correct (visitors from other towns were commonly identified by their town of origin), but is utterly inadequate in the Fourth Gospel. "Jesus the Nazarene" recalls Nathanael's initial skepticism of Jesus as a resident of Nazareth (1:45-46), the crowd's doubt that Jesus can be the Christ since he is from Galilee (7:41), the Pharisees' rejection of Jesus as the Prophet because he is from Galilee (7:52), and it foreshadows the mocking charges against Jesus on the *titulus* (19:19). In John, genuine disciples always address Jesus with an adequate title such as "rabbi" or "Lord" (and occasionally a more exalted title). The opponents of Jesus, as well as the uncertain crowds, never give him a title. The Pharisees pointedly refer to him as "this man" (οὗτος) or use no title at all, and Judas, in his only interaction with Jesus, uses no title.

Jesus responds to their inadequate title with his own lofty title: "I am" (ἐγώ εἰμι). John's play on words is clear by this point in the narrative.[6] While "I am" is a normal way to identify oneself in Greek (the blind man uses it in 9:9), Jesus has now used it twenty times to point to his multifaceted identity. This, Jesus' last use of the phrase in this Gospel, is reminiscent of his first two uses. When the Samaritan woman mentions the Christ, Jesus answers "I am, the one who speaks to you" (4:26). When the disciples fear Jesus as he walks on the water, he comforts them by saying "I am; do not be afraid" (6:20). Jesus' use of "I am" at the arrest reminds the readers that he is more than Jesus of Nazareth. He is the bread of life, the good shepherd, the true vine, and the way; ultimately he is the one who was with God and was God.

---

[6] See also Gary Burge, *John* (NIVAC; Grand Rapids, Mich.: Zondervan, 2000), 492; Keener, *John*, 1082; Andreas Köstenberger, *John* (BECNT; Grand Rapids, Mich.: Baker Academic, 2004), 507.

The Roman soldiers and the temple police respond to Jesus' words by "drawing back" (18:6), revealing again that Jesus is in charge of his own arrest. The narrator uses the phrase "they drew back" (ἀπῆλθον εἰς τὰ ὀπίσω) to compare the officers to the enemies of God in the LXX. The phrase εἰς τὰ ὀπίσω is repeatedly used to describe God shaming his enemies and forcing them to retreat (LXX Ps 9:4, 34:4, 39:15, 55:10, 69:3, 77:66, 128:5; cf. 1 Macc. 9:47).[7] John's use of this phrase in this military setting suggests that the officers are routed and shamed by the words of Jesus.

The temple police are not only routed; they also must give homage to Jesus. The phrase "they fell to the ground" recalls scenes of worship or obeisance in the LXX:

ἔπεσαν χαμαί (John 18:6)	Soldiers and police fall to the ground before Jesus.
πεσὼν χαμαὶ προσεκύνησεν (Job 1:20)	Job falls to the ground before God.
πεσὼν... χαμαὶ προσεκύνησε (Dan 2:46)[8]	Nebuchadnezzar falls to the ground before Daniel.

Both of these scenes (the only two scenes in the LXX to use this phrase) involve some volition on the part of the worshipper; in contrast, the worship of the temple police is completely involuntary.

Jesus' mastery over the temple police continues when he commands the release of his disciples. Peter's attack on Malchus constitutes an attack on the high priest (18:10); readers naturally expect that the temple police will function as agents of the chief priests and arrest Peter. But instead, the police obey Jesus' command to release Peter and the rest of the disciples (18:8). If the officers' retreat from and obeisance before Jesus were involuntary, then this obedience to Jesus seems equally involuntary.

Two final details confirm that the temple police are "double agents," working voluntarily on behalf of the antagonists and involuntarily on behalf of the protagonist. First, John informs the readers in a narrative aside that the temple police release the disciples "to fulfill the word that [Jesus] spoke, 'I lost not one of those whom you gave me'" (18:9; cf. 6:39, 17:12).[9] Second, Jesus' rebuke to

---

[7] In non-military contexts, εἰς τὰ ὀπίσω can refer merely to looking or turning back (Gen 19:26, 1 Sam 24:9, John 20:14). John uses the same phrase (ἀπῆλθον εἰς τὰ ὀπίσω) to refer to the false disciples who turn away from following Jesus (6:66). This may be coincidental, since the two scenes are quite different; or it may suggest that the false disciples, like the soldiers, are enemies of God.

[8] Similarly, Daniel falls to the ground in sleep at the words of Gabriel: ἐκοιμήθην ἐπὶ πρόσωπον χαμαί (Dan 8:18).

[9] Robert Alter suggests that statements by the narrator are the most explicit and certain means by which a narrator communicates information about a character. Of less certainty are, in decreasing order, the character's thoughts, words and actions. The narrative aside here thus communicates a high degree of certainty that the characters are unwittingly fulfilling Jesus' words (idem, *The Art of Biblical Narrative* [New York: Basic Books, 1981], 116–17).

Peter reminds the readers that Jesus' arrest and coming ordeal is "the cup that the Father has given me" (18:11). The temple police are ultimately carrying out the purposes of the main protagonists, Jesus and the Father.

The scene closes with some irony: the Roman soldiers and the temple police "arrested Jesus and bound him" (18:12). Every interaction between Jesus and the soldiers in this scene has demonstrated that Jesus is in charge of his arrest; the final arrest and binding of Jesus is clearly allowed by Jesus.

Scene 3: Interrogation (John 18:18–25)

The third scene involving the temple police takes place in the courtyard of the high priest. The Roman cohort departs, making the temple police somewhat more prominent, although now they act in concert with other people in the courtyard. The police continue to serve as agents of the chief priests; this is perhaps more clear in Greek, since "high priest" and "chief priest" are the same word (ἀρχιερεύς). While the scene is a coherent narrative unit, the point of view switches back and forth between Jesus and Peter.

Jesus' interaction with the temple police in this scene is brief. After Jesus asks Annas (the ἀρχιερεύς) to call witnesses, one of the officers strikes Jesus, accusing him of disrespect. Jesus challenges the officer to explain the attack (18:21–23). Ironically, Jesus' earlier words had commanded the officers' respect: "Never has a man spoken like this" (οὕτως, 7:46). Now, Jesus' words unfairly provoke an officer's abuse: "Do you answer the high priest like this (οὕτως, 18:22)?"

The officer's actions are a fulfillment of Jesus' words and Scripture (sometimes treated together in John; cp. 2:22). The officer fulfills Jesus' words from a few hours earlier: "…now they have seen and hated both me and my Father… it is written in their law: 'They hated me without cause'" (15:24–25). The officer is one who hates Jesus and thus hates the Father; his hatred is unjustified. This hatred is also a fulfillment of Scripture. Jesus' quote of Ps 68:5 LXX connects the unjust accusation against the psalmist with the officer's attack on Jesus. Jesus' challenge to the officer makes it clear that the slap is also "without cause." The officer's slap (ῥάπισμα) also draws the readers' attention to the only passage that uses the word in the LXX: "I gave my back to the whips and my cheeks to slaps (ῥαπίσματα); I did not turn my face away from the shame of spitting" (Is 50:6 LXX).[10] The officer thus unwittingly fulfills a role described in the Scriptures, like others who continue to abuse Jesus throughout these last scenes in John.

---

[10] Ῥάπισμα is only used in the NT to refer to the abuse of Jesus (John 18:22, 19:3; Mark 14:65).

Peter's interaction with the temple police occurs before and after Jesus' interrogation, inviting readers to compare the two encounters. The narrator closely connects Peter with the temple police: they are "standing and warming themselves" at the fire and Peter is "with them, standing and warming himself" (18:18, repeated in 18:25).[11] This apparent friendliness with the temple police contrasts sharply with the "hatred without cause" that Jesus experiences from one of the officers. Peter's vigorous denial of his identity also sharply contrasts him with Jesus. Peter's answer, "I am not" (οὐκ εἰμί, 18:25; cf. 18:17) is the opposite of Jesus' open affirmation, "I am" (ἐγώ εἰμι, 18:5, 6, 7; cf. 18:20). As R. Brown explains, "Jesus stands up before his questioners and denies nothing, while Peter cowers before his questioners and denies everything."[12] While the passage focuses on Jesus and Peter, the temple police provide the explicit contrast between them. Peter stands with the enemy in comfort, while Jesus stands against the enemy and suffers from their unjust hatred.

Scene 4: Crucify! (John 18:28–31, 19:6)

The final scene in which the temple police appear is the encounter between Pilate and the chief priests. Interestingly, the narrator is not specific about who brings Jesus to Pilate. He uses third-person verbs and pronouns such as "they brought Jesus to the praetorium," "they did not enter," and "Pilate went out to them" (18:28–30). The previous context indicates that "they" are the chief priests and the temple police, but they are primarily identified as "they" or "the Jews" in the conversation with Pilate (18:31, 38, 19:7).

The temple police are in the background; despite the generic "they," the narrative does not seem to depict them discussing the charges with Pilate. However, when Pilate presents Jesus in royal robes and crown, the narrator specifies that it is the chief priests and temple police who first cry out, "Crucify! Crucify!" Clearly the temple police act now in utter hostility to Jesus. They reject Pilate's declaration of innocence, and will not acknowledge even a mocking declaration of his kingship (19:5–7; cf. 19:15, 21). The officers' outcry (ἐκραύγασαν) links them with the other cries for violence against Jesus (18:40, 19:12, 19:15), and perhaps creates a contrast with those who cry out (ἐκραύγαζον) "Hosanna" to Jesus (12:13).

When Pilate questions Jesus about his kingdom, Jesus answers that his own officers (ὑπηρέται) are not fighting on his behalf, proving that Jesus' kingdom

---

[11] Peter "stands with Jesus' enemies" (Köstenberger, *John*, 515). Note the contrast with the disciples who were "with Jesus" (18:1-2) and the Beloved Disciple who entered "with Jesus" (18:15).

[12] Raymond E. Brown, *The Gospel According to John* (AB 29; New York: Doubleday, 1970), 842.

is not from the world (18:36). In this setting, Jesus' reference to his "officers" (the only time he ever refers to his followers by this title) is likely intended as a contrast with the temple officers. The violence and hostility of the temple police confirms that the kingdom they serve – a kingdom centered on the Temple and ruled by the chief priests – is a kingdom of the world.

In these final two scenes, the temple police act primarily as agents of the antagonists. While they are still ultimately carrying out the plans of Jesus and the Father, they do so as enemies; there is no sense of even grudging admiration or unwilling worship.

Conclusions

The temple police are *ficelles*, minor characters who serve primarily as plot functionaries and transitional agents between Jesus and the chief priests.[13] Their relative insignificance is confirmed by the way in which they blend in and are treated together with other character groups. In the first scene, they act much like the crowds and Nicodemus; in the second scene, they are treated together with the Roman cohort; and in the third and fourth scenes, they act in concert with the chief priests.

However, the temple police exhibit more roundedness than walk-on characters, as the narrator portrays them with some complexity, development, and penetration into inner life.[14] Their unwillingness or inability to arrest Jesus in the first scene gives some hint into their inner life. Their role as "double agents" gives them some complexity, since they serve the purposes of both the protagonist and the antagonists. There is a clear line of development in their characterization, but it is a development away from belief. In the first scene, the officers are impressed by Jesus and are sympathetic to him. Each successive scene shows them with greater conformity to the antagonists and greater hostility towards the protagonist. In scene two, they unwillingly bow to Jesus and obey him; in scene three, they abuse Jesus; and in scene four, they join with the chief priests in demanding Jesus' death. Ideal characters in John (as well as ideal readers) grow in their belief and loyalty to Jesus; the temple police grow in unbelief and hostility toward Jesus.

As with all other characters in John, the temple police serve as foils to Jesus. Willingly or unwillingly, the temple police attest to Jesus' words. In scene one, the temple police acknowledge the power of Jesus' words; they also unknow-

---

[13] Tolmie, *Narratology and Biblical Narratives*, 55–56, relying on Harvey, *Character and the Novel*.

[14] Joseph Ewen's three criteria for character roundedness (Tolmie, *Narratology and Biblical Narratives*, 56; citing Joseph Ewen, "The Theory of Character in Narrative Fiction," *Hasifrut* 3 [1974]: 1–30).

ingly serve Jesus' purposes as they cooperate with the "hour" of Jesus' arrest. In the second scene, they fulfill God's plans by arresting Jesus, and they unwillingly testify to Jesus' words by retreating and falling in worship when Jesus speaks. In the third and fourth scenes, the hostility of the temple police attests to the validity of Jesus' words: "they hated me without cause." Together with Jesus' other opponents, the temple police function as the darkness, and thus draw attention to the Light. Even as minor characters, the temple police help the narrator present the central choice of the Fourth Gospel to his readers: either to vainly try to overcome the Light, or to welcome the Light and thus receive his life.

The Greeks:
Jesus' Hour and the Weight of the World

Sherri Brown

In the Gospel according to John, the arrival of "the hour" of Jesus, an hour that was first introduced at the wedding feast in Cana (2:4) and that underscored the entirety of his public ministry, is marked by the coming of Greeks to Jesus (12:20–36).[1] Jesus himself announces the arrival of this hour when told by Philip and Andrew that "some Greeks" who had come up to worship at the Passover festival wished "to see" him (12:23). In the theological diction of the Fourth Evangelist, this active request by Greeks "to see Jesus" can be associated with a desire to believe.[2] The idea of Jesus' message reaching the Greeks in the diaspora had been earlier introduced by "the Jews" with some consternation at the festival of Tabernacles (7:35). Now following his entry into Jerusalem at this major Jewish festival, the coming of these Greek Gentiles to see Jesus punctuates the Pharisees' dismay at their futile attempts to restrict Jesus' effect since "the whole world has gone after him" (12:19).

The narrative force of the corporate character of the Greeks in the Gospel of John should not be underestimated.[3] Although the Greeks have little direct

---

[1] For the foreshadowing of the impending "hour" of Jesus' passion and glorification, see 2:4; 4:21, 23; 5:25, 28; 7:30; 8:20; 12:23, 27.

[2] For variations on the association of seeing with the intention of believing, see 1:50; 4:48; 6:30; 11:40; 20:25, 27.

[3] In the scholarly literature there is relatively little research on the corporate character of the Greeks in John. In 1970, Hendrik B. Kossen focused a study on the ethnicity of these characters (idem, "Who Were the Greeks of John xii 20?," in *Studies in John: Presented to Dr. J. N. Sevenster on the Occasion of His Seventieth Birthday* [NovTSup 24; ed. A. S. Geyser; Leiden: Brill, 1970], 97–110). In 1990, Johannes Beutler offered a review of the tradition history of this passage, and then examined the underlying theme of Isaiah's suffering servant (idem, "Greeks Come to See Jesus [John 12,20f]," *Bib* 71 [1990]: 333–47). In 1994, Jörg Frey contributed to the discussion in terms of the angst the arrival of the Greeks brought to Jesus and the narrative force of this encounter (idem, "Heiden–Griechen–Gotteskinder," in *Die Heiden: Juden, Christen und das Problem des Fremden* [ed. Reinhard Feldmeier and Ulrich Heckel; WUNT 70; Tübingen: Mohr Siebeck, 1994], 228–68. In 2000, Jonathan Draper revisited the question of ethnicity with reference to the Isaiah quotation (idem, "Holy Seed and the Return of the Diaspora in John 12:24," *Neot* 34 [2000]: 347–59). Other minor contributions include Thomas F. Torrance, "We Would See Jesus (John 12:21)," *EvQ* 23 (1951): 171–82; W. E. Moore, "Sir, We Wish to See Jesus: Was this an Occasion of Temptation?," *SJT* 20 (1967): 75–93; and Joseph Pathrapankal, "Jesus and the Greeks: Reflections on a Theology of Religious Identity," *Journal of Dharma* 10 (1985): 392–403. The bulk of scholarship on this

speech and no apparent dialogue with Jesus, their arrival confirms both the universal intent and result of Jesus' ministry. Further, their presence seems to provide Jesus affirmation for the fulfillment of his own promise for sheep not of the fold to join his flock (10:16). Indeed the coming of the Greeks marks the arrival of the hour that Jesus must lay down his life for that flock (12:23–36; see 10:14–18).

Setting the Scene: John 12

John 12 narrates the final moments of Jesus' public ministry and thereby concludes the so-called Book of Signs (1:19–12:50). At the same time, these crucial scenes, especially 12:20–36, transition the narrative into the Book of Glory and the passion and glorification of the Christ (13:1–20:31). The "hour" of vss. 23 and 27, so long coming in Jesus' mission, arrives and "now" (v. 31) is the appointed time of the death, resurrection, and exaltation of Jesus.[4] Characters, time, space, and dialogue combine with theological force to drive the plot forward.[5]

The first scene, 12:1–8, confirms the coming of the Passover introduced in 11:55, now in just six days, and concludes the climactic sign of chapter 11 and the raising of Lazarus from death (11:1–44; see 11:2). Mary anoints Jesus' feet with a costly ointment at a meal in Bethany where both her siblings and Jesus' disciples are also present (v. 3). Jesus affirms that her intimate action is preparation for his burial, but her anointing of his feet also serves the kingship motif that continues from Nathanael's early proclamation of Jesus as the "King of Israel" (1:49) and will come to a head in the passion (18:28–19:16, 19–21) through Jesus' lifting up and exaltation (12:32, 34), but on a cross. Judas's objection to Mary's act is characterized by his impending role as Jesus' betrayer (v. 4; see 6:64, 71; 13:11, 21; 18:2, 5). The anointing of this king, therefore, is an anointing of his body for burial.[6] Jesus' entry into Jerusalem is also

---

characterization is to be found as part of studies of larger issues such as Judith L. Kovacs, "'Now Shall the Ruler of this World be Driven Out': Jesus' Death as Cosmic Battle in John 12:20–36," *JBL* 114 (1995): 227–47; and Kiyoshi Tsuchido, "Tradition and Redaction in John 12.1–43," *NTS* 30 (1984): 609–19.

[4] On the eschatological nature of the hour, see the discussion in Kovacs, "Ruler," 228–29, 246–47. More generally, see also Raymond E. Brown, *The Gospel According to John (i–xii)* (AB 29; Garden City, N. Y.: Doubleday, 1966), 146; Rudolf Schnackenburg, *The Gospel According to St. John* (3 vols.; New York: Crossroad, 1987), 2:380.

[5] On the narrative force of this passage, see Francis J. Moloney, *The Gospel According to John* (SP 4; Collegeville, Minn.: Liturgical Press, 1998), 347–48. On the theological force, see Brown, *John*, 470.

[6] R. Alan Culpepper, *The Gospel and Letters of John* (Nashville: Abingdon, 1998), 193.

framed by references to Lazarus (vss. 9–11, 17–19), thus connecting these accolades to that sign as well as the condemnation by the Judean leadership that resulted from it (11:45–54). The narrator states that many "'Jews' were going away and believing in Jesus" (v. 11). This activity is confirmed in the narration of the actual entry, including the crowd's response to Jesus by way of Ps 118, and the narrator's characterization of the event through Zechariah 9:9 (vss. 12–15). This king and savior, however, will only be fully understood by his disciples after his passion and glorification (v. 16; see 2:22; 20:9). The crowd, and its potentially fickle nature, is here primarily because of that last sign when Jesus raised Lazarus from death (vss. 17–18) and their own messianic hopes. The Pharisees, for their part, are concerned that their efforts at eliminating Jesus have been fruitless, for the "whole world has gone after him" (v. 19). So many words are being fulfilled: those of Jesus (10:15–16), Caiaphas (11:50), and the narrator (11:52). If "the world" is going after Jesus, then the hour of his violent death must also be at hand (7:30; 8:20).[7]

There is, however, one ethnic group of "the world" – of sheep not of the Good Shepherd's fold for which he must also lay down his life – which has not yet arrived. The following scene resolves this tension with the arrival of "some Greeks" to see Jesus (vss. 20–21) which in turn brings about "the hour" (v. 23) of the Son of Man's lifting up and glorification (vss. 20–36).[8] In John's closest parallel to the agony in Gethsemane in the Synoptics, Jesus relates the human darkness of a troubled soul at facing this hour (v. 27).[9] However, through the metaphor of the grain of wheat, Jesus teaches that death brings new life (vss. 24–26) and the voice from heaven (v. 28) coupled with Jesus' response (vss. 30–32) point to the fulfillment of eschatological promises for the defeat of the ruler of this world and universal salvation (vss. 31–32; see 4:42).[10] The necessity is for Jesus' to die (v. 33); the appropriate response for the crowd is to turn away from the darkness, believe in the light, and thereby become children of the light (vss. 34–36; see 1:4–5, 9–12).

This climactic moment in the revelation of the Word to the world is followed by the narrator's longest exposition in the Gospel (vss. 37–43) which is supported with two quotations from Isaiah (55:1; 6:10).[11] In these words, the narrator provides an evaluation of Jesus' ministry to the world. The servant

---

[7] Moloney, *John*, 351.

[8] Moloney, *John*, 353, 359; Ignace de la Potterie, "L'exaltation du Fils de l'homme (Jn 12,31–36)," *Greg* 49 (1968): 461–62.

[9] See Mark 14:36 and parallels as well as Psalm 42/43. Frey, "Heiden," 228–68; Moloney, *John*, 353, 359; Schnackenburg, *John*, 2:387; Wilhelm Thüsing, *Die Erhöhung und Verherrlichung Jesu im Johannesevangelium* (NTAbh 21/1-2; 3d ed.; Münster: Aschendorff, 1979), 78–88.

[10] Kovacs, "Ruler," 227–47; Gail R. O'Day and Susan Hylen, *John* (Westminster Bible Companion; Louisville, Ky.: Westminster John Knox, 2006), 126.

[11] Culpepper, *Gospel and Letters*, 195.

nature of both Jesus' public ministry and the hour of his passion and glory are linked through these quotations and Isaiah 52:15, which tells of the arrival of the nations before the suffering servant.[12] Isaiah's pronouncement of judgment belies the authenticity of the faith of the crowds and sets the stage for Jesus' parting words (vss. 44–50).[13] This final speech summarizes and concludes the entirety of the ministry of John 1–12. The Word speaks without the boundaries of time and setting to any and all who would listen. The intimate relationship between God and the Word (1:1–2), Jesus and the Father (vss. 49–50), will culminate in this hour of Jesus' passion, death, and glorification, all suffered on behalf of the children of the light who believe in him (vss. 35–36, 44–45).

The Characters: John 12:20–36

The Greeks enter the stage at v. 20, where the mention of the feast (ἐν τῇ ἑορτῇ) connects this scene to the general context of the Passover which is the backdrop of this entire series. The lack of a clear temporal marker beyond the general connecting δέ situates this scene shortly following Jesus' entry into Jerusalem and likely in the Temple precincts where he often interacted and taught (2:14, 15; 5:14; 7:14, 28; 8:2, 20; 10:23). Some Greeks among those who have come up to worship wish to see Jesus. These Greeks, Ἕλληνές, are Greeks by birth, "God-fearers" or proselytes, who admire Judaism and live by its tenets as they are able. They are not Ἑλληνισταί, the term more appropriate for Greek-speaking Jews from the diaspora.[14] Therefore these Greeks serve as representatives of the Gentile world whose presence is underlined by Jesus' self-understanding as the one who is "drawing all to himself" (v. 32).[15] Again, the notion of "the Greeks" and the attractiveness of Jesus leaving his own country and bypassing the potential danger posed by his own people to teach in the diaspora were first introduced in 7:35, but this is their first appearance as agents who encounter Jesus.

These Greeks approach Philip who, the narrator reminds us, was from Bethsaida in Galilee (v. 21; see 1:43–44). Philip's Greek name and his background in the Gentile vicinity of the Galilee and the Decapolis ensure his role as a liaison to Jesus and underscore the arrival of the nations. The Greeks relay their wish "to see Jesus" (θέλομεν τὸν Ἰησοῦν ἰδεῖν). Although this desire to

---

[12] For a full discussion of the underlying Isaian suffering servant motif in this passage, see Beutler, "Greeks," 333–47.

[13] For other NT occurrences of this key quotation from the prophet Isaiah, see Mark 4:12; Matt 13:14; Luke 8:10; Acts 28:26; Rom 11:8. For discussion, see Culpepper, *Gospel and Letters*, 195.

[14] For full discussion of the ethnic identity of these characters, see Kossen, "Greeks," 97–110; More briefly, see Brown, *John*, 466; Moloney, *John*, 351.

[15] Beutler, "Greeks," 343; O'Day and Hylen, *John*, 126.

see may simply indicate the superficial sense "to meet," in the Johannine theological context it carries the more profound sense of the revelation of God and the Greeks' hope to believe in Jesus.[16] Philip responds by seeking out Andrew, the other disciple whose name is transmitted in its Greek form and who also comes from Bethsaida, and together they (Ἀνδρέας καὶ Φίλιππος) go to Jesus and share the news (v. 22; see 1:35–46). This abundance of Greek/Gentile characterization and action confirms the fear of the Pharisees that "the whole world has gone after him" (v. 19).

For his part, Jesus answers them not by directly responding to the Greek's request, rather by pointing to the significance of it, both theologically and narratively (vss. 23–36). He begins by acknowledging the arrival of the long-expected hour, "The hour has come for the Son of Man to be glorified" (v. 23). Through the remainder of the scene Jesus dialogues with his disciples, the voice from heaven, and the crowds to explain what the arrival of the hour will mean for himself, his followers across ethnicities, and "the Jews." The Greeks do not reappear or have any direct dialogue. They have faded from the stage as their part has been played. However, the themes of gathering those in and outside of Jesus' original fold that has been emerging since the Good Shepherd discourse of chapter 10 comes to the fore with their request, and the arrival of the hour signals the need for the Good Shepherd to lay down his life for the sheep (10:11). The Greeks serve primarily as actants whose purpose is to drive the plot forward; nonetheless the narrative force of these characters and the scene in which they encounter Jesus must not be undervalued.[17]

The Narrative Force of the Greeks in the Gospel of John

This overview of the setting and character of the Greeks and their encounter with Jesus in the Gospel of John provides a brief paradigm of traits.[18] Directly, these actants in the narrative are characterized as Greeks (Ἕλληνές), and therefore ethnically Gentile and part of the larger "world" with whom "the Jews" associate and of whom they are wary. Indirectly, their environment and actions in terms of their presence at the festival of Passover among the worshipers who have come up to Jerusalem (ἐκ τῶν ἀναβαινόντων ἵνα προσκυνήσωσιν ἐν τῇ ἑορτῇ) characterizes them as God-fearers with an active affinity for

---

[16] Brown, *John*, 466; Moloney, *John*, 352, 359.

[17] For more on this sort of actant, see Fred W. Burnett, "Characterization and Reader Construction of Characters in the Gospels," *Semeia* 63 (1993): 3–78, esp. 18–20.

[18] For a full discussion of compiling a trait paradigm, see D. Francois Tolmie, *Narratology and Biblical Narratives: A Practical Guide* (Bethesda, Md.: International Scholars Publications, 1999), 39–62. He notes that a trait is "any relatively stable or abiding personal quality associated with a character" (Tolmie, *Narratology*, 41). The process by which an implied author characterizes may be direct, indirect, or both (Tolmie, *Narratology*, 42–47).

Judaism and its beliefs and practices. In addition, their speech in terms of their request through the likely Greek-speaking disciples "to see Jesus" also indirectly characterizes them as faith-seekers, Gentiles who desire to encounter and believe in Jesus.

Although this trait paradigm is brief, it does allow for the classification of the corporate character of the Greeks, and thus also for the implication of their narrative force in the Gospel. The Greeks are background characters who are neither complex nor developed in the plot, and the reader is given only minor penetration into their inner lives.[19] Nonetheless, according to Greimas' actantial model, the Greeks can be classified as "senders" who initiate and/or enable an event in the advancement of the plot, in this case the crucial arrival of the hour of the passion, exaltation, and glorification of Jesus by God through the cross.[20] The coming of the Greeks to see Jesus and their implicit intent to believe in him and his mission signals to Jesus the advent of the necessary suffering for the servant who lays down his life for a flock that breaks ethnic boundaries and encompasses the world, but also the fulfillment of his own promise for universal and eschatological salvation as the Good Shepherd of that flock, as affirmed by the voice from heaven. Through the setting of John 12 during the Passover festival coupled with the death, burial, kingship, and glorification imagery across these scenes, the Greeks and their hope for Jesus are the initial fruition of that fulfilled mission.

---

[19] William J. Harvey uses the category of "background characters" (idem, *Character and the Novel* [London: Chatto & Windus, 1965]) and Joseph Ewen employs the three axes of complexity, development, and penetration (idem, "The Theory of Character in Narrative Fiction," *Hasifrut* 3 [1974]: 1–30). See the discussion in Tolmie, *Narratology*, 53–57.

[20] For Greimas' model of six general categories of actants in narrative texts, see Algirdas J. Greimas, *Sémantique structural: Recherche dé méthode* (Paris: Larousse, 1966), 172–91.

The Scribes and the Elders: Mirror Characterization of Jesus and His Opponents in the *Pericope Adulterae*

Chris Keith

In his groundbreaking *The Anatomy of the Fourth Gospel*, R. Alan Culpepper observes that, in John's Gospel, "Most of the characters appear on the literary stage only long enough to fulfill their role in the evangelist's representation of Jesus and the responses to him."[1] The scribes (γραμματεῖς) of John 8:3 are an interesting example of this facet of Johannine characterization. Their appearance on the scene is short and their narrative function is, as Culpepper suggests, primarily to characterize the protagonist Jesus. They are an interesting example of Johannine characterization, however, because their status as Johannine characters is questionable. They appear in the *Pericope Adulterae* (John 7:53–8:11), a passage that one could perhaps best describe as "quasi-Johannine," since it most likely was not in the original version of John's Gospel but appears there so frequently in the manuscript tradition that English Bibles continue to print it at John 7:53–8:11.[2] Scribes are, in fact, utterly absent elsewhere in the Fourth Gospel; they appear only in this later addition to the narrative.[3] The interpolator of the *Pericope Adulterae* is thus an early reader of the Johannine narrative who, in making a contribution to that narrative, reveals a characterization of Jesus and his opponents that is both similar to and dis-

---

[1] R. Alan Culpepper, *Anatomy of the Fourth Gospel: A Study in Literary Design* (Philadelphia: Fortress, 1983), 102. Further, "They exist to serve specific plot functions, often revealing the protagonist, and may carry a great deal of representative or symbolic value" (Culpepper, *Anatomy of the Fourth Gospel*, 104).

[2] Although the *Pericope Adulterae* appears in at least twelve narrative locations in the Gospels of John and Luke, 95.9% of Greek manuscripts that include the passage place it at John 7:53–8:11. See further Chris Keith, "The Initial Location of the *Pericope Adulterae* in Fourfold Tradition," *NovT* 51 (2009): 209–31, here 213–14; repr. in *The* Pericope Adulterae, *the Gospel of John, and the Literacy of Jesus* (NTTSD 38; Leiden: Brill, 2009), 120–23.

[3] One can therefore only wonder at the following statement of Larry J. Kreitzer, "'Revealing the Affairs of the Heart:' Sin, Accusation and Confession in Nathaniel Hawthorne's *The Scarlet Letter*," in *Ciphers in the Sand: Interpretations of the Woman Taken in Adultery (John 7.53–8.11)* (ed. Larry J. Kreitzer and Deborah W. Rooke; BS 74; Sheffield: Sheffield Academic Press, 2000), 139–213, here 162: "There is every indication that 'scribes and Pharisees' are representative opponents within the Gospel accounts, most particularly within the Gospel of John."

similar to the evangelist's characterization.[4] Similar to the evangelist, the interpolator portrays Jesus in a heated dispute with Jewish authorities over the interpretation of the Mosaic Law. Dissimilar to the evangelist, the interpolator attributes to Jesus grapho-literacy (John 8:6, 8) and includes scribes, practitioners of this rare literate skill, among his representative opponents.[5]

Before concentrating upon the scribes in 8:3, however, we should consider their relationship to "the elders" whom the interpolator later mentions. According to John 8:9, "those who heard" (οἱ ἀκούσαντες) Jesus' famous words concerning throwing the first stone (8:7) began to leave the scene ἀρξάμενοι ἀπὸ τῶν πρεσβυτέρων. It is not entirely clear whether one should understand this usage of πρεσβύτερος nominally or adjectivally. If understood nominally ("beginning with/from the elders;" so NAB, NRSV, CEB), then "those who heard" includes "the scribes and the Pharisees" (8:3) and "all the people" (8:2) with the former, "the elders," leaving first. If πρεσβύτερος is understood adjectivally ("beginning with/from the eldest;" so KJV, NEB, RSV, NKJV, NASB, NIV, NLT, ESV, TNIV), it would refer only to the most senior members of the listening audience. This understanding of πρεσβύτερος would not clarify, however, whether it means "the eldest" among "all the people" *and* "the scribes and the Pharisees" or only "the eldest" from among the latter group.

Further narrative clues do not resolve the confusion over the precise identity of "those who heard" and left the scene. For example, although the group's departure in apparent shame may suggest in favor of their synonymous identity with "the scribes and Pharisees" who initially challenged Jesus, the fact that Jesus is left alone with the woman (8:9) indicates that all present – that is, "all the people" and "the scribes and the Pharisees" – were among the departing audience. In short, since the precise identity of "those who heard" is not clear, it is also not clear whether the πρεσβύτεροι of 8:9 are the same collective character as "the scribes and the Pharisees" of 8:3. In light of this lack of certainty and the fact that the Pharisees are elsewhere treated in this volume, I will focus here upon the scribes of 8:3 while acknowledging the possibility that they are also part of the πρεσβύτεροι of 8:9.

---

[4] On the interpolator's insertion of the passage, see further Chris Keith, "A Performance of the Text: The Adulteress's Entrance into John's Gospel," in *The Fourth Gospel in First-Century Media Culture* (ed. Anthony Le Donne and Tom Thatcher; ESCO/LNTS 426; London: T&T Clark, 2011), 49–69.

[5] On the rarity of grapho-literacy and the fact that fewer could write than could read, see *inter alia*, Catherine Hezser, *Jewish Literacy in Roman Palestine* (TSAJ; Tübingen: Mohr Siebeck, 2001), 474–95; Chris Keith, *Jesus' Literacy: Scribal Culture and the Teacher from Galilee* (LHJS 8/LNTS 413; London: T&T Clark, 2011), 89–110. For the argument that John 8:6, 8 is indeed a claim for grapho-literacy, see Keith, *Pericope*, esp. 27–52, 175–202.

The Scribes, Moses, an Adulteress, and Jesus

The scribes appear alongside the Pharisees in John 8:3, and thus as representative of Torah authority. The group brings to Jesus a woman caught in adultery (8:3), informs him of her crime (8:4), and challenges Jesus to contradict the prescribed Mosaic punishment for such a crime (8:4; note the emphatic σύ). The narrator informs the reader of their ill intentions in this affair – "to test him" (8:6). This narratorial aside further confirms that their earlier attribution of the title "Teacher" to Jesus in 8:4 is disingenuous, which the astute reader may have already surmised from the fact that they are not part of the group that receives Jesus' teachings daily in the temple in 8:2. Upon hearing Jesus' words from 8:7, the scribes (and others) leave the scene in 8:9.

As was already noted, the interpolator's inclusion of the scribes is an augmentation of Jesus' enemies in the Fourth Gospel, where the Pharisees appear in similar episodes of confrontation, including the immediately preceding context (John 7:32, 45, 47, 48). This augmentation highlights not only the curious absence of scribes in the Fourth Gospel, but equally their presence in the *Pericope Adulterae*, and thus their unique contribution to the Johannine narrative once this passage is inserted. Along these lines, their contribution extends beyond their actions and words and includes their identities as grapho-literate Torah authorities. That is, the interpolator here buttresses Jesus' opponents with the most educated of Torah authorities in Second Temple Judaism.[6] When Jesus outwits his opponents, therefore, he not only bests the authorities, but the most authoritative of the authorities – those who copy the holy law.

The Purpose of Grapho-Literate Opponents – A Grapho-Literate Jesus

The addition of grapho-literate enemies of Jesus is not the only unique contribution that the interpolator makes to the Johannine narrative, however. He also includes a grapho-literate Jesus in John 8:6, 8. I have argued elsewhere in depth that the interpolator inserted the *Pericope Adulterae* at John 7:53–8:11 as a reaction to the previous context of John 7, where scribal-literate authorities question Jesus' literacy (John 7:15), claim that "the crowd" does not know the law (John 7:45), and mock Galileans' inability to search the holy text for themselves (John 7:52).[7] In response, the interpolator inserts the *Pericope Adulterae* and asserts not only that Jesus, a Galilean, is educated, but that he is as educated as the most educated of his interlocutors. Jesus, like scribes,

---

[6] This is not to claim that all Second Temple scribes were Torah experts. See Christine Schams, *Jewish Scribes in the Second Temple Period* (JSOTSup 291; Sheffield: Sheffield Academic Press, 1998).

[7] See esp. Keith, *Pericope*, 141–202, but also *Jesus' Literacy*, 147–56.

holds grapho-literacy. Confirming that Jesus' grapho-literacy is a particular emphasis of the narrator is the fact that no one in the narrative itself seems to care that he writes. The scribes and Pharisees ignore Jesus' actions by continuing to question him after the first act of writing (8:6–7) and leave only upon hearing (8:9) the words he spoke in 8:7; that is, not upon seeing his writing despite the fact that the second act of writing interrupts Jesus' statement in 8:7 and their response in 8:9.[8] Therefore, the inclusion of scribes as grapo-literate opponents in John 8:3 is ultimately in service of characterizing Jesus as, at least, an equally-authoritative interpreter of Torah,[9] and is the interpolator's answer to a question that the Johannine narrative raises in John 7:15 but does not itself answer.

Conclusion

The scribes of John 8:3 are therefore an example of what one might call "mirror characterization" since their characterization reflects the characterization of the protagonist Jesus. Furthermore, this example underscores the inherent correctness of historical narrative criticism. It may be the case that, once the *Pericope Adulterae* is inserted within the narrative world of John's Gospel, their implied authors or narrators are indistinguishable. It is nevertheless also the case that, at some point in history, a scribe or scribal school augmented John's Gospel with a separate tradition. The interpolator was not only a different entity, then, but functioning simultaneously as a reader of John's Gospel and a shaper of the Johannine narrative himself. To ignore this phenomenon by collapsing all forms of characterization into the literary world of the Gospel would be to fail to appreciate this interpolator's unique contributions to Johannine characterization.

---

[8] Further confirming that the attribution of grapho-literacy to Jesus is the narrator's motivation is that he seems only to care *that* Jesus wrote, not *what* he wrote, despite a lengthy interpretive history that includes at least thirty-eight speculations as to the content or meaning of the writing (see Keith, *Pericope*, 11–21).

[9] The precise usage of καταγράφω in John 8:6 and γράφω in 8:8 reveals a further claim, which is that Jesus' Torah authority is to be paralleled with God over Moses. Exod 32:15 LXX uses the same combination of verbs, in the same syntactical order, to describe God's authorship of the Decalogue, which addresses the adulteress's sin. Jesus' superiority to Moses is, of course, a sustained Johannine theme as well (for example, John 1:17–18, 6:32).

The Adulterous Woman:
Nameless, Partnerless, Defenseless

Peter Phillips

"Mind the gap," although a cliché in contemporary studies, might be a good subtitle for this aporic aporneia of a pericope, or, perhaps, this aporic porneia? A sex/sexy/sexist scandal caught in a non-Johannine gap?[1] Are there simply too many gaps to make sense of what is happening in this pericope, certainly to make any clear arguments about characterisation? This is, of course, the woman's pericope – *Pericope Adulterae*, γυνὴ ἐπὶ μοιχείᾳ, *mulier adultera, the adulteress, the Accused*,[2] *die Ehebrecherin*:[3] a woman known by a crime rather than a name ... (and surely even the most malestream of scholars must shudder at that as they realize with Gail O'Day that whatever title we choose represents "a decisive reshaping of the text" itself.[4])

The gathering of gaps around the woman reflects in some way the instability of this text within the Johannine corpus. While O'Day seeks to explore the meaning of the text before turning to questions about its status within a canonical gospel, that is surely putting too many carts before too few horses! There are so many questions before we can even read the passage to grasp some meaning. Should this pericope be here at all? It is so verbally non-Johannine, yet intrinsically Johannine; displaced, homeless, forcibly fostered into the Johannine text by the hand of later scribes?[5] The gaps simply multiply

---

[1] Andrew T. Lincoln, *The Gospel According to John* (BNTC; London: Continuum, 2005), 534; Robert Maccini, *Her Testimony is True: Women as Witnesses According to John* (JSNTSup 125; Sheffield: JSOT, 1996), 235.

[2] Leticia Guardiola-Sáenz calls for the pericope to be renamed "Jesus and the Accused:" "Border Crossing and its Redemptive Power in John 7:53–8:11: A Cultural Reading of Jesus and *The Accused*," in *Transformative Encounters: Jesus and Women Re-Viewed* (ed. Ingrid R. Kitzberger; Leiden: Brill, 2000), 267–91, here 282.

[3] Ulrich Becker, *Jesus und die Ehebrecherin: Untersuchungen zur Text- und Überlieferungsgeschichte von Joh. 7.53–8.11* (BZNW 28; Berlin: Walter de Gruyter, 1963).

[4] Gail O'Day, "John 7:53–8:11: A Study in Misreading," *JBL* 111 (1992): 631–40.

[5] For a concise overview see Andreas J. Köstenberger, *John* (BECNT; Grand Rapids, Mich.: Baker Academic, 2004), 245–49. Also, J. Martin C. Scott, "On the Trail of a Good Story: John 7.53–8.11 in the Gospel Tradition," in *Ciphers in the Sand: Interpretations of the Woman Taken in Adultery (John 7.53–8.11)* (ed. Larry J. Kreitzer and Deborah W. Rooke; Sheffield: Sheffield Academic Press, 2000), 53–82. John P. Heil's arguments for Johannine authenticity (see John P. Heil, "The Story of Jesus and the Adulteress (John 7,53–8,11) Reconsidered," *Bib* 72 [1991]: 182–91) are comprehensively critiqued by Daniel Wallace, "Reconsidering 'The

throughout the piece – what is the context; has she got a name; where is the man; what does Jesus write; does Jesus "write" at all; is it in Hebrew, Greek or just a doodle; what is the theology of the hidden (but public) dusty inscription; does he hint at judgement or mercy; is there a gap between inscription and vocalization; do the words in the dust match the words of his mouth?[6] And why are so many of these questions about the men in (or not in) the passage and not about the woman at all?

The truth of the matter, the elephant in the room, the unavoidable gap, is that there may not be anything here of concern to us in terms of Johannine characterization. The gaps in the manuscript tradition and in the internal evidence seem to suggest a pericope imported from a wholly other text (*The Gospel of the Hebrews* suggested Becker [{mis}following Papias' comments recorded in Eusebius],[7] and Becker is followed by almost everyone). Of course, there are other theories. Bart Ehrman argues for a double tradition – two pericopae, one hinted at in the third-century *Didascalia Apostolorum* (and probably Papias/Eusebius) and another referred to by Didymus the Greek in the fourth century.[8] These two traditions were then merged into the Johannine version and inserted, somehow, into the text in the fourth century or so. Or perhaps, as Chris Keith argues, the floating logion was given its Johannine makeover, not to enhance the characterization of the alleged adulteress, but to enhance the prestige of Jesus, and to fulfil the need for a superliterate founder for the Christian Church.[9]

William Petersen urges commentators to read their sources more carefully.[10] Noting verbal and form-critical parallels between the *Pericope Adul-*

Story of Jesus and the Adulteress Reconsidered,'" NTS 39/2 (1993): 290–96. Wallace (290) concurs with Ehrman's "overwhelming" and "unanimous" conclusion that the pericope "did not originally form part of the Fourth Gospel." See Bart D. Ehrman, "Jesus and the Adulteress," NTS 34/1 (1988): 24–44. In fact, Ehrman's view is more faithfully adapted in Chris Keith's monograph, *The* Pericope Adulterae, *the Gospel of John and the Literacy of Jesus* (Leiden: Brill, 2009).

[6] Lincoln, *John*, 534; Guardiola-Sáenz, "A Cultural Reading," 284.

[7] Becker, *Jesus und die Ehebrecherin*, 92–99. Having suggested that critics who only see Papias as referring to a version of Luke 7:36ff as absurd ("abwegig"), he concludes on p. 99: "Denn es spricht, wie wir zu zeigen versuchten, alles dafür, daß es sich bei dem Eusebzitat um eine Geschichte handelt, die mit der in Joh 7 53ff erzählten identisch ist. Wir halten deshalb die Existenz der Perikope von der Ehebrecherin schon für die erste Hälfte des 2. Jh.s für erwiesen: Papias ist ihr ältester Zeuge."

[8] Ehrman, "Jesus and the Adulteress," 24–44; Lincoln summarises this argument more concisely, *John*, 526.

[9] Keith, *The* Pericope Adulterae, 201–56. Although it seems strange that anyone would feel that the characterization of Jesus would need enhancing in the Fourth Gospel of all places!

[10] William Petersen, "ΟΥΔΕ ΕΓΩ ΣΕ [ΚΑΤΑ]ΚΡΙΝΩ. John 8:11, The *Protevangelium Jacobi*, and the history of the *Pericope Adulterae*," in *Sayings of Jesus: Canonical and Non-Canonical: Essays in Honour of Tjitze Baarda* (ed. William L. Petersen et al.; NovTSup 89; Leiden: Brill, 1997), 191–221. Petersen gives an excellent overview of the source critical issues

terae (*PA*) and the late second-century *Prot. Jas.* XVI.3, as well as between John 20 and *Prot. Jas.* XIX.3, Petersen argues that *PA* could possibly have its origin within a Johannine milieu or, at least, one that is much older than many commentators suppose. Of course, even Petersen agrees that such an outcome would raise as many questions as it provides answers. For *PA* to be definitely Johannine, argues Petersen, we would need to agree with Augustine's rather extreme suggestion that copyists wilfully excluded the passage from their versions of the Gospel out of fear for their wives' continued fidelity![11] Therefore, Petersen offers a less radical solution, namely that the story could have been part of another Judaic-Christian gospel or source, possibly even *Gos. Heb.* Whatever the source, Petersen is certain that the Papias/Eusebius tradition refers to a completely different narrative, most probably Luke's account of the anointing at Bethany (Luke 7:36–50), and that it is this narrative which Papias was saying could be found in *Gos Heb.*[12] Petersen's argument centres on Rufinus' harmonisation, in which he translated, or, rather, paraphrased, Eusebius' "γυναικὸς ἐπὶ πολλαῖς ἁμαρτίαις" with "*mulieris adulterae.*" Essentially, the question is whether this is a story about a "woman accused of many sins" (Papias/Eusebius and *Gos. Heb.*) or specifically about an "adulteress" (Rufinus)?[13] Rufinus clearly thought it was the latter, amended Eusebius and so provided the only absolute link to *Gos. Heb.* This created a provenance for the pericope which most 20th century scholarship has followed with alacrity (*pace* Ehrman and Barrett[14]).[15]

Whatever the background source, whether excised from its Johannine(?) roots by prurient copyists or transplanted from some other early (Judaic-) Christian source, this floating logion inveigled itself into the Johannine narrative flow assisted by such greats as Jerome, Augustine, Bede and Erasmus. However, the pericope's status in the text and worthiness for comment continue to be resisted by gap-averse editors and commentators who pass directly

---

related to the *Pericope* including an exhaustive summary of the manuscript evidence. Köstenberger provides a concise summary, *John*, 247–48.

[11] See Tom Oden (ed.), *Ancient Christian Commentary on Scripture: New Testament Volume IVa: John 1–10* (Downers Grove, Ill.: IVP Press, 2006), 272.

[12] Contra Becker, see fn. 7.

[13] See Petersen, "John 8:11," 199, fn. 33. It is interesting that Ehrman and Keith gloss over this change and have no hesitation in equating the "woman accused of many sins" with the adulteress. Becker makes the point that the clear problems with this identification have not prevented the majority of scholars from making it: Becker, *Jesus und die Ehebrecherin*, 93. However, he then proceeds to argue against those problems, 93–99.

[14] Ehrman does argue from Didymus' own introduction to the story that the story may have been known to him in different "gospels" and that elsewhere Didymus makes clear that he knew the *Gos. Heb.* However, it is a matter of conjecture that this logion appeared in that Gospel – Papias does not give enough detail to confirm the identification. Barrett argues that, despite the number of sins, "the correspondence is none the less fairly close," C. Kingsley Barrett, *The Gospel According to John* (2d ed.; London: SPCK, 1978), 588.

[15] Petersen, "John 8:11," 196–200; Lincoln, *John*, 526.

from 7:52 to 8:12, somewhat like the adulteress herself, *sans regard, sans voix*.[16]

Somehow, though, *Pericope Adulterae* has always stood against the gaps and against its detractors.[17] Bauer described it as "die hohe absolute Wahrheit"; von Soden as "Meisterstil".[18] In his monograph on the pericope, Chris Keith tells the story of Bart Ehrman's appearances on American cable TV where he called the pericope "the most popular story in the Gospels". On the other hand, Ambrose pointed to the disturbing nature of the pericope and, as we have seen, Augustine sees it as a victim of the unofficial censors.[19] Köstenberger states, almost with stone in hand, that the pericope "almost certainly was not part of the original Gospel and therefore should not be regarded as part of the Christian canon. Nor does inspiration extend to it."[20] On the other hand, Michaels argues: "regardless of when it may have been added to the Gospel, it becomes a kind of subtext to Jesus' Temple discourse at the Tent festival ... Hers is a story within a story, accenting the same truth within a more concise and limited sphere."[21]

---

[16] Guardiola-Sáenz links our textual preferences with our cultural agendas: "Explicitly or implicitly, our rejection or acceptance of the text shows the imprint of our cultural values, political agendas, and in sum, maps the borders of our subjectivities in the content of the our cultural conditions of consumption (readership)," "A Cultural Reading," 78. Amidst the confusing array of witnesses, there are some startling silences: such as Adele Reinhartz, *Befriending the Beloved Disciple* (London: Continuum, 2001); Sandra Schneiders avoids the pericope in her exploration of the role of women in the Gospel in *Written that You May Believe: Encountering Jesus in the Fourth Gospel* (New York: Herder & Herder, 1999); and Jerome Neyrey, despite having chapters on women and public space and also the trial motifs in John 7: *The Gospel of John in Cultural and Rhetorical Perspective* (Grand Rapids, Mich.: Eerdmans, 2009). Elizabeth Green catalogues the *lacunae* even within feminist scholarship, "Making her Case and Reading it Too: Feminist Readings of the Story of the Woman Taken in Adultery," in *Ciphers in the Sand* (ed. Kreitzer and Rooke), 240–67. Köstenberger points out that about half of commentators bother to comment on the passage (Carson, Laney, Lindars, Whitacre, Calvin and Westcott), while the other half refrain (Michaels, Talbert, Stibbe, Brodie, D. M. Smith), 249, fn. 11. His own commentary explores the evidence for the placement of the pericope and then "refrain[s] from further comment." Amongst others, Lincoln offers a longer exploration as an appendix to his commentary, *John*, 524–36, as did Barrett more briefly, *John*, 589–91; Michaels provides his own longer comments *en passant*, *John*, 493–500.

[17] For some explorations of the reception history of the pericope, see Kreitzer and Rooke (ed.), *Ciphers in the Sand*. Lincoln, *John*, 536: "It is not surprising that, despite its disputed status, this intriguing story has continued to function as a compelling witness to Jesus." In her cultural reading of the Pericope, Guardiola-Sáenz talks of the Bible as a whole, epitomized by this pericope, as a cultural text which is both consumed by culture and which itself creates further cultural dialogue: "A Cultural Reading," 275.

[18] Petersen, "John 8:11," 192.

[19] Petersen, "John 8:11," 199–200; O'Day, "John 7:53–8:11," 639.

[20] Köstenberger, *John*, 248; Lincoln, *John*, 528 warns his readers off interpreting the passage in terms of a canonical reading, while later affirming its popularity as a "compelling witness to Jesus" (536).

[21] J. Ramsey Michaels, *The Gospel of John* (NICNT; Grand Rapids, Mich.: Eerdmans, 2010), 500.

The truth of the pericope's reception history, of course, is complex. Despite being dragged into the public sphere to be stoned to silence, shielded or not by her protective textual bracketing, the pericope has always been an important part of Christian understanding of Jesus' approach to sinners, becoming a popular corrective to contemporary fundamentalisms with her emphasis on non-condemnatory acceptance.[22] Guardiola-Sáenz calls it "a hybridised, border-crossing story" and quotes Gail O'Day's assertion that the text should be read in its own light – "a story without time or place, a story to be read on its own terms without sustained reference to its larger literary context."[23]

I am not sure that such a reading is possible or necessary. I prefer to read the pericope in its present context despite all the gaps. In the end this is a jewel of a passage: or rather that kind of jewellery where the piercing enhances the whole – where the gaps are part and parcel of the wonder of the expertise which has crafted such a piece of beauty. This is gold filigree. *Pericope Adulterae* comes adorned with layers of ambiguity, both internal and external; with a shimmer of play about silence and absence; with names and no names; with issues about gender and seniority. It is no doubt time that we focussed less on the setting and more on the jewel itself.

Of course, it is important to remember what we are supposed to be doing. We have been beguiled by the mystery of where this logion comes from, but the actual focus of our attention should have been on the woman herself. She has been standing there in the middle, dishevelled, embarrassed, alone, and we have ignored her all this time. The controversy of the text has blinded us to the controversy of the woman. Is it not always so? How ironic for us to ignore this poor woman dragged in to prove a legal point, dragged in by men (we presume?) who are themselves, like us, obsessed with texts (or texts about sex?).[24] In what follows, we need to ensure that we focus on the woman herself rather than on her detractors, and indeed rather than on Jesus, who seems to draw everyone's attention all the time. Her detractors need to slink away, the eldest first. Jesus will remain. But, we are exploring the characterization of the woman not the messiah, although we shall soon see that the two may be

---

[22] Two interesting examples: firstly, the use of the pericope in the retelling of the York Mystery Plays in 2012 – including the extraordinarily symbolic effect of the sound of the stones falling from people's hands onto the wooden stage flooring; secondly, the possible use of the story in Lady Gaga's video, *Judas*, where the singer, dressed in white, is dragged into the middle of a courtyard and stoned – is there no room for non-condemnatory acceptance for the contemporary whore?

[23] Guardiola-Sáenz, "A Cultural Reading," 276; Gail O'Day, "John," in *The Women's Bible Commentary* (ed. Carol A. Newsom and Sharon H. Ringe; Louisville, Ky.: Westminster John Knox, 1992), 294–302, here 297.

[24] It should be noted that not all are seduced by the text/source-critical aspects of the story – see Holly Toensing, "Divine Intervention or Divine Intrusion? Jesus and the Adulteress in John's Gospel," in *A Feminist Companion to John: Volume 1* (ed. Amy-Jill Levine; Sheffield: Sheffield Academic Press, 2003), 159–72.

intrinsically linked, especially if in some way she represents him, is a narratological avatar for him.²⁵ But, first, we need to begin to see how she is characterized in this passage and what that characterization means to its readers.

The first thing we see is the scene being set. The venue is the Temple – a public place, a sacred space, indeed, as Green notes, a public sphere of male theological debate.²⁶ Not only is it ironic that it is here in this sacred place that these religious accusers drag the woman in order to confront/trap Jesus, it is also a violation of the sacred space which Jesus himself has constructed.²⁷ They are seeking to establish that at the heart of faith is a list of rules and regulations, to which judges must adhere in order to provide good judgements. They want Jesus to affirm their view. The cast is Jesus, seated, teaching, surrounded by "all the people" (v. 2). The scene is calm and serene and positive. Jesus is characterized in his normal teaching mode, content to be within the sacred space, which is so contested in the chapters now surrounding this text. There is an audience both for his teaching and for what is soon to happen. Indeed, it is important to remember that this is an observed event, not just a private altercation between Jesus and the Pharisees/Scribes, with a woman in attendance. This is a public act of humiliation for her (and potentially for him?) and a public test for both. Whether the public remain right through to the end depends on whether the phrase "until only Jesus was left" (μόνος v. 9) means "on his own" with her, or perhaps more interestingly whether it signifies that Jesus is the only one of a special category of people left ("sinless" ones – ones who have the right to cast stones?). The woman too remains, throughout, "in the middle" (ἐν μέσῳ v. 9) of the scene, watched by the crowd and by Jesus.²⁸

The second thing we see is the woman and those scribes and Pharisees dragging her into the sacred space – a lynch mob invading Jesus' space, invading the Temple. Although, set within the disputes of John 7–8, we might think it is Jesus who they intend to lynch rather than the poor woman. Indeed, within a few verses, the narrator will mention that that is indeed their intention (v. 6). The woman was always a way of getting at Jesus – there were already rumours of his championing of her sort (John 4, 11, 12, 20). Into this context, into the midst of the people, under public gaze, they drag the woman "caught in adultery:" not only suspected of adultery, not rumoured to be an adulteress, but, they say (v. 4), actually caught "in the very act of committing adultery."²⁹

---

[25] Michaels, *John*, 495.
[26] Green, "Making her Case," 261.
[27] Guardiola-Sáenz, "A Cultural Reading," 283–84.
[28] Toensing, "Divine Intervention or Divine Intrusion," 166–67; for an alternative view, see Michaels, *John*, 500.
[29] Lincoln, *John*, 529. In v. 4 her accusers describe her as: ἡ γυνὴ κατείληπται ἐπ' αὐτοφώρῳ μοιχευομένη; Toensing, "Divine Intervention or Divine Intrusion," 161–62, especially fn. 10 which explores some of the feminist readings of this accusation.

Neither the narrator nor any of the characters within his narrative reject this salacious accusation.[30] It conjures harsh images for the modern mind of scribes and Pharisees invading the private space of the woman and her partner.[31] Such images are hardly softened by the commentators' reminders that eye witnesses were required in order for the death penalty to be carried out in accordance with Deuteronomy 17:6 and 19:15 – and that such eye witnesses could not be malicious![32] If caught in the very act, then it would seem as though the woman was the victim of some form of entrapment, that apparently holy men were waiting for her: out of reputation, hers or his?

But could it be even worse? The woman is portrayed alone. But if she has been caught in the act, where is the man also engaged in this act? In fact, he is subject to the death penalty too (Lev 20:10). Has he run to escape from the punishment? Has he been allowed to run because of his social status or simply because "he was fleeter of foot than she"?[33] Indeed, where is the woman's husband seeking to defend (or accuse) her? Could it be that either her adulterous accomplice or even her husband was complicit in the entrapment plan?[34] Indeed, could it be even worse? Scholars have pointed out that the woman could have been an involuntary partner to the act, since this would still be seen as adultery under the Torah.[35] It may be that she has been trapped in more than one way – trapped into an illicit sex act, trapped to cry out in distress, trapped to thus reveal her own involuntary sin. Beasley-Murray and Carson even toy with (and eventually dismiss?) the ghastly possibility that the woman is a betrothed girl between the age of twelve and twelve and a half, since the ("more lenient," sic) punishment for

---

[30] Maccini, *Her Testimony is True*, 235.

[31] Guardiola-Sáenz, "A Cultural Reading," 284: "They have come to defend the territory that patriarchy has granted them, and do not hesitate to cross personal borders and invade the private space of the woman's house to bring her to trial."

[32] Lincoln, *John*, 529. For a contemporary exploration of the Old Testament background, see Deborah Rooke, "Wayward Women and Broken Promises: Marriage, Adultery and Mercy in the Old and New Testaments," in *Ciphers in the Sand* (ed. Kreitzer and Rooke), 17–52.

[33] Michaels, *John*, 496, fn. 157; Donald A. Carson, *The Gospel According to John* (Grand Rapids, Mich.: Eerdmans, 1991), 334. Rooke, "Wayward Women," 44.

[34] Guardiola-Sáenz, "A Cultural Reading," 285. Again, since she was caught alone, one reader of a draft of this chapter, Steven Hunt, asked whether the woman might have been caught masturbating and whether such sexual activity was considered adulterous behavior. I decided not to look into this possibility for a couple of reasons: firstly because there is so little evidence on whether female masturbation is associated with adultery in the first century; and secondly because it seems to deconstruct too severely the male condemnation aspect of the story. Why would the men accuse her of the more specific "adultery" (μοιχεία) rather than more general "sexual immorality" (πορνεία), which would more naturally include masturbation?

[35] Lincoln, *John*, 530.

a married woman would be strangling rather than stoning.[36] We simply do not know. Certainly, the woman is in much greater jeopardy than the man ever was.

The characterization of the woman has begun in dramatic form. Although so much of this is sheer speculation – the kind of instant gossip of the crowd before whom she is a spectacle. We are given no clues to stop the idle speculation going around in circles. We know only one thing, namely that the woman is totally defined by her involvement in a forbidden sex act. She is "the adulteress," or at least "the accused." She has been caught and, as we have seen, no one denies it. It is her involvement in a sexual sin which characterises her, although, of course, we do not know whether such involvement was voluntarily or not. The lack of any defending voices, Jesus' own warning to her to go and sin no more, suggests that she is not innocent. But what do we mean by innocence or guilt in a world where female sexuality is understood only within the terms of male sexual practice? Where even those who are raped are deemed to be guilty?

In the pericope, she is portrayed as a "type" of woman who deserves to be stoned (v. 5): "[the scribes' and Pharisees'] use of τὰς τοιαύτας indicates that they do not see the woman as an individual but as a kind of woman – the kind that categorically deserves death."[37] As Toensing points out, she is simply a pawn, which both sides seem willing to sacrifice in order to win a bigger prize.[38]

Objectification is an important aspect of the characterization of the woman. However much we may want to see this pericope as a liberal rejection of judgement,[39] it is clear that the woman is horribly objectified: "an object on display, given no name, no voice, no identity, apart from that for which she stands accused."[40] Nameless, partnerless, defenceless. Her stance and bearing are ignored. Her features and expression go un-noted. We are simply told that she stands. Indeed, such a description is too active. Instead we are told that she is placed, like a statue, "in the middle" (στησάντες αὐτὴν ἐν μέσῳ v. 3) – objectified, an almost inhuman, inanimate, unheard object in the masculine power game that is being played around her.[41]

There are, of course, other examples – too many – of women and men who have become pawns in biblical power games and Jayne Scott's article on this

---

[36] George R. Beasley-Murray, *John* (2d ed.; WBC 39; Nashville: Thomas Nelson, 1999), 145; Carson, *John*, 335.

[37] Toensing, "Divine Intervention or Divine Intrusion," 162.

[38] Toensing, "Divine Intervention or Divine Intrusion," 164; Rooke, "Wayward Woman," 48; Jayne Scott, "The One that Got Away," in *Ciphers in the Sand* (ed. Kreitzer and Rooke), 214–39, 223.

[39] If there is, perhaps, not too much anachronism in that phrase.

[40] O'Day, "John 7:53–8:11," 632.

[41] Guardiola-Sáenz, "A Cultural Reading," 286–87.

pericope maps those same games onto the contemporary experience of women.[42] Lincoln and others have seen similarities between the pericope and the apocryphal story of Susannah (Dan 13 LXX).[43] She, too, was brought into an assembly of the people, before her husband Joachim, and accused of adultery. Moreover, when Daniel reveals the treachery of her accusers, Susannah is exonerated. A falsely accused woman is decreed innocent before a crowd. However, the similarities remain relatively superficial, at least in terms of characterization. We are told so much detail about the saintly Susannah: about her beauty, her morality, her spirituality (vss. 2, 3, 27, 31, 35); about her understanding of the law and the support of her family (vss. 3, 30). We witness her innocence by being taken into the garden itself (vss. 15–27), having been warned already of the weak character of her accusers (vss. 8–14). When she is dragged before the assembly and her husband, she comes not alone but accompanied by her family and household (v. 30). We have no need of Daniel's wit, for we already know the truth about her innocence. The story about Susannah is as full of detail as this story is empty, as piously idealistic as *PA* is so horribly real.[44] Susannah is as rounded a character as this woman's is so crassly flattened. Susannah is personified; this woman objectified.

The Jewish leaders, like Susannah's accusers, represent a patriarchal order, which rests on the male control of women, epitomized by male control of female sexuality and sexual practice.[45] In these rules, a woman often did not have the luxury of innocence: "As in many societies around the world, so here: when it comes to sexual sins, the woman was much more likely to be in social and legal jeopardy than her paramour. The man could lead a 'respectable' life while masking the same sexual sins with a knowing wink."[46] For the woman accused of adultery, there was no such option. The woman is thus painted not only as an adulteress but, as part of her cultural and gender identity, as an implicit victim of the patriarchal system which dragged her into the middle of this scene.[47]

In fact, the accused, the adulteress, is more like the Levite's concubine, written about so brilliantly by Mieke Bal, or the man at the gravestones, whose role in the narrative as a repository of the community's sin was explored by Ched Myers.[48] The concubine and the man at the gravestones become representative

---

[42] J. Scott, "The One that Got Away," 216–17.
[43] Lincoln, *John*, 530, 534–36; Beasley-Murray, *John*, 146.
[44] Lincoln, *John*, 535.
[45] These issues are comprehensively explored in J. Scott, "The One that Got Away," 214–39 and Green, "Making her Case," 240–67.
[46] Carson, *John*, 336, 215.
[47] J. Scott, "The One that Got Away," 222; Green, "Making her Case," 248.
[48] Mieke Bal, "Body Politic," in *The Postmodern Bible Reader* (ed. Joblin et al.; Oxford: Blackwell, 2001), 142–58; Ched Myers, *Binding the Strong Man: A Political Reading of Mark's Story of Jesus* (Maryknoll, N. Y.: Orbis Books, 2003).

characters in some way bridging different communities and yet absorbing the sin of that community at the same time. Is this the role the woman plays here in this text – an objectification, an object, a symbol of the obsession with judgement at the heart of the Johannine narratives it interrupts? Is it/she a judgement upon that obsession (John 7:24, 8:15)?[49]

Or perhaps the story is a form of morality play – an enacted parable? Augustine hinted as such when he summarized the story as a confrontation between good and evil, between sin and mercy: "There remained alone they two, a wretch and mercy (*miseria et misericordia*)."[50] O'Day clearly objects to such dehumanizing of the woman, in that it limits her to being a cipher for sin, whilst it paints Jesus as a cipher for mercy. Instead, O'Day wants to point to the liberating power of the pericope: "The scribes and the Pharisees and the woman are invited to leave behind a world of judgement, condemnation, and death and enter a world of acquittal and life."[51] But could an Augustinian reading help us understand the stripped down characterization of this pericope so far? Perhaps the woman is not characterized, not humanized, precisely because she is a cipher, a literary device. This is where this pericope stands out as such a totally non-Johannine creation. The woman is known only by her sin. We know nothing else from the context or the background. She is not given the benefit of a long accusation or a mock trial like the man born blind (John 9). We have none of the detail even of the man at the pool of Bethzatha (John 5), never mind the biographical details around the Lazarus family (John 11–12) or the sheer depth of information we can glean from the conversation with the woman at the well (John 4). She is dragged out into the middle without anyone to defend her, without any words to make sense of what is happening, rendered absolutely powerless, her death seemingly of no concern to anyone.[52] You see, she is no one in particular; a mere narrative device; a player on a narrative substage. In these circumstances, characterization, as with Susannah, would turn this into a specific case study, or hagiography, rather than a morality play. The characterization here is almost parabolic, almost Synoptic. In other words, the characterization, or lack of it, seems to be affected not just by patriarchal power games but by the narratology of the passage itself.[53]

We have already noted that the introduction and indictment of the woman by the Jewish leaders may well remind the (experienced?) reader of Jesus' own experience within the wider narrative of the Gospel and within the immediate context of John 7–8. The woman caught in adultery may represent what the Jewish leaders want to do to Jesus himself – to drag him into a public place

---

[49] Michaels, *John*, 494–500.
[50] O'Day, "John 7:53–8:11," 634, citing Augustine, *Hom XXXIII*.
[51] O'Day, "John 7:53–8:11," 638.
[52] J. Scott, "The One that Got Away," 224.
[53] Green, "Making her Case," 262.

and stone him (John 10:31). Does the woman therefore represent Jesus in some way or act a narratological avatar for him?[54] Indeed, as a man present and in danger of being stoned, does Jesus stand alongside the woman as her co-accused? Guardiola-Sáenz points to the obvious links between the two: "This is a *crossroads-text* that depicts the existence and survival strategies of two border-crossers living at the crossroads ... Jesus is seen as sharing the experience of being on trial together with the accused woman ... the presence of the adulterer is neither important nor needed: Jesus, as a man, has symbolically taken his place."[55] We could take this much further asking whether the woman's experience in the present somehow prefigures Jesus' experience in the future. Does the arrest of the woman, the accusations, the humiliation of public display, the crowds looking on, her very silence, presage Jesus' own experience to come? Does her suffering and treatment represent what Jesus too will suffer? Is her liberation a foretaste of his resurrection? As Elizabeth Green concludes: "if Christ becomes symbolically female to redeem the victims of patriarchy, then the woman taken in adultery becomes an icon of the risen Christ."[56] Of course, there are limits to such images: Jesus is not her paramour, not the co-accused; unlike the woman, his innocence is reaffirmed throughout the text; his silence, even in John, is never as absolute as the woman's; his self-defence, even before the obvious power of Pilate, stands undaunted.

As the narrative continues, it becomes a male affair. She stands in the middle, exposed. The men argue around her, calling on Jesus to agree with the Law of Moses, calling on Jesus to agree to the stoning of the woman (v. 5). The entrapment has been changed – the woman is now bait in a trap prepared for Jesus. He stoops to "write" in the dust (v. 6). And the (mostly male) commentators feverishly provide endless explanations of anything that he may have written or scribbled or doodled. Obsessed by words, they let the woman languish in the middle, while they explore their vain attempts to determine that which can never be determined. As has often been pointed out, if what Jesus wrote was important, the text would have included it![57] The men in the story become impatient too. They see Jesus stooped to the ground and press him for an answer (v. 7). Jesus rises and speaks, calling on the one who is sinless to cast the first stone. Having spoken, he again stoops to "write" (v. 8).

Jesus seems to agree with the accusers. He calls anyone who regards themselves as sinless to throw the first stone. He does so without checking any facts of the case or asking the woman for her side of the story. This is Jesus operat-

---

[54] Michaels, *John*, 498–500.
[55] Guardiola-Sáenz, "A Cultural Reading," 276, 280.
[56] Green, "Making her Case," 264–65.
[57] See O'Day, "John 7:53–8:11," 635. Clearly Chris Keith has a specific angle here in thinking that the pericope was written to promote Jesus as a superliterate founder of the Church which was in desperate need for more writers. See Keith, *Pericope Adulterae*.

ing within patriarchy and many feminists have found this a difficult decision on his part. The woman remains silent, objectified, victimized. The text does not even consider how she feels. Is she terrified that Jesus has not saved her, not even addressed her, but only invited her death? It is true that he has placed a barrier for the accusers to cross – a formidable barrier. But he has all but sanctioned the woman's death: "Jesus directs the lens [of accusation] elsewhere, onto the would-be executioners. But, though he has made a move to avoid being trapped, he risks the woman's life to do so: if one among them has not sinned – or, if someone lies purposely or even inadvertently – the stoning of the woman begins … The woman's death is set up to be determined by the life of one man."[58]

There must be an astounding narrative silence between v. 8 and v. 9 as the narrator intensifies the dramatic tension. What will happen? Has Jesus succeeded in springing the trap? Will the woman be stoned? Into the silence comes the sound of footsteps as those who heard (just the scribes and the Pharisees or the crowd as well?) leave the scene, the eldest first. As their footsteps recede, Jesus is left alone with her. There has been a process of emptying out of the sacred space, a kenotic process. That which invaded that space has been found wanting and has left/been ejected. "Let the one who is without sin cast the first stone," he had said, and the only one who is without sin (ἀναμάρτητος v. 7), the only one worthy of passing judgement, is left behind to confront the woman.[59] He stands up, again, and speaks.

There is an interesting dynamic happening in these verses, which relates to Jesus' body posture and his speech: in both v. 6 and v. 8, Jesus stoops, rises and speaks, first to the accusers and then to the woman accused. In this context, riven with conflict, that is an intriguing response. Through his actions, Jesus seems to be rejecting the power dynamics of the scribes and Pharisees. He stoops in order to resist, or even to break, that power dynamic. When the accusers do not acknowledge this resistance, he re-asserts himself and gives his voice authority by rising and speaking. He stands and then pronounces. However, he then immediately chooses to stoop once again. He doesn't threaten the accusers with a show of defiance. He acts in a non-threatening, non-aggressive way offering them the opportunity to reflect upon their own identity and state of sin. He provides a (literal) space for reflection not dominated by his own presence but by the woman's. It is a rejection of the patriarchal conflict rules, which had been set up by the scribes and Pharisees as they set the trap. Jesus chooses a different way.[60] Interestingly, when he rises again (v. 10), he is able to address the woman for the first time and allows her to

---

[58] Toensing, "Divine Intervention or Divine Intrusion," 164–65; J. Scott, "The One that Got Away," 223.

[59] Toensing, "Divine Intervention or Divine Intrusion," 166; Michaels, *John*, 499.

[60] J. Scott, "The One that Got Away," 236–37; Green, "Making her Case," 264.

create her own boundaries of identity and she too is given a judgement (v. 11). Earlier surrounded, threatened by the voices and power of condemnation, she is now free.[61] In addressing her, Jesus transforms the woman from the "sex object" to which the action of the scribes and Pharisees had reduced her, to "acting human subject," now able to respond to Jesus' judgement/invitation.[62] His stooping opens up space for both his opponents and the accused to reflect upon their own identities.

O'Day notes the similarity between the two verses: Jesus stoops, rises and speaks, first to the accusers and then to the woman accused – but to both he speaks judgement.[63] As such, O'Day argues that "it is the equality of the woman and the scribes and Pharisees before Jesus that is at the heart of this story."[64] Both the accusers and the accused are treated identically. Jesus refuses to play the patriarchal game of objectifying the woman, or of treating her differently from the male characters in the pericope. Indeed, by revealing the chiastic relationship between v. 7b and v. 11b, O'Day is able to show how Jesus challenges both parties to give up previous sinful practice and to embrace a new future: "both stand under the power of old ways, the power of sin, to use the rhetoric of the text, but the present moment (ἀπὸ τοῦ νῦν) invites both to a new way of life."[65] For both parties, the narrative moves away from consideration of condemnation and death, to the hope of acquittal and life: "Go, and leave your life of sin" (v. 11).

Holly Toensing picks up on the equality between the accusers and the woman but suggests that the woman ends up trapped by Jesus.[66] When Jesus finally offers the woman the opportunity to speak, he confines her conversation to the subject of her former accusers. He doesn't give her a moment to speak for herself or to defend herself. He only offers her the opportunity to state the obvious – that no-one remains to condemn her (v. 11). It is true that he then states that neither will he. But this does suggest that he could – that he was the one without sin who could have cast that stone. Instead, he has chosen the path of no condemnation. He sends her on her way. She came in bonds; she goes free under her own volition. However, Jesus ensures that her departure has a sting in the tail. Despite his promise not to condemn, he still tells her to stop sinning. He thus confirms what we have suspected all the time – she was guilty from the start. Indeed, Toensing argues that he goes even further in his use of a present participle to suggest that her previous sin was habitual – "Go and leave this life of sin." As Carson argues: "the expression

---

[61] O'Day, "John 7:53–8:11," 633.
[62] Green, "Making her Case," 244.
[63] O'Day, "John 7:53–8:11," 633.
[64] O'Day, "John 7:53–8:11," 636.
[65] O'Day, "John 7:53–8:11," 637.
[66] Toensing, "Divine Intervention or Divine Intrusion," 167–70.

almost paints the woman as an habitual whore."[67] Our liberated woman, to whom we have taken pains to give the benefit of the doubt, is suddenly plunged back into some shadows. It is hoped that this will be the moment of transformation, the beginning of a new way of living for both her and her accusers.

In closing, it is worth exploring one further aspect of the woman's characterization contained in her objectification and representation. Both seem to point to the non-characterization of the woman, or to the probability that this of all the encounters in the Fourth Gospel is much more like a parabolic creation than an eyewitness record. The flattening of her character seems to be a narratological device, which allows her to represent any number of other things: "that sort of woman," or "that sort of sinner," or embodied sin, or even Jesus himself as we have seen. As such, whether there is any historical core to the story, in such a reading the woman becomes a voided avatar – an empty sign to be objectified all over again, denied her real existence in any other way than as a narratological device. She may be simply part of a morality play rather than someone who was once released from the threat of death by her Messiah. Ultimately, this would seem to go beyond the kind of characterization which we normally find in the Fourth Gospel. It is true that characters such as the Samaritan Woman and the man at the Pool of Bethzatha, or the man born blind all remain nameless and also act as a foil for some Messianic disclosure. But their characterization is usually much more full, much less ambiguous than the characterization of the woman caught in adultery and thus this would seem to be yet another argument for saying that this aporic aporneia must surely be a-Johannine, a-quartic (?) as well.

---

[67] Carson, *John*, 500; Toensing, "Divine Intervention or Divine Intrusion," 169.

The Devil:
Murderer, Liar, and Defeated Foe

Dave L. Mathewson

Although we usually associate characters in a story with human characters,[1] it is important to observe that supernatural characters should also be included. This is the case in the Fourth Gospel.[2] Besides God and angels (cf. 1:51; 20:12), the supernatural being which features most prominently in the Fourth Gospel is the Devil, or Satan, also called "the ruler of the world." These three designations are used of one of Jesus' main antagonists in the Fourth Gospel: διάβολος (6:70; 8:44; 13:2); σατανᾶς (13:27); ἄρχων τοῦ κόσμου (12:31; 14:30; 16:11). This study is an attempt to assess the character of the Devil in the Fourth Gospel by utilizing insights from participant reference in discourse analysis.

Discourse Analysis and Characterization

An important part of analyzing the characters (participants) in a discourse is a consideration of their function through the way they are referred to grammatically within the discourse.[3] For example, how the participant is encoded in a narrative can point to the role they play. Main characters seem to be introduced with full noun phrases identifying them, but then they usually receive reduced coding (pronouns) or zero coding (verb endings), but may still receive full encoding at times.[4] They are usually also activated over large stretches of narrative. Minor characters are activated more briefly in the narrative and are typically referred to with a full noun phrase identifying them, though at times

---

[1] The study of character in the Fourth Gospel by Cornelis Bennema does not include reference to the Devil: "A Theory of Character in the Fourth Gospel with Reference to Ancient and Modern Literature," *BibInt* 17 (2009): 375–421.

[2] One of the semantic domains included in Johannes P. Louw and Eugene A. Nida's *Greek-English Lexicon of the New Testament Based on Semantic Domains* (2 vols; New York: United Bible Society, 1988) is "Supernatural Beings and Powers" (domain 12).

[3] Stephen H. Levinsohn, *Discourse Features of New Testament Greek: A Coursebook on the Information Structure of New Testament Greek* (2d ed.; Dallas: SIL, 2000), 134–47; Jeffrey T. Reed, *A Discourse Analysis of Philippians* (JSNTSup 136; Sheffield: Sheffield Academic Press, 1997), 383.

[4] See Levinsohn, *Discourse Features*, 136.

they can play a crucial role in shorter stretches of narrative. A second important feature is the grammatical role played by the participants. Are they the subject of verbs in main clauses, performing the action, or are they only complements (receiving the action) or modifiers of other words? With what types of actions are they associated: material processes (activities), mental processes (verbs of perception), or relational processes (verbs of "being")? Are they found in the primary (independent) clauses, which function to carry the main storyline? Or are they found in secondary, supportive clauses, or in embedded clauses (participles or speeches)?[5] With which other participants do they interact, and how do they interact with them? The answers to these questions in relationship to the character or participant being analyzed can determine the role the participant plays within the discourse.

The rest of this study will analyze the three main "titles" used to refer to Jesus' antagonist of the Fourth Gospel: διάβολος, σατανᾶς, and ἄρχων τοῦ κόσμου.

The Proceeding Genesis of a Character: *Diabolos* and *Satanas* in the Making

The first term διάβολος occurs three times in 6:70, 8:44, and 13:2. In all three instances the Devil receives full encoding, though in 8:44 he is "referentially persistent" beyond the first clause and is referred to by pronouns or zero reference.[6] In 6:70 διάβολος occurs as a complement with a verb of relational process (ἐστίν) as an identification of Judas: Judas is identified as a/the devil.[7] Furthermore, it is important to see that this statement is embedded within a speech of Jesus, who identifies Judas with the Devil. Therefore, at this point the Devil only functions to identify the character of Judas and performs no activities, and is embedded within a speech of Jesus.

In 8:44, the "Höhepunkt dieses langen Streitgespräches,"[8] the first occurrence of the term διάβολος is "doubly nested" within the discourse.[9] First, it

---

[5] "Primary level clauses serve to provide the backbone of discourse, moving in the horizontal dimension. Secondary clauses, in contrast, function to provide further specification of information from a primary clause, thus functioning in the vertical dimension" (Matthew Brook O'Donnell, *Corpus Linguistics & the Greek of the New Testament* [Sheffield: Sheffield Phoenix, 2005], 454).

[6] For the concept of "referential persistence" see Reed, *Discourse Analysis*, 103.

[7] On the change in levels of narration here see Hartwig Thyen, *Das Johannesevangelium* (HNT 6; Tübingen: Mohr Siebeck, 2005), 383. The article is missing in the Greek text, creating some ambiguity as to whether it could be translated "a devil" or "the devil." In either case, the author is demonstrating the true source of Judas' activity and sets the stage for the Devil entering Judas in 13:2.

[8] Siegfried Schulz, *Das Evangelium nach Johannes* (NTD 4; Göttingen: Vandenhoeck & Ruprecht, 1972), 137. Schulz sees the conflict between God and the Devil here as part of a broader series of dualisms between belief and unbelief, light and darkness, and life and death.

occurs as a genitive modifier within a prepositional phrase: ἐκ τοῦ πατρὸς τοῦ διαβόλου which functions to identify the true familial origin of the religious leaders.[10] Second, once again this term is embedded within a speech of Jesus to the religious leaders (8:42). In other words, the Devil plays no role as an actor in the narrative itself, but is only spoken about by Jesus. The Devil is referred to in the rest of the verse with either πατήρ, since this is the issue in this section (who is the father of the religious leaders?)[11] or reduced reference in the form of a pronoun (ἐκεῖνος, αὐτῷ) or zero reference ἕστηκεν, ἐστίν, λαλῇ, λαλεῖ, since here the Devil is referentially persistent in this section of the discourse, playing an important role in this part of Jesus' speech in emphasizing the source of the religious leaders' activities. Again, it is instructive to note the types of verbs and clauses the Devil is associated with in v. 44. First he is the subject of a verb of relational process ἦν, identifying him as a murderer. Next, he is the subject of a verb that only indicates a state of standing: ἕστηκεν; he does not stand in the truth. Both are primary clauses and both function to contrast the Devil with Jesus. Whereas Jesus is characterized by giving life and speaking the truth, the Devil is a murderer and speaks lies.[12] The next two verbs attributed to the Devil are verbs of perception (speaking), λαλῇ, λαλεῖ, further associating the Devil with speaking lies, in contrast to Jesus who speaks the truth. The verb λαλεῖ functions in a primary clause, but is embedded within the speech of Jesus. Finally, in a causal clause (ὅτι) explaining why the Devil speaks lies he is the subject of a relational process (ἐστίν) further emphasizing his identity as a liar. Thus, the primary role that the Devil plays in this section is to indicate the origin and character of the religious leaders who oppose Jesus. Satan is identified as a murderer and one who, in contrast to Jesus, does not stand in the truth and whose characteristic activity is speaking lies, which is exactly what the religious leaders are doing: they are rejecting the truth spoken by Jesus and attempting to put him to death.[13] However, though he is referentially persistent in v. 44 and is sometimes the subject in primary clauses, Satan does not play a specific role in

---

[9] Brook O'Donnell notes that "participant references nested within the word group structure as modifiers play a less central role in the discourse than those functioning as head terms" (Brook O'Donnell, *Corpus Linguistics*, 421).

[10] For the familial metaphor that lies behind this see Jan G. van der Watt, *Family of the King: Dynamics of Metaphor in the Gospel According to John* (Leiden: Brill, 2000), 188–91. Perhaps 8:44 is anticipated in 1:12–13; 3:4–8.

[11] Cf. Craig Keener, *The Gospel of John: A Commentary* (2 vols.; Peabody, Mass.: Hendrickson, 2003), 1:756: "The notion of spiritual parentage drew on the standard conception that children reflect the nature of their parents ..."

[12] Joachim Gnilka, *Johannesevangelium* (NEchtB 4; Würzburg: Echter Verlag, 1989), 72, who says that "Lüge und Mord" contrasts with "Wahrheit und Leben."

[13] Ben Witherington III, *John's Wisdom: A Commentary on the Fourth Gospel* (Louisville, Ky.: Westminster John Knox, 1995), 178: "Throughout this whole discussion, the underlying assumption is that one's origins determine one's character."

advancing the plot of the narrative. His identification and activities are embedded with the speech of Jesus.[14]

The Devil reemerges in 13:2 with a full noun phrase (τοῦ διαβόλου), this time again in connection with Judas, the disciple who would betray Jesus. Here the Devil is not the subject of a main verb which advances the narrative, but is the subject of a participle in a genitive absolute construction. The main action of the narrative does not take place until v. 4 where Jesus is the main participant. That is, the Devil has already prompted Judas to betray Jesus in 13:2, but this only sets the stage and provides the backdrop for the activity of Jesus in v. 4 where he washes the disciples' feet.

It is not until 13:27 that the Devil, now identified as σατανᾶς, becomes an actual actor in the narrative as the subject of a verb of entering (εἰσῆλθεν) in a primary clause, the only time where the Devil plays such a role. The previous references to the Devil's relationship to Judas now reach their climax with Satan performing the action of entering Judas as an actor in the narrative.

In summary, so far in the narrative of the Fourth Gospel the Devil/Satan has played a minor and supporting role: he is not an actor in the narrative. He is the complement of a relational verb which identifies Judas who will betray Jesus; he is a modifier embedded in a prepositional construction where he functions to describe the origin and characteristics of the religious leaders who refuse Jesus' teaching and want to kill him; he is the subject of relational processes which identify his characteristic features, in contrast to Jesus, as murderer and liar; and he performs the action of speaking lies in a primary clause. All of these references to the Devil/Satan are further embedded with the speech of Jesus; that is, the Devil/Satan is not an actor in the narrative itself but is only spoken about by Jesus. At the same time, Jesus' speech functions to make clear the true underlying cause of hostility towards him by both Judas and the religious leaders, and the Devil/Satan plays a primary role in this section of Jesus' speech. The Devil is also the subject of a genitive absolute participle construction, which provides the backdrop for the activity of Jesus, the main participant. When the Devil/Satan finally plays a role in the narrative he is a subject of a verb of material process in a primary clause, he enters Judas (13:27). This analysis, then, suggests that the Devil/Satan is not a main character in the Gospel, but rather plays a supporting role within the narrative, inciting or providing the source for the actions of other human actors. He is the

---

[14] "Allerdings liegt es nicht im Interesse des Textes, grundsätzliche Aussagen über den Teufel zu machen, sondern seine Gegenwart zu erklären. Deshalb interessiert sich Johannes nur für die Rolle des Teufels im kosmischen Heilsdrama und nicht für seine Genese. Für Johannes steht der klare Gegensatz fest, dass Christus das Licht der Welt ist, während der Fürst dieser Welt, der durch die Sendung Jesu besiegt wurde (Joh 12,31), die Finsternis beherrscht." (Paul Metzger, Der Teufel [Wiesbaden: Marix Verlag, 2012], 54).

ultimate source of the disbelieving and murderous activities of the primary antagonists of Jesus: Judas and the religious leaders. "The plot is satanic."[15]

The Devil as the Ruler of the World

The final way that the Devil (Satan) is referred to is with the phrase "the ruler of this world" (ἄρχων τοῦ κόσμου) in 12:31; 14:30; 16:11. Again, it is instructive to note the verb types that are associated with the Devil here, and the grammatical role that he plays in relation to them. In 12:31, ἄρχων τοῦ κόσμου is the subject of a passive verb, ἐκβληθήσεται, the agent of the passive verb presumably being God. Here, the Devil as the ruler of this world is the object of God's judging activity on the world (τοῦ κόσμου) and is cast outside. That is, Satan does not perform an activity but plays a passive role (he is acted upon by God in judgment). Similarly, in 16:11 the ruler of this world is the grammatical subject of the verb, but it is also passive – κέκριται. Once again, as the ruler of this world the Devil is acted upon – he stands judged by God. In 14:30 the ruler of this world is the subject of two verbs of material processes, coming (ἔρχεται) and having (ἔχει). Yet the second verb is negated: the ruler of this world comes, but he does *not* have anything against Jesus.[16] His purposes are thwarted. Moreover, all three of these references to "the ruler of this world," though subjects of primary clauses, are embedded within the speech of Jesus; the ruler of this world is talked about by Jesus, but does not play a role in advancing the action of the narrative.

When the names attributed to this supernatural being – the Devil, Satan, and the ruler of this world – are examined in relationship to the other participants in the narrative with which they are associated, another interesting pattern emerges. The names the Devil and Satan are used in connection with other human antagonists of Jesus. That is, the Devil and Satan are associated with Judas and with the religious leaders. With the former, the Devil/Satan incites Judas to betray Jesus. This is consistent with the meaning of the two words, the Devil suggesting a slanderer, and Satan suggesting an adversary or enemy of God who now inspires Jesus' human enemies.[17] More importantly

---

[15] Charles H. Talbert, *Reading John: A Literary and Theological Commentary on the Fourth Gospel and the Johannine Epistles* (New York: Crossroad, 1992), 190. See also Raimo Hakola, *Identity Matters: John, the Jews and Jewishness* (NovTSup 118; Leiden: Brill, 2005), who goes even further and describes the entire narrative as a "cosmological tale that opens a framework for interpreting the whole narrative in light of Jesus' battle against the devil" (204).

[16] For ἐν ἐμοὶ οὐκ ἔχει οὐδέν meaning "he has nothing against me" (Jesus) see Rudolf Schnackenburg, *Das Johannesevangelium: Teil 3: Kommentar zu Kapitel 13–21* (HTKNT IV; Freiburg: Herder, 1977), 99–100.

[17] See similarly Donald A. Carson, *The Gospel According to John* (Grand Rapids, Mich.: Eerdmans, 1991), 304.

the latter name has its origin in the Genesis account (Gen 3) where Satan (cf. Rev 12:9) is the one who deceives humanity to sin and brought death into the world. His primary role in the Fourth Gospel is to deceive and incite human agents to oppose and ultimately kill Jesus by getting them to believe a lie.

By contrast, when the title "ruler of this world" is used it occurs only in association with God and Jesus. This may be because 1) the death of Jesus is seen in terms of a cosmic battle with the "ruler of this world;" in this case God and Jesus are more powerful and destroy the rule of Satan, rendering him powerless, demonstrating that the powers of evil were not able to thwart the divine will; 2) the title also functions to contrast with Jesus who is not of this world; Jesus' rule comes from elsewhere. Craig Keener also notes a further possible function. The term ἄρχων appears elsewhere in John with reference to the Jerusalem elites (3:1; 7:26, 48; 12:42).[18] If this is the case, then there is a further connection between the Devil who is the father of the religious leaders and the ruler of this world who stands behind the Jewish authorities who are hostile to Jesus. Furthermore, in 14:31, which occurs within the context of reference to Jesus' death, as the ruler of this world the Devil's power is destroyed and he is unseated ironically through the very death of Jesus that as the Devil and Satan he instigates through Judas and the Jewish leaders.[19]

In conclusion, the Devil stands behind and instigates the attempts of human beings to oppose and snuff out Jesus, thus playing an important but supporting role in the narrative; he is a minor (peripheral) rather than a major character. This can be observed by the fact that Satan plays a limited role in the narrative, and only plays a direct role within the narrative as a subject of a verb of material process in a primary clause in 13:27 where he enters Judas. The other references to the Devil, or Satan, or the ruler of this world, even when he is the subject of actions in a primary clause, are for the most part embedded within the speech of Jesus. Therefore, from time to time the Devil/Satan surfaces in the narrative as a reminder of the true source behind the activities of human characters who are the primary antagonists of Jesus. Thus the Devil plays a supporting role within the narrative of identifying the character and source of activities of others, and whose murderous and lying activity provide a contrast to Jesus who gives life and brings truth. The names given to the Devil also reveal a pattern of association with other participants. Devil and Satan are associated with human beings, namely Judas and the Jewish leaders, whereas "ruler of the world" is associated with God and Jesus. Thus, as the Devil/Satan he deceives and moves human agents to oppose and kill Jesus. But as ruler of this world he is also characterized as a defeated, powerless foe

---

[18] Keener, *John*, 2:985.

[19] Cf. also Craig Koester, *Symbolism in the Fourth Gospel. Meaning, Mystery, Community* (Minneapolis: Fortress, 2003), 233–44.

who is acted upon by God and Jesus, and who ironically seals his own fate by inciting and influencing human participants (Judas and the religious leaders) to kill Jesus which is the very means by which the Devil and the world are judged.

The Man Born Blind:
True Disciple of Jesus

Andy M. Reimer

Narrative critical methodology within the realm of biblical studies has its roots in modern language departments and the study of contemporary literature and film.¹ As such, there really is more tool there than is necessary for the relatively simple narratives of the biblical texts including Gospel narratives.² In John Ashton's opinion, "the sophisticated tools [narrative critics] wield have been designed for the dissection of works of a very different kind ... [leading to] ... needlessly bewildering complexity."³ Static and stereotyped characters with

---

¹ The ideological history of narrative criticism within biblical studies and its relationship to narratology and its theorists, especially Seymour Chatman and Gerard Genette, is told with some bite a short decade after its arrival by Stephen D. Moore, *Literary Criticism and the Gospels: The Theoretical Challenge* (New Haven: Yale University Press, 1989), esp. 47–55. Seymour Chatman's *Story and Discourse: Narrative Structure in Fiction and Film* (Ithaca, N. Y.: Cornell University Press, 1978) so influential in biblical studies in the 1980's was followed by *Coming to Terms: The Rhetoric of Narrative in Fiction and Film* (Ithaca, N. Y.: Cornell University Press, 1990). Gerard Genette's *Narrative Discourse: An Essay in Method* (trans. J. E. Lewin; Ithaca, N. Y.: Cornell University Press, 1980), frequently stripped of its poststructuralist conclusions (see Moore, *Literary Criticism and the Gospels*, 53), appears frequently amongst the first generation of narrative critics, as does Wayne Booth (*The Rhetoric of Fiction* [2d ed.; Chicago: University of Chicago Press, 1983], the "inventor" of the term "implied author," and Wolfgang Iser (*The Act of Reading: A Theory of Aesthetic Response* [Baltimore: Johns Hopkins University Press, 1978] and *The Implied Reader: Patterns of Communication in Prose Fiction from Bunyan to Beckett* [Baltimore: Johns Hopkins University Press, 1974]). Mark Allan Powell's *What is Narrative Criticism?* (Minneapolis: Fortress, 1990) provides a good synopsis of how these works have been appropriated by the end of the 1980's (esp. 1–21, but also in many chapter introductions). In the late 1990's Daniel Marguerat and Yvan Bourquin tell a similar story of the origins of the roots of "narrative criticism" in the narratology theorists of 1960–1980's (idem, *How to Read Bible Stories: An introduction to narrative criticism* [trans. J. Bowden; London: SCM Press, 1999], 3–17.

² Few have made this point with as sharp a tone as John Ashton in *Studying John: Approaches to the Fourth Gospel* (Oxford: Clarendon Press, 1994), 155–65. In particular, Ashton points out that stories such as those in the Gospels are among the most basic type and their narrative techniques more repetitive than worthy of extensive comment (157–59).

³ Ashton, *Studying John*, 162. On this point Moore's observation that narratology theorists typically draw from myriad examples from a broad range of literature (from pre- to postmodern) to illustrate their theories bears repeating (52). As such, it is not surprising that there is much more theory there than is required for critics intent on exegesis rather than the elaboration of narratological theory. This leaves Moore to point out the flip side of his equa-

minimally developed scenes and predictable plot lines are more the order of the day with biblical narrative. So whenever the narrative breaks out of this level of predictability, there is cause to take note. The character of the man born blind in John 9 does represent a rare development of character and plot twists that are intriguing and worth noting.[4] After over a decade of introducing students to the Gospel of John, I have found that John 9 and this character remain among of the most useful in helping students appreciate key narrative themes and narrative techniques deployed by our narrator across this Gospel.

Johannine Themes and Narrative Techniques

The narrator of the Gospel shows a marked preference for two person scenes. One could employ only two actors to execute most of the scenes in this Gospel. One of those actors would spend nearly all their time as Jesus. John 9 represents a slight adjustment of that pattern.[5] The two character scenes predominate, but in this case, other characters, including the man born blind, are given two character scenes in which Jesus is *not* present. As a result, the man born blind is one of only a handful of characters in this Gospel that even begin to approach character classifications such as "dynamic" or "round."[6] In particular, with the man born blind, special attention should be paid to the identification of parallel or contrasting characters as well as what is said (or perhaps unsaid by the character) – an interpretive technique that proves especially fruitful when applied to Hebrew Bible narratives. Jeffrey L. Staley offers a narrative critical analysis of the men healed in John 5 and John 9 that channels the interpretive spirits of well known Hebrew narrative analysts such as Robert Alter, Shimon Bar-Efrat, Adele Berlin, and Meir Stern-

---

tion – namely with biblical narrative critics, the priorities are reversed with a singular narrative providing the unity and the theoretical writings randomly sampled (52).

[4] Raymond E. Brown's commentary on this text includes such praise as: "... the story shows consummate artistry ...," "... Johannine dramatic skill at its best ...," "the care with which the evangelist has drawn his portraits ... is masterful ...," and "... vss. 24–34 is one of the most cleverly written dialogues in the NT" (idem, *The Gospel According to John I (i–xii)* [AB 29; New York: Doubleday, 1966], 376–77). Brown opines that "the blind man emerges from these pages in John as one of the most attractive figures in the Gospels" (377). For Ashton, the harshest of critics of the whole narrative critical endeavour, the healing of the man born blind, along with the passion narrative, do belong to the category of "well crafted," unlike the rest of the Gospel which is, from the point of view of narrative technique "as a whole ... unremarkable" (158).

[5] J. Louis Martyn, *History and Theology in the Fourth Gospel* (3d ed.; Louisville, Ky.: Westminster John Knox Press, 2003), 37.

[6] On these and other such terms to describe characters from a narrative critical perspective see Powell, *What is Narrative Criticism?*, 54–55, and Marguerat and Bourquin, *How to Read Bible Stories*, 60–61.

berg.[7] Staley's redeployment of their approach creates a fascinating portrait of both the poolside paralytic and the man born blind. In the final analysis, however, his interpretation of the man born blind is more convincing and satisfying than that of the poolside paralytic.[8] In Staley's reading, the poolside paralytic of John 5 emerges as a very positive figure – a reading that becomes even more odd when placed alongside that of the blind man of John 9. However, if one takes Staley's close reading of the man born blind and reads that rather as a *contrasting* character to the poolside paralytic (as per Culpepper), Staley's interpretation of John 9 becomes even more convincing.[9] Interpreting the man born blind as a parallel character with the (largely absent) Jesus equally produces interesting results. And once one reaches the conclusion, it is apparent that the blind man and the Pharisees serve as contrasting characters as well.

The story of the man born blind provides the narrator with the opportunity to improvise on techniques and themes one finds repeatedly in the Gospel. In addition to the use of parallel or contrasting characters already mentioned, this story contains ironic double entendre with terms that have multiple physical and spiritual connotations. And, as elsewhere in the Gospel, the narrator explores Jesus' character and identity by presenting multiple evaluations of Jesus by other characters. Andrew Lincoln's work on the Gospel of John drew attention to the forensic tone and lawsuit motif that pervades the Gospel.[10] Echoing the Hebrew Bible's use of the lawsuit motif (and the turning of tables during a lawsuit motif), the Gospel of John portrays Jesus on trial by "his own" and Jesus putting "his own" and "the world" on trial. In John 9 the man born blind presents the opportunity for another set of courtroom scenes and language.[11] In John 9, because the blind man "replaces" Jesus in quasi-judicial

---

[7] Jeffrey L. Staley, "Stumbling in the Dark, Reaching for the Light: Reading Character in John 5 and 9," *Semeia* 53 (1991): 55–80. The narrative critical works of the Hebrew Bible scholars mentioned above that shaped Staley's approach include Robert Alter, *The Art of Biblical Narrative* (New York: Basic Books, 1981) and *The Pleasure of Reading in an Ideological Age* (New York: Simon and Schuster, 1989); Shimon Bar-Efrat, *Narrative Art in the Bible* (Sheffield: Almond Press, 1989); Adele Berlin, *Poetics and Interpretation of Biblical Narrative* (Sheffield: Almond Press, 1983); and Meir Sternberg, *The Poetics of Biblical Narrative: Ideological Literature and the Drama of Reading* (Bloomington, Ind.: Indiana University Press, 1985).

[8] Staley's argument that the poolside paralytic represents a positive bold witness to Jesus is politely (and in my view correctly) dismissed by James M. Howard as not "the most natural intent behind John's presentation of the scene" (idem, "The Significance of Minor Characters in the Gospel of John," *BSac* [2006]: 71).

[9] R. Alan Culpepper, *Anatomy of the Fourth Gospel: A Study in Literary Design* (Philadelphia: Fortress, 1983), 139–40, and Staley, "Stumbling in the Dark," 60–64.

[10] See especially Andrew T. Lincoln, *Truth on Trial: The Lawsuit Motif in the Fourth Gospel* (Peabody, Mass.: Hendrickson, 2000).

[11] Lincoln, *Truth on Trial*, 96–105.

dispute scenes as a parallel character to Jesus, Jesus himself can "disappear" in this chapter without any loss to John's forensic themes.

The Blind Man Provokes a Dispute

As the chapter opens, the two person scene is that of Jesus and his disciples walking along. The man born blind is introduced, but he exists "outside" the dialogue that takes place between Jesus and his disciples. He is the object of the conversation, but clearly he is not party to the conversation. The disciples initiate a theoretical conversation with their question, "Who sinned, this man or his parents?" This transforms the usual Johannine pattern of exploring Jesus' character into one in which the blind man and his parents are critically examined. As the narrator's trustworthy and ideologically aligned character, Jesus' declaration of the innocence of the man born blind (as well has his parents' innocence) provides a key starting point. By the end of verse 5, the reader is fully aware that this man (who has yet to be brought into the narrative action in any meaningful way) is not culpable for his own blindness. However, it is equally apparent that this is likely to be a point of dispute.

Jesus' words here will prove significant in terms of the characterization of the blind man – "We must work the works of him who sent me while it is day; night is coming when no one can work. As long as I am in the world, I am the light of the world" (9:4–5 NRSV). The key here is that Jesus is the "sent one" who declares that, "I am the light ..." – a statement pregnant with Hebrew Bible allusions. Jesus is the one who brings light into an otherwise dark world that will get darker with the coming night.

With the disciples (and readers) having been informed that the man's blindness would provide opportunity to reveal the "works of God," the man's blindness is cured. Jesus performs "work" required by the one who sent him. Curiously, despite this miraculous transformation the emphasis will remain on the man's "blind from birth" status throughout. The very title of this chapter provides evidence for the staying power of this identity. Staley, following the lead of the Hebrew narrative specialists, considers it significant that the man is identified as "a beggar" (9:8) by the neighbours and "the one who had regained his sight" by the narrator when identifying his parents (9:18).[12] However, in 9:13, he is "the man formerly blind," in 9:17, "the blind man," and in 9:24, "the man who had been blind"; and repeatedly in conversations about the man, it is his former blindness that is at stake (9:18, 19, 20, 32). While the miracle of the man's reception of sight sparks the controversies that drive this chapter, what really matters in this dispute (as it pertains to the characteriza-

---

[12] Staley, "Stumbling in the Dark," 66.

tion of the blind man) is that he was "blind from birth." Both Jesus' disciples (a sympathetic but naive group character) and the Pharisees (the antagonist group character) take it as a given that a man born blind as such was "born into sin," his own or his parents, but either way fully tarnished and justly punished with blindness. Both Jesus and the narrator have their work cut out for them to convince their audiences otherwise.

The Miracle Scene

The very brief miracle scene itself has several curious features that will not be explored here (9:6–7). However, there are four observations worth noting.

First, the man shows himself to be blindly obedient – full pun intended. The man will continue to exhibit a certain childlike openness as the chapter progresses. However, in the words of his parents, "he is of age." Later in this chapter this childlike innocence will be put to subtle use in his dialogue with the Pharisees. In that exchange the man turns out to be more clever than expected. That raises the question of whether the man is ever quite as innocent as he appears. And this will require consideration of Staley's unique reading of the characterization of the man.

Second, the narrator offers an aside on the name of the pool used to complete the miracle. Clearly the narrator wants us to notice that Jesus "sent" the man to the "Pool of Sent." This takes us right back to Jesus' self-characterization as the "one sent" (9:4).[13] The one sent by the Father to bring light now sends another "to do the work" of bringing light to a dark world.[14] If the reader is being attentive to these verbal parallels, the stage is now set to see this blind man as a parallel character to Jesus. The reference to the pool will also spark a connection with the poolside paralytic of John 5. As such, it is worth noting that both Jesus and the paralytic as corresponding characters to the blind man are set up at this point.

Third, Raymond E. Brown has offered considerable evidence that the earliest readers of this Gospel used this text in baptismal contexts.[15] In 7:37–38

---

[13] Jörg Frey makes the intriguing point that the naming of the pool as "Sent" turns this into a sort of "distance healing" (*Fernheilung*), Jesus as the "sent one" present in the healing power of the pool with the same name; Jörg Frey, "Sehen oder Nicht-Sehen? (Die Heilung des blind Geborenen) Joh 9,1–41," in *Die Wunder Jesu* (ed. R. Zimmermann et al.; vol. 1 of *Kompendium der frühchristlichen Wundererzählungen*; Gütersloh: Gütersloher Verlagshaus, 2013), 725–41, here 729.

[14] Andrew T. Lincoln, *The Gospel According to Saint John* (BNTC; London: Continuum, 2006), 281–82.

[15] Brown, *John*, 380–82. Subsequent commentators such as Barrett have not necessarily been convinced the Gospel writer ever made this connection (C. Kingsley Barrett, *The Gospel According to St John: An Introduction with Commentary and Notes on the Greek Text* [2d ed.; London: SPCK, 1978], 355).

Jesus refers to himself as a source of life-giving water on the day water from the pool of Siloam was poured out in the Temple. If there are baptismal overtones here, again this lends credence to seeing parallels between our blind man and Jesus – both of whom will begin to face opposition after having being sent and then baptized.[16]

Fourth, it is tempting to read the healing ritual with Jesus' mud-making and anointing and the man's active participation through washing as implicating both Jesus and the man born blind as intentional "Sabbath-breakers."[17] Again, this creates a link to the paralytic (also implicated through the command to carry his mat), but one shouldn't miss the way it inextricably links Jesus and the blind man.

Development through Dialogue and Dispute

In Stibbe's groundbreaking work on John as storyteller, he cites Daiches' three ways of creating a character. It is the second type that Stibbe argues is most frequently applicable in this Gospel's narrative. Namely, "one can introduce a character as 'a shadowy and indeterminate creature' who only becomes a living, definable personality after responding to various events – 'the emergence of the complete character from the action.'"[18] Arguably, the man born blind is a classic case in point.

Upon the man's return from his appointed mission to the pool of Siloam, he becomes the object of controversy. As happens to Jesus throughout the Gospel, there is conflicting testimony about the man himself. Is he or isn't he the beggar blind from birth known to his neighbours and those who have watched him beg in the past? Again, there is a childlike quality to the man's answers, although in fairness this could be chalked up to the Gospel's use of a very simple narrative style and a narrow band of vocabulary. In response to the questions and counterclaims, he insists he is the man. He faithfully and simply recounts "the facts" of the actions of Jesus and himself and he claims

---

[16] This parallel presumes, of course, that the modern reader will follow the lead of ancient readers (familiar with the Jesus story) and read Jesus' baptism into the Baptist's recounting of the descending dove in 1:32.

[17] Frey's narrative analysis of this text suggests the Sabbath breaking is narrowly the kneading of the mud and one ought to read Jesus as the "sole actor" (Frey, "Sehen oder Nicht-Sehen," 734f.). However, as in John 5 where the man healed is commanded to act to complete the healing, so here too the man must engage in the Sabbath-breaking ritual for the healing to take place (and the specifics of the Sabbath breaking are not precisely explained in the text). Mark 3:2 provides evidence that at least some early Christian writers presumed that Judean Pharisees thought Sabbath healings of any sort were prohibited.

[18] Mark W. G. Stibbe, *John as Storyteller: Narrative Criticism and the Fourth Gospel* (Cambridge: Cambridge University Press, 1992), 25.

genuine ignorance about Jesus' whereabouts (9:8–12). However, as Lincoln points out, the man's actual words are ἐγώ εἰμι – "I am he." While Lincoln is quick to remove the divine connotations from these words at this point, clearly this is "Jesus-speak" in this Gospel.[19] Jesus may not appear for a while, but a tested and testifying "I am" will remain on the scene.

Only after this dispute concerning the man's identity does the catalyst for the controversy that will drive the remainder of the chapter emerge. The healing ritual, it turns out, was performed on a Sabbath (9:13–14). The elaborate components of the healing – the mud making, application and washing and perhaps too the travel to the pool – these serve to ensure the Sabbath-breaking qualities of the healing. This motif has already played itself out in John 5 where the inclusion of bed carrying in the healing rite by Jesus incites the same antagonists. These parallels provide a further incentive to draw a comparison between the man born blind here and the lame man in chapter 5.[20] But more on that in a moment. The parallels between characters within John 9 is between Jesus and the man born blind. Just as the question of the man's possible status as sinner generated this series of events, now Jesus' possible status as a sinner carry it forward. And just as there were counter claims on the man's identity one scene earlier, now there are counter claims on Jesus' identity as a sinner (9:16). This scene concludes like the previous one, with the man born blind asked questions and answering simply and faithfully. When asked what he believes about Jesus' status, he sides with those who have a positive assessment. Jesus is a prophet.

Given that characters in this Gospel appear to be assessed (theologically speaking at least) in terms of their comprehension and/or appreciation of Jesus' identity, this statement is important in establishing the narrator's evaluation of our character. From our character's point of view, all he knows is that Jesus is someone who has applied mud to his eyes and then sent him to wash the mud in the pool. Quirky rituals with instructions that must be strictly followed in order to produce a miraculous result are, as anyone familiar with the Hebrew scriptures knows, the *modus operandi* of the ancient prophet or "man of God." And never more so than with the two prophets of northern Israel, Elijah and Elisha (e. g., 2 Kgs 5:5–15). Our man born blind has not yet reached an understanding of Jesus that approaches that of the prologue. But given the information he has, he is on the right track in reading Jesus positively against the heroes of the ancient scriptures.

One more consideration needs to be made in terms of this scene. Staley argues that the healed man's statement in 9:15b is carefully crafted for a new hostile audience as compared to the man's statements in 9:11. He avoids nam-

---

[19] Lincoln, *John*, 282.
[20] On this especially see the list of parallels proposed by Culpepper, *Anatomy of the Fourth Gospel*, 139–40.

ing *Jesus*, the *making* of clay, and the *journey* to the pool.²¹ It is worth considering – especially in light of a less than innocent cleverness revealed in his speech in 9:25-32. The Pharisees' response suggests full knowledge of the healer and the Sabbath breaking qualities of the miracle. As such, Staley argues this knowledge must come about as a result of the report of the neighbours, not the man born blind. However, it is more likely that the brevity of the man's response is simply a literary device to avoid being overly repetitive given his full response only a few verses earlier.

In the next scene (9:18-23), the blind man is replaced onstage by his parents, although the blind man remains the subject of the dialogue. In this scene the first controversy is revisited. Was the blind man indeed blind? His parents affirm that he was. But when pressed about the miracle itself, they are less forthcoming than their son was. The narrator is at pains to attribute their reticence to fear of exclusion from the synagogue.²² As such, a strong contrast is created between the man's courage in the previous and subsequent scene, and his parents' lack of courage.

In the third scene involving the Pharisees, the division in the ranks of the Pharisees over the identity of Jesus apparent in the first scene is notably absent. Imperatives now replace any questioning. They appear to believe a miracle has occurred but the man is to attribute that to God and not Jesus the sinner. The rhetoric that follows shows the man born blind is not just courageous but nothing short of a clever rabbi himself.²³ As the man's scholarly opponents ironically admit in their final words, they have been "schooled" by the man born blind.²⁴ Given the stinging conclusion the man delivers, it is apparent that his speech throughout should be read as deliberately clever, not naive. The man begins coy, declaring uncertainty about Jesus' status as a sinner but reminding his opponents that a miracle has occurred. This is not exactly the response they had demanded. They take a more direct tact, trying to get the man to repeat the events which they believe establish Jesus as a sin-

---

²¹ Staley, "Stumbling in the Dark," 67.

²² The mention of synagogue exclusion creates an instinct on the part of contemporary biblical scholars to interpret the blind man against the backdrop of a much later era when Jewish (or Johannine?) Christians were no longer welcomed into synagogues (see for example, Barrett, *John*, 362; Lincoln, *John*, 284, and *Truth on Trial*, 97-98, and implicitly Culpepper, *Anatomy of the Fourth Gospel*, 140). As such, the blind man is rapidly extracted from this setting in the life of Jesus and becomes a paradigm of a much later disciple of Jesus who does not fear synagogue exclusion. While it may well function as such, this recontextualization of our character rather disrupts an analysis of this character within the actual plot and setting in which he is found in the Gospel.

²³ At this point I would certainly be in agreement with Staley's characterization (68) – and, in fairness this does count in favour of his argument to read earlier texts with a suspicion that the man is being more clever than first appears.

²⁴ Gail R. O'Day and Susan E. Hylen, *John* (Louisville, Ky.: Westminster John Knox Press, 2006), 101.

ner, as one who disregards the Sabbath. He comes back with the suggestion that they wish to hear it again because they are on the path to becoming Jesus' disciples. This allows the Pharisees to declare explicitly what has only become evident implicitly – the man born blind is, as they suggest with scorn, a "disciple of Jesus." If the Pharisees steadfastly refuse to acknowledge where Jesus "comes from," the man born blind will enlighten them. A worker of miracles such as this is "from God" and not a sinner. The Pharisees' response to this conclusion brings the story of the man born blind full circle. They march off declaring the man born blind was "born entirely into sins." For them the man who was once excluded as blind and believed to be tainted by sin is now clearly a man still "born blind" and excluded once again on the grounds of association with sin.

The Final Scene

In the first scene, Jesus is passive and it is the disciples' question that sets the action in motion. In this final scene this is replaced by an active Jesus seeking out of the formerly blind man in response to his exclusion. This is the second time that Jesus is portrayed reconnecting with a beneficiary of a Sabbath healing after their disputes with religious authorities. The contrast between the first beneficiary and this one is readily apparent in terms of what Jesus has to say to them.[25] This scene underscores what was implicit in the previous encounter between these two. This is a man willing and eager to listen and respond to whatever is told to him by Jesus. His faithfulness is about to be rewarded with full blown faith. Double entendre drip from the man's use of "lord" (κύριε). While possibly nothing more than a respectful address in 9:36, it becomes a theologically rich confession in 9:38.[26] As Jesus declares, this man has "seen" the Son of Man standing in front of him. This is true literally as a result of Jesus' miracle of restored sight. It is also spiritually true as a result of the man's faith. The man born blind is, as it were, the recipient of the sort of vision promised to Nathanael, the true Israelite, in chapter one. He is capable of seeing the divine "Son of Man" worthy of angelic attention. He responds with worship (προσεκύνησεν).

Jesus' summation then provides a transition to a final scene involving himself and the Pharisees, who overhear his concluding words regarding the provision of sight to the blind and blindness to those who see. As such, the Pharisees again serve as fully contrasting characters to the man born blind. Their journey from sight to blindness is as profound as the man's journey from

---

[25] Contra Staley.
[26] Lincoln, *John*, 286–87. So too Frey, "Sehen oder Nicht-sehen?," 732, 739.

blindness to sight. As Jesus promised to his disciples, the man born blind has indeed provided an occasion for the work of God to be revealed.

Creating a Round Character with Parallel and Contrast Characters

Within the confines of the narrative of this Gospel, the man born blind stands as a rare example of a somewhat round and dynamic character. Primarily, the characterization of this man is carried forward through a series of parallels and contrasts with other characters evoked in parallel scenes and two party dialogues. The disciples begin with the mistaken presumption that the man born blind is sinful or born into sin. Then, the man's neighbours are uncertain about his identity – is he really the man born blind? The Pharisees, upon encountering the man move the question about sin to the man's healer. Is Jesus a sinner? Given that some of their number raise the problem of a sinner performing such a sign, the matter turns from Jesus' identity back to that of the blind man. Where indeed is he from? His parents are called to testify as to his identity and to Jesus' identity as it turns out. Their failure to respond courageously then highlights the courage of the man born blind in answering the question of Jesus' origins and his denial of Jesus' status as a sinner. The Pharisees' concluding self-declared ignorance on where Jesus is from coincides with their conclusion that the man born blind is a sinner. The final scene then generates a contrast with the previous episode in which a man healed on the Sabbath is sought out by Jesus – only to be instructed to cease being a sinner. And throughout these twisting parallels and contrasts, the man born blind undergoes a double transformation. His reception of physical sight in the opening scene is matched by his full reception of spiritual sight in the concluding scene. This in turn sets up the final contrast between the man born blind and the Pharisees. Their failure to see their own blindness is, according to Jesus, the cause of their sin remaining. The supposedly sinful blind man sees and is shown not to be a sinner, while the seeing men are blind and so remain in sin. In an ironic twist on the disciples' question that opens the chapter, Jesus suggests the Pharisees too might have been shown to be the innocent blind had they but given up their claims to sight. In terms of Johannine theology, Lincoln concludes that "the blind man … [is] a representative of all humanity because there is a sense in which all are born blind and in darkness."[27]

---

[27] Lincoln, *Truth on Trial*, 98.

Conclusion

From a narrative critical perspective, the man born blind is not just given the gift of sight in John 9, he is also given the gift of speech and "screen time" that is rare in this Gospel. Indeed his speech has lived on in a way that neither the literary character nor his writer could ever have imagined in the words of the well known hymn, "Amazing Grace." Perhaps then it is not surprising that his journey chronicled in a series of dialogues has such close parallels to the character that holds the spotlight throughout this Gospel. He is, in the words of the Pharisees, a true disciple of Jesus. As such he shares in the experience of questions about his origins, accusations of being a sinner, abandonment by "his own" and ultimately persecution and exclusion. While methodologically narrative critical tools often exceed the demands of relatively simple biblical stories, here the tools do provide interesting, and arguably, meaningful results.

The Neighbors of the Man Born Blind: A Question of Identity

Matthew D. Montonini

Introduction

The neighbors of the man born blind play a crucial role in the narrative of John 9 despite their brief appearance (vss. 8–13).[1] They arrive on the scene as the man returns from the pool of Siloam following his healing (vss. 6–7). Their appearance serves as a surprise to the reader/hearer who might expect Jesus to be the first to greet the man subsequent to his healing. Instead, Jesus is conspicuous by his absence, as he will not reappear again until toward the end of the narrative in v. 35.[2] Structurally, their scene[3] forms a bridge[4] between the actual healing of the blind man (vss. 6–7) and his interaction with the Pharisees (vss. 15–17; 24–34). Further, the interaction between the neighbors and the man (vss. 8–12) prepares the reader for the interaction between the Pharisees and the man in vss. 15–17, 24–34. These interactions, as we shall discuss, will be centered on *identity*: first, the healed man's (vss. 8–9), and eventually, Jesus' (vss. 12; 15–17; 24–34), with the man answering for both parties.[5]

---

[1] Most commentators group vss. 8–12 together as a unit. In my opinion, this does not make the best sense of the scene, as the neighbors play a direct role in v. 13 when they deliver the man to the Pharisees. For a commentator who groups vss. 8–13 together as a unit, see Gary M. Burge, *John* (NIV Application Commentary; Grand Rapids, Mich.: Zondervan, 2000), 274.

[2] This marks the most prolonged absence of Jesus in the entire Gospel, a point noted by Paul D. Duke, *Irony in the Fourth Gospel* (Atlanta: John Knox Press, 1985), 119, and more recently by Gilbert Soo Hoo, *From Faith to Faith: Blindman's Bluff* (Eugene, Oreg.: Wipf & Stock, 2012), 73.

[3] J. Louis Martyn has declared this to be scene two in chapter nine. He proposes a seven-scene structure of John 9: 1) Jesus, his disciples, and the blind man (vss. 1–7); 2) The blind man and his neighbors (vss. 8–12); 3) The blind man and the Pharisees (vss. 13–17); 4) The Pharisees and the blind man's parents (vss. 18–23); 5) The Pharisees and the blind man (vss. 24–34); 6) Jesus and the blind man (vss. 35–38); 7) Jesus and the Pharisees (vss. 39–41). See *History and Theology of the Fourth Gospel* (3d ed.; Louisville, Ky.: Westminster John Knox, 2003), 37.

[4] Bennema refers to this scene (vss. 8–12) as an "interlude," explaining why the man is brought to the Pharisees. See Cornelis Bennema, *Encountering Jesus: Character Studies in the Gospel of John* (Milton Keynes: Paternoster, 2009), 138.

[5] Michaels aptly refers to the blind man as Jesus' "surrogate" and "stand-in." J. Ramsey Michaels, *The Gospel of John* (NICNT; Grand Rapids, Mich.: Eerdmans, 2010), 550.

Before evaluating the section at hand, a word concerning methodology is necessary. The model adopted here is one proposed by Cornelis Bennema.[6] Building on the work of Yosef Ewen,[7] Bennema proposes three continua or axes on which a character may be located: 1) *Complexity*: Characters can vary from singular traits to a nexus of traits and offer varying levels of complexity; 2) *Development*: Characters may vary from those who exhibit little to no development to those who exhibit a fully developed character; and 3) *Penetration into the inner life*: Some characters are seen from an outside perspective, with transparency difficult to detect, while others have their consciousness revealed from within. Based on these criteria, Bennema helpfully develops a four-fold *degree of characterization*[8] to plot along the continua: 1) an agent, actant, or walk on: These are characters who fill a plot function and produce no response to Jesus; 2) a type, stock, or flat character: These characters exhibit a single trait and show no development; 3) a character with personality: This character demonstrates a personality, but is not completely round; and 4) an individual or a person: These characters are the most developed and complex. Further, Bennema stresses that the *responses* of the characters also need classification,[9] based on the evaluative point of view of the Fourth Evangelist's dualistic worldview and the programmatic statement in John 20:31. According to these criteria, a character's response is viewed as adequate or inadequate.[10]

Setting the Stage: Jesus, the Disciples, and the Blind Man (9:1–7)

The narrative opens with Jesus walking along,[11] stating that he "saw a man" (εἶδεν ἄνθρωπον) congenitally blind (v. 1). This statement will anticipate the introduction of the neighbors in v. 8, as they are similarly recorded as "those

---

[6] Bennema outlines his approach in an article titled: "A Theory of Character in the Fourth Gospel with Reference to Ancient and Modern Literature," *BibInt* 17 (2009): 375–421. Further, he tests his methodology on characters in John in his *Encountering Jesus*.

[7] As Bennema notes, Ewen's work has only appeared in Hebrew, but, Shlomith Rimmon-Kenan has helpfully drawn attention to Ewen's work in her own in *Narrative Fiction: Contemporary Poetics* (2d ed.; London: Routledge, 2002).

[8] See Bennema, "Theory of Character," 407.

[9] Of course, this is a point of departure from Culpepper's model which ranks the belief responses of the various characters in John's Gospel. See R. Alan Culpepper, *Anatomy of the Fourth Gospel: A Study in Literary Design* (Philadelphia: Fortress, 1983), 146–48. Bennema insists that responses do not necessarily contribute to the whole portrayal of one's character with Peter being an obvious example, as he demonstrates both adequate and inadequate responses to Jesus throughout the Gospel; see Bennema, "Theory of Character," 418.

[10] Bennema, "Theory of Character," 410–19.

[11] Debate on whether to link this story with what precedes, namely, John 7–8 and the Feast of the Tabernacles continues to vex interpreters. I adopt the position of Moloney, who notes that no time change is indicated until 10:22, and the location remains Jerusalem (7:10, 14) while the temporal location is the Feast of Tabernacles (7:2). See Francis J. Moloney, *Signs*

who had seen him" (οἱ θεωροῦντες αὐτὸν) in the role of a beggar (cf. Mark 10:46). The disciples quickly question Jesus as to whether the man's blindness was due to his own sin or that of his parents (v. 2).[12] The reference to the man's parents will prepare the reader for their appearance in vss. 18–23. Jesus denies that "this man" (οὗτος; cf. v. 2) or his parents are the reason for the man's blindness. Rather, the man's blindness is the means by which God's works will be demonstrated in the man's life (v. 3). Jesus insists that while it is still day, he and the disciples must perform the works of the one who sent him and that with the impending arrival of "night" no more works will be performed (v. 4).[13] This proverb[14] should recall for the reader the revelation of God described as "light" in the prologue (1:4–9), and more immediately, Jesus as the "light of the world" (8:12; cf. 9:5). The impending darkness will signal the absence of Jesus, heightening the expediency for Jesus to act on the blind man's behalf in order to make God known.[15] Next, Jesus makes explicit, what was implicit in v. 4, restating that he is the "light of the world" (v. 5; cf. 8:12).

After this pronouncement story,[16] the miracle proper is performed (vss. 6–7). Jesus spits on the ground, makes mud, and places it on the man's eyes (v. 6). He is given the simple instruction to go and wash in the Pool of Siloam (v. 7a). The man formerly blind will recount this episode to the neighbors in v. 11, marking the most detailed retelling in the entire narrative (cf. 9:15, 27). The narrator adds the note, that Siloam means "sent." The reader will recall that Jesus is the "sent one" *par excellence*, with the result "... that blindness is removed with reference to and with the aid of the 'sent.'"[17] The man's subse-

---

and Shadows: Reading John 5–12 (Minneapolis: Fortress, 1996), 120. For a critique of Moloney's position, see Michaels, *John*, 538–39, fn. 1.

[12] This question reflects the notion that the sins of the father could be visited upon his children (e. g., Exod 20:5; Deut 5:9; Tobit 3:3–5). For a wide-ranging discussion on this principle in antiquity see Craig S. Keener, *The Gospel of John: A Commentary* (2 vols.; Peabody, Mass.: Hendrickson, 2003), 1:777–79. Contra the notion that a child is found guilty of his father's sins is the view of Ezek (18:14–20), as v. 20 states explicitly: "The person who sins shall die. A child shall not suffer for the iniquity of a parent, nor a parent suffer for the iniquity of a child; the righteousness of the righteous shall be his own, and the wickedness of the wicked shall be his own" (NRSV).

[13] I take the "we" (ἡμᾶς) along with most commentators, as referring to Jesus and the disciples. For a dissenting opinion, see Michaels, *John*, 542–43. Michaels intriguingly suggests that "we" refers to Jesus and the blind man, noting that the disciples play no role in the blind man's healing or his act of coming to faith (543).

[14] Craig Koester, *Symbolism in the Fourth Gospel: Meaning, Mystery, Community* (2d ed.; Minneapolis: Fortress, 2003), 162.

[15] Moloney, *Signs and Shadows*, 121. Also, recognized in the language of "night" and "dark" are the associations for Jesus' "hour" in John's Gospel. For a discussion of the latter, see: Michaels, *John*, 544.

[16] Jeffrey L. Staley, "Stumbling in the Dark, Reaching for the Light: Reading Character in John 5 and 9," *Semeia* 53 (1991): 55–80, esp. 64.

[17] Leon Morris, *The Gospel According to John* (rev. ed.; NICNT; Grand Rapids, Mich.: Eerdmans, 1995), 428.

quent actions, "went ... washed ... and came home ...," mirror the three-fold actions of Jesus in v. 6, with the result that the once blind man can now see (7b). Both parties, Jesus and the man, play a role in the man's healing.

The Absence of Jesus and the Nosy Neighbors (9:8–13)

Following the man's healing (v. 7), the reader might anticipate that Jesus would greet him, but instead the narrator introduces "his neighbors (γείτονες)," that is, "those who had seen him before as a beggar" (οἱ θεωροῦντες αὐτὸν τὸ πρότερον ὅτι προσαίτης) in v. 8.[18] The careful reader may note two details with the latter group's description. One, "seeing" operates on two levels in John's Gospel.[19] First, of course, is the physical attribute of sight, seen clearly in the restoration of the blind man's vision. Second, is the metaphorical attribute often expressed in terms of proper knowledge and linked to faith and discipleship.[20] Thus, the narrator might send the reader a clue that those who are familiar (i. e. "those who had seen") with the man formerly born blind will have difficulty seeing his new *identity*. The next detail suggests further that his identity will be the focus of the ensuing question and remarks (vss. 8–9). The man is described as a "beggar" (προσαίτης), marking the first time in the narrative that this description is used of him.[21] Hence, the neighbors see him according to his former status.

The first of their questions comes rapidly, "Is this not the man (οὗτος; vss. 2–3) who used to sit and beg?" Once more, the man's identity as a beggar is the focal point of the neighbors' reaction. Once the question is posed, division marks their response.[22] This division is marked by the reactions of "some"

---

[18] I take this latter descriptor epexegetically. Most commentators assume one group, while Morris offers a dissenting opinion when he writes, "There are two groups here, the man's neighbors and those who knew him as a beggar." See his *Gospel According to John*, 428.

[19] The participle used here in 9:8, οἱ θεωροῦντες, derives from the verb θεωρέω, a favorite in John's Gospel, as it is used some 24 occasions out of the 58 total uses in the NT (e. g., 2:23; 4:19; 6:2, 19, 40, 62; 7:3; 8:51; 10:12; 12:19, 45 [2x]; 14:17, 19 [2x]; 16:10, 16, 17, 19; 17:24; 20:6, 12, 14). For a good discussion on the varied uses of θεωρέω in John's Gospel, see J. M. Völkel, "θεωρέω," *EDNT* 2: 146–47.

[20] For a robust discussion on the act of "seeing" in John's Gospel, see the excellent article by Dorothy Lee, "The Gospel of John and the Five Senses," *JBL* 129/1 (2010): 115–127, here 117–120. See also the work of Clemens Hergenröder, *Wir schauten seine Herrlichkeit. Das johanneische Sprechen vom Sehen im Horizont von Selbsterschließung Jesu und Antwort des Menschen* (FB 80; Würzburg: Echter Verlag, 1996).

[21] Staley perceptively notes that descriptions referring to the man's former state of blindness highlight the dialogue in the next section with the Pharisees. He concludes: "Those with eyes to see do not have the ability to peer beneath the surface and find the person with true insight. Thus, from the perspective of the Pharisees, they never speak to anything more than an ignorant, 'blind' person (9:41)." See Staley, "Stumbling in the Dark," 66.

[22] As Michaels notes this is a common Johannine theme, recalling earlier "splits" in the crowd over the identity and activity of Jesus (7:12, 25–27, 40–43). Michaels, *John*, 548.

(ἄλλοι) who stated affirmatively that he was this individual (v. 9a), while "others" (ἄλλοι) insisted that he only resembled the man in question (v. 9b). The different reactions of the neighbors will prepare the reader for the following section, as it foreshadows the divided response of the Pharisees over the *identity* of Jesus (v. 16).[23] There, in response to the man's recollection of the healing, "some" (ἄλλοι) of the Pharisees claim that Jesus' is not an agent sent from God due to his non-observance of the Sabbath (v. 16a), while "others" (ἄλλοι) question how a "sinner" can perform these signs (v. 16b). The disagreement of the neighbors is answered definitively by the man himself with the statement: "I am" (ἐγώ εἰμι; v. 9c). In light of the previous chapter (ch. 8), and the narrator's successive uses of the ἐγώ εἰμι statements present there (8:12, 24, 28, 58) the reader cannot help but be struck by the irony of the man's self-declaration. The reader will remember that Jesus has been absent in the present narrative since v. 7a and will not appear again until near the end of the narrative in v. 35. Although Michaels admits that this remark is in the strictest sense a secular one, he writes: "… it creates an effect strangely similar to what it would have on Jesus' lips, for it confirms the reality of the miracle, and consequently the presence in Jerusalem of a miracle worker."[24] Thus, the man's declaration is intended to evoke the presence of the absent Jesus to the reader.

After the man's declaration, the once divided neighbors now ask in unison, "How were your eyes opened?" (v. 10). This same question will be echoed by the Pharisees later in the narrative (vss. 15, 26). The man's response is very familiar to the reader who will recall the voice of the narrator in v. 6, the instructions of Jesus in v. 7a, and the immediate results conveyed by the narrator in v. 7b. The added detail of Jesus' name in the man's near verbatim account serves to shift the focus back to the *identity* of the healer (v. 11). After all, "the man" (ὁ ἄνθρωπος) called Jesus (v. 11) echoes the beginning of the narrative where Jesus discovers "a man" (ἄνθρωπος) blind from birth (v. 1). This shift in identity will become the focus of the next section (esp. vss. 15–17, cf. v. 32), where ironically, Jesus will remain nameless much like the man born blind.[25]

---

[23] For a similar conclusion see J. Warren Holleran, "Seeing the Light: A Narrative Reading of John 9," *ETL* 49 (1993): 5–26, here 19.

[24] Michaels, *John*, 548. Brodie is more direct in his assessment: "… from a literary point of view, the man's *Egō eimi* is an echo of the divine *Egō eimi*" (348). Thomas L. Brodie, *The Gospel According to John: A Literary and Theological Commentary* (Oxford: Oxford University Press, 1993). Lindars notes that these successive uses "convey a deepening meaning." He would not agree, however with my interpretation of the man's use of ἐγώ εἰμι in 9:9c, opining that the statement lacks "the grand overtones which it has on the lips of Jesus in 8:58 and it is a mistake to read them into it" (334). Barnabas Lindars, *The Gospel of John* (NCB; Grand Rapids, Mich.: Eerdmans, 1982 [1972]).

[25] Staley surmises that this is due to a change in audience, and the man's unwillingness to disclose Jesus' identity. Further, he suggests that in light of the disclosure by the narrator in v. 14 that the healing took place on the Sabbath, the man changes the phrase "made mud"

After discovering the "how" of the man's healing, the neighbors want to know both the "who" and "where" of Jesus when they ask "Where is this man?" (ποῦ ἐστιν ἐκεῖνος; v. 12a). This question may seem innocuous at first, but this exact question was asked by the "Jews" at the beginning of the Tent Festival (7:11), "reminding the reader that Jesus is still wanted by the religious authorities, and that his life is still in danger."[26] Thus, the question provides a hint to the reader that the neighbors' role in the narrative is a negative one. The man's response is brief: "I do not know" (οὐκ οἶδα; v. 12b). Later in the narrative, in response to the Pharisees' accusation of Jesus as a "sinner" (v. 24c), the man pleads ignorance of knowing whether Jesus is a sinner or not with the identical phrase (οὐκ οἶδα), but quickly affirms "One thing I do know, that I was blind and now I see" (ἓν οἶδα ὅτι τυφλὸς ὢν ἄρτι βλέπω v. 25). Moreover, the ensuing narrative will reveal a growing understanding on the part of the healed man concerning Jesus as he refers to him as a prophet (v. 17) and as one sent from God (v. 32) before ultimately coming to a full understanding (v. 38).

The narrator records the last action of the neighbors in v. 13 when he writes, "They brought (ἄγουσιν) to the Pharisees him who was formerly blind." The only other time in John's Gospel where ἄγουσιν ("they brought") is used is in 18:28 when Jesus is being lead to the Praetorium to face interrogation by Pilate. This may also present indirect evidence in judging the neighbors negatively according to their actions here. Interestingly, in the *Pericope Adulterae* (7:53–8:11), the scribes and Pharisees "bring" (ἄγουσιν) the woman caught in adultery (8:3) so as to try, convict, and ultimately put her to death. Up until this verse, the neighbors could appear to be curious and innocent of any malicious intent towards the man born blind. However, this act of bringing the man to the authorities sends "ominous overtones."[27] This is reinforced by the narrative aside in v. 14 where the reader is reminded of the details of the healing in which Jesus "made mud" (πηλὸν ἐποίησεν; cf. vss. 6, 11, 15) and "opened eyes" (ἀνέῳξεν ... τοὺς ὀφθαλμούς; vss. 7, 11, 15) with the surprise remark that this took place on the Sabbath day. The reader will be reminded of the controversy of the lame man's healing on the Sabbath (5:9) ultimately kick-starting the murderous intent of the "Jews" toward Jesus (5:16, 18).[28]

(ἐποίησεν πηλόν; 9:6, 11) to "put mud" (πηλὸν ἐπέθηκέν). Staley, "Stumbling in the Dark," 67.

[26] Michaels, *John*, 549.

[27] Andrew T. Lincoln, *The Gospel According to John* (BNTC; Peabody, Mass.: Hendrickson, 2005), 282. Similarly, Michaels, *John*, 550.

[28] Asiedu-Peprah argues that this scene along with John 5 is a two-party juridical controversy, involving a dispute between two parties, the accuser and the accused, that does not involve outside mediation. The goal in this system is to come to peaceable terms before the case is sent to a trial. For a helpful outline of both John 5 and 9, see Martin Asiedu-Peprah, *Johannine Sabbath Conflicts as Juridical Controversy* (WUNT II/132; Tübingen: Mohr Siebeck, 2001), 24–25.

Character Matters: Evaluating the Neighbors

Returning to Bennema's criteria described above, we will first discuss how the neighbors measure on the axis of complexity, development, and penetration into their inner life. In terms of complexity, the neighbors are presented as curious as their questions demonstrate (vss. 8, 10, and 12). More ominously, however, they can also be classified as suspicious. Surely, the neighbors were aware when this healing took place, as the narrator points out (v. 14), and may have wondered about its legitimacy. To this latter point, one can add that their act of bringing the blind man to the authorities betrays their motive. Therefore, the neighbors' initial curiosity is best to be regarded more negatively, as they exhibit an air of suspicion which ultimately leads to their actions in v. 13. Consequently, the neighbors are not complex characters as they exhibit only two traits, curiosity and suspicion. Regarding development, the neighbors show very little, unless one would want to argue that the division that takes place in their responses as to the man's identity in v. 9a, b is replaced by their unification, demonstrated by their following questions in vss. 10, 12 and their act of bringing the man to the authorities in v. 13. Concerning the third criterion, penetration into their inner-life, the division in v. 9 is similar to a character's "self-talk." Here, the narrator informs the inner-monologue of the neighbors as they dispute the identity of the once blind man.[29]

Next, the neighbors probably fit most comfortably as a "type, stock, or flat character" in Bennema's four-fold degree of characterization model. Recalling that these characters display a single trait and demonstrate little to no development, the neighbors display a skeptical attitude towards the blind man as their questions and reactions reveal, ultimately leading them to bring him to the religious authorities in v. 13. Moreover, as noted above, their presence in this narrative foreshadows the Pharisees and the heightened disputes over Jesus' identity that is to follow. Finally, the response of the neighbors is seen as "inadequate." As Bennema argues, we must allow the Fourth Evangelist to set the terms to evaluate whether a character's response is positive or negative. In light of the dualistic worldview of the author and the programmatic statement of John 20:31: ("But these are written that you may believe that Jesus is the Messiah, the Son of God, and that by believing you may have life in his name"), all characters and their responses can be appropriately measured. In the case of the neighbors, their negative portrayal is clearly confirmed by their skepticism concerning the identity of Jesus (vss. 11–12) and when they hand the man over to the religious authorities (v. 13).

---

[29] For a host of examples of the narrator's role in portraying the inner-life of the Johannine characters, see Bennema, "Theory of Character," 405–406.

The Parents of the Man Born Blind: The Reason for Fear without True Reason*

Michael Labahn

Staying Anonymous

Within the Johannine narrative, the parents of the man born blind are only background characters. Like their son, who is the major figure in chap. 9, they have no names.[1] Further, the son is not defined in reference to his parents,[2] but rather the parents are defined in reference to their son and by the act of Jesus in giving sight: they are "the parents of him who could see again" (τοὺς γονεῖς αὐτοῦ τοῦ ἀναβλέψαντος). In contrast to their son, they behave (metaphorically speaking) as "no-names," individuals without a personality. They speak only after being asked to reply, and they do not demonstrate a sense of control over their own fate, but instead are motivated by a strong sense of fear of the possible actions of others (v. 22: "... they feared 'the Jews'" [ἐφοβοῦντο τοὺς Ἰουδαίους]; see below).

Refusing Answers

The significance of the appearance of the blind man's parents is indicated by the narrative setting. Verse 18 closes the first encounter of the man born blind with the religious authorities and introduces the interview of his parents. The interrogators are characterized as not believing that the man was formerly blind and, thus, as denying that Jesus had performed a "sign." Interestingly

---

* My thanks are extended to Tom Thatcher for checking the English in this essay and to the editors for their invitation to contribute and for their suggestions.

[1] Although the man born blind remains an anonymous character, he develops within the narrative from a blind beggar to one who gives fearless information about Jesus (as an example for readers of John, cf. Michael Labahn, "Der Weg eines Namenlosen – Vom Hilflosen zum Vorbild (Joh 9): Ansätze zu einer narrativen Ethik der sozialen Verantwortung im vierten Evangelium," in *Die bleibende Gegenwart des Evangeliums* [ed. Roland Gebauer and Martin Meiser; FS Otto Merk; MThSt 76; Marburg: Elwert, 2003], 63–80, esp. 72–76), who is finally found by Jesus and makes a confession (v. 38: πιστεύω).

[2] He is first called simply a "man" (ἄνθρωπον) who is blind from birth; he is never described as the son of someone in early scenes in this sequence.

enough, the son himself has already been interviewed before his parents are addressed (9:13–17). The legal interview of the parents consists of a short question by "the Jews" (v. 19) and a longer reply by the parents (vss. 20–21). A narrator's comment closes the episode by interpreting the parents' reply (vss. 22–23).

"The Jews'" question consists of two parts, one regarding the relationship of the healed man to the parents and another on the (debated) issue of how the blind man is now able to see. Taken together, these questions seem to assume some form of fraudulent collusion between Jesus and the man born blind, which perhaps could be unveiled by the parents identifying this individual as their son.[3] This reading is enhanced by the parents' assertion (v. 20) that their son was indeed born blind, which reflects the language of the interrogator's question (v. 19) and which appears to be an attempt to dispel any doubt concerning the son's identity or the basic facts of his life story.[4]

It is important for the characterization of the parents that their reply only partially answers the interrogators' question. In their response, the parents are careful to affirm only that which cannot be denied: the man is their son and he was born blind. Thereby, they confirm the identity of the man and his former physical status, but beyond this they are clearly reluctant to comment. As such, their answer clearly does not function as a reply to the issues raised by the question, but instead simply serves to refer "the Jews" back to the person they have asked about. Appropriately, then, they proceed to advise "the Jews" to have another direct encounter with their son: "ask him, he is old enough,[5] he shall speak for himself" (αὐτὸν ἐρωτήσατε ἡλικίαν ἔχει αὐτὸς περὶ ἑαυτοῦ λαλήσει). The reader is aware that such an interview has already taken place (v. 15; highlighted again in v. 27), and the basic content of that discussion is apparently presupposed by all characters within the episode. Nevertheless, this ambivalent statement by the parents functions to create a transition into the next sequence in the story, 9:24–33.

Self-Definition in Terms of Ignorance

Although the parents confirm the identity of the man born blind and his former physical status, they define themselves by their ignorance (twice they say, "we do not know" [… οὐκ οἴδαμεν … οὐκ οἴδαμεν·]). Even if they cannot

---

[3] E. g., Matthias Rein, *Die Heilung des Blindgeborenen (Joh 9): Tradition und Redaktion* (WUNT II/73; Tübingen: Mohr Siebeck, 1995), 143–44.

[4] E. g., Hartwig Thyen, *Das Johannesevangelium* (HNT 6; Tübingen: Mohr Siebeck, 2005), 466.

[5] In other words, he has reached the age of maturity; cf. Michael Labahn, *Jesus als Lebensspender: Untersuchungen zu einer Geschichte der johanneischen Tradition anhand ihrer Wundergeschichten* (BZNW 98; Berlin: de Gruyter, 1999), 361–62.

know what actually happened in 9:1–7 (since they were not present at that event), they notably portray themselves as people who only know what cannot be denied – that their son was their son and that he was born blind (v. 20). This does not really say anything at all about Jesus, as L. Schenke assumes: "Anders als die Juden … stellen sie denjenigen in den Mittelpunkt, der das Zeichen wirkte."[6]

We might label such a passive act of refusing to give a direct answer as a form of limited resistance that is prompted by the parents' analysis of the situation being developed in the narrative world. On the other hand, because the parents refuse to acknowledge the deeds of Jesus, the reader might lump them together with the opponents of Jesus who do not believe what happened and who oppose Jesus and his adherents (cf. v. 34).

Under Pressure

Even as anonymous background characters, the parents of the man born blind have had a significant career in recent Johannine research. Scholars who are interested in the social background of the Fourth Gospel often assume that these characters – normally in connection with the two-level drama model of J. Louis Martyn[7] – serve as a mirror of the Evangelist's extra-textual world: the parents represent a group of hidden Christian Jews who do not publically confess their belief and stay within the limits of their social and religious group.[8] Within such a diachronic interpretation, the parents function in the narrative as a negative foil in contrast to their son. While it may be true that the "first readers of the story, the Johannine Christians, also discovered their experience in the story"[9] – whatever that experience may have been – the rhetorical aim is to clearly encourage the reader not to behave like the parents but rather to imitate their sons' behavior, a call that would be valuable and relevant for many generations of readers.

The narrative setting clearly develops a social hierarchy that includes the parents: the parents are called to come (v. 18: ἐφώνησαν) by the opposing group.[10] Readers might be surprised by the passive and deferential reply of

---

[6] Ludger Schenke, *Johannes: Kommentar* (Kommentare zu den Evangelien; Düsseldorf: Patmos, 1998), 186.

[7] J. Louis Martyn, *History and Theology in the Fourth Gospel* (3d ed.; Louisville, Ky.: Westminster John Knox, 2003).

[8] Cf. Raymond E. Brown, *The Community of the Beloved Disciple: The Life, Loves, and Hates of an Individual Church in New Testament Times* (New York: Paulist Press, 1979), 71–73.

[9] Francis J. Moloney, *The Gospel of John* (SP 4; Collegeville, Minn.: Liturgical Press, 1988), 294.

[10] Craig Keener, *The Gospel of John: A Commentary* (2 vols.; Peabody, Mass.: Hendrickson, 2003), 787: "John probably uses … 'they called,' both as a scene change (cf. 9:24) and to signal the social power wielded by these leaders."

the parents, but the narrator gives an explanation for the behavior of his characters in terms of social power ([22] ταῦτα ... ὅτι ... [23] διὰ τοῦτο ...): the parents are afraid because the other group is a leading party that has power to exclude or to include people within the community.

In this case, the narrator only describes the parents' behavior without passing any explicit qualitative judgment on the behavior of his characters. Judgment is left to the reader, who knows that Jesus has the power to lose none of those who have been given to him by his Father (6:39; see also 10:29; 17:6). The readers will learn that the fearless confessor – the son, not his parents – will be called into the flock by Jesus, the "good shepherd" (10:3), who has found him (9:35) and who reveals himself to the man born blind. The readers could make further judgments on the grounds that the parents seem to know that a sign of Jesus has taken place (9:22), which the readers know should lead to belief (2:11; see also 11:47–48; 12:11). This is in accordance with the parents' self-introduction as people who have no knowledge about the events that have transpired (9:21), despite the fact that they are clearly aware of the potential consequences of involvement with Jesus and that the case at hand touches on this issue (v. 22). Their unwillingness to affirm any knowledge of Jesus associates them with the religious authorities, who also deny any knowledge of Jesus or his origins (9:29: "as for this man, we do not know [οὐκ οἴδαμεν] where he is from" ↔ v. 30).[11] By the narrative strategy of the text, the reader may be encouraged to conclude that the parents are on the side of the Jewish authorities. In any case, the parents are non-confessors who are not cast out from the synagogue, and who thus fall under the condemnation stated at 12:42: they love human glory more than glory from God (ἠγάπησαν γὰρ τὴν δόξαν τῶν ἀνθρώπων μᾶλλον ἤπερ τὴν δόξαν τοῦ θεοῦ; v. 43).

On Pragmatics

The parents function as narrative characters in a particular narrative setting. As such, they serve as a narrative link between the healing of their son (9:1–7) and the initial investigations of the Pharisees/Jews (9:8–17), and the interrogation of the healed one (9:24–34) on his way to a new encounter with his healer (9:35–38). They are characters who give *witness* to the dangers of confessing Jesus, the explicit motivation for their claim to limited knowledge (9:20). The narrator gives an explanation for their behavior: they "feared 'the Jews'" (ἐφοβοῦντο τοὺς Ἰουδαίους) because anyone who confesses Christ will be cast

---

[11] See Michael Labahn, "'Blinded by the Light': Blindheit und Licht in Joh 9 im Spiel von Variation und Wiederholung zwischen Erzählung und Metapher," in *Repetitions and Variations in the Fourth Gospel: Style, Text, Interpretation* (ed. Gilbert Van Belle et al.; BETL 223; Louvain: Peeters, 2009), 453–504, esp. 491.

out of the synagogue. This note shows that John 9:18–23 is referring to the following passage (9:24–34) and should read anew as the narrative progresses. Such a comment again sheds light on the behavior of the man born blind (see above). The fact that some characters "fear 'the Jews'" explains not only why the parents refuse to make a statement, but also highlights the portrayal of the son as a figure who gives a clear statement: "Weil seine Eltern als so kleinmütig trotzig beschrieben werden, wird der Mann ein Zeuge und ein Held."[12]

Put another way, the portrayal of the parents at 9:18–23 prepares the reader to better understand another character in the story: the man born blind. Although being in the same situation of danger, he acts without fear. Consequently, he is cast out by the religious and social community (9:34 referring to 9:22), but found as a believer (πιστεύω; 9:38) by the main hero (εὑρών; 9:35) of the Johannine text.

Summary

The figure of the parents is neither simply a mirror of an outside group, nor a mere foil for another character. They are part of the pragmatics of the story. The "parents of the man born blind" function as a character that invites the readers not to fear, but rather to give witness and thereby to confess Christ. By only accepting what is undeniable and by referring to their son, the parents illustrate to the reader how to act in relation to Jesus: not like these no-name characters whose passive act is only an act of limited resistance, but rather like the man born blind, who actively resists by confessing Jesus. The figure of the parents invites the reader to act differently and to behave fearlessly, like their son.

---

[12] Sjef van Tilborg, *Das Johannesevangelium: Ein Kommentar für die Praxis* (Stuttgart: Katholisches Bibelwerk, 2005), 133. In contrast to van Tilborg's paraphrase, I do not find a direct qualification of the parents in the narrator's comment.

The Believers Across the Jordan: On Location with Jesus

Ruben Zimmermann

The "Many Believers" – Within the Gospel Context

The "believers across the Jordan" should be regarded as a distinct group character.[1] Towards the end of John 10 the "many" (πολλοί) who come to Jesus and believe in him are mentioned twice (vss. 41, 42). The conceptual pair of "coming ... believing" in the parallel introductory phrases (v. 41a: καὶ πολλοὶ ἦλθον πρὸς αὐτόν; v. 42a: καὶ πολλοὶ ἐπίστευσαν εἰς αὐτόν) refers to the specific Johannine motif of "the way of faith" (e. g., John 1:46, 50; 4:30, 41; 11:45); the resumptive sentence (v. 42: "and many believed in him") in particular is used verbatim multiple times in the Gospel of John (see John 4:39; 7:31; 8:30; 11:45; 12:42; in John 2:23 with εἰς τὸ ὄνομα αὐτοῦ instead of εἰς αὐτόν). The semantic context therefore displays typically Johannine language, yet the verses contribute only marginally to establishing "many believers" as a distinct group character. Is the scarce textual information provided sufficient to speak of a group of characters *sui generis*? Unlike a mere structuralistic approach, Ralf Schneider and Fotis Jannidis consider characters as "mental models," which are generated in the act of reception.[2] The reader uses his/her knowledge about the narrated world to interlink and to augment the textual information about the characters.[3] Hence parallels, context, and indicators of interrelatedness figure prominently in the creation of a character. The following character analysis will follow this approach.

Let us focus for a moment on the parallel verses mentioned above, which immediately suggest a text comparison based on the verbatim sentence repetition. Some texts display structural similarities with John 10:39–42: In John 7:30–31 (see also 8:20, 30) a similar constellation of diametrically opposed

---

[1] See on the specifics of group characters, Uta Poplutz, *Erzählte Welt: Narratologische Studien zum Matthäusevangelium* (BThSt 100; Neukirchen-Vluyn: Neukirchener Verlag, 2008), 131–35.

[2] See Ralf Schneider, *Grundriß zur kognitiven Theorie der Figurenrezeption am Beispiel des viktorianischen Romans* (ZAA Studies 9; Tübingen: Stauffenburg-Verlag, 2000); Fotis Jannidis, *Figur und Person: Beitrag zu einer historischen Narratologie* (Narratologia 3; Berlin: de Gruyter, 2004).

[3] See Schneider, *Grundriß zur kognitiven Theorie*, 37–98; Jannidis, *Figur und Person*, 177–85.

reactions to Jesus is reported – a sub-group of the audience attempts to seize Jesus (John 7:30 = 10:39a: Ἐζήτουν οὖν αὐτὸν πιάσαι[4]), yet many others believe in him (John 7:30 = 10:42: καὶ πολλοὶ ἐπίστευσαν εἰς αὐτόν). In other texts, the faith of "the many" is characterized as deficient, as e. g., in John 8:30, in the context of the discussion about freedom and descent (John 8:31–59) or in John 12:42, in their refusal to confess to their faith (John 12:42–43). In John 4:9 the term "many" relates to believers among the non-Jewish Samaritans, and in John 10:41–42 "across Jordan" may either refer to the districts of Perea or Judea but also to the pagan region of the Decapolis. However, these similarities interlink the verses in a structural rather than in a functional way.

In the presentation of the characters diversity is prevalent: Who are the "many believers" within the Gospel? John 4:39 refers to the "many" Samaritans from Sychar; John 7:31 to the "many" in the crowd (Ἐκ τοῦ ὄχλου δὲ πολλοί); in John 8:30 "many" seems to refer to "the Jews" in the Temple (see 8:22, 31); in John 11:45 to the Jews who console Mary and Martha; and in John 12:42 to "many" of "the Jewish" authorities (ἐκ τῶν ἀρχόντων πολλοί). Hence, the "many" cannot be considered as a homogeneous group within the Gospel. The reasons attributed to the faith of the "many" are equally diverse, but they indicate a certain focus on "word" and "deed:" in John 4:39 the testimony of the Samaritan woman is mentioned as a reason for belief (διά), while in John 8:30 Jesus' prior discourse generates faith. The apodosis of John 7:31 refers to "signs" (σημεῖα), while John 11:45 explicitly recurs to the raising of Lazarus. In John 12:42 no direct causal connection is made. This illustrates that the Gospel of John uses the stereotypical sentence of the faith of the "many" in diverse contexts. It is the specific context and use of each occurrence of the term "many" that generates a specific profile of the "many believers" in each case.

Hence the textual parallels contribute to the clarification of the specific characteristics of the "many" in John 10:41–42. In this passage the familiar sentence is specified by a reference to the location: καὶ πολλοὶ ἐπίστευσαν εἰς αὐτὸν ἐκεῖ. And it is this localization ("there," ἐκεῖ) which attributes a certain autonomy to the group: the verse does not refer to just any believers, but those believers "there," "across Jordan." If we focus on this trait, the character analysis can be enhanced first and foremost by employing the semantics of space (2.), furthermore by analyzing the constellation of characters and connecting the believers with John the Baptist (3.), and finally by considering the larger context (John 9:39–10:42) and suggesting a christological interpretation (4.).

---

[4] The parallel use of the motif of hands also emphasizes the close relation of the verses; see John 7:30: "but no one laid hands on him" (καὶ οὐδεὶς ἐπέβαλεν ἐπ' αὐτὸν τὴν χεῖρα), John 10:39: "but he escaped from their hands" (καὶ ἐξῆλθεν ἐκ τῆς χειρὸς αὐτῶν).

Semantics of Space and Character Analysis in John 10:39–42

Space conveys meaning within a narrative:[5] a plot is dependent on the topography of narration in order to provide orientation and thus ensure the understanding of the reader. Space also helps to characterize the agents of the narrative. They are situated within a framework of spatial oppositions like here-there, high-low, inside-outside, etc. through which traits of character become noticeable or are enhanced. Therefore indications of space within a narrative have to be understood primarily as strategies of understanding, which attribute meaning and significance to an agent or an event within a plot. The presentation of geographical or topographical narrative spaces serves as a reference structure for socio-cultural spaces and non-spatial elements of meaning. As Jurij M. Lotman demonstrated in his narratological analysis of the semantics of space, topological (high-low, inside-outside, etc.) or topographical (mountain-valley, city-country) oppositions are often associated with non-topological semantic oppositions (e. g., good-bad; familiar-foreign) within narratives. The spatial model of the world becomes the "structuring element ..., around which non-spatial characteristics are organized."[6]

With regard to the Gospel of John, geographical spaces of the Jesus story (e. g., Galilee-Jerusalem) become spatial structures which can be associated with non-spatial fields of meaning (e. g., affirmation-rejection of Jesus) and contribute to the interpretation of Jesus' journey.[7] A significant example of the semantics of space can be found in the narration of the trial before Pilate (John 18:28–19:16), where the change of location (inside and outside of the praetorium) and the constant change in the constellation of agents (Pilate, Jesus, "Jews") initiates a process of interpretation, which inverts the parts of the characters involved in the trial.[8]

---

[5] See Gaston Bachelard, *Poetik des Raumes* (München: Hanser, 1960); Gerhard Hoffmann, *Raum, Situation, erzählte Wirklichkeit: poetologische und historische Studien zum englischen und amerikanischen Roman* (Stuttgart: Metzler, 1978); moreover Dietrich Jäger, *Erzählte Räume: Studien zur Phänomenologie der epischen Geschehensumwelt* (Würzburg: Königshausen & Neumann, 1998); Natascha Würzbach, "Erzählter Raum: Fiktionaler Baustein, kultureller Sinnträger, Ausdruck der Geschlechterordnung," in *Erzählen und Erzähltheorie im 20. Jahrhundert* (ed. Jörg Helbig; FS Wilhelm Füger; Heidelberg: Winter, 2001), 105–29.

[6] Jurij M. Lotman, *Die Struktur literarischer Texte* (4th ed.; München: Fink, 1993), 316: "zum organisierenden Element ..., um das herum sich auch die nichträumlichen Charakteristika ordnen."

[7] See Zbyněk Garský, *Das Wirken Jesu in Galiläa bei Johannes: Eine strukturale Analyse der Intertextualität des vierten Evangeliums mit den Synoptikern* (WUNT II/325; Tübingen: Mohr Siebeck, 2012).

[8] The judge Pilate is presented as wavering, "the Jews," who intend to remain "pure" because of the Passover lamb become guilty of blasphemy and do not recognize the "true Passover lamb:" for an analysis of the semantics of space in the trial before Pilate, see Ruben Zimmermann, "Deuten heißt 'Erzählen' und 'Übertragen': Narrativität und Metaphorik als zentrale Sprachformen historischer Sinnbildung zum Tod Jesu," in *Deutungen des Todes Jesu*

Details on geographical space hence play an essential role for the perception of the "many believers" as a group of characters in John 10:39–42. Let us therefore ask, which specific topology is being developed: "there" (v. 42) is located pointedly at the end of the passage and refers back to v. 40, where ἐκεῖ is also placed towards the end. Now it is Jesus, who remains "there." The static verb used here (μένειν) functions as a key word within John's Gospel to indicate "staying in a place." It stands in contrast with the two dynamic verbs used in the preceding text, the verbs ἐξῆλθεν (v. 39) and ἀπῆλθεν (v. 40), which signify a change of place: Jesus leaves the Temple (John 10:23) and Jerusalem (John 10:22) and goes to a place "across the Jordan." The reader is reminded of John 1:28 and 3:26 where the region πέραν τοῦ Ἰορδάνου has already been introduced. In John 1:28 we find an even more specific indication of place: "Bethany" (Βηθανία). Yet it is not the exact geographical information that matters to the narrator:[9] the key focus in John 10:40 is rather on the meaning which is ascribed to the place (τόπος) where John baptized, as well as on the temporal-spatial allusion to the beginning[10] of Jesus' ministry. Before Jesus sets out on his last journey to Jerusalem for his crucifixion (John 11:1) and before he travels to the "second" Bethany "near Jerusalem" for the raising of Lazarus (John 11:1, 18),[11] he returns to the beginning. Many exegetes therefore speak of an "extensive ring composition,"[12] as the first part of the Gospel is completed by the reference to Jesus and the Baptist first entering the stage (John 1–10), before the *leitmotifs* of death and resurrection (of Lazarus, John 11 and Jesus, John 18–20) introduce the second part of the Gospel. However, even if John 10:40–42 is considered a part of the Lazarus-pericope – cf., e. g., Michael Theobald[13] – the same can be stated: "The end recalls the beginning."[14] The verse functions as a hinge, which can imply either anaphoric or cataphoric reference.

---

im *Neuen Testament* (ed. Jörg Frey and Jens Schröter; WUNT 181; Tübingen: Mohr Siebeck, Studienausgabe 2011), 315–73, here 339–51.

[9] See, however, Rainer Riesner, *Bethanien jenseits des Jordan: Topographie und Theologie im Johannesevangelium* (Gießen: Brunnen-Verlag, 2002), 43–56.

[10] See John 10:40; τὸ πρῶτον βαπτίζων.

[11] See Ruben Zimmermann, "Vorbild im Sterben und Leben (Die Auferweckung des Lazarus) Joh 11,1–12,11," in *Die Wunder Jesu* (ed. Ruben Zimmermann et al., vol. 1 of *Kompendium der frühchristlichen Wundererzählungen*; Gütersloh: Gütersloher Verlag, 2013), 742–63, here 751.

[12] "Große Ringkomposition," see Hartwig Thyen, *Das Johannesevangelium* (HNT 6; Tübingen: Mohr Siebeck, 2005), 507. See also Klaus Wengst, *Das Johannesevangelium: 1. Teilband, Kapitel 1–10* (4 vols.; 2d ed.; ThKNT; Stuttgart: Kohlhammer, 2004) and all commentators, who support a two-part structure of the Gospel (John 1–10 and John 11–21).

[13] See Michael Theobald, *Das Evangelium nach Johannes: Kapitel 1–12* (RNT; Regensburg: Pustet, 2009), 705.

[14] Theobald, *Johannes*, 705: "Das Ende knüpft an den Anfang an."

Hence the spaces have unambigous connotations: While the dialogue in Jerusalem ends in conflict, with the accusation of blasphemy (John 10:33) and the attempt of stoning (John 10:31) and thus points to Jesus' imminent death, faith can be found with many "across the Jordan." Jerusalem or more generally the hill country of Judea are staged as the location of death (see also John 11:8), while "across Jordan" becomes the place of sanctuary (see John 14:2–3 τόπος), of salvation and truth.

Constellation of Characters: The Believers, Jesus and John the Baptist

In his study on narratological analysis, Sönke Finnern has presented a differentiated 6-step model of character analysis,[15] which I will draw on in a selective manner in the following analysis. If John 10:39–40 is included in the analysis because of its spatial relations with vss. 41–42, it is possible to distinguish between four characters or groups of characters within the text's agents ("*Figurenbestand*"): from the preceding text we can identify the characters of "the Jews," who aim to attack Jesus (v. 39), as well as "Jesus," even though only implicit verb forms and personal pronouns (v. 39) are employed. In vss. 40–42 the text mentions "the many" and "John" the Baptist, who is identified by his action (v. 40; βαπτίζων). John does not appear in the scene actively, but the text reports about him: the narrator comments on the place, where Jesus went "across Jordan," as the place where the Baptist first baptized (v. 40). In their direct speech the "many" say that John did not perform signs, but that his testimony about "this man" (περὶ τούτου), meaning Jesus, is true. The Baptist's action ("*Figurenhandlung*") is therefore most clearly described (he baptizes, he does not perform miracles, he speaks about Jesus), even though it is only referred to in a flashback within this scene. The action of "the Jews" consists in a renewed (πάλιν) attempt to seize Jesus, thus referring back to the attempt of stoning (v. 22) or – in verbatim re-occurrence – to the attempts to seize Jesus in John 7:30, 32, 44–45. But just as in John 8:20, the act of violence fails. Jesus is portrayed actively: he goes away (v. 39b), goes there (v. 40a) and stays (v. 40b). Apart from this centre of action he is the object of others' actions, whether in the attempt to seize him (negative action) or in it the testimony of the Baptist and the faith of the "many" (positive action). The "many" join Jesus' activities: their "coming" (ἔρχομαι; v. 41) corresponds with Jesus' action (although without prefix); their assumable remaining there (v. 40fin) is paral-

---

[15] Finnern distinguishes between 1. "Figurenbestand und -konfiguration;" 2. "Figurenmerkmale;" 3. "Figurenkonstellation;" 4. "Figur und Handlung;" 5. "Figurendarstellung" und 6. "Figurenkonzeption," see Sönke Finnern, *Narratologie und Biblische Exegese: Eine integrative Methode der Erzählanalyse und ihr Ertrag am Beispiel von Matthäus 28* (WUNT II/285; Tübingen: Mohr Siebeck, 2010), 125–63.

leled with "believing there" (v. 42), thus referring to the specific Johannine connection between "remaining" and "believing" (cf. John 4:40; 5:58; 8:51; 15:4–6, etc.).

While traits of character ("*Figurenmerkmale*") are hardly noticeable in the agents, especially in the many believers, an analysis of the constellation of characters ("*Figurenkonstellation*") is able to provide deeper insight into this group character. Finnern defines this step within character analysis as "the interrelation among the agents as the recipient perceives it."[16] Of central interest is the structure of interaction ("*Interaktionsstruktur*")[17] of the agents involved as well as the function and role of the agents within the developing plot.[18] According to Eder's categories the passage John 10:39–42 could be described as a "two-protagonist-narrative" or even better as a "two-protagonist-narrative miniature:"[19] Jesus enters the stage as first protagonist, with the hostile "Jews" as antagonists. The change of location is emphasized by the striking change of subject between v. 39a and v. 39b. In v. 41 the "many" enter the scene as second protagonist. This interpretation of the *Interaktionsstruktur* is supported by the parallel structure concerning the first and second protagonist with a view to the action, the scope of narration and the direct speech. The πολλοί are mentioned twice and are sided by John the Baptist, who is likewise mentioned twice, as their helper (*adjuvant*). For it is the testimony of the Baptist, which plays an important role in the development of faith. The "many" come to Jesus, but he remains passive and mute in this passage. They, however, remember during this meeting everything John said about Jesus (πάντα δὲ ὅσα εἶπεν Ἰωάννης περὶ τούτου) and acknowledge, that it is true (ἀληθή ἦν). The attentive reader is reminded of the testimony of the Baptist, which has already been mentioned in the prologue, and later more extensively in John 1:29–34 and 3:22–36. Moreover Jesus himself confirms the truth of the Baptist's testimony (John 5:32–33), and indeed surpasses it the testimony offered by his deeds, the Father and scripture (John 5:36–47). The servant role of the Baptist is also prevalent in John 10:40–42, as in contrast to Jesus himself he does not perform any signs. Does this imply that (i) Jesus performed signs while he was there, which they saw; or (ii) that they have heard of the signs that Jesus has performed? Or does it just mean (iii) that Jesus is superior to the Baptist, and that the implied author thus uses this group to underline Jesus' superiority to the Baptist?

---

[16] Finnern, *Narratologie*, 147: "das Verhältnis der Figuren untereinander … so wie der Rezipient es wahrnimmt."

[17] See Manfred Pfister, *Das Drama: Theorie und Analyse* (11th ed.; München: Fink, 2001), 227–35.

[18] Following on from the actantial model developed by Propp and Greimas, Jens Eder proposed a flexible heuristic model of eight actants ("Handlungsrollenmodell"), which can serve as a useful instrument to describe most existing constellations of actants, see Jens Eder, *Die Figur im Film: Grundlagen der Figurenanalyse* (Marburg: Schüren-Verlag, 2008), 492–500.

[19] See Eder, *Die Figur im Film*, 496–97.

Faith is hence aroused through the passing on of the witness to Christ as well as through the right point of view. The "second" protagonists stand in strong contrast to the antagonists concerning their relationship with Jesus. While the latter deny Jesus and attempt to seize him, the former come to believe in him.

However, all this leaves the readers somewhat perplexed when creating their mental image of the character. How can it be that the long Good Shepherd's discourse and the subsequent discussion seem lacking in effect with regard to the addressees, while the faith of the "many" happens unexpectedly and far from the place of the main action?

The Christ-belief of the "Many" and of the Readers

John 10:40–42 speaks of the faith of the "many," which ensues from the words of the Baptist and the meeting with Jesus. However, we are not told what the Baptist's actual words were; his testimony is valued as true, but regarding the content it remains indistinct. In order to determine the object of faith more closely, the verses have to be read within the preceding context. Detailed analyses of the structure have repeatedly highlighted the internal coherence of John 10:22–42.[20] It is possible to distinguish two separate discourses, each of which is composed of an introduction (vss. 22–24; vss. 32–33), Jesus' speech (vss. 25–30; vss. 24–38) and the audience's reaction (v. 31; vss. 39–42). In John 10:42 the Christological question is asked and not only answered positively (v. 25), but also surpassed by assertions of Jesus unity (v. 30) and reciprocal immanence (v. 38) with the Father. The motif of sheep (vss. 26–29) implies a close connection with John 10:1–18; it is therefore possible to describe John 9:39–10:42 as one large unity in four parts.[21]

A. John 9:39–10:21:   First Discourse
   1. Part (9:39–10:6)
      Introduction: Question of the Pharisees (9:39–41)
      Jesus' speech: Amen-Saying (v. 1a)
                         Parable of the shepherd (vss. 1b–5)
      Audience's reaction: Negative effect (v. 6): lack of understanding

---

[20] See for instance Francis J. Moloney, *Signs and Shadows: Reading John 5–12* (Minneapolis: Fortress, 1996), 143–53; Mary L. Coloe, *God Dwells With Us: Temple Symbolism in the Fourth Gospel* (Collegeville, Minn.: Liturgical Press, 2001), 147.

[21] See on the details Ruben Zimmermann, *Christologie der Bilder im Johannesevangelium: Die Christopoetik des vierten Evangeliums unter besonderer Berücksichtigung von Joh 10* (WUNT 171; Tübingen: Mohr Siebeck, 2004), 254–76, here 257; similarly Klaus Scholtissek, *In ihm sein und bleiben: Die Sprache der Immanenz in den johanneischen Schriften* (Herders biblische Studien 21; Freiburg: Herder, 2000), 322–24.

2. Part (vss. 7–21)	
Introduction:	(v. 7a)
Jesus' speech:	Amen-Saying (v. 7b)
	vss. 7–16: I am sayings (door, shepherd)
	vss. 17–18: christological conclusion
Audience's reaction:	Dividing effect (10:19–21)
	1. Reaction: demonization of Jesus (10:20)
	2. Reaction: reference to Jesus' sign (10:21)
B. John 10:22–42:	Second Discourse
3. Part (vss. 22–31)	
Introduction:	Indications of place and time (vss. 22–23)
	Quest for the Christ of "the Jews" (v. 24)
Jesus' speech:	vss. 25–30: aims at unity with the Father
Audience's reaction:	Negative effect (v. 31): attempt of stoning
4. Part (vss. 32–42)	
Introduction:	Question of Jesus (v. 32)
	Accusation of blasphemy (v. 33)
Jesus' speech:	vss. 34–38: aims at reciprocal immanence with the Father
Audience's reaction:	Dividing effect (vss. 39–42)
	1. Reaction: attempt to seize Jesus (v. 39)
	2. Reaction: faith of the "many" (vss. 40–42)

The two longer parts of the discourse reveal a striking parallel structure: in each of the two discourses two parts can be distinguished. Each of the four parts concludes with a note on the effect it creates on the audience: first the negative, non-verbal reaction is noted (v. 6: lack of understanding; v. 31: attempt of stoning), then the more elaborate dividing effect of Jesus' speech is narrated (vss. 20–21: many – others; vss. 39, 42: they – many). As there were "many" (πολλοί) in v. 20 who dismissed Jesus as possessed by demons, there are "many" (πολλοί) in v. 42 who come to believe in Jesus.

Through the embedding in the context the faith of the "many" seems like an answer to the previously debated christological questions. The central focus is on the quest for the Christ in the narrow sense, but a diverse spectrum of christological aspects is laid out like a mosaic.[22] Against this background facets of the content of the Baptist's testimony as remembered in John 10:40–42 become clearer. John the Baptist was – just like Jesus in John 10:24 – confronted with the Messianic question, which he negated twice (John 1:10–20; 3:28). In the parable of the bridegroom and his friend (John 3:29–30), however, Jesus is confirmed as the Messiah-bridegroom by the "many believers" who take the part of the "bride" (John 3:29).[23] The passage about the Mes-

---

[22] See Zimmermann, *Christologie der Bilder*, 379–83.

[23] See Mirjam and Ruben Zimmermann, "Der Freund des Bräutigams (Joh 3,29): Deflorations- oder Christuszeuge?," *ZNW* 90 (1999), 123–30; on the traditional background of the bridegroom-Messiah-metaphor see Ruben Zimmermann, "'Bräutigam' als frühjüdisches Messias-Prädikat? Zur Traditionsgeschichte einer urchristlichen Metapher," *BN* 103 (2000): 85–100.

siah-bridegroom is not only introduced by believers coming to Jesus (John 3:26 καὶ πάντες ἔρχονται πρὸς αὐτόν), it also explicitly mentions the place "across the Jordan" (John 3:26), linking it with John 10:40–41. What the Baptist promised by means of the parable in John 3:26–30 has been proved true. But also his testimony of the "Lamb of God" (John 1:29, 36) can be associated with the motif of sheep and shepherd in John 10. The sheep are to follow the shepherd in his exodus from the αὐλή or rather the Temple[24] (John 10:4), just as the "many" align their action to the action of Jesus. The notion that the flock of sheep is to be enlarged by "other sheep" (John 10:16) might be an indication of the integration of the believers "across the Jordan."

It is because of the testimony of the Baptist that historical exegesis has interpreted this in terms of mission or even absorption of the disciples of the Baptist.[25] However, the mention of the "many" in this passage would then have to be regarded as a motiveless addition, appended like an erratic block. If we remain on the level of the narration, the "many" can be defined more closely. Through the embedding in the narrow (John 10) and wider (John 1–3: Baptist) context, through the constellation of the agents and the semantics of space the character traits can be discovered in detail. Above all it is the reader, who has to draw these connecting lines in order to construct the mental model of the "many believers." In contrast to the rejection of Jesus (v. 39) it is this faith in Jesus displayed by the "many" (vss. 40–42), which has the potential to become a model for the reader to follow. Here the narrative crosses the Jordan river of history and hopes to find many current believers "across the Jordan."

---

[24] If one is to follow an interpretation, which assumes that the leading out of the sheep from the αὐλή (technical term for the forecourts of the Temple) and the spatial-temporal positioning of the passage in the Temple and during the Feast of Dedication (John 10:22–23) indicate a metaphorical substitution of the temple- and sacrificial cult in Jesus, then John 10 allows an understanding of the apodosis of the Baptist in John 1:29 concerning Jesus' bearing the sins of the world. While the sacrificial animals are led out and freed (John 10:3–4; see John 2:14–15.), Jesus himself is circled (John 10:24), led into the αὐλή (John 18:15) and finally sacrificed like the Passover lamb (John 19:1, 36). See for details Zimmermann, *Christologie der Bilder*, ch. 12.4, "Narrative Bildlichkeit in Joh 10: Jesus als Tempel," 355–71.

[25] See Knut Backhaus, *Die "Jüngerkreise" des Täufers Johannes: Eine Studie zu den religionsgeschichtlichen Ursprüngen des Christentums* (Paderborn: Schöningh, 1991); moreover Theobald, *Johannes*, 707: "Joh 10,40–42 ist eine sublime Vereinnahmung von konkurrierenden Täuferanhängern für die christliche Sache."

Lazarus:
"Behold a Man Raised Up by Christ!"

Marianne Meye Thompson

One of the best known, but also least developed, figures in the Gospel of John may well be Lazarus of Bethany, the brother of Mary and Martha, who was raised from the dead by Jesus. Typically, when titles or headings are given to various chapters or sections of the Gospel of John, its eleventh chapter is called "The Raising of Lazarus," even though Martha and Mary each figure more prominently in the narrative. But while Lazarus lends his name to the chapter, he does not play a role as an active agent in the narrative. He does not make a confession comparable to that which his sister Martha makes, since he never speaks at all, nor does he express lavish devotion to Jesus as his sister Mary subsequently does, since he is scarcely shown as acting at all. He figures in the narrative as the one called from death to life by Jesus. Not surprisingly, then, in his poetic treatment of the raising of Lazarus, Alfred Lord Tennyson (1809–1892), wrote these words:

> Behold a man raised up by Christ!
> The rest remaineth unreveal'd;
> He told it not; or something seal'd
> The lips of that Evangelist.[1]

Indeed much remains "unrevealed" about Lazarus, including his occupation, position in the family, marital status, age, appearance, habits, inner thoughts, and motivations. He neither speaks nor acts, so that nothing he says or does determines how he is known by the reader. Instead, he is presented entirely as one to whom things happen: he falls ill, dies, is mourned, raised to life, and becomes an object of both curiosity on the one hand and hostility on the other. In his silence and apparent passivity, Lazarus is somewhat unique in the Gospel. John the Baptist speaks at length about Jesus and baptizes with water; Nicodemus appears in three scenes to inquire of Jesus, defend his right to a hearing, and offer him a royal burial; the Samaritan woman comes to draw water at a well, converses at length with Jesus, and returns to her town to tell others about Jesus; a blind man washes in a pool, argues with Pharisees, and worships Jesus; and various disciples make confessions, converse with Jesus,

---

[1] From "In Memoriam XXXI."

bring others to him, fall away, defend Jesus, witness his death, and race to the tomb, among other things. Lazarus has the greatest affinities not with any of these disciples, but with the royal official's son (4:48–53). Indeed, this comparison is telling: here are two men, near death, whose families petition Jesus for help. Both the unnamed official's nameless son, and Lazarus, the brother of Mary and Martha, are examples of those who, subject to the power of death, are given life by Jesus.

Lazarus is presented in the Gospel entirely in terms of what happens to him and how others respond to him because of his mortality: because he is dying, his sisters solicit Jesus' help and, because he dies, Mary, Martha, Jesus and "the Jews" from Jerusalem mourn for him; because Jesus raises him from the dead, the curious wish to see him and therefore the chief priests seek his death; and ultimately and most significantly, because he dies, Jesus risks his own life, journeying to Bethany to bring the dead man back to life. This tension between life and death permeates the Gospel and the account of the raising of Lazarus, and determines the characterization of Lazarus. Mortal and frail, Lazarus represents all human beings faced with the threat of death; but as one who has received life, Lazarus represents all who are given life by the One who has and gives life.

Previous Studies of Lazarus

One of the first studies of the characters in John was undertaken by Raymond Collins, who argued that many of these characters were to be understood as representative of different faith responses to Jesus.[2] In brief, according to Collins, Lazarus represents "the disciple who has died but will be raised because of the glorification of Jesus."[3] Collins further suggests that the story of the raising of Lazarus likely circulated to address the problem of the delay of the parousia: Lazarus represents those who had died because of Jesus' delay in coming.[4]

---

[2] Raymond F. Collins, "John's Characters," in *These Things Have Been Written: Studies on the Fourth Gospel* (ed. idem; LThPM 2; Louvain: Peeters, 1990), 1–45. Collins names and discusses fifteen such characters: John the Baptist, Nathanael, the mother of Jesus, Nicodemus, the Samaritan woman, the royal official, the lame man, Philip, the man born blind, Lazarus, Judas, Mary Magdalene, Thomas, Peter and the Beloved Disciple. For a recent discussion of the characters as prototypes within social identity theory, see Philip F. Esler and Ronald Piper, *Lazarus, Mary and Martha: Social-Scientific Approaches to the Gospel of John* (Minneapolis: Fortress, 2006).

[3] Collins, *These Things Have Been Written*, 27. Collins' description of Lazarus might seem to minimize his individual, or distinctive, identity or significance. The relative lack of interest in Lazarus himself has been noted by others; see Francis J. Moloney, "Can Everyone Be Wrong? A Reading of Joh 11.1–12.8," *NTS* 49 (2003): 505–27, who writes, "John 11 shows little interest in Lazarus" (512).

[4] Collins, *These Things Have Been Written*, 26; he is followed here by R. Alan Culpepper,

Collins' study has cast a long shadow over much subsequent work on Johannine characterization. For example, Craig Koester's study of symbolism in John devoted a chapter to characterization with the heading "Representative Figures."[5] Under the subheading, "People who meet Jesus," Koester treats Mary, Martha and Lazarus. In Koester's view, Lazarus himself represents those who fulfill Jesus' words that "everyone who lives and believes in me shall never die" (11:25–26). Readers would also find an analogy with "their own stories, as they experienced sickness and death in a time when Christ was not visibly present, and as they turned to a seemingly absent Christ for help and received no timely answer."[6] These readers would thus identify with Lazarus in his mortality, in his dependence on Jesus and his life-giving power, and in the mystery of Jesus' apparent absence or delay in the face of great human need.

Alan Culpepper's seminal literary analysis of John, *Anatomy of the Fourth Gospel*, devoted a chapter to Johannine characters.[7] Although using somewhat different categories than Collins, Culpepper likewise argued that many of the characters in John were types, the "personification of a single trait," such as doubt, faith, perceptivity, and so on.[8] Furthermore, each of these traits is demonstrated in relationship to Jesus, with the result that the individuality of each character is "determined by their encounter with Jesus."[9] In Culpepper's discussion, Lazarus is identified as a disciple of Jesus by means of Jesus' description of him as a friend (11:11; cf. 15:13–15) and by the fact that Jesus, knowing that his action of raising Lazarus would lead to his own death (11:7, 8, 16), lays down his life for him (15:13). Lazarus thus "represents the disciple to whom life has been given and challenges the reader to accept the realization of eschatological expectations in Jesus."[10] Culpepper thus shows how the dra-

---

Anatomy of the Fourth Gospel: A Study in Literary Design (Philadelphia: Fortress, 1983), 140; and Craig R. Koester, *Symbolism in the Fourth Gospel: Meaning, Mystery, Community* (2d ed.; Philadelphia: Fortress, 2003), 65.

[5] Koester, *Symbolism*, 33–77. Brendan Byrne, S. J., argues that Lazarus' role in the narrative is "simply to be one loved by Jesus" and, precisely in that role, can "stand as a typical or representative figure – a character with whom anyone who reads the Gospel can identify" (idem, *Lazarus: A Contemporary Reading of John 11:1–46* [Collegeville, Minn.: Liturgical Press, 1990], 39, 85). But J. Frey observes that the sisters, together with Lazarus, appear as paradigms of those loved by Jesus (idem, *Die johanneische Eschatologie, Bd. III: Die eschatologische Verkündigung in den johanneischen Texten* [WUNT 117; Tübingen: Mohr Siebeck, 2000], 426).

[6] Koester, *Symbolism*, 65. See also Wilhelm Wuellner's rhetorical-critical study of the Lazarus narrative that takes seriously the past, present and future experience of the reader in engaging the text (idem, "Putting Life Back into the Lazarus Story and Its Reading: The Narrative Rhetoric of Joh 11 as the Narration of Faith," *Semeia* 53 [1991]: 113–32).

[7] Culpepper, *Anatomy of the Fourth Gospel*, 99–148.
[8] Culpepper, *Anatomy of the Fourth Gospel*, 102.
[9] Culpepper, *Anatomy of the Fourth Gospel*, 104.
[10] Culpepper, *Anatomy of the Fourth Gospel*, 141. In her study *Rhetoric and Reference in the Fourth Gospel*, Margaret Davies also devoted one chapter to characterization and, like Culpepper, argued that Johannine characters tend to have or represent a single trait; she

ma of life and death that runs throughout the Gospel finds concrete embodiment in the death and raising of Lazarus.

Mark Stibbe has argued that Johannine characters are less flat and more complex than earlier works have allowed.[11] He also stresses that the characters in the Gospel serve as foils to enhance the readers' understanding of Jesus. That is to say, characters are not introduced or developed for their own sake, but to underscore the identity of Jesus. Having said that, one of the most provocative, if not controversial, conclusions emerging from Stibbe's work is the proposal that Lazarus is "the disciple whom Jesus loved," i. e., the so-called "Beloved Disciple."[12] Stibbe believes that all the narrative clues add up to the identification of Lazarus as this otherwise unnamed disciple loved by Jesus. Stibbe also thinks that Lazarus' reminiscences lay behind a primitive gospel narrative, one of two narrative sources used by the Evangelist. The identification of Lazarus as the (Jerusalem based) Beloved Disciple allows Stibbe to "place" Lazarus at many scenes in the Gospel, including the calling of the first disciples, encounters in Jerusalem (for example, with Nicodemus); Jerusalem based miracles (chs. 5, 9); and most of the events commencing with the entrance to Jerusalem up to and including the account of the race to the tomb (ch. 20). The Beloved Disciple thus appears not only as a figure in the Gospel, but is actually responsible for many of the traditions that became "the Lazarus Gospel" and were taken up by the Evangelist into the Gospel as we now have it. Lazarus' significance thus extends beyond the boundaries of the written Gospel to the sources and even events behind the present Gospel and its literary forebear. Although in some senses a silent character in the narrative, Lazarus is nevertheless the one whose voice is heard in it.

"A Character Resurrected: Lazarus in the Fourth Gospel and Afterwards," by Raimo Hakola, appeared in the collection *Characterization in the Gospels*.[13] Hakola's discussion is a lengthy, detailed study of the narrative of John 11,

---

further emphasized that they are "flat" characters who show little development (idem, *Rhetoric and Reference in the Fourth Gospel* [JSNT 69; Sheffield: JSOT Press, 1992], 316–49).

[11] See Mark G. Stibbe, *John as Storyteller: Narrative Criticism and the Fourth Gospel* (SNTSMS 73; Cambridge: Cambridge University Press, 1992), 24–25; idem, "A Tomb With A View: John 11:1–44 in Narrative-Critical Perspective," *NTS* 40 (1994): 38–54.

[12] See, for example, Stibbe, *John as Storyteller*, 79–80, 168. That Lazarus is the Beloved Disciple is also argued by Steven A. Hunt, "Nicodemus, Lazarus, and the Fear of the 'the Jews' in the Fourth Gospel," in *Repetition and Variation in the Fourth Gospel: Style, Text, Interpretation* (ed. Gilbert Van Belle et al.; Louvain: Peeters, 2009), 199–212. If this were the case, then the characterization of Lazarus would need to be carried out through the rest of the Gospel, since the Beloved Disciple appears at the last supper lying next to Jesus (13:23), the cross (19:26), the empty tomb (20:8), and the Sea of Galilee during the last narrated resurrection appearance of Jesus (21:7, 20).

[13] Raimo Hakola, "A Character Resurrected: Lazarus in the Fourth Gospel and Afterwards," in *Characterization in the Gospels* (ed. David M. Rhoads and Kari Syreeni; London: T&T Clark, 1999), 223–63. For a somewhat different study, with a lengthy treatment of the influence of this narrative from the ancient to the modern periods, see also Jacob Kremer,

rather than an analysis of the character of Lazarus *per se*. Lazarus' character essentially "serves as a proof of Jesus' claims to be the giver of life whom the Father has sent into the world."[14] In spite of the minimal characterization of Lazarus, readers do learn Lazarus' name, of his friendship with Jesus, and a bit about his life after he was raised from death. But Hakola is particularly interested in another "afterlife" of Lazarus, namely, how John's account has been read and interpreted by subsequent generations of readers, not only biblical interpreters and patristic authors, but novelists, poets, and playwrights. Hakola notes that it is precisely because the Gospel tells the reader so little about Lazarus that subsequent interpreters exercise considerable freedom in imagining what Lazarus himself must have experienced or thought, or how he would have reacted to Jesus' bringing him back from the tomb. Lazarus, a "marginal agent" in the Gospel, moves toward "a genuine personality" in subsequent interpretation. Both the silence of the text – the absence of detail and description – and the change of point of view – from that of the narrator or the other characters in John's narrative to that of Lazarus himself in later plays and poems – allow for creative appropriation and retelling of the Johannine narrative. And, in this way, Lazarus lives on.

Most recently, in *Encountering Jesus: Character Studies in the Gospel of John*, the most comprehensive study of character in John to date, Cornelis Bennema protests against the inadequacy of previous studies on character in John, and particularly their description of the characters in John as "flat" or "types."[15] In describing Lazarus as portrayed in the Gospel of John, Bennema suggests that he is one of the "Jews," where "Jews" refers to "the (strict) Torah- and temple-loyalists who are mainly (but not exclusively) located in Jerusalem and Judea," and that Lazarus might well have been a wealthy nobleman.[16] But because Bennema thinks that character is often "inferred" from the text, and that "exegesis is the primary means for our character reconstruction,"[17] his study is to a large extent an analysis of the narrative of John 11 itself. In reading John 11 in the context of the Gospel as a whole, Bennema argues that characters in John should be classified by virtue of their response to Jesus "because John demands it."[18] That is to say, all characters must be evaluated

---

Lazarus: die Geschichte einer Auferstehung: Text, Wirkungsgeschichte und Botschaft von Joh 11,1–46 (Stuttgart: Katholisches Bibelwerk, 1985).

[14] Hakola, "A Character Resurrected," 247.

[15] Cornelis Bennema, *Encountering Jesus: Character Studies in the Gospel of John* (Milton Keynes: Paternoster, 2009); see also his earlier article, "A Theory of Character in the Fourth Gospel with Reference to Ancient and Modern Literature," *BibInt* 17 (2009): 375–421.

[16] Bennema, *Encountering Jesus*, 157–58.

[17] Bennema, *Encountering Jesus*, 21.

[18] Bennema, *Encountering Jesus*, 12. See also Moloney, "Can Everyone be Wrong?," who argues that one of the rhetorical functions of the narrative is to show that everyone misunderstands Jesus and errs in their confessions about him.

in light of John's statement of purpose in 20:30–31 to bring people to believe in Jesus so that they may have life. In that framework, Lazarus serves largely to allow Jesus to reveal an aspect of his own identity as "resurrection and life." Jesus thereby evokes both initial faith (on the part of "the Jews") and deepens existing faith (on the part of Martha and Jesus' disciples). In this context, it is Lazarus' *response* to Jesus, not his character *per se*, that should be called *typical*. While Bennema thus affirms the "representative value" of all the Johannine characters, he simultaneously resists their flattening into static "types."

Two points in particular emerge from these various studies. First, Lazarus is frequently described as a type or representative, usually representing the disciple who receives life from Jesus. But it remains curious that Lazarus himself is never explicitly described or presented as one who had faith in Jesus, although clearly his sisters express such trust. While Lazarus' death and return to life are occasions for *others* to express their faith in Jesus, Lazarus is not presented in terms of his own faith, but as one loved by Jesus. Given the fact that Lazarus is said to be loved by Jesus, and is called a "friend" by Jesus, he belongs among those who are Jesus' "own." One can, therefore, infer that Lazarus reciprocates Jesus' love, and is a disciple of Jesus, even as are his sisters, Martha and Mary. But it is not Lazarus' faith that is emphasized in this narrative; rather, it is his mortality and subsequent reception of life from Jesus. As argued earlier, Lazarus is characterized in the Gospel in terms of what happens to him and how others respond to him because of his mortality. Lazarus represents all human beings faced with the threat of death; but as one who has received life, Lazarus represents all who are given life by the One who is, has, and gives life.

Second, these various studies show how John characterizes Lazarus by means of his relationship to Jesus. In particular, in relationship to Lazarus Jesus is the one who has and gives life. While other aspects of Jesus' character and identity – he is the Messiah, Son of God, the One who gives the Spirit, the Good Shepherd, the Son of man, and so on – come to the fore in describing Jesus' relationship to other characters in the Gospel, the underlying attribute of Jesus, demonstrated time and again, is that he is the one in whom there is life. In the context of the raising of Lazarus, Jesus' identity is revealed in what he says – that he is resurrection and life (11:25–26) – and in what he does – he gives life to the dead. Jesus' word and deed thus emphasize the point that Lazarus represents human beings caught between the threat of death and the promise of life. We turn, then, to a closer look at the details of the characterization of Lazarus in the Gospel of John.

The Characterization of Lazarus

In his discussion of biblical characters, Robert Alter comments on the "sparse, even rudimentary means" through which the Bible presents its characters. Still, he notes that the literary techniques used by biblical authors are generated by their conceptions of God and human beings: the all-seeing God directs history, so that what happens expresses the divine purposes and will; but only this God knows the thoughts and hearts of every individual, which may not therefore always be disclosed or understood. Furthermore, every human being is created by this all-seeing God, and is made in the likeness of God, and given freedom, with the result that every individual also encompasses "the zenith and the nadir of the created world."[19]

Alter proposes a "scale of characterization," which moves from the least to the most explicit modes of characterization employed in a narrative. In increasing order of explicitness in setting forth the motives, attitudes, and moral nature of characters, the scale is as follows: (1) the report of actions of a character; (2) appearance, gestures, posture, or costume; (3) comments by another character; (4) direct speech by the character; (5) inward speech, whether summarized or quoted (i. e., as interior monologue); and finally (6) statements by the narrator about the character's attitudes and intentions.[20] One can see that this schema places the least emphasis on what the character does, since the understanding of actions remains open to a variety of interpretations, or what he or she looks like, and the greatest emphasis on various forms of speech, thought, or self-disclosure. As we move from the least explicit methods of characterization to the most explicit, from actions and appearance to speech and thought, we move from the way others see the character to the way the characters see or understand themselves, others, and the world.

The problems with using this scale to speak of the characterization of Lazarus are immediately apparent: the last three items on Alter's scale of categorization – direct speech; inward speech or interior monologue; and descriptions of the character's intentions and motives offered by the narrator – are missing from the Gospel's characterization of Lazarus. Still, Alter's scale serves as a useful heuristic device, for it quickly shows that the Gospel of John is not interested in what Lazarus thought or felt, as so many later poets and play-

---

[19] Robert Alter, *The Art of Biblical Narrative* (New York: Basic Books, 1981), 115. He is referring to the OT.

[20] Alter, *The Art of Biblical Narrative*, 116–17. Bennema uses the following categories to describe the character of Lazarus: Identity (titles, gender, age, marital status, occupation, socio-economic status, place of residence, relatives, and group affiliation); Speech and actions; Character classification (complexity, development, and inner life); Degree of characterization; and Response to Jesus (Bennema, *Encountering Jesus*, 163). It is noteworthy that a number of these items (age, marital status, occupation), as well as any hints of "development" or "inner life" are missing from Lazarus' portrayal in the Gospel of John.

wrights were, but in the fact that he is a dying man in need of a life-giving intervention. Other characters characterize Lazarus – and rightly! – as a man in desperate straits, as ill and dying, but Jesus raises Lazarus to life. As Alter pointed out, biblical characters encompass the nadir and zenith of human existence, and Lazarus might be said to represent the most extreme ends of the spectrum – he dies, but he lives again. In any case, it is not Lazarus', but Jesus' interpretation of this event that is significant in the Gospel. As is often the case in John, Jesus must reveal himself so that he may be rightly understood. Where others see only the power of death, Jesus has and gives the power of life, and he will demonstrate it in his own time, further declaring that he himself is that very life and resurrection. We shall use Alter's scale, or at least the first aspects of it, to describe the characterization of Lazarus, taking into account Alter's comments on the way in which biblical characterization reflects an understanding about God and human beings. First, however, we look briefly at the contexts in the Gospel in which Lazarus appears and the way in which he is introduced to the reader.

Lazarus appears in the Gospel primarily in two main narratives, namely, in the account of his illness, death, and restoration to life (11:1–44); and in the brief narrative of Mary's "anointing" of Jesus' feet, where Lazarus is found at table with Jesus (12:1–8). Additionally, the raising of Lazarus triggers the gathering of the chief priests and Pharisees to discuss what should be done with Jesus (11:45–53), leading to their resolve to put Jesus to death. We learn later that not only was Jesus attracting attention because of his signs, but a "great crowd of 'Jews'" wanted to see Lazarus, whom Jesus had raised from the dead (12:9). Because Lazarus' raising had become the occasion for many to believe in Jesus, the chief priests planned to put Lazarus to death as well (12:10). Finally, Lazarus is mentioned in passing when John refers to the witness borne by the crowd who had accompanied Jesus "when he called Lazarus out of the tomb" (12:17).

The first time Lazarus appears in the narrative, he is identified (1) by name and hometown (Bethany); and (2) as the brother of Mary and Martha. Lazarus is the Greek form of Eleazar, which means "God has helped." But there is little if any indication that John has in view the etymological significance of this name. Furthermore, as the studies of Tal Ilan have shown, Eleazar was the third most common male name among Palestinian Jews from 330 B.C.E. to 200 C. E.[21] In other words, the name is not distinctive, but common. That Lazarus is from Bethany suggests that he belongs among the "Jerusalem circle" of Jesus' disciples or admirers, as do also Lazarus' sisters, Nicodemus, Joseph of Arimathea, and the unnamed Beloved Disciple (if he is not Lazarus).

---

[21] See the statistics in *Lexicon of Jewish Names in Late Antiquity. Part I: Palestine 330 BCE–200 CE* (TSAJ 91; Tübingen: Mohr Siebeck, 2002).

Lazarus may have been a person of some wealth, as suggested by his sister's ability to procure a quantity of expensive perfume, the presence of many mourners "from Jerusalem," and his burial in a tomb, rather than in a simple ditch. These aspects of Lazarus' identity play no particular role in the narrative, but they are part of the indirect characterization of him. While he may have been a wealthy man, it is not his wealth but his ordinariness that serves to describe him: we learn he has a name, family, friends, lives in Bethany, and has taken ill. Nothing here particularly distinguishes him from a host of others. In order to explore the distinctive contours of the characterization of Lazarus, we turn to a closer analysis using the relevant aspects of Alter's scale.

(1) *The actions of a character.* In John 11–12, Lazarus becomes ill, dies, is buried, raised to life by Jesus, and subsequently enjoys table fellowship with Jesus. However, all this is assumed in the narrative or inferred by the reader, because there is no actual account of Lazarus' illness or dying. Neither his ailment nor the course of his illness, the moment of or circumstances surrounding his death, nor his actual burial is described. The reader can infer that these things have happened, but they are not presented as parts of the narrative.

But Lazarus' "return to life" is depicted. Standing in front of Lazarus' tomb, from which the stone has been removed, Jesus calls out with a "loud voice, 'Lazarus, come out!'" And, we read, "the dead man came out" (11:44). In all of the long narrative that comprises chapter 11, with its descriptions of what has happened to Lazarus – he has taken ill, died, and is buried – here is the one time when Lazarus is depicted as acting. In response to Jesus' command, Lazarus "came out" of the tomb (see also 12:17).[22] The raising of Lazarus demonstrates in narrative form earlier theological claims in the Gospel, namely, that the Son of God has the power to give life (5:25, 28). Note, however, that Lazarus is persistently described as "the dead man" (ὁ τεθνηκώς;

---

[22] Steven Hunt notes, "In ch. 11, Lazarus says nothing, and he does nothing, save walk out of a tomb" (Hunt, "Nicodemus, Lazarus, and the Fear of 'the Jews,'" 206). Bennema describes Lazarus' response as "obedience" (cf. Bennema, *Encountering Jesus*, 162–63). But while Lazarus does respond to Jesus' call to come out of the tomb, whether one should describe such a response as "obedience" might be contested, since it is problematic to picture dead persons as "obeying." In John 5:25, those who "hear" the voice of the Son of God "live." The Son calls them from death to life. Ruben Zimmerman maintains the tension between receptivity and response when he writes, "Lazarus 'simply' receives life through Jesus without any words or actions on his side and thus he becomes the prototype of the person of faith who, in the Johannine sense, correctly believes in the resurrection and thus in Jesus as the giver of life" (Ruben Zimmermann, "The Narrative Hermeneutics of Joh 11: Learning with Lazarus How to Understand Death, Life, and Resurrection," in *The Resurrection of Jesus in the Gospel of John* [ed. Craig R. Koester and Reimund Bieringer; WUNT 222; Tübingen: Mohr Siebeck, 2008], 75–101, here 96–97; more recently Ruben Zimmermann, "Vorbild im Sterben und Leben [Die Auferweckung des Lazarus] Joh 11,1–12,11," in *Kompendium der frühchristlichen Wundererzählungen, vol. 1: Die Wunder Jesu* [ed. Ruben Zimmermann et al., Gütersloh: Gütersloher Verlagshaus, 2013], 742–63). Esler and Piper suggest that Lazarus' "passivity" is not an obstacle to, but a feature of, his prototypicality (Esler and Piper, *Lazarus*, 75–112).

11:44) or "the one who had died" (τοῦ τετελευτηκότος; 11:39). In the first instance, Martha and Jesus are standing in front of the tomb; in the second instance, Lazarus is emerging from a tomb. He is, therefore, aptly characterized as "dead" – even though in the second instance he is actually alive! Still, he had been dead – for four days, as his sister points out – and thus needed the one who is resurrection and life to call him from the tomb. The persistent descriptions of Lazarus "as the one who had died" or "the dead man" show that Lazarus represents human beings both threatened by death and promised life by the one who is life.

Later, Lazarus is described as reclining (at table) with Jesus (12:2). In the course of the meal, no further attention is paid to Lazarus' presence at table. Rather, the focus shifts to the act of Mary, his sister, who anoints Jesus' feet with costly perfume. While Mary does that which is extraordinary, Lazarus participates in ordinary human behavior. But the description of Lazarus as *reclining at table with Jesus* paints in him stark contrast to the earlier descriptions of him as ill, dead, entombed, and wrapped in death's shroud. He has returned to life, and to the ordinary business of daily living. The raising of Lazarus also casts into narrative form the statement that Jesus' sheep know his voice, that as the good shepherd he calls them by name, and he leads them "in and out" to find abundant pasture, to find life in all its fullness (10:3, 10). Jesus calls Lazarus by name even as he is dead in the tomb and "leads him out" to life, where he shares a meal with Jesus.

(2) *Appearance, gestures, posture, or costume.*[23] Little is said about Lazarus' appearance, gestures, posture, or costume, although the indelible image that remains with the reader is of one who is ill, dead, and decaying in a tomb, from which he emerges bound in grave clothes. Lazarus is first and repeatedly described as ill (11:1, 2, 3, 6) and "asleep" (11:11, 12); and as having been in the tomb four days (11:17), having been laid there by his family (11:34). Each of these descriptions depicts Lazarus in a recumbent posture. The first time that Lazarus is seen doing anything, he walks out from the tomb – but still swathed in the trappings of death. This depiction of him with "hands and feet bound with strips of cloth, and his face wrapped in a cloth" has no doubt left a greater impression on readers and interpreters of the Gospel than the subsequent description of him eating with Jesus, but the contrast is important. First seen as ill, dead, entombed and bound, Lazarus is subsequently portrayed as walking, unbound, and eating. The reader "sees" Lazarus move from death to life. While on the one hand he is characterized by his mortality, on the other hand he is portrayed as one who has life from Jesus.

---

[23] On Bennema's scale, the elements of a character's "identity" (including gender, age, marital status, occupation, socio-economic status, place of residence and group affiliation) might fit here as well.

(3) *Comments by another character.* The reader encounters Lazarus primarily through what others say about him or what they do for or to him, whether those others are the disciples, Lazarus' sisters, the Jews, the chief priests, or Jesus. Lazarus is characterized first and foremost as the one who is loved by Jesus. In Mary and Martha's initial message to Jesus, informing Jesus of Lazarus' illness, they identify him not as their brother but as "the one whom you love" (ὃν φιλεῖς; 11:3). The assertion will be echoed by the comment of the Jews who see Jesus weeping at Lazarus' tomb, "See how he loved him!" (Ἴδε πῶς ἐφίλει αὐτόν; 11:36). In the same vein, Jesus also characterizes Lazarus as "friend" (φίλος; 11:11). Later in the Gospel, Jesus characterizes his friends (φίλοι) as those who do what he commands (15:14). While those who obey someone's commands might more aptly be thought of as "servants," Jesus paradoxically identifies them as his friends (φίλοι; 15:14). Since the command has to do with loving others (15:12), demonstrated above all in "laying down one's life for one's friends" (φίλοι; 15:13), Lazarus' designation as Jesus' friend may be a way of signaling that he, too, was a disciple of Jesus.

But it is clear from the narrative in John 11 that Jesus risks his life by returning to Judea to attend to the ailing Lazarus, and that the raising of Lazarus induces the authorities to move against Jesus. Jesus' description of Lazarus as "friend," when coupled with Jesus' later words about laying down one's life for one's "friends," indicates the depths and extent of Jesus' love for Lazarus, but also for all his disciples (see 13:1, "having loved his own who were in the world, he loved them to the utmost"). Lazarus might, then, be described as a representative character, but he represents how Jesus deals with or relates to his friends, to those whom he loves, since Lazarus' restoration to life demonstrates the shape of Jesus' love for his own.[24]

In the discussion of comments of another character, I will include also actions directed towards him, especially since these are often coupled with words about him. For example, Lazarus' sisters send news to Jesus regarding their brother and, presumably, have been responsible to see that he was buried. He is mourned not only by them, but by "'Jews' from Jerusalem" – and even by Jesus himself (11:31–33). More particularly, Jesus is described as "greatly disturbed in spirit" and "deeply moved" when Mary weeps at his feet (11:33). Subsequently, when standing in front of the tomb of the one whom he loved, Jesus himself weeps (11:35). Jesus then addresses the dead man in the tomb (11:43) and orders that he be unbound. Jesus' raising of this dead man leads

---

[24] Andrew T. Lincoln, "The Lazarus Story: A Literary Perspective," in *The Gospel of John and Christian Theology* (ed. Richard Bauckham and Carl Mosser; Grand Rapids, Mich.: Eerdmans, 2008), 211–32, here 215, calls Lazarus a "purely representative figure." Esler and Piper, *Lazarus*, 11, widen Lazarus' prototypical role as one "not of the world" (17:14–16), who lives anew (1:13; 3:3), as a "son of light" (12:36), having passed from death to life (5:24, 28–29). They write, "Lazarus' story typifies the anticipated experience of the follower of Jesus."

others to wish to see him, some to believe in Jesus (12:11), and the authorities to plot to take his life (12:10).

We learn as much about those who respond or react to him as we do about him: Jesus, Mary and Martha, and "the Jews" mourn his loss; the authorities mourn his return to life. Many believe in Jesus because of what he did to Lazarus; but, again, the authorities seek to undo the life-giving work of Jesus by returning Lazarus to death. These responses divide, even if not perfectly neatly, into two camps: those who respond favorably to Jesus and his life-giving work, and those who reject or refuse what Jesus has done. Lazarus belongs among those who respond favorably to Jesus, but it remains curious, especially in light of the Gospel's recurring emphasis on faith, that Lazarus is never explicitly said to believe in Jesus.[25]

The absence of such a characterization is perhaps not surprising, given that Lazarus is presented as ill, dead, and entombed. In John, many who are recipients of Jesus' generous acts are not explicitly said to have faith. For example, those who have the wine supplied for them at the wedding in Cana do not even know its origin, and are never said to believe; it is the disciples who see Jesus' glory. The man at the pool in John 5 demonstrates no faith at all. And it is not clear that the 5000 who were fed are depicted as having faith in Jesus.

But while the mere fact that Jesus calls Lazarus "friend," and the fact that Lazarus later appears at table with Jesus and that his life is sought by the authorities, imply that he is indeed a disciple of Jesus, he is not presented in the Gospel as a model of faith. Rather, he represents those who, in the ordinary course of life meets life's ordinary end, but, because he is loved by Jesus and is a friend of Jesus, also experiences the extraordinary gift of life. He is characterized by his mortality; his sisters, Jesus' disciples, and the Jews picture him primarily as dying and dead, and after he is raised to life the curious onlookers want to see him because he was once dead, and the authorities want to take his life away again. But even if death threatens Lazarus, that threat can never have the last word in the presence of the one who is life, since "the light shines in the darkness, and the darkness has never overcome it" (1:5). Although the Gospel elsewhere warns of the possibility of death facing Jesus' disciples (16:2), and foretells the coming death of Peter (21:19), it does not recount the final fate of Lazarus. One can assume that he belongs among those whom Jesus will take to be with him (14:3).

---

[25] Unless, of course, Lazarus is the Beloved Disciple, who "believed" upon seeing the linen wrappings in the empty tomb (20:8).

Death, Life, and the Character of Lazarus

The conflict between life and death permeates the account of the raising of Lazarus, as well as the entire Gospel of John. The deaths of both Lazarus and Jesus are in view almost from the beginning of the narrative in chapter 11. Jesus learns that Lazarus is ill (11:1–3), and subsequently, announces that Lazarus has died (11:10–14). He determines to go to Bethany, even though his life will be in danger. The disciples also anticipate that their own lives may be threatened by Jesus' decision to go to Bethany, but are determined to follow him to die with him there (11:7, 16). Knowing that his journey will lead to his own death, Jesus nevertheless travels to Bethany to bring life to Lazarus (11:4). Indeed, it is the raising of Lazarus, the climactic sign in the Gospel, that triggers the discussion in the Sanhedrin that leads to the decision that Jesus must be put to death to spare the people (ἔθνος) and the holy place (11:49–52). Not only does Jesus travel to Bethany, and raise Lazarus, at the cost of his own life, but Lazarus still remains subject to the threat of death, because those who seek Jesus' death also seek the death of Lazarus (12:9–11). In short, what brings life to Lazarus brings death to Jesus – but what brings death to Jesus brings life to the world. There is no life apart from death (10:18; 12:24).

The conflict between life and death also shapes the characterization of Lazarus who, in his mortality, represents all human beings faced with the threat of death; but as one loved by Jesus, Lazarus represents all who are given life by the One in whom there is life (1:4). The Gospel presents Lazarus as one whose identity is configured by the powerful realities of friendship, love, death, life. While his illness and death continue to mark him throughout the narrative, in the final analysis he is known not as the one who died and was placed in a tomb, but as the one who was called forth from the tomb to life by Jesus. Both aspects of his own personal story, however, must be held together describing his characterization in the Gospel of John. Ultimately, Lazarus, "the dead man," is characterized as the one who is given life by Jesus.

Mary (of Bethany):
The Anointer of the Suffering Messiah

Susan Miller

Introduction

Mary of Bethany is known for her act of anointing Jesus' feet with expensive perfume and then drying them with her hair but she first appears in chapter 11 when she and her sister send a message to Jesus about their brother's illness. Jesus, however, delays his journey to Bethany for two days, and Lazarus has died by the time Jesus arrives. Whereas Martha goes out to meet Jesus, and confesses her faith in him as the Messiah and Son of God, Mary remains at home with the mourners who have come from Jerusalem to comfort the sisters. When Mary also goes out to meet Jesus, she falls at his feet weeping, overcome by sorrow. Her grief prompts Jesus to weep, and he raises Lazarus from death. Some of those present report this sign to the Pharisees, and the council decides to arrest Jesus and put him to death. The anointing scene which follows depicts Mary's gift as a sign of her gratitude to Jesus for the life of her brother. Mary interrupts the dinner given at Bethany for Jesus to anoint him with expensive perfume and the fragrance spreads through the house. Judas criticises her action because the perfume could have been sold in order to help the poor but Jesus defends Mary saying that she has kept the perfume for the day of his burial.

The anointing of Jesus occurs in all Four Gospels with variations in the account of the woman who anoints Jesus and in the description of the setting. In Mark and Matthew a woman anoints the head of Jesus in the house of Simon the leper at Bethany (Mark 14:3–9; Matt 26:6–13). In Luke's Gospel a woman weeps at Jesus' feet and dries them with her hair before anointing them in the house of Simon the Pharisee (7:36–50). In our passage Mary anoints Jesus, and her sister Martha serves a meal while Lazarus reclines at the dinner with Jesus. The narrator describes Mary as a friend of Jesus, and John emphasises the love Jesus has for the family group of Mary, Martha, and Lazarus (11:3). John thus associates the anointing of Jesus with a woman who is one of his followers.

The character of Mary of Bethany has been interpreted as a model of discipleship. Elisabeth Schüssler Fiorenza compares Mary favourably to the character of Judas describing Mary as the "true disciple" and Judas as the "unfaithful disciple."[1] Raymond Collins proposes that John has selected individuals from his community's homiletic tradition to illustrate the ways in which faith in Jesus brings life.[2] R. A. Culpepper notes, moreover, that the minor characters often act as representatives of a range of positive and negative responses to Jesus, and he suggests that the character of Mary of Bethany represents "unlimited love and devotion."[3] Colleen Conway argues that the minor characters including Mary of Bethany should not be defined by a single character trait because their responses to Jesus are often ambiguous.[4] As Cornelis Bennema observes, some of the responses of the characters are depicted as "representative or typical" but this presentation does not mean that the characters themselves are to be interpreted as "types" since several characters such as Nicodemus, the Samaritan woman, Peter, and Judas are complex.[5] The work of these scholars raises the question of the extent to which Mary of Bethany is portrayed as an example of faith. We will also consider the ways in which the narrator presents Mary as a rounded character and assess the development of her character in the course of the Gospel.

Mary of Bethany is introduced as the one who anointed Jesus' feet and dried them with her hair at the beginning of the account of the raising of Lazarus before the anointing of Jesus has taken place. The narrator's reference to Mary's act of anointing Jesus suggests that the readers already know that she is the woman who anoints Jesus. Ernst Haenchen notes that characters are frequently defined by their actions.[6] Nicodemus is identified as the one who visited Jesus at night (7:50; 19:34) and Judas is described as the disciple who betrays Jesus (6:71). This literary technique suggests that the character of Mary of Bethany is defined by her act of anointing Jesus. The reference to the anointing of Jesus at the beginning of chapter 11 and the detailed description of the anointing in chapter 12 create a frame around the account of Jesus' act of raising Lazarus from death. The narrator presents a series of scenes depicting the meeting of Martha and Jesus, the meeting of Mary and Jesus, the raising of Lazarus and the report of some of the witnesses to the Pharisees, the decision of the Pharisees to put Jesus to death, and the anointing of Jesus by

---

[1] Elisabeth Schüssler Fiorenza, *In Memory of Her: A Feminist Theological Reconstruction of Christian Origins* (2d ed.; London: SCM, 1995), 330–31.
[2] Raymond F. Collins, "The Representative Figures of the Fourth Gospel – Part 1," *DRev* 94 (1976): 26–46, here 31.
[3] R. Alan Culpepper, *Anatomy of the Fourth Gospel: A Study in Literary Design* (Philadelphia: Fortress, 1983), 142.
[4] Colleen M. Conway, "Speaking through Ambiguity: Minor Characters in the Fourth Gospel," *BibInt* 10 (2002): 324–41.
[5] Cornelis Bennema, *Encountering Jesus: Character Studies in the Gospel of John* (Milton Keynes: Paternoster, 2009), 13–24.
[6] Ernst Haenchen, *John 2* (Philadelphia: Fortress, 1984), 57.

Mary. The presence of Lazarus at the dinner at Bethany acts as a confirmation of Jesus' power to raise the dead. The narrator brings the series of scenes to a conclusion with the description of the anointing of Jesus by Mary of Bethany.

In this article we will assess the character of Mary of Bethany in the context of the section of 11:1–12:8 as a literary unity. The narrator does not describe the inner thoughts and motives of Mary, and her character is revealed primarily through her actions. Our passage contains detailed portraits of several other characters including Martha, Judas, and Jesus. The mourners from Jerusalem also play a central role since they accompany Mary and witness the raising of Lazarus. We will examine the ways in which the interactions between Mary and the characters of Martha, Judas, Jesus, and the mourners provide insights into her character, and we will assess the significance of her act of anointing Jesus. In the final section we will examine the theological implications of our study of the character of Mary of Bethany.

The Meeting of Jesus with Martha and Mary

Chapter 11 begins with an account of the illness of Lazarus of Bethany, and the narrator identifies Bethany as the village of Mary and her sister Martha. The introduction is unusual since male characters are seldom identified through their relationships to women but Mary and Martha are presented as the leading characters in this account. The narrator's initial description suggests that Mary is the more prominent of the two sisters because she is the one who anointed Jesus' feet and dried them with her hair (11:1–2). There is no indication that the sisters and brother are married, and they appear to form an independent household. This situation is very unusual because most women married at a young age, and their marriages were often arranged by their parents.[7] The narrator does not include any information about the way in which Martha, Mary, and Lazarus met Jesus. The narrative gap may encourage the readers to believe that they became friends during one of Jesus' visits to Jerusalem. By the time of the illness of Lazarus, the women know Jesus well and they will have knowledge of the signs he has performed.

At the beginning of the narrative the sisters act together sending a word to Jesus about their brother's illness. The narrator summarises the message in the words of the sisters, "Lord, the one whom you love is ill" (11:3). The sisters do not make a direct request to Jesus but their message implies that they expect him to heal Lazarus. Their message recalls the portrayal of the mother of Jesus since she brings the lack of wine to Jesus' attention at the wedding at Cana by

---

[7] Tal Ilan, *Jewish Women in Greco-Roman Palestine* (Peabody, Mass.: Hendrickson, 1996), 62–69.

simply stating, "They have no wine" (2:3). The speech of the mother of Jesus implies that she would like Jesus to intervene to assist the wedding party, and despite his initial reluctance he transforms water into abundant wine. The women's statements heighten the authority of Jesus since they are unwilling to speak to him directly. In our passage the sisters' message also expresses a claim on Jesus based on their description of their brother as "the one whom Jesus loves" (11:3). The narrator suggests that Mary, Martha, and Lazarus have known Jesus for some time and have developed a close friendship with him.

The opening scene emphasises the unity of the characters of Mary and Martha but the sisters respond in different ways to the news that Jesus has arrived. Lazarus has been dead for four days, and the sisters are at home with some mourners who have come from Jerusalem to comfort them. Martha is the first sister to go out to meet Jesus while Mary sits in the house. Martha is portrayed as the more independent and active sister but it is possible that Mary has not been told that Jesus has arrived.[8] As D. M. Smith notes, one of the sisters would be expected to remain with the mourners, and he also points out that John focuses on the meeting of Jesus with individual characters.[9] Throughout the Gospel the narrator depicts a series of meetings of Jesus with a range of characters including Nicodemus (3:1–21), the Samaritan woman (4:1–42), Mary Magdalene (20:11–18), and Thomas (20:26–29). In these meetings Nicodemus struggles to understand Jesus, and the Samaritan woman wonders if Jesus could be the Messiah. Mary Magdalene is the first person to recognise the risen Jesus, and Thomas confesses his faith in Jesus. The narrator's presentation of the meetings of Jesus with Martha and Mary enables the readers to compare and contrast the sisters' responses to Jesus.

Martha addresses Jesus, "Lord, if you had been here, my brother would not have died" (11:21). She does not reproach Jesus since there is no indication that she is aware that Jesus has delayed his journey to Bethany. Her speech demonstrates her faith in Jesus despite the death of her brother.[10] Martha adds, "And even now I know that whatever you ask God, God will give you" (11:22). Then Jesus tells Martha that her brother will rise again, and she responds that Lazarus will rise again on the last day. Martha does not understand that Jesus is able to raise her brother before the last day. Jesus' reply, however, identifies himself as the resurrection and the life, and he states that whoever believes in him will live, though he or she dies, and whoever lives and believes in him will never die (11:26). Jesus asks Martha if she believes this, and she replies, "Yes, Lord, I believe that you are the Messiah, the Son of God, the one coming into the world" (11:27). Francis J. Moloney argues that Martha's confession of faith

---

[8] J. Ramsey Michaels, *The Gospel of John* (NICNT; Grand Rapids, Mich.: Eerdmans, 2010), 630.
[9] Dwight Moody Smith, *John* (Nashville: Abingdon, 1999), 221.
[10] George R. Beasley-Murray, *John* (WBC 36; Nashville: Thomas Nelson, 1999), 190.

is incomplete, and he proposes that the use of the perfect tense πεπίστευκα ("I believe") in this verse indicates that Mary has already believed in Jesus before the revelation of his identity.[11] The perfect tense, however, is also employed in Peter's confession of faith in Jesus as the Holy One of God (6:69). As Barnabas Lindars observes, Martha responds to Jesus' question, and her reply demonstrates that she believes Jesus' teaching about the resurrection.[12] Martha's confession of faith, moreover, expresses the purpose of the Gospel which is to lead John's readers to the belief that "Jesus is the Messiah and Son of God" (20:30–31).

After her confession of faith Martha returns to the house, and she tells Mary that Jesus is calling her (11:28). Jesus remains outside the village where he met Martha, and in this way Martha and Mary meet Jesus in the same place. Mary, moreover, addresses Jesus in the same words that were spoken by her sister, "Lord, if you had been here, my brother would not have died" (11:32). The meeting of the women with Jesus in the same location and the repetition of their speech suggest that the narrator encourages the readers to compare the responses of the two women to Jesus. Mary's speech reminds the readers of Martha's conversation and her confession of faith.[13] The narrator depicts a conversation between Martha and Jesus but Mary falls at Jesus' feet weeping, and she is silent after her initial address. The narrator portrays Martha as the more rational sister whereas Mary is overcome by her sorrow at her brother's death. As Peter Dschulnigg points out, Mary's act of falling at Jesus' feet may be interpreted as an indication of her grief and also as a sign of her devotion to Jesus.[14] In this way Martha and Mary both place their trust in Jesus even though he has not arrived in time to heal their brother.

The structure of the narrative, moreover, suggests that the account of the meetings of each sister with Jesus may be read together since there is a progression in the women's responses to Jesus. Martha comes to believe in Jesus as the "Messiah, the Son of God, the one coming into the world," and Jesus reveals his identity as the resurrection and the life. The juxtaposition of Martha's confession of faith with Mary's grief creates an expectation that Jesus will intervene to raise Lazarus to life. The account of Martha's confession of faith enables the readers to interpret Mary's grief in relation to the wider purposes of God who has power to bring life out of death.

Martha's confession of faith has led Jesus to reveal his identity to her as the resurrection and the life. Mary's emotional response prompts Jesus to express

---

[11] Francis J. Moloney, "Can Everyone Be Wrong? A Reading of John 11.1–12.8," *NTS* 49 (2003): 505–27, here 513–15.
[12] Barnabas Lindars, *The Gospel of John* (London: Marshall, Morgan & Scott, 1972), 396.
[13] Lindars, *John*, 397.
[14] Peter Dschulnigg, *Jesus begegnen: Personen und ihre Bedeutung im Johannesevangelium* (Münster: LIT, 2002), 201–203.

his own grief. When Jesus sees Mary weeping and the weeping of the mourners, he becomes "deeply indignant in spirit and troubled" (ἐνεβριμήσατο τῷ πνεύματι καὶ ἐτάραξεν ἑαυτόν, 11:33). The verb ἐμβριμάομαι is a strong verb associated with anger (cf. Dan 11:30 LXX; Matt 9:30; Mark 1:43). Rudolf Schnackenburg argues that Jesus is angry at the mourners because their weeping is an indication of their lack of faith.[15] Jesus' weeping, however, indicates that he does not condemn the weeping of Mary and the mourners. As Raymond Brown proposes, Jesus is angry at the power of death that is associated with the realm of Satan.[16] The second verb, ταράσσω ("trouble, disturb"), also points to Jesus' intense emotions, and Andrew Lincoln suggests that Jesus is distressed at the prospect of his own imminent death (12:27; 13:21).[17] In chapter 12 Jesus speaks of his sorrow as he prepares to face the hour of his passion, "My soul is troubled" (ἡ ψυχή μου τετάρακται, 12:27). He does not ask God to save him from this hour but he looks forward to the hour when he will cast out the ruler of the world (12:27–30). In the Farewell Discourse, moreover, Jesus is "troubled in spirit" (ἐταράχθη τῷ πνεύματι, 13:21), and he tells his disciples not to be distressed at his death (μὴ ταρασσέσθω ὑμῶν ἡ καρδία, 14:1, 27). The use of this verb links Jesus' emotions at the death of Lazarus with his forthcoming passion and his conflict with the power of evil.

The portrayal of Jesus' grief is unexpected since he has supernatural knowledge of the events which take place (2:23–25; 4:21–24; 13:1–4), and he rarely expresses his emotions. John does not given an account of the sorrow of Jesus as he struggles to follow the will of God in Gethsemane (cf. Mark 14:32–42). In Luke's Gospel he weeps over the city of Jerusalem (19:41) and his tears are described in Hebrews (5:7). In our narrative Mary's grief prompts the expression of Jesus' own sorrow at human suffering. When Jesus sees the tomb of Lazarus, he bursts into tears (ἐδάκρυσεν, 11:35). The description of Jesus' grief highlights the portrayal of Jesus as the word made flesh (1:14).[18] The mourners interpret Jesus' tears as a sign of his love for Lazarus (11:36). As D. M. Smith notes, their interpretation is correct since Jesus does love Lazarus, and the raising of Lazarus is a demonstration of God's love for humanity (3:16).[19] Mary's grief and the grief of the mourners lead Jesus to reveal his own love of human beings.

Many people come from Jerusalem to comfort Mary and Martha at their brother's death. The mourners are more closely aligned with Mary since they follow her when she goes out to meet Jesus because they think that she is going

---

[15] Rudolf Schnackenburg, *The Gospel according to St John* (3 vols.; London: Burns & Oates, 1980), 2:336.

[16] Raymond E. Brown, *The Gospel according to John* (2 vols.; AB 29A; New York: Doubleday, 1966), 1:435.

[17] Andrew T. Lincoln, *The Gospel according to Saint John* (BNTC 4; London: Continuum, 2005), 326–27.

[18] Lincoln, *John*, 327.

[19] Smith, *John*, 225.

to the tomb to weep there (11:31). Mary has a discipleship role since she inadvertently leads the mourners to Jesus. In the opening chapter Andrew leads his brother, Simon Peter, to Jesus (1:40–42) and Philip brings Nathanael to Jesus (1:45–51). The mourners are present at the conversation of Mary and Jesus, and they are also witnesses to the raising of Lazarus. J. Ramsey Michaels proposes that the presence of the mourners with Mary is "intrusive" and disrupts the scene.[20] The mourners, however, appear to have a similar role to that of the chorus in Greek tragedies since they represent the comments of the wider community on the private experiences of the family at Bethany. Adele Reinhartz highlights the positive portrayal of the people from Jerusalem who travel to Bethany to comfort Martha and Mary.[21] As Reinhartz points out, these people show no indication that they reject Martha and Mary on account of their belief in Jesus. The raising of Lazarus, however, changes this situation since it leads to a division in the crowd. Many mourners believe in Jesus but some mourners go to the Pharisees to let them know what Jesus has done.

The narrator does not include any account of the motivation of the people who inform the Pharisees about Jesus but they may know of the conflict between Jesus and the authorities. At the beginning of the narrative the disciples warned Jesus about the dangers of returning to Judea (11:8). In chapter 9 the Pharisees questioned the former blind man about his healing by Jesus and also questioned the man's parents. The parents did not wish to speak to the Pharisees about their son because they were afraid of being excluded from the synagogue (9:22). The mourners are aware that Jesus has healed the blind man (11:37) and may thus also know about the synagogue ban. In our passage the Pharisees are portrayed as the authorities within the community. The mourners may wish to defend Jesus or to inform the Pharisees that Jesus has returned to Judea. Mary has led some mourners to faith in Jesus but others have aligned themselves with his opponents. The chief priests and the Pharisees call a meeting of the council and the decision is made to arrest Jesus and put him to death. The narrator thus associates the death and raising of Lazarus with Jesus' own death and resurrection.

The narrator invites a comparison of the characters of Martha and Mary in the presentation of the meeting of each woman with Jesus. Martha and Mary address Jesus in the same way expressing their sorrow that he had not arrived in time to save their brother from death. The narrator then depicts the sisters' differing responses to Jesus. Martha is the more rational sister who confesses her faith in Jesus as the Messiah and Son of God whereas Mary is overcome by her emotions. As Ingrid Kitzberger points out, the narrator encourages the

---

[20] Michaels, *John*, 640.
[21] Adele Reinhartz, "From Narrative to History: The Resurrection of Mary and Martha," in *"Women Like This:" New Perspectives on Jewish Women in the Greco-Roman World* (ed. Amy-Jill Levine; Atlanta: Scholars Press, 1991), 161–84, here 178–79.

readers to assess the sisters in equal ways, and Jesus responds to each sister "in accordance with her personality."²² Our analysis, moreover, has noted that the sisters also prompt Jesus to reveal different dimensions of his character. Martha's confession of faith leads Jesus to reveal that he is "the resurrection and the life." The character of Mary leads Jesus to reveal his anger at the power of death and to share his grief with suffering humanity.

The Portrayal of Mary as a Prophetic Figure

Mary anoints Jesus' feet with perfume and then dries them with her hair, and the scent of the perfume spreads through the house. The narrator's portrait of Mary is disturbing since respectable women were not accustomed to loosen their hair in public (7:36–50; 1 Cor 11:2–16). Her act of anointing Jesus' feet is also shocking because she expresses her love of Jesus who is not one of her relatives at the public setting of a meal. Her gift demonstrates her devotion to Jesus and her gratitude at his restoration of her brother to life. Judas, however, objects to the cost of the gift, and he asks why the perfume could not have been sold for three hundred denarii and the money given to the poor (12:4). In Mark's Gospel some of those present criticize the woman, and in Matthew's Gospel the disciples are the ones who object to her gift. John's focus on Judas highlights the contrasting attitudes of Mary and Judas to Jesus. She is depicted as a faithful follower whereas he takes the role of the betrayer of Jesus.

Mary does not respond to the criticism of Judas, and she remains silent throughout the scene. Jesus defends Mary, and he provides a key to understanding the events that take place. His positive or negative response to the characters in the Gospel guides the responses of the readers. Jesus argues that Mary has kept the perfume for the day of his burial (τὴν ἡμέραν τοῦ ἐνταφιασμοῦ, 12:7). It was customary to anoint the dead before burial (2 Chr 6:14; Josephus, *Ant.* 17:199; *m. Sabb.* 23:5) but in our passage Jesus' explanation sounds odd because Mary does not anoint Jesus on the day of his burial. The term ἐνταφιασμός, however, may be translated as "preparation for burial" (cf. 19:40; Gen 50:2–3 LXX; Matt 20:12).²³ Jesus' reply suggests that Mary carries out a prophetic action to prepare his body for burial ahead of time. As Colleen Conway notes, Mary of Bethany is the first character to show significant insight into the imminence of Jesus' death.²⁴ Jesus refers to his imminent death

---

²² Ingrid Rosa Kitzberger, "Mary of Bethany and Mary of Magdala – Two Female Characters in the Johannine Passion Narrative: A Feminist, Narrative-Critical Reader-Response," NTS 41 (1995): 571–78.
²³ Lincoln, *Saint John*, 339.
²⁴ Colleen M. Conway, *Men and Women in the Fourth Gospel: Gender and Johannine Characterization* (Atlanta: Society of Biblical Literature, 1999), 151.

by saying that they will have the poor with them always but they will not always have him.

The interaction of Mary and Judas highlights the differences in social status between Mary and Judas. Judas is one of the twelve male disciples chosen by Jesus, and he is expected to have knowledge of Jesus' identity and purposes. He takes advantage of his role as a disciple to criticize Mary, and his mean attitude is contrasted with the generosity and self-giving of Mary.[25] Judas' concern for the poor masks his custom of helping himself to the common purse. Mary's expensive gift reveals her devotion to Jesus whereas Judas' protests conceal his plan to betray Jesus. Mary shows her love of Jesus while Judas, one of the Twelve, seeks to betray Jesus.

Jesus interprets Mary as a prophetic figure who anoints him as the Messiah before his death. In Mark and Matthew an anonymous woman anoints Jesus' head with perfume (Mark 14:3–9; Matt 26:6–13). In the Old Testament the anointing of the head is associated with the consecration of kings (1 Sam 9:15–10:1; 16:12–13; 1 Kgs 1:38–40). Prophets and priests carry out the act of anointing suggesting that Mary is presented in a role which is usually linked with men (1 Sam 10:1; 16:1; 1 Kgs 1:45). Raymond Brown notes that Mary of Bethany anoints Jesus' feet, and he proposes that she does not intend to anoint him as the royal Messiah.[26] On the other hand C. Kingsley Barrett argues that Mary anoints Jesus as the Messiah in preparation for his royal entry into Jerusalem.[27] After the anointing of Jesus he enters Jerusalem, and he is acclaimed as the King of Israel by the crowd (12:12–19).

The preceding events in the narrative imply that Mary knows that Jesus is the Messiah and Son of God. She has witnessed Jesus' ability to raise Lazarus from the dead, and she knows that the authorities are searching for him. The actions of Mary imply that she does intend to anoint Jesus as the Messiah. Mary loosens her hair, and women often wore their hair unbound during a period of mourning (Esth 4:17 LXX; *Jos. Asen.* 10:14). Charles Cosgrove notes that there are several references in Greco-Roman literature which associate the unbound hair of women with a time of mourning the dead (Plutarch, *Mor.* 267; Virgil, *Aen.* 3.65; Ovid, *Metam.* 583–99; Petronius, *Sat.* 111).[28] In our narrative Mary's appearance suggests that she is taking the role of one who mourns Jesus and who has knowledge of his imminent death.

---

[25] Margareta Gruber, "Die Zumutung der Gegenseitigkeit zur johanneischen Deutung des Todes Jesu anhand einer pragmatisch-intratextuellen Lektüre der Salbungsgeschichte Joh 12,1–8," in *The Death of Jesus in the Fourth Gospel* (ed. Gilbert Van Belle; Louvain: Leuven University Press, 2007), 647–60, here 649.

[26] Brown, *John*, 1:454.

[27] C. Kingsley Barrett, *The Gospel according to St John* (2d ed.; London: SCM, 1978), 409.

[28] Charles H. Cosgrove, "A Woman's Unbound Hair in the Greco-Roman World, with Special Reference to the Story of the 'Sinful Woman' in Luke 7:36–50," *JBL* 124 (2005): 675–92, here 682–83.

In the Old Testament the anointing of kings is linked with the bestowal of the power to rule. Mary's gift of expensive perfume prepares Jesus for his death in which he will give his life to bring life to others. She anoints Jesus' feet in order to prepare him for his mission of service.[29] Mary takes the role of a prophet since she anoints Jesus during a public meal when Martha, Lazarus, and the disciples are present whereas she could have anointed him on a less formal and public occasion. She wishes to carry out a prophetic action ahead of time to demonstrate her faith in him as the suffering Messiah. Mary's extravagant use of expensive perfume suggests that she intends to carry out a symbolic action pointing to the cost of Jesus' mission which will result in his death.

In chapter 11 Martha is presented as the more independent and active of the two sisters since she is the one who goes out to meet Jesus while Mary sits at home accompanied by the mourners. The narrator stresses the emotions of Mary since she falls at Jesus' feet weeping. Martha remains composed and in control of her actions whereas Mary is overcome by her grief. We see a development in Mary's character after Jesus has raised Lazarus from death. The narrator gives no indication that Martha or Lazarus is aware of Mary's plan to anoint Jesus, and Mary acts independently of her sister and brother at the dinner. Although she disrupts the dinner to anoint Jesus, she remains calm and in control of her actions. The narrator depicts a sharp contrast between the grief of Mary at the death of Lazarus and her composure when she anoints Jesus. The change in her character arises from her response to Jesus' restoration of her brother to life. The narrator describes Lazarus as he comes out of his tomb but there is no description of the emotions of the sisters. The gap in the narrative points to the miraculous power of Jesus to bring abundant life to human beings.

The sisters know that the threats against Jesus have increased on account of his act of raising their brother. Jesus is afraid to go about publicly, and he is taking a risk in visiting their house for a meal. In the opening scene Mary and Martha send a message to Jesus for his help but in the final scene Mary is the one who takes the initiative in doing something for Jesus. The narrator suggests that Mary has carefully planned her action of anointing Jesus by selecting the expensive perfume and waiting until the dinner has begun before she interrupts the meal to anoint Jesus' feet and dry them with her hair. She demonstrates her faith in Jesus as the Messiah before all the guests present at the meal. The development of her character reflects her understanding of Jesus' identity as the Messiah and her knowledge of his willingness to give his life for others.

---

[29] Beasley-Murray, *John*, 208–209.

The Theological Implications of the Anointing of Jesus by Mary of Bethany

Mary's act of anointing Jesus points to his identity as the Messiah and the Son of God. In the Fourth Gospel there is no Messianic Secret, and the first disciples recognize Jesus as the Messiah (1:41) and the Son of God (1:49). Jesus has supernatural knowledge of the thoughts of human beings, and has control over events. He tells his disciples that Lazarus' illness will not end in death since it is for the glory of God so that the Son of God may be revealed through it (11:4). This saying situates the raising of Lazarus within the wider purposes of God.[30] Martha, Mary, and Lazarus are friends of Jesus but he delays his journey to Bethany by two days. When Lazarus dies, moreover, he says that he is glad for the sake of the disciples that he was not there so that they may believe (11:14–15). Jesus' response is unexpected since he seems unconcerned about the grief and suffering of his friends. Ruben Zimmermann points out that the narrative develops through a technique of misunderstanding and correction which encourages the readers to seek the deeper meaning of Jesus' identity.[31] As he observes, the tension between sickness and death on the one hand with the glorification of God and Jesus on the other may only be resolved in relation to Jesus' own death and resurrection.

The raising of Lazarus is Jesus' final sign and it reveals his glory. The signs point forward to the glorification of Jesus at the time of his death (12:23, 27–28; 13:31–32; 17:1). Jesus' death is depicted as the time of the glorification of Jesus and God but our passage indicates that his glorification is deeply involved in human suffering. Mary's weeping and grief at her brother's death prompt Jesus to burst into tears. Jesus' sorrow contrasts with his calm demeanour in the opening verses of the narrative. The emotions of Mary reveal Jesus' own alignment with human suffering. The narrator's presentation of the divinity of Jesus is juxtaposed with his grief. In these passages the anguish of human beings in the face of death is not downplayed but the narrator emphasises that God's will prevails despite the present experience of suffering.

Mary's extravagant gift points to Jesus' identity as the Messiah and his glorification at the time of his death. Mary anoints Jesus' feet and dries them with her hair (ἐξέμαξεν, 12:3), and her action may be compared to Jesus' act of washing and drying the feet of his disciples (ἐκμάσσειν, 13:5). Jesus takes the role of a servant or slave in order to wash his disciples' feet in the middle of a meal. He teaches his disciples to follow his example and to wash one another's

---

[30] Lincoln, *Saint John*, 318–19.
[31] Ruben Zimmermann, "The Narrative Hermeneutics of John 11. Learning with Lazarus How to Understand Death, Life, and Resurrection," in *The Resurrection of Jesus in the Gospel of John* (ed. Craig R. Koester and Reimund Bieringer; WUNT 222; Tübingen: Mohr Siebeck, 2008), 75–101, here 82–84.

feet. Mary is portrayed as a disciple since she carries out a similar action. Jesus' act of washing his disciples' feet symbolizes the salvation that comes about through his death. He takes off his robe, washes his disciples' feet and then puts his robe on again. The verb τίθημι also occurs in Jesus' saying expressing his willingness to lay down his life (10:11, 15, 17, 18) and the verb λαμβάνω ("take") is also employed for the taking up of his life (10:17–18).[32] This description recalls the account of Jesus' willingness to lay down his life for others and to take his life up again.

Judas criticizes Mary's act of anointing, and he points out that the perfume could have been sold for three hundred denarii and the money given to the poor. Mary's extravagant gift raises the question of John's attitude towards poverty. The sum of three hundred denarii is equivalent to almost a year's wages of a labourer (cf. Matt 20:2). Judas objects to the cost of the perfume because he would like to have some of the money for himself. Nevertheless, Judas expects those present to agree with his criticism of Mary. In the Synoptic Gospels Jesus proclaims blessings on the poor (Matt 5:3; Luke 6:20) and he brings good news to the poor (Matt 11:5; Luke 4:18). In the Fourth Gospel Jesus' concern for the poor is illustrated by his healing of the man who has lain beside the pool of Bethesda for thirty-eight years (5:1–18) and his healing of the blind man who lived as a beggar (9:1–7).

The narrator highlights the theological significance of Mary's action by including the speech of Jesus. Jesus is presents as the authoritative voice who gives an assessment of Mary's action to the readers. Jesus defends Mary's expensive gift by contrasting the continual presence of the poor with his imminent death. In some rabbinic traditions the burial of the dead takes precedence over acts of charity (*t. Pe'ah* 4:19; *b. Sukkah* 49b).[33] In our passage Jesus takes precedence over the poor because he is facing death. Jesus, moreover, alludes to Deut 15:11 which refers to the continual presence of the poor in the land, and includes a commandment to care for the poor. His response to Judas, therefore, highlights the responsibility of the disciples to care for the poor in the period after his death.

The cost of the perfume, moreover, alludes to the cost of Jesus' life which is seen as an extravagant gesture of loss. The narrator emphasises the sacrificial nature of Jesus' death and suggests that his death brings abundant life. The anointing alludes to the deeper reality of the sacrificial nature of the love of God for the world. Jesus is sent into the world as an act of God's love. As Charles Giblin notes, the anointing of Jesus and the spread of the fragrance

---

[32] Brown, *John*, 2:551.
[33] David Daube, *The New Testament and Rabbinic Judaism* (London: Athlone Press, 1956), 315.

alludes to Jesus' death and his resurrection.[34] The expensive perfume points to the abundant life that Jesus brings to all human beings, both rich and poor.

The scent of perfume spreads through the house illustrating the extravagant nature of Mary's gift. This description is reminiscent of the imagery of fruitfulness in the signs of Jesus. At the wedding at Cana he transforms water into abundant wine (2:1–11) and he feeds the hungry crowd of five thousand people (6:1–14). Jesus offers living water to the Samaritan woman (4:14; cf. 7:37–38). Jesus is identified by the gifts he brings humanity. He is the bread of life (6:35) and the light of the world (8:12). He reveals his identity to Martha with an "I am" saying, "I am the resurrection and the life" (11:25). In our narrative Mary of Bethany recognises that Jesus' death brings abundant life. The spread of perfume through the house points to the abundance of the new age that comes about through Jesus' death. Jesus teaches his disciples that it is necessary for a seed to fall into the ground and die if it is to produce fruit (12:24). Mary's act of anointing Jesus illustrates this saying since the expensive perfume is dried from Jesus' feet while the scent remains spreading through the house.

Conclusion

The narrator provides more detailed information about Mary of Bethany than many other characters in the Fourth Gospel. We are also introduced to her sister Martha and her brother Lazarus, and the narrator depicts the women's concern at the illness of their brother and their grief at his death. Sandra Schneiders rightly proposes that the evangelist is concerned about the members of his community who have lost loved ones, and she argues that the characters of Martha, Mary, and Lazarus are employed to express the Johannine theology of eternal life.[35] Lazarus represents all the disciples who hope to be raised from death, and Mary represent the members of the community who mourn the loss of a loved one and trust in Jesus to reunite them.

The narrator highlights the ways in which the character of Mary of Bethany influences Jesus. Mary's grief prompts Jesus to express his own sorrow at the death of Lazarus. In this way Mary also represents those whose suffering touches Jesus. The love Jesus has for the sisters and brother illustrates the love he has for all his disciples. The family at Bethany are presented as the friends of Jesus, and he calls his disciples "friends" (15:15). The relationship between Martha, Mary and Jesus reveals the ability of Jesus to respond to the suffering of his disciples.

---

[34] Charles H. Giblin, "Mary's Anointing for Jesus' Burial-Resurrection (John 12,1–8)," *Bib* 73 (1992): 560–64.

[35] Sandra M. Schneiders, "Death in the Community of Eternal Life: History, Theology, and Spirituality in John 11," *Int* 41 (1987): 44–56.

The character of Mary is primarily conveyed through her act of anointing Jesus. Martha confesses her faith in Jesus as the Messiah and Son of God, and Mary dramatizes this belief by anointing Jesus as the suffering Messiah. Mary of Bethany is contrasted with Judas, one of the twelve male disciples. Her devotion to Jesus is expressed by her costly gift whereas Judas plots to betray Jesus. The character of Mary of Bethany develops in the course of the narrative. At first she falls at Jesus' feet overcome by grief but she becomes more composed and in control of her emotions after she has witnessed Jesus' power to raise Lazarus from death. The narrator does not describe the response of Mary to the raising of Lazarus, and this gap encourages the readers to imagine Mary's emotions at the restoration of her brother. The development in her character highlights the power of Jesus to strengthen the faith of his followers. Mary carries out a prophetic act to anoint Jesus as Messiah in public in order to communicate her faith in Jesus as the suffering Messiah, and the expensive perfume spreads through the house pointing to the abundant life that comes about through Jesus' death.

Martha:
Seeing the Glory of God

Gail R. O'Day

One of the most complicated issues in character study in biblical texts is maintaining the distinction between individuality and personality.[1] The construction of individuality – individual character traits, individual figures, the individual as character as distinct from the crowds – is a rhetorical practice in ancient texts.[2] The construction of personality, however, is extratextual and not a rhetorical practice. Whereas in other areas of literary critical study – the construction of plot or analysis of imagery, for example, scholars are clear that they are investigating the rhetorical features of the text, in character studies the distinction between rhetorical feature (character) and extratextual reality (personality) often is blurred.

When, for example, a scholar speaks of Martha in John 11 as "arrogant,"[3] the analytical focus seems to fall more on Martha's personality than on her contribution to Johannine rhetoric. "Arrogant" as a descriptor tends toward a psychological description,[4] rather than a rhetorical description. When an interpreter moves from first level analysis of characters (what are the component elements of John's rhetoric) to second level conclusions (what is the significance of this character in the larger story and for constructing meaning), there is a temptation to confuse the individuality of a character with personality.

Yet if one is to analyze characters from a literary critical perspective, it is crucial that rhetorical analysis takes the lead and that personality analysis is pushed to the background. Literary works have characters, not persons, even if the character in question is based on a historical personage;[5] the world has

---

[1] See Fred W. Burnett, "Characterization and Reader Construction of Characters in the Gospels," *Semeia* 63 (1993): 3–28; Gail R. O'Day, "The Citation of Scripture as a Key to Characterization in Acts," in *Scripture and Traditions: Essays on Early Judaism and Christianity in Honor of Carl R. Holladay* (ed. Patrick Gray and Gail O'Day; Leiden: Brill, 2008), 207–21.

[2] See, for example, the collection of essays, *Characterization and Individuality in Greek Literature* (ed. Christopher Pelling; Oxford: Clarendon, 1990).

[3] Francis J. Moloney, *Signs and Shadows: Reading John 5–12* (Minneapolis: Fortress, 1996), 180.

[4] Especially since the context for this comment is that Martha's serving at table in John 12:2 shows that her "previous arrogance has been transformed" (ibid.).

[5] For a good discussion of the how literary, historical, and ideological aspects intermingle in character study, see Petri Merenlahti and Raimo Hakola, "Reconceiving Narrative Criti-

persons, not characters. To take an example from recent contemporary fiction, one of the central characters in Geraldine Brooks's novel, *Caleb's Crossing*, is Caleb Cheeshahteaumauk, a member of the Wampanoag tribe of Noepe (Martha's Vineyard), who was the first Native American to graduate from Harvard College in 1665. Brooks writes an afterword to the novel that provides the facts of Caleb's life as they can be ascertained from archives and other sources.[6] While the basic outline of Caleb's life resembles the plot of the novel, the character of Caleb and his rhetorical function in propelling the novel's plot exists independently from the biographical sketch in the afterword. The character of Caleb, as distinct from the person of Caleb, has impact within the pages of the novel, and his impact derives from Brooks's rhetorical choices in constructing plot, theme, and character, not from the data Brooks provides about his life.

The move to turn characters into persons may be especially tempting in biblical texts because biblical characters are often seen as models or exemplars for the life of faith. But to read characters as if they were persons can deprive the literary character of its function and distinctive voice in its literary home:

> Certainly it is impossible to deny to readers any pleasure they may take in expanding character beyond its role in the literary work – in looking up from the page and pondering how the woman on the page is like the woman reading, and so on to inspired conjectures about what to do and how to live … All I ask is that such a reader admits that she has looked up and away from the story, and made use of it for something other than what it intrinsically is – that she has created her own illusion.[7]

This observation is about reading women characters in the novels of Henry James, but is pertinent to reading biblical characters as well, since character analysis in biblical studies often moves away from rhetorical function "to inspired conjectures about what to do and how to live." This observation may also be doubly pertinent for the analysis of women characters, where extratextual assumptions about women's conduct and women's capabilities often predetermine assessment of rhetorical function.

This is not to argue for pure formalism when reading literary characters. The rhetorical construction of a character depends on and reflects cultural and social conventions of both the author and the reader, as well as historical knowledge of the time when the literary work is set or was written. It is to suggest, however, that in the case of character study, analyses based primarily on rhetorical elements in the text often give way uncritically to conclusions

---

cism," in *Characterization in the Gospel: Reconceiving Narrative Criticism* (ed. David Rhoads and Kari Syreeni; Sheffield: Sheffield Academic Press, 1999), 13–48, here 44.

[6] Geraldine Brooks, *Caleb's Crossing* (New York: Viking, 2011).

[7] Mary Doyle Springer, *A Rhetoric of Literary Character: Some Women of Henry James* (Chicago: University of Chicago Press, 1978), 20.

based on assumptions of what may lie behind or in front of the text, to the detriment of rhetorical analysis.

Martha as ...

So when Martha heard that Jesus was coming, she went to meet him (Mary was in the house). Martha said to Jesus, "Lord, if you had been here, my brother would not have died, and even now I know that whatever you ask God, God will give you" (John 11:20–22).

The tendency to confuse character and personality is acute in the interpretation of Martha in the Gospel of John. Most interpreters of Martha seem always to be "looking up from the page and wondering how the woman on the page is like [or unlike] the woman [or more often, man] reading." A focal point in interpretations of Martha as character is her words and actions in John 11:20–22. The habit of assessing Martha as a person can be illustrated nicely by comparing three pre-modern readings of these verses: Augustine, Chrysostom, and Calvin.

Martha as Humble Interlocutor

Augustine interprets Martha's words in vss. 21–22 as an act of humility, not presuming on any outcome or decision that Jesus might make,

> She did not say, But even now I ask You to raise my brother to life again. For how could she know if such a resurrection would be of benefit to her brother? She only said, "I know that You can, and whatever You are pleased, You do: for Your doing it is dependent on Your own judgment, not on my presumption. But even now I know that, whatever You will ask of God, God will give it You."

In Augustine's view, Martha's words show the appropriate stance of humility, not impinging or presuming on divine initiative.[8] Augustine's assessment of Martha's words and behavior as non-presumptive hinges not on what she says, but on his approval of what she does not say.

Martha as Model of Appropriate Grief

John Chrysostom praises Martha (and Mary)[9] for being restrained in her grief. As with Augustine, his interpretation is primarily based on what Martha did not say, rather than what her words do say.

> See how great is the heavenly wisdom of the women, although their understanding be weak. For when they saw Christ, they did not break out into mourning and wailing and

---

[8] Augustine, Tractate 49 on John.
[9] The two women are undifferentiated in Chrysostom's interpretation, Homily 62 on John.

loud crying, as we do when we see any of those we know coming in upon our grief; but straightway they reverence their Teacher. So then both these sisters believed in Christ, but not in a right way ... For their affection to their Teacher did not allow them strongly to feel their present sorrow; so that the minds of these women were truly wise as well as loving.

Martha and Mary's knowledge may be inadequate and weak, but in their restrained grief, they show what to do and how to live:

But in our days, among our other evils there is one malady very prevalent among our women; they make a great show in their dirges and wailings, baring their arms, tearing their hair, making furrows down their cheeks. And this they do, some from grief, others from ostentation and rivalry, others from wantonness; and they bare their arms, and this too in the sight of men. Why do you, woman? Do you strip yourself in unseemly sort, tell me, you who are a member of Christ, in the midst of the market-place, when men are present there?

Martha as Example of Emotion Hindering Faith

Calvin's interpretation of Martha combines elements of both Augustine and Chrysostom, as he identifies Martha's request as modest, but he also focuses on the feelings that her grief engenders:

She begins with a lament, although in it she also modestly makes her wish known. It is as if she had said, "You could, by your presence, have saved my brother from death; and even now you can do it, for God does not deny you anything." But by speaking like this, she rather gives way to her feelings than restrains them under the rule of faith. I acknowledge that her words come from faith partly; but I say that disorderly passions were mixed up with them and carried her beyond proper bounds ... her faith, mixed up and entangled with unregulated desires, and even not completely free from superstition, could not shine with full brightness.[10]

Calvin's assessment of Martha is based on her emotional state, a mark of her personality, which he infers from her words. Because she makes a request of Jesus that seems to arise from her regret and grief that her brother died, her faith is suspect (in commenting on 11:23, Calvin refers back to Martha's request as "those faults of Martha that we have mentioned."). Calvin's views of the proper place of grief and of the measures of strong faith determine how he reads Martha's words and her place in the story.

Martha as ...

While it may be unfair to expect pre-modern readers to differentiate between character and person, the patterns of Martha's personality observed by these three interpreters remain dominant patterns that continue in contemporary,

---

[10] John Calvin, *John 11–21 and 1 John* (Calvin's New Testament Commentaries; trans. T. H. L. Parker; Grand Rapids, Mich.: Eerdmans, 1994), 7–9.

critical interpretation of Martha.[11] Scholarly assumptions about what Martha is "like," about the kind of woman that she is, about what she is feeling, shape discourse about Martha as character.

This approach to reading Martha is all the more striking since no adjectives or adverbs describe either Martha or her actions in John 11. John's narrative expresses no interest in Martha's personality. Her words and actions are building blocks in the story he is telling. Yet the temptation to interpret Martha as a person seems irresistible. Thomas Gardner, for example, in his recent book, *John in the Company of Poets,* writes of Martha's words in 11:21–22:

> This is a powerfully mixed set of statements. She knows he has power – he could have healed her brother – but she positions the power off to the side with the term "if" – if only he had been there, Lazarus would not have died. This is the sort of language we use when we try to make sense of trauma: if only this had happened, the terrible thing would not have occurred. She is stunned and casting about for words.[12]

This reading of Martha's response is not that different from Calvin's – Martha's grief is the touchstone for assessing the rhetoric of the verse.

The presupposition of this essay is that in order to understand the contribution of Martha to the rhetorical structure and aims of the Gospel of John, it is necessary to read Martha as a character in the narrative, not as a person in Jesus' life. This is not to deny the possibility of an external, historical referent for Martha (or her sister Mary and brother Lazarus). But for the interpreter, when "real life" resonances set the tone and scope of the interpretive conversation, Martha as character on the page disappears and only the Martha of "inspired conjecture" remains.

Rhetoric as Roadmap to Character Study

A recent essay illustrates the difference in approach to Martha as character when the focus is on the rhetoric of the Gospel and not on extratextual assumptions about Martha and women more generally.[13] In analyzing

---

[11] For example, see Turid Karlsen Seim, "Roles of Women in the Gospel of John," in *Aspects on the Johannine Literature* (ed. Lars Hartman and Birger Olsson; ConBNT 18; Uppsala: Almqvist & Wiksell, 1988), 70, for an interpretation similar to Augustine, and T. E. Pollard, "The Raising of Lazarus," in *Studia Evangelica,* VI (ed. Elizabeth A. Livingstone; Berlin: Akademie-Verlag, 1973), 434–43, for an interpretation that focuses on the sisters' emotions. See also Ingrid R. Kitzberger, "Mary of Bethany and Mary of Magdala – Two Female Characters in the Johannine Passion Narrative: A Feminist, Narrative-Critical Reader Response," *NTS* 41 (1995): 564–86.

[12] Thomas Gardner, *John in the Company of Poets: The Gospel in Literary Imagination* (Waco, Tex.: Baylor University Press, 2011), 108.

[13] Bart J. Koet and Wendy E. S. North, "The Image of Martha in Luke 10,38–42 and in John 11,1–12,8," in *Miracles and Imagery in Luke and John: Festschrift Ulrich Busse* (ed. Jozef Verheyden et al.; Louvain: Peeters, 2008), 47–66.

Martha's words to Jesus in 11:21–22, Koet and North interpret the content of Martha's words, not their imputed tone, as was often the case in the interpretations noted above:

> Perhaps we are intended to see here some hint of reproach ... Yet taken at face value, Martha's words do no more than state the case of the matter as far as she is concerned, namely, that she is facing the reality of the death of a loved one which, had Jesus been present, would not have occurred.[14]

Their rhetorical focus enables Koet and North to see that the repetition of these same words by Mary to Jesus in v. 35 underscores their content – death and bereavement – as a central theme in John 11.[15] The interpretive key to the repetition of the words about Jesus' absence and Lazarus' death is their rhetorical function, not the relative adequacy of the sisters' responses and faith.[16]

Koet and North also note the rhetorical function of 11:21–22 in engaging the reader in the story: "John has taken care to ensure that the readers themselves are in a more knowledgeable position than Martha at this stage." The readers know of Jesus' deliberate intention to stay away (11:6), Jesus' intention to "awaken" Lazarus (11:11), and the theophanic purpose of the illness (11:4). For the Gospel reader, "the fact that Martha remarks on Jesus' absence functions as a reminder that Jesus is in absolute control of events here and that grounds for hope exist, even if Martha herself is unaware of them." Martha's words have a role in moving the storyline forward.

Martha's words in 11:22 are also read rhetorically in Koet and North: "Martha goes on to affirm her certainty in words which anticipate the form Jesus' prayer will later take (vss. 41–42), that God will give Jesus whatever he asks."[17] John 11:22 shares the form of a common prayer logion (ask, and it will be given) that occurs repeatedly in the Farewell Discourse in Jesus' instruction

---

[14] Koet and North, "The Image of Martha," 62.

[15] Koet and North, "The Image of Martha," 62. See also Raimo Hakola, "A Character Resurrected: Lazarus in the Fourth Gospel and Afterwards," in *Characterization in the Gospels* (ed. Rhoads and Syreeni), 237–44; Sandra Schneiders, *Written that You May Believe: Encountering Jesus in the Fourth Gospel* (New York: Herder and Herder, 1999), 152–57; Andrew T. Lincoln, "The Lazarus Story: A Literary Perspective," in *The Gospel of John and Christian Theology* (ed. Richard Bauckham and Carl Mosser; Grand Rapids, Mich.: Eerdmans, 2008), 211–32, here 229–31; Eckart Reinmuth, "Lazarus und seine Schwestern – was wollte Johannes erzählen?," *TLZ* 124 (1999): 127–37; Ruben Zimmermann, "The Narrative Hermeneutics of Joh 11. Learning with Lazarus How to Understand Death, Life, and Resurrection," in *The Resurrection of Jesus in the Gospel of John* (ed. Craig R. Koester and Reimund Bieringer; WUNT 222; Tübingen: Mohr Siebeck, 2008), 75–101.

[16] So, e. g., Francis J. Moloney, "The Faith of Mary and Martha: A Narrative Approach to John 11,17–40," *Bib* 75 (1994): 471–93 and idem, "Can Everyone Be Wrong? A Reading of John 11.1–12.8," *NTS* 49 (2003): 505–27. Moloney's list of problems of incoherence in Martha's conversation with Jesus identifies a rhetorical problem, but he resolves the problem with a theological answer.

[17] Koet and North, "Image of Martha," 63.

on prayer (14:13-14; 15:7, 16; 16:23-26). The rhetorical form of Martha's words, not the strength of her personality, communicates her certainty and confidence in Jesus.[18]

The presenting question for the Koet/North essay, as its title indicates, is the image of Martha in the Gospel of John. Martha's image emerges out of the choices John has made in constructing the story, rather than being overly determined by extratextual presuppositions about how a woman of faith would, should, or could act. The rhetorical similarity between Martha's words to Jesus in 11:22 and a traditional Christian prayer logion, for example, establishes the narrative context in which readers can interpret Martha's words. Together the form and content of her words emphasize the confidence of her approach to Jesus. Martha's "personality" (arrogant, grief-stricken, humble, stunned) is irrelevant for interpreting the construction of confidence in the Gospel's rhetoric.

Martha appears as a character in John 11:1-44 and in 12:1-8. In the remainder of this essay, I will use three elements of the Gospel of John's rhetoric as a roadmap for reading these narratives with the aim of constructing Martha as character:

1. The narrator's comments about the character
2. The character's actions
3. The character's words

By focusing on these three elements of the Gospel's rhetoric, I intend to be rhetorically descriptive of Martha as a literary character, rather than prescriptive about her personality. An approach to character that stays focused on the rhetoric of character may allow Martha to emerge from John as a character who can engage the reader in the unfolding of the Gospel story rather than primarily as an extratextual model.

The Rhetorical Building Blocks of Martha as Character

Narrator's Comments about Martha

The narrator's comments about a character provide information directly to the reader through exposition.[19] The most basic way for the narrator to communicate this information is to concentrate it at the beginning of the story, providing the reader with the details he or she will need to assess the story as it

---

[18] Wendy E. Sproston North, *The Lazarus Story within the Johannine Tradition* (Sheffield: Sheffield Academic Press, 2001), 108-14.
[19] Meir Sternberg, *Expositional Modes and Temporal Ordering in Fiction* (Baltimore: Johns Hopkins University Press, 1978).

unfolds. The narrator can further shape the reader's perception of the flow of the story, and in the case of character, the reader's perception of the character, by varying from this basic pattern and providing exposition when the story is already underway.[20]

John 11:1–6

The heaviest concentration of the narrator's comments about Martha is in vss. 1–6. In each comment in this section, Martha is linked with her sister Mary:

Bethany, the village of Mary and her sister Martha (v. 1)
Jesus loved Martha and her sister and Lazarus (v. 5)

Martha never appears as an individual apart from her family unit in these opening verses, and no additional attributes or descriptors are given to Martha (cf. v. 2, where Mary is featured independently from Martha and she and Lazarus are further identified).

The reader learns two things about Martha from the narrator's comments – that she is defined by her family unit and that this family unit is loved by Jesus. Establishing Martha's place in the domestic sphere is an important element of this story, especially since this theme will recur in 12:1–8. That the family is described as the recipients of Jesus' love is also significant, since to this point in the Gospel narrative, no individuals have been identified in this way. The reader has learned of God's love for the world and of the Father's love for Jesus, but this is the first reference to Jesus' love for specific individuals.[21] These two sisters and their brother have a distinctive relationship to Jesus. No reason for Jesus' love of this family is provided, nor are the sisters explicitly described as reciprocating Jesus' love. As we will see below, the narrative does show the sisters exercising agency in response to Jesus' love, since Jesus' love for this family (at least his love for their brother) is part of the content of their message about Lazarus's illness in v. 3.

John 11:19

This verse widens Martha and Mary's sphere – from the family to their religious community. As in vss. 1–6, Martha is not featured independently of her sister.

---

[20] Sternberg, *Expositional Modes*, 98–99. See also the discussion of the expositional mode in R. Alan Culpepper, *Anatomy of the Fourth Gospel: A Study in Literary Design* (Philadelphia: Fortress, 1983), 18–20 and Peter Dschulnigg, *Jesus begegnen: Personen und ihre Bedeutung im Johannesevangelium* (Münster: LIT, 2000).

[21] In v. 3, *fileō* is used and in v. 5 *agapaō*, but there is no reason to ascribe significance to this vocabulary use. The Fourth Evangelist uses synonyms regularly, and both verbs are used to describe "the disciple whom Jesus loved" (see, e. g., 20:2 [*fileō*] and 19:26 [*agapaō*]).

This verse establishes the specifics of the religious community – the family is Jewish. The arrival of "Jews" to mourn with the sisters indicates that they are fully integrated into the life of their religious community.[22] The addition of this description of the sisters as co-mourners with "the Jews" midway through the story complicates the exposition of Martha's character and of the situation. In 11:8, "the Jews" have been mentioned as a threat to Jesus; here the same noun is used to describe a group who is supportive of the family whom Jesus loves (see also v. 31). The narrator provides this information immediately prior to Martha's private conversation with Jesus (vss. 21–27), positioning Martha's active involvement with her Jewish community as the backdrop for that conversation.

John 11:39

At Lazarus's tomb, the narrator describes Martha as "the sister of the dead man" (*hē adelphē tou teteleutekotos*). From the perspective of the reader's ability to recognize the character, this identification of Martha by the narrator is superfluous – it does not communicate any information that the reader does not already know (vss. 5, 21, 23). The rhetorical function of this comment, then, is more than expositional. The key to its rhetorical function is the verb form, *teteleutekotos*. This is the only occurrence of τελευτάω in John, and the use of the perfect tense here underscores that Lazarus's life is really "finished." Martha is the sister of a man who has died and who is dead (cf. the use of the perfect tense in v. 44).

The narrator's comment focuses the reader's attention on the reality of death and on Martha's intimate connection to that reality. This description of Martha provides the context for interpreting the words that she speaks at the tomb (see below). Martha is positioned as the tangible link to the death of Lazarus.

Martha's Actions

The narrator's comments about a character are the only explicit rhetorical markers of character development provided in the Gospel narrative. Everything else about a character must be inferred from the character's role in the unfolding of the Gospel story. A character's actions and speech are the principal ways that a character contributes to the story and as such are the principal lens into a character's rhetorical function.

---

[22] See Adele Reinhartz, "From Narrative to History: The Resurrection of Mary and Martha," in *"Women Like This": New Perspectives on Jewish Women in the Greco-Roman World* (ed. Amy-Jill Levine; Atlanta: Scholars Press, 1991), 161–84, here 178–80.

Two types of actions are associated with Martha: she either initiates an action or is the recipient of someone else's action.

The actions initiated by Martha in 11:1–44 and 12:1–8 can be outlined as follows:

1. She (and her sister, *hē adelphē*) *send a message* to Jesus (v. 3)
2. She *heard* that Jesus was coming (v. 20a)
3. She *went* and *met* Jesus (v. 20b)
4. She *spoke* to Jesus (v. 21)
5. She *speaks* to him [Jesus] (v. 24)
6. She *speaks* to him [Jesus] (v. 26)
7. (After *speaking*) she *returned* and
8. She *called* her sister Mary
9. *Speaking* privately (v. 28)
10. She *speaks* to Jesus (v. 39)
11. Martha *was serving* (12:2)[23]

The actions of which she is the recipient of someone else's initiative are:

1. Jesus *loved* Martha (and her sister and Lazarus) (v. 5)
2. Many of the Jews *had come* to Martha (and Mary) in order *to mourn with them* (v. 19)
3. Jesus *says to her* (v. 23)
4. Jesus *says to her* (vss. 25–26), including the direct question, "Do you believe (*pisteueis*) this?"
5. Jesus *says to her*, "Did I not tell you (*soi*) …?" (v. 40)

These two lists make clear that Martha is the initiator of action in this story much more than she is the recipient of others' initiatives. The dominant role assigned to her is that of communicating – eight times she is the subject of a verb of communication (vss. 3, 21, 24, 26, 28 [3x], 39). The main object of her communication is Jesus – she sends a message to Jesus, goes out to meet Jesus, and twice initiates conversation with Jesus (vss. 21, 39). Martha also is physically active in this narrative (11:20b, 28; 12:2), going from place to place, serving at the dinner table.

Five out of the six times when Martha is a recipient of someone else's action, she is the recipient of Jesus' action: Jesus loves Martha and her family and Jesus engages Martha directly in conversation. In a style that borders on

---

[23] Because this essay focuses on the rhetoric of Martha's character in John, Martha's service will be read in terms of what it contributes to the construction of Martha's character in John, not as part of a possible historical reconstruction of the "real" Martha and Mary, through the lens of Luke 10:38–42. See Koet and North, "Image of Martha," and Reinhartz, "From Narrative to History," for a comparison of the Lukan and Johannine stories and their representation of Martha and Mary.

the redundant, John's rhetoric keeps the reader's focus on the two characters of Martha and Jesus in their conversations. The direct object of each conversation partner's speech is mentioned explicitly each time a unit of speech is introduced ("Martha said to Jesus/him" and "Jesus said to her"). Jesus is the central character in all of the Gospel's rhetoric and narrative. That Martha receives as much of Jesus' attention as she gets in this story (both at her initiative and his) underscores her importance as a character.

Martha (and her sister) also receives an initiative of "the Jews" who come to mourn with them. "The Jews'" gestures toward the sisters highlight the reality of grief and bereavement that is a thread throughout the story. Just as the sisters are the recipients of Jesus' love, they are also the recipients of the consoling attention of their religious community. Their reception of "the Jews" as co-mourners reinforces the domestic and religious sphere that defines Martha and Mary and in which the drama of Lazarus's life and death is playing itself out.

Martha's Speech

The main rhetorical building block in constructing Martha's character is her speech. As the preceding discussion of Martha's actions shows, speech and communication is Martha's central action in John. Martha is given six speeches in the story (vss. 3, 21, 24, 26, 28, 39), and her speech is the catalyst for each of the major sections of John 11:

11:1–16: The sisters' message to Jesus about Lazarus's illness (v. 3) is the narrative catalyst for Jesus' teaching about the theophanic purpose of that illness (v. 4), of his decision to stay away from Bethany (v. 6), and provides the subject matter for his conversation with the disciples in vss. 7–16.

11:17–27: Martha speaks first to Jesus (v. 21) and her words are the catalyst for the conversation between her and Jesus.

11:28–37: Martha returns home and summons Mary to go and see Jesus (v. 28), and so sets in motion the exchange between Jesus and Mary. Interestingly, Mary goes to Jesus "at the place where Martha had met him," the narrator's comments making Martha present to the reader even after she has moved from the narrative center.

11:38–44: Martha's response to Jesus in v. 39 is the catalyst for Jesus' restatement of the theophanic purpose of the event.

Martha's speech in John 11:21–27: The sisters' message to Jesus in v. 3 is reprised in Martha's words in v. 21. When we read Martha's words in vss. 21–27 for their contribution to the movement and development of the narrative and its themes, instead of first assessing them for what they say about Martha's personality, an interesting pattern emerges:

Lord, Lazarus whom you love is ill. (v. 3)

Lord, if you had been here, my brother would not have died, and even now I know that whatever you ask God, God will give you. (v. 21)
I know that he will rise in the resurrection in the last day. (v. 24)
Yes, Lord, I believe that you are the Messiah, the Son of God who is coming into the world. (v. 26)

Martha's words move from complaint (v. 3) and petition (v. 21) to confidence (v. 24) and confession (v. 26). This movement mirrors the classic movement in Israel's psalms of lament, in which the petitioner begins with a plea that gives way to praise in the course of the psalm.[24]

In the plea section of a lament psalm, the petitioner addresses God directly and tells God how desperate the situation is. The petitioner then asks God for help, and to strengthen the petition may also provide God with reasons why God should act. Psalm 13 is one of the most succinct examples of the lament form: direct address to God ("How long, O Lord") and complaint ("must I bear pain in my soul") (vss. 1–2), followed by petition ("consider and answer me, O Lord my God") in v. 3, and motivation in v. 4 ("lest my enemy").

Just as in the classic lament psalms, Martha addresses Jesus directly (note the double use of *kuriē* in vss. 3 and 21), expresses her complaint (Lazarus is ill), which gives way to her petition in v. 21. Martha even provides Jesus with a motivation to act ("I know that whatever you ask God, God will give you"). Read in this light, the following outline emerges:

Address: Lord
Complaint: Lazarus is ill
Address: Lord
Complaint: If you had been here
Petition: But even now
Motivation: Whatever you ask, God will give you

Martha's words contain the basic elements of the lament prayer. Just as the psalmist can simultaneously complain about God's absence and ask for God's rescue, here Martha does the same. Martha's lament is not in a continuous prayer form but in an unfolding conversation. The reader knows from the narrator's commentary that Martha is an active participant in her religious community (v. 19), so for her to speak to Jesus in the cadences of Jewish lament is completely consistent with the way that her character has been presented.[25]

---

[24] For a classic analysis of the lament psalm, see Claus Westermann, *Praise and Lament in the Psalms* (Atlanta: John Knox Press, 1981). For an analysis of Matt 15:21–28 as a narrative enactment of a lament psalm, see Gail R. O'Day, "Surprised by Faith: Jesus and the Canaanite Woman," *Listening: Journal of Religion and Culture* 24 (1989): 290–301, reprinted in *A Feminist Companion to Matthew* (ed. Amy-Jill Levine; London: T&T Clark, 2001). Similar rhetorical patterns to those in the exchange between Jesus and the Canaanite woman can be identified in the exchange between Martha and Jesus in John 11.

Equally important for understanding Martha's speech, however, is that her words do not only mirror the complaint section of the lament psalm. They also mirror the praise section of that psalm form. In Ps 13, for example, the psalmist's complaints turn to trust and praise in vss. 5–6 ("I trusted in your steadfast love ... I will sing to the Lord"). The abrupt shift in tone is typical of the lament psalm and is normally explained by reference to the psalms as hymns in Israel's liturgy. In the context of the liturgy, a word of assurance may have been spoken that reminded the psalmist of God's promises,[26] enabling the psalmist to end with praise.

If we add Jesus' portion of the conversation into our analysis of Martha's speech, we find a similar dynamic. Verses 23–27 can be read as a double ending to Martha's "lament psalm," embodying the movement from plea to praise:

Words of assurance: Your brother will rise again (v. 23)
Words of praise and trust: I know my brother will rise again in the resurrection of the last day (v. 24)
Words of assurance: I am the resurrection and the life ... Do you believe this? (vss. 25–26)
Words of praise: Yes, Lord, I believe that you are the Messiah, the Son of God, and the one coming into the world. (v. 27)

Nothing in the exchange between Jesus and Martha indicates that Martha has not understood Jesus or that her understanding is limited because she can only envision a future resurrection for the dead.[27] On the contrary, when Martha's words are read in the context of the traditions of the prayers of the Jewish faithful, the full impact of her words emerges.[28] Jesus gives her two distinct words of assurance – one about her brother (v. 23) and one about himself (vss. 25–26) – and Martha responds affirmatively to both. She, like the psalmists before her, has moved from plea to praise, grounded in the assuring presence of God.

Martha's words of praise in v. 27, like those of the psalmist in Ps 13:5, take the form of trust and confession. It is regularly noted that Martha's words are

---

[25] Cf. Susan Hylen, *Imperfect Believers: Ambiguous Characters in the Gospel of John* (Louisville, Ky.: Westminster John Knox, 2009), 79: "In the midst of her sorrow, Martha cries out to God. Just as the psalmists state their knowledge of God's power and implore God to act, so Martha laments Jesus' absence and its results, even as she continues to believe in his power."

[26] See, e. g., Lam 3:55–57, where the assuring word is included in the lament form.

[27] As representative of this way of reading Martha's words in v. 27, see Raymond Brown, *The Gospel According to John (i–xii)* (AB 29; New York: Doubleday, 1966). More recently, Hylen, *Imperfect Believers*, 80.

[28] To read Martha's words in the context of Jewish prayer is a similar rhetorical strategy to North's reading of the prayer in light of a traditional Christian prayer logion, but grounds the rhetoric in what is known about Mary as character in the story (she is Jewish) rather than in later Christian traditions.

the fullest confession anywhere in the Gospel and that they anticipate the narrator's theological statement of purpose in 20:31 ("these are written so that you may come to believe that Jesus is the Messiah, the Son of God").[29] Yet scholars nonetheless debate whether this confession is adequate, whether Martha really meant or understood what she said. To engage in this debate, however, is to allow an extratextual assumption about what full faith looks like (and perhaps in whose voice it can be spoken) to diminish the Gospel's rhetoric. Martha has moved from lament and petition to praise and confession on the assurances of Jesus' promises. Her expressed faith is in Jesus as the Son of God. She moves from lament to praise not on the basis of a sign (which is still to come in this story), but on the basis of Jesus' self-revelation in vss. 25–26: "I am the resurrection and the life."

Martha's Words in John 11:39–40: After Jesus gives the instruction to take away the stone from Lazarus's tomb, Martha, "the sister of the dead man," says, "Lord, there will already be an odor, for it has been four days." These words are seen by most interpreters to undercut her confession of 11:27. Calvin's response to Martha's words is especially pointed,

> This is a sign of distrust, for she expects less from the power of Christ than she should have done. The root of evil lies in her measuring God's infinite and incomprehensible power by her carnal sense ... Certainly it was no thanks to Martha that her brother did not lie forever in the grave ...

Yet as extreme as Calvin's rhetoric may be, his words represent close to a consensus response to Martha's words here: her confession in v. 27 notwithstanding, her faith in Jesus is suspect.

To read v. 39 this way, however, is to ignore several rhetorical markers that the narrator has provided the reader. First, the narrative focus in vss. 38–44 shifts dramatically from that in vss. 17–27. In vss. 17–27, Lazarus's death is the presenting issue for the conversation between Martha and Jesus, but it is not the focus. In vss. 38–44, Lazarus's death is now the focus – indicated by the location of the conversation at Lazarus's tomb and Martha's designation as "the sister of the dead man."

The focus in vss. 17–27, as the parallels with the lament form help to highlight, is on the possibility of faith and confidence in God even in the face of death. Martha speaks her lament to Jesus and Jesus responds with the reassuring words that underscore his revelation of God, "I am the resurrection and the life." His words in vss. 25–26 do not promise the end of physical death; to the contrary, his words reinforce that death remains a reality ("even though one dies"). His words promise that God, as revealed through Jesus, will be pre-

---

[29] E. g., Raymond Collins, *These Things Have Been Written: Studies on the Fourth Gospel* (LTPM 2; Louvain: Peeters, 1990), 27; Culpepper, *Anatomy of the Fourth Gospel*, 141–42; Schneiders, *Written That You May Believe*, 158.

sent in life and death, and that death cannot reduce the life that Jesus brings. This promise grounds the assurance that moves Martha from lament to praise and confession.

That the particularity of Lazarus's death remains a reality, even in the face of Martha's confession, can be seen in vss. 28–37. The juxtaposition of Martha's confession in v. 27 and her summons of her sister to go and see Jesus (v. 28) shows that the domestic drama that began in vss. 1–5 is still being played out. The family's bereavement does not end, simply because Martha has confessed her faith in Jesus as the Son of God.[30] The dominant actions in vss. 28–37 are weeping and mourning.

Second, it is only in vss. 39–44 that the narrative finally turns to the miracle story proper. Much has intervened in the narrative since Jesus reported Lazarus's death in vss. 11–15. In that context, Martha's words serve a very basic function. They establish the situation of need that Jesus' miracle will overcome – Lazarus is dead. Martha's words focus the reader's attention on the tomb and the dead body inside it. In the rhetoric of the Gospel, she is stating a fact that is necessary to propel the storyline forward.

Third, in the rhetorical structure of John 11:1–44, Jesus' pronouncement that Lazarus "has fallen asleep, but I am going there to awaken him" (v. 11) was made to his disciples, not to Martha. Martha's words in v. 39 remind the reader that this promise of awakening was made outside of the domestic sphere that has so dominated most of the story. For the reader to see that Martha may not anticipate the miracle that Jesus will perform is perfectly consistent and appropriate for what her character knows. Jesus' words to Martha moved in a different direction than a particular miracle. His words of assurance proclaimed the character of God and Jesus as the revealer and embodiment of that character.

Jesus himself points the reader toward this reading of v. 39. In v. 40, Jesus responds to Martha's comment with the words, "Did I not tell you that if you believed you would see the glory of God?" Jesus speaks directly to Martha (the pronoun and verbs are all second person singular), calling her back to an earlier conversation, yet the teaching to which he alludes does not occur explicitly in vss. 21–27. Jesus spoke of glory in v. 4 ("This illness does not lead to death; rather it is for the glory of God, that the Son of Man might be glorified through it.") and nowhere else in the story.

In terms of the Gospel's rhetoric, the audience for Jesus' words in v. 4 is not clear. Jesus speaks of glory in response to hearing the sisters' message about Lazarus's illness (v. 3) and the words precede his decision to stay "two days longer in the place where he was" (vss. 5–6). But the Gospel narrative does not specify an audience for his words. Verse 7 supports the assumption that

---

[30] See Lincoln, "The Lazarus Story," 230–31.

the disciples are the audience for these words (as well as their parallel to Jesus' words to the disciples in 9:3). Yet in vss. 14–15 Jesus speaks directly to the disciples about the revelatory dimensions of Lazarus's death, as if they had not known of it before.

Jesus' words in v. 4 may best be understood as part of the narrator's rhetorical framing, rather than directly addressed to any set of characters. Its immediate narrative context supports this reading, because they are lodged in the story's introductory narrative exposition (vss. 1–6). As part of the exposition, v. 4 establishes the theophanic frame that shapes the whole story and to which Jesus returns in v. 40. Martha is the only character to this point in the story who has indeed seen the glory of God. Jesus revealed himself to her in his "I am" statement, and she embraced that fully in her confession. She saw the glory of God revealed in Jesus before and apart from the sign, as did the reader. The rest of the characters will now see the revelation of God's glory through Jesus' action in the miracle.

Importantly, John does not record Martha's response to the physical raising of Lazarus. She does not provide additional witness to the revelation of the glory of God. John 12:1–8 gives a glimpse of the restoration of the domestic sphere, but Martha is not at the center of that story. In her confession of Jesus as the Son of God in v. 27, Martha had already answered Jesus' question of v. 40 in the affirmative.

Martha and the Revelation of Jesus' Glory

In the preceding analysis, my goal has been to focus on the rhetorical function of Martha as character in the Gospel of John and not to offer conjectures about what she might be like off the page. Far from diminishing Martha's individuality as a character or reducing her significance for the Gospel of John, this approach highlights how attention to Martha as a character may show us more about her role and contribution to the Gospel story than interpretations that revolve around her projected personality.

The narrator's comments about Martha present her as a woman embedded in her family and her religious community. While both her family and her religious community may have extratextual significance, these two spheres as such are also pivotal for understanding the rhetorical strategy of John 11. Death is intensely personal in this story – Martha is the sister of a dead man, Martha is consoled by members of her religious community – and the narrator's comments about Martha help to bring the domestic intensity of death to the forefront.

But death is also more than personal in John 11, and Martha's actions and speech help advance this dimension of the story's rhetoric. Martha takes initiative with Jesus in action and word (vss. 21–27) and through her speech the reader is able to understand the extra-personal dimensions of death. Her words to Jesus are not simply personal complaint, lament, or petition, but mirror and embody the faithful speech of her religious community. By having Martha express both her grief and her hope in speech forms that recall the lament psalms, the Gospel shows her placing death in a larger theological context. Death is real, but so is the assuring promise of the presence of God.

Martha's speech also positions her in the forefront of all the other characters in this story. She is the reader's guide into the narrative. She accepts Jesus' words of assurance before there is a confirmatory miracle (v. 27), and she affirms the reality of death even with the confidence of that assurance (v. 39). Martha's words and actions guide the reader to see that the raising of Lazarus is the postscript to the core miracle of this story: the revelation of the glory of God in Jesus.

Thomas:
Question Marks and Exclamation Marks

Thomas Popp

The Gospel of John offers exclusive insight into Thomas' journey of faith. Thomas is one of the central figures in the Fourth Gospel. His name appears seven times and in four different scenes (11:16; 14:5; 20:24, 26, 27, 28; 21:2).[1] This distinctly characterized disciple is uniquely Johannine.

Thomas as Character: Varying Portrayals

The spectrum of interpretations given to the texts pertaining to Thomas in the Fourth Gospel is extremely wide. At his first appearance in the narrative, is he depicted as a faithful model of discipleship showing readiness for heroic action (11:16)?[2] Or does he appear as a fatalist[3] and doubter, whose characterization is qualified by skepticism, sarcasm, and defeatism?[4] These contradictory questions indicate that there is more than one way to understand the text. Thus, the Thomas texts are not conclusive but are, rather, through their polyvalence, open to diverse interpretive possibilities.[5] Our study's search for meaning in the Thomas texts will be undertaken with this hermeneutical presupposition in mind.

---

[1] See Peter Dschulnigg, *Jesus begegnen: Personen und ihre Bedeutung im Johannesevangelium* (Münster: LIT, 2000), 220; Eugen Ruckstuhl, "Θωμάς," *EWNT*² 2:408; A. Bauer, "Thomas," *Personenlexikon zum Neuen Testament* (ed. Josef Hainz et al.; Düsseldorf: Patmos, 2004), 304.

[2] See, for example, Udo Schnelle, *Das Evangelium nach Johannes* (THKNT 4; Leipzig: Evangelische Verlagsanstalt, 2004), 211, 331.

[3] See, for example, Josef Blank, *Das Evangelium nach Johannes II–III* (2d ed.; GSL.NT 4/3; Düsseldorf: Patmos, 1988), 265.

[4] For this more negative characterization of Thomas see Folker Siegert, *Das Evangelium des Johannes in seiner ursprünglichen Gestalt: Wiederherstellung und Kommentar* (SIJD 7; Göttingen: Vandenhoeck & Ruprecht, 2008), 435, 506, 613.

[5] According to Ruben Zimmermann, "Die Gleichnisse Jesu: Eine Leseanleitung zum Kompendium," in *Kompendium der Gleichnisse Jesu* (ed. idem; Gütersloh: Gütersloher Verlagshaus, 2007), 42, "… darf diese Offenheit der Interpretation nicht mit Beliebigkeit oder postmodernem Verstehensverlust verwechselt werden." For the possibility of differing readings, see also Thyen's remarks at the beginning of his commentary on John: "Ein objektiver Textsinn ist ein unauffindbares Phantom, Interpretation und Applikation sind untrennbar … Gewiss sind andere Arten der Lektüre möglich und die in diesem Kommentar unternommene ist nur eine."

The Composition of the Thomas Texts

The Thomas texts are placed purposefully in both the main section of the Gospel (John 1–12; 13–20) and in the epilogue (John 21). The reader encounters Thomas for the first time at the end of the first section of the Gospel (11:16); for the second time at the beginning of the farewell discourses (14:5–7); for the third time, in the final scene (20:24–29); and, for the last time, at the beginning of the supplemental chapter (21:2).

The key role that the beginning and the end of John's Gospel play in the structure and reception of the text already allows one to perceive Thomas' special role.[6] On the text–internal level, Thomas is led step-by-step on the path of salvation and is drawn into to the salvific acts of Jesus. On the text-external level, the narrator draws the readers into the story, thereby enabling them to be transformed by Thomas' journey of faith.

The Staging of Thomas' Journey

In order to arrive at an appropriate recognition of this key figure's character, the textual analysis of the three stages of Thomas' journey to Easter faith will progress through the following exegetical steps:[7]

(1) The narrative context in which Thomas is embedded will be described
(2) The constellation of characters in the scene will be investigated
(3) An interpretation drawing together various perspectives, especially those found in the character analysis, will be offered.

First Appearance (11:16)

As elsewhere in the Gospel of John, at the first appearance of Thomas all textual elements are artfully aligned with one another. Thomas emerges for the first time in the theologically loaded, richly symbolic story of Lazarus.

Contextual Framework (11:1–44)

The interpretation related to Thomas' character should be understood both in light of the entire context of the Lazarus account as well as in the immediate context of the four scenes in which he figures prominently. As the seventh sign

---

[6] For the vital significance of the beginning and the end of the text, see Thomas Popp, *Grammatik des Geistes: Literarische Kunst und theologische Konzeption in Johannes 3 und 6* (Arbeiten zur Bibel und ihrer Geschichte 3; Leipzig: Evangelische Verlagsanstalt, 2001), 54–57 (54, fn. 43 Lit.!).

[7] For methodical issues, see Popp, *Grammatik des Geistes*, 21–22, 45–57.

in the Fourth Gospel and the greatest miracle story in the New Testament, the story of Lazarus (11:1–44) marks the high point of the public ministry of Jesus (John 1–12).[8] At the same time, the raising of Lazarus is the major turning point in the Gospel, in particular as the story concludes by noting that this event led to the authorities' official decision to put Jesus to death (11:45–54). After the introduction to the story (11:1–5), Thomas appears in the disciples' dialogue with Jesus (11:6–10, 11–16). In it, Jesus reveals to them step by step that Lazarus has died. This announcement, as also the ensuing miracle, aims to lead the disciples, and with them the readers, to a deeper faith (πιστεύω; 11:15; see 11:42).[9] With the connection to the first miracle of Christ (2:1–11), where the emphasis likewise falls on the revelation of Jesus' glory and on faith (2:11), things have come full circle.[10] Thomas' decisive statement pointedly marks the end of the dialogue.

In the central scene (11:17–27), it is Martha, not Thomas, who takes on a key role. She responds fittingly (11:27) to Jesus' "I am" statement in the middle of this chapter on the resurrection (11:25–26). Through the encounter with Jesus, the faith Martha already has is deepened and grows (see 1:50–51), bursting forth in an exceptional confession, in which each word is truly spoken. For Thomas, such a confession is yet to come (see 20:28).

The Constellation of Characters

As in the entire Gospel, Jesus is the key figure in 11:1–44. The actions of all the other characters appearing in the scene are portrayed briefly in relationship to him.[11] Of all the disciples only Thomas is named as he makes his appearance, "called the Twin" (ὁ λεγόμενος Δίδυμος; 11:16a; see also 20:24; 21:2).[12] This

---

[8] See Jacob Kremer, *Lazarus: Die Geschichte einer Auferstehung: Text, Wirkungsgeschichte und Botschaft von Joh 11,1–46* (Stuttgart: Verlag Katholisches Bibelwerk, 1985); Thomas Popp, "Die konsolatorische Kraft der Wiederholung: Liebe, Trauer und Trost in den johanneischen Abschiedsreden," in *Repetitions and Variations in the Fourth Gospel: Style, Text, Interpretation* (ed. Gilbert Van Belle et al.; BETL 223; Louvain: Peeters, 2009), 528–32 (528, fn. 22 Lit.!).

[9] This point is clarified by Kremer, *Lazarus*, 354: "Der Glaube ist also kein fester Besitz, er bedarf einer ständigen Festigung und Vertiefung." For readings of the Lazarus story primarily in terms of this aspect of faith, see also 21, 25, 31, 36–38, 80–81.

[10] See Kremer, *Lazarus*, 21, 62, 354.

[11] See Ludger Schenke, *Johannes: Kommentar* (Düsseldorf: Patmos, 1998), 214–17.

[12] In the New Testament, this name is a special feature of the Gospel of John. The name Θωμᾶς (in contrast to Δίδυμος, not found in the older texts) is a translation of the Aramaic תְּאוֹמָא. See Ernst Haenchen, *Das Johannesevangelium: Ein Kommentar aus den nachgelassenen Manuskripten* (ed. Ulrich Busse; Tübingen: Mohr, 1980), 403; C. Kingsley Barrett, *Das Evangelium nach Johannes* (trans. H. Bald; KEK; Göttingen: Vandenhoeck & Ruprecht, 1990), 391; Hartwig Thyen, *Das Johannesevangelium* (HNT 6; Tübingen: Mohr Siebeck, 2005), 519. For a different opinion, see Judith Hartenstein, *Charakterisierung im Dialog: Maria Magdalena, Petrus, Thomas und die Mutter Jesu im Johannesevangelium im Kontext anderer frühchristlicher Darstellungen* (NTOA/SUNT 64; Göttingen: Vandenhoeck & Ruprecht, 2007), 213–14.

apposition "subtly challenges the audience. On the narrative, symbolic level, with whom is Thomas to be matched as a 'twin' character?"[13]

His entrance is unmediated and abrupt. He is suddenly present as an acting character and addresses his "fellow disciples" (συμμαθητής; 11:16a).[14] This description designates Thomas as a member of the group of disciples, thus also implying his obligation to follow Jesus.[15]

After 11:16 Thomas and his fellow disciples do not appear as active characters in the story; however, they are to be considered as constantly present (see, e. g., 6:22–59).[16]

The Decided One

First impressions are notably important as they shape and form subsequent perception. New characters are introduced to the readers of John's Gospel in a particular way and they are encouraged to take note of them attentively. At his first appearance Thomas is characterized in multiple ways:

(1) He is a man of words (εἶπεν οὖν; 11:16a).
(2) His second name is "Twin" (Δίδυμος; 11:16a).
(3) He is a disciple of Jesus (τοῖς συμμαθηταῖς; 11:16a).
(4) He repeats the collective call of Jesus (ἄγωμεν; 1:15d [see 11:7b] – 11:16b).[17]
(5) He acts as the spokesperson for the group of disciples (ἄγωμεν καὶ ἡμεῖς; 11:16b).
(6) As spokesperson, he indicates for the group the readiness to die with Jesus (ἵνα ἀποθάνωμεν μετ' αὐτοῦ; 11:16c).
(7) He is, in contrast to Jesus, not focused on Lazarus (ἄγωμεν πρὸς αὐτόν; 11:15d), but rather on Jesus (ἵνα ἀποθάνωμεν μετ' αὐτοῦ; 11:16c).[18]
(8) He does not know what Jesus, who knows in advance what is to come, has in mind (11:11–16).

---

[13] John Paul Heil, *Blood and Water: The Death and Resurrection of Jesus in Joh 18–21* (CBQMS 27; Washington: Catholic Biblical Association of America, 1995), 139–40.

[14] This New Testament *hapax* is accentuated in H. Rengstorf, "συμμαθητής" *TWNT* 4:464–65: "... die Gemeinschaft der μαθηταί mit Jesus und ihre in ihm gegründete Gemeinschaft untereinander in derselben Weise."

[15] See Kremer, *Lazarus*, 63.

[16] See Jörg Frey, *Die johanneische Eschatologie Bd. 3: Die eschatologische Verkündigung in den johanneischen Texten* (WUNT 117; Tübingen: Mohr Siebeck, 2000), 430; Christian Dietzfelbinger, *Das Evangelium nach Johannes* (ZBK 4; Zürich: TVZ, 2001), 343. On the absence of the "disciples" as presupposed in 6:22–59, see Popp, *Grammatik des Geistes*, 271, fn. 76.

[17] On the artful way in which this aspect is taken up further on, see Kremer, *Lazarus*, 58–59, 62–63.

[18] Regarding μετ' αὐτοῦ, see Kremer, *Lazarus*, 634, fn. 71; Thyen, *Das Johannesevangelium*, 520. For an opposite view, see Siegert, *Johannes*, 435, who interprets "with him" as referring to Lazarus. Sjef van Tilborg, *Das Johannesevangelium: Ein Kommentar für die Praxis* (Stuttgart: Katholisches Bibelwerk, 2005), 157, leaves it open whether Lazarus or Jesus is

Thomas' determination corresponds to that of Jesus (11:15; see 11:7) in that he himself has resolutely determined not to abandon him even if confronted with death (11:16).[19] By repeating Jesus' last request he appears "wie ein verlängerter Arm Jesu, der seine Anliegen weitervermittelt."[20] At the same time, however, he does not correctly understand the exhortation, as revealed by the contrast of the concluding phrases in 11:15b and 11:16c:

11:15b: ἵνα πιστεύσητε
11:16c: ἵνα ἀποθάνωμεν

Jesus has the faith of his disciples in view (11:15b) when he refers to the waking of Lazarus (11:11). Thomas does not understand this allusion. He is fixated on the earthly demise of Jesus and cannot comprehend the deeper meaning of Jesus' journey to Bethany (11:16).[21] On the text-internal pre-Easter level, he reacts appropriately to this journey. Even before departing, it was clear to the disciples that Jesus' journey to Judea would bring him into life-threatening circumstances (11:8). Discipleship, in this instance, would mean literally dying with Jesus. The further sequence of events in the text reveals that only Jesus will die (11:45–54; see 15:13).[22] In this decisive moment, Thomas indicates that he will remain with Jesus through the use of a hortatory subjunctive ἄγωμεν followed by an emphatic καὶ ἡμεῖς. He will remain loyal to the end.[23] Through an intra-textual perspective a "mirror effect" with Peter's confession of faith (6:67–69) is generated.[24] The use of such a literary technique joins, in a hardly coincidental manner, Peter and Thomas as the leading disciples of the Twelve (6:67; see 20:24).

6:68:   κύριε, πρὸς τίνα ἀπελευσόμεθα;
6:69:   καὶ ἡμεῖς πεπιστεύκαμεν
11:16: ἄγωμεν καὶ ἡμεῖς

---

meant. On this textual ambiguity, see also Peter G. Kirchschläger, *Nur ich bin die Wahrheit: Der Absolutheitsanspruch des johanneischen Christus und das Gespräch zwischen den Religionen* (Herders Biblische Studien 63; Freiburg: Herder, 2010), 206, fn. 1103.

[19] According to Dschulnigg, *Jesus begegnen*, 221, Thomas appears "verwegen mutig zu sein und fordert alle zum Martyrium mit Jesus auf."

[20] Hartenstein, *Charakterisierung im Dialog*, 216.

[21] See Kremer, *Lazarus*, 63; Frey, *Eschatologie III*, 430; Dschulnigg, *Jesus begegnen*, 221–22, 235; Glenn W. Most, *Der Finger in der Wunde: Die Geschichte des ungläubigen Thomas* (München: Beck, 2007), 94.

[22] See Haenchen, *Johannesevangelium*, 403; Craig Keener, *The Gospel of John: A Commentary* (2 vols.; Peabody, Mass.: Hendrickson, 2003), 842.

[23] On Thomas' loyalty in terms of the history of religions' background of the recognition scenes in Homer *Od.*, see Stan Harstine, "Un-Doubting Thomas: Recognition Scenes in the Ancient World," *PRSt* 33 (2006): 439–47.

[24] On the "mirror effect" as an inter-textual technique, see Margareta Gruber, "Berührendes Sehen: Zur Legitimation der Zeichenforderung des Thomas (Joh 20,24–31)," *BZ* 51 (2007): 61–83, here 69. With regard to 6:67–69, see Popp, *Grammatik des Geistes*, 408–21.

While Peter functions as the spokesperson for the disciples vis-à-vis Jesus, Thomas takes the initiative when compared to his fellow disciples (συμμαθητής).[25] Additionally, the words of Thomas (11:16) are reflected in the words of Peter at the beginning of Jesus' first farewell discourse (13:36–38). Both of them convey their readiness to die with Jesus. This correspondence suggests that Thomas does not represent skepticism and resignation in the Lazarus pericope,[26] but rather embodies a recognition of the present reality and a willingness to courageously follow as a disciple, even if this means giving up his own life (see 12:26; 13:37).[27] His words demonstrate more courage than is shown by Jesus' brothers (see 7:3–5); however, he, along with most of the other disciples, abandons Jesus in the hour of his arrest (see 16:31–32; 18:8).[28] Nevertheless, he is the only disciple who brings to expression Jesus' summons to die, thereby verbally presenting the proper understanding of the manner in which a disciple's fate is intertwined with that of Jesus. The truth encapsulated in this call to martyrdom must not be overlooked.[29] Thomas is, therefore, anything but naïve.[30] He actually embodies a radical link to Jesus even before possessing the full revelation that comes later.[31] The disciples as represented by Thomas, and in distinction to the readers or hearers of this Gospel, can "jetzt noch gar nicht ergreifen, selbst wenn sie in der 'Schule' Jesu auf dem Weg dahin sind."[32] It is for this reason that Jesus does not rebuke his disciples in

---

[25] See Michael Theobald, *Das Evangelium nach Johannes: Kapitel 1–12* (RNT; Regensburg 2009), 730.

[26] According to Jörg Frey, "Der zweifelnde Thomas (Joh 20,24–29) im Spiegel seiner Rezeptionsgeschichte," *Hermeneutische Blätter* 1 (2011): 5–32, here 11, "unverhohlene Skepsis gegenüber dem Zug Jesu in den Wirkungsbereich seiner Gegner" is evident in Thomas' statement in 11:16. Dietzfelbinger, *Das Evangelium nach Johannes 1*, 343, refers to Thomas' "tiefe Resignation." See also Haenchen, *Johannesevangelium*, 403; Blank, *Das Evangelium nach Johannes*, 265.

[27] See Kremer, *Lazarus*, 63; Schenke, *Johannes*, 214; Schnelle, *Johannes*, 211, 331; Keener, *John*, 842; Klaus Wengst, *Das Johannesevangelium: 2. Teilband: Kapitel 11–21* (THKNT 4; Stuttgart: Kohlhammer, 2007), 26; Gruber, "Berührendes Sehen," 63; Nicolas Farelly, *The Disciples in the Fourth Gospel: A Narrative Analysis of their Faith and Understanding* (WUNT II/290; Tübingen: Mohr Siebeck, 2010), 118, fn. 166; Cornelis Bennema, *Encountering Jesus: Character Studies in the Gospel of John* (Milton Keynes: Paternoster, 2009), 164–65, 169.

[28] See Keener, *John*, 842. On the inter-textual conjunction with 16:31–32 and 18:8, see Schenke, *Johannes*, 320.

[29] Cleverly contested by Rudolf Bultmann, *Das Evangelium des Johannes* (21st ed.; KEK 2; Göttingen: Vandenhoeck & Ruprecht, 1986), 305: "Des Thomas Wort, nicht mehr an Jesus, sondern an die Gefährten gerichtet, ist keine Warnung mehr, sondern bedeutet Ergebung in das den Jüngern mit Jesus gemeinsam drohende Schicksal. Zum erstenmal taucht hier die Wahrheit auf, dass die Jünger das Schicksal Jesu für sich übernehmen müssen." See also Thyen, *Das Johannesevangelium*, 520.

[30] For an opposite view, see Margaret M. Beirne, *Women and Men in the Fourth Gospel: A Genuine Discipleship of Equals* (JSNTSup 242; London: Sheffield Academic Press, 2003), 207.

[31] On this aspect of the *semeia* before Easter, see Gruber, "Berührendes Sehen," 67.

[32] Schenke, *Johannes*, 223.

the farewell discourses for the fact that they will abandon him on his way to the cross (16:32). The problem of the disciples not following Jesus, however, is a theme in Thomas' second appearance (14:5).[33]

Second Appearance (14:5)

Contextual Framework (13:31–14:31)

After first being mentioned in the important narrative concerning Lazarus (11:16), Thomas also appears at a prominent point in the artfully composed first farewell discourse (13:31–14:31).[34] The programmatic opening to the discourse (13:31–38) is verbally connected with the beginning of the Lazarus story (δοξάζω; 13:31–32; see 11:4; ὑπάγω; 13:33, 36; see 11:8). The promise of a new relationship with Jesus after his departure and glorification is explained in John 14 through a three-part discourse of comfort and exhortation:

(1) Jesus' departure to the Father as prelude to the post-Easter salvation era (14:1–14).
(2) The promise of the coming of the Spirit-Paraclete, the return of Jesus, and the indwelling of the Father and the Son (14:15–24).
(3) The conclusion to the discourse with a second promise of the Spirit-Paraclete (14:25–31).

Thomas makes his appearance in the first part (14:5). At the conclusion of the discourse, the ἄγωμεν found in the disciples' dialogue in the Lazarus story (11:7, 15–16) is taken up and employed.

11:7:   ἄγωμεν εἰς τὴν Ἰουδαίαν πάλιν
11:15: ἀλλὰ ἄγωμεν πρὸς αὐτόν
11:16: ἄγωμεν καὶ ἡμεῖς
14:31: ἄγωμεν ἐντεῦθεν

Both the disciples' dialogues during the Lazarus story and the first farewell discourse end with a call to depart. In this way, as far as the character analysis is concerned, Jesus and Thomas (explicitly in 14:5 and implicitly in 14:31) are brought into contact with one other.

---

[33] On the correlation of 14:5 and 16:31–32, Bultmann, *Johannes*, 456, points out: "Die Fragen des Petrus (13,36) und des Thomas (14,5) zeigen, daß darin die Schwierigkeit des Glaubens liegt, sich die scheinbare Verlassenheit deutlich zu machen, die Einsamkeit zu übernehmen, in die der Glaubende, der eschatologisch existieren will, innerhalb der Welt gestellt ist."

[34] On the composition of 13:31–14:31, see Popp, "Kraft der Wiederholung," 541–42 (541, fn. 79 Lit.!).

The Constellation of Characters

The immediate audience of the dialogue found in 13:31–14:31 is the community of the disciples, whereas in 15:1–16:33, the text-external readers and hearers are in view. In 13:31–38 Peter is the primary addressee, though starting in 14:1 all the disciples are once again addressed. In 14:1–31, Thomas (14:5) and Philip (14:8; see 1:43–45; 6:7; 12:21–22), along with "Judas (not Iscariot)" (14:22), appear by name. As was the case in his first appearance, Thomas takes the stage as an unmediated and central character.

The Questioning One

Thomas' character is multi-faceted. While at his first appearance he presents an emphatic call to his fellow disciples to depart with Jesus (11:16), at the beginning of the first farewell discourse he appears as the one questioning Jesus (14:5). The impetus for the question is the first statement of Jesus (14:1–4), culminating in the assertion in 14:4: "And you know the way to the place where I am going."[35] At this point a targeted, intentional semantic "gap" occurs which creates multiple meanings.[36] Jesus postulates as settled what is in fact still inconclusive and through his enigmatic ὁδός-statement provokes Thomas' question (14:5). This "Steilvorlage"[37] makes a further dialogical explanation possible (14:6–7).[38]

Thomas' further inquiry thus functions as the prelude to the solemnly formulated "I am" statement of Jesus (14:6).[39] After Peter's previous question about Jesus' destination (13:36), it is Thomas, who, with a hint of sorrow, interrupts Jesus with a question that once again takes up the keywords οἶδα, ὑπάγω and ὁδός (14:4–5; see 16:5): "Lord, we do not know where you are going. How can we know the way?"[40] He intervenes, just like Philip (14:8)

---

[35] On the one hand ὑπάγω (from 13:33, 36) and οἶδα (from 13:17–18; see 13, 1, 3, 7, 11) are picked up; on the other hand the lexeme ὁδός now appears for the first time. See ὁδοιπορία; 4:6; ὁδηγέω; 16:13.

[36] See Michael Theobald, *Herrenworte im Johannesevangelium* (Herders Biblische Studien 34; Freiburg: Herder, 2002), 305–306.

[37] Frey, "Der zweifelnde Thomas," 12.

[38] On the importance of dialogic presentation in the Gospel of John, see Hartenstein, *Charakterisierung im Dialog*; Georg Rubel, *Erkenntnis und Bekenntnis: Der Dialog als Weg der Wissensvermittlung im Johannesevangelium* (NTAbh 54; Münster: Aschendorff, 2009).

[39] On the rhetorical function of the disciples' questions, see Frey, *Eschatologie III*, 126; Kirchschläger, *Nur ich bin die Wahrheit*, 205–206.

[40] On the aspect of sorrow in 14:5, see Manfred Lang, "Johanneische Abschiedsreden und Senecas Konsolationsliteratur: Wie konnte ein Römer Joh 13,31–17,26 lesen?," in *Kontexte des Johannesevangeliums: Das vierte Evangelium in religions- und traditionsgeschichtlicher Perspektive* (ed. Jörg Frey and Udo Schnelle; WUNT 175; Tübingen: Mohr Siebeck, 2004), 395. In contrast, Judith Hartenstein regards Thomas' characterization, 218, as "in kritischer Distanz zu Jesus wie die anderen."

and Judas (14:22), as a representative of the group of disciples.[41] Unlike 11:16 Thomas now acts as Peter had (see 6:68–69), that is as the representative disciple speaking to Jesus.[42] As in his first appearance Thomas expresses his determination to follow Jesus;[43] though this time he articulates his wish to continue the journey with Jesus with a phrase that does not require an exclamation, but rather a question mark. He knows that Jesus will come to take him and his fellow disciples to the Father's house (14:2–3); yet, with this statement the possibility of him further following Jesus in the sense of a physical accompaniment seems to have come to an end.[44] The fact that Jesus himself *is* the way has not yet occurred to him.[45] In addition, he cannot yet know the goal of the journey, because according to the Johannine view no one except Jesus has seen the Father (see among others, 1:18; 6:46).[46] The goal of Jesus' journey had not been understood (7:33–34) or, alternatively, had not been stated (13:33).[47] That the way to Jesus' goal would lead through his death, has already (in typical Johannine irony) been stated by Thomas (11:16), even though Thomas himself was not aware of the deeper Christological meaning of his words.[48] That, in future, discipleship would take the form of Spirit-wrought faith in the crucified and risen divine revealer (14:1; see 11:15), is not yet clear to him at this point in the text. Once again, therefore, he appears here as someone who is not yet in a position to look beyond the boundaries of Jesus' death (see 11:16).[49] The hour of comprehending faith will only arrive after Easter in 20:24–29.

His current lack of understanding serves as an opportunity to provide a further Christological explanation. The "I am" statement of Jesus stands in

---

[41] This also explains the change from the singular (14:6) to the plural (14:7) in Jesus' answer. See also Kirchschläger, *Nur ich bin die Wahrheit*, 204–205.

[42] See Bennema, *Encountering Jesus*, 165.

[43] Aptly Schenke, *Johannes*, 284, remarks: "Nach wie vor anerkennt er, dass der Jünger Jesus zu folgen hat." See also Kirchschläger, *Nur ich bin die Wahrheit*, 205. For an opposite view, see Tilborg, *Johannesevangelium*, 207.

[44] See Schenke, *Johannes*, 284; Ulrich Wilckens, *Das Evangelium des Johannes* (NTD 4; Göttingen: Vandenhoeck & Ruprecht, 2000), 221.

[45] Referring to this, Theobald, *Herrenworte*, 305–306, states: "Vor allem aber scheint Thomas in seiner Antwort zwischen dem Weg und dem, der ihn begeht, Jesus, zu unterscheiden. Das dürfte bewusst vom Evangelisten so inszeniert worden sein, um im Kontrast dazu in v. 6 um so wirkungsvoller Jesus selbst als den Weg schlechthin proklamieren zu können." On 14:5 as a reading cue, see also Hans-Ulrich Weidemann, *Der Tod Jesu im Johannesevangelium: Die erste Abschiedsrede als Schlüsseltext für den Passions- und Osterbericht* (BZNW 122; Berlin: de Gruyter, 2004), 152.

[46] See Haenchen, *Johannesevangelium*, 475; Dietzfelbinger, *Das Evangelium nach Johannes 2*, 45.

[47] See Frey, *Eschatologie III*, 126.

[48] According to Johannes Neugebauer, *Die eschatologischen Aussagen in den johanneischen Abschiedsreden: Eine Untersuchung zu Johannes 13–17* (BWANT 140; Stuttgart: Kohlhammer, 1994), 103, Thomas had already partially answered his own question.

[49] See Dschulnigg, *Jesus begegnen*, 223; Frey, "Der zweifelnde Thomas," 12.

the center of the dialog with Thomas (14:6). This Johannine "Kompaktaussage"[50] augments the statement in 11:25 through a threefold self-identification. In fact, this "I am" statement can be seen as the summary of all the "I am" statements.[51] The semantic accent lies on "I am the way."[52] It is not Thomas who responds to Jesus' answer, but rather Philip (14:8). In comparison to Philip's objection, Thomas, with his question, appears to be more open to transformation.[53] Thus, Jesus does not respond to Thomas' question with a critical response as he does in his reply to Philip (14:9–10). However, Thomas' fitting reaction of faith continues to be missed (see 11:16).

Third Appearance (20:24–29)

Contextual Framework (20:1–31)

Thomas' three appearances are artfully correlated: both resurrection chapters, John 11 and 20, frame the Passion story.[54] The first farewell discourse provides the background for interpreting his appearance (13:31–14:31).[55]

The Easter story in John 20 is presented in four scenes, which are marked by an increase in tension and an amplification of the confession to Christ (20: [1–2], 3–10, 11–18, 19–23, 24–29).[56] As in the beginning chapter (1:35–51), the final chapter portrays Johannine characters coming to faith in a consecu-

---

[50] See Andreas Dettwiler, *Die Gegenwart des Erhöhten: Eine exegetische Studie zu den johanneischen Abschiedsreden (Joh 13,31–16,33) unter besonderer Berücksichtigung ihres Relecture-Charakters* (FRLANT 169; Göttingen: Vandenhoeck & Ruprecht, 1995), 165; in connection, Susanne Ruschmann, *Maria von Magdala im Johannesevangelium: Jüngerin – Zeugin – Lebensbotin* (NTAbh.NF 40; Münster: Aschendorff, 2002), 179. For a complete analysis of 14:6, see Theobald, *Herrenworte*, 305–22; Kirchschläger, *Nur ich bin die Wahrheit*, 207–14.

[51] See Wilckens, *Johannes*, 223–24.

[52] See Theobald, *Herrenworte*, 306–07, fn. 277.

[53] See Dschulnigg, *Jesus begegnen*, 226. For an opposite view, see Tilborg, *Johannesevangelium*, 207, who interprets this negatively in light of the repetition of Peter's question (13:36): "Kommunikativ bedeutet das, dass Thomas tut, als ob Jesus nicht auf die Frage des Petrus eingegangen sei, d. h.: er wird als jemand vorgestellt, der nicht gehorcht hat! Und sein Fragesatz offenbart, dass er sich sogar weigert, Jesus auf's Wort zu glauben. Um Nicht-bereitwillig-Sein und Widerwilligkeit geht es also." This interpretation ignores the literary technique that is used: a subtle forward movement in theological enlightenment through repetition, variation and amplification, as well as the didactic function of the questions (having a similar goal).

[54] See Kremer, *Lazarus*, 23. Concerning the context of 20:24–29, see also his "Hand," 2154–55.

[55] On the first farewell discourse as the key text for the Johannine Passion and Easter report, see Weidemann, *Der Tod Jesu*.

[56] On the subdivision of Joh 20 into scenes, see Schnelle, *Johannes*, 322–34; Rubel, *Erkenntnis und Bekenntnis*, 281–83; Jörg Frey, "'Ich habe den Herrn gesehen' (Joh 20,18): Entstehung, Inhalt und Vermittlung des Osterglaubens nach Johannes 20," in *Studien zu Matthäus und Johannes* (ed. Andreas Dettwiler and Uta Poplutz; ATANT 97; Zürich 2009), 267–84, 271.

tive, chain-like manner.⁵⁷ Mary Magdalene stands at the beginning of this chain (20:1-2, 11-18). John 20:17 is of special relevance in creating a mirror effect with Thomas' story. Whether Mary Magdalene touched the risen Christ or not depends upon the interpretation of the imperative μή μου ἅπτου (20:17a). This imperative should be translated as "don't hold on to me," not as a prohibition to touch him.⁵⁸ The first reason for having to let go of Jesus is his still incomplete ascension to the Father (20:17b; see 6:17, 62).⁵⁹ The second reason is his missionary assignment: Mary is to go and share the Easter message with his brothers (20:17c). In the narrative, Mary, the first witness, calls the Risen One κύριος (20:18). It remains unclear how the disciples reacted to Mary's news. Their initial fearful reaction in the following scene (20:19) indicates that hearing Mary's news without seeing and hearing for themselves did not immediately evoke faith.⁶⁰ This reaction of faith was only evoked in the encounter with the Crucified and Risen One on Easter Sunday (20:19-23). If one reads the mirror effect scene (6:16-21) in the context of the *lectio continua* of John 6, the reader is reminded of the celebration of Easter during the eucharist in the church service. This background should also be kept in mind in the case of the Sunday scene of 20:19-23 and its varied repetition in 20:24-29, a Johannine creation.⁶¹

---

⁵⁷ On the connection of John 1 and 20, see Martin Ebner, "Wer liebt mehr? Die liebende Jüngerin und der geliebte Jünger nach Joh 20,1-18," BZ 42 (1998): 39-55, here 50. On the Johannine interrelation between sight and belief in John 20, see Udo Schnelle, *Antidoketische Christologie im Johannesevangelium. Eine Untersuchung zur Stellung des vierten Evangeliums in der johanneischen Schule* (FRLANT 144; Göttingen: Vandenhoeck & Ruprecht, 1987), 156-61; Gruber, "Berührendes Sehen," 63-64.

⁵⁸ See Ruschmann, *Maria von Magdala*, 91-92; Michael Theobald, "Der johanneische Osterglaube und die Grenzen seiner narrativen Vermittlung (Joh 20)," in *Studien zum Corpus Iohanneum* (WUNT 267; Tübingen: Mohr Siebeck, 2010), 459-60; Weidemann, *Der Tod Jesu*, 460; Rubel, *Erkenntnis und Bekenntnis*, 267; Frey, "Entstehung, Inhalt und Vermittlung des Osterglaubens," 277-78; Gruber, "Berührendes Sehen," 75; Bennema, *Encountering Jesus*, 198-99.

⁵⁹ On the letting go of the previous community, see Ruschmann, *Maria von Magdala*, 196-97; Beate Kowalksi, "Der Gang zum leeren Grab (Joh 20,1-18) aus pragmatischer Sicht," *Geist und Leben* 73 (2000): 113-28, 115; Frey, "Entstehung, Inhalt und Vermittlung des Osterglaubens," 277-78. On the inter-textual relationship of 6:17, 62 and 20:17, see Popp, *Grammatik des Geistes*, 295, 394.

⁶⁰ See Ruschmann, *Maria von Magdala*, 95; Theobald, "Osterglaube," 466-67; Frey, "Entstehung, Inhalt und Vermittlung des Osterglaubens," 278.

⁶¹ The encounter of Thomas and the Risen One happens on the eighth day (20:26; see 20:19). In connection with the adverb πάλιν (20:26; see 11:8, 31, 44), this detail refers to the practice of Sunday church gatherings (see e. g. 1 Cor 16:2; Acts 1:10). See Rudolf Schnackenburg, *Das Johannesevangelium: Teil 3* (5th ed.; HTKNT IV; Freiburg: Herder, 1986), 394; Blank, *Das Evangelium nach Johannes* 4/3, 187-88; Schnelle, *Johannes*, 331; Wengst, *Das Johannesevangelium* 2, 316-17; Frey, *Eschatologie III*, 345; Jacob Kremer, "'Nimm deine Hand und lege sie in meine Seite!' Exegetische, hermeneutische und bibeltheologische Überlegungen zu Joh 20,24-29," in *The Four Gospels: Vol. 3 (FS F. Neiyrnck)* (ed. Frans van Segbroeck et al.; BETL 100; Louvain: Leuven University Press, 1992), 2153-81, 2163, 2168; Ebner, "Wer liebt

This passage is followed by the original book ending in 20:30–31. Taking into consideration contextual coherence, these verses serve as an indication of how to interpret the symbolic Thomas pericope.[62] This symbolic encounter story was also written down in order that "you may come to believe that Jesus is the Messiah, the Son of God, and that through believing you may have life in his name" (20:31).

Constellation of Characters

The constellation of characters in John 20 is purposefully configured. Thomas is one of the four explicitly named main characters within the narrative concept of the final chapter. After Mary Magdalene (20:1–2, 11–18), Peter, and the Beloved Disciple (20:3–10), he is the fourth and last individual disciple mentioned, and he is also the third character out of the circle of the Twelve (20:24–29). With Mary Magdalene he forms the sixth Johannine "gender pair."[63] As in the previous encounters, Jesus is the key figure in this concluding scene. As such, he is thematically connected with the disciples (20:26) and especially with Thomas (20:27–29).

The Believing One

The final encounter with the Risen One is introduced by Thomas' surprising contact with his fellow disciples (20:24–25).[64] He is described with the attribute "one of the Twelve" (ἑις ἐκ τῶν δώδεκα; 20:24). Because of this the readers are prompted to establish an association with the first appearance of the circle of Twelve. Except for John 20:24, this designation is only found in the key scene in John 6:67–71, which was already mentioned because of its correlation to John 11:16 and 14:5. It begins with a speech of Jesus to the "Twelve"

---

mehr?," 50; Rubel, *Erkenntnis und Bekenntnis*, 292. The use of the historical present and its reference to the Risen One (ἔρχεται; 20:26; λέγει; 20:27, 29) underlines the realization of the past as it was characteristic for church services. See Kremer, "Hand," 2156–57, 2163–64, 2167, 2169, 2172, fn. 57. On the connection with 20:19–23 and 20:24–29, see Schnelle, *Christologie*, 159; and, *Johannes*, 333–34; Dschulnigg, *Jesus begegnen*, 226–28; Rubel, *Erkenntnis und Bekenntnis*, 282–83, 293; Frey, "Der zweifelnde Thomas," 25–28.

[62] See Kremer, "Hand," 2155; Schnelle, *Johannes*, 331; Weidemann, *Der Tod Jesu*, 493–97; Gruber, "Berührendes Sehen," 80–82; Dschulnigg, *Jesus begegnen*, 229, 231; Bennema, *Encountering Jesus*, 167.

[63] On Mary Magdalene and Thomas as one of six "gender pairs" in the Gospel of John, see Beirne, *Women and Men*, 195–218 (see also Bennema, *Encountering Jesus*, 8–9). On the character combination, see also Dorothee A. Lee, "Partnership in Easter Faith: The Role of Mary Magdalene and Thomas in John 20," *JSNT* 58 (1995): 37–49; Heil, *Blood and Water*, 140–41; Werner Stenger, "Strukturale Lektüre der Ostergeschichte des Johannesevangeliums (Joh 19,31–21,25)," in *Strukturale Beobachtungen zum Neuen Testament* (ed. idem; NTTS 12; Leiden: Brill, 1990), 229–34; Weidemann, *Der Tod Jesu*, 508–10; Dietzfelbinger, *Das Evangelium nach Johannes 2*, 346; Most, *Finger in der Wunde*, 63–64.

[64] On the tension of the moment of surprise, see Dschulnigg, *Jesus begegnen*, 227–29.

(6:67) and ends with the assertion that Judas, one of the selected "Twelve," is a διάβολος (6:70–71). At the scene's conclusion Judas is pointedly designated as εἷς ἐκ τῶν δώδεκα. It is this singular reception of the phrase in John 20:24 that evokes the question of the relation between Judas and Thomas,[65] a question that can only be answered with the knowledge of the overall narrative.

Furthermore, the repetition of the attribute ὁ λεγόμενος Δίδυμος links back to the scene of Thomas' first appearance (20:24; see 11:16). First of all it is stated – without further reasoning or criticism – that Thomas was absent at the preceding epiphany (20:24).[66] This hint prepares the reader for Thomas' previously established special encounter with the Risen One. The other disciples, who are empowered and ready for mission, share the news with him "… im Wir-Stil der Wissenden,"[67] stressing the immediacy (οὖν): "*We* have seen the Lord" (20:25a; see 20:18).[68] This news *must* provoke a reaction from Thomas.[69] With his answer Thomas does not call into question their encounter with Christ.[70] He is, therefore, not a doubter.[71] He, who at his second appearance in the narrative recognized his lack of knowledge and wanted explanations (14:5), again in this scene, wants to know for himself.[72] He expects no more than what has been bestowed upon his fellow disciples and before them Mary Magdalene (20:25; see 20:18, 20).[73] He wants to ascertain through his

---

[65] See Dietzfelbinger, *Das Evangelium nach Johannes 2*, 342. For a different opinion, see Rubel, *Erkenntnis und Bekenntnis*, 288.

[66] On the Johannine stylistic technique of absence, see Thyen, *Das Johannesevangelium*, 768–69; Farelly, *Disciples in the Fourth Gospel*, 122.

[67] See Karl Löning and Erich Zenger, *Als Anfang schuf Gott: Biblische Schöpfungstheologien* (Düsseldorf: Patmos, 1997), 116.

[68] See Kremer, "Hand," 2158–59.

[69] See Stenger, "Strukturale Lektüre," 227–28.

[70] See Gruber, "Berührendes Sehen," 64, fn. 14, 79. For a different opinion, see William Bonney, *Caused to Believe: The Doubting Thomas Story at the Climax of John's Christological Narrative* (Biblical Interpretation Series 62; Leiden: Brill, 2002), 159; Theobald, "Osterglaube," 467; Farelly, *Disciples in the Fourth Gospel*, 123–25.

[71] See also Bennema, *Encountering Jesus*, 166. For an opposite view, see Frey, "Entstehung, Inhalt und Vermittlung des Osterglaubens," 280–81.

[72] For Blank, *Das Evangelium nach Johannes 4/3*, 187, Thomas appears "gleichsam als der 'erste Cartesianer vor Descartes,' als ein ausgesprochen 'moderner Mensch.'" According to Dschulnigg (*Jesus begegnen*, 231), Thomas is "fast wie ein verfrühtes Kind der Aufklärung." Dietzfelbinger, *Das Evangelium nach Johannes 2*, 342, states that Thomas did not want to believe simply because others believed. See also Roman Kühschelm, "Spiritualität aus dem Neuen Testament: Glaubenserfahrung und bleibende Christusbeziehung bei Paulus und Johannes," in *Spiritualität – mehr als ein Megatrend* (FS F. König) (ed. Paul M. Zulehner; Ostfildern: Schwabenverlag, 2004), 156–74, 171; Thyen, *Das Johannesevangelium*, 769; Farelly, *Disciples in the Fourth Gospel*, 122.

[73] See Schenke, *Johannes*, 379–80; Frey, "Entstehung, Inhalt und Vermittlung des Osterglaubens," 278, 280. Applicable is also Bennema, *Encountering Jesus*, 167: "Thomas simply demands what the others got – a first-hand experience of the risen Jesus – and it is graciously granted to him." According to Kremer, "Hand," 2161, fn. 22, this motif of being convinced by

own touch and sight that the Risen One is identical with the Crucified One.[74] Thomas is obstinate in a positive sense: He can only authentically believe through immediate sensory contact with the Risen One. In contrast to the previous appearances and experiences of Thomas, he now demands solid – tangible – proof in this scene (see 2:18; 4:48; 6:30).[75] Thus he carries the bodily concretization to the extreme.[76] The conditions for his belief are visual and tactile communication.[77] He does not only want to see, but also longs for palpable proof. He gives weight to this condition by using three negative particles in his answer: If he does not see (ἐὰν μή) in Jesus' hands (χεῖρες) the wounds of the nails and if he does not place his fingers in the holes of the nails and his hands in Jesus' side (πλευρά), he will "never ever" (οὐ μή) believe (20:25b). On the symbolic level this is a pneumatological-soteriological statement: the Spirit rests in the hand of Christ (see χείρ; 3:34–35) and flows out of his side (πλευρά; 19:34; see 20:20). Without the Spirit there is no faith (see 7:37–39).[78] In the emphatic οὐ μὴ πιστεύσω the semantic field of πίστις is taken up again and set in contrast with John 20:8: Thomas is correlated with the Beloved Disciple, who believed when merely faced with the empty tomb. Here a relationship is established with Thomas' first appearance: now the time has come for a definite answer – for Thomas (20:27–29a) as well as for the reader (20:29–31):[79]

---

sight is often found in pagan and Jewish literature (e. g., Philostratus *Vit. Apoll.* VIII,12; Midr Ruth 3:9).

[74] On the crucial aspects of the oneness of the Risen One with the Crucified One in 20:24–29, see Herbert Kohler, *Kreuz und Menschwerdung im Johannesevangelium: Ein exegetisch-hermeneutischer Versuch zur johanneischen Kreuzestheologie* (ATANT 72; Zürich: Theologischer Verlag, 1987), 159–91; Schnelle, *Christologie*, 156–61; Manfred Lang, *Johannes und die Synoptiker: Eine redaktionsgeschichtliche Analyse von Joh 18–20 vor dem markinischen und lukanischen Hintergrund* (FRLANT 182; Göttingen: Vandenhoeck & Ruprecht, 1999), 287–94; Frey, *Eschatologie III*, 280–82; Haenchen, *Johannesevangelium*, 573; Wengst, *Das Johannesevangelium 2*, 316–20; Gruber, "Berührendes Sehen," 64, fn. 64 (Lit.!), 78, 81–82.

[75] For the correlation with 2:18, 4:48 and 6:30, see Keener, *John*, 1208; Kremer, "Hand," 2163; Theobald, "Osterglaube," 467–71; Gruber, "Berührendes Sehen," 64–69. With regard to 4:48, see also Frey, "Der zweifelnde Thomas," 26.

[76] See Löning and Zenger, *Als Anfang schuf Gott*, 117.

[77] Heil, *Blood and Water*, 141–42, sees here an intensifying, individualizing, and contrasting development. One could also speak of a typical Johannine amplification.

[78] On Jesus as the giver of the Spirit in 3:34–35, see Popp, *Grammatik des Geistes*, 225–28. With regard to 7:37–39 and 19:34–35, see Heil, *Blood and Water*, 141; Kremer, *Lazarus*, 341; also, "Hand," 2161–62, 2178; Gruber, "Berührendes Sehen," 63, 75.

[79] Wengst, *Das Johannesevangelium 2*, 26–27 (with regard to 11:16) aptly comments: "Mit der Gestalt des Thomas spannt Johannes somit einen Bogen von der ersten Erwähnung in 11,16 bis fast zum Ende seines Evangeliums. Er beantwortet damit zugleich auch die Frage: 'Wann werden die Jünger wirklich glauben?' Sie hatte sich dadurch ergeben, dass zwar in V. 15 als Ziel des Handelns Jesu an Lazarus der Glaube seiner Schüler angegeben worden war, im Verlauf der Erzählung aber kein entsprechender Glaube festgestellt wird."

11:15:   ἵνα πιστεύσητε
20:25:   οὐ μὴ πιστεύσω
20:27:   μὴ γίνου ἄπιστος ἀλλὰ πιστός
20:29a: πεπίστευκας
20:29b: πιστεύσαντες
20:31:   ἵνα πιστεύ[σ]ητε

Faith is made possible through the coming of Jesus. He appears in the midst (μέσος) of his disciples and grants them all peace, including Thomas (20:26; see 20:19). Then he addresses Thomas in a special way. In a sense he offers him a private Easter experience.[80] The Risen One knows word for word what Thomas demanded in 20:25 (see 1:48; 2:24–25; 4:17–18).[81] He goes towards him (see ἔρχομαι; 20:26), thereby affirming Thomas' desire for an immediate, personal faith experience, and honors him with a private Christophany.[82] His affirmation of Thomas' three-fold demand is articulated unmistakably in five imperatives (φέρε; ἴδε; φέρε; βάλε; γίνου). Thomas is to stretch out his finger, to see Jesus' hands and stretch out his hand to put it (20:27a) in Jesus' side (πλευρά; see 19:34; 20:20, 25)[83].

With this invitation to a physical encounter with Christ – an eye-opening self-revelation of God – the fulfillment of both pre-Easter demands for signs in 2:18 and 6:30 is presented in an impactful narrative-symbolic form.[84] This is linked with the emphatic pneumatological-performative call from unbelief to belief (μὴ γίνου ἄπιστος ἀλλὰ πιστός; 20:27b; see οὐ μὴ πιστεύσω; 20:25b).[85] This coming to faith is a gift and an invitation. The Risen One gives to all what he has offered in a special lesson to Thomas (see 6:63). The character of Thomas may represent the "unbelief of believers."[86] In this way Thomas is an out-

---

[80] "... gewissermaßen sein eigenes Osterfest." See Rubel, *Erkenntnis und Bekenntnis*, 292.

[81] See Dietzfelbinger, *Das Evangelium nach Johannes 2*, 343; Kremer, "Hand," 2164. According to Bonney, *The Doubting Thomas Story*, 165–66, this wonderful foreknowledge of Jesus leads Thomas to faith.

[82] See Theobald, "Osterglaube," 468–69; also Michael Theobald, "'Wie mich der Vater gesandt hat, so sende ich euch' (Joh 20,21): Missionarische Gestalten im Johannesevangelium," in *Studien zum Corpus Iohanneum*, 485; Frey, "Entstehung, Inhalt und Vermittlung des Osterglaubens," 281; Wilfried Eisele, *Welcher Thomas? Studien zur Text- und Überlieferungsgeschichte des Thomasevangeliums* (WUNT 259; Tübingen: Mohr Siebeck, 2010), 58–59.

[83] According to Gruber, "Berührendes Sehen," 62, the inchoative aorist βάλε which expresses the intimacy of the scene prompts the readers to ask on a more profound level: "Zu welcher Berührung wird Thomas vom Auferstandenen aufgefordert? Welche Bedingung des Osterglaubens wird ihm dadurch erfüllt?"

[84] On this enlightening thesis, see Gruber, "Berührendes Sehen," 67–69.

[85] According to Weidemann, *Der Tod Jesu*, 490, Thomas' faith is evoked by the last imperative. On the constitution of his faith through the Risen One, see also Frey, "Entstehung, Inhalt und Vermittlung des Osterglaubens," 281–83.

[86] On this change, see Walter Rebell, *Gemeinde als Gegenwelt: Zur soziologischen und didaktischen Funktion des Johannesevangeliums* (BBET 20; Frankfurt: Lang, 1987); also Louis Walter, *L'incroyance des croyants selon Saint Jean* (LiBi 43; Paris: Editions du Cerf, 1976).

standing positive role model. The reader can test and validate his/her faith in the Risen One through identification with him.[87] Therefore this text is about awakening the faith of the believers and strengthening their responsibility to move towards mature faith.[88] It reveals the Christ event as a salvific, transformative event centering on a personal relationship. The leading disciple, who was not present at the first appearance (20:19–23) is now included in the saving events through the climactic exceptional appearance [of Christ]. The Crucified and Risen One draws Thomas to himself through his faith-generating (γίνου) words (see ἑλκύω; 6:44; 12:32).[89] Thomas accepts the invitation of the One who entered through closed doors (see 20:26) and he, in return, enters through Jesus, the door (see 10:9). This is expressed in his adequate Christ-centered testimony (20:28).[90] In contrast to Jesus' speech (λέγει; 20:27), it is not presented in the historical present, but in the aorist (ἀπεκρίθη). The narrative level of concurrency is again abandoned and, through the oscillation of the reader's perspective, the time difference is called into memory. Thomas' exemplary testimony has biblical connotations (ὁ κύριός μου καὶ ὁ θεός μου – ὁ θεός μου καὶ ὁ κύριός μου; Ps 34:23 LXX).[91] As indicated by the designation of time in 20:26 (see 20:19), this credo could stem from a liturgical Eucharistic context.[92]

---

[87] See Kremer, "Hand," 2170; Beate Kowalski, *Die Hirtenrede (Joh 10,1–18) im Kontext des Johannesevangeliums* (SBB 31; Stuttgart: Verlag Katholisches Bibelwerk, 1996), 218, fn. 164, 226–27, 333–34.

[88] See Klaus Scholtissek, "Mündiger Glaube: Zur Architektur und Pragmatik johanneischer Begegnungsgeschichten," in *Paulus und Johannes: Exegetische Studien zur paulinischen und johanneischen Theologie und Literatur* (ed. Dieter Sänger and Ulrich Mell; WUNT 198; Tübingen: Mohr Siebeck, 2006), 75–105; also Rubel, *Erkenntnis und Bekenntnis*, 348–50.

[89] See Kremer, "Hand," 2178–79.

[90] Bennema, *Encountering Jesus*, 170, also states that Thomas "eventually adequately believes" and classifies (Bennema, *Encountering Jesus*, 205–206) Thomas' reaction in terms of the following types of response: "acceptance (of Jesus and his revelation)," "open/public confession" and "signs-faith." According to Wilckens, *Johannes*, 318, Thomas comes "zum vollkommenen Glauben an Jesus." According to Dietzfelbinger, *Das Evangelium nach Johannes 2*, 346, he reacts "mit der höchsten der johanneischen Bekenntnisaussagen;" so too Kohler, *Kreuz und Menschwerdung*, 182; Frey, *Eschatologie III*, 280; and "Entstehung, Inhalt und Vermittlung des Osterglaubens," 281; and Frey, "Der zweifelnde Thomas," 5, 13; Schenke, *Johannes*, 370; Weidemann, *Der Tod Jesu*, 491, 493, 512; Andreas Leinhäupl-Wilke, *Rettendes Wissen im Johannesevangelium: Ein Zugang über die narrativen Rahmentexte (1,19–2,12 – 20,1–21,25)* (NTAbh 45; Münster: Aschendorff, 2003), 289–90; Thyen, *Das Johannesevangelium*, 769; Martina Kumlehn, *Geöffnete Augen - gedeutete Zeichen: Historisch-systematische und erzähltheoretisch-hermeneutische Studien zur Rezeption und Didaktik des Johannesevangeliums in der modernen Religionspädagogik* (Praktische Theologie im Wissenschaftsdiskurs 1; Berlin: de Gruyter, 2007), 321; Farelly, *Disciples in the Fourth Gospel*, 118, 126; Lang, *Kunst des christlichen Lebens*, 639.

[91] See Schnelle, *Christologie*, 158; and *Johannes*, 332; Kremer, "Hand," 2166; Weidemann, *Der Tod Jesu*, 491; Leinhäupl-Wilke, *Rettendes Wissen*, 290–91; Dschulnigg, *Jesus begegnen*, 229–30; Rubel, *Erkenntnis und Bekenntnis*, 308; Most, *Finger in der Wunde*, 80.

[92] Referring to 20:19–23, Barrett, *Das Evangelium nach Johannes*, 549, mentions the gath-

The conferral of God's attributes to Jesus may also be interpreted as a criticism of the imperial cult.[93] Domitian allowed himself the title *dominus et (ac) deus* (e. g., Suetonius *Dom.* 13:1–2; Mart. 5.8.1).[94] This arrogant claim is contradicted when Thomas uses the verbatim phrase from the context of early Christian liturgy in his fearlessly pronounced acknowledgment of faith. The two-fold use of the possessive pronoun μου – in amplification of Mary Magdalene's simple μου (20,13) – emphasizes the distinctly personal connotation of Thomas' words.[95]

As can be expected within the context of ancient rhetoric, the final confession of faith is both thematically and hermeneutically correlated with the beginning. It corresponds artfully with the Prologue (1:1–18). Thus the narrative alignment is organized in a linear way from beginning to end throughout the whole Gospel: Jesus represents God's exclusive manifestation on earth (1:1, 14, 18–20:28; see 10:30).[96] Thomas' credo constitutes the climax in the line of Johannine recognition sentences, which are primarily employed as climactic conclusions to the dialogue scenes (see 1:14–18; 1:49; 4:42; 6:69; 9:38; 16:30; 20:16, 18; see also 1 John 5:20–21).[97] The confessions of the Johannine church (1:18), of Nathanael (1:49) and Thomas form an *inclusion* which encompasses the whole Gospel:

---

ering on the Lord's Day, the gift of benediction and the Holy Spirit, as well as the promise of absolution, and aptly remarks with respect to 20:24–29: "Christus selbst ist gegenwärtig (dies können die Eucharistie und das gesprochene Wort Gottes nahe legen), und er trägt die Zeichen seiner Passion; er wird bekannt als Herr und Gott (vgl. Pliny the Younger, Ep. X,96,7, carmenque Christo quasi deo dicere)." According to Kremer also, "Hand," 2157, 2168, the acclamation of Thomas is borrowed from liturgy.

[93] See Schnelle, *Johannes*, 332; Tilborg, *Johannesevangelium*, 302, 306; Siegert, *Johannes*, 615–16; Keener, *John*, 1211–12; Bennema, *Encountering Jesus*, 166, fn. 10; cautiously Thyen, *Das Johannesevangelium*, 769. According to Dschulnigg, *Jesus begegnen*, 230, an anti-imperial connotation is not clearly stated. Schnackenburg, *Johannes 3. Teil*, 397, reckons that an attack on the imperial cult can hardly be assumed. See also Rubel, *Erkenntnis und Bekenntnis*, 309.

[94] See Most, *Finger in der Wunde*, 80; Thomas Popp, "Die Kunst der Wiederholung: Repetition, Variation und Amplifikation im vierten Evangelium am Beispiel von Johannes 6,60–71," in *Kontexte des Johannesevangeliums: Das vierte Evangelium in religions- und traditionsgeschichtlicher Perspektive* (ed. Jörg Frey and Udo Schnelle; WUNT 175; Tübingen: Mohr Siebeck, 2004), 246–47.

[95] On the personal tone in 20:28, see Rubel, *Erkenntnis und Bekenntnis*, 308, 339.

[96] See Schenke, *Johannes*, 415. For the clear reference of 20:28 back to 1:1, 18, see Schnelle, *Johannes*, 332; Wengst, *Das Johannesevangelium 2*, 318–19; Keener, *John*, 1208, fn. 366, 1211; Kremer, "Hand," 2167; Leinhäupl-Wilke, *Rettendes Wissen*, 289.

[97] See Popp, *Grammatik des Geistes*, 57, fn. 55 (Lit.!); Schnackenburg, *Johannes 3. Teil*, 397–98; Schenke, *Johannes*, 380; Dietzfelbinger, *Das Evangelium nach Johannes 2*, 346; Heil, *Blood and Water*, 143–44; Dschulnigg, *Jesus begegnen*, 229–31; Leinhäupl-Wilke, *Rettendes Wissen*, 289; Rubel, *Erkenntnis und Bekenntnis*, 310. On the correspondence with 1 John 5:20–21, see Thyen, *Das Johannesevangelium*, 769; Hans-Josef Klauck, *Der erste Johannesbrief* (EKKNT 23/1; Zürich: Benziger, 1991), 339; Georg Strecker, *Die Johannesbriefe* (KEK 14; Göttingen: Vandenhoeck & Ruprecht, 1989), 309–10; Weidemann, *Der Tod Jesu*, 491–92, fn. 199; Udo Schnelle, *Die Johannesbriefe* (THKNT 17; Leipzig: Evangelische Verlagsanstalt, 2010), 183–84; Frey, *Eschatologie III*, 90; Kremer, "Hand," 2167.

1:18: μονογενὴς θεός (see θεὸς ἦν ὁ λόγος; 1:1c)
1:49: ὁ υἱὸς τοῦ θεοῦ
20:28: ὁ κύριός μου καὶ ὁ θεός μου

The introduction and conclusion reveal an exact theological correspondence. Moreover, through the identification of Jesus as κυριός, John 20 generates a relationship between the confession of Mary Magdalene (20:18) and that of the disciples (20:25; see 20:20). In both cases, their sight was connected to an experience of physical contact (20:17, 22).[98] It is not narrated whether Thomas actually acts as Jesus demands and touches him.[99] Through the stimulation of the readers' power of imagination diverse possibilities of interpretation are created. Furthermore, because of the fictive nature of the Thomas-figure, this cannot be determined by a historical quest as to the first disciples' Easter experience, but rather by an "ein Abwägen narrativer Möglichkeiten."[100] If Thomas had shied away from touching Jesus, he would have been untrue to himself (see 20:25) and he would have been unfaithful to the call of the Risen One (see 20:27). The one who said that he would "never ever" (οὐ μή; 20:25b) believe without touching, becomes – through an experience of touching the Risen Crucified One – the one who utters the greatest Christological confession in the Fourth Gospel. The Thomas pericope thus presents the final amplification of touching of the Risen One in John 20.[101]

In the section following the Thomas credo (beginning without a connecting particle), the present Christ speaks again (λέγει; 20:29a). First he notes Thomas' faith resulting from sight (ὅτι ἑώρακάς με) by the perfect form πεπίστευκας (20:29a).[102] On macro- and micro-levels this is linked to Thomas' first and

---

[98] See Bultmann, *Johannes*, 539; Bennema, *Encountering Jesus*, 166–67.

[99] For the controversial interpretation of this gap, see Kremer, "Hand," 2153–81, who assumes that there was no actual physical contact; also Blank, *Das Evangelium nach Johannes 4/3*, 188–89; Schenke, *Johannes*, 380; Dietzfelbinger, *Das Evangelium nach Johannes 2*, 343; Siegert, *Johannes*, 614–15; Theobald, "Osterglaube," 468–69; Rubel, *Erkenntnis und Bekenntnis*, 307–308; Leinhäupl-Wilke, *Rettendes Wissen*, 287–88; Klaus Scholtissek, "Mystik im Johannesevangelium? Reflexionen zu einer umstrittenen Fragestellung," in *Pneuma und Gemeinde: Christsein in der Tradition des Paulus und Johannes (FS J. Hainz)* (ed. Jost Eckert et al.; Düsseldorf: Patmos, 2001), 321; Jean Zumstein, "Narratologische Lektüre der johanneischen Ostergeschichte," in *Kreative Erinnerung: Relecture und Auslegung im Johannesevangelium* (ATANT 84; Zürich: Theologischer Verlag, 2004), 283; Frey, "Entstehung, Inhalt und Vermittlung des Osterglaubens," 281; "Der zweifelnde Thomas," 32; Most, *Finger in der Wunde*, 85–87, 99–104, 135–36, 268. For an opposite interpretation, see Schnelle, *Johannes*, 332, fn. 48; Weidemann, *Der Tod Jesu*, 492; Gruber, "Berührendes Sehen," 61–83. On the possibilities of both options, see Schnackenburg, *Johannes 3. Teil*, 395–96.

[100] Frey, "Entstehung, Inhalt und Vermittlung des Osterglaubens," 281, fn. 70; see also "Der zweifelnde Thomas," 24–26.

[101] For the way in which the reader is guided step by step in John 20, see Gruber, "Berührendes Sehen," 74–76.

[102] This sentence is not to be understood as a question but rather as a statement. See Kremer, "Hand," 2167; Schnelle, *Johannes*, 333; Rubel, *Erkenntnis und Bekenntnis*, 311–12.

second appearance (πεπίστευκα; 11:27; καὶ ἑωράκατε αὐτόν; 14:7). Again this implies no reproach, but rather recognizes Thomas' faith explicitly.[103] Also the following Beatitude is no criticism of the last eyewitness, but rather directed at the readers as a group (μακάριοι; see 13:17), who have listened to Thomas' witness (20:29b). Together with the Beloved Disciple (see 19:35), Thomas is an exemplary representation of the Johannine community. The readers, born at a later stage, had to rely on their witness of the events (see 20:30–31; 1 John 1:1).[104] By means of the Spirit an experience of faith became a reality for them too, through a reading of the text and a recurring, deepening encounter with him (see 14:7 together with 14:15–26).[105] Herein the series of instructions for readers starting with 1:50–51 (see 1:49–20:28) comes to an end: as such, as the not seeing "and yet" (καί) believing, they are blessed (see e. g., 1 Peter 1:8).[106] The adversative καί is not to be interpreted as a negation of the importance of the actual touching of Christ, "sondern auf die vom Auferstandenen anerkannte und durch die Seligpreisung honorierte Schwierigkeit, ohne die Hilfe einer Erscheinung zum vollen Osterglauben zu gelangen."[107] If the concluding

---

[103] See Schnelle, *Johannes*, 332–33; Kohler, *Kreuz und Menschwerdung*, 190–91; Kremer, "Hand," 2167; Weidemann, *Der Tod Jesu*, 492; Rubel, *Erkenntnis und Bekenntnis*, 311–12; Frey, "Entstehung, Inhalt und Vermittlung des Osterglaubens," 280–81; also Frey, "Der zweifelnde Thomas," 30–31; Gruber, "Berührendes Sehen," 77–79. For an opposite interpretation, see Bultmann, *Johannes*, 539; Kühschelm, "Spiritualität aus dem Neuen Testament," 171; Dschulnigg, *Jesus begegnen*, 230, fn. 232. Also Bennema, *Encountering Jesus*, 167, regards 20:29 as a "mild rebuke directed at Thomas" and associates this disciple with those "who are pragmatic and want a tangible experience of Jesus in order to believe; loyal pragmatists who desire tangible experiences but who are encouraged to a steadier faith that is less dependent on the concrete and physical" (Bennema, *Encountering Jesus*, 210).

[104] See Kremer, "Hand," 2168, 2178. For the necessity of the message of the eyewitnesses, see also Schnelle, *Johannes*, 333–34; Wengst, *Das Johannesevangelium 2*, 314–15, 321; Heil, *Blood and Water*, 145; Bonney, *The Doubting Thomas Story*, 169–71; Bennema, *Encountering Jesus*, 168. For an opposite view, see Theobald, "Osterglaube," 469–71; Gruber, "Berührendes Sehen," 76–77. On the (possible) relation with 1 John 1:1, see Klauck, *Der erste Johannesbrief*, 61; Strecker, *Johannesbriefe*, 60; Kremer, "Hand," 2173, 2180; Beirne, *Women and Men*, 211. For an opposite view, see Schnelle, *Johannesbriefe*, 63–64.

[105] On the repeated reading of the Gospel of John as the fulfilling of the Beatitude, see Gruber, "Berührendes Sehen," 82. On the importance of the reading of the book as a medium of faith in the light of 20:30–31, see Thomas Söding, "Die Schrift als Medium des Glaubens: Zur hermeneutischen Bedeutung von Joh 20,30f.," in *Schrift und Tradition (FS J. Ernst)* (ed. Knut Backhaus and Franz G. Untergaßmair; Paderborn: Schöningh, 1996), 343–71; Weidemann, *Der Tod Jesu*, 496–97; Frey, "Entstehung, Inhalt und Vermittlung des Osterglaubens," 283–84. On the Johannine notion of the book as a means of communication offering evidence of saving knowledge, see Leinhäupl-Wilke, *Rettendes Wissen*; as well as his "Rettet ein Buch? Spurensuche in den Rahmenteilen des Johannesevangeliums," in *Rettendes Wissen: Studien zum Fortgang weisheitlichen Denkens im Frühjudentum und im frühen Christentum* (ed. Karl Löning and Martin Fassnacht; AOAT 300; Münster: Ugarit-Verlag, 2002), 269–315.

[106] On the adversative καί, see Kremer, "Hand," 2168, 2170; Gruber, "Berührendes Sehen," 77. On 1 Peter 1:8 and John 20:29, see also Keener, *John*, 1212; Popp, "Die Kunst der Wiederholung," 154.

[107] Gruber, "Berührendes Sehen," 77. For an opposite view, see Kremer, "Hand," 2168.

Beatitude of the Thomas pericope is read in terms of an intra-textual play with the first Beatitude (13:17), this encourages the readers to return to their own world.[108] Their faith in Jesus is constituted and stabilized through their reading of the recorded testimony of the eyewitnesses in the Gospel (see 20:30–31).

Fourth Reference (21:2)

In the supplemental chapter, John 21,[109] Thomas appears with the title of "twin" (see 11:16; 20:24) in the list of the seven disciples; after Simon Peter and before Nathanael, right in the second position (21:2). Through his prominent place in this list a strong correlation to the beginning (1:35–51) and to the end (20:24–29) of the original Gospel is established. Of the first five who were named (1:35–51) the only one not in the list of the seven disciples is Philip. He had his last appearance directly after Thomas and showed himself there as less open to change (see 14:5–11). He is substituted by Thomas. Through the "second chance" (20:24–29) offered to him, Thomas is also authorized for mission (see 20:19–23). He thus belongs to the same category as Peter and Nathanael – eyewitnesses and messengers of the Risen One.[110] To be sure, in the supplemental chapter, Thomas and the other disciples do not recognize the Risen One at first as they did in 20:24–29.[111] That which was indicated in 20:24–29 in connection with 6:22–59 and 13:1–20, is fulfilled explicitly in 21:1–14: faith by sight results in the Easter meal.[112]

Looking Back: Thomas – A Character that Could be Transformed

In the encounter with Jesus questions come to the fore and answers are found. This is shown in an exceptional way by Thomas' faith-biography – a biography illustrating an openness to transformation. This "man of extremes"[113] is one of the main characters in the Fourth Gospel. The way in which he is char-

---

[108] See Blank, *Das Evangelium nach Johannes 4/3*, 189; Jean Zumstein, "Die johanneische Ostergeschichte als Erzählung gelesen," ZNT 2 (1999): 12–13, 16, 18. On the intra-textual relation of 13:17 to 20:29, see Dschulnigg, *Jesus begegnen*, 230–31.

[109] For relative consensus about the secondary character of John 21, see Schnelle, *Johannes*, 339–40; Popp, *Grammatik des Geistes*, 79, fn. 168 (Lit.!). According to Gruber, "Berührendes Sehen," 74, fn. 47, the last word has not yet been spoken on this question.

[110] According to Dschulnigg, *Jesus begegnen*, 233, Thomas and Nathanael do not belong "mit zur idealen Siebenzahl von Jüngern, welche zur Mission aufbricht und darin ganz vom Wort und Auftrag Jesu abhängig bleibt." On the missionary dimension of 21:1–14, see Theobald, "Vater," 485–86; Hartenstein, *Charakterisierung im Dialog*, 223, 243.

[111] See Kremer, "Hand," 2155.

[112] See Martin Hasitschka, "Die beiden 'Zeichen' am See von Tiberias: Interpretation von Joh 6 in Verbindung mit Joh 21,1–14," SNTSU 24 (1999): 85–102; Gruber, "Berührendes Sehen," 68–69, 73–74, 76, 83.

[113] See Farelly, *Disciples in the Fourth Gospel*, 118, fn. 165.

acterized narratively by means of dialogues is an excellent example of Johannine individualization of persons, which ensures the uniqueness of persons without sacrificing the personal social nature of any individual.[114]

His poignant story is exciting from the beginning to the end. Because of the experiences which Thomas has throughout the course of the story, he is being changed. He is therefore not a static character; rather a complex character marked by growth.[115] He is formed and developed step by step. Thomas grows into Easter faith.

With this dynamic character sketch the readers are also involved in a didactic spiral, becoming more involved and thereby entering deeper into the mystery of the Christ event.[116] The pre-Easter relationship of Jesus and Thomas and the post-Easter relationship of Christ and the reader are thus effectively and simultaneously inter-related.

The process of change that Thomas undergoes creates an ambiguity (11:16; 14:5) in terms of both of his pre-Easter appearances. The situation here is precarious: The departure of Jesus is imminent. The first presentation of Thomas is "a positive illustration;"[117] he plays the role of a man who is determined to follow his own journey of faith. Thomas is thus the first one to grasp that, for the future community of Jesus, discipleship will imply a common destiny with Jesus, even though he still lacks some key notions if compared to the post-Easter community (11:16).

In a profound way Thomas' saying functions as a reformulation of Jesus' call to disciples to follow him to the cross, issued to "allen seinen 'Mitjüngern' bis heute."[118]

At the beginning of the first farewell discourse (13:31–14:31), Thomas again plays a prominent role as the spokesperson for the disciples. He is the first one to ask the pivotal question regarding the destination of the parting Jesus (14:5). This questioning "Bekenntnis der Unkenntnis"[119] again shows his readiness to

---

[114] On Johannine personalization and individualization as well as the avoidance of limited individual characterizations, see Popp, *Grammatik des Geistes*, 29–30, 53, fn. 39 (Lit.!), 91, 370, 429; Michael Theobald, "Wer ist Jesus für mich persönlich? Identifikationsangebote des Johannesevangeliums," in *Studien zum Corpus Iohanneum*, 678; Beirne, *Women and Men*, 205–206, 215–18.

[115] On the aspect of the development of faith in the case of Mary Magdalene and Thomas, see Beirne, *Women and Men*, 213–15, 218; for Thomas, see also Leinhäupl-Wilke, *Rettendes Wissen*, 291; Farelly, *Disciples in the Fourth Gospel*, 118. For an opposite view, see Bennema, *Encountering Jesus*, 170, 203. On the complex character of Thomas, see Bennema, *Encountering Jesus*, 170, 203; Farelly, *Disciples in the Fourth Gospel*, 118.

[116] On the spiral form of Johannine thought, see Popp, *Grammatik des Geistes*, 68–69 (fn. 117 Lit.!), 85–89, 127–28, 155–56, 179–80, 239, 250–51, 263, 318, 351, 354–55, 434–35, 444, 450, 466, 478. On the "didaktischen Spirale" in the Gospel of John, see also Jean Zumstein, "Das Johannesevangelium: Eine Strategie des Glaubens," in *Kreative Erinnerung*, 40.

[117] Keener, *John*, 842.

[118] Kremer, *Lazarus*, 355.

walk the road with Jesus. As was the case at his first appearance (11:16), the uncertainty of his question is caused by the limitations characteristic of the difference in time before and after Easter. This also makes possible a step-by-step development of his confession.[120] Thomas' lack of understanding, which is representative of the disciples' lack of understanding, serves to make the truth constantly clearer.[121] He is depicted as worthy of receiving a central "I am" saying of Jesus. The adequate faith response he will only offer at his third appearance.

Following a bold exclamation mark (11:16), Thomas travels from an understandable question mark (14:5), back to a bold exclamation mark (20:28), but one now informed by the post-Easter situation. This communicative learning process which he moves through climaxes in his special encounter with the Risen Crucified One (20:24–29). This example of narrative-dialogical Christology (see 11:1–44), that reads like a narrative realization of 1 John 1:1, creates the high and key points of the Easter story in chapter 20. Only in the third encounter does Jesus' focus on Thomas become explicit and have a great effect upon him. The arc thus reaches from the end of the first part to the end of the second part and the journey of Thomas builds to a grand finale. John 20:24–29 completes, with a perfect liturgical staging, the concluding, fitting faith-response of the Thomas-trilogy. Such individualizing staging strengthens the knowledge component in his faith. For the first time Jesus' action and Thomas' nonverbal and verbal reaction correspond. The unanswered dialogue of 14:5–7 is thus completed by 20:28 (see 6:20–26, 68–69). This dynamic dramatic composition of Thomas' character is expressed in the intense process of journeying from unbelief to experiential faith to confessing faith.[122]

At the end of Thomas' journey the readers are faced yet again with the question: Whose twin is Thomas or likewise who is his twin? In the textual references of the Fourth Gospel multiple cross-references between Thomas and other (individual) characters are established and have theological significance:[123]

1. A comparison with Nathanael is revealing: both at the beginning and at the end one sees a sympathetic skeptic, who does not want to believe blindly, reacting appropriately to Jesus. Thomas' confession surpasses that

---

[119] Kirchschläger, *Nur ich bin die Wahrheit*, 205.

[120] With regard to the function of this intended ambiguity in Thomas' question, see Dietzfelbinger, *Das Evangelium nach Johannes 2*, 45: "Aus ihm entwickelt sich die mehrschichtige Lösung des Problems. Sie erfolgt in deutlich erkennbaren Schritten." See also Kirchschläger, *Nur ich bin die Wahrheit*, 206.

[121] See Thyen, *Das Johannesevangelium*, 622.

[122] See Popp, *Grammatik des Geistes*, 419, fn. 731 (Lit.!). On the way in which faith is developed, see Rubel, *Erkenntnis und Bekenntnis*, 305.

[123] See for what follows amongst others Heil, *Blood and Water*, 140–45.

of Nathanael (1:49 – 20:28; see 21:2).[124] Both characters form a bridge between the Gospel and the readers (1:50–51–20:29; see 20:30–31).

2. The first lengthy conversation on faith is between the Jewish teacher Nicodemus and Jesus (3:1–21). With Thomas the circle between someone outside of the disciple community and someone from the inner circle of the twelve is closed (20:24–29): "Earthly" speech (see 3:31; 11:16), questions (see 3:4, 9; 14:5), and the longing for an immediate encounter with God (3:1–10; 20:24–29) connect Thomas with Nicodemus, who also appears three times in the narrative (3:1–10; 7:50–52; 19:38–42). Furthermore, both of them are linked to women testifying to faith (Nicodemus – Samaritan woman in John 3–4; Mary Magdalene – Thomas in John 20).

3. Also the relationship between Thomas' credo (20:28) and the confession of the Samaritans of Jesus as "Savior of the World" (4:42) may be intended. Mediated by other witnesses both of them discover faith by means of a direct encounter with Jesus.[125] In the case of the Samaritans, though, they came to faith through the word of a woman (see 4:39).[126]

4. The parallels to the confession of Peter (6:69 – 20:28) and his readiness to follow Jesus as demonstrated in his question (13:37 – 11:16; 14:5) have already been mentioned several times. Whereas Thomas at first does not perceive, Peter does not simply accept the suffering of Christ.[127] Neither of them can find faith without direct contact to the Risen One (20:6–7, 19:23–20:25).

5. Judas is, like Thomas, also one of the "Twelve" (6:71). Like Judas (13:30; 18:2–5), Thomas was also away from Jesus (20:24). In contrast to Judas, however, Thomas did not betray Jesus.

6. Thomas' confession may also be linked to the credo of the man born blind (9:38): both pray to Christ. If the blind man represents the Johannine com-

---

[124] On the correlation of Nathanael and Thomas, see Schnelle, *Johannes*, 332–34; Kremer, "Hand," 2155, 2166; Dschulnigg, *Jesus begegnen*, 233–34, 236; Theobald, "Vater," 485, fn. 661-664; Leinhäupl-Wilke, *Rettendes Wissen*, 288–89; Harstine, "Un-Doubting Thomas," 440–41; Kumlehn, *Geöffnete Augen*, 321–22; Manfred Lang, *Die Kunst des christlichen Lebens. Rezeptionsästhetische Studien zum lukanischen Paulusbild* (Arbeiten zur Bibel und ihrer Geschichte 29; Leipzig: Evangelische Verlagsanstalt, 2008), 640–41; Most, *Finger in der Wunde*, 81–82; Frey, "Der zweifelnde Thomas," 28–29.

[125] On the Johannine theological figure of thought used for conveying immediacy, see Klaus Scholtissek, *In ihm sein und bleiben: Die Sprache der Immanenz in den johanneischen Schriften* (Herders Biblische Studien 21; Freiburg: Herder, 2000), 361, also Klaus Scholtissek, "'Er kam in sein Eigentum – und die Eigenen nahmen ihn nicht auf' (Joh 1,11): Jesus – Mittler und Ort rettender vita communis in Gott nach dem Johannesevangelium," *GuL* 72 (1999): 450–51. With regard to the correlation to 4:42, see also Thyen, *Das Johannesevangelium*, 769; Theobald, "Osterglaube," 470; also his Jesus, 678–81; Frey, "Entstehung, Inhalt und Vermittlung des Osterglaubens," 283; Lang, *Kunst des christlichen Lebens*, 641.

[126] See Kühschelm, "Spiritualität aus dem Neuen Testament," 171.

[127] About this contrast, see R. Alan Culpepper, *Anatomy of the Fourth Gospel: A Study in Literary Design* (Philadelphia: Fortress, 1983), 123–24.

munity, then Thomas may be representative of the Johannine school (see 1:14–18).
7. In the first farewell discourse Thomas and Philip appear together (14:5–8; differently in 21:2). Both misunderstand Jesus, but Thomas appears to be more willing to change.
8. A relationship to the Beloved Disciple may also be identified. In contrast to Thomas the Beloved Disciple embodies the principle of 20:29 (20:8).[128]
9. With Mary Magdalene, Thomas shares an encounter with the Risen One through "sensory sight" (20:11–18 – 20:24–29).
10. The unique appearance of the Risen One to Thomas (20:24–29) is similar to his first appearance to the other disciples (20:19–23).

Thus, on the one hand, Thomas' actions are similar to those of the other characters mentioned above; on the other hand, he follows his own individual journey of faith, which climaxes in a unique encounter with the Risen One.[129] His proclamation of Jesus as God forms the concluding finale of this journey (20:28).[130] At this climax in the narrative the perspective from the point of view of his Lord and God is opened. In this sense Thomas is on the highest peak of the Christological mountain of the Fourth Gospel.

Thomas does not only function as the "twin" of the first readers who lacked confidence and were under pressure because of the Johannine schism and the imperial cult; he is also one of the central Johannine figures for all later readers, someone with whom they can identify because of his exclamation and question marks, as well as the overpowering encounter with the Risen One, as it was conveyed through the witness of his fellow disciples.[131] The biographic, narrative presentation of his character is a prime example of the communicative theology in the Fourth Gospel.[132] One characteristic that should be highlighted is the dialogical communication with the experience of the readers:

---

[128] Frey, "Der zweifelnde Thomas," 26–27, explains in detail that no fundamental contrast can be drawn between Thomas and the Beloved Disciple.
[129] See Heil, *Blood and Water*, 141.
[130] See Leinhäupl-Wilke, *Rettendes Wissen*, 289.
[131] Aptly put by Heil, *Blood and Water*, 142: "Indeed Thomas can be considered the 'Twin' to the individual reader, who has likewise not seen the risen Lord and must rely upon the witness of others to believe. Wishing to reinforce the witness of the group of disciples, Thomas will serve as a further, individual witness for the readers as individuals. Those who have not seen can come to believe through his seeing." See also Kremer, "Hand," 2169–70; Löning and Zenger, *Als Anfang schuf Gott*, 117; Leinhäupl-Wilke, *Rettendes Wissen*, 284; Theobald, "Osterglaube," 469, also fn. 664; Weidemann, *Der Tod Jesu*, 526; Rubel, *Erkenntnis und Bekenntnis*, 288–89, 314–17, 339, 347; Bennema, *Encountering Jesus*, 168–69, 212.
[132] On the theologically reflective biographic narration in the Fourth Gospel, see Eckart Reinmuth, "Biographisches Erzählen und theologische Reflexion im Johannesevangelium," *ZNT* 23 (2009): 36–45. On the Johannine communicative theology, see Rubel, *Erkenntnis und Bekenntnis*, 351–54.

"Thomas: das sind wir."[133] This identification is aimed at gaining life through faith (see 20:30–31): when looked at in the mirror of Thomas' story, our stories are interwoven with the Jesus story with such literary artistry and on such a high level of reflection, that it brings us to this decisive conclusion: Christ! He is our Lord and our God.

Wider Perspective: The Parallels and History of Reception

In comparison to the Fourth Gospel, the Synoptic Gospels and Acts only mention Thomas in the list of twelve (Mark 3:18; Matt 10:3; Luke 6:15; Acts 1:13); he is never depicted as an active character.[134]

In contrast to this, Thomas Didymos – in line with his prominent role in the Fourth Gospel – played a major role in the Syrian church under the name of "Judas Thomas" (see Gos. Thom.; Acts Thom.; Thom. Cont.).[135] The Gospel of Thomas developed the Johannine tradition further with its positive portrait of Thomas.[136] The Acts of Thomas moved Thomas, identified as Jesus' twin brother, to India, as missionary (see Acts Thom. 11; 31; 39).[137]

The third scene (20:24–29), in particular, has made Thomas famous in theology, liturgy, and representative art and writing.[138] It has been and will continue to be widely received and interpreted. In comparison to the apocryphal developments, the interpretation of the old church, up to the (Counter-)

---

[133] Most, *Finger in der Wunde*, 272. With regard to this orientation of the reader, see Lothar Steiger, *Erzählter Glaube: Die Evangelien* (Gütersloh: Mohn, 1978), 77: "Selber will er seine Erfahrung machen, will nicht glauben, weil andere erfahren haben. Diesen Thomas darf keiner sich schenken." See also Thyen, *Das Johannesevangelium*, 769.

[134] See Dschulnigg, *Jesus begegnen*, 220, 234; Theobald, *Johannes*, 730.

[135] See Rudolf Schnackenburg, *Das Johannesevangelium: Teil 2* (4th ed.; HTKNT IV; Freiburg: Herder, 1985) 410–11; Thyen, *Das Johannesevangelium*, 519–20; Theobald, *Johannes*, 730; Dschulnigg, *Jesus begegnen*, 234–35; H. J. W. Drijvers, "Thomas, Apostel," TRE 33:430–33; H. Attridge, "Thomas Didymus," RGG^4 8:367; Bauer, "Thomas," *Personenlexikon zum Neuen Testament*, 304.

[136] See Eisele, *Welcher Thomas?*, 58.

[137] See Schnackenburg, *Johannes 2. Teil*, 411, fn. 1 (Lit.!); Thyen, *Das Johannesevangelium*, 519; Theobald, *Johannes*, 730; Kremer, "Hand," 2158, fn. 10; Hartenstein, *Charakterisierung im Dialog*, 221, 228; Most, *Finger in der Wunde*, 129–34; Frey, "Der zweifelnde Thomas," 15–17; H. Balz, "Δίδυμος," $EWNT^2$ 1:771; Bauer, "Thomas," *Personenlexikon zum Neuen Testament*, 304; H. Jan Willem Drijvers, "Thomasakten," in *Neutestamentliche Apokryphen in deutscher Übersetzung, Bd. 2: Apostolisches. Apokalypsen und Verwandtes* (5th ed.; ed. Edgar Hennecke and Wilhelm Schneemelcher; Tübingen: Mohr, 1989), 289–367, 292. On the interpretation of Thomas as the twin brother of Jesus, see in detail Hartenstein, *Charakterisierung im Dialog*, 230–68, 295–307 (with a questionable characterization of the Johannine Thomas against the background of a possible pre-knowledge of the early Christian Thomas-tradition in the Syrian context); Most, *Finger in der Wunde*, 129–32.

[138] On the history of reception, see Most, *Finger in der Wunde*; Frey, "Der zweifelnde Thomas," 5–32.

Reformation, was more faithful to the text.[139] In art history the question whether Thomas had actually touched the Risen One and had put a hand in the wound in his side was almost always answered positively.[140] Since the high Middle Ages and especially since the Baroque period his touching of Jesus was painted in dramatic form for the viewer (e. g., Caravaggio [painted 1610]; Cantari [painted 1648]);[141] though one also finds alternative art historical interpretations (e. g., Rubens [d. 1640]; Rembrandt [d. 1669]).[142]

In Patrick Roth's Frankfurt poetry readings "Im Tal der Schatten" the revelation to Thomas appears on the very first page, in enchanting language: "Der Thomasfinger, den er da in die Wunde des Auferstandenen hält, in die tintenblutige Seite: lässt Jesus ihm auferstehen, macht Jesus dem Thomas lebendig … Der Körper, die Seitenwunde, in die Thomas seinen Realität heischenden Finger taucht, schreibt sich ihm in dieser Tat zu. Er schreibt: 'Das bist du, dieser Körper, tot und auferstanden. Tot bist du im Gesuchten, auferstanden im Gefundenen. Das Gesuchte hat dich gefunden.' Hier, in dieser Thomassekunde, sind Schreiben und Erleben noch ungetrennt … Schreiben ist Totenerweckung. Im Leser, im Autor."[143]

---

[139] See Most, *Finger in der Wunde*, 160–200; Frey, "Der zweifelnde Thomas, " 18–23.

[140] On Thomas in sacred art, see Most, *Finger in der Wunde*, 201–58.

[141] See Kremer, "Hand," 2153, 2172; Gruber, "Berührendes Sehen," 61, 83; Most, *Finger in der Wunde*, 206–12, 238–58, 295–98; Frey, "Der zweifelnde Thomas," 6–9.

[142] See Most, *Finger in der Wunde*, 250–51, 298 (Rubens); Frey, "Der zweifelnde Thomas," 9–10 (Rubens; Rembrandt).

[143] Patrick Roth, *Im Tal der Schatten: Frankfurter Poetikvorlesungen* (Frankfurt: Suhrkamp, 2002), 14.

Caiaphas and Annas:
The Villains of the Piece?

Adele Reinhartz

In popular retellings of the Jesus story, as well as in many historical studies, the high priest Caiaphas and his father-in-law, the former high priest Annas, play the role of the "bad guys" whose machinations lead directly to Jesus' condemnation and death on the cross.[1] This portrayal is grounded in great measure on two passages in the Gospel of John: John 11:49–52, which has Caiaphas explain to the council why it might be better to have one man die for the people than for the entire nation to be destroyed (11:50), and John 18:13, 19–24, in which Annas interrogates Jesus about his disciples and his teachings.[2]

A careful look at the Johannine portrayal of Caiaphas and Annas, however, challenges this portrait and requires a reevaluation of these characters and of the ways in which they are used to further the story. The general approach to be taken in this study is that of reader-response criticism. This approach views the narrative as a communication between an implied author (the image of the author constructed within and by the narrative) and an implied reader (the image of the reader constructed within and by the narrative) and considers how the portrayal of Caiaphas and Annas contributes to this communication.

Caiaphas is mentioned by name in 2 passages: 11:49–52, and 18:14, 24–28; Annas also appears in the latter passage. John 11:46–47 describes the dissension that occurred in the afternoon of Jesus' spectacular resurrection of his dead friend Lazarus. Many of those who witnessed this event believed in Jesus (11:45), but others "went to the Pharisees and told them what he had done" (11:46). The chief priests and Pharisees convened a meeting of the council to determine a course of action. Their concern was that "If we let him go on like this, everyone will believe in him, and the Romans will come and destroy both our holy place and our nation" (11:48).[3] At this point, "one of them, Caiaphas,

---

[1] For detailed discussion of the reception history of Caiaphas and Annas in scholarship and culture, see Adele Reinhartz, *Caiaphas the High Priest* (Studies on Personalities of the New Testament; Columbia: University of South Carolina Press, 2011). See also Rainer Metzner, *Kaiphas: der Hohepriester jenes Jahres: Geschichte und Deutung* (Leiden: Brill, 2010).

[2] The other passage that is crucial to this construction of the story is Matthew 26:57–68, in which the high priest tears his clothes and charges Jesus with blasphemy, and the council pronounces the death sentence.

[3] For discussion of the range of meanings of this reference, see Raymond E. Brown, *The*

who was high priest that year" spoke up: "You know nothing at all! You do not understand that it is better for you to have one man die for the people than to have the whole nation destroyed" (11:49-50).[4] The narrator then comments that Caiaphas "did not say this on his own, but being high priest that year he prophesied that Jesus was about to die for the nation, and not for the nation only, but to gather into one the dispersed children of God" (11:51-52). On these grounds, the council planned to put Jesus to death (11:53) and Jesus no longer went about openly among the Jews but withdrew to Ephraim, a town near the wilderness, and stayed there with his disciples (11:54).

From this first appearance of Caiaphas in this Gospel, a first-time implied reader would glean several pieces of information from which to begin building a portrait of this figure. 1. Caiaphas was a member of the council ("one of them"). 2. Caiaphas was high priest, a point that, along with the fact that he is the only one mentioned by name, begins to suggest his special status. 3. He was high priest that year. This latter point is ambiguous: does the implied author mean to suggest that Caiaphas was high priest for that year only, or that he was high priest at that specific time, without reference to the length of his term? Most commentators opt for the latter interpretation, on the basis of Josephus's chronology of the high priesthood, according to which Caiaphas was high priest from 18-36 or 37 C. E., a very long time especially when compared to some of his predecessors and successors, many of whom served for a year or less.[5] The implied reader, who has access only to the information provided in this Gospel in the order in which it is provided, is not aware of this historical point and thus may be left somewhat uncertain as Caiaphas's status. 4. Caiaphas feels free to chastise the group for being ignorant or unperceptive: "You know nothing at all!" This point bolsters the growing impression of Caiaphas as a person of some importance in the council, whether formal or informal.

What Caiaphas says next is shocking: "You do not understand that it is better for you to have one man die for the people than to have the whole nation destroyed." This comment provides several key pieces of information. First, Caiaphas here reinforces the point that his understanding and discern-

---

Gospel According to John (AB 29; Garden City: Doubleday, 1966), 439. Winter suggests that "our holy place" refers to the official status, position, or rank that Caiaphas and other members of the Sanhedrin held under the constitution granted by Rome to the representatives of the Jewish nation. This interpretation seems unlikely (Paul Winter, T. Alec Burkill, and Geza Vermes, *On the Trial of Jesus* [2d ed.; Berlin: de Gruyter, 1974], 54).

[4] On the sacrificial motif in this passage, see Raimo Hakola, "The Counsel of Caiaphas and the Social Identity of the Johannine Community (John 11:47-53)," in *Lux Humana, Lux Aeterna: Essays on Biblical and Related Themes in Honour of Lars Aejmelaeus* (ed. Antti Mustakallio et al.; Göttingen: Vandenhoeck & Ruprecht, 2005), 140-63.

[5] Craig Blomberg, *The Historical Reliability of John's Gospel: Issues & Commentary* (Downers Grove, Ill.: InterVarsity Press, 2002), 173.

ment in the current situation are superior to that of the council: while they do not know what to do (11:47) he does. Second, Caiaphas perceives the threat that "this man" poses to be so powerful that it can potentially result in the destruction of the entire nation. The reader would likely assume that "this man" is Jesus, but the fact that Jesus' name is not mentioned creates some distance between Caiaphas and Jesus: either the high priest does not know the troublemaker's name, or he does not attach importance to mentioning it. In either case, Caiaphas's words are a statement of general principle: "it is better for you that …" But for whom? The immediate context suggests that Caiaphas is articulating a situation that will work to the benefit of the council members whom he is addressing.

This point, like others already encountered in this short passage, remains ambiguous. Many commentators have suggested that it implies self-interest on the part of the council members: the death of one man instead of the nation is necessary in order to protect the personal power and wealth of the nation's leadership, the chief priests and Pharisees along with the council as a whole.[6] Readers less inclined to view the council in a sinister light, however, may opt for a more benign reading. Perhaps indeed the council is genuinely concerned for the survival and welfare of the nation and the temple, and wishes to avoid Roman reprisals, as they state in 11:48. It is true of course that their own lives and positions rest on the ongoing existence of the nation and temple, but their words do leave open the possibility that their concern for the nation overrides personal interest in what they perceive to be a dire situation. The implied reader is left with these two choices. While the council's concern appears to be hypothetical, the implied audience, whose "real-life" counterparts likely lived towards the end of the first century in a location in Asia Minor, may well have seen this as an allusion to the destruction of the Temple in 70 C. E. which occurred as a consequence of the Jewish revolt against Rome and which, according to some theories, was a factor in the relocation of the Johannine believers to the Diaspora.[7]

Caiaphas says no more in this passage, or, indeed, in the rest of the Gospel. The narrator, however, directs the implied reader to interpret his words in a particular light: as an inadvertent prophecy of Jesus' salvific death on behalf of Israel ("the nation") and for the sake of all children of God. This comment associates prophecy with the high priesthood, and also implies a positive assessment of Caiaphas, at least insofar as he becomes a mouthpiece for God by virtue of his position. Later real readers, such as Origen, will struggle with

---

[6] For this argument, see Helen K. Bond, *Caiaphas: Friend of Rome and Judge of Jesus?* (Louisville, Ky.: Westminster John Knox, 2004), 132.

[7] For detailed discussion of this historical scenario, see Raymond E. Brown, *The Community of the Beloved Disciple* (New York: Paulist, 1979).

the question of how it is possible for an evil person to utter a true prophecy, but this is not a concern of our implied author here.[8]

In repeating that Caiaphas was high priest "that year" the narrator also reintroduces the uncertainty as to the length and importance of Caiaphas's official status. Caiaphas is not important in and of himself, but only for his status as high priest at that time. But what is important in the passage is not what it says about the high priest but what it says about the implied audience. The narrator expresses the belief that Jesus' death will gather together the dispersed children of God. Implied readers familiar with Jewish messianic language would understand this as an allusion to the belief that the eschaton will be accompanied by the ingathering of believers who had been exiled from Jerusalem due to conquest. In the narrative context, the immediate allusion is to the Babylonian exile, which occurred as a consequence of the conquest of Solomon's temple in the sixth century B.C.E.; a late-first-century Diaspora readership, however, may well have been understand as a reference to the destruction of Herod's temple in 70 and the resultant exile. Furthermore, the phrase "and not for the nation only, but to gather into one the dispersed children of God" may imply that the implied audience includes not only those who are ethnically Jewish but also non-Jews who perceive themselves to be children of God, that is, believers in Jesus as the messiah and Son of God (cf. 1:12). The narrator concludes this passage by confirming the persuasive nature of Caiaphas's prophecy: The council took a specific lesson from the general principle articulated by the high priest: the way to avoid the possibility of destruction was to plan for Jesus' death.[9]

On the basis of this passage, how would the implied readers perceive Caiaphas? First, he is the high priest, and has an influential voice on the council. Second, he provides a general principle that the council uses to devise a plan that, from their perspective, addresses the problem that was brought before it in the aftermath of the raising of Lazarus. Third, he is a prophet who articulates a central tenet of Johannine theology. The implied author, whose views, in this case, are represented by the words of the narrator,[10] shares a secret with the implied audience to which the chief priests, Pharisees, and Caiaphas are not privy: Jesus' death, which the council believes will restore the status quo, will in fact transform it radically, for it will bring about salvation and broaden the covenant between God and Israel – currently represented by the nation

---

[8] For discussion, see Reinhartz, *Caiaphas the High Priest*, 59–62.

[9] Underlying this plan may have been the hope that Jesus would function as a "scapegoat" whose death would atone for the sins of the people (Jo-Ann Brant, *Dialogue and Drama: Elements of Greek Tragedy in the Fourth Gospel* [Peabody, Mass.: Hendrickson, 2004], 45).

[10] On the relationship between the narrator and the implied author, see R. Alan Culpepper, *Anatomy of the Fourth Gospel: A Study in Literary Design* (Philadelphia: Fortress, 1983), 16–17.

and the temple – to include all who believe. If we presume a correspondence between the implied audience and a "real" audience in the late first century, the passage conveys a further irony: the measure that the council undertakes will by no means avert Roman destruction of the nation and people. The implied author does not imply a direct connection between Jesus' death and the destruction of the temple[11] but using irony the implied author reinforces the ignorance and misguided behavior and intentions of the characters who refuse to believe in Jesus and would prevent others from doing so.

Annas is introduced in the Passion narrative. Immediately upon Jesus' arrest, "they" – presumably those who arrested him – "took him to Annas, who was the father-in-law of Caiaphas, the high priest that year" (18:13). This verse introduces Annas in relationship to Caiaphas, and reminds the implied reader of Caiaphas's status as the high priest of the time and, in the next verse, also reminds the readers of the earlier incident, by identifying Caiaphas as "the one who had advised the Jews that it was better to have one person die for the people" (18:14). The passage raises the question of why it is that Jesus is first brought to Annas, who apparently has no official high priestly standing, rather than to Caiaphas. The question is unresolved in the narrative. Scholars have attempted to fill this gap by suggesting that a former high priest retained some measure of high priestly authority,[12] but the implied readers would not have known this on the basis of the Gospel of John, or their own experience in the Diaspora after the destruction of the temple and the end of the institution of the high priesthood.

After a brief digression to describe Peter's first denial (18:15–18), the passage continues: "Then the high priest questioned Jesus about his disciples and about his teaching" (18:19). This brief notice adds additional confusion. The narrative context would imply that the one interrogating Jesus is Annas, who is merely the father-in-law of the high priest, yet the passage explicitly refers to the high priest as the one conducting the interrogation. This is another inconsistency that remains unresolved. The scene allows Jesus to defend himself against the charge that he has taught secretly: "I have spoken openly to the world; I have always taught in synagogues and in the temple, where all the Jews come together. I have said nothing in secret. Why do you ask me? Ask those who heard what I said to them; they know what I said" (18:20–21). The charge of secret teaching, it must be noted, is nowhere articulated, neither by Annas, nor by Caiaphas, nor the narrator. Jesus' defense is borne out by the

---

[11] For discussion, see Andreas J. Köstenberger, "The Destruction of the Second Temple and the Composition of the Fourth Gospel," *TrinJ* 26.2 (2005): 205–42.

[12] Josephus continues to refer to former high priests as "high priest" (see, for example, *J. W.* 2.441; *Ant.* 20.205; *Life* 193). For discussion, see James C. VanderKam, *From Joshua to Caiaphas: High Priests after the Exile* (Minneapolis: Fortress, 2004), 426.

Gospel as a whole, which does indeed present Jesus as speaking openly in synagogues and in the temple, up until the last supper and farewell discourses (John 13–17).

Jesus' response is construed as insolence: "When he had said this, one of the police standing nearby struck Jesus on the face, saying, 'Is that how you answer the high priest?'" (18:22). Jesus has a ready response to this question as well: "If I have spoken wrongly, testify to the wrong. But if I have spoken rightly, why do you strike me?" (18:23). How the high priest reacted to this is unknown, for the narrator concludes the scene abruptly: "Then Annas sent him bound to Caiaphas the high priest" (18:24).

Despite this comment, the narrator does not reveal whether Caiaphas also interrogated Jesus; the final reference to Caiaphas is similarly unrevealing: "Then they took Jesus from Caiaphas to Pilate's headquarters" (18:28). While some scholars argue that "they" were or at least included Caiaphas and Annas, in fact, neither of these priests appears again in the narrative.[13] Contrary to many of the movies about Jesus, the Gospel does not place the high priest or his father-in-law at the scene of the trial before Pilate, his sentencing, or at the foot of the cross.[14] While it is possible to infer their presence in the implied author's general references to the "chief priests" who *are* present during this part of the story, who clamor for his death (19:6, 15) and object to the wording on the *titulus* above Jesus' cross (19:21), they are not singled out in any way.

A close reading of the Gospel of John therefore does not support the portrait of Caiaphas and Annas as the ones who bear the moral responsibility for Jesus' death. The implied readers – or any real reader who has not read the other Gospels, watched the Jesus movies, or studied historical Jesus research or scholarly Gospel commentaries – would come away from a first reading of the Gospel of John with the impression that Caiaphas was high priest at the time of Jesus and had some role in the council, but such readers would not know how long he held this post or what his official position was in the council that made the decision to plan for Jesus' death. Implied readers would understand that Annas was Caiaphas's father-in-law but not what his official status was vis-à-vis the high priesthood; that high priests make true prophecies, even if neither they nor their immediate audience within the narrative understand the meaning of that prophecy, but not whether the high priest himself took an active role in ensuring that the prophecy came to pass; that the high priest considered the sacrifice of one person to be preferable to the destruction of the nation, but not whether the high priest had direct knowledge of Jesus or any opinions about him or his activities; that Annas appar-

---

[13] This is argued, for example, by Bond, *Caiaphas*, 138.
[14] On the portrayal of Caiaphas and Annas in film, see Reinhartz, *Caiaphas the High Priest*, 124–43.

ently had some interest in Jesus and some official role in the proceedings, but not why this was the case; that Jesus spent some time in Caiaphas's precinct before being led off to Pilate, but not what transpired during that time. Whether the Johannine tradition did not include a trial before Caiaphas, or whether the author(s) simply decided to omit it is impossible to say. The effect of the omission, however, is to distance Caiaphas from the judicial processes that resulted in Jesus' crucifixion.

The implied audience would be similarly uncertain about the characters and personalities of these two men. Implied readers would reasonably conclude, on the basis of Caiaphas's "prophecy" and his forthright chastisement of the council, that the high priest "that year" was, and saw himself as, shrewder than they were. Implied readers might even view Caiaphas as having provided the rationale for the course of behavior that the council took. But the absence of Caiaphas and Annas from the tragic and theologically-laden events leading to Jesus' death suggests that neither the implied author nor the implied readers saw them as major players in this drama. Caiaphas and Annas are not characters whose personalities emerge and develop throughout the course of the narrative. Rather, they are minor players whose knowledge of and attitudes towards Jesus are not of particular interest to the implied author, whose concern is to implicate the chief priests and Pharisees in the crime of crucifying the man whom he considered to be the Messiah and Son of God.

The Beloved Disciple: The Ideal Point of View

James L. Resseguie

The Beloved Disciple appears in the Fourth Gospel with the epithet "the one whom Jesus loved" at 13:23–26; 19:26–27; 20:2–10; 21:7, 20–23 and as an unnamed disciple at 1:35–40 and 18:15–16. The disciple is also the subject of narrative asides in 19:35 and 21:24. Recent scholarship has focused on the representative qualities of the disciple. He is seen as the ideal disciple, a paradigm of discipleship,[1] or as the ideal witness and ideal author.[2] The difficulty with identifying the Beloved Disciple as a model of discipleship is outlined by Richard Bauckham. Although the disciple may function as a paradigm of discipleship in the narrative – as do other disciples such as Nathanael and Mary Magdalene – it is misleading to view him as the disciple *par excellence*.[3] Bauckham's own characterization of the disciple as the ideal witness or ideal author is plausible as far as it goes, but he does not develop the narrative point of view and the Beloved Disciple's role as the voice of this point of view. This article fills that gap, arguing that the Beloved Disciple represents *the ideal point of view of the narrative*, the ideological perspective that the narrator wants the

---

[1] Craig Koester, *Symbolism in the Fourth Gospel: Meaning, Mystery, Community* (2d ed.; Minneapolis: Fortress, 2003), 242; Raymond F. Collins, "The Representative Figures of the Fourth Gospel," *DRev* 94 (1976), 24–46, 118–32, esp. 132, reprinted in *These Things Have Been Written: Studies on the Fourth Gospel* (ed. idem, LThPM 2; Louvain: Peeters, 1990), 1–45; R. Alan Culpepper, *Anatomy of the Fourth Gospel: A Study in Literary Design* (Philadelphia: Fortress, 1983), 121–23; William S. Kurz, "The Beloved Disciple and Implied Readers," *BTB* 19 (1989): 100–107; Brendan Byrne, "Beloved Disciple," *ABD*, 1:658–66, esp. 659.

[2] Richard Bauckham, *The Testimony of the Beloved Disciple: Narrative, History, and Theology in the Gospel of John* (Grand Rapids, Mich.: Baker Academic, 2007), 73–91; reprint of Bauckham, "The Beloved Disciple as Ideal Author," *JSNT* 49 (1993): 21–44. Cf. also Cornelis Bennema, *Encountering Jesus: Character Studies in the Gospel of John* (Milton Keynes: Paternoster, 2009), 171–82, who argues that he is the ideal eyewitness. Colleen M. Conway resists the representative approach and concludes that the Beloved Disciple is an ambiguous character that cannot be "flattened" to a single trait (idem, "Speaking Through Ambiguity: Minor Characters in the Fourth Gospel," *BibInt* 10 [2002]: 324–41).

[3] See Bauckham, *Testimony*, 82–85 for the reasons why he cannot be the paradigmatic disciple. Bauckham argues that the Beloved Disciple is characterized as superior to Peter not because he is the ideal disciple, but because he represents a different kind of discipleship from Peter's. Peter's discipleship role is characterized as active service and he models the role of chief under-shepherd. The Beloved Disciple, on the other hand, is the perceptive witness who sees the spiritual meaning of events and he models the role of ideal witness (e. g., 19:35; 20:8–9).

reader to adopt. The method of analysis is a close reading of the Beloved Disciple's sequential appearances in the Fourth Gospel with attention to characterization, narrative settings, literary devices and point of view.[4]

Point of view "signifies the way a story gets told."[5] The actions and dialogue of the characters, the literary devices, and settings are part and parcel of the narrator's perspective. What the narrator includes and the way it is expressed reveals a point of view. Boris Uspensky identifies four planes on which point of view is found in a narrative: phraseological (what words and phrases are used in the narrative?); spatial-temporal (where and when are events narrated?); psychological (what are the characters' thoughts and behaviors?); and ideological (what are the narrative's norms, values, and worldview?).[6] Of the four planes, ideological point of view is the most important, for it expresses the norms, values, and beliefs that the narrator wants the implied reader to adopt. In John, the ideological point of view is stated in the Prologue: "The Word became flesh (σάρξ) and lived among us, and we have seen his glory (δόξα), the glory as of a father's only son, full of grace and truth" (1:14).[7] While some characters in the Gospel see only flesh and stumble over Jesus' words and actions, others see the glory in the flesh. The ideological point of view of the Gospel is intended to convince the reader to see the glory in the flesh, the other worldly in the ordinary. Among the male disciples, the Beloved Disciple represents this ideal perspective.[8]

---

[4] On close readings of biblical narratives, see James L. Resseguie, *Narrative Criticism of the New Testament: An Introduction* (Grand Rapids, Mich.: Baker Academic, 2005). On point of view in the Fourth Gospel, see idem, *The Strange Gospel: Narrative Design and Point of View in John* (BIS 56; Leiden: Brill, 2001).

[5] Meyer H. Abrams, *A Glossary of Literary Terms* (7th ed.; Fort Worth, Tex.: Harcourt Brace College Publishers, 1999), s. v. "Point of View."

[6] Boris Uspensky, *A Poetics of Composition: The Structure of the Artistic Text and Typology of a Compositional Form* (trans. V. Zavarin and S. Wittig; Berkeley, Calif.: University of California Press, 1973). See also Susan Sniader Lanser, *The Narrative Act: Point of View in Prose Fiction* (Princeton, N. J.: Princeton University Press, 1981), 184–225; Resseguie, *The Strange Gospel*, 1–17.

[7] This is a development of Bultmann's observation: "The δόξα is not to be seen *alongside* the σάρξ, nor *through* the σάρξ as through a window; it is to be seen in the σάρξ and nowhere else. If man wishes to see the δόξα, then it is on the σάρξ that he must concentrate his attention, without allowing himself to fall a victim to appearances." See Rudolf Bultmann, *The Gospel of John: A Commentary* (trans. G. R. Beasley-Murray; Philadelphia: Westminster, 1971), 63. The "we" in 1:14 is not a group "we" but an authoritative "we" (Richard Bauckham, *Jesus and the Eyewitnesses: The Gospels as Eyewitness Testimony* [Grand Rapids, Mich.: Eerdmans, 2006], 380–381).

[8] Andrew T. Lincoln, "The Beloved Disciple as Eyewitness and the Fourth Gospel as Witness," *JSNT* 85 (2002): 3–26, esp. 10, argues that "the narrative's point of view is that God's relationship to the world is *like* a lawsuit." The Gospel is a cosmic trial in which God's claim on the world is presented through Jesus who is the chief witness and judge in the lawsuit. This point of view is part of the larger ideological point of view that the glory is seen in the incarnate Logos.

The Supper (13:23–26)

The first time the Beloved Disciple appears with the epithet "the one whom Jesus loved" is in 13:23. "One of his disciples – the one whom Jesus loved – was reclining next to him." The formal introduction of the Beloved Disciple is a "stunningly apparent" stroke of "narrative genius,"[9] for he is introduced immediately after Jesus demonstrates his love for the disciples in the act of washing the disciples' feet (13:1–20) and immediately before the commandment to "love one another just as I have loved you" (13:34). The framing device places the Beloved Disciple at "center stage,"[10] highlighting his importance in the Gospel and his special relationship with Jesus. His position next to Jesus (literally, the one "who is in the bosom of Jesus," 13:23) describes not only his proximity to Jesus at the supper but also his "closest communion" with him.[11] His intimacy recalls the Son's relationship to the Father in 1:18. "No one has ever seen God. It is God the only Son, who is close to the Father's heart [bosom] …"

During the supper, Jesus reveals that one of the disciples at the table will betray him (13:21) but all are unaware of his identity (13:22). Peter, therefore, motions to the anonymous disciple to ask Jesus who it is, and he learns that it is the one who takes the piece of bread that Jesus gives him (13:26). Yet it is uncertain whether the Beloved Disciple tells Peter this, and uncertain whether he understood any better than the other disciples the significance of Jesus' actions at the supper. No one at the table understood why Jesus told Judas, "Do quickly what you are going to do" (13:28). It is also an open question whether Peter is subordinated to the Beloved Disciple at the supper,[12] or the Beloved Disciple is directed by Peter, thus "reinforcing Peter's acknowledged authority and his intimacy and closeness to Jesus."[13] In fact, very little is learned about the Beloved Disciple in this scene apart from his unique epithet, "the one whom Jesus loved," and his place of intimacy with Jesus at the meal ("reclining next to Jesus"). What stands out in this scene is the Beloved Disciple's special relationship with Jesus which the verbal thread κόλπος (bosom) in 13:23 and 1:18 reinforces.

In the Gospel, Jesus' special relationship with God ("close to the Father's bosom [κόλπος]") enables him to see what others cannot see and to reveal

---

[9] James H. Charlesworth, *The Beloved Disciple: Whose Witness Validates the Gospel of John?* (Valley Forge, Pa.: Trinity Press International, 1995), 52.

[10] Charlesworth, *Beloved Disciple*, 52.

[11] BDAG, "κόλπος," 556–57.

[12] So Francis J. Moloney, *Glory not Dishonor: Reading John 13–21* (Minneapolis: Fortress, 1998), 20; Arthur H. Maynard, "The Role of Peter in the Fourth Gospel," NTS 30 (1984): 531–48, esp. 536–37.

[13] So Rudolf Schnackenburg, *The Gospel according to St. John* (3 vols.; New York: Crossroad, 1980–90), 3:30.

what only he could reveal. In literary terms, Jesus offers a unique point of view that is "not of this world" but is "from above" (8:23), an ideological perspective that is not restricted by human judgment. Jesus judges "with right judgment" and not according to "appearances" (7:24) or "by human standards" (lit. "according to flesh," 8:15). In the Gospel, Jesus' point of view contrasts with an opposing point of view that is "of this world" or "from below" (8:23). A below perspective judges by "appearances" and "according to the flesh" (7:24; 8:15), and seeks human glory rather than glory from God (5:44; 7:18; 12:43). The religious authorities in John are characterized by a below perspective, judging according to appearances. Nicodemus, for instance, is caught in the web of below thinking when he stumbles over Jesus' ambiguous statement that he must be born "from above"/"again" (3:3). He interprets the *double entendre* at a physical level and takes Jesus' statement in far too literal a way.[14] Yet the religious authorities are not alone in judging at a superficial level; other characters miss the deeper meaning of Jesus' statements. Peter is the spokesman for this point of view among the disciples. When Jesus wants to wash Peter's feet he at first refuses, and then goes further than Jesus intends and wants him to wash his hands and head also (13:6–9). Just as Nicodemus missed the deeper meaning of being born from above or again, Peter misses the deeper significance of Jesus' action in the washing of feet.

As Jesus sees what others do not see and represents an above point of view in the narrative, the Beloved Disciple sees what other disciples do not see and represents this ideal point of view in the narrative. He is able to see (as will be shown) the glory in the flesh: "And the Word became flesh and lived among us, and we have seen his glory" (1:14). While other characters may see only flesh and judge at the level of appearances, the Beloved Disciple demonstrates "right judgment," seeing the glory in the flesh. The Beloved Disciple, of course, is not the only character in the narrative to see beyond appearances and to exegete correctly. The man born blind, for instance, receives the gift of sight and with it a new point of view (9:1–41). While the religious authorities judge by appearance and conclude that Jesus is a sinner because his actions on the sabbath break conventions (9:24), the man born blind sees beyond appearances and sides with those who conclude that Jesus is "from God" (9:33). Among the male disciples, however, the Beloved Disciple stands alone as the one who sees beyond appearances and draws right conclusions. As he develops as a character in the narrative, his point of view is gradually unveiled as the ideal point of view in the narrative.

---

[14] See the character analysis in Resseguie, *The Strange Gospel*, 120–27; idem, *Narrative Criticism*, 244–54.

The Courtyard (18:15-18)

After the supper scene, the next appearance of the Beloved Disciple is in the courtyard of the high priest in John 18:15-18. Simon Peter is present also. Although it is by no means certain that the unnamed disciple is the Beloved Disciple, the identification is certainly possible.[15] In 20:2 "the other disciple," who is identified as the disciple whom Jesus loved, and Peter hear news of an empty tomb. The appearance of the definite article ("the other disciple") likely points back to the "other disciple" of 18:15.[16] If the anonymous disciple of 18:15-18 is the Beloved Disciple, then his appearance at Annas's courtyard augments his characterization as a faithful follower, especially if the courtyard scene is compared with the similar architectural setting found in 10:1-6. In John 10, Jesus tells a parable of the sheepfold (αὐλή), which is an enclosed space open to the sky[17] that protects the sheep from outside threats. Brigands and thieves lurk outside the fold, attempting to enter by subterfuge and steal the sheep (10:1). Wolves also attack the sheep from the outside (10:12). A gatekeeper (θυρωρός) opens the gate (θύρα) of the sheepfold for the shepherd (10:1, 2) and the sheep hear the shepherd's voice and follow him.

The courtyard scene echoes this architectural setting.[18] The word for courtyard (αὐλή) in 18:15 is the same word for sheepfold in 10:1; a gatekeeper (θυρωρός) is present in both accounts (10:3; 18:16, 17); characters or sheep go in and out through a gate (θύρα 10:1, 2; 18:16); and the good shepherd is pre-

---

[15] C. Kingsley Barrett, *The Gospel according to St. John: An Introduction with Commentary and Notes on the Greek Text* (2d ed.; Philadelphia: Westminster, 1978), 525 is cautious: "It is quite possible to identify him with the disciple 'whom Jesus loved,' but there is no definite ground for doing so." Several commentators identify the unnamed disciple with the Beloved Disciple. See George R. Beasley-Murray, *John* (WBC 36; Waco, Tex.: Word, 1987), 324; R. Alan Culpepper, *The Gospel and Letters of John* (Interpreting Biblical Texts; Nashville: Abingdon, 1998), 222; Charles H. Giblin, "Confrontations in John 18,1-27," *Bib* 65 (1984): 210-32, esp. 228; Donald Senior, *The Passion of Jesus in the Gospel of John* (Collegeville, Minn.: Liturgical Press, 1991), 63-64; Frans Neirynck, "The 'Other Disciple' in Jn 18,15-16," *ETL* 51 (1975): 113-41; Collins, *These Things Have Been Written*, 42; Kevin Quast, *Peter and the Beloved Disciple: Figures for a Community in Crisis* (JSNTSup 32; Sheffield: JSOT Press, 1989), 76-81. Thomas L. Brodie, *The Gospel according to John: A Literary and Theological Commentary* (New York: Oxford University Press, 1993), 529, and Charlesworth, *Beloved Disciple*, 342-59, suggest that the unnamed disciple is Judas which would explain his access to the high priest's house but raises problems of its own. Among others who do not identify the "other disciple" with the Beloved Disciple are: Bultmann, *John*, 645, fn. 4; Barnabas Lindars, *The Gospel of John* (London: Oliphants, 1972), 548; John J. Gunther, "The Relation of the Beloved Disciple to the Twelve," *TZ* 37 (1981): 129-48, esp. 147.

[16] Derek Tovey, *Narrative Art and Act in the Fourth Gospel* (JSNTSup 151; Sheffield: Sheffield Academic Press, 1997), 130-131.

[17] BDAG, "αὐλή," 150.

[18] See Mark W. G. Stibbe, *John as Storyteller: Narrative Criticism and the Fourth Gospel*, (SNTSMS 73; Cambridge: Cambridge University Press, 1972), 102-103, for similarities in the two passages. Also Resseguie, *Strange Gospel*, 64-71.

sent in both stories. There are differences, of course. Jesus is the gate for the sheepfold (cf. 10:7) but not in the courtyard scene. The anonymous disciple is the mediating character who goes in and out of the courtyard whereas Jesus fulfills that role in the parable of the sheepfold. Nevertheless, the similarities between the two scenes are too close to ignore.

In the sheepfold narrative, the good shepherd contrasts with hired hands. At the first sign of danger hired hands run away and abandon the sheep, while the good shepherd remains and even lays down his life to protect the sheep. The narrative also emphasizes that the sheep of this fold run away at "the voice of strangers" and respond only to the voice of the good shepherd (10:5). While both Simon Peter and the Beloved Disciple follow Jesus to the high priest's courtyard, only the unnamed disciple, who is known to the high priest, enters this space initially. Peter stands "outside at the gate" (18:16a). With Peter outside, the anonymous disciple speaks to the gatekeeper and brings Peter into the courtyard. (It is also possible that the gatekeeper brings Peter inside.) Mark Stibbe suggests that the similarity between the parable of the good shepherd and the courtyard scene lies in the distinction between the good shepherd and the hired hand. The good shepherd is the anonymous disciple who goes in and out of the courtyard, "whilst Peter functions as the hired hand who flees in the hour of danger (though Peter's flight is a metaphorical flight from confession, not a literal desertion). Peter is not yet a shepherd like his Master, willing to lay down his life for the sheep."[19] The hired hand analogy is possible but not likely. Peter does not flee; he enters the courtyard with the aid of the anonymous disciple. Rather the similarity in the architectural settings lies elsewhere. The actions within the common settings clarify the difference between the sheep that hears the master's voice and follows obediently and the sheep that regards the master as a stranger and denies him. In John 10, the sheep hear the shepherd's voice, follow him, and refuse to listen to the voice of a stranger (10:4, 5). Although both Peter and the unnamed disciple follow Jesus (18:15), only the Beloved Disciple willingly follows him into the courtyard. When Peter is given the opportunity to show that he is indeed a follower of Jesus, he treats him as a total stranger.

The spatial arrangement of characters in the courtyard further underscores the distinction between the faithful follower and the disciple that regards his master as a stranger. Once Peter enters the courtyard, he joins the slaves and the arresting posse around a charcoal fire (18:18b). A simple yet telling narrative aside highlights Peter's defection: "Peter also was standing with them" (18:18b). Peter's alignment with the arresting posse recalls Judas's stance in the garden with the soldiers and temple police: "Judas, who betrayed him, was standing with them" (18:5). The architectural setting and spatial arrangement

---

[19] Stibbe, *John as Storyteller*, 104.

of characters not only highlights Peter's defection as a follower of Jesus, but also enhances the characterization of the Beloved Disciple as a faithful follower. As a faithful follower of Jesus, the Beloved Disciple can best represent the ideal point of view of the narrative.

The Cross (19:26–27, 35)

The next appearance of the Beloved Disciple occurs in a brief and poignant scene at the cross. "When Jesus saw his mother and the disciple whom he loved standing beside her, he said to his mother, 'Woman, here is your son.' Then he said to the disciple, 'Here is your mother.' And from that hour the disciple took her into his own home" (19:26–27). Neither Jesus' mother nor the Beloved Disciple speaks in this scene; only Jesus speaks – to both, one at a time. To his mother he says, "Woman, here is your son." This could refer to himself, but the following words to the disciple, "here is your mother," leave little doubt that Jesus is naming the Beloved Disciple the son of his mother. Similarly, the Beloved Disciple is informed that Mary is his mother. With these words a new family is created as a result of Jesus' death on the cross.[20] The narrative descriptions and epithets for Jesus' mother (who is always unnamed in John) emphasize her dispossession as his mother. Initially, she is introduced as "his mother," i. e., Jesus' mother (19:25), and then, more generally, as "the mother" (19:26a twice). Jesus addresses Mary as "woman," which places distance between himself and his mother.[21] Finally when Jesus introduces his mother to the Beloved Disciple he calls her "your mother" (19:27). In the narrative descriptions, Mary progresses from "his mother" to "the mother" to "woman" to "your mother." Similarly, the Beloved Disciple is given a new relationship: he is the son of Jesus' mother and, as son, Jesus' brother. As Craig Koester notes, the Beloved Disciple is the first of many brethren.[22] Prior to this scene the epithet "brother" was used for those who are related to Jesus by blood (2:12; 7:3, 5); after the resurrection "brother" describes those who are related to Jesus by faith (20:17). The Beloved Disciple thus becomes the first of Jesus' brothers related by faith, reinforcing his special relationship to Jesus as the one who reclines in his bosom. He is also given superiority to the other disciples as the only male disciple present at the cross.

---

[20] Lindars, *John*, 578–80; Moloney, *Glory not Dishonor*, 145; Koester, *Symbolism*, 243. For symbolical interpretations of 19:25–27 see the listing in Quast, *Peter*, 89–97.

[21] On γύναι in John see David R. Beck, *The Discipleship Paradigm: Readers and Anonymous Characters in the Fourth Gospel* (BIS 27; Leiden: Brill, 1997), 55. The NRSV has "her" and "his mother" at 19:26 but the Greek has neither pronoun.

[22] Koester, *Symbolism*, 243.

A new point of view emerges from his presence at the cross. He faithfully follows and remains with Jesus and witnesses the key event of the Gospel: Jesus' glorification on the cross. But he is more than the ideal witness, as Bauckham calls him.[23] He sees the glory in the flesh which the narrative aside of 19:35 clarifies: "He who saw this has testified so that you also may believe. His testimony is true, and he knows that he tells the truth." Here the Beloved Disciple – as narrator – intrudes into the story with a parenthetical remark and addresses the reader directly ("that *you* also may believe").[24] This, of course, is not a direct reference to the Beloved Disciple but it is a probable reference. As the only male disciple present at Jesus' death, the disciple is likely the one who saw the blood and water flow from Jesus' pierced side (19:34).[25] By this direct address to the implied reader, the narrator draws the reader's attention to the significance of Jesus' death on the cross.[26] The water that flows from Jesus' side at the cross recalls Jesus' pronouncement in 7:38–9, which is a reference to the giving of the Spirit at Jesus' glorification. "Out of his belly[27] shall flow rivers of living water. Now he said this about the Spirit, which believers in him were to receive; for as yet there was no Spirit, because Jesus was not yet glorified." The hour of Jesus' death on the cross is also the moment at which life is given. The narrator's parenthetical remark at 19:35 calls the reader to take notice of the ideological point of view: the glory is seen in the flesh, life in death.[28]

The Tomb (20:2–10)

The Beloved Disciple is next found racing to the tomb with Peter in 20:2–10. After Mary Magdalene discovers that the stone has been rolled away, she runs to Simon Peter and "the other disciple, the one whom Jesus loved" and tells them the shocking news (20:2). Peter and the other disciple set out in a footrace to the tomb. The Beloved Disciple outruns Peter, arrives first (20:4), and looks into the tomb (20:5). Peter is the first to enter the tomb and see the linen

---

[23] Bauckham, *Testimony*, 82–87.

[24] See below on 21:23–24 for the argument that the Beloved Disciple is the narrator of the Gospel.

[25] Tovey, *Narrative Art and Act*, 134; Lincoln, "Beloved Disciple," 13–14. It is possible that one of the soldiers is the one who saw the blood and water, but it is unlikely.

[26] Lincoln, "Beloved Disciple," 14, 19. "As a literary device [the Beloved Disciple], his role once more allows the narrator to draw the implied readers into the story line, inviting them to share the perspective of this witness that Jesus' death was life giving" ("Beloved Disciple," 19).

[27] Literally in Greek; the NRSV has "out of the believer's heart," which, as Koester, *Symbolism*, 14, fn. 22 notes, obscures the Christological dimension of the text.

[28] The identity of the narrator as the Beloved Disciple is not made known here; it is withheld from the reader until the final two verses of the Gospel (21:24–25).

wrappings and the head wrapping (20:6, 7). Finally, the Beloved Disciple goes into the tomb and sees and believes (20:8).

The repetitions highlight the Beloved Disciple's arrival at the tomb first. In 20:4 the two are running together, but the Beloved Disciple outruns Peter and arrives at the tomb "first." A second time the narrator underscores the other disciple's presence at the tomb "first" (20:8). The repetition of "first" places the Beloved Disciple in the foreground,[29] while the narrative descriptions emphasize his overtaking of Peter. Peter appears first in the narrative in 20:2: Mary runs to "Simon Peter and the other disciple, the one whom Jesus loved." And as they set out for the tomb Peter is first: "Then Peter and the other disciple set out and went toward the tomb" (20:3). In the next verse, the two are on equal footing – "the two were running together" – but by the end of the verse the Beloved Disciple overtakes Peter in the narrative descriptions and is mentioned first. "But the other disciple outran Peter and reached the tomb first" (20:4b). From that point on, the Beloved Disciple is first with Peter lagging behind, which 20:6 italicizes: "Then Simon Peter came, *following him*, and went into the tomb."[30] Although Peter is the first to enter the tomb, the narrator resists drawing attention to that important event; instead he emphasizes the Beloved Disciple's arrival at the tomb *first* (20:4, 8). This emphasis on his priority sets the stage for his perceptive understanding at 20:8. He sees beyond the literal level – the physical evidence – and judges with "right judgment" (7:24). Unlike Mary who exegetes at the level of appearances and assumes that Jesus' body has been stolen (20:2, 13, 15; although Mary is awakened to a new point of view in 20:16–18), the Beloved Disciple exegetes correctly and believes (20:8). It may be argued that 20:9 qualifies this resurrection faith, but the verse states only that none of the disciples yet understood scripture's witness to the resurrection.

The Beloved Disciple represents the ideal point of view of the narrative, seeing beyond appearances and judging correctly (7:24). This is strengthened by the mutual confirmations of the two disciples. The Beloved Disciple arrives first at the tomb and sees the linen wrappings. Peter enters the tomb and confirms what the Beloved Disciple saw, but he sees something more: "the cloth that had been on Jesus' head, not lying with the linen wrappings but rolled up in a place by itself" (20:7). The Beloved Disciple also goes into the tomb and sees what Peter observed but goes a step further: he also believes (20:8). Peter sees but draws no conclusions;[31] the Beloved Disciple exegetes correctly.

---

[29] Cf. Schnackenburg, *John*, 3:310: "The precedence of the other disciple comes to the fore 'phonetically' with προέδραμεν and πρῶτος (vss. 4 and 8), and all the more through narrative development."

[30] Author's emphasis. In 21:20, however, the Beloved Disciple lags behind: "Peter turned and saw the disciple whom Jesus loved following them."

[31] Bultmann, *John*, 684 assumes that Peter also believes, but the narrative is silent about Peter's faith.

Although each disciple confirms what the other saw, the Beloved Disciple goes further and sees beyond appearances, from the naked evidence of abandoned clothes in an empty tomb to the reality of the resurrection.[32]

The fullness of names and descriptions at unexpected points in the narrative adds weight to the Beloved Disciple's point of view. The disciple is introduced in 20:2 with a full description – "the other disciple, the one whom Jesus loved" – and subsequently referred to as "the other disciple" (20:3, 4). But when the Beloved Disciple enters the tomb the narrator resorts to unexpected fullness of description – "the other disciple, who reached the tomb first" – which accents the importance of his role and prepares the reader for another "first." He is the first to believe (20:8).[33]

The Sea (21:7, 20–23)

The final appearance of the Beloved Disciple is at Jesus' third post-resurrection appearance in John 21. The physical and temporal settings underscore the disciples' distance from Jesus. Peter decides to go fishing and six others – Thomas, Nathanael, the sons of Zebedee, and two other disciples – tag along (21:2–3). Although they are not far from land, about two hundred cubits or a hundred yards, their physical distance highlights their distance from Jesus in other ways. Even though this was the third time that he appeared to them after the resurrection (21:14), they "did not know that it was Jesus" standing on the shore (21:4). The nighttime temporal setting adds to their imperceptiveness (21:3). Darkness or night may suggest imperceptivity in the Gospel. Nicodemus comes to Jesus at night (3:2) – a temporal notation that says as much about the opaqueness in his understanding as it does about the time of day.[34] Mary Magdalene comes to the tomb while "it was still dark" (20:1) – a descriptive backdrop for her imperceptivity concerning the resurrection.

The Beloved Disciple is one who sees what others do not see. His is the ideal point of view of the narrative, for he is able to interpret who the person is behind the miracle. After a night of failure ("they caught nothing," 21:3), Jesus appears on the shore at that suggestive time of day for awakenings – daybreak (20:4) – and commands them to cast their nets once more into the recalcitrant sea (20:6). The disciples' lack turns immediately to abundance just

---

[32] See Brendan Byrne, "The Faith of the Beloved Disciple and the Community in John 20," *JSNT* 23 (1985): 83–97 who argues that the position of the face veil acts as a "sign" for the Beloved Disciple.

[33] Similarly, Simon Peter's name swells at a key point in the narrative. He is introduced as "Simon Peter" (20:2) and then as "Peter" (20:3–4). But when he enters the tomb first his name swells again to "Simon Peter" (20:6).

[34] Barrett, *John*, 204–5; Koester, *Symbolism*, 9; Jouette M. Bassler, "Mixed Signals: Nicodemus in the Fourth Gospel," *JBL* 108 (1989): 635–46, esp. 638.

as their non-recognition turns to recognition. After casting the net into the sea, their haul was so abundant that they could not bring it aboard. The Beloved Disciple, who is given his favorite sobriquet ("whom Jesus loved"), is startled into recognition and exclaims to Peter, "It is the Lord!" (20:7). Just as he was the first to judge correctly the meaning of the abandoned grave clothes, he is the first to exegete correctly the significance of the miraculous catch of fish.

The remainder of the narrative is turned over to Peter whose point of view has not been ideal in the Gospel and serves as a foil to the Beloved Disciple's point of view. Whereas the Beloved Disciple judges correctly, Peter misspeaks and judges incorrectly. He wants to follow Jesus, but his words reveal his misunderstanding ("not my feet only but also my hands and my head," 13:9) and his eagerness to follow ("I will lay down my life for you," 13:37) gets in the way of following as Jesus intends. His insistence on following Jesus on his own terms ends in failure and bold denial (13:36–38; 18:15–27). Once more his eagerness is seen as he puts on clothes and jumps into the sea (21:7). But Peter's raw, eager attempts to follow Jesus on his own terms are remade in this story as he pledges himself to self-giving love and is commissioned shepherd of the sheep (21:15–17). He learns to follow Jesus on Jesus' terms (21:18–19).

The Ending (21:20–23, 24) and The Beginning (1:35–40)

The Beloved Disciple makes a final appearance in the Gospel where he follows both Peter and Jesus (21:20). This appears to put the Beloved Disciple in a subordinate role to Peter who is not only commissioned as shepherd of the sheep, but also leads with the Beloved Disciple lagging behind. Yet the narrative description of the Beloved Disciple is unexpectedly effusive at this point (even for a narrative transition). Whereas the narrator has been content to identify the Beloved Disciple as "the disciple whom Jesus loved" as recently as 21:20a, he now adds to this epithet a reminder of the supper scene, the disciple's privileged position at the table, and even the words he spoke at the meal. "He was the one who had reclined next to Jesus at the supper and had said, 'Lord, who is it that is going to betray you?'" (21:20b). The narrative commentary reinforces the Beloved Disciple's special relationship with Jesus that makes him especially qualified to voice the ideological point of view of the Gospel. Further placing doubt upon Peter's superior role in this scene is Jesus' command to him: "Follow me" (21:19, 22). Only as Peter is remade with a solemn pledge of love instead of denial is he in a position to follow as Jesus intends (21:15–17). Whereas his earlier following was on his own terms as seen in his insistence on following Jesus and even laying down his life for him (13:37), now he follows as Jesus intends. But even here a contrast is seen in Peter's following and the Beloved Disciples' following. On the one hand, Peter is only able to follow as Jesus intends after his restoration in 21:15–19; on the other, the Beloved Disciple has been faithfully following Jesus since 1:35–40.[35] The Beloved Disciple as faithful follower is reinforced with an *inclusio* at the beginning and ending of the Gospel.[36] In 1:35–40 two of John's disciples see Jesus and follow him. One of the disciples is later identified as Andrew, Simon Peter's brother, while the other unnamed disciple is possibly the Beloved Disciple.[37] The two disciples "follow" Jesus (1:37, 38) and "remain" with him (1:38, 39).[38] At the end of the Gospel the Beloved Disciple "follows" Peter and Jesus in 21:20, and Peter is told it is not his concern if he remains until Jesus comes again. "If it is my will that he remain until I come, what is it to you?" (21:22, 23). The Gospel is thus bracketed by the verbal threads "follow" in 1:37, 38 and 21:20, and "remain" in 1:38, 39 and 21:22, 23. The *inclusio* reinforces the Beloved Disciple's unique status among the disciples: he has followed and remained with Jesus from beginning to end.

The Beloved Disciple as a character in the narrative has remained distinct from the Beloved Disciple as writer of the narrative. This distinction is set aside in 21:24 with the movement from third person reporting to first person testimony: "This is the disciple who is testifying to these things and has written them, and we know that his testimony is true." The disciple referred to is the Beloved Disciple who is the subject of the previous verses, 21:20–23. He is the one responsible for the content and words of the Gospel account (if "these things" in 21:24 refers to the entire Gospel as 21:25 seems to require).[39] But is he also the narrator of the Gospel? The first person plural ("we know") seems to refer to a narrator as part of a group that is not the source of the Gospel. This plural ("we know," in 21:24b) – after a third person ("this is the disciple") and preceding a first person singular in 21:25 ("I suppose") – causes confusion. If, however, the role of the Beloved Disciple as a character in the narrative is distinguished from the Beloved Disciple as narrator, then the alternation in persons is clarified. The third-person reference was necessary for the writer to remain a character in the narrative without tipping his hand (even in 19:35 the Beloved Disciple does not reveal that he is the narrator). But now that the Beloved Disciple steps forward and reveals to the reader that he is the narrator, the third-person voice falls to the side and the first-person emerges. Yet the change from the "we know" of 21:24 to the "I suppose" of 21:25 remains some-

---

[35] Bauckham, *Testimony*, 84.
[36] Noted by Bauckham, *Jesus and the Eyewitnesses*, 390–393; Bennema, *Encountering Jesus*, 172.
[37] A case for the unnamed disciple as the Beloved Disciple is made by Bauckham, *Testimony*, 85 and Charlesworth, *Beloved Disciple*, 326–30. See also Tovey, *Narrative Art and Act*, 132–33.
[38] In the NRSV "remain" is translated as "stay" the first time and "remain" the second time.
[39] See Bauckham, *Jesus and the Eyewitnesses*, 358–63 who builds the case for the Beloved Disciple as author of the Gospel.

what puzzling. The confusion is mitigated if the first person plural is not taken as a true plural to refer to a group of persons, but as an authoritative plural to punctuate what is written.[40] As a substitute for the "I," the "we" gives added force to what is spoken or written (cf. also John 3:11). By resorting to this authoritative "we," the Beloved Disciple underscores the truth of his testimony and of the written narrative.

Conclusion

The development of the Beloved Disciple's characterization is static, even though he has a prominent role in voicing the ideal point of view of the Gospel. Unlike Peter, he does not stumble over Jesus' words or misinterpret his actions. He appears at key points in John: at the beginning (1:35–40); at the last supper (13:23–26); at Peter's denial (18:15–16); at the cross (19:26–27); at the tomb (20:2–10); and at Jesus' resurrection appearance at the Sea of Tiberias (21:7, 20–23). He seldom speaks in the narrative in contrast to Peter. At the supper he asks Jesus who his betrayer will be (13:25) and at the Sea of Tiberias he announces, "It is the Lord!" (21:7). Yet his actions speak louder than his own (tagged) speech. He faithfully follows and remains with Jesus from beginning to end (1:35–40; 21:20–23). He has a special relationship with Jesus that is underscored at the beginning and end of the Gospel's second half (13:23; 21:20). He not only follows Jesus into the courtyard of the high priest; he enables Peter who lags behind to enter the courtyard also (18:15–16). He is the only male disciple to witness Jesus' death on the cross and the first of a new spiritual family (19:26–27). He is the first to reach the tomb and the first to believe Jesus has risen from the dead (20: 4, 8). He is the first to recognize the risen Lord at the Sea of Tiberias (21:7). He is a perceptive witness who sees what other disciples do not see: the glory in the flesh. He sees the significance of Jesus' death on the cross and steps into the narrative to remind the reader of the importance of this event (19:35). He sees the significance of a tomb with linen wrappings and a *soudairan* rolled up in a place by itself, and he believes in the resurrection. And he sees the significance of a miraculous catch of fish and recognizes the Lord (21:7). He sees the glory in the flesh and wants the reader also to adopt this point of view.

---

[40] Bauckham, *Jesus and the Eyewitnesses*, 370–381 calls this the "we" of authoritative testimony and offers examples in the Gospel and three letters of John. Some understand the "we" to refer to the Johannine community. See R. Alan Culpepper, *John, the Son of Zebedee: The Life of a Legend* (Minneapolis: Fortress, 2000), 71.

Judas (not Iscariot): What's in a Name?

Catrin H. Williams

Among the numerous characters in the Fourth Gospel who make a fleeting appearance in the text to engage in conversation with Jesus is Judas "not Iscariot." He comes into sight during the farewell discourse, after Jesus' reassurance to his disciples that he will return to them (14:18); the world, in a little while, will no longer see Jesus, but the disciples will see him (14:19) because those who keep his commandments will be loved by him and he will reveal himself to them (14:21: καὶ ἐμφανίσω αὐτῷ ἐμαυτόν). Taking up Jesus' earlier contrast between the disciples and the world (14:19)[1] as well as his language about self-revelation (14:21), this other Judas, whose well-known namesake has already departed into the night (13:30), interjects to seek clarification about the exclusive nature of Jesus' promise of revelation: "Lord, how is it that you will reveal yourself to us (ὅτι ἡμῖν μέλλεις ἐμφανίζειν σεαυτὸν), and not to the world?" Given the strongly visual-theophanic focus often linked to the verb ἐμφανίζειν (Exod 33:13, 18 LXX; Wisdom 1:2),[2] Judas appears to envisage an event that will be visible to all. Jesus explains that only those who love him and keep his word can experience his self-manifestation, that is, through the coming of the Father and the Son to make their home with them (14:23).

Judas acts in this narrative as a one-dimensional character or "type" with only a single trait.[3] He displays no complexity, the implied reader is given no clues about his inner life, and, because he disappears as abruptly as he appears,[4] there is no development in his character(ization). In seeking to

---

[1] Cf. Barnabas Lindars, *The Gospel of John* (NCB; Grand Rapids, Mich.: Eerdmans, 1972), 482; Fernando F. Segovia, *The Farewell of the Word: The Johannine Call to Abide* (Minneapolis: Fortress, 1991), 101.

[2] Cf. C. Kingsley Barrett, *The Gospel According to St John: An Introduction with Commentary and Notes on the Greek Text* (2d ed.; London: SPCK, 1978), 465; Andreas Dettwiler, *Die Gegenwart des Erhöhten: Eine exegetische Studie zu den johanneischen Abschiedsreden (Joh 13,31–16,33) unter besonderer Berücksichtigung ihres Relecture-Charakters* (FRLANT 169; Göttingen: Vandenhoeck & Ruprecht, 1995), 196.

[3] Cf. D. Francois Tolmie, *Jesus' Farewell to the Disciples: John 13:1–17:26 in Narratological Perspective* (BIS 12; Leiden: Brill, 1995), 142; Cornelis Bennema, "A Theory of Character in the Fourth Gospel with Reference to Ancient and Modern Literature," *BibInt* 17 (2009): 375–412, here 407.

[4] See further Susan E. Hylen, *Imperfect Believers: Ambiguous Characters in the Gospel of John* (Louisville, Ky.: Westminster John Knox, 2009), 1.

define the contours of Judas' character trait, it has to be acknowledged that, although he acts as an individual, he fulfils a collective/representative role in his capacity as one of the disciples who interacts with Jesus during the first part of the farewell discourse (13:31–14:31): Peter (13:36–37), Thomas (14:5), Philip (14:8) and Judas himself (14:22). The inclusion of interrruptions by *four* disciples may, in this respect, be a deliberate evocation of the Jewish custom related to the youngest son who, within the context of the Passover meal, asks four questions of his father about the past and future significance of the exodus. Thus, following the departure of Judas Iscariot, Jesus addresses the remaining disciples as "little children" (13:33: τεκνία) in order to explain to them his own departure and return.[5] Judas' question bears striking similarity to the utterances of Peter (13:36–37), Thomas and Philip (14:5, 8): in all four cases the disciples address Jesus as "Lord" (κύριε), and the nature of their interjections point to a shared character trait, namely their inability to understand Jesus' words.[6] It is more difficult to identify precisely what underpins Judas' misunderstanding of Jesus: is it curiosity, surprise, doubt, or a combination of these features? Some commentators have noted the resemblance between Judas' question and the words of Jesus' brothers (7:3–4: "show yourself to the world"),[7] although the attempt to *challenge* Jesus is much more evident in the case of his brothers' demand.

The narrator provides no information as to whether Jesus' explanatory statement leads to comprehension on Judas' part. As with Thomas and Philip (14:6, 9), Jesus offers a direct reply (14:23) but the spotlight never returns to Judas for his own response. Indeed, the implied reader learns nothing more about him; his role as a character is to be a conduit for the elucidation of Jesus' earlier teaching and to act as yet another foil,[8] one whose ignorance contrasts sharply with Jesus' all-knowing pronouncements. This brief dialogue thus

---

[5] I am grateful to Steve Hunt, one of the editors of this volume, for alerting me to this possible explanation. On the four questions, see specifically Craig Keener, *The Gospel of John: A Commentary* (2 vols.; Peabody, Mass.: Hendrickson, 2003), 2:928. See further Annie Jaubert, "The Calendar of Qumran and the Passion Narrative in John," in *John and Qumran* (ed. James H. Charlesworth; London: Chapman, 1972), 67–68.

[6] See Tolmie, *Jesus' Farewell to the Disciples*, 135–36, 139; Christopher W. Skinner, *John and Thomas – Gospels in Conflict? Johannine Characterization and the Thomas Question* (PTMS 115; Eugene, Oreg.: Pickwick, 2009), 66–67, 142, 152–54.

[7] Cf. Joseph N. Sanders and Brian A. Mastin, *A Commentary on the Gospel According to St John* (BNTC 4; London: A&C Black, 1968), 332; Francis J. Moloney, *Glory not Dishonor: Reading John 13–21* (Minneapolis: Fortress, 1998), 45; Enno Edzard Popkes, *Die Theologie der Liebe Gottes in den johanneischen Schriften* (WUNT II/197; Tübingen: Mohr Siebeck, 2005), 340, fn. 41.

[8] William Harmon, *A Handbook to Literature* (11th ed.; Upper Saddle River: Prentice Hall, 2009), 232; James L. Resseguie, *Narrative Criticism of the New Testament: An Introduction* (Grand Rapids, Mich.: Baker Academic, 2005), 124. See also Andrew T. Lincoln, *The Gospel According to St John* (BNTC 4; London: Continuum, 2005), 396.

exemplifies the first part of the two-stage revelation presupposed by the narrative (cf. 13:37; 14:5, 8; 16:12, 29–33);[9] the disciples are exposed to private instruction during Jesus' earthly ministry, but only with further revelation – following the gift of the Spirit (14:26; cf. 7:38–39; 20:22) – do they fully grasp the meaning of his elusive words.

As to why Judas is the disciple named at this narrative juncture, some suggest that it arises from the author's "liking for variation,"[10] while others propose that his obscurity points to historical authenticity.[11] In fact it is Judas' identity rather than his characterization that usually receives scholarly attention: is he the Judas son of James included in Luke's list of the twelve (Luke 6:16; Acts 1:13)[12] or the Thaddaeus that is mentioned in other Synoptic lists (Mark 3:18; Matt. 10:3)[13]?

Given that "Judas" was a fairly common Jewish name,[14] the most striking aspect – narratologically speaking – of the three-word aside that accompanies his name (οὐχ ὁ Ἰσκαριώτης) is that he is the only character in the Fourth Gospel to be classified in terms of who he is *not*: he is not Judas Iscariot, the defector who betrayed Jesus. What is the narrative impact of the differentiation between this second Judas and the one in whom Satan is now said to reside (13:27)? As certain traits are undoubtedly collected under the proper name "Judas," which, in this case, are accentuated by the addition of the words "not Iscariot,"[15] the precisely worded "tagging" of this other Judas inevitably shapes the implied reader's response to him. The combination of some degree of alignment ("Judas") and distinction ("not Iscariot") means that the reader is encouraged to pair together these two characters for comparison – one of the Fourth Gospel's most consistent and striking techniques of characterization.[16] If Judas Iscariot has since disappeared into the dark-

---

[9] Robert G. Hall, *Revealed Histories: Techniques for Ancient Jewish and Christian Historiography* (JSPSup 6; Sheffield: Sheffield Academic Press, 1991), 231–32; John Ashton, *Understanding the Fourth Gospel* (2d ed.; Oxford: Oxford University Press, 2007), 315–17, 343–48.

[10] See Lindars, *The Gospel of John*, 482.

[11] Raymond E. Brown, *The Gospel According to John (xiii–xxi)* (AB 29; New York: Doubleday, 1966), 641: "If pure invention were involved, why would such an obscure disciple as this Judas be introduced?"

[12] Cf. Lincoln, *John*, 396; Klaus Wengst, *Das Johannesevangelium. 2. Teilband: Kapitel 11–21* (2d ed.; THKNT 4/2; Stuttgart: Kohlhammer, 2007), 141, fn. 161.

[13] Rudolf Schnackenburg, *The Gospel according to St. John* (3 vols.; trans. D. Smith and G. A. Kon; London: Burns & Oates, 1982), 3:80–81.

[14] Richard Bauckham, *Jesus and the Eyewitnesses: The Gospels as Eyewitness Testimony* (Grand Rapids, Mich.: Eerdmans, 2006), 85.

[15] On proper names as the locus for characterization, see Thomas Docherty, *Reading (Absent) Character: Towards a Theory of Characterization in Fiction* (Oxford: Clarendon, 1983), 73–74.

[16] See especially Michael W. Martin, *Judas and the Rhetoric of Comparison in the Fourth Gospel* (New Testament Monographs 25; Sheffield: Sheffield Phoenix Press, 2010).

ness, does his namesake's momentary dialogue with Jesus enables this Judas to move closer towards the light? The Johannine presentation of "Judas not Iscariot" may be too limited, too open-ended, for him to be viewed as the "replacement Judas," the one whose intervention opens the way for Jesus' self-revelation and future indwelling in the disciples.[17] Nevertheless, the implied reader is given no hint at all that this particular Judas is unwilling to persevere in his quest for revelation.

---

[17] Thomas L. Brodie, *The Gospel According to John: A Literary and Theological Commentary* (Oxford: Oxford University Press, 1993), 467.

The Roman Soldiers at Jesus' Arrest: "You Are Dust, and to Dust You Shall Return"

Steven A. Hunt

Introduction – In the Beginning

Before pursuing a specific reading related to the Roman soldiers who arrested Jesus in John 18, we must attend to one other matter. We do that in what follows as we briefly consider the substantial influence the book of Genesis has had on the story in the book of John.

The narrator of John's "spiritual Gospel"[1] invites intertextual readings of the work by beginning the first verse with a not-so-subtle allusion to the first verse of Genesis ("In the beginning ...").[2] The prologue (1:1–18) heightens the allusion, echoing Genesis' cosmogony by referring to the Word's role in the creation of "all things" (1:3–4; cf. Gen 1–2): "light" and "darkness" (1:4–5; cf. Gen 1:2–4, 14–18), "life" (1:4; cf. Gen 1:20–21, 24, 30; 2:7) and "the world" (1:9–10; cf. Gen 1:1; 2:4).[3] The creation theme continues on unabated once the narrative begins in 1:19, where the first scene takes place by a river (1:28; cf. Gen 2:10) and when readers get teased into counting a series of seven days, four plus three (1:29, 35, 43; 2:1; cf. Gen 1:5, 8, 13, 19, 23, 31; 2:2–3). After tracing some incidents from a three year ministry of the Word made flesh – Jesus – *in the world* (1:9–11, 14; cf. God in the garden in Gen 2:8–9 and 3:8), incidents which include among other things *seven* signs and *seven* "I Am" sayings (cf. with similar patterns of sevens in Genesis 1–3), the Gospel slows

---

[1] This is Clement of Alexandria's (d. 215 CE) famous description of the Gospel (*HE* 6.14.7 [NPNF² 1.261]).

[2] Cf. Jan A. du Rand, "The Creation Motif in the Fourth Gospel: Perspectives on Its Narratological Function Within a Judaistic Background," in *Theology and Christology in the Fourth Gospel* (ed. Gilbert Van Belle et al.; BETL 184; Louvain: Leuven University Press, 2005), 21–46, here 38–39. Unless otherwise noted, translations are from the NRSV. In addition, we assume John's use of the LXX translation of Genesis in our study.

[3] On the Prologue in John and Genesis 1, see esp. du Rand, "Creation Motif in the Fourth Gospel," 36–43; and Mary Coloe, "The Structure of the Johannine Prologue and Genesis 1," *ABR* 45 (1997): 40–55. On Genesis and John more generally, Calum M. Carmichael, *The Story of Creation: Its Origin and Its Interpretation in Philo and The Fourth Gospel* (Ithaca, N.Y.: Cornell University Press, 1996) and John Painter, "Earth Made Whole: John's Rereading of Genesis," in *Word, Theology, and Community in John* (ed. John Painter et al.; St. Louis, Mo.: Chalice Press, 2002), 65–84.

down, coming to its climax with yet another week beginning in 12:1, just before Jesus' Passion.

To be sure, all four of the Gospels allude to the cosmogony in Genesis in various ways[4] and show evidence of new creation themes especially in their Passion narratives and resurrection stories of Jesus. So, for example, in all of the Gospels, Jesus is questioned at his trials.[5] Might his questioning recall God's questions for the man and the woman in Genesis 3:9–13? Indeed, a lone comparison like this would not be very compelling. But given the connections which follow, perhaps there is more here than meets the eye. Consider, therefore, how each of the Gospels emphasize in their own way that the charges against Jesus are baseless,[6] whereas Genesis details the woman and man's obvious guilt in 3:14, 17. Compare also the crown of "thorns" Jesus wears in three of the Gospels[7] with the "thorns" that are part of the curse on the man in Genesis 3:18. Should the death sentence imposed on Jesus in the Gospels[8] be seen in light of the death sentence imposed on the man in Genesis 3:19 (cf. 2:17)? More obviously, note that each of the Gospels emphasize that Jesus' resurrection took place on "the first day of the week,"[9] a day clearly highlighted in the Genesis account (1:5) as well. And while Luke and John suggest that Jesus emerged from the tomb without his grave clothes (Luke 24:12; John 20:5–7), a detail that may relate to the importance placed on the man and the woman's nakedness in Gen 2:25 (cf. also 3:7, 10–11, 21), Matthew notes that two women "took hold of his feet" (28:9), and John observes that Jesus told Mary Magdalene, "do not hold on to me" (20:17), details which might both usefully be compared and contrasted to the Edenic image of "a man" who "clings to his wife" in Genesis 2:24.

Whatever one thinks of these details, and they may be fruitful as readings, consider now how allusions to the Genesis cosmogony and new creation multiply almost effortlessly in John's Passion narrative and resurrection stories, so that the story, like this sentence, teems with them. Among other things, consider the following uniquely Johannine additions to the story:

– Jesus gets arrested just outside a "garden" (18:1–12); clearly, the garden motif is important to the creation story in Genesis (2:8, 10, 15–16; 3:1–3, 8, 10, 23–24).[10]

---

[4] Cf., e. g., the language alluding to Genesis in Matt 1:1, 18 and Mark 1:1, or Jesus' genealogy, which goes back to Adam in Luke 3:38.
[5] Cf. Matt 26:57–68; 27:11–14; Mark 14:60–65; 15:1–5; Luke 22:67–71; 23:3–4, 8–9; John 18:19–24; 18:33–38; 19:9–11.
[6] Cf. Matt 26:59–60; 27:18–19, 22; Mark 14:56–59; 15:10, 14; Luke 23:4, 14–15, 22, 41, 47; John 18:38; 19:4, 6, 12.
[7] Cf. Matt 27:29; Mark 15:17; John 19:2, 5.
[8] Cf. Matt 26:66; Mark 14:64; Luke 22:71; 23:22, 24–25; John 18:30–31; 19:7, 15–16.
[9] Cf. Matt 28:1; Mark 16:2; Luke 24:1; John 20:1, 19.
[10] That John uses the word κῆπος for "garden" each time in his Gospel, while Genesis 2–3 employs παράδεισος, is not very significant: the terms are used synonymously in Eccl 2:5;

- Pilate asks Jesus specifically, "What have you done?" (τί ἐποίησας;) in 18:35,[11] in a manner reminiscent of when God asked the woman, "What is this that you have done?" (τί τοῦτο ἐποίησας;) in Genesis 3:13.
- Jesus is crucified in "between" (μέσον) two others (19:18), a place which may allude to the location of the two trees "in the middle" (ἐν μέσῳ) of the garden in Genesis 2:9 and 3:3.
- In John 19:25–27, while on the cross, Jesus speaks to his "mother," calling her "Woman," terms which figure prominently in Genesis 2:23 and 3:20 as well.[12]
- When Jesus says, "It is finished" (τετέλεσται) in 19:30, his language approximates the narrator's description of God's work at the end of the first creation story in Genesis 2:1–3 (συνετέλεσεν).
- While Jesus' spirit figures prominently in John 19:30, it is God's spirit which "swept over the face of the waters" in Genesis 1:2. And, of course, John already linked the spirit with water earlier in the narrative (7:37–39; cf. 3:5).
- John notes that soldiers "pierced his side" in 19:34; should readers consider this detail in light of the man's experience in Genesis 2:21–22?
- Similarly, John records that "water came out" of Jesus' side in 19:34; readers should probably consider this detail in light of the river that "flows out of Eden to water the garden" in Genesis 2:10.
- Interestingly, the river in Eden "divides and becomes four branches" (Gen. 2:10b). Should readers of John consider the four women "standing near the cross" (19:25b) in light of this detail? Given that three of the women play no role in the narrative that follows and that the Beloved Disciple emerges in the scene (19:26–27) apart from the listing of the four women, there may be more here than meets the eye.
- As he was arrested just outside a garden, so Jesus gets buried in a garden (19:41); see the discussion above.
- Jesus is mistaken for a gardener in John 20:15, a detail which conceivably alludes to the work of God who "planted a garden" and "made to grow every tree that is pleasant to the sight and good for food" in Genesis 2:8–9.
- Most obviously, when Jesus "breathed" (ἐνεφύσησεν) on his disciples in John 20:22, the language echoes precisely the critical moment when God "breathed" (ἐνεφύσησεν) into the man in Genesis 2:7.[13]

To be sure, not every one of these allusions is equally compelling. Taken together and in ordered patterns, however, the case for the narrator's use of Genesis in shaping his own story cannot ultimately be denied, except by those

---

κῆπος is used to refer to the garden of Eden in Ezek 36:35; and the narrator in John delights in the use of synonyms elsewhere. See the helpful discussion of Johannine symbolism relative to the garden in Ruben Zimmermann, "Symbolic Communication Between John and His Reader: The Garden Symbolism in John 19–20," in *Anatomies of Narrative Criticism: The Past, Present, and Futures of the Fourth Gospel as Literature* (ed. Tom Thatcher and Stephen D. Moore; Atlanta: Society of Biblical Literature, 2008), 221–35.

[11] Contrast this scene with Matt 27:23, Mark 15:14, and Luke 23:22, where Pilate asks Jesus' accusers what he has done.

[12] I am indebted for this observation to Mary Coloe, whose essay on Jesus' mother in John appears in this volume.

[13] See esp. the discussion of this text in du Rand, "Creation Motif in the Fourth Gospel," 43–46.

who refuse to see. Their sin remains (cf. 9:41)![14] In arguing this, of course, I am not suggesting that allusions to other texts are not here to be found (the narrator is clearly capable of polyvalence), or that John's text has no concern for historical matters. I am only arguing at this point that given the prominence of new creation themes in John, we should be open to them elsewhere, perhaps even in places where readers have not generally thought to look.

Arresting Jesus

In what follows, we will examine Jesus' arrest scene (18:1–12), studying the role of the "detachment" (hereafter, "Cohort") which comes to apprehend Jesus and how those soldiers play right into Jesus' (and the narrator's) hands. We will attempt first to set the scene in its narrative context. And then, after considering the Cohort's characterization in detail, we will attempt to show how the scene lends itself to an intertextual reading with the cosmogony in Genesis.

Narrative Context

In his final private discourse with his disciples (13:31–17:26), Jesus attempted to encourage them, knowing that the hour for which he had come loomed right in front of them and that the road ahead would be especially difficult without him: "Do not let your hearts be troubled," he said repeatedly (14:1; cf. 14:27). He warned them, "the world hates you" (15:19) and "will persecute you" (15:20). "Indeed," he said, "an hour is coming when those who kill you will think that by doing so they are offering worship to God" (16:1–2). And just when they thought they finally understood him (16:29–30), when they had steeled their resolve to face what he described, he responded, "Do you now believe? The hour is coming, indeed it has come, when you will be scattered, each one to his own home, and you will leave me alone" (16:31–32). Having pulled the rug out from under their self-confidence, he encouraged them one more time: "… In the world you face persecution. But take courage; I have conquered the world!" (16:33). Having then prayed for his disciples and for those who would follow after them (ch. 17), "He went out with his disciples across the Kidron valley to a place where there was a garden, which he and his disciples entered" (18:1). Only moments later – Jesus does not pray in the gar-

---

[14] Du Rand's assessment is more circumspect and, doubtless, more accurate: "the pretension is not that the creation motif is the only or even 'leading' perspective to interpret the structure of the Fourth Gospel, but that it is worth exploiting the reading of the Gospel according to John from such a viewpoint" (Du Rand, "Creation Motif in the Fourth Gospel," 21).

den before his arrest in John, as in the Synoptics – Judas, "who betrayed him" (v. 2), arrived with a Cohort of soldiers and Jewish police (v. 3). After a dramatic encounter (vss. 4–11), Jesus was arrested, bound, and taken to Annas (v. 12) for questioning (vss. 19–24). He would be crucified only hours later and dead soon thereafter.

The Cohort's Characterization – In Action and Speech (18:3–13)

As the Cohort only occurs in this scene and is an essentially flat corporate figure, we can summarize their characterization very briefly in terms of action and speech: as for actions, in their first narrative moment they are passive, being "brought" by Judas (v. 3). Arriving at the scene (v. 3), they are described simply as "standing" (v. 5); and in responding to Jesus' words, "they stepped back" and "fell to the ground" (v. 6); after this encounter, finally, they are part of the team that "arrested," "bound" (v. 12), and "took" Jesus to Annas (v. 13). In all of this, in true Roman military fashion, they move and act as one. When Jesus is sent to Caiaphas next (v. 24), however, they are not mentioned. Perhaps the narrator wants readers to presume that the Jewish police have taken custody of the still bound prisoner (v. 24), and the Cohort's service is no longer required. While "soldiers" will flog and abuse Jesus in 19:1–3, crucify him in 19:16–25a, and ensure his death (and that of the two co-crucified ones) in 19:32–34, they are never referred to as a Cohort and therefore will not figure into our discussion in this essay.[15] In terms of explicit action, then, the Cohort's only real activity in John comes at Jesus' arrest.

But they also speak – twice. In response to Jesus' twice repeated question about whom they sought, "they answered, 'Jesus of Nazareth'" in v. 5 and "they said, 'Jesus of Nazareth'" in v. 7. As in action, so in speech: they speak as one. Even though it is only the same three words, twice, a more literal translation proves helpful here, as they actually said, "Jesus the Nazorean" ('Ιησοῦν τὸν Ναζωραῖον) both times. This is probably significant, as we shall see below. We should note also that the narrator mentions explicitly that they have in their possession "lanterns," "torches," and "weapons" (v. 3), and, implicitly, something with which to bind Jesus (cf. v. 12). Finally, readers learn that this Cohort is led by an "officer" who also takes part in Jesus' arrest (v. 12). This is the only explicit and implicit information readers are given about the Cohort. But, as with all literature, enormous "gaps" remain. We attempt to fill in some of these in what follows.

---

[15] But see Michael Labahn's essay on the crucifying soldiers in this volume.

The Cohort's Lanterns, Torches, and Weapons (18:3)

The text infers that Jesus and his followers arrived in the garden sometime after sunset; actually, after midnight seems likely, as he stood before Pilate only some time later, "early in the morning" (18:28). It was dark in any case – as we have already noted, those who came to arrest him had both "lanterns and torches" (18:3). But how does this detail function? Should readers just assume that it is part of the story-teller's art, that it is simply descriptive of what they carried? On such a reading, the narrator might simply be trying to communicate that it was a dark night,[16] or that the arresting party, having been dispatched from the nearby Fortress Antonia,[17] needed light to find their way across the Kidron, or that they were concerned they would not be able to find Jesus if, upon their arrival, he hid in some shadowy corner of the garden. But given that the expression "lanterns and torches" is, first of all, a lovely example of literary redundancy[18] and that, secondly, neither source of light figures again in the narrative, readers should most likely consider other possibilities. Indeed, readers should understand these "lanterns and torches" as related to the broader "light and darkness" motif so common in this Gospel.[19] Read from this perspective, readers will recall (and, of course, sense the irony) that Jesus is the "light of the world" (8:12) and that "those who walk at night stumble, because the light is not in them" (11:10). In view of these earlier notices, it is no wonder the Cohort falls down in 18:6!

The Cohort carries weapons (ὅπλων) too.[20] While not redundant like the previous "torches" added to "lanterns," the notice is surely unnecessary. Soldiers always carried weapons. Again, since the narrator makes nothing of these weapons in this scene (but cf. 19:23, 34), even when Simon Peter pulls his own sword in v. 10, readers should be open to attaching some sort of symbolic meaning to them. If nothing else, perhaps weapons stand simply "in contrast to all that Jesus stands for, in contrast particularly to the gentleness of the foot-washing."[21] As instruments of darkness, they are designed solely to injure, to

---

[16] As noted by a number of scholars, given a full moon for Passover, the lanterns and torches may have been superfluous (see, e. g., Craig S. Keener, *The Gospel of John: A Commentary* [2 vols.; Peabody, Mass.: Hendrickson, 2003], 2:1078).

[17] On this fortress and its use by the Romans during the time of Jesus, see J. F. Hall, "Antonia, Tower Of," *ABD* 1:274.

[18] On this type of redundancy, some readers of this essay may recall that when Elwood of the "Blues Brothers" asked the woman tending bar "Uh, what kind of music do you usually have here?" she replied, "Oh, we got both kinds. We got Country and Western!"

[19] See especially, Craig R. Koester, *Symbolism in the Fourth Gospel: Meaning, Mystery, Community* (2d ed.; Minneapolis: Fortress, 2003), 141–73.

[20] On Roman military weapons specifically, see Jonathan C. N. Coulston, "Arms and Armour-Roman," in *The Oxford Companion to Classical Civilization* (ed. Simon Hornblower and Antony Spawforth; Oxford: Oxford University Press, 1998), 76–78.

[21] Thomas L. Brodie, *The Gospel According to John* (Oxford: Oxford University Press, 1993), 524.

kill, to destroy. Jesus, on the other hand, "came that they may have life, and have it abundantly" (10:10). Thus Jesus does not carry weapons or throw stones (7:53–8:11, 59; 10:31; 11:8)[22] and when Simon Peter brandishes a sword and strikes (18:10) in fulfillment of a promise (13:37) and presumably in Jesus' defense, he gets soundly rebuked (18:11).

The Cohort's Leadership

Judas "brought" (λαβών) the Cohort (18:3); but what ought readers to make of this observation? Was he merely the guide for the group or its leader? One could infer the former reading based on the fact that the narrator already communicated in v. 2 that "Judas ... also knew the place, because Jesus often met there with his disciples" (cf. Luke 21:37). In other words, when Judas "brought" them, he simply led them to a place they did not know, a place he knew Jesus was likely to be.[23] Two other details support this reading. First, while they are described in relation to Judas in v. 3, he is later described in relation to them in v. 5: he was standing "with them;"[24] if Judas was the leader of this group, perhaps the narrator would have pointed out that "the cohort was standing with Judas." Secondly, at the actual arrest in v. 12, the narrator introduces an "officer" as the leader of this Cohort.

On the other hand, Judas is not only the one who betrayed him (although he is that; see vss. 2, 5), he is also at this point in the story, "Satan-in-flesh," or, as Augustine put it, "the wolf in sheep's clothing."[25] Now, Jesus had already referred to Judas as "a devil" in 6:70; but in 13:2 "*the devil* had already put it into the heart of Judas ... to betray him" and, later, after he received the bread from Jesus, "Satan entered into him" (13:27). Almost certainly, the narrator thinks of this Satan as the "ruler of this world" who "now...will be driven out" (12:31) and who "has been condemned" (16:11). But immediately before Jesus' arrest, in the final discourse (ch. 14–17), he also said this to his disciples: "I will no longer talk much with you, *for the ruler of this world is coming*

---

[22] Although he makes and uses a whip on animals and perhaps even people in 2:15! On this issue, see Clayton N. Croy, "The Messianic Whippersnapper: Did Jesus Use a Whip on People in the Temple (John 2:15)?" *JBL* 128 (2009): 555–68.

[23] C. Kingsley Barrett concludes, "John probably means no more than that Judas acted as guide" (idem, *The Gospel According to St. John* [2d ed.; Philadelphia: Westminster, 1978], 518); and Raymond E. Brown notes, "no particular authority is [here] attributed to Judas" (idem, *The Gospel According to John (xiii–xxi)* [AB 29A; New York: Doubleday, 1970], 807); so also, Frederick F. Bruce, *The Gospel of John* (Grand Rapids, Mich.: Eerdmans, 1983), 340.

[24] Judas' being "with them" though may serve the more critical function of creating a contrast with the Beloved Disciple who later was "with Jesus" in 18:15, and a comparison with Peter who was "with" the guards warming himself by the fire in 18:18.

[25] Cited in Joel C. Elowsky, ed., *Ancient Christian Commentary on Scripture: John 11–21* (Downers Grove, Ill.: InterVarsity Press, 2007), 266.

(ἔρχεται). *He has no power over me*" (14:30). A good case can be made therefore that, on one level, when Judas "came" (18:3; ἔρχεται) bringing the Cohort and others to arrest Jesus, he incarnated the one who "is coming." And as "the ruler of this world," therefore, he clearly leads this Cohort. But when "the ruler of this world" (incarnate in Judas) fell to the ground when Jesus said "I Am"[26] in 18:6, Jesus struck the serpent's head, showing once and for all that Satan "has no power over me."[27]

The Size of the Cohort

How big was this Cohort? The term we have been translating as Cohort, σπεῖρα, can mean simply a "group of soldiers" – hence the NRSV's "detachment of soldiers" in v. 3.[28] Still, from the time of the Marian reforms to the Roman military in 107 B.C.E.,[29] which among other things instituted the maintenance of a standing army, the term σπεῖρα referred more specifically to one-tenth of a 6,000 man Roman legion – thus, six hundred men.[30] Given the narrator's penchant for the dramatic, that ancient readers (especially around the time of Trajan (98–117 C.E.) or Hadrian (117–138 C.E.), when the Roman military was at its height of power) may very well have read it as a technical military term, and that the Cohort's "officer" in v. 12 is described as a χιλίαρχος ("ruler of a thousand"),[31] readers ought at least to allow for the possibility that the narrator was describing six hundred professional soldiers, and not simply a smaller detachment from their number.[32] This reading becomes more credible still when the Cohort which goes out to arrest Jesus gets distinguished from the "soldiers" (στρατιῶται) who abuse and crucify Jesus and then confirm his death in ch. 19.

---

[26] On this translation, and its implications, see more below.
[27] Of course, on yet another level, when Jesus said, "He has no power over me" in 14:30b, he was also anticipating what he would say to Pilate, Caesar's representative, in 19:11.
[28] But why do they translate the same term simply as "soldiers" in v. 12?
[29] Le Bohec cautions against attributing to Marius too many reforms related to the Roman military, but notes that by the time of the "Social War" (91–88 B.C.E.), "the cohort had gained significantly in importance as a military unit" ("Armies," in *Brill's New Pauly: Encyclopaedia of the Ancient World* [ed. Hubert Cancik and Helmuth Schneider; Leiden: Brill, 2003], 2:11).
[30] Brown (*John*, 807–808), Barrett (*John*, 518) and others suggest that it could also refer to the subdivision of a cohort called a maniple, totaling two hundred men. Bruce, however, contends that "an auxiliary cohort, such as garrisoned the Antonia fortress northwest of the temple area, comprised a paper strength of 1,000 men (760 infantry and 240 cavalry)" (*John*, 340). For another variation on this understanding of the Roman Cohort, see the discussion in Le Bohec, "Armies," esp. 2:11–12. Note that in 2 Macc 8:22–23, the narrator uses the same word to describe Judas' division of his 6,000 man force into four 1,500 man cohorts.
[31] Cf. Brodie, *John*, 524 and Barrett, *John*, 518.
[32] Origen explains why "a great multitude was gathered against him with swords and staves" in his *Commentary on Matthew* (cited in Elowsky, *Ancient Christian Commentary*, 266–67).

The Cohort's Reinforcements?

On this reading then, six hundred well-armed, professionally-trained men,[33] also arrived with "police from the chief priests and the Pharisees" (18:3). Why the additional Jewish police? Were they all not simply looking for Jesus and possibly also his disciples (cf. 18:19)? In other words, a few day laborers and fishermen, perhaps some teenagers too? Had Judas given the soldiers faulty intelligence about their number or intentions? Did they expect trouble, some form of armed resistance? Given that Peter had a sword (v. 10), perhaps this substantial mobilization was just an ancient example of "shock and awe." Or does it speak to the authorities' level of frustration at several botched attempts to arrest and/or kill Jesus on other occasions?[34] Are these numbers of soldiers and police indicative of an attitude among the authorities that says, "He's not going to slip through our fingers again!"[35] Still, what if the narrator only intends to have a laugh at the Roman military's expense, suggesting that this battle-tested Cohort needed Jewish reinforcements! In any case, the size of the Cohort aside, it does seem at least possible that the narrator simply wants to suggest that Jews and Gentiles together arrested him (18:12) – "the world did not know him" (1:10) – and, therefore, that they together bear the responsibility for his death.[36] Again, the "gaps" in the narrative of John create far more questions than answers.

The Cohort's Mission – "Jesus, the Nazorean"

Whatever we are to make of these questions, one thing is clear: six hundred Roman soldiers heightens the drama at the critical scene when they get into a dialogue with Jesus. Readers should note Jesus' initiative in the scene and that his question, "Whom are you looking for?" in v. 4 and then again in v. 7 is unnecessary and redundant. Jesus knows everything in John[37] and undoubtedly knows for whom these soldiers are looking. To be sure, when they say,

---

[33] Brown (*John*, 808) describes the force which would have been available not long after Jesus' time through to the middle of the second century: "the Roman prefect or procurator in Palestine had at his disposal … a cohort (*Cohors Secunda Italica*) consisting of troops mustered in Italy and complemented by recruits from Samaria and Caesarea."

[34] Cf. 5:18; 7:1, 19, 30, 32, 44, 45–46; 8:20, 37, 59; 10:31–33, 39; 11:8, 16, 49–53, 57.

[35] Even with these numbers, readers may recall that five thousand men were not able to conscript Jesus to make him king, much less contain him, earlier in the story (6:10, 14–15).

[36] Keener writes: "John may be making a theological statement: both Romans and Jews bore responsibility for Jesus' arrest" (*John*, 2:1080). See also the ambiguity related to this matter at Jesus' sentencing and crucifixion in ch. 19.

[37] Cf. 1:42, 47–50; 2:24–25; 4:17–18; 6:6, 15, 64, etc.

"Jesus, the Nazorean" (Ἰησοῦν τὸν Ναζωραῖον) in v. 5 and v. 7 in response to Jesus' questions, on one level, they are only trying to identify Jesus, the one from Nazareth (cf. 1:45–46), hence the NRSV's translation. But the narrator's skillful use of language here is noteworthy, perhaps even startling – readers should not miss it.[38] So, when they say, "Jesus, the Nazorean" in v. 5, and then repeat this answer verbatim a second time in v. 7, the narrator tips his hand by means of the repetition.[39]

In short, in John's Gospel this name may be more than a name – it may be a title! The word "Nazorean" might very well be playing on the Jewish tradition related to "the Branch" (*netser* in Hebrew; cf. Isa. 11:1) especially as that tradition is developed in Zechariah 3:6–10 and 6:9–15.[40] If so, since "the Branch" will "build the temple of the LORD" (Zech 6:12), this scene anticipates the dénouement of the temple theme in the Fourth Gospel when Pilate's placard over Jesus' head identifies him as "Jesus, the Nazorean" (Ἰησοῦς ὁ Ναζωραῖος) in 19:19.[41] Pilate's inscription therefore unwittingly makes the point clear: "Jesus [is] the Branch, the King of the 'Jews.'" Readers will no doubt recall that Jesus said earlier in the story, "Destroy this temple, and in three days I will raise it up" (2:19) and that the narrator quickly added, "he was speaking of the temple of his body" (2:21). In his death on the cross, then, Jesus – the Branch – builds the true temple of God.[42]

The Cohort's Impotence, Unbelief and (implicit) Obedience!

When six hundred Roman soldiers "stepped back and fell to the ground" (v. 6) after Jesus pronounced the divine name "I Am" (ἐγὼ εἰμι), the scene becomes utterly surreal.[43] One moment an armed Cohort representing the mightiest

---

[38] A similar repetition playing on the word Nazareth occurs in Nathanael's story in 1:45–51. See my discussion of that text in my essay on Nathanael in this volume.

[39] On the importance of repetition in biblical narrative, see Robert Alter, *The Art of Biblical Narrative* (New York: Basic Books, 1981), 97–113.

[40] Brown briefly surveys this and other interpretive options related to the word "Nazorean" in *John*, 809–10.

[41] Note the differences with the Synoptics at this critical point (Matt 27:37; Mark 15:26; Luke 23:38).

[42] I discuss these conclusions in further detail in my essay on Nathanael in this volume. There, I also cite additional scholarly support for the position taken here.

[43] Most scholars understand ἐγὼ εἰμι to mean more than the NRSV's translation "I am he" suggests. Keener, for example, notes that ἐγὼ εἰμι "can mean simply 'I am (he),' that is, 'I am the one you are seeking.' But the reader of the Gospel by this point understands that the Jesus of this Gospel means more than this: he is declaring his divine identity" (Keener, *John*, 2:1082). He cites several others who affirm this reading as well. And we can add to his list, Brodie, *John*, 525–26; Brown, *John*, 818; Bruce, *John*, 341; and Andrew T. Lincoln, *The Gospel According to Saint John* (BNTC 4; London: Continuum, 2005), 444.

army the world had ever known stood ready to carry out their mission come what may, and, in the next, having heard nothing more than two words, they fell back, disarmed and undone. Powerless.[44] Had Jesus decided to walk out among them, disappearing back into Jerusalem or Bethany or even across the Jordan, they could have done nothing to stop him. Pilate's posturing in 19:10, declaring his power to release or to crucify Jesus, seems all the more ridiculous, all the more pathetic in light of our narrative – power indeed! Who is he kidding?

That the Cohort "stepped back" (ἀπῆλθαν εἰς τὰ ὀπίσω) before falling perhaps says something about them too. The narrator has used precisely this language once before in the Gospel. After Jesus' difficult discourse in the synagogue at Capernaum, many of his own disciples "turned back (ἀπῆλθον εἰς τὰ ὀπίσω) and no longer went about with him" (6:66). The language therefore intends "to express rejection of belief."[45] What if they fall not only because they have been overcome by the divine name, but because they refuse to believe as well? We will return to this question soon enough.

The Cohort only seems to recover when Jesus re-engages them "again" in v. 7, reminding them as it were of their business that dark night. And when Jesus initiates his own arrest here once more, readers understand even more clearly his earlier declaration with respect to his mission: "No one takes [my life] from me, but I lay it down of my own accord. I have power to lay it down, and I have power to take it up again" (10:18).[46]

As yet more evidence of Jesus' authority over this vanquished, prostrate Cohort, notice how they implicitly obey his command with reference to his disciples: "Let these men go," Jesus said in v. 8. And that is exactly what they do, despite the fact that one of them (Simon Peter) attacked and wounded the servant of the high priest (v. 10). Should not Simon Peter have been arrested also? Since Annas will question Jesus "about his disciples" directly in v. 19, thereby showing his interest in them and their activities too, one must wonder why Jesus' disciples were not arrested and bound as well, especially given the size of the Cohort marshalled against them. The only answer provided by the narrator relates to Jesus' authoritative command in v. 8 – "let these men go."

---

[44] Augustine writes: "With no other weapon than his own solitary voice uttering the words 'I am,' he knocked down, repelled and rendered helpless that great crowd, even with all their ferocious hatred and terror of arms" (cited in Elowsky, *Ancient Christian Commentary*, 268).

[45] Brodie, *John*, 526.

[46] So also, Lincoln, *John*, 444.

The Arrest and Fruitful Echoes of the Cosmogony in Genesis

Finally, returning to the point with which we began, how does an intertextual reading of this scene allude to the cosmological setting of Genesis? First, unlike the Synoptic Gospels, the arrest scene in John takes place near a garden (18:1; cf. also the burial and resurrection scenes in chs. 19–20). Obviously, the garden image, so important to the Gospel, creates a positive link between this narrative and the primeval narrative in Gen 1–3. And it did so for ancient readers as well. Cyril of Alexandria (*ca.* 375–444 C. E.) writes: "The place was a garden, typifying the paradise of old. For in this place as it were, all places were recapitulated and our return to humanity's ancient condition was consummated. For the troubles of humanity began in paradise, while Christ's sufferings, which brought us deliverance from all the evil that happened to us in times past, began in [this] garden."[47]

Given the connection ancient and modern readers have made between this garden and Eden, perhaps we can pursue this type of reading further. Observe then that the narrator makes a point of noting that Jesus "went out with his disciples" from some undisclosed location in or near Jerusalem (cf. 12:12) and that upon arriving at the garden, "he and his disciples entered" (18:1).[48] Are these clauses simply a narrative description of their movements, a way of showing that they went from point A to point B? Or is there something more here?

After the man and the woman's sin in Genesis, God "sent him forth from the garden of Eden … He drove out the man," placing cherubim "to guard the way to the tree of life" (3:23–24). The fact that the man and the woman were expelled from the garden and barred from returning to it in Genesis, may explain the narrator's use of language here. In our narrative, Jesus leads his disciples back *into the garden*. Perhaps as "the way, and the truth, and the life" (14:6), he is leading them back to the tree of life (again, in John only, he will be crucified in the "middle" (19:18), a location which alludes to the location of the tree of life in Genesis 2:9; 3:3). The narrator also observes that this garden was "across the Kidron valley," a valley just to the east of Jerusalem. If the original or implied readers were familiar with that geographical fact, they may have recalled that God "planted a garden in Eden, in the east" (Gen 2:8; cf. 3:24).

Second, Judas, the Cohort, and the police "came there" (ἔρχεται ἐκεῖ) – a point which, on this reading anyway, puts them at the very threshold of the garden, *but not in it*. The text does not say explicitly that they entered, as Jesus and his disciples did. In fact, the confrontation ensues when Jesus, initiating as

---

[47] Cited in Elowsky, *Ancient Christian Commentary*, 265.
[48] Gardens were often walled enclosures. That they "enter" the garden and Jesus exits in v. 4, "indicate it was a clearly defined enclosure" (Lincoln, *John*, 442).

he often does in this Gospel,[49] "went out" (NIV; ἐξῆλθεν) to address them. Note, Jesus could have just addressed them, but he did not; he moved toward them first. Ultimately, "knowing all that was to happen to him" (v. 4),[50] he exits the garden to meet the arresting party before they enter. Thus, he meets them on the edge of the garden, thereby protecting the garden and those in it (cf. vss. 8–11), perhaps like the cherubim in Gen 3:24.

Third, after the Christophanic exclamation, "I Am" (v. 5), the entire arresting party "stepped back" and "fell to the ground" (v. 6). As we have already noted, the Christophany clearly overpowers the *Roman* Cohort and *Jewish* police, as well as Judas – Satan-in-flesh and "the ruler of this world": Jesus has indeed "conquered the world!" (16:33). But is this all readers should see in this notice? If so, they could have simply fallen before him. The Cohort did not, however. First, they "stepped back" – thus rejecting him (cf. 6:66) and moving *further from the garden*, further from the one who offers life in this Gospel!

Lastly, if we pursue this type of cosmological reading here and take one more step with it, observe that the Cohort and the rest did not just fall. They did not fall at his feet (cf. Esther 8:3; Mark 5:22; Rev 1:17), or on their faces (cf. Gen 17:3, 17). Instead, they fell "to the ground," utilizing the locative adverb χαμαί.[51] In Genesis, God "formed man from the dust of the ground" (2:7; ἔπλασεν ὁ θεὸς τὸν ἄνθρωπον χοῦν ἀπὸ τῆς γῆς). Of course, the play on the words *adam* and *adamah* in the Hebrew version of this verse is well known. And later, after the man's sin, God cursed the man, saying: "You are dust, and to dust you shall return" (3:19; γῆ εἶ καὶ εἰς γῆν ἀπελεύσῃ). To be sure, the narrator of Genesis does not use the construction found in John to make any of these points, clearly preferring the noun γῆ for "ground/dust."[52] Interestingly, John's Gospel employs the noun γῆ thirteen times.[53] So why not just use it here in 18:6, so as to make the connection to Genesis more obvious?

---

[49] Cf. 1:38, 43, 47; 4:7, 16; 5:6; 6:5, etc.

[50] Despite its prevalence elsewhere in John, perhaps readers should also explore the themes related to Jesus' perfect knowledge here as well as his sense of responsibility later in this scene ("am I not to drink the cup the Father has given me," he says in v. 11). In Genesis, the primeval sin relates to knowledge and insofar as the man blames the woman, and the woman blames the serpent when they are discovered in it, they deny responsibility.

[51] Cf. 9:6; on this adverb's locative or dative force, see Archibald T. Robertson, *A Grammar of the Greek New Testament in the Light of Historical Research* (Nashville: Broadman, 1934), 295–96.

[52] In fact, the noun gets used over 40 times in Genesis 1–3 and over 350 times throughout Genesis. Note also that χοῦς ("dust") disappears from the text at this point.

[53] The narrator in John uses γῆ quite broadly: so, for example, the noun is used to refer to the "countryside" (3:22), a "field" (12:24), the "shore" of a lake (6:21; 21:8, 9, 11), and to the "earth" itself (3:31 [3x]; 12:32; 17:4); and, in exceptions which prove the rule (as they are not likely to be original to the Gospel), the narrator uses the noun twice when Jesus bends to write on the "ground" in 8:6, 8. Genesis employs the term broadly as well.

The answer could be as simple as this: the narrator clearly enjoys variation, seeming to know intuitively that a steady stream of perfect allusions makes for predictable literature, and limits polyvalent interpretations.

In view of the narrator's numerous allusions to Genesis elsewhere, then, perhaps χαμαί works just fine in this context. Indeed (and with apologies to Prof. Barr who delighted in deconstructing these kinds of arguments![54]), etymologically the word is related to both the Latin *humus* – "earth/ground" ("humble," "humiliate," "exhume," etc., all derive from this word) and *homo* – "human."[55] What gets implied therefore when the soldiers fell "to the ground"? Simply this: in "stepping back" from the Christophany, they participate in the "sin of the world" (1:29). And because they engage in this sin, refusing to do "the work of God" as described in this Gospel (6:29), they are therefore "condemned already" (3:18). Thus, in keeping with God's original judgment in Genesis, they are rightly returned to the ground – the dust – whence they came.

---

[54] James Barr, *The Semantics of Biblical Language* (Eugene, Oreg.: Wipf & Stock, 2004; repr. 1961).

[55] On the etymology of χαμαί, see the discussion of the hypothetical root *dhghem* in Calvert Watkins, *The American Heritage Dictionary of Indo-European Roots* (Boston: Houghton Mifflin, 2000), 20. On the word's use in Greek literature, see *LSJ*, 1975.

Malchus:
Cutting Up in the Garden

Christopher W. Skinner

Setting the Stage

Modern readers of the canonical gospels are well acquainted with the character identified in the Fourth Gospel as Malchus.[1] Known simply as the poor fellow who loses his ear to the sword of Peter, Malchus is for many, a narrative indicator of the tension that mounts just prior to Jesus' arrest in the garden. Though Malchus appears briefly and only in this pericope, several elements of his characterization stand out as important for what follows in the Johannine Passion. In this brief study we will employ a narrative-critical approach to examine the role Malchus plays in the story, with specific emphasis on how his presentation contributes to the developing plot and the presentation of other characters.

In his only scene, Malchus plays the role of an agent (or actant) – generally described as a character with little or no development that functions essentially to advance the plot.[2] He arrives on the scene as part of a nameless, faceless mob, remains silent, and as far as the reader knows, remains motionless. Yet the narrator has made it a point to include his name and his encounter with Peter and Jesus. Often in narrative literature anonymous characters serve as agents whose primary function is to advance the action of the story. Conversely, characters with names are generally the more important players. This trend is reversed in the Fourth Gospel; greater models of faith are left nameless while named characters continually reflect an improper response to Jesus.[3] Malchus fits the latter description. He appears briefly, stands in opposition to Jesus, and exists almost solely to advance the action of the narrative. Keeping

---

[1] A version of this story appears with minor variations in all four canonical Gospels: Mark 14:47–50; Matt 26:51–56; Luke 22:49–53; and John 18:1–11.

[2] For more on this, see Fred W. Burnett, "Characterization and Reader Construction of Characters in the Gospels," *Semeia* 63 (1993): 3–28, here 18–20. See also, Cornelis Bennema, "A Theory of Character in the Fourth Gospel with Reference to Ancient and Modern Literature," *BibInt* 17 (2009): 375–421.

[3] On this topic, see David Beck, *The Discipleship Paradigm: Readers and Anonymous Characters in the Fourth Gospel* (BIS 27; Leiden: Brill, 1997); and also idem, "The Narrative Function of Anonymity in the Fourth Gospel," *Semeia* 63 (1993): 143–58.

these things in mind, we proceed to a consideration of Malchus in the context of John 18:1-11.

John 18:1-11

At the beginning of John 18, Jesus and his disciples are departing across the Kidron valley for an unnamed olive grove. Once there, Jesus will be taken captive and transported first to the high priest and then to Pilate. The so-called "Farewell Discourse" (13:1-17:26) has just concluded and 18:1 opens with the words ταῦτα εἰπὼν Ἰησοῦς ἐξῆλθεν ("After he had spoken these things, Jesus departed"). Resuming the story *in medias res*, the reader finds this phrase to be a helpful reminder of the high priestly prayer of chapter 17, where Jesus prayed for himself (vss. 1-5), his disciples (vss. 6-19), and all future believers (vss. 20-26). The events of 18:1-11 set in motion the Johannine Passion and begin to fulfill the first part of Jesus' prayer (17:1-5) – that the Father would "glorify the Son." The Johannine agenda can only be accomplished by way of the cross, the ultimate means by which the Son will be glorified.

Along with Jesus and the disciples (v. 1), Judas Iscariot (v. 2), a Roman cohort (τὴν σπεῖραν = 600 soldiers), and a detachment of police from the Jewish leaders (v. 3) appear on the narrative stage of John 18. Malchus, our subject here, is a member of the Jewish delegation. Jesus now faces opposition from one of his own (Judas), the Jewish leaders, and new enemies in the form of Roman officials. This historically unlikely combination is a Johannine symbol for the powers of darkness arraying to oppose Jesus (cf. 1:5). In an ironic twist, the group comes under the cover of night, with lanterns (φανῶν) and torches (λαμπάδων), bringing their own illumination to take the light of humanity into their custody.[4]

Aware of what is about to happen, Jesus takes immediate control of the situation by identifying himself to his would-be captors (vss. 4-8a) and by securing release for his disciples (v. 8b). If Jesus is going to return to the Father, he must first be taken into custody by this delegation. In the process he does not intend to lose any of those whom the Father has entrusted to him (v. 9, cf. 6:39; 17:12). Instead of departing, however, Peter pulls his sword and strikes Malchus, the servant of the high priest, cutting off his right ear (v. 10). Jesus rebukes Peter for his impetuous action by commanding him to put his sword away and by making it clear that he intends to fulfill the will of the Father (v. 11).

In this brief scene the reader learns several things about Malchus. Since direct character description is rarely employed in the Fourth Gospel, most

---

[4] Cf. 1:4-9; 3:19-21; 9:5; 12:35-44.

characters are presented by the indirect means of speech or action. There is little narrative space within this scene for any character to be developed substantially. Consequently, Malchus becomes one of a small group of Fourth Gospel characters to receive a direct description. Three specific elements of his presentation by the narrator deserve further treatment.

1. His name is Malchus. Numerous suggestions have been set forth regarding the significance of the name Malchus.[5] Barrett suggests that the name derives from the Hebrew מֶלֶךְ ("king"), but he fails to comment on how this is significant for the present scene.[6] Guilding sees a reference to Zech 11:6 that was read as part of a Passover lectionary ("I will deliver each into the hand of his king," מַלְכּוֹ).[7] However, this explanation does not sufficiently account for what occurs in the scene, unless Peter's actions are regarded as a reversal of expectations raised by the intertextual reference.

The name itself probably has no specific meaning or outward significance. Rather, the presence of a named character (Malchus) face to face with another named character (Peter) is part of the Johannine presentation of character interaction. Also, named characters in the Fourth Gospel are associated with an improper understanding of or response to Jesus. That his name is given is a signal to the reader that Malchus represents spiritual incomprehension.[8] His association with the arresting party reinforces this interpretation.

2. He serves the high priest. Malchus is also described as τὸν τοῦ ἀρχιερέως δοῦλον, "the servant of the high priest" (v. 10). This detail connects Malchus to οἱ Ἰουδαῖοι, the Johannine opponents of Jesus who have by now become a fixture in the story.[9] Malchus' association with the Jewish leadership explicitly sets him in opposition to Jesus. His vocation as servant to the high priest also anticipates what will happen in the forthcoming interaction between Jesus and Annas (18:19–24).[10] As we approach the climax of the story, references to the Jewish leadership are intended to heighten the reader's sense of Jewish animos-

---

[5] Malchus was not an uncommon name during this period. Brown notes that, "'Malchus' is found five times in Josephus and is known from Palmyrene and Nabatean inscriptions (whence the suggestion that Malchus was an Arab)." See Raymond E. Brown, *The Gospel according to John (xiii–xxi)* (AB 29A: New York: Doubleday, 1970), 812.

[6] C. Kingsley Barrett, *The Gospel According to St. John* (2d ed.; London: SPCK, 1978), 522.

[7] Aileen Guilding, *The Fourth Gospel and Jewish Worship: A Study of the Relation of St. John's Gospel to the Ancient Jewish Lectionary System* (Oxford: Clarendon, 1960), 278–80.

[8] See my own treatment of Fourth Gospel characters where I suggest that misunderstanding is the primary category by which Johannine characters should be evaluated. Christopher W. Skinner, *John and Thomas – Gospels in Conflict? Johannine Characterization and the Thomas Question* (PTMS 115; Eugene, Oreg.: Pickwick, 2009).

[9] Here I have employed the Greek οἱ Ἰουδαῖοι rather than a translational equivalent (e. g., "the Jews") in an effort to avoid any potentially anti-Jewish sentiment.

[10] Caiaphas, the high priest, is also mentioned in this section (18:24, 28) but there is no scene where he and Jesus share a face to face encounter.

ity toward Jesus. Malchus thus represents opposition to Jesus, rejection of his message, and zeal for his demise.

This scene also provides the foundation for a contrast between Jesus, the "good shepherd" (cf. 10:11–18) and the high priest, the shepherd of Israel (cf. Jer 22:22–23:8). After Malchus is struck, Jesus admonishes Peter and corrects him with an explanation of his mission (τὸ ποτήριον ὃ δέδωκέν μοι ὁ πατὴρ οὐ μὴ πίω αὐτό; v. 11c). In 18:19–24 Jesus is struck by a minion of Annas. Not only does Annas not intervene but he sends Jesus bound to Caiaphas. By Johannine standards, neither Annas nor Caiaphas will qualify for the title of "good shepherd," since neither steps into to curb the violence or the sham prosecution.

3. *He is victimized by Peter.* Peter's actions with the sword contribute more to his own character development than to that of Malchus. This is probably the most important reason for Malchus' inclusion in the story. He further highlights Peter's reckless and impulsive behavior. In the fray Malchus loses his right ear, a detail the Johannine account shares with the Lukan version (cf. Luke 22:50).[11]

Several fanciful suggestions have been offered to explain the significance of Malchus losing his *right* ear. It has been suggested (1) that this detail is meant to portray Peter's attack as cowardly, (2) that damage on the right side of the body represents an indignity, or (3) that the detail confirms that Peter was left-handed.[12] These are interesting interpretive options but it seems more likely that the detail has been added to lend greater vividness to the scene. It is also interesting to note that the double diminutive ὠτάριον is used, rather than οὖς (the standard term) or ὠτίον (the simple diminutive form). It may be that ὠτάριον is intended as a reference to Malchus' earlobe rather than his entire ear.[13]

After he is rebuked by Jesus in 18:11 and the delegation takes Jesus away, Peter will follow the arresting party into the courtyard of the high priest where he will be confronted by a relative of Malchus.[14] In that moment Peter will deny ever knowing Jesus (18:26–27). Thus, in one scene Malchus is associated with Peter's intention to fight for and even die with Jesus. In another scene

---

[11] Because of this it has not been uncommon for commentators to suggest that the evangelist had access to or knowledge of the Lukan version of this story.

[12] See Raymond E. Brown's discussion of these interpretive options (idem, *The Death of the Messiah: From Gethsemane to the Grave: A Commentary on the Passion Narratives in the Four Gospels* [2 vols.; New York: Doubleday, 1994], 1:271–72).

[13] BDAG (p. 1107) defines ὠτάριον as "outer ear" but points out that in later Greek this form was used interchangeably with οὖς.

[14] Malchus is not mentioned by name in 18:26. The narrator refers to him as συγγενὴς ὢν οὗ ἀπέκοψεν Πέτρος τὸ ὠτίον, "a relative of the man whose ear Peter had cut off."

Malchus (by name rather than presence) is associated with Peter's shameful denial and inability to follow through on his earlier proclamation that he is willing to die alongside Jesus (cf. 13:37). Even as a minor player, Malchus adds theological depth to the narrator's presentation of Peter's contradictory character as well as the picture of Jesus' commitment to his mission.

Conclusion

The reading offered here suggests that the presence of Malchus in John 18 helps advance the action of the narrative and develop the story in three important ways. First, in placing Malchus alongside Peter, the narrator further highlights Peter's impetuous nature, his failure to comprehend Jesus' mission, and his inconsistency as a disciple. The narrative curtain will ultimately fall in John 20 without Peter fully realizing the promise expected in the changing of his name (1:42).[15] Only in the later material of ch. 21 is Peter restored to a place of prominence.[16] Second, in the Malchus scene, the narrator finds another opportunity to emphasize Jesus' commitment to fulfill his mission from the Father (v. 11). The Johannine mission consists of completing the Father's will and glorifying the Son. For this to happen, the Son must return to the Father and the παράκλητος must be sent. Third, the victimization of Malchus and Jesus' refusal to accept Peter's actions as legitimate further develops the Christological viewpoint of the Fourth Gospel. As χριστός (messiah), Jesus will defeat the powers of darkness by submission to the Father's will, not by force. The brief appearance of Malchus in the garden scene highlights these Johannine themes and pushes the Passion narrative one step closer to its climax at the cross.

---

[15] The changing of Peter's name from from Σίμων (Hebrew, "God has heard") to Κηφᾶς (Aramaic, "rock") is an early signal to the reader of Peter's importance. It holds the promise of strength and fortitude but that expectation is not met prior to John 21.

[16] Even here there is no little debate about Peter's significance in John 21. For a balanced approach to historical and literary issues, see Francis J. Moloney, "John 21 and the Johannine Story," in *Anatomies of Narrative Criticism: The Past, Present, and Futures of the Fourth Gospel as Literature* (ed. Tom Thatcher and Stephen D. Moore; SBLRBS 55; Atlanta: Society of Biblical Literature, 2008), 237–51.

People in the Courtyard: Escalating Darkness

Helen K. Bond

The high priest's courtyard contains a surprisingly large number of minor characters: a female doorkeeper, arresting officers and servants of the high priest. By any reckoning, their roles are small, representing nothing more than walk-on parts in a much grander narrative. Their purpose, as Alan Culpepper notes, is not to interact with one another but rather to allow the narrator to present a number of responses to Jesus, and to enable contrasts and comparisons to be drawn between more significant actors in the drama.[1] In this short essay we shall see that these characters allow the implied author to contrast Peter's failure with both the witness of Jesus before the high priest and the faithfulness of the Beloved Disciple.

Narrative Links

The courtyard scene has a number of narrative links with other passages in the Gospel. Most striking, given the high degree of shared vocabulary, is the discourse of John 10:1–17: There Jesus, the Good Shepherd, makes it clear that he will protect his "sheep" from thieves and robbers, and that he is willing to lay down his own life on their behalf (10:11, 15, 17, 18). All of this becomes a reality in the garden scene of 18:1–11 (another enclosed space, like the sheepfold[2]). As Judas and the arresting party approach, Jesus comes out to them and identifies himself clearly with the words "I am" (ἐγώ εἰμι; Deut 32:39, Isa 40–55). The identification is made three times in this scene (twice by Jesus and repeated once by the narrator) and will mirror Peter's three-fold denial in the courtyard. As the Good Shepherd, Jesus protects his sheep by commanding the officers to let his disciples go and offering his own life in return for theirs (John 18:8). The sheep theme will continue into the courtyard where the question is now whether Peter is truly one of Jesus' flock; will he continue to follow the Good Shepherd or be led astray?

---

[1] R. Alan Culpepper, *Anatomy of the Fourth Gospel: A Study in Literary Design* (Philadelphia: Fortress, 1983), 145–46.

[2] On this, see in particular Mark W. G. Stibbe, *John* (Sheffield: JSOT Press, 1993), 183–84.

There are also close connections between the courtyard scene and Jesus' preliminary hearing in front of the high priest, Annas. Peter's denials form two units which frame the trial narrative (18:19–24), suggesting that the author imagined them taking place concurrently. The narrative device invites the reader to make connections between Jesus, who answers the questions of the high priest with boldness and majesty, and Peter, who bows to pressure outside and denies everything. Peter's second and third denials take place as Jesus stands before Caiaphas, though the evangelist tells us nothing of what occurred at this trial (18:24, 28). Many commentators note that the whole of the first half of John's Gospel constitutes Jesus' trial before "the Jews," and that John has already used most of the traditions associated with Jesus' interrogation before Caiaphas earlier in the Gospel.[3] The effect of this, however, is that the contrast between Jesus and Peter now takes centre stage.

Setting

Peter's denials take place in the αὐλή of the high priest (the same word was used of the sheepfold in 10:1). Whereas the Synoptics imagine an accessible, open space, John presents an enclosed courtyard into which access can only be gained through a gate (see 10:1 again). Inside spaces are often places of security but the courtyard is quite the opposite.[4] The narrative takes place at night and the scene is replete with references to the "high priest," the supreme representative of "the Jews." The attentive reader might well suspect that, despite the charcoal fire, the courtyard will be a place of unbelief, denial and rejection.[5] Within this dark enclosure, Peter will be exposed to three challenges from members of the high priest's household, and it is to each of these that we now turn.

The "Other Disciple" and the Portress

The scene opens with the note that Simon Peter "followed" Jesus. Presumably more than simple movement is implied here, and the reader is to understand

---

[3] See Andrew T. Lincoln, "Trials, Plots and the Narrative of the Fourth Gospel," *JSNT* 56 (1994): 3–30, and Raymond E. Brown, "Incidents that are Units in the Synoptic Gospels but Dispersed in St John," *CBQ* 23 (1961): 143–52.

[4] See the discussion in James L. Resseguie, *The Strange Gospel: Narrative Design and Point of View in John* (BibInt 56; Leiden: Brill, 2001), 63–71.

[5] On Peter's role in this scene (which is beyond the scope of this present essay), see the discussion in Judith Hartenstein, *Charakterisierung im Dialog: Maria Magdalena, Petrus, Thomas und die Mutter Jesu im Johannesevangelium im Kontext frühchristlicher Darstellungen* (NTOA/SUNT 64; Göttingen: Vandenhoeck & Ruprecht, 2007), 192–94.

that Peter has remained faithful to Jesus (as he swore he would) and intends to stay with him to the end. The reader is also made aware at this point of the presence of "another disciple" who was "known to the high priest." This disciple was able to enter the courtyard while Peter was forced to remain outside.

The identity of this "other disciple" has been endlessly debated. A number of manuscripts add a definite article here – "the other disciple" – which would parallel the reference to the Beloved Disciple in 20:2, 4 and 8. Although there are difficulties with this particular disciple being "known" to the high priest, especially since the word γνωστός tends to indicate a close relationship,[6] this is perhaps the best identification.[7] The Beloved Disciple often appears in scenes with Peter (13:23–26, 20:2-10, 21:7, 20–23), and the author often adds him where the Synoptic tradition involves Peter alone (20:10, 21:1-14 [Luke 5:1-11]). His presence here prepares the way for his appearance later at the foot of the cross (19:26-27). He is thus the only male disciple to remain faithful to Jesus and, as Andrew Lincoln notes, guarantees the Johannine interpretation of events in this section.[8] His role at this point, however, is simply to allow Peter to gain access to the courtyard (after this he disappears from the scene). The full contrast between his enduring faithfulness and Peter's desertion will only become apparent later.

The "other disciple" appears not to have realised at first that Peter was unable to enter the courtyard. When he sees Peter's predicament he goes outside and speaks to the maid who allows his friend to enter. The girl presumably questions Peter as he crosses into the courtyard. Her simple question expects a negative response: "You are not also one of that man's disciples, are you?"[9] On one level, Peter's denial is expedient; a truthful answer would presumably not have gained him access to the courtyard. The first denial, then, is really a lie to enable him to proceed. Yet an attentive reader may well already begin to see Peter's disintegration. His clear "I am not" (οὐκ εἰμί) contrasts with Jesus' equally clear declaration of his identity in the garden, and his repudiation of his discipleship aligns him with Jesus' opponents in 9:27-29. Readers might well suspect that the darkness of the courtyard is poised to engulf Peter.

---

[6] So C. Kingsley Barrett, citing 2 Kgs 10:11 and Ps 54 (55):14 (idem, *The Gospel According to St John* [2d ed.; London: SPCK, 1978], 525–26).

[7] Scholars who see a reference to the Beloved Disciple here include: Donald A. Carson, *The Gospel According to John* (Grand Rapids, Mich.: Eerdmans, 1991), 582; Charles H. Talbert, *Reading John* (London: SPCK, 1992), 236; Stibbe, *John*, 181; and Andrew T. Lincoln, *The Gospel According to St John* (BNTC 4; London: Continuum, 2005), 449. Of the other possibilities, Judas is perhaps the most likely contender; see the detailed study of James H. Charlesworth, *The Beloved Disciple* (Valley Forge, Pa.: Trinity, 1995), 336–59.

[8] Lincoln, *John*, 449.

[9] The "too" here (καὶ σύ) is probably to be taken in a general way as it is in the Synoptics – "Are you a follower, like all the rest of the city?" – rather than a specific reference to the faith of the "other disciple."

Some interpreters obviously had difficulty imagining that a female portress would be on duty at the high priest's palace on such a night; a number of manuscripts have accordingly made her masculine, or transformed her into the (male) gatekeeper's maid. Yet female porters were not unknown and this whole section is clearly a Johannine reworking of a tradition in which a maid asked Peter the first question (see Mark 14:66–67 and par.).[10] The feminine questioner adds to the dramatic contrast between Peter and Jesus: the former was questioned by a lowly serving maid, a girl of no status or consequence. His lack of resolve before such a person contrasts strongly with Jesus' boldness before the high priest, a person of considerable power and standing.

Servants and Officers

The second group of questioners are drawn from the arresting party in the garden. The officers (ὑπηρέται) were first introduced in 18:3, where they are clearly Jewish guards, or perhaps Temple police. In 18:10 it is clear that servants (or slaves) of the high priest are also present. After delivering Jesus into the high priest's custody, both groups wait in the courtyard, presumably for their next orders.

Each reference to these men has some connection with fire or artificial light. The events of the passion narrative so far have all taken place at night (13:30); in the garden, the officers and soldiers bring "lanterns and torches and weapons" (18:4); later they light a charcoal fire to keep warm (18:18); and we are reminded of the fire in v. 25 by the repetition of the detail that Peter stood warming himself. Perhaps John intended an ironic contrast: Peter will abandon the true light that shines in the darkness (1:4–5) in favour of saving face before the lanterns, torches and fires of men. In any case, the reader is told that Peter stood "with them," just as Judas stood "with them" in the garden. Peter has already aligned himself with Jesus' enemies, and his subsequent denial will come as no great surprise.

The question of the servants and officers is exactly the same as that of the maid and once again elicits a straight-forward "I am not" from Peter. This time, however, the reader is specifically told that he denied his master. If his answer to the portress could claim a certain expediency, this is not the case now. Jesus' boldness before the high priest contrasts with Peter's inability to declare himself a follower. There is also a certain irony in Jesus' serene suggestion that the high priest question those who heard his teaching (18:21); the reader may well suspect that Peter will not be up to such a task. Peter had

---

[10] See 2 Sam 4:6 (LXX) and Rhoda in Acts 12:13.

wanted to accompany his master, to be with him to the end, but in the face of difficulty deserts him.

Malchus' Kinsman

The third questioner is one of the group of officers and servants, more specifically a relative of Malchus, the man whose ear Peter severed in the garden (18:10). His question firmly links events in the courtyard back to the garden: "I myself saw you in the garden, didn't I?" There is an escalation of danger here. No longer is Peter suspected of being an associate of Jesus, but now stands accused of violence by a relative of his victim (in this Gospel Jesus does not heal his ear, unlike Luke 22:50). Not surprisingly, perhaps, Peter denies his connection to Jesus a third time. He has saved his own skin, but at a high price.

In contrast to the Synoptic account of Peter's blustering denials and invocation of curses upon himself, the Johannine Peter's denials are simple and straightforward. The end of the scene, too, is all the more dramatic for its simplicity. John notes that the cock crowed, but allows readers to make the link with 13:37–38 themselves. There is no account of how Peter responded to the accusing cock-crow, whether he wept or felt any kind of remorse. It is left to chapter 21, generally regarded as an addition to the Gospel, to record his restoration in another scene involving a charcoal fire (ἀνθρακιά). There, Peter's three-fold declaration of his love for Jesus atones for his three-fold betrayal in the courtyard (21:15–17) and he is told that he will indeed suffer martyrdom for his master (21:18–19).

Final Remarks

In a setting evoking the sheepfold of chapter 10 and the garden of Jesus' arrest, the three questioners in the High Priest's courtyard each have their own character and identity, and each present Peter with an escalating threat. The first challenge is from a humble serving girl, the second from members of the arresting party, and the third from a relative of a man whom Peter had assaulted. Together they witness, and even contribute to, Peter's descent from faithful follower to one who (albeit temporarily) aligns himself with darkness and disbelief. The implied author's intention in crafting these characters is to allow them to act as foils to Peter who, at his lowest moment, is contrasted both with the ever-loyal Beloved Disciple (who remains faithful to the end) and also his sovereign master (who courageously speaks out before the High Priest).

Pontius Pilate:
Failing in More Ways Than One

D. Francois Tolmie

The characterization of Pontius Pilate in the Fourth Gospel has received a fair amount of attention, quite often resulting in widely divergent interpretations of this fascinating figure. Before presenting my own interpretation, I begin with a representative overview of research that has been conducted in this regard.

Research on the Characterization of Pilate in the Fourth Gospel

To *Alan Culpepper*,[1] the Pilate of the Fourth Gospel is a character who, like Nicodemus, the lame man and the blind man, is caught between "the Jews" and Jesus, and thus comprises the subject of a "study in the impossibility of compromise, the inevitability of decision, and the consequences of each alternative."[2] According to Culpepper, Pilate soon realizes that Jesus is innocent, but is nevertheless forced by "the Jews" to sanction the death of Jesus. He does attempt to secure Jesus' release, but in the end finds a clear-cut decision in Jesus' favor too costly and thus abandons what he senses to be the truth and instead condemns an innocent man. The events following Pilate's decision to have Jesus crucified (namely, the *titulus*; the permission to hasten the death of the crucified by having their legs broken; and the approval of a proper burial) are all interpreted by Culpepper as part of an attempt by Pilate to atone for his decision; but, in the end, all of this still represents worldly power, and Pilate thus remains on the side of the world. Culpepper regards this characterization of Pilate as an attempt by the evangelist to force the reader to make a decision regarding Jesus, since he uses this character in order to graphically portray the consequences of avoiding such a decision.

---

[1] R. Alan Culpepper, *Anatomy of the Fourth Gospel: A Study in Literary Design* (Philadelphia: Fortress, 1983), 142–43.
[2] Culpepper, *Anatomy of the Fourth Gospel*, 143.

Helen K. Bond[3] interprets Pilate in the Fourth Gospel as anything but a weak and indecisive figure, as many scholars perceive him to be. According to her, he takes Jesus' case seriously. He examines Jesus, but soon realizes that he is not a political threat. "He seizes on the opportunity, however, not only to mock the prisoner but also to ridicule 'the Jews' and their messianic aspirations."[4] He eventually puts Jesus to death, but in the process forces "the Jews" to renounce their messianic hopes and to accept the sovereignty of the Emperor. Bond also points out that, in this way Pilate aligns himself with the world, represented in the Gospel by "the Jews"; and, accordingly, on a deeper level both Pilate and "the Jews" are judged.

Charles H. Giblin[5] does not agree with Culpepper that John's Pilate capitulates under the pressure exerted by "the Jews." Instead, Giblin views Pilate as a "worldly man of power"[6] who is successful because he serves his own interests, even at the expense of an appropriate reaction to the truth and any consideration of justice. According to Giblin, Pilate makes one tactical error (when he offers to release Barabbas), but soon recovers from it, and then continues to bend "the Jews" to his own advantage, while still despising them. Giblin also points out that Pilate rejects Jesus' revelation to him and serves only his own political self-interest.

Dirk F. Gniesmer[7] points out two important aspects in the characterization of Pilate. First, he emphasizes that Pilate is what he calls a "hermeneutical figure." This refers to the fact that the purpose of the characterization of Pilate is not to provide a moral evaluation of the character as such, or even a psychological explanation of his behavior; instead, he functions hermeneutically, in the sense that his often repulsive and questionable behavior raises very important issues related to Jesus' person, claims, and innocence. Secondly, Gniesmer emphasizes Pilate's failure to act as a judge in the true sense of the word, which means that he is characterized as a failing judge ("[ein] scheiternder Anwalt Jesu").[8] Instead of acting independently and keeping his distance from the accusers, as a judge should, Pilate becomes a tool in the hands of "the Jews." Towards Jesus he attempts to remain distant and neutral, but as things develop it actually becomes clear that this is impossible. In the end Pilate loses his

---

[3] Helen K. Bond, *Pontius Pilate in History and Interpretation* (SNTSMS 100; Cambridge: Cambridge University Press, 1998), 174–93.

[4] Bond, *Pontius Pilate*, 192.

[5] Charles H. Giblin, "John's Narration of the Hearing before Pilate (John 18,28–19,16a)," *BTB* 67/2 (1986): 221–39.

[6] Giblin, "John's Narration," 239.

[7] Dirk F. Gniesmer, *In den Prozeß verwickelt: Erzähltextanalytische und textpragmatische Erwägungen zur Erzählung vom Prozeß Jesu vor Pilatus (Joh 18,28–19,16a.b)* (EHS: Theologie 23/688; Frankfurt: Lang, 2000), 370–74.

[8] Gniesmer, *Prozeß*, 373.

sovereignty as judge, and, instead of Jesus facing Pilate as judge, Pilate actually faces Jesus as the eschatological judge.

In his study of Pilate, *Martin C. de Boer*[9] first focuses on the portrayal of this character in the Gospel. In this regard he highlights the fact that Pilate is represented as being extremely reluctant to become involved in Jesus' trial. De Boer then asks why Pilate is characterized in this way. In his view, the answer relates to the fact that Jesus is portrayed repeatedly by Pilate as "the king of the Jews," a deliberate attempt by the author to affirm this fact. According to De Boer, the premise that Jesus died as "the king of the Jews" is one of the constraints placed upon the author by the tradition. However, this is exploited in an ironic way, in that "Jesus comes to function as the king *of the Jews* (emphasis De Boer) precisely in their successful campaign to have him killed on that very charge. John uses Pilate, the uncomprehending, unbelieving, and reluctant participant in the events leading to Jesus' crucifixion, as a narrative vehicle for this terrible and tragic irony."[10]

According to *Christopher M. Tuckett*,[11] the author of the Fourth Gospel shows no sympathy at all for Pilate, but rather portrays him as opposing everything for which Jesus stands. Tuckett points out that the author uses irony in a masterful way to achieve this objective. Some of the examples that Tuckett cites in this regard are as follows: The author presents Pilate as a character who uses sarcasm by asking "Am I a Jew?", implying that he is not; yet Pilate in the end ironically becomes a "Jew" in that he fails to believe in Jesus; Pilate asks Jesus in a dismissive, mocking way: "What is truth?", ironically totally unaware that Jesus is indeed the truth; and he tries to release Jesus from punishment by having him scourged, which, according to Tuckett, does not make sense at all. Tuckett concludes that Pilate in the end drives "the Jews" to a situation "where they deny their heritage and their God. He is the real instigator of the ultimate blasphemy."[12]

Cornelis Bennema[13] regards Pilate as one of the most complex characters in the Fourth Gospel. Bennema agrees with scholars who view Pilate as a strong character; but he is also of the opinion that they overrate the options available to him within this particular situation: "Pilate is a competent, calculating politician who wants to show 'the Jews' he is in charge while also trying to be

---

[9] Martin C. de Boer, "The Narrative Function of Pilate in John," in *Narrativity in Biblical and Related Texts. La narrativité dans la Bible et les textes apparentés* (ed. George J. Brooke and Jean-Daniel Kaestli; BETL 149; Louvain: Leuven University Press/Peeters, 2000), 141–58.

[10] De Boer, "Narrative Function of Pilate," 157.

[11] Christopher M. Tuckett, "Pilate in John 18–19: A Narrative-Critical Approach," in *Narrativity in Biblical and Related Texts* (ed. Brooke and Kaestli), 131–40.

[12] Tuckett, "Pilate in John," 139.

[13] Cornelis Bennema, *Encountering Jesus: Character Studies in the Gospel of John* (Milton Keynes: Paternoster, 2009), 187.

professional in handling Jesus' case."[14] However, Pilate does not succeed in achieving either of these two objectives, because he underestimates the determination of "the Jews." Although he realizes that Jesus is innocent, he is manipulated by "the Jews" into putting Jesus to death because he is afraid of losing his political power. Bennema also points out what he regards as indications of character development in Pilate, that is to say, that he at first does not try to release Jesus, but later attempts to do so; and the fact that he is surprisingly outmaneuvered by "the Jews."

From this brief overview, it is clear that there is no consensus regarding how the figure of Pilate should be understood. Is he primarily a weak and indecisive character forced by "the Jews" to do something he does not want to do? Or is he actually a shrewd figure, thinking only of his own political self-interest, manipulating "the Jews"? Does he ridicule them, and, if so, why? Is he a poor judge, or rather, perhaps, a character primarily used by the implied author[15] for the purpose of irony? To pretend that this study will offer the final answer to these questions would be presumptuous. Instead, its aim is more modest, namely to present my own interpretation of this character. This will be done in terms of an approach to characterization which, as far as I know, has not been utilized in describing the characterization of Pilate before, namely that of Seymour Chatman.[16] He advocates an easy, yet accurate approach towards interpreting the characterization of any particular character. It is based on the definition of characters in a narrative text in terms of *a paradigm of traits* – a trait being any relatively stable or abiding personal quality associated with a character. As such, the traits associated with a specific character may be unfolded or replaced, or may even disappear in the course of the nar-

---

[14] Bennema, *Encountering Jesus*, 188.
[15] Since the concepts "implied author" and "implied reader" are not always used in the same way, the way in which they are used in this study needs clarification. Following Jeff L. Staley, *The Print's First Kiss: A Rhetorical Investigation of the Implied Reader in the Fourth Gospel* (Atlanta: Scholars Press, 1988), 34, I use the concept "implied author" to refer to the organizing principle in the text, responsible for the total arrangement thereof. The concept "implied reader" is used to refer to the intratextual literary construct that functions as the counterpart of the implied author. The difference between the implied author and the implied reader is based upon the difference between the *linearity* and the *temporality* of the text. Whereas the implied author is defined in terms of the static overarching view of the text, the implied reader is defined in terms of the temporal quality of the text.
[16] Seymour Chatman, *Story and Discourse: Narrative Structure in Fiction and Film* (Ithaca, N. Y.: Cornell University Press, 1978), 119–33. For a more detailed overview, see D. Francois Tolmie, *Narratology and Biblical Narratives: A Practical Guide* (San Francisco: International Scholars Publications, 1999), 39–61. I have followed the same approach elsewhere: See my study of the characterization of Simon Peter in the Fourth Gospel: D. Francois Tolmie, "The (Not So) Good Shepherd: The Use of Shepherd Imagery in the Characterisation of Peter in the Fourth Gospel," in *Imagery in the Gospel of John: Terms, Forms, Themes, and the Theology of Johannine Figurative Language* (ed. Jörg Frey et al.; WUNT 200; Tübingen: Mohr Siebeck, 2006), 353–68.

rative. In practical terms this means that whenever a new character is introduced into the narrative world, a paradigm of traits to be associated with this particular character is opened by the implied reader. As soon as character appears again, the implied reader sorts through the paradigm of traits already associated with it in order to account for any new information provided in terms of the traits already identified. If the new information cannot be accounted for in terms of these traits, a new trait will be added or a given trait will be reformulated, replaced or removed. In this study, a paradigm of Pilate will be systematically drawn up as events in the part of the narrative in which he appears, unfold. The development of the plot will also be briefly touched upon, but from a particular angle, that is to say, with a focus on Pilate as a character.

A secondary aim of this study is to indicate the reasons for the disagreement among scholars on the characterization of Pilate. To my mind, this situation can be attributed to the following: First, Pilate is almost always characterized indirectly, i. e. by means of his words and deeds.[17] Accordingly, character traits should be deduced from his behavior, an objective which can often be achieved in more than one way. A second reason is the "empty spaces"[18] in the text. An "empty space" refers to a gap in the text which has to be filled in by the implied reader. Depending on the way in which such a gap is filled, different pictures of Pilate may result. In this study the primary focus will fall on a systematic identification of the traits associated with Pilate, but in the process I shall also attempt to identify other possible interpretations of Pilate's behavior. In a few instances, I shall also indicate open spaces in the text that are relevant for interpreting the characterization of Pilate.

The Characterization of Pilate in the Fourth Gospel

Following Raymond Brown[19] and others, John 18:28–19:16a is divided into seven scenes, alternating between "outside" and "inside" the *praetorium*.

---

[17] So, correctly, Cornelis Bennema, "A Theory of Character in the Fourth Gospel with Reference to Ancient and Modern Literature," *BibInt* 17 (2009): 375–421, here 397–98.

[18] On "empty spaces" in texts ("Leerstellen"), cf. Wolfgang Iser, *Der Akt des Lesens: Theorie ästhetischer Wirkung* (München: Fink, 1976), 257–355.

[19] Raymond E. Brown, *The Gospel According to John (xiii–xxi)* (AB 29A; London: Chapman, 1984), 858–59. In this regard Brown follows Albert Janssens de Varebeke, "La structure des scènes du récit de la passion en Joh. xviii–xix," *ETL* 38 (1962): 504–33, but does not agree with him that the other two divisions of the Passion Narrative also consist of seven episodes each. See Francis J. Moloney, *The Gospel of John* (SP 4; Collegeville, Minn.: Liturgical Press, 1998), 497–98, for a good discussion of this issue.

Scene One: John 18:28-32

Pilate is introduced into the narrative world without any detailed description,[20] which indicates that the implied author assumes that the implied reader already knows who this character is. With regard to the characterization in this scene, three actions of Pilate are narrated, on the basis of which traits may be inferred: Pilate goes out to "the Jews"; he asks them what accusation they bring against Jesus; and he tells them to judge Jesus by their own law. Depending on the way in which these actions are interpreted, different and even opposing traits may be deduced.

To complicate matters further, there are also empty spaces in this scene which can be filled in by the implied reader in more ways than one. The way in which these empty spaces are filled has a significant influence on how one understands the overall picture of Pilate. Some of the empty spaces can be formulated as follows: What should the implied reader assume that Pilate already knows at this stage about Jesus? What is the nature of the relationship between Pilate and "the Jews" at the beginning of this scene? To what extent is he aware of the intention of "the Jews" to have Jesus killed? To my mind, these empty spaces should be filled in as follows: According to John 18:3, Judas took a detachment of soldiers with him (together with the police supplied by the chief priests and the Pharisees), from which it may be deduced that Pilate must have had some knowledge of the arrest of Jesus and the reasons for it.[21] Furthermore, from Pilate's question later on in 18:33 ("Are you the king of the Jews?"), it is also clear that he is portrayed as having been informed of this accusation against Jesus beforehand.[22] Making a deduction regarding the nature of the relationship between Pilate and "the Jews" at the beginning of this scene is more difficult. To my mind, the insolent way in which they respond to Pilate in 18:30 may be taken as an indication that the relationship was strained from the outset.

Let us now consider the traits which may be inferred from each of the three actions of Pilate. According to v. 29, he goes out to "the Jews." This may be interpreted in several ways. A first possibility is that it could be an indication that he feels himself to be obliged to do as "the Jews" wish.[23] In this case, one could argue that the normal course of action for someone in a superior position, like Pilate, would have been to tell "the Jews" that they would have to come inside to him if they wished to discuss the matter. Going out to them

---

[20] Take note that the reference to the *praetorium* serves as an indication to the implied reader that the setting has now changed to the official residence of the governor.

[21] So, for example, Brown, *John*, 847, and Bond, *Pilate*, 175.

[22] So, correctly, among others, Bennema, *Encountering Jesus*, 184, and Andrew T. Lincoln, *The Gospel According to St John* (BNTC 4; London: Continuum, 2005), 461.

[23] Cf., for example, Culpepper, *Anatomy of the Fourth Gospel*, 143.

instead would then be a sign that he had succumbed to their pressure (thereby forfeiting his honor and ability to manipulate them). If Pilate's action is interpreted in this way, the underlying trait may be formulated as "finds it difficult to withstand the pressure of 'the Jews.'" A second possibility is to regard Pilate's action as indicative of wisdom, in the sense that he does not refuse to go out to meet "the Jews," because he is aware that they would be provoked by such a decision; instead, he acts wisely by going out to them.[24] Lastly, it may also be interpreted as being indicative of the trait of courtesy.[25] One could argue in favor of any of these interpretations; but to my mind, the fact that Pilate is portrayed later on in the narrative as succumbing to the pressure of "the Jews" may be taken as an indication that the first interpretation is probably the most plausible.

Pilate's second act in this scene is to ask "the Jews" what accusation they bring against Jesus. This may be interpreted in three ways, namely as a question indicating that Pilate is not yet (fully) informed about the matter;[26] as a way of formally opening the legal process;[27] or as a challenge to "the Jews," implying that they do not have enough evidence to charge Jesus.[28] Either of the first two interpretations may be accepted (the third one is not supported by the way in which the question is worded). Accordingly, the underlying trait may be formulated as: "attempts to fulfill his judicial role."

"The Jews" respond to Pilate's question sarcastically:[29] "If this man were not an evildoer, we would not have handed him over." Pilate's reply (that they should take Jesus and judge him according to their own law) is interpreted in different ways by scholars. Some interpret it in a positive sense, for example, as an indication that Pilate acts as a good governor should, in that a governor should not become involved in a case if the local authorities can handle it

---

[24] C. Kingsley Barrett, *The Gospel According to St John: An Introduction with Commentary and Notes on the Greek Text* (2d ed.; London: SPCK, 1978), 533.

[25] Bond, *Pilate*, 175. This might then also be the first stage of setting them up to be manipulated.

[26] Ernst Haenchen, *Das Johannesevangelium: Ein Kommentar aus den nachgelassenen Manuskripten herausgegeben von Ulrich Busse mit einem Vorwort von James M. Robinson* (Tübingen: Mohr Siebeck, 1980), 534. According to 18:33, Pilate is already aware that Jesus is accused of claiming to be the king of "the Jews," but this does not necessarily mean that he was fully informed about the matter.

[27] See, for example, Rudolf Schnackenburg, *Das Johannesevangelium: Teil 3* (HTKNT IV; Freiburg: Herder, 1979), 278; Mark W. G. Stibbe, *John as Storyteller: Narrative Criticism and the Fourth Gospel* (SNTSMS 73; Cambridge: Cambridge University Press, 1992), 106, and Gniesmer, *Prozeß*, 197.

[28] John P. Heil, *Blood and Water: The Death and Resurrection of Jesus in John 18–21* (CBQMS 27; Washington: Catholic Biblical Association of America, 1995), 48.

[29] So, most scholars. See, for example, Brown, *John*, 848; Barrett, *John*, 533; Bond, *Pilate*, 175. As pointed out above, I take this as an indication of the strained relationship between "the Jews" and Pilate.

themselves.[30] Although this principle might be true in general, it does not seem to fit this particular context. In this instance, "the Jews" have just acted in a very insolent way; and the assumption that Pilate's reaction indicates that he is simply handing back the case to them, does not constitute a feasible explanation. In any case, the mere fact that they have come to Pilate is already an indication to him that they cannot handle the matter in terms of their own law; otherwise they would not have been there in the first place. From the next scene, it is also clear that Pilate is already aware of the charge against Jesus, namely that he regards himself as the king of "the Jews"; and this is not the type of incident that a governor would summarily hand back to the local authorities. Thus, it cannot be accepted that Pilate really wants "the Jews" to handle the matter themselves. Hence, his words should be interpreted in another way, that is to say, as sarcasm.[31] By using sarcasm, he expresses his dislike for "the Jews," tries to humiliate them and reminds them of his superior position in relation to them. Furthermore, this sarcasm also expresses his reluctance to be involved in the matter at all[32] – although he realizes that he cannot avoid such involvement. The underlying trait relating to all of these aspects can be formulated as "dislikes 'the Jews.'"

"The Jews" respond to Pilate's sarcastic answer by stating that they are not allowed to kill anyone. In this way, they clearly indicate to Pilate their intention to have Jesus killed. Significantly, Pilate does not object to this. In fact, he does not say anything at all, but goes inside. This means that "the Jews" have the final word in this scene – a further illustration of one of Pilate's character traits, namely the fact that he finds it difficult to withstand the pressure exerted by "the Jews."

If the analysis presented above is correct, the paradigm of traits that the implied reader will associate with Pilate at the end of the first scene may be summarized as follows:

- Finds it difficult to withstand the pressure of "the Jews"
- Attempts to fulfill his judicial role
- Dislikes "the Jews"

How does the characterization of Pilate relate to the plot development in this scene? If one considers the course of events from Pilate's perspective, things do not go his way, because "the Jews" (whom he dislikes) not only force him to

---

[30] Sjef van Tilborg, *Reading John in Ephesus* (NovTSup 83; Leiden: Brill, 1996), 166. See also Gniesmer, *Prozeß*, 198–99.

[31] See, among others, Schnackenburg, *Johannesevangelium*, 3:279–80, and Bennema, *Encountering Jesus*, 184.

[32] See, for example, Culpepper, *Anatomy of the Fourth Gospel*, 143, and de Boer, "Narrative Function of Pilate," 143.

investigate the matter further, but also indicate the desired outcome: Jesus must be killed.

Scene Two: John 18:33–38a

This scene begins with Pilate asking Jesus if he is the King of "the Jews." This action again illustrates the trait, "attempts to fulfill his judicial role."[33] Jesus does not answer the question but responds with a question of his own, which gives rise to Pilate's indignant – and ironic[34] – retort: "Surely I am not 'a Jew'?" This reply confirms the trait, "dislikes 'the Jews,'" highlighted in the previous scene. The fact that Pilate still takes his judicial role seriously, is clear from his next question:[35] "What have you done?" After Jesus' rather lengthy response on the nature of his kingdom, Pilate steers the conversation back to what he regards as important, namely whether Jesus regards himself as a king. From Jesus' words he infers:[36] "So you are a king?" He is thus still trying to fulfill his judicial role.

To Jesus' answer (this time in terms of the nature of his kingship as it relates to truth),[37] Pilate responds briefly with "What is truth?" before he goes outside again. This question has been interpreted in quite different ways,[38] but as Johannine scholars nowadays agree,[39] it does not express a longing for the truth, nor does it signify any deep philosophical enquiry. The tone in which it is uttered may be interpreted in more than one way[40] (thus giving rise to another empty space in the text), but the function of the question is clear: It terminates the discussion on truth opened by Jesus, and, in fact, rejects Jesus as

---

[33] Heil, *Blood and Water*, 53, interprets Pilate's question as derisive, but this does not seem to be the case. It is possible that the question carries a note of incredulity (especially with the emphasis on σύ at the beginning), but this does not mean that it is deliberately derisive. See Brown, *John*, 851, and Gniesmer, *Prozeß*, 215.

[34] Μήτι presupposes a negative answer (see BDF 427), but, although Pilate is not "a Jew," he reacts in the same way as "the Jews" in that he eventually rejects Jesus, as many scholars point out. See, for example, Lincoln, *John*, 462, and Tuckett, "Pilate in John," 135.

[35] Pilate's words τὸ ἔθνος τὸ σὸν καὶ οἱ ἀρχιερεῖς παρέδωκαν σε ἐμοί may be an acknowledgement that he was pressured by "the Jews." So Rudolf Bultmann, *Das Evangelium des Johannes* (KEK 19; Göttingen: Vandenhoeck & Ruprecht, 1978), 506.

[36] This is the implication of οὐκοῦν here. See BDAG in this regard. οὐκοῦν is used only here in the New Testament.

[37] Jesus' words might be regarded as an offer to Pilate to receive the truth. So Moloney, *John*, 494.

[38] See Haenchen, *Johannesevangelium*, 536–37, for a good overview.

[39] I could not find any examples of a different interpretation by a contemporary Johannine scholar.

[40] Some examples: According to Culpepper, *Anatomy of the Fourth Gospel*, 142, the question has a "cynical ring"; Heil, *Blood and Water*, 57, detects a tone of "exasperation"; Stibbe, *Storyteller*, 106, describes it as a "frustrated exclamation"; Moloney, *John*, 494, calls it a "brusque refusal"; Tuckett, "Pilate in John," 135, views it as a "dismissive mocking question"; and Bennema, *Encountering Jesus*, 185, describes it as "dismissive."

the truth. Thus, contrary to what happened in the previous scene, Pilate does have the last word in this scene; however, what he says does not characterize him in a positive way at all. The new trait revealed by his words may be formulated as "rejects Jesus as the truth."

At the end of the second scene, the paradigm of traits that the implied reader associates with Pilate may thus be summarized as follows (traits that are repeated in this scene or revealed for the first time, are italicized):

– Finds it difficult to withstand the pressure of "the Jews"
– *Attempts to fulfill his judicial role*
– *Dislikes "the Jews"*
– *Rejects Jesus as the truth*

The plot development in this scene may be read on two levels. On one level, Pilate is fulfilling his judicial role, trying to determine whether the accusation against Jesus will stand up to scrutiny. On another level, he fails to grasp Jesus' true identity as king, as a witness to the truth, and, in fact, as *the* truth.

Scene Three: John 18:38b–40

Although this scene is rather brief, the characterization of Pilate in it is quite complex. The scene opens with Pilate's announcement that he finds no case[41] against Jesus. From this, it can be deduced that his examination of Jesus in the previous scene has brought him to the conclusion that Jesus is innocent.[42] The trait illustrated by this behavior is thus one that has already been identified earlier on, that is to say, "attempts to fulfill his judicial role." In this instance, one may even add "in a just way," since Pilate is clearly trying to act in a just manner by announcing publicly that Jesus is not guilty of the charges against him. However, this picture is tainted by what follows. Instead of immediately releasing Jesus as he should, he offers "the Jews" a choice between Jesus and Barabbas. The mere fact that this happens – regardless of the way in which one interprets Pilate's offer – indicates unjust behavior on his part. If Jesus is innocent, there should be no need for any further action except to release him. Thus, the trait "attempts to fulfill his judicial role in a just way" is thereby immediately negated. Furthermore, the fact that Pilate finds it necessary to negotiate with "the Jews" regarding the release of Jesus, is another illustration

---

[41] Αἰτία refers to the crime of which Jesus has been charged; so, correctly, Brown, *John*, 854. The interpretation of this as also signifying that Pilate finds no reason to become a believing disciple of Jesus, as Heil, *Blood and Water*, 59, claims, cannot be accepted. Why would he announce this to "the Jews"?

[42] *Contra* Schnackenburg, *Johannesevangelium*, 3:288, who finds no link between this announcement of Jesus' innocence and what happened in the previous scene.

of a trait already pointed out earlier, namely that he finds it difficult to withstand their pressure.

It is regularly noted by scholars that the choice that Pilate offers to "the Jews" is expressed in a strange way, since he refers to Jesus as "the king of the Jews." Explaining this presents quite a challenge. Why is Pilate portrayed as using these words, which would definitely not help to persuade "the Jews" to accept his offer? In terms of overall narrative strategy, the expression does play an important role, because Jesus' kingship is one of the dominant themes in this part of the narrative, and this is probably the reason why the implied author also portrays Pilate as using this expression here.[43] However, it also affects one's interpretation of the characterization of Pilate, but how? The easiest way out is to accept that Pilate's behavior does not make sense and that historical plausibility is not important to the implied author.[44] On the other hand, if one assumes that Pilate is portrayed as acting rationally[45] – as I do – his strange behavior needs to be explained. In this regard, one must first decide whether Pilate indeed wishes to set Jesus free. Some scholars assume that this is not really his intention, and explain his offer to "the Jews" as an attempt to ridicule or taunt them.[46] This would mean that Pilate is portrayed as being deliberately dishonest: either he does not think that Jesus is innocent, and lies about this when saying that he does not find a case against him; or he knows that Jesus is innocent, but has no intention of setting him free. In this case, he would be acting cruelly, both towards "the Jews" and Jesus. To my mind, it is rather difficult to substantiate such an interpretation on the basis of the text. That Pilate is portrayed as being dishonest about Jesus' innocence seems unlikely in the light of the fact that he makes the same claim further on, in 19:4 and 19:6. If Pilate is indeed convinced of Jesus' innocence, it is more likely that he would want to do something about it. Furthermore, since he is already aware that "the Jews" want Jesus dead (18:31), it can be assumed that because he finds it difficult to withstand the pressure exerted by them, he devises an alternative which makes it possible for them to opt out without losing face. This fails (with "the Jews" having the last word in this scene again), for two reasons. Firstly (and most importantly), "the Jews" will not be persuaded in any way whatsoever to let Jesus go. Secondly, the offer is made in a very clumsy way. This could be explained in more than one way. For example, one could surmise that it is intended by Pilate as an ironic overstatement, which

---

[43] See the thorough discussion of this issue by de Boer, "Narrative Function of Pilate," 146–48.

[44] See, for example, Gniesmer, *Prozeß*, 267.

[45] See Brown, *John*, 855–56: "Even though the evangelist is not interested in writing a psychological study of the prefect, we must suppose that Pilate is presented as acting rationally."

[46] So, for example, Bond, *Pilate*, 180; Lincoln, *John*, 464; Bennema, *Encountering Jesus*, 185.

goes wrong;⁴⁷ that he foresees that "the Jews" will not accept his offer and therefore expresses it in such a way that they will respond by implicitly renouncing their own expectation of a king of "the Jews";⁴⁸ that it is another manifestation of the trait "dislikes 'the Jews'"; or that it is merely indicative of incompetence. I would opt for either of the last two possibilities.

If the above interpretation is correct, the paradigm of traits that the implied reader associates with Pilate at the end of Scene 3 can be formulated as follows:

- *Finds it difficult to withstand the pressure of "the Jews"*
- *Attempts to fulfill his judicial role in a just way* ↔⁴⁹ *Fulfils his judicial role unjustly*
- *Dislikes "the Jews"*
- Rejects Jesus as the truth
- *Clumsy*

Viewed in terms of Pilate's role, the plot development in this scene may be summarized as follows: Pilate is convinced of Jesus' innocence, but fails to set him free.

Scene Four: John 19:1–3

This scene is situated inside the *praetorium* again.⁵⁰ Pilate has Jesus flogged and Jesus is then, ironically, mocked by the soldiers as "king of the Jews."⁵¹ Why does Pilate have Jesus flogged? Flogging was used by the Romans for several purposes: as part of the process of crucifixion, as a means of obtaining information from an accused, or as a form of punishment in itself.⁵² In the Fourth Gospel, the flogging of Jesus is not part of the crucifixion process. The other two possibilities must therefore be considered. In the next scene, after the flogging, Pilate brings Jesus out to "the Jews," announcing that he is bringing Jesus out to them so that they may know that he finds no crime in him. He is thus portrayed as linking the flogging of Jesus to a (possible) recognition of Jesus' innocence by "the Jews." To my mind, this could either mean that he has had Jesus punished and is still convinced of his innocence – which is con-

---

⁴⁷ Heil, *Blood and Water*, 59.
⁴⁸ Brown, *John*, 856.
⁴⁹ I use the sign ↔ to indicate Pilate's conflicting behavior in this regard: he decides that Jesus is innocent, but does not set him free immediately. As indicated in the discussion above, this can be ascribed to another trait, namely that he finds it difficult to withstand the pressure of "the Jews."
⁵⁰ Although this is not stated explicitly, Pilate is depicted in 19:4 as going out again.
⁵¹ The importance of the ironical portrayal of Jesus' kingship in this scene – the central scene in a series of seven – is discussed in more detail by many scholars. See, for example, Paul D. Duke, *Irony in the Fourth Gospel* (Atlanta: John Knox, 1985), 131–32, and Gniesmer, *Prozeß*, 277–86.
⁵² Schnackenburg, *Johannesevangelium*, 3:291–92.

firmed by the appearance of the flogged and humiliated Jesus, or that even the flogging has not revealed any new information disproving his conviction that Jesus is innocent.[53] Of these two options, the latter seems to me to be more feasible.

If so, Pilate's action should be viewed neither as a way of mocking Jesus,[54] nor primarily as an abuse of power,[55] but as an attempt to free Jesus in an indirect way;[56] not so much by creating sympathy for Jesus,[57] but rather by using the flogging as a proof of Jesus' innocence.

Which traits of Pilate are revealed by this event? Two traits which have already been revealed earlier on are illustrated again, namely that Pilate acts unjustly (even if his action comprises an attempt to free Jesus, it is still unjust, because Jesus is innocent), and that he finds it difficult to withstand the pressure of "the Jews": Instead of setting Jesus free immediately, he attempts to devise another scheme to bring about Jesus' release.

The paradigm of traits is thus still the same as it was at the end of Scene 3:

- *Finds it difficult to withstand the pressure of "the Jews"*
- Attempts to fulfill his judicial role in a just way ↔ *fulfils his judicial role unjustly*
- Dislikes "the Jews"
- Rejects Jesus as the truth
- Clumsy

The plot development in this scene may be summarized as follows: Convinced of Jesus' innocence, Pilate devises another scheme to set Jesus free.

---

[53] Bennema, *Encountering Jesus*, 185, who follows Jennifer A. Glancy, "Torture, Flesh, Truth, and the Fourth Gospel," *BibInt* 13 (2005): 107–36, here 121–22, in this regard believes that Pilate has Jesus flogged in order to extract a confession from him. However, there is no indication in the text that Pilate has changed his mind concerning Jesus' innocence; and therefore, it would be strange if he tried to extract a confession from him. Therefore I have followed a somewhat different approach to the formulation of the situation: Pilate does not have Jesus flogged because he regards Jesus as guilty. He does so, *although* he thinks Jesus is innocent, and then presents this as proof that nothing was revealed during the flogging to disprove his conviction that Jesus is innocent.

[54] Bond, *Pilate*, 182–85.

[55] Hartwig Thyen, *Das Johannesevangelium* (HNT 6; Tübingen: Mohr-Siebeck, 2005), 723, following Klaus Wengst, *Das Johannesevangelium. 2. Teilband* (THKNT IV/2; Stuttgart: Kohlhammer, 2001), 232, describes it as "Zynismus der Macht."

[56] So many scholars, for example, Bultmann, *Johannes*, 509–11; Culpepper, *Anatomy of the Fourth Gospel*, 142; de Boer, "Narrative Function of Pilate," 143.

[57] Haenchen, *Johannesevangelium*, 539.

Scene Five: John 19:4–8 [58]

This scene opens with Pilate announcing that he is bringing Jesus out.[59] Pilate then repeats that he finds no case against him, and refers to Jesus with the words:[60] ἰδοὺ ὁ ἄνθρωπος. This expression should be interpreted on two levels: Pilate, using it as part of his strategy to release Jesus, probably intends it in the sense of "How can this flogged, humiliated man be the King of the Jews?,"[61] but on a deeper level it is highly ironical,[62] because Jesus is much more than meets the eye.

Which trait is manifested by Pilate's actions in 19:4–6? If these actions are regarded as part of a strategy by Pilate to set Jesus free,[63] as I believe, a trait already revealed earlier on is illustrated again, that is to say, that Pilate attempts to fulfill his judicial role in a just way. Furthermore, the fact that he finds it necessary to use such a strategy, again illustrates that he finds it difficult to withstand the pressure of "the Jews."

To the demand of the chief priests and the officers to have Jesus crucified, Pilate responds that they should take him and crucify him, followed by a third declaration of Jesus' innocence. Although it is conceivable that the implied reader might conclude that the Jewish authorities could kill Jesus with the approval of the governor,[64] it seems more feasible to assume, in the light of

---

[58] This scene is sometimes demarcated as 19:4–7 (see, for example, Gniesmer, *Prozeß*, 286, and Bennema, *Encountering Jesus*, 186), but strictly speaking, v. 8 is still part of this scene, since Pilate only moves inside in v. 9.

[59] Although Pilate says that he is "bringing" Jesus out, Jesus "comes out" by himself (19:5), which is interpreted by Moloney, *John*, 495, as an indication that Jesus "is still master of his own destiny."

[60] The text does not explicitly state that Pilate is speaking these words, but this is the logical way to interpret the sentence. Occasionally, scholars interpret the statement as signifying that the words are spoken by Jesus, for example Friedheim Wessel. See the discussion (and rejection) of Wessel's proposal by Gniesmer, *Prozeß*, 288, fn. 871.

[61] The expression is interpreted in a wide variety of ways. In his survey, Charles Panackel, *ΙΔΟΥ Ο ΑΝΘΡΩΠΟΣ (Jn 19,5b): An Exegetico-Theological Study of the Text in the Light of the Use of the Term ΑΝΘΡΩΠΟΣ Designating Jesus in the Fourth Gospel* (Analecta Gregoriana 251; Roma: Editrice Pontificia Universita Gregoriana, 1988), 312–22, identifies the following interpretations offered by scholars: In terms of its primary meaning, it may indicate the ridiculousness of the Jewish charge, Pilate's contempt for either Jesus or "the Jews," an appeal to Jewish goodwill, the impression that Jesus has made on Pilate, or a formula of acquittal; in terms of its secondary meaning it may refer to Jesus as Son of Man, human par excellence, heavenly man, paradox of the Word incarnate, human being, Suffering Servant, or Son of God.

[62] On the use of irony and paradox in this scene, see, for example, Lincoln, *John*, 465–66, and Thyen, *Johannesevangelium*, 723–24.

[63] So many scholars, for example, Bultmann, *Johannes*, 509–11; Schnackenburg, *Johannesevangelium*, 3:245; Stibbe, *Storyteller*, 108. Another (to my mind, less plausible) way of interpreting these events, is to regard them as a mockery on Pilate's part, both of Jesus and of the nationalistic hopes of "the Jews." See Bond, *Pilate*, 185.

[64] De Boer, "Narrative Function of Pilate," 144, fn. 13.

18:31, that Pilate does not really want them to do so. The tone of his words is difficult to determine (another empty space in the text). It could be indicative of a taunt,[65] sarcasm,[66] exasperation[67] or irritation,[68] or perhaps a combination of some or all of these. In any case, the trait revealed by this behavior remains the same, namely that he dislikes "the Jews."

"The Jews" again have the final word in this scene: According to their law, Jesus has to die, because he has made himself the Son of God. Their words to Pilate are followed by one of the rare examples of internal focalization[69] in the Fourth Gospel: "Ὅτε οὖν ἤκουσεν ὁ Πιλᾶτος τοῦτον τὸν λόγον, μᾶλλον ἐφοβήθη. Because it has not been indicated earlier on that Pilate is afraid, some scholars interpret μᾶλλον in an elative sense ("very much afraid").[70] However, this cannot be accepted. The mere fact that he is not explicitly portrayed as being afraid earlier on, does not imply that one should interpret this expression as meaning something else than "he was more afraid." As Gniesmer[71] points out, something similar happens in 5:18, where "the Jews" are portrayed as seeking "all the more" to kill Jesus (μᾶλλον is also used in this instance), despite the fact that their desire to kill Jesus has not been explicitly indicated earlier in the Gospel. Furthermore, if one considers the way in which μᾶλλον is generally used in the New Testament, interpreting it as "very much" here does not seem a feasible option.[72]

Thus, it is retrospectively revealed to the implied reader that Pilate has been afraid all along. Afraid of whom? Two possibilities come to mind, namely that

---

[65] For example, Barrett, *John*, 541.
[66] For example, Schnackenburg, *Johannesevangelium*, 3:297.
[67] For example, Brown, *John*, 876.
[68] Gniesmer, *Prozeß*, 294.
[69] For a more detailed discussion of the aspect of focalization in biblical narratives, see Tolmie, *Narratology*, 29–38.
[70] For example, Barrett, *John*, 542, who refers to LS in this regard, and Bond, *Pilate*, 187, who claims that μᾶλλον indicates a change in attitude.
[71] Gniesmer, *Prozeß*, 317, fn. 952.
[72] Schnackenburg, *Johannesevangelium*, 3:300, fn. 78, disagrees with Barrett (see fn. 70 above), who refers to LS μάλα II in this regard. Schnackenburg correctly argues that the examples referred to in LS do not apply in the case of 5:18. LS II defines the meaning of μᾶλλον as follows: "more, more strongly; also rather," but not one of the examples cited reflects the meaning of the term as it is used in John 19:8. BDAG, μᾶλλον, provides three options for interpreting the word: "1. to a greater extent, *more*...; 2. for a better reason, *rather, all the more*...; 3. marker of alternative to someth., *rather* in the sense of *instead* (of someth.)." BDAG refers to all four of the instances in which μᾶλλον is used in the Fourth Gospel, classifying 5:18 and 19:8 as examples of 1, and 3:19 and 12:43 as examples of 3. In the lengthy entry for this word, BDAG never suggests "very much" as a translation for any occurrence of μᾶλλον in the New Testament. Also take note, that according to BDAG, in cases where μᾶλλον means "rather" (in the sense of "instead"), the alternative is either mentioned or easily inferred from the context (as in Matt 25:9), which is not the case in John 19:8. This, to my mind, makes it unlikely that μᾶλλον ἐφοβήθη would mean "instead, he became afraid," as Bond (see fn. 70 above) seems to claim.

he may be afraid of Jesus, or of "the Jews." Thus far there has not been any suggestion that Pilate is afraid of Jesus, but the fact that he finds it difficult to withstand the pressure of "the Jews" has been demonstrated more than once, which makes it more likely that he is being portrayed here as having been afraid of "the Jews" all along. Accordingly, the trait "finds it difficult to withstand the pressure of 'the Jews'" can be further defined as "afraid of 'the Jews.'"

Why does Pilate become "more afraid" in this scene? His fear is linked directly to the response of "the Jews" in the previous verse, which means that the increase in his fear could be linked to the fanaticism of "the Jews"; the possibility that his superiors in Rome might not be satisfied, since he does consider the religious feelings of "the Jews"; or the possibility that he now realizes that a deity/deities might be involved in this case, too.[73] To my mind, the fact that Pilate immediately goes inside and asks Jesus where he comes from, indicates that the last option should be accepted. If this is correct, his fear increases in the sense that, besides having been afraid of "the Jews" all along, he now also starts to fear Jesus, perhaps as a result of superstition. A new trait thus comes to the fore, which can be formulated as: "afraid of Jesus." Thus, the paradigm of traits is as follows at the end of this scene:

- *Finds it difficult to withstand the pressure of "the Jews"; afraid of "the Jews"*
- Attempts to fulfill his judicial role in a just way ↔ fulfils his judicial role unjustly
- *Dislikes "the Jews"*
- Rejects Jesus as the truth
- Clumsy
- *Afraid of Jesus*

Viewed in terms of Pilate's role, the plot development in this scene may be summarized as follows: Pilate's attempt to set Jesus free is thwarted by "the Jews."

Scene Six: John 19:9-11

From Pilate's behavior in this scene, two traits may be deduced – one of which has been revealed earlier on, that is to say, the fact that Pilate does not believe in Jesus, or – as this trait has been formulated earlier in this study – that he rejects Jesus as the truth. This is evident from the fact that although he (ironically[74]) asks the right question about Jesus ("Where do you come from?"), it is

---

[73] These three possibilities have already been outlined by Bauer in his commentary of 1933. See Thyen, *Johannesevangelium*, 725–26.

[74] Pilate seems to be portrayed here as employing the question as a way of determining whether Jesus really comes from a god (so, for example, Bultmann, *Johannes*, 512, and Stibbe, *Storyteller*, 109), without being aware that he is asking one of the most important questions

also clear that he does not believe in him. For this reason Jesus does not respond to his question.⁷⁵ Irritated by Jesus' lack of response, Pilate attempts to force Jesus into saying something by stressing his own authority, but Jesus has the final word on this issue: Pilate's authority over him actually comes "from above."⁷⁶ The new trait that is revealed here is that Pilate is unaware of the true nature of his authority over Jesus. Accordingly, at the end of this scene, the paradigm of traits associated with Pilate is as follows:

- Finds it difficult to withstand the pressure of "the Jews"; afraid of "the Jews"
- Attempts to fulfill his judicial role in a just way ↔ fulfils his judicial role unjustly
- Dislikes "the Jews"
- *Rejects Jesus as the truth*
- Clumsy
- Afraid of Jesus
- *Not aware of the true nature of his authority over Jesus*

In terms of plot development, two important aspects should be highlighted: First, Pilate fails to achieve his objective of determining Jesus' origin: He asks the right question, but does not draw the correct conclusion from Jesus' response. Secondly, he fails in his attempt to impress Jesus with his authority; instead he is confronted with the true nature of his own authority.

Scene Seven: John 19:12–16a

Because of Jesus' words,⁷⁷ Pilate seeks⁷⁸ to set him free, which is another illustration of the trait "attempts to fulfill his judicial role in a just way." This attempt, however, is thwarted by "the Jews," who force him to choose between being "a friend of Caesar"⁷⁹ and Jesus. This prompts Pilate to hand Jesus over,

---

regarding Jesus. Moloney, *John*, 495, calls it "the fundamental question of Johannine Christology." In fact, Pilate asks all the "right" questions about Jesus: "Are you the King of the Jews?," "What have you done?," "So you are a king?," "What is truth?," and "Where do you come from?"

⁷⁵ So, among others, Brown, *John*, 878, and Bond, *Pilate*, 188. Haenchen, *Johannesevangelium*, 538, also detects another motif: "Das Göttliche weist sich nicht direkt aus."

⁷⁶ Hans von Campenhausen, "Zum Verständnis von Joh 19,11," *ThLZ* 73 (1948): 387–92, here 388, puts it well: "[Jesus] ironisiert vielmehr das naive Machtgefühl, das der Landpfleger zur Schau trägt." See also Thyen, *Johannesevangelium*, 727, in this regard.

⁷⁷ Ἐκ τούτου is to be interpreted here in a causal rather than a temporal sense. See, for example, Schnackenburg, *Johannesevangelium*, 3:303. It may refer either to everything that Jesus has said to Pilate in the previous scene, or specifically to the implication that Pilate would (also) be guilty of sin in having Jesus executed. Another possibility is that Jesus' reference to "above" has been interpreted by Pilate as an indication that the gods are indeed involved.

⁷⁸ The imperfect suggests a series of attempts.

⁷⁹ The expression φίλος τοῦ Καίσαρος could denote a formal title, or it could be used in a

thus fulfilling his judicial role in an unjust way, but also manifesting a new trait, namely selfishness, since he opts to safeguard his own position instead of making any further attempt to set Jesus free. Pilate thus sits down[80] on the βῆμα, calling on "the Jews" to look at their king. This is neither another attempt to set Jesus free,[81] nor an appeal to a possible feeling of honor among "the Jews,"[82] but rather a form of sarcasm to get even with "the Jews."[83] Accordingly, it is another illustration of the trait "dislikes 'the Jews.'" Their response causes him to repeat his sarcasm ("Should I crucify your king?") before handing Jesus over to be crucified.

Thus, at the end of Scene 7, the paradigm of traits that the implied reader will associate with Pilate may be summarized as follows:

- *Finds it difficult to withstand the pressure of "the Jews";* afraid of "the Jews"
- Attempts to fulfill his judicial role in a just way ↔ *fulfils his judicial role unjustly*
- *Dislikes "the Jews"*
- Rejects Jesus as the truth
- Clumsy
- Afraid of Jesus
- Not aware of the true nature of his authority over Jesus
- *Selfish*

In terms of plot development, Pilate finally succumbs to the pressure of "the Jews."[84] They have achieved their objective; he has not achieved his. In this scene, they have the last word: "We have no king but Caesar."

---

general sense. To my mind, the second option is more feasible. See Thyen, *Johannesevangelium*, 727-28.

[80] There is an extensive debate on whether ἐκάθισεν should be interpreted in a transitive or an intransitive sense. For an exposition of the case for a transitive interpretation, see I. de la Potterie, "Jésus, roi et juge d'après Jn 19,13: ἐκάθισεν ἐπὶ βήματος," *Bib* 41 (1960): 217-47. Thorough overviews, as well as reasons why the intransitive sense should be accepted, are provided by Raymond E. Brown, *The Death of the Messiah: From Gethsemane to the Grave. A Commentary on the Passion Narratives in the Four Gospels* (Vol. 2; New York: Doubleday, 1994), 1388-93, and Gniesmer, *Prozeß*, 337-47. The text is definitely ambiguous; but strictly speaking, it cannot be regarded as having a double meaning, since, as Schnackenburg, *Johannesevangelium*, 3:305-6, points out, the reader cannot imagine both at the same time.

[81] *Contra* Schnackenburg, *Johannesevangelium*, 3:306.
[82] *Contra* Bultmann, *Johannes*, 514.
[83] So most scholars. Giblin, "John's Narration," 233, suggests that here, Pilate is capitalizing on his earlier blunder in this regard.
[84] The way in which "the Jews" force Pilate to do what they want him to is ironic. They want to see Jesus crucified more than they care about their confession that they have no King but Yahweh.

Aftermath

In the rest of the narrative, Pilate is mentioned a further three times: According to 19:19–22, the chief priests complain about the words "king of the Jews" on the inscription on the cross, but Pilate refuses to change the wording; according to 19:31–32, they ask him to have the legs of the three crucified men broken, to which he consents; and, according to 19:39, he is approached by Joseph of Arimathea, who asks to be allowed to take away the body of Jesus – a request which Pilate grants. Culpepper[85] interprets all of these instances as part of an attempt by Pilate to atone for his earlier concession to "the Jews"; but to my mind, this interpretation reads too much into these actions. Rather, they should be interpreted as follows: Pilate's refusal to change the wording on the title seems to be another manifestation of his contempt for "the Jews." The other two events can simply be regarded as a sensible response by Pilate to reasonable requests.

Conclusion

First, I trust that the analysis above has illustrated how Chatman's approach to characterization can be applied profitably in the interpretation of a character in a Biblical narrative. If the analysis above is correct, no fewer than eight traits are associated with Pilate, which is quite remarkable for a character who appears rather briefly in the Gospel. As a result of the relatively large number of traits, a fairly complex character emerges. Although I would not classify Pilate as a round character, he is definitely not a flat character. Perhaps one may call him a multi-layered character, since the traits that he embodies represent a fairly diverse group of characteristics: He finds it difficult to withstand the pressure of "the Jews," dislikes them, and is even afraid of them, but at the same time he also attempts to fulfill his judicial role in a just way, although he does not achieve this objective. Furthermore, he rejects Jesus as the truth and even becomes afraid of him. To my mind, all these traits form the core of the characterization of Pilate in the Fourth Gospel, with the conflict between the traits pertaining to "the Jews" on the one hand, and the trait pertaining to his judicial role on the other hand, comprising a predominant feature of the picture of Pilate. This picture is given some depth by a number of other, unrelated, traits, each of which only comes to the fore once in the narrative, namely his clumsiness, his ignorance of the true nature of his power over Jesus and his selfishness. Interestingly, his decision to hand Jesus over to "the Jews" (in the last scene) is motivated by one of these traits, that is to say, his selfishness.

---

[85] Culpepper, *Anatomy of the Fourth Gospel*, 143.

Secondly, the importance of empty spaces in the characterization of Pilate has been noted. As I have tried to show, the text has quite a number of these empty spaces, and the choices that one is forced to make in filling them determine one's interpretation of this character to a significant degree. This gives rise to another question: Why are there so many empty spaces in this regard? One could argue that this was done on purpose, i. e., that the implied author wished to create an ambiguous character. However, I do not believe this to be the case. Rather, the large number of empty spaces can probably be ascribed to the fact that Pilate is not really the focal figure in these chapters. As is the case in the rest of the Gospel, the focus falls primarily on Jesus, and the characterization of Pilate is a secondary issue in relation to that of Jesus. Pilate is only relevant insofar as he interacts with Jesus and "the Jews" who want to have Jesus killed; hence the fairly large number of empty spaces regarding his characterization.

Thirdly, if one considers the development of the plot in Chapters 18–19 in terms of Pilate's role therein, the most significant feature is that he keeps on failing to achieve his objectives. In Scene 1 he is forced by "the Jews" to investigate the matter further, although he clearly does not want to do so; in Scene 2 he is portrayed as failing to grasp Jesus' true identity; in Scene 3 he fails to set Jesus free; in Scenes 4 and 5 he fails in a further attempt to set Jesus free; in Scene 6 he fails to determine Jesus' origin, and also fails to impress Jesus with his authority, and in Scene 7 he finally succumbs to the pressure of "the Jews." One could thus say that he is portrayed as failing in more ways than one. This is also reflected by the fact that in most of the scenes the final words are not Pilate's: In Scenes 1, 3, 5 and 7 "the Jews" have the last word, while the final words in scene 6 are uttered by Jesus. It is only in Scene 2 that the final words belong to Pilate ("What is truth?"); but, even then, his words do not project a very positive picture of him, since they ironically reveal his failure to believe in Jesus.

Finally, the question arises as to how the characterization of Pilate fits into the overall objective of the implied author in the Gospel. In other words, how does the characterization of Pilate contribute to the plot of the Gospel as such? When the characterization of Pilate is considered from this perspective, at least two aspects should be mentioned: First, Pilate's repeated attempts to set Jesus free underline the fact that Jesus goes to the cross innocently and does not really deserve to die. Secondly, Pilate's failure to grasp Jesus' identity (again – as happens throughout the Gospel) emphasizes Jesus' true identity: He is the truth, the king of "the Jews" in the true sense of the word.

Barabbas:
A Foil for Jesus, the Jewish Leadership, and Pilate

David L. Mathewson

One of the most enigmatic figures in the Fourth Gospel is Barabbas, laconically referred to in 18:40 towards the end of Jesus' trial. This short study will apply insights from modern linguistics and participant reference in order to discuss the function of Barabbas within this section of the Gospel. More specifically, it will consider how Barabbas is encoded within the discourse, the grammatical role that Barabbas plays, and the processes assigned to him by the narrator. I will then briefly consider the function of Barabbas in relation to the other main participants in John 18.

One of the clues to understanding a character/participant's role within a discourse is how much encoding he/she receives.[1] Thus, main characters tend to be introduced and activated with a full noun phrase identifying them, but then receive reduced coding (pronouns) or zero coding (inflected endings of verbs).[2] They are also activated over large stretches of narrative.[3] Sometimes a main character will receive full reference (noun phrase) when he/she is reintroduced after an absence in the narrative, or to distinguish him/her from other participants on a "crowded stage," or to make the participant prominent, such as to draw out a contrast. Minor characters are activated only briefly in a narrative and typically are referred to with a noun phrase (unless they play a role over a stretch of narrative).[4] Second, the importance of a participant can also be determined by the grammatical role they play, whether they are subjects (and hence thematic) of the main clauses (which carry the story line), or whether they are only complements (receiving the action, as direct objects or indirect objects), or whether they are found only in supporting clauses, such as the object of a preposition, or whether in other embedded clauses (participles, or speeches). Third, the role of the participant is often indicated by the types of processes (verbs) with which they are associated: material process (actions);

---

[1] Stephen H. Levinsohn, *Discourse Features of New Testament Greek: A Coursebook on the Information Structure of New Testament Greek* (2d ed.; Dallas: SIL, 2000), 134–47.
[2] Jeffrey T. Reed, *A Discourse Analysis of Philippians* (JSNTSup 136; Sheffield: Sheffield Academic Press, 1997), 383.
[3] Levinsohn, *Discourse Features*, 134.
[4] Cf. Reed, *Discourse Analysis*, 384.

mental processes (verbs of perception, such as speaking); relational processes (verbs of "being").[5]

Barabbas is only mentioned here in John 18:40. He does not appear anywhere else in the Fourth Gospel.[6] Furthermore, both times he is mentioned in 18:40 he receives encoding with a full noun phrase (Βαραββᾶς, Βαραββᾶν), suggesting that he is not a main character in the Gospel or in this section. Furthermore, here in v. 40 grammatically Barabbas plays only the role of the direct object of the assumed verb ἀπολύω, and is further embedded as part of the speech of the crowd (ἐκραύασαν οὖν πάλιν λέγοντες). In the second reference Barabbas is the subject of a verb, ἦν, but in contrast to the surrounding verbs, it is not a verb of action which advances the story line, but one that simply identifies Barabbas as a λῃστής (on which see below). Therefore, the only verb type that Barabbas grammatically is the subject of is a relational verb (ἦν) – one which does not produce an action and advance the narrative. This stands in contrast to the other participants, Jesus, Pilate, and the crowds which all are subjects of verb types of actions and speeches. In other words, Barabbas is a passive participant in the narrative, not performing any actions which advance the narrative, and plays a minor role. He is the object of an action embedded in a speech, and is the subject of a relational process of identification.

In light of this, Barabbas seems to play a role within the narrative of functioning as a foil for three other key participants. First, he is a "Gegenfigur" to Jesus.[7] While Jesus is portrayed as innocent of the charges of political insurrection (note the ironic "King of the Jews" on the lips of Pilate), Barabbas is portrayed as a λῃστής, an insurrectionist and murderer.[8] In light of the combination of λῃστής with shepherd terminology in 10:1, 8, it becomes ironic that the guilty insurrectionist is released in exchange for the innocent shepherd of the people.[9] Second, Barabbas functions as a foil to highlight the irony of the action of the Jewish leadership.[10] Once again, the Jewish leadership exchanges

---

[5] Michael A. K. Halliday and Christian M. I. M. Matthiessen, *An Introduction to Functional Grammar* (3d ed.; London: Arnold, 2004), 170–75.

[6] For Synoptic references see Matt 27:16, 17, 20, 21, 26; Mark 15:7, 11, 15; Luke 23:18.

[7] Stephan Witetschek, "Ein Räuber: Barabbas im Johannesevangelium," in *The Death of Jesus in the Fourth Gospel* (ed. Gilbert Van Belle; BETL 200; Louvain: University Press, 2007), 805–15, here 811–15.

[8] BDAG, 594, followed by most commentaries, usually pointing to evidence from Josephus. *Contra* Witetschek, who argues that it is just a general term to refer to someone "der durch seine Taten und seine Lebensweise außerhalb der zivilisierten menschlichen Gemeinschaft steht" ("Ein Räuber," 815). Cf. Joachim Gnilka, *Johannesevangelium* (Würzburg: Echter Verlag, 1989), 140 ("ein Verbrecher").

[9] Andrew T. Lincoln, *Truth on Trial: The Lawsuit Motif in the Fourth Gospel* (Peabody, Mass.: Hendrickson, 2000), 26. Cf. also Witetschek, "Ein Räuber," 813–15, though Witetschek only thinks that Barabbas draws attention to the contrast between those who would destroy life, and Jesus who now gives his life in fullness.

[10] Most commentaries have noted the irony between the release of the guilty Barabbas in exchange for the innocent Jesus: e. g., Rudolf Bultmann, *The Gospel of John: A Commentary*

an innocent victim for a guilty bandit. They declare Barabbas' innocence, siding with a criminal, thus reflecting the thieves and robbers (λῃσταί) that come to kill and destroy (10:8, 10).[11] Finally, Barabbas is also a foil for Pilate, demonstrating his failure to dispense justice commensurate with his office, and instead his willingness to evade a decision (knowing full well that Jesus is innocent), fearing the world rather than the truth. By failing to give Jesus justice, Pilate "makes a travesty of justice" by releasing one who is guilty.[12] It is unlikely that Alan Culpepper is correct that the overt reference to Barabbas' identity as a λῃστής suggests that Barabbas was unknown.[13] Rather, it appears that the explicit identity of Barrabas as a λῃστής is for rhetorical effect to draw attention to the above ironies in comparison with Jesus, Pilate, and the Jewish leadership.

(trans. G. R. Beasley-Murray; Philadelphia: Westminster, 1971), 658; R. Alan Culpepper, *Anatomy of the Fourth Gospel: A Study in Literary Design* (Philadelphia: Fortress, 1983), 172; Raymond E. Brown, *The Gospel According to John (i–xii)* (AB 29; New York: Doubleday, 1966), 872; J. Ramsey Michaels, *The Gospel of John* (NICNT; Grand Rapids, Mich.: Eerdmans, 2010), 317; George M. Beasley-Murray, *John* (2d ed.; WBC 36; Nashville: Nelson, 1999), 333; Lincoln, *Truth on Trial*, 26, 130; Ben Witherington, III, *John's Wisdom: A Commentary on the Fourth Gospel* (Louisville, Ky.: Westminster John Knox, 1995), 292 (he refers to the "sarcasm and irony" throughout this section); Donald A. Carson, *The Gospel According to John* (Grand Rapids, Mich.: Eerdmans, 1991), 596.

[11] Cf. Witetschek, "Ein Räuber," 813–15.
[12] Brown, *John*, 872.
[13] Culpepper, *Anatomy of the Fourth Gospel*, 216.

The Soldiers Who Crucify: Fulfilling Scripture*

Michael Labahn

The Soldiers (στρατιῶται): Their Function and Presence in the Story

Within a crucifixion story, the normal function of soldiers is to lead a sentenced criminal to the cross and to oversee his/her execution outside a town. The anonymous soldiers of the Johannine narrative act according to these general rules by taking Jesus through a crowd to a place outside Jerusalem called Golgotha, serving to supervise the execution, and finally speeding the death of the victims and confirming their deaths.

The term στρατιῶται ("soldiers") appears for the first time in the Johannine text in 19:2. Here the term identifies a group of people who mock Jesus by hailing him as "king of the Jews." This mockery is one of several unwitting prophecies made by different *hostile characters* in the Johannine story.[1] The mocking of Jesus is part of a larger episode that leads to the decision to bring Jesus to death. The first mention of the soldiers as narrative characters helps the reader identify the group as *hostile unbelievers* who unwittingly give witness to Jesus' true character.

The term "soldier" re-appears in John 19:23–24 (three times) and in 19:32, 34. Each of these short episodes connects the soldiers to the fulfillment of Scripture: 19:24, 28, 36. As noted below, certain actions of the soldiers in relation to Jesus are interpreted in relation to Scripture, thereby showing that Jesus' fate is in accordance with God's will. In this respect, the soldiers as narrative characters serve the larger characterization of the main figure in the Johannine narrative, Jesus.

The soldiers are identified not only by the term στρατιῶται, but also, as appropriate, by the use of personal pronouns or plural verb forms. The analysis here is limited to the appearance of the soldiers under the cross and therefore to the episode in 19:18–37. Verse 18 refers to the act of crucifixion: αὐτὸν

---

* My thanks are extended to Tom Thatcher for checking the English in this essay and to the editors for their invitation to contribute and for their suggestions.

[1] E. g., Craig S. Keener, *The Gospel of John: A Commentary* (2 vols.; Peabody, Mass.: Hendrickson, 2003), 1120–1121; see also Hartwig Thyen, *Das Johannesevangelium* (HNT 6; Tübingen: Mohr Siebeck, 2005), 733.

ἐσταύρωσαν ("they crucified him"). The 3rd person plural verb probably refers to v. 16b, where it is mentioned that Jesus is handed over by Pilate to "them." It remains unclear who is meant by the 3rd person plural. As Craig Keener notes, this ambivalence could be intentional: on one hand, the reference might be to the Jewish authorities who are held responsible for the death of Jesus; on the other hand, v. 16 could refer to the (Roman) soldiers. Perhaps one could say that when Jesus is handed over to the soldiers he is also handed over "to the will of the Jewish leaders."[2]

The Soldiers under the Cross and Their Deeds in Relation to the Crucified Jesus

Pilate delivers Jesus to a group representing Roman power and the will of the Jewish leaders. However, within the narrative setting, the soldiers are identified by their relationship to the convicted Jesus, who is still the main acting character even in the Johannine crucifixion story. They clearly oppose Jesus, especially in the violent acts they commit against him, but finally become part of an ironic interplay. Unwittingly they serve God's will. With their hostility, they fulfill God's will.

From the start of the episode, the soldiers play only a very limited role. They "took Jesus" (v. 16b: παρέλαβον οὖν τὸν Ἰησοῦν), but Jesus in turn "takes" his own cross (v. 17: βαστάζων[3] ἑαυτῷ τὸν σταυρόν) and thereby turns the soldiers into bystanders. While it is a well-known fact that criminals carried their own crosses in the ancient world, this act is highlighted in the Johannine story so that Jesus, though being brought to crucifixion, is acting on his own power (see already 18:1–12) and in accordance with his own (and his Father's) will, as is further indicated by reference to Scripture's fulfillment. Such an act signals that the soldiers have only a limited power over Jesus.

The soldiers crucified Jesus (v. 18a: αὐτὸν ἐσταύρωσαν) and two other criminals, whose presence carries little meaning in the Johannine story.[4] By crucifixion Jesus is "lifted up" in the middle of these criminals to take his place on his throne as the "king of 'the Jews'" (vss. 19–22). The act of crucifixion itself is narrated concisely, although in fact it might have taken some time.

---

[2] Keener, *John*, 1132.

[3] The participle βαστάζων ("to carry," figuratively, "to suffer") may indicate that the narrator does not ignore the language and reality of suffering in his narrative. But against the backdrop of the Synoptic passion accounts, it becomes quite obvious that Jesus, not the soldiers, is the real actor in this scene.

[4] E. g., Manfred Lang, *Johannes und die Synoptiker: Eine redaktionsgeschichtliche Analyse von Joh 18–20 vor dem markinischen und lukanischen Hintergrund* (FRLANT 182; Göttingen: Vandenhoeck & Ruprecht, 1999), 213.

This indicates that the narrative is not interested in presenting a documentary about the soldiers' deeds, but rather in the significance of what they are doing in relation to their narrative counterpart, Jesus.

After the act of crucifixion, they took (ἔλαβον) Jesus' clothes (perhaps following ancient law and custom),[5] and divided them into four parts, one for each soldier (v. 23). Here the reader gains knowledge about the number of soldiers: they are four individuals – a small Roman military unit of four soldiers (cf. Acts 12:4) – who are responsible for torture. Parallel to them, and representing a contrasting sympathetic response, are the four women under the cross who seek to console Jesus.[6]

One part of Jesus' clothing, a seamless tunic, is not torn by the soldiers, but lots were cast for it "to fulfill Scripture" (ἡ γραφὴ πληρωθῇ; v. 24). This act by the soldiers "was their contribution to the plan of God"[7] and points to a deeper meaning behind the story which is revealed by the narrator and his commentary – or, more specifically, revealed by another "speaker," the Scriptures themselves.[8] Within the Johannine story-line, keeping the tunic whole and intact is not coincidental, but rather illustrates the relationships among Jesus' followers/family. The narrator's commentary offers an interpretation of the soldiers' action that also illuminates the next action of Jesus, referring to a relationship from above that also was not "split." Jesus establishes a new relationship by making the Beloved Disciple the son of his Mother who stands under his cross.[9]

The next act of the soldiers depends directly upon Jesus, their crucified victim. He understands that his soteriological duty[10] has been fulfilled (vss. 28, 30). As a final act, he refers the reader to the fulfillment of Scripture by stating, "I am thirsty." The soldiers reply by giving him a sponge full of vinegar upon a branch of hyssop. This is not an act of compassion. Jesus' thirst and the soldiers' offer of a drink correspond to each other as the fulfillment of Scripture, which can be understood by the immediate reference to Jesus' death as giving a poisoned drink. The verbal convergences (thirst, vinegar, drink) as well as the form and plot of the episode give evidence for the use of Ps 69(68):22 in John

---

[5] Michael Labahn, "'Verlassen' oder 'Vollendet': Ps 22 in der 'Johannespassion' zwischen Intratextualität und Intertextualität," in *Ps 22 und die Passionsgeschichten der Evangelien* (ed. Dieter Sänger; BThSt 88; Neukirchen-Vluyn: Neukirchener Verlag, 2007), 111–53, here 133 with fn. 68.

[6] Sjef van Tilborg, *Das Johannesevangelium: Ein Kommentar für die Praxis* (Stuttgart: Katholisches Bibelwerk, 2005), 286–87.

[7] Barnabas Lindars, *The Gospel of John* (NCB; Grand Rapids, Mich.: Eerdmans, 1982), 578.

[8] Michael Labahn, "Scripture *Talks* because Jesus *Talks*: The Narrative Rhetoric of Persuading and Creativity in John's Use of Scripture," in *The Fourth Gospel in First-Century Media Culture* (ed. Anthony Le Donne and Tom Thatcher; LNTS 426; London: T&T Clark, 2011), 133–54, esp. 152–53.

[9] Cf., e. g., Labahn, "'Verlassen' oder 'Vollendet,'" 137–40.

[10] Labahn, "'Verlassen' oder 'Vollendet,'" 129–30.

19:28–29.[11] When the Johannine Jesus accepts the drink, he drinks the cup given to him by his Father (18:11, 12:27–28):[12] the path to the cross turns into the way back to the Father; but Jesus' death also generates community (12:23–24) and devotion to his followers (10:11, 15; 11:50–51). What follows presents itself in the sense of Johannine irony,[13] which distinguishes between the intentions of the figures and the truth of their statements or of their actions. The thirst of the thirst-quencher is met with a poisonous drink, but this potion leads Jesus to the Father and leads the people to life while giving his life; with such an act, love reaches its goal (13:1) and brings the son to glorification (13:31–32; 17).[14]

Even after Jesus' death, Scripture is fulfilled and the soldiers act entirely in accordance with God's will as revealed in Scripture. The Johannine narrator explains that no corpse should remain exposed on the so-called "Great Sabbath"; therefore, the death of the crucified should be hastened by breaking their legs (vss. 31–32). In Jesus' case only, no leg was broken, because he was already dead (v. 33). To verify the death, the soldiers pierce his side with a spear so that blood and water pour out (v. 34). Through these actions the soldiers verify the death of Jesus, but within the narrative world the flow of blood and water from Jesus' side also institutes the Johannine rites of Eucharist and Baptism.[15] Finally, both acts – not breaking Jesus' legs and piercing his side – are fulfillments of Scripture.

Overall, the soldiers are placed in the typical narrative frame of a crucifixion story, but they do not function totally according to the expected role of this special literary frame. Within the Johannine story, it is clear from 19:2 on that the soldiers are a hostile and non-believing character. It also becomes clear that this group unwittingly gives witness to the true nature of the main character, Jesus, first through their mockery and then later by being part of Scripture's fulfillment. Within a story of crucifixion there is usually a clear hierarchy between the soldiers who are responsible for the execution and their victim(s). In all their deeds, however, it is shown that the soldiers are inferior to the Johannine Jesus, who is the sovereign of his own fate; in fact, the fulfillment of his mission is underscored by the narrated actions of the soldiers. The story does not deny the reality of the suffering of Jesus (e. g., nakedness, thirst),

---

[11] Robert L. Brawley, "An Absent Complement and Intertextuality in John 19:28–29," *JBL* 112 (1993): 427–43, here 437.

[12] Donald Senior, *The Passion of Jesus in the Gospel of John* (The Passion Series 4; Collegeville, Minn.: Liturgical Press, 2001), 116.

[13] Cf. Senior, *The Passion of Jesus*, 118.

[14] Labahn, "'Verlassen' oder 'Vollendet,'" 141–46.

[15] Michael Labahn, "Kreative Erinnerung als nachösterliche Nachschöpfung: Der Ursprung der christlichen Taufe," in *Ablution, Initiation, and Baptism: Late Antiquity, Early Judaism, and Early Christianity* (ed. David Hellholm et al.; BZNW 176; Berlin: de Gruyter, 2011), 337–76, here 360–361.

which is caused by his opponents and their narrative function. But the focus is not on suffering, but rather on the fulfillment of God's will and the supremacy of Jesus to carry out his mission to completion.

Intertextuality and "Character Building"

As already shown, the narrative role of the soldiers under the cross within the Johannine story is mostly related to an intertextual play. They do not serve Pilate or the will of the Jewish authorities, but rather serve the main characters of the story – God and Jesus – by fulfilling the Scripture. Space does not permit a detailed discussion of the reference texts behind this intertextual play,[16] but it is appropriate to briefly note here how nearly every narrated act of the soldiers under the cross relates in some way to Scripture and its fulfillment.

The soldiers' main action is to crucify Jesus, who takes his own cross (19:17). By that act they become part of the ultimate purpose behind God's sending of Jesus, as acknowledged by Jesus' cry τετέλεσται ("it is brought to its end;" 19:30), which is, according to the context of the Johannine story, in accordance with Scripture. Besides the crucifixion itself, every other act of the soldiers is explicitly related to Scripture. The distribution of the garments of the crucified Jesus (19:23–24) is related to Ps 22:19. Serving Jesus by fulfilling his demand for a drink (διψῶ) with vinegar on a branch of hyssop (19:27–28) is related to Ps 22:16 (and other passages from Scripture).[17] After the death of Jesus, the soldiers are asked to break the legs of the crucified but exclude Jesus, again in fulfillment of Scripture (19:31–37). To demonstrate his death, they pierce his side with a spear, which is again related to Scripture by the narrator: Ps 34:31 (combined with LXX Ex 12:10, 46; Num 9:12 in John 19:36)[18] and Zech 12:10 (John 19:37). Both passages related to the deeds of the Roman soldiers indicate that Jesus' soteriological mission leads him necessarily to the cross, so that his crucifixion could be widely seen to benefit his flock/followers (cf. John 10:11).

---

[16] See, e. g., Maarten J. J. Menken, *Old Testament Quotations in the Fourth Gospel: Studies in Textual Form* (CBET 15; Kampen: Kok Pharos, 1996); Bruce G. Schuchard, *Scripture Within Scripture: The Interrelationship of Form and Function in the Explicit Old Testament Citations in the Gospel of John* (SBLDS 133; Atlanta: Scholars Press, 1992).

[17] Cf., e. g., Labahn, "'Verlassen' oder 'Vollendet,'" 141–47.

[18] Menken, *Old Testament Quotations*, 147–66.

Summary

The main narrative function of the soldiers who crucify Jesus is to highlight that the crucifixion of Jesus is in accordance with God's will as revealed in Scripture. Although the soldiers are located in the narrative as a small, anonymous and negative figure that opposes the hero of the story, they play a crucial role in the Johannine interpretation of the crucifixion of Jesus and its significance to the readers' lives. They represent an ironical play in which they unintentionally act according to the will of God and to the mission of the story's hero. As a result of the soldiers' actions, at the cross Jesus brings his soteriological mission to completion – further, the soldiers' act of piercing Jesus' side directly refers to the Johannine rites of Eucharist and Baptism. However, their narrated acts mainly interpret Jesus' death, including aspects of his suffering, as part of God's will indicated in the Scriptures, which themselves speak of Jesus and his mission. In this way, the soldiers become *a character to fulfill Scripture*.

The Co-Crucified Men: Shadows by His Cross

Chelsea N. Revell and Steven A. Hunt

Introduction

At least in comparison to their portrayal in the Synoptic Gospels, the two men crucified on either side of Jesus in John appear to be relatively bland, insignificant extras. While Matthew and Mark describe them specifically as "bandits" (λῃσταί; Matt 27:38; Mark 15:27), and Luke describes them as "criminals" (κακούργοι; 23:32), in John they are merely "two others" (ἄλλους δύο; 19:18).[1] More interesting still, in Matthew and Mark the co-crucified men join with those who abuse Jesus, apparently taking time out from their final moments to taunt him (cf. Matt 27:44; Mark 15:32). Luke, meanwhile, brings these two into sharp disagreement with one another: one "kept deriding Jesus" while the other "rebuked him," acknowledged his guilt and Jesus' innocence, and then asked that Jesus remember him. Jesus responded to the penitent man directly, promising him a place in paradise (23:39–43). In John, on the other hand, the two co-crucified men do not act or speak, nor are they spoken to; in fact, far less than subjects, they are merely objectified in the scene.

The two men are mentioned twice in John: first in 19:18 as an introductory detail related to Jesus' crucifixion and again in 19:31–32 when the Jewish leaders request that the legs of the men be broken and their bodies taken down from the crosses. Aside from their placement on either side of Jesus and the fact that their legs get broken, they are not described in any way. Did they, too, carry their crosses to the place of execution? Or have family standing nearby when they took their last breath? Did they offer any final words? And while their death is presumed, not narrated, were they subsequently buried or left for wild animals?[2] The narrator's silence on these issues as well as others con-

---

[1] Scriptural quotations, unless otherwise noted, are from the NRSV.

[2] Since Deut 21:22–23 requires that the bodies of hanged men be buried, and since this text appears to stand behind John 19:31, perhaps implied readers would have read this narrative assuming that the men were buried. On the other hand, as Jerome H. Neyrey observes, victims of crucifixion in the Greco-Roman world were often "denied honorable burial; corpses were left on display and were devoured by carrion birds and scavenger animals" (idem, *The Gospel of John in Cultural and Rhetorical Perspective* [Grand Rapids, Mich.: Eerdmans, 2009], 413).

trasts markedly with the story about Jesus. Since there is so little detail related to them, it is virtually impossible to conclude whether they ought to be understood negatively (as in Matthew's and Mark's portrayals, or in Luke's portrayal of the derisive man) or positively (as in Luke's portrayal of the penitent man). Given Jesus' own death by execution, even the fact that they are crucified is no guarantee of a negative portrayal by the narrator, much less a negative understanding by implied readers.[3] One might assume they were "bandits" like Barabbas (who apparently got pardoned; 18:39–40), but John's narrative never commits to this detail. And one is left to wonder, as these men must have wondered, why "the Jews"[4] clamored for Barabbas' release rather than their own.[5] What was their crime? Were they really guilty of a capital offense? Or, like the one with whom they were crucified, were they innocent victims of Roman (or Jewish) oppression (cf. 18:38; 19:4, 6)?[6] Obviously, John's narrative creates questions quite easily with respect to these two men; answers remain positively elusive.

Clearly, the co-crucified men have little to offer as characters in their own right, but it is precisely their objectification, especially in contrast to the Synoptics,[7] that marks their role as literary foils in John – foils that further highlight the centrality of Jesus and his glorification through crucifixion. The narrator makes this point clear by only noting their location and broken legs,

---

[3] In his final discourse, Jesus forewarns his disciples about persecution (15:20) and martyrdom (16:2); and then in ch. 21, both Jesus and the narrator speak to the subject of Peter's martyrdom as the shepherd of Jesus' flock (vss. 15–19). In the face of such explicit warnings about persecution, perhaps the deaths of the two co-crucified men only serve to showcase Rome's total authority as well as their utterly capricious and brutal attitude towards life and death.

[4] On the use of "the Jews" in John, always in quotations in my work, see "And the Word Became Flesh – Again? Jesus and Abraham in John 8:31–59," in *Perspectives on Our Father Abraham* (ed. Steven A. Hunt; Grand Rapids, Mich.: Eerdmans, 2010), 85–86, fn. 14.

[5] Of course, this comment assumes their presence when Barabbas was pardoned. But the narrative does not speak to this possibility one way or another.

[6] The narrator does not record whether Pilate also placed inscriptions on the crosses of the co-crucified men. Such action would have been in keeping with the occasional Roman custom of publicly writing out a criminal's offense; see further, Raymond E. Brown, *The Gospel According to John (xiii–xxi)* (AB 29; New York: Doubleday, 1966), 2.901. Clearly, the narrator did not want to draw attention away from the placard on Jesus' cross, which functions on a number of levels, especially as yet another major example of irony: that is, on the placard Pilate unwittingly proclaimed Jesus' actual kingship (see esp. Paul D. Duke, *Irony in the Fourth Gospel* [Atlanta: John Knox Press, 1985], 136–37). As Brodie (*John*, 545) observes: "The result is that the crucifixion, instead of being a place of empty silence, becomes a scene of proclamation." While Jesus' death demands recognition, the deaths of the co-crucified ones then are marked by silence, meaninglessness.

[7] This essay will proceed assuming the author's use of the Synoptics when crafting the passion narrative. See further, Steven A. Hunt, *Rewriting the Feeding of Five Thousand: John 6.1–15 as a Test Case for Johannine Dependence on the Synoptic Gospels* (Studies in Biblical Literature 125; New York: Peter Lang, 2011).

and only then as a way of giving further meaning to Jesus' death. Remarkably then, Jesus' glory shines brighter due to their faceless shadows in this scene.

This essay will briefly explore several potential readings related to the narrator's use of these men to advance Christological themes, and will further pursue how these men might also contribute to the characterization of "the Jews," the Roman soldiers, as well as Jesus' family at the cross.[8]

"And with him *two* others ..."

After a dramatic confrontation between Pilate and the chief priests, the former handed Jesus over for crucifixion (19:16a). In a surprising departure from the Synoptic accounts, where Simon of Cyrene carries Jesus' cross (Matt 27:32; Mark 15:21; Luke 23:26), in John, Jesus carries the cross "by himself" to the place of execution (19:17).[9] And then, in a classic example of dramatic minimalism (especially given the narrative's drive towards this decisive moment), the narrator records simply, "they crucified him" (19:18a). It is immediately after this detail that readers are introduced to the two co-crucified men.

How might these two men contribute to our reading of the story of Jesus in John? First, ancient Christian readers often connected the idea that Jesus carried his own cross in John to the notion that Isaac bore the wood for the burnt offering in Genesis 22:6.[10] To be sure, these kinds of details are ripe for the picking, especially given John's connections to Genesis elsewhere.[11] What most

---

[8] On the rather "synthetic" methodology which follows, employing both diachronic and synchronic approaches to narrative criticism, see the introduction to my essay, "Nathanael: Under the Fig Tree on the Fourth Day," in this volume.

[9] In this omission, it appears that the narrator tells the traditional story through a different lens: thus, Jesus carries his own cross to further the theme of his determination to fulfill his mission (cf. Brodie, *John*, 544). Still, the notice also creates a sense of historical verisimilitude, since it was customary for a condemned man to carry his own cross beam to the place of execution (cf. Craig R. Koester, *Symbolism in the Fourth Gospel: Meaning, Mystery, Community* [2d ed.; Minneapolis: Fortress, 2003], 212; Edwyn C. Hoskyns, *The Fourth Gospel* [ed. Francis N. Davey; 2d ed.; London: Faber & Faber, 1950], 528). Of course, this historical background suggests that implied readers of John probably would have assumed that the co-crucified men also carried their crosses, despite the fact that the detail goes unmentioned.

[10] So, e. g., Clement of Alexandria, Tertullian, and Chrysostom all make a link between the two stories based on these details (see Joel C. Elowsky, ed., *Ancient Christian Commentary on Scripture: John 11–21* [Downers Grove, Ill.: InterVarsity Press, 2007], 308. They may have done so with good reason, since Jewish tradition came to view this story about Abraham as a story that testified also to Isaac's obedience to God. This sacrificial obedience was understood in some circles as a source of merit which could be passed on to others (cf. Josephus *Ant.* 1.232; 4 Macc. 13:12; 16:20), and was further associated with the Passover sacrifice in a number of Jewish texts (see, e. g., *Jub.* 18:3; 49:1; see further, Koester, *Symbolism*, 222).

[11] On these connections generally, see more below; in addition, I have pursued some of the connections between John and Genesis 22 in "And the Word Became Flesh – Again?," 81–109.

readers have not considered intertextually are the two extras in the two stories, and the fact that they are referred to three times in each. In our story, of course, it is precisely the two co-crucified men (19:18, 31, 32). But it is interesting to note that when Abraham set out in Genesis 22, "he took two of his young men with him" (v. 3). It is not entirely clear what purpose these two young men serve in the story. Their presence is merely noted in the first place (22:3), and then they are referred to again when Abraham addressed them and separated from them with Isaac to go on ahead to the place for the offering (v. 5). Finally, they are mentioned once more in the conclusion to the narrative when Abraham returned to them and they "arose" and "went together" to Beersheba (v. 19). Beyond noting the fact that two nameless men figure in both narratives three times – narratives which have, for other reasons entirely, often been drawn together by readers – we are not sure what to do with this observation.

Second, and more promising perhaps, readers ought to reflect on the two co-crucified men in light of earlier statements in the Gospel. For example, at a critical moment in the narrative Jesus promised, when lifted up, to draw all people to himself (12:32). In light of this, some have understood the two co-crucified men to be representative of the two groups that Jesus, now in position to draw all to himself, would bring to salvation. This line of thinking was developed as early as Cyril of Alexandria (d. 444 C. E.), who maintained that the two criminals by Christ's side symbolized the two nations – Israel and the Gentiles: "And why do we take condemned criminals as the type? Because the Jews were condemned by the Law, for they were guilty of trespassing it. And the Greeks were condemned by their idolatry, for they worshipped the creature more than the Creator ..."[12] Given the pervasive dualisms in the Fourth Gospel,[13] much less the basic sociological dualism of the ancient world,[14] there may be more to the fact that there are *two* crucified men (as opposed to three or four or whatever) than meets the eye.

Third, it is interesting to note also that John's crucifixion narrative in particular is sprinkled with other character couplets: the mother of Jesus and the Beloved Disciple (19:26–27); the one soldier who pierced Jesus' side and the Beloved Disciple (19:34–35); Joseph of Arimathea and Pilate (19:38); and, finally, Joseph of Arimathea and Nicodemus (19:39–42). The pattern doubles when one considers the four soldiers (19:23–25a) and the four women stand-

---

[12] Cited in Elowsky, *Ancient Christian Commentary*, 310.

[13] Not only is Jesus tried by both Jewish and Roman authorities, but recall too that it is only in John that Jesus is arrested by both Roman soldiers as well as Jewish police (18:2–13). On other dualisms in John, see the classic study of Rudolf Bultmann in *Theology of the New Testament* (London: SCM, 1955), 2.15–32; see further, John Ashton, *Understanding the Fourth Gospel* (Oxford: Clarendon Press, 1991), 205–37.

[14] Cf., for example, the distinction between Greeks and barbarians in Rom 1:14, or Jews and Greeks in Gal 3:28.

ing near the cross (19:25b).¹⁵ Perhaps it is also worth noting a major de-coupling in this narrative: 19:26–27 and 19:35 are the only instances in John's Gospel in which the Beloved Disciple appears without Peter.¹⁶

Of these character couplets, then, two sets are nearest to Jesus on the cross: the two co-crucified men "on either side" of Jesus (19:18) and the Mother of Jesus and the Beloved Disciple "standing beside her" (19:26). Comparing these two sets reinforces the idea that the former are simply literary foils in the crucifixion narrative. But now, we observe, not only in relation to Jesus: while the co-crucified ones were obviously close to Jesus physically – they were crucified "with him" (19:18; cf. v. 32)¹⁷ – it is the Mother of Jesus and the Beloved Disciple who are seen and addressed.¹⁸ While the former two remain flat characters, the latter two are further rounded out in the episode. Whereas in Luke one crucified man receives the promise of future life (23:39–43), in John Jesus gives nothing to the men hanging beside him; rather it is his Mother and the Beloved Disciple who are formed into a new community and, thereby, form the foundation of a new creation.

Perhaps there is another lesson embedded in the episode as well: what profit is it to be literally "with" Jesus (i. e., the co-crucified men) if one is not spiritually "near" him (i. e., the Mother of Jesus and the Beloved Disciple)? What benefit is there if one does not truly *see*, and is not truly *seen*? In a Gospel where *seeing* and *abiding* necessarily denote but also transcend simple perception and location, the one who truly *sees* and *abides* with Jesus is the one who receives life. Evidently, the Mother of Jesus and the Beloved Disciple are near the cross in more ways than one.

"... one on each side ..."

The Synoptics also note the specific location of the co-crucified men vis-à-vis Jesus: they were crucified "one on his right and one on his left" (Matt 27:38; Mark 15:27; Luke 23:33); the narrator of John's Gospel simplifies this description, observing that they were crucified with Jesus, "one on each side" (ἐντεῦθεν καὶ ἐντεῦθεν), but then quickly adds, "and Jesus in the middle" (μέσον δὲ τὸν Ἰησοῦν, 19:18; quotations from the NIV). The Johannine addi-

---

¹⁵ Of course, this comparison assumes four women at the cross, rather than three or even two women; these latter options are possible syntactically. See the discussion of the issue in Richard Bauckham, *Gospel Women: Studies of the Named Women in the Gospels* (Grand Rapids, Mich.: Eerdmans, 2002), 204–05.

¹⁶ Cf. 13:23–24; 18:15–16; 20:2–10; 21:7, 20–23; see further, Brodie, *John*, 550.

¹⁷ Cf. 18:5, 18, 26; cf. 18:15.

¹⁸ See further, Francis J. Moloney, *The Gospel of John* (SP 4; Collegeville, Minn.: The Liturgical Press, 1998), 503–504.

tion simultaneously marks the marginal position of the two co-crucified men while emphasizing the centrality of Jesus. To be sure, the detail lends itself to multiple interpretations.[19] At its basest level, however, it is simply descriptive, providing the relative position of the three crucified men on Golgotha. The notice therefore creates spatial symmetry, forcing readers to visualize the scene and focus on Jesus – the one in the "middle."[20]

But Jesus' centrality also complements the later notice related to the gathering of four women and the beloved disciple around the crucified Lord at the cross (19:25b–27), a detail which should be seen at least as a first installment on Jesus' word which, as we have already noted, promised that when he was lifted up, he would "draw all people" to himself (12:32). In Matthew and Mark, one will recall, "many women were also there, looking on *from a distance*" (Matt 27:55; cf. Mark 15:40) and Jesus' disciples, of course, were conspicuous only for their absence.[21] John's Gospel, however, in another major departure from the Synoptics, has the women and the beloved disciple "standing *near* the cross" (19:25b), close enough for conversation (19:26–27) and crucial eye-witness testimony (19:35). These later scenes as visual and visceral spectacles are made even more dramatic given Jesus' location "in the middle," his having been *centered* by the co-crucified ones "on each side."

At a more significant level, however, this spatial semantic with respect to Jesus should probably be understood in light of the Genesis cosmogony, which noted that the tree of life was "in the middle of the garden" (LXX Gen 2:9: ἐν μέσῳ τῷ παραδείσῳ; quotation from the NIV). Indeed, the narrator employs unique "garden" language front and center at Jesus' arrest (κῆπος; 18:1), burial (κῆπος; 19:41–42), and resurrection (κηπουρός; 20:15) in John.[22] And moreover, when water (i. e., the Spirit; cf. 3:5; 7:37–39) issues from Jesus' side in 19:34, the action builds on the idea, as much Jewish tradition does, of the "river" which "flows out of Eden to water the garden" in Genesis 2:10a.[23] Readers will recall that Jesus said to the Samaritan woman, "The water that I will give

---

[19] On the import of "spatial semantics" in John, see my colleague Ruben Zimmermann's essay, "The Believers Across the Jordan: On Location with Jesus," in this volume.

[20] Cf. J. Ramsey Michaels, *The Gospel of John* (NICNT; Grand Rapids, Mich.: Eerdmans, 2010), 949.

[21] Luke notes that "all his acquaintances, including the women ..., stood at a distance, watching these things" (23:49).

[22] That John uses the word κῆπος for "garden," where Gen 2–3 uses παράδεισος, is not very significant: the terms are used synonymously in Eccl 2:5; κῆπος is used to refer to the garden of Eden in Ezek 36:35; and the narrator in John delights in the use of synonyms elsewhere. See further, Ruben Zimmermann, "Symbolic Communication Between John and His Reader: The Garden Symbolism in John 19–20," in *Anatomies of Narrative Criticism: The Past, Present, and Futures of the Fourth Gospel as Literature* (ed. Tom Thatcher and Stephen D. Moore; Atlanta: SBL, 2008), 221–35.

[23] See further below, esp. at fn. 37.

will become in them a spring of water gushing up to eternal life" (4:14b). That four women are "standing near the cross" (19:25b) then may rightly be seen in light of Eden's river which "divides and becomes four branches" in Genesis 2:10b. The movement towards Jesus' cross in John is paralleled by the water – the Spirit – that flows from it. The entire scene, on this reading, simply anticipates the moment when Jesus, in the middle (εἰς τὸ μέσον) once again, gives the Holy Spirit to the disciples and "sends" them, as he has been sent (20:21–22). In any case, Jesus' position "in the middle" during his crucifixion must be more than just a detail related to location. Jesus' death on the cross in John most likely intends to allude in polyvalent ways to the cosmogony in Genesis.[24]

Highlighted such as it is by the co-crucified men on either side and the preliminary gathering which begins to emerge around it, perhaps the spatial centrality of Jesus' cross functions to reinforce the notion of Jesus' cosmic centrality. If the prologue of the Gospel, which insists that the Word was instrumental in the creation of all things, is not a prime example of this idea, certainly Jesus' promise in 1:51 is: "You will see heaven opened and the angels of God ascending and descending upon the Son of Man." As Neyrey has shown, the angels' ascent and descent functions at least to point "to the locus of the Son of man figure, viz., seated in the center of heaven."[25] As the true temple of God (cf. 2:21), therefore, Jesus' location here "in the middle" may relate to Jewish conceptions about the temple's cosmic centrality.[26]

"The soldiers came and broke the legs ..."

Since Jesus was crucified *between* the two other men, why is it that he is approached last by the soldiers who have been commissioned to break all of their legs? Would it not have been more logical for the soldiers to break the legs of the first man, then the legs of Jesus in the middle, and finally the legs of the third man? The narrator gives no explanation for this oddity, but perhaps there is a conceptual significance related to the fact that Jesus is in this moment encountered *third* and *last*: while in 19:18 it was important to establish Jesus as the *center* of three, it may have been important here (given Scriptural associations with the "third,"[27] our narrator's series of threes,[28] and

---

[24] I have explored these connections to Genesis and a number of others in my essay, "The Roman Soldiers at Jesus' Arrest: 'You are Dust, and to Dust You Shall Return,'" in this volume.

[25] Neyrey, *John in Cultural and Rhetorical Perspective*, 99–101.

[26] See the fine discussion of this topic in Gregory Stevenson, *Power and Place: Temple and Identity in the Book of Revelation* (BZNW 107; Berlin: de Gruyter, 2001), 154–57.

[27] See esp. the timing of the Sinai Theophany on "the third day" in Exod 19:9b–25.

[28] See in this regard the Johannine motif related to the lifting up of the Son of Man in

obvious reference to threes and thirds elsewhere[29]) that he be conceptually stationed – in this decisive Christophanic and Theophanic moment – as the *last* of three, as the final and climactic figure.[30]

That the co-crucified men's legs actually get broken also speaks to the characterization of "the Jews," and does so in two important ways. First, the narrator specifically notes that it was not Pilate but "the Jews" who initiated the action – the *crurifragium*. The narrator also details the reason for their request: "they did not want the bodies left on the cross during the Sabbath" (19:31). Thus, "the Jews" are concerned about *objects* which defile – "bodies" – because they are fastidious about ritual purity: that is, the Law forbids leaving a hanged man on a tree overnight, lest the land be defiled (Deut 21:22–23). The "men" are here objectified then, reduced to mere obstacles in a religious quest for purity. So, true to their overall characterization, "the Jews" attempt to have them removed by the soldiers. Earlier in the scene, readers will recall, they would not enter Pilate's headquarters "so as to avoid ritual defilement" (18:28). The whole section, therefore, "drips with Johannine irony, underlining a matter of serious religious incongruity: those who have falsely convicted Jesus and secured his execution now express piety concerning Sabbath observance."[31] In contrast to what motivated "the Jews" in this scene, in a number of other texts related to crucifixion in the ancient world, a crucified man's legs were broken simply to hasten death, perhaps even as a severe mercy – a *coup de grâce*, as it were – since crucifixions could otherwise last for several days.[32] Bringing these points together, clearly Jesus is not portrayed in John's Gospel as one hamstrung by Jewish notions of purity (e. g., 2:1–11; 4:1–42) or legal observance (e. g., 5:1–18; 9:1–41), and insofar as this is true of "the Jews" who demonstrate these very attitudes here (especially in the absence of mercy; cf. 7:53–8:11), they are portrayed poorly in the scene. As Jesus might have put it, since they preferred sacrifice to mercy (cf. Matt 9:13; 12:7), they ended up swallowing camels, even as they strained out the gnats (cf. Matt 23:24).

3:14, 8:28, and 12:32; or the three connected absolute "I Am" sayings in 18:4–9, especially as they are seen in light of two distinct sets of triple negations in 1:19–21 and 18:17, 25–27.

[29] See, e. g., 2:1, 19–20; 13:38; 21:14, 17.

[30] Cf. Michaels, *John*, 967.

[31] Craig Keener, *The Gospel of John: A Commentary* (2 vols.; Peabody, Mass.: Hendrickson, 2003), 2.1151.

[32] On crucifixion generally, as well as the practice of *crurifragium* as a means of hastening death, most commentators still cite the classic study of Martin Hengel, *Crucifixion in the Ancient World and the Folly of the Message of the Cross* (Philadelphia: Fortress, 1977). Some view *crurifragium* in terms of a mercy extended to victims of crucifixion; see, e. g., Archibald M. Hunter, *The Gospel According to John* (CBC; Cambridge: University Press, 1965), 181; cf. Frederick Dale Bruner, *The Gospel of John: A Commentary* (Grand Rapids, Mich.: Eerdmans, 2012), 1123. Interestingly, according to Suetonius, even *before* he had the pirates who kidnapped him crucified, Julius Caesar slit their throats as an act of mercy (*The Lives of the Twelve Caesars*, Julius Caesar, 74.1).

Second, as it is "the Jews" who ask Pilate to break the legs of all the men, at a narrative level their request shows that they are once again rejecting the testimony of John (the Baptist) with respect to Jesus. According to John, Jesus is "the lamb of God" (1:29, 36).[33] After this confession, Jesus himself directly accused "the Jews" of rejecting John's testimony (5:33–35), and the narrator suggests, significantly, that those on the other side of the Jordan do accept John's testimony about Jesus (10:40–42). Since Jesus – God's lamb – is being crucified on "the day of Preparation for the Passover" (19:14a; cf. 18:28; 19:31) and at a typical time for the Passover lambs to be slaughtered (19:14b),[34] readers should question why "the Jews" make such a request since the Law specifically forbids breaking the bones of the Passover lamb (Exod 12:46; cf. Num 9:12). Simply put, given the Law, why are they attempting to break the bones of God's Lamb? Ironically then, on a narrative level, it is Roman soldiers who know better! They broke the legs of the first two men, "but when they came to Jesus and saw that he was already dead, they did not break his legs" (19:33), despite Pilate's implied instruction to do so. Thus do the soldiers become conduits once again (cf. 19:23–24) for the fulfillment of Scripture. By not breaking the bones of God's Lamb, they fulfill the law in Exodus, as the narrator makes clear by means of a modified quotation in 19:36. And then by piercing Jesus' side (thus enabling the water of the Spirit to pour forth; cf. 7:37–39),[35] the one soldier in particular fulfills Zechariah 12:10, which the narrator cites in 19:37. In sum, at a narrative level, unwitting Roman soldiers are portrayed more positively than "the Jews" who deliberately reject the Baptist's testimony about Jesus by specifically requesting that Jesus' legs – the legs of God's Lamb – be broken. But perhaps the supreme irony of the passage is that Jesus, whose corpse was expected in the eyes of the Jewish leaders to defile the land (cf. Deut 21:22–23), becomes God's Paschal Lamb (cf. 1 Cor 5:7) who brings cleansing and deliverance; indeed, who "takes away the sin of the world" (1:29).[36]

Their broken legs apparently mark the end of the two co-crucified men; again, the narrative is not interested in whether they died at this point or even if they were subsequently buried. In light of their disappearance from the nar-

---

[33] On the inherent difficulties related to understanding this phrase in John's Gospel, see the extraordinarily helpful essay by Jesper Tang Nielsen, "The Lamb of God: The Cognitive Structure of a Johannine Metaphor" in *Imagery in The Gospel of John* (ed. Jörg Frey et al.; WUNT 200; Tübingen: Mohr Siebeck, 2006), 217–56.

[34] See the discussion of the timing of this sacrifice for Passover in Keener, *John*, 2.1130.

[35] No motivation for this soldier's action is provided by the narrative, but the act was apparently typical during crucifixions; see further, Koester, *Symbolism*, 210. On the soldier's action in John as a rewriting of the widely (and perhaps wrongly) discredited variant in Matt 27:49, see the helpful discussion in Michaels, *John*, 967–69.

[36] For additional connections to Passover in this scene (e. g., the hyssop in 19:29), see Hoskyns, *John*, 531.

rative, even these men, it seems, follow the Baptist's rule: "He must increase, but I must decrease" (3:30). So while the shattering of these men's legs presumably meant nothing more than death, the soldiers' treatment of Jesus, the one already dead, resulted in *life* as blood and water flowed from Jesus' side (19:34). Since Jesus' blood is "true drink" (6:55), and since the water refers to the Spirit (cf. 3:5; 7:37–39) which Jesus gives "without measure" (3:34), thereby filling vessels "to the brim" (2:7), and slaking thirst forever (cf. 4:14), the entire scene accentuates Jesus' glorification on the cross.[37] At a narrative level, then, the timely disappearance of the co-crucified men simply plays into this accentuation.

Readers of the Gospels will recall that in Luke one of the crucified men is promised a place in paradise with Jesus after death (23:43). As already noted above, our narrator omits this detail. In John, therefore, readers will assume that the co-crucified men were simply defeated by death, just like all of Adam's children. Their story draws on humankind's hopelessness when death knocks at the door. While the means by which men and women meet their end may differ, their end is the same. But the co-crucified men's humiliation while being *lifted up* to death in crucifixion becomes at the same moment glorification for the Son of Man and a new beginning for everything else. Thus do these two men die at precisely the moment when the incarnate God – the Word made flesh – began to recreate the world (cf. 1:3, 10). So, echoing a critical primeval moment, Jesus said, "It is finished" (19:30; cf. Gen 2:1–3). On one reading then, these co-crucified men are the last to die in that old world. They died just before a new creation greeted a new day "early on the first day of the week" (20:1; cf. v. 19; Gen 1:5).

Detour: The Co-Crucified Men and the Implied Author

Finally, should modern readers consider what such a dispassionate portrayal of these two men suggests about the implied author? After all, they were not merely the "co-crucified," they were crucified! Presumably, to the implied author these two were real, historical men who also hung on crosses, suffering

---

[37] On the primary motif related to water in the Fourth Gospel, see especially Koester, *Symbolism*, 175–206. The occurrence of water flowing from Jesus' side in 19:34 (the resolution of a plot-motif announced clearly in 7:37–39) very likely draws on foundational imagery in the Old Testament: Ezek 47:1–12 and Zech 14:8 offer prime examples of the connection between water and the Spirit of God. Since in Ezekiel and Zechariah the water flows from the temple and from Jerusalem, these texts (and others) contribute to a richer understanding of John 19:34 (as well as 7:37–39), one that accentuates Jesus' glorification on the cross by highlighting him as God's true temple and dwelling place. See further, Chelsea N. Revell in an unpublished essay entitled, "Second Temple Sukkot, Ezekiel 47, and Zechariah 14: Religio-Cultural and Textual Backgrounds of John 7:37–39." For copies, contact the author.

unimaginable agony, until they were dead. Instead of expressing any sympathy for these beaten and crucified men, men whose legs were broken, smashed by a heavy iron mallet, the implied author has noted their presence and inferred their ghastly deaths only in the service of his story about Jesus. Does such a portrayal suggest an implied author who is altogether too accustomed to and desensitized by Roman executions? Or does our narrative's lack of empathy suggest nothing more than an implied author whose eyes remain so fixed on Jesus that, while these men are crucified on the stage, their experience of crucifixion remains off-stage and out of sight?

Conclusion

This essay has argued that the striking objectification of the co-crucified men in the Fourth Gospel serves no other purpose than to illumine theological claims about Jesus and to create additional opportunities for intercharacterizational analysis with other significant figures in the narrative, including "the Jews," Jesus' family at the cross, and the Roman soldiers. We examined the centrality of Jesus in 19:18 from a number of perspectives, offering several interpretive possibilities for readers to consider. We further concentrated on the fact that the co-crucified men's legs get broken in the narrative when Jesus' do not. The scene clearly reflects on theological claims related to Jesus, but also speaks to the characterization of those who made the request, those ordered to carry it out, and the Beloved Disciple who bore faithful witness to the events themselves. Finally, we noted that by the end of the crucifixion narrative, the co-crucified men had vanished from the scene as quickly as they were introduced; indeed, our analysis shows that they were simply foils, extras in someone else's story. Two crucified shadows.

The Women by the Cross: Creating Contrasts

D. Francois Tolmie

The subject of this brief study is a group character – the group of women portrayed at the cross of Jesus in John 19:25. The way in which these women are characterized individually will not be dealt with here; the issue is considered elsewhere in this book, where the characterization of two of the women (the Mother of Jesus[1] and Mary Magdalene[2]) is discussed at length, along with that of another group character appearing in the next two verses (the Mother of Jesus and the Beloved Disciple[3]). In this study, it is the four women as a group character that will be investigated from a narrative perspective. Prior to this, a brief overview of the issues that normally receive attention when John 19:25 is discussed by scholars will be presented.

Issues That Normally Receive Attention in John 19:25

The issue that generally receives the most attention is the uncertainty as to exactly how many women are to be distinguished in this verse. This uncertainty arises from the fact that one can punctuate and interpret the text in three different ways.[4] These are as follows (for the sake of clarity, I have used Roman numerals to indicate the number of women distinguished according to each interpretation):

Two women: Εἱστήκεισαν δὲ παρὰ τῷ σταυρῷ τοῦ Ἰησοῦ (i) ἡ μήτηρ αὐτοῦ (ii) καὶ ἡ ἀδελφὴ τῆς μητρὸς αὐτοῦ, (i) Μαρία ἡ τοῦ Κλωπᾶ (ii) καὶ Μαρία ἡ Μαγδαληνή.

According to this interpretation, only two women are referred to, the Mother of Jesus and her sister, who are then identified in the next clause as

---

[1] Cf. the article of Mary Coloe elsewhere in this book.
[2] Cf. the article of Jaime Clark-Soles elsewhere in this book.
[3] Cf. the article of Jean Zumstein elsewhere in this book.
[4] This issue is mentioned and discussed in most commentaries on the Fourth Gospel. My discussion of the three options and the arguments used by scholars in each instance is based on Raymond E. Brown, *The Death of the Messiah: From Gethsemane to the Grave. A Commentary on the Passion Narratives in the Four Gospels. Vol. 2* (ABRL; New York: Doubleday, 1994), 1013–19, who provides a detailed exposition of the matter.

"Mary of Clopas" and "Mary Magdalene" respectively. This possibility is usually rejected by scholars on two grounds, namely that it is unlikely that Mary, the wife of Joseph, would be referred to as Mary of Clopas; and that, if Mary Magdalene were the sister of the Mother of Jesus, this would imply that their parents had given two of their daughters the same name, "Mary" (Miriam), which seems unlikely.[5] The interpretation of John 19:25 as referring to two women is an approach that is not popular among scholars nowadays; in fact, I could not find a single instance of any contemporary scholar who endorses this interpretation.[6]

Three women: Είστήκεισαν δὲ παρὰ τῷ σταυρῷ τοῦ Ἰησοῦ (i) ἡ μήτηρ αὐτοῦ καὶ (ii) ἡ ἀδελφὴ τῆς μητρὸς αὐτοῦ, (ii) Μαρία ἡ τοῦ Κλωπᾶ, καὶ (iii) Μαρία ἡ Μαγδαληνή.

If the text is interpreted in this way, three women are distinguished: the Mother of Jesus, her sister who is then further identified as "Mary of Clopas," and Mary Magdalene. This still leaves one with the problem of two sisters having the same name; and therefore, this interpretation is usually also rejected by most scholars. However, if one interprets ἀδελφή in a different way, for example, as "sister-in-law" instead of "sister," this objection can be overcome. Such an interpretation has been proposed by Richard Bauckham[7] in a thorough study of "Mary of Clopas" in the New Testament.

Four women: Είστήκεισαν δὲ παρὰ τῷ σταυρῷ τοῦ Ἰησοῦ (i) ἡ μήτηρ αὐτοῦ καὶ (ii) ἡ ἀδελφὴ τῆς μητρὸς αὐτοῦ, (iii) Μαρία ἡ τοῦ Κλωπᾶ, καὶ (iv) Μαρία ἡ Μαγδαληνή.

In the light of the objections raised against the first two interpretations outlined above, this option is favoured by most scholars, and is also the interpretation accepted in this study. If John 19:25 is interpreted in this way, four different women are to be distinguished, two of whom are identified by their relationship to Jesus (the Mother of Jesus and the sister of his mother), while the other two are referred to as Mary of Clopas and Mary Magdalene. The fact that the first two are only identified in terms of their relationship to Jesus,

---

[5] The fact that the Mother of Jesus is never named in the Gospel might mean that this objection loses some of its force.

[6] Josef Blinzler, *Die Brüder und Schwester Jesu* (SBS 21; Stuttgart: Verlag Katholisches Bibelwerk, 1967), 111, mentions some scholars from the nineteenth and twentieth centuries who supported this interpretation, namely M. Schwalb, H. J. Holtzmann and G. M. de la Garenne.

[7] Richard Bauckham, *Gospel Women: Studies of the Named Women in the Gospels* (Grand Rapids, Mich.: Eerdmans, 2002), 203–23. Cf. also Herman C. Waetjen, *The Gospel of the Beloved Disciple: A Work in Two Editions* (New York: T&T Clark International, 2005), 397; and Turid K. Seim, "Roles of Women in the Gospel of John," in *Aspects on the Johannine Literature: Papers Presented at a Conference of Scandinavian New Testament Exegetes at Uppsala, June 16–19, 1986* (ed. Lars Hartman and Birger Olsson; Stockholm: Almqvist & Wiksell, 1987), 56–73; here 57–58.

without their names being mentioned, is explained in various ways by scholars. For example, in the case of the Mother of Jesus, some argue that she is identified in this way because "Mother of Jesus" was regarded as an honorary title, whereas others propose that the title might have been used to underline the symbolic role that she fulfils in the Gospel. In the case of her sister, two suggestions are made: either that this was the way in which she was known in early Christianity, or that her name was not preserved in the tradition.[8]

A second issue that regularly turns up in the scholarly discourse is how one should relate the women mentioned in John 19:25 to the women mentioned in the Synoptic Gospels – who are portrayed as "standing afar" as Jesus dies, and not close to the cross as is the case in the Fourth Gospel. This is a complex issue, as the lists in the Synoptic Gospels do not correspond: Mark refers to Mary Magdalene, Mary, the mother of James the younger and of Joses, Salome, and "many other women" who had come up with Jesus to Jerusalem (Mark 15:40–41); Matthew alludes to "many women" who had followed Jesus from Galilee, including Mary Magdalene, Mary, the mother of James and of Joseph, and the mother of the sons of Zebedee (Matthew 27:55–56); while Luke makes a general reference to all those (masculine) known to Jesus, as well as the women who had followed him from Galilee (23:49; cf. Luke 8:1–3).[9] Some scholars attempt to harmonize the lists of women found in the four Gospels as far as possible, e. g., by arguing that Mary of Clopas (mentioned by John) refers to the same person as Mary the mother of James the younger and of Joseph/Joses (mentioned by Mark and Matt respectively), and that the sister of the Mother of Jesus (mentioned by John) is the same person as Salome (mentioned by Mark) and the mother of the sons of Zebedee (mentioned by Matt);[10] whereas others caution against such an approach.[11] Closely linked to this issue, is the matter of the source of the information in the Fourth Gospel. This is usually explained in one of two ways: 1) an independent tradition is reflected in this Gospel;[12] or 2) the author deliberately deviated from the Synoptic Gospels on this point.[13]

The last issue that should be highlighted is the question as to the function that the women fulfil in this scene. There is also a difference of opinion among

---

[8] Brown, *Death of the Messiah*, 1015.

[9] Brown, *Death of the Messiah*, 1017, provides a comprehensive table, summarizing all the data.

[10] For example, Brooke F. Westcott, *The Gospel According to St. John: The Authorized Version with Introduction and Notes* (repr.; Grand Rapids, Mich.: Eerdmans, 1971 [1881]), 275–76.

[11] For example, Rudolf Bultmann, *Das Evangelium des Johannes* (19th ed.; KEK 19; Göttingen: Vandenhoeck & Ruprecht, 1978), 520–521; and Rudolf Schnackenburg, *Das Johannesevangelium: Teil 3: Kommentar zu Kapitel 13–21* (3d ed.; HTKNT IV; Freiburg: Herder, 1979), 321–23.

[12] Bauckham, *Gospel Women*, 218.

[13] Hartwig Thyen, *Das Johannesevangelium* (HNT 6; Tübingen: Mohr Siebeck, 2005), 738.

scholars regarding this matter. The majority detect a contrast between the group of four women and the four soldiers who crucified Jesus[14] (we will return to this contrast later in the essay), but others are not so sure about this. For example, according to Rudolf Bultmann,[15] v. 25 was merely used as a transition to v. 26, and the evangelist was primarily interested in the Mother of Jesus.

Against this background, we will now turn to possible observations that can be made from a narrative perspective with regard to this group character.

The Women by the Cross From a Narrative Perspective

In narrative terms, a new group character, consisting of four female characters, is introduced into the narrative world in 19:25. The composition of this group character is noteworthy, since two of the four women play an important role elsewhere in the narrative world, whereas the other two are only encountered here, and do not play any role in the rest of the narrative. One could thus say that the group consists of two major characters and two minor characters. Of the two major characters, one has already been introduced earlier on in the narrative world (the Mother of Jesus, at the wedding of Cana, where she played an important role), whereas the other is introduced into the narrative world at this point for the first time, but will play an important role later on (Mary Magdalene). In a sense, then, these two major characters "meet" each other here in the narrative world, as has rightly been pointed out by Judith Lieu,[16] who also draws attention to the fact that both these women are addressed as γύναι by Jesus: "Thus, this scene (19:25–27) is a meeting point between the two women, the mother of Jesus, whom he addressed as γύναι before, and Mary, whom he will so address and will also name in his resurrection power."

To my mind, in view of the fact that this group character includes two major figures, it is unlikely that it does not actually play any real role in this scene, and that it only fulfils a transitory function – as some scholars, for example Bultmann, argue. Furthermore, there are certain clues in the way in which the women are introduced into the narrative world that give pause to the tendency to pass over their presence at the cross too quickly. The first clue lies in the use of the μέν ... δέ construction, which could be interpreted as an

---

[14] For example, Thyen, *Johannesevangelium*, 737; George R. Beasley-Murray, *John* (WBC 36; Waco, Tex.: Word Books, 1987), 348; and Mark W. G. Stibbe, *John* (Sheffield: JSOT Press, 1993), 194.
[15] Bultmann, *Johannes*, 520.
[16] Judith M. Lieu, "The Mother of the Son in the Fourth Gospel," *JBL* 117/1 (1998): 61–77, here 68.

indication to the reader that there is a contrast between the group of women and the group of soldiers who are mentioned directly before them:[17]

Οἱ μὲν οὖν στρατιῶται ταῦτα ἐποίησαν. Εἱστήκεισαν δὲ παρὰ τῷ σταυρῷ τοῦ Ἰησοῦ ἡ μήτηρ αὐτοῦ καὶ ἡ ἀδελφὴ τῆς μητρὸς αὐτοῦ, Μαρία ἡ τοῦ Κλωπᾶ καὶ Μαρία ἡ Μαγδαληνή.

(The nature of the contrast will be discussed in more detail later.)

A second clue to the reader is the way in which the description of the "action" performed by the four women is worded: They "stood" there, or more accurately, "were standing" there (all along). Take note of the use of the pluperfect here,[18] which may be interpreted as signifying that they had been standing there at the cross since the crucifixion began. When viewed from the perspective of the way in which temporal relations in a narrative are analyzed, the words "were standing there" could thus be classified as an analepsis, i. e., as being indicative of a situation where an action is narrated *after* it occurred and not at the point where it occurred;[19] or, in this instance, to be more precise, where an action is narrated some time after it had already started happening. The fact that the presence of the women by the cross is not merely noted here, but that care is taken to reveal retrospectively to the reader that they had been standing there at the cross all the time (since the events narrated in 19:18), may thus be taken as an indication that this event in itself is important. This is not merely a transition to a subsequent important event!

This leads us to the next question: If it is, in fact, the case that the women and the soldiers are contrasted, in what sense should the contrast be interpreted? To my mind, one can identify several layers of contrast:

At the most basic level, there is a contrast between what the soldiers and the women *do*. While the soldiers act in a most horrific way towards the Son of God, the four women are there, at his side, supporting him.[20] As Don Carson[21]

---

[17] This is noted by many scholars, e. g., Barnabas Lindars, *The Gospel of John* (NCB; Grand Rapids, Mich.: Eerdmans, 1981), 578.

[18] The use of the pluperfect is often noted by scholars. Cf. Brown, *Death of the Messiah*, 1013. Cf. also Jörg Frey, *Die johanneische Eschatologie II: Das johanneische Zeitverständnis* (WUNT 110; Tübingen: Mohr Siebeck, 1998), 115–16, who distinguishes between two uses of the pluperfect in the Fourth Gospel, namely, firstly, for the exposition of an event, and, secondly, for providing background information. The pluperfect in John 19:25 is classified as an example of the first use.

[19] For a detailed discussion of the way in which temporal relations in a narrative text may be analyzed, cf. D. Francois Tolmie, *Narratology and Biblical Narratives: A Practical Guide* (San Francisco: International Scholars Publication, 1999), 87–103.

[20] It is not literally said that they supported Jesus, but this may be deduced from the fact that they are at the cross. Furthermore the use of ἵστημι elsewhere in John (e. g., where John the Baptist "stands" as witness in 1:35; 3:29) could possibly also be cited in support of such an interpretation.

[21] Donald A. Carson, *The Gospel According to John* (Grand Rapids, Mich.: Eerdmans, 1991), 615.

puts it, "While the soldiers carry out their barbaric task and coolly profit from the exercise, the women wait in faithful devotion to the one whose death they can still only understand as tragedy."

Secondly, if one moves to a more abstract level, the mere fact that the women are present at the cross is significant, because it implies that they have *followed* Jesus there. Their presence thus stands in stark contrast to the absence of another group character, the disciples. The disciples should have been there, but have deserted him (except for the Beloved Disciple). In contrast to them, the women are indeed the "faithful few"[22] who have followed Jesus all the way and remain with him. In this regard, it is important to take note that the preposition παρά that is used here together with the verb "standing" suggests the notion of abiding – an important theme in the Fourth Gospel. Elsewhere this preposition is used several times on its own or together with μένειν to indicate the notion of abiding. Cf., for example, John 1:6 ("with God"), 1:14 ("with the Father") and 1:39 ("with him" = Jesus).

Thirdly – and this is an issue that is often overlooked by (mostly male) Johannine scholars[23] – the contrast pertaining to *gender* in this scene should not go unnoticed. It is the females who follow and support Jesus, while the males (with the exception of the Beloved Disciple) reject him: the disciples, the soldiers, Pilate, the religious leaders … One could even say that, in this scene, the respective responses of women and men to Jesus are portrayed in a manner that is typical of the Fourth Gospel. The difference between the way in which males and females typically respond to Jesus in the Fourth Gospel is superbly described by Sandra Schneiders:[24]

No woman is shown as resisting Jesus' initiatives, failing to believe, deserting him, or betraying him. This is in sharp contrast to John's presentation of men who are frequently presented as vain (13:37), hypocritical (12:4–6), fickle (13:38; 16.31–32), obtuse (3:10; 16.18), deliberately unbelieving (9:24–41; 20:24–25), or thoroughly evil (13:2, 27–30).

In our discussion thus far, the emphasis has fallen on the role that the four women play, i. e., on the women as subjects, and thus, on what they *do*: having followed Jesus to the cross, they continue to stand there. If one considers their role from the opposite perspective, i. e., if one views them not as subjects performing a certain action, but as objects that something is "being done to," a further aspect comes to the fore. As "objects," they find themselves at the foot

---

[22] Frederick D. Bruner, *The Gospel of John: A Commentary* (Grand Rapids, Mich.: Eerdmans, 2012), 1107.

[23] There are exceptions, e. g., Stibbe, *John*, 194.

[24] Sandra M. Schneiders, "Women in the Fourth Gospel," in *The Gospel of John as Literature: An Anthology of Twentieth-Century Perspectives* (ed. Mark W. G. Stibbe; NTTS 17; Leiden: Brill, 1993), 123–43; here 29. Cf. also Coleen M. Conway, *Men and Women in the Fourth Gospel: Gender and Johannine Characterization* (SBLDS 167; Atlanta: SBL, 1999), 205.

of the cross, because they have been drawn there by Jesus.²⁵ What he predicted in John 12:32 has come true: "When I am lifted up from the earth, I will draw all to myself." The four women by the foot of the cross are the first to be drawn to Jesus as he is being lifted up. Further on, in the scene between Jesus, the Mother of Jesus and the Beloved Disciple (19:26–27), the presence of the followers of Jesus at the cross is developed in terms of the notion of a new family. In verse 25, in which the presence of the four women is noted, the first inklings of this notion may already be seen: The fact that the first two women mentioned are part of the (biological) family of Jesus highlights the notion of family, which is then interpreted in a broader sense, in 26–27, to denote a new spiritual family that is constituted at the foot of the cross. It is even possible that the order in which the four women are introduced into the narrative world in 19:25 is significant for this theme:[26] The first two are directly related to Jesus; the last two are not, but they comprise part of the broader group following Jesus. Could the difference between the two pairs of women perhaps already be indicative of the new family? Could they perhaps be viewed as two concentric circles around the cross of Jesus, already suggesting the outward effect that he has on the gathering of the new spiritual family?

Finally, let us return to the issue of the number of women by the cross of Jesus, as discussed at the beginning of this article – but from a different angle this time. As has been pointed out earlier on in this study, scholars do not agree on the number of women who are listed in John 19:25. It may be two, three or four. I have also indicated that I agree with the majority of Johannine scholars who conclude that four women are distinguished here. However, it also needs to be pointed out that such an interpretation can only be reached after careful and prolonged consideration (and even then, some scholars sometimes still opt to refrain from making a decision on the number of women – for example, Hartwig Thyen![27]). The point is: If a decision in this regard can normally only be made by scholars after lengthy consideration, what does this imply for the way in which this part of the text would be read by a "normal" attentive reader? Would it be far-fetched to surmise that such a reader would take note of the ambiguity, pause, and read the sentence a second time?[28] Be

---

[25] Brown, *Death of the Messiah*, 1019, refers to this aspect, but does not develop the notion further.

[26] It is often noted by scholars that the fact that the Mother of Jesus is mentioned first is an indication of the important role she plays in the Gospel. Cf., e. g., Judith Hartenstein, *Charakterisierung im Dialog: Maria Magdalena, Petrus, Thomas und die Mutter Jesu im Johannesevangelium im Kontext anderer frühchristlicher Darstellungen* (NTOA/SUNT 64; Göttingen: Vandenhoeck & Ruprecht, 2007), 274.

[27] Thyen, *Johannesevangelium*, 738.

[28] In the case of a listener listening to someone reading the text to him/her, the effect of such an ambiguity might be similar. Even though the person reading the text might not stop to read the sentence again, a careful listener would be able to note the ambiguity and speculate about different ways of understanding it.

that as it may, the important aspect that should be noted here is that an ambiguity such as this normally has *a retarding effect* on the reading process – it slows the process down. To explain this effect, one might borrow a concept from Formalism (in particular, from Victor Shklovsky[29]), namely that of "defamiliarization." This refers to a situation where what has become automatic through habitual usage is made strange, becomes unfamiliar and is suddenly perceived differently. Applied to John 19:25: The ambiguity in the text may lead to the normal reading process being disrupted, thus causing the duration and difficulty of the perception to be increased. Why is it important to take note of this? Because a slowing down in the reading process will focus the attention of the reader more intensely on the content – in this instance, on the presence of a certain group of women by the cross and what they are doing there. Two, three or four women by the cross? And what are they doing there? Perhaps questions such as these might linger on in the mind of the "normal" reader for much longer than many Johannine scholars would suspect …

---

[29] For a good overview of Formalism and Shklovsky's idea of "defamiliarization," cf. W. Randolph Tate, *Interpreting the Bible: A Handbook of Terms and Methods* (Peabody, Mass.: Hendrickson, 2006), 138–44.

Mary Magdalene:
Beginning at the End

Jaime Clark-Soles

Mary Magdalene never fails to enthrall.[1] She appears in crucial roles in the Gospel of John, but only at the end and then suddenly. In John, Mary Magdalene is standing right at the foot of the cross and participates in the birth (or, perhaps more accurately, "creation"[2]) of the Johannine church as Jesus gifts his Mother and Beloved Disciple with one another. To be part of Johannine community is to be part of a family, to be home (cf. 1:11–13; 14:23).

> Meanwhile, standing near the cross of Jesus were his Mother, and his Mother's sister, Mary the wife of Clopas, and Mary Magdalene.[3] When Jesus saw his Mother and the disciple whom he loved standing beside her, he said to his Mother, "Woman, here is your son." Then he said to the disciple, "Here is your mother." And from that hour the disciple took her into his own home (John 19:25–27).

As if that were not a powerful enough scene, Mary Magdalene (MM) becomes the first person to encounter the risen Lord, by herself, and the first to announce the resurrection in Christian history. It is *she* who proclaims the resurrection of Jesus to the disciples. Had she appeared only in 19:25, the reader might notice her with momentary curiosity or a cursory gesture toward apparent historical accuracy (since she appears in each of the Gospel accounts at the crucifixion and tomb); but almost as soon as she enters the narrative in John, she commandeers it.

In the following essay, I offer a narratological study of MM drawing upon the practical guidelines provided by Tolmie.[4] Tolmie defines the implied author "in terms of the overall textual strategy" (including narrator, narratee,

---

[1] Mary Magdalene is a pop culture icon, appearing in books (such as Dan Brown's *The Da Vinci Code* and Jane Schaberg with Melanie Johnson-Debaufre's *Mary Magdalene Understood*), movies (such as *Jesus Christ Superstar* or *Jesus of Montreal*), paintings and music. She even appeared in an off-Broadway musical, *The Magdalene*, which debuted in 2011.

[2] See Deborah Sawyer, "John 19:34: From Crucifixion to Birth, or Creation?," in *A Feminist Companion to John, Volume II* (ed. Amy-Jill Levine with Marianne Blickenstaff; Cleveland: Pilgrim Press, 2003), 130–39.

[3] For a brief treatment that distinguishes all of the Marys and, in particular, Mary Magdalene, see Jaime Clark-Soles, *Engaging the Word: The New Testament and the Christian Believer* (Louisville, Ky.: Westminster John Knox, 2010), 35–42.

[4] D. Francois Tolmie, *Narratology and Biblical Narratives: A Practical Guide* (San Francisco: International Scholars Publications, 1999).

focalization, events, time, setting and character).[5] This strategy is revealed to the readers verse by verse as they experience the narrative.

Who is She? A Brief Background on Mary Magdalene

Before beginning the detailed literary analysis, however, it is important to clarify Mary Magdalene as a biblical character and a figure in history.[6] After all, she is often confused with other characters, notably the other Marys in the Gospels, and especially Mary of Bethany. Early in the history of interpretation, Mary of Bethany and Mary Magdalene became conflated and associated with the anointing woman of the Four Gospels. Mary of Bethany has good reason to be associated with the anointing woman, as she is actually recounted in John 12:1–8 as anointing Jesus. The anointing woman in Matt 26:6–13 and Mark 14:3–9 is unnamed. The woman described as a sinner in Luke 7:36–50 who anoints Jesus also lacks a name and performs this act far earlier in Jesus' ministry (the other anointings take place shortly before the crucifixion).

Despite the presence of distinct geographic markers in their names (Bethany and Magdalene), the two Marys become one, and unite with the anointing woman/women. This harmonization comes to a climax in a sermon given by Pope Gregory the Great in 591 when he proclaims, "She whom Luke calls the sinful woman, whom John calls Mary [of Bethany], we believe to be the Mary from whom seven devils were ejected according to Mark."[7] Unfortunately, inattentive exegesis has practically become doctrine in this case.

Mary Magdalene herself only appears in the Gospels as a disciple (Luke 8:2), at the foot of the cross (Matt 27:56; Mark 15:40; John 19:25), and at the tomb (Matt 27:61, 28:1–10; Mark 15:47–16:11; Luke 24:1–11; John 20:1–18). The only details provided about her life in the New Testament include her association with Magdala, that Jesus cast seven demons from her, and that she may have been a woman of means (implied in her bringing costly spices to the tomb in Mark). She does appear in extra-biblical works, notably as the legend-

---

[5] Tolmie, *Narratology*, 115.

[6] For further information on Mary Magdalene, see Jane Schaberg and Melanie Johnson DeBaufre, *Mary Magdalene Understood* (New York: Continuum, 2006); Judith Hartenstein, *Charakterisierung im Dialog: Die Darstellung von Maria Magdalena, Petrus, Thomas und die Mutter Jesu im Kontext anderer frühchristlicher Traditionen* (Göttingen: Vandenhoeck & Ruprecht, 2007); Robin Griffin-Jones, *Beloved Disciple: The Misunderstood Legacy of Mary Magdalene, the Woman Closest to Jesus* (New York: Harper One, 2008); Bruce Chilton, *Mary Magdalene: A Biography* (New York: Doubleday, 2005); Ann Graham Brock, *Mary Magdalene, the First Apostle: The Struggle for Authority* (Cambridge, Mass.: Harvard University Press, 2003).

[7] For further discussion about these points, see Clark-Soles, *Engaging*, 42; and Carl E. Olson and Sandra Miesel, *The Da Vinci Hoax: Exposing the Errors in the Da Vinci Code* (San Francisco: Ignatius, 2004), 82.

ary author of the Gospel of Mary. She is also mentioned in vss. 32 and 55 of the Gospel of Philip, first as Jesus' lover and then as the one Jesus loved most and kissed often. Whether this love included a sexual relationship, however, is at the very least ambiguous.

Mary, particularly the conflated Mary Magdalene/Bethany also shows up in legend as somewhat of a mystic who relocated to the South of France following the death of Jesus. These legends seem to have originated in the Middle Ages, however, and thus cannot claim to be historical. Mary of Bethany/Magdala can count a number of women followers, however, particularly during the Middle Ages.[8]

Narrator and Narratee

The implied author uses a reliable, extradiegetic (i. e., primary level narration) and heterodiegetic (i. e., not one of the characters in the story) narrator who narrates the story by means of ulterior narration (i. e., the story is narrated after the events have occurred). The narrator is overtly perceptible (especially in places such as 20:16 when translating "Rabbouni" or in 20:2 where the other disciple is further identified as "the one whom Jesus loved."). At times the implied author employs intradiegetic (i. e., embedded) narrators (Mary, angels, Jesus) and narratees (the disciples, Mary, Jesus).

The extradiegetic narrator's patterns are important. First, he compares and contrasts characters in order to highlight what is valuable and true theologically. Here MM is contrasted with the disciples who are found wanting in terms of abiding, comprehending discipleship. Second, the narrator uses dialogue to validate what is narrated here and elsewhere (e. g., that Jesus rose from the dead and ascended to the Father from whom he came and with whom he abides in intimate relationship). Third, the dialogue is energetic and moves the story at a rapid pace as the characters speak in short sentences (with the exception of the important information Jesus conveys in 20:17), and quickly go back and forth. Furthermore, there is redundancy in the speeches – both Jesus and the angels ask Mary, "Woman, why are you weeping?"

In 20:8–9, the narrator is used to provide the central theological kernel that drives the whole narrative of 20:1–18, namely that Jesus must rise from the dead as indicated by scripture. This clearly relates to 2:22: "After he was raised from the dead, his disciples remembered that he had said this; and they believed the scripture and the word that Jesus had spoken." Throughout the Fourth Gospel (FG), the reader is taught that coming, seeing, believing and

---

[8] Diane E. Peters, "The Legends of St. Mary of Bethany and their Dissemination in the Later Middle Ages," *ATLA Summary of Proceedings* 48 (1994): 154–57.

understanding scripture's testimony to the identity of Jesus are key traits of good discipleship. Here, Peter and the other disciple are presented positively insofar as they come and see. Then the reader learns that the other disciple "believes." But what, exactly, does he believe? Often it is assumed that he believes the central message of the narrative, namely, that Jesus has risen from the dead. But this cannot be accurate since the narrator immediately and starkly informs the reader that they did *not* understand. Therefore, the only thing that the "other disciple" believes at this point is MM's testimony that the tomb was empty.

The narrator then turns to the first character in the narrative who comes, sees the empty tomb, encounters the resurrected Son of God (20:17) and Lord (both titles which the implied author depends and insists upon in conveying his Christology) and testifies to his resurrection.

Attending to the function of intradiegetic narration also displays the importance of Mary's voice. The disciples never speak. The supernatural characters, Jesus and the angels, speak but Mary is the only human character to speak. She speaks far more than the angels (they get only three words in the NA27 text). Strikingly, she speaks more words than Jesus himself (MM speaks 43 words; Jesus speaks 38). Mary, as an intradiegetic narrator, has a recurring concern: much of her speech is about where Jesus has been laid and by whom, thereby highlighting the fact and the meaning of the empty tomb.

Furthermore, using intradiegetic narration is a vivid means for the implied author to convey the theological claims about the identity of Jesus and his intimate relationship with his followers. The technique is more immediate than extradiegetic narration and aligns with the implied author's admission that the aim is to persuade at the personal level: "But these are written so that you may come to believe that Jesus is the Messiah, the Son of God, and that through believing you may have life in his name" (20:31).

Time

The events in 20:1–18 are mostly narrated in the order in which they occurred but there are two important exceptions. At v. 9 we find a prolepsis that indicates a primary theological point of the implied author: "for as yet they did not understand the scripture, that he must rise from the dead." Second, there is an embedded analepsis at the other locus of theological import in the narrative, namely v. 18 where Mary proclaims the risen Lord and "told them that he had said these things to her" (presumably including at least the content narrated in v. 17). Who the exact recipients of her testimony are remains unclear.

The events in 20:1–18 appear to happen in a very brief period of time. The narrator indicates in 20:1 that the events occurred "early on the first day of the week [i. e., Sunday], while it was still dark" and then does not provide another time indicator until 20:19 where the reader learns that the next set of events happens that same [Sunday] evening. Regarding duration, note that the narrative about MM takes up more narrative space than both of the appearances to the male disciples combined.

Setting

The narrator informs the reader at 19:42 that it was the "Jewish day of Preparation;" the larger context is Passover (19:14). Placing Jesus' words and deeds in the context of Jewish feasts is, of course, a typical strategy of the implied author and contributes to the Christology of the Gospel. Jesus is the Lamb sent by God who takes away the sin of the world.

Scenically, based on 19:41 the reader knows that at 20:1 MM is in a garden, the garden of all gardens, as it turns out. At 20:15 the reader learns that she supposed Jesus to be *the* gardener (ὁ κηπουρός). The narrator notes that it is the *first* day, taking the reader back to the very beginning of creation (cf. John 1:1–5), the very *first* day with the creator and a garden and two human beings who are trying to work out personhood, and bodies, and gender and sex and earthliness/fallenness/grief/despair (descent?) and godliness/redemption/peace/joy (ascent?). Genesis allusions abound.[9] Fulfillment comes here, in the garden, and then *life* starts here – eternal life – in the garden. Creation has come to completion.

Focalization

Focalization answers the question: "Through whose eyes do we view the events that are being narrated to us?"[10] Tolmie uses the analogy of a movie camera (the locus of perception) and the way it causes the reader to view the various scenes. In this passage, the focalization is mostly external such that the narrated events are presented "as if they are perceived ('viewed') by an onlooker who does not play any role in the story himself/herself."[11] But there are times when the camera zooms in so closely that the readers feel that they are looking

---

[9] For Genesis allusions, see Ruben Zimmermann, "Symbolic Communication Between John and His Reader: The Garden Symbolism in John 19–20," in *Anatomies of Narrative Criticism: The Past, Present, and Futures of the Fourth Gospel as Literature* (ed. Tom Thatcher and Stephen D. Moore; Atlanta: SBL, 2008), 221–35. See also Steven Hunt's essay on the Roman soldiers at the arrest of Jesus in this volume.

[10] Tolmie, *Narratology*, 32.

[11] Tolmie, *Narratology*, 32.

through the eyes of one of the characters through internal focalization, especially because the narrator repeatedly tells the reader what the characters "saw" (1, 5, 6, 8, 11, 12, 14, 18; four different verbs are used: βλέπω, παρακύπτω, θεωρέω, and ὁράω). Almost every time that verbs for seeing appear, the object is either the empty tomb and the items in it or the risen Jesus. The disciples see only the empty-tomb paraphernalia (5, 6, 8); Mary sees much more: the empty tomb (1, 11), angels (12), and the risen Lord Jesus (14, 18). She sees because she abides (μένω). μένω occurs forty times in the Fourth Gospel (cf. three times in Matt.; twice in Mark; six times in Luke). Abiding is a signature mark of true discipleship in the Fourth Gospel and those who do so receive immense benefits (cf. 6:56–58; 15:4–7). MM is in no less pain than the disciples, but she abides and is richly rewarded for it.

The "camera" first shoots the empty tomb. Then it follows MM to the place where the disciples are gathered, wherever that may be. It then follows Peter and "the other disciple" back to the tomb. Though not explicitly narrated, it is clear that MM returns as well because she is there in v. 11. The reader then sees split screens: on one side the reader sees the disciples, again, shockingly self-absorbed (ἀπῆλθον οὖν πάλιν πρὸς αὐτούς, 20:10); on the other the reader sees Mary "weeping outside the tomb." She stays until v. 18. So, for the vast majority of the narrative time Mary stays at the tomb; the disciples run over momentarily and have no interest in remaining (they do not weep, wonder where the body is, etc.). She leaves the tomb only to speak to the disciples (vss. 2 and 18) who, one would think, would be at the tomb. Good things come to those who wait.

The focalized objects (i. e., the characters) include MM, the disciples, the angels, and Jesus. Notice that the camera focuses on MM in 10 of the 18 verses. The only focalized objects who receive internal focalization (the portrayal of the inner thoughts, feelings and knowledge of the characters)[12] are the disciples and Mary. At first neither they nor she have the requisite knowledge that matters so much to the narrator in v. 9. By the end of this passage, however, MM not only acquires this life-giving knowledge, but also immediately shares it (a trait highly valued by the narrator). Seasoned readers of the Fourth Gospel know that the narrator regularly uses intercharacterization technique; that is, the narrator develops characters by juxtaposing them one with another. This will be addressed further in what follows.

---

[12] Tolmie, *Narratology*, 33.

Detailed Analysis

A full discussion of the characterization of MM requires even more attention to the details of the narrative as it unfolds in linear fashion.

Jesus Gets Laid: 19:41–42

After MM's first appearance, Jesus goes on to die and has his body penetrated by violent men; finally, he is laid by Joseph of Arimathea and Nicodemus (ἔθηκαν τὸν Ἰησοῦν; 19:42) on "the Jewish day of Preparation." Concern for Jesus' laid body compels MM who appears in the very next verse, John 20:1.

Magdalene Takes Center Stage: Vss. 1–2

V. 1: "Early on the first day of the week, while it was still dark, Mary Magdalene came to the tomb and saw that the stone had been removed from the tomb."

Already the reader of the FG experiences shockwaves of various sorts and numerous questions arise. To begin, the first person to arrive on the scene, and early, is a character who was only introduced into the narrative as a whole a mere thirteen verses earlier. Surely the reader should expect the Beloved Disciple to appear first, or Jesus' Mother, or really *any* other character who appeared far earlier in the narrative.

Second, MM "comes" (ἔρχομαι) and "sees" (βλέπω). "Come and see" is a Johannine catchphrase used by characters who express the values and paradigmatic behavior championed by the narrator (cf. 1:46; 4:29). This should not be surprising since Jesus himself is identified as the one always "*coming* into the world" (1:9) and *coming* to his followers (14:23, 28) and revealing himself to them. MM is proactive, a trait valued by the author.

Intercharacterization

Third, the language of light and darkness indicates that MM is being juxtaposed to other characters in the Gospel. Recall that the narrator leads the reader forward sentence by sentence, character by character. By the time that the implied readers get to Mary they have met (and judged) numerous characters. "Intertextuality" is a prominent narrative strategy of the FG and is on vivid display with the "intercharacterization" that occurs often. That is, while characters can be understood in part individually, they are often only fully perceived by comparison with and contrast to other characters. Since this is a chief component of the characterization of Mary, it deserves special attention.

Characters whom the narrator regards most highly are related to light; those to be suspected or rejected are related to darkness. The narrator associates some would-be disciples with darkness. Nicodemus arrives at night not only in his first appearance (3:2) but also his last (19:39). The narrator explicitly indicates that Judas' betrayal occurred at night (13:30).

Mary comes at the start of day, πρωΐ. The only other occurrence of this word in the FG appears in 18:28: "Then they took Jesus from Caiaphas to Pilate's headquarters. It was early in the morning." The males with power, be it the religious establishment or the Roman Empire, deal with Jesus πρωΐ and decide against him unto death. MM, the next and only other person to act πρωΐ, decides for him unto life.

Furthermore, MM is being played off of the obviously-missing disciples, here Peter and the Beloved Disciple. She is the first one who takes the Jesus affair so seriously that she races to the tomb, and she is the first to grasp the full meaning of the resurrection. This is consistent with the narrator's noteworthy (if thoroughly offensive for his/her own time) insistence that the foundations of the kerygma rest in large part upon female characters.[13] As duly noted elsewhere, this pattern appears throughout the Gospel and is part of its situational irony (so that God works in mysterious ways that entail women as chief agents, witnesses, apostles, catalysts, and evangelists). The same pattern of female trust, insight, and proclamation inheres in the story of John 2, where the disciples are at the wedding but it is Jesus' Mother who proactively, if inchoately, indicates an understanding of Jesus' unique power and destiny. In ch. 4, the Samaritan woman, in direct contrast to Nicodemus' failed attempt to fully encounter Jesus, experiences a theophany (4:26) and evangelizes a city; she is boldly contrasted with the disciples who adopt a reluctant stance whereby they sit on a stump distracted by many ponderous thoughts about why Jesus is speaking with a woman and what kind of food Jesus might be hoarding (4:33). The compassionate reader feels rather awful for the disciples at this point, so dazzlingly is the Samaritan woman painted.[14]

MM is positively connected to Martha, Mary, and Jesus as they appear in chapter 11. Jesus' interactions with Mary and Martha precipitate one of his great revelatory statements: "I am the resurrection and the life. Those who believe in me, even though they die, will live" (11:25). Lazarus never says a word, but Jesus' interaction with the women eventuates in a testimony and an ejaculatory, kerygmatic proclamation by Martha: "Yes, Lord, I believe that you are the Messiah, the Son of God, the one coming into the world" (11:27).

---

[13] For further discussion, see Colleen M. Conway, *Men and Women in the Fourth Gospel: Gender and Johannine Characterization* (SBLDS 167; Atlanta: Society of Biblical Literature, 1999).

[14] Note that the Samaritan woman interacts with Jesus at the height of daylight, noon. Far from the tired, salacious interpretations that indicate she must come at noon because she is an alienated whore (none of which is substantiated by the text), the narrator depicts her as an elevated, perfect match for Jesus.

Recall that here Martha clearly conveys the conviction expressed by the implied author at 1:9: "The true light, which enlightens everyone, was coming into the world."

Furthermore, the fact that MM is a "Mary" who "weeps" outside a "tomb" cannot be lost on the reader of John 11 any more than can the mention of the stone that holds the dead Lazarus (11:38) and the one that held the dead Jesus (20:1). Mary of Bethany and Jesus both weep[15] appropriately for the loss of a loved one. Lazarus' restoration foreshadows weeping turned to joy later within the narrative. Again, both Mary of Bethany and Jesus are certainly positive figures, so the reader should view MM's weeping as entirely positive in this setting as it ties her to heroes of the narrative.

V. 2: "So she ran and went to Simon Peter and the other disciple, the one whom Jesus loved, and said to them, 'They have taken the Lord out of the tomb, and we do not know where they have laid him.'"

MM sees that the stone is gone in 20:1. The text does not say that she bothered to inspect further, but it assumes this fact when she indicates knowledge that the tomb is in fact empty by her statement: "they have taken him from the tomb." MM energetically hies[16] to two particular disciples, Simon Peter and the "other disciple whom Jesus loved" and thereby catalyzes the subsequent stages of the resurrection narrative. The narrator then turns to Peter and the Beloved Disciple for a short while (20:3–10). But the fact that the story returns to MM after eight verses cues the reader to understand that MM provides the framework of the story; it focuses on her rather than on them. They are a foil, just as the disciples are for the Samaritan woman in chapter 4. Same technique, different chapter. Since this essay is limited to MM, it cannot address the BD and Peter at length. In brief, Peter and the BD arrive, glance around, gather some initial information and then go back to "doing their own thing." The NRSV translation is problematic here. It translates 20:10 as: "Then the disciples returned to their homes," but neither the word οἶκος nor οἰκία appears here; rather, the phrase is: ἀπῆλθον οὖν πάλιν πρὸς αὐτοὺς οἱ μαθηταί. The disciples just turn inward and go back to their own way of life, much like they do after the stunning appearances of the resurrected Jesus after which they just go back to fishing and being absorbed by their own small interests (to such a degree that Jesus has to ask Peter whether he loves his fishing stuff more than Jesus in 21:15).

---

[15] Too much is usually made of the fact that a different verb is used for Jesus' weeping, but John is known for using a variety of words synonymously (see: βλέπω/ὁράω/θεωρέω; ἀγαπάω/φιλέω).

[16] The narrator highlights MM's intensity by doubling the verbs of action (τρέχω and ἔρχομαι). Furthermore, the use of the historic present adds to the dramatic excitement.

Mary's Angelophany: Vss. 11–13

But not so MM. They leave; she stays (μένω; cf. with Andrew and the other disciple in 1:39).[17] As she cries, she bends over to peer into the tomb; the phrase overtly calls us to compare her to Peter and the Beloved Disciple since the same verb is used for bending over (παρακύπτω; used only in 20:5 and 11). When *she* leans into the tomb, the same one that the now-revered disciples glance at, she has the supernatural, existential, holy, eschatological experience of a lifetime: she sees (θεωρέω) not one (as in Matthew 28:5) but two angels (ἄγγελος; in Mark 16:5, it is one young man; in Luke 24:4, two men) sitting there (καθέζομαι). This language is not accidental and depends upon intertextuality for the full impact of its meaning. Angels and the revelation of Jesus' identity cohere in John (cf. 1:51 and 12:29). Furthermore, the only other sitting that occurs in John is done by Jesus himself (4:6, presumably in direct imitation of Jacob at the well) and by Mary who sits while Martha runs off to meet Jesus (11:20). Those who sit tight (in an active, proclamatory, emotional fashion) apparently have a reasonable chance of encountering Jesus in a transformative way.

In v. 13, the angels in white appear. The reader should note that the word white (λευκός) appears elsewhere only, not surprisingly, in the story of the Samaritan woman, where Jesus declares that the fields are white for harvest (4:35); once again, the NRSV kills the moment, and, more importantly, the connection, by translating "white for harvest" as "ripe for harvest." The Samaritan woman is the first pre-resurrection evangelist in the narrative and MM is the first post-resurrection evangelist.

These angels in white ask MM why she is crying, at which point she almost reiterates what she said in v. 2 except that, this time, it becomes truly personal (and that is surely the point):

v. 2: "They have taken *the* Lord out of the tomb, and *we* do not know where they have laid him."
v. 13: "They have taken away *my* Lord, and *I* do not know where they have laid him."

The Turning Point: Mary's Christophany (vss. 14–17)

In v. 14 MM turns (στρέφω) and sees (θεωρέω), really *sees* Jesus in the Johannine sense of the word. Only when she can articulate her pain, her need, her hope in the most personal, vulnerable, honest sense does she receive a Christophany. As long as she speaks in the safe terms of "we," she can be among the cohort of people who serve as catalysts for the faith of others; but it is only

---

[17] That the contrast is intentional is indicated by the use of δέ at the beginning of the verse.

when she finds the courage and audacity to speak in terms of herself, "my" Lord and what "I" do and do not know, that she becomes a personality rather than a type. And what a personality! How many people have gone from a cipher, a type, a mere representative of this or that to a "person" in, say, five verses? In v. 13, we see MM express her fear, her despair, her finitude, her de-centeredness, and not-yet-knowing. But v. 14 signals a U-turn (ἐστράφη εἰς τὰ ὀπίσω) on her part. She has remained. She has wept. She has confessed that she does not have the necessary knowledge yet to be at peace. And this persistence, depth, humility, insistence, and would-be-despair keeps her in the game. It has to be called a "game" of sorts since Jesus does toy with her somewhat in v. 15. Maybe it is for her own good or maybe he is just flexing his post-resurrection muscle, or maybe it is both. Whatever the case, in v. 15 Jesus says the same thing the angels in white said (here one is clear that the angels are dressed in white, but what is Jesus wearing? Not his ὀθόνιον or σουδάριον, obviously): "Woman, why are you crying?" But then he proceeds to ask a very Johannine-Jesus question: "Whom do you seek?" In the Fourth Gospel, one's character is largely determined by whom or what one seeks (ζητέω; cf. 1:38; 7:1, etc.).

Mary's embryonic recognition begins with her perceiving Jesus to be the gardener. Not *a* gardener, but rather *the* (ὁ) gardener. Immediately the reader is transported back to the Garden of Eden, back to Genesis, where, in the beginning, God created (cf. John 1:1–5). A veritable pyrotechnic display of Johannine intertextual allusions and Old Testament allusions explodes onto the reader's scene. His initial question to her reminds the reader not only of the angels above but also of his conversation with his mother (who is never called Mary in John, for whatever reason) in the context of a wedding: "And Jesus said to her, 'Woman, what concern is that to you and to me? My hour has not yet come'" (2:4). He questions her and immediately makes an important theological and narrative statement about his "hour" (ὥρα). The same pattern inheres in 20:15; Jesus addresses MM as "woman" and makes a theological statement via a question about seeking (ζητέω), a favorite Johannine word. Clearly, Jesus is both seeker and the one who should be sought, according to the Fourth Gospel.

Furthermore, the garden scene reminds the reader of ch. 4 where Jesus interacts with a woman at a well, an OT site of betrothal. The scene in ch. 4 is laced with the notions of Jesus as bridegroom that arose in ch. 2. Here, Jesus seeks out Mary, who is longing for his body. The encounter achieves climax and both Jesus and Mary find satisfaction in the Garden. Creation has been restored, ecstasy has replaced agony. Where Adam and Eve experience the disintegration of intimacy, Jesus and MM exhibit reconciliation in the garden.

In v. 16, Jesus calls Mary by name (as Adam does of Eve and as Jesus does of his sheep in ch. 10) and, whereas Lazarus reacts to Jesus' voice by "coming out" (11:44), Mary responds to his voice by "coming to." She recognizes her Rabbi, her shepherd who knows his sheep and calls them by name (10:1–16). This Gospel iterates intimacy and is a remarkably tactual text (1:18; 9:6; 13:23; 20:27).[18] The text does not specifically narrate the moment that Mary begins touching Jesus, but it is clear that a) Jesus assumes that it would be natural for her to touch his body (which she has been aiming to do all through the passage – she is after his body, the concrete Jesus she can touch and know and experience as real) and b) that she is *already* touching him.[19] He asks her to stop touching him not because he is ascetic, puritanical, or aloof, but because the story needs to move forward so that he can ascend to the Father who initially sent him. From the start, the reader understands that Jesus' return to the Father, like all of his words and deeds, is finally inevitable. Jesus has come in accordance with the will of God and he marches through the Gospel accomplishing that will, always on cue. For instance, in ch. 12 he never requests a different fate (i. e., asking of the cup to pass from him as does the Synoptic Jesus); rather, he insists that he came patently for this fate (cf. 12:27, 32). Likewise, on the cross he does not express any sense of God-forsakenness; rather, he announces that he has completed the work the Father gave him (19:30: "It is finished"). No one and nothing can throw Jesus of course. He is the one who, after all, lays down his life of his own accord in order to take it up again (10:17–18). He is a motivated man with a compelling mission, always directing this God-drama and nothing and no one can impede him, not even Mary.

Jesus directs Mary as if he is directing a play whose plot must drive forward so that the narrative's goal as expressed by 20:31 might be accomplished. Jesus assuages her fears that their relationship is dying but indicates that it will be conducted in a new mode. None of this can be accomplished, however, unless she and Jesus play their parts to keep events moving. So, she must go to Jesus' brothers (and sisters)[20] and report his words: "'I am ascending to my Father and your Father, to my God and your God'" (20:17). Mary, therefore, is charged with announcing what the narrative has insisted upon all along: that God, Jesus, and Jesus' followers are intimately, inseparably related (14:1–23; 17:20–24). The copious use of intimate, familial language throughout the Gos-

---

[18] See Teresa Swan, "Re-membering the Body of Jesus," in *Problems in Translating Texts About Jesus: Proceedings from the International Society of Biblical Literature, 2008* (ed. Mishael Caspi and John T. Greene; Lewiston, N. Y.: Mellen Press, 2011), 19–41.

[19] For a review of the various interpretive possibilities related to this vexatious verse across the centuries, see Harold W. Attridge, "'Don't Be Touching Me': Recent Feminist Scholarship on Mary Magdalene," in *A Feminist Companion to John, Volume II* (ed. Amy-Jill Levine; New York: T&T Clark, 2003), 140–66.

[20] I disagree with the NRSV which here translates ἀδελφοί only as brothers instead of its usual custom of "brothers and sisters." It must assume that only the BD and Peter are the recipients of this news but I see no reason that this proclamation is not to be made to the larger community of disciples (including Jesus' Mother).

pel is striking – no model of intimate human relationships is omitted: parent/child, siblings, those partnered in marriage, friends. Apparently Jesus was serious about there being no distinction between the relationship he shares with God and which his followers share with God after his resurrection. Jesus even refers to the Father here as "my God." It is no accident, of course, that Thomas will, in just a few verses, call Jesus himself "my God" since the narrator indicates by means of 1:1 that this connection should be made if the narrative unfolds persuasively.

Jesus' Angel – Mary Magdalene's Big Announcement: V. 18

Without hesitation or question, MM immediately goes and announces (ἀγγέλλω) to the disciples (here called μαθηταί, not ἀδελφοί): "I have seen the Lord." As noted earlier, seeing is a crucial theme in John as is recognizing Jesus as Lord. She is the first Christian preacher insofar as she proclaims not only her own personal experience of the resurrected Christ but transmits "these things he had spoken to her" (presumably the words from v. 17 but maybe the whole dialogue).

Conclusion: Magdalene – What a Character

A careful investigation into the techniques used to characterize MM in the Fourth Gospel reveals that not only is she a major character (despite her late arrival in the narrative), but also a positively paradigmatic one. The extradiegetic and heterodiegetic narrator does not simply describe MM straightforwardly. Rather, her character is revealed through intercharacterization; her dialogue with various characters; time; setting; and focalization. In addition, irony, gender dynamics, and intertextuality shape the narrative. By such means, the reader recognizes Mary as one who exhibits attributes that are presented as desirable throughout the narrative. She is a proactive character who seeks Jesus. She is obedient to the will of Jesus, and, therefore, God. Her grief is turned to joy at the coming of the risen Lord after he is lifted up. She is one of Jesus' sheep whom he calls by name. She abides and, as a result, is rewarded with an angelophany and Christophany. She is the first character to see and proclaim the risen Christ; therefore, Sandra Schneiders is quite correct in naming her "the apostle of the apostles."[21] Others might call her an evangelist. She is depicted finally as one who is born from above, i. e., not "by means of the will of a husband, but of God" (1:12–13), sharing the same Father as Jesus (cf.

---

[21] *Contra* Cornelis Bennema who calls Schneiders' observation an "overstatement" without justifying his criticism or providing an exegetical rebuttal (idem, *Encountering Jesus: Character Studies in the Gospel of John* [Milton Keynes: Paternoster, 2009], 200, fn. 26).

20:17). Note that the narrator never comments on MM's age, appearance, or social standing.

My summary might imply that I take MM only to be a "representative" figure who simply exemplifies this or that trait. While this may be true of some characters in the Fourth Gospel, such an approach is probably too flat for this rich character who exudes personality and complexity.[22] A less sterile summary than above may psychologize a bit more in accord with clues from the text. Mary moves from faithfulness to belief in the resurrected Lord. Unlike any other character, her commitment brings her to the tomb early in the morning. Her boldness and deep connectedness to Jesus propel her to the tomb. Once there, she confronts the empty tomb and, in paradigmatic Johannine fashion, she relates her experience to the wider community. Like the woman of John 4, she proactively involves others in the seeking after truth, the seeking after Jesus. Her hunger, her persistence, and her longing plant her squarely at the last known place her Jesus was laid. Despite some belief in the eschatological resurrection, she feels the gaping hole left by death and lack of physical presence foreshadowed in ch. 14–17. This is reminiscent of the loss Jesus felt with the death of Lazarus which also caused anguish and weeping – despite an eschatological vantage point. Like Jesus, she weeps. Her grief, however, is immediately tended to by God in the form of an angelophany and Christophany. She first calls Jesus "Teacher," as Nicodemus does. The reader knows that this is an inadequate confession and within two verses the narrator has her call Jesus "Lord" and proclaim him risen, in accordance with the scriptures.

Whatever taxonomy or viewpoint one employs, MM must be interpreted as a "full-fledged character" (to use Berlin's system): she is "complex, manifesting a multitude of traits, and appearing" as a "real" person.[23] She is a personality, with the complicated, conflicting thoughts, emotions and actions that being a person entails.[24]

---

[22] Classicist Christopher Gill presents two aspects of characterization in ancient tragedy: what he calls the "character-viewpoint," on the one hand, which tends toward the moralistic and representational, and the "personality-viewpoint" on the other, which is more nuanced and complex. Christopher Gill, "The Question of Character and Personality in Greek Tragedy," *Poetics Today* 2 (1986): 251–73. See also Fred W. Burnett, "Characterization and Reader Construction of Characters in the Gospels," *Semeia* 63 (1993): 3–28. See also Jaime Clark-Soles, "Re(constructing) History: Characters who Count: The Case of Nicodemus," in *The Gospel of John and the Jesus of History: Engaging with C. H. Dodd on the Fourth Gospel* (ed. Tom Thatcher and Catrin Williams; Cambridge: Cambridge University Press, forthcoming).

[23] Tolmie, *Narratology*, 55.

[24] Though attention to characterization in the Fourth Gospel has increased since Culpepper's *Anatomy of the Fourth Gospel*, I find it surprising that Mary Magdalene is not treated more thoroughly. Sandra M. Schneiders' *Written That You May Believe* (New York: Crossroad, 2003), 211–23, is quite helpful as is Conway's aforementioned work. One might expect her to make a more powerful appearance in Craig Koester's seminal work, *Symbolism in the*

MM is a crucial part of the Johannine theological, ecclesiological web. Through a variety of narrative strategies, then, the narrator uses the narrative to create a personality to be encountered, not a morality lesson to be swallowed with some verbal castor oil. The Fourth Gospel is no *Pilgrim's Progress* when it comes to drawing characters.

I state this so emphatically because the author of the Fourth Gospel, not to mention MM, has been done a disservice through centuries of biblical interpretation insofar as the Gospel's characters have generally been viewed too flatly. Furthermore, the robust, rich, brilliant character that he or she has created in MM has often been tarnished and belittled by interpretations that rob her of her true character. Such interpretations are not supported by the Johannine text (and probably not the Synoptics either).

Even a Johannine scholar as astute and careful as Cornelis Bennema falls into the trap. Though he labels MM a "personality" (using a range of type, personality, and individuality) and notes that "Many scholars assess Mary negatively, but this is unwarranted,"[25] he immediately proceeds to perpetuate the problem. He calls her "dull" and her quest "earthly." Though on p. 201 he lists her as "obedient," she does not achieve his "obedient response" category on p. 206 (though both Lazarus and the invalid at the pool do). Also, he does not include her in his "open/public confession" type of response, though the man born blind, Martha, Thomas, Andrew, Philip, Nathanael and others do. How is her confession less public or open? He is content, however, to put her in the "thinking 'from below'" category with Nicodemus. Such a move is flawed, exegetically speaking.

MM first testifies that the resurrected Jesus Christ is a central fact of human history, even cosmic history. In so doing, she herself becomes a central fact of that history as well. What a character! What a personality!

Fourth Gospel (Minneapolis: Fortress, 1995). In chapter two, "Symbolic and Representative Figures," each of the following characters gets a separate named section: Jesus; Nicodemus and the Samaritan Woman; The Royal Official and the Invalid; The Crowds; The Man Born Blind and Martha, Mary, and Lazarus; and Jesus' Disciples. She appears briefly in his discussion of Jesus' Disciples on pp. 69–70. She appears in the "Notably Present Characters: Women" in Jo-Ann A. Brant's ovular work, *Dialogue and Drama: Elements of Greek Tragedy in the Fourth Gospel* (Peabody, Mass.: Hendrickson, 2004), 208–20.

[25] Bennema, *Encountering Jesus*, 200.

The Mother of Jesus and the Beloved Disciple: How a New Family is Established Under the Cross

Jean Zumstein[1]

The scene in John 19:25–27 introduces and establishes a group of people which can be labeled the "new family" of Jesus. How did this collective character take shape and how can it be characterized?[2] What is its role in the plot and theology of the Gospel of John?

The central question, posed by an analysis of the characters in 19:25–27, is best examined when broken into three components: first, we will consider the formation of one collective character out of two typical johannine characters. Second, we will observe that the individual figures only emerge when the symbolic language and the intertextual relationships within which they occur are decoded. Third, we will point out that the relationship between the Mother of Jesus and the Beloved Disciple is an issue that remains controversial in research.

Constellation of Characters

To begin, we will briefly describe *the configuration of the family*. The four women (v. 25), who are contrasted with the four enemy soldiers (v. 24b), embody the group of believers.[3] Verse 26 adds another follower, the Beloved Disciple. As the narrative proceeds, the focus centers on the Mother of Jesus and this disciple. Surprisingly, both of these figures are nameless. This peculiarity is not a manifestation of the author's ignorance of their names, but rather highlights his conscious intent, an intent seen in the expressions he uses to label both characters (ἡ μήτηρ αὐτοῦ [*his* mother]; ὁ μαθητὴς ὃν

---

[1] Translated by Sophia Buchanan.
[2] Compare R. Alan Culpepper, *Anatomy of the Fourth Gospel: A Study in Literary Design* (Philadelphia: Fortress, 1983), 99–148 (esp. for Jesus' Mother, pages 133–34; for the Beloved Disciple, 121–23); Daniel Marguerat and Yvan Bourquin, *How to Read Bible Stories* (London: SCM, 1999), 58–76.
[3] Though the belief of the four women is not expressly described, their presence by Jesus in the hour of his rejection is a narrative element which shows their belief. Compare Anton Dauer, *Die Passionsgeschichte im Johannesevangelium: Eine traditionsgeschichtliche und theologische Untersuchung zu Joh 18,1–19,30* (SANT 30; München: Kösel, 1972), 316–18.

ἠγάπα [the disciple *he* loved]) so as to clarify their relationships to Jesus. In each case the designations are characteristic of closeness, markers of intimacy. This scene, therefore, plays out between the crucified Jesus and those closest to him.

How is the *relationship between the characters* to be defined?[4] The johannine Jesus actively engages with sovereign wisdom through his words, while his Mother and Beloved Disciple remain fully passive and silent. Their only action consists in realizing and fulfilling the instructions that Jesus gives them from the cross. Jesus' last wish relates to the time after his death. In line with Jewish family law, he places his Mother under the protection of the Beloved Disciple. This disciple is prompted to take over the same role for Jesus' Mother that up to this point Jesus had filled. Only on the basis of the primary intention of the last wish of Jesus can the relationship between the Mother of Jesus and the Beloved Disciple be clarified. The Mother of Jesus is not asked to take up the care of the Beloved Disciple (a mariological interpretation[5]), nor should theirs be a relationship of mutual partnership. Only the Beloved Disciple is entrusted with a mission. He must take the Mother "into his home."

The *familia Dei* under the Cross

The terminology employed belongs to the semantic field of "family" (e. g., the pair of *mother* and *son*) and the central theme is the establishment of a new relationship within this family. That is to say, that at the hour of his death, Jesus lays the foundations for the new family in the time after his death. In other words, he establishes the post-Easter family. Thus both the characters of the Mother of Jesus and of the Beloved Disciple are transformed into one collective character. From now on they constitute and exemplify the core substance of the *familia Dei*.

As the characters of the Mother of Jesus and the Beloved Disciple are portrayed as the core image of the *familia Dei*, it is clear that the language used in this passage has a symbolic dimension.[6] That is, within the first meaning, a

---

[4] The relationship between the figures is constantly debated, mostly for dogmatic reasons. The narrative logic of John 19:25–27 was demonstrated in exemplary fashion in the work of Schürmann (cf. Heinz Schürmann, "Jesu letzte Weisung: Jo 19,26–27a, 13–28," in *Ursprung und Gestalt: Erörterungen und Besinnungen* [Düsseldorf: Patmos, 1990]).

[5] The mariological interpretation has been an ever present feature of the text's interpretive history. Detailed criticism of mariological exegesis can be found in Dauer, *Passionsgeschichte*, 323–26.

[6] The characterization of the figures plays with the symbolic language in this passage. Ricœur lays out how we are to understand and interpret such language (cf. Paul Ricœur, *De l'interprétation: Essais sur Freud* [L'ordre philosophique, Paris: Le Seuil, 1965], 20–27).

second meaning should be observed. This symbolic meaning, however, is to be seen primarily through an examination of the intertextual relationships in John 19:25–27.[7]

In this passage the Beloved Disciple is presented so matter-of-factly that the character only takes shape (in terms of meaning and consistency) when read in terms of the other texts which describe him.[8] All through chapters 13–20 the Beloved Disciple is displayed as the trusted companion of Jesus.[9] During the Last Supper (13:23–25), he lies at the bosom of Jesus. The term "bosom" indicates to readers that the disciple has the same status in relation to Jesus, that Jesus has in relation to God the Father (cf. 1:18). Just as Jesus' close relationship to the Father enables him to reveal the Father and interpret him for humankind, so also the Beloved Disciple's close relationship to Jesus enables him to bear witness to Jesus' words and interpret them for believers. John 13:23–25 confirms this view as from this point forward the Beloved Disciple plays an intermediary role between Jesus and Peter. If John 19:25 refers to the Beloved Disciple, then his presence at the cross ought to be interpreted as the presence of a witness. The Beloved Disciple is therefore the trustworthy witness and the authentic, first-hand interpreter of the key moment of revelation in the Gospel: the glorification of the Son. Chapter 20 completes this picture: The Beloved Disciple's victory during the puzzling race emphasizes his zeal (vss. 2–10); furthermore he is the only one who understands what happened (v. 8), although he restrains himself in respect of/in the presence of Peter. Chapter 21 configures the identity of the Beloved Disciple in a twofold manner. On the one hand, the relationship between Peter and the Beloved Disciple is set forth once again, but in a new way, and its meaning is presented for the church. On the other hand, the trustworthy witness and interpreter of Jesus becomes the author of a text – namely, the author of the Fourth Gospel.

Just as in the case of the Beloved Disciple, the scene at the foot of the cross offers virtually nothing which allows the role and the meaning of the *mother* to be explained.[10] The only possible hints in the narrative are found in the link to the earlier story of the Miracle at Cana (2:1–11). Four observations support this hypothesis: (a) in both scenes the Mother of Jesus is referred to with the

---

[7] On the issue of intertextuality, see Nathalie Piégay-Gros, *Introduction à l'intertextualité* (Paris: Dunod, 1996). I have written a detailed analysis of the intertextual relationships found in 19:25–27 (and the entire Gospel) in an earlier publication (Jean Zumstein, "Johannes 19,25–27," in *Kreative Erinnerung: Relecture und Auslegung im Johannesevangelium* [ATANT 84; Zürich: TVZ, 2004], 253–275).

[8] With Jürgen Becker, *Das Evangelium nach Johannes: Kapitel 11–21* (ÖTK 4/2; Gütersloh: Gütersloher Verlagshaus Mohn, 1991), 699.

[9] For the interpretation of the character of the Beloved Disciple, see Jean Zumstein, *L'Evangile selon Saint Jean (13–21)* (CNT IVb; Genève: Labor et Fides, 2007), passim.

[10] In reference to the portrayal of the Mother of Jesus, see Schürmann, "Jesu letzte Weisung," 20–22.

term ἡ μήτηρ (τοῦ Ἰησοῦ); (b) in both scenes Jesus speaks to her directly (using the vocative case γύναι); (c) in both scenes the theme of "the hour" is present (2:4 and 19:27b); and (d) in both scenes the Mother relates to her Son in a manner of intimacy and trust.

Hermeneutical Conclusion

How should this intertextual play be interpreted? The Mother of Jesus appears to play a significant role in the development of the plot not only in the first scene but also in the final act of revelation by her Son. She functions as a textual signal which marks the beginning and the end of the public ministry of Jesus. She alludes in both cases to a future, a future in which she herself will be involved. As the Johannine Jesus in Cana refers beyond the sign to a future hour, so on the cross does he point to the decisive hour referred to at Cana (19:27: ἀπ' ἐκείνης τῆς ὥρας), thus opening the door to the post-Easter future.

Should the Mother of Jesus be interpreted as a *typological* character? One literary detail is especially noteworthy: her natural and spiritual nearness (to Jesus). We can conclude therefore that she is a representation of faith. Two aspects of this interpretation must be specified further. On the one hand, it seems unlikely that Jesus' Mother represents the belief of the collective covenant people of Israel.[11] The contrast between Israel and Gentile does not play a decisive role in the way in which she is characterized. On the other hand, even if one accepts that she embodies a character of faith, it seems just as unlikely that she represents the church as such and that she takes over its responsibility for the entire body of believers, who are entrusted to her protection and intercessory care.[12] At the cross the Mother of Jesus stands with other women who likewise are bound to Jesus. Her future is determined by the fact that she is taken in by the Beloved Disciple in his household and that she finds protection and hospitality with him.

What is the architecture of meaning then which is constructed through this intertextual play? The analysis of the narrative logic from 19:25–27 has shown that while on the cross Jesus constructed a new family, giving the authority thereof to the Beloved Disciple. The Beloved Disciple is summoned to compensate for the inevitable absence of the Mother's Son. The intertextual play shows that the Mother, who is taken in by the Beloved Disciple, had faithfully

---

[11] In Cana, all the characters belong to Israel and even the disciples are described as believers (2:11). At the cross, the Mother of Jesus is part of a group of women who all have a relationship to Jesus. Accordingly, the Mother cannot be contrasted to the Beloved Disciple because she belongs to Israel.

[12] For example, see in Ignace de la Potterie, *La passion de Jésus selon l'évangile de Jean* (LiBi 73; Paris: Cerf, 1986), 144–65.

accompanied Jesus from Cana to the crucifixion. Furthermore, at the cross the post-Easter future of the pre-Easter companions is determined. The intertextual play shows also that the Beloved Disciple compensates for the absence of the Son because he turns the post resurrection time into a time during which the companions of Jesus have a place to stay (εἰς τὰ ἴδια). As a trustworthy witness and interpreter of the passion, death, and resurrection of Jesus, he is in a position to compensate for the loss of the crucified Jesus and to take under his protection the believing followers of Jesus, who are symbolized by the Mother of Jesus.

Joseph of Arimathea:
One of "the Jews," But with a Fearful Secret!

William John Lyons

Joseph of Arimathea in the Fourth Gospel

In the Gospel of John, Joseph of Arimathea only appears after Jesus' death on the cross and immediately disappears from view after the burial of the body (19:38–42). Described as "a disciple of Jesus, but secretly, for fear of 'the Jews'" in a narratorial aside (19:38), the otherwise status-less Joseph asks Pilate for Jesus' body and receives permission to take it. He is joined in the burying of the corpse by Nicodemus (19:39–42), a Pharisee and a leader of "the Jews" (cf. 3:1), who had once come to Jesus by night (3:1–21) and then tried to intercede with the chief priests and Pharisees on Jesus' behalf (7:45–52). Anointing the body with the "hundred pounds" of "myrrh and aloes" supplied by Nicodemus (19:39), the two men bind the body in a cloth in customary Jewish fashion and then lay it hurriedly (cf. 19:42) in a new tomb – a point emphasized by its near-redundant further description as a tomb where "no one had ever been laid" – in a nearby garden (19:41). Only in v. 38 does Joseph act alone, but even then he is initiating no new activity; he is merely echoing the request for the bodies already made to Pilate by "the Jews" in 19:31.

Despite his fleeting appearance to the implied audience of the Fourth Gospel, however, Joseph plays a pivotal role in the Johannine story of the "Word become flesh," being responsible – with Nicodemus for the actual burial – for Jesus' body as "it" moves/is moved between the cross and the tomb, for the time period between Jesus' death and his burial/resurrection. So what does that implied audience know about Joseph of Arimathea, when does it know it, and what does it see as his significance within the Johannine narrative?

The Implied Audience and Narrative Criticism

In R. A. Culpepper's ground breaking narrative-critical work, *Anatomy of the Fourth Gospel: A Study in Literary Design* (published in 1983),[1] the chapter on

---

[1] R. Alan Culpepper, *Anatomy of the Fourth Gospel: A Study in Literary Design* (Minneapolis: Fortress, 1983).

the "Implied Reader" was placed just before the conclusion; narrator and point of view, time, plot, characterization, and implicit commentary were all considered before the audience of the Gospel. The rationale for this was made early on: "By systematically collecting and analyzing [unexplained characters, places, customs and terms] one can construct a portrait of the Gospel's implied reader."[2] Culpepper's preface to the paperback makes clear that, while he considered his account of the implied reader an advance on previous studies, it was only a preliminary attempt at defining the relationship between the elements of the text and the reader that they evoked. Much still had to be done.[3]

There is something appealing about the idea that the implied reader – or better, in the case of the Fourth Gospel's oral milieu, the implied audience – can simply be read off the closed world of the text. As T. Thatcher has noted,[4] however, Culpepper's use of the reader-response theory of W. Iser was already hinting well beyond such a restricted view, towards the involvement of the "actual reader" in "actualizing" the text's meaning, in filling in its gaps.[5] The impact of one reader's decisions – i.e., those of Culpepper himself – on the implied audience went largely unremarked at the time, however. Over the next quarter century, Culpepper's "semi-formal" narrative criticism was co-opted by many biblical scholars as yet another tool in their methodological box,[6] though reverting to the closed world scenario is always a temptation for those who continue to ignore their own "presence" in their historical-critical works. The more creative possibilities of gap-filling have been explored in a number of the essays contained in *Anatomies of Narrative Criticism: The Past Present and Futures of the Fourth Gospel as Literature*, edited by T. Thatcher and S. D. Moore, and an explicit commemoration of the twenty-fifth anniversary of Culpepper's *Anatomy of the Fourth Gospel*.[7]

Yet Culpepper's Iserian model – his version of what Moore tells us has long been called "classical narratology"[8] – has been heavily criticized over the years, both by the radical reader-response criticism of such as Stanley E. Fish[9] and by the diverse post-structuralist developments within narratology.[10] For some

---

[2] Culpepper, *Anatomy of the Fourth Gospel*, 8.
[3] Culpepper, *Anatomy of the Fourth Gospel*, xii.
[4] Tom Thatcher, "Anatomies of the Fourth Gospel: Past, Present, and Future Probes," in *Anatomies of Narrative Criticism: The Past, Present, and Futures of the Fourth Gospel as Literature* (ed. Tom Thatcher and Stephen D. Moore; Atlanta: Society of Biblical Literature, 2008), 1–38, here 33–35.
[5] Culpepper, *Anatomy of the Fourth Gospel*, 209.
[6] Cf. Stephen D. Moore, "Afterword: Things Not Written in This Book," in *Anatomies of Narrative Criticism* (ed. Thatcher and Moore), 253–58, here 255.
[7] Thatcher and Moore, eds., *Anatomies of Narrative Criticism*.
[8] Moore, "Afterword," 255.
[9] Stanley E. Fish, *Doing What Comes Naturally: Change, Rhetoric, and the Practice of Theory in Literary and Legal Studies* (Oxford: Clarendon Press, 1989), 74–86.
[10] Moore, "Afterword," 255–58.

biblical scholars, myself included, the foundational notion of solid, formal, guiding elements, seemingly at the same time *both* unconstructed *and* context-free, is now passé. Narratology beyond semi-formalism may usefully choose to employ narrative-critical concepts and terms – e.g., narrator, time, plot, characterization, and implied audience – but it must acknowledge that their solidity is inextricably linked to the person who beholds them, a figure whose own unchanging mental permanence is now equally compromised. What we call the narrative-critical meaning of the Fourth Gospel is the end-product of a complex interaction between a number of *constructs*: the "structures" of the biblical texts, any "relevant extra-textual material" available relating to its milieu and use of language, and the "mind" of the narrative-critical exegete who "sees" the structures, "determines the relevance" of any extra-textual material, and "produces" the reading that is ascribed to the narrative text. The question of what the implied audience knows about a character like Joseph is not then likely to have a simple agreed answer.

Bennema's Joseph of Arimathea and Its Audience

In an important article on character, C. Bennema offers an approach in which the limited knowledge of characters ascribed to the implied audience in earlier narrative-critical work is left far behind. Instead Bennema focuses upon what a modern reader might know about the characters of the Gospel of John:

> The Fourth Gospel is non-fiction, and hence the dramatis personae in the Johannine story are also composites of real historical people. This almost demands that we also look outside the Fourth Gospel at other sources that can assist us in reconstructing the Johannine characters... Too often, narrative critics restrict themselves to the text of the gospel and the narrative world it evokes, thereby effectively reading the gospel as a fictional narrative that has no contact with reality. Instead, we need a form of historical narrative criticism, taking a text-centred approach but examining aspects of the world outside or "behind" the text if the text invites us to do so. In other words, we should reconstruct the Johannine characters from the information that the text of the Fourth Gospel provides *and* supplement it with relevant information from other sources.[11]

But rather than ask the obvious question – "relevant" in whose eyes? – let us look at Bennema's application of his approach to Joseph of Arimathea in the chapter entitled "Joseph of Arimathea – Faith and Fear" in his book *Encountering Jesus: Character Studies in the Gospel of John*,[12] and see if we are convinced by his overall approach to characterization.

---

[11] Cornelis Bennema, "A Theory of Character in the Fourth Gospel with Reference to Ancient and Modern Literature," *BibInt* 17 (2009): 375–421, here 399, 401–2 (his emphasis).

[12] Cornelis Bennema, *Encountering Jesus: Character Studies in the Gospel of John* (Milton Keynes: Paternoster, 2009), 190–95.

Bennema's chapter opens with a brief statement of "issues," the resolution of which will, he suggests, lead to a better understanding of the Johannine Joseph of Arimathea (introduced briefly in his earlier chapter on Nicodemus).[13] A two paragraph section entitled "The identity of Joseph of Arimathea"[14] summarizes the information that Bennema feels is relevant to the case, before he goes on to consider in detail how the character of Joseph is portrayed in the Fourth Gospel.[15]

In the first paragraph of the section on "identity," Bennema writes: "[W]e are presented with an enigmatic figure [in Joseph] since the information about him in John's Gospel (and other sources) seems contradictory."[16] A tension between John 19:31 ("the Jews" asked Pilate for the bodies) and 19:38 (Joseph asked Pilate for the body) is noted before Bennema introduces details from the "other sources," but now without brackets:[17]

- In Acts 13:27–29 unnamed "Jews" bury Jesus;
- In the Synoptic Gospels this act is attributed to Joseph (Matt 27:57–60; Mark 15:42–46; Luke 23:50–53);
- Joseph is portrayed by the Synoptics as a rich man from Arimathea and a respected member of the Sanhedrin who disagrees with the decision to kill Jesus (referencing Matt 27:57; Mark 15:43; Luke 23:50–51; cf. Nicodemus in John 7);
- He is also described by them as "a good and righteous man, who waits expectantly for the Kingdom of God (Mark 15.43; Luke 23.50–51), and even as a disciple of Jesus (Matt 27:57)."[18]

John's description of Joseph as a secret disciple for fear of "the Jews" (19:38) is finally added to the "other sources" mix. Unsurprisingly Bennema concludes that "[t]hese disparate portraits of Joseph are difficult to reconcile,"[19] adding that "it is also unclear whether Joseph is affiliated with 'the Jews' or with Jesus."[20]

In the second and final paragraph of the "identity" section, quoted here, Bennema offers what is effectively a fully reconciled Joseph:

Piecing together the available information I suggest the following profile of Joseph ... Joseph is probably a wealthy respected Jewish leader and a member of the Sanhedrin, making him either a notable Pharisee or a chief priest ... However, he apparently disagrees with the Sanhedrin's decision to have Jesus killed (11:47–53). Joseph probably

---

[13] Bennema, *Encountering Jesus*, 82–83.
[14] Bennema, *Encountering Jesus*, 190–91.
[15] Bennema, *Encountering Jesus*, 191–95.
[16] Bennema, *Encountering Jesus*, 190.
[17] Bennema, *Encountering Jesus*, 190.
[18] Bennema, *Encountering Jesus*, 190.
[19] Bennema, *Encountering Jesus*, 190–91.
[20] Bennema, *Encountering Jesus*, 191.

disagrees with them because he is a disciple of Jesus, albeit a secret one because he fears his colleagues. When the Jews want to have the body removed from the cross before the Sabbath starts, Joseph perhaps volunteers to go to Pilate and ask for permission. Joseph has a lot in common with Nicodemus. Nicodemus, a wealthy and prominent Pharisee, is also a member of the Sanhedrin ... Like Joseph, Nicodemus is sympathetic to Jesus (although we cannot call Nicodemus a disciple of Jesus). At an earlier meeting of the Sanhedrin, Nicodemus too disagrees with his colleagues' plans regarding Jesus. It is therefore not too surprising that Nicodemus pairs up with Joseph at Jesus' burial.[21]

Bennema's Joseph of Arimathea – A Critique

It seems to me that there is nothing to distinguish Bennema's description of Joseph from the many historical-critical portraits produced over the years by those attempting to reconcile the four canonical portraits of Joseph, most recently that of Pope Benedict XVI in his *Jesus of Nazareth: Holy Week*.[22] That conclusion is my basic problem with Bennema's proposed methodology. Given the disparate, even contradictory, details of the canonical accounts – including Matthew's claim that the tomb *belonged to Joseph* (27:60) which is left unmentioned by Bennema – surely there should be some difference between the kind of broad-based reconciliation of traditions available to a modern audience – an audience whose knowledge of the ancient world has its own limits – and the content of the narrative-critical Johannine Joseph? In the sparse account in John 19:39–42, Joseph is certainly not described as a Sanhedrin member (a label occurring only in Mark and Luke); nor is he described as "wealthy" (Matthew only) or as "respected" (Mark only). In what sense does the "identity" of Bennema's Joseph arise from the narrative structures of the Fourth Gospel?

In what follows, Bennema's broad-based methodological approach will be replaced by one targeted towards a somewhat narrower audience, one that is justified by recent historical-critical work on the setting of the Fourth Gospel. Richard Bauckham has offered a number of relevant arguments in his chapters in his edited volume *The Gospel for All Christians*.[23] First, he has argued that the Gospels were constructed with a wider audience in mind than a traditional Johannine community.[24] But second, and in contrast to Bennema, this audience is not a general modern one; it retains a certain historical specificity.[25] Third, Bauckham attacks the assumption that every single element of the nar-

---

[21] Bennema, *Encountering Jesus*, 191.
[22] Pope Benedict XVI, *Jesus of Nazareth: Holy Week* (San Francisco: Ignatius, 2011), 226–29.
[23] Richard Bauckham, "For Whom Were the Gospels Written?," in *The Gospel for all Christians* (ed. idem; Edinburgh: T&T Clark, 1998), 9–48; and idem, "John for Readers of Mark," in *The Gospel for all Christians*, 147–71.
[24] Bauckham, "For Whom Were the Gospels Written?," 26–44.
[25] Richard Bauckham, "Response to Philip Esler," *SJT* 51 (1998): 249–53.

rative must relate to the whole audience being addressed.²⁶ Finally, in a second essay in the volume, he argues that John includes two asides which indicate that John may have been written in the knowledge that certain members of the audience knew the Gospel of Mark,²⁷ a position which has received some criticism (e. g., D. C. Sim,²⁸ W. E. S. North,²⁹ and A. Reinhartz;³⁰ on Bauckham's general position, see the criticisms of P. Esler,³¹ E. van Eck,³² B. J. Incigneri,³³ and M. Mitchell;³⁴ cf. the summaries of E. W. Klink³⁵).

With these points in mind, I offer two narrative-critical accounts of the Johannine Joseph, the first according to the implied audience of the Gospel of John and the second, assuming the basic soundness of Bauckham's argument about John and Mark, according to the implied audience of these two Gospels alone.

Joseph of Arimathea and the Implied Audience of the Gospel of John

With the exception of Jeffrey L. Staley,³⁶ narrative critics have tended to agree that the Johannine narrator should be regarded as a reliable one, whose omniscience, omnipresence, and personal ideology (explicit in e. g., 13:1-6) are insufficiently troubling to the implied audience for it to question that figure's integrity or to reject the direction that is being offered to it.³⁷ Given that no direct speech is recorded for Joseph of Arimathea in the Fourth Gospel (or indeed in any other canonical text), he is characterized only in the narrator's "telling"; the short summary of events combined with clarifying/directive nar-

---

[26] Bauckham, "For Whom Were the Gospels Written?," 24–25.
[27] Bauckham, "John for Readers of Mark," 147–71.
[28] David C. Sim, "'The Gospel for All Christians': A Response to Richard Bauckham," *JSNT* 84 (2001): 3–27.
[29] Wendy E. S. North, "John for Readers of Mark? A Response to Richard Bauckham's Proposal," *JSNT* 25 (2003): 449–68.
[30] Adele Reinhartz, "Gospel Audiences: Variations on a Theme," in *The Audience of the Gospels: The Origin and Function of the Gospels in Early Christianity* (ed. Edward W. Klink; LNTS; London: T&T Clark, 2010), 134–52.
[31] Philip Esler, "Community and Gospel in Early Christianity: A Response to Richard Bauckham's *Gospel for All Christians*," *SJT* 51 (1998): 235–48.
[32] Ernest van Eck, "A Sitz for the Gospel of Mark: A Critical Reaction to Bauckham's Theory on the Universality of the Gospels," *HvTSt* 56 (2000): 200–35.
[33] Brian J. Incigneri, *The Gospel to the Romans: The Setting and Rhetoric of Mark's Gospel* (Leiden: Brill, 2003), 33–34.
[34] Margaret Mitchell, "Patristic Counter-Evidence to the Claim that 'The Gospels Were Written for All Christians,'" *NTS* 51 (2005): 36–79.
[35] Edward W. Klink, "The Gospel Community Debate: State of the Question," *CBR* 3 (2004): 60–85; and his edited volume, *The Audience of the Gospels*.
[36] Jeffrey L. Staley, *The Print's First Kiss: The Implied Reader in the Fourth Gospel* (Atlanta: Scholars, 1986).
[37] Culpepper, *Anatomy of the Fourth Gospel*, 24, 32–34.

ratorial asides that appears in John 19:38–42. Those asides include general clarifications for the audience (e. g., "as is the burial custom of 'the Jews'"), but also introduce reliable information about both Joseph (the inner detail that he "was a disciple of Jesus, but secretly, for fear of 'the Jews'") and about the man who joins him in burying Jesus, Nicodemus (e. g., the internal analeptic detail that he "had at first come to [Jesus] by night"). But no information is provided about Joseph's social standing and an explicit detailed statement about his relationship to the narrative's previous events is also lacking; the implied audience knows only what it can infer from the text so far.

Since there is no explicit reference to the narrative's plot in these verses either, the meaning of Joseph's role in the burial has to be inferred from the plot as it has been revealed in the preceding chapters. Finding M. W. G. Stibbe's view that the plot is focused on Jesus solely as the bringer of life unconvincing,[38] this account takes its lead from A. T. Lincoln's suggestion that the "darker" side of the Fourth Gospel must also be considered. For him, the plot revolves around the motif of a cosmic lawsuit launched by God against the world through the sending of Jesus which is then reflected back onto the bringer of the lawsuit by a world that seeks to prosecute him in turn.[39] The mission statement that Lincoln has proposed for the plot is not Stibbe's life-promising John 3:16,[40] but rather the challenge to the status quo that is uttered by Jesus in John 18:37:[41] "For this I was born, and for this I have come into the world, to bear witness to the truth. Everyone who is of the truth hears my voice."

A stark dualism of decision therefore permeates the overall structure of the text, focused upon the question of how each individual responds to Jesus' words; Pilate's "what is truth" is hardly what the narrator would consider an adequate response to the challenge. At the same time, however, there are numerous characters who do not offer sufficiently clear responses to Jesus for the implied audience to be certain of their final status in relation to the plot's structure; the "invalid" of John 5, for example, or, if we are dealing with the shape of the canonical text, the adulteress of John 7:53–8:11 (cf. Culpepper's list of responses that occur within the text: [1] rejection; [2] acceptance without open commitment; [3] acceptance of Jesus as wonder worker; [4] belief in words; [5] commitment with misunderstanding; [6] paradigmatic discipleship;

---

[38] Mark W. G. Stibbe, "Return to Sender: A Structuralist Approach to John's Gospel," *BibInt* 1 (1993): 189–206.
[39] Andrew T. Lincoln, "Trials, Plots and the Narrative of the Fourth Gospel," *JSNT* 56 (1994): 3–30; idem, *Truth on Trial*; idem, "The Beloved Disciple as Eyewitness and the Fourth Gospel as Witness," *JSNT* 85 (2002): 3–26; and idem, *The Gospel According to St John* (BNTC 4; London: Continuum, 2005).
[40] Stibbe, "Return to Sender," 193.
[41] Lincoln, "Trials," 8.

and [7] defection).[42] So how should the implied audience evaluate the narrator's portrayal of Joseph as a secret disciple and his response to Jesus' message?

The narrative background for evaluating Joseph's participation in events is the fact that his request to Pilate is not presented in the Fourth Gospel as either a bold act or as a unique one (*contra* the claim of G. R. O'Day and S. E. Hylen that "Joseph now is bold enough to ask Pilate for Jesus' body;"[43] see also G. Renz[44]). Pilate has already received a nearly identical request from "the Jews" for all of the crucified bodies (rather than just Jesus' body) in 19:31 and was willing to grant it; the subsequent breaking of the legs of those crucified was a consequence of his reaction to the Jewish need for the bodies to be removed before the Sabbath began. When Joseph makes his subsequent request, Pilate would doubtless have seen him merely as one of "the Jews," an individual simply reiterating the earlier request now that those crucified are actually dead. (Presumably his order in response to Joseph's request for the body of Jesus would have been to release all of the bodies, with others then dealing with the bodies of those crucified with Jesus.) Joseph's "fear" of "the Jews" – introduced in a narratorial aside in this verse! – is not obviously suggestive of his boldness before Pilate.

The result is a tension between the implied audience's easy agreement with Pilate that Joseph's actions simply mark him out as one of "the Jews" and the narrator's description of him a secret disciple, with the latter characterization also being further complicated by the negativity attached by the narrator to the silence of the believing Jewish leaders in 12:42–43.[45] For an audience already familiar with the Fourth Gospel's complex use of "the Jews" as a group who debate Jesus' identity until the resolution to kill him is finally reached at the close of his public ministry (12:50; cf. 12:10–11), this appearance of the term in close proximity to Joseph both rehearses those earlier disagreements about Jesus' identity and emphasizes the total invisibility of Joseph among the crowds who had heard Jesus speak. His combined "absence"/"presence" in the crowd leaves him relatively undefined; while he is not encountering Jesus for the first time as a corpse wholly divorced from the claims that he had made about his identity and the need for hearers to make a choice, neither is Joseph openly proclaiming his faith in the one sent by the Father. Joseph's decision for secrecy leaves him a disciple, but, as with so many other characters in the

---

[42] Culpepper, *Anatomy of the Fourth Gospel*, 146–48.

[43] Gail R. O'Day, *John* (Louisville, Ky.: Westminster John Knox, 2006), 190.

[44] Gabi Renz, "Nicodemus: An Ambiguous Disciple? A Narrative Sensitive Investigation," in *Challenging Perspectives on the Gospel of John* (ed. John Lierman; WUNT II/219; Tübingen: Mohr Siebeck, 2006), 255–81, here 275, 277.

[45] Jouette M. Bassler notes the contribution of burying Jesus according the Jewish customs (19:40) to this "disturbing but ambiguous element" (idem, "Mixed Signals: Nicodemus in the Fourth Gospel," *JBL* 108 [1989]: 642).

Fourth Gospel, it certainly does not make him the disciple that an audience predisposed by the plot towards black/white answers might expect him to be.

Nicodemus appears on the scene to help Joseph with the burial, but the interaction between them is largely functional. They do not discuss their task or the identity of the one whom they are burying. Neither does the large amount of myrrh and aloes that Nicodemus brings to anoint a body otherwise quickly buried ("a new tomb ... close at hand") occasion even a brief comment – whether surprised or otherwise – from Joseph (*pace* Culpepper[46] and P. Dschulnigg,[47] Jesus is not given a lavish kingly burial by *both* Joseph and Nicodemus because *only the latter actively seeks to do that*). Both work in a conspiracy of apparent and absolute silence. In contrast to those who claim that Jesus' death was a "catalyst for these two hesitant men to move to a more public expression of their devotion" (C. H. Talbert;[48] cf. also, e. g., Dschulnigg[49]), there is little to suggest a significant public aspect to the customary but speedy and localised burial of a crucified corpse. As some have noted, their activity suggests a finality to the burial unbecoming to believers (cf. Bassler's summary,[50] and Renz[51]); here Joseph's silence in response to the anointing makes him appear even less active a character.

The implied audience is left to contemplate the actions of these two contrasting characters. Nicodemus appears to have done more to warrant the audience's conclusion – having heard Jesus in person, having defended him against opponents, and having buried him so lavishly – that he has come to a public position on the identity of Jesus, though curiously nothing is explicitly said by either the man himself or the narrator. Yet it is Joseph, whose actions only either match those of "the Jews" of 19:41 or fall in line with the activities initiated by Nicodemus, who is the one explicitly described by the narrator as a "disciple" of Jesus, albeit a secret one. Even when combined in a single figure, however, the actions of Nicodemus and Joseph do not add up to the "ideal" of the disciple who openly proclaims Jesus in the manner envisaged in the Farewell discourses. True, this is perhaps a moment of hiatus before the Spirit, the Paraclete, is given in John 20:22, but the inevitable conclusion that arises from that for the implied audience is that both Joseph of Arimathea and Nicodemus are characters in transition, their possible futures only being defined somewhere beyond the edges of the surface chronology of the narrative. If the implied audience's experience of discipleship subsequent to the death and res-

---

[46] Culpepper, *Anatomy of the Fourth Gospel*, 96.

[47] Peter Dschulnigg, *Jesus begegnen: Personen und ihre Bedeutung im Johannesevangelium* (Münster: LIT, 2000), 118.

[48] Charles H. Talbert, *Reading John: A Literary and Theological Commentary on the Fourth Gospel and the Johannine Epistles* (London: SPCK, 1992), 246.

[49] Dschulnigg, *Jesus begegnen*, 118.

[50] Bassler, "Mixed Signals," 642–43.

[51] Renz, "Nicodemus," 278–79.

urrection of Jesus is that implied proleptically by the farewell discourses of John 14–17, they may legitimately expect positive affirmations for faith from both men who bury Jesus' body. But our text also gives sufficient examples of "those who had believed in him" falling away for doubt to remain as to their futures (Renz also concludes with a similar but not identical claim of readerly ambivalence[52]).

Joseph of Arimathea and the Implied Audience of the Gospels of John and Mark

If we add an awareness of the contents of the Gospel of Mark to the knowledge of *some* of our text's implied audience (as Bauckham helpfully suggests[53]), a number of subtle shifts in characterization may, arguably, take place as that implied audience effectively splits into two discrete entities. This mixing of the two narratives is a very complex phenomenon, however, and what follows is a brief sketch of some possible interactions between Mark and John in the minds of an implied audience who hears the latter in light of the former. Consideration of the myriad changes possible will focus on three elements whose shape is altered by the presence of the Second Gospel: (a) the help that Joseph receives in the burial, (b) the ascription of "boldness" to Joseph in asking Pilate for the body, and (c) the implied author of the Second Gospel's relatively ambivalent feelings – at least in comparison with those of the implied author of John – about his characters' open acknowledgment of the identity of Jesus.

In contrast to the Fourth Gospel, the Gospel of Mark portrays Joseph as the only person involved in the burial of Jesus' body; Nicodemus is wholly absent from the text (as he is indeed from the rest of the non-Johannine Joseph tradition). This is not to say that Joseph worked alone, but rather that he was the only person of significance involved. The effect of this on the implied audience of the Gospels of John and Mark is not to diminish the character of Nicodemus as he appears to that audience – his two earlier appearances in John 3 and 7 mean that he is too significant a Johannine character for that – but is rather to elevate Joseph the secret disciple by stressing his role in the act of burying Jesus' body over against that of his co-worker. Instead of appearing as a passive figure whose actions are given content as a result of Nicodemus's viewing Jesus as being apparently worthy of vast quantity of anointing materials, the Joseph of Arimathea who arises from these two differing portrayals now becomes – potentially at least – the more dominant of the two characters.

---

[52] Renz, "Nicodemus," 279.
[53] Bauckham, "For Whom Were the Gospels Written?," 24–25.

This shift in characterization is further strengthened by Mark's silence about an "earlier request" to Pilate for the bodies and his explicit description of Joseph as someone who "boldly" went to Pilate in marked contrast with his portrayal as one whose life is effectively ruled by fear in the Fourth Gospel. The stress on his personal bravery moves the depiction of the sole individual action taken by the Johannine Joseph – his request for the body – away from its being a mere repetition requiring no initiative or bravery at all, allowing the audience to downgrade the impact of Joseph's fear-dominated belief on its assessment of his character and behaviour. Instead of Joseph's actions being over-shadowed by those of Nicodemus and/or "the Jews," he increasingly moves towards the forefront of the narrative, even to the extent of potentially being considered the more likely of the two – Joseph/Nicodemus – to become something like the Fourth Gospel's exemplary disciple.

Mark's depiction of Joseph as an "esteemed councillor" and member of the Sanhedrin who condemned Jesus (15:43) serves to fill out his role as one of "the Jews" who were responsible for the death of Jesus, but his boldness in going to Pilate and the secret nature of his faith ameliorate the darker-side of his role in the crucifixion narrative (an interesting contrast to Luke's description of Joseph as someone who disagreed with the decision to kill Jesus [23:50–51]). But also contributing to the increasingly impressive behaviour of Joseph is the difference in the way that the interaction between non-disciples and disciples are depicted in the Second Gospel. The range of characterizations found in John can be viewed more positively after reading Mark because the latter uses just such a range as a series of critical but positive comparisons points against which to view the Markan disciples (e. g., C. C. Black;[54] E. S. Malbon[55]). When Culpepper compared Nicodemus to Mark's scribe (12:28–34), and wrote that while he was thus not far from the kingdom of God he remained outside, he was over-writing the positivity that Mark ascribes to those who are awaiting the Kingdom of God with the dualistic and jaundiced negativity contained within a Johannine plot that is unrealized even in the characterizations of the Fourth Gospel.[56] This is not to say that Mark simply sees such people as believers, however; he does not. Rather I suggest that the more favourable Markan usage of minor characters opens up the possibility of a less condemnatory approach by an implied audience familiar with both texts to a (now) bold individual who shows initiative in burying Jesus (with unimportant help) and whose secret faith appears stronger and stronger as the influence of Mark on that implied audience becomes stronger and stronger.

---

[54] C. Clifton Black, *The Disciples according to Mark: Markan Redaction in Current Debate* (Sheffield: JSOT Press, 1989), 45.

[55] Elizabeth S. Malbon, *In the Company of Jesus: Characters in Mark's Gospel* (Louisville, Ky.: Westminster John Knox, 2000), 221–25.

[56] Culpepper, *Anatomy of the Fourth Gospel*, 136.

Ironically, this Joseph appears more like the one we usually get from Johannine scholarship, as his passivity is swept away by the influence of Synoptic material (cf., e. g., Renz's negative reading of Joseph which still regards him as the burial scene's active character[57]).

Conclusion

The lesson of the history of exegesis of Joseph of Arimathea is that the multiple canonical accounts have produced a remarkably diverse and adaptable figure. Bennema's Joseph is effectively an attempt to cut that diversity by reducing Joseph to a single portrayal in the mind of a modern reader. Giving the Fourth Gospel its due while acknowledging the creative possibilities that arise from its "collision" with another Gospel in the minds of some of its readers, however, produces instead something rather more like the "creative" account I have tried to give here. Setting the "fearfulness" of the Johannine Joseph over against the "boldness" of the Markan Joseph, for example, opens up a range of possibilities for the implied audience of both these texts, and even more so for those of us with an even wider vision of Joseph at this end of history. We would do well, however, not to inflict that wide vision on either of these two earlier implied audiences indiscriminately. Sometimes less truly is more!

---

[57] Renz, "Nicodemus," 277.

The Angels:
Marking the Divine Presence

Jan van der Watt

The word "angel" (ἄγγελος) is used only three times in John (1:51; 12:29; 20:12[1]); the narrator does not develop or elaborate on themes related to this word in any of these texts. Only in one instance do angels feature as characters, namely in 20:12. In 1:51 and 12:29, they are merely referred to by other characters and do not play a role as characters themselves. To my knowledge, there is no existing analysis of angels as characters in the Gospel of John.[2]

The description of the angels in 20:12–13 is very brief:

And she saw two angels in white, sitting where the body of Jesus had been lying, one at the head and the other at the feet. They said to her, "Woman, why are you weeping?" She said to them, "They have taken away my Lord, and I do not know where they have laid him."

A comparison with the parallel passages in the Synoptic Gospels reveals significant differences. These differences – pertaining to the number of angels (one or two), where they sat, what they said,[3] as well as the length of the narratives – suggest strong redaction[4] in each case. Schnackenburg remarks that "we are

---

[1] Mention should also be made of the angel stirring the water in 5:4, but this is regarded as a later addition to the original text, on the basis of text-critical arguments. Cf. Charles H. Dodd, *Historical Tradition in the Fourth Gospel* (Cambridge: Cambridge University Press, 1963), 179; C. Kingsley Barrett, *The Gospel according to St John* (2d ed.; London: SPCK, 1978), 211; Leon Morris, *The Gospel according to John* (Grand Rapids, Mich.: Eerdmans, 1995), 302. Zane C. Hodges, "The Angel at Bethesda – John 5:4," *BSac* 136 (1979): 25–39, argues that this is not necessarily the case, and that the confidence of those who attempt to dismiss this text as a later addition is "seriously displaced" (39). In spite of the fact that he argues on text-critical, historical and theological grounds, his position is not particularly convincing. This verse will therefore not be considered here.

[2] For instance, in the detailed discussion of 1:51 by Alan R. Kerr, *The Temple of Jesus' Body: The Temple Theme in the Gospel of John* (JSNTSup 220; Sheffield: Sheffield Academic Press, 2002), 136–66, only a brief, casual reference is made to angels. This is typical of discussions of 1:51 and angels in general. In his book on characters in John, Cornelis Bennema does not even mention angels as characters (idem, *Encountering Jesus: Character Studies in the Gospel of John* [Milton Keynes: Paternoster, 2009]).

[3] Cf. Tobias Nicklas, "Angels in Early Christian Narratives on the Resurrection of Jesus. Canonical and Apocryphal Texts," in *Angels: The Concept of Celestial Beings – Origins, Development and Reception* (ed. Friedrich V. Reiterer et al.; Berlin: de Gruyter, 2007), 293–311, here 304.

[4] Raymond E. Brown, *The Gospel according to John* (2 vols.; AB 29A; New York: Double-

dealing here with an advanced tradition and a rather high degree of reflection."[5]

The description of the angels in 20:12–13 is brief: there is not much detail, and only three aspects are used to characterize them: a) their white garments; b) the fact that they were sitting in the tomb, one where the head and one where the feet of Jesus had been; and c) the brief words they spoke to Mary.

a) The first aspect that is narrated is that the two angels seen by Mary were dressed in white (ἐν λευκοῖς),[6] signifying that they were from the heavenly world. These were no ordinary men! As Beasley-Murray remarks, following Blank: "[S]hining white garments are the symbol of the heavenly world."

b) The narrator then relates that the two angels were sitting in the tomb where the body of Jesus had lain. The question as to why the angels sat where the feet and head of Jesus had been, has left commentators guessing, resulting in a variety of views.[7] The angels' positions can be interpreted in various ways. Possibly the two angels marked the place where Jesus had lain in order to emphasize that he was no longer there, since, according to 20:7, the cloths were spread out in the grave (i. e., the face cloth was separated from the other linen). However, this could not have been the main reason, since Mary already knew that Jesus' body was no longer there; there was no need for the angels to point this out. Another possibility is that their being there indicated a divine presence, a function that is evident elsewhere in the Gospel (1:51). Thus, although Jesus was no longer present in the tomb, the presence of the angels served to emphasize the heavenly "presence" in the empty tomb,[8] implying that God was active in whatever had happened there.

A further possibility that should be considered is that 20:12 may comprise an implicit comment on 1:51, in order to emphasize that the situation had changed. It could be that here the angels are elaborating on, or even "filling in" the remark in 1:51. Let us briefly entertain this possibility. In 1:51, the reference to angels symbolically marks the locus of the divine presence by means of their descending *on* Jesus. Here (20:12), they have descended *on*

---

day, 1966), 988; Rudolf Schnackenburg, *The Gospel according to St John* (3 vols.; London: Burns & Oats, 1982), 3:315; Barclay M. Newman and Eugene A. Nida, *A Handbook on the Gospel of John* (New York: United Bible Societies, 1993), 608; George R. Beasley-Murray, *John* (Dallas: Word, 2002), 374.

[5] Schnackenburg, *John*, 3:315.

[6] Cf. also Newman and Nida, *John*, 608; Brown, *John*, 989; Barnabas Lindars, *The Gospel of John* (Grand Rapids, Mich.: Eerdmans, 1987), 604. Cf. Ruth M. M. Tuschling, *Angels and Orthodoxy* (Tübingen: Mohr Siebeck, 2007), 106, on linen clothing and priestly service.

[7] Robert Jamieson, Andrew R. Fausset, and David Brown, *A Commentary: Critical and Explanatory, on the Old and New Testaments* (Oak Harbor: Logos Research Systems, 1997), ad loc., mention possibilities such as that the position of the sitting angels proclaimed that they had had the body, or that it emphasizes the confined space "within which the Lord of glory had contracted Himself." This is nothing more than guess-work.

[8] Beasley-Murray, *John*, 374.

him, but he is no longer there. At most, they can sit where his feet and head were.[9] This picture serves as a vivid preparation for the revelation of Jesus to Mary that directly follows. Jesus lives; and he himself is now ascending to the Father (20:17), and will return (as he promised in ch. 14). It is he who now "links" what is above with what is below through his presence as the risen Lord. This implies that the function of the angels has been accomplished; and thus, they are portrayed as being seated. The posture of being seated, rather than moving up and down as in 1:51, might thus suggest that their work is completed. Jesus now takes over. He is recognized as "my Lord and God" (20:28) and marks the location of the divine presence – angels are no longer necessary in order to do so.

It must be conceded that what happens in 20:12 is not exactly what was promised in 1:51. According to 1:51, angels would descend on Jesus; in 20:12 his body is no longer there, where the angels are present. This difference, however, precisely emphasizes the essence of what the implied author wants to say: Jesus supersedes the situation described in 1:51, where angels are needed to mark divine presence. However, the prediction made in 1:51 was not uttered in vain – it became a reality in 20:12, through the descent of the angels into the tomb of Jesus.

Apart from the fact that this interpretation is also in keeping with the theology of John, according to which Jesus takes over the function that would previously have been carried out by angels, there is also other support for this line of argumentation. Looking at the Gospel as narrative, this is the first and only instance in which angels are actually portrayed as characters in the narrative, and the only place where the possible fulfilment of 1:51 may realistically be found. In 1:51, the expectation was created that angels would be seen, and in 12:29 they are actually not present. It is only here, in 20:12, that they appear in the narrative world, at the place where the body of Christ formerly lay, but with an expanded message – the body is no longer there. Jesus is outside the tomb, as the Risen One.

By means of this interpretation, the references to angels in 1:51 and 20:12–13 are merged. This also highlights the functionality of angels in the Gospel of John. Although the angels identify the place of Jesus' burial as an area of divine significance, the way in which they are portrayed also seems to signify that they have been functionally replaced by Jesus (see also 12:29). The angels remained seated in the burial place.

---

[9] Beasley-Murray, *John*, 374, explains the angels' seated positions at the head and foot as follows: "Their position in the tomb ... is a reminder of the silent testimony of the grave clothes, but of another order; it witnesses that *God*, not robbers, has taken Jesus, for a purpose yet to be revealed." This is not convincing, since it does not really explain why the angels sit at the places where the feet and head were. His emphasis on their witness to the presence of the activity of God is, however, plausible.

c) Lastly, it is narrated that the angels asked Mary a question: γύναι, τί κλαίεις; ("Woman, why do you cry?"). Thus, they did not reveal anything directly to her, in the customary manner associated with angels.[10] Why this particular question? First, it should be noted that the angels did not appear to Peter and John, but only to Mary. This factor links them directly to the figure and actions of Mary. The appearance of the angels should thus be interpreted in terms of the characterization of Mary.[11] What is immediately striking is Mary's repetitious plea, addressed to the disciples (20:2), the angels (20:13) and Jesus (20:15), asking for the body of Jesus, since somebody "has taken" Jesus' body and she does not know where it is.[12] Her assumption is that Jesus is still dead and that his body is somewhere else. She entertains no other possibility, for instance, that Jesus has risen from the dead – not even after seeing the angels sitting in the tomb. Within this framework, the response of the angels becomes functional, challenging the perception of Mary and opening the way for an alternative perception. The angels' question – "Why do you cry?" – calls for a response from Mary. This highlights her restricted view that leaves her in tears instead of making her a witness.[13] The question also suggests that she should not be crying; there is no reason to do so. This prepares the reader for what follows: it intensifies the revelation to her of Jesus as the Risen One (20:14–17).[14] In the narrative, the function of the angels is thus limited to rhetorically highlighting Mary's misunderstanding, or lack of understanding, and emphasizing the revelation of Jesus. This indicates to the reader that their erstwhile function as divine messengers has no place here, since the task of explaining the empty tomb to humans does not devolve upon the angels – instead, they indirectly reveal to Mary that it is Jesus who truly reveals.[15]

Of course, this function of the two angels does correspond to some degree with the reference to the angel in 12:29, where the allusion to an angel also highlights misunderstanding and emphasizes the revelation by Jesus. In both cases, it is Jesus who reveals the truth that clears up the misunderstanding. The words of the angels can only point to the source of that truth.

---

[10] Cf. the Synoptic Gospels, where the angels have a revelatory function – a common perception regarding angels in ancient times. See D. Francis Watson, "Angels in the New Testament," *ABD* 1:254; Tuschling, *Angels*, 81–84; Beasley-Murray, *John*, 374.

[11] There is no ground for the thesis of Schnackenburg, *John*, 3:316, that the Johannine source originally did not contain the reference to the angels, but that it was added by the editor, who was then obliged to omit the Easter revelation of the angels (see the Synoptic Gospels).

[12] Schnackenburg, *John*, 3:316.

[13] So also Nicklas, *Angels*, 304.

[14] Schnackenburg, *John*, 3:315–16. Lindars, *John*, 604–05, contends that the true message of the angels was omitted for the sake of the climax in v. 17.

[15] Nicklas, *Angels*, 303–4.

In conclusion, the identity of the angels, as characters, could be described as that of heavenly beings who identify the place of Jesus' burial as an area of divine significance. They thereby serve as witnesses of the divine event that caused the empty tomb, marking heavenly or divine presence. They interact with Mary, in preparation for her revelatory meeting with the living Jesus whom she seeks among the dead. The angels are not complex characters at all. Their relative inactivity – sitting in the empty tomb and simply uttering three words – minimizes their role in favour of the overwhelming presence of the character of Jesus as the true revealer (1:18).

The Sons of Zebedee and Two Other Disciples: Two Pairs of Puzzling Acquaintances in the Johannine Dénouement

Christos Karakolis

In the Fourth Gospel's last chapter (21:2) the implied reader finds for the first and last time a reference to the sons of Zebedee followed by a reference to two other unnamed and thus unknown disciples. Although the information about these mysterious characters is minimal, there is still a certain amount of information to be extracted from the immediate context of 21:2, as well as from the Gospel narrative as a whole. This information will help us to understand the position, the function, and the traits, and even make some assumptions about the actual identity of these characters. To this end we will employ a narratological approach with an emphasis on characterization and on reader-response criticism.

The "Sons of Zebedee"

The first question related to the collective character[1] of the "sons of Zebedee" in John 21:2 that has to be answered is about its classification. Since they do not appear anywhere else in the Johannine narrative and they lack even the slightest active role in the story of the Gospel, they have to be classified as background characters or even as walk-ons.[2]

Nevertheless there are some interesting narrative elements that do connect them with the Johannine story. The sons of Zebedee are in the company of five other disciples of Jesus: Simon Peter, Thomas and Nathanael, as well as the two additional unnamed disciples.[3] All these disciples are not in Jerusalem

---

[1] See on the term Daniel Marguerat and Yvan Bourquin, *How to Read Bible Stories: An Introduction to Narrative Criticism* (London: SCM, 1999), 60.

[2] See on the term James L. Resseguie, *Narrative Criticism of the New Testament: An Introduction* (Grand Rapids, Mich.: Baker, 2005), 125; Sönke Finnern, *Narratologie und biblische Exegese: Eine integrative Methode der Erzählanalyse und ihr Ertrag am Beispiel von Matthäus 28* (WUNT II/285; Tübingen: Mohr Siebeck, 2010), 148.

[3] Joseph of Arimathea mentioned in 19:38 is a high official, a detail made clear by the fact that he can speak directly to Pilate in order to ask for the body of Jesus. Being also apparently an inhabitant of Jerusalem he should not be considered as being one of the seven disciples at the shore of the Galilean sea in ch. 21.

any more, as is the case in the previous chapter. They are now in Galilee, which is home to at least some of them, at the shore of the Galilean sea. Up to this point in the Johannine narrative the narrator has never mentioned that some of the disciples are fishermen,[4] a basic piece of information in the Synoptic tradition.[5] However, this information can be inferred from 21:3, in which Simon announces to the rest of the disciples that he is going fishing. All of them spontaneously agree to follow him and fish all night long (21:3–4). This information reveals in an indirect way that all disciples present, including the sons of Zebedee, share a fisherman's experience, although it is not clear whether this is their actual profession. Only thus can their spontaneous response be explained, a response in which everyone in the group immediately agrees to follow Peter in a nighttime fishing expedition on a rather unpredictable and dangerous lake.[6] A man without fishing experience would not have followed so willingly. Indeed if such a man wanted to join the group, the others may have rejected him, since his inexperience may have proved an obstacle to their success or even a potential threat to their safe return.

Thus, since the sons of Zebedee appear to have sufficient experience to embark on a fishing trip at night using a net on a fishing boat, they are likely considered by the implied author to be Galileans and part of the disciples' subgroup that travelled from Jerusalem to Galilee after the resurrection.[7]

On the basis of the information provided in the Gospel narrative, it should be taken for granted that the sons of Zebedee follow Jesus too throughout his travels, listen to his teaching, and witness his signs. They belong to the disciples who were not scandalized (6:60–71), listening to Jesus' words about eating his flesh and drinking his blood (6:48–58) and, therefore, do not abandon him (6:66). They are among those whose feet Jesus washed during the last supper (13:3–11) and who listened to his farewell discourse (13:31–16:33) and his last prayer (17:1–26). Along with the other disciples, they encounter the resurrected Jesus in Jerusalem, and receive the Holy Spirit, as well as the power over human sin (20:19–23). Their situation in chapter 21 is still a pre-missionary one. The disciples, including the sons of Zebedee, are gathered, but not occupied. They seem to be just waiting for another appearance of the "Lord" (cf.

---

[4] This could be deduced by the implied reader from the story in 6:16–21.

[5] Cf. Matt 4:18–22; Mark 1:16–20; Luke 5:1–11. Even the story of the call of the disciples in John is located in Bethany beyond the Jordan (1:28) and thus disassociated from Galilee and from anything that has to do with fishing.

[6] The unpredictability of the weather on the Galilean sea is witnessed to in the narrative world of John in 6:16–21. There it is implied that at least some of the disciples have an experience of navigating the sea, since they trust themselves to navigate late in the evening to the opposite shore. However, they are obviously not able to accurately predict the bad weather, as otherwise they would not have started this journey in the first place.

[7] In the Johannine narrative world the only body of water large enough for fishing on a fishing boat is the sea of Galilee.

21:7).[8] Lastly, like all other disciples, the sons of Zebedee also share the authority to take care of Jesus' sheep (cf. 21:15–17).[9]

This is quite a lot of information considering the fact that it refers to an unspecified number of men known only by their father's name. On the other hand, all of the experiences above are not unique to the sons of Zebedee. All of Jesus' disciples experienced these things, while the fishing trip described in ch. 21 was experienced by only the disciples of v. 2. Since however the sons of Zebedee do not stand out in any way earlier in the narrative compared to the other disciples, the question has to be raised with respect to why now, in this last chapter of the Gospel, they are expressly mentioned. Since unnamed characters – even disciples – are not an unusual occurrence in the Fourth Gospel, we have to assume that there must be a reason for mentioning the sons of Zebedee at this very point of the narrative.[10] Otherwise the implied author could have just mentioned any other number of anonymous disciples in addition to the three named ones and skipped mentioning the sons of Zebedee entirely.

Provided that indeed the reference to the sons of Zebedee bears some kind of narrative significance, their relationship with the other disciples of the list of 21:2 has to be more extensively considered. The three named disciples are the most complex or dynamic and round disciple characters in the Gospel (leaving aside the anonymous Beloved Disciple).[11] Peter often interacts with Jesus

---

[8] Had they already started their missionary activity (cf. 4:35–38), they would have dispersed and not gathered at the shore of the Galilean sea. On the other hand (contra Udo Schnelle, *Das Evangelium nach Johannes* [THKNT 4; Leipzig: Evangelische Verlagsanstalt, 1998], 314, 316), if they had just returned to their normal way of life, which in this case would be fishing (since any other kind of work would require them to sleep through the night and work during the day), the spontaneous dialogue between Peter and the other disciples in 21:3 would have been superfluous.

[9] This is a command that refers not only to pastoral care, but also or even mainly to missionary activity, since Jesus has other sheep too, sheep which need to be drawn to his own courtyard or sheepfold (10:16). In the dialogue between Jesus and Peter in 21:15–17, Peter does not receive a unique responsibility or office, as opposed to the other disciples. Due to his threefold denial he is simply restored to their state. This is evident by the structure of the dialogue, in which Jesus' command towards Peter to take care of his sheep depends upon Peter's declaration of love towards him. The love of the other disciples towards Jesus is never questioned and, therefore, their responsibility for Jesus' sheep does not have to be made explicit; contra Schnelle, *Evangelium*, 315. See the relevant discussion in George R. Beasley-Murray, *John* (2d ed.; WBC 36; Nashville: Nelson, 1999), 405–407.

[10] In ch. 1, one of the first two disciples remains anonymous (1:37, 40). The disciple who is acquainted with the high priest is also not mentioned by name (18:15–16). The Beloved Disciple is a further case of anonymity (13:23–26; 19:26–27; 20:2–8; 21:7, 20–24), although a special one.

[11] The Beloved Disciple is a special case, as he is identified with the author of the Gospel (21:24; cf. 19:35). As such he is at the same time a character of the narrative, the narrator, and a person who is supposed to be shaping the narrative from the outside. This explains his paradigmatic character. Cf. R. Alan Culpepper, *Anatomy of the Fourth Gospel: A Study in Literary Design* (Philadelphia: Fortress, 1983), 121–23.

demonstrating an inner development and complex character traits. He represents all other disciples by giving a confession to the uniqueness of Jesus (6:68–69) and declares his deep respect and love for his master, for whom he will willingly die (13:37). He is one of the two disciples who follow Jesus to his Jewish trial (18:15). On the other hand, he denies Jesus three times (18:17, 25–27), and he has to be reinstated by Jesus himself as a "shepherd" to take care of Jesus' "sheep" after having to declare his love for Jesus no less than three times (21:15–17). Similarly, Thomas would rather die alongside Jesus – although he does not understand why – than not follow him (11:16). After the resurrection he refuses to believe until he sees and touches Jesus (20:25). When he does see him, however, he offers the most theologically loaded confession in the Fourth Gospel (20:28). Nathanael is also wary at first about Jesus of Nazareth (1:46) who is presented to him by Philip as being the one prophesied by the law and the prophets (1:45). Only when Jesus interacts with him does Nathanael believe, whereupon he makes an impressive messianic confession of faith in Jesus (1:49).

It is striking that the three named disciples of 21:2 are the only disciples to have made a confession of faith referring directly to Jesus. According to Peter, Jesus speaks words of life and he is the Holy One of God (6:68–69). Thomas recognizes Jesus as his "Lord" and his "God" (20:28). Nathanael confesses that Jesus is the Son of God and the king of Israel (1:49). On the other hand, Jesus also addresses each of them with words carrying great narrative and theological weight. Simon receives from Jesus the name Peter and thus a renewed identity (1:42). In the end of the narrative he is reinstated and given the responsibility to take care of Jesus' sheep (21:15–17). Thomas is recognized by Jesus as a true believer, even if he had to see first in order to believe (20:27, 29). Nathanael is said to be a true Israelite without deceit (1:47) and is promised that he will see more than what he has already witnessed (1:50).

On the other hand, it is notable that Andrew and Philip are not mentioned, at least by name,[12] in the disciples' list of 21:2, although Andrew is the brother of Simon and both Andrew and Philip come from the same Galilean city – Bethsaida (1:44). Moreover, Andrew is obviously also a fisherman according to the indirect information about his brother Simon in 21:3–11.[13] Nevertheless, from a narratological point of view Andrew and Philip are rather flat characters compared to Peter, Thomas, and Nathanael. Readers do not have access to their inner life and do not see any development in their character in the Johan-

---

[12] Unless they would be identified with the two unnamed disciples referred to in the end of the list of 21:2.

[13] In rural antiquity brothers usually practiced the profession of their family; cf. Miriam Peskowitz, "Family/ies in Antiquity: Evidence from Tannaitic Literature and Roman Galilean Architecture," in *The Jewish Family in Antiquity* (ed. Shaye J. D. Cohen; Brown Judaic Studies 289; Atlanta: Scholars, 1993), 9–36 (28–34).

nine narrative. They are not presented as having ups and downs with regard to their faith in Jesus. Their relationship with Jesus is flat, expected and mainly limited to their role as those who introduce other characters to him.[14] Even the wish of Philip that Jesus show the Father to the disciples (14:8) is not a sign of character development. Philip's wish is only used as the occasion for Jesus to say that anybody who has seen him, has also seen his Father.[15]

According to our analysis so far it would seem that from a narratological point of view there is not much in common between the first three absolutely round and dynamic characters of the list of 21:2 and the sons of Zebedee about whom there is no information whatsoever except for what is valid for other disciples too. While Andrew and Philip are rather flat characters, the sons of Zebedee are walk-ons staying in the background and not having any active role in the narrative.

It is interesting however that the list of 21:2 seems to have an inner logic in the succession of the disciples it contains. First Simon Peter is mentioned by both his initial name and the one given to him by Jesus. He is the most round and dynamic disciple in the Gospel, the most prominent of the named disciples. Thomas and Nathanael, also two round characters, but not of Peter's prominence, follow next. Thomas is mentioned also by his Greek name, Didymus. In the case of Nathanael his city of origin, Cana, is mentioned. This additional information gives to the three named disciples of 21:2 an official character. Then follow the sons of Zebedee, disciples that are not mentioned by their own name, but only by the name of their father (which is as close to actually naming them as can be). Lastly, two other unnamed and thus totally unknown disciples complete the list. From a narratological point of view the list then moves from the most important to the most unimportant characters, from the most distinctive to the most colorless.

It is not common in the Gospel of John that a father's name is mentioned. Jesus' father Joseph is mentioned by Philip (1:45), as well as by the Galilean crowd (6:42). Simon Peter's father's name, John, is only mentioned once by Jesus himself during their first encounter (1:42) and then three more times in their final encounter (21:15-17). Simon happens to be the name of the father of Judas Iscariot and is only mentioned by the narrator (6:71; 13:2, 26). These three characters are crucial for the story. Jesus is obviously the protagonist of the story. Simon Peter is the most round disciple character with the possible exception of the Beloved Disciple. He is willing to fight (cf. 18:10) and die (13:37) for Jesus, but finally denies him out of fear (18:17, 25-27). In the end he is restored after declaring his love for him (21:15-17). Judas, on the other

---

[14] Andrew introduces his own brother Peter (1:40-42), as well as the child with the five loaves and the two fish to Jesus (6:8-9). Philip, on the other hand, introduces Nathanael (1:45-47), while both of them bring the Greeks to Jesus (12:20-22).

[15] The same applies also to the question of Judas (not Iscariot) in 14:22.

hand, is instrumental for the plot as a negative example of unbelief (cf. 6:71; 12:4–6), and the character who triggers Jesus' passion by betraying him (13:2, 26–30; 18:2–5).[16] Since no other fathers are mentioned by name in the Gospel, this character trait is significant, reserved for only a few.

In 21:2, however, a father's name is also used for the sons of Zebedee and in a peculiar and unique way within the Johannine narrative. There is no other case in the Fourth Gospel where only a father's name, not the actual name of a character is mentioned. Another peculiarity consists in that the word "sons" (υἱοί) is not used at all, but only implied by a unique syntactic feature within the Fourth Gospel: in the syntactic connection of two nouns with each other (the first one being in the nominative and the second one in the genitive) the governing noun in the nominative is omitted and only the dependent noun in the genitive as well as the two articles actually remain (οἱ [υἱοὶ] τοῦ Ζεβεδαίου).[17] A third peculiarity is that in our case no explanatory sentence or expression is used about who the sons of Zebedee actually are, while this is what we normally find in the Johannine narrative when named characters are introduced.[18] On the basis of these oddities we are forced to conclude that the implied author considers the sons of Zebedee to be well-known personalities to the implied readers, readers who are therefore expected to fill in missing pieces of information from their own knowledge base, whatever that might be.

According to James Resseguie, an implied reader is "thoroughly familiar with the repertoire of literary, historical, social, linguistic, and cultural assumptions of the authorial audience – that is the audience the author has in mind when he or she writes the work. This reader is guided by the clues of the text and reads the text as the implied author intended."[19] This leads us to question

---

[16] Culpepper, *Anatomy of the Fourth Gospel*, 124–25.

[17] The expression οἱ ἐν τοῖς μνημείοις (5:28) is not an exact parallel because a participle (and not a noun) is omitted (οἱ [ὄντες] ἐν τοῖς μνημείοις). The difference is that such a participle can be easily added by the reader, while an expression with an omitted noun is more ambivalent and therefore only used when the omitted noun is considered to be well known. In our case οἱ τοῦ Ζεβεδαίου could take on also other meanings, such as the friends, the soldiers, the slaves, the servants, the relatives and so on, of Zebedee. As readers of the Gospel we are absolutely certain that the reference is to the *sons* of Zebedee not due to intratextual, but to intertextual evidence derived from the Synoptic tradition. See for this grammatical phenomenon the excellent observation of Raphael Kühner, *Grammatik der griechischen Sprache* (2 vols.; 2d ed.; Hannover: Hahnsche Hofbuchhandlung, 1870), 285–86: "Oft hängt das Verständnis des Genitivs von historischer Kenntnis ab, so z. B. wenn eine Abstammung ausgedrückt wird." Kühner cites examples, among others from Homer, *Il.* 2,527 (Ὀϊλῆος [υἱὸς] ταχὺς Αἴας); Sophocles, *Phil.* 943 (ἱερὰ λαβὼν τοῦ Ζηνὸς Ἡρακλέους); *El.* 694 (Ὀρέστης τοῦ Ἀγαμέμνονος); *Aj.* 172 (Διὸς Ἄρτεμις), 450 (ἡ Διὸς γοργῶπις ἀδάματος θεά); Herodotus, *Hist.* 3,60 (Εὐπαλῖνος Ναυστρόφου).

[18] Cf. 1:6–8, 40, 42, 44, 47; 3:1; 6:71; 11:1–2, 16, 49; 14:22; 18:10, 13, 40; 19:38. Pilate (in 18:29) forms an exception to this rule, and is worthy of further examination from a narratological point of view.

[19] Resseguie, *Narrative Criticism*, 32.

what exactly the implied reader was meant to understand from the implied author's reference to the sons of Zebedee.

The implied reader should identify the Beloved Disciple, who makes his appearance later on in the narrative of this chapter, with either one of the sons of Zebedee or with one of the two unnamed disciples of 21:2. However, what seems like a riddle to the modern reader of the Gospel would probably have been obvious to the implied readers of the Gospel. According to Resseguie's reconstruction above, implied readers bring to the narrative their own knowledge of the issue at hand which may be beyond the content of the Gospel. We can at least be certain that implied readers understood that οἱ τοῦ Ζεβεδαίου indeed meant the sons of Zebedee. Otherwise the implied author would have written the word υἱοί. We can also safely conclude, therefore, that the implied readers knew the individual names of the sons of Zebedee.[20] We cannot be sure where they derived this knowledge from, but we can be certain that the implied author trusts them to know what goes unmentioned, as otherwise the implied author would probably have mentioned it. The tradition about the two sons of Zebedee and about the great importance of one of them, namely John, is very broadly witnessed in the New Testament and should be assumed to be widely known at the end of the first century C. E. when the Gospel of John was presumably written.[21]

Why then isn't there any mention of the names of the two sons of Zebedee within the Fourth Gospel? And why are they only mentioned as such at the end of the Gospel? The implied reader should be able to make all necessary connections and draw the relevant conclusions. While on the one hand the Beloved Disciple remains mysteriously unnamed, on the other hand the actual names of the sons of Zebedee are never mentioned. The Beloved Disciple is very close to Jesus and a person that is often compared to Peter and found to have a superior faith and a closer relationship to Jesus than Peter has.[22] From the perspective of the implied reader this person should therefore be a most significant apostle and not an unknown and insignificant character. From an historical point of view John of Zebedee was such a person.[23] Although this kind of argumentation ignores some important information from an historical

---

[20] Cf. Klaus Wengst, *Das Johannesevangelium: 2. Teilband: Kapitel 11–21* (TKNT 4; Stuttgart: Kohlhammer, 2001), 311; Hartwig Thyen, *Das Johannesevangelium* (HNT 6; Tübingen: Mohr Siebeck, 2005), 781.

[21] See a summary of the relevant discussion in Carl R. Holladay, *A Critical Introduction to the New Testament: Interpreting the Message and Meaning of Jesus Christ* (Nashville: Abingdon, 2005), 279.

[22] Cf. 13:23–26; 20:2–8; 21:7, 20–23, and perhaps also 18:15–16.

[23] Cf. Donald Guthrie, *New Testament Introduction* (3d ed.; London: InterVarsity, 1970), 245–49. For a detailed presentation of the relevant ancient Christian traditions, see R. Alan Culpepper, *John, the Son of Zebedee: The Life of A Legend* (Studies on Personalities of the New Testament; Columbia, SC: South Carolina University Press, 1994), 107–244.

point of view,[24] it does, however, make sense from the point of view of the interaction between the implied author and the implied reader. The implied reader should be able to draw the above conclusions, although these were perhaps not always drawn by real historical readers of the Fourth Gospel.

We cannot be sure about what the real author(s) of chapter 21 or – in case this chapter comes from the same author(s) as the rest of the Gospel – the real author of the Fourth Gospel wanted real historical readers to understand. This has to remain an open question. However, the implied reader could very well interpret the clue about the sons of Zebedee in a way that pointed to John of Zebedee as the unnamed Beloved Disciple of Jesus.[25]

If this assumption is correct, then the reference to the sons of Zebedee only at the end of the Gospel can be better explained from a narratological point of view. The Beloved Disciple has to remain obscure and only known to the implied reader. This is a strategy that the implied author of the Gospel chooses to follow from the beginning of the Gospel to its end. However, this does not mean that no traces are left for the implied reader to follow so as to ascertain the hidden identity of the Beloved Disciple. The anonymity of the Beloved Disciple and the lack of reference to John of Zebedee in the Gospel narrative as a whole is such a trace. This trace is reinforced by the reference to the sons of Zebedee in ch. 21. This is the first (and last) time in the Gospel that a disciples' list is utilized, even if only seven disciples are contained in it. The Beloved Disciple is part of this list and it is the first time that the sons of Zebedee are mentioned. James and John of Zebedee are absent from the preceding narrative, while Peter and Andrew of "John" (cf. 1:40–42) are present in the Gospel's story and influence the plot right from the beginning. The reference to the sons of Zebedee would in this sense bring balance to the antagonism between Peter and the Beloved Disciple. If the Beloved Disciple is indeed identified with John of Zebedee, then he also has a brother just like Peter, and his brother is also here referred to, if only by his father's name. Furthermore, mentioning the father's name of the Beloved Disciple adds to the significance of the Beloved Disciple in the Fourth Gospel's narrative.

Simon Peter is always mentioned in the Fourth Gospel by one of his two names or by both of them at the same time (namely his birth name and his second name, which was attributed to him by Jesus himself; 1:42). The Beloved Disciple is not identified by his name, but by his relationship to Jesus. This gives to the Beloved Disciple a special quality that we can only find in one other person in the Johannine narrative, namely the Mother of Jesus (2:3, 5,

---

[24] See summaries of the relevant discussion in Jean Zumstein, "L'Évangile selon Jean," in *Introduction au Nouveau Testament: Son histoire, son écriture, sa théologie* (ed. Daniel Marguerat; Le Monde de la Bible 41; Geneve: Labor et Fides, 2000), 362–63; Udo Schnelle, *Einleitung in das Neue Testament* (7th ed.; Göttingen: Vandenhoeck & Ruprecht, 2011), 505–11.

[25] Cf. Thyen, *Johannesevangelium*, 782.

12; 19:25–27), who is also identified not by her name, but by her relationship to Jesus. The disciple whom Jesus loved and the Mother of Jesus are not just ways to hide their real names. They have to be more than mere names, namely titles of honor.[26] By keeping the anonymity of the Beloved Disciple until the end of the narrative the implied author emphasizes the importance of his title. By naming him in 21:2 as a son of his father and not by his actual name the implied author remains faithful to this narrative strategy while at the same time giving an important hint about his identity.

In case the mysterious person of the Beloved Disciple can indeed be identified as John of Zebedee, the mention of his father's name and the implication that he has a brother provide the implied reader with proof that he was a real person who also existed outside of the narrative. This would be one more of the traces that can be found in the Fourth Gospel, witnessing to the historical existence of the Beloved Disciple.

"Two Others of His Disciples"

Notwithstanding the argument above, one cannot exclude the possibility of the implied reader identifying the Beloved Disciple with one of the two unnamed disciples referred to at the end of the list of 21:2.[27] The first question that has to be dealt with in this regard is why the implied author included two unnamed disciples at this final point of the Gospel in the first place. One obvious answer would be to include the Beloved Disciple among them, in case he is not to be understood by the implied reader as one of Zebedee's sons. The fact that the Beloved Disciple remains unnamed throughout the Gospel could lead the implied reader to the conclusion that he is one of the two unnamed disciples in the end of the list of 21:2. There are also some narrative details that could be understood as hints in this direction. One of them is the reference in the first chapter to the two disciples of John the Baptist who follow Jesus. One of these disciples is identified as Andrew, while the other one remains unnamed. This unknown disciple could very well be identified with the Beloved Disciple. In fact there does not seem to be any other plausible reason for this reference at this point of the narrative unless it is indeed a first concealed appearance of the Beloved Disciple.[28]

---

[26] Cf. a similar approach in William S. Kurz, "The Beloved Disciple and Implied Readers," *BTB* 19 (1989): 100–107 (101).

[27] Cf. Barnabas Lindars, *The Gospel of John* (NCB; London: Oliphants, 1972), 624–25; Wengst, *Johannesevangelium*, 311; Francis J. Moloney, *The Gospel of John* (SP 4; Collegeville, Minn.: Liturgical Press, 1998), 548–49.

[28] See the detailed argumentation of Michael Theobald, "Der Jünger, den Jesus liebte: Beobachtungen zum narrativen Konzept der johanneischen Redaktion," in *Frühes Christentum*

However, this does not necessarily mean that this unknown disciple should be understood as one of the two unnamed disciples of 21:2. Alternately, he could be one of the two sons of Zebedee. In this regard, the fact that the Beloved Disciple is mentioned as ὁ ἄλλος μαθητής (20:2–4, 8 and perhaps also 18:15–16[29]) is not an argument in favor of the Beloved Disciple's being one of the ἄλλοι ἐκ τῶν μαθητῶν αὐτοῦ δύο (21:2). Ὁ ἄλλος μαθητής is actually a terminus technicus referring to the Beloved Disciple as a specific round character, repeatedly mentioned in the Gospel narrative, and well-known to the implied reader, although unnamed. In an analogous way with ὁ μαθητὴς ὃν ἠγάπα ὁ Ἰησοῦς, the expression ὁ ἄλλος μαθητής is a means for covering the real identity of the Beloved Disciple, and referring to him at the same time. However, the mention of two other disciples in 21:2 is obviously no terminus technicus, as the Fourth Gospel nowhere else refers to two unnamed disciples as a pair. Even in the reference in 1:37 one of the two disciples is identified a little later as Andrew (1:40). Furthermore, there is no definite article in the case of 21:2, which would concretize the reference, as is the case with ὁ ἄλλος μαθητής in 20:2–4, 8. Lastly, there are no grammatical, syntactical or lexical peculiarities in the reference to the "two other" unnamed disciples that would call for the special attention of the implied reader, nothing that would force the implied reader to ascertain their significance and as a second step to identify one of them with the Beloved Disciple. Why then are these two unnamed disciples mentioned in the list of 21:2 in the first place? It could well be that they are needed in order for the disciples present in ch. 21 to reach the number seven.

In the Gospel of John the number seven plays an undeniable symbolic role:[30] the Johannine story is inititiated by a period of action that lasts seven days.[31] On a symbolic level there is a connection between these seven days and the seven days of creation implied in the prologue of the Gospel (cf. 1:1–3). While the time after this first week is not counted any more by days, but by Jewish festivals, seven days before Jesus' resurrection, time once again starts being counted by days (12:1).[32] Meanwhile, seven of Jesus' signs are narrated

---

(ed. Hermann Lichtenberger; vol. 3 of *Geschichte – Tradition – Reflexion: Festschrift für Martin Hengel zum 70. Geburtstag*; ed. Hubert Cancik et al.; Tübingen: Mohr Siebeck, 1996), 219–55, (220–22).

[29] Theobald, "Der Jünger, den Jesus liebte," 222–24.

[30] See the relevant discussion in Craig R. Koester, *Symbolism in the Fourth Gospel: Meaning, Mystery, Community* (2d ed.; Minneapolis: Fortress, 2003), 311–16.

[31] Cf. 1:29, 35, 43; 2:1, as well as T. Barrosse, "The Seven Days of the New Creation in St. John's Gospel," *CBQ* 21 (1959): 507–16; Donald A. Carson, *The Gospel According to John* (Grand Rapids, Mich.: Eerdmans, 1991), 167–68.

[32] Six days before the Passover in John means seven days before the resurrection, since the Passover in John is on the Sabbath (19:31), the Passion takes place on the preparation day (19:14) and the resurrection on the first weekday (20:1).

in a detailed way, although the implied reader becomes aware that there were many more signs performed by him.[33] Accordingly, there are seven groups of *ego-eimi* sayings in the Gospel narrative.[34] Five loaves of bread and two fish, a total of seven, is all that is needed for Jesus to feed a multitude of 5000 men (6:9-10). It is obvious that the number seven is important to the Johannine narrative as the number of "representative completeness."[35] However, the number twelve can take a similar meaning when referring to the number of the disciples closest to Jesus (6:67), to the number of the baskets with remnants gathered after the multiplication of the loaves and the fish (6:13), or even to the number of hours of daylight (11:9).[36] Why then are there only seven disciples at the shore of the Galilean sea?

It seems that from the end of ch. 6 onwards there are no disciples left who indeed follow Jesus other than the twelve (6:60-71).[37] In the narrative after Jesus' long sermon about the bread from heaven, "many of his disciples" were scandalized and did not walk with him any more (6:66). When Jesus asked the twelve if they also wanted to leave him (6:67), they affirmed their desire to stay through Peter's confession (6:68-69). The implied reader could very well deduce from this narrative that the twelve are the only disciples who continued to follow, while all the others left him, since Jesus does not turn to the remaining disciples in general, but specifically to the twelve (6:67). Had more disciples than the twelve remained close to Jesus, it would not have made any sense for Jesus to exclusively address the twelve, considering the fact that the twelve have not been mentioned at all up to this point in the Johannine narrative. One could go so far as to see at this point the constitution of the circle of the twelve in the Johannine narrative, as being the only disciples who continue to follow Jesus after ch. 6. This way of understanding the end of that chapter is supported by the evidence of 20:24. There, Thomas is presented as being one of the twelve, although he was absent, when the resurrected Jesus appeared to them. Since up to this point the implied author speaks about the disciples in general, while in 20:24 identifying the remaining disciples as the twelve, the implied reader could draw the conclusion that in the Johannine narrative after

---

[33] Cf. 2:23; 3:2; 5:36; 6:2; 7:31; 10:25, 32, 37-38; 11:47; 12:37; 14:10-12; 15:24; 20:30.

[34] As classified by Koester, *Symbolism*, 312, fn. 20, concerning "bread (6:35, 51), light (8:12; 9:5), door (10:7, 9), shepherd (10:11, 14), resurrection and life (11:25), way, truth, and life (14:6), and the vine (15:1, 5)."

[35] K. H. Rengstorf, "ἑπτά, ἑπτάκις ...," *TWNT* 2:624, notes about the symbolical meaning of the number seven in the Bible and its religious environment: "... daß sich mit der Sieben jeweils die Vorstellung eines geschlossenen und vollkommenen Ganzen verknüpft und sie also die gegebene Größe ist, wenn man ein derartiges Ganzes kurz und prägnant zum Ausdruck bringen will. Die Siebenzahl trägt somit den Charakter der Totalität, und zwar den der von Gott gewollten und geordneten Totalität."

[36] Cf. K. H. Rengstorf, "δώδεκα ...," *TWNT* 2:321-28.

[37] Cf. Culpepper, *Anatomy of the Fourth Gospel*, 117.

the end of ch. 6 the "twelve" and the "disciples" are one and the same group. Joseph of Arimathaea is no exception to this rule. He is nothing more than a hidden disciple due to his fear of "the Jews" (19:38). This means that he does not follow Jesus in the first place and is, therefore, not taken into consideration in ch. 6 and 20.[38]

In this context it is noteworthy that reference to the twelve in ch. 20 is only an indirect one, primarily referring to a character trait of Thomas and only secondarily playing the role of an attribute of the disciples as a group that witnessed the resurrected Jesus. This is due to the fact that the "twelve" disciples are not really twelve anymore, since they now miss Judas Iscariot. They are eleven.[39] Thus, the significant number twelve is no longer accurate, while the actual number of the disciples, namely eleven, does not have any symbolic meaning whatsoever. The implied author is obviously not interested in reconstituting the number twelve after Jesus' resurrection, as is the case for instance in the narrative of Acts (1:16–26). A possible further step would be for the implied author to reduce the number of the disciples to the next symbolically loaded number – seven. In this light, the two unnamed disciples at the end of the list of 21:2 would seem to fulfill one basic narrative function, namely to complete the disciples' list in such a way that their number is seven.[40]

It is noteworthy that in the Johannine narrative the implied reader never learns all the names of the twelve disciples. The only names the implied reader encounters are Andrew, Simon Peter, Philip, Nathanael, Thomas, Judas and Judas Iscariot. These are interestingly enough seven names. Of these seven disciples only three are mentioned by name in 21:2. The sons of Zebedee are an addition that raises the number of the disciples of 21:2 to five. However, for reaching the number seven the implied author needs two more disciples. It seems to be a conscious choice not to mention the names of these two disciples. However, since Peter and Nathanael are mentioned at the beginning of the list, the implied reader could infer that the two unnamed disciples at the end of the list are actually Andrew and Philip, the brother of Peter and the friend of Nathanael respectively.[41] These two disciples are well-known in the

---

[38] In ch. 20 the "twelve" disciples are hidden in a closed house because of their fear of "the Jews." On the other hand, Joseph was a hidden disciple because of his fear of "the Jews." In the first case the hiding of the twelve is temporary and begins after Jesus' arrest. In the second case it is a permanent character trait of Joseph.

[39] Cf. Raymond E. Brown, *The Gospel according to John (xiii–xxi)* (AB; Garden City, N. Y.: Doubleday, 1970), 1067.

[40] Cf. Rudolf Schnackenburg, *Das Johannesevangelium: 3. Teil: Kommentar zu Kapitel 13–21* (HTKNT IV; Freiburg: Herder, 1975) 420; Jean Zumstein, *L'Évangile selon Saint Jean (13–21)* (Commentaire du Nouveau Testament 2/4b; Genève: Labor et Fides, 2007), 305; Thyen, *Johannesevangelium*, 781.

[41] Cf. Brown, *Gospel*, 1068; contra Christian Dietzfelbinger, *Das Evangelium nach Johannes* (ZBK 4; Zürich: Theologischer Verlag, 2001), 352.

preceding narrative (1:40, 44), form a distinct narrative pair of characters in two separate scenes (6:5-10; 12:20-22), come from the Galilean Bethsaida, and could at least be expected by the implied reader to belong to the seven disciples who are at the shore of the Galilean sea and share a fishermen's experience. In this case the inclusio between the first and last chapter of John with regard to the disciples mentioned would become even stronger.

How then can the anonymity of the two last disciples of 21:2 be explained if they are indeed meant to be Andrew and Philip? A possible answer is that in giving the names of Andrew and Philip the implied author would disorient the implied reader, making it difficult to make the right connections and to draw the right conclusions from the preceding narratives: the implied reader is supposed to connect the three named disciples with their three impressive confessions of faith, addressed directly to Jesus, as a result of their character development. This is not the case with Andrew and Philip who are, as already mentioned, rather flat characters and therefore uninteresting for the story's dénouement. If, on the other hand, the implied reader could guess that Andrew and Philip are hidden behind the reference of the last two unnamed disciples, then the unnamed disciple of ch. 1 could be more strongly identified with one of the two sons of Zebedee mentioned in 21:2.

Provided that the above line of thinking is indeed plausible, the implied reader would end up with a new set of seven, post-resurrection, disciples. In this case the sons of Zebedee would replace Judas Iscariot the betrayer of Jesus, as well as the other Judas who is mentioned only once as a background character (14:22).

Conclusion

Summarizing the above, if we stick to the strictly narratological approach of the reference to the sons of Zebedee, we are bound to admit that their actual role in the narrative is next to nothing. Even if we may deduce a couple of character features from the rest of the Gospel narrative, these features are collective disciple traits and not particular traits of the sons of Zebedee. In this case the sons of Zebedee have to be classified as walk-ons with no inner life or development in the story of the Gospel.

However, a couple of peculiarities in the way these characters are mentioned lead us to the conclusion that their reference could be a clue for implied readers who should combine their own information with the text's in order to be able to decode their significance for the narrative. The implied readers would then possibly be led to the conclusion that Zebedee is the father of the Beloved Disciple who also has a brother. In this case the sons of Zebedee should not be classified as being walk-ons. At least one of them, the Beloved

Disciple, is both a round and a dynamic character within the narrative, as well as a character who from the outside shapes the narrative, according to the information provided by the narrator (21:24).

On the other hand, the two unnamed disciples at the end of 21:2 are also walk-ons who seem only to play the role of filling out the symbolically significant number seven with reference to the disciples' list. In case the implied reader would identify one of them with the Beloved Disciple, mentioning them would be crucial. However, there are no conclusive intratextual or intertextual elements that would plausibly lead the implied reader to this verdict. Although such an interpretation remains possible the odds are in favor of the identification of the Beloved Disciple with one of the sons of Zebedee.

This conclusion is of course not to be confused with the intentions of the real historical author and the understanding of the real historical readership. From that perspective the judgments of this present study are rather irrelevant.

List of Contributors

Paul N. Anderson (Professor of Biblical and Quaker Studies, George Fox University)
Mark Appold (Campus Pastor and Associate Professor of Religion, Truman State University)
Harold W. Attridge (The Reverend Henry L. Slack Dean of Yale Divinity School and Lillian Claus Professor of New Testament)
Cornelis Bennema (Senior Lecturer in New Testament at Wales Evangelical School of Theology, UK and Academic Associate of the Research Institute for Theology, University of South Africa)
Helen K. Bond (Senior Lecturer in New Testament, University of Edinburgh)
Martinus C. de Boer (Emeritus Professor of New Testament, VU University)
Sherri Brown (Assistant Professor of New Testament, Niagara University)
Jaime Clark-Soles (Associate Professor of New Testament, Perkins School of Theology, Southern Methodist University)
Mary L. Coloe (pbvm, Associate Professor, MCD University of Divinity and Honorary Fellow of the Australian Catholic University)
R. Alan Culpepper (Dean, McAfee School of Theology)
Steven A. Hunt (Professor of New Testament, Gordon College)
Susan E. Hylen (Associate Research Professor of New Testament, Candler School of Theology, Emory University)
Peter J. Judge (Associate Professor, Department of Philosophy & Religious Studies, Winthrop University)
Christos Karakolis (Associate Professor of New Testament, Faculty of Theology, University of Athens)
Chris Keith (Professor of New Testament and Early Christianity, and Director of the Centre for the Social-Scientific Study of the Bible, St. Mary's University College)
Edward W. Klink III (Associate Professor of New Testament, Talbot School of Theology, Biola University)
Michael Labahn (Professor of New Testament, Martin-Luther-University, Halle-Wittenberg, and Research Collaborator of North West University, South Africa)
Susanne Luther (Dr. theol., wiss. Mitarbeiterin, Protestant Faculty of Theology, Johannes Gutenberg-University of Mainz)
William John Lyons (Senior Lecturer in Biblical Interpretation, University of Bristol)

Gary T. Manning, Jr. (Associate Professor of New Testament, Talbot School of Theology, Biola University)
David L. Mathewson (Associate Professor of New Testament, Denver Seminary)
Mark A. Matson (Associate Professor of Bible, Milligan College)
J. Ramsey Michaels (Professor of Religious Studies Emeritus, Missouri State University)
Susan Miller (Tutor, University of Glasgow)
Matthew D. Montonini (PhD cand., New Testament Studies, Faculty of Theology, University of the Free State)
Joel Nolette (Research Assistant, Gordon College)
Gail R. O'Day (Dean, Divinity School, Wake Forest University)
Peter Phillips (Director of Research, CODEC Director of Research and Teaching Fellow in New Testament, St. John's College, Durham University)
Uta Poplutz (Professor of New Testament, Bergische University of Wuppertal)
Thomas Popp (Professor for Practical Theology, Lutheran University of Applied Sciences in Nürnberg; Privatdozent of New Testament, Martin-Luther-University, Halle-Wittenberg)
Andy M. Reimer (Sessional Lecturer, St. Mary's University College)
Adele Reinhartz (Professor, Department of Classics and Religious Studies, University of Ottawa)
James L. Resseguie (J. Russell Bucher Distinguished Professor of New Testament Emeritus, Winebrenner Theological Seminary)
Chelsea N. Revell (Research Assistant, Gordon College)
Dieter T. Roth (wiss. Mitarbeiter, Protestant Faculty of Theology, Johannes Gutenberg-University of Mainz and Research Associate of the University of Pretoria)
Christopher W. Skinner (Associate Professor of Religion, Mount Olive College)
Marianne Meye Thompson (George Eldon Ladd Professor of New Testament, Fuller Theological Seminary)
D. Francois Tolmie (Professor of New Testament, University of the Free State)
Derek Tovey (Theological Lecturer, The College of St. John the Evangelist; School of Theology, The University of Auckland)
Gilbert Van Belle (Professor, Research Unit Biblical Studies, Catholic University of Leuven)
Jan van der Watt (Professor of New Testament at the Faculty of Theology, Radboud University)
Catrin H. Williams (Senior Lecturer in New Testament Studies, University of Wales Trinity Saint David, Lampeter)
Ruben Zimmermann (Professor of New Testament at the Protestant Faculty of Theology, Johannes Gutenberg-University of Mainz and Research Associate of UNISA, South Africa)
Jean Zumstein (Emeritus Professor of New Testament, University of Zurich)

Index of References

Old Testament (including LXX)

Genesis
1–2	554
1–3	554
1:1	192, 210, 554
1:2–4	554
1:3–2:3	192
1:5	193, 554–55, 616
1:8	554
1:13	554
1:14	193–94
1:14–18	554
1:14–19	194
1:15	194
1:16	194
1:18	193–94
1:19	554
1:20–21	554
1:23	554
1:24	554
1:30	554
1:31	554
2	211–12
2:1–2	210
2:1–3	556, 616
2:2–3	554
2:3	210
2:4	554
2:7	193, 554, 556, 566
2:8	193, 555, 565
2:8–9	193, 554, 556
2:9	193, 211, 556, 565, 612
2:10	192, 554–56, 612–13
2:15	193
2:15–16	555
2:17	555
2:21–22	556
2:23	210–11, 556
2:24	555
2:25	555
3	26
3:1–3	555
3:3	556, 565
3:7	555
3:8	554–55
3:9–13	555
3:10–11	555
3:13	556
3:14	555
3:17	555
3:18	555
3:19	555, 566
3:20	210–11, 556
3:21	555
3:23–24	193, 555, 565
3:24	565–66
17:3	566
17:17	566
22	90, 610
22:3	610
22:5	610
22:6	609
22:19	610
24:11	271
27:35	198
29:2	271
32	199
32:28	198–99
32:30	199
34:13	198
37:30	358
38	290
50:2–3	480

Exodus
2:15	271
3:10–12	48
3:10–15	60
12:10	96, 605
12:46	96, 605, 615
14:31	218

15:24	249	22:28–29	287
16	86	24:1	286
16:2–12	249	24:1–4	286–87
16:7	218	25:5–6	283
17:3	86, 218	25:7–10	285
19	230–31	32:39	573
19–24	229		
19:8	229	Ruth	
19:11	229	3–4	283
19:16	230		
24	230	1 Samuel (1 Kingdoms)	
24:3	229	1:1	48
24:7	229	9:15–10:1	481
24:16	230	10:1	481
24:17	230	16:1	481
33:13	550	16:12–13	481
33:18	550		
38:6–26	283	1 Kings (3 Kingdoms)	
38:11	285	1:38–40	481
38:14	285	1:45	481
38:26	285	8:4–5	114
		17:8–24	316
Leviticus		17:17	316
19:2	265	17:18	316
20:10	413	17:20	316
21:7	287	17:20–21	316
21:14	287	17:21	316
		17:22	316
Numbers		17:23	316
9:12	605, 615		
14	86	2 Kings (4 Kingdoms)	
14:2	218	4:38	358
14:26–27	249	4:41	358
14:27	218	4:42–44	358
14:27–29	86	5:5–15	434
14:29	86	17:24	288
14:36	218		
19:11–22	285	Ezra	
		2:70	114
Deuteronomy		7:7	114
1:16	257	10:5	114
15:11	484		
17:4	257	Esther	
17:6	13	4:17	481
18:15–18	348	8:3	566
18:15–22	184		
19:15	413	Job	
19:16–18	257	1:20	392
21:22–23	614–15	3:1–19	285
22:13–19	287	28:22	366

Psalms

9:4	392
13	498
13:1–2	498
13:3	498
13:4	498
13:5	500
13:5–6	499
22:16	605
22:19	605
34:4	392
34:23	519
34:31	605
39:15	392
41:9	367
55:10	392
69:3	392
69:10	145
69 (68):22	603
77:66	392
82:6	92
118	399
128:5	392

Proverbs

5:15–18	274
15:11	366
27:20	366
31:10	287

Song of Solomon

4:12–15	274

Isaiah

6:8	48, 60
6:10	399
11:1	563
40–55	573
40:3	52, 112, 263
40:3–5	52
50:6	393
52:15	400
53:1	351
53:4	54
53:7	54
53:12	54
55:1	399
60:3	184

Jeremiah

22:22–23:8	571

Ezekiel

44:15	114

Daniel

2:46	392
11:30	478
13(LXX)	415
13:2	415
13:3	415
13:8–14	415
13:15–27	415
13:27	415
13:30	415
13:31	415
13:35	415

Joel

2:28–32	181

Micah

4:1–4	201

Zephaniah

3:15	83

Zechariah

3	201
3:6–10	563
3:9	201
3:10	201
6:9–15	563
6:12	201, 563
8:23	261
9:9	83, 399
9:9–10	350
11:6	570
12:10	605, 615
14	247
14:21	246

Malachi

3:3	265

Greek-Texts (LXX)

1 Maccabees
9:47   392

Sirach
25:26   286

Tobit
3:7–9   284
3:10–15   285

Wisdom
1:2   550

New Testament

Matthew
2:1   304
3:4   46
3:11   46
4:5–7   240
4:18   141
5:3   484
8:5–13   308
9:10–13   290
9:13   614
9:30   478
10:2   141
10:2–4   189
10:3   180, 243, 528, 552
10:17–20   179
11:5   484
11:9   46
11:19   290
12:7   614
13:37   310
13:54–58   238
13:55   243
14:3–9   481
14:13–21   146
14:26   217
15:32–39   146
16:18   142, 152
19:3–12   286
20:2   484
20:12   480
22:23–33   284
23:24   614
25   297
26:6–13   473, 481, 627
27:4–5   259
27:32   609
27:37   200
27:38   607, 611
27:44   607
27:55   612
27:55–56   620
27:56   627
27:57   649
27:57–60   649
27:60   65
27:61   627
28:1–10   627
28:5   635
28:9   555

Mark
1:4   46
1:6   46
1:14–15   56
1:16   141
1:16–20   141, 152
1:43   478
2:3–4   339
2:5   342
2:9   339
2:9–12   342
2:12   339
3:14   177
3:16–19   189
3:18   180, 243, 528, 552
5:22   566
5:43   338
6:1–6   238
6:2   255
6:3   243
6:4   304, 310
6:32–44   146
6:37   176, 184
6:45   176, 178
6:49   217
8:1–10   146

New Testament   683

8:22	176, 178
10:46	441
10:51	338
11:32	46
12:18–27	284
12:28–34	656
13:11	178
14:3–9	473, 627
14:32–42	478
14:47	160
14:66–67	576
15:21	609
15:26	200
15:27	607, 611
15:32	607
15:40	612, 627
15:40–41	620
15:42–46	649
15:43	649, 656
15:47–16:11	627
16:5	635

Luke

2:1–7	304
2:25	216
3:3	46
4:9–12	240
4:18	484
4:24	310
5:1–11	575
6:14	141, 180
6:14–16	189
6:15	528
6:16	552
6:20	484
7:1–10	308
7:28	264
7:36–50	290, 409, 473, 627
8:1–3	620
8:2	627
9:10–17	146
12:11–12	179
13:11	338
16:16	243
18:18	250
19:1–10	290
19:14	478
20:27–40	284
21:37	560
22:3	213
22:50	571, 577
23:13	304
23:26	609
23:32	607
23:33	611
23:38	200
23:39–43	607, 611
23:43	616
23:49	620
23:50–51	649, 656
23:50–53	649
24:4	635
24:12	555
27:1–11	627

John

1	76, 142, 146, 149, 154, 190–91, 196, 675
1–3	459
1–12	400, 505–06
1:1	49, 210, 254, 520
1:1–2	66, 400
1:1–3	672
1:1–5	48–49, 630, 636
1:1–13	49
1:1–18	63, 192, 324, 520, 554
1:1–4:54	324
1:3	63, 66, 326, 616
1:3–4	554
1:4	49, 66, 324, 331, 472, 554
1:4–5	194, 254, 399, 554, 576
1:4–9	441
1:5	63–64, 127, 263, 351, 391, 471, 569
1:6	48–49, 54, 57, 60, 110, 216, 254, 623
1:6–8	46–50, 110, 130
1:7	47, 49–50, 57
1:7–8	49
1:8	47, 49–50, 58, 131
1:8–9	57
1:9	194, 241, 254, 632, 634
1:9–10	554
1:9–11	554
1:9–12	399
1:10	63, 241–42, 326, 562, 616
1:10–11	63
1:10–13	127, 349
1:10–20	458
1:11	63, 209, 213, 243, 310

Reference	Pages
1:11–12	209
1:11–13	626
1:12	49, 66, 213, 234, 253, 533
1:12–13	127, 638
1:14	49, 66, 186, 193, 331, 478, 520, 538, 540, 554, 623
1:14–16	49
1:14–18	49, 520, 527
1:15	46–51, 56, 58–59, 507
1:16	186, 236
1:16–26	674
1:17	96
1:18	66, 69, 158, 199, 254, 512, 520–21, 539, 637, 643, 662
1:18–20	520
1:19	47–48, 51, 73, 84, 97–99, 104, 110–11, 113, 116–18, 120, 254, 312, 554
1:19–21	50
1:19–25	143
1:19–27	57
1:19–28	46, 50–51, 110, 114, 119, 131, 230
1:19–29	116
1:19–31	260
1:19–37	50
1:19–51	175, 194
1:19–2:12	230
1:19–12:50	398
1:20	52, 55, 58, 111–12
1:20–21	51, 113
1:20–36	194
1:21	52, 60, 111
1:22	112
1:23	52–53, 58, 60, 112, 263
1:24	84, 98, 112, 116, 118, 120, 122, 254, 312
1:24–26	53
1:25	54, 113, 263
1:25–28	335
1:26	53–54, 56, 115, 254, 263
1:26–27	113
1:27	50, 54, 58, 114
1:28	54, 57, 84, 114, 192, 195, 263, 454, 520, 554
1:28–42	300
1:29	51, 53–54, 60, 114, 141, 192, 198, 201, 241, 254, 342, 459, 554, 567, 615
1:29–34	46, 50–51, 53–54, 110, 230, 456
1:30	50–51, 54, 56, 58–59
1:31	47, 53–54, 184
1:32	47, 54, 60
1:32–33	60
1:33	47, 51, 54, 59–60, 263, 335
1:34	47, 51, 54, 60, 254
1:35	130, 133–36, 192, 554
1:35–36	51, 141, 400
1:35–37	46, 50, 141, 264
1:35–39	134
1:35–40	127, 134–36, 148, 537, 547–49
1:35–41	145
1:35–42	50, 55, 110, 137, 140, 148–49, 230
1:35–44	149
1:35–46	401
1:35–51	149, 262, 513, 523
1:36	50–51, 53–55, 152, 198, 254, 297, 459, 615
1:37	57, 128, 135, 141, 152, 297, 548, 672
1:37–39	141
1:38	55, 128, 134–35, 141, 195, 391, 548, 636
1:38–39	196
1:39	128, 131, 135, 141–42, 147, 150, 152, 176, 197–98, 297, 548, 623, 635
1:39–40	128
1:40	46, 55, 133, 136–37, 140–42, 148, 150, 151, 152, 672, 675
1:40–42	479, 670
1:40–44	196
1:41	115, 128, 142, 144–45, 147–50, 152, 194–96, 254, 342, 483
1:41–42	145, 196–97, 357
1:42	142, 151–52, 163, 195, 199, 297, 572, 666–67, 670
1:43	133, 143–45, 148–49, 176, 192, 194, 196, 297, 341–42, 554
1:43–44	300, 400
1:43–45	145, 196, 511
1:43–48	168
1:43–51	137, 144, 193, 230

1:44	137, 144–45, 147–48, 176, 178, 180, 194–95, 666, 675	2:12	114, 194, 207, 217, 238–39, 300, 315, 543, 670
1:44–45	199, 400	2:12–22	316
1:45	60, 147, 176, 185–86, 191, 195–96, 200, 342, 666–67	2:12–26	316
		2:13	72, 82, 85, 97, 190, 242
1:45–46	310, 391, 563	2:13–25	85, 324
1:45–51	142, 145, 190, 194, 200–01, 300, 479	2:13–3:21	263
		2:14	400
1:46	176, 195, 199–200, 297, 451, 666	2:15	400
		2:16	247, 261
1:47	145, 193, 198, 342, 666	2:18	247, 254, 517–18
1:48	145, 190, 196, 199, 201, 282, 518	2:18–20	113, 341
		2:19	563
1:49	55, 83, 176, 185, 191, 194, 199, 224, 254, 297, 398, 483, 520–21, 632, 666	2:19–21	255
		2:20	85, 231
		2:21	297, 563, 613
1:49–50	400	2:22	311, 393, 399, 628
1:50	145, 190, 194, 198–99, 201, 451, 666	2:23	242, 253, 300, 347, 451
		2:23–24	349
1:50–51	191, 194, 506, 522, 526	2:23–25	251, 253, 255, 301, 310, 317, 330, 354, 478
1:51	145, 147, 196, 421, 613, 635, 658–60		
		2:23–35	255
2	87, 245, 247, 301, 633, 636	2:24–25	300, 347–48, 353, 370, 386, 518
2:1	192, 195, 210–11, 300, 315, 554		
		2:25	253, 282
2:1–11	191, 234, 309, 315–16, 330, 335, 485, 506, 614, 643	3	76, 123, 247, 257, 312, 655
		3–4	526
2:1–12	230, 322, 324	3:1	73, 98, 120, 123, 253, 257, 300, 375, 426, 646
2:1–4:42	320		
2:1–4:45	318	3:1–2	310
2:1–4:54	315–16, 324	3:1–10	526
2:2	146, 148, 216	3:1–12	249, 253
2:3	204, 234, 316, 476, 670	3:1–21	262, 316, 330, 476, 526, 646
2:3–5	235	3:2	55, 253–55, 391, 546, 633
2:3–9	242	3:3	209, 311, 540
2:4	205, 210–11, 234, 316, 340, 397, 636, 644	3:4	236, 526
		3:5	209, 255, 325–26, 335, 556, 612, 616
2:5	206, 234, 242, 312, 316, 330, 560, 670		
		3:6	256
2:6	72, 82, 234, 265	3:7	324
2:7	616	3:8	256
2:7–8	228	3:8–10	254
2:8	235	3:9	250, 256, 526
2:9	233, 235	3:1	120, 265, 623
2:9–10	129	3:11	253, 549
2:10	207, 233	3:12	253
2:11	194, 196, 207, 217, 221, 239, 253, 300, 305, 311, 313, 316, 324, 33–31, 449, 506	3:14	148, 372
		3:15	160
		3:15–16	324
		3:16	241, 372, 478, 652

3:17	241	4:10	318
3:18	127, 242, 349, 567	4:11	318
3:18–20	127	4:11–15	223
3:19–21	226	4:12	284, 294, 296
3:20–21	239	4:13–14	325
3:21	127	4:14	325, 485, 613, 616
3:22	55, 217, 220, 263, 300, 315	4:16	282, 291
3:22–24	55	4:16–29	316
3:22–26	316	4:17	282
3:22–30	55, 260, 324	4:17–18	518
3:22–36	46, 456	4:18	282–84, 288, 342
3:23	130, 335	4:19	115, 282, 294, 296, 325
3:24	56, 59	4:19–25	335
3:25	55, 260, 262, 264	4:20	284, 294, 296
3:25–26	389	4:21	83, 212
3:25–30	127	4:21–24	478
3:26	50, 55–56, 114, 128–29, 260, 454, 459	4:22	74, 77, 83, 102, 105, 261, 293, 296
3:26–30	459	4:23	83
3:27	55	4:24	294, 297
3:27–30	55–56, 236	4:25	284, 345
3:28	50, 55, 58, 128, 143, 458	4:26	297, 391, 633
3:28–30	50, 207	4:27	220, 223, 288
3:29	56, 236, 267, 272, 290, 324, 365, 458	4:27–30	316
		4:29	198, 284, 289, 296–98, 632
3:29–30	58, 231, 458	4:29–30	294
3:30	56, 195, 236, 616	4:30	290–91, 451
3:31	56–57, 199	4:31	217
3:31–36	55–56, 324	4:33	216, 218, 223, 633
3:33	128	4:34	210
3:34	616	4:35	290
3:34–35	517	4:38	223
3:36	56, 130, 324, 327, 349	4:39	288–89, 291, 312, 451–52, 526
4	83, 268, 270–71, 309, 325–26, 316, 324, 333, 412, 416, 476, 614, 633–34, 636, 639	4:39–41	389
		4:39–42	220, 294–95, 301, 309, 316
4:1	55–56, 129, 312	4:40	290, 298, 456
4:1–3	300, 322	4:41	223, 291, 451
4:1–15	316	4:41–42	290, 311, 313, 326
4:2	55, 217, 335	4:42	105, 296–98, 399, 520, 526
4:3	72, 301	4:43	223, 290, 301, 310, 315
4:5–6	300	4:43–45	300–03, 316–17
4:6	635	4:43–46	322
4:6–7	288, 391	4:43–54	309, 315, 325
4:7	291	4:44	115, 310, 325
4:7–26	325–26	4:45	261, 299, 310–11, 320
4:8	217	4:46	315–23, 326, 329, 338–39
4:9	83, 90, 105, 261, 284, 293, 295, 452	4:46–47	317
		4:46–48	300

New Testament

4:46–54	191, 306, 314–20, 325, 330, 332	5:16	85, 96, 101, 106, 326, 345, 444
4:47	72, 311–12, 316–17, 319, 321–23, 326	5:16–18	341
		5:17	210
4:48	242, 300, 302, 305–06, 311, 316–17, 319–20, 322, 389, 517	5:18	85, 87, 90, 96, 101, 103–04, 106, 240, 346, 444, 592
		5:19	87, 257, 325
4:48–53	461	5:19–29	325
4:49	306, 312, 316–17, 319, 321–23, 326, 329	5:19–47	85, 325
		5:20	325
4:49–50	317	5:21	325
4:50	306, 311–12, 316–21, 323, 325–27, 329	5:22	325
		5:23	325
4:50–53	325	5:23–24	325
4:51	318, 321, 323, 326–27, 329	5:24	319
4:51–52	329	5:25	56, 318, 325, 468
4:51–53	317, 323	5:25–26	325
4:52	322, 323, 326, 329	5:26	325, 327
4:52–53	330	5:27	325
4:53	306, 311–13, 316–19, 321–23, 326–27, 330–31	5:28	468
		5:31–39	57
4:54	72, 114, 315, 318–19, 322, 330	5:32–33	456
		5:33	47, 50, 57, 98
5	76, 86–87, 103, 106–07, 263, 325–26, 333, 416, 429–30, 432, 434, 471, 652	5:33–35	58, 615
		5:33–36	46–47, 57
		5:34	47, 50, 57
5–12	97, 107	5:34–35	50
5:1	72, 97, 242, 263, 337	5:35	57–58
5:1–9	85	5:36	47, 210, 257
5:1–18	325, 484, 614	5:36–37	325
5:1–20	332	5:36–47	456
5:1–6:59	318	5:37	85
5:2	337	5:38	85
5:2–3	339	5:39	85, 191
5:3	332–33, 335–37, 339	5:40	85
5:4	337	5:41	310
5:5	337, 341, 344	5:42	85
5:6	338, 340, 342	5:43	85
5:7	338, 344	5:44	85, 351, 540
5:8	102, 339	5:45–47	96
5:9	338–40, 342, 444	5:46	60, 176
5:10	340	5:47	85
5:10–16	389	5:54	305
5:10–18	113	5:58	456
5:11	338, 341–42, 344–46	6	86, 101, 146, 149, 154–55, 158, 164, 172, 175–76, 178, 184, 217–18, 223, 265, 279, 325, 347, 350–52, 354, 358–59, 673–74
5:12	341, 345		
5:13	341		
5:14	196, 338, 341–42, 400		
5:15	326, 338, 342, 344		
5:15–16	99	6–7	354

6:1–2	347	6:31	86, 99, 348
6:1–3	357	6:31–58	218
6:1–14	137, 146, 149, 485	6:32	358
6:1–59	154	6:32–33	348
6:2	242, 332–33, 335–36, 348, 352	6:33	241
6:3	146, 148	6:34	348, 352
6:4	72, 82, 146, 190, 242	6:35	147, 325, 485, 635
6:5	146, 155, 186, 357	6:35–36	348
6:5–7	168, 176, 180	6:36	351–53
6:5–9	196	6:38	147
6:5–10	675	6:39	222, 449, 569
6:6	154, 282, 357	6:41	86, 101, 147, 305, 348–50
6:7	146, 154, 176, 184, 198, 357, 511	6:41–42	86, 199
6:7–8	133	6:41–59	86, 113, 348
6:8	137, 146, 148, 150, 154	6:42	99, 176, 198, 310, 667
6:8–9	149	6:43	86, 98, 222
6:9	146, 149, 154, 356–57, 359	6:44	86, 519
6:9–10	673	6:45	87
6:10	146, 357	6:46	86, 512
6:10–13	146	6:47	87
6:10–15	347	6:48–58	664
6:11	154, 357–59	6:49	86, 99, 102, 198
6:12	217	6:50	147
6:12–13	357	6:51	86, 241, 318, 372
6:13	673	6:52	86, 98, 101, 348
6:14	115, 146, 305, 348, 350, 352, 354, 357	6:53–58	147
		6:54	87
6:14–15	350, 352	6:55	616
6:15	146, 240, 348	6:56	87
6:16–17	217	6:56–58	86, 631
6:16–21	217, 514	6:57	318, 327
6:17	514	6:58	86–87, 319
6:19	217	6:59	114
6:20	217, 391	6:59–7:9	238
6:20–26	525	6:60	218–19
6:21	217–18	6:60–66	154
6:22–25	348, 352	6:60–69	365
6:22–59	507, 523	6:60–71	217–18, 665, 673
6:25–34	352	6:61	86, 218
6:25–40	348	6:62	389, 514
6:26	348, 350, 353, 358	6:63	518
6:27	147, 358	6:64	282, 353, 361, 364, 370, 386, 398
6:27–29	348		
6:28	352	6:66	86, 218, 239, 564, 566, 664, 673
6:28–31	354		
6:29	567	6:67	155, 190, 223, 508, 515, 673
6:30	350, 517–18	6:67–69	142, 508
6:30–31	348, 352	6:67–71	216, 515
		6:68	197, 508

6:68–69	151–52, 155, 512, 525, 666, 673	7:25–36	135
6:69	155, 223–24, 239, 265, 477, 508, 520, 526	7:26	241, 349, 373–76, 378, 426
		7:26–27	115
		7:27	353
6:70	155, 265, 360, 365, 370, 421–22, 560	7:27–29	199
		7:28	353, 373, 400
6:70–71	223, 361, 367–69, 516	7:28–29	249
6:71	155, 360–61, 364–66, 370, 398, 474, 526, 667–68	7:30	389, 399, 452, 455
		7:30–31	349, 352, 451
7	87, 241, 257, 325, 347, 349–52, 354, 649, 655	7:31	352, 354, 451–52
		7:32	88, 115, 120–22, 124, 349–50, 352, 383, 388, 405, 455
7–8	412, 416		
7–10	87–88, 122–23	7:33–34	512
7:1	72, 87, 103–04, 240, 305, 636	7:35	88, 98, 177, 397, 400
		7:35–36	87
7:1–4	64	7:36	88
7:1–7	62, 64, 69	7:36–50	480
7:1–9	238	7:37–38	325, 349, 432, 485
7:1–13	373	7:37–39	517, 556, 612, 615–16
7:2	82, 242	7:38	318
7:2–3	72	7:38–39	60, 552
7:3	72, 310, 543	7:40	115
7:3–4	551	7:40–41	352
7:3–5	239, 509	7:40–42	353
7:4	64, 239	7:40–43	135, 349, 352, 354
7:5	64, 543	7:40–44	302–03
7:6	64	7:40–53	123
7:7	64, 241	7:41	199, 391
7:8	389	7:41–42	310
7:10	242	7:43	98, 123–24, 223
7:11	87, 444	7:44	352, 389
7:11–13	349	7:44–45	455
7:11–53	113	7:45	87, 115, 374, 383, 405
7:12	223, 349–50, 352–53	7:45–49	388
7:12–13	349	7:45–52	120, 122, 374, 383, 646
7:13	87, 91, 103	7:46	123, 374, 389–90, 392
7:14	400	7:47	120, 122, 405
7:14–19	87	7:47–48	123, 374
7:14–36	373	7:47–49	389
7:14–10:39	87	7:48	124, 257, 373–76, 378, 405, 426
7:15	99, 101, 405–06		
7:15–16	88	7:49	349, 354, 374
7:19	87, 102–04	7:50	87, 120, 123, 257, 259, 474
7:20	103, 349–50, 352	7:50–51	123
7:21–23	343	7:50–52	128, 249, 257, 390, 526
7:23	343	7:51	121, 258
7:24	416, 540, 545	7:52	115, 135, 191, 199, 258, 302–03, 310, 391, 405
7:25	73, 87, 373		
7:25–27	352, 354	7:52–8:12	410
7:25–32	384	7:53–8:11	403, 405, 444, 560, 614, 652

8	76, 88, 90, 98, 119, 193, 276, 443	8:48	349–50
		8:48–59	88, 90
8:2	400, 404–05, 412	8:51	456
8:3	403–06, 413, 444	8:52	90, 103, 349–50
8:4	405, 412	8:53	90, 104
8:5	414, 417	8:56	60
8:6	404–05, 412, 417–18	8:57	90
8:6–7	406	8:58	90, 443
8:7	404–06, 417–19	8:59	101, 223, 242, 389, 560
8:8	404–05, 417–18	9	76, 90–92, 98, 257, 332, 327, 346, 351, 416, 429–30, 434, 438–39, 479, 540, 614
8:9	404–06, 412, 418		
8:10	418		
8:11	290, 418–19	9:1	338, 440, 443
8:12	141, 194, 351, 441, 443, 485, 559	9:1–7	440, 448–49, 484
		9:2	219, 343, 441
8:12–13	122	9:2–3	442
8:12–20	122	9:3	342–43, 441, 502
8:13	88, 119	9:4	254, 432, 441
8:13–19	119	9:4–5	431
8:14	199	9:5	431, 441
8:15	416, 540	9:6	441–44, 637
8:17	87	9:6–7	432, 439, 441
8:20	114, 389, 399–400, 451, 455	9:7	441–44
8:20–59	113	9:8	431, 440, 442, 445
8:21	88, 119, 342	9:8–9	439, 442
8:21–23	135	9:8–12	91, 434, 439
8:21–30	88	9:8–13	439, 442
8:22	103, 119, 452	9:8–17	449
8:23	88, 242, 540	9:9	443, 445
8:24	88, 343–44, 443	9:10	443, 445
8:27	88, 101	9:11	91, 256, 434, 441, 443–44
8:28	103, 119, 148, 443	9:11–12	445
8:30	88, 101, 451–52	9:12	439, 444–45
8:30–31	101	9:13	91, 431, 444–45
8:31	90–91, 104, 105, 223, 261, 452	9:13–14	434
		9:13–16	118, 121
8:31–47	88–89	9:13–17	91, 447
8:31–59	242, 452	9:13–41	119
8:33	89	9:14	444–45
8:34	343	9:15	91, 256, 434, 441, 443–44, 447
8:37	89–90, 101–03		
8:39	89–90	9:15–17	91, 439, 443
8:40	89–90, 101, 103	9:16	91, 98, 124, 254, 257, 434, 443
8:41	89		
8:42	89, 423	9:17	91, 115, 256, 431, 444
8:43	89, 101	9:18	91, 101, 121, 431, 446, 448
8:44	73, 89–90, 103–04, 365, 368, 421–23	9:18–23	435, 441, 450
		9:18–34	91
8:45–46	89	9:19	99, 431, 447
8:47	89	9:20	431, 447–49

New Testament

9:20–21	447
9:21	449
9:22	87, 91–92, 101, 103, 121, 374, 446, 449–50, 479
9:22–23	447
9:24	91, 121, 254, 431, 444, 540
9:24–33	447
9:24–34	91, 439, 449–50
9:24–41	623
9:25	91, 444
9:25–32	435
9:26	443
9:27	441, 447
9:27–29	105, 575
9:28	101, 106
9:29	101, 135, 449
9:30	91, 449
9:32	431, 443–44
9:33	91, 92, 540
9:34	101, 103–04, 124, 342, 389, 448, 450
9:34–35	92
9:34–38	105
9:35	196, 342, 344, 439, 443, 449–50
9:35–38	449
9:36	436
9:38	91, 436, 444, 450, 520, 526
9:39–41	124, 351, 457
9:39–10:6	457
9:39–10:21	92, 457
9:39–10:42	452, 457
9:40	91–92, 124
9:41	343, 557
9:54	114
10	58, 87, 92, 151, 368, 401, 451, 459, 541, 577, 636
10:1	366, 368, 457, 541, 574, 599
10:1–5	457
10:1–6	541
10:1–16	637
10:1–17	573
10:1–18	164, 457
10:2	541
10:2–5	222
10:3	222, 449, 469, 541
10:3–4	56
10:4	141, 222, 459, 542
10:5	542
10:6	457
10:7	458, 542
10:7–16	458
10:7–21	458
10:8	366, 368, 599–600
10:9	519
10:10	366, 368, 469, 560, 600
10:11	159–60, 165, 401, 484, 573, 604–05
10:11–18	571
10:12	541
10:14–18	398
10:15	160, 484, 573, 604
10:15–16	399
10:16	56, 398, 459
10:17	484, 573
10:17–18	458, 484, 637
10:18	472, 484, 564, 573
10:19	92, 98, 101
10:19–21	223, 458
10:19–42	113
10:20	458
10:20–21	458
10:21	257, 458
10:22	454–55
10:22–23	458
10:22–24	457
10:22–31	92, 458
10:22–42	92, 457–48
10:23	400, 454
10:24	92, 100–02, 115, 241, 458
10:24–38	457
10:25	92, 457
10:25–26	101
10:25–30	457–58
10:26–29	457
10:27	102, 141, 176
10:29	222, 449
10:30	92, 457, 520
10:31	93, 103, 241, 416, 455, 457–58, 560
10:31–33	101
10:32	458
10:32–33	457
10:32–42	92, 458
10:33	104, 455, 458
10:34	87
10:34–38	458
10:37	101
10:38	93, 106–07, 457
10:39	93, 103, 452, 454–56, 458–59

10:39–40	455	11:16	81, 195, 224, 240, 462, 472, 504–13, 515–16, 523–26, 666
10:39–42	451, 453–54, 456–58		
10:40	57, 114, 454–55		
10:40–41	459	11:17	469
10:40–42	46, 57–58, 454–59, 615	11:17–27	497, 500, 506
10:41	47, 50, 57–58, 105, 451, 455–56	11:18	82, 454
		11:19	82, 93, 103, 105, 121, 494, 496, 499
10:41–42	50, 57–58, 452, 455		
10:42	93, 107, 451–52, 454, 456–58	11:20	496, 635
11	122, 258, 326–27, 398, 412, 454, 463–64, 468, 470, 472–75, 482, 487, 491, 503, 513, 633–34	11:20–22	489
		11:21	476, 495–98
		11:21–22	489, 491–92
		11:21–27	495, 497, 501, 503
11–12	93, 101, 416, 468	11:22	476, 492–93
11:1	454, 469, 494	11:23	490, 495–96, 499
11:1–2	475	11:24	496–99
11:1–3	472	11:25	326, 485, 513, 633
11:1–5	501, 506	11:25–26	462, 465, 496, 499–500, 506
11:1–6	494, 502	11:26	476, 496–98
11:1–16	497	11:27	115, 476, 499–503, 506, 522, 633
11:1–44	398, 467, 493, 496, 501, 505–06, 525		
		11:28	477, 496–97
11:1–12:8	475	11:28–37	497, 501
11:2	338, 398, 469, 494	11:31	93, 105, 479, 495
11:3	469–70, 473, 475–76, 494, 496–98, 501	11:31–33	470
		11:32	477
11:4	472, 483, 492, 497, 501–02, 510	11:33	93, 104–05, 285, 470, 478
		11:34	198, 469
11:5	72, 494–95	11:35	93, 470, 478, 492
11:5–6	502	11:36	470, 478
11:6	469, 492, 496–97	11:37	93, 479
11:6–10	506	11:38	634
11:7	72, 462, 472, 502, 507–08, 510	11:38–44	66, 497
		11:39	469, 495–97, 500–01, 503
11:7–16	497	11:39–40	500
11:8	93, 101, 219, 240, 455, 462, 479, 495, 508, 510, 560	11:39–44	500–01
		11:40	496, 501–02
11:9	673	11:41–12	492
11:9–10	351	11:41–43	66
11:10	254, 559	11:42	506
11:10–14	472	11:43	470
11:11	462, 469–70, 492, 501, 508	11:44	326, 468–69, 495, 637
11:11–15	501	11:45	77, 93–94, 101, 104–05, 350, 384, 451–52, 530
11:11–16	506–07		
11:12	220, 469	11:45–46	98, 124, 389
11:12–13	219	11:45–47	119
11:13	220	11:45–53	118, 121, 383, 467
11:14	221	11:45–54	399, 506, 508
11:14–15	483, 502	11:45–57	66
11:15	506–08, 510, 512	11:46	93, 98, 105, 129, 345, 530

New Testament

11:46–47	530	12:15	83
11:47	115, 121, 383, 385, 532	12:16	220, 399
11:47–48	385–86, 449	12:17	467–68
11:47–53	345, 361, 385, 649	12:17–18	350, 399
11:48	129, 383, 530–31	12:17–19	399
11:49–50	531	12:18	350, 352
11:49–52	472, 530	12:18–19	350
11:49–53	389	12:19	62, 66–67, 69, 121, 178, 397, 399, 401
11:50	399, 530		
11:50–51	604	12:20	147, 400
11:51–52	531	12:20–21	147, 399
11:52	399	12:20–22	133, 675
11:53	122, 385–86, 531	12:20–23	177
11:54	531	12:20–26	137, 147, 149, 309
11:55	82, 350, 398	12:20–36	397–400
11:55–56	135	12:21	144–45, 149, 176, 178, 186, 302, 400
11:57	115, 118, 122, 383, 385		
12	146, 149, 177–78, 180, 183, 347, 350–52, 354, 368, 398, 402, 412, 474, 478, 637	12:21–22	198, 357, 511
		12:21–23	168, 196
		12:22	137, 147–49, 176, 180, 401
12–13	368	12:23	147, 178, 397–99, 401, 483
12:1	193, 555, 672	12:23–24	604
12:1–8	258, 368, 398, 467, 493–94, 496, 502, 627	12:23–36	398, 401
		12:24	147, 472, 485
12:1–19	66	12:24–26	399
12:2	469, 496	12:25–26	147
12:3	398, 483	12:26	141, 176, 509
12:3–8	66	12:27	398–99, 478, 637
12:4	360–61, 364, 368, 370, 398, 480	12:27–28	483, 604
		12:27–30	478
12:4–6	623, 668	12:27–40	350, 352
12:5	368	12:28	399
12:5–6	365, 371	12:29	635, 658, 660–61
12:6	80, 213, 360, 366, 368–71	12:29–30	350
12:7	480	12:30–32	399
12:7–8	368	12:31	194, 241, 398, 421, 425, 560
12:9	66, 94, 98, 107, 350, 352, 467	12:31–32	399
12:9–11	399, 472	12:31–36	351
12:9–50	175	12:32	147, 372, 398, 400, 519, 610, 612, 624, 637
12:10	115, 386, 467, 471		
12:10–11	350, 385, 653	12:32–33	165
12:11	94, 98–99, 101, 104–05, 107, 129, 384, 399, 449, 471	12:32–34	165
		12:33	89, 399
12:12	565	12:34	148, 354, 374, 398
12:12–13	350, 352	12:34–36	399
12:12–15	399	12:37	351
12:12–19	66, 350, 352, 481	12:37–42	399
12:13	83, 176, 394	12:39–41	351
12:13–14	352	12:41	60
12:14–15	350	12:42	92, 12–21, 124, 258, 351,

	354, 373–76, 378, 426, 449, 451–52	13:27–30	623
		13:28	156, 220, 539
12:42–43	118, 121, 452, 653	13:28–29	369
12:43	351, 449, 540	13:29	360
12:44–50	400	13:30	254, 367, 369, 526, 550, 576, 633
12:50	653		
13	156, 159, 166, 366	13:31–32	159, 483, 510, 604
13–17	64, 97, 106, 535, 569	13:31–38	510–11
13–20	398, 505, 643	13:31–14:31	510–11, 513, 524, 551
13:1	147, 156–57, 367, 470, 604	13:31–16:33	664
13:1–4	478	13:31–17:26	557
13:1–6	651	13:33	97, 99, 159, 510, 512, 551
13:1–20	265, 368, 523, 539	13:34	157, 226, 539
13:1–30	365	13:34–35	159
13:2	360–61, 364–67, 369–70, 421–22, 424, 560, 623, 667–68	13:36	141, 165, 224, 510–11
		13:36–37	159, 551
		13:36–38	142, 509, 547
13:2–4	156	13:37	159–60, 509, 526, 547, 552, 560, 572, 623, 666–67
13:3–11	664		
13:4	424	13:37–38	577
13:4–5	156	13:38	160, 162, 165, 623
13:5	483	14	175, 184, 510–11, 660
13:6	157	14–16	179, 184
13:6–9	540	14–17	185, 560, 639, 655
13:6–10	142, 156, 159	14:1	478, 511–12, 557
13:7	157	14:1–4	511
13:8	157	14:1–14	510
13:9	547	14:1–23	637
13:10	370	14:2–3	455, 512
13:10–11	366	14:3	471
13:11	353, 360–61, 364, 370, 386, 398	14:4	221, 511
		14:4–5	511
13:17	522–23, 604	14:5	216, 504, 510–11, 515–16, 524–26, 551–52
13:18	222, 367		
13:19	222	14:5–7	505, 525
13:20	158	14:5–8	527
13:21	158, 166, 220, 361, 364, 369–70, 398, 478, 539	14:5–11	523
		14:6	96, 326, 511, 513, 551, 565
13:21–30	158, 367	14:6–7	511
13:22	539	14:7–8	177
13:23	136, 158, 539, 549, 637	14:7	522
13:23–25	643	14:8	178, 186, 511, 513, 551–52, 667
13:23–26	58, 537, 539, 549, 575		
13:24	142, 153, 166	14:8–9	168
13:25	153, 549	14:8–14	198
13:26	360, 367, 539, 667	14:9	551
13:26–27	367, 369	14:9–10	513
13:26–30	668	14:13–14	493
13:27	213, 365, 367, 369, 421, 424, 426, 552, 560	14:15	67
		14:15–17	62, 67, 69

14:15–24	510	16:5	511
14:15–26	522	16:7	186
14:16	186	16:11	194, 421, 425, 560
14:17	68, 221	16:12	552
14:18	550	16:13	345
14:19	327, 550	16:16–19	220
14:19–20	222	16:17–18	219
14:21	550	16:18	623
14:22	243, 511–12, 551, 675	16:20	62, 68
14:23	367, 551, 626, 632	16:22	222
14:25–31	510	16:23–26	493
14:26	186, 222, 552	16:25	219
14:27	478, 557	16:27	214, 221
14:28	222, 632	16:27–28	214
14:29	222	16:27–32	215
14:30	421, 425, 561	16:29–30	214, 219, 557
14:31	426, 510	16:29–33	552
15	65	16:30	221, 253, 370, 386, 520
15–16	510–11	16:31	221
15–17	172	16:31–32	214–15, 219, 509, 557, 623
15:1–17	65	16:32	510
15:2	222	16:33	242, 244, 557, 566
15:3	265	17	65, 69, 265, 557, 569, 664
15:4	222	17:1	483
15:4–6	456	17:1–5	69, 569
15:4–7	631	17:2	222
15:4–10	129	17:3	115, 256
15:5	222	17:4	210
15:7	493	17:6	449
15:12	470	17:6–19	69, 569
15:13	160, 462, 470, 508	17:11	265
15:13–15	462	17:12	360, 365–66, 569
15:14	222, 470	17:14	65
15:14–15	186	17:14–15	62, 64, 69
15:15	222, 485	17:15	65
15:16	222, 493	17:17–19	265
15:18	65	17:20	135, 222
15:18–21	62, 64–65, 69	17:20–24	637
15:19	65, 222, 241–42, 557	17:20–26	69, 569
15:20	87, 557	17:21–23	367
15:20–21	65	17:22–23	226
15:22	343	17:24	69, 222
15:24–25	393	17:25	62, 69
15:25	87, 241	18	164, 200, 554, 569, 572, 598
15:26	186	18–19	597
15:27	135–36, 222	18–19	106, 365
15:29–30	241	18–20	454
15:32	87	18:1	211, 217, 557, 565, 569, 612
16:1–2	557	18:1–11	569, 573
16:2	92, 471	18:1–12	193, 364, 555, 557, 602

18:1–13	388	18:24	535, 558, 574
18:2	360–61, 364, 398, 558, 560, 569	18:24–28	530
		18:25	161, 394, 576
18:2–3	360, 389	18:25–27	142, 161, 666–67
18:2–5	526, 668	18:26–27	571
18:3	115, 120, 122, 200, 364, 370, 383, 390, 558–62, 569, 576, 583	18:27	162
		18:28	94–95, 444, 535, 559, 574, 614–15, 633
18:3–13	558	18:28–30	394
18:4	562, 566, 576	18:28–31	388
18:4–8	569	18:28–32	583
18:4–9	159–60	18:28–19:16	94, 398, 453, 582
18:4–11	558	18:29	101, 583
18:5	161, 199–201, 310, 360–61, 364–65, 394, 398, 542, 558, 560, 563, 566	18:30	361, 583
		18:31	94–95, 101, 588, 592
		18:31–19:42	113, 394
18:6	200, 392, 558–59, 561, 563, 566	18:33	83, 95, 583
		18:33–38	586
18:7	199–201, 310, 558, 562–64	18:35	95, 115, 361, 556
18:8	509, 564, 569, 573	18:36	94, 361, 391, 395
18:8–9	196	18:37	95, 652
18:8–11	566	18:38	94, 96, 391, 394, 608
18:9	569	18:38–40	587
18:10	195, 559–60, 562, 564, 569–70, 576–77	18:39	83, 95
		18:39–40	608
18:10–11	142, 160	18:40	598–99
18:11	160, 393, 560, 569, 571–72, 604	19	103, 106, 561
		19–20	97, 565
18:12	94, 391, 393, 558, 560–62	19:1	597
18:12–24	94	19:1–3	558, 589
18:13	530, 534, 558	19:2	597, 601, 604
18:14	391, 530, 534	19:3	83, 95, 597
18:15	136, 160–61, 165, 167, 541–42, 666	19:4	588, 597, 608
		19:4–6	591
18:15–16	537, 549, 672	19:4–8	94, 591
18:15–18	142, 161, 534, 541	19:5	95, 597
18:15–27	151, 160, 547	19:5–7	394
18:16	160, 161, 541–42	19:6	94, 115, 383, 385–86, 388, 394, 535, 588, 595, 597, 608
18:17	161, 394, 541, 666–67		
18:18	94, 161, 394, 542, 576	19:7	94–95, 394, 597
18:18–25	388, 393	19:9	135
18:19	534, 562, 564	19:9–11	593
18:19–21	398	19:10	564
18:19–24	161, 530, 558, 570–71, 574	19:11	94, 361
18:20	98–99, 222, 241, 394	19:12	94–95, 385, 394
18:20–21	534	19:12–16	594
18:21	576	19:14	54, 83, 94, 615, 630
18:21–23	393	19:15	83, 94–95, 115, 383, 385–86, 394, 535
18:22	94, 393, 535		
18:23	535	19:16	94, 103, 361, 602, 609

New Testament

19:16–25	558	19:38	87, 96, 103, 259, 610, 646, 649, 674
19:17	602, 605, 609		
19:17–18	211	19:38–42	258, 526, 646, 652
19:18	556, 565, 601–02, 607, 609–11, 613, 617, 622	19:39	120, 123, 254, 258–59, 596, 633, 646
19:18–37	601	19:39–42	249, 610, 646, 650
19:19	83, 95, 199–201, 310, 391, 563	19:40	82, 96, 480
		19:41	193, 211, 556, 630, 646, 654
19:19–22	596, 602	19:41–42	612, 632
19:19–42	96	19:42	82, 96, 630, 632, 646
19:20	96, 98	20	103, 162–63, 409, 412, 463, 513, 515, 521, 525–26, 572, 643, 674
19:20–21	106		
19:21	83, 94, 96, 115, 383, 385–86, 394, 535		
		20–21	225
19:23	559, 603	20:1	193, 285, 546, 616, 629–32, 634
19:23–24	601, 605, 615		
19:23–25	610	20:1–2	513–15, 632
19:23–20:25	526	20:1–18	627–29
19:24	601, 603, 641	20:2	136, 162, 541, 544–46, 575, 628, 631, 634–35, 661
19:25	210–11, 365, 543, 556, 611–13, 618–21, 624–27, 641, 643		
		20:2–4	672
		20:2–10	142, 162, 537, 544, 549, 643
19:25–27	556, 612, 621, 626, 641, 643–44, 671	20:3	545–46
		20:3–10	167, 513, 515, 634
19:26	208, 210–11, 543, 611, 621, 641	20:4	544–46, 549, 575
		20:4–5	156
19:26–27	159, 196, 243, 537, 543, 549, 556, 575, 610–12, 624	20:5	544, 631, 635
		20:5–7	555
19:27	208–09, 213, 543, 644	20:6	391, 545–46, 631
19:27–28	605	20:6–7	526
19:28	210, 601, 603	20:7	545, 547, 659
19:28–29	604	20:8	58, 163, 517, 527, 545–46, 549, 575, 631, 643, 672
19:29	54, 242		
19:30	208, 210, 361, 372, 556, 603, 605, 616, 637	20:8–9	628
		20:9	399, 545, 629, 631
19:31	95–96, 106, 210, 610, 614–15, 646, 649, 653	20:10	575, 631, 634
		20:11	631, 635
19:31–32	596, 604, 607	20:11–12	285
19:31–37	604	20:11–13	635
19.32	601, 610–11	20:11–18	476, 513–15, 527
19:32–34	558	20:12	421, 631, 658–60
19:33	604, 615	20:12–13	658–60
19:34	209, 474, 517–18, 544, 556, 559, 604, 612, 616	20:13	520, 545, 635–36, 661
		20:14	631, 635
19:34–35	610	20:14–17	635–36, 661
19:35	58–59, 139, 159, 261, 522, 537, 543–44, 548–49, 611–12	20:15	193, 212, 545, 556, 612, 630, 634, 636, 661
19:36	54, 96, 601, 605, 615	20:16	520, 628, 636
19:37	68, 261, 605, 615	20:16–18	545

20:17	389, 514, 521, 543, 555, 628–29, 637–39, 660	21:4–6	164
20:17–18	243	21:7	58, 136, 164, 537, 546–57, 549, 575, 665
20:18	514, 516, 520, 629, 631, 638	21:9	359
20:19	87, 96, 103, 193, 222, 514, 518–19, 630	21:11	164
		21:12	220, 226
20:19–23	153, 162, 164, 222, 513–14, 519, 523, 527, 664	21:13	359
		21:14	546
20:19–29	163	21:15–17	151, 165, 547, 577, 665–67
20:20	163, 217, 516–18, 521	21:15–19	153, 163–64, 167, 548
20:21–22	613	21:15–23	142
20:21–23	163	21:15–25	164
20:22	60, 162, 167, 193, 521, 552, 556, 654	21:16	165
		21:17	353, 370, 386
20:24	216, 504, 506, 508, 515–16, 523, 526, 673	21:18–19	160, 165, 547, 577
		21:19	141, 167, 176, 224, 471, 547
20:24–25	226, 515, 623	21:19–20	198
20:24–29	505, 512–15, 523, 525–28	21:20	166, 361, 547–49
20:25	219, 222, 516–18, 521, 666	21:20–23	166, 537, 546–49, 575
20:26	222, 225, 504, 515, 519	21:20–24	266
20:26–29	476	21:21–23	166
20:27	344, 504, 518–19, 521, 637, 666	21:22	141, 176, 547–48
		21:23	548
20:27–29	515, 517	21:24	58–59, 186, 224, 537, 547–48, 676
20:28	157, 224, 504, 506, 519, 521, 525–27, 660, 666		
		21:25	548
20:29	518, 521–22, 526–27, 666		
20:29–31	517	Acts	
20:30–31	307, 318–19, 324, 363, 465, 477, 515, 522–23, 526, 528	1	180–82
		1:9–14	180
20:31	115, 139, 171, 198, 202–03, 226, 228, 244, 326, 336, 345, 354–55, 370, 372, 387, 440, 445, 500, 515, 518, 629, 637	1:13	180, 243, 528, 552
		2:17	181
		3:2	338
		6	180, 182
21	97, 153, 160, 163, 166, 172, 215, 359, 505, 572, 577, 643, 664–65, 670, 672	6:1–7	181
		8	181–82
		8:5–13	181
21:1–3	222	8:14–25	181
21:1–7	136	8:26–31	181
21:1–14	142, 163, 523, 575	8:40	181
21:2	135, 164, 177, 190–91, 194–95, 267, 504–06, 523, 526–27, 663, 665–69, 671–72, 674–76	9:3–16	256
		9:33	338
		12:4	603
		13:27–29	649
21:2–3	151, 164, 546	21	181–82
21:3	130, 151, 153, 164, 254, 546, 664	21:8	181
		21:8–9	181
21:3–4	664	21:9	181
21:3–11	666	22:6–16	256
21:4	220, 546	26:12–18	256

Romans		1 Peter	
1:3	304	1:8	522

1 Corinthians		1 John	
1:22	255	1:1	522, 525
5:1	283	4:15	345
5:7	615	5:1	345
11:2–16	480	5:5	345
		5:12	327
2 Corinthians		5:20	327
6:14	480	5:20–21	520

Galatians		2 John	
4:19	210	1:9–10	185

Hebrews		Judas	
5:7	478	6:71	81

James		Revelation	
5:15	344	1:17	566
		12:9	426
		19:7	267

Jewish Literature

1QM		Mishna, Talmud, and Tosefta	
2:1	114	m. Sabb.	
5:6	114	23:5	480

1QH		b. Sanh.	
3:16	366	43a	190
3:19	366		
3:32	366	b. Sukkah	
		49b	484
Joseph and Aseneth			
10:14	481	b. Taanith	
		20a	250
Josephus, Jewish Antiquities			
17:199	480	t. Pe'ah	
18:27	178	4:19	484
18:108	178		
20:250–51	382		

Greco-Roman Literature

Martialis		Ovid, Metamorphoses	
5.8.1	520	538–99	481

Petronius, Satyricon
111   481

Plutarch, Moralia
267   481

Suetonius, Domitian
13:1–2   520

Virgil, Aeneid
3.65   481

Early Christian Literature

Acts of Peter
36–41   165

Acts of Thomas
11   528
31   528
39   528

Eusebius, Hist. Eccl.
2.25.8   165
3.1.2   165

Gospel of Philip (NHC II,3)
32   628
55   628

Gospel of Thomas (NHC II,2)
Gos. Thom. 528

Martyrdom of Polycarp
6:1   358
7:1   358

Protevangelium of James
16:3   409

Tertullian, Scorpiace
15:3   165

Index of Modern Authors

Abbott, H. P. 1, 47, 53, 58
Abrams, M. H. 10, 538
Adkisson, R. 129
Aitken, E. 272
Allison, D. C. 283-84
Allrath, G. 108
Alter, R. XII, 9, 201, 290, 377, 392, 430, 466, 563
Amit, Y. 12
Anderson, J. 17
Anderson, P. N. 168-69, 171-74, 176-77, 179-80, 186
Anderson, R. T. 284, 289, 296
Appold, M. 81
Arbeitman, Y. 360
Arav, R. 178
Ashton, J. 108, 173, 262, 299, 303, 428-29, 552, 610
Asiedu-Peprah, M. 444
Attridge, H. 528, 637

Bachelard, G. 453
Backhaus, K. 46-47, 127, 261, 459
Bacon, H. 293-95, 298
Bakhtin, M. 16, 171, 174
Bal, M. 5, 20, 53, 79, 81, 415
Balz, H. 528
Bar-Efrat, S. 10, 204, 228, 430
Barker, M. 211
Barr, J. 567
Barrett, C. K. 49, 56-57, 63, 69, 111, 133, 135, 143, 173, 191, 198, 200, 208, 212, 251, 261, 264, 289, 294, 298, 301, 303, 333, 358, 366, 409-10, 432, 435, 481, 506, 519-20, 541, 546, 550, 560-61, 570, 575, 584, 592, 658
Barrosse, T. 672
Barthes, R. G. 4
Bassler, J. M. 252, 546, 653-54
Bauckham, R. XV, 134, 176, 190, 250, 258, 266, 304, 320, 359, 537-38, 544, 548-49, 552, 611, 619-20, 650-51, 655

Bauer, A. 504, 528, 593
Bauer, D. R. 18
Beardsley, M. C. 171
Beasley-Murray, G. R. 231, 241-42, 296-97, 344, 414-15, 476, 482, 541, 600, 621, 659-661, 665
Beck, D. R. 30, 118, 131, 134-35, 169, 543, 568
Becker, J. 643
Becker, U. 407-09
Beckman, K. 361, 365, 367
Beekman, K. D. 2
Beirne, M. M. 29-30, 134, 509, 515, 522, 524
Benedict XVI. 650
Bennema, C. XII-XIII, XVI, 23, 27, 47-48, 59, 61-62, 65, 71, 73, 78, 80, 86, 97-98, 107-08, 119, 121, 129, 134, 137-38, 146, 149-50, 155, 157, 163, 165, 168, 170, 189-90, 192, 202-03, 216, 222, 224-25, 228, 233, 242, 252-53, 266, 268, 307-08, 312, 331, 348, 352, 362-63, 365, 375, 377, 381, 382-85, 421, 439-40, 445, 464, 466, 468-69, 474, 509, 512, 514-16, 519-22, 524, 527, 537, 548, 550, 568, 580-83, 585, 588, 590-91, 638, 640, 647-49, 658
Berger, K. 148
Berlin, A. XII, 9, 12, 76, 169, 334, 353, 369, 377-78, 386, 430
Bernard, J. H. 133, 250
Bernstein, C. 260
Beutler, J. 397, 400
Bittner, W. J. 315
Black, C. C. 656
Blaine, Jr., B. B. 133-34, 151, 153, 197
Blank, J. 504, 509, 514, 516, 521, 523
Blass, F. 143
Bligh, J. 271
Blinzer, J. 619
Blomberg, C. 531
Boers, H. 274

Boismard, M.-É. 113, 133, 211, 231, 318
Bond, H. K. 14, 532, 535, 579, 583–84, 588, 590–92, 594
Bonneau, N. R. 271
Bonney, W. 516, 518, 522
Booth, W. C. 50, 108, 428
Borgman, P. 22
Böttrich, C. 154
Bourquin, Y. 11–12; 299, 317, 356–57, 377, 428–29, 641, 663
Boyarin, D. 72, 382
Brant, J.-A. 32, 187, 270–71, 294, 378–79, 533, 640
Bratcher, R. G. 230
Brawley, R. L. 604
Brock, A. G. 627
Brodie, T. L. 52, 56, 111–12, 197, 201, 240–41, 333, 346, 356, 358, 410, 443, 541, 553, 559, 561, 563–64, 608–09, 611
Brooks, G. 488
Brown, D. 659
Brown, D. 626
Brown, R. E. 27, 51, 95, 111–13, 133, 135, 138, 144–45, 158, 172, 191, 197–98, 201, 208–09, 222–23, 231, 239, 241–42, 251, 263–64, 268, 270–71, 275–76, 289, 301–02, 304, 311, 346, 366, 394, 398, 400–01, 429, 432, 448, 478, 481, 484, 499, 530–32, 552, 560–63, 570–71, 574, 582–84, 586–89, 592, 594–95, 600, 608, 618, 620, 622, 624, 658–59, 674
Brown, T. G. XIII
Brown, J. K. 211
Brownson, J. V. 365–66, 368, 371
Bruce, F. F. 199, 560–61, 563
Brumlik, M. 74
Bruner, F. D. 324, 614, 623
Buch-Hansen, G. XIII
Bühner, J.-A. 114
Bultmann, R. 23, 75, 113, 144, 174, 214–15, 250, 264, 303, 329, 349–50, 366, 382, 509–10, 521–22, 538, 541, 545, 586, 590–91, 593, 595, 599–600, 610, 620–21
Burge, G. M. XIII, 133, 135, 193, 391, 439
Burkill, T. A. 531
Burnett, F. W. 17, 27, 377, 401, 487, 568, 639

Burridge, R. A. 187
Busse, U. 153
Byrne, B. 462, 537, 546

Cahill, P. J. 271
Calvin, J. 242, 410, 490
Camp, C. V. 287
Campenhausen, H. von 594
Cane, A. 361, 366–67
Carmichael, C. M. 204, 271, 274, 554
Caron, G. 31, 75–76, 88
Carson, D. A. 133, 171, 221, 366, 410, 413, 415, 420, 425, 575, 600, 622, 672
Chapman, D. W. 288
Charlesworth, J. H. 148, 266, 539, 541, 548, 575
Chatman, S. XII, 4–6, 10–12, 29–30, 55, 79, 108, 117–18, 246, 335, 352, 364, 377, 384, 428, 581
Chaucer, G. 282
Chilton, B. 627
Clark-Soles, J. 618, 626–27, 639
Clivaz, C. 20
Collins, R. F. 23–24, 46–47, 52, 59, 170, 192, 286, 306–07, 314, 367, 379–80, 461, 474, 500, 537, 541
Coloe, M. L. 56, 195, 200–01, 204, 207, 209, 211, 229, 231, 457, 554, 556, 618
Conway, C. M. 25–26, 29, 47, 58, 133, 152, 169, 238, 373, 380–81, 474, 480, 537, 623, 633, 639
Cosgrove, C. H. 481
Coulot, C. 214
Coulston, J. C. N. 559
Croy, C. N. 245, 560
Cullmann, O. 360
Culpepper, R. A. XIII, XV, 24, 46, 75, 85, 99, 116, 118, 127, 129, 131, 137–40, 146, 149–50, 151, 163, 169–70, 192, 209, 214–15, 224–26, 229, 234, 258–59, 306–07, 324–25, 346, 347, 354–55, 356–57, 360, 367, 371–72, 378–80, 382, 398–400, 403, 430, 434–35, 440, 461–62, 474, 494, 526, 533, 537, 541, 549, 573, 578, 583, 585–86, 590, 596, 600, 639, 641, 646–47, 651, 653–54, 656, 665, 668–69, 673
Cuvillier, É. 223

Danker, F. W. 313, 321–22
Danove, P. 16
Darr, J. A. 18–19, 30, 303
Daube, D. 284, 484
Dauer, A. 641–42
Davies, M. 24, 365, 370, 462–63
Davies, W. D. 283–84
Dawsey, J. M. 19
Day, J. N. 269, 272–74
De Boer, M. C. 100, 138, 147–48, 580, 585, 588, 590–91
De Goedt, M. 208
De Jonge, M. 258
De la Garenne, G. M. 619
De la Potterie, I. 399, 595, 644
De Varebeke, A. J. 582
Debrunner, A. 143
Delitzsch, F. 250
Dettwiler, A. 513, 550
Diefenbach, M. 32
Dietzfelbinger, C. 507, 509, 512, 515–16, 518–21, 525, 674
Dionne, C. 21–22
Docherty, T. 552
Dodd, C. H. 50, 110, 240, 260, 338, 658
Donaldson, T. L. 252
Draper, J. A. 52, 397
Drijvers, H. J. W. 528
Dschulnigg, P. XIII, 24–25, 157, 160, 163, 165, 249, 254, 257, 259, 260, 318, 372, 477, 494, 504, 508, 512–13, 515–16, 519–20, 522–23, 526, 528, 654
Du Toit, D. S. 16
Duke, P. D. 170–71, 191, 195, 249, 439, 589, 608
Dunn, J. D. G. 297

Ebner, M. 16, 514–15
Eder, J. 1, 8, 80, 362, 380, 456
Edwards, R. 29
Ehrman, A. 360
Ehrman, B. 408–09
Eisele, W. 518, 528
Eisen, U. 22–23
Elowsky, J. 131, 210, 239, 560–61, 564–65, 609–10
Ernst, J. 46, 50, 59
Esler, P. F. 461, 468, 470, 651
Eslinger, L. 271, 274, 362, 370–71

Ewen, J. XII, 6, 12, 27, 30, 80, 115, 130, 170, 308, 363, 395, 402, 440

Farelly, N. 170, 355, 367–68, 370–71, 509, 516, 519, 523–24
Fausset, A. R. 659
Fehribach, A. 29, 170, 233, 269, 272, 274, 277
Fenske, W. 190, 366
Feuillet, A. 315, 325
Fewell, D. N. 10–11, 271–72
Finnern, S. 13, 79–80, 107, 362, 375, 455–56, 663
Fish, S. E. 647
Fleddermann, H. T. 362
Fokkelman, J. 11
Fontaine, C. R. 287
Fontijn, J. 2
Forster, E. M. XII, 1–2, 10–12, 30, 47–48, 191, 215, 246, 307, 334–35, 369, 373
Freed, E. D. 321
Frei, H. 20
Freund, R. A. 178
Frey, J. 72, 91, 102, 123, 397, 399, 432–33, 436, 462, 507, 509, 511–22, 526–29, 622
Fuller, R. 354
Funk, R. W. 143

Gardner, T. 491
Garský, Z. 453
Gathercole, S. 361
Gench, F. T. XIII, 26, 170
Genette, G. 79, 428
Giblin, C. H. 311, 485, 541, 579, 595
Gibson, S. 264
Giles, T. 284, 289, 296
Gill, C. 639
Glancy, A. 590
Glasson, T. F. 53
Gniesmer, D. F. 96, 579, 584–86, 588–89, 591–92, 595
Gnilka, J. 423
Godet, F. L. 250
Gosling, F. A. 361
Gossip, A. J. 356, 358
Gowler, D. B. 215, 303
Green, E. 410, 412, 415–19
Greimas, A. J. 3, 5, 11–12, 30, 115, 357, 376, 402, 456

Griffin-Jones, R. 627
Gruber, M. 481, 508-09, 514-18, 521-23, 529
Guardiola-Sáenz, L. 407-08, 410-14, 417
Guilding, A. 570
Gunn, D. 10-11
Gunther, J. J. 541
Guthrie, D. 669

Haenchen, E. 94, 264, 333, 474, 506, 508, 512, 517, 584, 586, 590, 594
Hahn, F. 73
Hakola, R. 31, 72, 89, 202-03, 354, 425, 463-64, 487-88, 492, 531
Hall, J. F. 559
Hall, R. G. 552
Halliday, M. A. K. 599
Hanhart, K. 190
Harker, J. W. 109
Harmon, W. 551
Harstine, S. XIV, 62, 169, 508, 526
Harstock, C. 21
Hartenstein, J. 26-27, 53, 60, 79-80, 151-52, 154, 161, 163, 215, 506, 508, 511, 523, 528, 574, 624, 627
Hartin, P. J. 151
Harvey, A. E. 51-52
Harvey, W. J. XII, 3, 12, 30, 115, 130, 215, 334, 389, 395, 402
Hasitschka, M. 164, 523
Heil, J. P. 407, 507, 515, 517, 520, 522, 525, 527, 584, 586-87, 589
Hengel, M. 210, 266, 614
Hergenröder, C. 442
Heyd, T. 109
Hezser, C. 404
Hill, C. E. 190
Hochman, B. 5, 29, 377-78
Hodges, Z. C. 658
Hoegen-Rohls, C. 157
Hof, R. 108
Hoffman, G. 453
Hogan, L. P. 332
Holladay, C. R. 669
Holleran, J. W. 443
Holtzmann, H. J. 619
Holzmeister, U. 190
Hoo, G. S. 439
Hooker, M. D. 49
Hopkins, A. 129, 131, 390

Horsley, R. A. 52
Hoskyns, E. C. 223, 609, 615
Howard, J. K. 332
Howard, J. M. 32-33, 430
Howell, J. R. 15
Hunt, S. A. XIII, 90, 101, 103, 161, 176, 194, 238, 249, 257-58, 290, 297, 304, 333, 348, 358, 365, 413, 463, 468, 551, 608-09, 630
Hunter, A. M. 614
Hur, J. 20
Hylen, S. E. 33, 78, 86, 101, 105, 133, 216-18, 224, 226, 244, 252, 258, 293, 301-02, 399-400, 435, 499, 550

Ilan, T. 467, 475
Incigneri, B. J. 651
Instone-Brewer, D. 286
Iser, W. 428, 582

Jäger, D. 453
James, H. 1
Jamieson, R. 659
Jannidis, F. 1, 4, 7-8, 74, 81, 119, 357, 362, 451
Jaubert, A. 271, 551
Jebb, S. 205
Jeremias, J. 383
Johnson-Debaufre, M. 626-27
Jones, L. P. 274
Judge, P. J. 308

Keener, C. S. 158, 192, 234, 264, 272-73, 278, 280-81, 284-86, 288, 310, 367, 389, 391, 423, 426, 441, 448, 508-09, 517, 520, 522, 524, 551, 559, 562-63, 601-02, 614-15
Keith, C. 403-06, 408-09, 417
Kellogg, R. 3-4, 380
Kerr, A. R. 658
Kierspel, L. 31, 61-62, 71, 98
Kilpatrick, G. D. 243, 321
Kim, D. 365-68, 372
Kindt, T. 108
Kingsbury, J. D. 119
Kirchschläger, P. G. 508, 511-13, 525
Kittel, G. 230
Kitzberger, I. R. 30-31, 204, 209, 212, 293, 480, 491
Klassen, W. 360-61, 365-66, 368-69, 371

Klauck, H.-J. 321, 365-66, 369, 371, 520, 522
Klink, III., E. W. 234, 651
Koch, T. 118
Koester, C. R. 26, 73, 141, 170-71, 190-93, 289, 311, 325, 347-48, 350, 371, 380, 426, 441, 462, 537, 543-44, 546, 559, 609, 615-16, 639-40, 672-73
Koet, B. J. 491-92, 496
Kohler, H. 517, 519, 522
Kokkinos, N. 178
Kopas, J. 206
Köppe, T. 108
Kossen, H. B. 397, 400
Köstenberger, A. 66, 129, 133, 141, 241, 297-98, 360, 391, 394, 407, 409-10, 534
Kovacs, J. L. 398-99
Kowalksi, B. 514, 519
Krafft, E. 23-24, 367
Kreitzer, L. J. 403
Kremer, J. 464-64, 506-09, 513-24, 526-29
Kügler, J. 151, 158
Kühner, R. 668
Kühschelm, R. 516, 521, 526
Kumlehn, M. 519, 526
Kundsin, K. 263
Kurz, W. S. 537, 671
Kysar, R. 75, 261

Labahn, M. XIV, 91, 154, 156, 161, 163-64, 356, 446-47, 449, 558, 603-05
Lamouille, A. 211, 318
Landis, S. 321
Lang, M. 511, 517, 519, 526, 602
Lanser, S. S. 538
Le Bohec, Y. 561
Lee, D. 20, 209-10, 442, 515
Leidig, E. 190
Leinhäupl-Wilke, A. 519-22, 524, 526-27
Léon-Dufour, X. 274
Leslie, R. C. 273
Levine, A.-J. 169
Levinsohn, S. H. 421, 598
Lieu, J. M. 204, 207, 621
Lightfoot, J. 250, 303
Lightfoot, R. H. 312
Lim, S. U. 293, 296
Lincoln, A. T. 49, 52, 58-59, 89, 93, 193-94, 199, 289, 292, 294, 296-98, 301-02, 345, 355, 367, 371-72, 386, 407-10, 412-13, 415, 430, 432, 434-37, 444, 470, 478, 480, 483, 492, 501, 538, 544, 551-52, 563-65, 574-75, 583, 586, 588, 591, 599, 652
Lindars, B. 135, 172-73, 231, 238, 242, 321-23, 346, 410, 443, 477, 541, 543, 550, 552, 603, 622, 659, 661, 671
Link, A. 269
Liptay, F. 108
Loader, W. 286
Löning, K. 516-17, 527
Louw, J. P. 321, 333, 421
Lowe, M. 72
Lotman, J. M. 4, 95, 453
Lützelberger, E. C. J. 148
Lyons, W. J. 299, 303

Maccini, R. G. 28-29, 294-95, 407, 413
Malbon, E. S. 15, 169, 202, 656
Malina, B. J. 234, 353, 363
Manning, Jr., G. T. XIV
Manns, F. 211, 231
Margolin, U. XII, 6-7, 334, 377
Marguerat, D. 11-12, 299, 317, 356-57, 377, 428-29, 641, 663
Marrow, S. B. 61
Martin, M. W. 132, 372, 552
Martyn, J. L. 72, 92, 138, 142-43, 145, 147, 249, 251, 429, 439, 448
Mason, S. N. 383
Mastin, B. A. 551
Matson, M. 247
Matthews, C. R. 182
Matthiessen, M. I. M. 599
Mattila, T. 18
Maynard, A. H. 151, 205, 539
McHugh, J. F. 322
McRay, J. 147
McWhirter, J. 233
Meeks, W. A. 251, 258, 278
Meier, J. P. 309, 344
Meiser, M. 361, 372
Menken, M. J. J. XV, 60, 112, 605
Merenlahti, P. 14-15, 183, 202-05, 213, 377, 487-88
Metzger, B. M. 143, 239
Metzger, P. 424
Metzner, R. 530
Meyer, R. 349-50

Michaels, J. R. 107, 121, 190, 195–97, 240, 242–43, 288, 297–98, 309, 324, 328, 410, 412–13, 416–17, 439, 441–44, 476, 479, 600, 612, 614–15
Michaud, J.-P. 205
Michie, D. 15
Miesel, S. 627
Minear, P. S. 359
Mitchell, M. 651
Moloney, F. J. 57, 66, 68, 73, 83, 92, 111, 113, 138, 158, 191, 204, 223, 229–30, 273–76, 278, 309–13, 315–17, 321, 323, 329–30, 366, 370, 398–401, 440–41, 448, 457, 461, 464, 477, 487, 492, 539, 543, 551, 572, 582, 586, 591, 594, 611, 671
Moore, S. D 189, 277, 292, 299, 363, 428–29, 647
Moore, W. E. 397–98
Most, G. W. 508, 515, 519–21, 526, 528–29
Morris, L. 89, 231, 289, 441–42, 658
Motyer, S. 76–77, 382
Moule, C. F. D. 190
Müller, C. G. 21
Müller, U. B. 46, 57
Müller, W. 30
Myers, C. 415

Neirynck, F. 133, 311, 318, 321, 323, 541
Neubrand, M. 71, 89
Neugebauer, J. 512
Neusner, J. 261
Newman, B. M. 333, 659
Neyrey, J. H. 55, 190, 198, 271, 296, 298, 362, 410, 607, 613
Nicklas, T. 31–32, 51, 76, 153, 190, 197, 262, 309, 312, 315, 331, 658, 661
Nicol, W. 318
Nida, E. A. 321, 333, 421, 659
Nielsen, J. T. 615
North, W. E. S. 491–93, 496, 499, 651
Nünning, A. 108–09
Nuttall, A. D. 255

O'Day, G. R. XIII, 169–70, 217, 223, 275, 292, 301–02, 327, 368, 399–400, 407, 410–11, 414, 416–17, 419, 435, 487, 498, 653
Oden, T. 409

O'Donnell, M. B. 422–23
Öhler, M. 322
Okorie, A. M. 19–20
Okure, T. 269
Olsen, C. E. 627
Olsson, B. 229, 274
O'Neill, J. C. 108
Osten-Sacken, P. von der 74
Ottillinger, A. 54

Paffenroth, K. 370–71
Painter, J. 169, 177, 311, 554
Panackel, C. 591
Pancaro, S. 257–58
Parsenios, G. 270
Parson, M. C. 21
Pathrapankal, J. 398
Pedersen, J. 169
Pedersen, S. 169
Pelling, C. 487
Pesch, R. 201
Peskowitz, M. 666
Peters, D. E. 628
Petersen, W. 408–10
Peterson, N. R. 169, 174
Pfister, M. 79, 117, 456
Phelan, J. 7
Phillips, G. A. 271–72
Piégay-Gros, N. 643
Pilch, J. 332–33, 336
Piper, R. 461, 468, 470
Pollard, T. E. 491
Popkes, E. E. 551
Poplutz, U. 18, 79, 81, 84, 91, 116–18, 375, 451
Popp, T. 505–08, 510, 514, 517, 520, 522–25
Porter, S. E. 221
Powell, M. A. 10, 17, 50, 127, 129, 202, 262, 299, 375, 388, 428–29
Pratscher, W. 361
Propp, V. J. 2–3, 11, 456

Quast, K. 133, 541, 543
Quek, T.-M. 54

Rad, G. von 230
Rebell, W. 518
Reed, J. T. 421–22, 598
Rein, M. 447

Reinhartz, A. 74, 76, 104, 131, 410, 479, 495–96, 530, 533, 535, 651
Reinmuth, E. 492, 527
Rengstorf, K. H. 507, 673
Rensberger, D. K. 249, 251
Renz, G. 252, 258–59, 653–55, 657
Resseguie, J. XII, 12–14, 25, 50, 52, 55–56, 79, 117, 130, 132, 134, 203, 212, 228, 323, 334–35, 347, 353, 364, 369–72, 373, 377–78, 384–85, 538, 540–41, 551, 574, 663, 668
Revell, C. 616
Rhees, R. 191
Rhoads, D. 15
Ricœur, P. 642
Ridderbos, H. N. 57
Riesner, R. 454
Rimmon-Kenan, S. 5–6, 12, 20, 30, 47–48, 53, 79, 117, 308, 363, 369, 440
Rinke, J. 51, 53
Ritt, H. 269
Robertson, A. T. 113, 566
Robinson, B. P. 323
Robinson, J. A. T. 112, 250
Rohrbaugh, R. L. 234
Rooke, D. 413–14
Roth, P. 529
Rowland, C. 190
Rubel, G. 511, 513–16, 518–22, 525, 527
Ruckstuhl, E. 24, 318
Ruschmann, S. 513–14
Rylaarsdam, J. C. 230

Saldarini, A. J. 118, 122, 126
Sanders, E. P. 246
Sanders, J. N. 551
Sandnes, K. O. 212, 256
Sasse, H. 61
Sawyer, D. 626
Schaberg, J. 626–27
Schaff, B. 125
Schams, C. 405
Schenk, W. 318
Schenke, L. 87, 95, 161, 218, 270, 448, 506, 509, 512, 516, 519–21
Schmidl, M. 253
Schnackenburg, R. 48, 73, 120, 191, 195, 198, 214, 251, 264, 282, 286, 289, 327, 368, 398–99, 425, 478, 514, 520–21, 528, 539, 545, 552, 584–85, 587, 589, 591–92, 594–95, 620, 659, 661, 674
Schneider, R. 1, 451
Schneiders, S. M. 27–28, 252, 269, 287, 289, 293–94, 296, 298, 307, 410, 485, 492, 623, 638–39
Schnelle, U. 73, 77, 97, 102, 156, 158–59, 166, 189, 379, 504, 509, 513–15, 517, 519–23, 526, 665, 670
Scholes, R. 3–4, 380
Scholtissek, K. 159, 208–09, 212, 457, 519, 521, 526
Schrenk, G. 383
Schröder, J.-M. 309
Schröter, J. 159
Schuchard, B. G. 605
Schultheiß, T. 151–53, 155, 157, 159, 162
Schulz, S. 422
Schürmann, H. 642–43
Schüssler-Fiorenza, E. 28, 269, 473–74
Schwalb, M. 619
Schweizer, E. 318
Scott, J. M. C. 407, 414–16, 418
Seesemann, H. 343
Segovia, F. 169–70, 214–15, 225, 550
Seim, T. K. 28, 491, 619
Senior, D. 541, 604
Sevrin, J. M. 252, 258
Shklovsky, V. XII, 625
Siegert, F. 504, 507, 520–21
Sim, D. C. 651
Simon, L. 151
Skinner, C. W. XVI, 33, 551, 570
Smalley, S. S. 325
Smith, A. 16
Smith, D. M. 382, 410, 476, 478
Söding, T. 163, 522
Spicq, C. 230
Springer, M. D. 488
Staley, J. L. 169, 272, 346, 430–31, 435–36, 441–44, 581, 651
Stare, M. 86
Steiger, A. 191
Steiger, L. 528
Stenger, W. 515–16
Stephen, L. 1
Sternberg, M. 9–10, 203, 233–34, 430, 493–94
Stevenson, G. 613

Stibbe, M. W. G. XII, XIII, 24, 50–51, 54, 142, 146, 169, 238, 244, 270–71, 315, 320–22, 410, 433, 463, 541, 573, 575, 584, 586, 591, 593, 621, 623, 652
Stowasser, M. 49, 56–57
Strange, J. F. 145
Strecker, G. 520, 522
Sturdevant, J. XIII
Swan, T. 637
Sylva, D. D. 259

Talbert, C. H. 192, 410, 425, 575, 654
Tannen, D. 205–06
Tate, W. R. 625
Tennyson, A. L. 460
Thatcher, T. 151, 155, 157, 189, 370, 446, 601, 647
Theobald, M. XIV, 49, 51, 53, 86, 88–89, 92, 118, 134, 374–75, 454, 459, 509, 511–14, 516–18, 521–24, 526–28, 671–72
Thomas, J. C. 333, 335
Thompson, M. M. XIII, 314, 325
Thompson, R. P. 22
Thüsing, W. 399
Thyen, H. 48, 271, 275, 335, 359, 374, 378, 422, 447, 454, 506–07, 509, 516, 519–20, 525–26, 528, 590–91, 593–95, 601, 620–21, 624, 669–70, 674
Toensing, H. 411–12, 414, 418–20
Tolmie, D. F. XIII, XV, 12, 30, 47–48, 59, 77, 84–85, 87, 95, 100, 114–15, 130, 153, 159, 162, 262, 363, 370, 378, 389, 395, 401–02, 550–51, 581, 592, 622, 626–27, 630–31, 639
Tolstoy, L. 290
Torrance, T. F. 397
Tovey, D. 135–36, 541, 544, 548
Traets, C. 319
Tsuchido, K. 185, 398
Tuckett, C. M. 580, 586
Tuschling, R. M. M. 659, 661

Uspensky, B. 17, 538

Van Belle, G. 105, 310–11, 315, 318–20, 324–26
Van der Merwe, D. G. 110
Van der Watt, J. G 208–09, 315, 358, 423
Van Eck, E. 651

Van Iersel, B. M. F. 113
Van Tilborg, S. 28, 134, 136, 450, 507–08, 512–13, 520, 585, 603
VanderKam, J. C. 230, 534
Vermes, G. 261, 531
Vökel, J. M. 442
Von Wahlde, U. C. 71–73, 87, 89, 108, 116, 120, 170, 192, 376

Waetjen, H. 619
Wallace, D. B. 112, 407–408
Walter, L. 518
Warren, A. 2–3
Watkins, C. 567
Watson, D. F. 661
Wead, D. 169
Webb, G. R. 16–17
Webster, J. 292
Weidemann, H.-U. 512–15, 518–22, 527
Wellek, R. 2–3
Wengst, K. 57, 71–72, 94, 374, 454, 509, 514, 517, 520, 522, 552, 590, 669
Wessel, F. 288, 591
Westcott, B. F. 250, 321, 410, 620
Westermann, C. 498
Wiarda, T. 14, 151, 160
Wilckens, U. 512–13, 519
Wilder, T. 339
Williams, C. H. 53, 60
Williams, J. F. 15–16, 356
Williams, R. H. 205
Wilson, J. 56
Wimsatt, Jr., W. K. 171
Winter, B. W. 287
Winter, J. 231
Winter, P. 531
Witetschek, S. 599–600
Witherington, III, B. 423, 600
Witherup, R. D. 19
Wolf, Y. 108
Wright, N. T. 297
Wright, W. M. 362, 370–71
Wuellner, W. H. 273, 462
Wucherpfennig, A. 151
Wünsche, A. 231
Würzbach, N. 453

Zahn, T. 250, 292
Zenger, E. 516–17, 527

Zimmermann, M. 56, 59, 267, 272, 288, 290, 293, 298, 458
Zimmermann, R. XIII, XV, 54, 56, 59, 92–93, 95, 114, 193, 209, 211, 219, 229, 231–32, 236, 245–46, 267, 272, 274, 288, 290, 293, 298, 314, 366, 453–54, 457–59, 468, 483, 492, 504, 556, 612, 630
Zumstein, J. 164, 208, 213, 521, 523–24, 618, 643, 670

Index of Subjects

Aaron 243
Abel 243
Abraham 89–90, 100, 102–03, 194, 383, 609–10
Absence (of Characters) 46, 57–58, 167, 189, 239, 243, 320, 403, 405, 411, 430, 442–43, 462, 492, 498–99, 507, 516, 536, 598, 612, 623, 644–45, 653, 670, 673
Actant → Classification of Characters
Actantial Model 3, 30, 115, 357, 376, 402, 456
Actions
- Actions of Characters (in John) 28, 32, 47–48, 53, 66, 82, 84–86, 88–89, 93, 95, 99–102, 106, 117, 128, 130, 132, 157, 165, 174, 191–92, 206–07, 217–18, 222–23, 231, 245, 247–48, 258, 297–98, 311–12, 317, 344, 346, 350, 356–59, 365, 370–71, 378–80, 390, 393, 398, 401, 405–06, 418–19, 424–26, 431, 433, 436, 442, 444–46, 455–56, 459, 462, 468, 470, 473–75, 480–84, 489, 491, 493, 495–97, 501–04, 506, 525, 527, 530, 538–42, 549, 558, 568–72, 583–87, 590–91, 596, 601, 603, 614–15, 622–23, 634, 642, 653–56, 661, 672
- Actions of Characters (Theoretical Issues) 1, 3, 5–6, 9–10, 13, 17, 20, 26, 78, 80, 117, 172, 175, 216, 233, 246, 295, 307, 356, 364, 376, 378, 392, 422, 433, 466, 474, 568, 570, 598
Actor → Classification of Characters
Actual Reader → Reader
Adam 193, 211, 555–66, 616, 636
Adonijah 243
Adulterous Woman 26, 40, 212, 276, 343, 405–06, 407–20, 444, 652
Adultery 285, 288, 413, 415
Agent → Classification of Characters
Aggression 99, 101, 160, 352–53, 418
Ahithophel 367

Allegory 8, 209, 267, 276, 288–89
Ambiguity 23, 25, 33, 78, 104–05, 109, 119, 129, 140, 144, 151–67, 182, 205–06, 212, 216, 222, 225–26, 233, 238, 241, 251–53, 269, 272, 292, 308–09, 346, 377, 379–81, 390, 411, 420, 422, 474, 508, 524–25, 531–32, 537, 540, 562, 595, 597, 624–25, 628, 653
Ambrose 410
Anachrony 16
Analepsis 55, 59, 622, 652
Analogy 6, 20, 144, 280, 462, 542, 672
Ananias (in Acts) 19
Andrew (in John) 33, 35, 127–32, 133–36, 137–50, 152, 154, 168, 176–78, 180, 183–84, 186, 193–98, 230, 254, 264, 298, 300, 320, 342, 357–58, 389, 397, 401, 479, 548, 635, 640, 666–67, 670–76
Angel/Angels (in John) 45, 145, 337, 421, 613, 628–29, 631, 635–36, 638, 658–62
Animal Sellers 37, 245–248 (→ also Money Changers)
Annas 44, 382, 393, 530–36, 541, 558, 564, 57-1, 574
Anointing 66, 123, 258, 304, 344, 398, 409, 433, 467, 469, 473–75, 480–86, 627, 646, 654–55
Anonymity 23, 30, 35, 81, 97, 129–36, 141–43, 148–49, 152, 160, 237, 260–67, 292, 320, 355, 388–89, 446, 448, 481, 539, 541–42, 568, 601, 606, 665, 670–71, 675
Anonymous Disciple (in John) 80, 133–36, 142, 152, 320, 389, 665
Anonymous Judean/a "Jew" 38, 127, 260–67
Another Disciple → Beloved Disciple
Antagonist → Classification of Characters
Anti-Judaism 31–32, 74, 76, 261
Antipathy 10, 129, 380, 388, 390
Anti-Semitism → Anti-Judaism
Apostasy 18, 364–68, 370–72

Apostle 137, 180–82, 267, 269, 280, 296, 298, 633, 638, 669
Appearance (Physical Appearance of Characters) 6–7, 9–10, 20, 46, 466, 469, 540, 639
Aristotle 1, 246, 280, 362
Arrest (of Jesus) 94, 103, 122, 160–61, 193, 200, 211, 217, 240, 340, 349, 364, 369, 371, 374, 384, 388–96, 473, 479, 509, 534, 542, 554–68, 570–71, 573, 576–77, 583, 610, 612–13, 630, 674
Arrogance 273, 276, 487, 493, 520
Artefact → Classification of Characters
Ascent 145, 180, 209, 243, 322, 389, 514, 613, 628, 630, 637, 660
Aside → Narrative Aside
Auctorial Narrator → Narrator
Augustine 239, 389, 409–10, 416, 489–91, 560, 564
Author
- Ideal Author (in John) 134, 266, 537
- Implied Author (in John) 77, 88, 99, 107–09, 135–36, 261, 456, 531, 533–34, 536, 573, 583, 588, 597, 616–17, 628–30, 634, 655, 660, 664–65, 668–71, 673–76
- Implied Author (Theoretical Issues) 10, 114, 138–40, 374, 401, 428, 530, 533, 581, 626, 668
- Real Author (in John) 68, 72, 80, 89, 125, 128–31, 137–38, 140, 160, 172, 244, 251, 262, 264, 266, 311, 330, 339, 363, 376, 391, 422, 445, 536, 548, 574–75, 580, 617, 632, 640, 643, 665, 670
- Real Author (Theoretical Issues) 6–7, 48, 74, 109, 137–39, 170, 233, 363, 372, 488, 668
Authority/Authorities
- Authority/Authorities (in John) 40, 51, 71–74, 78, 87, 98, 102, 104, 106, 108, 112–14, 117–18, 120–24, 156, 158, 166–67, 240, 247, 257, 260, 262, 308, 312, 325, 329, 340–41, 345–46, 349–51, 354, 361–62, 364, 371–72, 373–81, 382–83, 404–06, 418, 426, 436, 444–46, 449, 452, 470–71, 476, 479, 481, 484, 506, 539–40, 549, 560, 562, 564, 584–85, 591, 594–97, 602, 605, 608, 610, 644, 655, 676
- Authority/Authorities (in Mark) 15
- Authority/Authorities (in Matthew) 18

Background Character → Classification of Characters
Background Information 118, 120, 622
Baptism 47, 53–55, 57, 113, 120, 127, 181, 195, 210, 217, 230, 255, 260, 262–65, 275, 300, 335, 432–33, 454–55, 460, 604, 606
Baptist → John the Baptist/Baptizer
Barabbas 44, 579, 587, 598–600, 608
Bar-Jesus (in Luke) 21
Bartholomew (in Synoptics) 180, 190
Bartimaeus (in Luke) 338
Beggar 41, 343, 431, 433, 441–42, 446, 484
Believers across the Jordan 42, 451–59
Beloved Disciple 23, 29, 33, 43, 58–59, 63, 131, 133–36, 138, 142, 148, 153, 156, 158–64, 166, 168, 172, 186, 196–97, 208–09, 211, 213, 224, 243, 359, 367, 394, 461, 463, 467, 471, 515, 517, 522, 527, 537–49, 556, 560, 573, 575, 577, 603, 610–12, 617–19, 623–24, 626–27, 632–35, 641–45, 665, 667, 669–72, 675–76
Bethany
- Bethany 26, 28–29, 32, 42, 94, 105, 107, 398, 409, 460–61, 467–68, 472–86, 494, 497, 508, 564, 627–28, 634, 664
- Bethany (across the Jordan) 84, 114, 263, 300, 454
Bethesda 66, 85, 337, 484 (→ also Bethzatha)
Bethlehem 283, 302, 304
Bethsaida 144–45, 147–48, 168, 176–80, 185, 187, 194–95, 300, 302, 337, 400–01, 666, 675
Bethzatha 34, 39, 337, 416, 420 (→ also Bethesda)
Betray/Betrayal/Betrayer 17, 40, 70, 151, 155, 158, 190, 213, 220, 223–24, 345, 360–372, 390, 398, 424–25, 474, 480–81, 486, 526, 539, 542, 547, 549, 552, 558, 560, 577, 623, 633, 668, 675 (→ also Judas)
Betrothal 229, 272, 288, 290, 297–98, 413, 636

Birth → Born from Above
Blasphemy 83, 90, 95, 104, 383, 453, 455, 458, 530, 580
Blind Man (in Luke) 21
Blind Man (in John) → Man Born Blind
Blood 79, 104, 209–10, 327, 543–44, 604, 616, 664
Bold/Boldness 49, 51, 58, 159, 174, 220, 223–24, 274, 351, 357, 430, 525, 547, 550, 574, 576, 639, 653, 655–57 (→ also Courage)
Born from Above 209, 212, 249, 255–59, 324, 342, 540, 638
Boy with Loaves and Fish 39, 146, 149, 177, 183, 314, 356–59, 667
Branch (*Netzer*) 190, 200–01, 563
Bread
- Bread (Physical) 86, 154–55, 186, 217, 356–59, 367, 539, 560, 673
- Bread (Jesus as Bread) 147, 154–55, 174, 241, 265, 318–19, 348, 358, 391, 485, 673

Breathe Upon 193, 210–11, 556
Bride 194, 267, 269, 272, 297, 458, 636
Bridegroom
- Bridegroom 29, 36–37, 56, 131, 194, 205, 207, 228, 230–32, *233–37*, 267, 269, 272, 290, 297, 334, 458–59, 636
- Friend of the Bridegroom 56, 231, 267, 458
- Mother of the Bridegroom 207

Bridging Function 51, 60, 168, 179–80, 182–83, 187, 294, 315, 416, 526
Brother
- Brother (Beloved Disciple as Brother of Jesus) 208, 543
- Brothers (Biological, General) 42, 82, 128, 133, 140, 142–54, 161, 196, 198, 283–85, 290, 300, 460–61, 467, 470, 473, 475–86, 489–91, 494, 498–500, 528, 548, 666–67, 671, 675
- Brothers of Jesus (Biological) 37, 64, 87, 207, *238–44*, 300, 509, 514, 543, 551
- Brothers of Jesus (Spiritual) 208–09, 212, 243–44, 372, 514, 637

Burial 82–83, 96, 162, 193, 249, 252, 258–59, 398, 402, 460, 468, 473, 480, 484, 565, 578, 607, 612, 646–57, 660, 662

Caesar 178, 387, 594–95, 614 (→ also Emperor)
Caiaphas 43, 94, 127, 362, 382, 389, 399, *530–36*, 558, 570–71, 574, 633
Cain 243
Calvin 242, 410, 489–91, 500
Cana 82, 191, 194–95, 204–07, 210–13, 228–39, 242, 265, 300, 302, 306, 312, 315–18, 321–25, 330, 335, 337, 397, 471, 475, 485, 506, 621, 643–45, 667
Canaanite Woman (in Matthew) 18, 498
Capernaum 144, 207, 238–39, 300, 306, 308–09, 317, 321–323, 326, 329, 339, 348, 564
Card → Classification of Characters
Caricature → Classification of Characters
Carnival → Classification of Characters
Center → Middle
Cephas → Peter
Characterization
- Characterization in Acts 13–14, 19–22, 118, 137, 179–82, 187, 243, 256, 303, 338, 528, 649
- Characterization in John *passim*
- Characterization in Luke 14, 18–23
- Characterization in Mark 15–17
- Characterization in Matthew 14, 17–18
- Direct Characterization 1, 6, 9–12, 20, 22, 26, 32, 48, 79–80, 82–85, 88, 90, 99, 101–02, 106, 108, 114, 117, 215–16, 401, 493, 570
- Indirect Characterization 1, 6, 10, 12, 20, 22, 26, 79–80, 82, 84, 86, 90, 100–01, 104, 106, 108, 114, 117, 191, 215–16, 401–02, 468, 570, 582, 590, 664, 666
- Techniques of Characterization 9–10, 12–14, 22, 29, 48, 50, 100, 119, 137, 154, 233, 270, 376–78, 380–81, 429–30, 466, 474, 483, 508, 513, 516, 552, 629, 631, 634, 638
- Theories on Characterization 1–12, 17–19, 26, 29–30, 33, 48, 80, 117, 137, 139, 169–70, 189, 202–03, 216, 299, 302–03, 305, 308, 334, 351, 362, 384, 428, 433, 440, 455, 466, 487–89, 648

Characters
- Characters and Action → Actions
- Constellation of Characters 13, 26, 80,

84, 91, 95, 97, 106, 114–15, 452–53, 455–56, 459, 505–06, 511, 515, 641
- Evaluation of Characters 11–12, 27, 30, 32–33, 46, 49–50, 59, 66, 77, 95, 109, 129, 166, 203, 215, 222, 224, 351–55, 362–64, 370–72, 374, 378, 380, 384, 386–87, 399, 430, 434, 440, 445, 464, 570, 579, 653,
- Relationship between Characters 1, 5, 13, 15, 21–22, 28, 31, 62, 81, 97–99, 103, 119, 141, 158, 161, 164, 175, 195, 205–08, 212–13, 216, 221–23, 241, 267, 283, 285, 287–88, 291, 294–97, 312, 327, 364, 371, 375–76, 381, 400, 404, 424, 447, 457, 462, 465, 475, 485, 494, 506, 510, 519, 521, 524, 526–27, 534, 539, 543, 547, 549, 575, 583–84, 602–03, 619, 628–29, 637–38, 641–44, 665, 667, 669–71
- Traits of Characters 2, 4–7, 12–15, 18–19, 21–22, 24, 30, 33, 47–48, 50–52, 59, 63, 75, 77, 80–81, 84–85, 87–88, 90–91, 96, 101–04, 106–08, 114–15, 119, 123, 125, 129, 134–35, 149, 191–92, 215, 246, 251, 307–08, 312, 334, 351–53, 362–65, 368–70, 372–73, 377–81, 384–86, 401–02, 440, 445, 452–53, 456, 459, 462, 474, 487, 537, 550–52, *581–97*, 629, 631–32, 639, 663, 666, 668, 674–75 (→ also Paradigm of Traits)

Chief Priests 40, 78, 95–96, 116–18, 120–25, 129, 249, 304, 345, 349, 372, 374–76, 379, *382–87*, 388, 390–95, 461, 467, 470, 479, 530, 532–33, 535–36, 562, 583, 591, 596, 609, 646, 649

Children of God 89, 127–28, 208–09, 212–13, 253, 259, 314, 531–33

Chorus 32, 80, 93, *292–98*, 479

Christ → Messiah

Christology 32, 60, 90, 100, 104, 106, 111, 113, 141, 155–56, 254, 265, 327, 365, 452, 457–58, 512, 521, 525, 527, 544, 572, 594, 609, 629–30

Christophany 518, 566–67, 614, 635, 638–39

Chronotype → Classification of Characters

Chrysostom 239, 288, 389, 489–90, 609

Church 22, 158, 166–67, 179–82, 185, 187, 244, 250, 293, 337, 372, 408, 417, 514–15, 520, 528, 626, 640, 643–44

Cipher 158, 202, 249, 307, 416, 636

Classification of Characters
- Actant 3, 114–15, 174, 182, 187, 228, 363, 376, 401–02, 440, 456, 568
- Actor 3, 5, 32, 107, 252, 423–24, 433, 602
- Agent 11, 16, 27, 58, 76, 130–31, 135, 207, 228, 233, 235–37, 246, 331, 352, 362–63, 384, 388, 390, 392–93, 395, 440, 453, 455–56, 459–60, 568
- Antagonist 1, 70, 129, 305, 344, 376, 388–90, 302, 395, 421–22, 425–26, 432, 434, 456, 457
- Artefact 8
- Background Character 3, 115, 334, 336, 402, 446, 448, 663, 675
- Bakhtinian Categories 16, 171, 174
- Card 3, 334
- Caricature 2, 24, 159, 293–94
- Carnival 16–17
- Chronotope 16–17
- Complex Character 2, 5–6, 10, 32, 47, 59, 76, 104, 106–07, 115, 149, 151, 166, 264, 307, 352–53, 363–64, 370, 373, 377–79, 381, 384–86, 402, 440, 445, 463, 474, 524, 580, 587, 596, 639, 653 (→ also Complexity)
- Connective Character *168–88*
- Corporate Character 107, 114–15, 216–19, 223, 351–54, 382, 385–86, 397, 402, 558,
- Dominant Character 13, 379, 655
- Double Agents *388–96*
- Dynamic Character 2, 12, 80, 107, 363, 373, 378–79, 381, 429, 437, 665, 667, 676
- Elderly 3
- *Ficelle* 3, 130, 135, 215, 307, 334, 395
- Flat Character 1–2, 4, 9, 11–13, 20, 24–25, 29–30, 32–33, 47, 76, 106–07, 149, 170, 173, 191–92, 215, 228, 246, 283, 307, 331, 334–35, 344, 359, 362–63, 370, 373, 380, 415, 420, 440, 445, 463–65, 537, 558, 596, 611, 639–40, 666–67, 675
- Full-Fledged Character 9, 639
- Functionary 9, 30, 130, 334, 336, 395
- Group Character 31, 78, 81, 83–84,

714 Index of Subjects

97, 102, 107, 116–20, 123, 295, 299–300, 305, 332, 334–35, 432, 451, 456, 618, 621, 623
- Helper 2–3, 5, 18, 357, 359, 456
- Hermeneutical Character 579
- Hero 2, 156, 158, 160, 167, 198, 213, 272, 434, 450, 606, 634
- Ideal Character 395
- Individual/Individuality 27, 80, 134, 192, 313, 352, 362–63, 370, 384, 440, 487
- *Ingénue* 3
- Intermediary Character 20, 168, 181, 185, 334
- Juvenile 3
- Main Character 1, 12–13, 17, 80, 119, 166, 181, 245, 320, 421, 424, 515, 523, 598–99, 604–05
- Major Character 18, 376, 379, 426, 621, 638
- Marginal Character 376, 378–79, 381, 464
- Minor Character 15–16, 18, 23–25, 32, 80, 110, 170, 228, 232, 292, 314, 323, 334, 356, 359, 373, 376, 380–81, 395–96, 421, 474, 573, 598, 621, 656
- Monochromic Character 47
- Multichromatic Character 7
- Multi-Dimensional Character 8, 80, 260–61
- Multi-Layered/Multi-Leveled Character 59, 171, 596
- One-Dimensional Character 28, 47, 80, 149, 265, 362, 370, 550
- Opponent 3, 5, 18, 107, 116, 118–19, 125, 156, 161–62, 194, 365, 376–77, 379, 391, 396, 403–06, 419, 435, 448, 479, 570, 575, 605, 654
- Personality 27, 47, 58, 107, 117, 269, 308, 352–53, 362–63, 384, 386, 433, 440, 464, 636, 639–40
- Protagonist 1, 3, 23, 60, 80, 83, 116, 135, 175, 182, 295, 307, 334, 388, 390–93, 395, 403, 406, 456–57, 667
- Pseudo-Hero 156, 158, 160
- Receiver 3, 5, 363,
- Representative Character 7, 18, 28, 30, 59, 64, 67, 75, 98, 120, 154, 166, 170, 209, 214, 223, 225, 250, 253–54, 269, 289, 296, 306–08, 320–21, 365, 372, 379–81, 400, 403–04, 415, 437, 461–62, 465, 470, 474, 512, 525, 537, 551, 610, 636, 639, 673
- Round Character 1–2, 9, 11–13, 47, 107, 170, 191–92, 215, 295, 307, 334–35, 362–63, 373, 429, 437, 440, 596, 665, 667, 672, 676
- Sender 3, 5, 115, 402
- Simple Character 10, 107, 356, 363
- Static Character 2, 4, 12, 15, 80, 107, 127, 213, 249, 308, 363, 379, 381, 428, 465, 524, 549
- Stereotype 293, 344, 428
- Stock Character 4, 10, 12, 335, 344, 363, 440, 445
- Subsidiary Character 10, 13
- Types 2, 9, 12, 27, 32, 47, 59, 74–76, 119, 135, 149, 192, 213, 228, 238, 251, 268, 306–08, 313, 334, 352, 362–63, 379–81, 384, 414, 440, 445, 462, 464–65, 474, 550, 636, 640
- Walk-On 12, 80, 228, 334–36, 363, 395, 573, 663, 667, 675–76

Cleansed Leper in Mark 17
Cleansing of the Temple 66, 85, 220, 245–48, 297, 560
Clement of Alexandria 554, 609
Climax 527, 555, 614, 636
Co-Crucified 45, 558, *607–17*
Cognitivistic Approach 74, 79, 109
Cohort 44, 200, 361, 364, 390, 393, 395, *554–67*, 569, 635
Comparison of Characters → Characters, Relationship
Complex Character → Classification of Characters
Complexity (of Characters) 5–6, 14, 22, 27, 47, 80, 104, 115, 130, 170, 215, 233, 268, 308, 312, 351–53, 362–64, 370, 373, 377, 384–86, 395, 402, 440, 445, 466, 550, 580, 639 (→ also Classification of Characters)
Concubine (Levite's Concubine) 415
Connective Character → Classification of Characters
Constellation of Characters → Characters, Constellation
Continuum (of Characterization) 5, 19, 27, 223, 308, 351, 353, 362–63, 368, 370, 384–86

Contrast 6, 9, 11, 16, 20, 58, 65, 69, 88, 91, 99, 128–29, 132, 143, 154, 176, 198–99, 218, 241, 265, 296, 310, 325–26, 335, 339, 344, 346, 378, 392, 394–95, 423–24, 435, 437, 446, 456, 469, 476, 482, 517, 526–28, 547, 549–50, 559–60, 571, 573–76, 599, 621–22, 632–33, 644 (→ also Juxtaposition)
Corporate Character → Classification of Characters
Cosmogony 192–93, 554–55, 557, 565, 612–13 (→ also Creation)
Cosmology 192–93, 425, 565–66 (→ also Creation)
Council → Sanhedrin
Courage 158–161, 167, 244, 251, 435, 437, 509, 557, 577, 637 (→ also Boldness)
Courtyard 44, 16–61, 164, 166, 388, 393, 411, 542, 571, 573–75
Creation 193–94, 204, 210, 211, *541–42*, 549, 554, 571, *573–77*, 665 (→ also Cosmology/Cosmogony)
Cross-Cultural 177–83, 185–87
Crowd (in John) 14–15, 18, 25, 39, 58, 64, 66–67, 73, 84, 86–87, 94, 98, 107, 120, 149, 154, 168, 176–78, 184, 218, 223, 238, 240–42, 257, 300–05, 330, 332–33, 335–36, 341, *347–55*, 357, 374, 389–91, 395, 399–01, 405, 412, 414–15, 417–18, 442, 452, 467, 479, 481, 485, 487, 564, 599, 601, 653, 667
Crowd (in Mark/Matthew) 15
Cry → Weep
Crucifixion 17, 66, 68, 82, 88–89, 94, 96, 103–04, 119, 162, 162, 165, 193, 208–09, 210–12, 214, 225, 243, 304, 385, 388, 394, 454, 536, 556, 558, 561–62, 564–65, 578, 580, 589, 591, 595–96, *601–06, 607–17*, 621–22, 626–27, 642, 645, 653–54, 656
Cyril of Alexandria 565, 610

Dark/Darkness 31, 49, 63, 65, 88, 122, 127–28, 193, 201, 226, 249, 254, 345, 351, 354, 367–69, 372, 378, 391, 396, 399, 422, 431–32, 437, 441, 471, 546, 552, 554, 559, 564, 569, 572, *573–77*, 630, 632–33, 652
David, King 9, 243, 367

Defamiliarization 14, 625
Denouement 288, 317, 357, 563, 663, 675 (→ also Resolution)
Development (of Characters) 2, 6, 24, 27, 30, 47, 77–78, 80, 104, 107–08, 115, 130, 149, 153, 162, 167, 170–71, 173, 192, 213, 233, 249, 269, 308, 312, 334, 344, 351, 353, 362–63, 365, 368–70, 372, 377, 379, 384–86, 395, 402, 429, 433, 440, 445, 463, 466, 474, 482, 486, 495, 524–25, 549–50, 568, 571, 581, 666–67, 675
Devil 41, 73, 89, 103–04, 155–56, 241, 360–73, *421–27*, 516, 560
Devotion 195, 350, 367–68, 460, 474, 477, 480–81, 486, 604, 623, 654
Diachronic Approach 26, 75, 189, 448, 609
Diaspora 88, 177, 262, 397, 400, 532–34
Didymus (Thomas Didymus) 528, 667
Didymus the Greek 408–09
Diogenes Laertius 251
Diotima 280
Direct Characterization → Characterization
Disbelief 33, 167, 174, 221, 223–25, 316–17, 351, 577 (→ Unbelief)
Disciples
– Disciples of Jesus (in John) *212–227, passim*
– Disciples of Jesus (in Luke) 19–20
– Disciples of Jesus (in Mark) 15–16
– Disciples of Jesus (in Matthew) 17–18
– Disciples of John the Baptist/Baptizer (in John) 35, 51, 55–56, *127–32*, 133, 194–96, 260, 262, 389, 671
Dishonesty 364, 368–70, 588
Dishonor → Shame/Honor
Disloyal/Disloyalty 364, 368, 37–71, 385
Dispute 93–94, 129–30, 261, 264–65, 300, 346, 404, 410, 412, 431, 433–34, 436, 444–45
Division 75, 86, 98, 101, 107, 123–24, 126, 154, 218, 223, 257, 349, 354–55, 435, 442, 445, 479
Dominant Character → Classification of Characters
Domitian 185, 520
Doorkeeper → Portress
Double Agents → Classification of Characters

Double *Entendre* 63, 260, 274–75, 389, 430, 436, 540
Drama 26, 32, 72, 77, 87, 93, 97, 119, 201, 234, *268–81*, 292, 294–95, 298, 378, 448, 573
Dramatic Irony → Irony
Dualism 26–27, 65, 127–28, 193, 224, 226, 238, 256, 380–81, 386, 422, 440, 445, 610, 652, 656
Dynamic Character → Classification of Characters

Eden 211, 556, 565, 612–13, 636
Elderly → Classification of Characters
Eleazar 467
Eliab 243
Elijah 51–52, 111–12, 145, 263, 303, 316, 434
Elisha 303, 358, 434
Empathy 10, 129, 380, 388–89, 617
Emperor 83, 95, 104, 178, 385, 579 (→ also Caesar)
Empty Spaces (in Texts) → Gaps
Enemy/Enemies 132, 341, 343, 345, 371, 391–92, 394–95, 405, 425, 498, 569, 576, 641
Epithet 5, 10, 17, 21, 80, 293, 360, 365–66, 537, 539, 543, 547
Erasmus 409
Erotic Tone 272, 274–75, 277, 280
Esau 243
Eschatology 16, 60, 112–13, 163, 200, 223, 226, 236, 278, 324, 398–99, 402, 462, 510, 533, 580, 635, 639
Ethiopian Eunuch (in Acts) 181
Eucharist 275, 514, 519–20, 604, 606
Eusebius 165, 179, 182, 187, 408–09
Evaluation of Characters → Characters
Eve 209–10, 636
Exclusion (from Synagogue) 91–92, 111, 374, 435–36, 438, 479 (→ also Expulsion)
Exodus 86, 99, 218, 230, 615
Explicit Characterization → Characterization
Expulsion (from Synagogue) 98, 101, 103, 125–26, 351 (→ also Exclusion)

Family 26, 207–09, 212, 234, 238, 242, 244, 285–86, 297–98, 306, 312–13, 316–17, 320–22, 326–27, 329, 331, 339, 358, 360, 370–71, 415–16, 423, 460, 468–69, 473, 475, 479, 485, 494–96, 501–02, 543, 549, 574, 603, 607, 609, 617, 624, 626, *641–45*, 666
Fear 16, 87, 91–92, 96, 101, 103, 106, 121, 124, 147, 217, 222, 249, 287, 290, 349, 351, 374, 377–78, 380, 384, 391, 401, 409, 435, 446, 449–50, 463, 514, 592–93, 600, 636–37, 646, 649–50, 652–53, 656–57, 667, 674
Feeding of the Five Thousand 146, 149, 168, 176, 178, 183–84, 217, 305, 347–48, 356–58, 471, 485, 673
Female Servants (in Matthew) 18
Feminism 29, 269, 410, 412, 418
Ficelle → Classification of Characters
Figures → Character
Flat Character → Classification of Characters
Focalization
– Focalization 5, 12, 48, 53–55, 79, 83, 357, 363, 592, 627, 630, 638
– Character-Bound Focalization 53
– External Focalization 53, 55, 357, 630
– Focalized 12
– Focalized Object 631
– Focalizer 54–55
– Focalizing Marker 54
– Internal Focalization 53, 357, 592, 631
– Zero Focalization 357
Foil 12, 29, 76, 91, 104–05, 131, 149, 163, 260, 268, 335, 395, 420, 448, 450, 463, 547, 551, 577, *598–600*, 608, 611, 617, 634
Foot-Washing 156–59, 265, 366–67, 373, 413, 483–84, 539–40, 559
Friend of the Bridegroom → Bridegroom
Friendship 159, 212, 371, 464, 472, 476
From Above 56, 61, 66, 69–70, 88, 174, 195, 199, 249, 255–57, 259, 303, 311, 324, 342, 540, 594, 603, 638
From Below 56, 88, 174, 243, 256–57, 348, 526, 540, 640
Full-Fledged Character → Classification of Characters
Functionary → Classification of Characters

Index of Subjects

Gabriel 31
Galileans 38, 73, 184, 261, *299–305*, 309–12, 317, 320, 348, 405, 664
Gaps (Semantic Gaps in Texts) 58–59, 163, 191, 194, 203, 205, 207, 250, 252, 283, 304, 335, 407–11, 475, 482, 486, 511, 521, 534, 537, 558, 562, 582–83, 586, 592, 597, 647
Garden 160–61, 193, 211–12, 217, 388, 415, 542, 554–57, 559, 565–66, *568–72*, 573, 575–77, 612, 630, 636, 646
Gardener 193, 211, 556, 630, 636
Gate 161, 541–42, 574
Gatekeeper → Portress
Gender 18, 23, 27–31, 205, 411, 415, 417, 466, 469, 515, 576, 623, 630, 638
Genesis 190, 192–94, 198–99, 204, 209, 211, 426, 554–57, 565–67, 609–13, 630, 636
Gentiles 22, 140, 147, 177, 185, 297, 302, 309, 400–02, 562, 610, 644
Gesture 5, 9, 158, 273–74, 367, 466, 469, 484, 497, 626
Gideon (Sons of) 243
God
- God (in Acts) 21–22
- God (in John) *passim*
- God (in Mark) 16
- God (in Matthew) 17
Good Shepherd 103, 159, 162, 164–65, 391, 399, 401–02, 449, 457, 465, 469, 541–42, 571, 573, 581, 637
Gospel of Mary 628
Gospel of Philip 628
Gospel of the Hebrews 408–09
Gospel of Thomas 528
Grapho-Literacy *404–06*
Greek Literature 24, 26–27, 32, 213, 292–94, 298, 378, 479, 639
Greeks 40, 88, 101, 147–49, 168, 177–78, 180, 183, 185, 302, 309, *397–402*, 610, 667
Gregory the Great 627
Group Character → Classification of Characters

Hadrian 561
Haemorrhaging Woman (in Synoptic Gospels) 15
Hatred 64–66, 127, 241–42, 393–94, 396

Helper → Classification of Characters
Hermeneutical Character → Classification of Characters
Hero → Classification of Characters
Herod 16, 19, 178, 289, 308–09, 320, 533
High Priest 43–44, 73, 93–94, 98–99, 160–61, 164, 166, 382–83, 388, 392–93, *53–36*, 541–42, 549, 564, 570–72, *573–77*, 665
Holy Spirit (in John) 30, 51, 54, 59–60, 62, 67–68, 162–63, 167, 174, 177–79, 181, 184–86, 193, 208–11, 222, 225, 249, 255–56, 263, 275, 278, 294, 325–26, 335, 342, 345, 361, 465, 510, 512, 517, 520, 522, 544, 552, 612–13, 615–16, 664 (→ also Paraclete)
Holy Spirit (in Luke–Acts) 20, 22
Homer 508, 668
Honor/Shame 85, 157–58, 164, 230, 234, 236–37, 272, 279–80, 287, 300–01, 305, 310, 368, 393, 404, 584, 595, 671
Hostility 64–65, 72, 75, 78, 85–86, 93–94, 99, 101–04, 106–07, 127–28, 240–42, 262, 305, 348, 351, 354, 382, 385–86, 388, 390–91, 394–96, 424, 426, 434, 456, 460, 601–02, 604
Household → Family
Humiliation 412, 417, 567, 585, 590–91, 616
Humility 47, 192, 368, 489, 636
Husbands of the Samaritan Woman → Samaritan Woman
Hyperbole 67, 92
Hypocrisy 364, 368, 370, 623

Ideal Author → Author
Ideal Character → Classification of Characters
Ideal Disciple 128–29, 190, 389, 537
Ideal Witness 134, 537, 544
Ignorance 59, 62, 66–69, *233–37*, 241, 254, 275, 296–97, 354, 434, 437, 444, 447, 534, 551, 596, 641
Ill/Sick (at Pool of Bethzatha) 39, *332–36*, 337, 416, 420,
Immorality 276, 284, 287–89, 292–93, 413
Imperial Cult 185, 520, 527
Implicit Characterization → Characterization

Implied Audience/Reader → Reader
Inclusio 51, 135–36, 155, 209, 213, 316, 520, 548, 675
Indirect Characterization → Characterization
Individual → Classification of Characters
Ingénue → Classification of Characters
Inner Life of Characters → Penetration
Inner Monologue 80, 353, 377, 455, 466
Innocence 14, 32, 95, 394, 414–15, 417, 431–32, 435, 437, 444, 578–79, 581, 587–91, 597, 599–600, 607–08
Intended Reader → Reader
Interaction between Characters → Characters, Relationship
Intercharacterizational Approach 189, 617, 631–32, 638
Interior Monologue → Inner Monologue
Intermediary Character → Classification of Characters
Intertextuality 30, 189–90, 246–47, 268, 270, 358–59, 453, 554, 557, 565, 570, 605, 610, 632, 635–36, 638, 641, 643–45, 668, 676
Intimacy 28, 68, 123, 158, 164, 206–07, 367, 369, 371, 398, 400, 495, 518, 539, 628–29, 636–38, 642, 644
Invalid (at the Pool) 23, 25, 29, 32, 39, 85, 99, 127, 129, 325–26, 336, *337–46*, 389, 420, 430, 432, 434–44, 461, 471, 578, 640
Irony 11, 63, 78, 88, 90, 101, 103, 126, 135, 139, 157, 164, 17–71, 173–75, 177, 195, 200, 229, 231, 234–36, 239, 242, 254, 256, 258, 260, 270, 274–75, 293, 302, 305, 335, 354, 391, 393, 411–12, 426–27, 430, 435, 437, 443, 512, 534, 559, 576, 580–81, 586, 588–89, 591, 593–95, 597, 599–600, 604, 606, 608, 614–15, 633, 638, 657
Isaac 198, 243, 609–10
Isaiah 52, 60, 112, 200, 263, 351, 397, 399–400
Ishmael 243
Israelite 73, 86, 102, 145, 191–94, 198–99, 218, 229, 342, 348, 436, 666

Jacob 190, 198–99, 243, 271, 273–74, 294, 296, 300, 635
Jacob of Sarug 210

James of Alphaeus 190
Jerome 409
Jesus
– Jesus (in Four Gospels) 15
– Jesus (in John) *passim*
– Jesus (in Luke–Acts) 19, 22, 303–04
– Jesus (in Mark) 15–17
– Jesus (in Matthew) 17–18
– Jesus' Mother → Mother of Jesus
Jewish Leaders (in Matthew) 17
Jewish Police → Temple Police
"Jews"
– "Jew"/"Jews" (in John) *71–109, 260–67, passim*
– "Jews" (in Matthew) 17
Joachim 415
Job 285, 365
Johannine Community 27, 29, 65, 72, 111, 125–26, 186, 298, 372, 522, 549, 626, 650
John
– John and History 71, 78–79, 125, 138, 156, 158, 170, 184–85, 187, 244, 250, 262, 308–09, 552, 588
– John and Synoptics 30, 46, 94, 112, 118, 121–22, 133, 141, 146, 152–54, 160, 168, 172–73, 176–77, 179, 184, 187, 189–90, 195, 211–12, 217, 238–41, 243, 250, 259, 264, 266–67, 304, 308–10, 321, 332–33, 338–40, 343, 375, 399, 409, 473, 478, 480–81, 484, 528, 552, 555–56, 558, 563, 565, 568, 571, 574–75, 577, 607–12, 616, 620, 627, 635, 637, 649–51, 655, 657–58, 661, 664
– John the Baptist/Baptizer (in Gospel of John) 23, 29, 34, *46–60*, 84, 99, 104, 106, 110–16, 119, *127–32*, 135, 141–45, 148, 152–53, 174, 184, 191, 194–96, 198, 201, 207, 216, 231, 254, *260–67*, 316, 335, 452, 454–61, 615–16, 622, 671
– John the Baptist/Baptizer (in Matthew) 17
– John the Baptist/Baptizer (in Mark) 16–17
Jordan 42, 84, 97, 114, 128, 178, 191, 195, 263, 300, *451–59*, 564, 615, 664
Joseph 243, 283, 300
Joseph of Arimathea 45, 96, 103–04, 106,

249, 258–59, 379, 467, 596, 610, 632, *646–57*, 663
Josephus 14, 72, 178, 195, 276, 289, 308, 354, 361, 383, 467, 480, 531, 534, 570, 599, 609
Judas
- Judas Iscariot (in Four Gospels) 15, 213
- Judas Iscariot (in John) 29, 25, 29, 40, 80–81, 127, 129, 155–56, 158–61, 223, 259, *360–72*, 384, 388–91, 398, 422–27, 461, 473–75, 480–81, 484, 486, 516, 526, 539, 541–42, 558, 560–62, 565–66, 569, 573, 575–76, 583, 633, 667, 674–75
- Judas Iscariot (in Luke) 15, 20
- Judas Iscariot (in Mark) 15
- Judas Iscariot (in Matthew) 15
- Judas Thomas 528
- Judas, not Iscariot (in John) 33, 43, 243, 511–12, *550–53*, 667, 675
Judean 72, 78, 102, 108, 176–77, 184, *26–67*, 300, 305, 309–10, 350, 399, 433
Judith 285
Julias 178
Juvenile → Classification of Characters
Juxtaposition 197, 230, 239, 339, 365, 477, 501, 632 (→ also Contrast)

King
- King of Israel 83, 102, 145, 176, 199, 201, 398, 666
- King of the "Jews" 83, 96, 104, 200, 563, 580, 583, 589, 591, 594, 596, 599, 601–02

Lame Man → Invalid
Lazarus 42, 66, 93–94, 101, 105, 121, 176, 219–20, 242, 258, 304, 326–27, 345, 350, 368, 383–86, 389, 398–99, 416, 452, 454, *460–72*, 473–86, 491–92, 494–98, 500–03, 505–10, 530, 533, 633–34, 636, 639–40
Levites 35, 73, 84, 98, *110–15*, 116–17, 131, 265, 312
Little People (in Mark) 15
Location → Setting
Loyal/Loyalty 47, 56, 59, 159–60, 166–67, 365, 371, 374, 376, 379, 385, 395, 508, 577

LXX (Use of LXX in John) 54, 90, 112, 193–94, 198–99, 201, 205, 211, 218, 230, 316, 358, 361, 365, 392–93, 406, 415, 478, 480–81, 519, 550, 554, 576, 603, 605, 612

Main Character → Classification of Characters
Major Character → Classification of Characters
Malchus
- Malchus 44, 392, *568–72*
- Relative of Malchus 577
Man Born Blind (in John)
- Man Born Blind 23–26, 29, 32, 41, 66, 90–92, 99–101, 106, 121, 124, 128–29, 132, 219, 256, 268, 327, 338, 342–44, 346, 351, 389, 391, 416, 420, *428–48*, 450, 460–61, 479, 484, 526, 540, 578, 640
- Neighbors of the Man Born Blind 41, 91, 100, 437, *439–45*
- Parents of the Man Born Blind 41, 91, 100, 103, 435, 437, 441, 444, *446–50*
Marginal Character → Classification of Characters
Marginalized Characters → Classification of Characters
Martha (in John) 28–29, 32–33, 42, 62, 82, 93, 128, 304, 350, 452, 460–86, *487–503*, 506, 633–35, 640
Mary
- Mary Magdalene 25–26, 28–29, 45, 162, 209, 211–12, 243, 391, 514–16, 520–21, 524, 526–27, 537, 544–46, 555, 618–25, *626–40*, 659–62
- Mary of Bethany 28–29, 32–33, 42, 62, 66, 82, 93, 101, 121, 304, 350, 368, 398, 452, 460–72, *473–86*, 487–503, 627–28, 633–34, 640
- Mary of Clopas 45, *618–25*, 626
- Mary, Mother of Jesus (in John) → Mother of Jesus
- Mary, Mother of Jesus (in Luke) 31
Master of the Banquet → Steward
Men of the Samaritan Woman → Samaritan Woman
Metaphor/Metaphorical 28, 33, 54, 56, 92, 114, 141, 208–09, 212, 217–18,

221–23, 229, 236, 255, 274, 287, 293, 314, 358, 399, 423, 442, 446, 458–59
Middle 193, 211, 411–12, 414–17, 556, 565, 602, 611–13
Minor Character → Classification of Characters
Minor Characters (in Mark/Matthew) 15–16, 18
Miraculous Catch of Fish 163–64, 547, 549
Miriam 243
Misunderstanding 33, 63–64, 66, 88, 100–01, 105, 153, 156–57, 159, 162, 167, 217–20, 225, 229, 303, 348, 350–52, 355, 483, 547, 551, 570, 652, 661
Moab 360
Model Disciple 154–55, 167
Model Reader → Reader
Money Changers 37, 81, *245–48*, 341 (→ also Animal Sellers)
Monochromic Figure → Classification of Characters
Moses 16, 60, 62, 85, 102, 106, 112, 144–45, 147, 173–74, 176, 185–86, 195, 197, 199, 218, 229–30, 243, 283–86, 348, 383, 405–06, 417
Mother of Jesus 26, 28–29, 32, 36, 45, 196, *202–13*, 229, 231, 234–35, 243, 306, 316, 543, 603, 610–11, 618–21, 624, 626, 632, 641–45, 671
Mother of the Bridegroom → Bridegroom
Mourning 68, 460–61, 468, 470–71, 473, 475–76, 478–79, 481–82, 485, 489, 495–97, 501
Multichromatic/Multi-Dimensional Character → Classification of Characters

Naqdimon ben Gurion 250
Narratalogy 5, 13, 20, 22–26, 30, 32, 49–50, 53, 55, 74–81, 92, 100, 108, 116, 123, 172–73, 270, 412, 416–17, 420, 428, 453, 455, 522, 626, 647–48, 663, 666–70, 675
Narrated World 46, 71, 74, 76, 81, 97, 118, 451
Narratee 138–40, 302–3, 626, 628
Narrative Aside 113, 172, 198, 220, 242, 304, 318, 392, 405, 432, 444, 537, 542, 544, 552, 646, 651–53,

Narrative Space → Setting
Narrator
- Auctorial Narrator 80, 378
- Extradiegetic Narrator 628–29, 638
- Heterodiegetic Narrator 628, 638
- Intradiegetic Narrator 629
- Narrator in John *passim*
- Omniscient Narrator 166, 338, 377
Nathanael 36, 142, 144–45, 149, 168, 176, 180, 184–86, *189–201*, 224, 230, 254, 300, 320, 342, 357, 391, 398, 436, 461, 479, 520, 523, 525–26, 537, 546, 563, 640, 663, 666–67, 674
Nazarene/Nazorean 200, 391, 558, 562–63 (→ also Branch)
Neighbors of the Man Born Blind → Man Born Blind
Netzer → Branch
New Birth → Born From Above
Nicodemus 23, 25–26, 29, 31, 33, 38, 62, 64, 87, 98, 104, 120–21, 123–26, 128, 197, 238, 247, *249–59*, 262, 268, 296, 300, 310–12, 316, 325–26, 330, 342, 375–79, 390, 395, 460–61, 463, 467, 474, 476, 526, 540, 546, 578, 610, 632–33, 639–40, 646, 649–50, 652, 654–56
Night → Darkness

Obedience 20, 255, 284, 286, 291, 312, 392, 432, 468, 542, 563–64, 609, 638, 640
Objectification 414–16, 418, 420, 607–08, 614, 617
Officer → Temple Police
Old Testament → LXX, Scripture
Omniscient Narrator → Narrator
One-Dimensional Character → Classification of Characters
Opponent → Classification of Characters
Origen 239, 276, 288, 532, 561
Other Disciple → Anonymous Disciple
Outsider 18, 161, 289, 296

Papias 266, 408–09
Paraclete 60, 67–70, 162–63, 167, 510, 572, 654 (→ also Holy Spirit)
Paradigm of Traits 5–6, 12, 55, 114–15, 401–02, *581–95* (→ also Character, Traits)
Paralytic → Invalid

Parents of the Man Born Blind → Man Born Blind
Participant Reference 421–23, 598
Paul (in Acts) 19, 21–23, 181, 256
Penetration (Inner Life of Characters) 5–7, 9–10, 27, 30, 59, 80, 115, 130, 149, 170, 192, 233, 269, 308, 312, 351, 353, 362–63, 369–70, 377, 384–86, 395, 402, 440, 445, 466, 550, 675
Peniel 199
People in the Court Yard 44, 393, *573–77*
People Selling Cattle, Sheep and Doves in Temple → Animal Sellers
Pericope Adulterae 177, *403–20*, 444
Peripheral Characters (in Matthew) 18
Personality → Classification of Characters
Peter
- Peter (in Acts) 23
- Peter (in Four Gospels) 15
- Peter (in John) *151–67, passim*
- Peter (in Luke–Acts) 14–15, 22
- Peter (in Mark) 14–15
- Peter (in Matthew) 14–15, 17
Pharisees
- Pharisee(s) (in John) *116–26, passim*
- Pharisees (in Acts) 303
Philip
- Philip (in John) 33, 36, 129, 133, 142, 144–49, 154, *168–88*, 189, 191, 194–99, 230, 254, 298, 300, 302, 320, 341–42, 357, 397, 400–01, 421, 461, 479, 513, 523, 527, 551, 598, 640, 666–67, 674–75
- Philip (in Eusebius) 179, 182, 187
- Philip (in Synoptics & Acts) 179–80, 187
- Philip II 178
Philo 14, 354
Photeine/Photina 269
Pilate
- Pilate (in John) 14, 24, 26, 29, 44, 81, 83, 94–95, 97, 100–01, 103, 200, 238, 258, 261, 341, 361, 383–86, 388, 394, 417, 444, 453, 535–36, 556, 559, 561, 563–64, 569, *578–97*, 598–600, 602, 605, 608–10, 614–15, 623, 633, 646, 649–50, 652–53, 656, 663, 668
- Pilate (in Synoptics) 14
- Pilate's Wife (in Matthew) 18
Place → Setting

Plato 280, 295
Pliny the Younger 520
Plot *passim*
Plutarch 481
Point of View 5, 25, 27, 50, 79, 139, 203, 228, 292, 329, 352, 362–64, 372, 384, 393, 457, 464, 527, 647
- Evaluative Point of View 10, 12, 49, 59, 66, 129, 203, 354, 364, 370, 387, 440
- Ideal Point of View 537–549
- Ideological Point of View 24, 139, 203–04, 211, 213, 228, 363
- Material Point of View 25
- Phraseological Point of View 17, 139, 203, 212, 538
- Psychological Point of View 203, 538
- Spatial Point of View 139, 203
- Spatial-Temporal Point of View 538
- Temporal Point of View 139, 203
Police → Temple Police
Polycrates 266
Pontius Pilate → Pilate
Portress 44, 161, 541–42, 573, *574–76*
Posture 9, 157, 418, 466, 469, 660
Praetorium 94–95, 394, 444, 453, 582–83, 589
Pragmatics 109
Praise 327, 351, 500–01
Priests 35, 73, 81, 84, 98, *110–15*, 116, 131, 287, 312, 481
Prochorus (in Acts) 181
Prolepsis 16, 63, 207, 629, 655
Protagonist → Classification of Characters
Pseudo-Hero → Classification of Characters
Psychological Approach 20, 71, 79, 162, 167, 250, 273, 338, 487, 579, 588, 639

Quinary Scheme 317–18, 356–57

Reader
- Implied Reader *passim*
- Intended Reader 78, 139–140
- Model Reader 7
- Real Reader 138–39, 158, 270, 301, 305, 532
Reader-Response Criticism 18, 24, 31, 76, 172, 193, 283, 530, 647, 663
Real Reader → Reader

Rebuke 123, 128, 160, 257, 276, 311, 317, 322, 365, 374, 388, 392, 509, 522, 560, 569, 571, 607
Receiver → Classification of Characters
Relecture → Re-Reading
Reliable Narration 3, 7, 9, 11, 17, 71, 85, *107–09*, 215, 225, 431, 628, 651
Religious Leaders (in Matthew) 17–18
Repetition 5–6, 16–17, 20, 22, 51, 55, 130, 165, 200–01, 219, 253–54, 318, 323, 326, 330, 451, 477, 492, 513–14, 516, 545, 563, 576, 656
Re-Reading 129, 136, 160, 163–64, 191, 293
Resolution 235, 264–65, 280, 317, 372, 616, 649 (→ also *Denouement*)
Representative Character → Classification of Characters
Retarding Effect 625
Rhetoric 7, 22, 28, 90, 111, 132, 156, 162, 167, 171–75, 182–83, 185, 187, 203–04, 253, 260, 363, 372, 376, 419, 435, 448, 462, 464, 487–89, 491–503, 511, 520, 600, 661
Rhoda (in Acts) 576
Roman Centurion (in Mark) 16
Roman Officer (in Matthew) 18
Roman Soldiers → Cohort
Round Character → Classification of Characters
Royal Official
– Royal Official 29, 32, 38, 300, 302, *306–13*, 316–17, 320, 322–23, 327, 329, 330–31, 342, 461
– Slaves of the Royal Official 39, *329–31*, 330–31
– Son of the Royal Official 39, *314–28*, 339, 342, 461
Ruler of this World 41, 194, 378, 399, *421*, *425–27*, 560–61, 566
Ruth 283

Samaritan Woman
– Men of the Samaritan Woman 38, 276–77, *282–91*, 342
– Samaritan Woman 23, 26, 28–29, 33, 38, 83, 128–29, 132, 176, 212, 220, 223, *261–81*, 282–98, 316, 326, 335, 342, 344–45, 389, 391, 420, 452, 460–61, 474, 476, 485, 526, 612, 633–35, 640

Samaritans 38, 83, 105, 181, 268, 272, 276–78, 284–86, 288–89, *292–98*, 300, 309, 311–13, 316, 326, 452, 526
Sanhedrin 121–22, 257, 345, 349, 374–76, 383, 472–73, 479, 530–36, 649–50, 656
Sarah 284, 285
Sarcasm 296, 504, 580, 584–85, 592, 595, 600
Satan 41, 213, 240–41, 369–72, *421–27*, 478, 552, 560–61, 566
Saul, King Saul 9
Savior of the World 279, 290–91, 295, 298, 326, 526
Scribe (in Matthew) 18
Scribes (in John) 40, 116–18, 122, 125, 239, 375, *403–06*, 407, 412–14, 416, 418–19, 444
Scripture (Use of Scripture in John) 52, 54, 83, 86, 92, 96, 112, 184, 245–47, 251, 257, 261, 263, 358, 365, 367, 392–93, 399–400, 430, 441, 484, 519, 570, 603, 605–07, 636
Secret Believer/Disciple 249, 251, 258–59, 351, 354–55, 378–89, 649–50, 653–56
Selfishness 275, 344, 595
Semantics of Space 452–534
Sender → Classification of Characters
Septuagint → LXX
Servant(s)
– Servants 18, 120–21, 123, 157, 358, 374, 402, 470, 483, 668
– Servants at Cana 37, 206–07, *228–32*, 235, 237, 306, 312
– Servants of the High Priest 160–61, 564, 569–70, 573, *576–77*
– Servants of the Royal Official → Royal Official
Setting 2, 19, 48, 52, 55, 57, 114, 124, 161, 164, 189, 192, 197, 201, 203, 206, 216, 229, 253, 260, 271, 300, 334–35, 339–40, 347–49, 351, 364, 395, 398, 400–02, 411, 435, 440, 446–49, 466, 473, 480, 538, 541–42, 546, 565, 574, 577, 583, 602, 627, 630, 638
Seven Deacons (in Acts) 181
Sex 28, 275–76, 281, 288–90, 293, 407, 411, 413–15, 419, 628, 630, 636
Showing 10, 12, 15, 50, 58, 79–80, 82, 84, 99, 128–29, 364, 377, 384

Sick (at the Pool of Bethzata) → Ill/Sick
Siloam 433, 439, 441
Simeon (in Luke) 215
Simon Peter → Peter
Simple Character → Classification of Characters
Sister of the Mother of Jesus 45, *618–25*, 626
Slaves of the Royal Official → Royal Official
Socrates 280
Soldiers
- Soldiers (in Matthew) 18
- Soldiers who Arrested Jesus (in John) 361, 364, 388, 390, 392–93, 542, *554–67*, 569, 576, 583, 589, 610, 615, 622, 630, 668
- Soldiers who Crucified Jesus (in John) 45, *601–06*, 610, 613–17, 621–23, 641
Solomon 533
Son of Perdition 360, 365, 370
Son of the Royal Official → Royal Official
Sons of Zebedee 45, 81, 143, 546, 620, *663–76*
Space → Setting
Speech (Characterization through Speech) 5–6, 9–11, 46–47, 51, 54, 100, 111, 123, 175, 197, 218–19, 221–22, 378, 418, 438, 466, 476, 497–500, 503, 507, 519, 549, 558, 597, 628–29, 651
Spirit → Holy Spirit/Paraclete
Spokesperson 19, 142, 151–53, 155, 158–59, 162–63, 167, 242, 257, 293, 507, 509, 524, 540
Static Character → Classification of Characters
Stephen (in Acts) 181
Stereotype → Classification of Characters
Steward at Cana 37, 207, *228–33*, 235–36
Stocks → Classification of Characters
Subsidiary Character → Classification of Characters
Suetonius 520, 614
Superiority 49–50, 53, 56–57, 153, 157–58, 166, 195, 237, 260, 266–67, 406, 456, 537, 543, 547, 583, 604, 616
Susannah (in Tobit) 415–16
Sychar 271, 282–98, 315–16, 452
Symbol/Symbolism 20, 26, 31, 52, 61, 69, 75, 139, 153, 156–57, 163, 165–66, 171, 192–93, 208–11, 229, 231, 248, 251, 254, 265, 269, 274, 289, 296, 307, 323, 325, 327, 335, 367, 372, 380–81, 403, 411, 416–17, 462, 482, 484, 505, 507, 515, 517–18, 556, 559, 569, 610, 62, 641–45, 659, 672, 674, 676
Sympathy 10, 16, 123, 287, 312, 331, 352, 375, 395, 432, 525, 580, 590, 603, 617, 650
Synchronic Approach 26, 32, 75, 79, 189, 609
Synoptics and John → John and Synoptics
Syrophroenician Woman (in Mark) 16, 177

Telling 10, 12, 15, 48, 50, 58, 60, 79, 80, 82, 84, 102, 107, 128, 364, 377, 384, 651
Temple Police 81, 87, 94, 103, 120, 349, 361, 364, 384, *388–96*, 535, 542, 558, 562, 565–66, 568, 576, 583, 610
Tertullian 165, 609
Testimony *passim*
Thecla 280
Theodore 240
Theophilus 270
Thief 213, 360, 366, 368–69, 371, 541, 573, 600
Thomas 26, 29, 33, 43, 81, 157, 177–78, 216, 222, 224, 266, 335, 344, 461, 476, *504–29*, 546, 551, 638, 640, 663, 666–67, 673–74
Thomas Didymos 528, 667
Titulus 83, 391, 535, 578, 596, 608
Tobit 284–85
Touch 348, 514, 517, 521–22, 529, 555, 637, 666
Traits → Characters
Trajan 561
Transformation 23, 69, 186, 241, 268, 279–80, 298, 317, 330, 357, 419–20, 431, 437, 505, 513, 519, 523, 635, 642
Twelve 33, 37, 127, 137, 142, 146, 149, 154–55, 177–78, 180–81, 184, 189–90, 216, 223, 266–67, 357, 360, 365, 370, 481, 486, 508, 515–16, 526, 528, 552, 673–74
Twin 43, 506–07, 523, 525, 527–28
Types → Classification of Characters

Unbelief 25–26, 32, 75, 89, 101, 105, 107, 130, 167, 174, 218, 226, 242–44, 261, 301, 342, 344, 348, 350–54, 365, 374, 380, 390, 395, 422, 518, 525, 563–64, 566, 574, 577, 668 (→ Disbelief)
Unreliable Narration → Reliable Narration
Use of Scripture in John → Scripture, Use

Virgil 481

Walk-On → Classification of Characters
Wedding at Cana 194, *202–13, 228–37*, 265, 302, 312, 315–16, 318, 330, 335, 397, 471, 485, 506, 643–45
Weep 68, 93, 176, 470, 473, 477–79, 482–83, 501, 628, 631, 634–36, 639, 658
Widow of Nain (in Luke) 31
Witness *passim*
Woman Accused of Adultery → Adulterous Woman
Woman Who Guarded Gate → Portress
Women
- Women (in John) 27–28, 30–31
- Women (in the Synoptics) 30–31
- Women at the Tomb (in Matthew) 18
- Women by the Cross (in John) 45, 556, 603, 611–13, *618–25*
- Women by the Cross (in Matthew) 18
- Women Sent to the Disciples (in Matthew) 18
World 31, 34, 54, *61–70*, 73, 75, 88, 98, 105, 121–22, 131, 141, 174, 178–79, 195, 241, 201, 222, 238–39, 241–44, 300, 318, 342, 347, 372, 382, 397, 399, 401, 430–32, 459, 472, 484, 494, 534, 538, 550–51, 557, 562, 579, 615, 630
Worship 83, 114, 147, 177–78, 277–78, 293–94, 296–97, 337, 392, 395–97, 400–01, 436, 460, 557, 610
Writing → Grapho-Literacy

Xenophon 280

Young Ruler (in Luke) 250

Zacchaeus (in Luke) 21
Zarephath 316
Zechariah 200
Zero Focalization → Focalization

www.ingramcontent.com/pod-product-compliance
Lightning Source LLC
Chambersburg PA
CBHW031537300426
44111CB00006BA/85